S0-BII-053

...Extreme Pets...

RATS

Deborah Chancellor

A+
Smart Apple Media

Smart Apple Media is published by Black Rabbit Books
P.O. Box 3263, Mankato, Minnesota 56002

Printed in the United States

Published by arrangement with the Watts Publishing Group Ltd, London.

Editors: Rachel Tonkin and Julia Bird
Designer: Proof Books
Picture researcher: Diana Morris

Picture credits:
A1Pix: 4; Arco Images/Alamy: 5, 6, 13, 25; Krys Bailey/Marmotta-PhotoArt: 17; Vladimir Georgievsky: 22; Elena Kenunen: 9; Jean Michel Labat/Ardea: 26; PetStockBoys: front cover, 1, 29; Steiner/Arco Images/Alamy: 12, 21.

All other photography: Andy Crawford

With thanks to Jan Bell and Lucy Milne, and Lucy's pet rats, Nipper and Rafferty.

Library of Congress Cataloging-in-Publication Data
Chancellor, Deborah.
Rats / Deborah Chancellor.
p. cm.—(Smart Apple Media. Extreme pets)
Summary: "Advice for kids on how to choose and care for a pet rat, including housing, diet, and keeping rats healthy"—Provided by publisher.
Includes index.
ISBN-13: 978-1-59920-236-5
1. Rats as pets—Juvenile literature. I. Title.
SF459.R3C43 2009
636.935'2—dc22

2007035385

9 8 7 6 5 4 3 2 1

Contents

What Is a Rat?

Rats have been bred and kept as pets for many years and make fantastic family pets. Anyone who has ever kept pet rats will tell you so. But sadly, some people confuse domestic rats with wild rats and do not like the idea of rats as pets. This is a mistake, because wild rats are very different from domestic ones.

Pet Rats

Pet rats are the same species as the wild brown rat, but this is where the similarity ends. Pet rats are much less aggressive than wild rats and bond very well with their human owners. They are bred for their pretty looks and friendly temperament.

Wild rats are often found in garbage dumps or in sewers. These unwelcome pests can spread disease.

Bucks

Male rats are called bucks. They are larger and lazier than female rats, with a coarser coat and a musky smell. Bucks like to mark out their territory with a few drops of their urine. This habit is known as "scent-marking."

Does

Female rats are called does. They are smaller and more active than males. They have a softer coat and don't smell musky like male rats. About once every five days, a female rat is "in heat" for about 12 hours. This is when she is looking for a male partner. During this time, she is more jumpy and active than normal.

Baby rats are born blind and rely on their mother to feed them for the first four weeks of their life.

In the Family

Rats are rodents. The rodent family includes many other small furry pets, such as hamsters, gerbils, and mice.

Having Kittens

A female rat is pregnant for 21-24 days before having a litter of between 2 and 20 babies. The tiny babies are called kittens, and they are born bald and blind. They need to drink their mother's milk for at least four weeks.

Blind As a Rat

Rats first open their eyes when they are two weeks old, and they do not have great eyesight. However, their senses of hearing and smell are very sharp—much better than a human's.

Questions & Answers

* **Is it better to have male or female pet rats?**
  Rats should be kept in same sex pairs or groups. It is up to you to choose whether you want to keep males or females—they behave slightly differently, but both are just as good to keep as pets.
* **Can you smell a rat's scent-markings?**
  No, because a male rat only uses a few small drops of urine to mark out his territory. Humans can't smell this, but other rats can.
* **Can I keep a wild rat as a pet?**
  No. It is against the law to keep wild rats as pets because they are classified as vermin.

Do You Really Want Rats?

Rats make excellent pets because they have lots of character and personality, and are very friendly. They are not particularly expensive to buy or feed. But it is hard work caring for rats for their entire lives. Before you buy pet rats, you must be sure you can give them the time and care they need.

Playmates

Just like dogs, rats can be affectionate to their owners. If you are kind and attentive to your pet rats, they will bond with you and will be lots of fun to play with. They will easily repay all the attention and affection you are prepared to give them. But your pets will quickly become unhappy if you don't take the time to play with them every day.

Free Time

Rats need time to roam outside their cages every day, or they soon will become bored and unhappy. Before you decide to get pet rats, you must check with your family to make sure you will be allowed to let your rats roam.

If you spend time playing with your rats, you will enjoy each other's company.

Be Prepared!

If you have pet rats, you can't have a day off just because you feel like it. You must be prepared to clean their cage regularly, give them food and water every day, and spend time each day playing with them. If you don't think you will be able to do this, then you should not keep pet rats.

Celebrity Rat

Beatrix Potter, the famous children's author and illustrator, had a white pet rat called Sammy.

Living Space

Rats need to live indoors, because they can get too hot or cold outside. This means that you must have enough space and a suitable place for a big rat cage in your home.

Do Your Homework

It is important to find out a lot about rats before you decide to get a pair or small group of them. Read a few books and look at some good Web sites (see page 31). If you can, talk to people you know who keep rats. You and your family must be prepared before you buy your new pets.

Questions & Answers

- **How long do I need to play with my rats every day?**
  Most rats need about an hour's play outside their cages each day.
- **Can rats learn tricks?**
  Yes. Rats are intelligent enough to learn simple tricks. For example, you can teach a rat to find the quickest way through a maze. Build the maze with books or bricks, and place a tasty treat at the other end for your rat to find.
- **Will my pet rats recognize me?**
  Yes, and they will quickly learn to enjoy being with you. When they see you coming, they will run to the front of their cage to meet you.

Do your research with someone in your family, so you can learn about rats together.

Choosing Your Rats

Before you buy your pet rats, you must get their cage ready for them. Make sure you have all the food, bedding, and accessories that they will need when they come home with you (see pages 18–19). Go to a good rat breeder or a high-quality pet shop to choose your rats. If the rats for sale have been well cared for, they will be healthy and sociable.

Breeders Are Best

It is best to buy rats from a rat breeder. This is because the baby rats won't have had the stress of moving from their birthplace to a pet shop. Also, a rat breeder can show you your chosen rats' parents and siblings. If the whole rat family is healthy, your chosen rats probably will be as well.

Which Ones?

Choose a pair of rats that are curious about you and do not seem nervous when you approach their cage. Baby rats should be handled from a very young age and should be used to human contact by the time they are bought. As a general rule, never buy a rat if it looks unwell or if any of its family members look sick.

Try to choose active and friendly rats. They will soon get used to you.

Leaving the Nest

Baby rats must stay with their mother for the first four to five weeks of their life. Rats that are taken away from their mother sooner than this can become unhappy and sickly. Your rats should be more than six weeks old when you take them home. The person who sells you your rats should be able to say exactly how old they are.

Fancy rats are named after the color of their fur. A "chocolate" fancy rat (left) is a soft brown color.

Fancy That!

Pet rats are called "fancy rats," and a group of rats is called a "mischief."

Young Mother?

If you want to get a pair of female rats, make sure that they were separated from their brothers at five weeks old. This is the age that rats can become parents! If your pair stayed with the whole litter for more than five weeks, one or both of them could be pregnant when you buy them.

Give a Rat a Home

Some people don't think carefully before they buy rats and decide they don't want to keep them after a while. The American Fancy Rat and Mouse Association Society can give you details of how to "adopt" a homeless rat. It is better to do this if you have owned rats before and are already confident about caring for them.

Questions & Answers

* **What colors are rats?**
  Rats come in lots of different colors, such as pink-eyed white, black-eyed cream, cinnamon, and chocolate.

* **Can I buy a rat by myself?**
  No. You will need to take an adult with you to buy a rat. Responsible rat breeders and pet shops will not sell to a child under the age of 16.

* **What is the best age to buy?**
  It is best to buy a baby rat that is around six weeks old. Older rats take longer to get used to you, and younger ones are too young to leave their mothers.

Handling Your Rats

When you bring your new rats home, give them as much attention as you can and handle them as often as possible. The more you hold and cuddle your rats, the more fun you will have with them. Don't forget to wash your hands with soap and water after playing with your pets.

Take Your Time

When you first put your rats in their new cage, give them some time to get used to their new surroundings. Don't pick them up right away. Put one of your old, unwashed T-shirts in their nest box (see page 19) so that they can get used to your smell. Talk to your pets to let them get used to the sound of your voice.

Holding Rats

To pick up your rat, put one hand on its back and scoop up its bottom and back legs with your other hand. Hold your pet against your body for comfort and warmth. Never pick up your rat by its tail or squeeze its body—this will really hurt it.

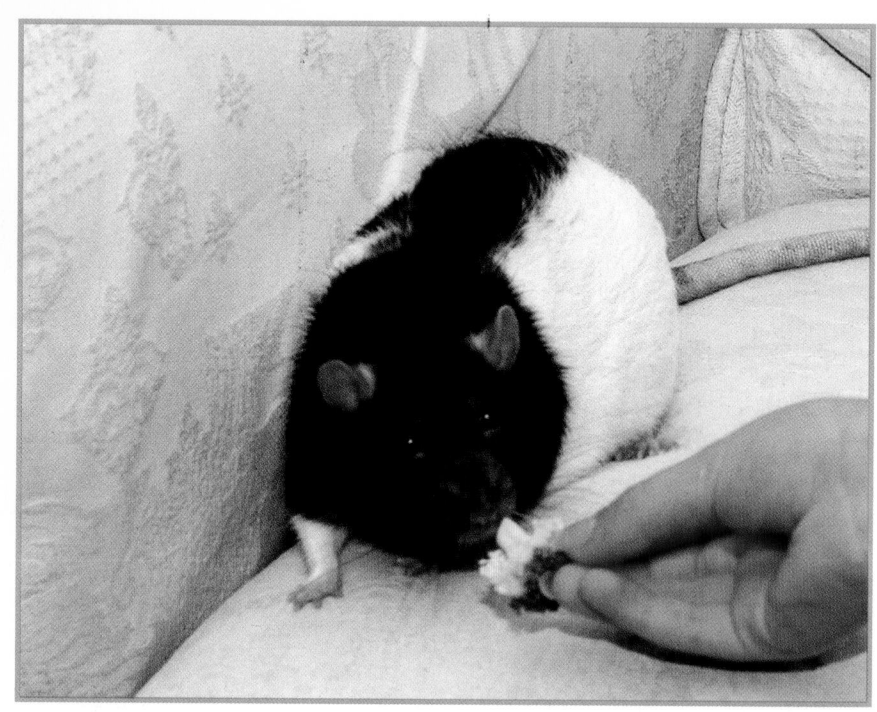

Let your rat get used to you before you give it food from your hand. Try not to feed it snacks too often or it may gain too much weight.

The First Time

Your rat may be a little nervous the first time you pick it up, and may start to wriggle. Hold it calmly and firmly. Don't make any sudden movements or you will frighten your pet. Don't give up if things aren't easy at first. Remember that the more you handle your pet rat, the quicker it will become really tame.

Friendly Rats

It is important to handle rats when they are very young. If rats are handled a lot when they are tiny, they will bond quickly with their owners.

Good Friends

You can never give your rats too much attention. Once you start handling your rats, they will soon get used to you and enjoy being with you. They may play with your hair and even lick your face!

Questions & Answers

* **Why can't I pick up my rats as soon as I get them home?**
  Your rats need to get over the shock of moving away from their first home and get used to their new environment. Leave them for a couple of hours before you pick them up.

* **How do I know when my rats are ready to be held?**
  Once your rats have learned to recognize your voice and smell, they will be happy to let you pick them up. They should be confident enough to take food from your hand when you offer it.

* **How long should I spend holding my rats every day?**
  There is no set amount of time. The more the better!

Will It Bite?

Don't worry that your rat might bite you. Biting is very unusual, and only happens if a rat has been taken by surprise or is very frightened and defensive. Some "teenage" male rats or pregnant and nursing females will bite if provoked. If a rat continues to bite, you may have to take it to a vet to be neutered. Most aggression is hormonal and can be treated in this way.

Rats like riding on your shoulder.

Rat Companions

Rats are extremely sociable animals. They like the company of other rats and enjoy life more if they are kept together in pairs or a small group. Keeping two rats is just as easy as keeping one, and the pair will be much happier and more interesting for you to watch.

These two brothers have been together since birth and are great friends.

Family Group

It is best to keep rats in groups of two or more of the same sex, preferably brothers or sisters from the same litter. They will already know each other well and will be used to one another's company.

Breeding Rats

Female rats can have babies when they are just four weeks old, and males can father babies at five weeks old. But it's not advisable for rats to breed so young. If you are serious about breeding your rats, wait until they are older (about six months), and ask a respected rat breeder for advice.

Old Friends

Try to introduce rats to each other before they are ten weeks old. Older rats take longer to get used to new rats. To introduce two older rats, clean out their cages to get rid of the territorial scent. Then, dab both rats with scent (such as vanilla essence) and let them play together on neutral ground. After a week, you can put them in the same cage. If they fight a lot, you may have to give up—not all rats get along.

Rats are very clean animals, and spend a lot of time grooming each other.

Out at Night

A rat's most active time is in the middle of the night. You will be asleep, so your rat needs the company of other rats at this time!

Play Time

Rats are fun to watch as they play. Sometimes, young "teenage" bucks (four to six months old) may have a fight, but only to figure out who is the boss—this isn't usually a serious fight. Does rarely fight with each other.

Time Out

If two rats are having a fight, never put your hand in their cage to separate them. They may bite you by accident or in self-defense. Instead, spray both animals with water, or throw a light towel over them. When they have stopped fighting, separate them so they can calm down. Then put them back together in their cage.

Questions & Answers

✶ **Will two rats bond with each other and become less tame with me?**
No. A pair of rats is much more content and confident than a single rat. As a result, the pair will be very easy to tame.

✶ **How big a cage will a pair of rats need if I keep them together?**
You should allow a minimum of two square feet (60 sq cm) per rat.

✶ **What if my rats have babies?**
They won't if you have been told the correct sex of your rats and you keep males and females apart. But if one of your female rats was pregnant when you bought her, she will have babies. If this happens, contact your pet shop or rat breeder for advice.

Housing Rats

Your pet rats should live indoors in your home, but if this is not possible, they could also live in your shed or garage. They need to be kept inside so they don't get too hot or cold and are not exposed to wild animals or disease.

Behind Bars

Cages with metal bars are best for rats. They allow fresh air to circulate in the cage, and your rats will enjoy experiencing the sounds and smells that come their way. A wire cage also provides an excellent climbing frame for your playful pets. You can stroke your rats through the bars and feed them treats every now and then.

Rats need lots of room, and will make good use of all the space you give them.

Choosing a Cage

Get a tall and roomy wire cage with a plastic or metal tray underneath that is easy to clean. The bars should be close together, so your rats can't escape. For the same reason, make sure that all the panels and doors are secure. A wooden hutch is not a good idea because your rats will chew the wood. Plastic tanks are not recommended because their ventilation is poor.

Bigger Is Better

The bigger the cage the better it is—rats can't have too much room to play. Each of your rats needs at least two square feet (60 sq cm) of living space. Check the exact size of a cage before you buy it, because every bit of space makes a difference to a rat. Make sure you have enough room at home for your cage before you buy it.

Hot and Cold

The ideal temperature for a rat is between 45°F and 75°F (7°C and 24°C). Your rats may become ill if they are colder or hotter than this.

Questions & Answers

* **Is it OK to buy a second-hand rat cage?**
  Yes, but make sure you disinfect, rinse, and dry it thoroughly before you put your new rats in it.
* **Can I keep my rats in a hamster cage?**
  No. Not even three-story hamster cages are big enough for rats, and they don't give your rats enough chances to climb.
* **Isn't a wire cage too drafty for my rats?**
  No. They need the ventilation, but they will also need a warm, sheltered nest box (see page 19) to sleep in.

Too Hot or Cold?

Rats don't like to be too hot or too cold, but they usually find it harder to cope with very high temperatures. If it gets hotter than 86°F (30°C) rats can die from heat stroke. Make sure your rats' cage is out of direct sunlight and away from radiators. Remember that your rats don't like cold either, so keep their cage away from drafts. If it gets very cold, give them extra warm bedding.

Keep your rats somewhere in your home where they can become part of the family. Always make sure the cage is securely closed.

Prime Position

Think carefully about where to put your rats' cage. If you can, place it up high on a table or chest of drawers in a busy part of your home, such as the living room. This will make it easy for you and your family to see your rats and interact with them. Rats are sociable creatures, so they will also enjoy being able to see you and your family.

Roaming Rats

Rats are intelligent animals, so they quickly get bored with their cage and need to go exploring. Let your rats roam free outside their cage every day. You will need to make a few small changes to the room you let them loose in, but it is well worth the trouble you take to give your rats this exciting experience.

Rat Room

Choose a room in your home that your rats can roam around in safely. Ask an adult to help you "rat-proof" the room. You will have to remove or cover anything that could be a danger to your pets. You may also need to protect your furniture. Male rats scent-mark their territory with drops of urine, so you may decide to cover some furniture.

Electric Danger

All rats like to chew, so you must ask an adult to move all electrical cables out of your pets' reach. If one of your rats chews through a wire, it could die from an electric shock. If it isn't possible to move all the cables out of the way, cover them with hosepipe or aquarium tubing.

Don't let a roaming rat get under blankets or inside furniture, or someone might sit on it by accident!

Getting Ready

When you "rat-proof" a room, move all your precious items out of the way, including clothes, books, and fragile ornaments. Remove all houseplants as well, because some plants are poisonous to rats. Your rats could also make a big mess by digging into the plant pots!

Rats will take a liking to any small objects that they can carry off to chew.

Rat's-Eye View

It may help to lie on the floor and look around, imagining that you are as small as a rat. Can you see any rat-sized holes or good hiding places? You will need to "rat-proof" these. Ask an adult to seal any cracks in the baseboards or floorboards. Finally, close all the doors and windows to the room, so that there are no escape routes.

Stay Indoors

Only let your rats loose in a room that has been specially prepared for this purpose. Never allow your rats to roam free outside the house. If they got lost, they would quickly starve or be killed by wild animals.

Roaming Time

Rats need to roam free for at least an hour every day.

Questions & Answers

* **Can I leave the room when my rats are roaming free?**
  Rats can easily get into trouble, so it's best not to leave them on their own. If you do need to leave the room for an urgent reason, ask someone in the family to watch them while you are gone.
* **Should I take my shoes off when my rats are roaming?**
  Yes, because you may step on your pets by accident and hurt them.
* **Can my rats play with my other pets?**
  Don't let your rats loose near a cat or dog—either of these animals could kill your rats if they wanted to. Take great care introducing your pets to each other, and never leave them alone together. You must also be aware that rats are predators. Don't let them get close to any other small animals or birds.

Litter and Bedding

Rats like to have a nice, cozy place to sleep. You must put clean, soft bedding in your rats' nest box, so they have a warm, secure bed to rest in. Your rats enjoy eating and drinking, but this means they will wet and soil their cage. You will need to put special litter at the bottom of their cage to soak up the mess and prevent odors.

Rat Litter

Buy the right kind of litter to line the bottom of your rats' cage. It is best to use shredded cardboard or paper-based litters. Put enough litter in to cover the entire base to a thickness of about 1 inch (2-3 cm).

The Right Type

Make sure that the litter you use is not too fine or dusty, or it may hurt your rats' eyes and get up their noses, making it hard to breathe. Don't use paper bedding or wood shavings that have been treated with aromatic oils—this is sometimes called "deodorized bedding." There can be chemicals called phenols in these types of bedding that will harm your rats' respiratory (breathing) system.

The litter you use will absorb the moisture from your rats' urine and droppings.

Make a Nest Box

Rats need nest boxes to sleep in. You can buy these in pet shops, but you can also make your own from an ice cream tub or a small plastic bucket. Your rats will be happy to share a nest box, but you may want to put two or more in their cage.

Cozy Bed

You will need to fill your rats' nest box with the right kind of bedding, which will soak up any moisture and make a snug bed. You can buy rat bedding material from pet shops or use paper towels or toilet paper rolls from home. Don't use cotton wool for bedding; your rats could choke on this if they swallowed it.

Bed Wetters

Rats are clean animals, but they do have a habit of wetting their nest boxes. Check your rats' nest box every day and remove wet bedding if necessary.

Paper Shredder

If you give your rats paper towel for bedding material, don't bother to tear it up first. Your rats will have lots of fun shredding it all by themselves, and this will save you time and effort!

Most types of shredded paper will make good bedding for your rats' nest box.

Questions & Answers

* **Can I put cat litter in my rat cage?**
  Yes, but be careful which type you use. Only recycled paper cat litter is suitable for rats.
* **Can I use newspaper as bedding?**
  Yes, but only if it is printed with non-toxic ink. If the ink runs when it is wet, then it is vegetable-based and safe for your rats—but be aware that it could stain the fur of light-colored rats.
* **Can I use straw or hay as bedding?**
  Yes, and some people like to do this. However, it is not very good at getting rid of smells and soaking up liquid. If you do buy hay or straw, get it from a pet shop and not a farm, or it might have ticks and fleas that could make your rats ill.

Rat Toys

Rats are playful and inquisitive, so it is very important for them to have a variety of things to play with. Most pet shops sell a good range of rat toys. You can also make your own toys or use things that you find around the house.

Good Toys

Baby and young rats really enjoy playing with toys. Suitable toys include bits of plastic drainpipe, large glass jars, cardboard boxes, and even old clothes. Hamster and gerbil toys are also good for small rats to play with. However, you must make sure the toys you give your rats are not too small, or they could swallow them.

Use your imagination to create an interesting home for your pets.

Playground

Your rats' cage can be made into an exciting adventure playground for your pets. Simply attach ropes, hammocks, ladders, or branches to the sides of the cage. You could also place small flowerpots and plastic tunnels on the cage floor to make a maze.

Climbing High

If you have a tall cage, don't forget to make good use of all the space. You can make extra shelves by sliding wipe-clean boards between the bars of the cage. Your rats will use these to climb on. You may need to attach a safety net under the shelves, in case your rats fall off them. Check first that the net is strong enough to hold your rats' weight.

Your rats will enjoy the challenge of an obstacle course in a rat-proofed room.

Play Time

Older rats are not as interested in toys, but still like to play games with their cage mates. They also love human contact, so you must play with them. Let them run up your sleeves and rest on your shoulders. Have some fun by laying out obstacle courses for your rats—you could use cardboard tubes, ladders, mirrors, and balls.

Balancing Act

Rats use their tails to keep their balance. A rat's tail can be as long as its body.

Wheel Problem

It is not a good idea to put a wire exercise wheel in your rats' cage. They are too small for adult rats. If a rat catches its tail between the bars, it will get a painful injury. Plastic wheels are also dangerous for rats, because they may chew the plastic and reach the sharp metal spikes beneath.

Questions & Answers

* **Can my rats have too many toys?** Yes. Be careful not to fill the cage with so many toys that your rats don't have any space left to run around.

* **Will my rats chew their toys?** Yes. Rats chew almost everything! Give your rats a chew toy from a pet shop to help keep their teeth short.

* **If I put branches in my rats' cage, should I take the bark off?** No. Bark will help to keep your rats' nails short. However, you should make sure that any branches you put in the cage haven't been sprayed with pesticides. Pesticides can harm your rat.

Food and Diet

Rats are omnivores, which means they eat all kinds of food. It is best to give your rats fresh, wholesome food to eat. Don't give too much of any one thing—your rats' diet should be varied and healthy, just like yours should be. Don't overfeed your rats or they will become fat.

Pet Shop Food

You can buy ready-mixed rat food from pet shops. Often, your rats will like one part of the mix more than the rest, and they may try to leave the bits they don't like. Give your rats a small amount of the mix at a time, and only give them more when the first portion is all eaten. You should also put a mineral lick in your rats' cage to give them nutrients that may be missing from their diet.

Fruit and vegetables are an essential part of a healthy diet for rats.

Fruit and Vegetables

Your rats need fiber in their diet, so they must eat fresh fruit and vegetables. Avoid acidic fruits like oranges, but try other fruits such as apples and bananas. Your rats will enjoy trying different vegetables such as carrots and curly kale. Don't give them too much fruit or too many vegetables, or your rats may get upset stomachs. It's best to offer your rats fruit and vegetables every other day.

Treats

You can give your rats healthy, tasty treats to spice up their diet. They will enjoy many different foods, including low protein dog biscuits, cooked bones, cooked legumes (such as lentils), live yogurt, unsweetened cereals, brown pasta, brown bread, and brown rice. Don't offer your rats sweet or salty snacks, such as chocolate, cakes, ice cream, or chips. These snacks are bad for their health.

Fresh Water

It is very important to give your rats fresh, cool water every day, preferably in a water bottle. Scrub the bottle with a bottlebrush once a week to keep it clean. Remember to replace the bottle with a new one every few months.

Substitute Care

When you go on vacation, make sure the person who is going to care for your rats knows what to feed them and when. You will probably need to write down some instructions. You should also leave details of someone to call in case of an emergency.

Don't let your rats run out of drinking water, especially on hot days.

Questions & Answers

* **When should I feed my rats?**
  Rats are most active in the evening. It is often best to feed them then.

* **How much food should I give my rats?**
  It is a good idea to give food in small amounts, and then give more if necessary. If your rats are leaving a lot of food, you are probably over-feeding them.

* **How often should I give my rats a food treat?**
  Save treats until after your rats have eaten their main food. Don't give too much—just a taste, such as a few dog biscuit crumbs or a small spoonful of live yogurt.

Regular Routine

Rats like to have a regular routine. Feed your rats at the same time every day. They will soon learn when to expect food and will be waiting for you.

Keeping Clean

You must remember to clean your rats' cage regularly, or it will become an unpleasant and unhealthy place for them to live. The cage will begin to smell and your family will probably start to complain! Cleaning out your rats' cage isn't difficult, and it won't take you long to do.

Cleaning your rats' cage should become part of your regular weekly routine. Always remember to wash your hands afterwards.

Clean Cage

When you clean your rats' cage, first take out the toys and throw away the litter and bedding. Wipe down the surfaces with a mild disinfectant bought from a pet shop. Remember to wipe the toys and branches too. Then wash off the disinfectant with water. When everything is dry, put fresh bedding back into the cage. Don't forget to wear plastic gloves when you clean your rats' cage.

Daily Check

You should also do a small clear-out every day. Remove any droppings and unwanted food scattered about the cage floor. Check that the bedding is clean and dry, scooping out any wet material and replacing it with fresh bedding. Wash the food bowl and remember to clean the water bottle if necessary.

Bath Time

Rats spend a lot of time grooming themselves and each other. You shouldn't have to wash your rats' coats to keep them clean. However, if you want to enter your rats in a show, you may need to bathe them. Use lukewarm water and small-animal shampoo when you do this.

Water Fun

Every now and again, give your rats some water in a bowl. A dog water bowl is best, because it is too heavy for them to tip over. Your rats will like to use the water for washing. You could encourage them to play in the water by putting in a few frozen peas. Your rats will get very wet!

Great Groomers

Rats spend about one third of their waking life grooming themselves.

Tail Trouble

Some rats don't clean their tails very well. You can remove stains on your rats' tails by brushing them with a soft toothbrush and some small–animal shampoo. Wet the tail first, then carefully brush away from the body towards the tip. Be very gentle—rough brushing will hurt your rats.

Rats are naturally very clean animals.

Questions & Answers

* **How often should I clean my rats' cage?**
  You should clean your rats' cage once or twice a week. Don't clean it every day, or your rats will feel insecure—rats don't like it when their own smell is removed too often. Male rats will scent-mark more frequently if you "overclean" their cage.
* **Where should I put my rats when I am cleaning their cage?**
  You could put them in a rat-proofed room with someone to watch them. Or, you can buy a rat carrier. These are very handy for trips to the vet and are also a good place to put your rats when you're cleaning their cage.
* **What is the best way to bathe my rat?**
  Fill two bowls with lukewarm water. Use one for washing your rat with small-animal shampoo and the other for rinsing your rat. Have a soft towel on hand to gently dry your rat after its bath.

Health Check

You need to check your rats regularly to make sure that they are keeping fit and well. A healthy rat should be lively, alert, and interested in its food. It should have a shiny and well-groomed coat and clean ears and tail. Its droppings shouldn't be too hard or too runny, and there should be no bumps or swellings on its body.

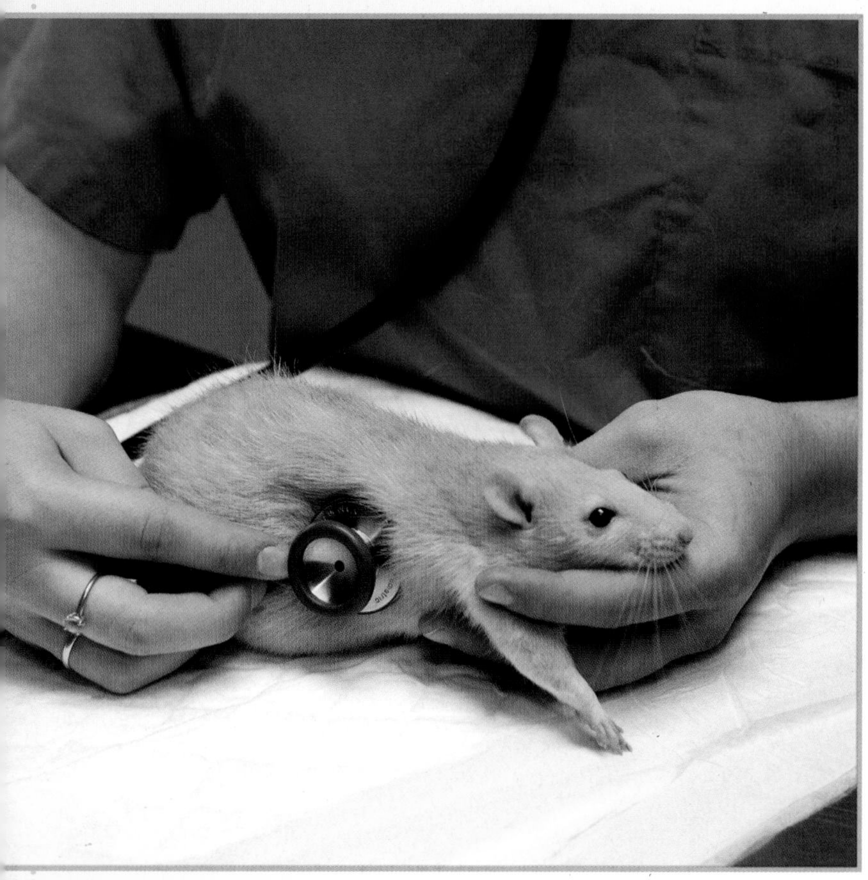

A good vet will tell you what to do if your rat gets ill.

Get a Vet

Rats are small animals, which means if they get ill, they can go downhill very fast. Make sure you find a good local vet as soon as you get your rats. This way, you will know where to go quickly if one of your rats becomes ill.

Warning Signs

It is not a good sign if one of your rats is hunched up in its cage and looks too tired to move. Listen to your rat's breathing, and take note if it is wheezy. If your rat loses interest in you and its food, or its coat starts to look scruffy, you must take it to the vet.

Body Language

Keep an eye on how your rat moves around in the cage. If it has a limp, it may be injured and in pain. If it holds its head on one side, it may have an ear problem. In both cases, you should go straight to the vet.

Long in the Tooth

A rat's teeth never stop growing. Rats need to gnaw and chew things to keep their teeth short.

Tooth and Nail

A rat with overgrown teeth won't be able to eat properly and can even starve. If your rat's teeth don't meet properly, they will need regular trimming by a vet to stop them from growing too long. Check your rat's teeth often, and get them trimmed if they look overgrown. It is also important to have your rat's nails clipped regularly. Get a vet or an adult to do this for you, using small animal nail clippers.

You can check your rat's nails and teeth when you are playing with your pet.

Weight Problem

Once your rats are adults, they should stay at about the same weight. If they suddenly lose or gain weight, they could be ill. Don't overfeed your rats—fat rats live shorter lives and are more likely to get sick. Healthy does should be lean and sleek, and bucks should be strong and muscular.

Questions & Answers

* **What should I do if my rat looks ill?**
  First of all, talk about it with an adult. Then, ask if they can take you and your pet to the vet. You may have to give your rat antibiotics to clear up an infection.
* **Will my rat get better?**
  Rats can get ill quickly, but given the right treatment, they can also make good recoveries. Recovery also depends on exactly what is wrong with your rat, and only a vet will know that.
* **How do I know if my rat's teeth and nails are too long?**
  If your rat's teeth are too long, they won't bite food properly and your rat will find it hard to eat. If your rat's nails are too long, it will scratch you when you pick it up.

Old Age

Rats need company, exercise, and a healthy diet to live a full and happy life. Sadly, however well and carefully you look after your rats, they will still grow old. As rats get older, they slow down, get weaker, and become prone to illness. You need to give your old rats a quiet life with lots of gentle care and affection.

If your rat gets heat stroke, cover it carefully with a damp towel.

Catching a Cold

Just like you, rats are prone to catching colds, and they are more likely to do this in old age. Watch for a runny nose, red eyes, wheezes, and sneezes. If your rat gets a cold, keep it warm and give it lots of water to drink. Take it to the vet, since it probably won't get better on its own.

Watch the Heat

It is always important to watch the temperature, especially for older rats. If your rat gets too hot, it could get heat stroke. You will need to wrap your rat in a damp towel to cool it down.

Keeping Warm

If your old rat gets cold, it could also become ill. You can revive your rat by slipping it under your clothes to warm it up with your body heat.

Some older rats can't see very well and are not as active as they used to be.

Head for Heights

Old rats become less agile and their eyesight may deteriorate. Some rats may also lose their sense of balance. It is a good idea to remove any ladders, branches, or climbing toys from their cage, so that they won't fall off and hurt themselves.

A Rat's Life

Most rats live for about two and a half years, but some can live up to four years.

Saying Goodbye

Many rats die naturally of old age. But if your rat is very sick, it may be kindest to talk to your vet about having it put to sleep. This is completely painless for your rat and a peaceful, gentle way to say goodbye to your old friend.

Questions & Answers

* **Will my rat look old?**
  When your rat is about two years old, it will start to look old. Its coat will get thinner, and it will begin to move more stiffly.

* **Should I bury my pet when it dies?**
  Some people find that it helps them to make a special burial place in the yard for their pet.

* **How can I remember my rat?**
  Take lots of photos of your rat throughout its life. Make a scrapbook, and label the pictures. You will enjoy looking at the photos and remembering the fun you had with your pet.

Glossary

alert
Lively, watchful, and interested in everything.

antibiotics
Medicines used to treat infectious diseases.

bedding
Soft material used to provide a warm, comfortable bed.

breed
To have babies.

bucks
Male rats are called bucks.

diet
The food that animals usually eat. Rats should have a varied and healthy diet.

does
Female rats are called does.

fancy rats
Pet rats are called fancy rats. Unlike wild rats, fancy rats have special colors or patterns on their fur.

grooming
Grooming is cleaning an animal's coat. Rats spend lots of time grooming themselves and each other.

hormonal
Controlled by hormones, the chemicals made in the bodies of plants and animals that affect their actions and responses.

kittens
Baby rats are called kittens.

litter
A litter is a group of baby rats born at the same time, with the same mother. Litter is also the material you use to line the bottom of your rats' cage.

mineral lick
A solid block for your rats to lick, containing nutrients that could be missing from their diet.

nest box
A snug place for your rats to rest and sleep that is both warm and secure.

nursing female
A female rat that is feeding milk to her newborn babies.

omnivores
Animals that eat all kinds of food, both plants and meat.

predator
An animal that hunts other animals.

put to sleep
To give a sick animal an injection to help it die peacefully.

rodents
A group of small, gnawing animals that includes rats, mice, hamsters, gerbils, squirrels, and beavers.

scent-marking
A male rat's habit of marking territory with a few drops of his urine.

species
A group of one type of animal or plant.

territory
An area that belongs to a single individual.

vermin
Vermin are animals that cause problems for people, often by carrying diseases. Pet rats are not vermin, but wild rats are.

Further Information

If you want to learn more about types of rats, buying rats, caring for rats, or if you would like to get involved in animal welfare, these are some helpful Web sites:

American Fancy Rat and Mouse Association
AFRMA promotes and encourages the breeding and exhibition of fancy rats and mice. It gives useful information on how to care for them.
Web site: www.afrma.org

North American Rat and Mouse Club, International
A club for rat and mouse owners, NARMCI educates the general public on how wonderful rats and mice are as well as debunks the negative myths surrounding them.
Web site: http://narmci.8k.com/index.html

People for the Ethical Treatment of Animals
The largest animals rights group in the world. Contains information promoting the safety and responsible treatment of animals.
Web site: www.peta.org

Rat Care: The 411
A site for kids run by the American Society for the Prevention of Cruelty to Animals (ASPCA) with information on how to care for rats.
Web site: http://www.aspca.org/site/PageServer?pagename=kids_pc_rat_411

The Rat Fan Club
A Web site for people who enjoy rats as pets. Includes information on caring for rats, locating breeders, and finding veterinarians.
Web site: http://www.ratfanclub.org/

Rat and Mouse Club of America (RMCA)
Good source of information about keeping fancy rats. The club hosts regular rat keeping events.
Web site: www.rmca.org

Note to parents and teachers: Every effort has been made by the publishers to ensure that these Web sites are suitable for children, that they are of the highest educational value, and that they contain no inappropriate or offensive material. However, because of the nature of the Internet, it is impossible to guarantee that the contents of these sites will not be altered. We strongly advise that Internet access is supervised by a responsible adult.

Index

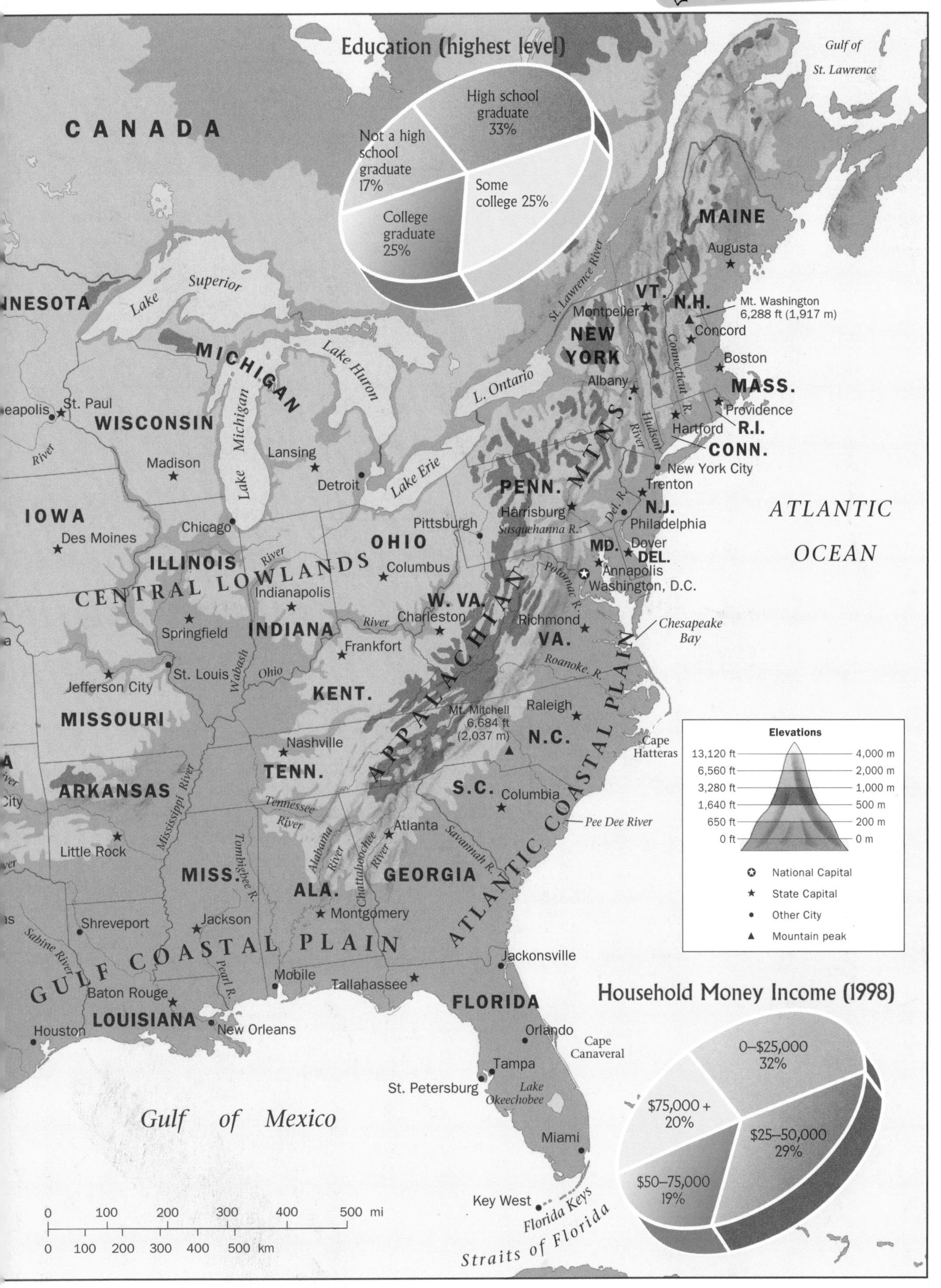
Education (highest level)
High school graduate 33%
Not a high school graduate 17%
Some college 25%
College graduate 25%
CANADA
Gulf of St. Lawrence
MAINE
Augusta
VT.
N.H.
Mt. Washington 6,288 ft (1,917 m)
Montpelier
Concord
NEW YORK
Boston
MASS.
Albany
Providence
R.I.
Hartford
CONN.
New York City
Trenton
N.J.
Philadelphia
PENN.
Harrisburg
Susquehanna R.
Del. R.
Hudson River
Connecticut R.
St. Lawrence River
L. Ontario
Lake Erie
Lake Huron
Lake Superior
Lake Michigan
MINNESOTA
Minneapolis
St. Paul
WISCONSIN
Madison
MICHIGAN
Lansing
Detroit
IOWA
Des Moines
Chicago
ILLINOIS
CENTRAL LOWLANDS
Pittsburgh
OHIO
Columbus
MD.
Dover
DEL.
Annapolis
Washington, D.C.
Potomac R.
ATLANTIC OCEAN
Indianapolis
Springfield
INDIANA
W. VA.
Charleston
Richmond
VA.
Chesapeake Bay
Frankfort
St. Louis
Jefferson City
Ohio River
Wabash
KENT.
Roanoke. R.
APPALACHIAN MTNS.
MISSOURI
Mt. Mitchell 6,684 ft (2,037 m)
Raleigh
N.C.
Cape Hatteras
Nashville
TENN.
ARKANSAS
Mississippi River
S.C.
Columbia
Tennessee River
Atlanta
Savannah R.
Pee Dee River
Little Rock
Tombigbee R.
Alabama River
Chattahoochee River
MISS.
ALA.
GEORGIA
ATLANTIC COASTAL PLAIN
Montgomery
Shreveport
Jackson
Sabine River
Pearl R.
GULF COASTAL PLAIN
Mobile
Tallahassee
Jacksonville
Baton Rouge
LOUISIANA
New Orleans
Houston
FLORIDA
Orlando
Cape Canaveral
Tampa
St. Petersburg
Lake Okeechobee
Gulf of Mexico
Miami
Key West
Florida Keys
Straits of Florida
Elevations
13,120 ft — 4,000 m
6,560 ft — 2,000 m
3,280 ft — 1,000 m
1,640 ft — 500 m
650 ft — 200 m
0 ft — 0 m
National Capital
State Capital
Other City
Mountain peak
Household Money Income (1998)
0–$25,000 32%
$75,000 + 20%
$25–50,000 29%
$50–75,000 19%
0 100 200 300 400 500 mi
0 100 200 300 400 500 km

GOVERNMENT IN AMERICA

GOVERNMENT IN AMERICA

PEOPLE, POLITICS, AND POLICY

Tenth Edition

GEORGE C. EDWARDS III
Texas A & M University

MARTIN P. WATTENBERG
University of California, Irvine

ROBERT L. LINEBERRY
University of Houston

New York San Francisco Boston
London Toronto Sydney Tokyo Singapore Madrid
Mexico City Munich Paris Cape Town Hong Kong Montreal

Vice President/Publisher: Priscilla McGeehon
Senior Acquisitions Editor: Eric Stano
Development Editor: Adam Beroud
Senior Marketing Manager: Megan Galvin-Fak
Supplements Editor: Kelly Villella
Production Manager: Denise Phillip
Project Coordination, Text Design, and Electronic Page Makeup: WestWords, Inc.
Cover Designer/Manager: John Callahan
Cover Photo: © PhotoDisc
Photo Researcher: Photosearch, Inc.
Senior Manufacturing Buyer: Dennis J. Para
Printer and Binder: Quebecor World
Cover Printer: Phoenix Color Corp.

For permission to use copyrighted material, grateful acknowledgment is made to the copyright holders on pp. 740–742 , which are hereby made part of this copyright page.

Library of Congress Cataloging-in-Publication Data

Edwards, George C.
Government in America : people, politics, and policy / George C. Edwards III, Martin P. Wattenberg, Robert L. Lineberry.—10th ed.
p. cm.
Includes bibliographical references and index.
ISBN 0-321-08777-1
1. United States—Politics and government. I. Wattenberg, Martin P. II. Lineberry, Robert L. III. Title.
JK274 .L573 2002
320.973—dc21 2001020389

Please visit our website at http://www.ablongman.com

ISBN 0-321-08777-1

1 2 3 4 5 6 7 8 9 10—RNV—04 03 02 01

Brief Contents

Part 3 The Policymakers

Part 4 Policies

Part 5 State and Local Government

Detailed Contents

3 Federalism 64

4 Civil Liberties and Public Policy 94

5 Civil Rights and Public Policy 136

Part 2
People and Politics

Part 3 The Policymakers

Part 5 State and Local Government

Preface

POLITICS MATTERS. THAT IS THE CORE MESSAGE OF THIS BOOK. The national government provides important services, ranging from retirement security and health care to recreation facilities and weather forecasts. The national government may also send us to war or negotiate peace with our adversaries, expand or restrict our freedom, raise or lower our taxes, and increase or decrease aid to education. As we enter the twenty-first century, decision makers of both political parties are facing difficult questions regarding American democracy and the scope of our government. Students need a framework for understanding these questions.

Focus

We write *Government in America* to provide our readers with a better understanding of our fascinating political system. This tenth edition of *Government in America* continues to frame its content with a public policy approach to government in the United States. We continually ask—and answer—the question, "What difference does politics make to the policies governments produce?" It is one thing to describe the Madisonian system of checks and balances and separation of powers or the elaborate and unusual federal system of government in the United States; it is something else to ask how these features of our constitutional structure affect the policies that governments generate.

We find that this focus engages students' interest. Students, like their instructors, quickly recognize that the principal reason for studying politics is to understand why government produces the policies it does. What many see as "dry" subjects become interesting when they are tied to outcomes that directly affect each of us. Even introductory students feel comfortable in asking, "So what?" To reinforce this interest, we have a feature in the margins entitled **"Why does it matter?"** in which we ask students to think critically about some aspect of our system and how things might be if it worked differently.

We do not discuss policy at the expense of politics, however. We provide extensive coverage of five core subject areas: constitutional foundations, patterns of political behavior, political institutions, public policy outputs, and state and local government, but we try to do so in a more analytically significant—and interesting—manner. We take special pride in introducing students to relevant work from current political scientists, such as the role of PACs or the impact of divided government—something we have found instructors appreciate.

It is not enough to arouse students' interest, however. To be a useful teaching tool, a text must be accessible to students and enjoyable to read. We believe that a principal reason for the success of *Government in America* is its high level of readability. To ensure that the material is not only clearly presented but also meaningful, we make special efforts to illustrate points with interesting examples to which students can relate. The ability of Congress to indirectly regulate behavior in the states becomes more meaningful when the power is illustrated with a discussion of raising the drinking age. In addition, this is neither a conservative nor a liberal book. Instead, we make every effort to present material in an evenhanded manner. As a result, over the years we have received many letters in which students have told us how much they enjoyed reading the book. Needless to say, we find this response very gratifying.

Two Themes

To render the policy focus in concrete terms, two important themes appear throughout the book: the nature of democracy and the scope of government. Each chapter begins with a preview of the relevancy of these themes to the chapter's subject, refers to the themes at points within the chapter, and ends with specific sections on the two themes under the heading "Understanding . . ." that show how the themes illuminate the chapter's subject matter.

The first great question central to governing, a question that every nation must answer is *How should we govern?* In the United States, our answer is "democracy." Yet democracy is an evolving and somewhat ambiguous concept. In Chapter 1, we define democracy as a means of selecting policymakers and of organizing government so that policy represents and responds to citizens' preferences. As with previous editions, we continue to incorporate theoretical issues in our discussions of different models of American democracy. We try to encourage students to think analytically about the theories and to develop independent assessments of how well the American system lives up to citizens' expectations of democratic government. To help them do this, in every chapter we raise questions about democracy. For example, does Congress give the American people the policies they want? Is a strong presidency good for democracy? Does our mass media make us more democratic? Are powerful courts that make policy decisions compatible with democracy?

A common complaint about the national government is that it cannot respond to the needs of its citizens, that it suffers from *gridlock*. A subtheme to our discussion of democracy is whether America's diversity and the openness of our political system have the drawback of incapacitating government. The diversity of the American people is reflected in the variety of political interests represented in the political system. This system is so open that many different interests find access to policymakers. In our system of checks and balances, opposition by one set of policymakers can sometimes frustrate the will of the majority. We leave it to the reader to determine whether the difficulty of achieving policy change, be it the Clinton health care reform plan or the Republicans' tax cut, is a positive feature of our system. Our goal is to promote understanding of the consequences of the American democratic system and to provoke discussion about these consequences. We find that students are especially interested in why government does not "do something."

The second theme, the scope of government, focuses on another great question of governing: *What should government do?* Here we discuss alternative views concerning the proper role and size for American government and how this scope is influenced by the workings of institutions and politics. The government's scope is the core question around which politics revolves in contemporary America, pervading many crucial issues: To what degree should Washington impose national standards such as speed limits on state policies? How high should taxes be? Do elections encourage politicians to promise more governmental services? Questions about the scope of government are policy questions and thus obviously directly related to our policy approach. Since the scope of government is *the* pervasive question in American politics today, students will have little problem finding it relevant to their lives and interests.

A subtheme of the scope of government is the role of *individualism* in American political life. The people who immigrated to America may have been diverse, but many adopted a common dream of America as a place where people could make it on their own without interference from government. Today, individualism remains a powerful influence in the United States. Americans' strong preference for free markets and limited government has important consequences for public policy. For example, it substantially constrains efforts to intervene in the economy, efforts that have long been the norm in other developed democracies.

At the same time, a central contest in American politics has been between two kinds of individualism. Economic individualism embraces the doctrines of capitalism. The purpose of government is to protect the creativity of entrepreneurs and markets, which leads to well being. Democratic individualism appeals to government to redress the social inequalities that result from economic individualism. Puritans, abolitionists, agrarian populists, prohibitionists, civil rights crusaders, feminists, and the contemporary religious right have preached collective purpose against individualism. Thus, we often employ the concept of individualism in our analysis of the scope of government.

We hope that students—long after reading *Government in America*—will employ these perennial questions about the nature of our democracy and the scope of our government when they examine political events. The specifics of policy issues will change, but questions about whether the government is responsive to the people or whether it should expand or contract its scope will always be with us.

Features

You Are the Policymaker

Six features appear throughout *Government in America:* (1) **You Are the Policymaker/Judge;** (2) **America in Perspective;** (3) **Making a Difference;** (4) **Why Does It Matter?;** (5) **How You Can Make a Difference;** and (6) **Career Profile.** Each of the features plays a particular role in the text to support our approach to American government.

We believe it is important that students recognize and think critically about difficult policy choices they must face as citizens. "**You Are the Policymaker**" asks students to read arguments on both sides of a specific current issue, such as whether we should prohibit PACs, and then to make a policy decision. In Chapters 4 and 5 (Civil Liberties and Civil Rights), this feature is titled "**You Are the Judge**" and presents the student with an actual court case. This feature directly supports our policy approach.

You Are the Judge

There are many ways to teach lessons, and many instructors find that employing a comparative approach helps them to make their points more effectively. Our "**America in Perspective**" feature examines how the United States compares to other countries in areas such as tax rates, voter turnout, and the delivery of public services. Through reading these boxes and comparing the United States to other nations, students can obtain a better perspective on the size of our government and the nature of our democracy.

America in Perspective

In "**Making a Difference**" we focus on an individual who became involved in government and politics and made a difference as a result. Our goal is simple: to show students that individuals, ordinary people, can—and do—make a difference in what government does. This feature nicely complements our increased focus on the relevance of government to our lives.

Making a Difference

We mentioned earlier our feature that appears several times in each chapter's margins entitled "**Why Does It Matter?**" Here we encourage students to think critically about an aspect of government, politics, or policy and ask them to consider the impact—usually on themselves—if things worked differently.

How You Can Make a Difference

Two new features appear in the tenth edition. First, **How You Can Make a Difference** provides students with information on how they can get involved with issues in order to influence how government works or what policies are established. We feel this feature is a natural extension of the "Making a Difference" boxes, which made their first appearance in our last edition. **Career Profile,** our second new feature, focuses on careers in

government by providing profiles of average people employed in areas of government and politics relevant to each chapter. We present details about salaries and benefits and where readers can find additional information about the career. We are confident that this information will help make the material even more relevant—and practical—for students.

Each chapter ends with a contemporary bibliography, a listing of key terms, and Internet resources relevant to the chapter. (The URLs included at the end of each chapter were current when the book went to press. However, changes or updates may have been made to the site at the discretion of the individual site owner or webmaster.)

Finally, as an additional study aid, we also define key terms in the margins of the text when they are first introduced.

Currency

This tenth edition of *Government in America* is completely up to date and incorporates the best recent scholarship on U.S. government. Our emphasis in each chapter on the scope of government is also very timely, as it remains at the core of debates about taxation, regulating tobacco products, campaign finance, and access to health care. We provide comprehensive coverage of the 2000 presidential, congressional, and state elections—both the campaigns and the results—in Chapters 8–10 and 12–13. We also include the latest Supreme Court decisions from 2001 on federalism, civil liberties, civil rights, and other relevant topics. From the numbers for the 2000 census to the backgrounds of President Bush's cabinet members, the text, tables, and figures reflect the most recent available data. Naturally, we devote considerable attention to the new Bush administration in Chapter 13 and to the efforts of both the president and Congress to deal with the budget (Chapter 14), which has become central to American politics and policy.

Graphics play an important role in textbooks, and we have substantially upgraded our figures, graphs, tables, and charts in this edition. We have employed more vibrant colors and worked to make all our graphics easier and more interesting to read. We also provide a brief guide to using graphics following this preface.

It is worth noting here that the website for the tenth edition of *Government in America* (www.aolonline.com/edwards) includes a section of "updates." These updates provide the latest information on campaign finance, voter turnout, and other matters as soon as the data become available. These allow us to offer the most current information between editions and to provide new links to sources of information useful to both students and faculty.

Appendix

The Appendix continues to include the Constitution and the Declaration of Independence, *Federalist Papers No. 10* and *No. 51*, tables on presidents and presidential elections, party control of the presidency and Congress in the twenty-first century, Supreme Court justices serving in the last century, and a glossary of key terms. We continue to provide a list of key terms in Spanish.

Supplements

Print and Technology Supplements for Instructors

Online Course Management

Longman offers comprehensive online course management systems such as CourseCompass, WebCT, and Blackboard in conjunction with this text. These systems provide complete content, class roster, online quizzing and testing, grade administration, and more, over the Internet. Please contact your local Allyn & Bacon/Longman representative for more information.

Instructor's Manual by Jan Leighley of Texas A&M University

The Instructor's Manual includes a list of pedagogical features, learning objectives, chapter outlines, narrative chapter overviews, key terms and definitions, suggestions for further study, media suggestions, and ideas for class discussion.

Test Bank by Jan Leighley of Texas A&M University

The Test Bank has been completely revised and contains thousands of challenging multiple choice, true-false, short answer, and essay questions along with a page-referenced answer key.

Computerized Test Bank on CD-ROM

The printed Test Bank is also available on a cross-platform CD-ROM through our fully networkable computerized testing system, TestGen-EQ. The program's friendly graphical interface enables instructors to view, edit, and add questions; transfer questions to tests; and print tests in a variety of fonts and forms. Search and sort features help instructors locate questions quickly and arrange them in a preferred order. Six question formats are available, including short answer, true-false, multiple choice, essay, matching, and bimodal.

Active Learning Guide

This innovative guide provides instructors with a variety of thoughtful active learning projects for their classrooms. The exercises address important concepts in American government and follow the organization of the text. The simulations and group projects encourage students to get actively involved in course material and to evaluate different perspectives on American government.

PowerPoint® CD-ROM

This PowerPoint® presentation CD includes a lecture outline of the new edition along with graphics from the book.

Transparencies

A set of four-color acetate transparencies includes figures, graphs and tables from the text.

American Government Instructor Presentation Library CD-ROM

This complete multimedia presentation tool provides: a built-in presentation-maker, 200 photographs, 200 figures and graphs from Longman texts, 20 minutes of audio clips, 20 video clips, and links to over 200 websites. Media items can be imported into PowerPoint® presentation programs.

Companion Website (CW) www.ablongman.com/edwards

This online course companion provides a wealth of resources for instructors using *Government in America*. Instructors will have access to lecture outlines, website links, and downloadable visuals from the text. Additionally, instructors can take advantage of Syllabus Builder, an easy-to-use tool that allows them to put their syllabus and assignments on the Web.

American Government Interactive Video

This video includes 27 segments dealing with provocative issues in contemporary American politics. Topics include the school prayer amendment, welfare reform, the role of the Internet in elections, and many more.

Politics in Action Video

Eleven "Lecture Launchers" covering broad topics such as social movements, campaigns, and the passage of a bill, are examined through narrated videos, interviews, edited documentaries and political ads. *Politics in Action* is accompanied by an extensive User's Manual, which provides background, links to topics in our American government texts, and discussion questions.

Longman Video Program

Longman offers a variety of videos to qualified adapters. Ask your local Allyn & Bacon/Longman representative for more information.

Technology Supplements for Students

LongmanParticipate.com

FREE six-month subscription with every new copy of the text. More interactive, more comprehensive, and more in-depth than any American government website currently available, *LongmanParticipate.com* offers instructors and students an exciting new resource for teaching and learning about our political system that's easy to integrate into any course.

For each major topic in American Government there are: *Simulations* that put students in the role of a political actor; *Visual Literacy* exercises that get students interpreting, manipulating, and applying data; *Interactive Timelines* through which students experience the evolution of an aspect of government; *Participation* activities that get students involved; and *Comparative* exercises in which students compare aspects of our system to those of other countries. In addition to activity sets for each major topic, the site also includes: political knowledge quizzes, an interactive research and writing primer, a comprehensive list of links to news and magazine websites, and a daily look back at politically significant events.

Companion Website (CW) www.ablongman.com/edwards

This online course companion provides a wealth of resources for students using *Government in America.* Students will find interactive exercises tied to text material, practice tests, links to related American government sites, a complete guide to conducting research on the Internet, updates to the text from the authors, and more!

Interactive Edition CD-ROM for *Government in America*

FREE when packaged with the text, this unique CD-ROM takes students beyond the printed page and offers them a complete multimedia learning experience. It contains the full text of the book on CD-ROM, with contextually placed media icons—audio, video, web links, activities, practice tests, primary sources, and more—that link students to additional content directly related to key concepts in the text.

ContentSelect™ Research Database

Longman and EBSCO Publishing, leaders in the development of electronic journal databases, have exclusively collaborated to develop the Political Science ContentSelect™ Research Database. Pincodes to access the database can be packaged for *free* with *Government in America*, giving students unlimited access to a customized, searchable collection of 25,000+ discipline-specific articles from top tier academic publications and journals. EBSCO's ContentSelect™ Database lets students do research anywhere and anytime they have an Internet connection.

StudyWizard CD-ROM by Charles Matzke

This computerized student tutorial program, now available on CD-ROM, helps students review and master key concepts in the text. Using chapter and topic summaries, practice test questions, and a comprehensive glossary, *StudyWizard* supplements the text by allowing students the opportunity to explore new topics and test their understanding of terms and ideas already presented in the reading assignments. Students receive immediate feedback on test questions in the form of answer explanations and page references to the text. In addition, the program allows students to print chapter outlines, difficult vocabulary, missed test questions, or a diagnostic report, which includes suggestions for further study.

Print Supplements for Students

Study Guide by Charles Matzke

The Study Guide helps students reinforce themes and concepts they encounter in the text. It includes chapter outlines, key terms, multiple choice, fill-in-the-blank, and essay questions, and exercises that help students test their understanding of the material with real-world applications.

NEW! Discount Subscription to Newsweek Magazine

Available only through Longman, your students can receive 12 issues of *Newsweek* at more than 80 percent off the regular subscription price! Also included in this offer is an instructor's manual prepared by *Newsweek*. The reduced rate subscription cards come shrink-wrapped with *Government in America*—ask your local Allyn & Bacon/ Longman representative how to take advantage of this offer.

Penguin-Putnam Paperback Titles at a Significant Discount

Longman offers 25 Penguin titles discounted more than 60 percent when packaged with *Government in America*. It's a unique offer and a wonderful way to enhance students' understanding of concepts in American government. Ask your local representative for a full listing of discounted Penguin titles and for information on how to order these books for your classes.

Ten Things Every American Government Student Should Read by Karen O'Connor

FREE when packaged with the text. We asked American Government instructors across the country to vote for the 10 things beyond the text—essays, documents, articles—that they believed every American government student should read. The top vote-getters in each of 10 categories were put into this unique and useful reader by Karen O'Connor of The American University.

Getting Involved: A Guide to Student Citizenship

FREE when packaged with the text, this practical handbook guides students through political participation with concrete advice and extensive sample material—letters, telephone scripts, student interviews, and real-life anecdotes. The aim of this exciting new guide is to generate student enthusiasm for political involvement and then help students to get connected, set goals and strategies, experiment with tactics, build networks, anticipate obstacles, and make a difference in their lives and communities.

Guide to the Internet for American Government, Second Edition

FREE when packaged with the text, this guide introduces students and instructors to ways in which the Internet can be used to explore American government. It includes practical information about the Internet, critical thinking exercises to reinforce students' application of Internet-based skills, and a glossary of Internet terms. In addition, the guide offers dozens of relevant websites that allow students to discover firsthand how the Web can be used as a resource for research.

Writing in Political Science, Second Edition by Diane Schmidt

Available at a significant discount when packaged with the text, writing in political science requires a distinct set of skills, vocabulary, sources, and methods of inquiry. This guide takes students step by step through all the aspects of writing for political science courses. With an abundance of samples from actual students, the guide also features a section on how to address writing problems and a new section on how to evaluate and cite Internet sources.

California State Supplement

FREE when packaged with the text, this 64-page supplement on state and local issues in California was created for use in the American government course. It introduces students to California's basic governmental structures and explores the political effects of California's Progressive tradition.

Texas State Supplement

FREE when packaged with the text, this is a brief primer on state and local issues in Texas for use in the American government course. This supplement includes discussion of the Constitution, the major branches of government, public policy, and other aspects of Texas politics.

Acknowledgments

Many, many colleagues have kindly given us comments on the drafts of the tenth edition of *Government in America.* They are:

Valentine J. Belfiglio, Texas Woman's College

Craig Bauer, Orr Lady of Holy Cross College

Myles L. Clowers, San Diego City College

Sara Trowbridge Combs, Virginia Highlands Community College

Forest Grieves, University of Montana

Haroon A. Khan, Henderson State University

Lisa Langenbach, Middle Tennessee State University

Michael Leuy, Southeast Missouri St. University

Cecilia G. Manrique, University of Wisconsin—La Crosse

Amy S. Patterson, Elmhurst College

Joseph Romance, Drew University

Harry L. Wilson, Roanoke College

A number of editors have provided valuable assistance in the production of this tenth edition of *Government in America.* Adam Beroud was a superb developmental editor, coordinating every aspect of the book. Production manager Denise Phillip deftly guided the production process. Editor Eric Stano provided valuable guidance. We are grateful to all of them. Finally, we owe a special debt of gratitude to Professor Donald Haider-Markel of the University of Kansas, who did an excellent job drafting Chapter 21, and Professors Paul Fessler of Culver-Stockton College and Lisa Langenbach of Middle Tennessee State University for their work on the new features *How You Can Make a Difference* and *Career Profile.*

George C. Edwards III
Martin P. Wattenberg
Robert L. Lineberry

A Student Guide to Reading Charts and Graphs

Information such as voting turnout in the last election, the president's job approval rating, or expenditures on national defense is often presented in quantitative form—that is, through the use of numbers. To help you understand this information, we employ charts and graphs. These figures provide a straightforward, visual representation of quantitative information. Yet charts and graphs can be confusing if you do not understand how to read them.

When you come across one of the charts and graphs in this book, you should ask three questions: First, *what is being measured?* This could be money, public opinion, seats in Congress, or a wide range of other subjects. Second, *what is the unit of measurement?* Is it 50 Americans or 50 percent of Americans? Obviously, it makes a difference. Finally, *what is the purpose of the figure?* Does it show changes over time? Does it compare two or more groups of people or countries? In most instances, captions are provided to explain the purpose of a figure.

After answering these general questions, you should examine the specific type of figure. This text relies on three main types of figures: pie charts, bar graphs, and line graphs. A *pie chart* is a circle divided into wedge-shaped "slices," or segments. Pie charts show the relative sizes of the segments to one another and to the whole. For example, by glancing at the following chart, you can quickly see that the federal government spends more of its funds on Social Security (23 percent) than on Medicare and Medicaid (19 percent). The area of each segment is the same percent of the total circle as the number it represents is of the sum of all the numbers in the chart. Since Social Security accounts for 23 percent of federal expenditures, its corresponding segment covers 23 percent of the area of the pie chart.

Federal Revenues and Expenditures

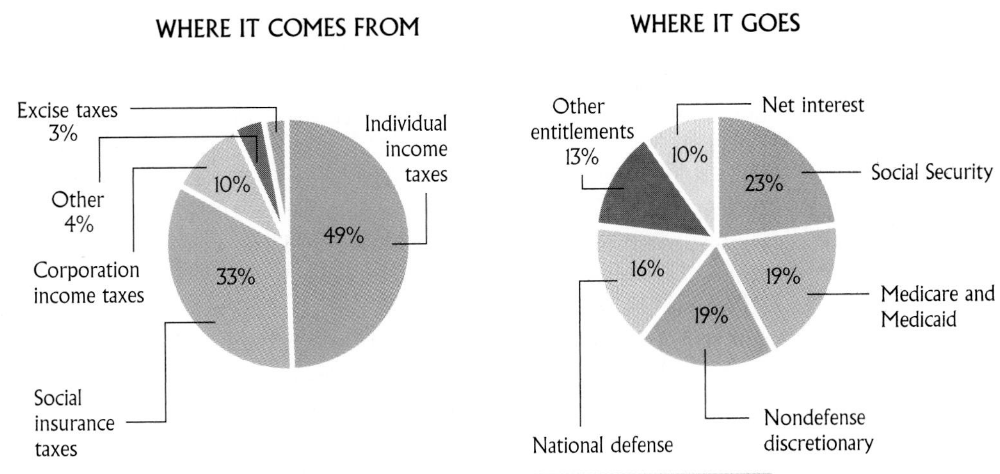

Source: Budget of the United States Government, Fiscal Year 2002 A Citizen's Guide to the Federal Budget, (Washington, D.C.: U.S. Government Printing Office, 2001), 5,9.

The second kind of figure, a *bar graph,* displays quantitative information by using rectangles (bars) set within two perpendicular lines, a vertical axis and a horizontal axis. Bar graphs are most frequently used to show and compare the values of multiple entities at a given point in time. Categories (such as groups of people or countries) are set along one axis and a scale (time or numbers, for example) is on the other axis. The length of each bar corresponds to its value on the scale. This makes it easy to visually contrast the values for multiple entities. For example, in the bar graph shown here, which uses a scale measuring poverty rates, you can see that the bars representing persons of African American origin, young people, and unmarried females are the longest, indicating that they are the most likely to be living in poverty. The characteristics of people are on the vertical axis and on the bars themselves, and the scale representing the percentage of people in poverty is on the horizontal axis.

Poverty Rates for Persons With Selected Characteristics

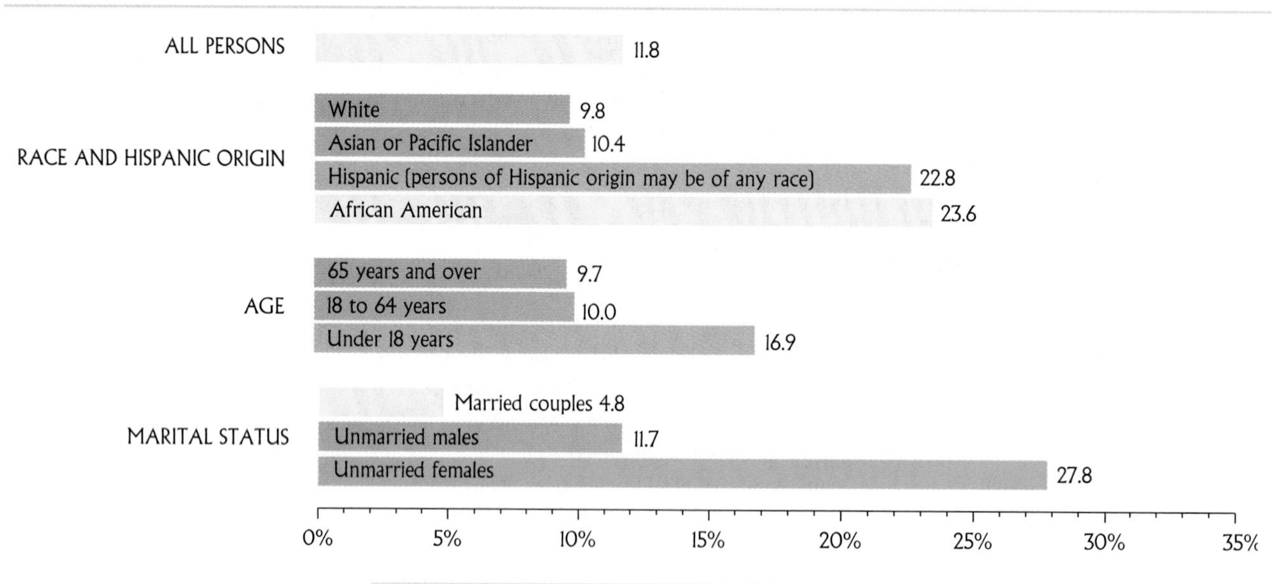

Source: U.S. Census Bureau.

The third type of figure, a *line graph,* illustrates quantitative information by means of lines. Typically, the vertical axis of a line graph represents a quantitative scale (such as percentages) and the horizontal axis represents a category (such as presidents or a sequence of dates). Specific numbers are represented as points on the graph between the two axes and are connected with a line. Sometimes there is more than one line on a graph, as when numbers are shown for two different sets of information—for example, elections for both the House and Senate, state and federal expenditures, or exports and imports. The two lines can be compared to each other, or, in some cases, the distance between the two lines can be analyzed. In the following line graph, which charts a single set of quantitative information, the percentage of the voting age population that actually voted is shown on the vertical axis, and the horizontal axis represents years of presidential elections. The falling line indicates that turnout has declined since 1892.

The Decline of Turnout in Presidential Elections, 1892–2000

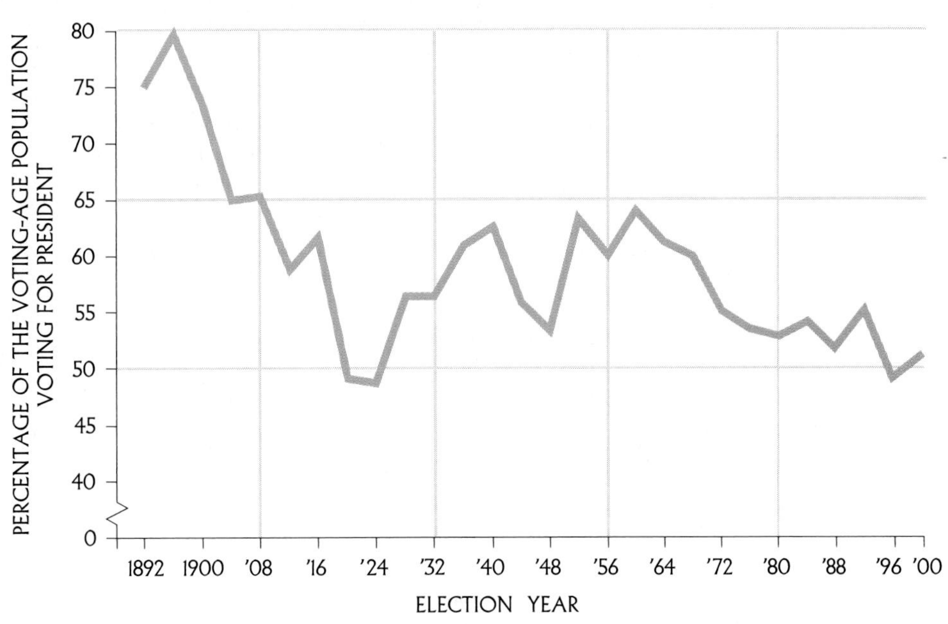

Sources: For data up to 1968, *Historical Statistics of the United States,* (Washington, D.C.: Government Printing Office, 1975), part 2, 1071. For 1972–1988, *Statistical Abstract of the United States,* 1990 (Washington, D.C.: Government Printing Office, 1990), 264. 1992, 1996, and 2000 data are from news reports.

By remembering these key features of charts and graphs, you can more accurately assess the information presented in *Government in America,* as well as interpret such figures wherever you encounter them—in other textbooks, in newspapers and magazines, or on the Web.

About the Authors

George C. Edwards III is distinguished professor of political science at Texas A&M University and director emeritus of the Center for Presidential Studies. He also holds the Jordan Professorship in Liberal Arts and has held visiting appointments at the U.S. Military Academy at West Point, Peking University in Beijing, Hebrew University of Jerusalem, and the University of Wisconsin in Madison.

When he determined that he was unlikely to become shortstop for the New York Yankees, he turned to political science. Today, he is one of the country's leading scholars of the presidency and has authored dozens of articles and has written or edited 16 books on American politics and public policy making, including *At the Margins: Presidential Leadership of Congress*, *Presidential Approval*, *Presidential Leadership*, *National Security and the U.S. Constitution*, and *Implementing Public Policy*.

Professor Edwards has served as president of the Presidency Research Section of the American Political Science Association and is editor of *Presidential Studies Quarterly*. He has also received the Decoration for Distinguished Civilian Service from the U.S. Army. A frequent speaker at universities around the country, he often lectures abroad as well.

Professor Edwards also applies his scholarship to practical issues of government. In 1988, he went to Brasilia to advise those writing the new constitution for Brazil. He was an issue leader for the National Academy of Public Administration's Project on the 1988 Presidential Transition, providing advice to the new president. In 1993, he spent six weeks in China lecturing on democracy. In 1994, he was a consultant to Russian democratic leaders on building a political party system in that country. Most recently, he was heavily involved in studies for the presidential transition in 2001.

When not writing, speaking, or advising, he prefers to spend his time with his wife, Carmella, sailing, skiing, scuba diving, traveling, or attending art auctions.

Martin P. Wattenberg is professor of political science at the University of California, Irvine. His first regular paying job was with the Washington Redskins, from which he moved on to receive a Ph.D. at the University of Michigan.

While at Michigan, Professor Wattenberg authored *The Decline of American Political Parties* (Harvard University Press), currently in its sixth edition. He is also the author of *The Rise of Candidate-Centered Politics*. In addition, he has contributed many professional articles to journals such as the *American Political Science Review*, *American Journal of Political Science*, *American Politics Quarterly*, and *Public Opinion Quarterly*.

Professor Wattenberg has lectured about American politics on all of the inhabited continents. His travels have led him to become interested in electoral politics around the world. He recently coedited two books—one on party systems in the advanced industrialized world, and the other on the recent trend toward mixed-member electoral systems.

Robert L. Lineberry is professor of political science at the University of Houston and has been its senior vice president. He served from 1981 to 1988 as dean of the College of Liberal Arts and Sciences at the University of Kansas in Lawrence.

A native of Oklahoma City, he received a B.A. degree from the University of Oklahoma in 1964 and a Ph.D. in political science from the University of North Carolina in 1968. He taught for seven years at Northwestern University.

Dr. Lineberry has been president of the Policy Studies Section of the American Political Science Association and is currently the editor of *Social Science Quarterly*. He is the author or coauthor of numerous books and articles in political science. In addition, for the past 35 years he has taught regularly the introductory course in American government.

He has been married to Nita Lineberry for 35 years. They have two children, Nikki, who works in Denver, Colo., and Keith, who works in Houston, Texas. They have three grandchildren—Lee, Callie, and Hunter.

Introducing Government in America

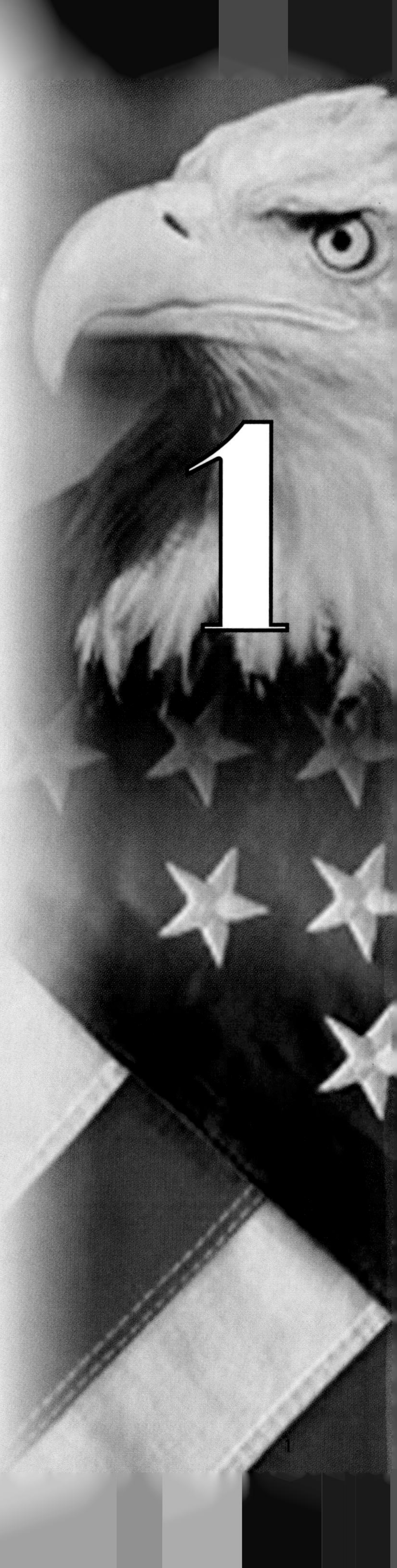

1

Chapter Outline

Government

Politics

The Policymaking System

Democracy

The Scope of Government in America

Summary

Politics and government matter—that is the single most important message of this book. Consider, for example the following list of ways that government and politics may have already impacted your life:

- Any public schools you attended were prohibited by the federal government from discriminating against females and minorities, and from holding prayer sessions led by school officials. Municipal school boards regulated your education, and the state certified and paid your teachers.
- The ages at which you could get your driver's license, drink alcohol, and vote were all determined by state and federal governments.
- Before you could get a job, the federal government had to issue you a Social Security number and you have been paying Social Security taxes every month in which you have been employed. If you worked at a relatively low-paying job, your starting wages were determined by state and federal minimum wage laws.
- As a college student, you may be drawing student loans financed by the government. Government even dictates certain school holidays.
- Federal policy makes it possible for you to drive long distances relatively cheaply. This is because taxes on gasoline are relatively low compared to most other advanced industrialized nations.
- If you have ever rented an apartment, federal law prohibits landlords from discriminating against you because of your race or religion.

Yet, many Americans—especially young people—are apathetic about politics and government. For example, before his recent historic return to space, Senator John Glenn remarked that he worried "about the future when we have so many young people who feel apathetic and critical and cynical about anything having to do with politics. They don't want to touch it. And yet politics is literally the personnel system for democracy."[1]

Stereotypes can be found to be mistaken; unfortunately this is one case where widely held impressions are overwhelmingly supported by solid evidence, which will be reviewed briefly here. It is important to note that this is not to say that young people are inactive in American society. Nearly three of four college freshmen surveyed in 1999 reported volunteering for a community group during their senior year in high school. It is only when it comes to politics that young people seem to express indifference about getting involved. Whether because they feel they can't make a difference, the political system is corrupt, or they just don't care, young Americans are clearly apathetic about public affairs. And while political apathy isn't restricted to

College students, like all Americans, are impacted by governmental policies. Yet, today's generation of young people does not seem to think that politics matters. The political apathy of today's youth can be seen in low levels of voter turnout, interest in politics, and knowledge of political affairs. This lack of political participation does not mean that this is a generation of couch potatoes, however. In fact, their level of volunteerism in community affairs is very high.

Figure 1.1 The Political Disengagement of College Students Today

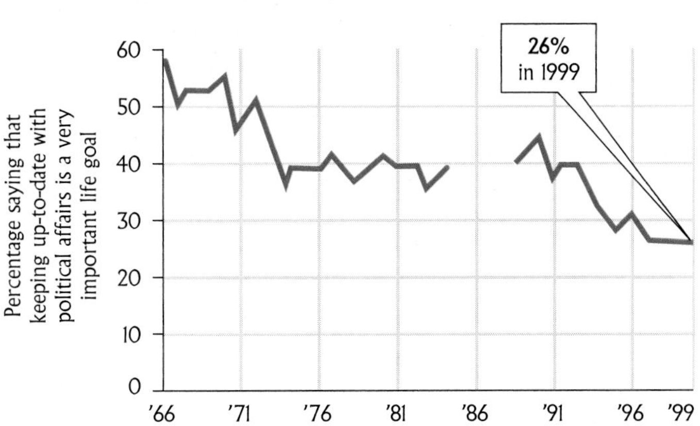

Source: UCLA Higher Education Research Institute

young people, a tremendous gap has opened up between the young (defined as under age 25) and the elderly (defined as over 65) on measures of political interest, knowledge, and participation.

An annual nationwide study of college freshmen recently found that among the class of 2003 only 26 percent said that "keeping up with politics" was an important priority for them, compared to 58 percent among the class of 1970—their parents' generation (see Figure 1.1). In addition, political interest among young people as a whole is quite low. In 2000, the National Election Study asked a nationwide sample about their general level of interest in politics. Only 26 percent of young people interviewed said they followed politics most or some of the time compared to 73 percent of senior citizens. Yet, there was no generation gap in terms of political interest when 18- to 20-year-olds first became eligible to vote in 1972. Back then, 69 percent of young people expressed at least some interest in politics compared to 65 percent of the elderly.

Because they pay so little attention to public affairs, American youth are less likely to be well informed about politics and government. Study after study in the 1990s has shown a substantial generation gap in terms of political knowledge. Perhaps the most comprehensive set of questions was asked in the 1994 National Election Study, and the results for young and elderly people can be seen in Table 1.1. Regardless of whether the question concerned identifying current leaders, basic civics, or current events, the result was the same: Young people were clearly less knowledgeable than the elderly. On average, respondents under 25 years old came up with the right answer only 35 percent of the time compared to 59 percent for senior citizens.

participation
You Are Part of the Political Landscape

Table 1.1 Political Knowledge of the Young and Elderly (In Percents)

QUESTION	YOUNG (18–24)	ELDERLY (65+)
Identified the vice president	68	84
Identified the chief justice of the Supreme Court	2	5
Identified the president of Russia	35	49
Identified the Speaker of the House	8	49
Knew that the Supreme Court decides if a law is constitutional	40	64
Knew that the president nominates judges to the federal courts	39	62
Knew which party held the majority in the House prior to the election	47	81
Knew which party held the majority in the Senate prior to the election	41	74
Average correct	35	59

Source: 1994 National Election Study.

Thomas Jefferson once said that there has never been, nor ever will be, a people who are politically ignorant and free. If this is indeed the case, write Stephen Bennett and Eric Rademacher, then "we can legitimately wonder what the future holds if Xers remain as uninformed as they are about government and public affairs."[2] While this may well be an overreaction, there definitely are important consequences when citizens lack political information. In *What Americans Know About Politics and Why It Matters*, Michael Delli Carpini and Scott Keeter make a strong case for the importance of staying informed about public affairs. Political knowledge, they argue: (1) fosters civic virtues, such as political tolerance; (2) helps citizens to identify what policies would truly benefit them and then incorporate this information in their voting behavior; and (3) promotes active participation in politics.[3] If you've been reading about the debate on health care reform, for example, you'll be able to understand proposed legislation on managed care and patient's rights. This knowledge will then help you identify and vote for candidates whose views agree with yours.

Lacking such information about political issues, however, fewer young Americans are heading to the polls compared to previous generations. This development has pulled the nationwide turnout rate down substantially in recent years. In 1996, presidential election turnout fell below the 50 percent mark for the first time since the early 1920s, when women had just received suffrage and not yet begun to use it as frequently as men. Young people have always had the lowest turnout rates, perhaps the reason why there was relatively little opposition in 1971 to lowering the voting age to 18. But even the most pessimistic analysts could not have foreseen the record low participation rates of young people in the recent years.

Why does voter turnout matter? As you will see throughout this book, those who participate in the political process are more likely to benefit from government programs and policies. Young people often complain that the elderly have far more political clout than they do—turnout statistics make it clear why this is the case. As shown in Figure 1.2, the voter turnout rate for people under 25 has fallen from 50 percent in 1972 to just 32 percent in 1996. By contrast, turnout among people over 65 has actually gone up slightly over the same period. Political scientists used to write that the frailties of old age led to a

Figure 1.2 Presidential Election Turnout Rates by Age, 1972–1996

Source: U.S. Census Bureau Current Population Surveys. Data can be found at *www.census.gov/population/www/socdemo/voting.html*

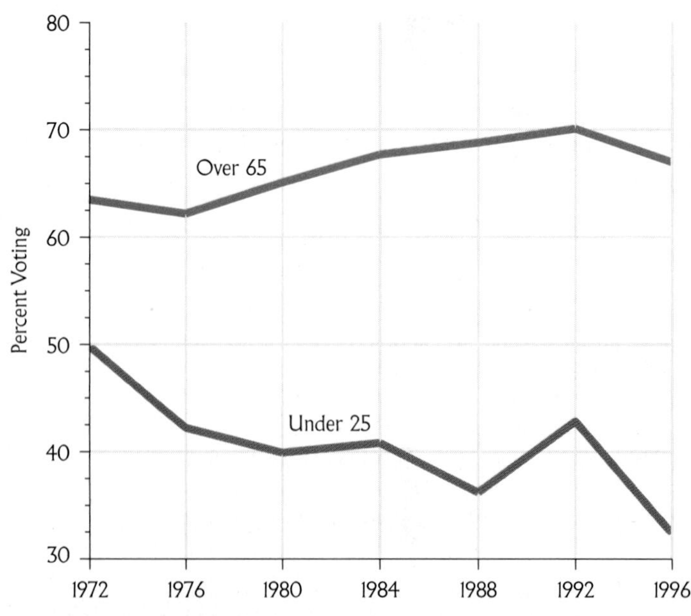

The narrow 537-vote margin by which George W. Bush carried the state of Florida in 2000 proved the old adage that every vote counts. Here, an election official strains to figure out how to interpret a voter's punch in the tedious process of recounting ballots by hand.

decline in turnout after age 60; now such a decline occurs only after 80 years of age. Greater access to medical care provided to today's elderly population because of the passage of Medicare in 1965 must surely be given some of the credit for this change. Who says politics doesn't make a difference?

Of course, today's youth has not had any policy impact them the way that Medicare has benefited their grandparents or that the draft and the Vietnam War affected their parents. However, the cause of young people's political apathy probably runs deeper. A broader reason is that today's youth have grown up in an environment in which public affairs news has not been as readily visible as it has been in the past. It has become particularly difficult to convince a generation that has channel surfed all their lives that politics really does matter.

Major political events were once shared national experiences. However, the current generation of young people has been the first to grow up in a media environment in which there are few such shared experiences. When CBS, NBC, and ABC dominated the airwaves, their blanket coverage of presidential speeches, political conventions, and presidential debates sometimes left little else to watch on TV. As channels have proliferated over the last two decades, though, it has become much easier to avoid exposure to politics altogether by simply grabbing the remote control. Whereas President Nixon got an average rating of 50 for his televised addresses to the nation (meaning that half the population was watching), President Clinton averaged only about 30 in his first term.[4] Political conventions, which once received more TV coverage than the Summer Olympics, have been relegated to an hour per night and draw abysmal ratings. The 2000 presidential debates drew a respectable average rating of 28, but this was only half the typical level of viewers drawn by debates held between 1960 and 1980. In sum, young people have never known a time when most citizens paid attention to major political events. As a result, most of them have yet to get into the habit of following and participating in politics.

Major Events that Changed the Political Landscape

The revolutionary expansion of channels and websites presents both opportunities and challenges for political involvement in the future, especially for today's youth. Some optimistic observers see these developments as offering "the prospect of a revitalized democracy characterized by a more active and informed citizenry."[5] Political

The Internet has opened up a new world of opportunities for computer-savvy young people to learn about politics. But with so many websites for so many specific interests, it remains to be seen whether many people will take advantage of the wide range of political information that is now available.

junkies will certainly find more political information available than ever before, and electronic communications will make it easier for people to express their political views in various forums and directly to public officials. However, with so many websites for so many specific interests, it will also be extraordinarily easy to avoid the subject of public affairs. Why read and discuss the president's latest speech when you can personalize your browser to display only the news you care most about, go into a chat room about movies, or download a new game?

It is our hope that after reading this book, you will be persuaded that paying attention to politics and government is important. As noted at the beginning of this chapter, government has a substantial impact on all our lives. But it is also true that we have the opportunity to have a substantial impact on government. In each chapter, we will present an example of someone whose involvement in politics has made a difference. We hope that their examples will spark some ideas of your own. Concerned about the environment? Participate in a group that lobbies for environmental protection, as Danny Seo has done (Chapter 11). Think the tax system is unfair? Take part in a state campaign to change it, as Barbara Anderson did (Chapter 10). Worried about your city's programs for affordable housing and public transportation? Consider running for a local elected office, as Charlene Marshall did (Chapter 21). Whether in positions of power, like Governor Jesse Ventura (Chapter 8), or simply as a private citizen making a statement about campaign finance, like Granny D (Chapter 6), Americans have countless opportunities to influence their government.

Government

government

The institutions and processes through which **public policies** are made for a society.

The institutions that make authoritative decisions for any given society are collectively known as **government.** In our own national government, these institutions are Congress, the president, the courts, and federal administrative agencies ("the bureaucracy"). Thousands of state and local governments also make policies that influence our lives. There are roughly 500,000 elected officials in the United States; that means that policies that affect you are being made almost constantly.

Because government shapes how we live, it is important to understand the process by which decisions are made, as well as what is actually decided. Two fundamental questions about governing will serve as themes throughout this book:

In the United States, the transfer of power is achieved through peaceful means. Though the 2000 election was heavily disputed, as evidenced by these protests on inauguration day, the transition from Bill Clinton to George W. Bush took place smoothly and without incident on January 20, 2001.

How should we govern? Americans take great pride in calling their government democratic. This chapter examines the workings of democratic government; the chapters that follow will evaluate the way American government actually works compared to the standards of an "ideal" democracy. We will continually ask, "Who holds power and who influences the policies adopted by government?"

What should government do? This text explores the relationship between *how* American government works and *what* it does. In other words, "Does our government do what we want it to do?" Debates over this question concerning the scope of government are among the most important in American political life today. Some people would like to see the government take on more responsibilities; others believe it already takes on too much and that America needs to promote individual responsibility instead.

While citizens often disagree about what their government should do for them, all governments have certain functions in common. National governments throughout the world perform the following functions:

Maintain a national defense. A government protects its national sovereignty, usually by maintaining armed forces. In the nuclear age, some governments possess awesome power to make war through highly sophisticated weapons. The United States spends about $275 billion a year on national defense.

Provide public services. Governments in this country spend billions of dollars on schools, libraries, weather forecasting, halfway houses, and dozens of other public policies. Some of these services, like highways and public parks, can be shared by everyone and cannot be denied to anyone. These kinds of services are called **public goods.** Other services, such as a college education or medical care, can be restricted to individuals who meet certain criteria, but may be provided by the private sector as well. Governments typically provide these services to make them accessible to people who may not be able to afford privately available services.

public goods

Goods, such as clean air and clean water, that everyone must share.

Preserve order. Every government has some means of maintaining order. When people protest in large numbers, governments may resort to extreme measures to restore order. For example, the National Guard was called in to stop the looting and arson after rioting broke out in Los Angeles after the 1992 Rodney King verdict.

Socialize the young. Most modern governments pay for education and use it to instill national values among the young. School curricula typically offer a course on the philosophy and practice of the country's government. Rituals like the daily Pledge of Allegiance seek to foster patriotism and love of country.

Governments are responsible for preserving order in society. The worst riots in modern U.S. history began when outnumbered police were faced down by crowds angered by the acquittals of four white police officers accused in the videotaped beating of Rodney King. Here, an L.A. police officer holds a shotgun on two looting suspects as a California state trooper puts handcuffs on them.

Many American public schools begin each day by reciting the Pledge of Allegiance. Like most governments around the world, the U.S. government uses the public schools to socialize its children. Required civics courses help ensure that the young understand and support the American system of government.

Collect taxes. Approximately one out of every three dollars earned by an American citizen was used to pay national, state, and local taxes—money that was used to pay for the public goods and services provided by the government.

All these governmental tasks add up to weighty decisions that must be made by our political leaders. For example, how much should we spend on national defense as opposed to education? How high should taxes for Medicare and Social Security be? The way we answer such questions is through politics.

Politics

politics

The process by which we select our governmental leaders and what policies these leaders pursue. Politics produces authoritative decisions about public issues.

Politics determines whom we select as our governmental leaders and what policies these leaders pursue. Political scientists often cite Harold D. Lasswell's famous definition of politics: "Who gets what, when, and how."[6] It is one of the briefest and most useful definitions of politics ever penned. Admittedly, this broad definition covers a lot of ground (office politics, sorority politics, and so on) in which political scientists are

Pro-life and pro-choice groups are single-minded and usually uncompromising. Few issues stir up as much passion as whether abortion should be permitted, and if so under what conditions.

not interested. They are interested primarily in politics related to governmental decision making.

The media usually focus on the *who* of politics. At a minimum, this includes voters, candidates, groups, and parties. *What* refers to the substance of politics and government—benefits, such as medical care for the elderly, and burdens, such as new taxes. *How* people participate in politics is important, too. They get what they want through voting, supporting, compromising, lobbying, and so forth. In this sense, government and politics involve winners and losers.

The ways in which people get involved in politics make up their **political participation.** Many people judge the health of a government by how widespread political participation is. America does quite poorly when judged by its voter turnout, with one of the lowest rates of voter participation in the world. Low voter turnout has an effect on who holds political power. Because so many people do not show up at the polls, voters are a distorted sample of the public as a whole. Groups such as the elderly benefit by having a high turnout rate, whereas others such as young people lack political clout because of their low likelihood of voting.

political participation

All the activities used by citizens to influence the selection of political leaders or the policies they pursue. The most common, but not the only, means of political participation in a **democracy** is voting. Other means include **protest** and **civil disobedience.**

Voting is only one form of political participation. (See Chapter 6 for a discussion of other forms of participation). For a few Americans politics is a vocation rather than an avocation. They run for office, and some even earn their livelihood from holding political office. In addition, there are also many Americans who treat politics as critical to their interests. Many of these people are members of **single-issue groups:** groups so concerned with one issue that members cast their votes on the basis of that issue only, ignoring a politician's stand on everything else. Groups of activists dedicated either to outlawing abortion or to preserving abortion rights are good examples of single-issue groups.

single-issue groups

Groups that have a narrow interest, tend to dislike compromise, and often draw membership from people new to politics. These features distinguish them from traditional **interest groups.**

When the Supreme Court handed down its decision in the case of *Webster v. Reproductive Health Services* in 1989, it narrowed abortion rights by allowing states to decide whether to provide funds to women who want abortions but cannot afford them. People on the pro-choice and the pro-life sides (note the loaded label each uses for itself) have turned to state politics to achieve their goals. Pro-lifers attempted to convince their legislators to restrict abortion funding by picketing abortion clinics and lobbying legislatures in many states. Pro-choicers have encouraged legislators to keep the right to abortion as broad as possible. Neither group considers a middle course. For this reason, many politicians feel that such single-issue groups get in the way of effective policymaking. Single-issue groups have little taste for compromise, an approach that most politicians view as essential to their job. The influence of single-issue groups on voters and elected officials complicates efforts to seek the middle ground on various issues.

Individual citizens and organized groups get involved in politics because they understand that the public policy choices made by governments affect them in significant ways. Will all those who need student loans receive them? Will everyone have access to medical care? Will people be taken care of in their old age? Is the water safe to drink? These and other questions tie politics to policymaking.

The Policymaking System

policymaking system

The process by which policy comes into being and evolves over time. People's interests, problems, and concerns create political issues for government policymakers. These issues shape policy, which in turn impacts people, generating more interests, problems, and concerns.

Americans frequently expect government to do something about their problems. For example, the president and members of Congress are expected to keep the economy humming along; voters will penalize them at the polls if they do not. The **policymaking system** reveals the way our government responds to the priorities of its people. Figure 1.3 shows a skeletal model of this system. The rest of this book will flesh out this model, but for now it will help you understand how government policy comes into being and evolves over time.

People Shape Policy

The policymaking system begins with people. All Americans have interests, problems, and concerns that are touched upon by public policy. Some people may think the government should help train people for jobs in today's new technological environment;

Figure 1.3 The Policymaking System

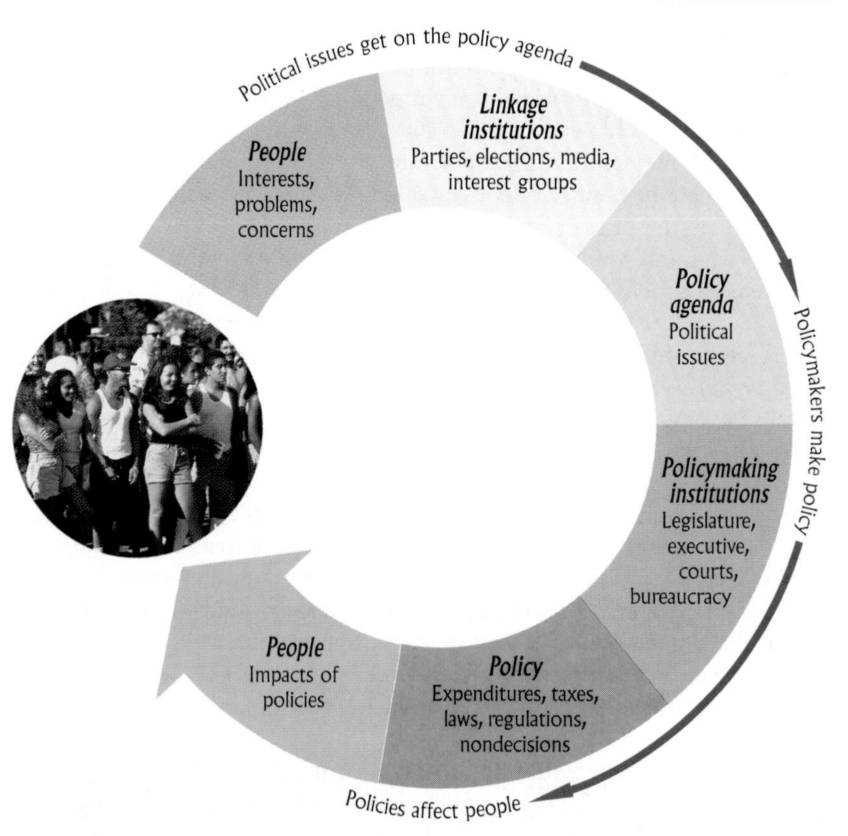

others may think that their taxes are too high and that the country would be best served by a large tax cut. Some people may expect government to do something to curb domestic violence; others may be concerned about prospects that the government may make it much harder to buy a handgun.

What do people do to express their opinions in a democracy? There are numerous avenues for action, such as voting for candidates who represent their opinions, joining political parties, posting messages to Internet chat groups, and forming interest groups. In this way, people's concerns enter the **linkage institutions** of the policymaking system. Linkage institutions transmit the preferences of Americans to the policymakers in government. Parties and interest groups strive to ensure that their members' concerns receive appropriate political attention. The media investigates social problems and informs people about them. Elections allow citizens the chance to make their opinions heard by choosing their public officials.

linkage institutions

The political channels through which people's concerns become political issues on the policy agenda. In the United States, linkage institutions include elections, political parties, interest groups, and the media.

All these institutions help to shape the government's **policy agenda,** which consists of the issues that attract the serious attention of public officials and other people actively involved in politics at any given time. Some issues will be considered, and others will not. If politicians want to get elected, they must pay attention to the problems that concern the voters. When you vote, you are partly looking at whether a candidate shares your agenda. If you are worried about rising health care costs and unemployment, and a certain candidate talks only about America's moral decay and ending legalized abortions, you will probably support another candidate.

policy agenda

The issues that attract the serious attention of public officials and other people actually involved in politics at any given point in time.

A government's policy agenda changes regularly. When jobs are scarce and business productivity is falling, economic problems occupy a high position on the government's agenda. If the economy is doing well and trouble spots around the world occupy the headlines, foreign policy questions are bound to dominate the agenda. In general, bad news—particularly about a crisis situation—is more likely than good news to draw sufficient media attention to put a subject on the policy agenda. As they say in journalism schools, "Good news is no news." When unemployment rises sharply it leads the news; when jobs are plentiful, the latest unemployment report is much less of a news story. Thus, the policy agenda responds more to societal failures than successes. The question politicians constantly ask is "How can we as a people do better?"

People, of course, do not always agree on what government should do. Indeed, one group's concerns and interests are often at odds with those of another group. A **political issue** is the result of people disagreeing about a problem or about the public policy needed to fix it. There is never a shortage of political issues; government, however, will not act on any issue until it is high on the policy agenda.

political issue

An issue that arises when people disagree about a problem and how to fix it.

Policymakers stand at the core of the political system, working within the three **policymaking institutions** established by the U.S. Constitution: the Congress, the presidency, and the courts. Policymakers scan the issues on the policy agenda, select those that they consider important, and make policies to address them. Today, the power of the bureaucracy is so great that most political scientists consider it a fourth policymaking institution.

policymaking institutions

The branches of government charged with taking action on political issues. The U.S. Constitution established three policymaking institutions—the Congress, the presidency, and the courts. Today, the power of the bureaucracy is so great that most political scientists consider it a fourth policymaking institution.

Very few policies are made by a single policymaking institution. Environmental policy is a good example. Some presidents have used their influence with Congress to urge clean-air and clean-water policies. When Congress responds by passing legislation to clean up the environment, bureaucracies have to implement the new policies. The bureaucracies, in turn, create extensive volumes of rules and regulations that define how policies are to be implemented. In addition, every law passed and every rule made can be challenged in the courts. Courts make decisions about what the policies mean and whether they conflict with the Constitution.

Policies Impact People

Every decision that government makes—every law it passes, budget it establishes, and ruling it hands down—is **public policy.** There are many types of public policies. Table 1.2 lists some of the most important types.

public policy

A choice that **government** makes in response to a political issue. A policy is a course of action taken with regard to some problem.

Table 1.2 Types of Public Policies

TYPE	DEFINITION	EXAMPLE
Congressional statute	Law passed by Congress	Social Security Act
Presidential action	Decision by president	American war planes sent to Kosovo
Court decision	Opinion by Supreme Court or other court	Supreme Court ruling that school segregation is unconstitutional
Budgetary choices	Legislative enactment of taxes and expenditures	The federal budget
Regulation	Agency adoption of regulation	Food and Drug Administration approval of a new drug

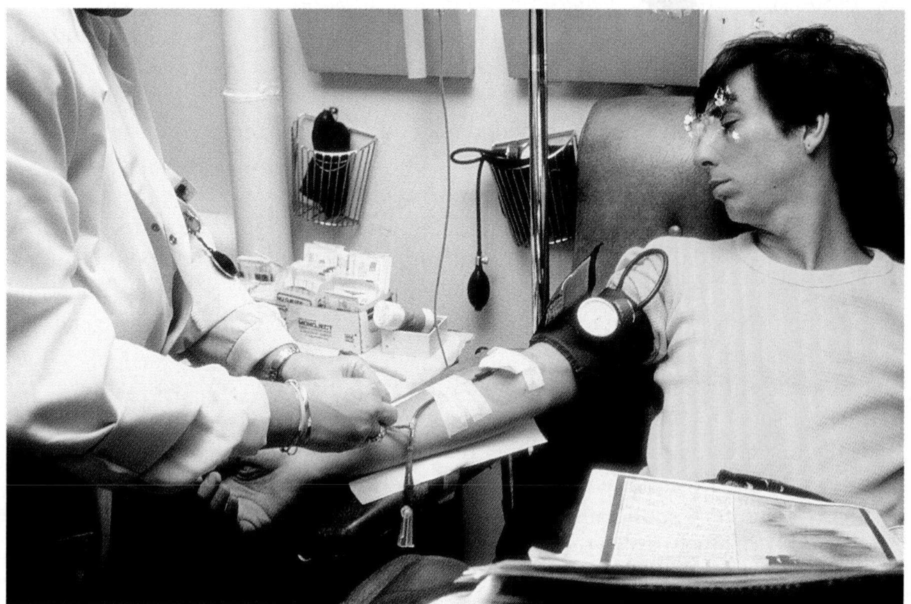

AIDS was relatively low on the political agenda until well-known celebrities started to die from the disease. AIDS activists have found, however, that getting the problem on the agenda is only half the political battle. Getting the government to take aggressive action to find and approve new treatments has proved to be at least as difficult.

Policies can also be established through inaction as well as action. Doing nothing—or nothing different—can prove to be a very consequential governmental decision. Reporter Randy Shilts' book traces the staggering growth in the number of people with AIDS and reveals how governments in Washington and elsewhere did little or debated quietly about what to do.[7] Shilts claims that, because politicians viewed AIDS as a gay person's disease, they were reluctant to support measures to deal with it, fearful of losing the votes of antigay constituents. The issue thus remained a low priority on the government's policy agenda until infections started to spread to the general population, including celebrities like basketball star Magic Johnson.

Once policies are made and implemented, they affect people. Policy impacts are the effects that a policy has on people and on society's problems. People want policy that addresses their interests, problems, and concerns. A new law, executive order, bureaucratic regulation, or court judgment doesn't mean much if it doesn't work. Environmentalists want an industrial emissions policy that not only claims to prevent air pollution but also does so. Minority groups want a civil rights policy that not only promises them equal treatment but also ensures it.

Having a policy implies a goal. Whether we want to reduce poverty, cut crime, clean the water, or hold down inflation, we have a goal in mind. Policy impact analysts ask how well a policy achieves its goal—and at what cost. The analysis of policy impacts carries the political system back to its point of origin: the concerns of the people. Translating people's desires into effective public policy is crucial to the workings of democracy.

Democracy

In 1848, Karl Marx and Friedrich Engels published *The Communist Manifesto*, one of the most famous political documents ever written. It began with these words: "A specter is haunting Europe. It is the specter of communism." Today one could write, "A specter is haunting the world. It is the specter of democracy."

From the Russia[illegible] in 1917 through the recent end of the Cold War, America[illegible] with preventing the spread of communism. This wa[illegible]ly after World War II, when the Soviet Union expanded its sphere of influence throughout Eastern Europe. As Winston Churchill warned, an "Iron Curtain" had descended across Europe. From then on, a cold war existed between the United States and the Soviet Union, a struggle between democracy and communism for control of governments around the world. In one famous televised encounter, Soviet Premier Nikita Khrushchev predicted to then Vice President Richard Nixon that Nixon's grandchildren would be communists. Nixon naturally responded that Khrushchev's grandchildren would live in a democracy. Nixon later recalled that at the time he was sure that Khrushchev would be wrong about America but that he was unsure whether his prediction about the Soviet Union would ever be realized. Over three decades later, it was. All the countries that once were part of the Soviet empire now practice democracy, holding regular elections and permitting freedom of speech.

Resounding demands for democracy have recently been heard in many corners of the world. In Argentina, Brazil, and other South American countries, one-party or military regimes gave way to competitive party systems and civilian governments. Over three centuries of White rule ended in South Africa in 1994 as a result of the first election open to all races. In Mexico, over seven decades of one-party rule and fraudulent elections came to an end in 2000 with the presidential election of Vincente Fox. Yet despite this global move toward democracy, not everyone defines democracy the way Americans do—or think they do.

comparative
Comparing Political Landscapes

In 1959, then Vice President Nixon journeyed to Moscow to meet with Soviet Premier Khrushchev. Outside an exhibit of a model kitchen of the future, Nixon and Khrushchev had an impromptu debate in front of reporters as to which system—capitalism or communism—was the best course for a prosperous future.

Defining Democracy

democracy

A system of selecting policymakers and of organizing government so that policy represents and responds to the public's preferences.

Democracy is a means of selecting policymakers and of organizing government so that policy reflects citizens' preferences. Today, the term *democracy* takes its place among terms like *freedom, justice,* and *peace* as a word that seemingly has only positive connotations. Yet the writers of the U.S. Constitution had no fondness for democracy, as many of them doubted the ability of ordinary Americans to make informed judgments about what government should do. Roger Sherman, a delegate to the Constitutional Convention, said the people "should have as little to do as may be with the government." Only much later did Americans come to cherish democracy and believe that all citizens should actively participate in choosing their leaders.

Most Americans would probably say that democracy is "government by the people." This phrase, of course, is part of Abraham Lincoln's famous definition of democracy from his Gettysburg Address: "government of the people, by the people, and for the people." How well each of these aspects of democracy is being met is a matter crucial to evaluating how well our government is working. Certainly, government has always been "of the people" in the United States, for the Constitution forbids the granting of titles of nobility. On the other hand, it is a physical impossibility for government to be "by the people" in a society of 280 million people. Therefore, our democracy involves choosing people from among our midst to govern. Where the serious debate begins is whether political leaders govern "for the people," as there always are significant biases in how the system works. Democratic theorists have elaborated a set of more specific goals for evaluating this crucial question.

Traditional Democratic Theory

Traditional democratic theory rests upon a number of key principles that specify how governmental decisions are made in a democracy. Robert Dahl, one of America's leading theorists, suggests than an ideal democratic process should satisfy the following five criteria:

Equality in voting. The principle of "one person, one vote" is basic to democracy. Voting need not be universal, but it must be representative.

Effective participation. Citizens must have adequate and equal opportunities to express their preferences throughout the decision-making process.

Enlightened understanding. A democratic society must be a marketplace of ideas. A free press and free speech are essential to civic understanding. If one group monopolizes and distorts information, citizens cannot truly understand issues.

Citizen control of the agenda. Citizens should have the collective right to control the government's policy agenda. If wealthy individuals or groups distort the agenda, the people cannot make government address the issues they feel are most important.

Inclusion. The government must include, and extend rights to, all those subject to its laws. Citizenship must be open to all within a nation if the nation is to call itself democratic.[8]

Only by following these principles can a political system be called "democratic." Furthermore, democracies must practice **majority rule,** meaning that in choosing among alternatives, the will of over half the voters should be followed. At the same time, most Americans would not want to give the majority free reign to do anything they can agree on. Restraints on the majority are built into the American system of government in order to protect those in the minority. Basic principles such as freedom of speech and assembly are inviolable **minority rights,** which the majority cannot infringe upon.

In a society too large to make its decisions in open meetings, a few will have to look after the concerns of the many. The relationship between the few leaders and the many followers is one of **representation.** The literal meaning of representation is to make present once again. In politics, this means that the desires of the people should be replicated in government through the choices of elected officials. The closer the correspondence between representatives and their constituents, the closer the approximation to an ideal democracy. As might be expected for such a crucial question, theorists disagree widely about the extent to which this actually occurs in America.

majority rule

A fundamental principle of **traditional democratic theory.** In a democracy, choosing among alternatives requires that the majority's desire be respected. See also **minority rights.**

minority rights

A principle of **traditional democratic theory** that guarantees rights to those who do not belong to majorities and allows that they might join majorities through persuasion and reasoned argument. See also **majority rule.**

representation

A basic principle of **traditional democratic theory** that describes the relationship between the few leaders and the many followers.

Three Contemporary Theories of American Democracy

Theories of American democracy are essentially theories about who has power and influence. All, in one way or another, ask the question, "Who really governs in our nation?" Each focuses on a key aspect of politics and government, and each reaches a somewhat different conclusion.

Pluralist theory. One important theory of American democracy, **pluralist theory,** states that groups with shared interests influence public policy by pressing their concerns through organized efforts.

The National Rifle Association (NRA), the National Organization for Women (NOW), and the United Auto Workers (UAW) are examples of groups of people who share a common interest. Because of open access to various institutions of government and public officials, organized groups can compete with one another for control over policy, and yet no one group or set of groups dominates. Given that power is dispersed in the American form of government, groups that lose in one arena can take their case to another. For example, civil rights groups faced congressional roadblocks in the 1950s but were able to win the action they were seeking from the courts.

Pluralists are generally optimistic that the public interest will eventually prevail in the making of public policy through a complex process of bargaining and compromise. They believe that rather than speaking of majority rule we should speak of groups of minorities working together. Robert Dahl expresses this view well when he writes that in America "all active and legitimate groups in the population can make themselves heard at some crucial stage in the process."[9]

Group politics is certainly as American as apple pie. Writing in the 1830s, Alexis de Tocqueville called us a "nation of joiners," and pointed to the high level of associational activities as one of the crucial reasons for the success of American democracy. The recent explosion of interest group activity can therefore be seen as a very positive development from the perspective of pluralist theory. Interest groups and their lobbyists—the groups'

pluralist theory

A theory of government and politics emphasizing that politics is mainly a competition among groups, each one pressing for its own preferred policies. Compare **elite and class theory, hyperpluralism,** and **traditional democratic theory.**

representatives in Washington—have become masters of the technology of politics. Computers, mass mailing lists, sophisticated media advertising, and hard-sell techniques are their stock-in-trade. As a result, some observers believe that Dahl's pluralist vision that all groups are heard via the American political process is more true now than ever before.

On the other hand, Robert Putnam argues that many of the problems of American democracy today stem from a decline in group-based participation.[10] Putnam theorizes that advanced technology, particularly television, has served to increasingly isolate Americans from one another. He shows that membership in a variety of civic associations, such as Parent-Teacher Associations, the League of Women Voters, the Elks, Shriners, and Jaycees have been declining for decades. Interestingly, Putnam does not interpret the decline of participation in civic groups as meaning that people have become "couch potatoes." Rather, he argues that Americans' activities are becoming less tied to institutions and more self-defined. The most famous example he gives to illustrate this trend is the fact that membership in bowling leagues has dropped sharply at the same time that more people are bowling—indicating that more and more people must be bowling alone. Putnam believes that participation in interest groups today is often like bowling alone. Groups that have mushroomed lately, such as the American Association of Retired Persons (AARP), typically just ask their members to write a check from the comfort of their own home as their participation. If people are indeed participating in politics alone rather than in groups, then pluralist theory is becoming less descriptive of American politics today.

Elite and Class Theory. Critics of pluralism believe that it paints too rosy a picture of American political life. By arguing that almost every group can get a piece of the pie, they say, pluralists miss the larger question of how the pie is distributed. The poor may get their food stamps, but businesses get massive tax deductions worth far more. Some governmental programs may help minorities, but the income gap between African Americans and Whites remains wide.

elite and class theory

A theory of government and politics contending that societies are divided along class lines and that an upper-class elite will rule, regardless of the formal niceties of governmental organization. Compare **hyperpluralism, pluralist theory,** and **traditional democratic theory.**

Elite and class theory contends that our society, like all societies, is divided along class lines and that an upper-class elite pulls the strings of government. Wealth—the holding of assets such as property, stocks, and bonds—is the basis of this power. Over a third of the nation's wealth is currently held by just one percent of the population. Elite and class theorists believe that this one percent of Americans controls most policy decisions because they can afford to finance election campaigns and control key institutions, such as large corporations. According to elite and class theory, a few powerful Americans do not merely influence policymakers—they *are* the policymakers.

At the center of all theories of elite dominance is big business. Around the turn of the century, President Woodrow Wilson charged that "the masters of the Government of the United States are the combined capitalists and manufacturers of the United States." President Calvin Coolidge expressed a more favorable attitude, stating "The business of America is business." No recent president has tried harder to help big business than Ronald Reagan, and many elite theorists believe that he succeeded beyond all expectations. As Kevin Phillips wrote in his best-seller *The Politics of Rich and Poor,* "The 1980s were the triumph of upper America—an ostentatious celebration of wealth, the political ascendancy of the richest third of the population and a glorification of capitalism, free markets and finance."[11]

It is doubtful that anything like this will be written about the Clinton administration. However, journalist Bob Woodward's account of Clinton's first year in office argues that many promises made in Clinton's "Putting People First" program were sacrificed to satisfy the demands of Wall Street.[12] Reflecting on the source of *real* power, Clinton's 1992 campaign manager, James Carville, reportedly told Woodward that, "I used to think if there was reincarnation, I wanted to come back as the president or the pope or a .400 baseball hitter. But now I want to come back as the bond market. You can intimidate everybody."[13] Elite theorists maintain that who holds office in Washington is of marginal consequence; the corporate giants always have the power.

visual literacy
Understanding the Distribution of Wealth in America

Hyperpluralism. A third theory, hyperpluralism, offers a different critique of pluralism. Hyperpluralism is pluralism gone sour. In this view, groups are so strong that government is weakened, as the influence of many groups cripples government's ability to make policy. **Hyperpluralism** states that many groups—not just the elite ones—are so strong that government is unable to act.

hyperpluralism

A theory of government and politics contending that groups are so strong that government is weakened. Hyperpluralism is an extreme, exaggerated, or perverted form of **pluralism.** Compare **elite and class theory, pluralist theory,** and **traditional democratic theory.**

Whereas pluralism maintains that input from groups is a good thing for the political decision-making process, hyperpluralism asserts that there are *too* many ways for groups to control policy. Our fragmented political system containing governments with overlapping jurisdictions is one major factor that contributes to hyperpluralism. Too many governments can make it hard to coordinate policy implementation. Any policy requiring the cooperation of the national, state, and local levels of government can be hampered by the reluctance of any one of them.

According to hyperpluralists, groups have become sovereign and government is merely their servant. Groups that lose policymaking battles in Congress these days do not give up the battle; they carry it to the courts. Recently, the number of cases brought to state and federal courts has soared. Ecologists use legal procedures to delay construction projects they feel will damage the environment; businesses take federal agencies to court to fight the implementation of regulations that will cost them money; labor unions go to court to secure injunctions against policies they fear will cost them jobs. The courts have become one more battleground in which policies can be effectively opposed as each group tries to bend policy to suit its own purposes.

These powerful groups divide the government and its authority. Hyperpluralist theory holds that government gives in to every conceivable interest and single-issue group. When politicians try to placate every group, the result is confusing, contradictory, and muddled policy—if politicians manage to make policy at all. Like elite and class theorists, hyperpluralist theorists suggest that the public interest is rarely translated into public policy.

Challenges to Democracy

Regardless of which theory is most convincing, there are a number of continuing challenges to democracy. Many of these challenges apply to American democracy as well as to the fledgling democracies around the world.

Increased Technical Expertise. Traditional democratic theory holds that ordinary citizens have the good sense to reach political judgments and that government has the capacity to act on those judgments. Today, however, we live in a society of experts, whose technical knowledge overshadows the knowledge of the general population. What, after all, does the average citizen—however conscientious—know about eligibility criteria for welfare, agricultural price supports, foreign competition, and the hundreds of other issues that confront government each year? Alexander Hamilton, the architect of the American economic system and George Washington's secretary of the treasury, once said that every society is divided into the few and the many. He argued that the few will rule; the many will be ruled. Years ago, the power of the few—the elite—might have been based on property holdings. Today, the elite are likely to be those who command knowledge, the experts. Even the most rigorous democratic theory does not demand that citizens be experts on everything; but as human knowledge has expanded, it has become increasingly difficult for individual citizens to make well-informed decisions.

Limited Participation in Government. When citizens do not seem to take their citizenship seriously, democracy's defenders worry. There is plenty of evidence that Americans know little about who their leaders are, much less about their policy decisions, as we will discuss at length in Chapter 6. Furthermore, Americans do not take

Many federal employees were furloughed in late-1995 and early-1996 when President Clinton vetoed the budget plans of the Republican Congress. Here, federal employees in Kansas City protest being put in this difficult position of not knowing when they could do their work and receive their next paycheck. Ultimately, such protests led Republican leaders to back down in the confrontation over the budget, as public opinion tended to sympathize with the federal employees and blame the GOP for their plight.

full advantage of their opportunities to shape government or select its leaders. Limited participation in government challenges the foundation of democracy. In particular, because young people represent the country's future, their abysmal turnout rates point to an even more serious challenge to democracy on the horizon.

Escalating Campaign Costs. Many political observers worry about the close connection between money and politics, especially in congressional elections. Winning a House seat these days usually requires a campaign war chest of *at least* half a million dollars, and Senate races are even more costly. Candidates have become increasingly dependent on Political Action Committees (PACs) to fund their campaigns because of the escalation of campaign costs. These PACs often represent specific economic interests, and they care little about how members of Congress vote on most issues—just the issues that particularly affect them. Critics charge that when it comes to the issues the PACs care about, the members of Congress listen, lest they be denied the money they need for their reelection. When democracy confronts the might of money, the gap between democratic theory and reality widens further.

Diverse Political Interests. The diversity of the American people is reflected in the diversity of interests represented in the political system. As will be shown in this book, this system is so open that interests find it easy to gain effective access to policymakers. Moreover, the distribution of power within the government is so decentralized that access to a few policymakers may be enough to determine the outcome of public policy battles.

When interests conflict, which they often do, no coalition may be strong enough to form a majority and establish policy. But each interest may use its influence to thwart those whose policy proposals they oppose. In effect, they have a veto over policy, creating what is often referred to as **policy gridlock.** In a big city, gridlock occurs when there are so many cars on the road that no one can move; in politics it occurs when each policy coalition finds its way blocked by others. This political problem is magnified when voters choose a president of one party and congressional majorities of the other party, as has often been the case in recent years.

policy gridlock

A condition that occurs when no coalition is strong enough to form a majority and establish policy. The result is that nothing may get done.

The result is that nothing may get done, even if action is widely desired by a clear majority of voters. For example, in the early 1990s, most people in the United States felt that the country faced a crisis in health care. Yet President Clinton was unable to overcome the opposition of various interests to fashion a comprehensive proposal that could pass Congress—even with Democratic majorities in both the House and Senate in 1993–1994.

Democracy is not necessarily an end in itself. For many, evaluations of democracy depend on what democratic government produces. Thus, a major challenge to democracy in America is to overcome the diversity of interests and fragmentation of power in order to deliver policies that are responsive to citizens' needs.

Preview Questions about Democracy

Throughout *Government in America* you will be asked to evaluate American democracy. The chapters that follow will acquaint you with the development of democracy in the United States. For example, the next chapter will show that the U.S. Constitution was not originally designed to promote democracy but has slowly evolved to its current form. Much of America's move toward greater democracy has centered on the extension of civil liberties and civil rights that we review in Chapters 4 and 5. Probably the most important civil right is the right to vote. Upcoming chapters will examine voting behavior and elections and ask the following questions about how people form their opinions and to what extent they express these opinions via elections:

- Are people knowledgeable about matters of public policy?
- Do they apply what knowledge they have to their voting choices?
- Are American elections designed to facilitate public participation?

Linkage institutions, such as interest groups, political parties, and the media, help translate input from the public into output from the policymakers. When you explore these institutions, consider the extent to which they either help or hinder democracy.

- Does the interest group system allow for all points of view to be heard, or do significant biases give advantages to particular groups?
- Do political parties provide voters with clear choices, or do they intentionally obscure their stands on issues in order to get as many votes as possible?
- If there are choices, do the media help citizens understand them?

It is up to public officials to actually make the policy choices because American government is a representative democracy. For democracy to work well, elected officials must be responsive to public opinion.

- Is the Congress representative of American society, and is it capable of reacting to changing times?
- Does the president look after the general welfare of the public, or has the office become too focused on the interests of the elite?

These are some of the crucial questions you will address in discussing the executive and legislative branches of government. In addition, the way our nonelected institutions function—the bureaucracy and the courts—is crucial to evaluating how well American democracy works. These institutions are designed to implement and interpret the law, but bureaucrats and judges often cannot avoid making public policy as well. When they do so, are they violating democratic principles for policy decisions, given that neither institution can be held accountable at the ballot box?

All of these questions concerning democracy in America have more than one answer. A goal of *Government in America* is to offer different ways to evaluate and answer these questions. One way to approach all of the preceding questions is to address one of the most important questions facing modern American democracy: Is the scope of government responsibilities too vast, just about right, or not comprehensive enough?

The Scope of Government in America

In his first presidential address to Congress in 1993, Bill Clinton stated, "I want to talk to you about what government can do because I believe government must do more." Toward this end, President Clinton later proposed a comprehensive government program to require businesses to provide a basic level of health insurance for their employees. Congressional Republicans lined up solidly against Clinton's plan for national health insurance, arguing that government intervention in the affairs of individual citizens and businesses does more harm than good.

Those who are inclined to support government involvement in matters such as health care argue that intervention is the only means of achieving important goals in American society. How else, they ask, can we ensure that everyone has enough to eat, clean air and water, and affordable housing? How else can we ensure that the disadvantaged are given opportunities for education and jobs and are not discriminated against? Opponents of widening the scope of government agree that these are worthwhile goals but challenge whether involving the federal government is an effective way to pursue them. Dick Armey, a key Republican leader in the House, expresses this view well when he writes, "There is more wisdom in millions of individuals making decisions in their own self-interest than there is in even the most enlightened bureaucrat (or congressman) making decisions on their behalf."[14] Or as President George W. Bush regularly told supporters during the 2000 presidential campaign: "Our opponents trust the government; we trust the people."

How Active Is American Government?

gross domestic product

The sum total of the value of all the goods and services produced in a nation.

In terms of dollars spent, government in America is vast. Altogether, our governments—national, state, and local—spend about one out of every three dollars of our **gross domestic product,** the total value of all goods and services produced annually by the United States. Government not only spends large sums of money but also employs large numbers of people. About 18 million Americans work for one of our governments, mostly at the state and local level as teachers, police officers, university professors, and so on. Consider some facts about the size of our national government:

- It spends about $2 trillion annually (printed as a number, that's $2,000,000,000,000 a year).
- It employs nearly 5 million people.
- It owns one-third of the land in the United States.
- It occupies 2.6 billion square feet of office space, more than four times the office space located in the nation's 10 largest cities.
- It owns and operates over 400,000 nonmilitary vehicles.

How does the American national government spend $2 trillion a year? National defense takes about one-sixth of the federal budget, a much smaller percentage than it did three decades ago. Social Security consumes more than one-fifth of the budget. Medicare is another big-ticket item, requiring a little over one-tenth of the budget. State and local governments also get important parts of the federal government's budget. The federal government helps fund highway and airport construction, police departments, school districts, and other state and local functions.

When expenditures grow, tax revenues must grow to pay the additional costs. When taxes do not grow as fast as spending, a budget deficit results. The federal government ran a budget deficit every year from 1969 through 1997. In 1998, however, there was a surplus of $69 billion, and in 1999 a $124 billion surplus was recorded. The immediate outlook is that surpluses could be the norm in the early twenty-first century. However, years of deficits have left the country with a national debt of about $5.5 trillion, which will continue to pose a problem for policymakers for decades to come.

Whatever the national problem—pollution, AIDS, earthquake relief, homelessness, hunger, sexism—many people expect Congress to solve it with legislation. Thus, American government certainly matters tremendously in terms of dollars spent, persons employed, and laws passed. Our concern, however, is less about the absolute size of government and more about whether government activity is what we want it to be.

A Comparative Perspective

A useful way to think about political issues, such as the scope of government, is to compare the United States with other countries, especially other democracies with developed economies. For example, it is possible to compare the size of the gross domestic product spent by all levels of government in the United States with similar expenditures in other prosperous nations. Compared to most other economically developed nations, the United States devotes a smaller percentage of its resources to government. As we will see in Chapter 14, the tax burden on Americans is small compared to other democratic nations.

Further, most advanced industrial democracies have a system of national insurance that provides most health care; the United States does not, though President Clinton unsuccessfully tried to establish such a system. In other countries, national governments have taken it upon themselves to start up airline, telephone, and communications companies. Governments have built much of the housing in most Western nations, compared to only a small fraction of the housing in America. Thus, in terms of its impact on citizens' everyday lives, government in the United States actually does less than the governments of similar countries.

Former President Ronald Reagan and former British Prime Minister Margaret Thatcher were close both personally and politically. Both leaders were great supporters of free-market policies and were opposed to government interventionism, and both effected major changes in their countries to this end.

American Individualism

individualism

The belief that individuals should be left on their own by the government. One of the primary reasons for the comparatively small scope of American government is the prominence of this belief in American political thought and practice.

One reason for the comparatively small scope of American government is the prominence of **individualism**—the belief that people can and should get ahead on their own—in American political thought and practice. The immigrants who founded American society may have been diverse, but many shared a common dream of America as a place where one could make it on one's own without interference from government. Louis Hartz's *The Liberal Tradition in America* is a classic analysis of the dominant political beliefs during America's formative years.[15] Hartz argues that the major force behind limited government in America is that it was settled by people who fled from the feudal and clerical oppressions of the Old World. Once in the New World, they wanted little from government other than for it to leave them alone.

Another explanation for American individualism is the existence of a bountiful frontier—at least up until the turn of the twentieth century. Thus, not only did many people come to America to escape from governmental interference, but the frontier allowed them to get away from government almost entirely once they arrived. Frederick Jackson Turner's famous work on the significance of the frontier in American history argues that "the frontier is productive of individualism."[16] According to Turner, being in the wilderness and having to survive on one's own left settlers with an aversion to any control from the outside world—particularly from the government.

The results of these historical influences are evident in American politics today. Individualism remains highly valued in the United States, with the public policy consequences being a strong preference for free markets and limited government. The importance of individualism in American politics will be a recurring topic in our analysis of the scope of government.

Preview Questions about the Scope of Government

Debate over the scope of government is central to contemporary American politics, and it is a theme this text will examine in each chapter. Our goal is not to determine for you the proper role of the national government. Instead, you will explore the implications of the way politics, institutions, and policy in America affect the scope of government. By raising questions such as those listed in the next few paragraphs, you may draw your own conclusions about the appropriate role of government in America. Part One of *Government in America* examines the constitutional foundations of American government. A concern with the proper scope of government leads to a series of questions regarding the constitutional structure of American politics, including

- What role did the Constitution's authors foresee for the federal government?
- Does the Constitution favor a government with a broad scope, or is it neutral on this issue?
- Why did the functions of government increase, and why did they increase most at the national rather than the state level?
- Has bigger, more active government constrained freedom?
- Or does the increased scope of government serve to protect civil liberties and civil rights?

Part Two focuses on those who make demands on government, including the public, political parties, interest groups, and the media. Here you will seek answers to questions such as

- Does the public favor a large, active government?
- Do competing political parties predispose the government to provide more public services?

- Do elections help control the scope of government, or do they legitimize an increasing role for the public sector?
- Are pressures from interest groups necessarily translated into more governmental regulations, bigger budgets, and the like?
- Has media coverage of government enhanced government's status and growth, or have the media been an instrument for controlling government?

Governmental institutions themselves obviously deserve close examination. Part Three discusses these institutions and asks

- Has the presidency been a driving force behind increasing the scope and power of government (and thus of the president)?
- Can the president control a government with so many programs and responsibilities?
- Is Congress, because it is subject to constant elections, predisposed toward big government?
- Is Congress too responsive to the demands of the public and organized interests?

The nonelected branches of government, which are also discussed in these chapters, are especially interesting when we consider the issue of the scope of government. For instance,

- Are the federal courts too active in policymaking, intruding on the authority and responsibility of other branches and levels of government?
- Is the bureaucracy too acquisitive, constantly seeking to expand its budgets and authority, or is it simply a reflection of the desires of elected officials?
- Is the bureaucracy too large, and thus a wasteful menace to efficient and fair implementation of public policies?

The next 20 chapters will search for answers to these and many other questions regarding the scope of government and why it matters. You will undoubtedly add a few questions of your own as you seek to resolve the issue of the proper scope of government involvement.

Summary

Evidence abounds that young people today are politically apathetic. But they shouldn't be. Politics and government matter a great deal to everyone, affecting many aspects of life. If nothing else, we hope this text will convince you of this.

Government consists of those institutions that make authoritative public policies for society as a whole. In the United States, four key institutions make policy at the national level: Congress, the presidency, the courts, and the bureaucracy. Politics is, very simply, who gets what, when, and how. People engage in politics for a variety of reasons, and all their activities in politics are collectively called political participation. The result of government and politics is public policy. Public policy includes all of the decisions and nondecisions made by government.

The first question central to governing is "How should we govern?" Americans are fond of calling their government democratic. Democratic government includes, above all else, a commitment to majority rule and minority rights. This text will help you compare the way American government works with the standards of democracy and will continually address questions about who holds power and who influences the policies adopted by government.

The second fundamental question regarding governing is "What should government do?" One of the most important issues about government in America has to do with its scope. Conservatives often talk about the evils of intrusive government; liberals see the national government as rather modest in comparison both to what it could do and to the functions governments perform in other democratic nations.

Key Terms

government
public goods
politics
political participation
single-issue groups
policymaking system
linkage institutions
policy agenda
political issue
policymaking institutions
public policy
democracy
majority rule
minority rights
representation
pluralist theory
elite and class theory
hyperpluralism
policy gridlock
gross domestic product
individualism

For Further Reading

Bok, Derek. *The State of the Nation: Government and the Quest for a Better Society.* Cambridge, MA: Harvard University Press, 1996. An excellent analysis of how America is doing, compared to other major democracies, on a wide variety of policy aspects.

Dahl, Robert A. *Democracy and Its Critics.* New Haven, CT: Yale University Press, 1982. An excellent work by one of the world's most articulate advocates of pluralist theory.

de Tocqueville, Alexis. *Democracy in America.* New York: Mentor Books, 1956. This classic by a nineteenth-century French aristocrat remains one of the most insightful works on the nature of American society and government.

Hartz, Louis. *The Liberal Tradition in America.* New York: Harcourt, Brace, 1955. A classic analysis of why the scope of American government has been more limited than in other democracies.

Kettl, Donald F. *Sharing Power: Public Governance and Private Markets.* Washington, D.C.: Brookings Institution, 1993. Explores the problems with contracting out government services to the private sector.

Kingdon, John W. *Agendas, Alternatives, and Public Policies,* 2nd ed. New York: HarperCollins, 1995. One of the first efforts by a political scientist to examine the political agenda.

Putnam, Robert. *Bowling Alone: The Collapse and Revival of American Community.* New York: Simon & Schuster, 2000. Putnam's highly influential work shows how Americans have become increasingly disconnected from one another since the early 1960s.

Smith, Hedrick. *The Power Game: How Washington Works.* New York: Ballantine, 1988. A good introduction to the political life of our nation's capital.

Stanley, Harold W., and Richard G. Niemi. *Vital Statistics on American Politics, 1999–2000.* Washington, D.C.: Congressional Quarterly Press, 2000. Useful data on government, politics, and policy in the United States.

Internet Resources

www.policy.com
Contains a discussion of major policy issues of the day and links to resources about them.

www.vote-smart.org/reference/histdocs/fedlist
The complete collection of *The Federalist Papers.*

www.c-span.org/alexis
Information and discussion about Tocqueville's classic work, *Democracy in America.*

www.bowlingalone.com
A site designed to accompany Robert Putnam's work, which contains information concerning the data he used and projects he is working on to reinvigorate American communities.

www.yahoo.com/Government
The place to go to search for information about government and politics.

Notes

1. "The Soul of a Senator." *Time,* August 10, 1998.
2. Stephen Earl Bennett and Eric W. Rademacher, "The Age of Indifference Revisited: Patterns of Political Interest, Media Exposure, and Knowledge among Generation X." In Stephen C. Craig and Stephen Earl Bennett, eds., *After the Boom: The Politics of Generation X* (Lanham, MD: Rowman and Littlefield, 1997), 39.
3. Michael X. Delli Carpini and Scott Keeter, *What Americans Know About Politics and Why It Matters* (New Haven, CT: Yale University Press, 1996), chap. 6.
4. Samuel Kernell, *Going Public: New Strategies of Presidential Leadership,* 3rd ed. (Washington, D.C.: Congressional Quarterly Press, 1997), 132.
5. Anthony Corrado, "Elections in Cyberspace: Prospects and Problems," in Anthony Corrado and Charles M. Firestone, eds., *Elections in Cyberspace: Toward a New Era in American Politics* (Washington, D.C.: The Aspen Institute, 1996), 29.
6. Harold D. Lasswell, *Politics: Who Gets What, When, and How* (New York: McGraw-Hill, 1938).

7. Randy Shilts, *And the Band Played On: Politics, People, and the AIDS Epidemic* (New York: Penguin Books, 1987).
8. Robert A. Dahl, *Dilemmas of Pluralist Democracy* (New Haven, CT: Yale University Press, 1982), 6.
9. Robert A. Dahl, *A Preface to Democratic Theory* (Chicago: University of Chicago Press, 1956), 137.
10. Robert Putnam, *Bowling Alone: The Collapse and Revival of American Community* (New York: Simon & Schuster, 2000). Putnam's famous first article on the subject can be found on the Web at *http://muse.jhu.edu/demo/journal_of_democracy/v006/putnam.html.*
11. Kevin Phillips, *The Politics of Rich and Poor: Wealth and the American Electorate in the Reagan Aftermath* (New York: Random House, 1990), 1.
12. Bob Woodward, *The Agenda: Inside the Clinton White House* (New York: Simon & Schuster, 1994).
13. Woodward, *The Agenda*, 145.
14. Dick Armey, *The Freedom Revolution* (Washington, D.C.: Regnery, 1995), 316.
15. Louis Hartz, *The Liberal Tradition in America* (New York: Harcourt, Brace, 1955).
16. Frederick Jackson Turner, *The Significance of the Frontier in American History* (New York: Readex Microprint, 1966), 221.

2 The Constitution

Chapter Outline

Gregory Lee Johnson knew little about the Constitution, but he knew he was upset. He felt that the buildup of nuclear weapons in the world threatened the planet's survival, and he wanted to protest presidential and corporate policies concerning nuclear weapons. Yet, he had no money to hire a lobbyist or purchase an ad in a newspaper. So he, along with some other demonstrators, marched through the streets of Dallas, chanting political slogans and stopping at several corporate locations to stage "die-ins" intended to dramatize the consequences of nuclear war. Gregory carried an American flag as he marched. The demonstration ended in front of Dallas City Hall, where Gregory unfurled the American flag, doused it with kerosene, and set it on fire.

Burning the flag violated the law, and Gregory was convicted of "desecration of a venerated object," sentenced to one year in prison, and fined $2,000. He appealed his conviction, claiming

the law that prohibited burning the flag violated his freedom of speech. The U.S. Supreme Court agreed in the case of *Texas v. Gregory Lee Johnson*.

Gregory was pleased with the Court's decision, but he was nearly alone. The public howled its opposition to the decision, and President George Bush called for a constitutional amendment authorizing punishment of flag desecraters. Many public officials vowed to support the amendment, and organized opposition to the amendment was scarce. However, an amendment to prohibit burning the American flag did not obtain the two-thirds vote in each house of Congress necessary to send a constitutional amendment to the states for ratification.

Instead, Congress passed a law—the Flag Protection Act—that outlawed the desecration of the American flag. The next year, however, in *United States v. Eichman*, the Supreme Court found the act an impermissible infringement on free speech.

After years of political posturing, legislation, and litigation, little has changed. Burning the flag remains a legally protected form of political expression despite the objections of the overwhelming majority of the American public. Gregory Johnson did not prevail because he was especially articulate; nor did he win because he had access to political resources such as money or powerful supporters. He won because of the nature of the Constitution.

Understanding how an unpopular protestor like Gregory Lee Johnson could prevail against the combined forces of the public and its elected officials is central to understanding the American system of government. The Constitution supersedes ordinary law, even when the law represents the wishes of a majority of citizens. The Constitution not only guarantees individual rights but also decentralizes power. Even the president, "the leader of the free world," cannot force Congress to act, as George Bush could not force Congress to start the process of amending the Constitution. Power is not concentrated efficiently in one person's hands, such as the president's. Instead, there are numerous checks on the exercise of power and many obstacles to change. Some complain that this system produces stalemate, while others praise the way it protects minority views. Both positions are correct.

Gregory Johnson's case raises some important questions about government in America. What does democracy mean if the majority does not get its way? Is this how we should be governed? And is it appropriate that the many limits on the scope of government action, both direct and indirect, prevent action desired by most people?

constitution

A nation's basic law. It creates political institutions, assigns or divides powers in government, and often provides certain guarantees to citizens. Constitutions can be either written or unwritten. See also **U.S. Constitution.**

A **constitution** is a nation's basic law. It creates political institutions, allocates power within government, and often provides guarantees to citizens. A constitution is also an unwritten accumulation of traditions and precedents that have established acceptable styles of behavior and policy outcomes.

A constitution sets the broad rules of the game of politics, allowing certain types of competition among certain players. *These rules are never neutral,* however. Instead, they give some participants and some policy options advantages over others in the policymaking process. This is why understanding these rules is so important to understanding government and to answering questions about how we are governed and what government does.

The Origins of the Constitution

In the summer of 1776, a small group of men met in Philadelphia and passed a resolution that began an armed rebellion against the government of the most powerful nation on earth. The resolution was, of course, the Declaration of Independence; the armed rebellion was the American Revolution.

The attempt to overthrow a government forcibly is a serious and unusual act. It is considered treasonous everywhere, including in the United States. Typically, it is punishable by death. A set of compelling ideas drove our forefathers to take such drastic and risky action. It is important to understand these ideas in order to understand the Constitution.

The Road to Revolution

By eighteenth-century standards, life was not bad for most people in America at the time of the Revolution (slaves and indentured servants being major exceptions). In fact, White colonists "were freer, more equal, more prosperous, and less burdened with cumbersome feudal and monarchical restraints than any other part of mankind."[1] Although the colonies were part of the British Empire, the king and Parliament generally confined themselves to governing America's foreign policy and trade. Almost everything else was left to the discretion of individual colonial governments. Although commercial regulations irritated colonial shippers, planters, land speculators, and merchants, these rules had little influence on the vast bulk of the population, who were self-employed farmers or artisans.

As you can see in Figure 2.1, Britain obtained an enormous new territory in North America after the French and Indian War (also known as the Seven Years' War) ended

Figure 2.1 European Claims in North America

Following its victory in the French and Indian War in 1763, Britain obtained an enormous new territory to govern. To raise revenues to defend and administer the territory, it raised taxes on the colonists and tightened enforcement of trade regulations.

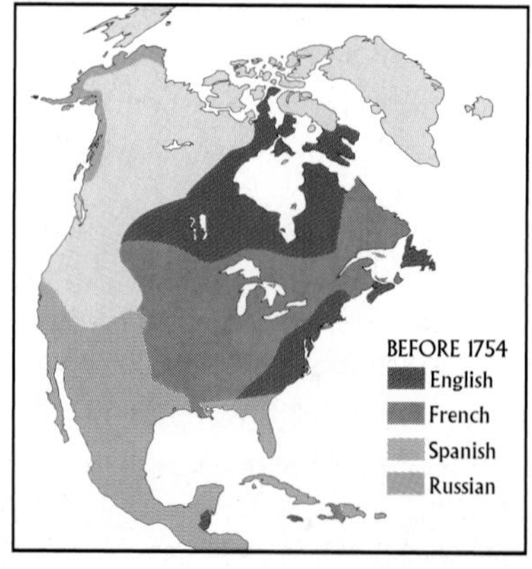

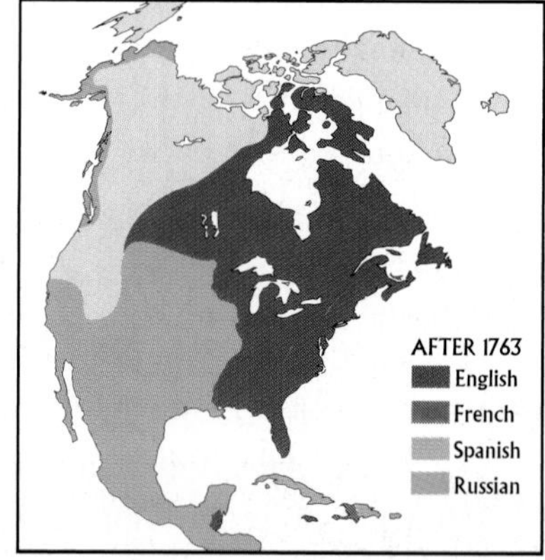

in 1763. The cost of defending this territory against foreign adversaries was large, and Parliament reasoned that it was only fair that those who were the primary beneficiaries—the colonists—should contribute to their own defense. Thus, in order to raise revenue for colonial administration and defense, the British legislature passed a series of taxes on official documents, newspapers, paper, glass, paint, and tea. Britain also began tightening enforcement of its trade regulations, which were designed to benefit the mother country, not the colonists.

Colonists resented these taxes, especially because they were imposed while the colonists lacked direct representation in Parliament. They protested, boycotted the taxed goods, and as a symbolic act of disobedience even threw 342 chests of tea into Boston Harbor. Britain reacted by applying economic pressure through a naval blockade of the harbor, further fueling the colonists' anger. The colonists responded by forming the First Continental Congress in September 1774, sending delegates from each colony to Philadelphia to discuss the future of relations with Britain.

Declaring Independence

As colonial discontent with the English festered, the Continental Congress was in almost continuous session during 1775 and 1776. Talk of independence was common among the delegates. Virginia, as it often did in those days, played a leading role at the Philadelphia meeting of the Congress. It sent seven delegates to join the serious discussion of repudiating the rule of King George III. These delegates were joined later by a last-minute substitute for Peyton Randolph, who was needed back in Williamsburg to preside over Virginia's House of Burgesses.

The substitute, Thomas Jefferson, was a young, well-educated Virginia lawmaker who had just written a resolution in the Virginia legislature objecting to new British policies. Jefferson brought to the Continental Congress his talent as an author and his knowledge of political philosophy. He was not a rabble-rousing pamphleteer like Thomas Paine, whose fiery tract *Common Sense* had appeared in January 1776 and fanned the already hot flames of revolution. Jefferson was steeped in the philosophical writings of European moral philosophers, and his rhetoric matched his reading.[2]

In May and June of 1776, the Continental Congress began debating resolutions about independence. On June 7, Richard Henry Lee of Virginia moved "that these United States are and of rights ought to be free and independent states." A committee composed of Thomas Jefferson of Virginia, John Adams of Massachusetts, Benjamin Franklin of Pennsylvania, Roger Sherman of Connecticut, and Robert Livingston of New York was formed to draft a document to justify the inevitable declaration. On July 2, Lee's motion to declare independence from England was formally approved. The famous **Declaration of Independence,** written primarily by Jefferson, was adopted two days later, on July 4.

Declaration of Independence
The document approved by representatives of the American colonies in 1776 that stated their grievances against the British monarch and declared their independence.

The Declaration of Independence quickly became one of the most widely quoted and revered documents in America. Filled with fine principles and bold language, it can be read as both a political tract and a philosophical treatise. (It is reprinted in the Appendix of this book.)

Politically, the Declaration was a polemic, announcing and justifying a revolution. Most of the document—27 of its 32 paragraphs—listed the ways the king had abused the colonies. George III was accused of all sorts of evil deeds, even though he personally had little to do with Parliament's colonial policies. King George was even blamed for inciting the "merciless Indian savages" to make war on the colonists. The king received the blame because the Convention delegates held that Parliament lacked authority over the colonies.

The Declaration's polemical aspects were important because the colonists needed foreign assistance to take on the most powerful nation in the world. France, which was engaged in a war with Britain, was a prime target for the delegates' diplomacy and eventually provided aid that was critical to the success of the Revolution.

John Adams (from right), Roger Sherman, Robert R. Livingston, Thomas Jefferson, and Benjamin Franklin submit the Declaration of Independence to Continental Congress President John Hancock. Legend has it that Hancock remarked, "We must be unanimous; there must be no pulling different ways; we must hang together," to which Franklin replied, "We must indeed all hang together, or, most assuredly, we shall hang separately."

Today, the Declaration of Independence is studied more as a statement of philosophy than as a political call to arms. In just a few sentences, Jefferson set forth the American democratic creed, the most important and succinct statement of the philosophy underlying American government—as applicable in the year 2001 as it was in 1776.

The English Heritage: The Power of Ideas

Philosophically, the Jeffersonian pen put on paper ideas that were by then common knowledge on both sides of the Atlantic, especially among those people who wished to challenge the power of kings. Franklin, Jefferson, James Madison of Virginia, Robert Morris of Pennsylvania, Alexander Hamilton of New York, and other intellectual leaders in the colonies were learned and widely read men, familiar with the works of English, French, and Scottish political philosophers. These leaders corresponded about the ideas they were reading, quoted philosophers in their debates over the Revolution, and applied those ideas to the new government they formed in the framework of the Constitution.

John Locke was one of the most influential philosophers read by the colonists. His writings, especially *The Second Treatise of Civil Government* (1689), profoundly influenced American political leaders. His work was "the dominant political faith of the American colonies in the second quarter of the eighteenth century. A thousand pulpits thundered with its benevolent principles; a hundred editors filled their pages with its famous slogans."[3]

natural rights

Rights inherent in human beings, not dependent on governments, which include life, liberty, and property. The concept of natural rights was central to English philosopher John Locke's theories about government, and was widely accepted among America's founding fathers.

The foundation upon which Locke built his powerful philosophy was a belief in **natural rights**—rights inherent in human beings, not dependent on governments. Before governments arise, Locke held, people exist in a state of nature in which there are no formal laws or governments. Instead, the laws of nature govern people, laws determined by people's innate moral sense. This natural law brings natural rights, including life, liberty, and property. Natural law can even justify a challenge to the rule of a tyrannical king, because it is superior to human law.

Government, Locke argued, must be built on the **consent of the governed;** in other words, the people must agree on who their rulers will be. It should also be a **limited government;** that is, there must be clear restrictions on what rulers can do. Indeed, the sole purpose of government, according to Locke, was to protect natural rights. The idea that certain things were beyond the realm of government contrasted sharply with the traditional notion that kings had been divinely granted absolute rights over subjects.

consent of the governed

The idea that government derives its authority by sanction of the people.

limited government

The idea that certain restrictions should be placed on government to protect the **natural rights** of citizens.

Two limits on government were particularly important to Locke. First, governments must provide standing laws so that people know in advance whether their acts will be acceptable. Second, and Locke was very forceful on this point, "the supreme power cannot take from any man any part of his property without his consent." To Locke, "the preservation of property was the end of government." The sanctity of property was one of the few ideas absent in Jefferson's draft of the Declaration of Independence. Even though Jefferson borrowed from and even paraphrased Lockean ideas, he altered Locke's phrase "life, liberty, and property" to "life, liberty, and the pursuit of happiness." We shall soon see, though, how the Lockean idea of the sanctity of property figured prominently at the Constitutional Convention. James Madison, the most influential member of that body, directly echoed Locke's view that the preservation of property is the purpose of government.

In an extreme case, said Locke, people have a right to revolt against a government that no longer has their consent. Locke anticipated critics' charges that this right would lead to constant civil disturbances. He emphasized that people should not revolt until injustices become deeply felt. The Declaration of Independence accented the same point, declaring that "governments long established should not be changed for light and transient causes." But when matters went beyond "patient sufferance," severing these ties was not only inevitable but also necessary.

Jefferson's Handiwork: The American Creed

There are some remarkable parallels between Locke's thought and Jefferson's language in the Declaration of Independence (see Table 2.1). Jefferson, like Locke, finessed his way past the issue of how the rebels knew men had rights. Jefferson simply declared that it was "self-evident" that men were equally "endowed by their Creator with certain unalienable rights," including "life, liberty, and the pursuit of happiness." Because it was the purpose of government to "secure" these rights, if it failed to do so, the people could form a new government.[4]

Locke represented only one element of revolutionary thought from which Jefferson borrowed. In the English countryside, there was also a well-established tradition of opposition to the executive power of the Crown and support for recovering the rights of the people. An indigenous American republicanism—stressing moral virtue, patriotism, relations based on natural merit, and the equality of independent citizens—intensified the radicalism of this "country" ideology and linked it with older currents of European thought stretching back to antiquity.

It was in the American colonies that the powerful ideas of European political thinkers took root and grew into what Seymour Martin Lipset has termed the "first new nation."[5] With these revolutionary ideas in mind, Jefferson claimed in the Declaration of Independence that people should have primacy over governments, that they should rule instead of be ruled. Moreover, each person was important as an individual, "created equal" and endowed with "unalienable rights." Consent of the governed, not divine rights or tradition, made the exercise of political power legitimate.

No government had ever been based on these principles. Ever since 1776, Americans have been concerned about fulfilling the high aspirations of the Declaration of Independence.

Table 2.1 Locke and the Declaration of Independence: Some Parallels

LOCKE	DECLARATION OF INDEPENDENCE
Natural Rights	
"The state of nature has a law to govern it" "life, liberty, and property"	"Laws of Nature and Nature's God" "life, liberty, and the pursuit of happiness"
Purpose of Government	
"to preserve himself, his liberty, and property"	"to secure these rights"
Equality	
"men being by nature all free, equal and independent"	"all men are created equal"
Consent of the Governed	
"for when any number of men have, by the consent of every individual, made a community, with a power to act as one body, which is only by the will and determination of the majority"	"Governments are instituted among men, deriving their just powers from the consent of the governed."
Limited Government	
"Absolute arbitrary power, or governing without settled laws, can neither of them consist with the ends of society and government." "As usurpation is the exercise of power which another has a right to, so tyranny is the exercise of power beyond right, which nobody can have a right to."	"The history of the present King of Great Britain is a history of repeated injuries and usurpations."
Right to Revolt	
"The people shall be the judge. . . . Oppression raises ferments and makes men struggle to cast off an uneasy and tyrannical yoke."	"Prudence, indeed, will dictate that Governments long established should not be changed for light and transient causes. . . . But when a long train of abuses and usurpations, pursuing invariably the same Object evinces a design to reduce them under absolute Despotism, it is their right, it is their duty, to throw off such Government."

IN CONGRESS. JULY 4, 1776.

The unanimous Declaration of the thirteen united States of America.

Winning Independence

The pen may be mightier than the sword, but declaring independence did not win the Revolution—it merely announced its beginning. John Adams wrote to his wife Abigail, "You will think me transported with enthusiasm, but I am not. I am well aware of the toil, blood, and treasure that it will cost us to maintain this Declaration, and support and defend these states." Adams was right. The colonists seemed little match for the finest army in the world, whose size was nearly quadrupled by hired guns from the German state of Hesse and elsewhere. In 1775, the British had 8,500 men stationed in the colonies and had hired nearly 30,000 mercenaries. Initially, the colonists had only

5,000 men in uniform, and their number waxed and waned as the war progressed. Nevertheless, in 1783, the American colonies won their war of independence. How they eventually won is a story best left to history books. How they formed a new government, however, will be explored in the following sections.

The "Conservative" Revolution

Revolutions such as the 1789 French Revolution, the 1917 Russian Revolution, and the 1978–1979 Iranian Revolution produced great societal change—as well as plenty of bloodshed. The American Revolution was different. Although many people lost their lives during the Revolutionary War, the Revolution itself was essentially a conservative movement that did not drastically alter the colonists' way of life. Its primary goal was to restore rights the colonists felt were already theirs as British subjects.

American colonists did not feel the need for great social, economic, or political upheavals. They "were not oppressed people; they had no crushing imperial shackles to throw off."[6] As a result, the Revolution did not create class conflicts that would split society for generations to come. The colonial leaders' belief that they needed the consent of the governed blessed the new nation with a crucial element of stability—a stability the nation would need.

The Government That Failed: 1776–1787

The Continental Congress that adopted the Declaration of Independence was only a voluntary association of the states. In 1776, the Congress appointed a committee to draw up a plan for a permanent union of the states. That plan, our first constitution, was the **Articles of Confederation.**[7]

Articles of Confederation

The first constitution of the United States, adopted by Congress in 1777 and enacted in 1781. The Articles established a national legislature, the Continental Congress, but most authority rested with the state legislatures.

The Articles of Confederation

The Articles established a government dominated by the states. The United States, according to the Articles, was a confederation, a "league of friendship and perpetual union" among 13 states. The Articles established a national legislature with one house; states could send as many as seven delegates or as few as two, but each state had only one vote. There was no president and no national court, and the powers of the national legislature—the Congress—were strictly limited. Most authority rested with the state legislatures because the new nation's leaders feared a strong central government would become as tyrannical as British rule.

Because unanimous consent of the states was needed to put the Articles into operation, the Articles adopted by Congress in 1777 did not go into effect until 1781, when laggard Maryland finally ratified them. In the meantime, the Continental Congress barely survived, lurching from crisis to crisis. At one point during the war, some of Washington's troops threatened to create a monarchy with him as king unless Congress paid their overdue wages.

Even after the Articles were ratified, many logistical and political problems plagued the Congress. State delegations attended haphazardly. Thomas Jefferson, a delegate to a meeting of the Congress, complained to his friend and fellow Virginian James Madison on February 20, 1784:

> *We cannot make up a congress at all. There are eight states in town, six of which are represented by two members only. Of these, two members of different states are confined by gout, so that we cannot make . . . a quorum. We have not sat above three days, I believe, in as many weeks. Admonition after admonition has been sent to the states to no effect. We have sent one today. If it fails, it seems as well we should all retire.*[8]

Why does it matter?

One of the central features of the Constitution is the creation of a strong national government. How might things be different if the framers had retained a weak national government, as under the Articles of Confederation? For example, how would the American economy be affected if Congress lacked the power to regulate interstate commerce? How would racial policy be different if the federal courts could not issue orders to protect civil rights? Would you be comfortable if some states still had segregated universities?

The Congress had few powers outside maintaining an army and navy—and little money to do even that. It had to request money from the states because it had no power to tax. If states refused to send money (which they often did), Congress did without. In desperation, Congress sold off western lands (land east of the Mississippi and west of the states) to speculators, issued securities that sold for less than their face value, or used its own presses to print money that was virtually worthless. Congress also voted to disband the army, despite continued threats from Britain and Spain.

Congress lacked the power to regulate commerce, which inhibited foreign trade and the development of a strong national economy. It did, however, manage to develop sound policies for the management of the western frontiers, passing the Northwest Ordinance of 1787 that encouraged the development of the Great Lakes region.

In general, the weak and ineffective national government could take little independent action. All government power rested in the states. The national government could not compel the states to do anything, and it had no power to deal directly with individual citizens. The weakness of the national government prevented it from dealing with the hard times that faced the new nation. There was one benefit of the Articles, however: When the nation's leaders began to write a new Constitution, they could look at the provisions of the Articles of Confederation and know some of the things they should avoid.

Changes in the States

What was happening in the states was more important than what was happening in the Congress. The most important change was a dramatic increase in democracy and liberty, at least for White males. Many states adopted bills of rights to protect freedoms, abolished religious qualifications for holding office, and liberalized requirements for voting. Expanded political participation brought a new middle class to power.

This middle class included farmers who owned small homesteads rather than manorial landholders, and artisans instead of lawyers. Before the Revolution, almost all members of New York's assembly were either urban merchants or wealthy landowners. In the 1769 assembly, for example, 43 percent of the legislators were farmers even though nearly 95 percent of New Yorkers were farmers. But after the Revolution, a major power shift occurred. With expanded voting privileges, farmers and craftworkers became a decisive majority, and the old elite of professionals, wealthy merchants, and large landholders saw its power shrink. The same change happened in other states as power shifted from a handful of wealthy individuals to a more broad-based group (see Table 2.2). After a careful examination of the economic backgrounds of pre- and post-Revolutionary legislators, Jackson Turner Main concluded,

> *The voters had ceased to confine themselves to an elite, but were selecting instead men like themselves. The tendency to do so had started during the colonial period, especially in the North, and had now increased so dramatically as almost to revolutionize the legislatures.*[9]

Democracy was taking hold everywhere.

The structure of government in the states also became more responsive to the people. Power was concentrated in the legislatures because legislators were considered closer to the voters than governors or judges. Governors were often selected by the legislatures and were kept on a short leash, with brief tenures and limited veto and appointment powers. Legislatures overruled court decisions and criticized judges for unpopular decisions.

The idea of equality was driving change throughout the nation. Although the Revolutionary War itself did not transform American society, it unleashed the republi-

Table 2.2 Power Shift: Economic Status of State Legislators Before and After the Revolutionary War

After the Revolution, power in the state legislatures shifted from the hands of the wealthy to those with more moderate incomes, and from merchants and lawyers to farmers. This trend was especially evident in the northern states.

	Three Northern States[a]		Three Southern States[b]	
STATUS OF LEGISLATORS	PREWAR	POSTWAR	PREWAR	POSTWAR
Wealthy	36%	12%	52%	28%
Well to do	47%	26%	36%	42%
Moderate Income	17%	62%	12%	30%
Merchants and lawyers	43%	18%	23%	17%
Farmers	23%	55%	12%	26%

[a]New York, New Jersey, and New Hampshire.
[b]Maryland, Virginia, and South Carolina.
Source: From Jackson Turner Main, "Government by the People: The American Revolution and the Democratization of the Legislatures," *The William and Mary Quarterly*, 3rd ser. 23 (July 1966): Reprinted by permission of the Omohandro Institute of Early American History and Culture.

can tendencies in American life. Americans were in the process of becoming "the most liberal, the most democratic, the most commercially minded, and the most modern people in the world."[10] Members of the old colonial elite found this turn of affairs quite troublesome because it challenged their hold on power.

Economic Turmoil

After the Revolution, James Madison observed that "the most common and durable source of factions [special interests] has been the various and unequal division of property."[11] The post-Revolutionary legislatures epitomized Madison's argument that economic inequality played an important role in shaping public policy. At the top of the political agenda were economic issues. A postwar depression had left many small farmers unable to pay their debts and threatened them with mortgage foreclosures. Now under control of people more sympathetic to debtors, the state legislatures listened to the demands of small farmers. A few states, notably Rhode Island, demonstrated their support of debtors, passing policies favoring them over creditors. Some printed tons of paper money and passed "force acts" requiring reluctant creditors to accept the almost worthless money. Debtors could thus pay big debts with cheap currency.

Shays' Rebellion

Policies favoring debtors over creditors did not please the economic elite who had once controlled nearly all the state legislatures. They were further shaken when, in 1786, a small band of farmers in western Massachusetts rebelled at losing their land to creditors. Led by Revolutionary War Captain Daniel Shays, this rebellion, called **Shays' Rebellion,** was a series of armed attacks on courthouses to prevent judges from foreclosing on farms. Farmers in other states—though never in large numbers—were also unruly. Jefferson was not distressed at this behavior, calling the attack a "little rebellion," but it remained on the minds of the economic elite. They were scared at the thought that people had taken the law into their own hands and violated

Shays' Rebellion

A series of attacks on courthouses by a small band of farmers led by Revolutionary War Captain Daniel Shays to block foreclosure proceedings.

Shays' Rebellion, in which farmers physically prevented judges from foreclosing on farms, helped spur the birth of the Constitution. News of the small rebellion quickly spread around the country, and some of the Philadelphia delegates thought a full-fledged revolution would result. The event reaffirmed the framers' belief that the new federal government needed to be a strong one.

the property rights of others. Neither Congress nor the state was able to raise a militia to stop Shays and his followers, and a privately paid force was assembled to do the job, which further fueled dissatisfaction with the weakness of the Articles of Confederation system.

The Aborted Annapolis Meeting

In September 1786, a handful of leaders assembled at Annapolis, Md., to discuss problems with the Articles of Confederation and suggest solutions. The assembly was an abortive attempt at reform. Only five states—New York, New Jersey, Delaware, Pennsylvania, and Virginia—were represented at the meeting; the 12 delegates were few enough in number to meet around a dinner table. Called to consider commercial conflicts that had arisen among the states under the Articles of Confederation, the Annapolis delegates decided that a larger meeting and a broader proposal were needed to organize the states. Holding most of their meetings at a local tavern, this small and unofficial band of reformers issued a call for a full-scale meeting of the states in Philadelphia the following May—in retrospect, a rather bold move by so small a group. Their request was granted, however; the Continental Congress called for a meeting of all the states. In May 1787, what we now call the Constitutional Convention got down to business in Philadelphia.

Making a Constitution: The Philadelphia Convention

Representatives from 12 states came to Philadelphia to heed the Continental Congress' call to "take into consideration the situation in the United States." Only Rhode Island, a stronghold of paper-money interests, refused to send delegates. Virginia's Patrick Henry (the colonial firebrand who had declared, "Give me liberty or give me death!"), fearing a centralization of power, also "smelled a rat" in the developments in Philadelphia and did not attend.

The delegates were ordered to meet "for the sole and express purpose of revising the Articles of Confederation." The Philadelphia delegates did not pay much attention

Alexander Hamilton, a New York delegate to the Convention, favored a strong central government; in fact, he favored an elected king. Hamilton was less influential at the Convention than he would be later as an architect of the nation's economic policy.

to this order, however, because amending the Articles required the unanimous consent of the states, which they knew would be impossible. Thus, the 55 delegates ignored their instructions and began writing what was to become the **U.S. Constitution.**

U.S. Constitution

The document written in 1787 and ratified in 1788 that sets forth the institutional structure of U.S. government and the tasks these institutions perform. It replaced the Articles of Confederation.

Gentlemen in Philadelphia

Who were these 55 men? They may not have been "demigods," as Jefferson, perhaps sarcastically, called them, but they were certainly a select group of economic and political notables. They were mostly wealthy planters, successful (or once-successful) lawyers and merchants, and men of independent wealth. Many were college graduates and most had practical political experience. Most were coastal residents, rather than residents of the expanding western frontiers, and a significant number were urbanites, rather than part of the primarily rural American population.

Philosophy into Action

The delegates in Philadelphia were an uncommon combination of philosophers and shrewd political architects. The debates moved from high principles on the big issues to self-interest on the small ones.[12] The first two weeks were mainly devoted to general debates about the nature of republican government (government in which ultimate power rests with the voters). After that, practical and divisive issues sometimes threatened to dissolve the meeting.

Obviously, these 55 men did not share the same political philosophy. Democratic Benjamin Franklin held very different views from aristocratic Alexander Hamilton, who hardly hid his disgust for democracy. Yet, at the core of their ideas, even those of Franklin and Hamilton, existed a common center. The group agreed on questions of

(1) human nature, (2) the causes of political conflict, and (3) the object, and (4) nature of a republican government.

Human Nature. In his famous work entitled *Leviathan* written in 1651, Thomas Hobbes argued that man's natural state was war and that a strong absolute ruler was necessary to restrain man's bestial tendencies. Without a strong government, Hobbes wrote, life would be "solitary, poor, nasty, brutish, and short." The delegates were not convinced of the need for a monarch, but they did hold a cynical view of human nature.

People, they thought, were self-interested. Franklin and Hamilton, poles apart philosophically, both voiced this sentiment. Said Franklin, "There are two passions which have a powerful influence on the affairs of men: the love of power and the love of money." Hamilton agreed in his characteristically blunt manner: "Men love power." The men at Philadelphia believed that government should play a key role in containing the natural self-interest of people.[13]

Political Conflict. Of all the words written by and about the delegates, none have been more widely quoted than these by James Madison: "The most common and durable source of factions has been the various and unequal distribution of property." In other words, *the distribution of wealth* (land was the main form of wealth in those days) *is the source of political conflict.* "Those who hold and those who are without property," Madison went on, "have ever formed distinct interests in society." Other sources of conflict included religion, views of governing, and attachment to various leaders.[14]

factions

Interest groups arising from the unequal distribution of property or wealth that James Madison attacked in **Federalist Paper** # 10. Today's parties or interest groups are what Madison had in mind when he warned of the instability in government caused by factions.

Arising from these sources of conflict are **factions,** which we might call parties or interest groups. A majority faction might well be composed of the many who have little or no property; the minority faction, of those with property. If unchecked, the delegates thought, one of these factions would eventually tyrannize the other. The majority would try to seize the government to reduce the wealth of the minority; the

Pennsylvania delegate Gouverneur Morris was a man of considerable means and, like Hamilton, an extreme antidemocrat primarily concerned with protecting property holders. He was responsible for the style and wording of the Constitution.

minority would try to seize the government to secure its own gains. Governments that are run by factions, the Founders believed, are prone to instability, tyranny, and even violence. The effects of factions had to be checked.

Objects of Government. To Gouverneur Morris of Pennsylvania, the preservation of property was the "principal object of government." Morris was outspoken and plainly overlooked some other objects of government, including security from invasion, domestic tranquillity, and promotion of the general welfare. However, Morris's remark typifies the philosophy of many of the delegates. John Locke (who was, remember, the intellectual patron saint of many of the delegates) had said a century before that "The preservation of property is the end of government." Few of these men would have disagreed. As property holders themselves, these delegates could not imagine a government that did not make its principal objective an economic one: the preservation of individual rights to acquire and hold wealth. A few (like Morris) were intent on shutting out the propertyless altogether. "Give the votes to people who have no property," Morris claimed, "and they will sell them to the rich who will be able to buy them."

Nature of Government. Given their beliefs about human nature, the causes of political conflict, the need to protect property, and the threat of tyranny by a faction, what sort of government did the delegates believe would work? They answered in different ways, but the message was always the same. Power should be set against power, so that no one faction would overwhelm the others. The secret of good government is "balanced" government. They were influenced in their thinking by writings of a French aristocrat, Baron Montesquieu, who advocated separate branches of government with distinct powers and the ability to check the other branches. The Founders agreed, concluding that a limited government would have to contain checks on its own power. So long as no faction could seize the whole of government at once, tyranny could be avoided. A complex network of checks, balances, and separation of powers would be required for a balanced government.

The Agenda in Philadelphia

The delegates in Philadelphia could not merely construct a government from ideas. They wanted to design a government that was consistent with their political philosophy, but they also had to meet head-on some of the thorniest issues confronting the fledgling nation at the time—issues of equality, the economy, and individual rights.

The Equality Issues

The Declaration of Independence states that all men are created equal; the Constitution, however, is silent on equality. Nevertheless, some of the most important issues on the policy agenda in Philadelphia concerned equality. Three issues occupied more attention than almost any others: whether the states were to be equally represented, what to do about slavery, and whether to ensure political equality.

Equality and Representation of the States. One crucial policy issue was how the new Congress would be constituted. The **New Jersey Plan,** proposed by William Paterson of New Jersey, called for each state to be equally represented in the new Congress. The opposing strategy, suggested by Edmund Randolph of Virginia, is usually called the **Virginia Plan.** It called for giving each state representation in Congress based on the state's share of the American population.

New Jersey Plan

The proposal at the Constitutional Convention that called for equal **representation** of each state in Congress regardless of the state's population.

Virginia Plan

The proposal at the Constitutional Convention that called for **representation** of each state in Congress in proportion to that state's share of the U.S. population.

Connecticut Compromise

The compromise reached at the Constitutional Convention that established two houses of Congress: the House of Representatives, in which **representation** is based on a state's share of the U.S. population, and the Senate, in which each state has two representatives.

The delegates resolved this conflict with a compromise devised by Roger Sherman and William Johnson of Connecticut. The solution proposed by this **Connecticut Compromise** was to create two houses in Congress. One body, the Senate, would have two members from each state (the New Jersey Plan), and the second body, the House of Representatives, would have representation based on population (the Virginia Plan). The U.S. Congress is still organized in exactly the same way. Each state has two senators, and the state's population determines its representation in the House.

Although the Connecticut Compromise was intended to maximize equality between the states, it actually gives more power to people who live in states with small populations than to those who live in more heavily populated states. Every state has two senators and at least one member of the House, no matter how small its population. To take the most extreme case, Wyoming and California have the same number of votes in the Senate (two), although Wyoming has less than 2 percent of California's population. Thus, a citizen of Wyoming has more than 50 *times* the representation in the Senate as does a citizen of California.[15]

Why does it matter?

You have seen that the Senate overrepresents states with small populations. What would be the consequences if there were only one house of Congress and it were based solely on population? Would the government be more efficient if bills only had to pass in one house? Would certain interests be less likely to get their way? If your family were farmers, would you favor equality of representation? Would you favor it if you depended on public transportation in a large city?

Because it is the Senate, not the House, that ratifies treaties, confirms presidential nominations, and hears trials of impeachment, citizens in less populated states have a greater say in these key tasks. In addition, the Electoral College (which is the body that actually elects the president and is discussed in Chapter 10) gives small states greater weight. If no presidential candidate receives a majority in the Electoral College, the House of Representatives make the final decision—with each state having one vote. In such a case (which has not occurred since 1824), the votes of citizens of Wyoming would again carry over 50 times as much weight as those of Californians.

Whether representation in the Senate is "fair" is a matter of debate. What is not open to question is that the delegates to the 1787 convention had to accommodate various interests and viewpoints in order to convince all the states to join an untested union.

Some experts have described the conflict as a struggle between big and small states (that is, states with large and small populations), each presumably looking for a plan that would maximize its representation. The votes in Philadelphia do not support this interpretation. Eight states voted on the New Jersey Plan (Georgia's delegation was split and did not vote), which supposedly favored the small states. In fact, three big states (New York, Maryland, and Connecticut) lined up with two small states

DOONESBURY Garry Trudeau

When the Constitution was written, many Northern and Southern delegates assumed that slavery, being relatively unprofitable, would soon die out. A single invention—Eli Whitney's cotton gin—made it profitable again. Although Congress did act to control the growth of slavery, the slave economy became entrenched in the South.

(Delaware and New Jersey) to support equal representation of the states. The two Carolinas, small states at the time, voted against the New Jersey Plan.[16] It was not a sharp cleavage of small versus large. Rather, the vote depended on different views about how to achieve equality of representation, one side favoring equal representation of the states and the other favoring equal representation of people.

Slavery. The second equality issue was slavery. The contradictions between slavery and the sentiments of the Declaration of Independence are obvious, but slavery was legal in every state except Massachusetts. It was concentrated in the South, however, where slave labor was commonplace in agriculture. Some delegates, like Gouverneur Morris, denounced slavery in no uncertain terms. But the Convention could not accept Morris' position in the face of powerful Southern opposition led by Charles C. Pinckney of South Carolina. The delegates did agree that Congress could limit *future importing* of slaves (they allowed it to be outlawed after 1808), but they did not forbid slavery itself. The Constitution, in fact, inclines toward recognizing slavery; it stated that persons legally "held to service or labour" (referring to slaves) who escaped to free states had to be returned to their owners.

Another difficult question about slavery arose at the Convention. How should slaves be counted in determining representation in Congress? Southerners were happy to see slaves counted toward determining their representation in the House of Representatives (though reluctant to count them for apportionment of taxation). Here the result was the famous *three-fifths compromise*. Representation and taxation were to be based on the "number of free persons," plus three-fifths of the number of "all other persons." Everyone, of course, knew who those other persons were.

Political Equality. The delegates dodged one other issue on equality. A handful of delegates, led by Franklin, suggested that national elections should require universal manhood suffrage (that is, a vote for all free adult males). This still would have left a majority of the population disenfranchised, but for those still smarting from Shays' Rebellion and the fear of mob rule, the suggestion was too democratic. Many delegates wanted to put property qualifications on the right to vote. Ultimately, as the debate wound down, they decided to leave the issue to the states. People qualified to vote in state elections could also vote in national elections (see Table 2.3).

Table 2.3 How Three Issues of Equality Were Resolved: A Summary

PROBLEM	SOLUTION
Equality of the States	
Should states be represented equally (the New Jersey Plan) or in proportion to their population (the Virginia Plan)?	Both, according to the Connecticut Compromise. States have equal representation in the Senate, but representation in the House is proportionate to population.
Slavery	
What should be done about slavery?	Although Congress was permitted to stop the importing of slaves after 1808, the Constitution is mostly silent on the issue of slavery.
How should slaves be counted for representation in the House of Representatives?	Count each slave as three-fifths of a person.
Political Equality	
Should the right to vote be based on universal manhood suffrage, or should it be very restricted?	Finesse the issue. Let the states decide qualifications for voting.

The Economic Issues

The Philadelphia delegates were deeply concerned about the state of the American economy. Economic issues were high on the Constitution writers' policy agenda. People disagreed (in fact, historians still disagree) as to whether the postcolonial economy was in a shambles. Advocates of the Constitution, called Federalists, stressed the economy's "weaknesses, especially in the commercial sector, and Anti-Federalists (those opposed to a strong national government, and thus opposed to a new constitution) countered with charges of exaggeration."[17] The writers of the Constitution, already committed to a strong national government, charged that the economy was indeed in disarray. Specifically, they claimed that the following problems had to be addressed:

- The states had erected tariffs against products from other states.
- Paper money was virtually worthless in some states, but many state governments, which were controlled by debtor classes, forced it on creditors anyway.
- The Congress was having trouble raising money because the economy was in a recession.

Understanding something about the delegates and their economic interests gives us insight into their views on political economy. They were, by all accounts, the nation's postcolonial economic elite. Some were budding capitalists. Others were creditors whose loans were being wiped out by cheap paper money. Many were merchants who could not even carry on trade with a neighboring state. Virtually all of them thought a strong national government was needed to bring economic stability to the chaotic union of states that existed under the Articles of Confederation.[18]

It is not surprising, then, that the framers of the Constitution would seek to strengthen the economic powers (and thus the scope) of the new national government. One famous historian, Charles A. Beard, claimed that their principal motivation for doing so was to increase their personal wealth. The framers, he said, not only were propertied, upper-class men protecting their interests but also held bonds and investments whose value would increase if the Constitution were adopted. The best evidence, however, indicates that although they were concerned about protecting property rights, the Founders' motivations were in the broad sense of building a strong economy rather than in the narrow sense of increasing their personal wealth.[19]

The delegates made sure that the Constitution clearly spelled out the economic powers of Congress (see Table 2.4). Consistent with the general allocation of power in the Constitution, Congress was to be the chief economic policymaker. It could obtain revenues through taxing and borrowing. These tools, along with the power to appropriate funds, became crucial instruments for influencing the economy (as we will see in Chapter 17). By maintaining sound money and guaranteeing payment for the national debt, Congress was to encourage economic enterprise and investment in the United States. Congress was also given power to build the nation's infrastructure by constructing post offices and roads and to establish standard weights and measures. To protect property rights, Congress was charged with punishing counterfeiters and pirates, ensuring patents and copyrights, and legislating rules for bankruptcy. Equally important (and now a key congressional power, with a wide range of implications for the economy) was Congress's new ability to regulate interstate and foreign commerce. In sum, the Constitution granted Congress the power to create the conditions within which markets could flourish.

In addition, the framers prohibited practices in the states that they viewed as inhibiting economic development, such as maintaining individual state monetary systems, placing duties on imports from other states, and interfering with lawfully contracted debts. Moreover, the states were to respect civil judgments and contracts made in other states, and they were to return runaway slaves to their owners. (This last protection of "property" rights is now, of course, defunct as a result of the Thirteenth Amendment, which outlawed slavery.) To help the states, the national government guaranteed them "a republican form of government" to prevent a recurrence of Shays' Rebellion, in which violence, instead of legislation and the courts, was used to resolve commercial disputes.

The Constitution also obligated the new government to repay all the public debts incurred under the Continental Congress and the Articles of Confederation—debts that totaled $54 million. Although this requirement may seem odd, there was sound economic reason for it. Paying off the debts would ensure from the outset that money would flow into the American economy and would also restore the confidence of investors in the young nation. Even today, people trade in government debt (in the form of bonds) just as they do in the stocks of corporations. Thus, the Constitution helped to spur a capitalist economy.

Table 2.4 Economics in the Constitution

Powers of Congress

1. Levy taxes.
2. Pay debts.
3. Borrow money.
4. Coin money and regulate its value.
5. Regulate interstate and foreign commerce.
6. Establish uniform laws of bankruptcy.
7. Punish piracy.
8. Punish counterfeiting.
9. Create standard weights and measures.
10. Establish post offices and post roads.
11. Protect copyrights and patents.

Prohibitions on the States

1. States cannot pass laws impairing the obligations of contract.
2. States cannot coin money or issue paper money.
3. States cannot require payment of debts in paper money.
4. States cannot tax imports or exports from abroad or from other states.
5. States cannot free runaway slaves from other states (now defunct).

Other Key Provisions

1. The new government assumes the national debt contracted under the Articles of Confederation.
2. The Constitution guarantees a republican form of government.
3. The states must respect civil court judgments and contracts made in other states.

The Individual Rights Issues

There was another major item on the Constitutional Convention agenda; the delegates had to design a system that would preserve individual rights. There was no dispute about the importance of safeguarding individualism, and the Founders believed that this would be relatively easy. After all, they were constructing a limited government that, by design, could not threaten personal freedoms. In addition, they dispersed power among the branches of the national government and between the national and state governments so that each branch or level could restrain the other. Also, most of the delegates believed that the various states were already doing a sufficient job of protecting individual rights.

As a result, the Constitution says little about personal freedoms. The protections it does offer are as follows:

writit of habeas corpus

A court order requiring jailers to explain to a judge why they are holding a prisoner in custody.

- It prohibits suspension of the **writ of habeas corpus** (except during invasion or rebellion). Such a court order enables persons detained by authorities to secure an immediate inquiry into the causes of their detention. If no proper explanation is offered, a judge may order their release. (Article I, Section 9)
- It prohibits Congress or the states from passing bills of attainder (which punish people without a judicial trial). (Article I, Section 9)
- It prohibits Congress or the states from passing *ex post facto* laws (which punish people or increase the penalties for acts that were not illegal or not as punishable when the act was committed). (Article I, Section 9)
- It prohibits the imposition of religious qualifications for holding office in the national government. (Article VI)
- It narrowly defines and outlines strict rules of evidence for conviction of treason. To be convicted, a person must levy war against the United States or adhere to and aid its enemies during war. Conviction requires confession in open court or the testimony of *two* witnesses to the *same* overt act. The framers of the Constitution would have been executed as traitors if the Revolution had failed, and they were therefore sensitive to treason laws. (Article III, Section 3)
- It upholds the right to trial by jury in criminal cases. (Article III, Section 2)

The delegates were content with their document. When it came time to ratify the Constitution, however, there was widespread criticism of the absence of specific protections of individual rights, such as free expression and the rights of the accused.

The Madisonian Model

The framers believed that human nature was self-interested and that inequalities of wealth were the principal source of political conflict. Regardless, they had no desire to remove the divisions in society by converting private property to common ownership; they also believed that protecting private property was a key purpose of government. Their experience with state governments under the Articles of Confederation reinforced their view that democracy was a threat to property. Many of them felt that the nonwealthy majority—an unruly mob—would tyrannize the wealthy minority if given political power. Thus, the delegates to the Constitutional Convention were faced with the dilemma of reconciling economic inequality with political freedom.

Thwarting Tyranny of the Majority

James Madison was the principal architect of the government's final structure, and his work still shapes our policymaking process[20] (see "Making a Difference: James Madison"). He and his colleagues feared both majority and minority factions. Either could take control of the government and use it to their own advantage. Factions of the minority, however, were easy to handle; the majority could simply out-vote them. Factions of the majority were harder to handle. If the majority united around some pol-

Making a Difference

James Madison

James Madison was an unlikely hero. The oldest of 10 children, he was born in Virginia in 1751. An excellent scholar though frail and sickly in his youth, he graduated from the College of New Jersey (later Princeton) in 1771, where he demonstrated special interest in government and the law. Considering the ministry for a career, however, he stayed on for a year of post-graduate study in theology. His health was too frail to fight in the Revolution in 1776, but at age 29 Madison was chosen to represent Virginia in the Continental Congress in 1780. Although originally the youngest delegate, he played a major role in the deliberations of that body. He wrote extensively about deficiencies in the Articles of Confederation, and he was highly instrumental in the convening of the Constitutional Convention in 1787.

Madison was not a great orator, nor was he a man of great wealth. He was a careful student of politics and government. Relying on the force of his intellect, he was clearly the preeminent figure at the Constitutional Convention—a gathering that included Benjamin Franklin, George Washington, and other giants of American history who were many years his senior. Though many of his proposals were rejected, he tirelessly advocated a strong government. Despite his poor speaking capabilities, he took the floor more than 150 times, third only to Gouverneur Morris and James Wilson. Ultimately, the Constitution reflected his thinking more than that of any other delegate. His journal of the convention is the best single record of the event.

Playing a lead in the ratification process in Virginia, too, Madison defended the document against such powerful opponents as Patrick Henry, George Mason, and Richard Henry Lee. In New York, where Madison was serving in the Continental Congress, he collaborated with Alexander Hamilton and John Jay in a series of essays that appeared in the newspapers in 1787–1788 and were soon published in book form as *The Federalist* (1788). This set of essays is a classic of political theory and a lucid exposition of the republican principles that dominated the framing of the Constitution.

Elected to the new House of Representatives in 1789, Madison helped frame and ensure passage of the Bill of Rights. He also assisted in organizing the executive department and creating a system of federal taxation. As leaders of the opposition to Hamilton's policies, he and Thomas Jefferson founded the Democratic-Republican Party.

Madison went on to become secretary of state and then succeeded Jefferson as president. He is best remembered, however, as a young man who fought for his ideas and, as a result, became the father of the Constitution.

icy issue, such as the redistribution of wealth, they could oppress the minority, violating the latter's basic rights.[21]

As Madison would later explain:

> *Ambition must be made to counteract ambition. . . . If men were angels, no government would be necessary. If angels were to govern men, neither external nor internal controls would be necessary. In framing a government which is to be administered by men over men, the great difficulty lies in this: you must first enable the government to control the governed; and then in the next place oblige it to control itself.*[22]

To prevent the possibility of a tyranny of the majority, Madison proposed the following:

1. Place as much of the government as possible beyond the direct control of the majority.
2. Separate the powers of different institutions.
3. Construct a system of checks and balances.

Limiting Majority Control. Madison believed that to thwart tyranny by the majority, it was essential to keep most of the government beyond their power. His plan placed only one element of government, the House of Representatives, within direct control of the votes of the majority. In contrast, state legislatures were to elect senators and special electors were to select the president; in other words, government officials would be elected by a small minority, not by the people themselves. Judges were to be nominated by the president (see Figure 2.2). Even if the majority

Figure 2.2 The Constitution and the Electoral Process: The Original Plan

Under Madison's plan, which was incorporated in the Constitution, voters' electoral influence was limited. Only the House of Representatives was directly elected. Senators and presidents were indirectly elected, and judges were nominated by the president. Over the years, Madison's original model has been substantially democratized. The Seventeenth Amendment (1913) established direct election of senators by popular majorities. Today, the Electoral College has become largely a rubber stamp, voting the way the popular majority in each state votes.

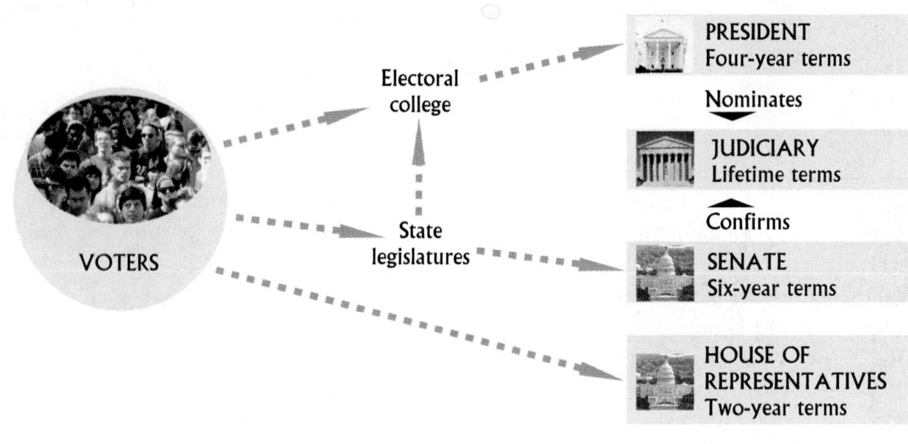

seized control of the House of Representatives, they still could not enact policies without the agreement of the Senate and the president. To further insulate governmental officials from public opinion, judges were given lifetime tenure and senators were given terms of six years, with only one-third elected every two years, compared with the two-year election intervals of all members of the House of Representatives.

separation of powers

A feature of the Constitution that requires each of the three branches of government—executive, legislative, and judicial—to be relatively independent of the others so that one cannot control the others. Power is shared among these three institutions.

Separating Powers. The Madisonian scheme also provided for a **separation of powers.** Each of the three branches of government—executive (the president), legislative (Congress), and judicial (the courts)—would be relatively independent of one another so that no single branch could control the others. The president, Congress, and the courts were all given independent elements of power. Power was not divided absolutely, however; rather, it was *shared* among the three institutions.

checks and balances

Features of the Constitution that limit government's power by requiring that power be balanced among the different governmental institutions. These institutions continually check one another's activities.

Creating Checks and Balances. Because powers were not completely separate, each branch required the consent of the others for many of its actions. This created a system of **checks and balances** that reflected Madison's goal of setting power against power to constrain government actions. He reasoned that if a faction seized one institution, it still could not damage the whole system. The system of checks and balances was an elaborate and delicate creation. The president checks Congress by holding veto power; Congress holds the purse strings of government and must approve presidential appointments.

The courts also figured into the system of checks and balances. Presidents could nominate judges, but their confirmation by the Senate was required. The Supreme Court itself, in *Marbury v. Madison* (1803), asserted its power to check the other branches through judicial review: the right to hold actions of the other two branches unconstitutional. This right, which is not specifically outlined in the Constitution, considerably strengthened the Court's ability to restrain the other branches of government. For a summary of separation of powers and the checks and balances system, see Figure 2.3.

visual literacy
The American System of Checks and Balances

Establishing a Federal System. As we will discuss in detail in Chapter 3, the Founders also established a federal system of government that divided the power of government between a national government and the individual states. Most government activity at the time occurred in the states. The framers of the Constitution anticipated that this would be an additional check on the national government.

Figure 2.3 Separation of Powers and Checks and Balances in the Constitution

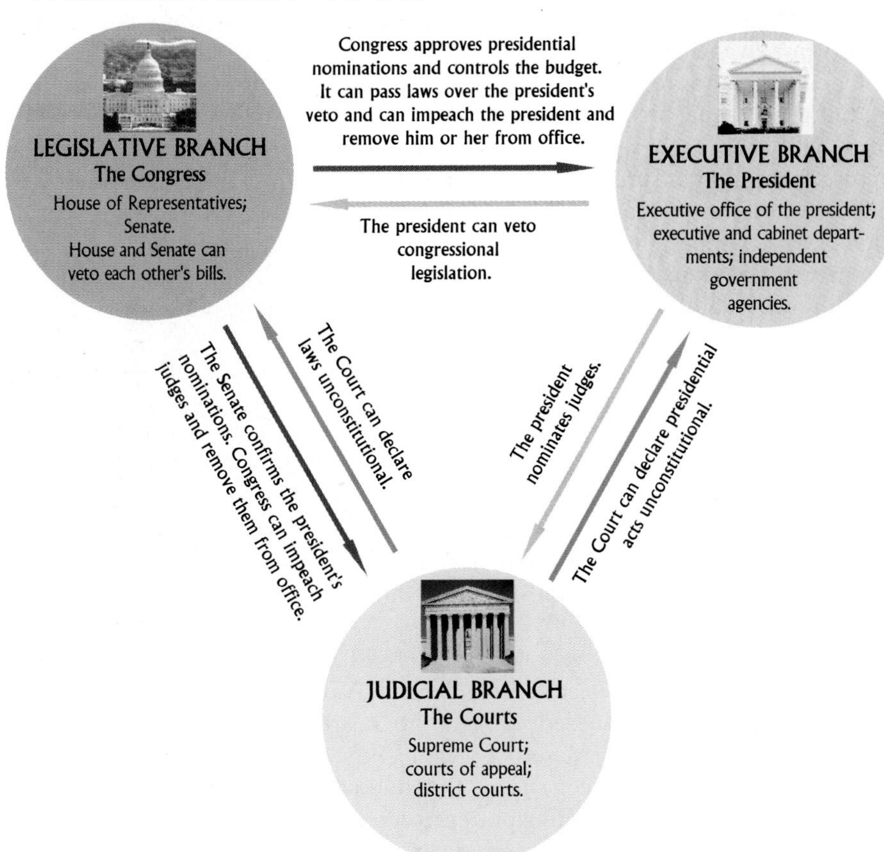

The doctrine of separation of powers allows the three institutions of government to check and balance one another. Judicial review—the power of courts to hold executive and congressional policies unconstitutional—was not explicit in the Constitution, but was asserted by the Supreme Court in *Marbury v. Madison.*

The Constitutional Republic

When asked what kind of government the delegates had produced, Benjamin Franklin is said to have replied, "A republic . . . if you can keep it." Because the Founders did not wish to have the people directly make all decisions (as in a town meeting where everyone has one vote), and because even then the country was far too large for such a proposal to be feasible, they did not choose to create a direct democracy. Their solution was to establish a **republic**: a system based on the consent of the governed in which representatives of the public exercise power. This deliberative democracy required and encouraged reflection and refinement of the public's views through an elaborate decision-making process.

The system of checks and balances and separation of powers favors the status quo. People who desire change must usually have a sizable majority, not just a simple majority of 51 percent. Those opposed to change need only win at one point in the policymaking process—say in obtaining a presidential veto—whereas those who favor change must win *every* battle along the way. Change usually comes slowly, if at all. As a result, the Madisonian system encourages moderation and compromise and slows change. It is difficult for either a minority or a majority to tyrannize; and both property rights and personal freedoms (with only occasional lapses) have survived.

Franklin was correct that such a system is not easy to maintain. It requires careful nurturing and balancing of diverse interests. Some critics argue that the policymaking process lacks efficiency, preventing effective responses to pressing matters. We will examine this issue closely throughout *Government in America.*

republic

A form of government in which the people select representatives to govern them and make laws.

Why does it matter?

The checks and balances in the Constitution favor the status quo. Is this a problem? Would it be better for America if there were less gridlock and policymakers could act swiftly to bring about change? For example, would you prefer a narrow majority in Congress to be able to reinstate the military draft, or would you prefer that the draft could only become law with the support of a large majority?

The End of the Beginning

On the 109th day of the meetings, in stifling heat made worse because the windows of the Pennsylvania statehouse were closed to ensure secrecy, the final version of the Constitution was read aloud. Then Dr. Franklin rose with a speech he had written, but was so enfeebled he had to ask James Wilson to deliver it. In it, Franklin noted that "There are several parts of this Constitution of which I do not at present approve, but I am not sure that I shall never approve them." He then offered a few political witticisms, defended their handiwork, and concluded by saying, "On the whole, Sir, I cannot help expressing a wish that every member of the Convention who may still have an objection to it, would with me on this occasion, doubt a little of his own infallibility—and make manifest our unanimity, put his name to this instrument."

Nonetheless, Edmund Randolph of Virginia rose to announce apologetically that he did not intend to sign. Gouverneur Morris of Pennsylvania stated his reservations about the compromises but called the document the "best that was to be attained" and said he would "take it with all its faults." Alexander Hamilton of New York again made a plea for unity, but Elbridge Gerry of Massachusetts was adamant in opposition. Taking Franklin's remarks personally, he "could not but view them as levelled against himself and the other gentlemen who meant not to sign." He bluntly predicted that a "civil war may result from the present crisis of the United States."

On Franklin's motion, a vote was taken. Ten states voted yes, and none voted no, but South Carolina's delegates were divided. As the records so quaintly put it, "The Members then proceeded to sign the instrument." Edmund Randolph, Elbridge Gerry, and George Mason of Virginia, however, refused to sign. Franklin then made another short speech, saying that the sun pictured on the chair of convention president George Washington represented the new nation and was rising, not setting. Then (quoting the records again) "the Constitution being signed . . . the convention dissolved itself by Adjournment." The members then adjourned to a tavern. The experience of the last few hours, when conflict intermingled with consensus, reminded them that implementing this new document would be no small feat.

George Washington presides over the signing of the Constitution. "The business being closed," he wrote, "the members adjourned to the City Tavern, dined together and took cordial leave of each other."

Ratifying the Constitution

The Constitution did not go into effect once the Constitutional Convention in Philadelphia was over. It had to be ratified by the states. Our awe of the Founders sometimes blinds us to the bitter politics of the day. There is no way of determining the public's feelings about the new document, but as John Marshall (who later became Chief Justice) suggested, "It is scarcely to be doubted that *in some of the adopting states, a majority of the people were in opposition.*" (Italics ours.)[23] The Constitution itself required that only 9 of the 13 states approve the document before it could be implemented, ignoring the requirement that the Articles of Confederation be amended only by unanimous consent.

Federalists and Anti-Federalists

Throughout the states, a fierce battle erupted between the **Federalists,** who supported the Constitution, and the **Anti-Federalists,** who opposed it. Newspapers were filled with letters and articles, many written under pseudonyms, praising or condemning the document. In praise of the Constitution, three men—James Madison, Alexander Hamilton, and John Jay—wrote a series of articles under the name Publius. These articles, known as the ***Federalist Papers,*** are second only to the Constitution itself in characterizing the framers.

Beginning on October 27, 1787, barely a month after the Convention ended, the *Federalist Papers* began to appear in New York newspapers as part of the ratification debate in New York. Eighty-five were eventually published. They not only defended the Constitution detail by detail but also represented an important statement of political philosophy. (The essays influenced few of the New York delegates, however, who voted to ratify the Constitution only after New York City threatened to secede from the state if they did not.)

Federalists

Supporters of the **U.S. Constitution** at the time the states were contemplating its adoption.

Anti-Federalists

Opponents of the American Constitution at the time when the states were contemplating its adoption.

Federalist Papers

A collection of 85 articles written by Alexander Hamilton, John Jay, and James Madison under the name "Publius" to defend the Constitution in detail.

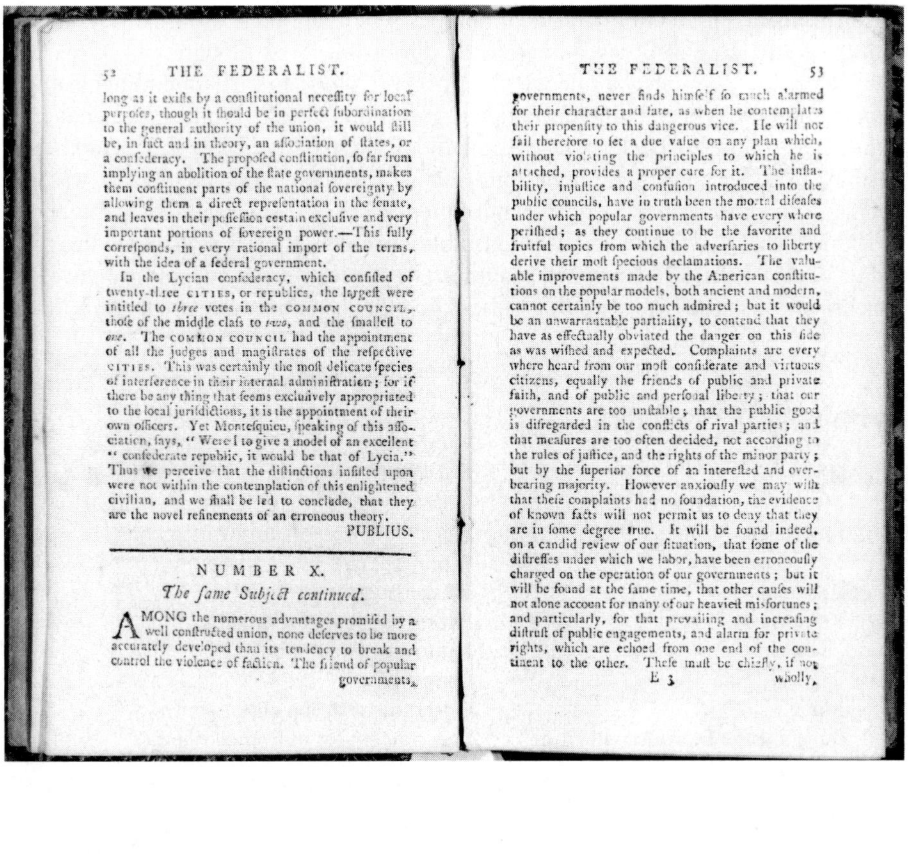

52 THE FEDERALIST.

long as it exiſts by a conſtitutional neceſſity for local purpoſes, though it ſhould be in perfect ſubordination to the general authority of the union, it would ſtill be, in fact and in theory, an aſſociation of ſtates, or a confederacy. The propoſed conſtitution, ſo far from implying an abolition of the ſtate governments, makes them conſtituent parts of the national ſovereignty by allowing them a direct repreſentation in the ſenate, and leaves in their poſſeſſion certain excluſive and very important portions of ſovereign power.—This fully correſponds, in every rational import of the terms, with the idea of a federal government.

In the Lycian confederacy, which conſiſted of twenty-three CITIES, or republics, the largeſt were intitled to *three* votes in the COMMON COUNCIL, thoſe of the middle claſs to *two*, and the ſmalleſt to *one*. The COMMON COUNCIL had the appointment of all the judges and magiſtrates of the reſpective CITIES. This was certainly the moſt delicate ſpecies of interference in their internal adminiſtration; for if there be any thing that ſeems excluſively appropriated to the local juriſdictions, it is the appointment of their own officers. Yet Monteſquieu, ſpeaking of this aſſociation, ſays, "Were I to give a model of an excellent "confederate republic, it would be that of Lycia." Thus we perceive that the diſtinctions inſiſted upon were not within the contemplation of this enlightened civilian, and we ſhall be led to conclude, that they are the novel refinements of an erroneous theory.

PUBLIUS.

NUMBER X.

The ſame Subject continued.

AMONG the numerous advantages promiſed by a well conſtructed union, none deſerves to be more accurately developed than its tendency to break and control the violence of faction. The friend of popular governments,

THE FEDERALIST. 53

governments, never finds himſelf ſo much alarmed for their character and fate, as when he contemplates their propenſity to this dangerous vice. He will not fail therefore to ſet a due value on any plan which, without violating the principles to which he is attached, provides a proper cure for it. The inſtability, injuſtice and confuſion introduced into the public councils, have in truth been the mortal diſeaſes under which popular governments have every where periſhed; as they continue to be the favorite and fruitful topics from which the adverſaries to liberty derive their moſt ſpecious declamations. The valuable improvements made by the American conſtitutions on the popular models, both ancient and modern, cannot certainly be too much admired; but it would be an unwarrantable partiality, to contend that they have as effectually obviated the danger on this ſide as was wiſhed and expected. Complaints are every where heard from our moſt conſiderate and virtuous citizens, equally the friends of public and private faith, and of public and perſonal liberty; that our governments are too unſtable; that the public good is diſregarded in the conflicts of rival parties; and that meaſures are too often decided, not according to the rules of juſtice, and the rights of the minor party; but by the ſuperior force of an intereſted and overbearing majority. However anxiouſly we may wiſh that theſe complaints had no foundation, the evidence of known facts will not permit us to deny that they are in ſome degree true. It will be found indeed, on a candid review of our ſituation, that ſome of the diſtreſſes under which we labor, have been erroneouſly charged on the operation of our governments; but it will be found at the ſame time, that other cauſes will not alone account for many of our heavieſt misfortunes; and particularly, for that prevailing and increaſing diſtruſt of public engagements, and alarm for private rights, which are echoed from one end of the continent to the other. Theſe muſt be chiefly, if not

E 3 wholly,

As an explanation and defense of the Constitution, the *Federalist Papers* were often discussed at dinner parties and debated in public places. Despite today's high literacy rates, it is doubtful that a similar set of documents, so rich in political philosophy, would be so widely read in modern America.

Far from being unpatriotic or un-American, the Anti-Federalists sincerely believed that the new government was an enemy of freedom, the very freedom they had just fought a war to ensure. Adopting names like Aggrippa, Cornelius, and Monteczuma, the Anti-Federalists launched bitter, biting, even brilliant attacks on the Philadelphia document. They frankly questioned the motives of the Constitution writers.

One objection was central to the Anti-Federalists' attacks: The new Constitution was a class-based document, intended to ensure that a particular economic elite controlled the public policies of the national government. The following quotations are from three Anti-Federalist critics of the Constitution.

> *This government will commence in a moderate aristocracy; it is at present impossible to foresee whether it will, in its operation, produce a monarchy, or a corrupt, oppressive aristocracy.*
>
> —*George Mason*

> *Thus, I conceive, a foundation is laid for throwing the whole power of the federal government into the hands of those who are in the mercantile interest; and for the landed, which is the great interest of this country to lie unrepresented, forlorn and without hope.*
>
> —*"Cornelius"*

> *These lawyers, men of learning, and moneyed men . . . expect to get into Congress themselves . . . so they can get all the power and all the money into their own hands.*
>
> —*Amos Singletary of Massachusetts*[24]

Remember that these charges of conspiracy and elitism were being hurled at the likes of Washington, Madison, Franklin, and Hamilton.

The Anti-Federalists had other fears. Not only would the new government be run by a few, but it would also erode fundamental liberties. James Lincoln was quoted in the records of the South Carolina ratifying convention as saying that he "would be glad to know why, in this Constitution, there is a total silence with regard to the liberty of the press. Was it forgotten? Impossible! Then it must have been purposely omitted; and with what design, good or bad, I leave the world to judge." You can compare the views of the Federalists and Anti-Federalists in Table 2.5.

These arguments were persuasive. To allay fears that the Constitution would restrict personal freedoms, the Federalists promised to add amendments to the document specifically protecting individual liberties. They kept their word; James Madison introduced 12 constitutional amendments during the First Congress in 1789. Ten were ratified by the states and took effect in 1791. These first 10 amendments to the Constitution, which restrain the national government from limiting personal freedoms, have come to be known as the **Bill of Rights** (see Table 2.6). Another of Madison's original 12 amendments, one dealing with congressional salaries, was ratified 201 years later as the Twenty-seventh Amendment (see the Appendix in this book).

Bill of Rights

The first 10 amendments to the **U.S. Constitution,** drafted in response to some of the **Anti-Federalist** concerns. These amendments define such basic liberties as freedom of religion, speech, and press and guarantee defendants' rights.

Opponents also feared that the Constitution would weaken the power of the states (which it did). Patrick Henry railed against strengthening the federal government at the expense of the states. "We are come hither," he told his fellow delegates to the Virginia

Table 2.5 Federalists and Anti-Federalists Compared

	ANTI-FEDERALISTS	FEDERALISTS
Backgrounds	Small farmers, shopkeepers, laborers	Large landowners, wealthy merchants, professionals
Government Preferred	Strong state government	Weaker state governments
	Weak national government	Strong national government
	Direct election of officials	Indirect election of officials
	Shorter terms	Longer terms
	Rule by the common man	Government by the elite
	Strengthened protections for individual liberties	Less concern for individual liberties

Table 2.6 The Bill of Rights (Arranged by Function)

Protection of Free Expression	
Amendment 1:	Freedom of speech, press, and assembly Freedom to petition government
Protection of Personal Beliefs	
Amendment 1:	No government establishment of religion Freedom to exercise religion
Protection of Privacy	
Amendment 3:	No forced quartering of troops in homes during peacetime
Amendment 4:	No unreasonable searches and seizures
Protection of Defendants' Rights	
Amendment 5:	Grand-jury indictment required for prosecution of serious crime No second prosecution for the same offense No compulsion to testify against oneself No loss of life, liberty, or property without due process of law
Amendment 6:	Right to a speedy and public trial by a local, impartial jury Right to be informed of charges against oneself Right to legal counsel Right to compel the attendance of favorable witnesses Right to cross-examine witnesses
Amendment 7:	Right to jury trial in civil suit where the value of controversy exceeds $20
Amendment 8:	No excessive bail or fines No cruel and unusual punishments
Protection of Other Rights	
Amendment 2:	Right to bear arms
Amendment 5:	No taking of private property for public use without just compensation
Amendment 9:	Unlisted rights are not necessarily denied
Amendment 10:	Powers not delegated to the national government or denied to the states are reserved for the states or the people

ratifying convention, "to preserve the poor commonwealth of Virginia."[25] Many state political leaders feared that their own power would be diminished as well.

Finally, not everyone wanted the economy to be placed on a more sound foundation. Creditors opposed the issuance of paper money because it would produce inflation and make the money they received as payment on their loans decline in value. Debtors favored paper money, however. Their debts (such as the mortgages on their farms) would remain constant, but if money became more plentiful, it would be easier for them to pay off their debts.

Ratification

Federalists may not have had the support of the majority, but they made up for it in shrewd politicking. They knew that many members of the legislatures of some states were skeptical of the Constitution and that state legislatures were populated with political leaders who would lose power under the Constitution. Thus, the Federalists specified that the Constitution be ratified by special conventions in each of the states—not by state legislatures.

Delaware was the first to approve, on December 7, 1787. Only six months passed before New Hampshire's approval (the ninth) made the Constitution official. Virginia and New York then voted to join the new union. Two states were holdouts: North Carolina and Rhode Island made the promise of the Bill of Rights their price for joining the other states.

With the Constitution ratified, it was time to select officeholders. The framers of the Constitution assumed that George Washington would be elected the first president of the new government—even giving him the Convention's papers for safekeeping—and they were right. The general was the unanimous choice of the Electoral College for president. He took office on April 30, 1789, in New York City, the first national capital. New Englander John Adams became "His Superfluous Excellence," as Franklin called the vice president.

Constitutional Change

"The Constitution," said Jefferson, "belongs to the living and not to the dead." The U.S. Constitution is frequently—and rightly—referred to as a living document. It is constantly being tested and altered.

Generally, constitutional changes are made either by formal amendments or by a number of informal processes. Formal amendments change the letter of the Constitution. There is also an unwritten body of tradition, practice, and procedure that, when altered, may change the spirit of the Constitution. In fact, not all nations, even those that we call democratic, have written constitutions (see "America in Perspective: Democracy *Without* a Constitution?").

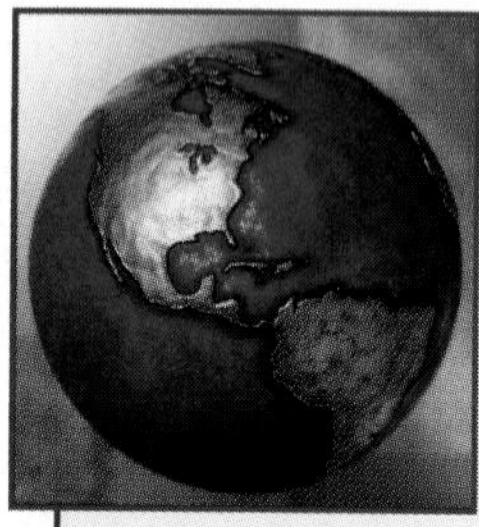

America in Perspective

Democracy *Without* a Constitution

Sometimes it is difficult for Americans to understand that constitutions can be both *written* and *unwritten*. They may be surprised to learn that Great Britain—often called "the cradle of democracy"—has no written constitution at all. The unwritten constitution of Britain is a mixture of acts of Parliament, judicial pronouncements, customs, and conventions about the rules of the political game. A number of documents are British constitutional landmarks, including the Magna Carta (the Great Charter), which King John accepted at Runnymeede in 1215 and which limited the power of the monarch. None of these documents, however, outlines Britain's entire governmental system, as does the U.S. Constitution for the United States.

Although in theory the British monarch has the power to overrule laws passed by Parliament (the British legislature), the last time the monarch did so was in 1707, when Queen Anne vetoed the Scottish Militia bill. Today, it is unthinkable that the British monarch would veto an act of Parliament. Thus, in Great Britain, there is no way to argue that an act of Parliament is *unconstitutional*, since there is no written constitution to which one can appeal. If Parliament passes a law, it remains a law.

Nevertheless, Britain is undeniably a democracy. The political system allows free speech, open and free elections, vigorously competing political parties, and all the other characteristics generally associated with democracy. British politicians simply have not had a need to produce a single constitutional document.

Britain has never experienced a sharp break with tradition—as in the American Revolution—forcing politicians to think about the basis of authority and the allocation of power, and then to write down how the country should be governed. As long as there is a basic consensus on how governing should take place, the British system works fine. When such a consensus is lacking, no government, whether it has a written or an unwritten constitution, can endure.

Figure 2.4 How the Constitution Can Be Amended

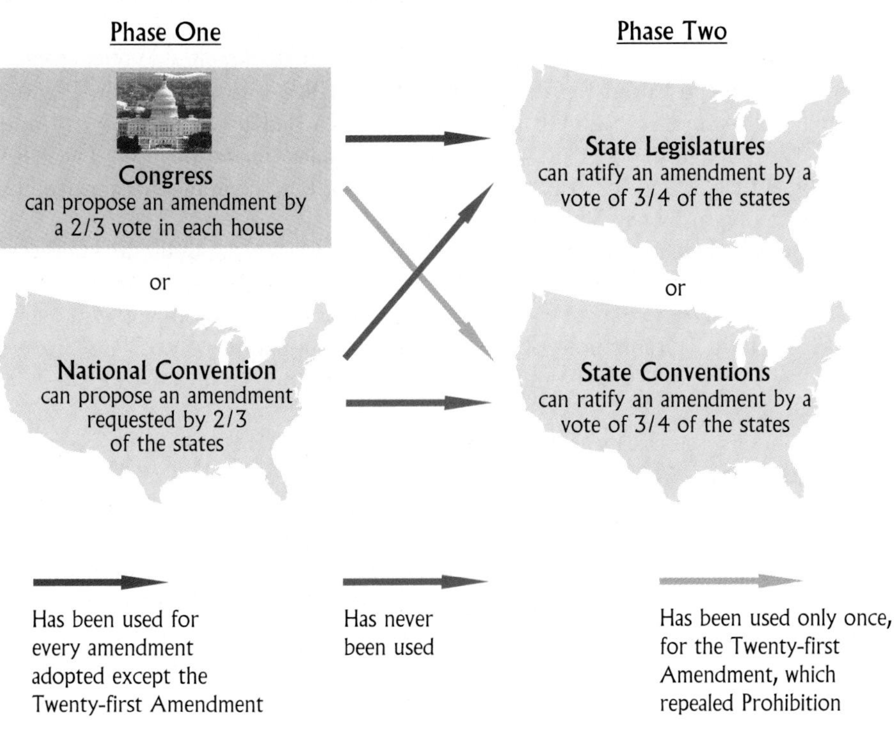

Has been used for every amendment adopted except the Twenty-first Amendment

Has never been used

Has been used only once, for the Twenty-first Amendment, which repealed Prohibition

The Constitution sets up two alternative routes for proposing amendments and two for ratifying them. Only one of the four combinations has been used in every case but one.

The Formal Amending Process

The most explicit means of changing the Constitution is through the formal process of amendment. Article V of the Constitution outlines procedures for formal amendment. There are two stages to the amendment process—proposal and ratification—and each stage has two possible avenues (see Figure 2.4). An amendment may be proposed either by a two-thirds vote in each house of Congress or by a national convention called by Congress at the request of two-thirds of the state legislatures. An amendment may be ratified either by the legislatures of three-fourths of the states or by special state conventions called in three-fourths of the states. The president has no formal role in amending the Constitution, although the chief executive may influence the success of proposed amendments.

comparative
Comparing Constitutions

All but one of the successful amendments to the Constitution have been proposed by Congress and ratified by the state legislatures. The exception was the Twenty-first Amendment, which repealed the short-lived Eighteenth Amendment—the prohibition amendment that outlawed the sale and consumption of alcohol. The amendment was ratified by special state conventions rather than by state legislatures. Because proponents of repeal doubted that they could win in conservative legislatures, they persuaded Congress to require that state conventions be called.

Unquestionably, formal amendments have made the Constitution more egalitarian and democratic. The emphasis on economic issues in the original document is now balanced by amendments that emphasize equality and increase the ability of a popular majority to affect government. The amendments are headed by the Bill of Rights (see Table 2.6), which Chapter 4 will discuss in detail. Later amendments, including the Thirteenth Amendment abolishing slavery, have forbidden various political and social inequalities based on race, gender, and age (these amendments will be discussed in Chapter 5). Other amendments, discussed later in this chapter, have democratized the political system, making it easier for voters to influence the government. Only one existing amendment specifically addresses the economy—the

Sixteenth, or "income tax," Amendment. Overall, it is clear that the most important effect of these constitutional amendments has been to expand liberty and equality in the United States.

Equal Rights Amendment

A constitutional amendment passed by Congress in 1972 stating that "equality of rights under the law shall not be denied or abridged by the United States or by any state on account of sex." The amendment failed to acquire the necessary support from three-fourths of the state legislatures.

Some amendments have been proposed but not ratified. The best known of these in recent years is the **Equal Rights Amendment**, or **ERA.** First proposed in 1923 by the nephew of suffragist Susan B. Anthony, the ERA had to wait 49 years—until 1972—before Congress passed it and sent it to the states for ratification. The ERA stated simply that "Equality of rights under the law shall not be denied or abridged by the United States or by any State on account of sex."

This seemingly benign amendment sailed through Congress and the first few state legislatures. The Hawaiian legislature, in fact, arranged for Senator Daniel Inouye's office to signal when the Senate passed the ERA so that Hawaii could be the first state to ratify.[26] Public opinion polls showed substantial support for the ERA. Surveys revealed that even people who held traditional views of women's roles still supported the ERA.[27]

Nevertheless, the ERA was not ratified. It failed, in part, because of the system of checks and balances. The ERA had to be approved not by a national majority but by three-fourths of the states. Many conservative Southern states opposed it, thus exercising their veto power despite approval by a majority of Americans.

timeline

The History of Constitutional Amendments

Proponents of other constitutional amendments have been especially active in recent years. You can consider the issue of frequently amending the Constitution in "You Are the Policymaker: How Frequently Should We Amend the Constitution?"

You Are the Policymaker

How Frequently Should We Amend the Constitution?

Since the ratification of the Bill of Rights in 1791, there have been only 16 amendments to the Constitution—an average of one amendment every 13 years. It is now common, however, for political activists—and even political party platforms—to call for amendments. Some recent examples include prohibiting the burning of the American flag, permitting prayer in the public schools, making abortions unconstitutional, requiring a balanced national budget, limiting the length of congressional terms, and protecting victims' rights—as well as guaranteeing women's rights (the ERA).

Conservatives have been in the forefront of most recent calls for amendments (the ERA being an exception); many of the proposals for constitutional change are designed to overcome liberal Supreme Court decisions. Liberals, quite naturally, have opposed these amendments. There is a larger question here than just the particular changes that advocates of amending the Constitution support, however. The big question is, How frequently should we change the fundamental law of the land?

Those who support amending the Constitution argue that the Constitution should reflect the will of the people. If the overwhelming majority of the public wants to prohibit burning the American flag, for example, why shouldn't the Constitution reflect their preference? There is little possibility that a minority or even a narrow majority will be able to impose its will on the people, they argue, because the Constitution requires an extraordinary majority to ratify an amendment. So why should we be reluctant to test the waters of change?

Opponents of changing the Constitution frequently have their own arguments. It is ironic, they say, that conservatives, who typically wish to preserve the status quo, should be in the forefront of fundamental change. They argue that the Constitution has served the United States very well for more than two centuries with few changes. Why should we risk altering the fundamentals of the political system? And if we do, will we be setting a dangerous precedent that will encourage yet more change in the future? Will such changes undermine the very nature of a constitution that is designed to set the basic rules of the game and be above the political fray?

What do *you* think? Are the arguments simply a reflection of ideologies? Should the Constitution reflect the current sentiment of the public and be changed whenever that opinion changes? Or should we show more caution in amending the Constitution no matter how we feel about a specific amendment?

The Informal Process of Constitutional Change

The members of the Constitutional Convention preserved the written document called The Constitution. They hired Jacob Shallus, a German immigrant in Philadelphia, to write out the Constitution and paid him the handsome sum of $30 to do so. The Convention was disbanding, having finished its work, and needed a rush job. On September 15, 1787, the conventioneers gave Shallus only 40 hours to copy the Constitution itself. Prepared on four pieces of parchment made from lamb or calf skin and written with a quill pen in Shallus' elegant script, the actual document bounced from capital to capital during the early days of the Republic. Today it sits at the National Archives, bathed in helium and under the watchful eye of an electronic camera.

Of course, the written Constitution itself is never changed, even when we pass a constitutional amendment. We do not haul out Shallus' old parchment and then write in some lines to abolish slavery or to create an income tax; the amendments, too, are deposited in the National Archives. Think for a moment of all the changes in American government that have taken place without altering a word or a letter of the written document. In fact, there is not a word in the Constitution that would lead us to suspect any of the following developments:

How You Can Make A Difference

Amending the Constitution

Today, it's not likely that anyone could have the kind of impact that James Madison had on the Constitution. Nevertheless, there are opportunities for average Americans to influence this enduring but malleable document. If you can't write the original document, you at least have a chance to change it! Every year advocates propose and champion new constitutional amendments. Some never get noticed while others keep percolating year after year. Inevitably, every advocate of a proposed amendment generates a vocal opponent. This is evident in two proposals gaining prominent attention in recent years: the Flag Protection Amendment and the Victims' Rights Amendment.

The drive for the Flag Protection Amendment began in the 1990s after the Supreme Court ruled that state and national laws that prohibited flag desecration were unconstitutional. A constitutional amendment seemed the only alternative to proponents of flag protection. In 1995, 1997, and 2000, only close votes in the Senate prevented the passage of such resolutions. If it passes both the House and the Senate, it appears extremely likely that it would be ratified by the states. Advocates of this amendment like the Citizens Flag Alliance (www.cfa-inc.org) argue that the flag deserves to be protected as the nation's most significant and important symbol of unity. Opponents like the ACLU (www.aclu.org) counter that this amendment would limit freedom of speech and squelch dissent in America.

The Victims' Rights Amendment, another recent proposal, evokes a similar split in public opinion. This amendment would guarantee victims of crime specific rights including restitution and an increased role in criminal proceedings. The National Victims' Constitutional Amendment Network (www.ncvan.org) claims that this amendment would restore balance to a criminal justice system without restricting the rights due to those accused of crimes. Opponents of this amendment come from a wide spectrum of American political thought. Fears of undermining the Bill of Rights drives the ACLU's opposition to this amendment while the libertarian Cato Institute (www.cato.org) argues that the federal government has no responsibility to address criminal problems. Like the Flag Protection Amendment, however, widespread public support within the states make eventual ratification of this amendment a distinct possibility if it ever passes both the House and the Senate.

You can make a difference in the battle for or against either of these proposed amendments by contacting the organizations listed and volunteering to take part in their advocacy efforts. You can also influence the shaping and interpretation of the Constitution by using more informal methods. Voting for presidential candidates that mirror your constitutional positions will enhance the likelihood that future Supreme Court justices and federal judges will interpret the Constitution along similar lines.

- The United States has the world's oldest two-party system, wherein almost every member of Congress and every president since Washington has declared, "I am a Democrat (or Republican, or Federalist, or Whig, or whatever)."
- Abortions through the second trimester of pregnancy (when the fetus cannot live outside the mother's womb) are legal in the United States.
- Members of the Electoral College consider themselves honor bound (and in some places even legally bound) to follow the preference of their state's electorate.
- Proceedings of both the Senate and the House are on TV; TV influences our political agenda and guides our assessments of candidates and issues.
- Government now taxes and spends about one-third of our gross domestic product, an amount the Convention delegates might have found gargantuan.

None of these things is "unconstitutional." The parties emerged, television came to prominence in American life, first technology and then the law permitted abortions—all without having to tinker with the Founders' handiwork. These developments could occur because the Constitution changes *informally* as well as formally. There are several ways in which the Constitution changes informally: through judicial interpretation, through political practice, and as a result of changes in technology and changes in the demands on policymakers.

Judicial Interpretation. Disputes often arise about the meaning of the Constitution. If it is the "supreme law of the land," then someone has to decide how to interpret the Constitution when disputes arise. In 1803, in the famous case of ***Marbury v. Madison,*** the Supreme Court decided it would be the one to resolve differences of opinion (Chapter 16 discusses this case in detail). It claimed for itself the power of **judicial review.** Implied but never explicitly stated in the Constitution,[28] this power gives courts the right to decide whether the actions of the legislative and executive branches of state and national governments are in accord with the Constitution.

Marbury v. Madison

The 1803 case in which Chief Justice John Marshall and his associates first asserted the right of the **Supreme Court** to determine the meaning of the **U.S. Constitution.** The decision established the Court's power of **judicial review** over acts of Congress, in this case the Judiciary Act of 1789.

judicial review

The power of the courts to determine whether acts of Congress, and by implication the executive, are in accord with the **U.S. Constitution.** Judicial review was established by John Marshall and his associates in ***Marbury v. Madison.***

Judicial interpretation can profoundly affect how the Constitution is understood because the Constitution usually means what the Supreme Court says it means. For example, in 1896 the Supreme Court decided that the Constitution allowed racial discrimination despite the presence of the Fourteenth Amendment. Fifty-eight years later it overruled itself and concluded that segregation by law violated the Constitution. In 1973, the Supreme Court decided that the Constitution protected a woman's right to an abortion during the first two trimesters of pregnancy when the fetus is not viable outside the womb—an issue the Founders never imagined. (These cases will be discussed in Chapters 4 and 5.)

Changing Political Practice. Current political practices also change the Constitution—stretching it, shaping it, and giving it new meaning. Probably no changes are more important than those related to parties and presidential elections.

Political parties as we know them did not exist when the Constitution was written. In fact, its authors would have disliked the idea of parties, which encourage factions. Regardless, by 1800 a party system had developed, and it plays a key role in making policy today. American government would be radically different if there were no political parties, even though the Constitution is silent about them.

Changing political practice has also altered the role of the Electoral College, which has now been reduced to a clerical one in selecting the president. The writers of the Constitution, eager to avoid giving too much power to the uneducated majority, intended that there be no popular vote for the president; instead, state legislatures or the voters (depending on the state) would select wise electors who would then choose a "distinguished character of continental reputation" (as the *Federalist Papers* put it) to be president. These electors formed the Electoral College. Each state would have the same number of electors to vote for the president as it had senators and representatives in Congress.

In 1796, the first election in which George Washington was not a candidate, electors scattered their votes among 13 candidates. By the election of 1800, domestic and foreign policy issues had divided the country into two political parties. To avoid dissipating their support, the parties required electors to pledge in advance to vote for the candidate who won their state's popular vote, leaving electors with a largely clerical function.

Although electors are now rubber stamps for the popular vote, nothing in the Constitution prohibits an elector from voting for any candidate. Every so often, electors have decided to cast votes for their own favorites; some state laws require electors to vote for the candidate chosen by a plurality of their state's citizens, but such laws have never been enforced. The idea that the Electoral College would exercise wisdom independent of the majority of people is now a constitutional anachronism, changed not by formal amendment but by political practice.

Technology. The Constitution has also been changed greatly by technology. The media have always played an important role in politics—questioning governmental policies, supporting candidates, and helping shape citizens' opinions. Modern technology, however, has spurred the development of a *mass* media that can rapidly reach huge audiences, something unimaginable in the eighteenth century. The bureaucracy has grown in importance with the development of computers, which create new potential for bureaucrats to serve the public (such as writing over 40 million Social Security checks each month)—and, at times, create mischief. Electronic communications and the development of atomic weapons have given the president's role as commander in chief added significance, increasing the power of the president in the constitutional system.

Increasing Demands on Policymakers. The significance of the presidency has also grown as a result of increased demands for new policies. The United States' evolution in the realm of international affairs—from an insignificant country that kept to itself to a superpower with an extraordinary range of international obligations—has concentrated additional power in the hands of the chief executive, who is designated to take the lead in foreign affairs. Similarly, the increased demands of domestic policy have positioned the president in a more prominent role in preparing the federal budget and a legislative program.

The Importance of Flexibility

The Constitution, even with all 27 amendments, is a short document containing fewer than 8,000 words. It does not prescribe in detail the structure and functioning of the national government. Regarding the judiciary, Congress is told simply to create a court system as it sees fit. The Supreme Court is the only court required by the Constitution, and even here the number of justices and their qualifications are left up to Congress. Similarly, many of the governing units we have today—such as the executive departments, the various offices in the White House, the independent regulatory commissions, and the committees of Congress, to name only a few examples—are not mentioned at all in the Constitution.

It is easy to see that the document the framers produced over 200 years ago was not meant to be static, written in stone. Instead, the Constitution's authors created a flexible system of government, one that could adapt to the needs of the times without sacrificing personal freedom. The framers allowed future generations to determine their own needs. As muscle grows on the constitutional skeleton, it inevitably gives new shape and purpose to the government. This flexibility has helped ensure the Constitution's—and the nation's—survival. Although the United States is young compared to other Western nations, it has the oldest functioning Constitution. France, which experienced a revolution in 1789, the same year the Constitution took effect,

has had 12 constitutions over the past two centuries. Despite the great diversity of the American population, the enormous size of the country, and the extraordinary changes that have taken place over the nation's history, the U.S. Constitution is still going strong.

Understanding the Constitution

As the body of rules that govern our nation, the Constitution has an impact on our everyday lives. A nation that prides itself on being "democratic" must evaluate the Constitution according to democratic standards. Our theme of the scope of government runs throughout this chapter, which focuses on what the national government can and cannot do. The following section will examine the Constitution in terms of democracy.

The Constitution and Democracy

Although the United States is often said to be one of the most democratic societies in the world, the Constitution itself is rarely described as democratic. This paradox is hardly surprising, considering the political philosophies of the men who wrote it. Among eighteenth-century upper-class society, democratic government was generally despised. If democracy was a way of permitting the majority's preference to become policy, the Constitution's authors wanted no part of it. The American government was to be a government of the "rich, well-born, and able," as Hamilton said, a government where John Jay's wish that "the people who own the country ought to govern it" would be a reality. Few people today would consider these thoughts democratic.

The Constitution did not, however, create a monarchy or a feudal aristocracy. It created a republic, a representative form of democracy modeled after the Lockean tradition of limited government. Thus, the undemocratic—even antidemocratic—Constitution established a government that permitted substantial movement toward democracy.

One of the central themes of American history is the gradual democratization of the Constitution. What began as a document characterized by numerous restrictions on direct voter participation has slowly become much more democratic. Today, few people share the Founders' fear of democracy. The expansion of voting rights has moved the American political system away from the elitist model of democracy and toward the pluralist model.

The Constitution itself offered no guidelines on voter eligibility, leaving it to each state to decide. As a result, only a small percentage of adults could vote; women and slaves were excluded entirely. Of the 17 constitutional amendments passed since the Bill of Rights, 5 have focused on the expansion of the electorate. The Fifteenth Amendment (1870) prohibited discrimination on the basis of race in determining voter eligibility (although it took the Voting Rights Act of 1965, discussed in Chapter 5, to make the amendment effective). The Nineteenth Amendment (1920) gave women the right to vote (although some states had already done so). The Twenty-third Amendment (1961) accorded the residents of Washington, D.C. the right to vote in presidential elections. Three years later, the Twenty-fourth Amendment prohibited poll taxes (which discriminated against the poor). Finally, the Twenty-sixth Amendment (1971) lowered the voter eligibility age to 18.

Not only are more people eligible to vote, but voters now have more officials to elect. The Seventeenth Amendment (1913) provided for direct election of senators. Presidential elections have been fundamentally altered by the development of political parties. By placing the same candidate on the ballot in all the states and requiring members of the electoral college to support the candidate who receives the most votes, parties have increased the probability that the candidate for whom most Americans vote will also receive a majority of the electoral college vote. According to the Constitution, the United States selects its president through an Electoral College, but in practice American citizens now directly elect the president. (For more on the Electoral College, see Chapter 10.) Nevertheless, it is possible for the candidate who receives the most popular votes to lose the election, as occurred in 1824, 1876, 1888, and 2000.

Technology has also diminished the separation of the people from those who exercise power. Officeholders communicate directly with the public through television, radio, and targeted mailings. Air travel makes it easy for members of Congress to commute regularly between Washington and their districts. Similarly, public opinion polls, the telephone, and e-mail enable officials to stay apprised of citizens' opinions on important issues. Even though the American population has grown from fewer than 4 million to 281 million people since the first census was taken in 1790, the national government has never been closer to those it serves.

participation
Democracy and the Internet

The Constitution and the Scope of Government

The Constitution created political institutions and the rules for politics and policymaking. Many of these rules limit government action. This limiting function is what the Bill of Rights and related provisions in the Constitution are all about. No matter how large the majority, for example, it is unconstitutional to establish a state-supported church.

Most of these limitations are designed primarily to protect liberty and to open the system to a broad range of participants. The potential range of action for the government is actually quite wide. Thus it is constitutionally permissible, although highly unlikely, for the United States either to abolish Social Security payments to the elderly or to take over ownership of the oil industry or the nation's airlines.

Yet the system of government created by the Constitution has profound implications for what the government does. On the one hand, individualism is reinforced at every turn. The separation of powers and the checks and balances established by the Constitution allow almost all groups some place in the political system where their demands for public policy can be heard. Because many institutions share power, groups can usually find at least one sympathetic ear in government. Even if the president opposes the policies a particular group favors, Congress, the courts, or some other institution can help the group achieve its policy goals.

In the early days of the civil rights movement, for example, African Americans found Congress and the president unsympathetic, so they turned to the Supreme

Court. Getting their interests on the political agenda would have been much more difficult if the Court had not had important constitutional power.

On the other hand, the Constitution encourages hyperpluralism. By providing effective access for so many interests, the Founders created a system of policymaking in which it is difficult for the government to act. The separation of powers and the system of checks and balances promote the politics of bargaining, compromise, and playing one institution against another. The system of checks and balances implies that one institution is checking another. *Thwarting, blocking,* and *impeding* are synonyms for checking. But if I block you, and you block someone else, and that person blocks me, none of us is going to accomplish anything, and we have gridlock.

Some scholars suggest that so much checking was built into the American political system that effective government is almost impossible. The historian and political scientist James MacGregor Burns has argued that

> *We have been too much entranced by the Madisonian model of government . . . The system of checks and balances and interlocked gears of government . . . requires the consensus of many groups and leaders before the nation can act; . . . we underestimate the extent to which our system was designed for deadlock and inaction.*[29]

If the president, Congress, and the courts all pull in different directions on policy, the result may be either no policy at all (gridlock) or an inadequate, makeshift policy. The outcome may be nondecisions when hard decisions are needed. If government cannot respond effectively because its policymaking processes are too fragmented, then its performance will be inadequate. Perhaps the Madisonian model has reduced the ability of government to reach effective policy decisions. Certainly, radical departures from the status quo are atypical in American politics.

Summary

The year 1787 was crucial in building the American nation. The 55 men who met in Philadelphia created a policymaking system that responded to a complex policy agenda. Critical conflicts over equality led to key compromises in the New Jersey and Virginia Plans, the three-fifths compromise on slavery, and the decision to leave the issue of voting rights to the states. There was more consensus, however, about the economy. These merchants, lawyers, and large landowners believed that the American economy was in a shambles, and they intended to make the national government an economic stabilizer. The specificity of the powers assigned to Congress left no doubt that Congress was to forge national economic policy. The delegates knew, too, that the global posture of the fledgling nation was pitifully weak. A strong national government would be better able to ensure its own security and that of the nation.

Madison and his colleagues were less clear about the protection of individual rights. Because they believed that the limited government they had constructed would protect freedom, they said little about individual rights in the Constitution. However, the ratification struggle revealed that protection of personal freedoms was much on the public's mind. As a result, the Bill of Rights was proposed. These first 10 amendments to the Constitution, along with the Thirteenth and Fourteenth Amendments, provide Americans with protection from governmental restraints on individual freedoms.

It is important to remember that 1787 was not the only year of nation building. The nation's colonial and revolutionary heritage shaped the meetings in Philadelphia. Budding industrialism in a basically agrarian nation put economic issues on the Philadelphia agenda. What Madison was to call an "unequal division of property" made equality an issue, particularly after Shays' Rebellion. The greatest inequality of all, that between slavery and freedom, was so contentious an issue that it was simply avoided at Philadelphia.

Career Profile

Position: Senior Archivist
Salary Range: $41,952-$54,538
Benefits: Health and life insurance and retirement benefits
Qualifications: A bachelor's degree is required with a master's degree in history, political science, or library science preferred. Candidates should have a minimum of 18 units in history and/or political science as undergrads. An ability to communicate effectively in oral and written form is required.

Real People on the Job: Bob Holzweiss

Want a job that involves deciphering constitutional decisions, top-secret documents, and pivotal moments in the history of American government and politics? If so, consider becoming an archivist within the presidential library system and the National Archives. This is exactly what Bob Holzweiss does.

Bob is the senior archivist at the George Bush Presidential Library at Texas A&M University. Working with other investigators, Bob searches for original documents and artifacts concerning the significant events of the Bush presidency. Events like the Gulf War, the Clarence Thomas hearings, U.S. involvement in Somalia and Panama, and the fall of the Berlin Wall come under Bob's purview. The job requires a great deal of detective work. After Bob and his team finally track down the documents they're looking for, they spend time carefully analyzing them. Some material contains top-secret information, confidential advice to the president, or other restricted data, so part of Bob's job is to decide whether or not the material can be released to the public. He relies upon criteria outlined by President Bush, the Presidential Records Act of 1986, and the Freedom of Information Act. Bob and his fellow archivists often know far more about the pivotal events in U.S. history than historians and political scientists do.

This job's wide range of activities and responsibilities ensure that a day at the office is never boring! Bob uses his computing skills to create interactive and informative websites. He plays a crucial role in designing exhibits at the museum by offering suggestions about which documents to include and writing detailed explanations of the content. Once every four weeks, Bob works directly with outside researchers and coordinates their efforts to use the library's resources. At times, his job involves meeting with current and former public officials ranging from former President George Bush and Supreme Court Justice Clarence Thomas to former directors of the CIA and foreign heads of state.

For further information about getting a job as an archivist, contact the National Archives and Records Administration that oversees 11 presidential libraries and museums, 17 regional NARA offices nationwide, and four national offices in the Washington, D.C. area. Call 1-800-234-8861 or see www.nara.gov for employment information.

Nor did ratification of the Constitution end the nation-building process. Constitutional change—both formal and informal—continues to shape and alter the letter and the spirit of the Madisonian system.

Because that system includes separate institutions sharing power, it results in many checks and balances. Today, some Americans complain that this system has created a government too responsive to too many interests and too fragmented to act. Others praise the way it protects minority views. In Chapter 3, we will look at yet another way in which the Constitution divides governmental power: between the national and the state governments.

Key Terms

Constitution
Declaration of Independence
natural rights
consent of the governed
limited government
Articles of Confederation
Shays' Rebellion
U.S. Constitution
factions
New Jersey Plan
Virginia Plan
Connecticut Compromise
writ of habeas corpus
separation of powers
checks and balances
republic
Federalists
Anti-Federalists
Federalist Papers
Bill of Rights
Equal Rights Amendment
Marbury v. Madison
judicial review

For Further Reading

Bailyn, Bernard. *The Ideological Origins of the American Revolution.* Cambridge, MA: Harvard University Press, 1967. A leading work on the ideas that spawned the American Revolution.

Becker, Carl L. *The Declaration of Independence: A Study in the History of Political Ideas.* New York: Random House, 1942. Classic work on the meaning of the Declaration.

Hamilton, Alexander, James Madison, and John Jay. *The Federalist Papers.* 2nd ed., Roy P. Fairfield, ed. Baltimore: Johns Hopkins University Press, 1981. Key tracts in the campaign for the Constitution and cornerstones of American political thought.

Higginbotham, A. Leon, Jr. *In the Matter of Color: Race and the American Legal Process, The Colonial Period.* New York: Oxford University Press, 1978. Chronicles how colonial governments established the legal foundations for the enslavement of African Americans.

Jensen, Merrill. *The Articles of Confederation.* Madison: University of Wisconsin Press, 1940. Definitive and balanced treatment of the Articles.

Jillson, Calvin C. *Constitution Making: Conflict and Consensus in the Federal Convention of 1787.* New York: Agathon, 1988. Sophisticated analysis of the drafting of the Constitution.

Lipset, Seymour Martin. *The First New Nation.* New York: Basic Books, 1963. Political sociologist Lipset sees the early American experience as one of nation building.

Maier, Pauline. *American Scripture.* New York: Knopf, 1997. Argues the Declaration was the embodiment of the American mind and historical experience.

McDonald, Forrest B. *Novus Ordo Seclorum: The Intellectual Origins of the Constitution.* Lawrence: University Press of Kansas, 1986. Discusses the ideas behind the Constitution.

Morris, Richard B. *The Forging of the Union, 1781–1789.* New York: Harper & Row, 1987. Written to coincide with the bicentennial of the Constitution, this is an excellent history of the document's making.

Norton, Mary Beth. *Liberty's Daughters.* Boston: Little, Brown, 1980. Examines the role of women during the era of the Revolution and concludes that the Revolution transformed gender roles, setting women on the course of equality.

Rossiter, Clinton. *1787: The Grand Convention.* New York: Macmillan, 1966. A well-written study of the making of the Constitution.

Storing, Herbert J. *What the Anti-Federalists Were For.* Chicago: University of Chicago Press, 1981. Analysis of the political views of those opposed to ratification of the Constitution.

Wood, Gordon S. *The Creation of the American Republic.* Chapel Hill: University of North Carolina Press, 1969. In-depth study of American political thought prior to the Constitutional Convention.

Wood, Gordon S. *The Radicalism of the American Revolution.* New York: Vintage, 1993. Shows how American society and politics were thoroughly transformed in the decades following the Revolution.

Internet Resources

www.law.emory.edu/FEDERAL/
The Declaration of Independence, the Constitution, and the *Federalist Papers.* Also allows you to search the Constitution and *Federalist Papers* using keywords.

www.nara.gov/exhall/charters/constitution/confath.html
Biographies of the Founders.

www.earlyamerica.com/earlyamerica/milestones/articles/text.html
The Articles of Confederation. Also provides access to a wide range of documents from the founding period.

Notes

1. Gordon S. Wood, *The Radicalism of the American Revolution* (New York: Vintage, 1993), 4.
2. Garry Wills, *Inventing America: Jefferson's Declaration of Independence* (New York: Doubleday, 1978), 13, 77.
3. Clinton Rossiter, *1787: The Grand Convention* (New York: Macmillan, 1966), 60.
4. On the Lockean influence on the Declaration of Independence, see Carl L. Becker, *The Declaration of Independence: A Study in the History of Political Ideas* (New York: Random House, 1942).
5. Seymour Martin Lipset, *The First New Nation* (New York: Basic Books, 1963).
6. Gordon S. Wood, *The Creation of the American Republic, 1776–1787* (Chapel Hill, NC: University of North Carolina Press, 1969), 3.
7. On the Articles of Confederation, see Merrill Jensen, *The Articles of Confederation* (Madison: University of Wisconsin Press, 1940).
8. Letter from Jefferson to Madison, reprinted in George Bancroft, *The History of the Formation of the Constitution of the United States of America* (New York: Appleton, 1900), 342–343.
9. Jackson Turner Main, "Government by the People: The American Revolution and the Democratization of the Legislatures," *The William and Mary Quarterly*, 3rd ser. 23 (July 1966): 405. Main's article is also the source of the data on New York.
10. Wood, *The Radicalism of the American Revolution*, 6–7.
11. "Federalist #10," in Alexander Hamilton, James Madison, and John Jay, *The Federalist Papers*, 2nd ed., Roy P. Fairfield, ed. (Baltimore: Johns Hopkins University Press, 1981), 18.
12. Calvin C. Jillson and Cecil L. Eubanks, "The Political Structure of Constitution-Making: The Federal Convention of 1787," *American Journal of Political Science* 28 (August 1984): 435–458. See also Calvin C. Jillson, *Constitution Making: Conflict and Consensus in the Federal Convention of 1787* (New York: Agathon, 1988).
13. See Arthur Lovejoy, *Reflections on Human Nature* (Baltimore: Johns Hopkins University Press, 1961), 57–63.
14. "Federalist #10," *The Federalist Papers.*
15. This representation may have practical consequences. See Frances E. Lee, "Representation and Public Policy: The Consequences of Senate Apportionment for the Geographic Distribution of Federal Funds," *Journal of Politics* 60 (February 1998): 34–62; and Daniel Wirls, "The Consequences of Equal Representation—The Bicameral Politics of NAFTA in the 103rd Congress," *Congress and the President* 25 (Autumn 1998): 129–145.
16. Paul Eidelberg, *The Philosophy of the American Constitution* (New York: Free Press, 1968), 82.
17. Cecelia M. Kenyon, ed., *The Antifederalists* (Indianapolis: Bobbs-Merrill, 1966), xxxv.
18. Rossiter, *1787.*
19. See Charles A. Beard, *An Economic Interpretation of the Constitution of the United States* (New York: Macmillan, 1913); Robert E. Brown, *Charles Beard and the Constitution* (Princeton, NJ: Princeton University Press, 1956); Forrest B. McDonald, *We the People: The Economic Origins of the Constitution* (Chicago: University of Chicago Press, 1958); and Forrest B. McDonald, *Novus Ordo Seclorum: The Intellectual Origins of the Constitution* (Lawrence: University Press of Kansas, 1986).
20. A brilliant exposition of the Madisonian model is found in Robert A. Dahl, *A Preface to Democratic Theory* (Chicago: University of Chicago Press, 1956).
21. "Federalist #10," *The Federalist Papers.*
22. "Federalist #51," *The Federalist Papers.*
23. Quoted in Beard, *An Economic Interpretation of the Constitution of the United States*, 299.
24. The three quotations are from Kenyon, *The Antifederalists*, 195, liv, and 1, respectively.
25. Jackson Turner Main, *The Antifederalists* (Chapel Hill: University of North Carolina Press, 1961). For more on the Anti-Federalists, see Herbert J. Storing, *What the Anti-Federalists Were For* (Chicago: University of Chicago Press, 1981).
26. The early attempts at ratification of the ERA are recounted in Janet Boles, *The Politics of the Equal Rights Amendment* (New York: Longman, 1978).
27. Jane J. Mansbridge, *Why We Lost the ERA* (Chicago: University of Chicago Press, 1986).
28. See "Federalist #78," *The Federalist Papers.*
29. James MacGregor Burns, *The Deadlock of Democracy* (Englewood Cliffs, NJ: Prentice-Hall, 1963), 6.

Federalism

3

Chapter Outline

Alfonso Lopez, Jr. was a senior at Edison High School in San Antonio, Texas. One day he arrived at school carrying a concealed .38 caliber handgun. School authorities, alerted by an anonymous tip, confronted Alfonso, who admitted he was carrying the weapon. He was arrested and charged under Texas law with firearm possession on school premises. The next day, the state charges were dismissed after federal agents charged him with violating the Gun-Free School Zones Act of 1990.

A grand jury then indicted Alfonso for violating federal law. Alfonso's lawyers had an ace up their sleeves, however. They moved to dismiss his federal indictment on the grounds that the Gun-Free School Zones Act was unconstitutional because Congress had no power to legislate control over public schools, which are under state control. Congress had relied on its authority to regulate interstate commerce to pass the law, and, Alfonso's lawyers argued, this case had nothing to do with commerce.

Nevertheless, the trial court found Alfonso guilty of violating the law and sentenced him to six months of imprisonment and two years of supervised release. On appeal, Alfonso's lawyers challenged his conviction based on the claim that the law exceeded federal jurisdiction. The court of appeals agreed and reversed Alfonso's conviction. The case then went to the Supreme Court, which ultimately found in *United States v. Lopez* that the Gun-Free School Zones Act did in fact exceed Congress's authority to regulate commerce among the states.

The issue was not whether it was a good idea to prohibit guns in public schools. Almost everyone agreed with that goal. Instead, the issue was establishing boundaries between federal and state—an issue over which America has fought a civil war. The fact that it took the Supreme Court to resolve this seemingly straightforward criminal case illustrates how federalism is at the center of important public policy battles. Indeed, the issue of federalism and the delegation of responsibility to different levels of government is a crucial political battleground—policymakers' answers to the questions of how we should be governed (in this case, by the states or by the federal government) and what should be the scope of the national government shape public policies.

It is important to understand American federalism, the complex relationships between different levels of government in the United States. We will be especially attentive to our themes of democracy and the scope of government. Does federalism, the vertical division of power, enhance democracy in the United States? Does the additional layer of policymakers make government more responsive to public opinion or merely more complicated? Does it enhance the prospects that a national majority of Americans have their way in public policy? And what are the implications of federalism for the scope of the national government's activities? Why has the national government grown so much in relation to state governments, and has this growth been at the expense of the states?

The relationships between governments at the local, state, and national levels often confuse Americans. Neighborhood schools are run by locally elected school boards but also receive state and national funds, and with those funds come state and national rules and regulations. Local airports, sewage systems, pollution control systems, and police departments also receive a mix of local, state, and national funds, so they operate under a complex web of rules and regulations imposed by each level of government.

Sometimes this complex system is almost impossible to understand, especially given the size of the country and the large number of governmental units within it. Even the national government has difficulty keeping track of more than $350 billion in federal aid distributed each year to states and cities.[1] In 1972, when the U.S. Treasury Department first sent revenue-sharing checks to 50 states and 38,000 local governments, some 5,000 checks were returned, marked "addressee unknown," by the Postal Service. If the Postal Service has trouble keeping up with all the governments in America, it's no wonder citizens do, too.

Defining Federalism

Federalism is a rather unusual system for governing, with particular consequences for those who live within it. This section explains the federal system and how it affects Americans living in such a system.

What Is Federalism?

federalism

A way of organizing a nation so that two or more levels of government have formal authority over the same land and people. It is a system of shared power between units of government.

Federalism is a way of organizing a nation so that two or more levels of government have formal authority over the same area and people. It is a system of shared power between units of government. For example, the state of California has formal authority over its inhabitants, but the national government can also pass laws and establish policies that affect Californians. We are subject to the formal authority of both the state and the national governments.

Although federalism is not unique to the United States, it is not a common method of governing. Only 11 of the 190 or so nations of the world have federal systems, and these countries, which include Germany, Mexico, Argentina, Canada, Australia, India, and the United States, share little else (see "America in Perspective: Why Federalism?").

unitary governments

A way of organizing a nation so that all power resides in the central government. Most governments today are unitary governments.

Most governments in the world today are not federal but **unitary governments,** in which all power resides in the central government. If the French Assembly, for instance, wants to redraw the boundaries of local governments or change their forms of government, it can (and has). However, if the U.S. Congress wants to abolish Alabama or Oregon, it cannot.

American states are unitary governments with respect to their local governments. Local governments get their authority from the states; they can be created or abolished by the states. States also have the power to make rules for their own local governments. They can tell them what their speed limits will be, the way in which they should be organized, how they can tax people, what they can spend money on, and so forth. States, however, receive their authority not from the national government, but *directly* from the Constitution.

comparative
Comparing Federal and Unitary Systems

There is a third form of governmental structure, a *confederation*. The United States began as such, under the Articles of Confederation. In a confederation, the national government is weak and most or all the power is in the hands of its components—for example, the individual states. Today, confederations are rare except in international organizations such as the United Nations (see Chapter 20). Table 3.1 provides a summary of the authority relations in the three systems of government.

intergovernmental relations

The workings of the federal system—the entire set of interactions among national, state, and local governments.

The workings of the federal system are sometimes called **intergovernmental relations.** This term refers to the entire set of interactions among national, state, and local governments.[2]

Table 3.1 Authority Relations in Three Systems of Government

	UNITARY	CONFEDERATE	FEDERAL
Central government	• holds primary authority • regulates activities of states	• limited powers to coordinate state activities	• shares power with states
State government	• little or no powers • duties regulated by central government	• sovereign • allocate some duties to central government	• shares power with central government
Citizens	• vote for central government officials	• vote for state government officials	• vote for both state and central government officials

Why Is Federalism So Important?

The federal system in America *decentralizes our politics*. Senators are elected as representatives of individual states, not of the entire nation. On election day in November, there are actually 51 presidential elections, one in each state and one in Washington, D.C. (see Chapter 10). It is even possible—as happened in 2000—for a candidate who receives the most popular votes in the country to lose the election because of the way the electoral votes are distributed by state.

The federal system decentralizes our politics in more fundamental ways than our electoral system. With more layers of government, more opportunities exist for political participation. With more people wielding power, there are more points of access in government and more opportunities for interests to have their demands for public policies

National campaigns for the presidency actually take place in the states; candidates must talk about oil prices in Texas, Social security benefits in Florida, and federal aid to cities in New York. Here, Republican Presidential candidate George W. Bush campaigns before the presidential election.

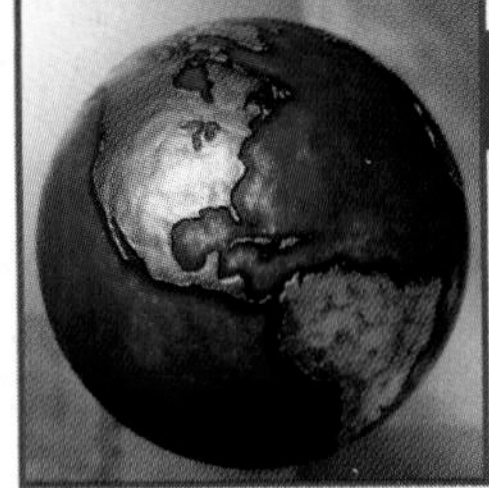

America in Perspective

Why Federalism?

Only 11 countries have federal systems. Trying to determine why these particular nations chose a federal system is an interesting but difficult task. All three North American nations have federal systems, but the trend does not continue in South America, where only two nations have federal systems. Countries large in size—such as Canada and Australia—or large in both size and population—such as India, the United States, Brazil, and Mexico—tend to have federal systems, which decentralize the administration of governmental services. Nevertheless, China and Indonesia—two large and heavily populated countries—have unitary governments, and tiny Malaysia and Switzerland have federal systems.

NATION	POPULATION	AREA (THOUSAND) SQUARE MILES	DIVERSITY (ETHNIC, LINGUISTIC, AND RELIGIOUS)
Argentina	36,955,182	1,072	Low
Australia	19,169,083	2,966	Low
Austria	8,131,111	32	Low
Brazil	172,860,370	3,286	Medium
Canada	31,281,092	3,852	High
Germany	82,797,408	137	Low
India	1,014,003,817	1,222	High
Malaysia	21,793,293	127	High
Mexico	100,349,766	762	Low
Switzerland	7,262,372	16	Medium
United States	275,562,673	3,615	Medium

Source: Central Intelligence Agency, *The World Factbook*, 2000.

A nation's diversity may also play a role in the development of a federal system. Brazil, Canada, India, Malaysia, Switzerland, and the United States have large minority ethnic groups that often speak different languages and practice different religions. Many nations with unitary systems, however, ranging from Belgium to most African countries, are also replete with ethnic diversity.

Most federal systems are democracies, although most democracies are not federal systems. Authoritarian regimes generally do not wish to disperse power away from the central government. Both the former Soviet Union and the former Yugoslavia, perhaps reflecting the extraordinary diversity of their populations, had federal systems—of a sort. In both countries, the central government, until recently, retained ultimate power. As democracy swept through these countries, their national governments dissolved and several smaller nations were formed.

satisfied. With more decisions made in the states, there are fewer sources of conflict at the national level.

As we will see, federalism also enhances judicial power. Dividing government power and responsibilities necessitates umpires to resolve disputes between the two levels of government. In the American system, judges serve as the umpires. Thus, when the national government places prohibitions or requirements on the states, inevitably issues arise for the courts to decide.

The federal system not only decentralizes our politics but also *decentralizes our policies*. The history of the federal system demonstrates the tension between the states and the national government about policy: who controls it and what it should be. In the past, people debated whether the states or the national government should regulate the railroads, pass child labor laws, or adopt minimum-wage legislation. Today, people debate whether the states or the national government should regulate abortions, enforce school desegregation, determine speed limits on highways, or tell 18-year-olds they cannot drink alcohol.[3]

Policies about equality, the economy, the environment, and other matters are subject to both the centralizing force of the national government and the dispersing force of the states. The overlapping powers of the two levels of government mean that most of our public policy debates are also debates about federalism.

States are responsible for most public policies dealing with social, family, and moral issues. The Constitution does not give the national government the power to pass laws that *directly* regulate drinking ages, marriage and divorce, or speed limits. These policy prerogatives belong to the states. They become national issues, however, when aggrieved or angry groups take their cases to Congress or the federal courts in an attempt to use the power of the national government to *influence* states or to get federal courts to find a state's policy unconstitutional. A good example of this process is the federal requirement that states raise their drinking age to 21 in order to receive highway funds (see "Making a Difference: Candy Lightner").

The American states have always been policy innovators.[4] The states overflow with reforms, new ideas, and new policies. From clean-air legislation to welfare reform, the states constitute a national laboratory to develop and test public policies and share the results with other states and the national government. Almost every policy the national government has adopted had its beginnings in the states. One or more states pioneered child labor laws, minimum-wage legislation, unemployment compensation, antipollution legislation, civil rights protections, and the income tax. More recently, states have been active in reforming health care, education, and welfare—and the national government is paying close attention to their efforts.

Why does it matter?

The Constitution guarantees you many rights. Your state constitution also offers protections for your liberty. Look up your state constitution. Would you feel comfortable if your freedom were only protected by your state constitution?

Making a Difference

Candy Lightner

Candy Lightner was no politician. She was a California real estate broker and, more important, a mother suffering from a tragedy: Her 13-year-old daughter, Cari, was killed by a drunk driver. The agony associated with children's deaths caused by drunk drivers is real. When the drunk driver is a teenager, inexperienced at both drinking and driving, passions heat further. Ms. Lightner was not content to grieve the loss of her child. She decided to do something about it.

Her first step was to form Mothers Against Drunk Driving (MADD). This group was the seed from which sprouted hundreds of local MADD chapters, as well as offshoots like Students Against Drunk Driving (SADD). MADD had no trouble rousing sentiments against the carnage of deaths caused by drunk drivers. No politician wants to be accused of supporting drunks on the road who are aiming two-ton vehicles at defenseless children. Lightner's lobbyists inundated state capitals to get the drinking age raised. Between 1976 and 1983, 19 states raised their drinking age, typically to age 21.

There were still 31 states that allowed people under 21 to drink, however. Ms. Lightner and her MADD supporters had to become political strategists. They realized that it was much easier to get a national law passed once than to lobby each of 50 state legislatures separately. Therefore, in 1983, at a press conference on the steps of the Capitol, Lightner and Secretary of Transportation Elizabeth Dole, Senator John Danforth (R-MO), Senator Richard Lugar (R-IN), and Senator Frank Lautenberg (D-NJ) announced their intention to support a nationally standard drinking age. Because they could not pass a bill directly setting the drinking age in the states, however, they proposed using federal highway funds as an incentive for the states to pass their bills.

The legislation stemming from the Lightner–Dole–Danforth–Lautenberg–Lugar press conference was an amendment to the Surface Transportation Act of 1982. The federal government could not legislate drinking ages, so it relied on a carrot-and-stick strategy: Congress would withhold 10 percent of all federal highway aid from states that did not raise their legal drinking age to 21 by 1988. The legislation sailed through Congress (the Senate passed it by a vote of 81 to 16, presumably few Senators wanted their votes construed as tolerating teenage drunken driving). President Reagan—a staunch opponent of federal regulations—signed the legislation in October 1984. By the end of 1989, every state had a legal drinking age of 21. Candy Lightner had made a difference.

How You Can Make A Difference

Drinking Age Laws

Do you agree with Candy Lightner's attempts to use the federal government to force states to raise their drinking ages to 21? Although virtually no one would argue against Ms. Lightner's goal of reducing drunk driving, many college-age men and women disagree with the methods advocated by MADD and SADD. Have you ever asked "If I can vote, drive, die for my country and otherwise be considered a legal adult at 18, then what right does the federal government have to restrict my right to drink alcohol until I'm 21?"

If you've pondered this situation, then perhaps you can make a difference in finding a new solution to drunk driving. RALLY (Realistic Alcohol Laws for Legal Youth), a nationwide student-run organization founded in 1995, believes that the first step remains lowering the drinking age to 18. At the same time, college-age students should become active in promoting alcohol awareness programs in their dorms, schools, cities, and states. Such programs coupled with an emphasis on strong individual responsibility can have a strong impact on reducing alcohol abuse among 18- to 21-year-olds without relying upon discriminatory laws. If you agree with RALLY, then you should start your own chapter on your college campus. Visit their web site at www.rallyusa.org and get advice and strategy on how to make a direct impact on your college and state.

Finally, however, perhaps you endorse Ms. Lightner's and the federal government's approach to this serious problem. SADD (www.sadd.org) strongly believes that these laws have saved thousands of lives and averted millions of dollars in property damage. You can also become active in keeping the drinking age at 21 by forming SADD chapters on your own campus or joining existing chapters. SADD and other similar organizations are strongly opposed to RALLY's efforts.

Federalism is an important key to unlocking the secrets of the American political system. Which president is elected, which policy innovations are developed, at what age young men and women can legally drink, and many other issues are profoundly affected by the workings of the federal system.

The Constitutional Basis of Federalism

The word *federalism* is absent from the Constitution, and not much was said about it at the Constitutional Convention. Eighteenth-century Americans had little experience in thinking of themselves as Americans first and state citizens second. In fact, loyalty to state governments was so strong that the Constitution would have been resoundingly defeated had it tried to abolish them. In addition, a central government, working alone, would have had difficulty trying to govern eighteenth-century Americans. The people were too widely dispersed, and the country's transportation and communication systems too primitive to allow governing from a central location. There was no other practical choice in 1787 but to create a federal system of government.

The Division of Power

The Constitution's writers carefully defined the powers of state and national governments (see Table 3.2). Although they favored a stronger national government, the framers still made states vital cogs in the machinery of government. The Constitution guaranteed states equal representation in the Senate (and even made this provision unamendable in Article V). It also made states responsible for both state and national elections—an important power. Further, the Constitution virtually guaranteed the continuation of each state; Congress is forbidden to create new states by chopping up old ones, unless a state's legislature approves (an unlikely event).

Table 3.2 The Constitution's Distribution of Powers

SOME POWERS GRANTED BY THE CONSTITUTION		
To the National Government	**To Both the National and State Governments**	**To the State Governments**
Coin money Conduct foreign relations Regulate commerce with foreign nations and among states Provide an army and a navy Declare war Establish courts inferior to the Supreme Court Establish post offices Make laws necessary and proper to carry out the foregoing powers	Tax Borrow money Establish courts Make and enforce laws Charter banks and corporations Spend money for the general welfare Take private property for public purposes, with just compensation	Establish local governments Regulate commerce within a state Conduct elections Ratify amendments to the federal Constitution Take measures for public health, safety, and morals Exert powers the Constitution does not delegate to the national government or prohibit the states from using
SOME POWERS DENIED BY THE CONSTITUTION		
To the National Government	**To Both the National and State Governments**	**To the State Governments**
Tax articles exported from one state to another Violate the Bill of Rights Change state boundaries	Grant titles of nobility Permit slavery (Thirteenth Amendment) Deny citizens the right to vote because of race, color, or previous servitude (Fifteenth Amendment) Deny citizens the right to vote because of gender (Nineteenth Amendment)	Tax imports or exports Coin money Enter into treaties Impair obligations or contracts Abridge the privileges or immunities of citizens or deny due process and equal protection of the law (Fourteenth Amendment)

The Constitution also created obligations of the national government toward the states; it is to protect states against violence and invasion, for example. At times, though, the states find the national government deficient in meeting its obligations, as we will discuss later in this chapter.

In Article VI of the Constitution, the framers dealt with what remains a touchy question: In a dispute between the states and the national government, which prevails? The answer that the delegates provided, often referred to as the **supremacy clause**, seems clear enough. They stated that the following three items were the supreme law of the land:

1. the Constitution
2. laws of the national government (when consistent with the Constitution)
3. treaties (which can be made only by the national government)

Judges in every state were specifically told to obey the U.S. Constitution, even if their state constitutions or state laws directly contradicted it. Today, all state executives, legislators, and judges are bound by oath to support the Constitution.

The national government, however, can operate only within its appropriate sphere. It cannot usurp the states' powers. But what are the boundaries of the national government's powers? According to some commentators, the **Tenth Amendment** provides part of the answer. It states that the "powers not delegated to the United States by the Constitution, nor prohibited by it to the states, are reserved to the states respectively, or to the people." To those advocating states' rights, the amendment clearly

supremacy clause

Article VI of the Constitution, which makes the Constitution, national laws, and treaties supreme over state laws when the national government is acting within its constitutional limits.

Tenth Amendment

The constitutional amendment stating that "The powers not delegated to the United States by the Constitution, nor prohibited by it to the states, are reserved to the states respectively, or to the people."

means that the national government has only those powers specifically assigned to it by the Constitution. The states or people have supreme power over any activity not mentioned there. Despite this interpretation, in 1941 the Supreme Court (in *United States v. Darby*) called the Tenth Amendment a constitutional truism, a mere assertion that the states have independent powers of their own—not a declaration that state powers are superior to those of the national government.

The Court seemed to backtrack on this ruling in favor of national government supremacy in a 1976 case, *National League of Cities v. Usery*, in which it held that extending national minimum-wage and maximum-hours standards to employees of state and local governments was an unconstitutional intrusion of the national government into the domain of the states. In 1985, however (in *Garcia v. San Antonio Metro*), the Court overturned the *National League of Cities* decision. The Court held, in essence, that it was up to Congress, not the courts, to decide which actions of the states should be regulated by the national government. Once again, the Court ruled that the Tenth Amendment did not give states power superior to that of the national government for activities not mentioned in the Constitution.

Occasionally, issues arise in which states challenge the authority of the national government. In the late 1980s, the governors of several states refused to allow their state National Guards to engage in training exercises in Central America. National Guards are state militias, but the Constitution provides that the president can nationalize them. In 1990, the Supreme Court reiterated the power of the national government by siding with the president. Similarly, South Dakota sued the federal government over its efforts to raise states' drinking-age laws and over its efforts to mandate a 55-mph speed limit on highways. The state lost both cases. (In 1995, however, Congress changed the law on speed limits.)

Federal courts can order states to obey the Constitution or federal laws and treaties. However, in deference to the states the *Eleventh Amendment* prohibits individual damage suits against state officials (such as a suit against a police officer for violating one's rights) and protects state governments from being sued against their consent by private parties in federal courts or in state courts.[5] In 2001, the Court voided the application of the Americans with Disabilities Act to the states, finding it a violation of the Eleventh Amendment (*Board of Trustees of University of Alabama, et at v. Garrett, et al*). Cases arising under the Fourteenth Amendment (usually cases regarding racial discrimination) are an exception.[6] Suits may also be brought by the federal government against states in federal courts, and by individuals against state officials seeking to prohibit future illegal actions.

You are a Federal Judge

Recently the Supreme Court has made it easier for citizens to control the behavior of local officials. The Court ruled that a federal law passed in 1871 to protect newly freed slaves permits individuals to sue local governments for damages or seek injunctions against any local official acting in an official capacity who they believe has deprived them of any right secured by the Constitution or by federal law.[7] Such suits are now common in the federal courts.

Establishing National Supremacy

Why is it that the federal government has gained power relative to the states? Four key events have largely settled the issue of how national and state powers are related: (1) the elaboration of the doctrine of implied powers, (2) the definition of the commerce clause, (3) the Civil War, and (4) the long struggle for racial equality.

McCulloch v. Maryland

An 1819 Supreme Court decision that established the supremacy of the national government over state governments. In deciding this case, Chief Justice John Marshall and his colleagues held that Congress had certain **implied powers** in addition to the **enumerated powers** found in the Constitution.

Implied Powers. As early as 1819, the issue of state versus national power came before the Supreme Court in the case of ***McCulloch v. Maryland.*** The new American government had moved quickly on many economic policies. In 1791, it created a national bank, a government agency empowered to print money, make loans, and engage in many other banking tasks. A darling of Alexander Hamilton and his allies, the bank was hated by those opposed to strengthening the national government's control of the economy. Those opposed—including Thomas Jefferson, farmers, and state legislatures—saw the bank as an instrument of the elite. The First Bank of the United States was allowed to expire, but then the Second Bank was created during the presidency of James Madison, fueling a great national debate.

Railing against the "Monster Bank," the state of Maryland passed a law in 1818 taxing the national bank's Baltimore branch $15,000 a year. The Baltimore branch refused to pay, whereupon the state of Maryland sued the cashier, James McCulloch, for payment. When the state courts upheld Maryland's law and its tax, the bank appealed to the U.S. Supreme Court. John Marshall was chief justice when two of the country's most capable lawyers argued the case before the Court.

Daniel Webster, widely regarded as one of the greatest senators in U.S. history, argued for the national bank, and Luther Martin, a delegate to the Constitutional Convention, argued for Maryland. Martin maintained that the Constitution was very clear about the powers of Congress (as outlined in Article I). The power to create a national bank was not among them. Thus, Martin concluded, Congress had exceeded its powers, and Maryland had a right to tax the bank. On behalf of the bank, Webster argued for a broader interpretation of the powers of the national government. The Constitution was not meant to stifle congressional powers, he said, but rather to permit Congress to use all means "necessary and proper" to fulfill its responsibilities.

Marshall, never one to sidestep a big decision, wrote his ruling in favor of the bank before the arguments ended—some said before they even began. He and his colleagues set forth two great constitutional principles in their decision. The first was the *supremacy of the national government over the states.* Marshall wrote that "If any one proposition could command the universal assent of mankind, we might expect it to be this—that the government of the United States, though limited in its power, is supreme within its sphere of action." As long as the national government behaved in accordance with the Constitution, said the Court, its policies took precedence over state policies. Accordingly, federal laws or regulations, such as many civil rights acts and rules regulating hazardous substances, water quality, and clean air standards, *preempt* state or local laws or regulations and thus preclude their enforcement.

The other key principle of *McCulloch* was that *the national government has certain implied powers that go beyond its enumerated powers.* The Court held that Congress was behaving consistently with the Constitution when it created the national bank. It was true, Marshall admitted, that Congress had certain **enumerated powers,** powers *specifically* listed in Article I, Section 8 of the Constitution. Congress could coin money, regulate its value, impose taxes, and so forth. Creating a bank was not enumerated. But the Constitution added that Congress has the power to "make all laws necessary and proper for carrying into execution the foregoing powers." That, said Marshall, gave Congress certain **implied powers.** It could make economic policy consistent with the Constitution in a number of ways.

Today, the notion of implied powers has become like a rubber band that can be stretched without breaking; the "necessary and proper" clause of the Constitution is often referred to as the **elastic clause.** Hundreds of congressional policies involve powers not specifically mentioned in the Constitution, especially in the domain of economic policy. Federal policies to regulate food and drugs, build interstate highways, protect consumers, clean up dirty air and water, and do many other things are all justified as implied powers of Congress.

Commerce Power. The Constitution gives Congress the power to regulate interstate and international commerce. American courts have spent many years trying to define commerce. In 1824, the Supreme Court, in deciding the case of ***Gibbons v. Ogden,*** defined commerce very broadly to encompass virtually every form of commercial activity. Today, commerce covers not only the movement of goods, but also radio signals, electricity, telephone messages, the Internet, insurance transactions, and much more.

enumerated powers

Powers of the federal government that are specifically addressed in the Constitution; for Congress, these powers are listed in Article I, Section 8, and include the power to coin money, regulate its value, and impose taxes.

implied powers

Powers of the federal government that go beyond those enumerated in the Constitution. The Constitution states that Congress has the power to "make all laws necessary and proper for carrying into execution" the powers enumerated in Article I.

elastic clause

The final paragraph of Article I, Section 8, of the Constitution, which authorizes Congress to pass all laws "necessary and proper" to carry out the enumerated powers.

Gibbons v. Ogden

A landmark case decided in 1824 in which the Supreme Court interpreted very broadly the clause in Article I, Section 8, of the Constitution giving Congress the power to regulate interstate commerce, encompassing virtually every form of commercial activity.

The Supreme Court's decisions establishing the national government's implied powers (*McCulloch v. Maryland*) and a broad definition of interstate commerce (*Gibbons v. Ogden*) created a source of national power as long as Congress employed its power for economic development through subsidies and services for business interests. In the latter part of the nineteenth century, however, Congress sought to use these same powers to regulate the economy rather than to promote it. The Court then interpreted the interstate commerce power as giving Congress no constitutional right to regulate local commercial activities such as establishing safe working conditions for laborers or protecting children from working long hours.

When the Great Depression hit, new demands were placed on the national government. Beginning in 1933, the New Deal of President Franklin D. Roosevelt produced an avalanche of regulatory and social welfare legislation, much of which was voided by the Supreme Court (see Chapter 16). But in 1937 the Court reversed itself and ceased trying to restrict the efforts of the national government to regulate commerce at any level. In 1964, Congress prohibited racial discrimination in places of public accommodation such as restaurants, hotels, and movie theaters on the basis of its power to regulate interstate commerce. Thus, regulating commerce is one of the national government's most important sources of power.

In recent years the Supreme Court has scrutinized the use of the commerce power with a skeptical eye, however. As we saw in the opening to this chapter, in 1995 the Court held in *United States v. Lopez* that the federal Gun-Free School Zones Act of 1990, which forbid the possession of firearms in public schools, exceeded Congress's constitutional authority to regulate commerce. Guns in a school zone, the majority said, have nothing to do with commerce. Similarly, in 2000 the Court ruled in *United States v. Morrison* that the power to regulate interstate commerce did not provide Congress with authority to enact the 1994 Violence Against Women Act, which provided a federal civil remedy for the victims of gender-motivated violence. Gender-motivated crimes of violence are not, the Court said, in any sense economic activity.

The Supreme Court announced another limitation on the commerce power in 1996. In *Seminole Tribe of Florida v. Florida*, the Court dealt with the case of a right Congress had given Indian tribes to sue state officials to force good faith negotiations (in this case over a license to run a casino). Contrary to previous decisions, the Court declared the Eleventh Amendment prohibits Congress from using the interstate commerce power to revoke states' immunity from such lawsuits by private parties. The principal effect of the decision will be to limit suits seeking to enforce rights granted by Congress within its authority under the Commerce Clause (which encompasses much of modern federal regulation).

Several other recent cases have had important implications for federalism. In *Printz v. United States* and *Mack v. United States* (1997), the Supreme Court voided the congressional mandate in the Brady Handgun Violence Prevention Act that the chief law enforcement officer in each local community conduct background checks on prospective gun purchasers. According to the Court, "The federal government may neither issue directives requiring the states to address particular problems, nor commend the states' officers, or those of their political subdivision, to administer or enforce a federal regulatory program.

The Civil War. What *McCulloch* pronounced constitutionally, the Civil War (1861–1865) settled militarily. The Civil War is often thought of mainly as a struggle over slavery; but it was also, and perhaps more important, a struggle between states and the national government. In fact, Abraham Lincoln announced in his 1861 inaugural address that he would willingly support a constitutional amendment guaranteeing slavery if it would save the Union. Instead, it took a bloody civil war for the national government to assert its power over the Southern states' claim of sovereignty.

In 1963, Alabama Governor George Wallace made a dramatic stand at the University of Alabama to resist integration of the all-White school. Federal marshals won this confrontation, and since then the federal government in general has been able to impose national standards of equal opportunity on the states.

The Struggle for Racial Equality. A century later, conflict between the states and the national government again erupted over states' rights and national power. In 1954, in *Brown v. Board of Education*, the Supreme Court held that school segregation was unconstitutional. Southern politicians responded with what they called "massive resistance" to the decision. When a federal judge ordered the admission of two African-American students to the University of Alabama in 1963, Governor George Wallace literally blocked the school entrance to prevent federal marshals and the students from entering the admissions office. Despite Wallace's efforts, the students were admitted, and throughout the 1960s the federal government enacted laws and policies to end segregation in schools, housing, public accommodations, voting, and jobs. In 1979 (after African Americans began voting in large numbers in Alabama), George Wallace himself said of his stand in the schoolhouse door: "I was wrong. Those days are over and they ought to be over." The conflict between states and the national government over equality issues was decided in favor of the national government. National standards of racial equality prevailed.

Federalism over Time

The national government is supreme within its sphere, but the sphere for the states remains a large and important one.

States' Obligations to Each Other

Federalism involves more than relationships between the national government and state and local governments. The states must deal with each other as well, and the Constitution outlines certain obligations that each state has to every other state.

Full Faith and Credit. Suppose that, like millions of other Americans, a person divorces and then remarries. For each marriage this person purchases a marriage license, which registers the marriage with a state. On the honeymoon for the second marriage, the person travels across the country. Is this person married in each state passed through, even though the marriage license is with only one state? Can the person be arrested for bigamy because the divorce occurred in only one state?

The answer, of course, is that a marriage license and a divorce, like a driver's license and a birth certificate, are valid in all states. Article IV of the Constitution requires that states give **full faith and credit** to the public acts, records, and civil judicial proceedings of every other state. This reciprocity is essential to the functioning of society and the economy. Without the full faith and credit clause, people could avoid their obligations, say, to make payments on automobile loans simply by crossing a state

full faith and credit clause

A clause in Article IV, Section 1, of the Constitution requiring each state to recognize the official documents and civil judgments rendered by the courts of other states.

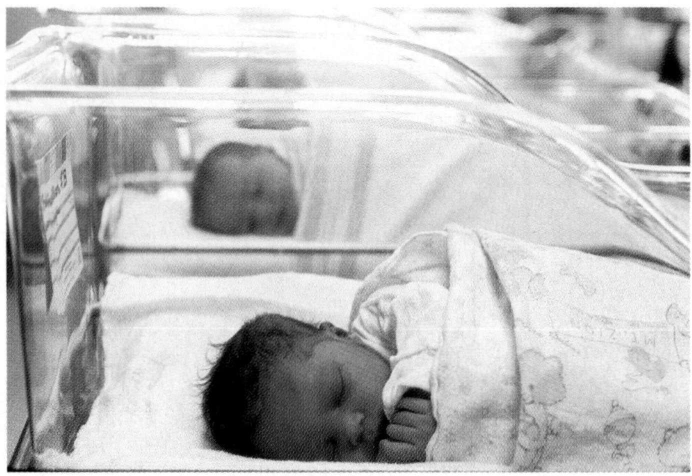

Because of the full faith and credit clause of the Constitution, these babies' birth certificates are valid in every state. They are also entitled to most of the benefits—and subject to most of the obligations—of citizenship in any state they visit, thanks to the privileges and immunities clause.

boundary. In addition, because contracts between business firms can be enforced across state boundaries, firms incorporated in one state can do business in another.

Usually, the full faith and credit provision in the Constitution poses little controversy. An exception occurred in 1996 when courts in Hawaii recognized same-gender marriages. What would happen in other states that did not recognize Hawaiian marriages between same-gender partners? Congress answered with the Defense of Marriage Act, which permits states to disregard gay marriages, even if they are legal elsewhere in the United States. Hawaii has since overturned recognition of gay marriage, but in 2000 Vermont accorded legal status to gay civil unions. It remains to be seen whether Congress has the power to make exceptions to the full faith and credit clause.

Extradition. What about criminal penalties? Almost all criminal law is state law. If someone robs a store, steals a car, or commits a murder, the chances are that this person is breaking a state, not a federal, law. The Constitution says that states are required to return a person charged with a crime in another state to that state for trial or imprisonment, a practice called **extradition.** Although there is no way to force states to comply, they usually are happy to do so, not wishing to harbor criminals and hoping that other states will reciprocate. Thus, a lawbreaker is prevented from avoiding punishment by simply escaping to another state.

extradition

A legal process whereby an alleged criminal offender is surrendered by the officials of one state to officials of the state in which the crime is alleged to have been committed.

privileges and immunities

A clause in Article IV, Section 2, of the Constitution according citizens of each state most of the privileges of citizens of other states.

Privileges and Immunities. The most complicated obligation among the states is the requirement that citizens of each state receive all the **privileges and immunities** of any other state in which they happen to be. The goal of this constitutional provision is to prohibit states from discriminating against citizens of other states. If, for example, a Texan visits California, the Texan will pay the same sales tax and receive the same police protection as residents of California.

There are many exceptions to the privileges and immunities clause, however. Many of you attend public universities. If you reside in the same state as your university, you generally pay a tuition substantially lower than that paid by your fellow students from out of state. Similarly, only residents of a state can vote in state elections. States often attempt to pass the burdens of financing the state government to those outside the state, such as through taxes on minerals mined in the state but consumed elsewhere or special taxes on hotel rooms rented by tourists.

The Supreme Court has never clarified just which privileges a state must make available to all Americans and which privileges can be limited to its own citizens. In general, the more fundamental the rights—such as owning property or receiving police protection—the less likely it is that a state can discriminate against citizens of another state. In 1999, the Supreme Court held in *Saenz v. Roe* that California could not require a new resident to wait a year before becoming eligible for welfare benefits that exceeded those available in the state from which the new resident came.

Intergovernmental Relations Today

The past two centuries have seen dramatic changes in American federalism. These changes are apparent in two main areas. First, there has been a gradual shift from a dual federalism to a cooperative federalism, which emphasizes power sharing between two levels of government.[8] The second major change has been the rise of fiscal federalism, the elaborate assortment of federal grants-in-aid to the states and localities.

From Dual to Cooperative Federalism

One way to understand the changes in American federalism over the past 200 years is to contrast two types of federalism. The first type is called **dual federalism,** in which both the national government and the states remain supreme within their own spheres. The states are responsible for some policies, the national government for others. For example, the national government has exclusive control over foreign and military policy, the postal system, and monetary policy. States are exclusively responsible for schools, law enforcement, and road building. In dual federalism, the powers and policy assignments of the layers of government are distinct, as in a layer cake, and proponents of dual federalism believe that the powers of the national government should be interpreted narrowly.

dual federalism

A system of government in which both the states and the national government remain supreme within their own spheres, each responsible for some policies.

Most politicians and political scientists today argue that dual federalism is outdated. They are more likely to describe the current American federal system as one of **cooperative federalism,** where powers and policy assignments are shared between states and the national government.[9] Instead of a layer cake, they see American federalism as more like a marble cake, with mingled responsibilities and blurred distinctions between the levels of government.

cooperative federalism

A system of government in which powers and policy assignments are shared between states and the national government. They may also share costs, administration, and even blame for programs that work poorly.

Before the national government began to assert its dominance over state governments, the American federal system leaned toward dual federalism. The American system, however, was never neatly separated into purely state and purely national responsibilities. For example, education was usually thought of as being mainly a state and local responsibility, yet even under the Articles of Confederation, Congress set aside land in the Northwest Territory to be used for schools. During the Civil War, the

Cooperative federalism began during the Great Depression of the 1930s. In this photo, Works Progress Administration workers, paid by the federal government, build a local road in New York. In subsequent decades, the entire interstate highway system was constructed with a combination of national and state dollars.

national government adopted a policy to create land grant colleges. Important American universities such as Wisconsin, Texas A&M, Illinois, Ohio State, North Carolina State, and Iowa State owe their origins to this national policy.

In the 1950s and 1960s, the national government began supporting public elementary and secondary education. In 1958 Congress passed the National Defense Education Act, largely in response to Soviet success in the space race. The act provided federal grants and loans for college students and financial support for elementary and secondary education in science and foreign languages. In 1965, Congress passed the Elementary and Secondary Education Act, which provided federal aid to numerous schools. Although these policies expanded the national government's role in education, they were not a sharp break with the past.

Today, the federal government's presence is felt in every schoolhouse. Almost all school districts receive some federal assistance. To do so, they must comply with federal rules and regulations. They must, for example, maintain desegregated and nondiscriminatory programs. In addition, as we will see in Chapter 4, federal courts have ordered local schools to implement elaborate desegregation plans and have placed constraints on school prayers.

Highways are another example of the movement toward cooperative federalism. In an earlier era, states and cities were largely responsible for building roads, although the Constitution does authorize Congress to construct "post roads." In 1956, Congress passed an act creating an interstate highway system. Hundreds of red, white, and blue signs were planted at the beginnings of interstate construction projects. The signs announced that the interstate highway program was a joint federal–state project and specified the cost and sharing of funds. In this and many other areas, the federal system has promoted a partnership between the national and state governments.

Cooperative federalism today rests on several standard operating procedures. For hundreds of programs, cooperative federalism involves:

- *Shared costs.* Washington foots part of the bill, but states or cities that want to get their share must pay part of a program's costs. Cities and states can get federal money for airport construction, sewage treatment plants, youth programs, and many other programs, but only if they pay some of the costs.
- *Federal guidelines.* Most federal grants to states and cities come with strings attached. Congress spends billions of dollars to support state highway construction, for example, but to get their share, states must adopt and enforce limits on the legal drinking age.
- *Shared administration.* State and local officials implement federal policies, but they have administrative powers of their own. The U.S. Department of Labor, for example, gives billions of dollars to states for job retraining, but states have considerable latitude in spending the money.

The cooperation between the national government and state governments is such an established feature of American federalism that it persists even when the two levels of government are in conflict on certain matters. For example, in the 1950s and 1960s, Southern states cooperated well with Washington in building the interstate highway system, while they clashed with the national government over racial integration.

In his first inaugural address, Ronald Reagan argued that the states had primary responsibility for governing in most policy areas, and he promised to "restore the balance between levels of government." Few officials at either the state or the national level agreed with Reagan about ending the national government's role in domestic programs. However, Reagan's opposition to the national government's spending on domestic policies and the huge federal deficits of the 1980s forced a reduction in federal funds for state and local governments, and shifted some responsibility for policy back to the states. Despite Reagan's move toward a more dual federalism, most Americans embrace a pragmatic view of governmental responsibilities, seeing the national government as more capable of—and thus responsible for—handling some issues, while they view state and local governments as better at managing others (see Table 3.3).

The Republican majorities that captured Congress in 1995 for the first time in four decades have been equally pragmatic in their approach to federalism. The Republicans often referred to a "revolution" in public policy, one aimed primarily at restricting the scope of the national government. They passed bills to give the states more authority over social and environmental programs that have long been in the realm of the national government. An overhaul of welfare policy was designed to allow states to devise innovative ways to lift people out of poverty, while reducing federal spending and cutting some benefits for the poor. Another bill, aimed at making it more difficult to enact new environmental protection legislation, prevented the federal government from imposing requirements on states without providing money to pay for them. Congress also repealed national speed limits and made it more difficult for prisoners to challenge the constitutionality of their sentences in federal court or to appeal to federal officials for relief from poor prison conditions.

participation
Federal Regulations and Mandates

At the same time, Republicans found turning to the federal government the most effective way to achieve many of their policy objectives. In an effort to reduce government interference in the marketplace and protect businesses from a patchwork of state requirements more stringent than federal ones, Republicans designated the federal government the sole regulator of products as diverse as mutual funds and agricultural chemicals. They also nullified state laws that had restricted telecommunications competition and set national standards requiring insurers to cover at least 48 hours of hospitalization for mothers and newborns.

To control immigration, Congress required state and local officials to meet new federal antifraud specifications for birth certificates and driver's licenses. And to combat crime, the legislature extended federal criminal penalties to cover crimes such as stalking, domestic terrorist activities, and rape during carjacking. Congress also threatened to cut off federal grants to states that failed to keep criminals behind bars for about 85 percent of their sentences or to increase arrests of violent criminals.

Table 3.3 A Pragmatic Federalism

The public has a pragmatic view of governmental responsibilities, seeing the national government as more capable of—and thus responsible for—handling some issues, while they view state and local government as better at managing others such as crime, welfare, and education. The founders did not give much thought to civil rights, environmental protection, or the health care system. Today, Americans frequently turn to Washington for help in dealing with these and other problems, including maintaining a strong economy. These are the results of a 1995 public opinion poll.

Which level of government should have more responsibility for . . .

	FEDERAL GOVERNMENT	STATE GOVERNMENTS
Protecting civil rights	67%	26%
Strengthening the economy	64	24
Protecting the environment	50	38
Improving the health care system	48	41
Providing assistance to the poor	40	44
Reforming welfare	42	46
Providing job training	31	55
Reducing crime	24	68
Improving public education	22	72

Source: NBC News/*Wall Street Journal* Polls, December 1994 and January 1995.

In addition, the new welfare bill imposed penalties on states that fail to meet new federal targets for placing welfare recipients in jobs. The states must also meet other requirements, such as creating registries to track child-support orders, or face a considerable loss of federal funds. Similarly, a clean drinking water bill required states to study local drinking water sources, map certain watersheds, and publish annual reports on drinking water violations.

Fiscal Federalism

fiscal federalism

The pattern of spending, taxing, and providing grants in the federal system; it is the cornerstone of the national government's relations with state and local governments.

The cornerstone of the national government's relations with state and local governments is **fiscal federalism:** the pattern of spending, taxing, and providing grants in the federal system. Subnational governments can influence the national government through local elections for national officials, but the national government has a powerful source of influence over the states—money. Grants-in-aid, federal funds appropriated by Congress for distribution to state and local governments, are the main instrument the national government uses for both aiding and influencing states and localities.

Despite the policy of the Reagan administration to reduce aid to states and cities, federal aid (including loan subsidies) still amounted to about $350 billion in 2002. Figure 3.1 illustrates the growth in the amount of money spent on federal grants. Federal aid, covering a wide range of policy areas (see Figure 3.2), accounts for about

Figure 3.1 Fiscal Federalism: Federal Grants to State and Local Governments

Federal grants to state and local governments have grown rapidly in recent decades and now amount to more than $350 billion per year.

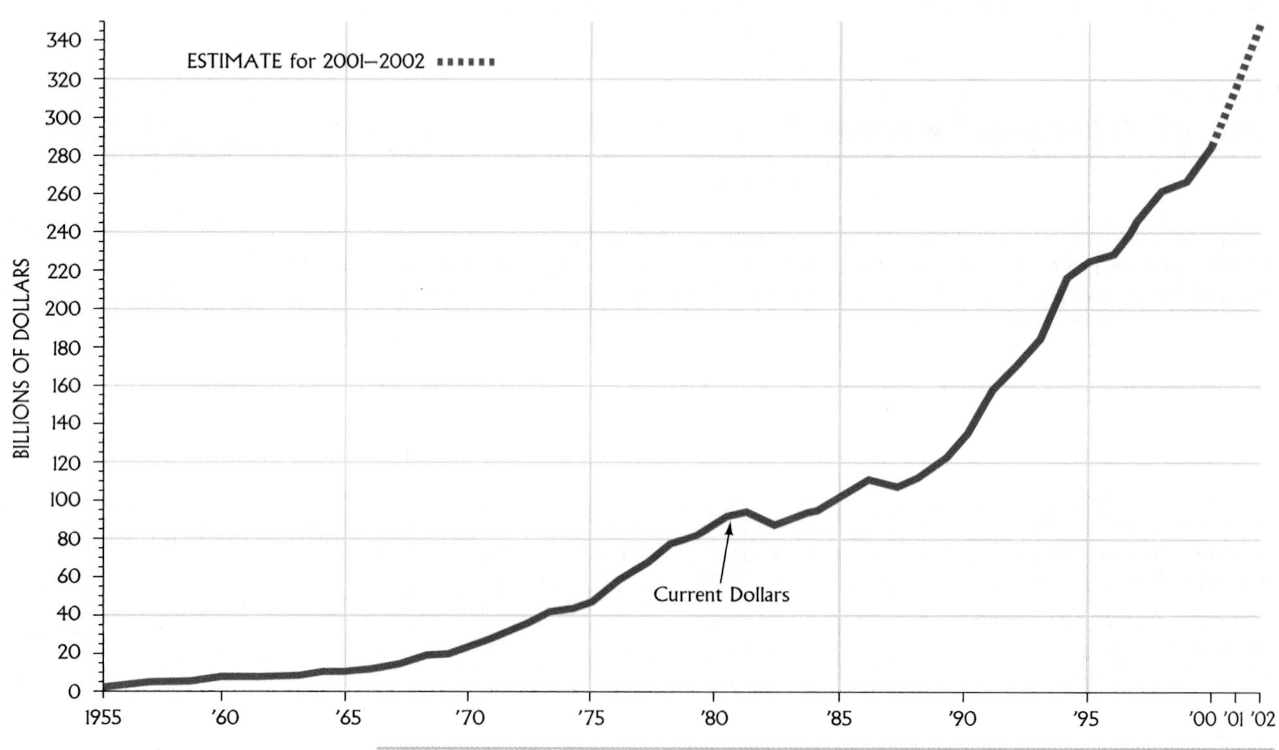

Source: Office of Management and Budget, *Budget of the United States Government, Fiscal Year 2002: Historical Tables* (Washington, D.C.: U.S. Government Printing Office, 2001), Table 12.2.

Figure 3.2 Functions of Federal Grants

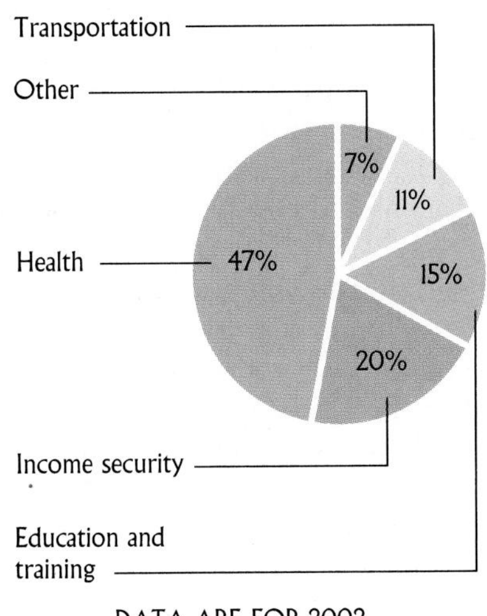

Health care receives the largest percentage of federal grants, followed by income security, education and training, and transportation.

Source: Office of Management and Budget, *Budget of the United States Government, Fiscal Year 2002: Historical Tables* (Washington, D.C.: U.S. Government Printing Office, 2001), Table 12.2.

The federal government often uses grants-in-aid as a carrot and stick for the states. For example, aid has been withheld from some cities until police departments have been racially and sexually integrated.

one-fourth of all the funds spent by state and local governments and for about 17 percent of all federal government expenditures.[10]

The Grant System: Distributing the Federal Pie. The national government regularly publishes the *Catalogue of Federal Domestic Assistance*, a massive volume listing the federal aid programs available to states, cities, and other local governments. The book lists federal programs that support energy assistance for the elderly poor, housing allowances for the poor, drug abuse services, urban rat control efforts, community arts programs, state disaster preparedness programs, and many more.

There are two major types of federal aid for states and localities: categorical grants and block grants. **Categorical grants** are the main source of federal aid to state and local governments. These grants can be used only for one of several hundred specific purposes, or categories, of state and local spending.

categorical grants

Federal grants that can be used only for specific purposes, or "categories," of state and local spending. They come with strings attached, such as nondiscrimination provisions. Compare **block grants.**

Why does it matter?

The federal system of grants-in-aid takes revenues obtained from federal taxes and sends it to state and local governments. Would you prefer to pay more in state and local taxes—such as property taxes, sales taxes, and income taxes—and perhaps less in federal income taxes to provide public services for your own state and city?

Because direct orders from the federal government to the states are rare (an exception is the Equal Opportunity Act of 1982, barring job discrimination by state and local governments), most federal regulation is accomplished in a more indirect manner. Instead of issuing edicts that tell citizens or states what they can and cannot do, Congress attaches conditions to the grants that states receive. The federal government has been especially active in appending restrictions to grants since the 1970s.

One string commonly attached to categorical and other federal grants is a nondiscrimination provision, stating that aid may not be used for purposes that discriminate against minorities, women, or other groups. Another string, a favorite of labor unions, is that federal funds may not support construction projects that pay below the local union wage. Other restrictions may require an environmental impact statement for a federally supported construction project or provisions for community involvement in the planning of the project.

The federal government may also employ *cross-over sanctions*—using federal dollars in one program to influence state and local policy in another, such as when funds are withheld for highway construction unless states raise the drinking age to 21 or establish highway beautification programs.

Cross-cutting requirements occur when a condition on one federal grant is extended to all activities supported by federal funds, regardless of their source. The grandfather of these requirements is Title VI of the 1964 Civil Rights Act (see Chapter 5), which bars discrimination in the use of federal funds because of race, color, national origin, gender, or physical disability. For example, if a university discriminates illegally in one program—such as athletics—it may lose the federal aid it receives for all its programs. There are also cross-cutting requirements dealing with environmental protection, historic preservation, contract wage rates, access to government information, the care of experimental animals, the treatment of human subjects in research projects, and a host of other policies.

project grants

Federal **categorical grants** given for specific purposes and awarded on the basis of the merits of applications.

formula grants

Federal **categorical grants** distributed according to a formula specified in legislation or in administrative regulations.

block grants

Federal grants given more or less automatically to states or communities to support broad programs in areas such as community development and social services.

There are two types of categorical grants. The most common type is a **project grant.** A project grant is awarded on the basis of competitive applications. National Science Foundation grants obtained by university professors are examples of project grants.

As their name implies, **formula grants** are distributed according to a formula. These formulas vary from grant to grant and may be computed on the basis of population, per capita income, percentage of rural population, or some other factor. A state or local government does not apply for a formula grant; a grant's formula determines how much money the particular government will receive. As a result, Congress is the site of vigorous political battles over the formulas themselves. The most common formula grants are those for Medicaid, child nutrition programs, sewage treatment plant construction, public housing, community development programs, and training and employment programs.

Applications for categorical grants typically arrive in Washington in boxes, not envelopes. Complaints about the cumbersome paperwork and the many strings attached to categorical grants led to the adoption of the other major type of federal aid, **block grants.** These grants are given more or less automatically to states or communities, which then have discretion within broad areas in deciding how to spend the money. First adopted in 1966, block grants are used to support programs in areas like community development and social services. The percentage of federal aid to state and local governments in the form of block grants began increasing in 1995 as the new Republican majority in Congress passed more federal aid in the form of block grants, including grants for welfare programs.

The Scramble for Federal Dollars. With more than $350 billion in federal grants at stake, most states and many cities have established full-time staffs in Washington.[11] Their task is to keep track of what money is available and to help their state or city get some of it. There are many Washington organizations of governments—the U.S.

Conference of Mayors and the National League of Cities, for example—that act like other interest groups in lobbying Congress. Senators and representatives regularly go to the voters with stories of their influence in securing federal funds for their constituencies. They need continued support at the polls, they say, so that they will rise in seniority and get key posts to help "bring home the bacon."

A general rule of federalism is that the more money there is at stake, the more fervently people will argue about its distribution. There are some variations in the amount of money that states give to, and get back from, the national government. On the whole, however, federal grant distribution follows the principle of *universalism:* something for everybody. The vigilance of senators and representatives keeps federal aid reasonably well spread among the states. Indeed, federal aid to states and cities is more equitably distributed than most other things in America, including income, access to education, and taxes.

This equality makes good politics, but it also may undermine public policy. Chapter 1 of the 1965 Elementary and Secondary Education Act is the federal government's principal endeavor to assist public schools. The primary intent of Chapter 1 was to give extra help to poor children. Yet the funds are allocated to 95 percent of all the school districts in the country. President Clinton's proposal to concentrate Chapter 1 funds on the poorest students failed when it ran into predictable opposition in Congress.

The Mandate Blues. States and localities are usually pleased to receive aid from the national government, but there are times when they would just as soon not have it. For example, say Congress decides to extend a program administered by the states and funded, in part, by the national government. It passes a law requiring the states to extend the program if they want to keep receiving aid, which most states do. Requirements that direct states or local governments to comply with federal rules under threat of penalties or as a condition of receipt of a federal grant are called *mandates.* Congress usually (though not always) appropriates some funds to help pay for the new policy, but either way, the states suddenly have to budget more funds for the project just to receive federal grant money.

Medicaid, which provides health care for poor people, is a prime example of a federal grant program that puts states in a difficult situation. Administered by the states, Medicaid receives wide support from both political parties. The national government pays between 50 and 83 percent of the bill, and the states pick up the rest. Since 1984, Congress has moved aggressively to expand Medicaid to specific populations, requiring the states to extend coverage to certain children, pregnant women, and elderly poor. Congress also increased its funding for the program a whopping 146 percent in the 1980s. Increased federal spending for Medicaid meant increased spending for the states as well. In 1989, troubled by the drain on their states' budgets, 49 of the 50 governors called for a two-year moratorium on mandated expansions of Medicaid.

A related problem arises when Congress passes a law creating financial obligations for the states but provides no funds to meet these obligations. For example, in 1990 Congress passed the Americans with Disabilities Act. States were required to make

facilities, such as state colleges and universities, accessible to individuals with disabilities but were allocated no funds to implement such a policy. Similarly, the Clean Air Act of 1970 established national air quality standards but requires states to administer them and to appropriate funds for their implementation.

In 1995, the newly elected Republican majorities in Congress made limiting unfunded and underfunded mandates on state and local governments a high priority. Congress passed, and President Clinton signed, a law that requires both chambers to take a separate, majority vote in order to pass any bill that would impose unfunded mandates of more than $50 million on state and local governments. The law also requires the Congressional Budget Office to estimate the costs of all bills that impose such mandates. All antidiscrimination legislation and most legislation requiring state and local governments to take various actions in exchange for continued federal funding (such as grants for transportation) are exempt from this procedure.

Federal courts also create unfunded mandates for the states. In recent years, federal judges have issued states orders in areas such as prison construction and management, school desegregation, and facilities in mental health hospitals, sometimes even temporarily taking them over. These court orders often require states to spend funds to meet standards imposed by the judge.

A combination of federal regulations and inadequate resources may also put the states in a bind. The national government requires that a local housing authority build or acquire a new low-income housing facility for each one it demolishes. But for years Congress has provided little money for the construction of public housing. As a result, a provision intended to help the poor by ensuring a stable supply of housing actually hurts them because it discourages local governments from demolishing unsafe and inadequate housing.

The federal government may also unintentionally create financial obligations for the states. In 1994, California, New York, Texas, Florida, and other states sued the federal government for reimbursement for the cost of health care, education, prisons, and other public services that the states provide to illegal residents. The states charged that the federal government's failure to control its borders was the source of huge new demands on their treasuries and that Washington, not the states, should pay for the problem. Although the states did not win their cases, their point is a valid one.

Understanding Federalism

The federal system is central to politics, government, and policy in America. The division of powers and responsibilities among different levels of government has implications for both the themes of democracy and the scope of government.

Why does it matter?

One of the great debates in the United States focuses on the role of the federal government. Does the fact that state and local governments are physically closer to the people they serve make them more responsive to the public? Do you think that the government officials in your state and city are more competent than federal government officials (such as those in the military or the Social Security Administration) in serving citizens?

Federalism and Democracy

One of the reasons the founders established a federal system was to allay the fears of those who believed that a powerful and distant central government would tyrannize the states and limit their voice in government. By decentralizing the political system, federalism was designed to contribute to democracy—or at least to the limited form of democracy supported by the founders. Has it done so?

Advantages for Democracy. The more levels of government, the more opportunities there are for participation in politics. State governments provide thousands of elected offices for which citizens may vote and/or run.

Additional levels of government also contribute to democracy by increasing access to government. Because different citizens and interest groups will have better access to either state-level governments or the national government, the two levels increase the opportunities for government to be responsive to demands for policies. For example, in

You Are the Policymaker

Should *Whether* You Live Depend on *Where* You Live?

Because the federal system allocates major responsibilities for public policy to the states, policies often vary with the different views of the population in different locations. The differences among public policies are especially dramatic in the criminal justice system.

A conviction for first-degree murder in 38 states may well mean the death penalty for the convicted murderer. In 12 other states, first-degree murderers only spend time behind bars. In Arizona, the minimum age for the death penalty is 14; it is 16 in 11 other states. Eight states have no minimum age at all.

Some people see diversity in public policy as one of the advantages of federalism. Others may argue that citizens of the same country ought to be subject to uniform penalties. What do *you* think? Should *whether* you live depend on *where* you live?

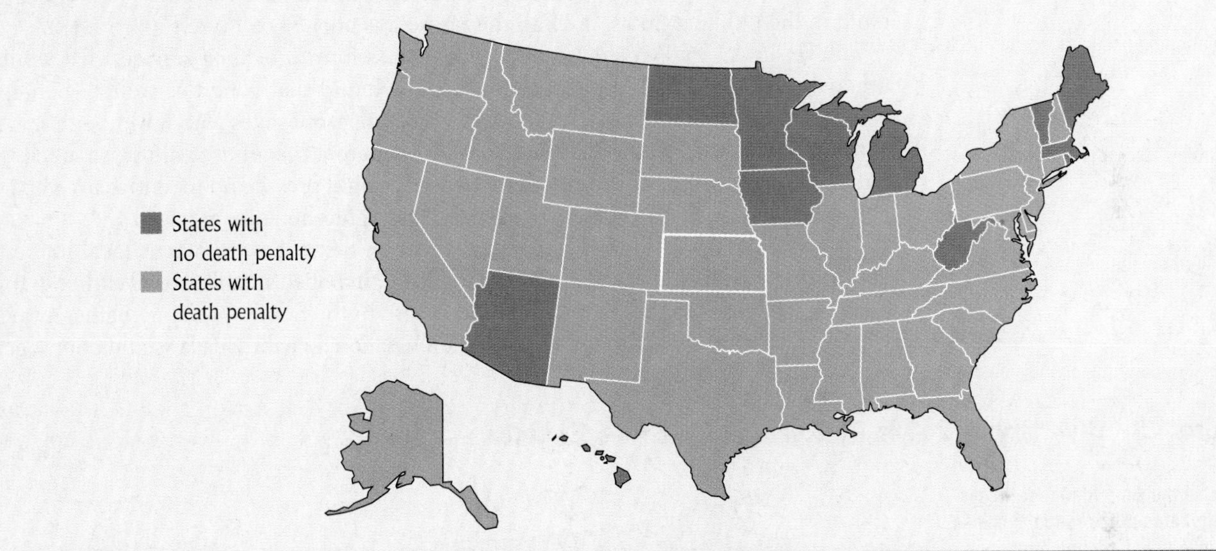

the 1950s and 1960s when advocates of civil rights found themselves stymied in Southern states, they turned to the national level for help in achieving racial equality. Business interests, on the other hand, have traditionally found state governments to be more responsive to their demands. Organized labor is not well established in some states, but it can usually depend on some sympathetic officials at the national level who will champion its proposals.

Different economic interests are concentrated in different states: oil in Texas, tobacco farming in Virginia, and copper mining in Montana, for example. The federal system allows an interest concentrated in a state to exercise substantial influence in the election of that state's officials, both local and national. In turn, these officials promote policies advantageous to the interest in both Washington and the state capital. This is a pluralism of interests that James Madison, among others, valued within a large republic.

State and local bases have another advantage. Even if a party loses at the national level, it can rebuild in its areas of strength and develop leaders under its banner at the state and local levels. As a result, losing an election becomes more acceptable, and the peaceful transfer of power is more probable. This was especially important in the early years of the nation before our political norms had become firmly established.

Because the federal system assigns states important responsibilities for public policies, it is possible for the diversity of opinion within the country to be reflected in different public policies among the states. If the citizens of Texas wish to have a death penalty, for example, they can vote for politicians who support it, whereas those in Wisconsin can vote to abolish the death penalty altogether (see "You Are the Policymaker: Should *Whether* You Live Depend on *Where* You Live?"). Similarly, there are large differences in the amounts that states provide for the poor, ranging from $923 per month for a family of three in Alaska to $170 per month in Mississippi (see Figure 3.3).

By handling most disputes over policy at the state and local level, federalism also reduces decision making and conflict at the national level. If every issue had to be resolved in Washington, the national government would be overwhelmed.

Disadvantages for Democracy. Despite its advantages for democracy, relying on states to supply public services has some drawbacks. States differ in the resources they can devote to services like public education. Thus, the quality of education a child receives is heavily dependent on the state in which the child's parents happen to reside. In 1998, New Jersey state and local governments spent an average of $10,420 for each child in the public schools; in Utah the figure was only $4,059 (see Figure 3.4).

Diversity in policy can also discourage states from providing services that would otherwise be available. Political scientists have found that generous welfare benefits can strain a state's treasury by attracting poor people from states with lower benefits. As a result, states are deterred from providing generous benefits to those in need. A national program with uniform welfare benefits would provide no incentive for welfare recipients to move to another state in search of higher benefits.[12]

Federalism may also have a negative effect on democracy insofar as local interests are able to thwart national majority support of certain policies. As discussed earlier in this chapter, in the 1960s the states—especially those in the South—became battlegrounds when the national government tried to enforce national civil rights laws and court deci-

Figure 3.3 Diversity in Public Policy: State Welfare Benefits

Because the American federal system allocates major responsibilities for public policy to the states, policies often vary in different locations. This figure shows that for the emotionally charged issue of welfare, different states have adopted quite different policies.

[a] Figures are for New York City only.

[b] Figures are for Wayne County, which includes Detroit.

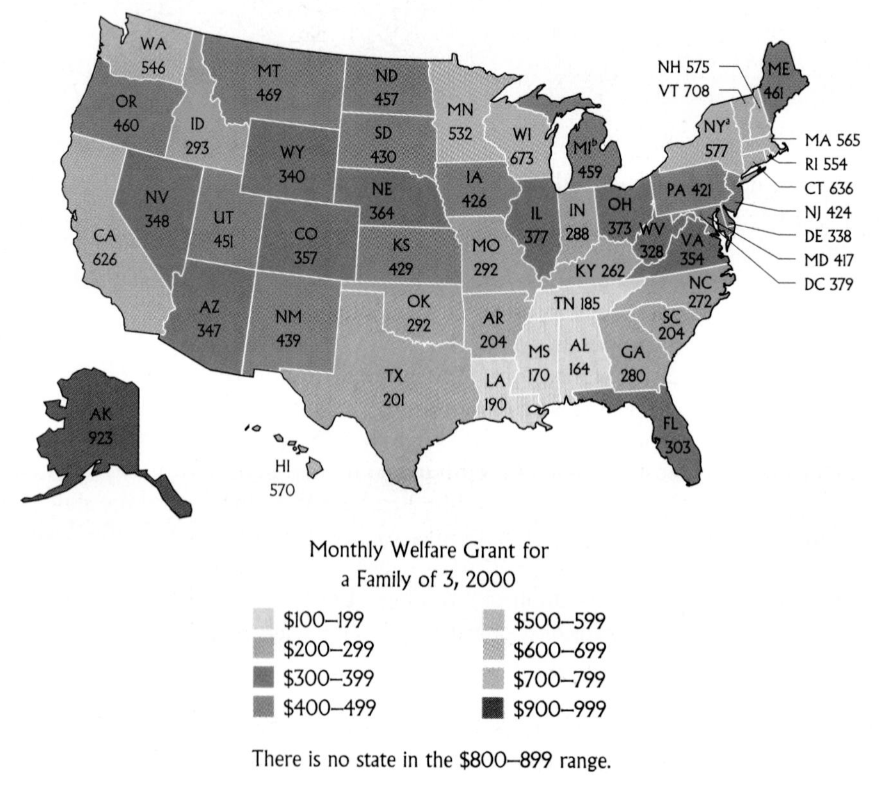

Source: House Ways and Means Committee; 2000 *Green Book.*

Figure 3.4 The Downside of Diversity: Spending on Public Education

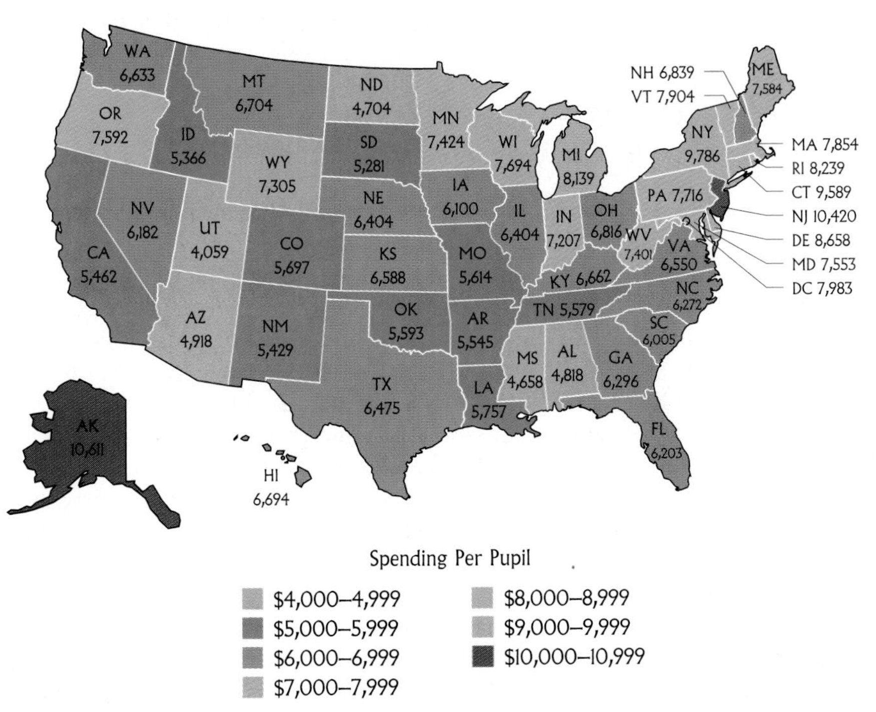

The downside of the public policy diversity fostered by federalism is that states are largely dependent on their own resources for providing public services; these resources vary widely from state to state. This map shows the wide variation among the states in the money spent on each child in the public schools.

1999 Average: $6,734

Source: U.S. Department of Commerce, *Statistical Abstract of the United States, 2000* (Washington, D.C.: U.S. Government Printing Office, 2001), 172.

sions. Federalism complicated and delayed efforts to end racial discrimination because state and local governments were responsible for public education and voting eligibility, for example, and because they had passed most of the laws supporting racial segregation.

Finally, the sheer number of governments in the United States is, at times, as much a burden as a boon to democracy. Program vendors at baseball games say that "You can't tell the players without a scorecard"; unfortunately, scorecards are not available for local governments, where the players are numerous and sometimes seem to be involved in different games. The U.S. Bureau of the Census counts not only people but also governments. Its latest count revealed an astonishing 87,504 American governments (see Table 3.4).

Certainly, 87,000 governments ought to be enough for any country. Are there too many? Americans speak eloquently about their state and local governments as grassroots

Table 3.4 The Number of Governments in America

	NUMBER OF GOVERNMENTS
U.S. government	1
States	50
Counties	3,043
Municipalities	19,372
Townships or towns	16,629
School districts	13,726
Special districts	34,683
Total	**87,504**

Source: U.S. Department of Commerce, *Statistical Abstract of the United States, 2000* (Washington, D.C.: U.S. Government Printing Office, 2001), 299.

governments, close to the people. Yet having so many governments makes it difficult to know which governments are doing what. Exercising democratic control over them is even more difficult; voter turnout in local elections is often less than 20 percent.

Federalism and the Scope of the National Government

One of the most persistent questions in American politics has been the scope of the national government relative to that of the states. To understand the relative roles of the two levels of government we must first understand why the national government grew and then ask whether this growth was at the expense of the states or whether it occurred because of the unique capabilities and responsibilities of the national government.

President Ronald Reagan negotiated quotas on imports of Japanese cars in order to give advantages to the American auto industry, raising the price of all automobiles in the process. At the behest of steel companies, President George Bush exercised his authority to continue Reagan's quotas on the amount of steel that could be imported (thereby making steel products more expensive). The first major piece of legislation the Bush administration sent to Congress was a bailout plan for the savings and loan industry, which had gotten into financial trouble through a combination of imprudent loans, declining property values, deregulation of banking, incompetence, and corruption. President Clinton proposed that the Pentagon spend nearly $600 million to fund the development of a U.S. industry in "flat-panel displays" used for laptop computers, video games, and advanced instruments.

In each of these cases and dozens of others, the national government has involved itself (some might say interfered) in the economic marketplace with quotas and subsidies intended to help American businesses. As Chapter 2 explained, the national government took a direct interest in economic affairs from the very founding of the republic. As the United States changed from an agricultural to an industrial nation, new problems arose and with them new demands for governmental action. The national government responded with a national banking system, subsidies for railroads and airlines, and a host of other policies that dramatically increased its role in the economy.

The industrialization of the country raised other issues as well. With the formation of large corporations in the late nineteenth century—Cornelius Vanderbilt's New York Central Railroad and John D. Rockefeller's Standard Oil Company, for example—came the potential for such abuses as monopoly pricing. If there is only one railroad in town, it can charge farmers inflated prices to ship their grain to market. If a single company distributes most of the gasoline in the country, it can set the price at which gasoline sells. Thus, many interests asked the national government to restrain monopolies and to encourage open competition.

There were additional demands on the national government for new public policies. Farmers sought services such as agricultural research, rural electrification, and price supports. Unions wanted the national government to protect their rights to organize and bargain collectively and to help provide safer working conditions, a minimum wage, and pension protection. Along with other groups, labor unions supported a wide range of social welfare policies, from education to health care. As the country became more urbanized, new problems arose in the areas of housing, welfare, the environment, and transportation. In each case, the relevant interest turned to the national government for help.

Why not turn to the state governments instead? In most cases, the answer is simple: A problem or policy requires the authority and resources of the national government. The Constitution forbids states from having independent defense policies.

Each state could have its own space program, but it is much more efficient for the states to combine their efforts in one national program. The same principle applies to economic security and to a host of other important programs.

And even if it did not, how many states would want to take on a responsibility that represents more than half of the federal work force and about one-sixth of federal expenditures?

It is constitutionally permissible, but not sensible, for the states to handle a wide range of other issues. It makes little sense for Louisiana to pass strict controls on polluting the Mississippi River if most of the river's pollution occurs upstream, where Louisiana has no jurisdiction. Rhode Island has no incentive to create an energy policy because no natural energy reserves are located in the state. Similarly, how effectively can a state regulate an international conglomerate such as General Motors? How can each state, acting individually, manage the nation's money supply?

Each state could have its own space program, but it is much more efficient if the states combine their efforts in one national program. The largest category of federal expenditures is that for economic security, including the Social Security program. Although each state could have its own retirement program, how could state governments determine which state should pay for retirees who move to Florida or Arizona? A national program is the only feasible method of ensuring the incomes of the mobile elderly of today's society.

Figure 3.5 shows that the national government's share of American governmental expenditures has grown rapidly since 1929; most of this growth occurred during the Great Depression. At that time, the national government spent an amount equal to only 2.5 percent of the size of the economy, the gross domestic product (GDP); today, it spends about 20 percent of our GDP (this includes grants to states and localities). The proportion of our GDP spent by state and local governments has grown less rapidly than the national government's share. States and localities spent 7.4 percent of our GDP in 1929; they spend about 9 percent today (not including federal grants).[13]

Figure 3.5 demonstrates that the states have not been supplanted by the national government; indeed, they carry out virtually all the functions they always have. Instead, with the support of the American people (see Table 3.3), the national government has taken on new responsibilities. In addition, the national government has added programs to help the states meet their own responsibilities.

Figure 3.5 Fiscal Federalism: The Public Sector and the Federal System

The federal government's spending increased rapidly during the Great Depression and World War II. In recent years, the role of both federal and state governments has declined slightly.

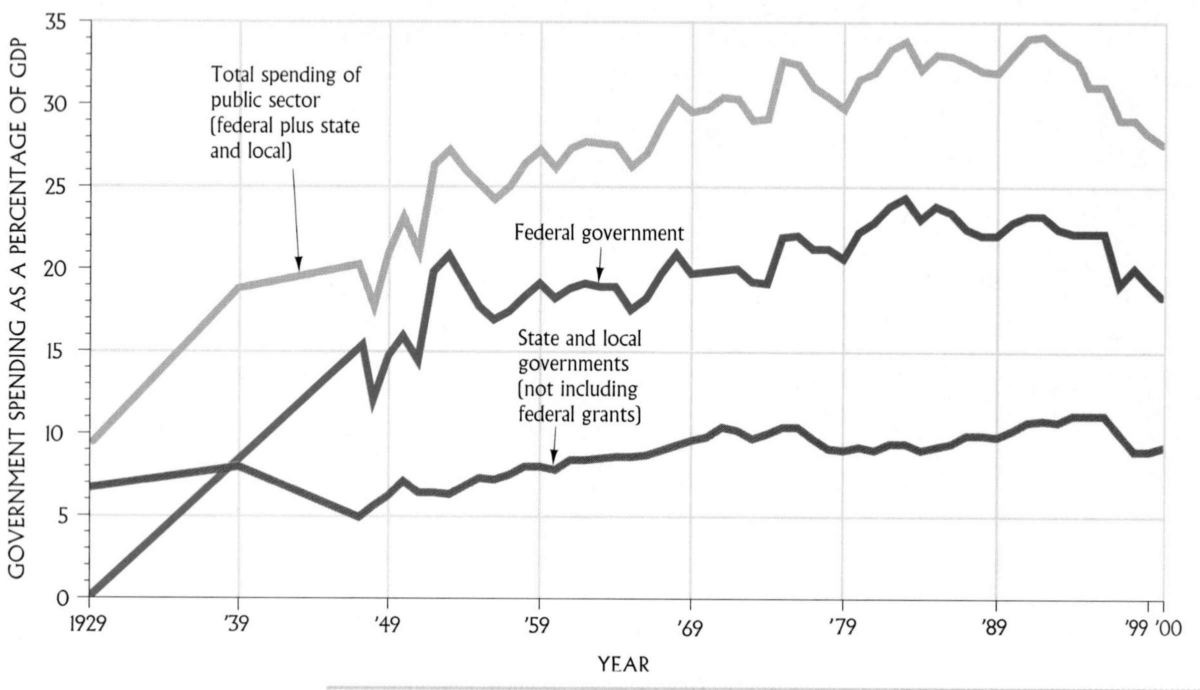

Source: Office of Management and Budget, *Budget of the United States Government, Fiscal Year 2002: Historical Tables* (Washington, D.C.: U.S. Government Printing Office, 2001), Table 15.3.

Summary

Federalism is a governmental system in which power is shared between a central government and other governments. Federalism is much less common than are the unitary governments typical of most parliamentary democracies. American federalism consists of 50 state governments joined in an "indestructible union" (as the Supreme Court once called it) under one national government. Today, federal power over the states is indisputable; the Supreme Court cases *McCulloch v. Maryland* and *Gibbons v. Ogden*, the Civil War, and the struggle for racial equality all helped to determine national supremacy. The federal government often uses its fiscal leverage to influence state and local policies.

The United States has moved from a system of dual federalism to one of cooperative federalism, in which the national and state governments share responsibility for public policies. Fiscal federalism is of great help to states. Even after the Reagan administration reductions, the federal government distributes more than $350 billion in federal funds to states and cities each year.

Federalism was instituted largely to enhance democracy in America, and it strengthens democratic government in many ways. At the same time, diverse state policies and the sheer number of local governments cause problems as well. Demands for new policies and the necessity for national policy on certain issues have contributed to the growth of national government relative to state governments. Yet the state governments continue to play a central role in governing the lives of Americans.

Although American federalism concerns state power and national power, it is not a concept removed from most Americans' lives. Federalism affects a vast range of social and economic policies. Slavery, school desegregation, abortion, and teenage drinking have all been debated in terms of federalism.

Career Profile

Position: Emergency Management Specialists
Employer: Federal Emergency Management Agency (FEMA)
Starting Salary Range: $28,000-34,000
Benefits: 401K, life and health insurance, and mentoring programs
Eligibility/Qualifications: Though a bachelor's degree is not required, it is highly recommended unless one has extensive experience in the field. Customer service skills are crucial.

Real People on the Job: Carol Coleman

Carol Coleman, an Emergency Management Specialist and the Human Services Branch Chief for FEMA, is usually one of the first federal employees on a disaster scene after state officials have requested federal assistance and that assistance has been approved. Working out the FEMA Midwest branch headquarters in Kansas City, Mo., Carol has dealt with floods in Missouri and Iowa and tornadoes across the region. She and her teams remain at the site of a disaster anywhere from three weeks to two months at a time.

In the aftermath of an earthquake, tornado, flood, or hurricane, stricken citizens quickly forget debates over the nuances of federalism and the role of the federal government. At such times, their biggest concerns are finding shelter, food, and medical attention. FEMA strives to ensure that emergency relief efforts run smoothly by coordinating efforts among state, federal, and private organizations to alleviate suffering and devastation.

Perhaps the most exciting aspect of Carol's job remains its ever-changing nature. All floods and tornados are not the same, says Carol, because each disaster event has its own character and its own needs. Every flood, hurricane, earthquake, or tornado occurs in a specific neighborhood with different people from different backgrounds requiring a tailored approach for every incident.

Regardless of where a disaster occurs, FEMA's primary goal remains constant: to help people as quickly and efficiently as possible. The people always come first. Although computerization and telecommunication advances have streamlined FEMA's response time, it is still vital to have specialists and operatives on the ground to meet people face to face. If a community seems to be badly shaken in the aftermath of a disaster, Carol and her coworkers establish crisis-counseling centers to help them deal with the shock and loss. On-site inspectors and specialists examine houses and disseminate relief information throughout the community. Thus, FEMA disaster teams function much like a caring, well-organized family during a time of crisis. It is this trait, more than any other, that makes Carol proud to work at FEMA.

If you think you might be interested in making FEMA part of your career future, the organization offers student internships in nearly every office at the FEMA headquarters in Washington, D.C., including the Office of Congressional Affairs. FEMA also needs workers to perform temporary, on-call disaster work for its CORE force (Cadre of Response/Recovery Employees). Similar to many other government agencies, qualified computer programmers and technicians are constantly in demand at FEMA. For information about career opportunities at FEMA, check out its web site at www.fema.org.

Key Terms

federalism	enumerated powers	dual federalism
unitary governments	implied powers	cooperative federalism
intergovernmental relations	elastic clause	fiscal federalism
supremacy clause	*Gibbons v. Ogden*	categorical grants
Tenth Amendment	full faith and credit	project grant
McCulloch v. Maryland	extradition	formula grants
	privileges and immunities	block grants

For Further Reading

Anton, Thomas. *American Federalism and Public Policy.* Philadelphia: Temple University Press, 1989. An overview of how the national, state, and local governments share responsibility for policies.

Beer, Samuel H. *To Make a Nation: The Rediscovery of American Federalism.* Cambridge, MA: Harvard University Press, 1993. An excellent study of the philosophical bases of American federalism.

Conlan, Timothy J. *From New Federalism to Devolution: Twenty-Five Years of Intergovernmental Reform.* Washington, D.C.: Brookings Institution, 1998. An analysis of the efforts to restructure intergovernmental relations since the late 1960s.

Dye, Thomas R. *American Federalism: Competition Among Governments.* Lexington, MA: Lexington Books, 1990. Analyzes competitive federalism, in which states and local governments compete to offer public services at low costs.

Elazar, Daniel J. *American Federalism: A View from the States,* 3rd ed. New York: Harper & Row, 1984. A well-known work surveying federalism from the standpoint of state governments.

Kettl, Donald F. *The Regulation of American Federalism.* Baltimore: Johns Hopkins University Press, 1987. Examines the regulations that the national government imposes on state and local governments.

Peterson, Paul E. *The Price of Federalism.* Washington, D.C.: Brookings Institution, 1995. A current assessment of the costs and benefits of federalism.

Peterson, Paul, Barry G. Rabe, and Kenneth K. Wong. *When Federalism Works.* Washington, D.C.: Brookings Institution, 1986. Examines federal grants-in-aid programs and explains why they are implemented better in some areas than in others.

Walker, David B. *The Rebirth of Federalism.* Chatham, NJ: Chatham House, 1995. A history of American federalism and an analysis of its current condition.

Wright, Deil S. *Understanding Intergovernmental Relations,* 3rd ed. Belmont, CA: Brooks/Cole, 1988. A review of the relations among the local, state, and national levels of government.

Internet Resources

www.cfda.gov
Allows you to search through the hundreds of federal grants.

www.ncsl.org/statefed/afipolcy.htm
Information and discussion of issues on federal–state relations.

www.census.gov/statab/www/
The *Statistical Abstract of the United States,* containing a wealth of data on state public policies.

www.statesnews.org
Council of State Governments web site with information on states and state public policies.

www.thirteen.org/federalist
Discussions of the *Federalist Papers* and short articles and debates on issues regarding federalism.

Notes

1. Thomas Anton, *Moving Money* (New York: Oxford University Press, 1982).
2. One useful introduction to federalism and intergovernmental relations is Deil S. Wright, *Understanding Intergovernmental Relations,* 3rd ed. (Belmont, CA: Brooks/Cole, 1988). Another is David B. Walker, *The Rebirth of Federalism* (Chatham, NJ: Chatham House, 1995).
3. For a study of how different states enforce federal child support enforcement, see Lael R. Keiser and Joe Soss, "With Good Cause: Bureaucratic Discretion and the Politics of Child Support Enforcement," *American Journal of Political Science* 42 (October 1998): 1,133–1,156.
4. On the states as innovators, see Jack L. Walker, "The Diffusion of Innovations in the American States," *American Political Science Review* 63 (September 1969): 880–899; Virginia Gray, "Innovation in the States: A Diffusion Study," *American Political Science Review* 67 (December 1973): 1,174–1,185; and Richard P. Nathan and Fred C. Doolittle, *Reagan and the States* (Princeton, NJ: Princeton University Press, 1987).

5. *Alden v. Maine* (1999). See also *College Savings Bank v. Florida Prepaid Postsecondary Education Expense Board* (1999); and *Florida Prepaid Postsecondary Education Expense Board v. College Savings Bank* (1999).
6. The Fourteenth Amendment was passed *after* the Eleventh Amendment.
7. *Monroe v. Pape*, 1961; *Monell v. New York City Department of Social Welfare*, 1978; *Owen v. Independence*, 1980; *Maine v. Thiboutot*, 1980; *Oklahoma City v. Tuttle*, 1985; *Dennis v. Higgins*, 1991.
8. The transformation from dual to cooperative federalism is described in Walker, *The Rebirth of Federalism*, chap. 4.
9. The classic discussion of cooperative federalism is found in Morton Grodzins, *The American System: A New View of Governments in the United States*, Daniel J. Elazar, ed. (Chicago: Rand McNally, 1966).
10. Office of Management and Budget, *Budget of the United States Government, Fiscal Year 2002: Analytical Perspectives* (Washington, D.C.: U.S. Government Printing Office, 2001), Table 9.2.
11. On intergovernmental lobbying, see Donald H. Haider, *When Governments Go to Washington* (New York: Free Press, 1974); and Anne Marie Commisa, *Governments as Interest Groups: Intergovernmental Lobbying and the Federal System* (Westport, CT: Praeger, 1995).
12. Paul E. Peterson and Mark Rom, "American Federalism, Welfare Policy, and Residential Choices," *American Political Science Review* 83 (September 1989): 711–728. Some states are now limiting welfare payments to new residents.
13. Office of Management and Budget, *Budget of the United States Government, Fiscal Year 2002: Historical Tables* (Washington, D.C.: U.S. Government Printing Office, 2001), Table 15.3.

Civil Liberties and Public Policy

4

Chapter Outline

The Board of Regents of the University of Wisconsin System requires students at the University's Madison campus to pay a segregated activity fee. The fee supports various campus services and extracurricular student activities. In the University's view, such fees enhance students' educational experience by promoting extracurricular activities, stimulating advocacy and debate on diverse points of view, enabling participation in campus administrative activity, and providing opportunities to develop social skills, all consistent with the University's broad educational mission. Registered student organizations (RSOs) engaging in a number of diverse expressive activities are eligible to receive a portion of the fees, which are administered by the student government subject to the University's approval.

Both sides in the case agreed that the process for reviewing and approving RSO applications for funding is administered in a viewpoint-neutral fashion. RSOs may also obtain funding through a student referendum. Some students, however, sued the University, alleging that the activity fee violated their First Amendment rights, and that the University must grant them the choice not to fund RSOs that engage in political and ideological expression offensive to their personal beliefs.

In 2000, the Supreme Court held in a unanimous decision in *Board of Regents of University of Wisconsin System v. Southworth* that if a university determines that its mission is well served if students have the means to engage in dynamic discussion on a broad range of issues, it may impose a mandatory fee to sustain such dialogue. The Court recognized that it was all but inevitable that the fees will subsidize speech that some students find objectionable or offensive. Thus, the Court required that a university provide some protection to its students' First Amendment interests by requiring viewpoint neutrality in the allocation of funding support.

The University of Wisconsin case is the sort of complex controversy that shapes American civil liberties. Debates about the right to abortion, the right to bear arms, the rights of criminal defendants, and similar issues are constantly in the news. Some of these issues arise from conflicting interests. The need to protect society against crime often conflicts with society's need to protect the rights of people accused of crime. Other conflicts derive from strong differences of opinion about what is ethical, moral, or right. To some Americans, abortion is murder, the taking of a human life. To others, a woman's choice whether to bear a child, free of governmental intrusion, is a fundamental right. Everyone, however, is affected by the extent of our civil liberties.

Deciding complex questions about civil liberties requires balancing competing values, such as maintaining an open system of expression while protecting individuals from the excesses such a system may produce. As we learned in Chapter 1, civil liberties are essential to democracy. How could we have free elections without free speech, for example? But does it follow that critics of officials should be able to say whatever they want, no matter how untrue? And who should decide the extent of our liberty? Should it be a representative institution such as Congress or a judicial elite such as the Supreme Court?

The role of the government in resolving civil liberties controversies is also the subject of much debate. Conservatives usually advocate narrowing the scope of government, yet many strongly support government-imposed limits on abortion and government-sanctioned prayers in the public schools. They also want government to be less hindered by concern for defendants' rights. Liberals, who typically support a broader scope of government, usually want to limit government's role in prohibiting abortion and encouraging religious activities and to place greater constraints on government's freedom of action in the criminal justice system.

Issues of civil liberties present many vexing problems for the courts to resolve. For example, is burning the American flag desecration of a sacred patriotic symbol, or is it an expression of opposition to government policy that is protected by the Constitution?

civil liberties

The legal constitutional protections against government. Although our civil liberties are formally set down in the **Bill of Rights,** the courts, police, and legislatures define their meaning.

Bill of Rights

The first 10 amendments to the **U.S. Constitution,** which define such basic liberties as freedom of religion, speech, and press and guarantee defendants' rights.

Civil liberties are individual legal and constitutional protections against the government. Americans' civil liberties are set down in the **Bill of Rights,** the first 10 amendments to the Constitution. At first glance, many questions about civil liberties look easy. The Bill of Rights' guarantee of a free press seems straightforward; either Americans can write what they choose, or they cannot. In the real world of American law, however, these issues are subtle and complex.

Disputes about civil liberties often end up in court. The Supreme Court of the United States is the final interpreter of the content and scope of our liberties; this ultimate power to interpret the Constitution accounts for the ferocious debate over presidential appointments to the Supreme Court.

Throughout this chapter you will find special features entitled "You Are the Judge." Each feature describes an actual case brought before the courts and asks you to apply your sense of fairness and your standards to arrive at a judgment.

To understand the specifics of American civil liberties, we must first understand the Bill of Rights.

The Bill of Rights—Then and Now

By 1787, all state constitutions had bills of rights, some of which survive, intact, to this day. Although the new U.S. Constitution had no bill of rights, the states made its inclusion a condition of ratification. The Bill of Rights was passed as a group by the First Congress in 1789 and sent to the states for ratification. In 1791, these amendments became part of the Constitution.

The Bill of Rights ensures Americans' basic liberties, such as freedom of speech and religion, and protection against arbitrary searches and being held for long periods without trial (see Table 4.1). The Bill of Rights was passed when British abuses of the colonists' civil liberties were still a fresh and bitter memory. Newspaper editors had been jailed; citizens had been arrested without cause, detained, and forced to confess at gunpoint or worse. Thus, the first 10 amendments enjoyed great popular support.

Table 4.1 The Bill of Rights

(These amendments were passed by Congress on September 25, 1789, and ratified by the states on December 15, 1791.)

Amendment I—Religion, Speech, Assembly, Petition
Congress shall make no law respecting an establishment of religion, or prohibiting the free exercise thereof; or abridging the freedom of speech, or of the press; or the right of the people peaceably to assemble, and to petition the Government for a redress of grievances.

Amendment II—Right to Bear Arms
A well-regulated militia, being necessary to the security of a free State, the right of the people to keep and bear arms, shall not be infringed.

Amendment III—Quartering of Soldiers
No Soldier shall, in time of peace be quartered in any house, without the consent of the owner, nor in time of war, but in a manner to be prescribed by law.

Amendment IV—Searches and Seizures
The right of the people to be secure in their persons, houses, papers, and effects, against unreasonable searches and seizures, shall not be violated, and no warrants shall issue, but upon probable cause, supported by oath or affirmation, and particularly describing the place to be searched, and persons or things to be seized.

Amendment V—Grand Juries, Double Jeopardy, Self-Incrimination, Due Process, Eminent Domain
No person shall be held to answer to a capital, or otherwise infamous crime, unless on a presentment or indictment of a Grand Jury, except in cases arising in the land or naval forces, or in the militia, when in actual service in time of war or public danger: nor shall any person be subject for the same offense to be twice put in jeopardy of life or limb; nor shall be compelled in any criminal case to be a witness against himself, nor be deprived of life, liberty, or property, without due process of law; nor shall private property be taken for public use, without just compensation.

Amendment VI—Criminal Court Procedures
In all criminal prosecutions, the accused shall enjoy the right to a speedy and public trial, by an impartial jury of the State and district wherein the crime shall have been committed, which district shall have been previously ascertained by law, and to be informed of the nature and cause of the accusation; to be confronted with the witnesses against him; to have compulsory process for obtaining witnesses in his favor, and to have the assistance of counsel for his defense.

Amendment VII—Trial by Jury in Common-Law Cases
In Suits at common law, where the value in controversy shall exceed twenty dollars, the right of trial by jury shall be preserved, and no fact tried by a jury, shall be otherwise reexamined in any Court of the United States.

Amendment VIII—Bails, Fines, and Punishment
Excessive bail shall not be required, nor excessive fines imposed, nor cruel and unusual punishments inflicted.

Amendment IX—Rights Retained by the People
The enumeration in the Constitution, of certain rights, shall not be construed to deny or disparage others retained by the people.

Amendment X—Rights Reserved to the States
The powers not delegated to the United States by the Constitution, nor prohibited by it to the States, are reserved to the States respectively, or to the people.

Political scientists have discovered that people are devotees of rights in theory but that their support wavers when it comes time to put those rights into practice.[1] For example, Americans in general believe in freedom of speech, but many citizens would not let the Ku Klux Klan speak in their neighborhood or allow their public schools to teach about atheism or homosexuality. Few rights are absolute; we cannot avoid the difficult questions of balancing civil liberties and other individual and societal values.

The Bill of Rights and the States

Take another look at the **First Amendment.** Note the first words: "Congress shall make no law . . ." The Bill of Rights was written to restrict the powers of the new national government. In 1791, Americans were comfortable with their state governments; after all, every state constitution had its own bill of rights. Thus, a literal reading of the First Amendment suggests that it does not prohibit a state government from passing a law prohibiting the free exercise of religion, free speech, or freedom of the press.

What happens, however, if a state passes a law violating one of the rights protected by the federal Bill of Rights and the state's constitution does not prohibit this abridgment of freedom? In 1833, the answer to that question was "nothing." The Bill of Rights, said the Court in ***Barron v. Baltimore,*** restrained only the national government, not states and cities.

First Amendment
The constitutional amendment that establishes the four great liberties: freedom of the press, of speech, of religion, and of assembly.

Barron v. Baltimore
The 1833 Supreme Court decision holding that the **Bill of Rights** restrained only the national government, not the states and cities.

Almost a century later, however, the Court ruled that a state government must respect some First Amendment rights. The 1925 ruling in ***Gitlow v. New York*** relied not on the First Amendment but on the Fourteenth—the second of three "Civil War Amendments" that ended slavery, gave former slaves legal protection, and ensured their voting rights. Ratified in 1868, the **Fourteenth Amendment** declared:

> *No state shall make or enforce any law which shall abridge the privileges or immunities of citizens of the United States nor shall any state deprive any person of life, liberty, or property, without due process of law; nor deny to any person within its jurisdiction the equal protection of the laws.*

Gitlow v. New York

The 1925 Supreme Court decision holding that freedoms of press and speech are "fundamental personal rights and liberties protected by the **due process clause** of the **Fourteenth Amendment** from impairment by the states" as well as the federal government. Compare ***Barron v. Baltimore.***

Fourteenth Amendment

The constitutional amendment adopted after the Civil War that states, "No State shall make or enforce any law which shall abridge the privileges or immunities of citizens of the United States; nor shall any state deprive any person of life, liberty, or property, without due process of law; nor deny to any person within its jurisdiction the **equal protection** of the laws." See also **due process clause.**

incorporation doctrine

The legal concept under which the **Supreme Court** has nationalized the **Bill of Rights** by making most of its provisions applicable to the states through the **Fourteenth Amendment.**

In *Gitlow*, the Court announced that freedoms of speech and press "were fundamental personal rights and liberties protected by the due process clause of the Fourteenth Amendment from impairment by the states." In effect, the Court interpreted the Fourteenth Amendment to say that states could not abridge the freedoms of expression protected by the First Amendment. This decision began the development of the **incorporation doctrine,** the legal concept under which the Supreme Court has nationalized the Bill of Rights by making most of its provisions applicable to the states through the Fourteenth Amendment. However, not everyone agreed that the Fourteenth Amendment incorporated parts of the Bill of Rights into state laws. For example, Edwin Meese, who served as attorney general under Ronald Reagan, strongly criticized *Gitlow* and called for "disincorporation" of the Bill of Rights.

Initially, only parts of the First Amendment were held binding on the states as a result of *Gitlow.* Gradually, especially during the 1960s when Earl Warren was Chief Justice, the Supreme Court applied most of the Bill of Rights to the states (see Table 4.2). "One by one," wrote constitutional scholar Samuel Krislov, "the provisions of the Bill of Rights have been held to apply to the states, not in their own right, but as implicit in the Fourteenth Amendment."[2] Many of the court decisions that empowered the Bill of Rights were controversial, but today the Bill of Rights guarantees individual freedoms against infringement by state and local governments as well as by the national government. Only the Second, Third, and Seventh Amendments, the grand jury requirement of the Fifth Amendment, and the prohibition against excessive fines and bail in the Eighth Amendment have not been applied specifically to the states.

Freedom of Religion

The First Amendment contains two elements regarding religion and government. These elements are commonly referred to as the establishment clause and the free exercise clause. The **establishment clause** states that "Congress shall make no law respecting an establishment of religion." The **free exercise clause** prohibits the abridgment of citizens' freedom to worship, or not to worship, as they please. Sometimes these freedoms conflict. The government's practice of providing chaplains on military bases is one example of this conflict; some accuse the government of establishing religion in order to ensure that members of the armed forces can freely practice their religion. Usually, however, establishment clause and free exercise clause cases raise different kinds of conflicts.

establishment clause

Part of the **First Amendment** stating that "Congress shall make no law respecting an establishment of religion."

free exercise clause

A **First Amendment** provision that prohibits government from interfering with the practice of religion.

The Establishment Clause

Some nations, such as Great Britain, have an established church that is officially supported by the government and recognized as a national institution. A few American colonies had official churches, but the religious persecutions that incited many colonists to move to America discouraged any desire for the First Congress to establish a national church in the United States. Thus, an established national religion is prohibited by the First Amendment.

Table 4.2 The Nationalization of the Bill of Rights

DATE	AMENDMENT	RIGHT	CASE
1925	First	Freedom of speech	*Gitlow v. New York*
1931	First	Freedom of the press	*Near v. Minnesota*
1937	First	Freedom of assembly	*De Jonge v. Oregon*
1940	First	Free exercise of religion	*Cantwell v. Connecticut*
1947	First	Establishment of religion	*Everson v. Board of Education*
1958	First	Freedom of association	*NAACP v. Alabama*
1963	First	Right to petition government	*NAACP v. Button*
	Second	Right to bear arms	Not incorporated[a]
	Third	No quartering of soldiers	Not incorporated[b]
1949	Fourth	No unreasonable searches and seizures	*Wolf v. Colorado*
1961	Fourth	Exclusionary rule	*Mapp v. Ohio*
1897	Fifth	Guarantee of just compensation	*Chicago, Burlington, and Quincy RR v. Chicago*
1964	Fifth	Immunity from self-incrimination	*Mallory v. Hogan*
1969	Fifth	Immunity from double jeopardy	*Benton v. Maryland*
	Fifth	Right to grand jury indictment	Not incorporated
1932	Sixth	Right to counsel in capital cases	*Powell v. Alabama*
1948	Sixth	Right to public trial	*In re Oliver*
1963	Sixth	Right to counsel in felony cases	*Gideon v. Wainwright*
1965	Sixth	Right to confrontation of witnesses	*Pointer v. Texas*
1966	Sixth	Right to impartial jury	*Parker v. Gladden*
1967	Sixth	Right to speedy trial	*Klopfer v. North Carolina*
1967	Sixth	Right to compulsory process for obtaining witnesses	*Washington v. Texas*
1968	Sixth	Right to jury trial for serious crimes	*Duncan v. Louisiana*
1972	Sixth	Right to counsel for all crimes involving jail terms	*Argersinger v. Hamlin*
	Seventh	Right to jury trial in civil cases	Not incorporated
1962	Eighth	Freedom from cruel and unusual punishment	*Robinson v. California*
	Eighth	Freedom from excessive fines or bail	Not incorporated
1965	Ninth	Right of privacy	*Griswold v. Connecticut*

[a]The Supreme Court has upheld limits on the rights of private citizens to bear arms.
[b]The quartering of soldiers has not occurred under the Constitution.

It is much less clear, however, what else the first Congress intended to be included in the establishment clause. Some people argued that it meant only that the government could not favor one religion over another. In contrast, Thomas Jefferson argued that the First Amendment created a "wall of separation" between church and state, forbidding not just favoritism but also any support for religion at all. These interpretations continue to provoke argument, especially when religion is mixed with education.

Debate is especially intense over aid to church-related schools and prayers in the public schools. Proponents of *parochiaid* (short for "aid to parochial schools") argue that the aid does not favor any particular religion. Opponents claim that the Roman Catholic Church has by far the largest religious school system in the country and gets most of the aid. It was Protestant Lyndon Baines Johnson who obtained the passage of the first substantial aid to parochial elementary and secondary schools in 1965. He argued that aid went to students, not schools, and thus should go wherever the students were, including parochial schools.

In ***Lemon v. Kurtzman*** (1971), the Supreme Court declared that aid to church-related schools must

1. Have a secular legislative purpose.
2. Have a primary effect that neither advances nor inhibits religion.
3. Not foster an excessive government "entanglement" with religion.

Lemon v. Kurtzman

The 1971 Supreme Court decision that established that aid to church-related schools must (1) have a secular legislative purpose; (2) have a primary effect that neither advances nor inhibits religion; and (3) not foster excessive government entanglement with religion.

Why does it matter?

The Constitution prohibits the establishment of religion. What if it did not? Would public education, health care, and other important aspects of public policy be different if some religions had official sanction and received direct governmental support? How would you feel if you were not a member of the sanctioned religions?

Since that time the Court has had to draw a fine line between aid that is permissible and aid that is not. For instance, the Court has allowed religiously affiliated colleges and universities to use public funds to build buildings. Tax funds may also be used to provide students in parochial schools with textbooks, computers and other instructional equipment, lunches, transportation to and from school, and to administer standardized testing services. Public funds cannot, however, be used to pay teacher salaries or to provide transportation for students on field trips. The theory underlying these decisions is that it is possible to determine that buildings, textbooks, lunches, school buses, and national tests are not used to support sectarian education. However, determining how teachers handle a subject in class or focus a field trip may require complex and constitutionally impermissible regulation of religion.

In an important loosening of its constraints on aid to parochial schools, however, the Supreme Court decided in 1997 in *Agostini v. Felton* that public school systems could send teachers into parochial schools to teach remedial and supplemental classes to needy children. Decisions such as this one provide momentum for the drive to legalize the use of government vouchers to pay students' tuition at religious schools.

Controversy over aid to schools is not limited to Roman Catholic schools or any other single religion. In 1994, the Supreme Court ruled in *Kiryas Joel v. Grumet* that New York state had gone too far in favoring religion when it created a public school district for the benefit of a village of Hasidic Jews.

At the same time, the Supreme Court has been opening public schools to religious activities. The Court decided that public universities that permit student groups to use their facilities must allow student religious groups on campus to use the facilities for religious worship.[3] In the 1984 Equal Access Act, Congress made it unlawful for any public high school receiving federal funds (almost all of them do) to keep student groups from using school facilities for religious worship if the school opens its facilities for other student meetings.[4] Similarly, in 1993 the Court required public schools that rent facilities to organizations to do the same for religious groups.[5] In 1995, the Court held that the University of Virginia was constitutionally required to subsidize a student religious magazine on the same basis as other student publications.[6]

The threshold of constitutional acceptability becomes higher when public funds are used in a more direct way to support education. Thus, school authorities may not permit religious instructors to come into the public school buildings during the school day to provide religious education,[7] although they may release students from part of the compulsory school day to receive religious instruction elsewhere.[8] In 1980, the Court also prohibited the posting of the Ten Commandments on the walls of public classrooms.[9]

School prayer is perhaps the most controversial religious issue. In 1962 and 1963, the Court aroused the wrath of many Americans by ruling that voluntary recitations of prayers or Bible passages, when done as part of classroom exercises in public schools, violated the establishment clause. In ***Engel v. Vitale*** and ***School District of Abington Township, Pennsylvania v. Schempp*** the justices observed that "the place of religion in our society is an exalted one, but in the relationship between man and religion, the State is firmly committed to a position of neutrality."

Engel v. Vitale

The 1962 Supreme Court decision holding that state officials violated the **First Amendment** when they wrote a prayer to be recited by New York's schoolchildren.

School District of Abington Township, Pennsylvania v. Schempp

A 1963 Supreme Court decision holding that a Pennsylvania law requiring Bible reading in schools violated the **establishment clause** of the **First Amendment.**

It is *not* unconstitutional, of course, to pray in public schools. Students may pray silently as much as they wish. What the Constitution forbids is the sponsorship or encouragement of prayer, directly or indirectly, by public school authorities. Thus, in 1992 the Court ruled that a school-sponsored prayer at a public-school graduation violated the constitutional separation of church and state.[10] In 2000, the Court held that student-led prayer at football games was also unconstitutional.[11] Three Alabama laws—passed in 1978, 1981, and 1982—authorized schools to hold one-minute periods of silence for "meditation or voluntary prayer," but the Court rejected this approach in 1985 because the state made it clear that the purpose of the statute was to return prayer to the schools. The Court did indicate, however, that a less clumsy approach would pass its scrutiny.[12]

One of the most controversial issues regarding the First Amendment's prohibition of the establishment of religion is prayers in public schools. Although students may pray on their own, school authorities may not sponsor or encourage prayers.

Political scientist Kenneth D. Wald observes that the last few years have been marked by great ferment in the relationship between religion and American political life. Religious issues and controversies have assumed much greater importance in political debate than they commanded before.[13] Much of this new importance is due to fundamentalist religious groups that have spurred their members to political action. Many school districts have simply ignored the Supreme Court's ban on school prayer and continue to allow prayers in their classrooms. Some religious groups and many members of Congress, especially conservative Republicans, have pushed for a constitutional amendment permitting prayer in school. A majority of the public consistently supports school prayer.

Fundamentalist Christian groups have pressed some state legislatures to mandate the teaching of "creation science"—their alternative to Darwinian theories of evolution—in public schools. Louisiana, for example, passed a Balanced Treatment Act requiring schools that taught Darwinian theory to teach creation science, too. Regardless, the Supreme Court ruled in 1987 that this law violated the establishment clause.[14] The Court had already held in a 1968 case that states cannot prohibit Darwin's theory of evolution from being taught in the public schools.[15]

The Supreme Court's struggle to interpret the establishment clause is also evident in areas other than education. For example, displays of religious symbols during the holidays have prompted considerable controversy. In 1984, the Court found that Pawtucket, R.I., could set up a Christmas nativity scene on public property—along with Santa's house and sleigh, Christmas trees, and other symbols of the Christmas season.[16] Five years later, the Court extended the principle to a Hanukkah menorah, placed next to a Christmas tree. The Court concluded that these displays had a secular purpose and provided little or no benefit to religion. At the same time, the Court invalidated display of the nativity scene without secular symbols in a courthouse because, in this context, the county gave the impression of endorsing the display's religious message.[17]

In this case, the Court said the Constitution does not require complete separation of church and state; it mandates accommodation of all religions and forbids hostility toward any. At the same time, the Constitution forbids government endorsement of religious beliefs. Drawing the line between neutrality toward religion and promotion of it is not easy; this dilemma ensures that cases involving the establishment of religion will continue to come before the Court.

The Free Exercise Clause

The First Amendment also guarantees the free exercise of religion. This guarantee seems simple enough. Whether people hold no religious beliefs, practice voodoo, or go to church, temple, or mosque, they should have the right to practice religion as they choose. The matter is, of course, more complicated. Religions sometimes forbid actions that society thinks are necessary; or, conversely, religions may require actions that society finds unacceptable. For example, what if a religion justifies multiple marriages or the use of illegal drugs? Muhammad Ali, the boxing champion, refused induction into the armed services during the Vietnam War because, he said, military service would violate his Muslim faith. Amish parents often refuse to send their children to public schools. Jehovah's Witnesses and Christian Scientists may refuse to accept blood transfusions and certain other kinds of medical treatment for themselves or their children.

Consistently maintaining that people have an inviolable right to *believe* what they want, the courts have been more cautious about the right to *practice* a belief. What if, the Supreme Court once asked, a person "believed that human sacrifices were a necessary part of religious worship?" In *Employment Division v. Smith* (1990), the Court discarded its previous requirement for a "*compelling interest*" before a government could even indirectly limit or prohibit religious practices. In *Smith,* the Court decided that state laws interfering with religious practices but not specifically aimed at religion are constitutional. As long as a law does not single out and ban religious practices because they are engaged in for religious reasons, or only because of the religious belief they display, a general law may be applied to conduct even if the conduct is religiously inspired (denying people unemployment compensation is an exception). In *Smith,* the state of Oregon was allowed to prosecute persons who used the drug peyote as part of their religious rituals.

Even before this decision, the Supreme Court had never permitted religious freedom to be an excuse for any and all behaviors. The Court had upheld laws and regu-

The free exercise of religious beliefs sometimes clashes with society's other values or laws, as when the Amish—who prefer to lead simple, traditional lives—refused to send their children to public schools. The Supreme Court eventually held in favor of the Amish, arguing that Amish children, living in such a close-knit community, were unlikely to become dependent on the state.

You Are the Judge

The Case of Animal Sacrifices

The church of Lukumi Babalu Aye, in Hialeah, Fla., practiced Santeria, a Caribbean-based mix of African ritual, voodoo, and Catholicism. Central to Santeria is the ritual sacrifice of animals—at birth, marriage, and death rites, as well as ceremonies to cure the sick and initiate new members.

Offended by these rituals, the city of Hialeah passed ordinances prohibiting animal sacrifices in religious ceremonies. The church challenged the constitutionality of these laws, claiming they violated the free exercise clause of the First Amendment because the ordinances essentially barred the practice of Santeria. The city, the Santerians claimed, was discriminating against a religious minority. Besides, many other forms of killing animals were legal, including fishing, using animals in medical research, selling lobsters to be boiled alive, and feeding live rats to snakes.

You Be the Judge: Do the Santerians have a constitutional right to sacrifice animals in their religious rituals? Does the city's interest in protecting animals outweigh the Santerians' requirement for animal sacrifice?

Answer: In 1993, the Court overturned the Hialeah ordinances that prohibited the use of animal sacrifice in religious ritual. In *Church of the Lukumi Babalu Aye, Inc. v. City of Hialeah*, the justices concluded that governments that permit other forms of killing of animals may not then ban sacrifices or ritual killings. In this instance, the Court found no compelling state interest that justified the abridgment of the freedom of religion.

lations forbidding polygamy, outlawing business activities on Sunday as applied to Orthodox Jews, denying tax exemptions to religious schools that discriminate on the basis of race,[18] approving building a road through ground sacred to some Native Americans, and even prohibiting a Jewish air force captain from wearing his yarmulke (Congress later intervened to permit military personnel to wear yarmulkes).

Other religiously motivated practices have been granted protection under the free exercise clause. The Court allowed Amish parents to take their children out of school after the eighth grade. Reasoning that the Amish community was well established and that its children would not burden the state, the Court held that religious freedom took precedence over compulsory education laws.[19] More broadly, although a state can compel parents to send their children to an accredited school, parents have a right to choose religious schools rather than public schools for their children's education. A state may not require Jehovah's Witnesses or members of other religions to participate in public-school flag-saluting ceremonies. Congress has also ruled, and the courts have upheld, that people can become conscientious objectors to war on religious grounds. You can examine another free exercise case in "You Are the Judge: The Case of Animal Sacrifices."

In the Religious Freedom Restoration Act of 1993, Congress attempted to overturn the principle the Court articulated in *Smith*. It conferred on all persons the right to perform their religious rituals unless the government can show that the law or regulation in question is narrowly tailored and in pursuit of a "compelling interest." In 1997, however, the Supreme Court declared this act an unconstitutional intrusion by Congress into the states' prerogatives for regulating the health and welfare of citizens.[20]

Freedom of Expression

A democracy depends on the free expression of ideas. Thoughts that are muffled, speech that is forbidden, and meetings that cannot be held are the enemies of the democratic process. Totalitarian governments know this, which is why they go to enormous trouble to limit expression.

Americans pride themselves on their free and open society. Freedom of conscience is absolute; Americans can *believe* whatever they want. The First Amendment plainly forbids the national government from limiting freedom of *expression*—that is, the right to say or publish what one believes. Is freedom of expression, then, like freedom of conscience, also *absolute?* Supreme Court Justice Hugo Black thought so; he was fond of pointing out that the First Amendment said Congress shall make *no* law. "I read no law abridging to mean no law abridging." In contrast, Justice Oliver Wendell Holmes offered a classic example of impermissible speech in 1919: "The most stringent protection of free speech would not protect a man in falsely shouting 'fire' in a theater and causing a panic."

The courts have been called upon to decide where to draw the line separating permissible from impermissible speech. In doing so, judges have had to balance freedom of expression against competing values like public order, national security, and the right to a fair trial. Currently, one of the most controversial freedom of expression issues surrounds so-called hate speech. Advocates of regulating hate speech, such as Stanford Law Professor Charles R. Lawrence, forcefully argue that racial insults, like fighting words, are "undeserving of First Amendment protection because the perpetrator's intent is not to discover the truth or invite dialogue, but to injure the victim."[21] In contrast, critics of hate speech policy, such as Ira Glasser of the ACLU, argue that "sacrificing free speech rights is too high a price to pay to advance the cause of equality."[22] In 1992, the Supreme Court ruled that legislatures and universities may not single out racial, religious, or sexual insults or threats for prosecution as "hate speech" or "bias crimes."[23]

The courts have also had to decide what kinds of activities do and do not constitute *speech* (or press) within the meaning of the First Amendment. Holding a political rally to attack an opposing candidate's stand on important issues gets First Amendment protection. Obscenity and libel, which are also expressions, do not. To make things more complicated, certain forms of nonverbal speech, such as picketing, are considered symbolic speech and receive First Amendment protection. Other forms of expression, such as fraud and incitement to violence, are considered action rather than speech. Government can limit action more easily than it can limit expression.

The one thing all freedom of expression cases have in common is the question of whether a certain expression receives the protection of the Constitution.

Prior Restraint

One principle stands out clearly in the complicated history of freedom of expression laws: Time and time again, the Supreme Court has struck down prior restraint on speech and the press. **Prior restraint** refers to a government's actions that prevent material from being published; in a word, prior restraint is censorship. In the United States, the First Amendment ensures that even if the government frowns on some material, a person's right to publish it is all but inviolable. A landmark case involving prior restraint is ***Near v. Minnesota*** (1931). A blunt newspaper editor called local officials a string of names including "grafters" and "Jewish gangsters." The state closed down his business, but the Supreme Court ordered the paper reopened.[24] Of course, the newspaper editor—or anyone else—could later be punished for violating a law or someone's rights *after* publication.

prior restraint

A government preventing material from being published. This is a common method of limiting the press in some nations, but it is usually unconstitutional in the United States, according to the **First Amendment** and as confirmed in the 1931 Supreme Court case of ***Near v. Minnesota.***

Near v. Minnesota

The 1931 Supreme Court decision holding that the **First Amendment** protects newspapers from **prior restraint.**

The extent of an individual's or group's freedom from prior restraint does depend in part, however, on who that individual or group is. In 1988, the Supreme Court ruled that a high school newspaper was not a public forum and could be regulated in "any reasonable manner" by school officials.[25]

Restrictions on the right to publish have also been upheld in the name of national security. Wartime often brings censorship to protect classified information. These restrictions often have public support; few would find it unconstitutional if a newspaper, for example, were hauled into court for publishing troop movement plans during a war.

You Are the Judge

The Case of the Purloined Pentagon Papers

During the Johnson administration, the Department of Defense had amassed an elaborate secret history of American involvement in the Vietnam War. Hundreds of documents, many of them secret cables, memos, and war plans, were included. Many documented American ineptitude and South Vietnamese duplicity. One former Pentagon official, Daniel Ellsberg, who had become disillusioned with the Vietnam War, managed to retain access to a copy of these Pentagon papers. Hoping that revelations of the Vietnam quagmire would help end American involvement, he decided to leak the Pentagon papers to the *New York Times.*

The Nixon administration pulled out all the stops in its effort to embarrass Ellsberg and prevent publication of the Pentagon papers. Nixon's chief domestic affairs advisor, John Ehrlichman, approved a burglary of Ellsberg's psychiatrist's office, hoping to find damaging information on Ellsberg. (The burglary was bungled, and it eventually led to Ehrlichman's conviction and imprisonment.) In the courts, Nixon administration lawyers sought an injunction against the *Times* that would have ordered it to cease publication of the secret documents. Government lawyers argued that national security was being breached and that the documents had been stolen from the government by Ellsberg. The *Times* argued that its freedom to publish would be violated if an injunction were granted. In 1971 the case of *New York Times v. United States* was decided by the Supreme Court.

You Be the Judge: Did the *Times* have a right to publish secret, stolen Department of Defense documents?

Answer: In a 6-to-3 decision, a majority of the justices agreed that the "no prior restraint" rule prohibited prosecution before the papers were published. The justices also made it clear that if the government brought prosecution for theft, the Court might be sympathetic. No such charges were filed.

Critics of the press during the Persian Gulf War complained that press reporting might have helped to pinpoint locations of SCUD missile attacks, knowledge of which could be used to aim future missiles more precisely. Defenders of the freedom of the press complained that never before had the press been as "managed" as in that conflict: Reporters could get to the field only in the company of official Pentagon press representatives—and some who tried other ways of getting in the field were captured by the Iraqis.

Prior restraint of a different sort was demanded and secured by the national government for books written by former CIA agents Victor Marchetti and Frank Snepp. The government sued Snepp for failing to have his book about Vietnam, *A Decent Interval,* submitted to the agency for censorship, even though the book revealed no classified information.[26] Both men had signed agreements allowing the CIA to clear their future writings about the agency.

Nevertheless, the courts are reluctant to issue injunctions prohibiting the publication of material even in the area of national security. The most famous case involving prior restraint and national security involved the publication of stolen Pentagon papers. We examine this case in "You Are the Judge: The Case of the Purloined Pentagon Papers."

Free Speech and Public Order

Not surprisingly, government has sometimes been a zealous opponent of speech that opposes government policies. In wartime and peacetime, the biggest conflict between press and government has been about the connection between a free press and the need for public order. During World War I, Charles T. Schenck, the secretary of the American Socialist Party, distributed thousands of leaflets urging young men to resist the draft. Schenck was charged with impeding the war effort. The Supreme Court upheld his conviction in 1919 (***Schenck v. United States***). Justice Holmes declared that government could limit speech if it provokes a clear and present danger of

Schenck v. United States

A 1919 decision upholding the conviction of a socialist who had urged young men to resist the draft during World War I. Justice Holmes declared that government can limit speech if the speech provokes a "clear and present danger" of substantive evils.

"The way I see it, the Constitution cuts both ways. The First Amendment gives you the right to say what you want, but the Second Amendment gives me the right to shoot you for it."

The prevailing political climate often determines what limits the government will place on free speech. During the early 1950s, Senator Joseph McCarthy's persuasive—if unproven—accusations that many public officials were Communists created an atmosphere in which the courts placed restrictions on freedom of expression—restrictions that would be unacceptable today.

substantive evils. Only when such danger exists can government restrain speech. It is difficult to say, of course, when speech becomes dangerous rather than simply inconvenient for the government.

The courts confronted the issue of free speech and public order during the 1950s. In the late 1940s and early 1950s there was widespread fear that communists had infiltrated the government. American anticommunism was a powerful force, and the national government was determined to jail the leaders of the Communist Party. Senator Joseph McCarthy and others in Congress were persecuting people they thought subversive, based on the Smith Act of 1940, which forbade advocating the violent overthrow of the American government. In *Dennis v. United States* (1951), the Supreme Court upheld prison sentences for several Communist Party leaders for conspiring to advocate the violent overthrow of the government—even in the absence of evidence that they actually urged people to commit specific acts of violence. Although the activities of this tiny, unpopular group resembled yelling "Fire!" in an empty theater rather than a crowded one, the Court ruled that a Communist takeover was so grave a danger that government could squelch their threat. Free-speech advocates were unable to stem the relentless persecution of the 1950s; the Supreme Court, as in the *Dennis* case, valued national security over First Amendment rights at the time.

Soon the political climate changed, however, and the Court narrowed the interpretation of the Smith Act, making it more difficult to prosecute dissenters (see "America in Perspective: Civil Liberties in Britain"). In later years, the Court has found that it is permissible to advocate the violent overthrow of the government in the abstract, but not actually to incite anyone to imminent lawless action (*Yates v. United States*, 1957; *Brandenburg v. Ohio*, 1969).

comparative
Comparing Civil Liberties

The 1960s brought waves of protest that strained and expanded the constitutional meaning of free speech. Among the unrest over political, economic, racial, and social issues, the Vietnam War was the source of the most bitter controversy. Many people saw military service as a duty and war as an issue that government should decide. Others felt that citizens should not be asked to die or pay for conflicts that they felt were unjust. Organized protests on college and university campuses became common. People burned draft cards, seized university buildings, marched, and demonstrated against the Southeast Asian conflict.

Americans today live in relatively less turbulent times, yet many people still engage in public demonstrations. Courts have been quite supportive of the right to protest, pass out leaflets, or gather signatures on petitions—as long as it is done in public places. Campaign literature may even be distributed anonymously.[27]

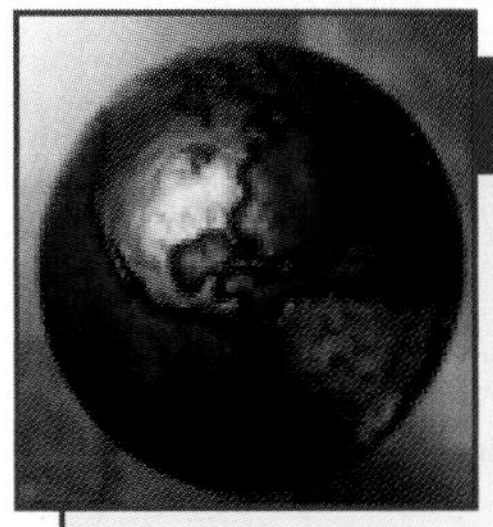

America in Perspective

Civil Liberties in Britain

As discussed in Chapter 2, Great Britain has an unwritten constitution, a set of understood principles that limits governmental power—most of the time. For example, it would be "unconstitutional" to punish someone for an act that is not forbidden by law or for the prime minister to restrict the sovereign's access to government documents. There is no equivalent, however, to the First Amendment to the U.S. Constitution that provides grounds for a lawsuit if someone disapproves of a restriction on freedom of expression. No court in Britain would overturn an act of Parliament for violating someone's freedom of speech.

Freedom of expression is generous in Great Britain, but there are some restrictions there that differ from those in the United States. British libel laws, for instance, are stricter than ours.

In November 1988, the government of Prime Minister Margaret Thatcher imposed a restriction that was too much for many British subjects. It forbade the broadcasting of any radio or television interviews with members of the Irish Republican Army or its legal political organization in Northern Ireland. A group of 200 British journalists, judges, and academics issued a plea for an act of Parliament that would guarantee freedom of expression. No such guarantee has been enacted, however. Of course, the Parliament to which they appealed was led by the same government that had imposed the restrictions.

What would happen if the administration tried something similar in the United States? The Pentagon papers case in 1971 has some similarities to Prime Minister Thatcher's gag rule. However, the U.S. Supreme Court refused to stop the publication of these classified documents, even though the president said it would harm national security.

The United States has not always been ahead of Britain in permitting free speech and press. Remember the imprisonment of American Communists such as Dennis and his associates in the 1950s. When they used the First Amendment to challenge the Smith Act, the Court ruled in favor of the government. Even where written constitutions exist, judges may rely on their own views of political necessity—which are often shared with the legislative and executive branches that developed the civil liberties policies—to determine the scope of individual rights.

Constitutional protections diminish once a person steps on private property, for example, most shopping centers. The Supreme Court has held that federal free-speech guarantees did not apply when a person was on private property.[28] However, it upheld a state's power to include politicking in shopping centers within its own free-speech guarantee,[29] and in 1994, the Supreme Court ruled that cities cannot bar residents from posting signs on their own property.[30]

Free Press and Fair Trials

The Bill of Rights is an inexhaustible source of potential conflicts among different types of freedoms. One is the conflict between the right of the press to print what it wants and the right to a fair trial. The quantity of press coverage given the trial (and pretrial hearings) of football star O. J. Simpson, accused of murdering his wife and her friend, surpassed that given the Super Bowl, and little of it was sympathetic to Simpson. Does such extensive media coverage compromise the fairness of the trial? Defense attorneys argue that such publicity can inflame the community—and potential jurors—against defendants. It may very well. The trouble is that the Constitution's guarantee of freedom of the press entitles journalists to cover every trial.

In addition to arguing that the public has a "right to know," some journalists hope to capitalize on their coverage of lurid crime stories to sell newspapers, gain ratings, or attract advertisers. Those motivations have prompted newspapers to challenge courts' restrictions on media coverage of trials. When a Nebraska judge issued a gag order forbidding the press to report any details of a particularly gory murder (or even to report the gag order itself), the outraged Nebraska Press Association took the case to the Supreme Court. The Court sided with the editors and revoked the gag order.[31] In 1978, the Court reversed a Virginia judge's order to close a murder trial to the public and the press. "The trial of a criminal case," said the Court, "must be open to the public."[32] A pretrial hearing, though, is a different matter. A 1979 case permitted a closed hearing on the grounds that pretrial publicity might compromise the defendant's right to fairness.

Although reporters always want access to trials, they do not always want the courts to have access to their files. Occasionally a reporter withholds some critical evidence that either the prosecution or the defense wants in a criminal case. Reporters argue that "pro-

Fundamental rights are sometimes in conflict. Press coverage of the murder trial of O. J. Simpson, pictured here with one of his lawyers, made it very difficult to impanel a jury whose members had not reached conclusions about his guilt before the trial began.

"Since you have already been convicted by the media, I imagine we can wrap this up pretty quickly."

Drawing by Richter; © 1991 The New Yorker Magazine Inc.

tecting their sources" should exempt them from revealing notes from confidential informants. More than one reporter has gone to jail for this principle, arguing that they had no obligation to produce evidence that might bear on the guilt or innocence of a defendant.

Some states have passed *shield laws* to protect reporters in these situations. In most states, though, reporters have no more rights than other citizens once a case has come to trial. The Supreme Court ruled in *Branzburg v. Hayes* (1972) that in the absence of shield laws, the right of a fair trial preempts the reporter's right to protect sources. This issue came to a head in one celebrated case involving the student newspaper at Stanford University. After a violent confrontation with student protestors, the police got a search warrant and marched off to the *Stanford Daily*, which they believed to have pictures of the scene from which they could make arrests. The paper argued that its files were protected by the First Amendment, but the decision in ***Zurcher v. Stanford Daily*** (1976) sided with the police, not the paper.

Zurcher v. Stanford Daily

A 1978 Supreme Court decision holding that a proper **search warrant** could be applied to a newspaper as well as to anyone else without necessarily violating the **First Amendment** rights to freedom of the press.

It is one thing to attempt to obtain the press's cooperation in trials and quite another to limit the press's coverage of judicial proceedings. The balance between a free press and a fair trial is not an even one. The Court has *never* upheld a restriction on the press in the interest of a fair trial. Ultimately, the only feasible measure the judicial system can take against the influence of publicity in high profile cases is to sequester the jury, thereby isolating it from the media and public opinion.

Obscenity

In *The Brethren*, a gossipy portrayal of the Supreme Court, Bob Woodward and Scott Armstrong recount the tale of Justice Thurgood Marshall's lunch with some law clerks. Glancing at his watch at about 1:50 P.M., the story goes, Marshall exclaimed, "My God, I almost forgot. It's movie day, we've got to get back."[33] Movie day at the Court was an annual event when movies brought before the Court on obscenity charges were shown in a basement storeroom.

Several justices boycotted these showings, arguing that obscenity should never be banned and so how "dirty" a movie is has no relevance. In 1957, however, the majority held that "obscenity is not within the area of constitutionally protected speech or press" (***Roth v. United States***). The doctrine set forth in this case still prevails. Deciding what is obscene, though, has never been an easy matter. In a line that would

Roth v. United States

A 1957 Supreme Court decision ruling that "obscenity is not within the area of constitutionally protected speech or press."

haunt him for the rest of his life, Justice Potter Stewart once remarked that although he could not define obscenity, "I know it when I see it." During the Supreme Court's movie day, law clerks echoed Stewart's line, punctuating particularly racy scenes with cries of "That's it! That's it! I know it when I see it."

Efforts to define obscenity have perplexed the courts for years. Obviously, public standards vary from time to time, place to place, and person to person. Much of today's MTV would have been banned a decade or two ago. What might be acceptable in Manhattan's Greenwich Village would shock residents of some other areas of the country. Works that some people call obscene might be good entertainment or even great art to others. At one time or another, the works of Aristophanes, those of Mark Twain, and even the "Tarzan" stories by Edgar Rice Burroughs were banned. The state of Georgia banned the acclaimed film *Carnal Knowledge*—a ban the Supreme Court struck down in 1974.[34]

Miller v. California

A 1973 Supreme Court decision that avoided defining obscenity by holding that community standards be used to determine whether material is obscene in terms of appealing to a "prurient interest" and being "patently offensive" and lacking in value.

The Court tried to clarify its doctrine by spelling out what could be classified as obscene and thus outside First Amendment protection in the 1973 case of ***Miller v. California.*** Then Chief Justice Warren Burger wrote that materials were obscene if:

1. The work, taken as a whole, appealed "to a prurient interest in sex."
2. The work showed "patently offensive" sexual conduct that was specifically defined by an obscenity law.
3. The work, taken as a whole, lacked "serious literary, artistic, political, or scientific value."

Decisions regarding whether material was obscene, said the Court, should be based on average people (in other words, juries) applying the contemporary standards of local—not national—communities.

The Court did provide "a few plain examples" of what sort of material might fall within this definition of obscenity. Among these examples were "patently offensive representations of ultimate sexual acts, . . . actual or simulated," "patently offensive representations of masturbation or excretory functions," or "lewd exhibition of the genitals." Cities throughout the country duplicated the language of *Miller* in their obscenity ordinances. The difficulty remains in determining what is *lewd* or *offensive*. Laws must satisfy these qualifying adjectives to prevent communities from banning anatomy texts, for example, as obscene.

Another reason why obscenity convictions can be difficult to obtain is that no nationwide consensus exists that offensive material should be banned—at least not when it is restricted to adults. In many communities the laws are lenient regarding pornography, and prosecutors know that they may not get a jury to convict, even when the disputed material is obscene as defined by *Miller*. Thus, obscene material is widely available in adult bookstores, video stores, and movie theaters.

Regulations aimed at keeping obscene material away from the young, who are considered more vulnerable to its harmful influences, are more popular, and courts have consistently ruled that states may protect children from obscenity. The rating scheme of the Motion Picture Association of America is one example, as is the recent TV ratings system. Equally popular are laws designed to protect the young against pornographic exploitation. It is a violation of federal law to receive sexually explicit photographs of children through the mail, and in 1991 the Supreme Court upheld Ohio's law forbidding the possession of child pornography.[35]

Advances in technology have created a new wrinkle in the obscenity issue. The Internet and the World Wide Web make it easier to distribute obscene material rapidly, and a number of online information services have taken advantage of this opportunity. Congress, especially concerned with protecting minors from exposure to pornography, has recently decided that the Internet is not the electronic equivalent of the printing press and thus does not deserve the free-speech protection of the First Amendment. Instead, it regards the Internet as a broadcast medium, subject to government regulation (discussed later in this chapter).

Although the Supreme Court ruled, in *Roth v. United States,* that obscenity is not protected by the First Amendment, determining just what is obscene has proven difficult. Rapper Eminem has been accused of promoting hate and violence in his song lyrics and performances. Some communities have debated whether they should—or could—ban performances by Eminem and other controversial musicians.

In 1996, Congress passed the Communications Decency Act, banning obscene material and criminalizing the transmission of indecent speech or images to anyone under 18 years of age. The new law made no exception for material that has serious literary, artistic, political, or scientific merit as outlined in *Miller v. California.* In 1997, the Supreme Court overturned this law as being overly broad and vague and a violation of free speech.[36] Apparently the Supreme Court views the Internet similarly to print media, with similar protections against government regulation. In 1999, however, the Court upheld prohibitions on obscene e-mail and faxes.

Despite the Court's best efforts to define obscenity and determine when it can be banned, state and local governments continue to struggle with the application of these rulings. In one famous case, a small New Jersey town tried to get rid of a nude dancing parlor by using its zoning power to ban all live entertainment. The Court held that the measure was too broad and thus unlawful.[37] But the Court has upheld laws banning nude dancing when their effect on overall expression was minimal.[38] Jacksonville, Fl., tried to ban drive-in movies containing nudity. We will examine the Court's reaction in "You Are the Judge: The Case of the Drive-in Theater."

visual literacy
What Speech Is Protected by the Constitution?

Other attempts to restrict obscenity have been proposed by some women's groups, which claim that pornography degrades and dehumanizes women. Legal scholar Catherine MacKinnon claims that "pornography is an . . . industry of rape and battery and sexual harassment."[39] Some cities, at the urging of an unusual alliance of conservative Christians and feminists, have passed antipornography ordinances on the grounds that pornography harms women. So far, however, courts have struck these ordinances down on First Amendment grounds. No such case has reached the Supreme Court—yet.

You Are the Judge

The Case of the Drive-in Theater

Almost everyone concedes that *sometimes* obscenity should be banned by public authorities. One instance might be when a person's right to show pornographic movies clashes with another's right to privacy. Presumably, no one wants hard-core pornography shown in public places where schoolchildren might see it. Showing dirty movies in an enclosed theater or in the privacy of your own living room is one thing. Showing them in public is something else. Or is it?

The city of Jacksonville, Fla., wanted to limit the showing of certain kinds of movies at drive-in theaters. Its city council reasoned that drive-ins were public places and that drivers passing by would be involuntarily exposed to movies they might prefer not to see. Some members of the council argued that drivers distracted by steamy scenes might even cause accidents. So the council passed a local ordinance forbidding movies showing nudity (defined in the ordinance as "bare buttocks . . . female bare breasts, or human bare pubic areas") at drive-in theaters. Arrested for violating the ordinance, a Mr. Erznoznik challenged the constitutionality of the ordinance. He claimed that the law was overly broad and banned nudity, not obscenity. The lawyers for the city insisted that the law could be squared with the First Amendment. The government, they claimed, had a responsibility to forbid a "public nuisance," especially one that might cause a traffic hazard.

You Be the Judge: Did Jacksonville's ban on nudity in movies at drive-ins go too far or was it a constitutional limit on free speech?

Answer: In *Erznoznik v. Jacksonville* (1975) the Supreme Court held that Jacksonville's ordinance was unconstitutionally broad. The city council had gone too far; it could end up banning movies that might not be obscene. The ordinance would, said the Court, ban a film "containing a picture of a baby's buttocks, the nude body of a war victim or scenes from a culture where nudity is indigenous." Said Justice Powell for the Court: "Clearly, all nudity cannot be deemed obscene."

Libel and Slander

libel

The publication of false or malicious statements that damage someone's reputation.

Another type of expression not protected by the First Amendment is **libel**: the publication of false statements that are malicious and damage a person's reputation. *Slander* refers to spoken defamation, whereas libel refers to written defamation. Of course, if politicians could collect damages for every untrue thing said about them, the right to criticize the government—which the Supreme Court termed "the central meaning of the First Amendment"—would be stifled. No one would dare be critical for fear of making a factual error.

New York Times v. Sullivan

Decided in 1964, this case established the guidelines for determining whether public officials and public figures could win damage suits for libel. To do so, individuals must prove that the defamatory statements were made with "actual malice" and reckless disregard for the truth.

To encourage public debate, the Supreme Court has held in cases such as ***New York Times v. Sullivan*** (1964) that statements about public figures are libelous only if made with malice and reckless disregard for the truth. Public figures have to prove to a jury, in effect, that whoever wrote or said untrue statements about them knew that the statements were untrue and intended to harm them. This standard makes libel cases difficult for public figures to win because it is difficult to prove that a publication was intentionally malicious.[40]

Private individuals have a lower standard to meet for winning libel lawsuits. They need show only that statements made about them were defamatory falsehoods and that the author was negligent. Nevertheless, it is unusual for someone to win a libel case; most people do not wish to draw attention to critical statements about themselves.

Libel cases must balance freedom of expression with respect for individual reputations. If public debate is not free, there can be no democracy. On the other hand, some reputations will be damaged, or at least bruised, in the process. In one widely publicized case, General William Westmoreland, once the commander of American troops in South Vietnam, sued CBS. On January 23, 1982, the network broadcast a documentary called "The Uncounted Enemy." It claimed that American military leaders in Vietnam, including Westmoreland, systematically lied to Washington about their success there to

General William Westmoreland's aborted lawsuit against CBS demonstrates the difficulty public figures have winning libel convictions. Even though Westmoreland (shown here at a Vietnam briefing) could show that CBS had knowingly made factual errors, he realized that it would be impossible to prove that the networks had been intentionally malicious He dropped the suit in return for a statement from CBS calling him "patriotic."

make it appear that the United States was winning the war. All the evidence, including CBS's own internal memoranda, showed that the documentary made errors of fact. Westmoreland sued CBS for libel. Ultimately, the power of the press—in this case, a sloppy, arrogant press—prevailed. Fearing defeat at the trial, Westmoreland settled for a mild apology.[41]

An unusual case that explored the line between parody and libel came before the Supreme Court in 1988, when Reverend Jerry Falwell sued *Hustler* magazine. *Hustler* editor Larry Flynt had printed a parody of a Campari Liquor ad about various celebrities called "First Time" (in which celebrities related the first time they drank Campari, but with an intentional double meaning). When *Hustler* depicted the Reverend Jerry Falwell having had his "first time" in an outhouse with his mother, Falwell sued. He alleged that the ad subjected him to great emotional distress and mental anguish. The case tested the limits to which a publication could go to parody or lampoon a public figure. The Supreme Court ruled that they can go pretty far—all nine justices ruled in favor of the magazine.

Why does it matter?

It is difficult for public figures to win libel cases. Public figures will likely lose even if they can show that the defendant made defamatory falsehoods about them. Is this fair? Should freedom of speech guarantee your right to publicly say anything you want about someone, whether true or false? If a person made false and damaging remarks about you in a newspaper, in what way would you expect the legal system to protect your reputation?

Symbolic Speech

Freedom of speech, more broadly interpreted, is a guarantee of freedom of expression. In 1965, Mary Beth Tinker and her brother John were suspended from school in Des Moines, Iowa, when they wore black armbands to protest the Vietnam War. The Supreme Court held that the suspension violated the Tinkers' First Amendment rights. The right to freedom of speech, said the Court, went beyond the spoken word.[42]

Texas v. Johnson

A 1989 case in which the Supreme Court struck down a law banning the burning of the American flag on the grounds that such action was **symbolic speech** protected by the **First Amendment.**

symbolic speech

Nonverbal communication, such as burning a flag or wearing an armband. The Supreme Court has accorded some symbolic speech protection under the **First Amendment.**

When Gregory Johnson set a flag on fire at the 1984 Republican National Convention in Dallas to protest nuclear arms buildup, the Supreme Court decided that the state law prohibiting flag desecration violated the First Amendment (***Texas v. Johnson,*** 1989). Burning the flag, the Court said, constituted speech and not just dramatic action.[43] When Massachusetts courts ordered the organizers of the annual St. Patrick's Day parade to include the Irish-American Gay, Lesbian, and Bisexual Group of Boston, the Supreme Court declared that a parade is a form of protected speech and thus that the organizers are free to include whomever they want.

Wearing an armband, burning a flag, and marching in a parade are examples of **symbolic speech:** actions that do not consist of speaking or writing but that express an opinion. Court decisions have classified these activities somewhere between pure speech and pure action. The doctrine of symbolic speech is not precise; for example, although burning a flag is protected speech, burning a draft card is not.[44] The relevant cases make it clear, however, that First Amendment rights are not limited by a rigid definition of what constitutes speech.

Commercial Speech

commercial speech

Communication in the form of advertising. It can be restricted more than many other types of speech but has been receiving increased protection from the Supreme Court.

Not all forms of communication receive the full protection of the First Amendment. **Commercial speech,** such as advertising, is restricted far more extensively than expressions of opinion on religious, political, or other matters. The Federal Trade Commission (FTC) decides what kinds of goods may be advertised on radio and television and regulates the content of such advertising. These regulations have responded to changes in social mores and priorities. Thirty years ago, for example, tampons could not be advertised on TV, whereas cigarette commercials were everywhere. Today the situation is just the reverse.

The FTC attempts to ensure that advertisers do not make false claims for their products, but "truth" in advertising does not prevent misleading promises. For example, when ads imply that the right mouthwash or deodorant will improve one's love life, that dubious message is perfectly legal.

Nevertheless, commercial speech on the airwaves is regulated in ways that would clearly be impossible in the political or religious realm—even to the point of forcing a manufacturer to say certain words. For example, the makers of Excedrin pain reliever were forced to add the words "on pain other than headache" in their commercials describing tests that supposedly supported the product's claims of superior effectiveness. (The test results were based on the pain experienced after giving birth.)

Although commercial speech is regulated more rigidly than other types of speech, the courts have been broadening its protection under the Constitution. For years, many states had laws that prohibited advertising for professional services—such as legal and engineering services—and for certain products ranging from eyeglasses and prescription drugs to condoms and abortions. Advocates of these laws claimed that they were designed to protect consumers against misleading claims, while critics charged that the laws prevented price competition. In recent years, the courts have struck down many such restrictions as violations of freedom of speech. In 1989 the Supreme Court overturned restrictions on advertising casino gambling in states where such gambling is legal.[45]

Regulation of the Public Airwaves

The Federal Communications Commission (FCC) regulates the content, nature, and very existence of radio and television broadcasting. Although newspapers do not need licenses, radio and television stations do. A licensed station must comply with regulations, including the requirement that they devote a certain percentage of broadcast time to public service, news, children's programming, political candidates, or views other than those its owners support. The rules are more relaxed for cable channels, which can specialize in a particular type of broadcasting because consumers pay for, and thus have more choice about, the service.

This sort of governmental interference would clearly violate the First Amendment if it were imposed on the print media. For example, the state of Florida passed a law requiring newspapers in the state to provide space for political candidates to reply to newspaper criticisms. The Supreme Court, without hesitation, voided this law (***Miami Herald Publishing Company v. Tornillo***, 1974). Earlier, in ***Red Lion Broadcasting Company v. Federal Communications Commission*** (1969), the Court upheld similar restrictions on radio and television stations, reasoning that such laws were justified because only a limited number of broadcast frequencies were available.

Miami Herald Publishing Company v. Tornillo

A 1974 case in which the Supreme Court held that a state could not force a newspaper to print replies from candidates it had criticized, illustrating the limited power of government to restrict the **print media.**

Red Lion Broadcasting Company v. FCC

A 1969 case in which the Supreme Court upheld restrictions on radio and television broadcasting. These restrictions on the **broadcast media** are much tighter than those on the **print media** because there are only a limited number of broadcasting frequencies available.

One FCC rule regulating the content of programs restricts the use of obscene words. Comedian George Carlin has a famous routine called "Seven Words You Can Never Say on Television." A New York City radio station tested Carlin's assertion by airing his routine. The ensuing events proved Carlin right. In 1978, the Supreme Court upheld the Commission's policy of barring these words from radio or television when children might hear them.[46]

Similarly, in 1992 the FCC fined New York disc jockey Howard Stern $600,000 for indecency. It is especially interesting that if Stern's commentaries had been carried by cable or satellite instead of the airwaves, he could have expressed himself with impunity. Technological change has blurred the line between broadcasting and private communications between individuals. With cable television now in about two-thirds of American homes, the Supreme Court is now faced with ruling on the application of free-speech guidelines to cable broadcasting.

Section 505 of the Telecommunications Act of 1996 requires cable television operators providing channels "primarily dedicated to sexually-oriented programming" either to "fully scramble or otherwise fully block" those channels or to limit their transmission to hours when children are unlikely to be viewing, set by administrative regulation as between 10 P.M. and 6 A.M. The Playboy Entertainment Group pointed out that banning transmission restricts sexually oriented programming even to households without children. It challenged the law as an unconstitutional violation of the First Amendment free-speech guarantee, arguing that Congress had less restrictive ways to accomplish its goals.

In 2000 in *United States v. Playboy Entertainment Group*, the Supreme Court agreed. It held that although government had a legitimate right to regulate sexually oriented programming, any such regulation must be narrowly tailored to promote a compelling government interest. If a less restrictive alternative would serve the government's purpose, Congress must use that alternative. The Court concluded that targeted blocking, in which subscribers can ask their cable companies to block a signal to their homes, is less restrictive than banning and is a feasible and effective means of furthering its compelling interests. Thus, the more restrictive option of banning a signal for most of the day cannot be justified.

Freedom of Assembly

The last of the great rights guaranteed by the First Amendment is the freedom to "peaceably assemble." This freedom is often neglected alongside the more trumpeted freedoms of speech, press, and religion, yet it is the basis for forming interest groups, political parties, and professional associations, as well as for picketing and protesting.

Right to Assemble. There are two facets of the freedom of assembly. First is the literal right to assemble—that is, to gather together in order to make a statement. This freedom can conflict with other societal values when it disrupts public order, traffic flow, peace and quiet, or bystanders' freedom to go about their business without interference. Within reasonable limits, called *time, place,* and *manner restrictions,* freedom of assembly includes the rights to parade, picket, and protest. Whatever a group's cause, it has the right to demonstrate, but no group can simply hold a spontaneous demonstration anytime, anywhere, and anyway it chooses. Usually, a group must apply to the local city government for a permit and post a bond of a few hundred dollars—a little like making a security deposit on an apartment. The governing body must grant a permit as long as the group pledges to hold its demonstration at a time and place that allows the police to prevent major disruptions. There are virtually no limitations on the content of a group's message. In one important case, the American Nazi Party applied to the local government to march in the streets of Skokie, Ill., a Chicago suburb with a sizable Jewish population, including many survivors of Hitler's death camps. You can examine the Court's response in "You Are the Judge: The Case of the Nazis' March in Skokie."

The balance between freedom and order is tested when protest verges on harassment. Protestors lined up outside abortion clinics are now a common sight. Members of groups such as "Operation Rescue" try to shame clients into staying away and may harass them if they do visit a clinic. Rights are in conflict in such cases: A woman seeking to terminate her pregnancy has the right to obtain an abortion; the demonstrators have the right to protest the very existence of the clinic. The courts have acted to restrain these protestors, setting limits on how close they may come to the clinics and upholding damage claims of clients against the protestors. In 1994, Congress passed a law enacting broad new penalties against abortion protestors. Pro-life demonstrators in a Milwaukee suburb paraded outside the home of a physician who was reported to perform abortions. The town board forbade future picketing in residential neighborhoods. In 1988, the Supreme Court agreed that the right of residential privacy was a legitimate local concern and upheld the ordinance.[47]

Right to Associate. The second facet of freedom of assembly is the right to associate with people who share a common interest, including an interest in political change. In a famous case at the height of the civil rights movement, Alabama tried to

You Are the Judge

The Case of the Nazis' March in Skokie

Hitler's Nazis slaughtered 6 million Jews in death camps like Bergen-Belsen, Auschwitz, and Dachau. Many of the survivors migrated to the United States, and many settled in Skokie, Ill. Skokie, with 80,000 people, is a suburb just north of Chicago. In its heavily Jewish population are thousands of survivors of German concentration camps.

The American Nazi Party was a ragtag group of perhaps 25 to 30 members. Their headquarters was a storefront building on the West Side of Chicago, near an area of an expanding African-American population. After being denied a permit to march in an African-American neighborhood of Chicago, the American Nazis announced their intention to march in Skokie. Skokie's city government required that they post a $300,000 bond to get a parade permit. The Nazis claimed that the high bond was set in order to prevent their march and that it infringed on their freedoms of speech and assembly. The American Civil Liberties Union (ACLU), despite its loathing of the Nazis, defended the Nazis' claim and their right to march. The ACLU lost half its Illinois membership because it took this position.

You Be the Judge: Do Nazis have the right to parade, preach anti-Jewish propaganda, and perhaps provoke violence in a community peopled with survivors of the Holocaust? What rights or obligations does a community have to maintain order?

Answer: A federal district court ruled that Skokie's ordinance did restrict freedom of assembly and association. No community could use its power to grant parade permits to stifle free expression. In *Collins v. Smith* (Collins was the Nazi leader and Smith was the mayor of Skokie), the Supreme Court let this lower-court decision stand. In fact, the Nazis did not march in Skokie, settling instead for some poorly attended demonstrations in Chicago.

White supremacists and antiwhite supremacists square off. The Supreme Court has generally upheld the right of any group, no matter how controversial or offensive, to peaceably assemble, as long as the group's demonstrations remain on public property.

harass the state chapter of the National Association for the Advancement of Colored People (NAACP) by requiring it to turn over its membership list. The Court found this demand an unconstitutional restriction on freedom of association (***NAACP v. Alabama***, 1958).

NAACP v. Alabama

The Supreme Court protected the right to assemble peaceably in this 1958 case when it decided the NAACP did not have to reveal its membership list and thus subject its members to harassment.

The four freedoms guaranteed by the First Amendment—religion, speech, press, and assembly—are one key part of Americans' civil liberties. When people confront the American legal system as criminal suspects, they also have certain rights under the Constitution. Even suspected and convicted criminals are guaranteed some rights, which regulate how they can be investigated, interrogated, tried, and punished.

Defendants' Rights

The Bill of Rights contains only 44 words that guarantee the freedoms of religion, speech, press, and assembly. Most of the remaining words concern the rights of people accused of crimes. These rights were originally intended to protect the accused in *political* arrests and trials; British abuse of colonial political leaders was still fresh in the memory of American citizens. Today the protections in the Fourth, Fifth, Sixth, Seventh, and Eighth Amendments are mostly applied in criminal justice cases.

It is useful to think of the stages of the criminal justice system as a series of funnels decreasing in size. Generally speaking, a *crime* is (sometimes) followed by an *arrest*, which is (sometimes) followed by a *prosecution*, which is (sometimes) followed by a *trial*, which (usually) results in a *verdict* of innocence or guilt. The funnels get smaller and smaller, each dripping into the next. Many more crimes occur than are reported; many more crimes are reported than arrests are made (the ratio is about five to one); many more arrests are made than prosecutors prosecute; and many more prosecutions occur than jury trials. At each stage of the criminal justice system, the Constitution protects the rights of the accused (see Table 4.3).

Interpreting Defendants' Rights

The Bill of Rights sets out civil liberties that American citizens have if they are arrested or brought to court. At every stage of the criminal justice system, police, prosecutors, and judges must behave in accordance with the Bill of Rights. Any misstep may invalidate a conviction.

Table 4.3 The Constitution and the Stages of the Criminal Justice System

Although our criminal justice system is complex, it can be broken down into stages. The Constitution protects the rights of the accused at every stage.

STAGE	PROTECTIONS
1. Evidence gathered	"Unreasonable search and seizure" forbidden (Fourth Amendment)
2. Suspicion cast	Guarantee that "writ of habeas corpus" will not be suspended, forbidding imprisonment without evidence (Article I, Section 9)
3. Arrest made	Right to have the "assistance of counsel" (Sixth Amendment)
4. Interrogation held	Forced self-incrimination forbidden (Fifth Amendment)
	"Excessive bail" forbidden (Eighth Amendment)
5. Trial held	"Speedy and public trial" by an impartial jury required (Sixth Amendment)
	"Double jeopardy" (being tried twice for the same crime) forbidden (Fifth Amendment)
	Trial by jury required (Article III, Section 2)
	Right to confront witnesses (Sixth Amendment)
6. Punishment imposed	"Cruel and unusual punishment" forbidden (Eighth Amendment)

The language of the Bill of Rights comes from the late 1700s and is often vague. For example, just how speedy is a "speedy trial"? How "cruel and unusual" does a punishment have to be in order to violate the Eighth Amendment? The courts continually must rule on the constitutionality of actions by police, prosecutors, judges, and legislatures—actions that a citizen or group could claim violate certain rights. Defendants' rights, just like those rights protected by the First Amendment, are not clearly defined in the Bill of Rights.

One thing is clear, however. The Supreme Court's decisions have extended specific provisions of the Bill of Rights—one by one—to the states as part of the general process of incorporation discussed earlier. Virtually all the rights discussed in the following sections affect the actions of both the national and state authorities.

Searches and Seizures

Police cannot arrest a citizen without reason. They need evidence to arrest, and courts need evidence to convict. Before making an arrest, police need what the courts call **probable cause,** reasonable grounds to believe that someone is guilty of a crime. Often police need to get physical evidence—a car thief's fingerprints, a snatched purse—to use in court. The Fourth Amendment is quite specific in forbidding **unreasonable searches and seizures.** To prevent abuse of police power, the Constitution requires that no court may issue a **search warrant** unless probable cause exists to believe that a crime has occurred or is about to occur. These written warrants must specify the area to be searched and the material sought in the police search.

A warrant is not a constitutional requirement for a reasonable police search, however. Most searches in this country take place without warrants. Such searches are valid if probable cause exists, if the search is necessary to protect an officer's safety, or if the search is limited to material relevant to the suspected crime or within the suspect's immediate control.

Normally, if police find anything in a search, they find what they have probable cause to believe is there. In two cases involving Fourth Amendment issues, authorities used aerial searches to secure the evidence they needed. The first case involved a marijuana grower named Ciraolo. When police, responding to a tip, went to look at his place, it was surrounded by 10-foot fences. The police then rented a private plane, took pictures of the crop, and secured a conviction. Environmental Protection Agency officials took a similar aerial photo of Dow Chemical's Midland, Mich., plant and located environmental violations. Both Ciraolo and Dow sued, claiming they were the victims

probable cause

The situation occurring when the police have reason to believe that a person should be arrested. In making the arrest, the police are allowed legally to search for and seize incriminating evidence.

unreasonable searches and seizures

Obtaining evidence in a haphazard or random manner, a practice prohibited by the Fourth Amendment. **Probable cause** and/or a **search warrant** are required for a legal and proper search for and seizure of incriminating evidence.

search warrant

A written authorization from a court specifying the area to be searched and what the police are searching for. The Fourth Amendment requires a search warrant to prevent **unreasonable searches and seizures.**

of unconstitutional search and seizure. Both lost, however, when their cases came before the Supreme Court. Since then, the Court has also upheld roadside checkpoints in which police randomly examine drivers for signs of intoxication.[48] The Court has, however, voided more general vehicle checkpoints.[49]

Ever since 1914, the Supreme Court has used an **exclusionary rule** to weigh evidence in criminal cases. This rule prevents illegally seized evidence from being introduced in court, but until 1961 the rule applied only to the federal government. The Supreme Court broadened the application in the case of a Cleveland woman named Dollree Mapp, who was under suspicion for illegal gambling activities. The police broke into her home looking for a fugitive, and while there, they searched the house and found a cache of obscene materials. Mapp was convicted of possessing them. She appealed her case to the federal courts, claiming that the exclusionary rule should be made a part of the Fourth Amendment. Since the local police had no probable cause to search for obscene materials—only for materials related to gambling—she argued, the evidence should not be used against her. In an important decision (***Mapp v. Ohio***, 1961), the Supreme Court ruled that the evidence had been seized illegally and the Court reversed Mapp's conviction. Since then, the exclusionary rule has been part of the Fourth Amendment and has been incorporated within the rights that restrict the states, as well as the federal government.

Critics of the exclusionary rule, including some Supreme Court justices, argue that its strict application may permit guilty persons to go free because of police carelessness or innocent errors. The guilty, they say, should not go free because of a "technicality." Supporters of the exclusionary rule respond that the Constitution is not a technicality and that—because everyone is presumed innocent until proven guilty—defendants' rights protect the *accused*, not the guilty. You can examine one contemporary search-and-seizure case in "You Are the Judge: The Case of Ms. Montoya."

exclusionary rule

The rule that evidence, no matter how incriminating, cannot be introduced into a trial if it was not constitutionally obtained. The rule prohibits use of evidence obtained through **unreasonable search and seizure.**

Mapp v. Ohio

The 1961 Supreme Court decision ruling that the Fourth Amendment's protection against **unreasonable searches and seizures** must be extended to the states as well as the federal government.

You Are the Judge

The Case of Ms. Montoya

Rose Elviro Montoya de Hernandez arrived at the Los Angeles International Airport on Avianca Flight 080 from Bogotá, Colombia. Her first official encounter was with U.S. Customs Inspector Talamantes, who noticed that she spoke no English. Interestingly, Montoya's passport indicated eight recent quick trips from Bogotá to Los Angeles. She had $5,000 in cash but no pocketbook or credit cards.

Talamantes and his fellow customs officers were suspicious. Stationed in Los Angeles, they were hardly unaware of the fact that Colombia was a major drug supplier. They questioned Montoya, who explained that her husband had a store in Bogotá and that she planned to spend the $5,000 at Kmart and JC Penney, stocking up on items for the store.

The inspector, somewhat wary, handed Montoya over to female customs inspectors for a search. These agents noticed what the Supreme Court later referred to delicately as a "firm fullness" in Montoya's abdomen. Suspicions, already high, increased. The agents applied for a court order to conduct pregnancy tests, X rays, and other examinations, and eventually they found 88 balloons containing 80 percent pure cocaine in Montoya's alimentary canal.

Montoya's lawyer argued that this constituted unreasonable search and seizure and that her arrest and conviction should be set aside. There was, he said, no direct evidence that would have led the officials to suspect cocaine smuggling. The government argued that the arrest had followed from a set of odd facts leading to reasonable suspicion that something was amiss.

You Be the Judge: Was Montoya's arrest based on a search-and-seizure incident that violated the Fourth Amendment?

Answer: Justice Rehnquist wrote the majority opinion, holding that U.S. Customs agents were well within their constitutional authority to search Montoya. Even though collection of evidence took the better part of two days, Justice Rehnquist remarked wryly that "the rudimentary knowledge of the human body which judges possess in common with the rest of mankind tells us that alimentary canal smuggling cannot be detected in the amount of time in which other illegal activities may be investigated through brief . . . stops."

An increasingly conservative Court made some exceptions to the exclusionary rule beginning in the 1980s. The Court allowed the use of illegally obtained evidence when this evidence led police to a discovery that they eventually would have made without it.[50] The justices also decided to establish the good-faith exception to the rule; evidence could be used if the police who seized it mistakenly thought they were operating under a constitutionally valid warrant.[51] In 1995, the Court held that the exclusionary rule does not bar evidence obtained illegally as the result of clerical errors.[52] The Court even allowed evidence illegally obtained from a banker to be used to convict one of his customers.[53] The current Supreme Court, with its conservative orientation, may make even more exceptions in the future.

Why does it matter?

One of the most controversial aspects of the courts' efforts to uphold defendants' rights has been their use of the exclusionary rule in which they disregard evidence obtained illegally. Does the exclusionary rule serve the interests of justice? If you were a defendant, would you view the exclusionary rule as a technicality or as an appropriate restraint on police power?

However, a case decided in 1998 offers more protection against searches. An Iowa police officer stopped Patrick Knowles for speeding and issued him a citation rather than arresting him. The officer then conducted a full search of the car, without either Knowles' consent or probable cause, found marijuana and a "pot pipe," and arrested Knowles. The Supreme Court held that the search of Knowles' car violated the Fourth Amendment. The Court said that although officers may order a driver and passengers out of a car while issuing a traffic citation and may search for weapons to protect themselves from danger, Knowles presented no threat to the officer's safety and thus provided no justification for the intrusion of a search of his car.[54] Similarly, in *Florida v. J. L.* (2000), the Supreme Court ruled that an anonymous tip that a person is carrying a gun is not sufficient justification for a police officer to stop and frisk that person.

Self-incrimination

Suppose that evidence has been gathered and suspicion directed toward a particular person, and the police are ready to make an arrest. In the American system, the burden of proof rests on the police and the prosecutors. Suspects cannot be forced to help with their own conviction by, say, blurting out a confession in the stationhouse. The **Fifth Amendment** forbids forced **self-incrimination,** stating that no person "shall be compelled to be a witness against himself." Whether in a congressional hearing, a courtroom, or a police station, suspects need not provide evidence that can later be used against them. Under law, though, the government may guarantee suspects *immunity*—exemption from prosecution in exchange for suspects' testimony regarding their own and others' misdeeds.

Fifth Amendment

The constitutional amendment designed to protect the rights of persons accused of crimes, including protection against double jeopardy, **self-incrimination,** and punishment without due process of law.

self-incrimination

The situation occurring when an individual accused of a crime is compelled to be a witness against himself or herself in court. The **Fifth Amendment** forbids self-incrimination.

Miranda v. Arizona

The 1966 Supreme Court decision that sets guidelines for police questioning of accused persons to protect them against **self-incrimination** and to protect their right to counsel.

You have probably seen television shows in which an arrest is made and the arresting officers recite, often from memory, a set of rights to the arrestee. These rights are authentic and originated from a famous court decision—perhaps the most important modern decision in criminal law—involving an Arizona man named Ernesto Miranda.[55]

Miranda was picked up as a prime suspect in the rape and kidnapping of an 18-year-old girl. Identified by the girl from a police lineup, Miranda was questioned for two hours. During this time, he was told of neither his constitutional right against self-incrimination nor his right to counsel. In fact, it is unlikely that Miranda had even heard of the Fifth Amendment. He said enough to lead eventually to a conviction. The Supreme Court reversed his conviction on appeal, however. In ***Miranda v. Arizona*** (1966), the Court established guidelines for police questioning. Suspects must be told that:

- they have a constitutional right to remain silent and may stop answering questions at any time;
- what they say can be used against them in a court of law;
- they have a right to have a lawyer present during questioning and that the court will provide an attorney if they cannot afford their own lawyer.

Police departments throughout the country were originally disgruntled by *Miranda.* Officers felt that interrogation was crucial to any investigation. Warning sus-

One of the most important principles of constitutional law is that defendants in criminal cases have rights. Here a police officer reads a suspect his rights based on the Supreme Court's decision in *Miranda v. Arizona.*

pects of their rights and letting them call a lawyer were almost certain to silence them. Most departments today, however, seem to take *Miranda* seriously and usually read a *Miranda* card advising suspects of their rights. Ironically, when Ernesto Miranda himself was murdered, the suspect was read his rights from a *Miranda* card.

In the decades since the *Miranda* decision, the Supreme Court has made a number of exceptions to its requirements. In 1991, for example, the Court held that a coerced confession introduced in a trial does not automatically taint a conviction. If other evidence is enough for a conviction, then the coerced confession is a "harmless error" that does not necessitate a new trial.[56] Nevertheless, in 2000 in *Dickerson v. U.S.*, the Court made it clear that it supported the *Miranda* decision and that Congress was not empowered to change it.

The Fifth Amendment prohibits not only coerced confessions but also coerced crimes. The courts have overturned convictions based on *entrapment*—when law enforcement officials encourage persons to commit crimes (such as accepting bribes or purchasing illicit drugs) that they otherwise would not commit. "You Are the Judge: The Case of the Dirty Old Man" addresses this issue.

THE WIZARD OF ID

You Are the Judge

The Case of the Dirty Old Man

In 1984, Keith Jacobson, a 56-year-old farmer who supported his elderly father in Nebraska, ordered two magazines and a brochure from a California adult bookstore. He expected nude photographs of adult males, but instead found photographs of nude boys. He ordered no other magazines.

Three months later the federal law was changed to make the receipt of such materials illegal. Finding his name on the mailing list of the California bookstore, two government agencies repeatedly enticed Jacobson through five fictitious organizations and a bogus pen pal with solicitations for sexually explicit photographs of children. After 26 months of enticement, Jacobson finally ordered a magazine and was arrested for violating the Child Protection Act.

He was convicted of receiving child pornography through the mail, which he undoubtedly did. Jacobson claimed, however, that he had been entrapped into committing the crime.

You Be the Judge: Was Jacobson an innocent victim of police entrapment, or was he a dirty old man seeking child pornography?

Answer: The Court agreed with Jacobson. In *Jacobson v. United States* (1992), it ruled that the government had overstepped the line between setting a trap for the "unwary innocent" and the "unwary criminal" and failed to establish that Jacobson was independently predisposed to commit the crime for which he was arrested. Jacobson's conviction was overturned.

The Right to Counsel

One of the most important of the *Miranda* rights is the right to secure counsel. Even lawyers who are taken to court hire another lawyer to represent them. (There is an old saying in the legal profession that a lawyer who defends himself has a fool for a client.) Although the **Sixth Amendment** has always ensured the right to counsel in federal courts, this right was not extended to people tried in state courts until the 1960s. Winning this right for poor defendants was a long fight. Until the 1930s, individuals were tried and sometimes convicted for capital offenses (those in which the death penalty could be imposed) without a lawyer. In 1932, the Supreme Court ordered the states to provide an attorney for indigent (poor) defendants accused of a capital crime (*Powell v. Alabama*).

Sixth Amendment

The constitutional amendment designed to protect individuals accused of crimes. It includes the right to counsel, the right to confront witnesses, and the right to a speedy and public trial.

Most crimes are not capital crimes, however, and most crimes are tried in state courts. It was not until 1963, in ***Gideon v. Wainwright***,[57] that the Supreme Court extended the right to an attorney for everyone accused of a felony in a state court (see "Making a Difference: Clarence Gideon" for more about this case). Subsequently, the Court went a step further than *Gideon* and held that whenever imprisonment could be imposed, a lawyer must be provided for the accused (*Argersinger v. Hamlin*, 1972).

Gideon v. Wainwright

The 1963 Supreme Court decision holding that anyone accused of a felony where imprisonment may be imposed, however poor he or she might be, has a right to a lawyer. See also **Sixth Amendment**.

Trial by Jury

Television's portrayal of courts and trials is almost as dramatic as its portrayal of detectives and police officers—both often vary from reality. Highly publicized trials are dramatic, but rare. The murder trial of O. J. Simpson made headlines for months. Cable News Network even carried much of the pretrial and trial live. But in reality, most cases, even ones in which the evidence is solid, do not go to trial.

If you visit a typical American criminal courtroom, you will rarely see a trial complete with judge and jury. In American courts, 90 percent of all cases begin and end with a guilty plea. Most cases are settled through a process called **plea bargaining.** A plea bargain results from an actual bargain struck between a defendant's lawyer and a

plea bargaining

An actual bargain struck between the defendant's lawyer and the prosecutor to the effect that the defendant will plead guilty to a lesser crime (or fewer crimes) in exchange for the state's promise not to prosecute the defendant for a more serious (or additional) crime.

Making a Difference

Clarence Gideon

Clarence Earl Gideon was a frail, poorly educated, 51-year-old ex-convict who had served four sentences for gambling and theft. One day he was arrested for breaking into the Bar Harbor Poolroom in Panama City, Fla., with the intent to rob it. Gideon was too poor to hire a lawyer, so he asked the court to appoint one for him. The court refused, citing the Supreme Court precedent of *Betts v. Brady* that a court-appointed attorney was only required by law in cases where the defendant was facing capital punishment.

Put to trial before a jury, Gideon conducted his defense as well as could be expected. He made an opening statement to the jury, cross-examined the state's witnesses, presented witnesses in his own defense, declined to testify himself, and made a short argument emphasizing his innocence. Nevertheless, the jury returned a guilty verdict, and Gideon was sentenced to serve five years in the state prison.

While in prison, Gideon taught himself law in the prison library. Subsequently, he filed a habeus corpus petition in the Florida Supreme Court attacking his conviction and sentence on the ground that the trial court's refusal to appoint counsel for him denied him rights guaranteed by the Constitution. The Florida Supreme Court denied Gideon's claim.

Using the prison's law books, he then filed a handwritten *pauper's petition* and sent it to the U.S. Supreme Court. Much to his surprise, the Court agreed to hear his case. Equally important, the Court appointed a counsel for him—Abe Fortas, one of the finest attorneys in the country (Fortas later served on the Supreme Court). Gideon did not get to leave prison to hear his case argued before the Supreme Court, but he certainly heard the result. In *Gideon v. Wainwright* (1963), the Court overruled *Betts v. Brady* and held that defendants in all felony cases had a right to counsel.

Gideon was released, retried (this time with a public defender handling his case), and acquitted. More than a thousand of Gideon's fellow Florida prisoners, plus thousands more who had been convicted in other states without benefit of counsel, were also released. One man, without friends or funds, who had lost neither his sense of injustice nor his passion for freedom, had made a difference.

prosecutor to the effect that a defendant will plead guilty to a lesser crime (or fewer crimes) in exchange for a state's not prosecuting that defendant for a more serious (or additional) crime.

Critics of the plea-bargaining system believe that it permits many criminals to avoid the full punishment they deserve. The process, however, works to the advantage of both sides; it saves the state the time and money that would otherwise be spent on a trial, and it permits defendants who think they might be convicted of a serious charge to plead guilty to a lesser one.

Whether plea bargaining serves the ends of justice is much debated. To its critics, plea bargaining benefits defendants. David Brereton and Jonathan Casper, studying sentencing patterns in three California counties, discovered that a larger proportion of defendants who went to trial (rather than plea bargained) ended up going to prison, compared with those who pleaded guilty and had no trial. In answer to their question "Does it pay to plead guilty?" these authors give a qualified yes.[58] Good or bad, plea bargaining is a practical necessity. Only a vast increase in resources devoted to the court system could cope with a trial for every defendant.

The defendants in the 300,000 cases per year that actually go to trial are entitled to many rights, including the Sixth Amendment's provision for a speedy trial by an impartial jury. These days, defendants (those who can afford it, at least) do not leave jury selection to chance. A sophisticated technology of jury selection has developed. Jury consultants—often psychologists or other social scientists—develop profiles of jurors likely to be sympathetic or hostile to a defendant. Lawyers for both sides spend hours questioning prospective jurors in a major case.

The Constitution does not specify the size of a jury; in principle, it could be anywhere from one or one hundred people. Tradition in England and America has set jury

How You Can Make A Difference

Defendants' Rights

Protecting the rights of the accused and the imprisoned presents a special challenge. Often these rights are overlooked or even frowned on by the public because most people have little sympathy for those charged with or guilty of crimes. Outrage at criminal behavior can easily blind people to the fundamental importance of defendants' rights within a democracy. As we've already shown, Clarence Gideon's case failed to generate any public sympathy or recognition. Obviously, crime is an emotionally charged issue. If you want to make a difference, you must prepare yourself for possible hostility and opposition from the public, victims of crime, and even the accused themselves.

Many activist groups ranging from the religious to the secular would eagerly welcome your help in protecting the rights of the accused and imprisoned. The American Friends (Quakers) run a national network of regional chapters devoted not only to protecting civil liberties but also to providing comfort to those in prison (www.afsc.org). Though international in scope, both the Human Rights Watch (www.hrw.org) and Amnesty International (www.amnesty.org) have specific efforts focused on criminal law and the prison system in the United States. For more detailed listings of similar organizations, check out CURE (www.cure.org) on the Internet.

Sometimes those passionate about the rights of the accused and imprisoned may be tempted to glorify a person who may have had their rights abridged and turn that person into a hero or celebrity despite evidence of wrongdoing. Some argue that this is the case with the recent worldwide celebrity accorded Mumia Abu Jamal, an African-American political activist on death row for murdering a police officer. In cases like this, distinguishing between a person's civil liberties and a person's responsibility for criminal actions can be difficult for both the criminal justice system *and* rights activists to determine. Because of such confusion, some groups, such as the Criminal Justice Legal Foundation (www.cjlf.org), believe that a *balance* should be restored between the rights of crime victims and rights of the criminally accused.

No matter which stance you find more compelling, most people involved in this debate agree that guaranteeing the civil liberties of the accused and imprisoned remains necessary in order to preserve every citizen's civil liberties.

size at 12, although in petty cases 6 jurors are sometimes used. Whereas traditionally a jury had to be unanimous in order to convict, the Supreme Court eroded those traditions, permitting states to use fewer than 12 jurors and to convict with a less than unanimous vote. Federal courts still employ juries of 12 persons and require unanimous votes for a criminal conviction.

Cruel and Unusual Punishment

Eighth Amendment

The constitutional amendment that forbids **cruel and unusual punishment,** although it does not define this phrase. Through the **Fourteenth Amendment,** this **Bill of Rights** provision applies to the states.

cruel and unusual punishment

Court sentences prohibited by the **Eighth Amendment.** Although the Supreme Court has ruled that mandatory death sentences for certain offenses are unconstitutional, it has not held that the death penalty itself constitutes cruel and unusual punishment.

Citizens convicted of a crime can expect some punishment ranging from mild to severe, the mildest being some form of probation and the most severe, of course, being the death penalty. The **Eighth Amendment** forbids **cruel and unusual punishment,** although it does not define the phrase. Through the Fourteenth Amendment, this provision of the Bill of Rights applies to the states.

Almost the entire constitutional debate over cruel and unusual punishment has centered on the death penalty (an exception can be found in "You Are the Judge: The Case of the First Offender"). Nearly 3,000 people are currently on death row, about a quarter of them in Florida and Texas. In 1968, the Court overturned a death sentence because opponents of the death penalty had been excluded from the jury at sentencing (*Witherspoon v. Illinois*), a factor that stacked the cards, said the Court, in favor of the extreme penalty.

The Court first confronted the question of whether the death penalty is inherently cruel and unusual punishment in *Furman v. Georgia* (1972). Although *Furman* sent a message, it was a confusing one. Four justices said that the death penalty was not cruel and unusual punishment, yet the Court overturned Georgia's death penalty law

You Are the Judge

The Case of the First Offender

Ronald Harmelin of Detroit was convicted of possessing 672 grams of cocaine (a gram is about one-thirtieth of an ounce). Michigan's mandatory sentencing law required the trial judge to sentence Harmelin, a first-time offender, to life imprisonment without possibility of parole. Harmelin argued that this was cruel and unusual punishment because it was "significantly disproportionate," meaning that, as we might say, the "punishment did not fit the crime." Harmelin's lawyers argued that many other crimes more serious than cocaine possession would net similar sentences.

You Be the Judge: Was Harmelin's sentence cruel and unusual punishment?

Answer: The Court upheld Harmelin's conviction in *Harmelin v. Michigan* (1991), spending many pages to explain that severe punishments were quite commonplace, especially when the Bill of Rights was written. Severity alone does not qualify a punishment as "cruel and unusual." The severity of punishment was up to the legislature of Michigan, which, the justices observed, knew better than they the conditions on the streets of Detroit.

because its imposition was "freakish" and "random." Warned by *Furman*, 35 states passed new laws permitting the death penalty. Some states, to prevent arbitrariness in punishment, went to the other extreme, mandating death penalties for some crimes. In *Woodson v. North Carolina* (1976), the Supreme Court ruled against mandatory death penalties.

Since then the Court has come down more clearly on the side of the death penalty. Troy Gregg had murdered two hitchhikers and was awaiting execution in Georgia's state prison. Gregg's attorney argued that the death penalty was cruel and unusual punishment. In ***Gregg v. Georgia*** (1976), the Court disagreed. "Capital punishment," it said, "is an expression of society's outrage at particularly offensive conduct. . . . It is an extreme sanction, suitable to the most extreme of crimes."

A divided Court rebuffed the last major challenge to the death penalty in ***McCleskey v. Kemp*** (1987) when it refused to rule that the penalty violated the equal protection of the law guaranteed by the Fourteenth Amendment. Although social scientists testified that minority defendants and murderers whose victims were White were disproportionately likely to receive death sentences, the Court insisted that this fact did not violate the Fourteenth Amendment because there was no evidence that juries intended to discriminate on the basis of race. Not everyone is convinced, however. Shortly before retiring from the bench, Justice Harry Blackmun declared that the administration of the death penalty "fails to deliver the fair, consistent and reliable sentences of death required by the Constitution."[59]

Nevertheless, today the death penalty is a part of the American criminal justice system, and more than 600 persons have been executed since the Court's decision in *Gregg v. Georgia*. In 1989, the Court held that it is constitutionally acceptable to execute even 16- or 17-year-olds and mentally retarded persons. More recently, the Court has made it more difficult for death row prisoners to file habeas corpus petitions that would force legal delays and appeals to stave off their appointed executions. The Court has also allowed "victim impact" statements detailing the character of murder victims and their families' suffering to be used against a defendant.

On the other hand, Governor George Ryan of Illinois energized the debate over the death penalty when he declared a moratorium on executions in his state after 13 people were released from death row upon proving their innocence. In addition, attorneys have employed DNA evidence in a number of states to obtain the release of

Gregg v. Georgia

The 1976 Supreme Court decision that upheld the constitutionality of the death penalty, stating that "It is an extreme sanction, suitable to the most extreme of crimes." The court did not, therefore, believe that the death sentence constitutes **cruel and unusual punishment.**

McCleskey v. Kemp

The 1987 Supreme Court decision that upheld the constitutionality of the death penalty against charges that it violated the **Fourteenth Amendment** because minority defendants were more likely to receive the death penalty than were White defendants.

visual literacy
Race and the Death Penalty

dozens of other prisoners. The debate over the death penalty is likely to continue to be intense.

The Right to Privacy

The members of the First Congress who drafted the Bill of Rights and enshrined American civil liberties would never have imagined that Americans would go to court to argue about wiretapping, surrogate motherhood, abortion, or pornography. New technologies have raised ethical issues unimaginable in the eighteenth century. Today, one of the greatest debates concerning Americans' civil liberties lies in the emerging area of privacy rights.

Is There a Right to Privacy?

right to privacy

The right to a private personal life free from the intrusion of government.

Nowhere does the Bill of Rights say that Americans have a **right to privacy.** Clearly, however, the First Congress had the concept of privacy in mind when it crafted the first 10 amendments. Freedom of religion implies the right to exercise private beliefs; protections against "unreasonable searches and seizures" make persons secure in their homes; private property cannot be seized without "due process of law." In 1928, Justice Brandeis hailed privacy as "the right to be left alone—the most comprehensive of the rights and the most valued by civilized men."

The idea that the Constitution guarantees a right to privacy was first enunciated in a 1965 case involving a Connecticut law forbidding the use of contraceptives. It was a little-used law, but a doctor and family planning specialist were arrested for disseminating birth control devices. The state reluctantly brought them to court, and they were convicted. The Supreme Court, in the case of *Griswold v. Connecticut*, wrestled with the privacy issue. Seven justices finally decided that various portions of the Bill of Rights cast "penumbras" (or shadows)—unstated liberties implied by the explicitly stated rights—protecting a right to privacy, including a right to family planning between husband and wife. Supporters of privacy rights argued that this ruling was reasonable enough, for what could be the purpose of the Fourth Amendment, for example, if not to protect privacy? Critics of the ruling—and there were many of them—claimed that the Supreme Court was inventing protections not specified by the Constitution.

The most important application of privacy rights, however, came not in the area of birth control but in the area of abortion. The Supreme Court unleashed a constitutional firestorm in 1973 that has not yet abated.

Controversy over Abortion

Roe v. Wade

The 1973 Supreme Court decision holding that a state ban on all abortions was unconstitutional. The decision forbade state control over abortions during the first trimester of pregnancy, permitted states to limit abortions to protect the mother's health in the second trimester, and permitted states to protect the fetus during the third trimester.

In the summer of 1972, Supreme Court Justice Harry Blackmun returned to Minnesota's famous Mayo Clinic, where he had once served as general counsel. The clinic lent him a tiny desk in the corner of a librarian's office, where he worked quietly for two weeks. His research during this short summer vacation focused on the medical aspects of abortion. Blackmun had been assigned the task of writing the majority opinion in one of the most controversial cases ever to come before the Court. The judge was chronically tardy in his opinion writing; this decision was no exception. Later, back in Washington, Blackmun finished his draft opinion and sent it to his impatient colleagues.

The opinion, in ***Roe v. Wade*** (1973), has been called both radical and temperate. "Jane Roe" was the pseudonym of a Texas woman, Norma McCorvey, who sought an abortion. She argued that the state law allowing the procedure only to save the life of a mother was unconstitutional. Texas argued that states had the power to regulate moral behavior, including abortions.

Blackmun's decision followed medical authorities in dividing pregnancy into three equal trimesters. *Roe* forbid any state control of abortions during the first trimester; it permitted states to allow regulated abortions, but only to protect the mother's health, in the second trimester; and it allowed the states to ban abortion during the third trimester, except when the mother's life or health was in danger. This decision unleashed a storm of protest. The Court's staff needed extra mailboxes to handle the correspondence, some of which contained death threats.[60] Eventually, states adjusted to the new decision, doctors and hospitals cooperated, and, however awkward the reasoning or controversial the result, the decision governed public policy. Since *Roe v. Wade*, about 1.5 million legal abortions have been performed annually.

Yet the furor has never subsided. Congress has passed numerous statutes forbidding the use of federal funds for abortions. Many states have passed similar restrictions. Missouri went as far as any other state, forbidding the use of state funds or state employees to perform abortions. A clinic in St. Louis challenged the law as unconstitutional, but in *Webster v. Reproductive Health Services* (1989), the Court upheld the law. It has also upheld laws requiring minors to notify one or both parents or a judge before obtaining an abortion.

In 1991, the conservative Court went even further in upholding restrictions on abortions. In *Rust v. Sullivan*, the Court found that a Department of Health and Human Services ruling—specifying that family planning services receiving federal funds could not provide women any counseling regarding abortion—was constitutional. This decision was greeted by a public outcry that the rule would deny many poor women abortion counseling and limit the First Amendment right of a medical practitioner to counsel a client. On his third day in office, President Clinton lifted the ban on abortion counseling.

In 1992, in ***Planned Parenthood v. Casey***, the Court changed its standard for evaluating restrictions on abortion from one of "strict scrutiny" of any restraints on a "fundamental right" to one of "undue burden" that permits considerably more regulation. The Court upheld a 24-hour waiting period, a parental or judicial consent requirement for minors, and a requirement that doctors present women with information on the risks of the operation. The Court struck down a provision requiring a married woman to tell her husband of her intent to have an abortion. At the same time, the majority also affirmed their commitment to the basic right of a woman to obtain an abortion. In 2000,

Planned Parenthood v. Casey

A 1992 case in which the Supreme Court loosened its standard for evaluating restrictions on abortion from one of "strict scrutiny" of any restraints on a "fundamental right" to one of "undue burden" that permits considerably more regulation.

Passions sometimes rule in the debate over abortion. Paul Hill went so far as to murder a physician who performed abortions, arguing that he had a right to do so to save the lives of the unborn. The jury did not agree, and Hill was sentenced to death.

Figure 4.1 The Abortion Debate

In few areas of public opinion research do scholars find more divided opinion than on abortion. Some people feel very strongly about the matter, enough so that they are "single-issue voters" unwilling to support any candidate who disagrees with them on abortion. Most take a middle position, one that supports the principle of abortion but that also accepts restrictions on access to abortions.
"Now, on the issue of abortion: Do you think abortions should be legal under any circumstances, legal only under certain circumstances, or illegal in all circumstances?"

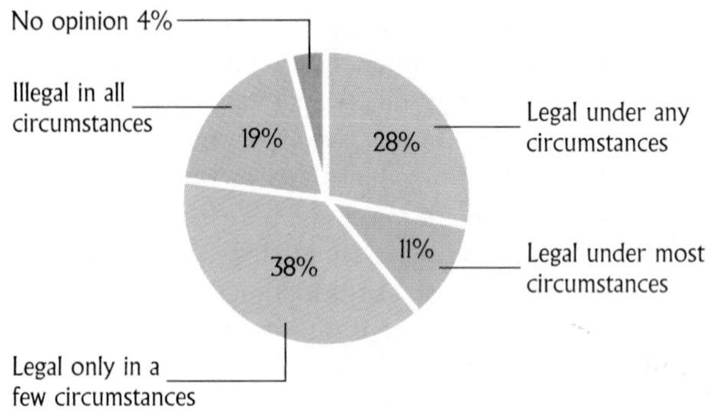

Source: Gallup/CNN/*USA Today Poll*, January 13–16, 2000.

the Court held in *Sternberg v. Carhart* that Nebraska's prohibition of "partial birth' abortions was unconstitutional because it placed an undue burden on women seeking an abortion by limiting their options to less safe procedures and because the law provided no exception for cases where the health of the mother was at risk.

Americans are deeply divided on the issue of abortion (see Figure 4.1). Polls can be found indicating strong support for a woman's right to choose, whereas other polls indicate strong majorities opposing unlimited abortion. Proponents of choice believe that access to abortion is essential if women are to be fully autonomous human beings. Opponents call themselves pro-life because they believe that the fetus is fully human; therefore, an abortion deprives a fetus of the right to life. These positions are irreconcilable, making abortion a politician's nightmare. Wherever a politician stands on this divisive issue, a large number of voters will be enraged.

Because passions run so strongly on the issue, advocates may take extreme action. In the last decade a number of abortion clinics have been bombed. Opponents of abortion murdered two physicians who performed abortions in Pensacola, Fla.

Efforts to protect women's access to clinics sometimes clash with protesters' rights to free speech and assembly. In 1994, the Court consolidated the right to abortion established in *Roe* with the protection of a woman's right to enter an abortion clinic to exercise that right. Citing the government's interest in preserving order and maintaining women's access to pregnancy services, the Court upheld a state court's order of a 36-foot buffer zone around a clinic in Melbourne, Fla.[61] That same year Congress passed the Freedom of Access to Clinic Entrances Act, which makes it a federal crime to intimidate abortion providers or women seeking abortions. In 2000 it upheld a 100-foot restriction in Colorado.[62] In another case, the Court decided that abortion clinics could invoke the federal racketeering law to sue violent antiabortion protest groups for damages.[63]

A Time To Live and a Time To Die

The idea of rights to live, die, or have children were all but meaningless before the twentieth-century revolution in medicine and biotechnology. Today, medical science can continue certain life functions, especially respiration and blood circulation, in the absence of other vital signs, such as brain activity. State laws struggle to define death. At the same time, in vitro fertilization, frozen embryos, and artificial insemination complicate efforts to define birth by separating reproduction from sexual intercourse and the parent-child relationship. Do people have rights to use these new technologies—or to refuse them? May people make these decisions for their parents or children?

Many of the issues surrounding birth and death were crystallized in two "Baby Doe" cases. Baby Doe was born in Indiana with Down syndrome, a genetic defect causing mental retardation. Baby Jane Doe was born in New York with spina bifida (in which the spine fails to close properly), a condition that can cause serious mental and physical defects. Doctors for both babies told the parents that the children would die without surgery. The Indiana parents decided against surgery, at which point the hospital went to court to get permission for it. The hospital's efforts were unsuccessful, and the baby died.

In Baby Jane Doe's case, the parents and the doctors unanimously decided against surgery. However, Lawrence Washburn, an attorney who frequently intervened in lawsuits to prevent abortions, sued the hospital and parents, claiming that their decision constituted discrimination against a disabled person and violated federal law. New York courts upheld the decision of the parents and the hospital. The Justice Department then filed suit, threatening to cut off the $20 to $25 million that the hospital received each year in federal funds if it refused to release its records regarding babies with serious physical disabilities. Eventually, the Supreme Court affirmed parents' rights to make medical decisions for their children.[64] Baby Jane Doe did survive.

Mary Sue Davis and Junior Davis had another kind of conflict over the beginnings of life. At their divorce hearing in Tennessee, they argued about seven fertilized embryos. The embryos had been produced through a technique known as in vitro fertilization, in which sperm and ovum are joined outside a woman's body and frozen for later implantation in the uterus. Mary Sue argued that the embryos were alive and should be released to her. Junior's lawyer argued that life begins at birth; therefore, the embryos were not living things and should be destroyed. The judge gave Mary Sue custody of the embryos, but another judge prohibited her from ever using them.

Similar conflicts led to the famous "Baby M" case in New Jersey. When Elizabeth Stern, a physician, developed health problems that made pregnancy risky, she and her husband William sought help from an agency. Mary Beth Whitehead agreed to become what the press has labeled a "surrogate mother"; she was artificially inseminated with William's sperm in order to bear a child for the Sterns. Nine months later, Whitehead gave birth to a girl, called Baby M in court records. Whitehead soon decided that she did not want to give up her baby. The state supreme court gave parental rights to both natural parents: Mary Beth Whitehead and William Stern.

Experts estimate that one in every six American couples who want children will experience difficulty in having them. In vitro fertilization and surrogate motherhood are techniques that can compensate for several kinds of fertility problems. As a result, the Davis and Whitehead cases are a foretaste of more legal quandaries to come.

At the other end of the life spectrum is the issue of the right of adults to choose to die—and to receive help in doing so. Most states have legislated against suicide and those who would assist suicide. In *Cruzan v. Director, Missouri Department of Health* (1990) the Supreme Court recognized a limited constitutional right for patients to refuse unwanted medical treatment, a form of suicide.

What about those who would help terminally ill patients end their lives? Dr. Jack Kervorkian has become a household name as the result of helping terminally ill patients commit suicide and the numerous trials in which he has faced charges for violating the law. In 1999, he was convicted of second degree murder. In 1997, the Supreme Court ruled that there is no constitutional right to physician-assisted suicide

The History of the Right to Privacy

One of the most difficult issues facing our high-tech society is whether there is a right to choose to die. Dr. Jack Kervorkian has been dubbed the "suicide doctor" because of his efforts to help terminally ill patients end their lives. Because not everyone approves of assissted suicide, Kevorkian has spent a great deal of time in court defending his actions. Here, Kervorkian and his sister leave a Michigan courtroom in 1999, following his conviction of second-degree murder.

and that states may prohibit it if they wish.[65] They may also pass laws legalizing it, as Oregon has done, so the decision is back in the hands of the state legislatures.

Understanding Civil Liberties

American government is both democratic and constitutional. America is democratic because it is governed by officials who are elected by the people and, as such, are accountable for their actions. The American government is constitutional because it has a fundamental organic law, the Constitution, that limits the things government may do. By restricting the government, the Constitution limits what the people can empower the government to do. The democratic and constitutional components of government can produce conflicts, but they also reinforce one another.

Civil Liberties and Democracy

The rights ensured by the First Amendment—the freedoms of speech, press, and assembly—are essential to a democracy. If people are to govern themselves, they need access to all available information and opinions in order to make intelligent, responsible, and accountable decisions. If the right to participate in public life is to be open to all, then Americans—in all their diversity—must have the right to express their opinions.

Individual participation and the expression of ideas are crucial components of democracy, but so is majority rule, which can conflict with individual rights. The majority does not have the freedom to decide that there are some ideas it would rather not hear, although at times, the majority tries to enforce its will upon the minority. The conflict is even sharper in relation to the rights guaranteed by the Fourth, Fifth, Sixth, Seventh, and Eighth Amendments. These rights protect all Americans, but they also make it more difficult to punish criminals. It is easy, though misleading, for the majority to view these guarantees as benefits for criminals at the expense of society.

simulation
You are the Police Officer

Career Profile

Position: Executive Director of the ACLU of Kansas and Western Missouri
Salary Range: $45,000-$65,000
Benefits: health insurance, retirement plan, liberal vacation and sick leave
Qualifications: strong affinity for civil liberties issues, good verbal and written language skills, interpersonal and media skills.

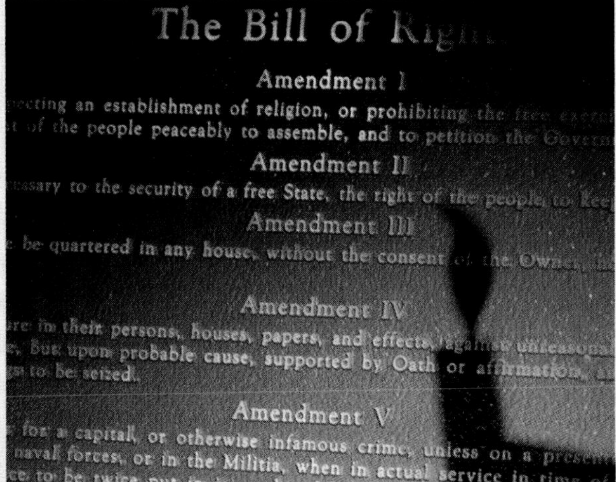

Real Person on the Job: Dick Kurtenbach

Because public perception of the American Civil Liberties Union largely centers around controversial court cases, you may be surprised to know that not all senior ACLU personnel possess law degrees. Instead, most, like Dick Kurtenbach, an executive director at the regional office in Kansas City, have a background in managing nonprofit advocacy organizations and electoral politics. Dick's road to his current position began with managing U.S. Senate and House campaigns. After sharpening his skills in politics, Dick started working for the ACLU affiliates in Nebraska and in Cincinnati before he finally moved to his current location.

The ACLU is an advocate on behalf of civil liberties guaranteed by the Constitution, particularly the Bill of Rights. In the course of a single month, Dick's office receives over 500 phone calls requesting ACLU aid in specific cases. Because of limited resources, Dick, along with his staff and legal director, continually face the task of choosing which cases to pursue. The criteria used to make these decisions include: the cases's nature as a constitutional issue, availability of resources (lawyers and funds), chances of prevailing, and a case's potential precedent value. Most requests are rejected due to lack of funds and time. Telling people that his office can't help them is definitely the worst part of Dick's job. Some of the recent cases Dick's branch has taken on include school prayer in Augusta, Kan., the decision by the Kansas State Board of Education to place limits on the teaching of evolution, and racial profiling by traffic police in the Kansas City area.

Working 55–60 hours a week, Dick's job requires the patience and wisdom of an administrator, tenacity of a master fundraiser, and savvy of a public spokesperson. Dick charts a course for his staff to follow. He spends nearly a quarter of his time on the phone with potential donors to raise funds to carry out his office's priorities. Dick also handles the seemingly endless requests for interviews from reporters. He said that perhaps the most enjoyable aspect of his job is trying to convey to the general public the mission of ACLU and the nature of the various cases he has chosen to pursue.

The ACLU is constantly looking for qualified accountants, lawyers, computer programmers, and administrative coordinators from various backgrounds at the National Headquarters in New York City, the National Offices in Washington, D.C., the Southern Regional Offices in Atlanta, and the various regional affiliate offices. For a more complete list of these jobs, check out their website at www.aclu.org.

With some notable exceptions, the United States has done a good job in protecting the rights of diverse interests to express themselves. There is little danger that a political or economic elite will muffle dissent. Similarly, the history of the past four decades is one of increased protections for defendants' rights, and defendants are typically not among the elite. Ultimately, it has been the courts that have decided what constitutional guarantees mean in practice. Although federal judges, appointed for life, are not directly accountable to popular will,[66] it is "elitist" courts that have often protected civil liberties from the excesses of majority rule.

Civil Liberties and the Scope of Government

Civil liberties in America are both the foundation for and a reflection of our emphasis on individualism. When there is a conflict between an individual or a group attempting to express themselves or worship as they please and an effort by a government to constrain them in some fashion, the individual or group usually wins. If protecting the freedom of an individual or group to express themselves results in inconvenience or even injustice for the public officials they criticize or the populace they wish to reach, so be it. Every nation must choose where to draw the line between freedom and order. In the United States, we generally choose liberty.

Today's government is huge and commands vast, powerful technologies. Americans' Social Security numbers, credit cards, driver's licenses, and school records are all on giant computers to which the government has immediate access. It is virtually impossible to hide from the police, the FBI, the Internal Revenue Service, or any governmental agency. Because Americans can no longer avoid the attention of government, strict limitations on governmental power are essential. The Bill of Rights provides these vital limitations.

Thus, in general, civil liberties limit the scope of government. Yet substantial government efforts are often required to protect the expansion of rights that we have witnessed in this century. Those seeking abortions may need help reaching a clinic; defendants may demand that lawyers be provided them at public expense; advocates of unpopular causes may require police protection; litigants in complex lawsuits over matters of birth or death may rely on judges to resolve their conflicts. It is ironic, but true, that an expansion of freedom may require a simultaneous expansion of government.

Summary

Civil liberties are an individual's protection against the government. The Bill of Rights makes it clear that American government is a constitutional democracy in which individual rights limit government. Disputes about civil liberties are frequent because the issues involved are complex and divisive. Legislatures and courts are constantly defining in practice what the Bill of Rights guarantees in theory.

In a way, the notion that government can protect people from government is contradictory. Thomas Jefferson wrote in the Declaration of Independence that all people "are endowed by their creator with certain unalienable rights." Jefferson's next "self-evident truth" was that "to secure these rights, governments are instituted." People, said Jefferson, do not get their rights from government. Instead, rights precede government, which then gets its power to rule from the people. The Bill of Rights does not give Americans freedom of religion or the right to a fair trial; these amendments merely recognize that these rights exist. People often speak, however, as though rights are things that government gives them.

The First Amendment guarantees freedoms of religion, expression, and assembly. The Bill of Rights also contains protections that are especially important to those accused or convicted of crimes. Together, these rights provide Americans with more liberty than that enjoyed by most other people on earth.

One task that government must perform is to resolve conflicts between rights. Often, First Amendment rights and rights at the bar of justice exist in uneasy tension; a newspaper's right to inform its readers may conflict with a person's right to a fair trial. Today, most of the rights enjoyed under the U.S. Constitution have been extended to the states.

Today's technologies raise key questions about ethics and the Constitution. Although the Constitution does not specifically mention a right to privacy, the Supreme Court found this right implied by several guarantees in the Bill of Rights. The most controversial application of privacy rights has been in abortion cases. And if the right to life is a political and legal issue, so, equally, is the right to die.

Key Terms

civil liberties
Bill of Rights
First Amendment
Fourteenth Amendment
incorporation doctrine
establishment clause
free exercise clause
prior restraint
libel
symbolic speech
commercial speech
probable cause
unreasonable searches and seizures
search warrant
exclusionary rule
Fifth Amendment
self-incrimination
Sixth Amendment
plea bargaining
Eighth Amendment
cruel and unusual punishment
right to privacy

Key Cases

Barron v. Baltimore (1833)
Gitlow v. New York (1925)
Lemon v. Kurtzman (1971)
Engel v. Vitale (1962)
School District of Abington Township, Pennsylvania v. Schempp (1963)
Near v. Minnesota (1931)
Schenck v. United States (1919)
Zurcher v. Stanford Daily (1976)
Roth v. United States (1957)
Miller v. California (1973)
New York Times v. Sullivan (1964)
Texas v. Johnson (1989)
Miami Herald Publishing Company v. Tornillo (1974)
Red Lion Broadcasting Company v. Federal Communications Commission (1969)
NAACP v. Alabama (1958)
Mapp v. Ohio (1961)
Miranda v. Arizona (1966)
Gideon v. Wainwright (1963)
Gregg v. Georgia (1976)
McCleskey v. Kemp (1987)
Roe v. Wade (1973)
Planned Parenthood v. Casey (1992)

For Further Reading

Adler, Renata. *Reckless Disregard.* New York: Knopf, 1986. The story of two monumental conflicts between free press and individual reputations.

Baker, Liva. *Miranda: The Crime, the Law, the Politics.* New York: Atheneum, 1983. An excellent book-length treatment of one of the major criminal cases of our time.

Craig, Barbara Hickson, and David M. O'Brien. *Abortion and American Politics.* Chatham, NJ: Chatham House, 1993. Provides a history of the abortion issue since 1973.

Garrow, David J. *Liberty and Sexuality.* New York: Macmillan, 1994. The most thorough treatment of the development of the law on the right to privacy and abortion.

Irons, Peter. *The Courage of Their Convictions: Sixteen Americans Who Fought Their Way to the Supreme Court.* New York: Penguin Books, 1990. Accounts of 16 Americans over a period of 50 years who took their cases to the Supreme Court in defense of civil liberties.

Levy, Leonard W. *The Emergence of a Free Press.* New York: Oxford University Press, 1985. A major work on the framers' intentions regarding freedom of expression.

Levy, Leonard W. *The Establishment Clause: Religion and the First Amendment.* New York: Macmillan, 1986. The author argues that it is unconstitutional for government to provide aid to any religion.

Lewis, Anthony. *Make No Law: The Sullivan Case and the First Amendment.* New York: Random House, 1991. A well-written story of the key case regarding American libel law and an excellent case study of a Supreme Court case.

Rosenblatt, Roger. *Life Itself: Abortion in the American Mind.* New York: Random House, 1992. The author seeks to reconcile the clash of absolutes in the abortion controversy with scholarly analysis and interview data.

Internet Resources

www.freedomforum.org
Background information and recent news on First Amendment issues.

www.eff.org
Website concerned with protecting online civil liberties.

www.aclu.org
Home page of the American Civil Liberties Union offering links to many other sites concerned with civil liberties.

w3.trib.com/FACT/1st.religion.html
Overview of freedom of religion in the United States.

www.law.cornell.edu/topics/criminal.html
The text of the landmark cases on criminal justice and background material.

www.law.cornell.edu/topics/first_amendment.html
The text of the landmark cases on freedom of religion, speech, press, and assembly and background material.

www.cc.org/
Christian Coalition home page containing background information and discussion of current events.

Notes

1. James W. Prothro and Charles M. Grigg, "Fundamental Principles of Democracy: Bases of Agreement and Disagreement," *Journal of Politics* 22 (1960): 276–294; and John L. Sullivan et al., "The Sources of Political Tolerance: A Multivariate Analysis," *American Political Science Review* 75 (1981): 100–115.
2. Samuel Krislov, *The Supreme Court and Political Freedom* (New York: Free Press, 1968), 81.
3. *Widmar v. Vincent* (1981).
4. *Westside Community Schools v. Mergens* (1990).
5. *Lamb's Chapel v. Center Moriches Union Free School* (1993).
6. *Rosenberger v. University of Virginia* (1995).
7. *Illinois ex rel McCollum v. Board of Education* (1948).
8. *Zorach v. Clauson* (1952).
9. *Stone v. Graham* (1980).
10. *Lee v. Weisman* (1992).
11. *Santa Fe School District v. Doe* (2000).
12. *Wallace v. Jaffree* (1985).
13. Kenneth D. Wald, *Religion and Politics in the United States*, 3rd ed. (Chatham, NJ: Chatham House, 1997).
14. *Edwards v. Aguillard* (1987).
15. *Epperson v. Arkansas* (1968).
16. *Lynch v. Donelly* (1984).
17. *County of Allegheny v. American Civil Liberties Union* (1989).
18. *Bob Jones University v. United States* (1983).
19. *Wisconsin v. Yoder* (1972).
20. *Boerne v. Flores* (1997).
21. Charles R. Lawrence III, "If He Hollers Let Him Go: Regulating Racist Speech on Campus," in Mari J. Matsuda, Charles R. Lawrence III, Richard Delgado, and Kimberle Crenshaw, *Words that Wound: Critical Race Theory, Assaultive Speech, and the First Amendment* (Boulder, CO: Westview, 1993), 67–68.
22. Ira Glasser, "Introduction," in Henry Louis Gates, Jr. ed., *Speaking of Race, Speaking of Sex: Hate Speech, Civil Rights, and Civil Liberties* (New York: New York University Press, 1994), 8.
23. *R.A.V. v. St. Paul* (1992). However, states may impose longer prison terms on people convicted of "hate crimes" (crimes motivated by racial, religious, or other prejudice) without violating their rights to free speech.
24. See Fred W. Friendly, *Minnesota Rag* (New York: Random House, 1981).
25. *Hazelwood School District v. Kuhlmeier* (1988).
26. The Supreme Court upheld the government's suit in *United States v. Snepp* (1980).
27. *McIntyre v. Ohio Elections Commission* (1995).
28. *Hudgens v. National Labor Relations Board* (1976).
29. *Pruneyard Shopping Center v. Robins* (1980).
30. *City of Ladue v. Gilleo* (1994).
31. *Nebraska Press Association v. Stuart* (1972).
32. *Richmond Newspapers v. Virginia* (1978).
33. Bob Woodward and Scott Armstrong, *The Brethren* (New York: Avon, 1979), 233.
34. *Jenkins v. Georgia* (1974).
35. *Osborne v. Ohio* (1991).
36. *Reno v. ACLU* (1997).
37. *Schad v. Mount Ephraim* (1981).
38. *Barnes v. Glen Theater, Inc.* (1991); *Erie v. Pap's A.M.* (2000).
39. Catherine MacKinnon, *Feminism Unmodified* (Cambridge, MA: Harvard University Press, 1987), 198.
40. The story of this case is told in Anthony Lewis, *Make No Law: The Sullivan Case and the First Amendment* (New York: Random House, 1991).
41. Renata Adler, *Reckless Disregard* (New York: Knopf, 1986).
42. *Tinker v. Des Moines Independent School District* (1969).
43. After Congress passed the Flag Protection Act of 1989 outlawing desecration of the American flag, the Supreme Court also found the act an impermissible infringement on free speech in *United States v. Eichman* (1990).
44. *United States v. O'Brien* (1968).
45. *Greater New Orleans Broadcasting, Inc. v. United States.*
46. *FCC v. Pacifica Foundation* (1978).
47. *Frisby v. Schultz* (1988).
48. *Michigan v. Sitz* (1990).
49. *Indianapolis v. Edmond* (2000).
50. *Nix v. Williams* (1984).
51. *United States v. Leon* (1984).
52. *Arizona v. Evans* (1995).
53. *United States v. Payner* (1980).
54. *Knowles v. Iowa* (1998).
55. On the *Miranda* case, see Liva Baker, *Miranda: The Crime, the Law, the Politics* (New York: Atheneum, 1983).
56. *Arizona v. Fulminante* (1991).
57. The story of Gideon is eloquently told by Anthony Lewis, *Gideon's Trumpet* (New York: Random House, 1964).

58. David Brereton and Jonathan D. Casper, "Does It Pay to Plead Guilty? Differential Sentencing and the Function of the Criminal Courts," *Law and Society Review* 16 (1981–1982): 45–70.
59. *Callins v. Callins* (1994).
60. Woodward and Armstrong, *The Brethren,* 271–284.
61. *Madsen v. Women's Health Center* (1994). In 1997, the Court also upheld a 15-foot buffer zone.
62. *Hill v. Colorado* (2000).
63. *National Organization for Women v. Scheidler* (1994).
64. *Bowen v. American Hospital Association,* 476 U.S. 610 (1985).
65. *Vacco v. Quill* (1997) and *Washington v. Glucksberg* (1997).
66. Though, as Chapter 16 on the judiciary will show, there is indirect accountability.

5 Civil Rights and Public Policy

Chapter Outline

A 42-year-old seamstress named Rosa Parks was riding in the "colored" section of a Montgomery, Ala., city bus on December 1, 1955. A White man got on the bus and found that all the seats in the front, which were reserved for Whites, were taken. He moved on to the equally crowded colored section. J. F. Blake, the bus driver, then ordered all four passengers in the first row of the colored section to surrender their seats because the law prohibited Whites and African Americans from sitting next to or even across from one another.

Three of the African Americans hesitated and then complied with the driver's order. But Rosa Parks, a politically active member of the NAACP, said no. The driver threatened to have her arrested, but still she refused to move. He then called the police, and a few minutes later two officers boarded the bus and arrested her.

At this moment the civil rights movement was born. There had been substantial efforts, and some important successes, to use the

courts to end racial segregation, but Rosa Parks' refusal to give up her seat led to extensive mobilization of African Americans. Protestors employed a wide range of methods to end segregation, including nonviolent resistance. A new preacher in town, Martin Luther King, Jr., of Atlanta, organized a boycott of the city buses. He was jailed, his house was bombed, and his wife and infant daughter were almost killed, but neither he nor the African-American community wavered. Finally, the city relented. On December 21, 1956, Rosa Parks boarded a Montgomery city bus for the first time in over a year. She sat near the front.

Americans have never fully come to terms with equality. Most Americans favor equality in the abstract—a politician who advocated inequality would not attract many votes—yet the concrete struggle for equal rights under the Constitution has been our nation's most bitter battle. It pits person against person, as in the case of Rosa Parks and the nameless White passenger, and group against group. Those people who enjoy privileged positions in American society have been reluctant to give them up.

Individual liberty is central to democracy. So is a broad notion of equality, such as that implied by the concept of "one person, one vote." Sometimes these values conflict, as when individuals or a majority of the people want to act in a discriminatory fashion. How should we resolve such conflicts between liberty and equality? Can we have a democracy if some citizens do not enjoy basic rights to political participation or suffer discrimination in employment? Can we or should we try to remedy past discrimination against minorities and women?

In addition, many people have called on government to protect the rights of minorities and women, increasing the scope and power of government in the process. Ironically, this increase in government power is often used to *check* government, as when the federal courts restrict the actions of state legislatures. It is equally ironic that society's collective efforts to use government to protect civil rights are designed not to limit individualism but to enhance it, freeing people from suffering from prejudice. But how far should government go in these efforts? Is an increase in the scope of government to protect some people's rights an unacceptable threat to the rights of yet other citizens?

The phrase "all men are created equal" is at the heart of American political culture; yet implementing this principle has proved to be one of our nation's most enduring struggles. Throughout our history, issues involving African Americans, women, and other minorities have raised constitutional questions about slavery, segregation, equal pay, and a host of other issues. Their rallying cry has been **civil rights,** which are policies designed to protect people against arbitrary or discriminatory treatment by government officials or individuals.

civil rights

Policies designed to protect people against arbitrary or discriminatory treatment by government officials or individuals.

The resulting controversies have been fought in the courts, Congress, and the bureaucracy, but the meaning of *equality* remains as elusive as it is divisive. Today's equality debates center on these key types of inequality in America:

- *Racial discrimination.* Two centuries of discrimination against racial minorities have produced historic Supreme Court and congressional policies that seek to eliminate racial discrimination from the constitutional fabric. Issues such as the appropriate role of affirmative action programs have yet to be resolved, however.
- *Gender discrimination.* The role of women in American society has changed substantially since the 1700s. However, equal rights for women have yet to be constitutionally guaranteed. The Equal Rights Amendment was not ratified, and women continue to press for equality and to seek protection from sexual harassment.
- *Discrimination based on age, disability, sexual orientation, and other factors.* As America is "graying," older Americans, too, are demanding a place under the civil rights umbrella. People with disabilities are among the newest claimants for civil rights. Also seeking constitutional protections against discrimination are groups such as gays and lesbians, people with AIDS, and the homeless.

Two Centuries of Struggle

The struggle for equality has been a persistent theme in our nation's history. Slaves sought freedom; free African Americans fought for the right to vote and to be treated as equals; women pursued equal participation in society; and the economically disadvantaged called for better treatment and economic opportunities. This fight for equality affects all Americans. Philosophically, the struggle involves defining the term *equality.* Constitutionally, it involves interpreting laws. Politically, it often involves power.

Conceptions of Equality

What does *equality* mean? Jefferson's statement in the Declaration of Independence that "all men are created equal" did not mean that he believed that everybody was exactly alike or that there were no differences among human beings. Jefferson insisted throughout his long life that African Americans were genetically inferior to Whites. The Declaration went on to speak, however, of "inalienable rights" to which all were equally entitled. A belief in *equal rights* has often led to a belief in *equality of opportunity;* in other words, everyone should have the same chance. What individuals make of that equal chance depends on their abilities and efforts.

American society does not emphasize *equal results* or *equal rewards;* few Americans argue that everyone should earn the same salary or have the same amount of property. In some other countries, such as the Scandinavian nations, for example, the government uses its taxing power to distribute resources much more equally than in the United States. These countries thus have much less poverty. On the other hand, critics of these more egalitarian countries often complain that emphasis on the equal distribution of resources stifles initiative and limits opportunity.

Early American Views of Equality

More than 200 years ago, Virginia lawyer Richard Bland proclaimed, "I am speaking of the rights of a people, rights imply equality." Bland's interpretation of the meaning of the American Revolution was not widely shared. Few colonists were eager to defend slavery, and the delegates to the Constitutional Convention did their best to avoid facing the tension between slavery and the principles of the Declaration of Independence. Women's rights got even less attention than slavery at the Convention. John Adams, for instance, was uncharacteristically hostile to his wife Abigail's feminist opinions. Abigail's claim that "if particular care and attention is not paid to the ladies, we are determined to foment a rebellion" prompted her husband to reply, "I cannot but laugh."[1]

Statements like Bland's were ahead of their times in America but were not unheard of elsewhere. The aspirations of people on this side of the Atlantic were similar to those of people on the other side, such as the French, who were soon to start their own revolution with cries of "liberty, equality, fraternity." Whereas in the French Revolution the king lost his head in the name of equality, in the American Revolution the king lost his colonies in the name of independence.

The Constitution and Inequality

Perhaps the presence of conflicting views of equality in eighteenth-century America explains why the word *equality* does not appear in the original Constitution. In addition, America in 1787 was a place far different from contemporary America, with far different values. The privileged delegates to the Constitutional Convention would have been baffled, if not appalled, at discussions of equal rights for 12-year-old children, deaf students, gay soldiers, or female road dispatchers. The delegates created a plan for government, not guarantees of individual rights.

Not even the Bill of Rights mentions equality. It does, however, have implications for equality in that it does not limit the scope of its guarantees to specified groups within society. It does not say, for example, that only Whites have freedom from compulsory self-incrimination or that only men are entitled to freedom of speech. The First Amendment guarantees of freedom of expression, in particular, are important because they allow those who are discriminated against to work toward achieving equality. This kind of political activism, for instance, led to the constitutional amendment that enacted a guarantee of equality, the Fourteenth Amendment.

The first and only place in which the idea of equality appears in the Constitution is in the **Fourteenth Amendment,** one of the three amendments passed after the Civil War. (The Thirteenth abolishes slavery, and the Fifteenth extends the right to vote to African Americans.) The Fourteenth Amendment forbids the states from denying to anyone "equal protection of the laws." Those five words represent the only reference to the idea of equality in the entire Constitution, yet within them was enough force to begin ensuring equal rights for all Americans. The full force of the amendment was not felt for nearly 100 years, for it was not until the mid-twentieth century that the Fourteenth Amendment was used as an instrument for unshackling disadvantaged groups. Once dismissed as "the traditional last resort of constitutional arguments," the equal protection clause now has few rivals in generating legal business for the Supreme Court.

But what does **equal protection of the laws** mean? The Fourteenth Amendment does not say that "the states must treat everybody exactly alike" or that "every state must promote equality among all its people." Presumably, it means, as one member of Congress said during the debate on the amendment, "equal protection of life, liberty, and property" for all. Thus, a state cannot confiscate an African American's property

Fourteenth Amendment

The constitutional amendment adopted after the Civil War that states, "No State shall make or enforce any law which shall abridge the privileges or immunities of citizens of the United States; nor shall any state deprive any person of life, liberty, or property, without due process of law; nor deny to any person within its jurisdiction the **equal protection of the laws.**" See also **due process clause.**

equal protection of the laws

Part of the **Fourteenth Amendment** emphasizing that the laws must provide equivalent "protection" to all people.

The African-American struggle for equality paved the way for civil rights movements by women and other minorities. Here, civil rights leaders Roy Wilkins, James Farmer, Martin Luther King, Jr.,and Whitney Young meet with President Lyndon B. Johnson.

under the law while letting Whites keep theirs, or otherwise give Whites privileges denied to African Americans. Some members of Congress interpreted the clause to be a much more lavish protection of rights than this interpretation. But shortly after the amendment was ratified in 1868, the narrow interpretation won out in the courts. In *Strauder v. West Virginia* (1880), the Supreme Court invalidated a law barring African Americans from jury service, but the Court refused to extend the amendment to remedy more subtle kinds of discrimination.

Over the last 100 years, however, the equal protection clause has become the vehicle for more expansive constitutional interpretations. In order to determine whether a particular form of discrimination is permissible, the Supreme Court developed three levels of scrutiny, or analysis, called standards of review (see Table 5.1). The Court has ruled that most classifications that are *reasonable*—that bear a rational relationship to some legitimate governmental purpose—are constitutional. The person who challenges these classifications has the burden of proving that they are arbitrary. Thus, for example, the states can restrict the right to vote to people over the age of 18; age is a reasonable classification and hence a permissible basis for determining who may vote. A classification that is arbitrary—a law singling out, say, people with red hair or blue eyes for inferior treatment—is invalid.

The Court has also ruled that racial and ethnic classifications are *inherently suspect*. These classifications are presumed to be invalid and are upheld only if they serve a "compelling public interest" and there is no other way to accomplish the purpose of the law. In this case, the burden of proof is on the state. Classifications by race and ethnicity, such as for college admissions, may be acceptable if they are made in laws seeking to remedy previous discrimination. However, as we will see in our discussion of affirmative action, the future of such laws is in doubt.

Classifications based on gender fit *somewhere between* these two extremes; they are presumed neither to be constitutional nor to be unconstitutional. A law that discriminates on the basis of gender must bear a substantial relationship to an important legislative purpose. If these three levels of judicial scrutiny (reasonable, inherently suspect, and somewhere in between) appear confusing, indeed they are—even judges and legal scholars struggle to interpret these standards.

Table 5.1 Supreme Court's Standards for Classifications Under the Equal Protection Clause of the Fourteenth Amendment

BASIS OF CLASSIFICATION	STANDARD OF REVIEW	APPLYING THE TEST
Race	Inherently suspect (difficult to meet)	Is the classification necessary to accomplish a compelling governmental purpose and the least restrictive way to reach the goal?
Gender	Intermediate standard (moderately difficult to meet)	Does the classification bear a substantial relationship to an important governmental goal?
Other (age, wealth, etc.)	Reasonableness (easy to meet)	Does the classification have a rational relationship to a legitimate governmental goal?

Today the equal protection clause is interpreted broadly enough to forbid racial segregation in the public schools, prohibit job discrimination, reapportion state legislatures, and permit court-ordered busing and affirmative action. Conditions for women and minorities would be radically different if it were not for the "equal protection" clause.[2] The next three sections show how equal protection litigation has worked to the advantage of minorities, women, and other groups seeking protection under the civil rights umbrella.

Race, the Constitution, and Public Policy

Throughout American history, African Americans have been the most visible minority group in the United States. These individuals have blazed the constitutional trail for securing equal rights for all Americans. Three eras delineate African Americans' struggle for equality in America: (1) the era of slavery, from the beginnings of colonization until the end of the Civil War in 1865, (2) the era of reconstruction and resegregation, from roughly the end of the Civil War until 1953, and (3) the era of civil rights, roughly from 1954 to the present.

The Era of Slavery

The first African immigrants to America were kidnap victims. Most African Americans lived in slavery for the first 250 years of American settlement. Slaves were the property of their masters. They could be bought and sold, and they could neither vote nor own property. The Southern states, whose plantations required large numbers of unpaid workers, were the primary market for slave labor.

During the slavery era, any public policy of the slave states or the federal government had to accommodate the property interests of slave owners. The Supreme Court got into the act, too, along with the legislative and executive branches (see Table 5.2). The boldest decision supporting slavery was ***Dred Scott v. Sandford*** (1857), wherein Chief Justice Taney bluntly announced that a black man, slave or free, was "chattel" and had no rights under a White man's government and that Congress had no power to ban slavery in the western territories. This decision invalidated the hard-won Missouri Compromise, which allowed Missouri to become a slave state on the condition that northern territories would remain free of slavery. As a result, the *Dred Scott* decision was an important milestone on the road to the Civil War.

The Union victory in the Civil War and the ratification of the **Thirteenth Amendment** ended slavery. The promises implicit in this amendment and the other

Dred Scott v. Sandford
The 1857 Supreme Court decision ruling that a slave who had escaped to a free state enjoyed no rights as a citizen and that Congress had no authority to ban slavery in the territories.

Thirteenth Amendment
The constitutional amendment ratified after the Civil War that forbade slavery and involuntary servitude.

Table 5.2 Toward Racial Equality: Milestones in the Era of Slavery

1600–1865
Slavery takes hold in the South, comes to characterize almost all relations between African Americans and Whites, is constitutionally justified, and finally abolished.

1619	Slaves from Africa are brought to Jamestown and sold to planters.
1776	The Continental army enlists African Americans to fight the British after the British offer freedom to slaves who would fight on their side.
1787	The Constitution provides for a slave to be counted as three-fifths of a person in representation and taxation, and permits Congress to forbid the importation of new slaves after 1808.
1808	Congress prohibits importation of slaves.
1857	The *Dred Scott v. Sandford* decision holds that slaves may not gain freedom by escaping to a free state or territory; it upholds the constitutionality of the slave system.
1862	President Lincoln issues the Emancipation Proclamation.
1865	The Thirteenth Amendment abolishes slavery and involuntary servitude.

two Civil War amendments introduced the era of reconstruction and resegregation in which these promises were first honored and then broken.

The Era of Reconstruction and Resegregation

After the Civil War ended, Congress imposed strict conditions on the former confederate states before they could be readmitted to the Union. No one who had served in secessionist state governments or in the Confederate Army could hold state office; the legislatures had to ratify the new amendments; and the military would govern the states like "conquered provinces" until they complied with the tough federal plans for reconstruction. Many African-American men held state and federal offices during the 10 years following the war. Some government agencies, such as the Freedmen's Bureau, provided assistance to former slaves who were making the difficult transition to independence.

To ensure his election in 1876, Rutherford Hayes promised to pull the troops out of the South and let the old slave states resume business as usual. This done, Southerners lost little time reclaiming power and imposing a code of *Jim Crow laws*, or segregational laws, on African Americans. ("Jim Crow" was the name of a stereotypical African American in a nineteenth-century minstrel song.) These laws relegated African Americans to separate public facilities, separate school systems, and even separate restrooms. Most Whites lost interest in helping former slaves. And what the Jim Crow laws mandated in the South was also common practice in the North. In this era, racial segregation affected every part of life, from the cradle to the grave. African Americans were delivered by African-American physicians or midwives and buried in African-American cemeteries.

Plessy v. Ferguson

An 1896 Supreme Court decision that provided a constitutional justification for segregation by ruling that a Louisiana law requiring "equal but separate accommodations for the White and colored races" was constitutional.

The Supreme Court provided a constitutional justification for segregation in the 1896 case of ***Plessy v. Ferguson.*** The Louisiana legislature required "equal but separate accommodations for the White and colored races" in railroad transportation. Although Homer Plessy was seven-eighths White, he had been arrested for refusing to leave a railway car reserved for Whites. The Court upheld the law, saying that segregation in public facilities was not unconstitutional as long as the separate facilities were substantially equal. In subsequent decisions, the Court paid more attention to the "separate" than to the "equal" part of this principle. For example, Southern states were allowed to maintain high schools and professional schools for Whites even when there were no such schools for African Americans. A measure of segregation in both the South and the North existed as late as the 1960s; nearly all the African-American physicians in the United States were graduates of two medical schools, Howard University in Washington, D.C., and Meharry Medical College in Tennessee.

Nevertheless, some progress on the long road to racial equality was made in the first half of the twentieth century. The Supreme Court and the president began to prohibit a few of the most egregious practices of segregation (see Table 5.3), paving the way for a new era of civil rights.

The Era of Civil Rights

After searching carefully for the perfect case to challenge legal school segregation, the Legal Defense Fund of the National Association for the Advancement of Colored People (NAACP) selected the case of Linda Brown. An African-American student in Topeka, Kans., Brown was required by Kansas law to attend a segregated school. In Topeka, the visible signs of education—teacher quality, facilities, and so on—were substantially equal between African-American and White schools. Thus, the NAACP chose the case in order to test the *Plessy v. Ferguson* doctrine of "separate but equal." The Court would be forced to rule directly on whether school segregation was inherently unequal and thereby violated the Fourteenth Amendment's requirement that states guarantee "equal protection of the laws."

President Eisenhower had just appointed Chief Justice Earl Warren. So important was the case that the Court had already heard one round of arguments before Warren joined the Court. The justices, after hearing the oral arguments, met in the Supreme Court's conference room. Believing that a unanimous decision would have the most impact, the justices negotiated a broad agreement and then determined that Warren himself should write the opinion.

In ***Brown v. Board of Education*** (1954), the Supreme Court set aside its precedent in *Plessy* and held that school segregation was inherently unconstitutional

Brown v. Board of Education

The 1954 Supreme Court decision holding that school segregation in Topeka, Kans., was inherently unconstitutional because it violated the **Fourteenth Amendment's** guarantee of **equal protection.** This case marked the end of legal segregation in the United States.

Table 5.3 Toward Racial Equality: Milestones In The Era Of Reconstruction And Resegregation

1866–1953

Segregation is legally required in the South and sanctioned in the North; lynchings of African Americans occur in the South; civil rights policy begins to appear.

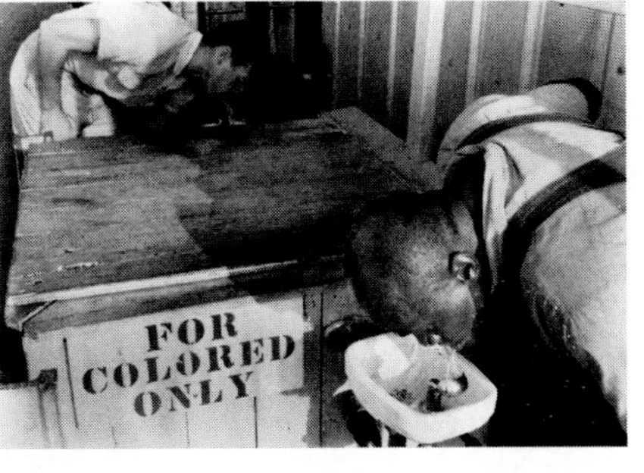

1868 The Fourteenth Amendment makes African Americans U.S. citizens and guarantees "equal protection of the law." This guarantee is widely ignored for nearly a century.

1870 The Fifteenth Amendment forbids racial discrimination in voting, although many states find ways to prevent or discourage African Americans from voting.

1877 End of Reconstruction. African-American gains made in the South (such as antidiscrimination laws) are reversed as former Confederates return to power. Jim Crow laws flourish, making segregation legal.

1883 In the *Civil Rights Cases* the Supreme Court rules that the Fourteenth Amendment does not prohibit discrimination by private businesses and individuals.

1896 The *Plessy v. Ferguson* decision permits "separate but equal" public facilities, providing a constitutional justification for segregation.

1910 The National Association for the Advancement of Colored People (NAACP) is founded by African Americans and Whites.

1915 *Guinn v. United States* bans the grandfather clause that had been used to prevent African Americans from voting.

1941 Executive order forbids racial discrimination in defense industries.

1944 The *Smith v. Allwright* decision bans all-White primaries.

1948 President Truman orders the armed forces desegregated.

1950 *Sweatt v. Painter* finds the "separate but equal" formula generally unacceptable in professional schools.

because it violated the Fourteenth Amendment's guarantee of equal protection. Legal segregation had come to an end.

A year after its decision in *Brown*, the Court ordered lower courts to proceed with "all deliberate speed" to desegregate public schools. Desegregation began, and proceeded slowly in the South, however. A few counties threatened to close their public schools; enrollment in private schools by Whites soared. In 1957, President Eisenhower had to send troops to desegregate Central High School in Little Rock, Ark. In 1969, 15 years after its first ruling that school segregation was unconstitutional and in the face of continued massive resistance, the Supreme Court withdrew its earlier grant of time to school authorities and declared that "Delays in desegregating school systems are no longer tolerable" (*Alexander v. Board of Education*). In 1964, under the Civil Rights Act, Congress prohibited federal aid to schools that remained segregated. Thus, after nearly a generation of modest progress, Southern schools were suddenly integrated (see Figure 5.1).

The Court found that if schools were legally segregated before, authorities had an obligation to overcome past discrimination. This could include the distribution of students and pupils on a racial basis. Some federal judges ordered the busing of students to achieve racially balanced schools, a practice upheld (but not required) by the Supreme Court in *Swann v. Charlotte-Mecklenberg County Schools* (1971).

Not all racial segregation is what is called *de jure* ("by law") segregation. *De facto* ("in reality") segregation results, for example, when children are assigned to schools near their homes, and those homes are in neighborhoods that are racially segregated for social and economic reasons. Sometimes the distinction between *de jure* and *de facto* segregation has been blurred by past official practices. Because minority groups

Why does it matter?

In *Brown v. Board of Education*, the Supreme Court overturned its decision in *Plessy v. Ferguson*. How would your life be different if the Court had upheld segregation in public facilities and services like education?

Figure 5.1 Percentage of Black Students Attending School With any Whites in Southern States[a]

Despite the Supreme Court's decision in *Brown v. Board of Education* in 1954, school integration proceeded at a snail's pace in the South for a decade. Most Southern African-American children entering the first grade in 1955 never attended school with White children. Things picked up considerably in the late 1960s, however, when the Supreme Court insisted that obstruction of implementation of its decision in *Brown* must come to an end.

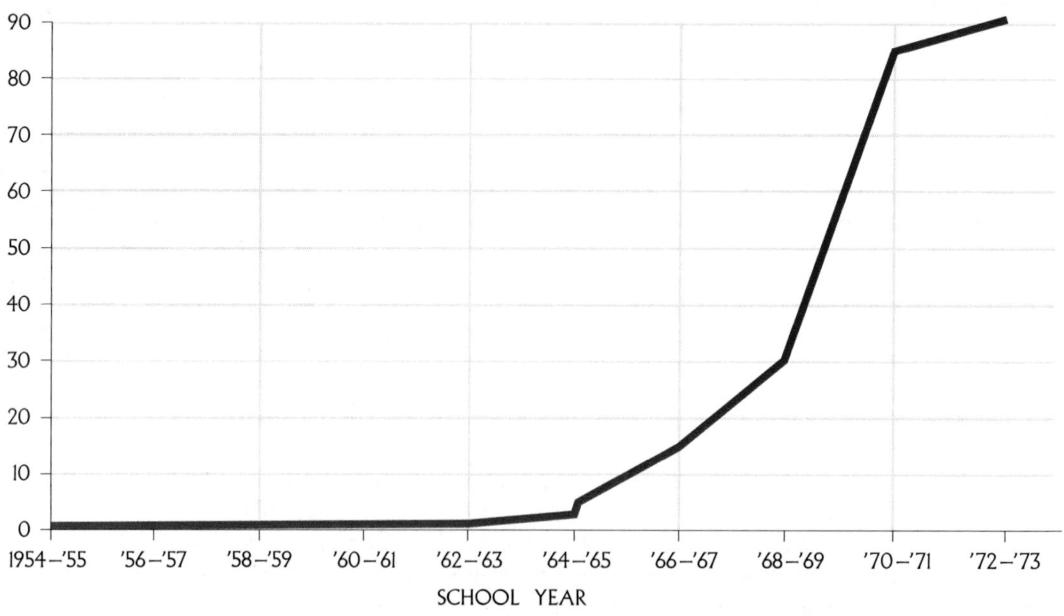

Source: Lawrence Baum, *The Supreme Court,* 6th ed. (Washington, D.C.: Congressional Quarterly, 1998), 233.

[a]Elementary and secondary students in 11 Southern states, including: Virginia, North Carolina, South Carolina, Georgia, Alabama, Mississippi, Louisiana, Texas, Arkansas, Tennessee, and Florida.

On September 25, 1957, troops of the 101st Airborne Division escorted nine African-American children to Central High School in Little Rock, Ark. A court had ordered the school's desegregation in response to *Brown v. Board of Education,* but Arkansas Governor Orville Faubus fought the ruling. President Eisenhower used the National Guard to provide continuing protection for the students.

and federal lawyers demonstrated that Northern schools, too, had purposely drawn district lines to promote segregation, school busing came to the North as well. Denver, Boston, and other cities instituted busing for racial balance, just as Southern cities did.

Busing, one of the least popular remedies for discrimination, has been opposed by majorities of both Whites and African Americans. In recent years, it has become less prominent as a judicial instrument.

Courts do not have the power to order busing between school districts; thus, school districts that are largely composed of minorities must rely on other means to integrate. Kansas City, Mo., spent years and $1.5 billion under federal court orders to attract White students from the city's suburbs, but with limited success. In 1995, in *Missouri v. Jenkins,* the Supreme Court indicated that it would not look favorably on continued federal control of the district.

The civil rights movement organized both African Americans and Whites to end the policies and practices of segregation. As we learned earlier, the movement began in 1955 when Rosa Parks, an African-American woman, refused to give up her seat in a Montgomery, Ala., bus to a White man. This incident prompted a bus boycott led by a local minister, Martin Luther King, Jr., who became the best-known civil rights activist.

Sit-ins, marches, and civil disobedience were key strategies of the civil rights movement, which sought to establish equal opportunities in the political and economic sectors and to end policies that put up barriers between people because of race. The movement's trail was long and sometimes bloody. Its nonviolent marchers were attacked by police dogs in Birmingham, Ala. Other activists were murdered in Meridian, Miss., and Selma, Ala. Fortunately, the goals of the civil rights movement appealed to the national conscience. By the 1970s, overwhelming majorities of White Americans supported racial integration.[3] Today, the principles established in *Brown* have near universal support.

It was the courts, as much as the national conscience, that put civil rights goals on the nation's policy agenda. *Brown v. Board of Education* was only the beginning of a string of Supreme Court decisions holding various forms of discrimination unconstitutional. *Brown* and these other cases gave the civil rights movement momentum that was to grow in the years that followed (see Table 5.4).

As a result of national conscience, the courts, the civil rights movement, and the increased importance of African-American voters, the 1950s and 1960s saw a marked increase in public policies seeking to foster racial equality. These innovations included policies to promote voting rights, access to public accommodations, open housing, and

Table 5.4 Toward Racial Equality: Milestones In The Era Of Civil Rights

1954–2001

Integration becomes a widely accepted goal; the civil rights movement grows, followed by urban racial disorders in the 1960s; African-American voting increases; attention shifts to equal results and affirmative action.

1954	*Brown v. Board of Education* holds that segregated schools are inherently unequal and violate the Fourteenth Amendment's equal protection clause.
1955	Martin Luther King, Jr., leads a bus boycott in Montgomery, Ala.
1957	Federal troops enforce desegregation of a Little Rock, Ark., high school.
1963	Civil rights demonstrators numbering 250,000 march on Washington, D.C.
1964	The Civil Rights Act forbids discrimination in public accommodations and employment.
	The Twenty-fourth Amendment ends the poll tax in federal elections.
1965	The Voting Rights Act sends federal registrars to Southern states and counties to protect African Americans' right to vote and gives registrars the power to impound ballots in order to enforce the act.
	Executive order requires companies with federal contracts to take affirmative action to ensure equal opportunity.
	Riots occur in Watts, Calif., and other cities and reappear every summer in various cities for the next five years.
1966	*Harper v. Virginia* holds that the Fourteenth Amendment forbids making payment of a tax a condition of voting in any election.
1967	Cleveland becomes the first major city to elect an African-American mayor (Carl Stokes).
1968	The *Jones v. Mayer* decision and the Civil Rights Act of 1968 make all racial discrimination in the sale or rental of housing illegal.
	Martin Luther King, Jr. is assassinated.
1971	The *Swann v. Charlotte-Mecklenberg County Schools* decision approves busing as a means of combating state-enforced segregation.
1978	*California Board of Regents v. Bakke* forbids rigid racial quotas for medical school admissions but does not forbid considering race as a factor when deciding admissions.
1979	*United Steelworkers of America v. Weber* permits an affirmative action program to favor African Americans if the program is designed to remedy past discrimination.
	Dayton Board of Education v. Brinkman upholds school busing to remedy Northern school segregation.
1980	Jesse Jackson becomes the first serious African-American candidate for president.
1984	*Grove City College v. Bell* forbids the federal government from withholding all federal funds from a college that refuses to file forms saying that it does not discriminate. (Only a specific program risked its federal funds.)
1988	Congress rewrites the Civil Rights Act to "overturn" the implications of *Grove City College.*
1991	After three years of conflict, Congress enacts the Civil Rights and Women's Equity in Employment Act, which counters the effects of several Supreme Court decisions making it more difficult for workers to bring and win job discrimination suits.
1995	*Adarand Constructors v. Pena* holds that affirmative action programs must undergo strict scrutiny to determine that they are narrowly tailored to serve a compelling governmental interest.

Civil Rights Act of 1964

The law that made racial discrimination against any group in hotels, motels, and restaurants illegal and forbade many forms of job discrimination.

nondiscrimination in many other areas of social and economic life. The **Civil Rights Act of 1964:**

- made racial discrimination illegal in hotels, motels, restaurants, and other places of public accommodation
- forbade discrimination in employment on the basis of race, color, national origin, religion, or gender[4]
- created the Equal Employment Opportunity Commission (EEOC) to monitor and enforce protections against job discrimination
- provided for withholding federal grants from state and local governments and other institutions that practiced racial discrimination
- strengthened voting rights legislation
- authorized the U.S. Justice Department to initiate lawsuits to desegregate public schools and facilities

The Voting Rights Act of 1965 (discussed next) was the most extensive federal effort to crack century-old barriers to African-American voting in the South. The

Open Housing Act of 1968 took steps to forbid discrimination in the sale or rental of housing.

So many congressional and judicial policies were instituted after 1954 that virtually every type of segregation was attacked by a legislative or judicial policy. By the 1980s, few, if any, forms of racial discrimination were left to legislate against. Efforts for legislation were successful, in part, because by the mid-1960s federal laws effectively protected the right to vote, in fact as well as on paper; members of minority groups thus had some power to hold their legislators accountable.

timeline
The Fourteenth Amendment

Getting and Using the Right To Vote

When the Constitution was written, no one thought about extending the right to vote to African Americans (most of whom were slaves) or to women. The early Republic limited **suffrage,** the legal right to vote, to a handful of the population—mostly property-holding White males. Only after the Civil War was the right to vote extended, slowly and painfully, to African-American males and then to other minority groups.

suffrage

The legal right to vote, extended to African Americans by the **Fifteenth Amendment,** to women by the **Nineteenth Amendment,** and to people over the age of 18 by the **Twenty-sixth Amendment.**

The **Fifteenth Amendment,** adopted in 1870, guaranteed African Americans the right to vote—at least in principle. It said, "The right of citizens to vote shall not be abridged by the United States or by any state on account of race, color, or previous condition of servitude." The gap between these words and their implementation, however, remained wide for a full century. States seemed to outdo one another in developing ingenious methods of circumventing the Fifteenth Amendment.

Fifteenth Amendment

The constitutional amendment adopted in 1870 to extend **suffrage** to African Americans.

Oklahoma and other Southern states used a *grandfather clause* to deny African Americans the right to vote. These states required potential voters to complete literacy tests before registering to vote. The grandfather clause, however, exempted persons whose grandfathers were eligible to vote in 1860 from taking these tests. This exemption did not apply, of course, to the grandchildren of slaves, but did allow illiterate

The Voting Rights Act of 1965 produced a major increase in the number of African Americans registered to vote in Southern states. The ability to vote gave African Americans more political clout: In the 20 years following enactment of the law, more than 2,500 African Americans were elected to state and local offices in that region.

Whites to vote. The law was blatantly unfair; it was also unconstitutional, said the Supreme Court in the 1915 decision *Guinn v. United States.*

To exclude African Americans from registering to vote, most Southern states also relied on **poll taxes,** which were small taxes levied on the right to vote that often fell due at a time of year when poor sharecroppers had the least cash on hand. To render African-American votes ineffective, most Southern states also used the **White primary,** a device that permitted political parties in the heavily Democratic South to exclude African Americans from voting in primary elections, thus depriving them of a voice in the most important contests and letting them vote only when it mattered least. The Supreme Court declared White primaries unconstitutional in 1944 in *Smith v. Allwright.*

The civil rights movement put suffrage high on its political agenda; one by one, the barriers to African-American voting fell during the 1960s. Poll taxes in federal elections were prohibited by the **Twenty-fourth Amendment,** which was ratified in 1964. Two years later, the Supreme Court voided poll taxes in state elections in *Harper v. Virginia State Board of Elections.*

Many areas in the South employed fraudulent or sham voter registration tests—requiring literacy or an understanding of the Constitution, for example—in a discriminatory fashion. Voting registrars would declare literate African Americans to be illiterate and thus ineligible to register to vote, while allowing illiterate Whites to register. The **Voting Rights Act of 1965** prohibited any government from using voting procedures that denied a person the vote on the basis of race or color and abolished the use of literacy requirements for anyone who had completed the sixth grade. Federal election registrars were sent to areas with long histories of discrimination, and these same areas had to submit all proposed changes in their voting laws or practices to a federal official for approval. As a result of these provisions, hundreds of thousands of African Americans registered in Southern states.

The effects of these efforts were swift and certain, as the civil rights movement turned from protest to politics.[5] When the Voting Rights Act was passed in 1965, only 70 African Americans held public office in the 11 Southern states. By the early 1980s, more than 2,500 African Americans held elected offices in those states, and the number has continued to grow. There are currently about 12,000 African-American elected officials in the United States.[6]

The Voting Rights Act of 1965 not only secured the right to vote for African Americans but also ensured that their votes would not be diluted through racial gerrymandering (drawing district boundaries to advantage a specific group). For example, majority White districts frequently elected members of a city council in at-large seats (in which council members were elected from the entire city) and prevented a geographically concentrated minority from electing a minority council member. When Congress amended the Voting Rights Act in 1982, it further insisted that minorities be able to "elect representatives of their choice" when their numbers and configuration permitted. Thus, redrawing district boundaries was to avoid discriminatory *results* and not just discriminatory *intent.* In 1986, the Supreme Court upheld this principle in *Thornburg v. Gingles.*

Officials in the Justice Department, which was responsible for enforcing the Voting Rights Act, and state legislatures that drew new district lines interpreted these actions as a mandate to create minority-majority districts. Consequently, when congressional district boundaries were redrawn following the 1990 census, several states, including Florida, North Carolina, Texas, Illinois, New York, and Louisiana, created odd-shaped districts that were designed to give minority-group voters a numerical majority. Fourteen new U.S. House districts were drawn specifically to help elect African Americans to Congress, and six districts were drawn to elect new Hispanic members (these efforts worked, as we will see in Chapter 12).

However, in 1993, the Supreme Court heard a challenge to a North Carolina congressional district that cut in places no wider than a superhighway, with an African-American majority winding snakeline for 160 miles. In its decision in *Shaw v. Reno,* the Court decried the creation of districts based solely on racial composition, as well

poll taxes

Small taxes, levied on the right to vote, that often fell due at a time of year when poor African-American sharecroppers had the least cash on hand. This method was used by most Southern states to exclude African Americans from voting registers. Poll taxes were declared void by the **Twenty-fourth Amendment** in 1964.

White primary

One of the means used to discourage African-American voting that permitted political parties in the heavily Democratic South to exclude African Americans from primary elections, thus depriving them of a voice in the real contests. The Supreme Court declared White primaries unconstitutional in 1941.

Twenty-fourth Amendment

The constitutional amendment passed in 1964 that declared **poll taxes** void in federal elections.

Voting Rights Act of 1965

A law designed to help end formal and informal barriers to African-American **suffrage.** Under the law, hundreds of thousands of African Americans were registered and the number of African-American elected officials increased dramatically.

as the district drawers' abandonment of traditional redistricting standards such as compactness and contiguity. Thus, the Court gave legal standing to challenges to any congressional map with an oddly shaped minority-majority district that may not be defensible on grounds other than race (such as shared community interest or geographical compactness). The next year in *Johnson v. DeGrandy*, the Court ruled that a state legislative redistricting plan does not violate the Voting Rights Act if it does not create the greatest possible number of districts in which minority-group votes would make up a majority.

In 1995 in *Miller v. Johnson*, the Court rejected the efforts of the Department of Justice to achieve the maximum possible number of minority districts. It held that the use of race as a "predominant factor" in drawing district lines should be presumed to be unconstitutional. The next year, in *Bush v. Vera* and *Shaw v. Hunt*, the Supreme Court voided three convoluted districts in Texas and one in North Carolina on the grounds that race had been the primary reason for abandoning compact district lines and that the state legislatures had crossed the line into unconstitutional racial gerrymandering.

In yet another turn, in 1999 the Court declared in *Hunt v. Cromartie* that conscious consideration of race is not automatically unconstitutional if the state's primary motivation was potentially political rather than racial. We can expect continued litigation concerning this question over the next few years in the wake of the 2000 census.

African Americans are not the only racial group that has suffered legally imposed discrimination. Even before the civil rights struggle, Native Americans, Asians, and Hispanics learned how powerless they could become in a society dominated by Whites. The civil rights laws for which African Americans fought have benefited members of these groups as well. In addition, social movements tend to beget new social movements; thus, the African-American civil rights movement of the 1960s spurred other minorities to mobilize to protect their rights.

Why does it matter?

In passing the Voting Rights Act of 1965, Congress enacted an extraordinarily strong law to protect the rights of minorities to vote. How would America be different if the law had not been passed? Would officials in your state pay as much attention to minorities? Would as many members of minority groups be elected to high public office in your state?

Other Minority Groups

As we discuss in Chapter 6, America is heading toward a *minority majority*: a situation in which minority groups will outnumber Caucasians of European descent. As of 2001 African Americans are no longer the largest minority group in the United States. Yet many of these other groups—Native Americans, Hispanics, and Asians—have been affected by the African-American civil rights movement of the 1960s.

Native Americans. The earliest inhabitants of the continent, the American Indians, are, of course, the oldest minority group. Nearly 2 million people identify themselves as Native Americans. The history of poverty, discrimination, and exploitation experienced by American Indians is a long one. Not until 1924 were American Indians made citizens of the United States, a status that African Americans had achieved a half-century before. Not until 1946 did Congress establish the Indian Claims Act to settle financial disputes arising from lands taken from the American Indians.[7] Today, most Native Americans still live in poverty and ill health, almost half on or near a reservation. American Indians know, perhaps better than any other group, the significance of the gap between public policy and private realization regarding discrimination.

But progress is being made. The civil rights movement of the 1960s created a more favorable climate for Native Americans to secure guaranteed access to the polls, to housing, and to jobs and to reassert their treaty rights. The Indian Bill of Rights was adopted as Title II of the Civil Rights Act of 1968, applying most of the provisions of the Constitution's Bill of Rights to tribal governments. In *Santa Clara Pueblo v. Martinez* (1978), the Supreme Court strengthened the tribal power of individual tribe members and furthered self-government by Indian tribes.

American Indian activists such as Dennis Means of the American Indian Movement (AIM), Vine Deloria, and Dee Brown drew attention to the plight of the

American Indian tribes. Several Native Americans seized Alcatraz Island in San Francisco Bay in 1969 to protest the loss of Indian lands. In 1973, armed members of AIM seized 11 hostages at Wounded Knee, S.D.—the site of an 1890 massacre of 200 Sioux (Lakota) by U.S. cavalry—and remained there for 71 days until the federal government agreed to examine Indian treaty rights. Ben Nighthorse Campbell was elected a U.S. senator from Colorado in 1992, the first Native American elected to Congress.

Equally important, Indians began to use the courts to protect their rights. The Native American Rights Fund (NARF), founded in 1970, has won important victories concerning hunting, fishing, and land rights. Native Americans are also retaining access to their sacred places and have had some success in stopping the building of roads and buildings on ancient burial grounds or other sacred spots. Several tribes have won court cases protecting them from taxation of tribal profits.

As in other areas of civil rights, the preservation of Native American culture and the exercise of Native American rights sometimes conflict with the interests of the majority. For example, there is conflict over special rights that some tribes have to fish and even hunt whales. Anglers concerned with the depletion of fishing stock and environmentalists worried about the loss of whale population have voiced protests. Similarly, Native American rights to run businesses denied to others by state law and to avoid taxation on tribal lands have made running gambling casinos a lucrative option for Indians. This has irritated both those who oppose gambling and those who are offended by the tax-free competition.

Hispanic Americans. Hispanic Americans (or Latinos, as some prefer to be called)—chiefly from Mexico, Puerto Rico, and Cuba but also from El Salvador, Honduras, and other countries in Central America—have displaced African Americans as the largest minority group. Today they compose about 13 percent of the U.S. population.

The first major efforts on behalf of civil rights for Hispanics date only from the mid-1960s. Hispanic leaders drew from the tactics of the African-American civil rights movement and sit-ins, boycotts, marches, and related activities to draw attention to their cause. Inspired by the NAACP's Legal Defense Fund, they also created the Mexican American Legal Defense and Education Fund (MALDEF) in 1968 to help argue their cause in court. In addition, Hispanic groups began mobilizing in other ways to protect their interests. An early prominent example was the United Farm Workers, led by Cesar Chavez, who publicized the plight of migrant workers, a large proportion of whom are Hispanic.

The growing numbers of Hispanic Americans will soon make them the largest minority group in the United States. Their political power is reflected in Mel Martinez's selection for President George W. Bush's cabinet and in the 19 members of the U.S. House of Representatives, such as Loretta Sanchez of California.

One of the low points in the protection of civil rights in the United States occurred during World War II when more than 100,000 Americans of Japanese descent were moved to internment camps.

Like Native Americans, Hispanic Americans benefit from the nondiscrimination policies originally passed to protect African Americans. Provisions of the Voting Rights Act of 1965 covered San Antonio, Texas, and thereby permitted Hispanic voters to lend weight to the election of Mayor Henry Cisneros. There are now about 6,000 elected Hispanic officials in the United States,[8] and Hispanic Americans play a prominent role in the politics of such major cities as Houston, Miami, Los Angeles, and San Diego. In 1973, Hispanics won a victory when the Supreme Court found that multimember electoral districts (in which more than one person represents a single district) in Texas discriminated against minority groups because they decreased the probability of a minority being elected.[9] Nevertheless, poverty, discrimination, and language barriers continue to depress Hispanic voter registration and turnout.

participation
Statehood for Puerto Rico and the District of Colombia

Asian Americans. Asian Americans are the fastest growing minority group; their representation in the American population rose from 0.5 percent to 4 percent from 1960 to 2000. Asian Americans suffered discrimination in education, jobs, and housing, as well as restrictions on immigration and naturalization for more than a hundred years prior to the civil rights acts of the 1960s. Discrimination was especially egregious during World War II when the U.S. government, beset by fears of a Japanese invasion of the Pacific Coast, rounded up more than 100,000 Americans of Japanese descent and herded them into encampments. These internment camps were, critics claimed, America's concentration camps. The Supreme Court, however, in ***Korematsu v. United States*** (1944), upheld the internment as constitutional. Congress has since authorized benefits to the former internees. Today, Americans of Chinese, Japanese, Korean, Vietnamese, and other Asian cultures have assumed prominent positions in U.S. society.

Korematsu v. United States
A 1944 Supreme Court decision that upheld as constitutional the internment of more than 100,000 Americans of Japanese descent in encampments during World War II.

The struggle for equal rights has not been limited to racial minorities, however. Political activity on behalf of women has been so energetic and so far-reaching that a separate section is needed to examine this struggle for equality.

Women, the Constitution, and Public Policy

Abigail Adams may have been practically alone in her feminist views in the 1770s, but the next century brought significant feminist activity. The first women's rights activists were products of the abolitionist movement, where they often encountered sexist opposition. Two of these women, Lucretia Mott and Elizabeth Cady Stanton, organized a meeting at Seneca Falls in upstate New York. They had much to discuss. Not only were women denied the vote, but they were also subjected to patriarchal (male-dominated) family law and denied education and career opportunities. The legal doctrine known as *coverture* deprived married women of any identity separate from that of their husbands; wives could not sign contracts or dispose of property. Divorce law was heavily biased in favor of husbands. Even abused women found it almost impossible to end their marriages, and men had the legal advantage in securing custody of the children.

The Battle for the Vote

On July 19, 1848, 100 men and women signed the Seneca Falls Declaration of Sentiments and Resolutions. Patterned after the Declaration of Independence, it proclaimed, "The history of mankind is a history of repeated injuries and usurpations on the part of man toward woman, having in direct object the establishment of an absolute tyranny over her." Thus began the movement that would culminate in the ratification of the **Nineteenth Amendment** 72 years later, giving women the vote. Charlotte Woodward, 19 years old in 1848, was the only signer of the Seneca Falls Declaration who lived to vote for the president in 1920.

Nineteenth Amendment

The constitutional amendment adopted in 1920 that guarantees women the right to vote. See also **suffrage.**

The battle for women's suffrage was fought mostly in the late nineteenth and early twentieth centuries. Leaders like Stanton and Susan B. Anthony were prominent in the cause, which emphasized the vote but also addressed women's other grievances. The suffragists had considerable success in the states, especially in the West. Several states allowed women to vote before the constitutional amendment passed. The feminists lobbied, marched, protested, and even engaged in civil disobedience.[10]

The "Doldrums": 1920–1960

Winning the right to vote did not automatically win equal status for women. In fact, the feminist movement seemed to lose rather than gain momentum after winning the vote, perhaps because the vote was about the only goal on which all feminists agreed. There was considerable division within the movement on other priorities.

Many suffragists accepted the traditional model of the family. Fathers were breadwinners, mothers bread bakers. Although most suffragists thought that women should have the opportunity to pursue any occupation they chose, many also believed that women's primary obligations revolved around the roles of wife and mother. Many suffragists had defended the vote as basically an extension of the maternal role into public life, arguing that a new era of public morality would emerge when women could vote. These *social feminists* were in tune with prevailing attitudes.

Public policy toward women continued to be dominated by protectionism rather than by the principle of equality. Laws protected working women from the burdens of overtime work, long hours on the job, and heavy lifting. The fact that these laws also protected male workers from female competition received little attention. State laws tended to reflect—and reinforce—the traditional family roles. These laws concentrated on limiting women's work opportunities outside the home so that they could concentrate on their duties within it. In most states, husbands were legally required to support their families (even after a divorce) and to pay child support, though divorced fathers did not always pay. When a marriage ended, mothers almost always got custody of the children, although husbands had the legal advantage in custody battles. Public policy was designed to preserve traditional motherhood and hence, supporters claimed, to protect the family and the country's moral fabric.[11]

Making a Difference

Sally Reed

Sally and Cecil Reed adopted a son, Richard Lynn Reed. Sally and Cecil separated, and on March 29, 1967, Richard died in Ada County, Idaho. Richard was a minor without a will. Approximately seven months after Richard's death, Sally filed a petition in the probate court seeking appointment as administrator of her son's estate, which she estimated as consisting of a few items of personal property and a small savings account. Shortly thereafter, Cecil filed a competing petition seeking to have himself appointed administrator of his son's estate.

The probate court held a hearing and then named Cecil to be administrator of Richard's estate because Idaho law stated specifically that "males must be preferred to females" in cases where the parents otherwise had equal claims. In reaching the conclusion, the probate judge gave no indication that he had attempted to determine the relative capabilities of Sally and Cecil to administer Richard's estate. The decision was made without regard to their individual qualifications.

The total value of the estate was less than $1,000, but there was a principle at stake. Sally Reed appealed the probate court order all the way to the U.S. Supreme Court. Along the way she picked up some vital support. The American Civil Liberties Union's new National Women's Rights Project handled her case before the high court. A Columbia University law professor named Ruth Bader Ginsburg, who would join the Court as an associate justice 22 years later, headed the project.

In 1971 Chief Justice Warren Burger delivered the unanimous opinion of the Court. The historic decision in *Reed v. Reed* found that the arbitrary preference established in favor of males in the Idaho law violated the Equal Protection Clause of the Fourteenth Amendment. This was the first time that any law had been voided on the basis of gender discrimination.

Following the decision, telegrams and congratulations from women poured in on Mrs. Reed, who was soon contending with a lawn full of reporters. "We never dreamed it would go this far," she said of the case's modest origins. "I just cared about the principle of the thing.... Instead of complaining about the way things are, we've got to go into the courts and get them changed." The Supreme Court is a long way from Ada County. Yet the struggle of one woman for equal rights established an essential milestone on the path to gender equality in the United States.

Source: "First No to Sex Bias," *Time*, December 6, 1971, p. 71.

Only a minority of feminists challenged these assumptions. Alice Paul, the author of the original **Equal Rights Amendment (ERA),** was one activist who claimed that the real result of protectionist law was to perpetuate gender inequality. Simply worded, the ERA reads, "Equality of rights under the law shall not be denied or abridged by the United States or by any state on account of sex." Most people saw the ERA as a threat to the family when it was introduced in Congress in 1923. It gained little support. In fact, women were less likely to support the amendment than men were.

Equal Rights Amendment

A constitutional amendment originally introduced in Congress in 1923 and passed by Congress in 1978, stating that "equality of rights under the law shall not be denied or abridged by the United States or by any state on account of sex." Despite public support, the amendment failed to acquire the necessary support from three-fourths of the state legislatures.

The Second Feminist Wave

The civil rights movement of the 1950s and 1960s attracted many female activists, some of whom also joined student and antiwar movements. These women often met with the same prejudices as had women abolitionists. Betty Friedan's book *The Feminine Mystique*, published in 1963, encouraged many women to question traditional assumptions and to assert their own rights. Groups such as the National Organization for Women (NOW) and the National Women's Political Caucus were organized in the 1960s and 1970s.

Before the advent of the contemporary feminist movement, the Supreme Court upheld virtually any instance of gender-based discrimination. The state and federal governments could discriminate against women—and, indeed, men—as they chose. In the 1970s, the Court began to take a closer look at gender discrimination. In ***Reed v. Reed*** (1971), the Court ruled that any "arbitrary" gender-based classification violated the equal protection clause of the Fourteenth Amendment (see "Making a Difference: Sally Reed"). This was the first time the Court declared any law unconstitutional on the basis of gender

Reed v. Reed

The landmark case in 1971 in which the Supreme Court for the first time upheld a claim of gender discrimination.

Table 5.5 Toward Gender Equality: Public Policy Milestones

1969–2001	
1969	Executive order declares that offering equal opportunities for women at every level of federal service is to be national policy and establishes a program for implementing the policy.
1971	In *Reed v. Reed,* the Supreme Court invalidates a state law preferring men to women in court selection of an estate's administrator.
1972	Provisions of Title VII of the Civil Rights Act of 1964 are extended to cover the faculty and professional staffs of colleges and universities.
	The Education Act forbids gender discrimination in public schools (with some exceptions for historically single-gender schools).
	The ERA is proposed by Congress and sent to the states for ratification.
1974	A woman—Ella Grasso of Connecticut—is elected governor for the first time without succeeding her husband to the office.
1975	Congress opens armed services academies to women.
1976	Courts strike down an Oklahoma law setting different legal drinking ages for men and women.
1977	Supreme Court voids arbitrary height and weight requirements for employees in *Dothard v. Rawlinson.*
1978	The deadline for ratification of the ERA is extended.
	Congress passes the Pregnancy Discrimination Act.
1981	The Supreme Court rules that males-only military draft registration is constitutional.
	Sandra Day O'Connor becomes the first woman Supreme Court Justice.
1982	The ERA ratification deadline passes without ratification of the amendment.
1984	Geraldine Ferraro is nominated as the first woman vice-presidential candidate of a major party.
1988	The Supreme Court unanimously upholds a 1984 New York City law aimed primarily at requiring the admission of women to large, private clubs that play an important role in professional life.
1991	After three years of conflict, Congress enacts the Civil Rights and Women's Equity in Employment Act, which counters the effects of several Supreme Court decisions making it more difficult for workers to bring and win job discrimination suits.
1992	California becomes the first state to be represented by two female U.S. senators.
1993	Supreme Court in *Harris v. Forklift Systems* lowers the threshold for proving sexual harassment in the workplace.
1994	48 women elected to U.S. House and 8 to the Senate, the most in history.
1996	In *United States v. Virginia et al.*, the Supreme Court declares categorical exclusion of women from state-funded colleges unconstitutional.
1997	Madeline Albright appointed Secretary of State, the first woman to serve in that role.

Craig v. Boren

In this 1976 ruling, the Supreme Court established the "medium scrutiny" standard for determining gender discrimination.

discrimination. Five years later, ***Craig v. Boren*** established a "medium scrutiny" standard: Gender discrimination would be presumed to be neither valid nor invalid. The courts were to show less deference to gender classifications than to more routine classifications, but more deference than to racial classifications. Table 5.5 lists important policy milestones on gender equality.

The Supreme Court has struck down many laws and rules for discriminating on the basis of gender. For example, the Court voided laws giving husbands exclusive control over family property.[12] The Court also voided employers' rules that denied women equal monthly retirement benefits because they live longer than men.[13]

In fact, many of the litigants in cases raising constitutional questions about gender discrimination have been men seeking equality with women in their treatment under the law. For example, the Court has voided laws that

- provided for alimony payments to women only (*Orr v. Orr,* 1979)
- closed a state's nursing school to men (*Mississippi v. Hogan,* 1982)
- set a higher age for drinking for men than for women (*Craig v. Boren,* 1976)
- set a higher age for reaching legal adult status for men than for women (*Stanton v. Stanton,* 1975)

Men have not always prevailed in their efforts for equal treatment, however. The Court upheld a statutory rape law applying only to men[14] and the male-only draft, which we will discuss shortly. The Court also allowed a Florida law giving property tax exemptions only to widows, not to widowers.[15]

Contemporary feminists have suffered defeats as well as victories. The ERA was revived when Congress passed it in 1972 and extended the deadline for ratification until 1982. Nevertheless, the ERA was three states short of ratification when time ran out. Paradoxically, the defeat of the ERA had just the opposite effect of that which the 1920 suffrage victory had on feminism. Far from weakening the movement, losing the ERA battle has stimulated vigorous feminist activity. Proponents have vowed to keep reintroducing the amendment in Congress (without success so far) and continue to press hard for state and federal action on women's rights.

Women in the Workplace

One reason why feminist activism persists has nothing to do with ideology or other social movements. The family pattern that traditionalists sought to preserve—father at work, mother at home—is becoming a thing of the past. The female civilian labor force amounts to 65 million (as compared to 75 million males), representing 60 percent of adult women. Sixty–two percent of these women are married. There are also 30 million female-headed households (8 million of which include children), and about two-thirds of American mothers who have children below school age are in the labor force.[16] As conditions have changed, public opinion and public policy demands have changed, too. Protectionism is not dead. Women still assume more duties inside the home than men do, and debates over policies like the "mommy track" (reduced work responsibilities for women workers with children) parental leaves to women reflect this social phenomenon. Demands for equality, however, keep nudging protectionism into the background.

Congress has made some important progress, especially in the area of employment. The Civil Rights Act of 1964 banned gender discrimination in employment. The protection of this law has been expanded several times. For example, in 1972, Congress gave the Equal Employment Opportunity Commission (EEOC) the power to sue employers suspected of illegal discrimination. Title IX of the Education Act of 1972 forbade gender discrimination in federally subsidized education programs, including athletics. The Pregnancy Discrimination Act of 1978 made it illegal for employers to exclude pregnancy and childbirth from their sick leave and health benefits plans. The Civil Rights and Women's Equity in Employment Act of 1991 shifted the burden of proof in justifying hiring and promotion practices to employers, who must show that employment practices are related to job performance and that they are consistent with "business necessity" (an ambiguous term, however).

The Supreme Court also weighed in against gender discrimination in employment and business activity. In 1977, it voided laws and rules barring women from jobs through arbitrary height and weight requirements (*Dothard v. Rawlinson*). Any such prerequisites must be directly related to the duties required in a particular position. Women have also been protected from being required to take mandatory pregnancy leaves from their jobs[17] and from being denied a job because of an employer's concern for harming a developing fetus.[18] Many commercial contacts are made in private business and service clubs, which often have excluded women from membership. The Court has upheld state and city laws that prohibit such discrimination.[19]

Education is closely related to employment. Title IX of the Education Act of 1972 forbids gender discrimination in federally subsidized education programs (which include almost all colleges and universities). But what about single-gender schooling? In 1996, the Supreme Court declared that Virginia's categorical exclusion of women from education opportunities at the state-funded Virginia Military Institute (VMI) violated women's rights to equal protection of the law.[20] A few days later, The Citadel, the nation's only other state-supported all-male college, announced that it would also admit women.

Women have made substantial progress in their quest for equality, but debate continues as Congress considers new laws. Three of the most controversial issues that

Why does it matter?

Women have made substantial gains in entering careers formerly occupied almost entirely by men. Have your employment opportunities changed as a result of the laws and Supreme Court decisions striking down barriers to employment for women?

As women have become more active in politics, they have begun to assume more leadership roles. Here, Dianne Feinstein and Barbara Boxer celebrate their 1992 victories in the U.S. Senate races in California, marking the first time a state has been represented in the Senate by two female senators.

legislators will continue to face are wage discrimination, the role of women in the military, and sexual harassment.

Wage Discrimination and Comparable Worth

Traditional women's jobs often pay much less than men's jobs that demand comparable skill; a female secretary often earns far less than a male accounts clerk with the same qualifications. Median annual earnings for full-time women workers are only about three-fourths of those of men.[21]

In 1983, the Washington State Supreme Court ruled that its state government had discriminated against women for years by denying them equal pay for jobs of **comparable worth.** The U.S. Supreme Court has remained silent so far on the merits of this issue. The executive branch under Ronald Reagan consistently opposed the idea of comparable worth. The late Clarence Pendleton, Reagan's appointee as head of the U.S. Civil Rights Commission, argued that lawsuits based on comparable worth would interfere with the free market for wages by reducing incentives for women to seek higher-paying, traditionally male jobs. Pendleton called comparable worth "the craziest idea since Looney Tunes." Ridicule has not made this serious dispute go away, however.

comparable worth

The issue raised when women who hold traditionally female jobs are paid less than men for working at jobs requiring comparable skill.

Women in the Military

Military service is another controversial aspect of gender equality. Women have served in every branch of the armed services since World War II. Originally, they served in separate units such as the WACS (Women's Army Corps), the WAVES (Women Accepted for Volunteer Emergency Service in the navy), and the Nurse Corps. The military had a 2 percent quota for women (which was never filled) until the 1970s. Now women are part of the regular service. They make up 11 percent of the armed forces (14 percent of the army), and compete directly with men for promotions.

Congress opened all the service academies to women in 1975. Women have done well, including graduating first at the U.S. Naval Academy in Annapolis and serving as First Captain of the Corps of Cadets at West Point.

Two important differences between the treatment of men and that of women persist in military service. First, only men must register for the draft when they turn 18 (see "You Are the Judge: Is Male-Only Draft Registration Gender Discrimination?"). Second, statutes and regulations also prohibit women from serving in combat. A breach exists between policy and practice, however, as the Persian Gulf War showed. Women piloted helicopters at the front and helped to operate antimissile systems; some were taken as prisoners of war. Women are now permitted to serve as combat pilots in the navy and air force and to serve on navy warships. However, they are still not permitted to serve in ground combat units in the army or marines.

These actions have reopened the debate over whether women should serve in combat. Some experts insist that because women, on the average, have less upper-body strength than men, they are less suited for combat. Others argue that men will not be able to fight effectively beside wounded or dying women. Critics of these views point out that some women surpass some men in upper-body strength and that we do not know how well men and women will fight together. This debate is not only a controversy about ability; it also touches on the question of whether engaging in combat is a burden or a privilege. Clearly some women—and some who would deny them combat duty—take the latter view.

Sexual Harassment

Whether in the military, on the assembly line, or in the office, women have voiced concern about sexual harassment for years, which, of course, does not affect only women. In 1986, the Supreme Court articulated this broad principle: Sexual harassment that is so pervasive as to create a hostile or abusive work environment is

In the past few years, women have overcome many obstacles to serving in the military, performing well in a variety of nontraditional roles such as piloting helicopters.

You Are the Judge

Is Male-Only Draft Registration Gender Discrimination?

There is no military conscription at present (the United States has had a volunteer force since 1973), but President Jimmy Carter asked Congress to require both men and women to register for the draft after the Soviet Union invaded Afghanistan in 1979. Registration was designed to facilitate any eventual conscription. In 1980, Congress reinstated registration for men only, a policy that was not universally popular. Federal courts ordered registration suspended while several young men filed a suit. These men argued that the registration requirement was gender-based discrimination that violated the due process clause of the Fifth Amendment.

You Be the Judge: Does requiring only males to register for the draft unconstitutionally discriminate against them?

Answer: The Supreme Court displayed its typical deference to the elected branches in the area of national security when it ruled in 1981 in *Rostker v. Goldberg* that male-only registration did not violate the Fifth Amendment. The Court found that male-only registration bore a substantial relationship to Congress's goal of ensuring combat readiness and that Congress acted well within its constitutional authority to raise and regulate armies and navies when it authorized the registration of men and not women. Congress, the Court said, was allowed to focus on the question of military need, rather than "equity."

a form of gender discrimination, which is forbidden by the 1964 Civil Rights Act.[22] In 1993, in *Harris v. Forklift Systems*, the Court reinforced its decision. No single factor, the Court said, is required to win a sexual harassment case under Title VII of the 1964 Civil Rights Act. The law is violated when the workplace environment "would reasonably be perceived, and is perceived, as hostile or abusive." Thus, workers are not required to prove that the workplace environment is so hostile as to cause them "severe psychological injury" or that they are unable to perform their jobs. The protection of federal law comes into play before the harassing conduct leads to psychological difficulty.

In 1998 the Supreme Court again spoke expansively about sexual harassment in the workplace. In *Faragher v. City of Boca Raton* the Court made it clear that employers are responsible for preventing and eliminating harassment at work. They can be held liable for even those harassing acts of supervisory employees that violate clear policies and of which top management has no knowledge. In *Burlington Industries, Inc. v. Ellreth*, the Court found that an employee could sue for sexual harassment even without being able to show job-related harm. Victims must have availed themselves of effective complaint policies and other protection offered by the company first, however. The Court also made it clear that the law also prevents sexual harassment by people of the same gender (*Oncale v. Sundower Offshore Services*).

In 1999, the Court turned its attention to sexual harassment in public schools. It held that school districts can be held liable for sexual harassment in cases of student-on-student harassment where the school district has knowledge of the harassment or is deliberately indifferent to it. The harassment must be so severe, pervasive, and objectively offensive that it can be said to deprive the victims of access to the educational opportunities or benefits provided by the school (*Davis v. Monroe County Board of Education*).

Sexual harassment can occur anywhere but may be especially prevalent in male-dominated occupations such as the military. A 1991 convention of the Tailhook Association, an organization of naval aviators, made the news after reports surfaced of drunken sailors jamming a hotel hallway and sexually assaulting female guests, including naval officers, as they stepped off the elevator. After the much-criticized initial failure of the navy to identify the officers responsible for the assault, heads rolled, including those of several admirals and the secretary of the navy. In 1996 and 1997, a number of army officers and noncommissioned officers had their careers ended, and some went to prison, for sexual harassment of female soldiers in training situations. Behavior that was once viewed as simply male high jinks is now recognized as intolerable.

The push for gender equality is a worldwide phenomenon (see "America in Perspective: Mrs. In-the-Back-of-the-House Goes to Parliament"). Many women are asserting their civil rights for the first time.

comparative
Comparing Civil Rights

Newly Active Groups Under the Civil Rights Umbrella

Racial and ethnic minorities and women are not the only Americans who can claim civil rights; policies enacted to protect one or two groups can be applied to others. Four recent entrants into the civil rights arena are aging Americans, young Americans, people with disabilities, and homosexuals. All these groups claim equal rights, as racial minorities and women do, but represent different challenges to mainstream America.

Civil Rights and the Graying of America

America is aging rapidly. People in their 80s make up the fastest growing age group in this country. John Glenn, a 77-year-old senator from Ohio, made history in October 1998 as the oldest person in space when he accompanied a crew of six other astronauts aboard the space shuttle Discovery.

When the Social Security program began in the 1930s, 65 was the retirement age. Although this age was apparently chosen arbitrarily, it soon became the mandatory retirement age for many workers. Although many workers might prefer to retire while they are still healthy and active enough to enjoy leisure, not everyone wants or can

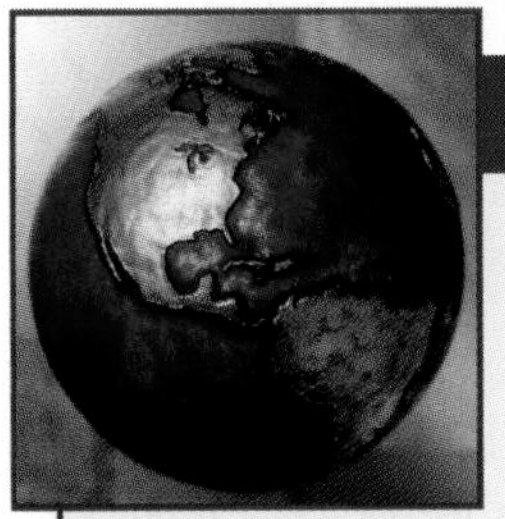

America in Perspective

Mrs. In-the-Back-of-the-House Goes to Parliament

In Japan, married women are often supposed to stay at home to clean the house and raise the children. In fact, the Japanese word for wife means "Mrs. In-the-Back-of-the-House." There are even legal incentives to encourage married women to quit full-time jobs, and a married couple is legally required to use the same last name—almost always the husband's.

Such an environment presents immense obstacles for women to overcome in order to transform themselves into a meaningful force in Japanese politics. Women find it difficult to be taken seriously by voters, facing prejudice such as that reflected in one male candidate's taunt, "Women can't do anything. They should just shut up." Many of the women who are elected to Parliament are actresses or other celebrities.

Thus, we should not be surprised that in the Japanese Parliament elected in 1996, women composed only 4 percent of the more powerful lower house. (In the United States, as we discuss in Chapter 12, women constitute 13 percent of the Senate and 14 percent of the House.) Most of the women who are elected represent opposition parties and thus have little influence.

Despite these cultural barriers, women in Japan are making progress. The number of women in local town and county assemblies has increased over the last decade, bringing attention to issues such as environmental and food safety. It remains to be seen whether the base in local government will be sufficient to propel more women into positions of power at the national level.

Source: From Sherly WuDunn, "23 Women Break Into a Male Citadel," in the *New York Times*, October 26, 1996, 4.

afford to do so. Social Security is not, and was never meant to be, an adequate income, and not all workers have good pension plans.

Although many elderly people wished to work, employers routinely refused to hire people over a certain age. Graduate and professional schools often rejected applicants in their 30s on the grounds that their professions would get fewer years, and thus less return, out of them. This policy had a severe impact on housewives and veterans who wanted to return to school.

As early as 1967, Congress banned some kinds of age discrimination. In 1975, civil rights law denied federal funds to any institution discriminating against people over the age of 40 because of their age. The Age Discrimination in Employment Act was amended in 1978 to raise the general compulsory retirement age to 70. Now compulsory retirement has been phased out altogether. No one knows what other directions the *gray liberation movement* may take as its members approach the status of a minority majority. In 1976 the Supreme Court, however, declared that it would not place age in the suspect classification category when it upheld a state law requiring police officers to retire at the age of 50. Age classifications would fall under the rational basis test.[23]

Job bias is often hidden, and proving it depends on inference and circumstantial evidence. The Supreme Court made it easier to win cases of job bias in 2000 when it held in *Reeves v. Sanderson* that a plaintiff's evidence of an employer's bias, combined with sufficient evidence to find that the employer's asserted justification is false, may permit juries and judges to conclude that an employer unlawfully discriminated. Thus, employees can win lawsuits without direct evidence of an employer's illegal intent. The impact of the decision is likely to extend beyond questions of age discrimination to the litigation of race and gender discrimination cases brought under Title VII of the Civil Rights Act of 1964 as well as cases brought under the Americans With Disabilities Act.

Are the Young a Disadvantaged Group, Too?

Older Americans are not the only victims of age discrimination. The young, too, have suffered from inferior treatment under the law. The case discussed in Chapter 4 in which the Supreme Court declared that a high school newspaper was not a public forum and thus could be regulated by school officials[24] is one example of such treatment. Will there soon be an autonomous children's rights movement? There are obvious difficulties in organizing such a movement, but these obstacles do not mean that young people are silent in asserting their rights.

Walter Polovchak of Chicago is one example. In 1980, when Walter was 12, his family emigrated from the Ukraine. His parents, quickly disillusioned, decided to return. Walter, however, wanted to stay in Chicago; he ran away to live with relatives in the area. The law was on his parents' side; so were groups such as the American Civil Liberties Union. Court after court ordered the boy returned to his parents. But what Shakespeare called "the law's delay" was Walter's best ally. When he reached his eighteenth birthday and was no longer answerable to his parents, he was still in Chicago. He remains there today, an American citizen.[25]

In 1992, a precocious 12-year-old boy in Florida went to court and "divorced" his family so that he could be adopted by foster parents. Several similar cases followed, guaranteeing that children's rights will continue to occupy legal scholars.

Civil Rights and People With Disabilities

Americans with disabilities have suffered from both direct and indirect discrimination. They have often been denied rehabilitation services (a kind of affirmative action), education, and jobs. Many people with disabilities have been excluded from the workforce and isolated without overt discrimination. Throughout most of

Americans with disabilities are among the successors to the 1960s civil rights activists. In recent years they have been active in demanding government benefits.

American history, public and private buildings have been hostile to the blind, deaf, and mobility-impaired. Stairs, buses, telephones, and other necessities of modern life have been designed in ways that keep these individuals out of offices, stores, and restaurants. As one slogan said, "Once, blacks had to ride at the back of the bus. We can't even get on the bus."

The first rehabilitation laws were passed in the late 1920s, mostly to help veterans of World War I. Accessibility laws had to wait another 50 years. The Rehabilitation Act of 1973 (twice vetoed by Richard Nixon as "too costly") added people with disabilities to the list of Americans protected from discrimination. Because the law defines an inaccessible environment as a form of discrimination, wheelchair ramps, grab bars on toilets, and Braille signs have become common features of American life. The Education of All Handicapped Children Act of 1975 entitled all children to a free public education appropriate to their needs. The **Americans with Disabilities Act of 1990 (ADA)** strengthened these protections, requiring employers and administrators of public facilities to make "reasonable accommodations" and prohibiting employment discrimination against people with disabilities.

Americans with Disabilities Act of 1990

A law passed in 1990 that requires employers and public facilities to make "reasonable accommodations" for people with disabilities and prohibits discrimination against these individuals in employment.

Determining who is "disabled" has generated controversy. Are people with acquired immune deficiency syndrome (AIDS) entitled to protections? In 1998 the Supreme Court answered yes. It ruled that the ADA offered protection against discrimination to people with AIDS.[26] What about people with bad eyesight or high blood pressure? In 1999 the Supreme Court ruled that people with physical impairments who can function normally when they wear glasses or take their medicine cannot be considered disabled and thus do not fall under the ADA's protection against employment discrimination.[27]

Nobody wants to oppose policies beneficial to people with disabilities. After all, people like Helen Keller and Franklin Roosevelt are popular American heroes. Nevertheless, civil rights laws designed to protect the rights of these individuals have met with vehement opposition and, once passed, with sluggish enforcement. The source of this resistance is the same concern that troubled Nixon: cost. Budgeting for such programs is often shortsighted, however. People often forget that changes allowing people with disabilities to become wage earners, spenders, and taxpayers are a gain, rather than drain, on the economy.

Gay and Lesbian Rights

Gay and lesbian activists may face the toughest battle for equality. The reluctance to appear hostile to the elderly or to women, which bridles the tongue of many potential opponents, has no apparent equivalent with respect to gay and lesbian Americans.

Moreover, gays and lesbians rarely enjoy even the formal—if often condescending—praise that women, older people, children, and people with disabilities receive. Few positive stereotypes are commonly associated with homosexuality—contrast the feminine virtues attributed to women, the wisdom of the old, the innocence of children, and the courage of people with disabilities—that can counter the impact of the negative stereotyping that gays and lesbians face.

Homophobia—fear and hatred of homosexuals—has many causes; some are very powerful. Some religions, for instance, condemn homosexuality. Such attitudes continue to characterize a large segment of the American public despite some changes over the past few years (see Table 5.6). Homophobia appeared to be the motive for the brutal 1998 killing of Matthew Shepard, a 21-year-old political science freshman at the University of Wyoming. Shepard was attacked after attending a meeting for Gay Awareness Week events on campus. He was found tied to a fence, where he had been hit in the head with a pistol 18 times and kicked repeatedly in the groin.

Even by conservative estimates, several million Americans are homosexual, representing every social stratum and ethnic group. Of particular concern to the gay community is the AIDS virus, which has had an especially devastating effect on male homosexuals. For some segments of the population, the fear of the disease has provided a convenient excuse for suspicion and outright bigotry. Not only is homosexual activity illegal in some states, but homosexuals often face discrimination in hiring, education, access to public accommodations, and housing.

A notorious incident in a New York City bar in 1969 stimulated the growth of the gay rights movement. The Stonewall bar, frequented by gay men, was raided by the police. Unwarranted violence, arrests, and injury to persons and property resulted. Both gay men and lesbians organized throughout the 1970s and 1980s in an effort to protect their civil rights. During this time, they developed political skills and formed powerful interest groups.

Despite setbacks, including *Bowers v. Hardwick* (1986), which allowed states to ban homosexual relations; rulings permitting the armed forces to exclude homosexuals; and the efforts of some states to prohibit homosexuals from receiving protection against discrimination, gay activists have won important victories. Seven states, including California, and more than 100 communities have passed laws protecting homosexuals against some forms of discrimination.[28] The state of Vermont recognizes gay "civil unions." Most colleges and universities now have gay rights organizations on campus. In 1996, in *Romer v. Evans,* the Supreme Court voided a state constitutional amendment approved by the voters of Colorado that denied homosexuals protection against discrimination. The Court found that the Colorado amendment violated the U.S. Constitution's guarantee of equal protection of the law. In November, 1998, the Georgia Supreme Court overturned the state's controversial antisodomy law on the grounds that it was an unconstitutional intrusion of the right to privacy guaranteed by the Georgia Constitution.[29]

In the summer of 1993, after months of negotiation with the Pentagon and an avalanche of criticism, President Clinton announced a new policy that barred the Pentagon from asking military recruits or service personnel to disclose their sexual orientation. Popularly known as the "don't ask, don't tell" policy, it also reaffirmed the Defense Department's strict prohibition against homosexual conduct. Service members who declare their homosexuality face discharge unless they can prove they will remain celibate, and they are barred from even disclosing to a friend in private conversation that they are gay or bisexual. The new policy also requires commanders to have "credible information" that the policy is being violated before launching an inves-

Table 5.6 Discrimination Against Homosexuals

Homosexuals face opposition to entering many common occupations from a substantial percentage of the American public, but this opposition seems to be decreasing.

Do you think homosexuals should or should not be hired for each of the following occupations?

	% Saying "Yes"		
	1992	1996	1999
Salesperson	82%	90%	90%
Armed forces	57%	65%	70%
Doctors	53%	69%	75%
High school teachers	47%	60%	61%
Clergy	43%	53%	54%
Elementary school teachers	41%	55%	54%

Source: Gallup Poll, April 1999.

tigation. As you might expect, the policy is currently facing many challenges in the courts. In a clear setback for gays and lesbians, the Supreme Court held in a decision in 2000 that the Boy Scouts could exclude a gay man from being an adult member because homosexuality violates the organization's principles.[30]

Affirmative Action

The public policy paths for women and minorities have not been identical. However, they have converged in the debate about affirmative action to overcome the effects of past discrimination. Some people argue that groups that have suffered invidious discrimination require special efforts to provide them access to education and jobs. **Affirmative action** involves efforts to bring about increased employment, promotion, or admission for members of such groups. The goal is to move beyond *equal opportunity* (in which everyone has the same chance of obtaining good jobs, for example) toward *equal results* (in which different groups have the same percentage of success in obtaining those jobs). This goal might be accomplished through special rules in the public and private sectors that recruit or otherwise give preferential treatment to previously disadvantaged groups. Numerical quotas that ensure that a portion of government contracts, law school admissions, or police department promotions go to minorities and women are the strongest and most controversial form of affirmative action.

affirmative action

A policy designed to give special attention to or compensatory treatment of members of some previously disadvantaged group.

The constitutional status of affirmative action is not clear. New state and federal laws have discriminated *in favor of* these previously disadvantaged groups. Some state governments adopted affirmative action programs to increase minority enrollment, job holding, or promotion. Eventually, the federal government mandated that all state and local governments, as well as each institution receiving aid from or contracting with the federal government, adopt an affirmative action program.

One such program was introduced at the University of California at Davis. Eager to produce more minority physicians in California, the medical school set aside 16 of a total 100 places in the entering class for "disadvantaged groups." One White applicant who did not make the freshman class was Allan Bakke. After receiving his rejection letter from Davis for two straight years, Bakke learned that the mean scores on the Medical College Admissions Test of students admitted under the university's program were the 46th percentile on verbal tests and the 35th on science tests. Bakke's scores on the same tests were at the 96th and 97th percentiles, respectively. He decided to sue

How You Can Make A Difference

Influencing Affirmative Action

For college students, affirmative action remains an important issue regardless of your race or gender. In one way or another, affirmative action impacts college admission policies, financial aid packages, graduate school prospects, and job opportunities. Emotions can run deep when debating this issue. There is even considerable disagreement over the precise definition of affirmative action. It is possible, however, to get involved in this issue without generating hostility or assailing the character of your opponents.

In the decades following the Civil Rights Movement and the federal intervention in the 1960s and 1970s, the drive for racial and gender equality made big strides. Legal forms of discrimination have all but disappeared as a result of increased government oversight and heightened public awareness. While few dispute that disparities still remain, there now exists a divide over how to best address these inequalities and ensure civil rights for all in twenty-first century America. This divide manifests itself most clearly in the debate over affirmative action.

Do you believe that affirmative action is needed to preserve the advances made in civil rights since the 1950s? The NAACP (www.naacp.org), Americans United for Affirmative Action (www.auaa.org), and the American Association of University Women (www.aauw.org) stand out as organizations that can offer you ways to support the policies of affirmative action. Perhaps you believe that the affirmative action policies might actually undermine the effort to ensure civil rights for all. If so, you should contact organizations such as Campaign for a Color-Blind America (www.equalrights.com), the American Civil Rights Institute (www.acri.org), and the Center for Equal Opportunity (www.ceousa.org) to see how you can participate in their causes.

Regardless of which view you hold, college students can make a difference in how their university, city, and state respond to affirmative action. You can make your views known through letter and e-mail campaigns, voter registration drives, and even student protests.

UC-Davis, claiming that it had denied him equal protection of the laws by discriminating against him because of his race.

Regents of the University of California v. Bakke

A 1978 Supreme Court decision holding that a state university could not admit less qualified individuals solely because of their race.

The result was an important Supreme Court decision in Bakke's favor, ***Regents of the University of California v. Bakke*** (1978).[31] The Court ordered Bakke admitted, holding that the UC-Davis Special Admissions Program did discriminate against him because of his race. Yet the Court refused to order UC-Davis never to use race as a criterion for admission. A university could, said the Court, adopt an "admissions program where race or ethnic background is simply one element—to be weighed fairly against other elements—in the selection process." It could *not,* as UC-Davis Special Admissions Program did, set aside a quota of spots for particular groups.

Although Bakke ended up in medical school, Brian Weber did not get into an apprenticeship program he wanted to enter in Louisiana. In *United Steelworkers of America, AFL-CIO v. Weber* (1979), the Court found that the Kaiser Aluminum Company's special training program, which employed a quota for minorities, was intended to rectify years of past employment discrimination at Kaiser. Thus, said the Court, a voluntary union- and management-sponsored program to take more African Americans than Whites did *not* discriminate against Weber.

Until 1995, the Court was more deferential to Congress than to local government in upholding affirmative action programs. In 1989, the Court found a Richmond, Va. plan that reserved 30 percent of city subcontracts for minority firms to be unconstitutional.[32] In 1980, on the other hand, the Court upheld a federal rule setting aside 10 percent of all federal construction contracts for minority-owned firms.[33] In 1990, the Court agreed that Congress may require preferential treatment for minorities to increase their ownership of broadcast licenses.[34] This event marked the first time the Supreme Court upheld a specific affirmative action program that was not devised to remedy past discrimination.

Things changed in 1995, however. In ***Adarand Constructors v. Pena,*** the Court overturned the decision regarding broadcast licenses and cast grave doubt on its holding regarding contracts set aside for minority-owned firms. It held that federal programs that classify people by race, even for an ostensibly benign purpose such as expanding opportunities for members of minorities, should be presumed to be unconstitutional. Such programs must be subject to the most searching judicial inquiry and can survive only if they are "narrowly tailored" to accomplish a "compelling governmental interest." In other words, the Court applied criteria for evaluating affirmative action programs similar to those it applies to other racial classifications, the less benign suspect classifications we discussed earlier in the chapter. These are also the same criteria the Court has applied to state affirmative action programs since 1989. Although *Adarand Constructors v. Pena* did not void federal affirmative action programs in general, it certainly limits their potential impact.

Adarand Constructors v. Pena

A 1995 Supreme Court decision holding that federal programs that classify people by race, even for an ostensibly benign purpose such as expanding opportunities for minorities, should be presumed to be unconstitutional.

On other matters, the Court has approved preferential treatment of minorities in promotions;[35] and it has also ordered quotas for minority union memberships.[36] We examine a case of a public employer using affirmative action promotions to counter underrepresentation of women and minorities in the workplace in "You Are the Judge: The Case of the Santa Clara Dispatcher."

On the other hand, the Court has ruled that affirmative action does not exempt recently hired minorities from traditional work rules specifying the "last hired, first fired" order of layoffs.[37] In 1986, the Court found unconstitutional an effort to give preference to African-American teachers in layoffs, because this policy punished innocent White teachers and the African-American teachers had not been the actual victims of past discrimination.[38]

Not everyone agrees that affirmative action is a wise or fair policy. There is little support from the general public for programs such as those that set aside jobs or employ quotas for members of minority groups (see Table 5.7). Opposition is especially strong when people view affirmative action as *reverse discrimination*—as in the case of individuals like

You Are the Judge

The Case of the Santa Clara Dispatcher

For four years, Diane Joyce patched asphalt with a Santa Clara county road crew around San Jose, Calif., and its suburbs. She applied for a promotion, hoping to work in the less strenuous and better-paid position of dispatcher. Another applicant for the job was Paul Johnson, a White male who had worked for the agency for 13 years.

Like Diane, Paul did well on the exam given to all applicants; in fact, the two scored among the top six applicants, Diane with a score of 73, and Paul with 75. Knowing that Paul's score was a shade better and his work experience longer, the supervisor decided to hire him. The county's affirmative action officers overruled the supervisor, however, and Diane got the job. Paul decided to get a lawyer.

Paul's lawyer argued that Diane's promotion violated Title VII of the Civil Rights Act of 1964. This law, originally passed to guarantee minority access to jobs and promotions, makes it unlawful for an employer to deprive any individual of employment opportunities because of their race, color, religion, gender, or national origin.

You Be the Judge: Should Diane Joyce have been promoted?

Answer: In *Johnson v. Transportation Agency, Santa Clara County* (1987), the Supreme Court held that public employers may use carefully constructed affirmative action promotion plans, designed to remedy specific past discriminations, to counter women's and minorities' underrepresentation in the workplace. Thus, Diane Joyce kept her job. In a stinging dissent, Justice Scalia complained that the Court was "converting [the law] from a guarantee that race or sex will not be a basis for employment determinations, to a guarantee that it often will."

Table 5.7 Affirmative Action

Although Americans in general support nondiscrimination in employment and education, most Americans oppose "reverse discrimination" programs and quotas that give advantages to women and minorities.

Do you favor or oppose…?

	FAVOR	OPPOSE
Hiring a minority applicant who is *less* qualified than a White applicant, when filling a job in a business that has few minority workers?	12%	85%
Making a certain number of scholarships at public colleges and universities available only to minorities and women?	31	67
Establishing quotas requiring businesses to hire a certain number of minorities and women?	34	64
Establishing quotas requiring schools to admit a certain number of minorities and women as students?	38	58
Requiring a certain percentage of government contracts to be awarded to businesses owned by minorities and women?	48	48
Favoring a well-qualified minority applicant over an *equally* qualified White applicant, when filling a job in a business that has few minority workers?	50	42
Making special efforts at companies to find qualified minorities and women and encouraging them to apply for jobs with that company?	74	24
Providing job training programs for minorities and women to make them qualified for better jobs?	82	17

Source: Gallup Poll, March 1995.

Allan Bakke who are themselves blameless—and less qualified individuals are hired or admitted to educational or training programs because of their minority status.

Critics of reverse discrimination argue that any race or gender discrimination is wrong, even when its purpose is to rectify past injustices rather than to reinforce them. After all, Bakke and Johnson could no more help being White and male than Diane Joyce could help being a woman. Opponents of affirmative action believe that merit is the only fair basis for distributing benefits. Bakke and Johnson found that the rules by which institutions operated had suddenly changed—and they suffered as a result. It is easy to sympathize with them.

In 1996, California voters passed Proposition 209, which banned state affirmative action programs based on race, ethnicity, or gender in public hiring, contracting, and educational admissions (Washington state passed a similar ban in 1998). Opponents immediately filed a lawsuit in federal court to block enforcement of the law, claiming that it violated the Fourteenth Amendment. Ultimately, the U.S. Supreme Court will have to resolve the issue, but there is little question that support for Proposition 209 represents a widespread skepticism about affirmative action programs. A federal court of appeals placed a similar ban on universities in Texas, Oklahoma, and Mississippi.

On the other hand, the case for affirmative action is also persuasive. Proponents of these policies argue that what constitutes merit is highly subjective and can embody prejudices of which the decision maker may be quite unaware. Experts suggest that a man can "look more like" a road dispatcher and thus get a higher rating from interviewers than a woman might. Affirmative action supporters believe that increasing the number of women and minorities in desirable jobs is such an important social goal that it should be considered when determining an individual's qualifications. They claim that what White males lose from affirmative action programs are privileges to which they were never entitled in the first place; after all, nobody has the right to be a doctor or a road dispatcher.

Understanding Civil Rights and Public Policy

The original Constitution is silent on the issue of equality. The only direct reference is in the Fourteenth Amendment, which forbids the states to deny "equal protection of the laws." Those five words have been the basis for major civil rights statutes and scores of judicial rulings protecting the rights of minorities and women. These laws and decisions, granting people new rights, have empowered groups to seek and gain still more victories. The implications of their success for democracy and the scope of government are substantial.

Civil Rights and Democracy

Equality is a basic principle of democracy. Every citizen has one vote because democratic government presumes that each person's needs, interests, and preferences are neither any more nor any less important than the needs, interests, and preferences of every other person. Individual liberty is an equally important democratic principle, one that can conflict with equality.

Equality tends to favor majority rule. Because under simple majority rule everyone's wishes rank equally, the policy outcome that most people prefer seems to be the fairest choice in cases of conflict. What happens, however, if the majority wants to deprive the minority of certain rights? In situations like these, equality threatens individual liberty. Thus, the principle of equality can invite the denial of minority rights, whereas the principle of liberty condemns such action.[39]

Majority rule is not the only threat to liberty. Politically and socially powerful minorities have suppressed majorities as well as other minorities. Women have long outnumbered men in America, about 53 percent to 47 percent. In the era of segregation, African Americans outnumbered Whites in many Southern states. Inequality persisted, however, because customs that reinforced it were entrenched within the society and because inequality often served the interests of the dominant groups. When slavery and segregation existed in an agrarian economy, Whites could get cheap agricultural labor. When men were breadwinners and women were homemakers, married men had a source of cheap domestic labor.

Both African Americans and women made many gains even when they lacked one essential component of democratic power: the vote. They used other rights—such as their First Amendment freedoms—to fight for equality. When Congress protected the right of African Americans to vote in the 1960s, the nature of Southern politics was changed dramatically. The democratic process is a powerful vehicle for disadvantaged groups to press their claims.

Civil Rights and the Scope of Government

Civil rights laws increase the scope and power of government. These laws regulate the behavior of individuals and institutions. Restaurant owners must serve all patrons regardless of race. Professional schools must admit women. Employers must accommodate people with disabilities and make an effort to find minority workers, whether they want to or not. Those who want to reduce the scope of government are uneasy with these laws, if not downright hostile to them.

The founders might be greatly perturbed if they knew about all the civil rights laws the government has enacted; these policies do not conform to the eighteenth-century idea of limited government. But the founders would expect the national government to do whatever is necessary to hold the nation together. The Civil War showed that the original Constitution did not adequately deal with issues like slavery that could destroy the society the Constitution's writers had struggled to secure.

Career Profile

Position: Federal Investigator with the Equal Employment Opportunity Commission (EEOC)
Salary Range: $32,000-42,000 to start
Benefits: Health, life, and medical insurance. Retirement pension plan.
Qualifications: Mature decision-making ability, superior writing and analytical skills, and interpersonal communication expertise. While no educational requirement is stated, successful applicants usually have at least a bachelor's degree.

Real People on the Job: Karen McDonough

A middle-aged woman working at a automobile factory discovers that her male co-workers are receiving higher pay for the same work even though she has superior qualifications and has worked at the plant for a longer time. Who's she going to call? Chances are that she will probably contact a Federal Investigator like Karen McDonough at the Equal Employment Opportunity Commission (EEOC).

Working out of the Philadelphia District Office of the EEOC enforcement unit, Karen handles these and other claims of discrimination. Before making any judgments on the validity of a claim, Karen conducts a two-hour "intake" session and interview with the claimant to gather all relevant information. During the intake session, Karen must discern the claim's credibility and decide whether it falls under the jurisdiction of the EEOC. Making this type of judgment call is not always an easy or straightforward task. She must interpret and apply the laws that govern the EEOC's jurisdiction—Title VII of the 1964 Civil Rights Act, the Age Discrimination in Employment Act, the Americans with Disabilities Act, and the Equal Pay Act. In essence, the EEOC can only investigate further if someone has been discriminated against on the basis of race, sex, color, national origin, religion, age, or disability. Sometimes, the harassment is based on a personality conflict or other issues outside Karen's jurisdiction.

Though she handles all types of claims, Karen's background as a statistician allows her to specialize in class action cases that involve more than three people. After determining to proceed with a case, EEOC investigators often conduct an on-site investigation to gather company records and interview the parties involved. Statistical analysis of a company's employment and disciplinary records can help determine whether a pattern of discrimination exists. Each investigator handles between 30 to 60 cases, depending on the cases' complexity. Class action suits, for example, require far more time and attention than individual cases. If it is an individual case, then Karen's job is to try and reach a settlement between the employer and employee in order to avoid litigation. In class action cases, Karen must sift through the evidence, determine the costs involved (punitive, emotional, etc), and assign a dollar figure that the offending company must pay. Only if conciliation and settlement fail does the EEOC move forward with litigation.

According to Karen, her investigative position combines excitement, variety, and intellectual stimulation—rare traits for any job. Although a good portion of her time is spent in front of the computer analyzing statistical trends, Karen's job also incorporates plenty of opportunities to get out of the office and into the field. Most of all, she treasures the sense of accomplishment she gets from being able to affect positive change in discriminatory working environments. If you would like to consider an investigative position at the EEOC, please go to the federal government's job website at www.usajobs.opm.gov.

However, civil rights, like civil liberties, is an area in which increased government activity in protecting basic rights can lead to greater checks on government by those who benefit from such protections. Remember that much of segregation was *de jure*, established by governments. Moreover, government action in the area of civil rights can be viewed as the protection of individualism. Basic to the notion of civil rights is that individuals are not to be judged according to characteristics they share with a group. Thus, civil rights protect the individual against collective discrimination.

The question of where to draw the line in the government's efforts to protect civil rights has received different answers at different points in American history, but few Americans want to turn back the clock to the days of *Plessy v. Ferguson* and Jim Crow laws or to the exclusion of women from the workplace.

Summary

Racial minorities have struggled for equality since the very beginning of the Republic. In the era of slavery, the Supreme Court upheld the practice and denied slaves any rights. After the Civil War and Reconstruction ended, legal segregation was established. For a time, the Supreme Court sanctioned the Jim Crow laws, but in 1954, the *Brown v. Board of Education* case held that *de jure* racial segregation violated equal protection of the laws, which was guaranteed by the Fourteenth Amendment. This event marked the beginning of the era of civil rights. *Brown* inaugurated a movement that succeeded in ending virtually every form of legal discrimination against minorities.

Although feminists have not ignored the courts, the struggle for women's equality has emphasized legislation over litigation. Women won the right to vote in 1920, but the Equal Rights Amendment has not yet been ratified. This defeat did not kill the feminist movement, however. Comparable worth, women's role in the military, sexual harassment, and the balance between work and family are among the many controversial women's issues that are still being debated.

The interests of women and minorities have converged on the issue of affirmative action—that is, policies requiring special efforts on behalf of disadvantaged groups. In the *Bakke* case and in decisions like *Johnson v. Santa Clara*, the Court ruled that affirmative action plans were both legal and constitutional. However, there is substantial opposition to what many see as reverse discrimination.

The civil rights umbrella is a large one. Increasing numbers of groups seek protection for their rights. Older and younger Americans, people with disabilities, and homosexuals have used the laws to ensure their equality. People with AIDS and other chronically ill people may mount battles yet to be fought in the political arena. It is difficult to predict what controversies the twenty-first century will bring, when minority groups will outnumber the current majority.

Key Terms

civil rights
Fourteenth Amendment
equal protection of the laws
Thirteenth Amendment
Civil Rights Act of 1964
suffrage
Fifteenth Amendment
poll taxes
White primary
Twenty-fourth Amendment
Voting Rights Act of 1965
Nineteenth Amendment
Equal Rights Amendment
comparable worth
Americans with Disabilities Act of 1990
affirmative action

Key Cases

Dred Scott v. Sandford (1857)
Plessy v. Ferguson (1896)
Brown v. Board of Education (1954)
Korematsu v. United States (1944)
Reed v. Reed (1971)
Craig v. Boren (1976)
Regents of the University of California v. Bakke (1978)
Adarand Constructors v. Pena (1995)

For Further Reading

Baer, Judith A. *Women in the Law: The Struggle Toward Equality from the New Deal to the Present,* 2nd ed. New York: Holmes and Meier, 1996. An excellent analysis of women's changing legal status.

Berger, Raoul. *Government by Judiciary: The Transformation of the Fourteenth Amendment.* Cambridge, MA: Harvard University Press, 1977. Berger is not one who favors use of the Fourteenth Amendment to expand equality.

Bergman, Barbara R. *In Defense of Affirmative Action.* New York: Basic Books, 1996. An argument on behalf of affirmative action policies.

Berry, Mary F. *Why ERA Failed.* Bloomington: Indiana University Press, 1986. An excellent account of public policies affecting women, with particular attention to the demise of the Equal Rights Amendment.

Brown, Dee. *Bury My Heart at Wounded Knee: An Indian History of the American West.* New York: Holt, Rinehart and Winston, 1970. History from an American Indian perspective.

Bullock, Charles S., III, and Charles M. Lamb. *Implementation of Civil Rights Policy.* Monterey, CA: Brooks/Cole, 1984. Focuses on the difficulty of turning the goals of civil rights policies into reality.

Greenberg, Jack. *Crusader in the Courts.* New York: Basic Books, 1994. The story of litigation in the civil rights era as told by one of the chief participants.

Hatamiya, Leslie T. *Righting a Wrong: Japanese Americans and the Passage of the Civil Liberties Act of 1988.* Stanford, CA: Stanford University Press, 1993. An analysis of the passage of the Civil Liberties Act of 1988 and its impact on Japanese Americans.

Kluger, Richard. *Simple Justice.* New York: Knopf, 1976. The story of the *Brown* case.

Mansbridge, Jane. *Why We Lost the ERA.* Chicago: University of Chicago Press, 1986. The politics of women's rights.

McClain, Paula D., and Joseph Stewart. *"Can't We All Get Along?"* Boulder, CO: Westview, 1995. Racial and ethnic minorities in American politics.

McGlen, Nancy, and Karen O'Connor. *Women's Rights: The Struggle for Equality in the Nineteenth and Twentieth Centuries.* New York: Praeger, 1983. A good account of the struggle for equal rights for women.

Urofsky, Melvin I. *A Conflict of Rights: The Supreme Court and Affirmative Action.* New York: Scribner's, 1991. A case study of the issues, people, and events surrounding the case of *Joyce v. Johnson.*

Verba, Sidney, and Gary R. Orren. *Equality in America: The View from the Top.* Cambridge, MA: Harvard University Press, 1985. An examination of the views of the American elite on equality.

Wilkinson, J. Harvie, III. *From* Brown *to* Bakke. New York: Oxford University Press, 1979. The political and legal history of civil rights policies between Brown and Bakke.

Woodward, C. Vann. *The Strange Career of Jim Crow,* 2nd ed. New York: Oxford University Press, 1966. Examines the evolution of Jim Crow laws in the South.

Internet Resources

www.law.cornell.edu/topics/equal_protection.html
The text of the landmark cases on equal protection and background material.

www.usdoj.gov/crt/
Home page of the Civil Rights Division of the U.S. Department of Justice containing background information and discussion of current events.

www.usdoj.gov/crt/ada/adahom1.htm
Home page of the Americans with Disabilities Act of the U.S. Department of Justice containing background information and discussion of current events.

www.naacp.org/
Home page of the NAACP containing background information and discussion of current events.

Notes

1. Bland is quoted in Sidney Verba and Gary R. Orren, *Equality in America: The View from the Top* (Cambridge, MA: Harvard University Press, 1985), 25. The Adams' quotes are from Judith A. Baer, *Equality Under the Constitution: Reclaiming the Fourteenth Amendment* (Ithaca, NY: Cornell University Press, 1983), 44–47.

2. For opposing interpretations of the Fourteenth Amendment, see Baer, *Equality under the Constitution*; and Raoul Berger, *Government by Judiciary: The Transformation of the Fourteenth Amendment* (Cambridge, MA: Harvard University Press, 1977).
3. D. Garth Taylor, Paul B. Sheatsley, and Andrew M. Greeley, "Attitudes Toward Racial Integration," *Scientific American* 238 (June 1978): 42–49; Richard G. Niemi, John Mueller, and John W. Smith, *Trends in Public Opinion* (Westport, CT: Greenwood Press, 1989), 180.
4. There are a few exceptions. Religious institutions such as schools may use religious standards in employment. Gender, age, and disabilities may be considered in the few cases where such occupational qualifications are absolutely essential to the normal operations of a business or enterprise, as in the case of a men's restroom attendant.
5. On the implementation of the Voting Rights Act, see Richard Scher and James Button, "Voting Rights Act: Implementation and Impact," in *Implementation of Civil Rights Policy*, Charles Bullock III and Charles Lamb, ed. (Monterey, CA: Brooks/Cole, 1984); Abigail M. Thernstrom, *Whose Votes Count?* (Cambridge, MA: Harvard University Press, 1987); and Chandler Davidson and Bernard Groffman, eds., *Quiet Revolution in the South: The Impact of the Voting Rights Act, 1965–1990* (Princeton, NJ: Princeton University Press, 1994).
6. U.S. Department of Commerce, *Statistical Abstract of the United States, 2000* (Washington, D.C.: U.S. Government Printing Office, 2001), 287. See David Lublin, *The Paradox of Representation: Racial Gerrymandering and Minority Interests in Congress* (Princeton, NJ: Princeton University Press, 1997) on how racial redistricting helped increase the number of minority representatives in Congress.
7. See Dee Brown, *Bury My Heart at Wounded Knee: An Indian History of the American West* (New York: Holt, Rinehart and Winston, 1970).
8. *Statistical Abstract of the United States, 2000*, 287.
9. *White v. Register* (1973).
10. See Eleanor Flexner, *Century of Struggle* (New York: Atheneum, 1971).
11. See J. Stanley Lemons, *The Woman Citizen: Social Feminism in the 1920s* (Urbana: University of Illinois Press, 1973).
12. *Kirchberg v. Feenstra* (1981).
13. *Arizona Governing Committee for Tax Deferred Annuity and Deferred Compensation Plans v. Norris* (1983).
14. *Michael M. v. Superior Court* (1981).
15. *Kahn v. Shevin* (1974).
16. *Statistical Abstract of the United States, 2000*, 54–55, 404–405, 409–410.
17. *Cleveland Board of Education v. LaFleur* (1974)
18. *United Automobile Workers v. Johnson Controls* (1991)
19. *Roberts v. United States Jaycees* (1984); *Board of Directors of Rotary International v. Rotary Club of Duarte* (1987); and *New York State Club Association v. New York* (1988).
20. *United States v. Virginia et al.*, (1996).
21. *Statistical Abstract of the United States, 2000*, 437.
22. *Meritor Savings Bank v. Vinson* (1986).
23. *Massachusetts Board of Retirement v. Murgia* (1976).
24. *Hazelwood School District v. Kuhlmeier* (1988).
25. Walter Polovchak with Kevin Klose, *Freedom's Child* (New York: Random House, 1988).
26. *Bregdon v. Abbott* (1998).
27. *Sutton v. United Air Lines* (1999), *Albertsons v. Kirkingburg* (1999), and *Murphy v. United Parcel Service* (1999).
28. Kenneth D. Wald, James W. Button, and Barbara A. Rienzo, "The Politics of Gay Rights in American Communities: Explaining Antidiscrimination Ordinances and Policies," *American Journal of Political Science* 40 (November 1996):1,152–1,178, examines why some communities adopt antidiscrimination ordinances and policies that include sexual orientation and others do not.
29. *Powell v. State* (1998).
30. *Boy Scouts of America v. Dale* (2000).
31. On the affirmative action issues raised by *Bakke* and other cases, see Allan P. Sindler, *Bakke, De Funis and Minority Admissions* (New York: Longman, 1978).
32. *Richmond v. J.A. Croson Co.* (1989).
33. *Fullilove v. Klutznick* (1980).
34. *Metro Broadcasting, Inc. v. Federal Communications Commission* (1990).
35. *Local Number 93 v. Cleveland* (1986), and *United States v. Paradise* (1987).
36. *Local 28 of the Sheet Metal Workers v. EEOC* (1986).
37. *Firefighters v. Stotts* (1984).
38. *Wygant v. Jackson Board of Education* (1986).
39. See Barbara S. Gamble, "Putting Civil Rights to a Popular Vote," *American Journal of Political Science* 41 (January 1997): 245–269.

6 Public Opinion and Political Action

Chapter Outline

One of the biggest issues of the 2000 presidential race revolved around income tax cuts. George W. Bush made his plan to cut taxes for everyone the centerpiece of his campaign. This proposal tapped straight into the fundamental issue of the scope of government. Bush's plan was based on the premise that the federal budget surplus was due to taxes being higher than necessary for the government to carry out its functions. On the other side, Al Gore saw much to criticize in the Bush plan. He decided to strongly attack the Bush's proposal by pointing out that a big percentage of the benefits would go to the wealthiest Americans—a point he made repeatedly in the presidential debates.

Both Bush and Gore, however, faced the usual problem of getting the public to take notice of their stands. Throughout the campaign, Harvard University's Vanishing Voter project regularly asked a random sample of the public the following question: "Do you happen to know whether Bush favors or opposes a large cut in personal income taxes?"

In October 2000, 45 percent of respondents said that he favored a cut, 12 percent said he did not, and 43 percent admitted that they did not know. Public knowledge about the most publicized issue of the campaign was not impressive.

Public opinion polling has become a major growth industry in recent years. Each of the national evening news broadcasts and almost every major newspaper now commissions their own regular polls. Polls are great investments for the media because they provide a timely story that can be billed as exclusive. If there is nothing new in their findings, journalists can always fall back on one sure pattern: the lack of public attention to politics. Whether it's George W. Bush's tax-cut plan, the McCain-Feingold campaign finance reform bill, or the question of American military involvement in Kosovo, the safest expectation that a public opinion analyst can make is that many people will be unaware of the policy issue.

In a democracy, the people are expected to guide public policy. But do people pay enough attention to public affairs to fulfill their duty as citizens? As we shall see in this chapter, there is much reason to be concerned about the level of political information among the American public. This is particularly the case for complex issues that involve the scope of government.

It is common for politicians and columnists to intone the words "the American people . . ." and then claim their view as that of the citizenry. Yet it would be hard to find a statement about the American people—who they are and what they believe—that is either 100 percent right or 100 percent wrong. The American people are wondrously diverse. There are about 280 million Americans, forming a mosaic of racial, ethnic, and cultural groups. America was founded on the principle of tolerating diversity and individualism, and it remains one of the most diverse countries in the world today. Most Americans view this diversity as one of the most appealing aspects of their society.

public opinion

The distribution of the population's beliefs about politics and policy issues.

The study of American **public opinion** aims to understand the distribution of the population's belief about politics and policy issues. Because there are many groups with a great variety of opinions in the United States, this is an especially complex task. This is not to say that public opinion would be easy to study even if America were a more homogeneous society; as you will see, measuring public opinion involves painstaking interviewing procedures and careful wording of questions. Further complicating the task is the fact that people are often not well informed about the issues. The least informed are also the least likely to participate in the political process, a phenomenon that creates imbalances in who takes part in political action.

For American government to work efficiently and effectively, the diversity of the American public and its opinions must be faithfully channeled through the political process. This chapter reveals just how difficult a task this is.

The American People

demography

The science of population changes.

census

A valuable tool for understanding demographic changes. The Constitution requires that the government conduct an "actual enumeration" of the population every 10 years.

One way of looking at the American public is through **demography**—the science of human populations. The most valuable tool for understanding demographic changes in America is the **census.** The U.S. Constitution requires that the government conduct an "actual enumeration" of the population every 10 years. The first census was conducted in 1790.

The Census Bureau tries to conduct the most accurate count of the population humanly feasible. It isn't an easy job, even with the allocation of billions of federal dollars to the task. After the 1990 census was completed, the Bureau estimated that 4.7 million people were not counted. Furthermore, they found that members of minority groups were disproportionately undercounted, as they were apparently more suspicious of government

Responding to criticisms that many minority groups had been undercounted in the previous census, the Census Bureau launched special advertising campaigns to improve cooperation rates in these communities in 2000. Here you can see a poster in Detroit targeted at the large number of Iraqi immigrants in the city.

and thus less willing to cooperate with census workers. In order to correct for such an undercount in 2000, the Clinton Administration approved a plan to scientifically estimate the characteristics of those people who failed to respond to the census forms and follow-up visits from census workers, and then incorporate this information into the official count. Conservatives maintain that such a procedure would be subject to manipulation, less accurate than a traditional head count, and unconstitutional. In the 1999 case of *Department of Commerce v. U.S. House of Representatives*, the Supreme Court ruled that sampling could not be used to determine the number of congressional districts each state is entitled to. However, the Court left the door open for the use of sampling procedures to adjust the count for other purposes, such as the allocation of federal grants to states. In the end, the Bush Administration decided not to do this.

Getting a question included on the census form is a highly competitive enterprise, as groups of all different kinds seek to be counted.[1] Once a group can establish its numbers, it can then ask for federal aid in proportion to its size. In 1990, advocates for the disabled won out when the census added a question designed to count people who have difficulty taking care of themselves or getting where they need to go. The census also responded to complaints that the homeless were being left out of the count by sending out 15,000 workers one night to count them—the final tally came to 228,621.

Changes in the U.S. population, as reflected in these census figures, impact our culture and political system in numerous ways, which will be examined in the next few sections.

The Immigrant Society

The United States has always been a nation of immigrants. As John F. Kennedy said, America is "not merely a nation but a nation of nations." All Americans except Native Americans are either descended from immigrants or are immigrants themselves. Today, federal law allows up to 800,000 new immigrants to be legally admitted to the country every year. This is equivalent to adding a city with the population of Washington, D.C., every year. And in recent years, illegal immigrants have outnumbered legal immigrants.

There have been three great waves of immigration to the United States.

- Prior to the late nineteenth century, northwestern Europeans (English, Irish, Germans, and Scandinavians) constituted the first wave of immigration.

- During the late nineteenth and early twentieth century, southern and eastern Europeans (Italians, Jews, Poles, Russians, and others) made up the second wave. Most of these passed through Ellis Island in New York (now a popular museum) as their first stop in the new world.
- In recent decades, a third wave of immigrants has consisted of Hispanics (from Cuba, Central America, and Mexico) and Asians (from Vietnam, Korea, the Philippines, and elsewhere). The 1980s saw the second largest number of immigrants of any decade in American history, and these groups are continuing to immigrate in large numbers.

Immigrants bring with them their aspirations, as well as their own political beliefs. For example, Cubans in Miami, who nearly constitute a majority of the city's population, first came to America to escape Fidel Castro's Marxist regime and have brought their anti-Communist sentiments with them. Similarly, the Vietnamese came to America after a Communist takeover there. Cubans and Vietnamese are just two recent examples of the many types of immigrants who have come to America over the years to flee an oppressive government. Other examples from previous periods of heavy immigration include the Irish in the first wave and the Russians in the second. Throughout American history, such groups have fostered a great appreciation for individualism in American public policy by their wish to be free of governmental control.

melting pot

The mixing of cultures, ideas, and peoples that has changed the American nation. The United States, with its history of immigration, has often been called a melting pot.

minority majority

The emergence of a non-Caucasian majority, as compared with a white, generally Anglo-Saxon majority. It is predicted that by about 2060, Hispanic Americans, African Americans, and Asian Americans together will outnumber white Americans.

The American Melting Pot

With its long history of immigration, the United States has often been called a **melting pot.** This phrase refers to a mixture of cultures, ideas, and peoples. As the third wave of immigration continues, policymakers have begun to speak of a new **minority majority,** meaning that America will eventually cease to have a white, generally Anglo-Saxon majority. The 2000 census data found an all-time low in the percentage of non-Hispanic White Americans—just over 69 percent of the population. African Americans made up 12 percent of the population, Hispanics 13 percent, Asians 4 percent, and Native Americans slightly less than 1 percent. Between 1980 and 1990, minority populations grew at a much faster rate than the white population. As you can see in Figure 6.1, the

Figure 6.1 The Coming Minority Majority

Based on the basis of current birth rates and immigration rates, the Census Bureau estimates that the demographics of the country should change as shown in the accompanying graph. Extend the lines a bit beyond the year 2050, and it is clear that the minority groups will soon be in the majority nationwide.
Of course, should rates of birth and immigration change, so will these estimates. But already there are 65 congressional districts with a minority majority, about 85 percent of which are represented in the House by an African American, a Hispanic, or an Asian American. These numbers are bound to increase as we move into the twenty-first century.

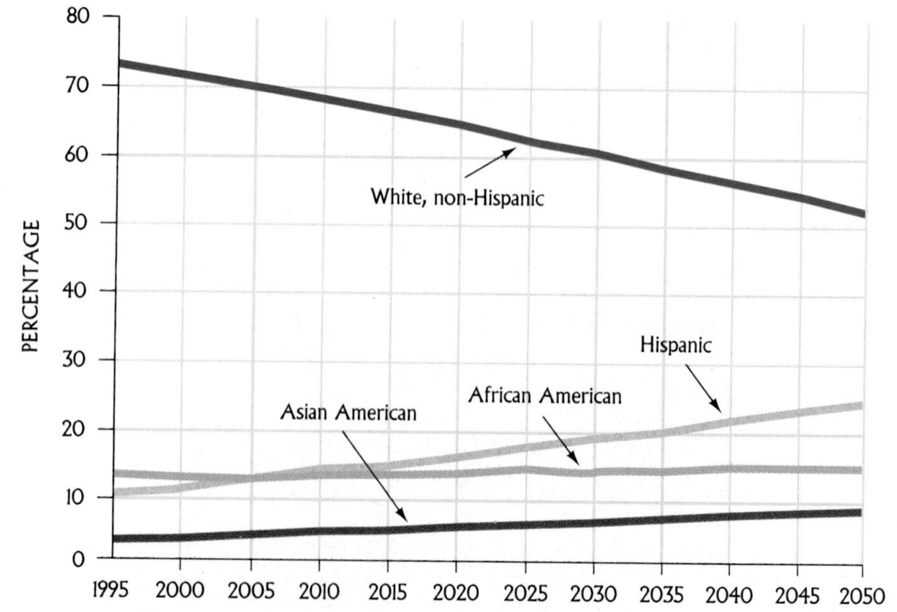

Census Bureau estimates that by the middle of the twenty-first century, Whites will represent only 52 percent of the population.

Until recently, the largest minority group in the country has been the African-American population. One in eight Americans is a descendent of these reluctant immigrants: Africans who were brought to America by force as slaves. As in Chapter 5, a legacy of racism and discrimination has left a higher proportion of the African-American population economically and politically disadvantaged than the white population. About 27 percent of African Americans currently live below the poverty line, compared to about 11 percent of Whites.

Despite this economic disadvantage, African Americans have recently been exercising a good deal of political power. African Americans have been elected as mayors of many of the country's biggest cities, including Los Angeles, New York, and Chicago. In 1989, Douglas Wilder of Virginia became the nation's first elected African-American governor, and in 1992, Carol Moseley-Braun of Illinois became the first African-American woman to be elected to the U.S. Senate. The number of African-American elected officials has increased by over 500 percent since 1970.[2]

The familiar problems of African Americans sometimes obscure the problems of other minority groups, such as Hispanics (composed largely of Mexicans, Cubans, and Puerto Ricans). The 2000 Census reported that for the first time the Hispanic population outnumbered the African-American population. Like African Americans, Hispanics are concentrated in cities. Hispanics are rapidly gaining power in the Southwest, and cities such as San Antonio and Denver have elected mayors of Hispanic heritage. In recent years, the state legislatures of New Mexico, Texas, Arizona, Colorado, Florida, California, and Connecticut all had at least 5 percent Hispanic representation.

An issue of particular concern to the Hispanic community is what to do about the problem of illegal immigration. The Simpson-Mazzoli Act, named after its congressional sponsors, requires that employers document the citizenship of their employees. Whether people are born in Canton, Ohio, or Canton, China, they must prove that they are either U.S. citizens or legal immigrants in order to work. Civil and criminal penalties can be assessed against employers who knowingly employ undocumented immigrants. This law has raised concern among leaders of immigrant groups, who worry that employers may simply decline to hire members of such groups rather than take any chances. There has been little evidence of this so far, however. In fact, many believe that the provisions of the Simpson-Mazzoli Act have proved to be inadequate in stopping illegal immigration from Mexico. One proposed solution that has been very controversial in recent years involves denying all benefits from government programs to people who cannot prove that they are legal residents of the United States (see "You Are the Policymaker: Should Illegal Immigrants Receive Benefits from Government Programs?").

Just north of San Diego, the problem of illegal immigration from Mexico has taken a dangerous turn. Seeking to make their way around a freeway checkpoint, immigrants sometimes attempt to cross the busy San Diego freeway. After a number of people had been hit by cars, authorities posted signs like these to warn motorists to look out for people crossing the freeway.

You Are the Policymaker

Should Illegal Immigrants Receive Benefits from Government Programs?

Americans have traditionally welcomed immigrants with open arms. However, some immigrants have recently become less welcome: those who are in the country illegally. In states such as Texas and California, where many illegal immigrants from south of the border reside, there is concern that providing public services to these people is seriously draining state resources. This became the topic of heated debate when Californians voted on Proposition 187 in 1994. Labeled by its proponents as the "save our state initiative," this measure sought to cut illegal immigrants off from public services, such as the right of their children to attend public schools, and medical assistance for people with low incomes. According to its advocates, not only would Proposition 187 save the state treasury, but it would also cut down on the number of illegal immigrants—many of whom, they argued, had come mostly to take advantage of the free goods offered in America.

Opponents replied that although illegal immigration is surely a problem, the idea of cutting off public services could easily do more harm than good. They pointed out the risks to public health of denying illegal immigrants basic health care, such as immunizations that help control communicable diseases. And by throwing the children of illegal immigrants out of school, they argued that many would inevitably turn to crime with nothing to do all day. Besides, though they may be here illegally, these immigrants have to pay sales taxes on everything they buy and pay rent—a portion of which indirectly goes to the state when their landlords pay their property taxes. Given that they contribute to the tax base that pays for public services, opponents of Proposition 187 argued that they should in all fairness be entitled to make use of them.

The proponents of Proposition 187 won at the ballot box. However, so far they have lost in their attempts to get the measure enforced. The courts have consistently ruled that the proposition violated the rights of illegal immigrants as well as national laws concerning eligibility for federally funded benefits. Overall, the proposition was held to be an unconstitutional state scheme to regulate immigration.

Although the courts have held that states cannot deny public services to illegal aliens, in some cases it may be possible for the federal laws to do so. The 1996 Republican Party platform stated that "Illegal aliens should not receive public benefits other than emergency aid, and those who become parents while illegally in the United States should not be qualified to claim benefits for their offspring." What do you think? Would you support the sort of national laws that the Republicans proposed? What do you think would be the likely consequences if such laws were passed on the national level?

Unlike Hispanics who have come to America to escape poverty, the recent influx of Asians has been driven by a new class of professional workers looking for greater opportunity. Asians who have come to America since the 1965 Immigration Act[3] opened the gate to them make up the most highly skilled immigrant group in American history, as Ronald Takaki documents.[4] Indeed, Asian Americans have often been called the superachievers of the minority majority. This is especially true in the case of educational attainment—42 percent of Asian Americans over the age of 25 hold a college degree, almost twice the national average. As a result, their median family income has already surpassed that of non-Hispanic Whites. Although still a very small minority group, Asian Americans have had some notable political successes. In 1996, Gary Locke (a Chinese American) was elected governor of Washington and in 2000 Norman Mineta (a Japanese American) was appointed to be secretary of commerce.

Whereas Asian Americans are the best off of America's minority groups, by far the worst off is the one indigenous minority, known today as Native Americans. Before Europeans arrived in America, 12 to 15 million Native Americans lived here. War and disease reduced their numbers to a mere 210,000 by 1910. About 1.8 million Americans currently list themselves as being of Native American heritage. Statistics show that they are the least healthy, the poorest, and the least educated group in the American melting pot. Only

Asian Americans have been labeled as the "superachievers" of the coming minority majority due to their high levels of educational achievement and income. The proportion of Asian-American students currently exceeds 40 percent at some campuses of the University of California.

a handful of Native Americans have found wealth; even fewer have found power. Some tribes have discovered oil or other minerals on their land and have used these resources successfully. Most Native Americans, though, remain economically and politically disadvantaged in American society. The 1990 census found that in the Dakotas, site of the largest Sioux reservations, over half the Native Americans lived below the poverty line.

Americans live in an increasingly multicultural and multilingual society. Yet, regardless of ethnic background most Americans share a common **political culture**—an overall set of values widely shared within a society. For example, there is much agreement among ethnic groups about what truly makes an American, as shown in Table 6.1. Minority groups have assimilated many basic American values, such as the principle of treating all equally. Yet, not all observers view this recent wave of immigration without concern. Ellis Cose has written that "racial animosity has proven to be both an enduring American phenomenon and an invaluable political tool." Because America has entered a period of rapid ethnic change, Cose predicts immigration will be a magnet for conflict and hostility."[5]

political culture

An overall set of values widely shared within a society.

The emergence of the minority majority is just one of several major demographic changes that have altered the face of American politics. In addition, the population has been moving and aging.

Table 6.1 What Makes Someone an American?

A field poll of California asked a representative sample about different characteristics that many people think makes someone an American. Here you can see how different racial groups in California responded.

CHARACTERISTIC	ANGLOS	AFRICAN AMERICANS	HISPANICS	ASIANS
Treating all equally	89	94	81	93
Trying to get ahead	77	69	67	56
Speaking English	77	85	67	70
Voting	78	71	69	70
Speaking up for the country	51	63	54	43
Believing in God	36	65	48	35

Source: "American Identity and the Politics of Ethnic Change" by Jack Citrin, Beth A. Reingold, and Donald P. Green from *Journal of Politics*, 52:4, pp. 424–454.

The Regional Shift

For most of American history, the most populous states have been concentrated in the states north of the Mason-Dixon line and east of the Mississippi River. As you can see in Figure 6.2, though, over the last 60 years, much of America's population growth has been centered in the West and South. In particular, the populations of Florida, California, and Texas have grown rapidly as people moved to the Sunbelt. From 1990 to 2000, the rate of population growth was 24 percent in Florida, 14 percent in California, and 23 percent in Texas. In contrast, population growth in the Northeast was a scant 5 percent.

Demographic changes are associated with political changes. States gain or lose congressional representation as their population changes, and thus power shifts as well. This **reapportionment** process occurs once a decade, after every census. After each census, the 435 seats in the House of Representatives are reallocated to the states on the basis of population changes. Thus, as California has grown throughout this century, its representation in the House has increased from just 7 in 1900 to 53 as of 2002. New York, on the other hand, has lost about one-third of its delegation over the last 50 years.

reapportionment

The process of reallocating seats in the House of Representatives every 10 years on the basis of the results of the census.

The Graying of America

One of the three megastates, Florida, has grown in large part as a result of its attractiveness to senior citizens. Nationwide, the fastest growing age group in America is composed of citizens over 65. Not only are people living longer as a result of medical advances, but the birthrate has dropped substantially. About 60 percent of adult Americans living today grew up in families of four or more children. If the current "baby bust" continues, this figure will eventually be cut to 30 percent.[6]

By the year 2020, as the post-World War II baby boom generation reaches senior citizen status, there will be just two working Americans for every person over the age of 65, which will put tremendous pressure on the Social Security system. Begun under the New Deal, Social Security is exceeded only by national defense as America's most costly public policy. The current group of older Americans and those soon to follow can lay claim to roughly $5 trillion guaranteed by Social Security. They also hold title to roughly $1 trillion in public and private pension plans. There is a political message in these numbers: People who have been promised benefits expect to collect them, especially benefits for which they have made monthly contributions. Thus both political parties have long treated Social Security benefits as sacrosanct.

As the population has aged, new political interests have mobilized. Once discounted as no longer productive, the elderly now claim "gray power."[7] In Florida, the state's senior citizens typically vote against referenda for school taxes, much to the dismay of younger parents. They have also managed to secure tax breaks and service benefits for older people from the Florida legislature. Senior citizens have thus discovered an old political dictum: There is strength in numbers. A growing and potent group, the elderly have one advantage that no other group has—everyone can anticipate eventually reaching senior citizen status.

Why does it matter?

America is changing demographically. What difference does it make that there will probably be a minority majority in your lifetime? How may demographic changes likely impact policy? For example, how will an increase in the number of elderly citizens affect programs like Social Security and Medicare? In what ways might demographic changes alter your own interaction with government?

How Americans Learn About Politics: Political Socialization

As the most experienced segment of the population, the elderly have undergone the most **political socialization.** Political socialization is "the process through which an individual acquires his or her particular political orientations—his or her knowledge, feelings, and evaluations regarding his or her political world."[8] As people become more socialized with age, their political orientations grow firmer. It should not be surprising

political socialization

According to Richard Dawson, "the process through which an individual acquires his [or her] particular political orientations—his [or her] knowledge, feelings, and evaluations regarding his [or her] political world."

Figure 6.2 Shifting Population

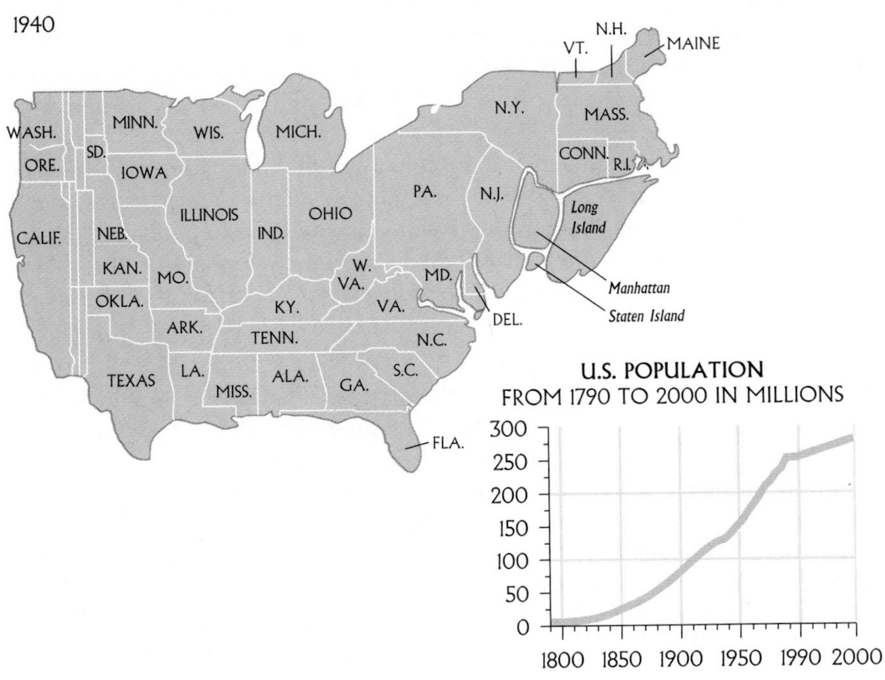

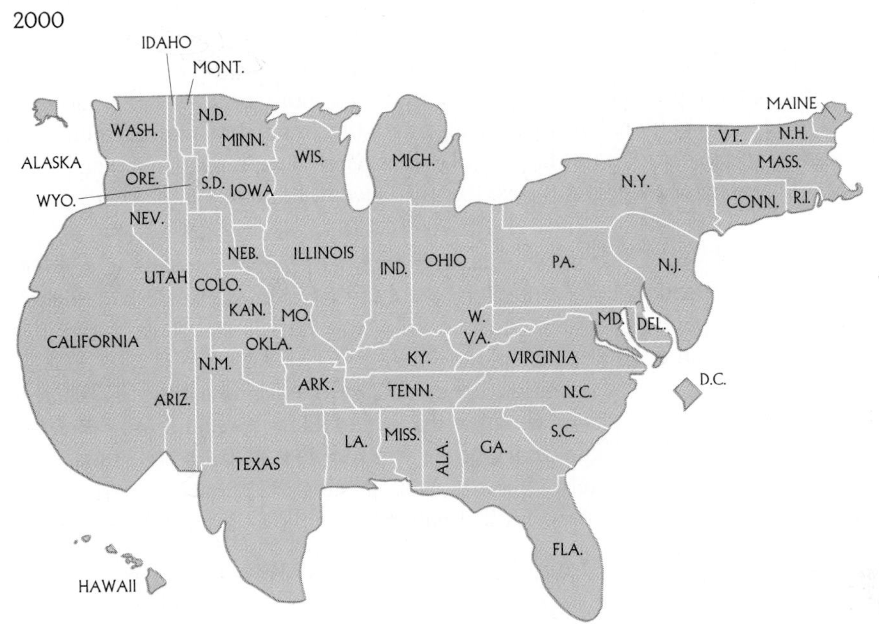

These maps paint a population portrait of the United States over the last six decades. The states are drawn to scale on the basis of population. In 1940, the most populous states were concentrated east of the Mississippi River. New York, Pennsylvania, and Illinois stand out. By 2000 the national population picture—and the map—had changed considerably. Today the country's 281 million citizens are scattered more widely, and though large concentrations of population still dominate the East, there has been huge growth on the West Coast, in Texas, and in Florida.

Source: The 1940 map was the work of the National Opinion Research Center, University of Denver, as printed in John Gunther's 1946 book *Inside U.S.A.*

that governments aim their socialization efforts largely at the young, not the elderly. Authoritarian regimes are particularly concerned with indoctrinating their citizens at an early age. For example, youth groups in the former Soviet Union were organized into the Komsomols, the Young Communist League. Membership in these groups was helpful in gaining admission to college and entering certain occupations. In the Komsomols, Soviet youths were taught their government's view of the advantages of communism (though apparently not well enough to keep the system going). In contrast, socialization is a much more subtle process in the United States.

The Process of Political Socialization

Only a small portion of Americans' political learning is formal. Civics or government classes in high school teach citizens some of the nuts and bolts of government—how many senators each state has, what presidents do, and so on. But such formal socialization is only the tip of the iceberg. Americans do most of their political learning without teachers or classes.

Informal learning is really much more important than formal, in-class learning about politics. Most informal socialization is almost accidental. Few parents sit down with their children and say, "Johnny, let us tell you why we're Republicans." Words like *pick up*, *absorb*, and *acquire* perhaps best describe the informal side of socialization. The family, the media, and the schools all serve as important agents of socialization.

The Family. The family's role in socialization is central because of its monopoly on two crucial resources in the early years: time and emotional commitment. The powerful influence of the family is not easily undermined. Most students in an American government class like to think of themselves as independent thinkers, especially when it comes to politics. Yet one can predict how the majority of young people will vote simply by knowing the political leanings of their parents. Table 6.2 shows how well people's party identification corresponds with that of their parents.

As children approach adult status, though, some degree of adolescent rebellion against parents and their beliefs often takes place. Witnessing the outpouring of youthful rebellion in the late 1960s and early 1970s, many people thought a generation gap was opening up. Radical youth supposedly condemned their backward-thinking parents. Though such a gap did exist in a few families, the overall evidence for it was slim. Eight years after Jennings and Niemi first interviewed a sample of high school seniors and their parents in the mid-1960s, they still found far more agreement than disagreement across the generational divide. Moving out of the family nest and into adulthood, the offspring did become somewhat less like their parents politically, however.[9] Other socialization agents had apparently exerted influence in the intervening years.

The Mass Media. The mass media are "the new parent" according to many observers. Average grade-school youngsters spend more time each week watching television than they spend at school. And television now displaces parents as the chief source of information as children get older.

Unfortunately, today's generation of young adults is significantly less likely to watch television news and read newspapers than their elders. A recent study attributed the relative lack of political knowledge of the youth of the 1990s to their media consumption, or more appropriately, to their lack of it.[10] In 1965, Gallup found virtually no difference between age categories in frequency of following politics through the

Table 6.2 How Party Identification is Passed Down From One Generation to the Next

The National Election Study has often asked respondents whether their parents thought of themselves as Democrats, Independents, or Republicans when they were growing up. In the most recent available data, 87 percent of those who could identify the partisanship of both parents reported that their parents agreed on partisan choice. In the following data, you can see how these respondents have generally followed in their parents' footsteps politically.

	DEMOCRAT	INDEPENDENT	REPUBLICAN	TOTAL
Both Parents Democrats	59	29	13	100%
Both Parents Independents	17	67	16	100%
Both Parents Republicans	12	29	59	100%

Source: Authors' analysis of 1992 National Election Study data.

media. By the 1990s, a considerable gap had opened up, though, with older people paying the most attention to the news and young adults the least. If you have ever turned on the TV news and wondered why all the commercials seem to be for Geritol, laxatives, or denture cream, now you know why.

School. Political socialization is as important to a government as it is to an individual. This is one reason why governments (including America's) often use schools to promote loyalty to the country and support for its basic values. In most American schools, the day begins with the Pledge of Allegiance. During the 1988 presidential campaign, George Bush argued that teachers should be required to lead students in the Pledge. His opponent, Michael Dukakis, had vetoed a bill to require this in Massachusetts, claiming that it was unconstitutional. Underlying Bush's argument was the assumption that proper socialization in the schools was crucial to the American political system—a position that Dukakis disagreed with more in terms of means than in ends.

Governments throughout the world use schools to attempt to raise children committed to the basic values of the system. For years, American children have been successfully educated about the virtues of capitalism and democracy. In the hands of an unscrupulous government, though, educational socialization can sometimes be a dangerous tool. For example, in Nazi Germany, textbooks were used to justify murderous policies. Consider the following example from a Nazi-era math book:

> *If a mental patient costs 4 Reichsmarks a day in maintenance, a cripple 5.50, and a criminal 3.50, and about 50,000 of these people are in our institutions, how much does it cost our state at a daily rate of 4 Reichsmarks—and how many marriage loans of 1,000 Reichsmarks per couple could have been given out instead?*[11]

These children—the faces of the coming minority majority population—suggest the unique problem of American political socialization: transforming people of diverse cultural backgrounds and beliefs into participating American citizens.

One can only imagine how the constant exposure, in schools, to this kind of thinking warped the minds of some young people growing up in Nazi Germany.

Both authoritarian and democratic governments care that students learn the positive features of their political system because it helps ensure that youth will grow up to be supportive citizens. David Easton and Jack Dennis have argued that "those children who begin to develop positive feelings toward the political authorities will grow into adults who will be less easily disenchanted with the system than those children who early acquire negative, hostile sentiments."[12] Of course, this is not always the case. Well-socialized youths of the 1960s led the opposition to the American regime and the war in Vietnam. It could be argued, however, that even these protestors had been positively shaped by the socialization process, for the goal of most activists was to make the system more democratically responsive rather than to change American government radically.

Today, education is often the issue that people cite as the most important to them, and there is no doubt that educational policy matters a great deal. Most American schools are public schools, financed by the government. Their textbooks are often chosen by the local and state boards, and teachers are certified by the state government. Schooling is perhaps the most obvious intrusion of the government into Americans' socialization. Education exerts a profound influence on a variety of political attitudes and behavior. Better-educated citizens are more likely to vote in elections, they exhibit more knowledge about politics and public policy, and they are more tolerant of opposing (even radical) opinions.

The payoffs of schooling extend beyond better jobs and better pay. Educated citizens also more closely approximate the model of a democratic citizen. A formal civics course may not make much difference, but the whole context of education does. As Albert Einstein once said, "Schools need not preach political doctrine to defend democracy. If they shape men and women capable of critical thought and trained in social attitudes, that is all that is necessary."

Political Learning Over a Lifetime

Political learning does not, of course, end when one reaches 18, or even when one graduates from college. Politics is a lifelong activity. Because America is an aging society, it is important to consider the effects of growing older on political learning and behavior.

Aging increases political participation, as well as strength of party attachment. Young adults (those 18 through 25) lack experience with politics. Because political behavior is to some degree learned behavior, there is some learning yet to do. Political participation rises steadily with age until the infirmities of old age make it harder to participate, as can be seen in the data presented in Figure 6.3. Similarly, strength of party identification also increases as one grows older and often develops a pattern for usually voting for one party or another.

participation
Which Are You: Liberal or Conservative

Politics, like most other things, is thus a learned behavior. Americans learn to vote, to pick a political party, and to evaluate political events in the world around them. One of the products of all this learning is what is known as public opinion.

Measuring Public Opinion and Political Information

Before examining the role that public opinion plays in American politics, it is essential to learn about the science of public opinion measurement. How do we really know the approximate answers to questions such as what percentage of young people favor abortion rights, how many African Americans supported Clinton's reelec-

Figure 6.3 Turnout by Age, 2000

This graph shows how turnout in the 2000 presidential election was related to age.

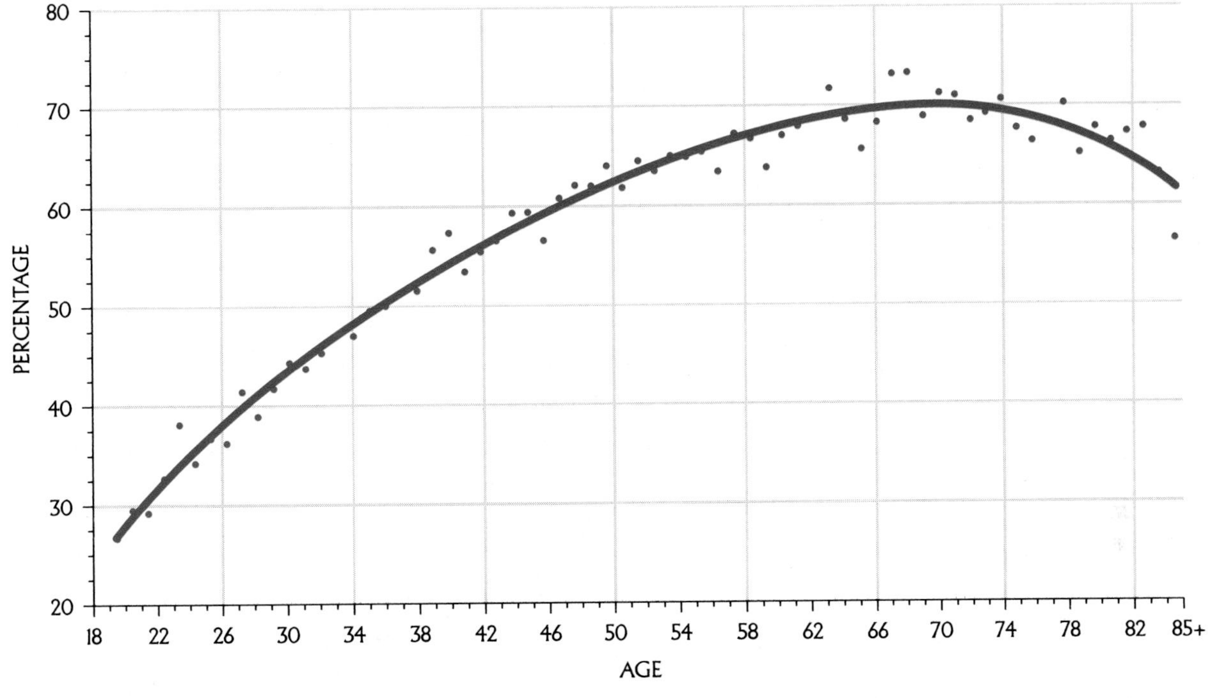

Source: Authors' analysis of 2000 Census Bureau Data.

tion, or what percentage of the public favored impeaching Clinton because of the Lewinsky scandal? Polls provide these answers, but there is much skepticism about polls. Many people wonder how this can be done by only interviewing 1,000 or 1,500 people around the country. This section provides an explanation of how polling works, which will hopefully enable you to become a well-informed consumer of polls.

How Polls Are Conducted

Public opinion polling is a relatively new science. It was first developed by a young man named George Gallup, who initially did some polling for his mother-in-law, a longshot candidate for secretary of state in Iowa in 1932. With the Democratic landslide of that year, she won a stunning victory, thereby further stimulating Gallup's interest in politics. From that little acorn the mighty oak of public opinion polling has grown. The firm that Gallup founded spread throughout the democratic world, and in some languages, *Gallup* is actually the word used for an opinion poll.[13]

It would be prohibitively expensive and time consuming to ask every citizen his or her opinion on a whole range of issues. Instead, polls rely on a **sample** of the population—a relatively small proportion of people who are chosen to represent the whole. Herbert Asher draws an analogy to a blood test to illustrate the principle of sampling.[14] Your doctor does not need to drain a gallon of blood from you to determine whether you have mononucleosis, AIDS, or any other disease. Rather, a small sample of blood will reveal its properties.

sample

A relatively small proportion of people who are chosen in a survey so as to be representative of the whole.

In public opinion polling, a sample of about 1,000 to 1,500 people can accurately represent the "universe" of potential voters. The key to the accuracy of opinion

QUALITY TIME Gail Machlis

I know I'd be completely devastated if he grew up and registered for another political party.

random sampling

The key technique employed by sophisticated survey researchers, which operates on the principle that everyone should have an equal probability of being selected for the sample.

sampling error

The level of confidence in the findings of a public opinion poll. The more people interviewed, the more confident one can be of the results.

polls is the technique of **random sampling,** which operates on the principle that everyone should have an equal probability of being selected as part of the sample. Your chance of being asked to be in the poll should therefore be as good as that of anyone else—rich or poor, African American or White, young or old, male or female. If the sample is randomly drawn, about 12 percent of those interviewed will be African American, slightly over 50 percent female, and so forth, matching the population as a whole.

Remember that the science of polling involves estimation; a sample can represent the population with only a certain degree of confidence. The level of confidence is known as the **sampling error,** which depends on the size of the sample. The more people interviewed in a poll, the more confident one can be of the results. A typical poll of about 1,500 to 2,000 respondents has a sampling error of ± 3 percent. What this means is that 95 percent of the time the poll results are within 3 percent of what the entire population thinks. If 60 percent of the sample say they approve of the job the president is doing, one can be pretty certain that the true figure is between 57 and 63 percent.

In order to obtain results that will usually be within sampling error, researchers must follow proper sampling techniques. In perhaps the most infamous survey ever, a 1936 *Literary Digest* poll underestimated the vote for President Franklin Roosevelt by 19 percent, erroneously predicting a big victory for Republican Alf Landon. The well-established magazine suddenly became a laughingstock and soon went out of business. Although the number of responses the magazine obtained for its poll was a staggering 2,376,000, its polling methods were badly flawed. Trying to reach as many people as possible, the magazine drew names from the biggest lists they could find: telephone books and motor vehicle records. In the midst of the Great Depression, the people on these lists were above the average income level (only 40 percent of the public had telephones then; fewer still owned cars) and were more likely to vote

simulation
You are a Polling Consultant

Republican. The moral of the story is this: Accurate representation, not the number of responses, is the most important feature of a public opinion survey. Indeed, as polling techniques have advanced over the last 50 years, typical sample sizes have been getting smaller, not larger.

The newest computer and telephone technology has made surveying less expensive and more commonplace. Until recently, pollsters needed a national network of interviewers to traipse door-to-door in their localities with a clipboard of questions. Now most polling is done on the telephone with samples selected through **random-digit dialing.** Calls are placed to phone numbers within randomly chosen exchanges (for example, 512–471-xxxx) around the country. In this manner, both listed and unlisted numbers are reached at a cost of about one-fifth that of person-to-person interviewing. There are a couple of disadvantages, however. Seven percent of the population does not have a phone, and people are somewhat less willing to participate over the telephone than in person—it is easier to hang up than to slam the door in someone's face. These are small trade-offs for political candidates running for minor offices, for whom telephone polls are the only affordable method of gauging public opinion.

random digit dialing

A technique used by pollsters to place telephone calls randomly to both listed and unlisted numbers when conducting a survey.

From its modest beginning with George Gallup's 1932 polls for his mother-in-law in Iowa, polling has become a big business. Public opinion polling is one of those American innovations, like soft drinks and fast food restaurants, that has spread throughout the world. From Manhattan to Moscow, from Tulsa to Tokyo, people want to know what other people think.

The Role of Polls in American Democracy

Polls help political candidates detect public preferences. Supporters of polling insist that it is a tool for democracy. With it, they say, policymakers can keep in touch with changing opinions on the issues. No longer do politicians have to wait until the next election to see whether the public approves or disapproves of the government's course. If the poll results suddenly turn, then government officials can make corresponding midcourse corrections. Indeed, it was George Gallup's fondest hope that polling could contribute to the democratic process by providing a way for public desires to be heard at times other than elections.

Critics of polling, by contrast, think it makes politicians more concerned with following than leading. Polls might have told the constitutional convention delegates that the Constitution was unpopular or might have told President Thomas Jefferson that people did not want the Louisiana Purchase. Certainly they would have told William Seward not to buy Alaska, a transaction known widely at the time as "Seward's Folly." Polls may thus discourage bold leadership, like that of Winston Churchill, who once said,

> *Nothing is more dangerous than to live in the temperamental atmosphere of a Gallup poll, always taking one's pulse and taking one's temperature. . . . There is only one duty, only one safe course, and that is to try to be right and not to fear to do or say what you believe.*[15]

Recent research by Jacobs and Shapiro argues that the common perception of politicians like Bill Clinton pandering to the results of public opinion polls may be mistaken. Their examination of major policy debates in the 1990s finds that political leaders "track public opinion not to make policy but rather to determine how to craft their public presentations and win public support for the policies they and their supporters favor."[16] Staff members in both the White House and the Congress repeatedly remarked that their purpose in conducting polls was not to set policies, but rather the keywords and phrases with which to "sell" policies. Thus, rather than using polls to identify centrist approaches that will have the broadest popular appeal, Jacobs and Shapiro argue that elites use them to formulate strategies that enable them to avoid compromising on what they want to do.

Public opinion polls these days are mostly done over the telephone. Interviewers, most of whom are young people (and frequently college students), sit in front of computer teriminals and read the questions that appear on the screen to randomly chosen individuals who they have reached on the phone. They then enter the appropriate coded responses directly into the computer database. Such efficient procedures make it possible for analysts to get survey results very quickly.

Polls can also weaken democracy by distorting the election process. They are often accused of creating a *bandwagon effect*. The wagon carrying the band was the centerpiece of nineteenth-century political parades, and enthusiastic supporters would literally jump on it. Today, the term refers to voters who support a candidate merely because they see that others are doing so. Although only 2 percent of people in a recent CBS/*New York Times* poll said that poll results had influenced them, 26 percent said they thought others had been influenced (showing that Americans feel "It's always the other person who's susceptible"). Beyond this, polls play to the media's interest in who's ahead in the race. The issues of recent presidential campaigns have sometimes been drowned out by a steady flood of poll results.

exit polls

Public opinion surveys used by major media pollsters to predict electoral winners with speed and precision.

Probably the most widely criticized type of poll is the election-day **exit poll.** For this type of poll, voting places are randomly selected around the country. Workers are then sent to these places and told to ask every tenth person how they voted. The results are accumulated toward the end of the day, enabling the television networks to project the outcomes of all but very close races before the polls even close. In the presidential elections of 1980, 1984, 1988, and 1996, the networks declared a national winner while millions on the West Coast still had hours to vote. Critics have charged that this practice discourages many people from voting and thereby affects the outcome of some state and local races. Although many voters in the Western states have been outraged by this practice, careful analysis of survey data shows that few voters have actually been influenced by exit-poll results.[17]

In 2000, the exit polls received much of the blame for the media's inaccurate calls of the Florida result on election night. But contrary to common perception, the exit polls deserve only a portion of the blame for the networks' election night fiasco. Because the Florida exit poll showed a small advantage for Gore, the networks could not have called the election based on this information alone. Inaccurate reports and estimates of the actual votes threw off the network prognostications most. The early call for Gore was apparently largely caused by underestimating the size of the absentee vote, which favored Bush. In addition, there was also a serious mistake in the early reporting of the vote in Duval County. Amazingly, the Voter News Service had entered in 95 percent for Gore in this Republican county, which naturally threw off their projection. Then, near the end of the counting on election night, they estimated that there were only about 180,000 votes left when there were actually twice as many left. Hence, they prematurely gave the state (and the presidency) to Bush, not realizing how much of a chance there was for Gore to close the gap.

Perhaps the most pervasive criticism of polling is that by altering the wording of a question, pollsters can usually get the results they want. Sometimes subtle changes in question wording can produce dramatic differences. For example, a month before the start of the Gulf War, the percentage of the public who thought we should go to war was 18 percentage points higher in the ABC/*Washington Post* poll than in the CBS/*New York Times* poll. The former poll asked whether the United States should go to war "at some point after January 15 or not," a relatively vague question; in contrast, the latter poll offered an alternative to war, asking whether the "U.S. should start military actions against Iraq, or should the U.S. wait longer to see if the trade embargo and other economic sanctions work."[18] It is therefore important to evaluate carefully how questions are posed when reading public opinion data.

Polling sounds scientific with its talk of random samples and sampling error; it is easy to take results for solid fact. But being an informed consumer of polls requires more than just a nuts-and-bolts knowledge of how they are conducted. You should think about whether the questions are fair and unbiased before making too much of the results. The good—or the harm—that polls do depends on how well the data are collected and how thoughtfully the data are interpreted.

What Polls Reveal About Americans' Political Information

Abraham Lincoln spoke stirringly of the inherent wisdom of the American people: "It is true that you may fool all of the people some of the time; and you can even fool some of the people all of the time; but you can't fool all of the people all the time." Obviously, Lincoln recognized the complexity of public opinion.

Thomas Jefferson and Alexander Hamilton had very different views about the wisdom of common people. Jefferson trusted people's good sense and believed that education would enable them to take the tasks of citizenship ever more seriously. Toward that end, he founded the University of Virginia. Hamilton held a contrasting view. His infamous words "Your people, sir, are a great beast" do not reflect confidence in people's capacity for self-government.

If there had been polling data in the early days of the American republic, Hamilton would probably have delighted in throwing some of the results in Jefferson's face. If public opinion analysts agree about anything, it is that the level of public knowledge about politics is dismally low. As discussed, this is particularly true for young people, but the overall levels of political knowledge are not particularly encouraging either. For example, in the 2000 National Election Study conducted by the University of Michigan, a random sample was asked to identify the position held by some prominent political leaders. The results were as follows:

- 51 percent knew Janet Reno was attorney general of the United States
- 30 percent knew Tony Blair was prime minister of the United Kingdom
- 9 percent knew William Rehnquist was chief justice of the Supreme Court
- 7 percent knew that Trent Lott was the Republican leader in the U.S. Senate

With all the results taken into account, the study found that less than half of the population could identify three of these four leaders.

No amount of Jeffersonian faith in the wisdom of the common people can erase the fact that Americans are not well informed about politics. Polls have regularly found that less than half the public can name their representative in the House, much less say how he or she generally votes. Asking most people to explain their opinion on

Why does it matter?

Does the average American lack the political knowledge required to be a citizen of true democracy? How much political knowledge is enough? Do your family and friends know enough? Do you? How might politics be different if more people were better informed?

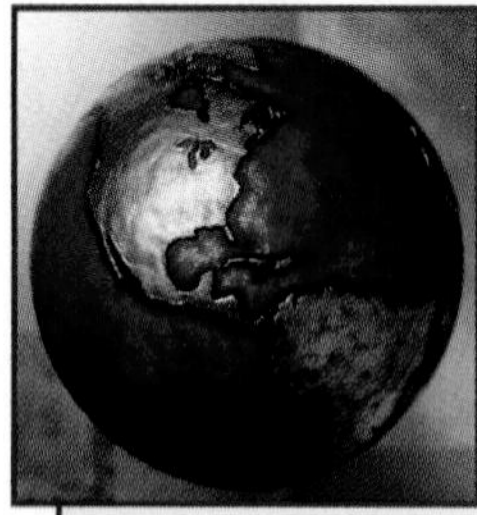

America in Perspective

Citizens Show Little Knowledge of Geography

In a major cross-national study, over 12,000 people in 10 nations were asked to identify 16 places on the following world map. The average citizen in the United States could identify barely more than half. Believe it or not, 14 percent of Americans could not even find their own country on the map. Despite years of fighting in Vietnam, 68 percent could not locate this Southeast Asian country. Such lack of basic geographic knowledge is quite common throughout the world. Here is the average score for each of the 10 countries in which the test was administered:

COUNTRY	AVERAGE SCORE
Sweden	11.6
West Germany	11.2
Japan	9.7
France	9.3
Canada	9.2
United States	**8.6**
Great Britain	8.5
Italy	7.6
Mexico	7.4
Soviet Union	7.4

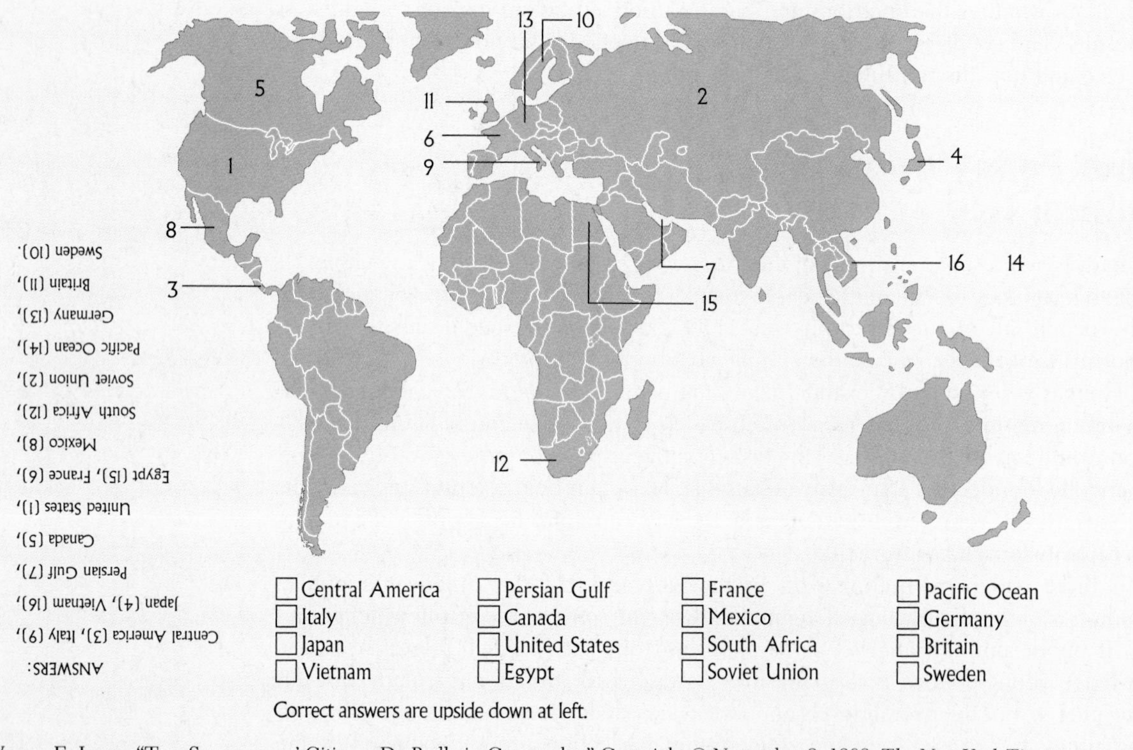

Correct answers are upside down at left.

Source: Warren E. Leary, "Two Superpowers' Citizens Do Badly in Geography." Copyright © November 9, 1989, *The New York Times.*

whether trade policy toward China should be liberalized, the proposed "Star Wars" missile defense system, or whether the strategic oil reserve should be tapped when gasoline prices skyrocket often elicits blank looks. When trouble flares in a far-off country, polls regularly find that people have no idea where that country is. In fact, surveys show that citizens around the globe lack a basic awareness of the world around them (see "America in Perspective: Citizens Show Little Knowledge of Geography.")

As Lance Bennett points out, these findings provide "a source of almost bitter humor in light of what the polls tell us about public information on other subjects."[19] He notes that more people know their astrological sign (76 percent) than know the name of their representative in the House. Slogans from TV commercials are better recognized than famous political figures. Few people knew President Bush's stand on the capital gains tax, but 75 percent of the public could name the vegetable he did not like (broccoli).

How can Americans, who live in the most information-rich society in the world, be so ill-informed about politics? Some blame the schools. E. D. Hirsch, Jr. criticizes schools for a failure to teach "cultural literacy."[20] People, he says, often lack the basic contextual knowledge—for example, where Africa is, what the Vietnam War was about, and so forth—necessary to understand and use the information they receive from the news media or from listening to political candidates. Indeed, it has been found that increased levels of education over the last four decades have scarcely raised public knowledge about politics.[21] Despite the apparent glut of information provided by the media, Americans do not remember much about what they are exposed to through the media. (Of course, there are many critics who say that the media fail to provide much meaningful information, a topic that will be discussed in Chapter 7.)

The "paradox of mass politics," says Russell Neuman, is that the American political system works as well as it does given the discomforting lack of public knowledge about politics.[22] Part of the reason for this phenomenon is that people may not know the ins and outs of policy questions or the actors on the political stage, but they know what basic values they want upheld.

The Decline of Trust in Government

Sadly, the American public has become increasingly dissatisfied with government over the last four decades, as you can see in Figure 6.4. In the late 1950s and early 1960s about three quarters of Americans said that they trusted the government in Washington to do the right thing always or mostly. Following the 1964 election, however, researchers started to see a precipitous drop in public trust in government. First Vietnam and then Watergate shook the people's confidence in the federal government. The economic troubles of the Carter years and the Iran hostage crisis helped continue the slide; by 1980, only a quarter of the public thought the government could be trusted most of the time or always. During the Reagan years, public cynicism abated a

Figure 6.4 The Decline of Trust in Government

This graph shows how people have responded over time to the following question: How much of the time do you think you can trust the government in Washington to do what is right—just about always, most of the time, or only some of the time.

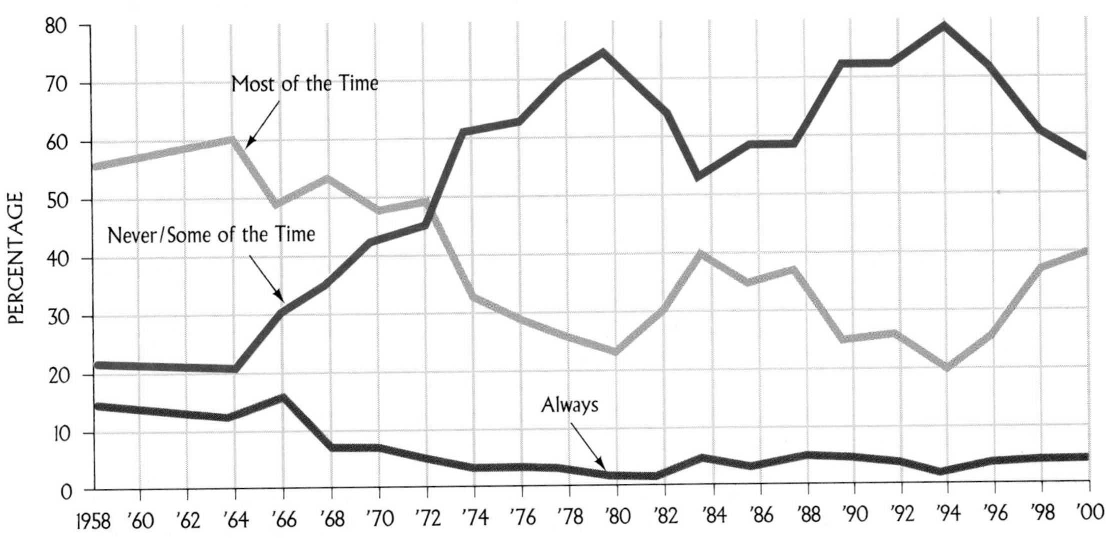

Source: Authors' analysis of 1958–2000 American National Election Study data.

bit, but by 1994, trust in government had plummeted again to another all-time low. Since 1994, trust in government has improved somewhat, but it seems unlikely that we will see trust return to the optimistic levels of the Kennedy years any time soon.

Some analysts have noted that a healthy dose of public cynicism helps to keep politicians on their toes. Others, however, note that a democracy is based on the consent of the governed and that a lack of public trust in the government is a reflection of their belief that the system is not serving them well. When people feel that government is not working according to the values they subscribe to, the sleeping giant of public opinion may be stirred to action. Examining these values is thus of great importance.

What Americans Value: Political Ideologies

political ideology

A coherent set of beliefs about politics, public policy, and public purpose. It helps give meaning to political events, personalities, and policies. See also **liberalism** and **conservatism.**

A coherent set of values and beliefs about public policy is a **political ideology.** Liberal ideology, for example, supports a wide scope for the central government, often involving policies that aim to promote equality. Conservative ideology, in contrast, supports a less active scope of government that gives freer reign to the private sector. Table 6.3 attempts to summarize some of the key differences between liberals and conservatives.

Who Are the Liberals and Conservatives?

Overall, more Americans consistently choose the ideological label of **conservative** over **liberal.** Combining data from the 1996 and 1998 National Election Studies (in order to have more cases to analyze), we found that of those who labeled themselves, 42 per-

Table 6.3 How to Tell a Liberal From a Conservative

Liberal and *conservative*—these labels are thrown around in American politics as though everyone knows what they mean. Here are some of the political beliefs likely to be preferred by liberals and conservatives. This table, to be sure, is oversimplified.

	LIBERALS	CONSERVATIVES
FOREIGN POLICY:		
Military spending	Believe we should spend less	Believe we should maintain peace through strength
Use of force	Less willing to commit troops to action, such as in the Persian Gulf War	More likely to support military intervention around the world
SOCIAL POLICY:		
Abortion	Support "freedom of choice"	Support "right to life"
Prayer in schools	Are opposed	Are supportive
Affirmative action	Favor	Oppose
ECONOMIC POLICY:		
Scope of government	View government as a regulator in the public interest	Favor free-market solutions
Taxes	Want to tax the rich more	Want to keep taxes low
Spending	Want to spend more on the poor	Want to keep spending low
CRIME:		
How to cut crime	Believe we should solve the problems that cause crime	Believe we should stop "coddling criminals"
Defendants' rights	Believe we should guard them carefully	Believe we should stop letting criminals hide behind laws

cent were conservatives, 34 percent were moderates, and just 25 percent were liberals. The predominance of conservative thinking in America is one of the most important reasons for the relatively restrained scope of government activities compared to most European nations.

Yet, there are some groups that are more liberal than others, and thus would generally like to see the government do more. Among people under the age of 30, there are just as many liberals as conservatives (see Table 6.4). The younger the individual, the less likely that person is to be a conservative. The fact that younger people are also less likely to vote, therefore means that conservatives are overrepresented at the polls.

In general, groups with political clout tend to be more conservative than groups whose members have often been shut out from the halls of political power. This is because excluded groups have often looked to the government to rectify the inequalities they have faced. For example, African Americans benefited from government activism in the form of the major civil rights bills of the 1960s to bring them into the mainstream of American life. Many African-American leaders currently place a high priority on retaining social welfare and affirmative action programs in order to assist their progress. It should come as little surprise then that African Americans are more liberal than the national average. Similarly, Hispanics also are less conservative than Whites, and if this pattern continues into the twenty-first century the influx of many more Hispanics into the electorate will move the country in a slightly liberal direction.

Women are not a minority group, making up about 54 percent of the population, but they have nevertheless been politically and economically disadvantaged. Compared to men, women are more likely to support spending on social services and to oppose the higher levels of military spending, which conservatives typically advocate. It is these issues concerning the priorities of government rather than the issue of abortion—on which men and women actually differ very little—that leads women to be significantly less conservative than men. This ideological difference between men

Table 6.4 The Political Ideology of Various Demographic Groups

The following table shows the percentage of liberals, moderates, and conservatives among each demographic group. Those who said they didn't usually think of themselves in these terms, or didn't know, are excluded. (Numbers may not always add up to 100 due to rounding.)

	LIBERAL	MODERATE	CONSERVATIVE
Women	27	36	37
Men	22	30	47
18–29	34	32	34
30–44	25	34	41
45–64	23	31	46
65+	16	38	47
White	24	33	43
African-American	31	37	32
Hispanic	27	37	36
lower third in family income	25	37	38
middle third in family income	26	37	37
upper third in family income	24	28	49
Protestant	18	34	49
Catholic	25	35	41
Jewish	63	20	18
No religion	39	36	25

Source: Authors' analysis of 1996 and 1998 American National Election Study data combined.

gender gap

A term that refers to the regular pattern by which women are more likely to support Democratic candidates. Women tend to be significantly less conservative than men and are more likely to support spending on social services and to oppose higher levels of military spending.

and women has led to the **gender gap,** which refers to the regular pattern by which women are more likely to support Democratic candidates. Bill Clinton carried the women's vote while Bob Dole was preferred among men in 1996, making Clinton the first president who can be said to be elected via the support of only one gender. In 2000, exit polls showed that women were about 12 percent more likely to support Al Gore than men.

The gender gap is a relatively new predictor of ideological positions, dating back only to 1980, when Ronald Reagan was first elected. A much more traditional source of division between liberals and conservatives has been financial status, or what is often known as social class. But as you can see in Table 6.4, the relationship between family income and ideology is now relatively weak. As a result, social class has become much less predictive of political behavior than it used to be.[23]

The role of religion in influencing political ideology has also changed greatly in recent years. Catholics and Jews, as minority groups who struggled for equality, have long been more liberal than Protestants. Today, Jews remain by far the most liberal demographic group in the county.[24] However, the ideological gap between Catholics and Protestants is now smaller than the gender gap. Ideology is now determined more by religiosity—that is, the degree to which religion is important in one's life—than by religious denomination. What is known as the new Christian Right consists of Catholics and Protestants who consider themselves fundamentalists or "born again." The influx of new policy issues dealing with matters of morality and traditional family values has recently tied this aspect of religious beliefs to political ideology. Those who identify themselves as "born again" Christians are currently the most conservative demographic group. On the other hand, people who say they have no religious affiliation (roughly one-tenth of the population) are more liberal than conservative.

visual literacy
Who Are Liberals and Conservatives? What's the Difference?

Just as some people are very much guided by their religious beliefs whereas others are not, the same is true for political ideology. It would probably be a mistake to assume that when conservative candidates do better than they have in the past that this necessarily means people want more conservative policies, for not everyone thinks in ideological terms.

Do People Think in Ideological Terms?

The authors of the classic study *The American Voter* first examined how much people rely on ideology to guide their political thinking.[25] They divided the public into four groups, according to ideological sophistication. Their portrait of the American electorate was not flattering. Only 12 percent of the people showed evidence of thinking in ideological terms and thus were classified as *ideologues.* These people could connect their opinions and beliefs with broad policy positions taken by parties or candidates. They might say, for example, that they liked the Democrats because they were more liberal or the Republicans because they favored a smaller government. Forty-two percent of Americans were classified as *group benefits* voters. These people thought of politics mainly in terms of the groups they liked or disliked; for example, "Republicans support small business owners like me" or "Democrats are the party of the working person." Twenty-four percent of the population were *nature of the times* voters. Their handle on politics was limited to whether the times seemed good or bad to them; they might vaguely link the party in power with the country's fortune or misfortune. Finally, 22 percent of the voters were devoid of any ideological or issue content in their political evaluations. They were called the *no issue content* group. Most of them simply voted routinely for a party or judged the candidates solely by their personalities. Overall, at least during the 1950s, Americans seemed to care little about the differences between liberal and conservative politics.

There has been much debate about whether this portrayal accurately characterizes the public today. Nie, Verba, and Petrocik took a look at the changing American voter from 1956 to 1972 and argued that voters were more sophisticated in the 1970s than in the 1950s.[26] Others, though, have concluded that people only seemed more informed and ideological because the wording of the questions had changed.[27] If the exact same methods are used to update the analysis of *The American Voter* through more recent elections, one finds some increase in the proportion of ideologues, but not much. The last time these methods were employed was in 1988, and then just 18 percent were classified as ideologues, as compared to 12 percent in 1956. Given that George Bush continually labeled his 1988 opponent Michael Dukakis as "that liberal Governor from the most liberal state in the country," it is striking how few people actually evaluated the parties and candidates in ideological terms.

These findings do not mean that the vast majority of the population does not have a political ideology. Rather, for most people the terms *liberal* and *conservative* are just not as important as they are for the political elite such as politicians, activists, journalists, and the like. Relatively few people have ideologies that organize their political beliefs as clearly as shown in Table 6.3. Thus, the authors of *The American Voter* concluded that to speak of election results as indicating a movement of the public either left (to more liberal policies) or right (to more conservative policies) is not justified because most voters do not think in such terms. Furthermore, those who do are actually the least likely to shift from one election to the next.

The American Voter argued persuasively that Republican Dwight Eisenhower's two election victories did not represent a shift in the conservative direction during the 1950s. In the 1980s, the issue of whether public opinion had undergone a major rightward change was once again raised in the wake of the victories of Ronald Reagan, who campaigned vigorously against intrusive government.

Has There Been a Turn Toward Conservatism?

Ronald Reagan was clearly the most conservative president since the New Deal. During his eight years as president, he pressed ahead with a thoroughly conservative agenda that included:

- Reduced levels of government spending on domestic programs such as welfare and federal aid to education
- Increased defense spending, and support for foreign political movements that claimed to be fighting communism
- A 25 percent across-the-board reduction in federal income tax rates
- Support for a conservative social agenda, including prayer in schools, stronger law enforcement, and antiabortion legislation

With Reagan's landslide reelection victory in 1984, some political observers felt that a conservative wildfire had swept the country. Numerous Democratic leaders warned party members not to be left out on a liberal limb. "Don't be the party of more taxing and spending," they cautioned fellow Democrats. In 1992, Bill Clinton followed this advice, saying that his vision for government was "not tax and spend, but invest, educate, innovate, a partnership between government and business."[28]

Despite Reagan's victories throughout the 1980s, scholarly analyses included the common theme that people liked Reagan but not his policies. With the exception of a rise in support for military spending during the 1980 campaign, public opinion specialists were unable to document any shift toward conservative attitudes during the 1980s. As Ferguson and Rogers concluded, "If American public opinion drifted anywhere over Reagan's first term, it was toward the left, not the right, just the opposite of the turn in public policy."[29] Asked to assess Reagan's time in office, the 1988 electorate was evenly split on the wisdom of defense increases, and was generally unaware and unsupportive of domestic cuts.[30]

If so many people disagreed with Reagan, why was he such a popular president, and why was George Bush able to run successfully on his record in 1988? The answer is simply that many swing voters, those whom *The American Voter* classified as *nature of the times* voters, care more about results than ideology.[31] The 1980 election was more about voting Carter out of office than voting Reagan into it. In 1984 and 1988, the Republicans had a record of relative peace and prosperity on their side, which was the key to victories for Reagan and Bush. With the economic downturn in 1992, these same swing voters decided that it was time for a change and propelled Bill Clinton into the White House.

Clinton's time in the White House marked a return to largely centrist policies. His major success has been to eliminate the budget deficit without cutting social programs. He did increase taxes somewhat in his first yearly budget, but not by nearly as much as most liberals would have liked. Clinton's only real venture into advocating liberal programs was a complex scheme to eventually guarantee health care coverage to all Americans. This ambitious proposal proved to be the biggest policy failure of his presidency, and never really got off the ground in Congress—due in part to strong opposition from many political activists concerned with health care policy (see Chapter 19 for further details).

www.longmanparticipate.com
timeline
Public Opinion and Presidential Approval

How Americans Participate in Politics

In politics, as in many other aspects of life, the squeaky wheel gets the grease. The way citizens "squeak" in politics is to participate. Americans have many avenues of political participation open to them.

- Mrs. Jones of Iowa City goes to a neighbor's living room to attend her local precinct's presidential caucus.
- Demonstrators against abortion protest at the Supreme Court on the anniversary of the *Roe v. Wade* decision.
- Parents in Alabama file a lawsuit to oppose textbooks that, in their opinion, promote "secular humanism."
- Mr. Smith, a Social Security recipient, writes to his senator to express his concern about a possible cut in his cost-of-living benefits.
- Over 100 million people vote in a presidential election.

political participation

All the activities used by citizens to influence the selection of political leaders or the policies they pursue. The most common, but not the only, means of political participation in a **democracy** is voting. Other means include **protest** and **civil disobedience.**

All these activities are types of political participation. **Political participation** encompasses the many activities in which citizens engage to influence the selection of political leaders or the policies they pursue.[32] Participation can be overt or subtle. The mass protests throughout Eastern Europe in the Fall of 1989 represented an avalanche of political participation, yet quietly writing a letter to your congressperson also represents political participation. Political participation can be violent or peaceful, organized or individual, casual or consuming.

Generally, the United States has a culture that values political participation. Citizens express pride in their nation: 87 percent say they are very proud to be Americans.[33] Nevertheless, just 51 percent of adult Americans voted in the presidential election of 2000, and only 36 percent turned out for the 1998 midterm elections. At the local level, the situation is even worse, with elections for city council and school board often drawing less than 10 percent of the eligible voters. (For more on voter turnout and why it is so low, see Chapter 10.)

Conventional Participation

Although the line is hard to draw, political scientists generally distinguish between two broad types of participation: conventional and unconventional. Conventional participation includes many widely accepted modes of influencing government—voting, trying to persuade others, ringing doorbells for a petition, running for office, and so on. In contrast, unconventional participation includes activities that are often dramatic, such as protesting, civil disobedience, and even violence.

For a few, politics is their lifeblood; they run for office, work regularly in politics, and live for the next election. The number of Americans for whom political

There are many ways of participating in politics beyond voting. One conventional form of participating is to sign a petition concerning a political issue. Here, some New York residents are shown signing a petition demanding stricter control of water pollution.

activity is an important part of their everyday life is minuscule; they number at most in the tens of thousands. To these people, policy questions are as familiar as slogans on TV commercials are to the average citizen. They are the political elites—activists, party leaders, interest group leaders, judges, members of Congress, and other public officials. (Part 3 of this book will discuss the political elite in detail.)

Millions take part in political activities beyond simply voting. In two comprehensive studies of American political participation conducted by Sidney Verba and his colleagues, samples of Americans were asked in 1967 and 1987 about their role in various kinds of political activities.[34] Included were voting, working in campaigns, contacting government officials, and working on local community issues. Voting was the only aspect of political participation that a majority of the population reported engaging in, but also the only political activity for which there is evidence of a decline in participation in recent years. Substantial increases in participation were found on the dimensions of giving money to candidates and contacting public officials, and small increases are evident for all the other activities. Thus, although the decline of voter turnout is a development Americans should rightly be concerned about (see Chapter 10), a broader look at political participation reveals some positive developments for participatory democracy.

Protest as Participation

From the Boston Tea Party to burning draft cards, to demonstrating against abortion, Americans have engaged in countless political protests. **Protest** is a form of political participation designed to achieve policy change through dramatic and unconventional tactics. The media's willingness to cover the unusual can make protests worthwhile, drawing attention to a point of view that many Americans might otherwise never encounter. For example, when an 89-year-old woman decided to try to walk across the country to draw attention to the need for campaign finance reform, she put this issue onto the front page of newspapers most everywhere she traveled (see "Making a Difference: Granny D and Her Walk for Campaign Finance Reform"). Using much more flamboyant means, the AIDS activist group appropriately called "ACT-UP" interrupts political gatherings to draw attention to the need for AIDS research. In fact, protests today are often orches-

protest

A form of **political participation** designed to achieve policy change through dramatic and unconventional tactics.

Making a Difference

Granny D and Her Walk for Campaign Finance Reform

Doris Haddock was tired of hearing in the media that people didn't really care about campaign finance reform. She cared deeply about this issue, and she thought the majority of Americans agreed with her. On her web site (www.grannyd.com) she announced that: "My goal is to convince Congress that We, The People, do care about Campaign Finance Reform."

At the beginning of 1999, this New Hampshire woman resolved to do something unusual that would draw the attention of the media and the politicians to her cause. On New Year's Day she traveled to the Rose Bowl in Pasadena, Calif. to begin a cross-country walk to Washington, D.C. to protest how political campaigns are financed. Her web site announced that, "I shall travel as a pilgrim, seeking not your money, but food, shelter, and signatures on my petition. My petition will read: "We the people of the United States of America request our congress to enact with all due speed meaningful campaign finance reform."

Doris Haddock was hardly the first person to traverse the country on behalf of a cause, but she was a most unlikely candidate for such a task. What made her pilgrimage remarkable was the fact that Doris Haddock was then 89 years old and a great-grandmother. She figured the media could hardly ignore such a story, and she was right.

Moving at a pace of 10 miles per day, Granny D—the nickname Mrs. Haddock assumed for publicity purposes—soon encountered desert heat and wind that would discourage most young and healthy people from continuing. Near the California-Arizona border she became so exhausted and run down by the flu that she required hospitalization. Many of her family and friends felt it was too risky for her to continue. But Granny D was soon back on the road with a support team and equipment provided by Common Cause, a public interest group that has long urged campaign finance reform.

In February 2000, Granny D finally made it all the way to Washington, D.C., accompanied by 2,000 fellow walkers as she approached the Capitol. Along the way, she had publicized her cause through numerous media interviews and met with various members of Congress in their local offices. Tens of thousands of ordinary citizens had come out to see her, sign her petition, and sometimes walk along with her for a while. The National Association of Secretaries of State issued a resolution commending her "for showing that one person can make a difference."

trated to provide television cameras with vivid images. Demonstration coordinators steer participants to prearranged staging areas and provide facilities for press coverage.

civil disobedience

A form of **political participation** that reflects a conscious decision to break a law believed to be immoral and to suffer the consequences.

Throughout American history, individuals and groups have sometimes used **civil disobedience** as a form of protest; that is, they have consciously broken a law that they thought was unjust. In the 1840s, Henry David Thoreau refused to pay his taxes as a protest against the Mexican War and went to jail; he stayed only overnight because his friend Ralph Waldo Emerson paid the taxes. Influenced by India's Mahatma Gandhi, Reverend Martin Luther King, Jr. won a Nobel Peace Prize for his civil disobedience against segregationist laws in the 1950s and 1960s. His "Letter from a Birmingham Jail" is a classic defense of civil disobedience.[35]

Sometimes political participation can be violent. The history of violence in American politics is a long one—not surprising, perhaps, for a nation born in rebellion. The turbulent 1960s included many outbreaks of violence. African-American neighborhoods in American cities were torn by riots. College campuses were sometimes turned into battle zones as protestors against the Vietnam War fought police and National Guard units. At a number of campuses, demonstrations turned violent; students were killed at Kent State and Jackson State in 1970. Although supported by few people, violence has been a means of pressuring the government to change its policies throughout American history.

Class, Inequality, and Participation

The rates of political participation are unequal among Americans. Virtually every study of political participation has come to the conclusion that "citizens of higher social economic status participate more in politics. This generalization . . . holds true

Unconventional protest techniques are the trademark of ACT-UP, an AIDS awareness protest group. Here, members of the group are lying down near the White House, defying police orders to disperse. Members of ACT-UP believe that such dramatic protests are necessary to keep the issue of AIDS in the public eye.

Perhaps the best-known image of American political violence from the late-1960s to early-1970s period: A student lies dead on the Kent State campus, one of four killed when members of the Ohio National Guard opened fire on anti-Vietnam War demonstrators.

whether one uses level of education, income, or occupation as the measure of social status."[36] Figure 6.5 presents recent evidence on this score. Note that not only are people with higher incomes more likely to donate money to campaigns, but also to participate in other ways that do not even require financial resources. Theorists who believe that America is ruled by a small, wealthy elite make much of this fact to support their view.

The participation differences between African Americans and Hispanics and the national average are no longer enormous, however. For African Americans, participation in 1996 was a mere 4 percentage points below the national average; for Hispanic

Nonviolent civil disobedience was one of the most effective techniques of the civil rights movement in the American South. Young African Americans sat at "Whites only" lunch counters to protest segregation. Photos such as this drew national attention to the injustice of racial discrimination.

Figure 6.5 Political Participation by Family Income

The following graph shows, by their income status, the percentage of the adult population who said they participated in various forms of political activity.

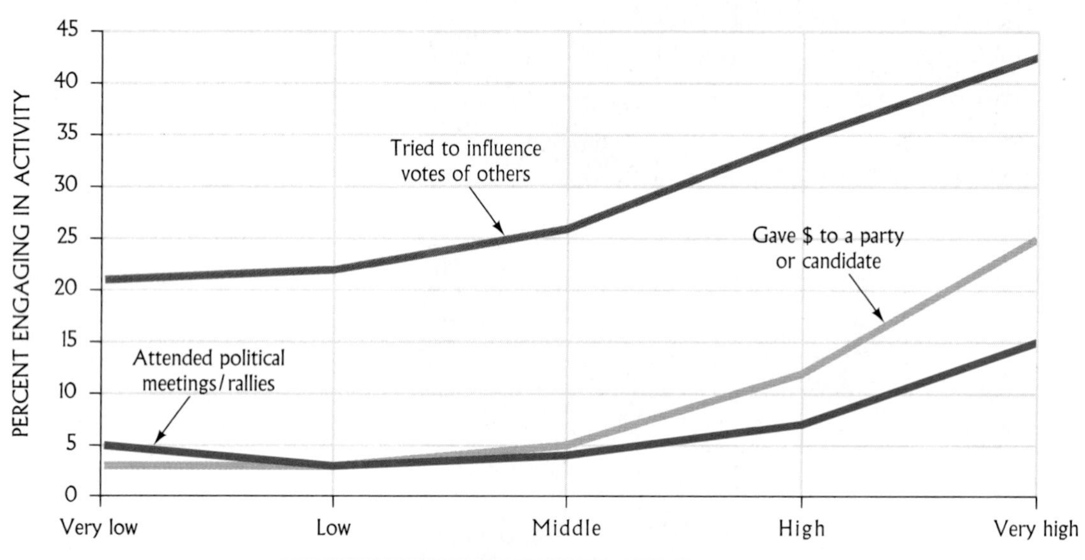

Source: Authors' analysis of 1996 National Election Study data.

citizens it was 10 percent. One reason for this smaller-than-expected participation gap is that minorities have a group consciousness that gives them an extra incentive to vote. In fact, when African Americans, Hispanics, and Whites of equal income and education are compared, the minorities participate more in politics.[37] In other words, a poor Hispanic or African American is more likely to participate than a poor White. In general, lower rates of political participation among these minority groups are linked with lower socioeconomic status.

People who believe in the promise of democracy should definitely be concerned with the inequalities of political participation in America. Those who participate are easy to listen to; nonparticipants are easy to ignore. Just as the makers of denture cream do not worry too much about people with healthy teeth, many politicians don't concern themselves much with the views of groups with low participation rates, such as the young and people with low incomes. Who gets what in politics therefore depends in part on who participates.

Why does it matter?

Is inequality in political participation a problem? How so? How would politics be different if people of all age, ethnic, and income groups participated equally? Do you participate in politics? If not, why?

How You Can Make a Difference

Whether it's campaign finance reform, or any other issue you feel strongly about, there are ways that you, too, can make a difference. First, if you have not done so already, immerse yourself in the issues. Learn the ins and outs of existing laws pertaining to the issue you are concerned about. If the issue is campaign finance, learn about the role of political action committees (PACs), campaign finance laws, and soft money. Similarly, develop a basic understanding of the corrective legislation that has been proposed to deal with these problems, such as the McCain-Feingold bill. For information on these topics, including lists of books, federal resources, interest groups, etc., go to http://campaignfinance.homestead.com or go to www.commoncause.org for an amazing amount of easily understood and well-organized information on campaign finance reform.

Another thing to do is to join an interest group that represents your position on the issue, and if you can't find one, start your own!

Find out where your congressperson and senators stand on the issue. Write, call, or e-mail their offices informing them of your position and asking them to support or introduce appropriate legislation. Keep up the letter writing campaign until your representative promises results.

If feasible, organize an event to garner media exposure for your views. An effective event can be anything from a classic protest march to something more original like a mock auction of congressional votes, a controversial art exhibit on special interests, or in the case of Granny D, a walk across the country. Be creative, but stay within the bounds of the law unless you are willing to pay the consequences.

Volunteer your time to help support candidates who promise to legislate for the issue you hold dear. If you live in a state that allows public initiatives, start or get involved with a group to place an initiative on the ballot.

On Election Day, send a clear signal by voting for those who support what you favor.

Understanding Public Opinion and Political Action

In 1989, people protested for democracy throughout much of the communist world. Many said they wanted their political system to be just like America's, even though they had only a vague idea of how American democracy works. As this chapter has shown, there are many limits on the role Americans play in their political system. The average person is not very well informed about political issues, including the crucial issue of the scope of government.

Public Attitudes Toward the Scope of Government

Central to the ideology of the Republican Party is the belief that the scope of American government has become too wide-ranging. According to Ronald Reagan, probably the most admired Republican in recent history, government was not the solution to society's problems—it was the problem. He called for the government to "get off the backs of the American people."

Reagan's rhetoric about an overly intrusive government was reminiscent of the 1964 presidential campaign rhetoric of Barry Goldwater, who lost to Lyndon Johnson in a landslide. Indeed, Reagan first made his mark in politics by giving a televised speech on behalf of the embattled Goldwater campaign. Although the rhetoric was much the same when Ronald Reagan was first elected president in 1980, public opinion about the scope of government had changed dramatically. In 1964, only 30 percent of the population thought the government was getting too powerful; by 1980, this figure had risen to 50 percent.

For much of the population, however, questions about the scope of government have consistently elicited no opinion at all. Indeed, when this question was last asked in the 2000 National Election Study, 42 percent of those interviewed said they had not thought about the question (among those under 25 years of age, this figure was 60 percent). The question of government power is a complex one, but as *Government in America* will continue to emphasize, it is one of the key controversies in American politics today. Once again, it seems that the public is not nearly so concerned with political issues as would be ideal in a democratic society.

Nor does public opinion on different aspects of the same issue exhibit much consistency. Thus, although more people today think the government is too active, a plurality has consistently called for more spending on such programs as education, health care, aid to big cities, protecting the environment, and fighting crime. Many political scientists have looked at these contradictory findings and concluded that Americans are ideological conservatives but operational liberals—meaning that they oppose the idea of big government in principle but favor it in practice. The fact that public opinion is often contradictory in this respect contributes to policy gridlock because it is hard for politicians to know which aspect of the public's attitudes to respond to.

Democracy, Public Opinion, and Political Action

Remember, though, that American democracy is representative rather than direct. As *The American Voter* stated many years ago, "The public's explicit task is to decide not what government shall do but rather who shall decide what government shall do."[38] When individuals under communist rule protested for democracy, what they wanted most was the right to have a say in choosing their leaders. Americans can—and often do—take for granted the opportunity to replace their leaders at the next election. Protest is thus directed at making the government listen to specific demands, not overthrowing it. In this sense, it can be said that American citizens have become well socialized to democracy.

If the public's task in democracy is to choose who is to lead, we must still ask whether it can do so wisely. If people know little about where candidates stand on issues, how can they make rational choices? Most choose performance criteria over policy criteria. As Morris Fiorina has written, citizens typically have one hard bit of data to go on: "They know what life has been like during the incumbent's administration. They need not know the precise economic or foreign policies of the incumbent administration in order to see or feel the results of those policies."[39] Thus, even if they are only voting according to the nature of the times, their voices are clearly being heard—holding public officials accountable for their actions.

Summary

American society is amazingly varied. The ethnic makeup of America is changing to a minority majority. Americans are moving toward warmer parts of the country and growing older as a society. All these changes have policy consequences. One way of understanding the American people is through demography—the science of population changes. Demography, it is often said, is destiny.

Another way to understand the American people is through examination of public opinion in the United States. What Americans believe—and what they believe they know—is public opinion, the distribution of people's beliefs about politics and policy issues. Polling is one important way of studying public opinion; polls give us a fairly accurate gauge of public opinion on issues, products, and personalities. On the positive side for democracy, polls help keep political leaders in touch with the feelings of their constituents. On the negative side, polls may lead politicians "play to the crowds" instead of providing leadership.

Polls have revealed again and again that the average American has a low level of political knowledge. Far more Americans know their astrological sign than know the names of their representatives in Congress. Ideological thinking is not widespread in the American public, nor are people necessarily consistent in their attitudes. Often they are conservative in principle but liberal in practice; that is, they are against big government but favor more spending on a wide variety of programs.

Acting on one's opinions is political participation. Although Americans live in a participatory culture, their actual level of participation is less than spectacular. In this country, participation is a class-biased activity; certain groups participate more than others. Those who suffer the most inequality sometimes resort to protest as a form of participation. Perhaps the best indicator of how well socialized Americans are to democracy is that protest typically is aimed at getting the attention of the government, not overthrowing it.

Career Profile

Position: Project Director
Employer: Hamilton Beattie and Staff, a political polling firm
Salary Range: $38,000–$58,000
Benefits: health, 401k, profit sharing
Qualifications: bachelor's degree in politics, statistics, sociology or history, and an interest in and knowledge of politics and political campaigns. Attention to detail a must. Knowledge of survey research techniques also needed. A master's degree in political science, statistics, political campaigning, or similar field is helpful but not required.

Real People on the Job: Maggie Ryner

Maggie Ryner is a project director at Hamilton Beattie and Staff, one of the oldest political polling firms in the United States. Since 1964, HB&S has conducted over 10,000 surveys for over 400 political campaigns in all 50 states and 22 different countries. Their clients include political parties, candidates, the media, interest groups, and major corporations. Their polls have helped elect U.S. senators, U.S. congressmen and women, governors, and state legislators. Past clients include U.S. Representative Thomas P. (Tip) O'Neill, David Wu, Bella Abzug, and Claude Pepper; U.S. Senators Lloyd Bentsen, Bob Graham, and John Glenn; and Governors Bruce Babbitt and Martha Layne Collins.

Maggie's job at HB&S involves designing and constructing polling questionnaires, supervising the administration of surveys (including the computer programming and data analysis), and overseeing quality control. She also coordinates focus groups. In addition to working with domestic clients, she is responsible for coordinating field services with international clients in Eastern Europe and Scandinavia. She has also traveled to many Caribbean nations, where she's conducted research operations on the ground, work that involved coordinating personal interviews, cross-tabulating data, and sending the results back to the analysts in Washington, D.C.

If you would like to work for a political polling firm, make sure you agree with the party positions or ideology of the firm's clients. There are firms that only work for Democrats or for Republicans. To make yourself marketable to a polling firm, you should have some knowledge of politics and campaigns, preferably hands-on experience. Volunteer for a campaign. Election years are a great time to get this experience since every campaign needs extra hands. Campaign experience looks good on your résumé when you go job hunting and it allows you to meet the players on the field before you get up to bat. Additionally, there are some good graduate programs in campaigning, public opinion, and statistical methodology.

Key Terms

public opinion
demography
census
melting pot
minority majority
political culture
reapportionment
political socialization
sample
random sampling
sampling error
random-digit dialing
exit poll
political ideology
liberalism
conservatism
gender gap
political participation
protest
civil disobedience

For Further Reading

Asher, Herbert. *Polling and the Public: What Every Citizen Should Know,* 4th ed. Washington, D.C.: Congressional Quarterly Press, 1998. A highly readable introduction to the perils and possibilities of polling and surveys.

Campbell, Angus, et al. *The American Voter.* New York: Wiley, 1960. The classic study of the American voter, based on data from the 1950s.

Conway, M. Margaret. *Political Participation,* 3rd ed. Washington, D.C.: Congressional Quarterly Press, 2000. A good review of the literature on political participation.

Delli Carpini, Michael X., and Scott Keeter. *What Americans Know About Politics and Why It Matters.* New Haven: Yale University Press, 1996. The best study of the state of political knowledge in the electorate.

DeSipio, Louis. *Counting on the Latino Vote.* Charlottesville: University of Virginia Press, 1996. An examination of the current state of Latino public opinion, and how more Latinos could be politically mobilized in the future.

Jacobs, Lawrence R., and Robert Y. Shapiro. *Politicians Don't Pander.* Chicago: University of Chicago Press, 2000. Contrary to popular notions that politicians hold their fingers to the wind and try to follow the polls, Jacobs and Shapiro argue that politicians use polls to figure out how to best persuade the public to support their preferred policies.

Jennings, M. Kent, and Richard G. Niemi. *Generations and Politics: A Panel Study of Young Adults and Their Parents.* Princeton, NJ: Princeton University Press, 1981. A highly influential study of the class of 1965, their parents, and how both generations changed over the course of eight years.

Nie, Norman H., Jane Junn, and Kenneth Stehlik-Barry. *Education and Democratic Citizenship in America.* Chicago: University of Chicago Press, 1996. An in-depth investigation of the role of education in fostering political tolerance and participation.

Page, Benjamin I., and Robert Y. Shapiro. *The Rational Public: Fifty Years of Trends in Americans' Policy Preferences.* Chicago: University of Chicago Press, 1992. The authors argue that the public, as a whole, responds in a reasonable fashion to changing political circumstances and information.

Tate, Katherine. *From Protest to Politics: The New Black Voters in American Elections.* Cambridge, MA: Harvard University Press, 1994. An excellent examination of public opinion and participation among the African-American community.

Verba, Sidney, and Norman H. Nie. *Participation in America.* New York: Harper & Row, 1972. A landmark study of American political participation.

Verba, Sidney, Kay Lehman Schlozman, and Henry E. Brady. *Voice and Equality: Civic Voluntarism in American Politics.* Cambridge, MA: Harvard University Press, 1995. A worthy update and extension to *Participation in America.*

Internet Resources

www.census.gov
The census is the best source of information on America's demography. Go to the list of topics to find out the range of materials that are available.

www.gallup.com
The Gallup poll regularly posts reports about their political surveys at this site.

www.census.gov/statab/www/
The *Statistical Abstract of the United States* contains a wealth of demographic and political information and is available in Adobe Acrobat format off the Internet.

www.demographics.com/publications/ad/index.htm
American Demographics magazine publishes many interesting stories summarizing how America's population is currently changing.

Notes

1. See Margo Anderson, *The American Census: A Social History* (New Haven, CT: Yale University Press, 1988).
2. See *Statistical Abstract of the United States, 1999* (Washington, D.C.: U.S. Government Printing Office, 2000), 298.
3. On the details of the 1965 Immigration Act and its unintended consequences, see Steven M. Gillon, *That's Not What We Meant to Do: Reform and Its Unintended Consequences in Twentieth-Century America* (New York: Norton, 2000), chap. 4.

4. Ronald T. Takaki, *Strangers from a Different Shore* (Boston: Little, Brown, 1989), chap. 11.
5. Ellis Cose, *A Nation of Strangers: Prejudice, Politics, and the Populating of America* (New York: William Morrow and Company, 1992), 219.
6. Judith Blake, *Family Size and Achievement* (Berkeley: University of California Press, 1989).
7. See Henry J. Pratt, *The Gray Lobby* (Chicago: University of Chicago Press, 1977).
8. Richard Dawson et al., *Political Socialization*, 2nd ed. (Boston: Little, Brown, 1977), 33.
9. See M. Kent Jennings and Richard G. Niemi, *Generations and Politics: A Panel Study of Young Adults and Their Parents* (Princeton, NJ: Princeton University Press, 1981).
10. "The Age of Indifference." Report of the Times Mirror Center for the People and the Press, June 28, 1990.
11. Quoted in Sabine Reichel, *What Did You Do in the War Daddy? Growing Up German* (New York: Hill & Wang, 1989), 113.
12. David Easton and Jack Dennis, *Children in the Political System* (New York: McGraw-Hill, 1969), 106–107.
13. Jean M. Converse, *Survey Research in the United States: Roots and Emergence, 1890–1960* (Berkeley: University of California Press, 1987), 116. Converse's work is the definitive study on the origins of public opinion sampling.
14. Herbert Asher, *Polling and the Public: What Every Citizen Should Know* (Washington, D.C.: Congressional Quarterly Press, 1988), 59.
15. Quoted in Norman M. Bradburn and Seymour Sudman, *Polls and Surveys: Understanding What They Tell Us* (San Francisco: Jossey-Bass, 1988), 39–40.
16. Lawrence R. Jacobs and Robert Y. Shapiro, *Politicians Don't Pander* (Chicago: University of Chicago Press, 2000), p. xiii.
17. For a good summary of the evidence, see Seymour Sudman, "Do Exit Polls Influence Voting Behavior?" *Public Opinion Quarterly* 50 (Fall 1986): 331–339.
18. David W. Moore, *The Superpollsters: How They Measure and Manipulate Public Opinion in America* (New York: Four Walls Eight Windows, 1992), 353–354.
19. W. Lance Bennett, *Public Opinion and American Politics* (New York: Harcourt Brace Jovanovich, 1980), 44.
20. E. D. Hirsch, Jr., *Cultural Literacy* (Boston: Houghton Mifflin, 1986).
21. Michael X. Delli Carpini and Scott Keeter, *What Americans Know About Politics and Why It Matters.* (New Haven, CT: Yale University Press, 1996), chap. 3.
22. W. Russell Neuman, *The Paradox of Mass Politics: Knowledge and Opinion in the American Electorate* (Cambridge, MA: Harvard University Press, 1986).
23. See Ronald Inglehart, *Modernization and Postmodernization* (Princeton, NJ: Princeton University Press, 1997), 254–255. Inglehart also shows that the decline of class voting is a general trend throughout Western democracies.
24. See Seymour Martin Lipset and Earl Raab, *Jews and the New American Political Scene* (Cambridge, MA: Harvard University Press, 1995), chap. 6.
25. Angus Campbell et al., *The American Voter* (New York: John Wiley, 1960), chap. 10.
26. Norman H. Nie, Sidney Verba, and John R. Petrocik, *The Changing American Voter* (Cambridge, MA: Harvard University Press, 1976), chap. 7.
27. See, for example, John L. Sullivan, James E. Pierson, and George E. Marcus, "Ideological Constraint in the Mass Public: A Methodological Critique and Some New Findings," *American Journal of Political Science* 22 (May 1978): 233–249; and Eric R.A.N. Smith, *The Unchanging American Voter* (Berkeley: University of California Press, 1989).
28. Sar Fritz, "Clinton Rejects Bush's Charges He Is Tax-and-Spend Democrat," *Los Angeles Times*, September 26, 1992, A20.
29. Thomas Ferguson and Joel Rogers, *Right Turn* (New York: Hill & Wang, 1986), 28; for a longer-term perspective on the movement of public opinion in a largely liberal direction, see Benjamin I. Page and Robert Y. Shapiro, *The Rational Public: Fifty Years of Trends in Americans' Policy Preferences* (Chicago: University of Chicago Press, 1992).
30. Martin P. Wattenberg, *The Rise of Candidate-Centered Politics: Presidential Elections of the 1980s* (Cambridge, MA: Harvard University Press, 1991).
31. This theory is carefully developed in Morris P. Fiorina, *Retrospective Voting in Presidential Elections* (New Haven, CT: Yale University Press, 1981).
32. This definition is a close paraphrase of that in Sidney Verba and Norman H. Nie, *Participation in America* (New York: Harper & Row, 1972), 2.
33. Russell J. Dalton, *Citizen Politics in Western Democracies* (Chatham, NJ: Chatham House, 1988), 237.
34. See Verba and Nie, *Participation in America;* and Sidney Verba, Kay Lehman Schlozman, and Henry E. Brady, *Voice and Equality: Civic Voluntarism in American Politics* (Cambridge, MA: Harvard University Press, 1995).
35. This letter can be found in Juan Williams, *Eyes on the Prize: America's Civil Rights Years, 1954–1965* (New York: Viking, 1987), 187–189.
36. Verba and Nie, *Participation in America,* 125.
37. On African Americans, see Verba and Nie, *Participation in America,* chap. 10; on Hispanics, see Raymond E. Wolfinger and Steven J. Rosenstone, *Who Votes?* (New Haven, CT: Yale University Press, 1980), 92.
38. Campbell et al., *The American Voter,* 541.
39. Fiorina, *Retrospective Voting,* 5.

The Mass Media and the Political Agenda

7

Chapter Outline

In Washington's Smithsonian Museum, the television console used by President Lyndon Johnson in the mid-1960s can be seen on permanent display. Not wanting to miss anything on TV, Johnson asked for three screens to be installed in one console so he could monitor CBS, NBC, and ABC all at the same time. White House technicians rigged up a special remote control for the president, enabling him to switch the audio easily from one network to another. According to many observers, whenever he saw his picture appear, he immediately turned on the audio from that screen to hear what was being said about him.

As a piece of genuine Americana, LBJ's triple TV set symbolizes the tremendous importance that television had assumed in U.S. politics by the mid-1960s. Interestingly, Al Gore completed his senior thesis at Harvard on the impact of television on the conduct of the presidency the same year that Lyndon Johnson left the White House. The essence of Gore's thesis was that TV had an

inherent bias toward individuals over institutions that over time would bring more attention to the president at the expense of the other branches of government. With a president's power increasingly stemming from his ability to dominate the airwaves, Gore's thesis argued that the ability to communicate well through the visual medium of television was becoming crucial to governing. Ironically for a politician who regularly joked that the difference between himself and his Secret Service agents is that "he's the stiff one," the young Gore speculated that future presidents would have to have personalities that play well to the TV cameras.

The rise of television has had a profound impact on the two central questions we emphasize in this text—*How should we govern?* and *What should government do?* Television has brought an immediacy to how we govern, removing the filter of time from events. Whatever the problem or event, it is happening now—live on the TV screen. People thus have more reason than ever to expect immediate governmental responses. However, the Founding Fathers designed a very deliberative governing process, in which problems would be considered by multiple centers of political power and acted upon only after lengthy give and take. Given the difficulties of getting quick action through the American political system, it is no wonder that the public has come to be more dissatisfied with our government in the television age.

In some cases, though, television has set the stage for leaders to take quick action affecting the scope of government. Lyndon Johnson was watching his triple screen TV set when NBC interrupted its airing of "Judgment at Nuremburg" to show film that had just become available of civil rights demonstrators being brutally attacked by police in Selma, Alabama. Sensing the public outrage at this violence and injustice, Johnson soon proposed and pushed through the historic Voting Rights Act of 1965 (see Chapter 5). If President George W. Bush takes strong action on some important policy problem, television will no doubt set the stage by focusing attention on the issue and putting it high on the policy agenda.

high-tech politics

A politics in which the behavior of citizens and policymakers and the political agenda itself are increasingly shaped by technology.

mass media

Television, radio, newspapers, magazines, the Internet, and other means of popular communication.

The American political system has entered a new period of **high-tech politics**—a politics in which the behavior of citizens and policymakers, as well as the political agenda itself, is increasingly shaped by technology. The **mass media** are a key part of this technology. Television, radio, newspapers, magazines, the Internet, and other means of popular communication are called *mass media* because they reach and profoundly influence not only the elites but also the masses. This chapter examines media politics, focusing on:

- The rise of modern media in America's advanced technological society.
- The making of the news and its presentation through the media.
- The biases in the news.
- The impact of the media on policymakers and the public.

This chapter also reintroduces the concept of the policy agenda, in which the media play an important role.

The Mass Media Today

media events

Events purposely staged for the media that nonetheless look spontaneous. In keeping with politics as theater, media events can be staged by individuals, groups, and government officials, especially presidents.

Whether promoting a candidate, drawing attention to a social issue, or generating a government program, effectively communicating a message is critical to political success. The key is gaining control over the political agenda, which involves getting one's priorities presented at the top of the daily news. Politicians have learned that one way to guide the media's focus successfully is to limit what they can report on to carefully scripted events. A **media event** is staged primarily for the purpose of being covered. If the media were not there, the event would probably not happen or would have little significance. For example, on the eve of the 2000 New Hampshire primary, Al Gore went door-to-door in a middle-class neighborhood with TV crews in tow. The few dozen people he met could scarcely have made a difference, but Gore was not really there to win votes by personal contact. Rather, the point was to get pictures of him reaching out to ordinary people on TV. Getting the right image on TV news for just 30 seconds can easily have a greater payoff than a whole day's worth of handshaking. Whereas once a candidate's G.O.T.V. program stood for "Get Out the Vote," today it is more likely to mean "Get on TV."

In addition, a large part of today's so-called 30-second presidency is the slickly produced TV commercial. Approximately 60 percent of presidential campaign spending is now devoted to TV ads. In recent presidential elections, about two-thirds of the prominently aired ads were negative commercials.[1] Many people are worried that the tirade of accusations, innuendoes, and countercharges in political advertising is poisoning the American political process and possibly even contributing to declining turnout.[2] Other democracies typically allocate their parties free air time for longer ads that go into more depth than is possible than with the American-style 30-second ad (see "America in Perspective: How Campaign Advertising Compares Across Five Nations").

visual literacy
What's in an Ad?

Image making does not stop with the campaign; it is also a critical element in day-to-day governing. Politicians' images in the press are seen as good indicators of their clout. Image is especially important for presidents, who in recent years have devoted much attention to maintaining a well-honed public image, as shown in the following internal White House memo written by President Nixon.

> *When I think of the millions of dollars that go into one lousy 30-second television spot advertising a deodorant, it seems to me unbelievable that we don't do a better job in seeing that presidential appearances always have the very best professional advice whenever they are to be covered on TV. . . . The President should never be without the very best professional advice for making a television appearance.*[3]

comparative
Comparing News Media

Few, if any, administrations devoted so much effort and energy to the president's media appearance as did Ronald Reagan's. It has often been said that Reagan played to the media as he had played to the cameras in Hollywood. According to

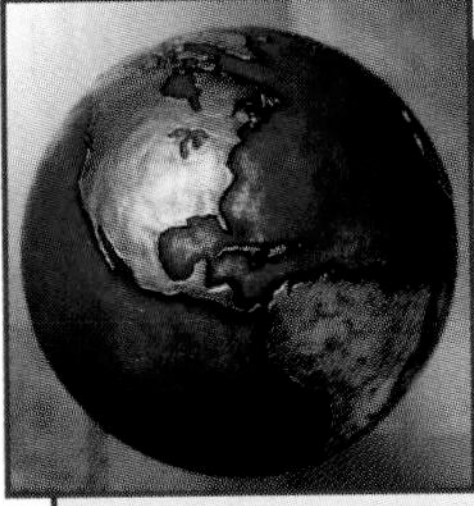

America in Perspective

How Campaign Advertising Compares Across Five Nations

Campaign advertising in the United States differs greatly from that in other democracies. Most other countries have party-sponsored ads, provided by the state, with limits on both ad number and length.

	UNITED STATES	BRITAIN	FRANCE	GERMANY	ISRAEL
Sponsorship	mostly candidate	party	party	party	party
Method of allocating ads	purchase	allocated by the state	allocated by the state	allocated by the state	allocated by the state
Limitations on number of ads	No	Yes	Yes	Yes	Yes
Duration of ads	unlimited, but typically only 30 seconds	2–3 minutes	up to 4 minutes	2 1/2 minutes	5 minutes

Source: Lynda Lee Kaid and Christina Holtz-Bacha, eds., *Political Advertising in Western Democracies: Parties and Candidates on Television* (Thousand Oaks, CA: Sage, 1995).

The Reagan Administration carefully—and masterfully—controlled the president's image as presented by the media. To avoid having Reagan give unrehearsed answers, for example, his advisors would place the media at a distance and rev a helicopter engine so that the president could not hear reporters' questions.

Television enables many more people to see candidates for elected office than would ever be possible in person. In fact, people have become so accustomed to seeing politicians' faces when they speak that giant TV screens are now often used to enable those attending political events to see the speakers' facial expressions.

Mark Hertsgaard, news management in the Reagan White House operated on the following seven principles: (1) plan ahead, (2) stay on the offensive, (3) control the flow of information, (4) limit reporters' access to the president, (5) talk about the issues you want to talk about, (6) speak in one voice, and (7) repeat the same message many times.[4]

Michael Deaver, who occupied the office right outside the Oval Office, was responsible for advising the president on image making, as former Secretary of the Treasury Donald Regan recalls:

> *It was Deaver who identified the news story of the day at the eight o'clock staff meeting, and coordinated plans for dealing with it, Deaver who created and approved photo opportunities. . . . He saw—designed—each presidential action as a one-minute or two-minute spot on the evening network news, or a picture on page one of the Washington Post or the New York Times and conceived every presidential appearance in terms of camera angles.*[5]

To Ronald Reagan, the presidency was often a performance, and aides like Deaver helped to choreograph his public appearances. Perhaps there will never again be a president so concerned with public relations as Reagan, but for a president to ignore the power of image and the media would be perilous. In today's high-tech age, presidents can hardly lead the country if they cannot communicate effectively with it.

The Development of Media Politics

Lyndon Johnson was one of two recent American presidents (the other was Richard Nixon) who felt that he was hounded out of office by the press. A year after leaving the White House, Johnson was asked in a televised memoir what had been the biggest change in politics during his long career. "You guys," said Johnson. "All you guys in the media. All of politics has changed because of you. You've broken all the machines and the ties between us in Congress and the city machines. You guys have given us a new kind of politician."[6] Today, most scholars would agree with Johnson that the mass media have changed the face of American politics.

The media were not always so important, of course. There was virtually no daily press when the First Amendment was written during Washington's presidency. The daily newspaper is largely a product of the mid-nineteenth century; radio and television have been around only since the first half of the twentieth century. As recently as the presidency of Herbert Hoover (1929–1933), reporters submitted their questions to the president in writing, and he responded in writing—if at all. As Hoover put it, "The President of the United States will not stand and be questioned like a chicken thief by men whose names he does not even know."[7]

Hoover's successor, Franklin D. Roosevelt (1933–1945), practically invented media politics. To Roosevelt, the media were a potential ally. Roosevelt promised reporters two **press conferences**—presidential meetings with reporters—a week, resulting in about 1,000 press conferences during his 12 years in the White House. FDR was also the first president to use radio, broadcasting a series of reassuring "fireside chats" to the Depression-ridden nation. Roosevelt's crafty use of radio helped him win four presidential elections. Theodore White tells the story of the time in 1944 when FDR found out that his opponent, Thomas E. Dewey, had purchased 15 minutes of air time on NBC immediately following FDR's address. Roosevelt spoke for 14 minutes and then left 1 minute silent. Thinking that the network had experienced technical difficulties, many listeners changed their dials before Dewey came on the air.[8]

press conferences

Meetings of public officials with reporters.

Another of Roosevelt's talents was knowing how to feed the right story to the right reporter. He used presidential wrath to warn reporters off material he did not want covered, and he chastised news reports he deemed inaccurate. His wrath was rarely invoked, however, and the press revered him, never even reporting to the American public that the president was confined to a wheelchair. The idea that a political leader's private life might be public business was alien to journalists in FDR's day.

When someone becomes an instant political celebrity it takes a police escort to get them through the hordes of cameras and reporters. Here, Monica Lewinsky leaves a federal courthouse amid much commotion after providing evidence for the special prosecutor's investigation into charges of wrongdoing by President Clinton.

This relatively cozy relationship between politicians and the press lasted through the early 1960s. ABC's Sam Donaldson said that when he first came to Washington in 1961, "Many reporters saw themselves as an extension of the government, accepting, with very little skepticism, what government officials told them."[9] The events of the Vietnam War and the Watergate scandal, though, soured the press on government. Today's newspeople work in an environment of cynicism. To them, politicians rarely tell the whole story; the press sees ferreting out the truth as their job. No one has demonstrated this attitude better in recent years than Donaldson, who earned a hard-nosed reputation by regularly shouting unwanted questions at President Reagan. In his book, *Hold On, Mr. President!*, Donaldson wrote,

> *If you send me to cover a pie-baking contest on Mother's Day, I'm going to ask dear old Mom whether she used artificial sweetener in violation of the rules, and while she's at it, could I see the receipt for the apples to prove she didn't steal them. I maintain that if Mom has nothing to hide, no harm will have been done. But the questions should be asked.*[10]

investigative journalism

The use of detective-like reporting to unearth scandals, scams, and schemes, putting reporters in adversarial relationships with political leaders.

Many political scientists are critical of **investigative journalism**—the use of detective-like reporting methods to unearth scandals—which often pits reporters against political leaders. There is evidence that TV's fondness for investigative journalism has contributed to greater public cynicism and negativity about politics.[11]

In his analysis of media coverage of presidential campaigns since 1960, Thomas Patterson found that news coverage of presidential candidates has become increasingly less favorable. His tally of *Time* and *Newsweek* stories about the campaigns reveals that favorable references about Kennedy and Nixon outnumbered unfavorable ones by a three-to-one margin. In contrast, in 1992 there were three negative references regarding Clinton and Bush for every two favorable references. Patterson's careful analysis uncovers several aspects of the trend toward more negative media coverage of the candidates over the last three decades. First, he finds that the emphasis of campaign reporting has changed dramatically from "what" to "why." Patterson's content analysis of front-page *New York Times* stories revealed that in 1960 over 90 percent of news stories employed a descriptive framework, whereas by 1992 less than 20 percent did so. Second, the type of interpretative story that has become more prominent is hard-biting analysis of political maneuvering and the horse race. Such reporting tends toward unfavorable impressions of the candidates because the unstated assumption behind much of today's coverage of the issues has shifted from policy statements to campaign controversies. Coverage of such issues as Al Gore's fundraising at a

The White House press room is often the scene of much activity, with daily briefings on the president's activities each day the president is in residence. Contrary to the image that is often presented on television, reporters work in a cramped environment at the White House.

Buddhist Temple or George W. Bush's youthful indiscretions are not likely to draw favorable references.

Whether or not such media coverage is ultimately in the public's best interest is much debated. The press maintains that the public is now able to get a complete, accurate, and unvarnished look at the candidates. Critics of the media charge that they overemphasize the controversial aspects of the campaign at the expense of an examination of the major issues.

Scholars distinguish between two kinds of media: the **print media,** which include newspapers and magazines, and the **broadcast media,** which include radio, television, and the Internet. Each has reshaped political communication at different points in American history. It is difficult to assess the likely impact of the Internet at this point, but there is at least some reason to believe that political communication is being reshaped once again.

print media

Newspapers and magazines, as compared with **broadcast media.**

broadcast media

Television and radio, as compared with **print media.**

The Print Media

The first American daily newspaper was printed in Philadelphia in 1783, but such papers did not proliferate until the technological advances of the mid-nineteenth century. The ratification of the First Amendment in 1791, guaranteeing freedom of speech, gave even the earliest American newspapers freedom to print whatever they saw fit. This has given the media a unique ability to display the government's dirty linen, a propensity that continues to distinguish the American press today.

Rapid printing and cheap paper made possible the "penny press," which could be bought for a penny and read at home. In 1841, Horace Greeley's *New York Tribune* was founded, and in 1851 the *New York Times* began. By the 1840s, the telegraph permitted a primitive "wire service," which relayed news stories from city to city faster than ever before. The Associated Press, founded in 1849, depended heavily on this new technology.

At the turn of the century, newspaper magnates Joseph Pulitzer and William Randolph Hearst ushered in the era of "yellow journalism." This sensational style of reporting focused on violence, corruption, wars, and gossip, often with a less than scrupulous regard for the truth. On a visit to the United States at that time, young Winston Churchill said that "the essence of American journalism is vulgarity divested of truth."[12] In the midst of the Spanish-American conflict over Cuba, Hearst once boasted of his power over public opinion by telling a news artist "You furnish the pictures and I'll furnish the war."

Newspapers consolidated into **chains** during the early part of the twentieth century. Today's massive media conglomerates (Gannett, Knight-Ridder, and Newhouse are the largest) control newspapers with 78 percent of the nation's daily circulation.[13] Thus, three of four Americans now read a newspaper owned not by a fearless local editor but by a corporation headquartered elsewhere. Often these chains control television and radio stations as well.

chains

Newspapers published by massive media conglomerates that account for almost three-quarters of the nation's daily circulation. Often these chains control **broadcast media** as well.

Among the press there is, of course, a pecking order. Almost from the beginning, the *New York Times* was a cut above most newspapers in its influence and impact; it is the nation's "newspaper of record" and can be found on line at www.nytimes.com. Its clearest rival in government circles is the *Washington Post* (www.washingtonpost.com), offering perhaps the best coverage inside Washington and a sprightlier alternative to the *Times*. Papers such as the *Chicago Tribune* (www.chicagotribune.com) and the *Los Angeles Times* (www.latimes.com), as well as those in Atlanta, Boston, and other big cities, are also major national institutions. For most newspapers in medium-sized and small towns, though, the main source of national and world news is the Associated Press wire service, whose stories are reprinted in small newspapers across the country.

Ever since the rise of TV news, however, newspaper circulation rates have been declining, as you can see in Figure 7.1. Most political scientists who have studied the role of media in politics believe this is an unfortunate trend, as studies invariably find that regular newspaper readers are better informed and more likely to vote.[14] It remains to be

Figure 7.1 The Decline of Newspaper Circulation

Following is the average number of newspapers sold daily per 1,000 Americans over the age of 18. Whereas one newspaper was sold for every two adults in 1960, by 1998 only slightly more than one paper was sold for every four adults.

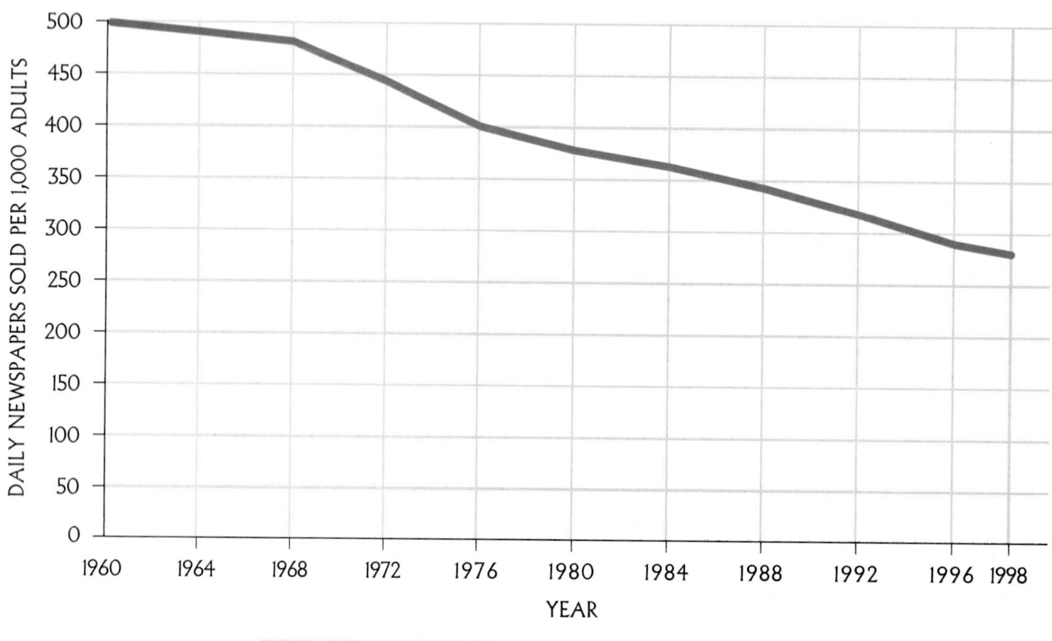

Source: Editor and Publisher; U.S. Census Bureau.

seen whether the availability of most newspapers on the web will lead more people to look at them in the future, or rather will prove to be a desperate gasp for a fading business.

Magazines, the other component of the print media, are also struggling in the Internet age, especially when it comes to the few that are heavily concerned with political events. The so-called newsweeklies—mainly *Time, Newsweek,* and *U.S. News and World Report*—rank well behind such popular favorites as the *Reader's Digest, TV Guide,* and *National Geographic.* Although *Time*'s circulation is a bit better than that of the *National Enquirer, Playboy* and *People* edge out *Newsweek* in sales competition. Serious magazines of political news and opinion tend to be read by the educated elite; magazines such as the *New Republic,* the *National Review,* and the *Atlantic Monthly* are outsold by American favorites such as *Hot Rod, Weightwatchers Magazine,* and *Organic Gardening.*

The Broadcast Media

Gradually, the broadcast media have displaced the print media as Americans' principal source of news and information. By the middle of the 1930s, radio ownership had become almost universal in America, and during World War II, radio went into the news business in earnest. The 1950s and early 1960s were the adolescent years for American television. During those years, the political career of Richard Nixon was made and unmade by television. In 1952, while running as Dwight Eisenhower's vice-presidential candidate, Nixon made a famous speech denying that he took gifts and payments under the table. He did admit accepting one gift—his dog, Checkers. Noting that his daughters loved the dog, Nixon said that regardless of his political future, they would keep it. His homey appeal brought a flood of sympathetic telegrams to the Republican National Committee, and party leaders had little choice but to leave him on the ticket.

In 1960, Nixon was again on television's center stage, this time in the first televised presidential debate against Senator John F. Kennedy. Nixon blamed his poor appearance in the first of the four debates for his narrow defeat in the election. Haggard from a week in the hospital and with his five o'clock shadow and perspiration clearly visible, Nixon looked awful compared to the crisp, clean, attractive Kennedy. The poll results from this debate illustrate the visual power of television in American politics; people listening on the radio gave the edge to Nixon, but those who saw the debate on television thought Kennedy won. Russell Baker, who covered the event for the *New York Times*, writes in his memoirs that "television replaced newspapers as the most important communications medium in American politics" that very night.[15]

Just as radio had taken the nation to the war in Europe and the Pacific during the 1940s, television took the nation to the war in Vietnam during the 1960s. TV exposed governmental naïveté (some said it was outright lying) about the progress of the war. Napoleon once said that "Four hostile newspapers are more to be feared than a thousand bayonets." Lyndon Johnson learned the hard way that three television networks could be even more consequential. Every night, in living color, Americans watched the horrors of war on television. President Johnson soon had two wars on his hands, one in faraway Vietnam and the other at home with antiwar protesters—both covered in detail by the media. In 1968, CBS anchor Walter Cronkite journeyed to Vietnam for a firsthand look at the state of the war. In an extraordinary TV special, Cronkite reported that the war was not being won, nor was it likely to be. Watching from the White House, Johnson sadly remarked that if he had lost Cronkite, he had lost the support of the American people.[16]

With the growth of cable TV, particularly the Cable News Network (CNN), television has recently entered a new era of bringing the news to people—and to political leaders—as it happens. President Bush and his aides regularly watched CNN during the Gulf War, as did the Iraqi leadership. Marlin Fitzwater, Bush's press secretary, stated that "CNN has opened up a whole new communications system between governments in terms of immediacy and directness. In many cases it's the first communication we have."[17] A frequent response from U.S. officials to reporters' questions during the Gulf War was "I don't know any more than what you saw on CNN."[18]

Since 1963, surveys have consistently shown that more people rely on TV for the news than any other medium. Furthermore, by a regular two-to-one margin, people think television reports are more believable than newspaper stories.[19] (Consider the old sayings "Don't believe everything you read" and "I'll believe it when I see it.") Whereas people are predisposed to be skeptical about what they read in a newspaper, with television seeing is believing. Young people are particularly likely to rely on television as opposed to newspapers for news, as you can see in Table 7.1.

Why does it matter

When Samuel Morse sent the first telegraph message from the U.S. Capitol building, he tapped out a question, "What hath God wrought?" The answer back was, "What is the news from Washington?" Ever since then, the transmission of news via electronic means has become faster and faster. How has the increasing speed by which the news is conveyed changed American politics? Have the changes been good or bad for democracy?

Narrowcasting: Cable TV and the Internet

The future of political communication seems destined to bring more and more choices regarding what we can see about our government. About two-thirds of the American public currently subscribes to cable television, thereby giving them access to dozens of channels. Sometime in the twenty-first century it is expected that most cable systems will offer 500 channels. How will this explosion of TV channels impact political communication? Our best guess, based on developments with cable TV to date, is that information about politics will be presented in a way that appeals to a narrow and specific audience rather than to the public at large.

The first major networks—ABC, NBC, and CBS—adopted the term "broadcasting" in the names of their companies because their signal was being sent out to a broad audience. As long as these networks dominated the industry, each would have to deal with general topics that the public as a whole was concerned with, such as politics and government. But with the development of cable TV, market segmentation has taken

Table 7.1 Spending Time With the News

In May of 1998, the Pew Research Center asked a representative sample of the population how much time they spent during an average day getting the news from TV, newspapers, and radio. This table shows the results, broken down by age. Notice that young people spend less time following the news via these means. One might think that their greater reliance on the Internet makes up for this, but only 38 percent reported turning to the Internet for news.

	Spending Time With the News (Avg. Minutes Yesterday*)				
	PAPER	TV	RADIO	TOTAL	NO NEWS YESTERDAY
18–24	9	26	13	48	25%
25–29	11	23	16	50	17%
30–34	11	24	19	54	15%
35–49	16	28	19	63	14%
50–64	21	34	16	71	14%
65+	33	44	19	96	6%

*All averages are estimated.
Source: Reprinted by permission of the Pew Research Center for the People & Press from their website: http://www.people-press.org/medsec3.htm.

hold. Sports buffs can watch ESPN all day, music buffs can tune to MTV or VH1, history buffs can glue their dial to the History Channel, and so forth. If you are interested in politics, you can channel surf between C-SPAN, C-SPAN2, CNN, CNN Headline News, and other news stations. Rather than appealing to a general audience, channels such as ESPN, MTV, and C-SPAN focus on a narrow particular interest. Hence, their mission can be termed **"narrowcasting,"** rather than the traditional "broadcasting." This is even more true for websites, which require far less start-up costs than a TV channel and hence can be successful with a very small and specific audience.

narrowcasting

Media programming on cable TV or the Internet that is focused on one topic and aimed at a particular audience. Examples include MTV, ESPN, and C-SPAN.

As the number of channels and websites proliferates, it is clear that political junkies will find more political information readily available than ever before. Rumors that once were carefully verified by careful journalists are now immediately disseminated around the world electronically (see "Making A Difference: Matt Drudge"). But with so many readily available sources of information for so many specific interests, it will also be extremely easy for those who are not very interested in politics to completely avoid news and public affairs. The result could well be a growing inequality of political information, with the politically interested becoming more knowledgeable while the rest of the public slips further into political apathy. That's what some scholars are worried will happen in the potentially information-rich media environment of the twenty-first century.

timeline
300 Years of U.S. Media

Reporting the News

As every journalism student will quickly tell you, news is what is timely and different. It is a man biting a dog, not a dog biting a man. An oft-repeated speech on foreign policy or a well-worn statement on fighting drug abuse is less newsworthy than an odd episode. The public rarely hears about the routine ceremonies at state dinners, but when President Bush threw up all over the Japanese prime minister in 1992, the world's media jumped on the story. In its search for the unusual, the news media can give the audience a peculiar view of events and policymakers.

Making a Difference

Matt Drudge

Matt Drudge was 30 years old when he broke his first story about Monica Lewinsky's relationship with President Clinton, which would become the biggest political scandal of the 1990s. Drudge had never been trained in journalism nor hired by any media outlet. He had neither verified the story nor done any extensive research on it. All he had to go on was the rumor that *Newsweek* had been working on this story and had decided not to print it in that week's issue. But for Drudge, a rumor was good enough to report on. No editor was going to tell him that he needed confirmation because Drudge worked on his own. He didn't have to worry about the damage to his publication because he didn't have one; he relied instead on getting the "Drudge Report" out through an e-mail list and by posting it on his website(www.drudgereport.com). When Drudge hit the enter button on his computer to post the Lewinsky story, he knew his life would be changed forever, and for quite some time so would the nation's.

Matt Drudge and his brand of cyber reporting have changed the whole news cycle in America. Journalists who are working on a scoop know they can quickly lose an exclusive story if someone like Drudge gets wind of it and posts the headline on the Internet. As a result, a number of newspapers immediately post their most important stories on their website rather than waiting until the next morning. The *Dallas Morning News* made big headlines when they rushed a story onto the web about a White House steward testifying that he had seen President Clinton and Monica Lewinsky in a compromising position. The next day the paper had egg on its face, however, when the steward's lawyer strongly denied the story and the paper was forced to retract it. Similarly, Drudge found himself in trouble when he accused White House aide Sidney Blumenthal of spouse abuse. He quickly pulled the story and apologized when he realized it was planted by politically motivated Republican operatives, but not before Blumenthal hit him with a $30 million libel suit.

Opinions on Matt Drudge and his reporting techniques vary widely. Because of his penchant for reporting rumors and gossip, the *New York Times* has called him "the nation's chief mischief maker." Others have dubbed him the first Internet superstar and praised how he has paved the way for communication power to be transferred from media giants to anyone with a modem. However one views him, it is clear that Matt Drudge has made a difference. What do you think? Has the "Drudge Report" been a positive or negative development for democracy in America?

Millions of new and different events happen every day; journalists must decide which of them are newsworthy. No one has taken a more careful look at the definition and production of news than Edward J. Epstein, who, given the unique opportunity to observe NBC's news department for a year, wrote *News from Nowhere*, a classic inside account of the TV news business.[20] Epstein found that in their pursuit of high ratings, news shows are tailored to a fairly low level of audience sophistication. To a large extent, TV networks define news as what is entertaining to the average viewer.

Regardless of the medium, it cannot be emphasized enough that news reporting is a business in America. Striving for the bottom line, profits, shapes how journalists define what is newsworthy, where they get their information, and how they present it. Because some types of news stories attract more viewers or readers than others, certain biases are inherent in what the American public sees and reads.

Finding the News

Americans' popular image of correspondents or reporters somehow uncovering the news is accurate in some cases, yet most news stories come from well-established sources. Major news organizations assign their best reporters to particular **beats**—specific locations from which news often emanates, such as Congress. For example, during the Persian Gulf War, more than 50 percent of the lead stories on the TV newscasts came from the White House, Pentagon, and State Department beats.[21] Numerous

beats

Specific locations from which news frequently emanates, such as Congress or the White House. Most top reporters work a particular beat, thereby becoming specialists in what goes on at that location.

How You Can Make A Difference

The Internet and Political Action

Until very recently, the average citizen had little voice within the mass media beyond the opinion pages in newspapers. The advent of the Internet, however, has changed this—as the story of Matt Drudge breaking the Monica Lewinsky story clearly demonstrates. With the modest exception of small low-frequency radio stations and low-cost alternative newspapers that reached relatively few people, before the Internet no media allowed ordinary people to so immediately and powerfully affect public opinion and to challenge politicians and governments.

In fact, the meaning of grass-roots activism has changed as the world has become increasingly web savvy. In the comfort of a dorm room, today's college students can help topple foreign governments and pressure domestic government agencies into action. The governments in China, Malaysia, and Mexico have all been targets of Internet activists pressing for improved human rights. For example, the small and largely ineffectual Zapatista National Liberation Army led by the ski-masked Subcommandante Marcos has used the Internet to raise funds and convince thousands in Europe, North America and Latin America to picket Mexican consulates in support of autonomy for the indigenous people of Chiapas. Jagdish Parikh of Human Rights Watch notes that ". . . what is making the difference is that ordinary people are now coming to this medium." This is especially true in the more technically advanced United States where the Internet and computers have become a necessity rather than a luxury. In the late 1990s, Internet postings and e-mail from civil liberty groups convinced the Federal Deposit Insurance Corporation to maintain strict privacy rules. According to *Business Week*, the FDIC got 205,000 e-mails opposing any loosening of their privacy policy compared to less than 100 in favor of a change.

Some observers note that many of the accepted rules of politics expressed in this textbook may become obsolete as the power of the Internet grows and changes the political landscape. While other pundits caution that the impact of the Internet can be exaggerated especially outside the United States, Jagdish Parikh wisely considers, "How many people in China have Internet access? Not many. But then why is the government there rushing to make laws restricting access? It's because the Internet makes people realize that they should have the legal, codified right to information."

How can you become part of this new online activist movement? First, you need to have a clearly defined issue to publicize. Secondly, you need to put together the tools, strategy, and research necessary to make your online campaign effective. You should begin by going to One Northwest website at www.onenw.org/toolkit. This organization provides a handbook and strategy guide to help you become a successful online activist.

Sources: Pete Engardio, Richard Dunham, Heidi Dawley, Irene Kunji, and Elisabeth Malkin. "Activists Without Borders," *Business Week* (October 4, 1999): 144–149.

studies of both the electronic and the print media show that journalists rely almost exclusively on such established sources to get their information.[22]

trial balloons

An intentional **news leak** for the purpose of assessing the political reaction.

Those who make the news depend on the media to spread certain information and ideas to the general public. Sometimes they feed stories to reporters in the form of **trial balloons:** information leaked to see what the political reaction will be. For example, a few days prior to President Clinton's admission that he had an "inappropriate relationship" with Monica Lewinsky, top aides to the president leaked the story to Richard Berke of the *New York Times*. The timing of the leak was obvious; the story appeared just before Clinton had to decide how to testify before Kenneth Starr's grand jury. When the public reacted that it was about time he admitted this relationship, it was probably easier for him to do so—at least politically.

Reporters and their official sources have a symbiotic relationship. Newsmakers rely on journalists to get their message out at the same time that reporters rely on public officials to keep them in the know. When reporters feel that their access to information is being impeded, complaints of censorship become widespread. During the Gulf War, reporters' freedom of movement and observation was severely restricted. After the fighting was over, 15 influential news organizations sent a letter to the secretary of defense complaining that the rules for reporting the war were designed more to

Viewers around the world tuned in to CNN to learn of events in the Persian Gulf War. President Bush reportedly told other world leaders, "I learn more from CNN than I do from the CIA."

Bob Woodward (left) and Carl Bernstein, two obscure local reporters for the *Washington Post*, painstakingly uncovered the first details of the Watergate scandal. Watergate signaled a new era in the relationship between journalists and politicians; journalists assumed that politicians had something to hide, and politicians assumed that reporters were out to embarrass them.

control the news than to facilitate it.[23] Although the signers of the letter vowed not to let this happen again, there is probably little they can do about it. Official sources who have the information usually have the upper hand over those who merely report it.

Despite this dependence on familiar sources, an enterprising reporter occasionally has an opportunity to live up to the image of the crusading truth seeker. Local reporters Carl Bernstein and Bob Woodward of the *Washington Post* uncovered important evidence in the Watergate case in the early 1970s. Columnists such as Jack Anderson regularly expose the uglier side of government corruption and inefficiency. Such reporting is highly valued among the media elite.

Pulitzer prizes typically go to reporters whose stories make a difference in politics and government. For example, in 1997 the *New York Times* won a Pulitzer for their in-depth reports on how a proposed gold mining operation threatened the environment of part of Yellowstone National Park. When President Clinton vacationed at nearby Jackson Hole, he decided to go up and see the mine because he had been reading about it in the *New York Times*. Soon afterward, the project was stopped and the government gave the owners of the property a financial settlement.

Presenting the News

Once the news has been "found," it has to be neatly compressed into a 30-second news segment or fit in among the advertisements in a newspaper. If you had to pick a single word to describe news coverage by the print and broadcast media, it would be *superficial*. "The name of the game," says former White House press secretary Jody Powell, "is skimming off the cream, seizing on the most interesting, controversial, and unusual aspects of an issue."[24] Editors do not want to bore or confuse their audience. TV news, in particular, is little more than a headline service. According to CBS anchor Dan Rather, "You simply cannot be a well-informed citizen by just watching the news on television."[25]

Except for the little-watched, but highly regarded "Newshour" on PBS and ABC's late-night "Nightline," analysis of news events rarely lasts more than a minute. Patterson's study of campaign coverage (see Chapter 9) found that only skimpy attention was given to the issues during a presidential campaign. Clearly, if coverage of political events during the height of an election campaign is thin, coverage of day-to-day policy questions is even thinner. Issues such as reforming the Medicare system, adjusting how the consumer price index is calculated, and deregulating the communications industry are highly complex and difficult to treat in a short news clip. A careful study of media coverage of President Clinton's comprehensive health care proposal early in his first term found that the media focused much more on strategy and who was winning the political game than on the specific policy issues involved.[26]

Strangely enough, as technology has enabled the media to pass along information with greater speed, news coverage has become less thorough.[27] Newspapers once routinely reprinted the entire text of important political speeches; now the *New York Times*

Figure 7.2 The Incredible Shrinking Sound Bite

Following is the average length of time a presidential candidate was shown speaking uninterrupted on the evening network news from 1968 to 2000.

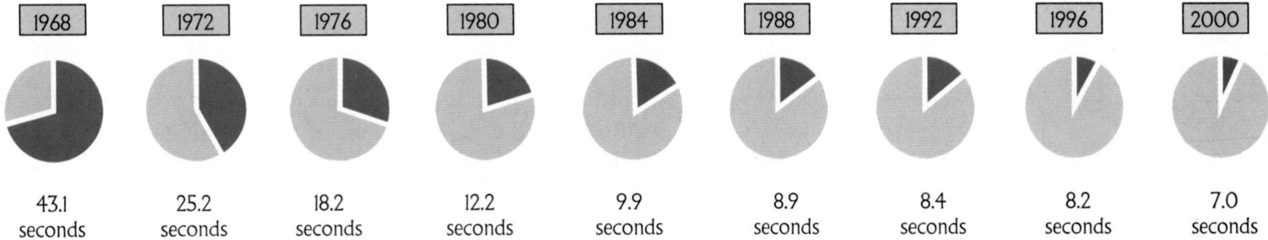

Source: Daniel Hallin, "Sound Bite News: Television Coverage of Elections," *Journal of Communications,* Spring 1992; 1992 to 2000 data from studies by the Center for Media and Public Affairs.

is virtually the only paper that does so—and even the *Times* has cut back sharply on this practice. In place of speeches, Americans now hear **sound bites** of 15 seconds or less on TV. As you can see in Figure 7.2, the average length of time that a presidential candidate has been given to talk uninterrupted on the TV news has declined precipitously since the late 1960s. Responding to criticism of sound-bite journalism, in 1992 CBS News briefly vowed that it would let a candidate speak for at least 30 seconds at a time. However, CBS found this to be unworkable and soon dropped the threshold to 20 seconds, noting that even this was flexible.[28] In 2000, the average sound bite of a candidate shown talking on the nightly news once again averaged less than 10 seconds.

sound bites

Short video clips of approximately 15 seconds; typically all that is shown from a politician's speech or activities on the nightly television news.

Even successful politicians sometimes feel frustrated by sound-bite journalism. A year after his election to the presidency, Jimmy Carter told a reporter that

> *. . . it's a strange thing that you can go through your campaign for president, and you have a basic theme that you express in a 15- or 20-minute standard speech, . . . but the traveling press—sometimes exceeding 100 people—will never report that speech to the public. The peripheral aspects become the headlines, but the basic essence of what you stand for and what you hope to accomplish is never reported.*[29]

Rather than presenting their audience with the whole chicken, the media typically give just a McNugget. Why should politicians work to build a carefully crafted case for their point of view when a catchy line will do just as well? As former CBS anchor Walter Cronkite writes, "Naturally, nothing of any significance is going to be said in seven seconds, but this seems to work to the advantage of many politicians. They are not required to say anything of significance, and issues can be avoided rather than confronted."[30] Cronkite and others have proposed that in order to force candidates to go beyond sound bites they should be given blocks of free air time for a series of nights to discuss their opposing views (see "You Are the Policymaker: Should the Networks Have To Provide Free Air Time To Presidential Candidates?").

Bias in the News

Many people believe that the news is biased in favor of one point of view. During the 1996 presidential campaign, Bob Dole often charged that the press was against him. "Annoy the Media—Elect Dole" became one of his favorite lines. The charge that the media have a liberal bias has become a familiar one in American politics, and there is some limited evidence to support it. A lengthy study by the *Los Angeles Times* in the mid-1980s found that reporters were twice as likely to call themselves liberal as the general public.[31] A 1992 survey of 1,400 journalists found that 44 percent identified

simulation
You are the News Editor

You Are the Policymaker

Should the Networks Have To Provide Free Air Time to Presidential Candidates?

In 1996, a group of prominent political and media figures proposed the idea of a series of free prime time television appearances for presidential candidates to address the issues. The Coalition for Free Air Time called upon the networks to turn over two to five minutes a night to the candidates in the month before the presidential election. Furthermore, the coalition suggested that these segments should be "roadblocked"—shown simultaneously on all networks, PBS, and interested cable stations so that people watching prime-time entertainment would be sure to see the candidates. The coalition hoped that this format would promote a nightly dialogue on the issues, with candidates making news with their replies to each other's previous segments. The only requirement would be that the candidates look straight into the camera and talk. There would be no manipulation of images or unseen narrators—just candidates making their case directly to the biggest potential audience every night.

Most of the networks did eventually grant the candidates some free time in 1996, but the approach was a scattershot one. The segments varied from one to two-and-a-half minutes, and each network chose a different time to broadcast them. A survey done by the Annenberg School of Communication immediately after the election found that only 22 percent of registered voters even knew that the free-time effort existed. Virtually everyone involved was disappointed with the results. The results from the 2000 election were similarly disheartening, as once again the networks adopted different approaches and the audiences tended to be relatively small.

Many observers believe that the experience of the last two presidential elections has demonstrated the necessity of adopting a common format and time for all networks; some even advocate using the government's regulatory powers to force the networks to adopt this approach. Others point to the poor ratings of the televised debates as an example of the ineffectiveness of roadblocking political dialogue when the public just isn't interested. You be the policymaker. Is this an experiment that the government should mandate in future presidential elections?

themselves as Democrats, compared to just 16 percent who said they were Republicans.[32]

However, there is little reason to believe that journalists' personal attitudes sway their reporting of the news. The vast majority of social science studies have found that reporting is not systematically biased toward a particular ideology or party.[33] Most stories are presented in a "point/counterpoint" format in which two opposing points of view (such as liberal versus conservative) are presented, and the audience is left to draw its own conclusions. A number of factors explain why the news is typically characterized by such political neutrality. Most reporters strongly believe in journalistic objectivity, and those who practice it best are usually rewarded by their editors. In addition, media outlets have a direct financial stake in attracting viewers and subscribers and do not want to lose their audience by appearing biased—especially when multiple versions of the same story are readily available. It seems paradoxical to say that competition produces uniformity, but this often happens in the news business.

To conclude that the news contains little explicit partisan or ideological bias is not to argue that it does not distort reality in its coverage. Ideally, the news should mirror reality; in practice there are far too many possible stories for this to be the case. Journalists must choose which stories to cover and to what degree. The overriding bias is toward stories that will draw the largest audience. Surveys show that people are most fascinated by stories with conflict, violence, disaster, or scandal, as can be seen in Table 7.2. Good news is unexciting; bad news has the drama that brings in big audiences.

Television is particularly biased toward stories that generate good pictures. Seeing a **talking head** (a shot of a person's face talking directly to the camera) is boring; view-

Why does it matter

In his book *Understanding Media,* Marshall McLuhan coined the famous phrase, "The medium is the message." By this, McLuhan meant that the way we communicate information can be more influential than the information itself. In the United States, news is a commodity controlled by the media, not a public service. How do you think the media's profit motive affects the reporting of the news?

talking head

A shot of a person's face talking directly to the camera. Because this is visually unappealing, the major commercial networks rarely show a politician talking one-on-one for very long.

Conservative Republicans often criticize the media for being biased against them. Studies have indeed shown that TV and newspaper reporters are more likely to be liberals than conservatives. However, there is little evidence that the personal views of reporters influence their coverage.

ers will switch channels in search of more interesting visual stimulation. For example, during an unusually contentious and lengthy interview of George Bush by Dan Rather concerning the Iran-Contra scandal, CBS's ratings actually went down as people tired of watching two talking heads argue for an extended period of time.[34] A shot of ambassadors squaring off in a fistfight at the United Nations, on the other hand, will increase the ratings. Such a scene was shown three times in one day on CBS. Not once, though, was the cause of the fight discussed.[35] Network practices like these have led observers such as Lance Bennett to write that "the public is exposed to a world driven into chaos by seemingly arbitrary and mysterious forces."[36]

participation
Where Do You Get Your News, and How Reliable is It?

The News and Public Opinion

How does the threatening, hostile, and corrupt world often depicted by the news media shape what people believe about the American political system? This question is difficult to answer. Studying the effects of the news media on people's opinions and behaviors is a difficult task. One reason is that it is hard to separate the media from other influences. When presidents, legislators, and interest groups—as well as news organizations—are all discussing an issue, it is not easy to isolate the opinion changes that come from political leadership from those that come from the news. Moreover, the effect of one news story on public opinion may be trivial; the cumulative effect of dozens of news stories may be important.

For many years, students of the subject tended to doubt that the media had more than a marginal effect on public opinion. The "minimal effects hypothesis" stemmed from the fact that early scholars were looking for direct impacts—for example, whether the media affected how people voted.[37] When the focus turned to how the media affect *what Americans think about*, more positive results were uncovered. In a series of controlled laboratory experiments, Shanto Iyengar and Donald Kinder subtly manipulated the stories participants saw on the TV news.[38] They found that they could significantly affect the importance people attached to a given problem by splicing a few stories

Table 7.2 Stories Citizens Have Tuned in and Stories they Have Tuned Out

Since 1986, the monthly survey of the Pew Research Center for the People and the Press has asked Americans how closely they have followed major news stories. As one would expect, stories involving disaster or human drama have drawn more attention than complicated issues of public policy. A representative selection of their findings is presented here. The percentage in each case is the proportion who reported following the story "very closely."

The explosion of the space shuttle *Challenger*	80%
San Francisco earthquake	73%
Los Angeles riots	70%
Rescue of baby Jessica McClure from a well	69%
Crash of TWA 800	69%
Littleton, Colo. school shootings	68%
Iraq's invasion of Kuwait	66%
Hurricane Andrew	66%
Summer 2000 increases in gasoline prices	58%
Explosion during Atlanta Olympics	57%
Supreme Court decision on flag burning	51%
Opening of the Berlin Wall	50%
Arrest of O. J. Simpson	48%
Nuclear accident at Chernobyl	46%
Attack on ice skater Nancy Kerrigan	45%
Controversy over whether Elian Gonzalez should have to return to Cuba	39%
2000 Presidential Election outcome	38%
Iran-Contra hearings	33%
Impeachment trial of President Clinton in the Senate	31%
Congressional debate about NAFTA	21%
2000 New Hampshire primary	18%
Passage of the Communications Deregulation Bill	12%
Election of Ariel Sharon in Israel in 2001	9%
Discussion and debate about expanding NATO into Eastern Europe	6%

Source: The Pew Research Center for the People and the Press.

about it into the news over the course of a week. Iyengar and Kinder do not maintain that the networks can make something out of nothing or conceal problems that actually exist. But they do conclude that "what television news does, instead, is alter the priorities Americans attach to a circumscribed set of problems, all of which are plausible contenders for public concern."[39]

This effect has far-reaching consequences. By increasing public attention to specific problems, the media influence the criteria by which the public evaluates political leaders. When unemployment goes up but inflation goes down, does public support for the president increase or decrease? The answer could depend in large part on which story the media emphasized. The fact that the media emphasized the country's slow economic growth in 1992, rather than the good news of low inflation and interest rates, was clearly helpful to Bill Clinton's first campaign for the presidency.

In another study, Page, Shapiro, and Dempsey examined public opinion polls on the same issues at two points in time, carefully coding the news coverage of these issues on the networks and in print during the interim. People's opinions did indeed shift with the tone of the news coverage. Presidential statements prompted some opinion change, though this varied with the popularity of the president. Not surprisingly, popular presidents were much more effective than unpopular ones in changing people's opinions. In contrast, interest groups seemed to have a negative impact on opinion

change, which suggests that interest groups' overt activities on behalf of a certain policy position may in fact discourage support for that position. Of all the influences on opinion change that these researchers examined, news commentators had the strongest impact. If Page and his colleagues are correct, the news media today are one of the most potent, perhaps the most potent, engine of public opinion change in America.[40]

Much remains unknown about the effects of the media and the news on American political behavior. Enough is known, however, to conclude that the media are a key political institution. The media control much of the technology that in turn controls much of what Americans believe about politics and government. For this reason, it is important to look at the American policy agenda and the media's role in shaping it.

The Media's Agenda-Setting Function

Someone who asks you, "What's your agenda?" wants to know something about your priorities. As discussed in Chapter 1, governments also have agendas. John Kingdon defines **policy agenda** as "the list of subjects or problems to which government officials, and people outside of government closely associated with those officials, are paying some serious attention at any given time."[41] Interest groups, political parties, individual politicians, public relations firms, bureaucratic agencies—and, of course, the president and Congress—are all pushing for their priorities to take precedence over others. Health care, education, unemployment, welfare reform—these and scores of other issues compete for attention from the government.

Political activists depend heavily on the media to get their ideas placed high on the governmental agenda. Political activists are often called **policy entrepreneurs**—people who invest their political "capital" in an issue (as an economic entrepreneur invests capital in an idea for making money). Kingdon says that policy entrepreneurs can "be in or out of government, in elected or appointed positions, in interest groups or research organizations."[42] Policy entrepreneurs' arsenal of weapons includes press

policy agenda

The issues that attract the serious attention of public officials and other people actively involved in politics at the time.

policy entrepreneurs

People who invest their political "capital" in an issue. According to John Kingdon, a policy entrepreneur "could be in or out of government, in elected or appointed positions, in interest groups or research organizations."

releases, press conferences, and letter writing; convincing reporters and columnists to tell their side; trading on personal contacts; and, in cases of desperation, resorting to the dramatic.

The staging of political events to attract media attention is a political art form. Dictators, revolutionaries, prime ministers, and presidents all play to the cameras. When Henry Kissinger, Nixon's top foreign policy advisor, arranged Nixon's famous trip to China, he was reminded that domestic appearances were as important as foreign policy gains. Meeting with Kissinger and Nixon, White House Chief of Staff Bob Haldeman "saw no sense in making history if television were not there to broadcast it."[43] The three men then had a lengthy discussion of how to obtain plentiful, favorable media coverage. Orchestrated minute by minute, Nixon's 1972 trip to China was perhaps the biggest media event of all time. Chinese officials were cooperative, knowing that good press coverage would help their government establish relations with the United States. They even bought the satellite transmitter the networks needed to broadcast the visit live to America. In the end, Nixon's trip to China was presented to the American public as a TV miniseries. As befits the art form that it was, years later the trip became the subject of a successful opera production.

The media are not always monopolized by political elites; the poor and downtrodden have access to them too. Civil rights groups in the 1960s relied heavily on the media to tell their stories of unjust treatment. Many believe that the introduction of television helped to accelerate the movement by showing Americans—in the North and South alike—just what the situation was.[44] Protest groups have learned that if they can stage an interesting event that attracts the media's attention, at least their point of view will be heard. Radical activist Saul Alinsky once dramatized the plight of one neighborhood by having its residents collect rats and dump them on the mayor's front lawn. The story was one that local reporters could hardly resist.

Conveying a long-term, positive image via the media is more important than a few dramatic events. Policy entrepreneurs—individuals or groups, in or out of government—depend on good will and good images. Sometimes it helps to hire a public relations firm that specializes in getting a specific message across. Groups, individuals, and

Richard Nixon's 1972 trip to China was carefully planned for the benefit of the viewing audience back home. The image of Nixon as a world statesman and peacemaker boosted his popularity and aided his reelection bid.

even countries have hired public relations firms to improve their image and their ability to peddle their issue positions.[45]

Understanding the Mass Media

The media act as key linkage institutions between the people and the policymakers, and have a profound impact on the political policy agenda. Bernard Cohen goes so far as to say that "no major act of the American Congress, no foreign adventure, no act of diplomacy, no great social reform can succeed unless the press prepares the public mind."[46] If Cohen is right, then the growth of government in America would have been impossible without the need for it being established through the media.

Why does it matter

Studies show that the media's primary influence on public opinion is through identifying issues of concern. As such, the media plays an indirect rather than direct role in the making of public policy. The media may lack the ability to tell people *how* to think, but by deciding *what* people think about, it can influence the course of history. How powerful is this role of the media? In what ways does it define or overlook the issues that are important to you?

The Media and the Scope of Government

The watchdog function of the media helps to restrict politicians. Many observers say that the press is biased against whoever holds office at the moment and that reporters want to expose officeholders. Reporters, they argue, hold disparaging views of most public officials, believing that they are self-serving, hypocritical, lacking in integrity, and preoccupied with reelection. Thus, it is not surprising that journalists see a need to debunk public officials and their policy proposals.

As every new proposal is met with much skepticism, regular constraints are placed on the scope of what government can do. The watchdog orientation of the press can be characterized as neither liberal nor conservative, but reformist. Reporters often see their job as crusading against foul play and unfairness in government and society. This focus on injustice in society inevitably encourages enlarging the scope of government. Once the media identify a problem in society—such as poverty, inadequate medical care for the elderly, or poor education for certain children—reporters usually begin to ask what the government is doing about the problem. Could it be acting more effectively to solve the problem? What do people in the White House and Congress, as well

When the TV networks projected Al Gore to be the winner in Florida early on Election Night 2000, most observers thought he was well on his way to being declared the President-elect. When it became clear that these projections were based on faulty data and that the race was too close to call, as shown in these newspaper headlines, the national media were incredibly embarrassed. Some members of Congress have suggested regulations to prevent the media from making such erroneous projections in the future, but First Amendment considerations probably make this impossible to accomplish.

as state and local government, have to say about it? In this way, the media portray government as responsible for handling almost every major problem. Though skeptical of what politicians say and do, the media report on America's social problems in a manner that often also encourages government to take on more and more tasks.

Individualism and the Media

More than any other development in the twentieth century, the rise of television broadcasting has reinforced and furthered individualism in the American political process. Candidates are now much more capable of running for office on their own by appealing to people directly through television. Individual voters can see the candidates "up close and personal" for themselves, and they have much less need for political parties or social groups to help them make their decisions.

Television finds it easier to focus on individuals than on groups. As a result, parties have declined, and candidate personality is more important than ever. Congress is difficult to cover on television because there are 535 members, but there is only one president; thus, as Al Gore predicted in his senior thesis (see chapter opening) the presidency has increasingly received more exposure than the Congress. Doris Graber's study of nightly news broadcasts found that 60 percent of the coverage devoted to the three branches of government was devoted to the president as compared to 37 percent for the Congress. The Supreme Court, which does not allow TV cameras to cover its proceedings and whose members rarely give interviews, is almost invisible on TV newscasts, receiving only a mere 3 percent of the coverage.

Democracy and the Media

As Ronald Berkman and Laura Kitch remark, "Information is the fuel of democracy."[47] Widespread access to information could be the greatest boon to democracy since the secret ballot, yet most observers think it has fallen far short of this potential. Noting the

What'll it be—entertainment news or entertainment

vast increase in information available through the news media, Berkman and Kitch state that "If the sheer quantity of news produced greater competency in the citizenry, then we would have a society of political masters. Yet, just the opposite is happening."[48] The rise of the "information society" has not brought about the rise of the "informed society."

Whenever the media are criticized for being superficial, their defense is to say that this is what people want. Network executives remark that if people suddenly started to watch in-depth shows such as PBS's "Newshour," then they would gladly imitate them. If the American people wanted serious coverage of the issues, networks would be happy to give it to them. Network executives claim that they are in business to make a profit and that to do so, they must appeal to the maximum number of people. As Matthew Kerbel observes, "the people who bring you the evening news would like it to be informative *and* entertaining, but when these two values collide, the shared orientations of the television news world push the product inexorably toward the latter."[49] It is not their fault if the resulting news coverage is superficial, network executives argue; blame capitalism, or blame the people—most of whom like news to be more entertaining than educational. Thus, if people are not better informed in the high-tech age, it is largely because they do not care to hear about complicated political issues. In this sense, one can say that the people really do rule through the media.

Summary

Plenty of evidence points to the power of the media in American politics. The media are ubiquitous. There is evidence that the news and its presentation are an important—perhaps the most important—shaper of public opinion on political issues. The media are an important ingredient in shaping the policy agenda, and political entrepreneurs carefully use the media for this purpose.

Gradually, the broadcast media have replaced the print media as the principal source of news. Recently, the development of cable TV channels and websites has led to narrowcasting—appealing to specific segments of the mass public rather than to the

Career Profile

Position: Press Secretary to Governor Don Sundquist (R-TN)
Employer: State of Tennessee
Salary Range: $60,000-$80,000 year
Benefits: Life and health insurance, retirement plan
Qualifications: College graduate with thorough knowledge of the media and politics, willingness to travel with the governor, and be on call 24 hours a day/7 days a week.

Real People on the Job: Beth Fortune

In early 1994, Beth Fortune was a public affairs manager at the Nashville Airport Authority. She'd recently earned her master's degree in journalism and public affairs and was looking for a new challenge. She found it by working in media relations for the gubernatorial campaign of Don Sundquist. After Sundquist won the election later that year, he offered Beth the job of press secretary, a position she retained after he was elected to a second term in 1998.

As press secretary, Beth is the primary spokesperson for the governor and his administration. She handles all media inquiries, makes herself available for interviews, and generally speaks for the governor on a daily basis. She also oversees and manages the media operations for the 22 departments of the state government. She frequently travels with Governor Sundquist, joining him at many of the meetings and events he attends.

The most important part of her job is to effectively communicate the governor's message and agenda to the people of Tennessee. This isn't always an easy task. Recently she had to present the governor's unpopular proposal for a state income tax in a favorable light and answer the pointed questions of people hostile to the plan. The job has its rewards, however. As a key player in the administration and the first woman to hold the job of press secretary in the history of Tennessee, Beth knows that she's making history.

If you are interested in being a press secretary, it helps to have experience as a political reporter and in political campaigns. You must have an awareness of public relations and a sensitivity to politics. You also need to be able to handle the press on a daily basis. Like many jobs, becoming a press secretary is partly what you know and how well you do it, and partly who you know. Get out there and volunteer on campaigns to show people what you are capable of doing.

entire population. The media largely define "news" as people and events out of the ordinary. Because of economic pressures, the media are biased in favor of stories with high drama that will attract people's interest, instead of extended analyses of complex issues. With the media's superficial treatment of important policy issues, it should be no surprise that the incredible amount of information available to Americans today has not visibly increased their political awareness or participation.

Key Terms

high-tech politics	print media	trial balloons
mass media	broadcast media	sound bites
media event	chains	talking head
press conferences	narrowcasting	policy agenda
investigative journalism	beats	policy entrepreneurs

For Further Reading

Dautrich, Kenneth, and Thomas H. Hartley. *How the News Media Fail American Voters: Causes, Consequences and Remedies.* New York: Columbia University Press, 1999. A highly critical look at how the news media covered the 1996 presidential election.

Epstein, Edward J. *News from Nowhere: Television and the News.* New York: Random House, 1973. Although dated, this account still provides an excellent view of network news.

Frantzich, Stephen, and John Sullivan. *The C-SPAN Revolution.* Norman: University of Oklahoma Press, 1996. An account of the network for political junkies.

Graber, Doris A. *Mass Media and American Politics*, 5th ed. Washington, D.C.: Congressional Quarterly Press, 1996. The standard textbook on the subject.

Hertsgaard, Mark. *On Bended Knee: The Press and the Reagan Presidency.* New York: Farrar, Straus & Giroux, 1988. An in-depth look at how the press treated Reagan, and vice versa.

Iyengar, Shanto, and Donald R. Kinder. *News That Matters.* Chicago: University of Chicago Press, 1987. Two political psychologists show how the media can affect the public agenda.

Jamieson, Kathleen Hall. *Eloquence in an Electronic Age.* New York: Oxford University Press, 1988. A noted communications scholar takes a look at how television has altered political discourse.

Kingdon, John W. *Agendas, Alternatives, and Public Policy*, 2nd ed. New York: HarperCollins, 1995. The best overall study of the formation of policy agendas.

Neuman, W. Russell, Marion R. Just, and Ann N. Crigler. *Common Knowledge: News and the Construction of Political Meaning.* Chicago: University of Chicago Press, 1992. An interesting study arguing that television is reasonably effective in promoting learning about the issues.

Patterson, Thomas E. *Out of Order.* New York: Knopf, 1993. A highly critical and well-documented examination of how the media covers election campaigns.

Smith, Hedrick, ed. *The Media and the Gulf War: The Press and Democracy in Wartime.* Washington, D.C.: Seven Locks Press, 1992. A diverse set of readings concerning how the Gulf War was reported.

West, Darrell M. *Air Wars: Television Advertising in Election Campaigns, 1952–1996*, 2nd ed. Washington, D.C.: Congressional Quarterly Press, 1997. An analysis of how TV campaign ads have evolved over the last four decades and what impact they have had on elections.

Internet Resources

www.people-press.org
The Pew Center for the People and the Press regularly surveys people regarding their attitudes toward the media's coverage of politics, and measures which news events people follow most closely.

www.appcpenn.org

The Annenberg Public Policy Center conducts studies that analyze the content of TV coverage of politics, which they post at this site.

www.n-net.com
Listings for newspapers all over the country, including web links where available.

www.cmpa.com
The Center for Media and Public Affairs posts their studies of the content of media coverage of politics at this site.

www.ammi.org/livingroomcandidate/
A great collection of classic political commercials from 1952 through 2000.

Notes

1. See Darrell M. West, *Air Wars: Television Advertising in Election Campaigns, 1952–1992* (Washington, D.C.: Congressional Quarterly Press, 1993), 48.
2. Stephen Ansolabehere and Shanto Iyengar, *Going Negative* (New York: Free Press, 1995).
3. December 1, 1969, memo from Nixon to H. R. Haldeman in Bruce Oudes, ed., *From: The President—Richard Nixon's Secret Files* (New York: Harper & Row, 1988), 76–77.
4. Mark Hertsgaard, *On Bended Knee: The Press and the Reagan Presidency* (New York: Farrar, Straus & Giroux, 1988), 34.
5. Donald T. Regan, *For the Record* (New York: Harcourt Brace Jovanovich, 1988), 247–248.
6. The Johnson interview is recounted in David Halberstam, *The Powers That Be* (New York: Dell Books, 1979), 15–16.
7. Quoted in David Brinkley, *Washington Goes to War* (New York: Knopf, 1988), 171.
8. Theodore H. White, *The Making of the President, 1972* (New York: Atheneum, 1973), 250.
9. Sam Donaldson, *Hold On, Mr. President!* (New York: Random House, 1987), 54.
10. *Ibid.*, 20.
11. See the classic report by Michael J. Robinson, "Public Affairs Television and the Growth of Political Malaise: The Case of 'The Selling of the Pentagon'," *American Political Science Review* 70 (June 1976): 409–432. Also see Joseph Cappella and Kathleen Hall Jamieson, *Spiral of Cynicism: The Press and the Public Good* (New York: Oxford, 1997).
12. William Manchester, *The Last Lion: Winston Churchill, Visions of Glory, 1874–1932* (Boston: Little, Brown, 1984), 225.
13. Doris A. Graber, *Mass Media and American Politics*, 4th ed. (Washington, D.C.: Congressional Quarterly Press, 1993), 44.
14. See, for example, Michael X. Delli Carpini and Scott Keeter, *What Americans Know About Politics and Why It Matters* (New Haven, CT: Yale University Press, 1996) and Ruy A. Teixeira, *The Disappearing American Voter* (Washington, D.C.: Brookings Institution, 1992).
15. Russell Baker, *The Good Times* (New York: William Morrow, 1989), 326.
16. See Walter Cronkite, *A Reporter's Life* (New York: Knopf, 1996), 257–258.
17. Maureen Dowd, "Where Bush Turns for the Latest," the *New York Times*, August 11, 1989, A11.
18. Lewis A. Friedland, *Covering the World: International Television News Services* (New York: The Twentieth Century Fund, 1992), 8.
19. See Harold W. Stanley and Richard G. Niemi, *Vital Statistics on American Politics*, 5th ed. (Washington, D.C.: Congressional Quarterly Press, 1995), 68.
20. Edward J. Epstein, *News from Nowhere: Television and the News* (New York: Random House, 1973).
21. Steven Ansolabehere, Roy Behr, and Shanto Iyengar, *The Media Game: American Politics in the Television Age* (New York: Macmillan, 1993), 53.
22. For example, see Leon V. Sigal, *Reporters and Officials: The Organization and Politics of News Reporting* (Lexington, MA: D.C. Heath, 1973), 122.
23. This letter can be found in Hedrick Smith, ed., *The Media and the Gulf War: The Press and Democracy in Wartime* (Washington, D.C.: Seven Locks Press, 1992), 378–380. Smith's book contains an excellent set of readings on media coverage of the war.
24. Jody Powell, "White House Flackery," in Peter Woll, ed., *Debating American Government*, 2nd ed. (Glenview, IL: Scott, Foresman, 1988), 180.
25. Dan Rather, quoted in Hoyt Purvis, ed., *The Presidency and the Press* (Austin, TX: Lyndon B. Johnson School of Public Affairs, 1976), 56.
26. Kathleen Hall Jamieson and Joseph N. Capella, "The Role of the Press in the Health Care Reform Debate of 1993–1994," in Doris Graber, Denis McQuail, and Pippa Norris, eds., *The Politics of News, the News of Politics* (Washington, D.C.: Congressional Quarterly Press, 1998), 118–119.
27. This point is well argued in Kathleen Hall Jamieson, *Eloquence in an Electronic Age* (New York: Oxford University Press, 1988).
28. For a discussion of CBS's failed attempt to lengthen candidate sound bites in 1992, see S. Robert Lichter and Richard E. Noyes, *Good Intentions Make Bad News*, 2nd ed. (Lanham, MD: Rowman & Littlefield, 1996), 246–250.
29. Quoted in Austin Ranney, *Channels of Power* (New York: Basic Books, 1983), 116.
30. Walter Cronkite, *A Reporter's Life*, 376–377.
31. William Schneider and I. A. Lewis, "Views on the News," *Public Opinion* 8 (August/September 1985): 6–11.
32. William Glaberson, "More Reporters Leaning Democratic, Study Says," the *New York Times*, November 18, 1992, A13.
33. See Michael J. Robinson and Margaret A. Sheehan, *Over the Wire and on TV: CBS and UP in Campaign '80* (New York: Russell Sage Foundation, 1983); and C. Richard Hofstetter, *Bias in the News: Network Television Coverage of the 1972 Election Campaign* (Columbus: Ohio State University Press, 1976).
34. Michael J. Robinson and Margaret Petrella, "Who Won the George Bush-Dan Rather Debate?" *Public Opinion 10* (March/April 1988): 43.
35. Robinson, "Public Affairs Television," 428.
36. W. Lance Bennett, *News: The Politics of Illusion*, 2nd ed. (New York: Longman, 1988), 46.
37. See Paul F. Lazarsfeld et al., *The People's Choice* (New York: Columbia University Press, 1944).
38. Shanto Iyengar and Donald R. Kinder, *News That Matters* (Chicago: University of Chicago Press, 1987).
39. *Ibid.*, 118–119.
40. See Benjamin I. Page, Robert Y. Shapiro, and Glenn R. Dempsey, "What Moves Public Opinion?" *American Political Science Review* 81 (March 1987): 23–44.
41. John W. Kingdon, *Agendas, Alternatives, and Public Policies* (Boston: Little, Brown, 1984), 3.
42. *Ibid.*, 3.
43. Henry A. Kissinger, *White House Years* (Boston: Little, Brown, 1979), 757.
44. See the interview with Richard Valeriani in Juan Williams, *Eyes on the Prize* (New York: Viking, 1987), 270–271.

45. For an interesting study of how hiring a public relations firm can help a nation's TV image, see Jarol B. Manheim and Robert B. Albitton, "Changing National Images: International Public Relations and Media Agenda Setting," *American Political Science Review* 78 (September 1984): 641–657.
46. Bernard Cohen, *The Press and Foreign Policy* (Princeton, NJ: Princeton University Press, 1963), 13.
47. Ronald W. Berkman and Laura W. Kitch, *Politics in the Media Age* (New York: McGraw-Hill, 1986), 311.
48. *Ibid.*, 313.
49. Matthew Robert Kerbel, *Edited for Television: CNN, ABC, and the 1992 Presidential Campaign* (Boulder, CO: Westview Press, 1994), 196.

Political Parties

8

Chapter Outline

Three hundred and sixty-seven Republican candidates for the House of Representatives stood on the steps of the U.S. Capitol in late September of 1994 to sign a document they entitled "Contract with America." This document outlined the reforms the Republicans promised to pass on the first day of the new Congress, as well as 10 bills they agreed would be brought to the floor for a vote within the first 100 days of the new Republican-controlled House of Representatives. The contract was the brainchild of Newt Gingrich and Richard Armey, both of whom were college professors before they were elected to Congress. Gingrich and Armey thought that the Republicans needed a stronger message in 1994 than simply saying they opposed President Clinton's policies. The contract was an attempt to offer the voters a positive program for reshaping American public policy and reforming how Congress works. Without actually knowing much about the individual

candidates themselves, voters would know what to expect of the signers of the contract and would be able to hold them accountable for these promises in the future. In this sense, the contract endeavored to make politics user-friendly for the voters.

America's Founding Fathers were more concerned with their fear that political parties could be forums for corruption and national divisiveness than they were with the role that parties could play in making politics user-friendly for ordinary voters. Thomas Jefferson spoke for many when he said, "If I could not go to heaven but with a party, I would not go there at all." In his farewell address, George Washington also warned of the dangers of parties.

Today, most observers would agree that political parties have contributed greatly to American democracy. In one of the most frequently—and rightly—quoted observations about American politics, E. E. Schattschneider said that "political parties created democracy . . . and democracy is unthinkable save in terms of the parties."[1] Political scientists and politicians alike believe that a strong party system is desirable and bemoan the weakening of American political parties in recent decades.

The strength of the parties has an impact not only on how we are governed but also on what government does. The major historical developments in the expansion or contraction of the scope of government have generally been accomplished through the implementation of one party's platform. Currently, the Democrats and Republicans differ greatly on the issue of the scope of government. If either party were to gain control of both the presidency and the Congress for an extended period of time, that circumstance would have a profound impact on the scope of government. However, as we shall see in this chapter, during the past few decades the Congress was usually controlled by one party and the White House by the other. This lack of unified party control has largely stifled any major changes in the scope of government in America.

As you read this chapter, consider whether you would prefer to see a single party in firm control of the government, and what difference such control would make.

party competition

The battle of the parties for control of public offices. Ups and downs of the two major parties are one of the most important elements in American politics.

The alternating of power and influence between the two major parties is one of the most important elements in American politics. **Party competition** is the battle between Democrats and Republicans for the control of public offices. Without this competition there would be no choice, and without choice there would be no democracy. Americans have had a choice between two major political parties since the early 1800s, and this two-party system remains intact almost two centuries later.

The Meaning Of Party

political party

According to Anthony Downs, a "team of men [and women] seeking to control the governing apparatus by gaining office in a duly constituted election."

Almost all definitions of political parties have one thing in common: Parties try to win elections. This is their core function and the key to their definition. By contrast, interest groups do not nominate candidates for office, though they may try to influence elections. For example, no one has ever been elected to Congress as the nominee of the National Rifle Association, though many nominees have received the NRA's endorsement. Thus, Anthony Downs defined a **political party** as a "team of men [and women] seeking to control the governing apparatus by gaining office in a duly constituted election."[2]

The word *team* is the slippery part of this definition. Party teams may not be so well disciplined and single-minded as teams fielded by top football coaches. Party teams often run every which way (sometimes toward the opposition's goal line) and are difficult to lead. Party leaders often disagree about policy, and between elections the party organizations seem to all but disappear. So who are the members of these teams? A widely adopted way of thinking about parties in political science is as "three-headed political giants." The three heads are (1) the party in the electorate, (2) the party as an organization, and (3) the party in government.[3]

The *party in the electorate* is by far the largest component of an American political party. Unlike many European political parties, American parties do not require dues or membership cards to distinguish members from nonmembers. Americans may register as Democrats, Republicans, Libertarians, or whatever, but registration is not legally binding and is easily changed. To be a member of a party, you need only claim to be a member. If you call yourself a Democrat, you are one—even if you never talk to a party official, never work in a campaign, and often vote for Republicans.

The *party as an organization* has a national office, a full-time staff, rules and bylaws, and budgets. In addition to a national office, each party maintains state and local headquarters. The party organization includes precinct leaders, county chairpersons, state chairpersons, state delegates to the national committee, and officials in the party's Washington office. These are the people who keep the party running between elections and make its rules. From the party's national chairperson to its local precinct captain, the party organization pursues electoral victory.

The *party in government* consists of elected officials who call themselves members of the party. Although presidents, members of Congress, governors, and lesser officeholders may share a common party label, they do not always agree on policy. Presidents and governors may have to wheedle and cajole their own party members into voting for their policies. In the United States, it is not uncommon to put personal principle—or ambition—above loyalty to the party's leaders. These leaders are the main spokespersons for the party, however. Their words and actions personify the party to millions of Americans. If the party is to translate its promises into policy, the job must be done by the party in government.

Political parties are everywhere in American politics—present in the electorate's mind, as an organization, and in government offices—and one of their

The major parties have different demographic bases of support. Of all social groups, African Americans tend to be the most solidly aligned with one party. Ever since the Civil Rights Act of 1964, they have voted overwhelmingly for Democratic candidates. In 2000, African-American voters cast 89 percent of their votes for Al Gore, 8 percent for George W. Bush, and 2 percent for Ralph Nader.

major tasks is to link the people of the United States to their government and its policies.

Tasks of the Parties

The road from public opinion to public policy is long and winding. All 280 million Americans cannot raise their voices to government and indicate their policy preferences in unison. In a large democracy, **linkage institutions** translate inputs from the public into outputs from the policymakers. Linkage institutions sift through all the issues, identify the most pressing concerns, and put these onto the governmental agenda. In other words, linkage institutions help ensure that public preferences are heard loud and clear. In the United States, there are four main linkage institutions: parties, elections, interest groups, and the media.

linkage institutions
The channels through which people's concerns become political issues on the government's policy agenda. In the United States, linkage institutions include elections, political parties, interest groups, and the media.

Kay Lawson writes that "parties are seen, both by the members and by others, as agencies for forging links between citizens and policymakers."[4] Here is a checklist of the tasks parties perform, or should perform, if they are to serve as effective linkage institutions:

Parties Pick Candidates. Almost no one above the local level (and often not even there) gets elected to a public office without winning a party's endorsement.[5] A party's endorsement is called a *nomination*. Up until the early twentieth century, American parties chose their candidates with little or no input from the voters. Progressive reformers led the charge for primary elections, in which citizens would have the power to choose nominees for office. The innovation of primary elections spread rapidly, transferring the nominating function from the party organization to the party identifiers.

Parties Run Campaigns. Through their national, state, and local organizations, parties coordinate political campaigns. However, television has made it easier for candidates to campaign on their own, without the help of the party organization. For example, Ross Perot received 18.9 percent of the presidential vote in 1992 and 8.5 percent in 1996 with hardly any organizational support at all.

party image

The voter's perception of what the Republicans or Democrats stand for, such as **conservatism** or **liberalism**.

Parties Give Cues to Voters. Most voters have a **party image** of each party; that is, they know (or think they know) what the Republicans and Democrats stand for. Liberal, conservative, probusiness, prolabor—these are some of the elements of each party's image. Even in the present era of weakened parties, many voters still rely on a party to give them cues for voting.

Why does it matter?

Parties perform many important tasks in American politics. Yet, 30 percent of the respondents to the 1998 National Election Study felt that parties were no longer needed. What do you think? Would you like to see the parties disbanded and have every candidate for office run completely on his or her own? How would this change American politics?

Parties Articulate Policies. Within the electorate and within the government, each political party advocates specific policy alternatives. For example, the Democratic Party has clearly supported abortion rights, and the Republican Party has repeatedly called for restrictions on abortion.

Parties Coordinate Policymaking. In America's fragmented government, parties are essential for coordination among the branches of government. Virtually all major public officials are also members of a party. When they need support to get something done, the first place they look is to their fellow partisans.

The importance of these tasks makes it easy to see why most political scientists accept Schattschneider's famous assertion that modern democracy is unthinkable without competition between political parties.

Parties, Voters, and Policy: The Downs Model

rational-choice theory

A popular theory in political science to explain the actions of voters as well as politicians. It assumes that individuals act in their own best interest, carefully weighing the costs and benefits of possible alternatives.

The parties compete, at least in theory, as in a marketplace. A party is in the market for voters; its products are its candidates and policies. Anthony Downs has provided a working model of the relationship among citizens, parties, and policy, employing a rational-choice perspective.[6] **Rational-choice theory** "seeks to explain political processes and outcomes as consequences of purposive behavior. Political actors are assumed to have goals and to pursue those goals sensibly and efficiently."[7] Downs argues that (1) voters want to maximize the chance that policies they favor will be adopted by government, and (2) parties want to win office. Thus, in order to win office, the wise party selects policies that are widely favored. Parties and candidates may do all sorts of things to win—kiss babies, call opponents ugly names, even lie and cheat—but in a democracy they will primarily use their accomplishments and policy positions to attract votes. If Party A figures out what the voters want more accurately than does Party B, then Party A should be more successful.

The long history of the American party system has shown that successful parties rarely stray far from the midpoint of public opinion. In the American electorate, a few voters are extremely liberal and a few are extremely conservative, but the majority are in the middle (see Figure 8.1). If Downs is right, then centrist parties will win, and extremist parties will be condemned to footnotes in the history books. Indeed, occasionally a party may misperceive voters' desires or take a risky stand on a principle—hoping to persuade voters during the campaign—but in order to survive in a system where the majority opinion is middle-of-the-road, parties must stay near the center.

We frequently hear criticism that there is not much difference between the Democrats and the Republicans. Given the nature of the American political market,

Figure 8.1 The Downs Model: How Rational Parties Match Voters' Policy Preferences

In 1998, the National Election Study asked a sample of the American electorate to classify themselves on a 7-point scale from extremely liberal to extremely conservative. The graph shows how the people located themselves in terms of ideology and how they perceived the ideology of the parties.

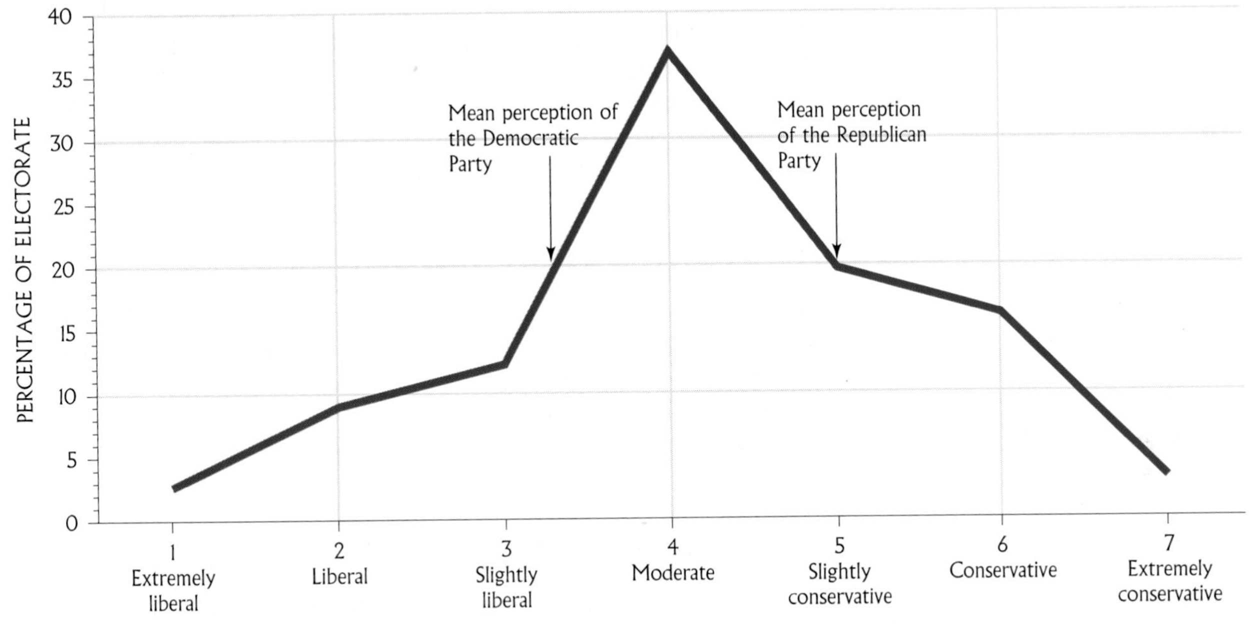

Source: From the National Election Studies conducted by the University of Michigan, Center for Political Studies, 1998.

Figure 8.2 Do People See Differences Between the Parties?

Over the years, the National Election Studies have repeatedly asked nationwide samples whether they thought there were major differences between the Democrats and the Republicans. Since Ronald Reagan first became the Republican Party's nominee in 1980, and moved the GOP further toward conservatism, more people have said that they see substantial differences between the parties.

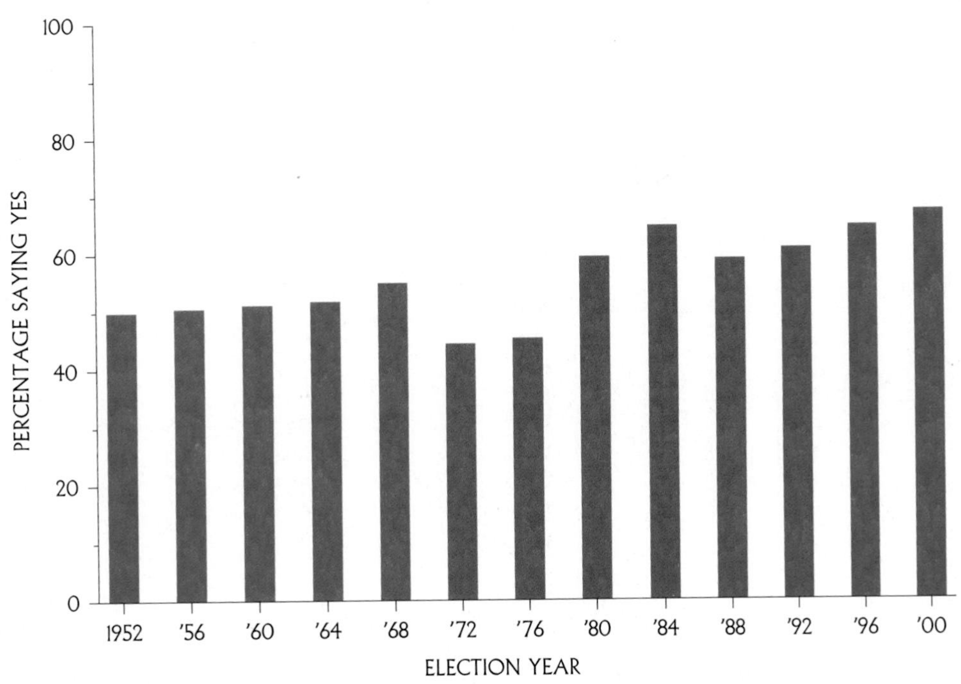

Source: From the National Election Studies conducted by the University of Michigan, Center for Political Studies.

however, these two parties have little choice. We would not expect two competing department stores to locate at opposite ends of town when most people live on Main Street. Downs also notes, though, that from a rational-choice perspective, one should expect the parties to differentiate themselves at least somewhat. Just as Chrysler tries to offer something different from and better than General Motors in order to build buyer loyalty, so Democrats and Republicans have to forge different identities to build voter loyalty. Two-thirds of the the population currently believes that important differences do exist between the parties, as you can see in Figure 8.2. When asked what those differences are, respondents most frequently comment that the Republicans favor lower taxes and less domestic spending, whereas Democrats favor more government programs to help the middle class and less-advantaged Americans.

The Party in the Electorate

In most European nations, being a party member means formally joining a political party. You get a membership card to carry around, you pay dues, and you vote to pick your local party leaders. In America, being a party member takes far less work. There is no formal "membership" in the parties at all. If you believe you are a Democrat or a Republican, then you are a Democrat or a Republican. Thus the party in the electorate consists largely of symbolic images and ideas. For most people the party is a psychological label. They may never go to a party meeting, but they have images of the parties' stances on issues and of which groups the parties generally favor or oppose.

party identification

A citizen's self-proclaimed preference for one party or the other.

Party images help shape people's **party identification**, the self-proclaimed preference for one party or the other. Because many people routinely vote for the party they identify with (all else being equal), even a shift of a few percentage points in the distribution of party identification is important. Since 1952, the National Election Study surveys have asked a sample of citizens, "Generally speaking, do you usually think of yourself as a Republican, a Democrat, or an Independent?" Repeatedly asking this question permits political scientists to trace party identification over the past four decades (see Table 8.1). The clearest trend has been *the decline of both parties and*

Table 8.1 Party Identification in the United States, 1952–2000[a]

YEAR	DEMOCRATS	INDEPENDENTS	REPUBLICANS
1952	48.6	23.3	28.1
1956	45.3	24.4	30.3
1960	46.4	23.4	30.2
1964	52.2	23.0	24.8
1968	46.0	29.5	24.5
1972	41.0	35.2	23.8
1976	40.2	36.8	23.0
1980	41.7	35.3	23.0
1984	37.7	34.8	27.6
1988	35.7	36.3	28.0
1992	35.8	38.7	25.5
1996	39.3	32.9	27.8
2000	34.8	41.0	24.2

[a]In percentage of people; the small percentage who identify with a minor party or who cannot answer the question are excluded.

Source: From the 1952–2000 National Election Studies conducted by the University of Michigan, Center for Political Studies.

resultant upsurge of independence (mostly at the expense of the Democrats). In 2000, 41 percent of the population called themselves Independents.

Virtually every major social group—Catholics, Jews, poor Whites, Southerners, and so on—has moved toward a position of increased independence. The major exception has been African-American voters. A decade of Democratic civil rights policy in the 1960s moved African Americans even more solidly into the Democratic Party. Currently, only about 5 percent of African Americans identify themselves as Republicans.[8]

For many white Americans, though, the abandonment of either party for a non-partisan stance is well advanced. This abandonment occurred at all age levels in the electorate, but it was most pronounced for younger voters, who have always had the weakest party ties. The baby boom and the lowering of the voting age to 18 contributed to the rising tide of independence during the 1970s. Young people are usually the most likely to call themselves Independents.

Not only are there more Independents now, but those who still identify with a party are no longer so loyal in the voting booth. In recent years, **ticket-splitting**—voting with one party for one office and the other for other offices—has reached record proportions.[9] An examination of a random sample of over 8,000 actual 1994 ballots from Los Angeles County compiled by Anthony Salvanto reveals that only 30 percent cast a complete and straight vote for all 11 partisan offices contested that year.[10] The result of voters failing to make an across-the-board choice between the parties has often been divided party government, at both the federal and state levels.

ticket-splitting

Voting with one party for one office and with another party for other offices. It has become the norm in American voting behavior.

The Party Organizations: From the Grass Roots to Washington

An organizational chart is usually shaped like a pyramid, with those who give orders at the top and those who carry them out at the bottom. In drawing an organizational chart of an American political party, you could put the national committee and national convention of the party at the apex of the pyramid, the state party organizations in the middle, and the thousands of local party organizations at the bottom. Such a chart, however, would provide a misleading depiction of an American political party. The president of General Motors is at the top of GM in fact as well as on paper. By contrast, the chairperson of the Democratic or Republican national committee is on top on paper, but not in fact.

As organizations, American political parties are decentralized and fragmented. As Paul Allen Beck writes, party organizations in the United States "lack the hierarchical control and efficiency, the unified setting of priorities and strategy, and the central responsibility we often find in parties in other nations."[11] One can imagine a system in which the national office of a party resolves conflicts among its state and local branches, states the party's position on the issues, and then passes orders down through the hierarchy. One can even imagine a system in which the party leaders have the power to enforce their decisions by offering greater influence and resources to officeholders who follow the party line and by punishing those who do not. Many European parties work just that way, but in America the formal party organizations have little such power. Candidates in the United States can get elected on their own. They do not need the help of the party most of the time, and hence the party organization is relegated to a comparatively limited role.

Local Parties

The urban political party was once the main political party organization in America. From the late nineteenth century through the New Deal of the 1930s, scores of cities were dominated by **party machines.** A machine is a kind of party organization, very

party machines

A type of political party organization that relies heavily on material inducements, such as patronage, to win votes and to govern.

different from the typical fragmented and disorganized political party in America today. It can be defined as a party organization that depends on rewarding its members in some material fashion.

patronage

One of the key inducements used by party machines. A patronage job, promotion, or contract is one that is given for political reasons rather than for merit or competence alone.

Patronage is one of the key inducements used by party machines. A patronage job is one that is awarded for political reasons rather than for merit or competence alone. In the late nineteenth century, political parties routinely sold some patronage jobs to the highest bidder. Party leaders made no secret of their corruption, openly selling government positions to raise money for the party. Some of this money was used to buy votes, but a good deal went to line the pockets of the politicians themselves. The most notable case was that of Boss Tweed of New York, whose ring reportedly made between $40 million and $200 million from tax receipts, payoffs, and kickbacks.

At one time, urban machines in Albany, Chicago, Philadelphia, Kansas City, and elsewhere depended heavily on ethnic group support. Some of the most fabled machine leaders were Irish politicians, including New York's George Washington Plunkett, Boston's James Michael Curley, and Chicago's Richard J. Daley. Daley's Chicago machine was the last survivor, steamrolling its opposition amid charges of racism and corruption. Even today there are remnants of the Chicago machine, particularly in white and ethnic neighborhoods. The survival of machine politics in Chicago can be traced to its ability to limit the scope of reform legislation. A large proportion of city jobs were classified as "temporary" even though they had been held by the same person for decades, and these positions were exempted from the merit system of hiring. At its height, the Daley machine in Chicago dispensed 40,000 patronage jobs, the recipients of which were expected to deliver at least 10 votes each on election day and to kick back 5 percent of their salary in the form of a donation to the local Democratic Party.[12]

Urban party organizations are also no longer very active as a rule. Progressive reforms that placed jobs under the merit system rather than at the machine's discretion weakened the machines' power. Regulations concerning fair bidding on government contracts also took away much of their ability to reward the party faithful. As ethnic integration occurred in big cities, the group loyalties that the machines often relied on no longer seemed very relevant to many people.

Partly filling in the void created by the decline of the inner-city machines has been a revitalization of party organization at the county level—particularly in affluent suburbs. Table 8.2 demonstrates how county party organizations in the early 1990s were more likely to have the characteristics of permanent institutions than those of just a dozen years earlier. These county organizations distribute yard signs and campaign literature, get out the vote on election day, and help state and local candidates any way they can. To candidates who have ample resources of their own, the county organization is probably not of great consequence; as you can see, most still have no regular paid staff. However, to candidates for less visible offices who often work on shoestring budgets, the local party organization can provide crucial assistance.

The 50 State Party Systems

American national parties are a loose aggregation of state parties, which are themselves a fluid association of individuals, groups, and local organizations. There are 50 state party systems, and no two are exactly alike. In a few states, the parties are well organized, have sizable staffs, and spend a lot of money. Pennsylvania is one such state. In other states, however, parties are weak. California, says Kay Lawson, "has political parties so weak as to be almost nonexistent; it is the birthplace of campaigning by 'hired guns'; and it has been run by special interests for so long that Californians have forgotten what is special about that."[13]

You Are the Policymaker

Was the Blanket Primary A Good Idea?

In the 1996 California primary, voters were presented with an initiative to change the state's closed primary process to a blanket primary. Proponents of this initiative argued that a closed primary system favors the election of party hard-liners, contributes to legislative gridlock, and stacks the deck against moderate problem solvers. By opening up the primary process to allow voters to vote for any set of candidates they like regardless of partisanship, advocates of the blanket primary argued that politicians would be encouraged to focus on the median voter rather than a narrow group of partisans. They also noted that participation in primary elections would increase by allowing Independents a chance to take part, and by giving minority party voters in noncompetitive districts a real say in selecting their representatives.

Both the Democratic and Republican state parties of California came out strongly against this initiative. They argued that the blanket primary would be an invitation to political mischief, with political consultants and special interests manipulating the system to help the candidate they'd most like to face in November get the other party's nomination. A frequently used analogy during the campaign was that allowing members of one party a large voice in choosing another party's nominee was like letting UCLA's football team choose USC's head coach. Rather than seeing this reform as giving voters more choice, opponents argued that it would diminish choice in the long run by muddling the differences between major parties.

In the end, the voters approved the blanket primary by a margin of 60 to 40. The exit polls showed that the initiative was supported by Democrats and Republicans alike. However, the party organizations immediately took the case to federal court, arguing that the blanket primary infringed on their constitutional rights of freedom of association by giving nonmembers a say in their activities. U.S. District Judge David Levy listened to a variety of testimony from political consultants, party leaders, and political scientists (including one of the coauthors of this book). In *Democratic Party et al. v. Jones* he ruled that although the blanket primary weakened the parties it was what the voters wanted and shouldn't be overruled by the courts. Subsequently, the 9th Circuit Court of Appeals upheld the ruling. But the Supreme Court had the final word in June of 2000, ruling that the blanket primary violated the parties' right to freedom of association. Writing for the majority, Justice Antonin Scalia stated that the blanket primary forces the parties "to adulterate their candidate-selection process—the basic function of a political party—by opening it up to persons wholly unaffiliated with the party."

Upon hearing of the Supreme Court decision, California's Democratic governor and Republican secretary of state both pledged to try to retain a blanket primary system by making primary elections nonpartisan, as currently practiced in Louisiana. In his opinion, Justice Scalia indicated that such a system is constitutional because party nominees are not chosen through such a process; indeed, sometimes this system leads to a general election between two members of the same party. It would be ironic if the parties' court victory led them to be excluded from the primary process in some states altogether. You be the policymaker: Should the Supreme Court have outlawed California's blanket primary? Is the nonpartisan blanket primary an idea that should now be tried in a number of states?

Table 8.2 Organizational Characteristics Of Parties At The County Level (in percents)

	Democrats		Republicans	
	1979–1980	1992	1979–1980	1992
Year-Round Office	12	45	14	64
Paid Full-Time Staff	3	22	4	26
Maintain a Campaign Office	55	85	60	65

Source: Adapted from Paul Allen Beck, *Party Politics in America*, 8th edition (New York: Longman, 1997), 79.

closed primaries

Elections to select party nominees in which only people who have registered in advance with the party can vote for that party's candidates, thus encouraging greater party loyalty.

open primaries

Elections to select party nominees in which voters can decide on election day whether they want to participate in the Democratic or Republican contests.

blanket primaries

Elections to select party nominees in which voters are presented with a list of candidates from all the parties. Voters can then select some Democrats and some Republicans if they like.

The states are allowed wide discretion in the regulation of party activities, and how they choose to organize elections influences the strength of the parties profoundly. Some states give parties greater power than others to limit who can participate in their nomination contests. In **closed primaries** only people who have registered in advance with the party can vote in its primary, thus encouraging greater party loyalty. In contrast, **open primaries** allow voters to decide on election day whether they want to participate in the Democratic or Republican contests. And most antiparty of all are **blanket primaries,** which present voters with a list of candidates from all the parties and allow them to pick some Democrats and some Republicans if they like. (See "You are the Policymaker: Was the Blanket Primary A Good Idea?")

When it comes to the general election, some states promote voting according to party by listing the candidates of each party down a single column, whereas others place the names in random order. About a third of the states currently have a provision on their ballots that enables a voter to cast a vote for all of one party's candidates with a single act. This option clearly encourages straight-ticket voting and makes the support of the party organization more important to candidates in these states.

Organizationally, state parties are on the upswing throughout the country. As recently as the early 1960s, half of the state party organizations did not even maintain a permanent headquarters; when the state party elected a new chairperson, the party organization simply shifted its office to his or her hometown.[14] In contrast, almost all state parties today have a physical headquarters, typically in the capital city or the largest city. State party budgets have also increased. In the early 1960s, more than half the parties had an annual budget of less than $50,000. With the development of permanent headquarters, professional staffs, and high-tech equipment, this figure has risen substantially. A 1984 survey found that the average Democratic state party budget was $260,000; the Republican state parties were much better off with an average budget of $795,000.[15]

Why does it matter?

Some state party organizations are much more active and influential than others. What about your state—do you think the party organizations play an important role? Why do you think they are either weak or strong in your state? What might the consequences be if these state party organizations become better funded in the future?

Though no study of state parties has been conducted recently, it is almost certain that their financial resources have increased. In the 1996 case of *Colorado Republican Campaign Committee v. Federal Election Commission* the Supreme Court ruled that the government may not restrict the amount that the state or national parties spend on behalf of candidates through independent expenditures. This ruling opened the floodgates for a good deal of money to be spent through the state parties, much of it transferred down from the national party organization. In 1996, these transfers to the state parties amounted to $76 million for the Democrats and $66 million for the Republicans.

In terms of headquarters and budgets, state parties are better organized than they used to be. Nevertheless, as John Bibby points out, they mostly serve to supplement the candidates' own personal campaign organizations; thus, state party organizations rarely manage campaigns. The job of the state party, writes Bibby, is merely "to provide technical services" within the context of a candidate-centered campaign.[16]

national convention

The meeting of party delegates every four years to choose a presidential ticket and write the party's platform.

national committee

One of the institutions that keeps the party operating between conventions. The national committee is composed of representatives from the states and territories.

national chairperson

The national chairperson is responsible for the day-to-day activities of the party and is usually hand-picked by the presidential nominee.

The National Party Organizations

The supreme power within each of the parties is its **national convention.** The convention meets every four years, and its main task is to write the party's platform and then nominate its candidates for president and vice president. (Chapter 9 will discuss conventions in detail.) Keeping the party operating between conventions is the job of the **national committee,** composed of representatives from the states and territories. Typically, each state has a national committeeman and a national committeewoman as delegates to the party's national committee. The Democratic committee also includes assorted governors, members of Congress, and other party officials.

Day-to-day activities of the national party are the responsibility of the party's **national chairperson.** The national party chairperson hires the staff, raises the money, pays the bills, and attends to the daily duties of the party. When asked what their biggest organizational challenge was at a 1998 joint appearance, the chairs of the Democratic and Republican parties both promptly responded "money."[17]

The chairperson of the party that controls the White House is normally selected by the president. In the early 1970s, two of the people who served for a while as chair of the Republican Party at the request of President Nixon were Bob Dole and George Bush, both of whom used this position as a means of political advancement.

The Party in Government: Promises and Policy

Which party controls which of America's many elected offices matters because each party and the elected officials who represent it generally try to turn campaign promises into action. As a result, the party that has control over the most government offices will have the most influence in determining who gets what, where, when, and how.

However, because candidates are now less dependent on parties to get nominated and elected, that "control" is much less fixed than it was when George W. Bush took political science classes at Yale University in the 1960s. Presidents are now less likely to play the role of party leader, and members of Congress are less amenable to being led.

When George W. Bush ran for the presidency in 2000, he rarely made reference to the need for a Republican Party majority in Congress. In contrast, John Kennedy often made the point in 1960 that he wanted more members of his party elected to Congress. Presidents have always had a tendency to bypass parties on occasion by appealing to the national interest and the people as a whole. However, with the growth of communications technology, such a strategy has become far more feasible and potentially rewarding. Presidents no longer need the party machinery to get their message out; they can go on TV at any time to appeal directly to the American public. Nor do members of Congress feel that they owe any great loyalty to presidents of their own party. Few members of Congress these days feel that their reelection is strongly tied to the president's success or failure. Like the president, most congressional candidates can expect to run on their own personal record rather than the party's.

Voters are attracted to a party in government by its performance and policies. What a party has done in office, and what it promises to do greatly influences who will join its **coalition**—a set of individuals and groups supporting it. Sometimes voters suspect that political promises are made to be broken. To be sure, there are notable instances in which politicians have turned—sometimes 180 degrees—from their policy promises. Lyndon Johnson repeatedly promised in the 1964 presidential campaign that he would not "send American boys to do an Asian boy's job" and involve the United States in the Vietnam War, but he did. In the 1980 campaign, Ronald Reagan asserted that he would balance the budget by 1984, yet his administration quickly ran up the largest deficit in American history. Throughout the 1988 campaign George Bush proclaimed, "Read my lips—no new taxes," but he reluctantly changed course two years later when pressured on the issue by the Democratic majority in Congress. Bill Clinton promised a tax cut for the middle class during the 1992 campaign, but after he was elected he backed off, saying that first the deficit would have to be substantially reduced.

coalition

A group of individuals with a common interest upon which every political party depends.

It is all too easy to forget how often parties and presidents do exactly what they say they will do. For every broken promise, many more are kept. When he first ran for president, Bill Clinton promised to support bills providing for family leave, easing voting registration procedures, and tightening gun control that had been vetoed by President Bush. He lobbied hard to get these measures through Congress again and proudly

Table 8.3 Party Platforms, 2000

Although few people actually read party platforms, they are one of the best written sources for what the parties believe in. A brief summary of some of the contrasting positions in the Democratic and Republican platforms of 2000 illustrates major differences in beliefs between the two parties.

REPUBLICANS	DEMOCRATS
Credit Claiming Inspired by Presidents Reagan and Bush, Republicans hammered into place the framework for today's prosperity and surpluses. We cut tax rates, simplified the tax code, deregulated industries, and opened world markets to American enterprise. The result was the tremendous growth in the 1980s that created the venture capital to launch the technology revolution of the 1990s.	**Credit Claiming** In 1992, Americans elected Bill Clinton and Al Gore with a mandate to turn America around. And that's just what they did. . . . Eight years later the record is clear: the longest economic expansion in American history. The most jobs ever created under a single administration. The first real wage growth in 20 years.
Abortion The unborn child has a fundamental individual right to life that cannot be infringed.	**Abortion** The Democratic Party stands behind the right of every woman to choose, consistent with *Roe v. Wade*, and regardless of ability to pay.
The Environment The way current laws have been implemented has often fostered costly litigation and discouraged personal innovation in environmental conservation. . . . We condemn the current administration's policy of resorting to confrontation first.	**The Environment** We have worked for eight years to produce the cleanest environment in decades: with cleaner air, cleaner water, and a safer food supply; a record number of toxic waste dumps cleaned up; new smog and soot standards so that children with asthma and the elderly would be able to live better lives; and a strong international treaty to begin combating global warming.
Health Care We will promote a health care system that supports, not supplants, the private sector; that promotes personal responsibility in health care decision making; and that ensures the least intrusive role for the federal government.	**Health Care** We must redouble our efforts to bring the uninsured into coverage step-by-step and as soon as possible. We should guarantee access to affordable health care for every child in America. We should expand coverage to working families, including more Medicaid assistance to help with the transition from welfare to work.
Taxes Budget surpluses are the result of overtaxation of the American people. . . . When the average American family has to work more than four months out of every year to fund all levels of government, it's time to change the tax system, to make it simpler, flatter, and fairer for everyone.	**Taxes** The Bush tax slash would let the richest one percent of Americans afford a new sports car and middle-class Americans afford a warm soda. It would undermine the American economy and undercut our prosperity. Democrats want to give middle-class families tax cuts they can use.
Defense Spending Republicans are the party of peace through strength. . . . Republicans will restore the health of a defense industry weakened by a combination of neglect and misguided policies.	**Defense Spending** With Bill Clinton and Al Gore in the White House, Democrats reversed a decline in defense spending that began under President Bush, boosted pay and allowances, and provided the funding for a new generation of weapons.
Education We endorse the principles of Governor Bush's education reforms, which will: Raise academic standards through increased local control and accountability to parents, shrinking a multitude of federal programs into five flexible grants in exchange for real, measured progress in student achievement.	**Education** The Republicans refuse to invest in America's crumbling schools and crowded classrooms—spending 100 times more on tax cuts than on education. When it comes to education, Democrats want to invest more and aim higher, the Republicans invest too little and aim too low.
Social Security Personal savings accounts must be the cornerstone of restructing. Each of today's workers should be free to direct a portion of their payroll taxes to personal investments for their retirement future.	**Social Security** To build on the success of Social Security, Al Gore has proposed the creation of Retirement Savings Plus—voluntary, tax-free, personally controlled, privately managed savings accounts with a government match that would help couples build a nest egg of up to $400,000.
Affirmative Action We believe rights inhere in individuals, not in groups. We will attain our nation's goal of equal opportunity without quotas or other forms of preferential treatment.	**Affirmative Action** Al Gore has strongly opposed efforts to roll back affirmative action programs. He knows that the way to lift this nation up is not by pulling the weakest down, but by continuing to expand opportunities for everyone who wants to achieve.

Source: Excerpts from party platforms as posted on the websites of each organization.

signed them into law once they arrived on his desk. Ronald Reagan promised to step up defense spending and cut back on social welfare expenditures, and within his first year in office he did just that. He promised a major tax cut and provided one. He promised less government regulation and quickly set about deregulating natural gas prices and occupational safety and environmental policies. In sum, the impression that politicians and parties never produce policy out of promises is largely erroneous.

In fact, the parties have done a fairly good job over the years of translating their platform promises into public policy. Gerald Pomper has shown that party platforms are excellent predictors of a party's actual policy performance in office. He tabulated specific pledges in the major parties' platforms over a number of years, tabulating 3,194 specific policy pronouncements. Pomper then looked to see whether the party that won the presidency actually fulfilled its promises. Nearly three-fourths of all promises resulted in policy actions. Others were tried but floundered for one reason or another. Only 10 percent were ignored altogether.[18]

If parties generally do what they say they will, then the party platforms adopted at the national conventions represent blueprints, however vague, for action. Consider what the two major parties promised the voters in 2000 (see Table 8.3). There is little doubt that the election of Bush over Gore will direct the government in a course different from the one it would have taken if the outcome had been reversed.

visual literacy
Comparing Political Party Platforms

Party Eras in American History

While studying political parties, remember the following: *America is a two-party system and always has been.* Of course, there are many minor parties around—Libertarians, Socialists, Reform, Greens—but they rarely have a chance of winning a major office. In contrast, most democratic nations have more than two parties represented in their national legislature. Throughout American history, one party has been the dominant majority party for long periods of time. A majority of voters identify with the party in power; thus this party tends to win a majority of the elections. Political scientists call these periods **party eras.** The majority party does not, of course, win every election; sometimes it suffers from intraparty squabbles and loses power. Sometimes it nominates a weak candidate, and the opposition cashes in on the majority party's misfortune.

Punctuating each party era is a **critical election.**[19] A critical election is an electoral earthquake: fissures appear in each party's coalition which begins to fracture; new issues appear, dividing the electorate. Each party forms a new coalition—one that endures for years. A critical election period may require more than one election before change is apparent, but in the end, the party system will be transformed.

This process is called **party realignment**—a rare event in American political life that is akin to a political revolution. Realignments are typically associated with a major crisis or trauma in the nation's history. One of the major realignments, when the Republican Party emerged, was connected to the Civil War. Another was linked to the Great Depression of the 1930s, when the majority Republicans were displaced by the Democrats. The following sections look more closely at the various party eras in American history.

party eras

Historical periods in which a majority of voters cling to the party in power, which tends to win a majority of the elections.

critical election

An electoral "earthquake" where new issues emerge, new coalitions replace old ones, and the majority party is often displaced by the minority party. Critical election periods are sometimes marked by a national crisis and may require more than one election to bring about a new party era.

party realignment

The displacement of the majority party by the minority party, usually during a **critical election** period.

1796–1824: The First Party System

In the *Federalist Papers,* James Madison warned strongly against the dangers of "factions," or parties. But Alexander Hamilton, one of the coauthors of the *Federalist Papers,* did as much as anyone to inaugurate our party system.[20] Hamilton was the nation's first secretary of the treasury, for which service his picture appears on today's $10 bill. To garner congressional support for his pet policies, particularly a national bank, he needed votes. From this politicking and coalition building came the rudiments of the Federalist

Aaron Burr dealt a near-death blow to the Federalist Party when he killed its leader, Alexander Hamilton, in this 1804 duel. Burr, then vice president, challenged Hamilton to the duel after the former treasury secretary publicly called him a traitor.

party, America's first political party. The Federalists were also America's shortest-lived major party. After Federalist candidate John Adams was defeated in his reelection bid in 1800, the party quickly faded. The Federalists were poorly organized, and by 1820 they no longer bothered to offer up a candidate for president. In this early period of American history, most party leaders did not regard themselves as professional politicians. Those who lost often withdrew completely from the political arena. The ideas of a loyal opposition and rotation of power in government had not yet taken hold.[21] Each party wanted to destroy the other party, not just defeat it—and such was the fate of the Federalists.

timeline
Patterns of Presidential Elections: Realignment and Dealignment

The party that crushed the Federalists was led by Virginians, Jefferson, Madison, and Monroe, each of whom was elected president for two terms in succession. They were known as the Democratic-Republicans, or sometimes as the Jeffersonians. The Democratic-Republican Party derived its coalition from agrarian interests rather than from the growing number of capitalists who supported the Federalists. This made the party particularly popular in the largely rural South. As the Federalists disappeared, however, the old Jeffersonian coalition was torn apart by factionalism as it tried to be all things to all people.

1828–1856: Jackson and the Democrats Versus the Whigs

More than anyone else, General Andrew Jackson founded the modern American political party. In the election of 1828, he forged a new coalition that included Westerners as well as Southerners, new immigrants as well as settled Americans. Like most successful politicians of his day, Jackson was initially a Democratic-Republican, but soon after his ascension to the presidency his party became known as simply the Democratic Party, which continues to this day. The "Democratic" label was particularly appropriate for Jackson's supporters because their cause was to broaden political opportunity by eliminating many vestiges of elitism and mobilizing the masses.

Whereas Jackson was the charismatic leader, the Democrats' behind-the-scenes architect was Martin Van Buren, who succeeded Jackson as president. Van Buren's one term in office was relatively undistinguished, but his view of party competition left a lasting mark. He "sought to make Democrats see that their only hope for maintaining the purity of their own principles was to admit the existence of an opposing party."[22] A realist, Van Buren argued that a party could not aspire to pleasing all the people all the time. He argued that a governing party needed a loyal opposition to represent parts of society that it could not. This opposition was provided by the Whigs. The Whig Party included such notable statesmen as Henry Clay and Daniel Webster, but it was able to win the presidency only when it nominated aging but popular military heroes, such as William Henry Harrison (1840) and Zachary Taylor (1848). The Whigs had two distinct wings—Northern industrialists and Southern planters—who were brought together more by the Democratic policies they opposed than by the issues on which they agreed.

1860–1928: The Two Republican Eras

In the 1850s, the issue of slavery dominated American politics and split both the Whigs and the Democrats. Slavery, said Senator Charles Sumner, an ardent abolitionist, "is the only subject within the field of national politics which excites any real interest."[23] Congress battled over the extension of slavery to the new states and territories. In *Dred Scott v. Sandford*, the Supreme Court of 1857 held that slaves could not be citizens and that former slaves could not be protected by the Constitution. This decision further sharpened the divisions in public opinion, making civil war increasingly likely.

The Republicans rose in the late 1850s as the antislavery party. Folding in the remnants of several minor parties, in 1860 the Republicans forged a coalition strong enough to elect Abraham Lincoln president and to ignite the Civil War. The "War Between the States" was one of those political earthquakes that realigned the parties. After the war, the Republican Party thrived for more than 60 years. The Democrats controlled the South, though, and the Republican label remained a dirty word in the old Confederacy.

A second Republican era was initiated with the watershed election of 1896, perhaps the most bitter battle in American electoral history. The Democrats nominated William Jennings Bryan, populist proponent of "free silver" (linking money with silver, which was more plentiful than gold, and thus devaluing money to help debtors). The Republican Party made clear its positions in favor of the gold standard, industrialization, the banks, high tariffs, and the industrial working classes, as well as its positions against the "radical" western farmers and "silverites." "Bryan and his program were greeted by the country's conservatives with something akin to terror."[24] The *New York Tribune* howled that Bryan's Democrats were "in league with the Devil." On the other side, novelist Frank Baum lampooned the Republicans in his classic novel, *The Wizard of Oz*. Dorothy follows the yellow brick road (symbolizing the gold standard) to the Emerald City (representing New York) only to find that the Wizard (whose figure resembles McKinley) is powerless. But by clicking on her *silver* slippers (the color was changed to ruby for technicolor effect in the movie), she finds that she can return home.

Political party conventions have changed dramatically as a result of technological progress. When Franklin Roosevelt appeared at the Democratic Convention of 1932, it marked the first time that a nominee's acceptance speech was broadcast live across the nation via radio.

Political scientists call the 1896 election a realigning one because it shifted the party coalitions and entrenched the Republicans for another generation. (For more on the election of 1896, see Chapter 10.) For the next three decades the Republicans continued as the nation's majority party, until the stock market crashed in 1929. The ensuing Great Depression brought about another fissure in the crust of the American party system.

1932–1964: The New Deal Coalition

President Herbert Hoover's handling of the Depression turned out to be disastrous for the Republicans. He solemnly pronounced that economic depression could not be cured by legislative action. Americans, however, obviously disagreed, and voted for Franklin D. Roosevelt, who promised the country a *New Deal.* In his first 100 days as president, Roosevelt prodded Congress into passing scores of anti-Depression measures. Party realignment began in earnest after the Roosevelt Administration got the country moving again. First-time voters flocked to the polls, pumping new blood into the Democratic ranks and providing much of the margin for Roosevelt's four presidential victories. Immigrant groups in Boston and other cities had been initially attracted to the Democrats by the 1928 campaign of Al Smith, the first Catholic to be nominated by a major party for the presidency.[25] Roosevelt reinforced the partisanship of these groups, and the Democrats forged the **New Deal coalition.**

New Deal Coalition

A coalition forged by the Democrats, who dominated American politics from the 1930s to the 1960s. Its basic elements were the urban working class, ethnic groups, Catholics and Jews, the poor, Southerners, African Americans, and intellectuals.

The basic elements of the New Deal coalition were:

- *Urban dwellers.* Big cities such as Chicago and Philadelphia were staunchly Republican before the New Deal realignment; afterward, they were Democratic bastions.
- *Labor unions.* FDR became the first president to support unions enthusiastically, and they returned the favor.
- *Catholics and Jews.* During and after the Roosevelt period, Catholics and Jews were strongly Democratic.
- *The poor.* Though the poor had low turnout rates, their votes went overwhelmingly to the party of Roosevelt and his successors.
- *Southerners.* Ever since the pre-Civil War days, white Southerners had been Democratic loyalists. This alignment continued unabated during the New Deal.
- *African Americans.* The Republicans freed the slaves, but under FDR the Democrats attracted the majority of African Americans.
- *Intellectuals.* Small in number, prominent intellectuals provided a wealth of new ideas that fueled Roosevelt's New Deal policies.

As you can see in Figure 8.3, many of the same groups that supported FDR's New Deal continue to shape the party coalitions today.

The New Deal coalition made the Democratic Party the clear majority party for decades. Harry S Truman, who succeeded Roosevelt in 1945, promised a Fair Deal. World War II hero and Republican Dwight D. Eisenhower broke the Democrats' grip on power by being elected president twice during the 1950s, but the Democrats regained the presidency in 1960 with the election of John F. Kennedy. His New Frontier was in the New Deal tradition, with platforms and policies designed to help labor, the working classes, and minorities. Lyndon B. Johnson, picked as Kennedy's vice president because he could help win Southern votes, became president upon Kennedy's assassination and was overwhelmingly elected to a term of his own in 1964. Johnson's Great Society programs included a major expansion of government programs to help the poor, the homeless, and minorities. His War on Poverty was reminiscent of Roosevelt's activism in dealing with the Depression. Johnson's Vietnam War policies, however, tore the Democratic Party apart in 1968, leaving the door to the presidency wide open for Republican candidate Richard M. Nixon.

Figure 8.3 Party Coalitions Today

The two parties continue to draw support from very different social groups, many of which have existed since the New Deal era. This figure shows the percentage of Democrats and Republicans with various characteristics.

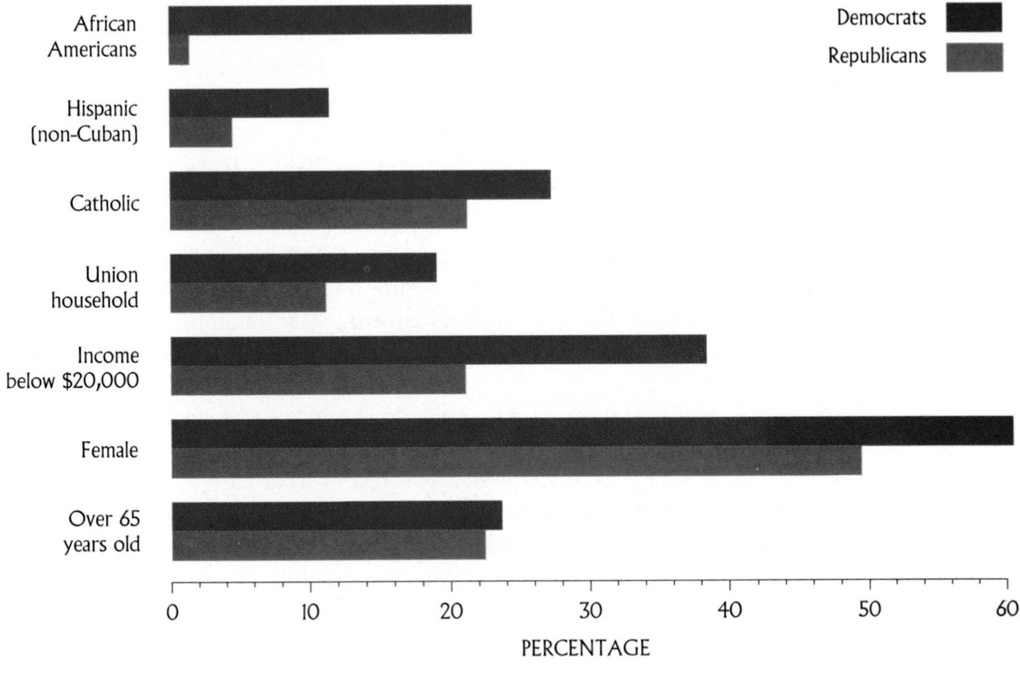

Source: From the National Election Studies conducted by the University of Michigan, Center for Political Studies, 1996.

1968–Present: The Era of Divided Party Government

Throughout most of American history, newly elected presidents have routinely swept a wave of their fellow partisans into office with them. For example, the Democrats gained 62 seats in the House when Woodrow Wilson was elected in 1912 and 97 when FDR was elected in 1932. The first time in the twentieth century that a newly elected president moved into the White House without having his party in control of both houses of Congress was when Nixon won the 1968 election. Nixon's election was not to be an exception, however, but rather the beginning of a common pattern—repeated in the presidential elections won by Reagan and Bush. For a time, it seemed that the normal state of affairs in Washington was to have a Republican president and a Democratic Congress.

timeline
Parties that made American History

Bill Clinton's election in 1992 briefly restored united party government until the Republicans won both houses of Congress in the 1994 elections. After the 1994 elections, Republican leaders were optimistic that they were at last on the verge of a new Republican era in which they would control both the presidency and Congress simultaneously. On the other side, Democratic leaders were hopeful that voters would not like the actions of the new Republican Congress and would restore unified Democratic control of the government. In the end, the ambitions of both sides were frustrated as voters opted to continue divided party government.

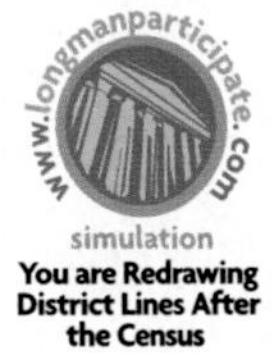

simulation
You are Redrawing District Lines After the Census

With fewer voters attached to the two major parties, it will be difficult for either one to gain a strong enough foothold to maintain simultaneous control of both sides of Pennsylvania Avenue for very long. All told, both houses of Congress and the presidency have been simultaneously controlled by the same party for just 6.3 of the 34 years from 1969 to 2002.[26] The discrepancy between the patterns of presidential and congressional voting during this era of divided party government is unprecedented in American history.

Divided party government is frequently seen not only at the federal level but at the state level as well. As Morris Fiorina shows, the percentage of states that have unified party control of the governorship and the state legislature has steadily declined for over four decades.[27] Whereas 85 percent of state governments had one party controlling both houses of the legislature and the governorship in 1946, by 2001 this was the case in only 42 percent of the states (see Figure 8.4). Divided government, once an occasional oddity in state capitols, is now commonplace.

party dealignment

The gradual disengagement of people and politicians from the parties, as seen in part by shrinking party identification.

The recent pattern of divided government has caused many political scientists to believe that the party system has dealigned rather than realigned. Whereas realignment involves people changing from one party to another, **party dealignment** means that people are gradually moving away from both parties. When your car is realigned, it is adjusted in one direction or another to improve its steering. Imagine if your mechanic were to remove the steering mechanism instead of adjusting it—your car would be useless and ineffective. This is what many scholars fear has been happening to the parties.

party neutrality

A term used to describe the fact that many Americans are indifferent toward to two major political parties.

In the parties' heyday, it was said that people would vote for a yellow dog if their party nominated one. Now, more than 90 percent of all Americans insist that "I always vote for the person whom I think is best, regardless of what party they belong to."[28] Rather than reflecting negative attitudes toward the parties, the recent dealignment has been characterized by a growing **party neutrality.** For example, 30 percent of the 1996 National Election Study respondents answered as follows to a set of four open-ended questions about the parties:

> *Q. Is there anything in particular that you like about the Democratic Party?*
> A. No.
> *Q. Is there anything in particular that you don't like about the Democratic Party?*
> A. No.

The Democratic National Committee meets to consider a new party symbol.

The Republican National Committee meets to consider a new party symbol.

Figure 8.4 Partisan Control of State Governments: 2001

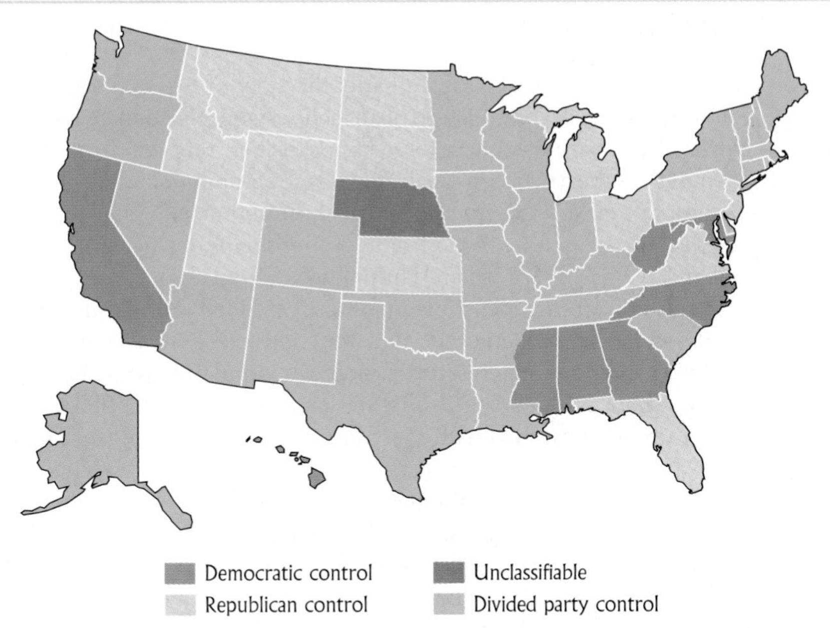

The following map shows which states as of 2001 were totally under Democratic or Republican control—that is, had one party controlling both Houses of the legislature as well as the Governorship. Divided party control means that either one or both Houses of the legislature are controlled by a party different than the Governor. Nebraska has a nonpartisan legislature and hence cannot be classified.

Q. Is there anything in particular that you like about the Republican Party?
A. No.
Q. Is there anything in particular that you don't like about the Republican Party?
A. No.

When these questions were first asked in the 1950s, only about 10 percent of respondents answered in this neutral way, generally indicating that they were not following politics at all. Now, many of those who say nothing about the parties are quite aware of the candidates. Lacking any party anchoring, though, they are easily swayed one way or the other. As a result, they are often referred to as "the floating voters." More than any other group, it is these independent-minded voters who will determine the ups and downs of party fortunes in the twenty-first century.

Why does it matter?

The partisan era since 1969 has been characterized by divided party government. How has this made recent American politics different from previous partisan eras? In what ways has divided party government affected policymaking and policy implementation?

One's party affiliation is an important part of one's political identity. Although clubs of college Republicans and college Democrats are common on campuses around the country, roughly half of college-age Americans do not have a party affiliation, preferring to call themselves Independents.

Third Parties: Their Impact on American Politics

third parties

Electoral contenders other than the two major parties. American third parties are not unusual, but they rarely win elections.

The story of American party struggle is primarily the story of two major parties, but **third parties** are a regular feature of American politics and occasionally attract the public's attention. Third parties come in three basic varieties. First are parties that promote certain causes—either a controversial single issue (prohibition of alcoholic beverages, for example) or an extreme ideological position such as socialism or libertarianism. Second are splinter parties, which are offshoots of a major party. Teddy Roosevelt's Progressives in 1912, Strom Thurmond's States' Righters in 1948, and George Wallace's American Independents in 1968 all claimed they did not get a fair hearing from Republicans or Democrats and thus formed their own new parties. Finally, some third parties are merely an extension of a popular individual with presidential aspirations. Both John Anderson in 1980 and Ross Perot in 1992 and 1996 offered voters who were dissatisfied with the Democratic and Republican nominees another option.

Although third party candidates almost never win office in the United States, scholars believe they are often quite important.[29] They have brought new groups into the electorate and have served as "safety valves" for popular discontent. The Free Soilers of the 1850s were the first true antislavery party; the Progressives and the Populists put many social reforms on the political agenda. George Wallace told his supporters in 1968 they had the chance to "send a message" to Washington—a message of support for tougher law and order measures, which is still being felt to this day. Ross Perot used his saturation of the TV airwaves in 1992 to ensure that the issue of the federal deficit was not ignored in the campaign. In 1998, a former professional wrestler stunned the political world when he won the governorship of Minnesota as a third party candidate (see "Making a Difference: Jesse "The Body" Ventura"). And in 2000 Green Party candidate Ralph Nader forced more attention on environmental issues, and ultimately probably cost Gore the presidency by drawing away a small percentage of the liberal votes.

Despite the regular appearance of third parties, the two-party system is firmly entrenched in American politics. Would it make a difference if America had a multiparty system, as so many European countries have? The answer is clearly yes. The most obvious consequence of two-party governance is the moderation of political conflict. If America had many parties, each would have to make a special appeal in order to stand

Ralph Nader challenged the two-party system in 2000 by running for president on the ticket of the Green Party. Exit polls show his voters preferred Gore over Bush by a margin of five to two. With the margin being as close as it was in 2000, it seems readily apparent that Nader's presence in the race influenced the outcome.

Making a Difference

Jesse "The Body" Ventura

Few people thought former professional wrestler Jesse "The Body" Ventura had much of a chance when he entered the race for governor of Minnesota on the ticket of the Reform Party. For starters, no member of the party founded by Ross Perot had ever been elected to a major office. Although an imposing figure at 6'4" and 250 pounds, Jesse Ventura hardly seemed like the man to make the Reform Party's first breakthrough. His only political experience had been as mayor of Brooklyn Park, a Minneapolis suburb, and it seemed unlikely he could raise nearly as much money as the Democratic and Republican nominees. He could count on virtually no help from the Reform Party organization, as the newly formed party had very few members. And perhaps most important, he would have to change the common perception that supporting a third-party candidate was a wasted vote.

On his campaign web site, Jesse Ventura posted a message to all Minnesota voters explaining how he could win. He listed three major factors that he wanted people to consider. First, he pointed out that the candidate with the most money doesn't always win. Second, he noted that his opponents were "boring." And finally, he said that he had a "secret weapon" that the pundits were ignoring: Many people who would turn out to vote for him normally wouldn't vote.

Ventura's opponents were not worried. In fact, Democratic nominees Hubert Humphrey III, heir to the most famous political name in Minnesota history, refused to participate in any televised debate unless Ventura were included. He reasoned that Ventura's antitax message would siphon more votes away from the Republican candidate than from him. The former professional wrestler joked that he would "body slam" his opponents in the debates, and in the end he stole the show, using his talent for ad-libbing and performing. He appealed to young people and blue-collar workers with his candor, compassion, and antiestablishment rhetoric. The major party candidates ignored Ventura, spending most of their time hurling accusations at one another.

Ventura's strong showing in the debates brought him recognition as a serious candidate and therefore some supporters. Volunteers started to sign up via his web site, and through an e-mail list an organization was stitched together to help out at campaign events around the state. Money also started to come in, giving Ventura enough funds to start advertising on television. His low-budget, irreverent ads used the theme from "Shaft" as his campaign song, portrayed children playing with a Jesse Ventura action figure who battles Evil Special Interest Man, and featured Ventura posing as Rodin's "The Thinker."

The final statewide poll had Ventura in third place, but only 8 percent behind. Few people expected him to win, but neither did they consider that a vote for this third party candidate would necessarily be "wasted." On election day, Ventura's "secret weapon" actually materialized, and he won with 37 percent of the vote. Turnout in Minnesota was the highest in the nation at 59 percent, far above the national rate of 36 percent. Young people made up a larger percentage of the electorate in Minnesota than anywhere else, and their strong support for Ventura put him over the top. Approximately 150,000 voters aged 18 to 29 voted for Ventura, who won by just 57,000 votes.

The shocking victory of Jesse Ventura was one of the biggest stories of 1998, proving that Democrats and Republicans don't necessarily have a lock on all American elections. Would you like to see more third party candidates like Jesse Ventura in order to give people a wider range of choice in American elections?

out from the crowd. It is not hard to imagine what a multiparty system might look like in the United States. Quite possibly, African-American groups would form their own party, pressing vigorously for more civil rights legislation. Environmentalists could constitute another party, vowing to clean up the rivers, oppose nuclear power, and save the wilderness. America could have religious parties, union-based parties, farmers' parties, and all sorts of others. As in some European countries, there could be half a dozen or more parties represented in Congress (see "America in Perspective: Multiparty Systems in Other Countries").

The American two-party system contributes to political ambiguity. Why should parties risk taking a strong stand on a controversial policy if doing so will only antagonize many voters? Ambiguity is a safe strategy,[30] as extremist candidates Barry Goldwater in 1964 and George McGovern in 1972 found out the hard way. The two-party system thus throttles extreme or unconventional views.

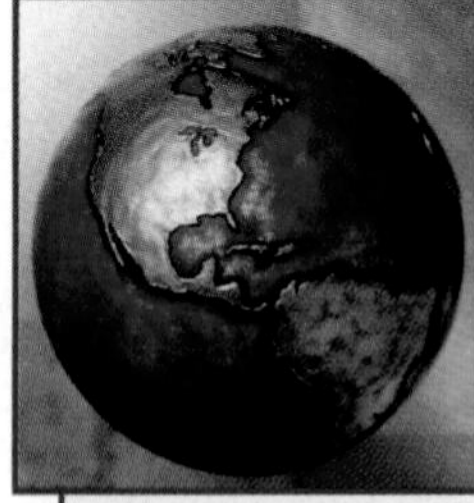

America in Perspective

Multiparty Systems in Other Countries

One of the major reasons why the United States has only two parties represented in government is structural. America has a **winner-take-all system,** in which whoever gets the most votes wins the election. There are no prizes awarded for second or third place. Suppose there are three parties; one receives 45 percent of the vote, another 40 percent, and the third 15 percent. Though it got less than a majority, the party that finished first is declared the winner. The others are out in the cold. In this way, the American system discourages small parties. Unless a party wins, there is no reward for the votes it gets. Thus, it makes more sense for a small party to form an alliance with one of the major parties than to struggle on its own with little hope. In this example, the second- and third-place parties might merge (if they can reach an agreement on policy) to challenge the governing party in the next election.

In a system that employs **proportional representation,** however, such a merger would not be necessary. Under this system, which is used in most European countries, legislative seats are allocated according to each party's percentage of the nationwide vote. If a party wins 15 percent of the vote, then it receives 15 percent of the seats. Even a small party can use its voice in Parliament to be a thorn in the side of the government, standing up strongly for its principles. Such has often been the role of the Greens in Germany, who are ardent environmentalists. In 1998, they entered the government for the first time when they formed a **coalition government** along with Germany's Social Democratic Party. Together the coalition controls over half the seats. Coalition governments are common in Europe. Italy has regularly been ruled by a coalition since the end of World War II, for example.

Even with proportional representation, not every party gets represented in the legislature. To be awarded seats, a party must always achieve a certain percentage of votes, which varies from country to country. Israel has one of the lowest thresholds at 1.5 percent. This explains why there are always so many parties represented in the Israeli Knesset. The founders of Israel's system wanted to make sure that all points of view were represented, but sometimes this has turned into a nightmare, with small extremist parties holding the balance of power.

Parties have to develop their own unique identities to appeal to voters in a multiparty system. This requires strong stands on the issues, but after the election compromises must be made to form a coalition government. If an agreement cannot be reached on the major issues, the coalition is in trouble. Sometimes a new coalition can be formed; other times the result is the calling of a new election. In either case, it is clear that proportional representation systems are more fluid than the two-party system in the United States.

winner-take-all system

An electoral system in which legislative seats are awarded only to the candidates who come in first in their constituencies. In American presidential elections, the system in which the winner of the popular vote in a state receives all the electoral votes of that state.

proportional representation

An electoral system used throughout most of Europe that awards legislative seats to political parties in proportion to the number of votes won in an election.

coalition government

When two or more parties join together to form a majority in a national legislature. This form of government is quite common in the multiparty systems of Europe.

Understanding Political Parties

Political parties are considered essential elements of democratic government. Indeed, one of the first steps taken toward democracy in Eastern Europe was the formation of competing political parties to contest elections. After years of one-party totalitarian rule, Eastern Europeans were ecstatic to be able to adopt a multiparty system like those that had proved successful in the West. In contrast, the founding of the world's first party system in the United States was seen as a risky adventure in the then uncharted waters of democracy. Wary of having parties at all, the founders designed a system that has greatly restrained their political role to this day. Whether American parties should continue to be so loosely organized is at the heart of today's debate about their role in American democracy.

Democracy and Responsible Party Government

Ideally, in a democracy candidates should say what they mean to do if elected and, once they are elected, should be able to do what they promised. Critics of the American party system lament that this is all too often not the case, and have called for a "more responsible two-party system."[31] Advocates of the **responsible party model** believe the parties should meet the following conditions:

1. Parties must present distinct, comprehensive programs for governing the nation.

How You Can Make a Difference

Volunteering for Political Campaigns

If you do not support either major political party, why not join one of the smaller political parties such as the Green Party, the Libertarian Party, or the Reform Party? Sometimes minor parties can win, such as when Jesse Ventura won the gubernatorial race in Minnesota in 1998. Minor parties suffer at the polls due to restrictive ballot access laws and lack of money. Many states will not let minor parties be on the ballot unless they demonstrate a lot of support in that state. Most states require a certain number of signitures of registered votes on petitions to allow a minor party on the ballot. You can help these parties get on the ballot in your state by carrying petitions and getting signatures. You can also help register new members of the party, distribute leaflets, write letters to the editors of newspapers, or in any other way your local party leaders need. There are statewide organizations for most of the smaller political parties, and many local chapters, as well. You can find the nearest one by checking the party's web site.

Green Party: www.greens.org. The Green Party is a progressive party that supports environmentalism, grassroots democracy, social justice, and peace/ nonviolence. Ralph Nader was the Green Party candidate for the 2000 Presidential Elections. Many believe his candidacy influenced the final outcome.

Libertarian Party: www.lp.org. The Libertarian party is both very liberal and very conservative. It favors absolute freedom in both the economic realm (free trade, nonintervention in foreign affairs, unrestricted free market, no government programs such as Social Security, welfare, interstate highways, or public schools) and in social/personal issues (no restrictions on abortions, drug use, prostitution, and so forth).

Reform Party: www.reformparty.org. The Reform Party was started by Ross Perot and his followers in the early 1990s and reflects concerns such as favoring a balanced federal budget, campaign finance reform, a new tax system, and trade that protects American workers.

Other lesser known minor parties include:

Christian Alliance (formerly the Puritan Party): www.christianalliance.com. This is a very conservative, religious party that seeks to call Christians to act politically and according to their faith.

Communist Party USA: www.hartford-hwp.com/cp-usa/. This party is a Marxist-Leninist working-class party that believes capitalism has failed and is angry at the continuing injustices and suffering they say it brings. They work for a socialist economy that puts people before profits and for full equality of all races and both genders.

Constitution Party (formerly U.S. Taxpayers Party) www.USTaxpayers.org. This conservative group wishes to return the U.S. government to its constitutional boundaries and limitations by restricting much current government activity.

U.S. Pacifist Party: www.geocities.com/CapitolHill/Lobby/4826. This party is opposed to all military power and says that it is the root of most major social evils such as war, poverty, the arms race, and political oppression.

2. Each party's candidates must be committed to its program and have the internal cohesion and discipline to carry out its program.
3. The majority party must implement its programs, and the minority party must state what it would do if it were in power.
4. The majority party must accept responsibility for the performance of the government.

responsible party model

A view favored by some political scientists about how parties should work. According to the model, parties should offer clear choices to the voters, who can then use those choices as cues to their own preferences of candidates. Once in office, parties would carry out their campaign promises.

A two-party system operating under these conditions would make it easier to convert party promises into governmental policy. A party's officeholders would have firm control of the government, so they would be collectively, rather than individually, responsible for their actions. Voters would therefore know whom to blame for what the government does and does not accomplish.

As this chapter has shown, American political parties fall far short of these conditions. They are too decentralized to take a single national position and then enforce it. Most candidates are self-selected, gaining their nomination by their own efforts rather than the party's. Virtually anyone can vote in party primaries; thus, parties do not have control over those who run under their labels. In 1991, for example, a former grand wizard of the Ku Klux Klan, David Duke, became the Republican nominee for governor of Louisiana despite denunciations from

President Bush, who ultimately said he preferred the Democratic nominee. Had Duke won the election, the Republican Party would have been powerless to control his actions in office.

In America's loosely organized party system, there simply is no mechanism for a party to discipline officeholders and thereby ensure cohesion in policymaking. As David Mayhew writes, "Unlike most politicians elsewhere, American ones at both legislative and executive levels have managed to navigate the last two centuries of history without becoming minions of party leaders."[32] Thus, it is rare to find congressional votes in which over 90 percent of Democrats vote in opposition to over 90 percent of Republicans. Indeed, Mayhew's analysis of historic legislation from 1946 to 1990 failed to uncover a single case in which a major law was passed by such a clearly partisan vote.[33] The 1998 vote in the House to impeach President Clinton was unparalleled in recent times, with 98 percent of each party's members sticking to the party line.

Not everyone thinks that America's decentralized parties are a problem, however. Critics of the responsible party model argue that the complexity and diversity of American society are too great to be captured by such a simple model of party politics. Local differences need an outlet for expression, they say. One cannot expect Texas Democrats always to want to vote in line with New York Democrats. In the view of those opposed to the responsible party model, America's decentralized parties are appropriate for the type of limited government the founders sought to create and most Americans wish to maintain.[34]

Individualism and Gridlock

The Founding Fathers were very concerned that political parties would trample on the rights of individuals. They wanted to preserve individual freedom of action by various elected officials. With America's weak party system, this has certainly been the case. Individual members of Congress and other elected officials have great freedom to act as they see fit rather than toeing the party line.

One frequently cited consequence of this allowance for individualism, however, is gridlock in American policymaking. The lack of a strong party structure makes it easier for politicians to pass the buck than bite the bullet. In particular, the divided

America's decentralized political parties have little control over candidates, as shown by the Senate nomination of Oliver North, who figured prominently in the Iran-Contra scandal. North obtained the Republican nomination in Virginia despite being denounced by the state's senior Republican Senator, John Warner, as well as by former Presidents Reagan and Bush.

government of the Reagan-Bush era allowed Republican leaders to blame budget deficits on congressional unwillingness to cut social programs, while Democratic leaders put the blame on what they viewed as the president's excessive military spending and tax cuts for the wealthy. With neither party really in charge and each pointing a finger at the other, it is no wonder that little was done to resolve the budget deficit. With the situation reversed in 1995–1996, the new Republican majority in Congress found their agenda frustrated by a Democratic president. Although both sides agreed on the importance of passing a plan to balance the budget, the two sides could not reach an agreement, and at two points during the budget controversy, unprecedented shutdowns of parts of the federal government occurred.

When one party has simultaneous control of the executive and legislative branches, there is much less open conflict. Nevertheless, the party in control typically has a hard time maintaining sufficient unity to accomplish major changes. When President Clinton had the chance to work with Democratic majorities in the House and Senate in 1993 and 1994, he found it hard to get the support he needed from other Democrats. Gridlock was clearly evident on such issues as health care, campaign finance reform, and welfare reform during the first two years of the Clinton presidency.

American Political Parties and the Scope of Government

The lack of disciplined and cohesive European-style parties in America goes a long way to explain why the scope of governmental activity in the United States is not as broad as it is in other established democracies. The absence of a national health care system in America provides a perfect example. In Britain, the Labour Party had long proposed such a system, and after it won the 1945 election, all of its members of Parliament voted to enact national health care into law. On the other side of the

Atlantic, President Truman also proposed a national health care bill in the first presidential election after War World II. But even though he won the election and had majorities of his own party in both houses of Congress, his proposal never got very far. The weak party structure in the United States allowed many congressional Democrats to oppose Truman's health care proposal. Over four decades later, President Clinton again proposed a system of universal health care and had a Democratic-controlled Congress to work with. His experience in 1994 was much the same as Truman's; the Clinton health care bill never even came up for a vote in Congress because of the President's inability to get enough members of his own party to go along with him. Thus substantially increasing the scope of government in America is not something that can be accomplished through the disciplined actions of one party's members, as is the case in other democracies.

On the other hand, because no single party in the United States can ever be said to have firm control over the government, the hard choices necessary to cut back on existing government spending are rarely addressed. A disciplined and cohesive governing party would have the power to say no to various demands on the government. In contrast, America's loose party structure makes it possible for individual politicians to focus their efforts on getting more from the government for their own constituents.

Is the Party Over?

The key problem for American political parties is that they are no longer the main source of political information, attention, and affection. The party of today has rivals that appeal to voters and politicians alike, the biggest of which is the media. With the advent of television, voters no longer need the party to find out what the candidates are like and what they stand for. The interest group is another party rival. As Chapter 11 will discuss, the power of interest groups has grown enormously in recent years. Interest groups, not the parties, pioneered much of the technology of modern politics, including mass mailings and sophisticated fund-raising.

The parties have clearly been having a tough time lately, but there are indications that they are beginning to adapt to the high-tech age. Although the old city machines are largely extinct, state and national party organizations have become more visible and active than ever. More people are calling themselves Independents and splitting their tickets, but the majority still identify with a party, and this percentage seems to have stabilized.

For a time, some political scientists were concerned that parties were on the verge of disappearing from the political scene. A more realistic view is that parties will continue to play an important, but significantly diminished, role in American politics. Leon Epstein sees the situation as one in which the parties have become "frayed." He concludes that the parties will "survive and even moderately prosper in a society evidently unreceptive to strong parties and yet unready, and probably unable, to abandon parties altogether."[35]

Summary

Even though political parties are one of Americans' least beloved institutions, political scientists see them as a key linkage between policymakers and the people. Parties are pervasive in politics; for each party there is a *party in the electorate*, a *party organization*, and a *party in government*. Political parties affect policy through their platforms. Despite much cynicism about party platforms, they are taken seriously when their candidates are elected.

America has a two-party system. This fact is of fundamental importance in understanding American politics. The ups and downs of the two parties constitute party competition. In the past, one party or the other has dominated the government for long periods

Career Profile

Position: State Party Chair
Employer: Iowa Democratic Party
Salary and Benefits: None, this is a volunteer position
Qualifications: College degree, commitment to the political party, interest in politics and public policy, management skills

Real People on the Job: Rob Tully

Rob Tully gets paid nothing to do an awful lot of work. As party chair of the Iowa Democratic Party, it's his job is to run the day-to-day operations of the state party, serve as the party's chief spokesperson to the local media, help recruit candidates to run for office, raise money for their campaigns, and decide how to spend the money. He estimates that at least half his time is spent fund-raising, perhaps more.

The party chair's most important job is to help elect and to keep in office Democratic candidates for a variety of government positions, ranging all the way from city dogcatcher to president of the United States. This job requires long hours, especially during election season, and great dedication to the cause. There is almost always a campaign going on that needs money and assistance. It is the party chair's job to make sure each Democratic race is successful.

In Iowa, the Democratic party chair has a unique responsibility since Iowa conducts the first presidential caucus in the country. Rob says that this makes Iowa the best state to be a party chair in because he gets to meet face to face with all the candidates and comes to know each one of them as individuals. He recalls meeting with Bill Bradley during the presidential nomination process for the 2000 election. Bradley had just finished walking in a Fourth of July parade and the two of them sat down under a big shade tree and talked for more than an hour about politics, policy, and Bradley's chances in Iowa. For someone who had grown up hearing of Bradley's prowess as a basketball player, Rob was impressed to be sitting down "like real people" with the former athlete and presidential candidate.

There are many jobs in political parties, and they vary somewhat by state and by party. Some are paid while others are not. Local parties have ward or precinct chairpersons (an easy position to get in most places–just show enthusiasm and ask). The city or county party will usually have a central committee, composed of volunteers who have shown an interest in the party over a number of years and who have worked on a number of campaigns. Beyond this is the state party central committee and state party chairperson. The national parties have central committees and a national chairperson.

of time. These periods were punctuated by critical elections, in which party coalitions underwent realignment. Since 1968, however, American government has experienced a unique period of party dealignment. Although parties are currently weaker at the mass level, they are somewhat stronger and richer in terms of national and state organization. Some would have them be far more centralized and cohesive, following the responsible party model. The loose structure of American parties allows politicians to avoid collective responsibility but also promotes individualism that many Americans value.

Key Terms

party competition
political party
linkage institutions
party image
rational-choice theory
party identification
ticket-splitting
party machines
patronage
closed primaries
open primaries
blanket primaries
national convention
national committee
national chairperson
coalition
party eras
critical election
party realignment
New Deal coalition
party dealignment
party neutrality
third parties
winner-take-all system
proportional representation
coalition government
responsible party model

For Further Reading

Beck, Paul Allen. *Party Politics in America,* 8th ed. New York: Longman, 1997. The standard textbook on political parties.

Black, Earl, and Merle Black. *Politics and Society in the South.* Cambridge, MA: Harvard University Press, 1987. An excellent examination of the transformation of party politics in the South.

Cox, Gary W., and Samuel Kernell, eds. *The Politics of Divided Government.* Boulder, CO: Westview Press, 1991. A set of readings that addresses both the causes and the consequences of divided party government.

Downs, Anthony. *An Economic Theory of Democracy.* New York: Harper & Row, 1957. An extremely influential theoretical work that applies rational-choice theory to party politics.

Epstein, Leon. *Political Parties in the American Mold.* Madison: University of Wisconsin Press, 1986. Epstein demonstrates the remarkable persistence of both parties during a century of profound social change.

Green, John C., and Daniel M. Shea. *The State of the Parties,* 3rd ed. Lanham, MD: Rowman & Littlefield, 1999. A diverse set of articles on numerous aspects of party politics, with an emphasis on how well the party system is working.

Maisel, L. Sandy, ed. *The Parties Respond: Changes in the American Parties and Campaigns,* 3rd ed. Boulder, CO: Westview Press, 1998. A good collection of readings on how parties have adapted to changes in the political system.

Rosenstone, Steven, Roy Behr, and Edward Lazarus. *Third Parties in America,* 2nd ed. Princeton, NJ: Princeton University Press, 1996. An analytical study of why third parties appear, when they do, and what effect they have.

Sabato, Larry. *The Party's Just Begun: Shaping Political Parties for America's Future.* Glenview, IL: Scott, Foresman/Little, Brown, 1988. A spirited prescription for strengthening the parties.

Sundquist, James L. *Dynamics of the Party System,* rev. ed. Washington, D.C.: Brookings Institution, 1983. One of the best books ever written on the major realignments in American history.

Tarrance, V. Lance Jr., and Walter DeVries with Donna L. Mosher. *Checked and Balanced: How Ticket-Splitters Are Shaping the New Balance of Power in American Politics.* Grand Rapids, MI: Eerdmans, 1998. A good basic presentation of trends in ticket-splitting, which also contains in-depth interviews that shed light on the meaning of such votes.

Wattenberg, Martin P. *The Decline of American Political Parties, 1952–1996.* Cambridge, MA: Harvard University Press, 1998. An account of the decline of parties in the electorate.

White, John Kenneth, and Jerome M. Mileur. *Challenges to Party Government.* Carbondale, IL: Southern Illinois University Press, 1992. A collection of essays that examines the responsible party model from the perspective of politics in the 1990s.

Internet Resources

www.rnc.org
The official site of the Republican National Committee.

www.democrats.org
The Democratic Party online.

www.lp.org
Although Libertarians rarely get more than a few percent of the vote, they are consistently getting many of their candidates on the ballot for many offices. You can learn more about their beliefs at this official site.

www.reformparty.org
The official web site for the party founded by Ross Perot, which nominated Pat Buchanan for president in 2000.

Notes

1. E. E. Schattschneider, *Party Government* (New York: Farrar and Rinehart, 1942), 1.
2. Anthony Downs, *An Economic Theory of Democracy* (New York: Harper & Row, 1957).
3. Paul Allen Beck, *Party Politics in America,* 8th ed. (New York: Longman, 1997), 12.
4. Kay Lawson, ed., *Political Parties and Linkage: A Comparative Perspective* (New Haven, CT: Yale University Press, 1980), 3.

5. The major exception to this rule is nominations for the one-house state legislature in Nebraska, which is officially non-partisan. In addition, Bernard Sanders has represented Vermont in the House as an Independent since 1990, and in 1994 Angus King was elected governor of Maine as an Independent.
6. Downs, *Economic Theory*.
7. Morris P. Fiorina, *Congress: Keystone of the Washington Establishment*, 2nd ed. (New Haven, CT: Yale University Press, 1989), 101.
8. See Katherine Tate, *From Protest to Politics: The New Black Voters in American Elections* (Cambridge, MA: Harvard University Press, 1993).
9. Martin P. Wattenberg, *The Decline of American Political Parties*, 1952–1996 (Cambridge, MA: Harvard University Press, 1998), chap. 10.
10. We wish to thank Anthony Salvanto of the University of California, Irvine for making this finding available to us prior to its publication.
11. Beck, *Party Politics in America*, 8th ed., 103.
12. See Adam Cohen and Elizabeth Taylor, *American Pharaoh* (Boston: Little, Brown, 2000), 155–163.
13. Kay Lawson, "California: The Uncertainties of Reform," in Gerald Pomper, ed., *Party Renewal in America*, (New Brunswick, NJ: Praeger, 1980), chap. 8.
14. John F. Bibby et al., "Parties in State Politics," in Virginia Gray, Herbert Jacob, and Kenneth Vines, eds., *Politics in the American States*, 4th ed. (Boston: Little, Brown, 1983), 76–79.
15. John F. Bibby, *Politics, Parties, and Elections in America*, 2nd ed. (Chicago: Nelson-Hall, 1992), 102.
16. John F. Bibby, "State Party Organizations: Coping and Adapting to Candidate-Centered Politics and Nationalization," in L. Sandy Maisel, ed., *The Parties Respond*, 3rd ed. (Boulder, CO: Westview, 1998), 34.
17. Comments of Roy Romer and Jim Nicholson at the Bulen Symposium on American Politics, December 1, 1998, as noted by Martin Wattenberg.
18. Gerald M. Pomper, *Elections in America* (New York: Longman, 1980), 161. Another study of presidential promises from Kennedy through Reagan also reaches the conclusion that campaign pledges are taken seriously. See Jeff Fishel, *Presidents and Promises* (Washington, D.C.: Congressional Quarterly Press, 1985).
19. The term is from V. O. Key. The standard source on critical elections is Walter Dean Burnham, *Critical Elections and the Mainsprings of American Politics* (New York: Norton, 1970).
20. On the origins of the American party system, see William N. Chambers, *Political Parties in a New Nation* (New York: Oxford University Press, 1963).
21. See Richard Hofstader, *The Idea of a Party System: The Rise of Legitimate Opposition in the United States, 1780–1840* (Berkeley: University of California Press, 1969).
22. James W. Ceaser, *Presidential Selection: Theory and Development* (Princeton, NJ: Princeton University Press, 1979), 130.
23. Quoted in James L. Sundquist, *Dynamics of the Party System*, rev. ed. (Washington, D.C.: Brookings Institution, 1983), 88. Sundquist's book is an excellent account of realignments in American party history.
24. *Ibid.*, 1955.
25. On Boston, see Gerald H. Gamm, *The Making of New Deal Democrats: Voting Behavior and Realignment in Boston, 1920–1940* (Chicago: University of Chicago Press, 1989).
26. For a good collection of readings on the causes and consequences of divided party government, see Gary W. Cox and Samuel Kernell, eds., *The Politics of Divided Government* (Boulder, CO: Westview, 1991).
27. See Morris P. Fiorina, *Divided Government* (New York: Macmillan, 1992).
28. Larry Sabato, *The Party's Just Begun: Shaping Political Parties for America's Future* (Glenview, IL: Scott, Foresman/Little, Brown, 1988), 133.
29. Steven J. Rosenstone, Roy L. Behr, and Edward H. Lazarus, *Third Parties in America* (Princeton, NJ: Princeton University Press, 1984).
30. For discussion of political ambiguity as a strategy, see Kenneth A. Shepsle, "The Strategy of Ambiguity: Uncertainty and Electoral Competition," *American Political Science Review* 66 (June 1972): 555–568; and Benjamin I. Page, *Choices and Echoes in Presidential Elections* (Chicago: University of Chicago Press, 1978), chap. 6.
31. The classic statement on responsible parties can be found in "Toward a More Responsible Two-Party System: A Report of the Committee on Political Parties, American Political Science Association," *American Political Science Review* 44 (1950): supplement, number 3, part 2.
32. David R. Mayhew, *Divided We Govern: Party Control, Lawmaking, and Investigations, 1946–1990* (New Haven: Yale University Press, 1991), 199.
33. *Ibid.*, 126.
34. See Evron M. Kirkpatrick, "Toward a More Responsible Party System: Political Science, Policy Science, or Pseudo-Science?" *American Political Science Review* 65 (1971): 965–990.
35. Leon Epstein, *Political Parties in the American Mold* (Madison: University of Wisconsin Press, 1986), 346.

9 Nominations and Campaigns

Chapter Outline

Campaigning for any major office has become a massive undertaking in today's political world. Consider George W. Bush's grueling schedule for March 28–29, 2000, a relatively low-key period of the presidential campaign:

- The governor begins his day with an early morning flight from his home in Austin, Texas, to Dulles Airport in Northern Virginia.
- Upon landing in Virginia, Bush goes to a reception to raise money for his campaign. After lunch, he goes to the headquarters of Sallie Mae, a corporation that helps students finance educational expenses, to give a speech about his views on government and higher education.
- Governor Bush then boards his campaign plane again for a flight to Newark, N.J., where he participates in another fundraiser and gives his standard campaign speech at dinner. After dinner, he goes to Manville, N.J., to address the Somerset County Republican Party convention.

Finally, after 15 hours of traveling and campaigning, his day ends when he checks in at the Newark Hilton at 9:30 P.M.

- The next morning, Bush goes to the North Star Academy Charter school in Newark to give another speech on education. He then rides in a limousine to New York City to give a lunch speech on foreign affairs.
- After this quick stop in New York, Bush flies to Baltimore, Md. to meet with the local press, attend a youth rally, and deliver his standard campaign speech yet again at a dinner event. Finally, Bush takes his fourth flight in two days—this time to Eau Claire, Wis., where he arrives after 14 hours on the go.

It is often said that the presidency is the most difficult job in the world, but getting elected to the position may well be tougher. It is arguable that the long campaign for the presidency puts candidates under more continuous stress than they could ever face in the White House.

The current American style of long and arduous campaigns has evolved from the belief of reformers that the cure for the problems of democracy is more democracy. Whether this approach is helpful or harmful to democracy is a question that arouses much debate with respect to American political campaigns. Some scholars believe it is important that presidential candidates go through a long and difficult trial by fire. Others, however, worry that the system makes it difficult for politicians with other responsibilities—such as incumbent governors and senior senators—to take a run at the White House.

The consequences for the scope of government are also debatable. Anthony King argues that American politicians do too little governing because they are always "running scared," in today's perpetual campaign.[1] From King's perspective, the campaign process does not allow politicians the luxury of trying out solutions to policy problems that might be initially unpopular but would work well in the long run. The scope of government thus stays pretty much as is, given that politicians are usually too concerned with the next election to risk fundamental change. Of course, many analysts would argue that having officeholders constantly worrying about public opinion is good for democracy and that changes in the scope of government shouldn't be undertaken without extensive public consultation.

As you read this chapter, consider whether today's nomination and campaign process provides *too much* opportunity for interaction between the public and candidates for office. Also, consider whether the entire process takes too much time and costs *too much* money—two very important topics of debate in American politics today.

With about half a million elected officials in this country, there is always someone somewhere running for office. This chapter will focus mainly on the campaign for the world's most powerful office: the presidency of the United States. On some topics that are broadly generalizable, such as money and campaigning, we will include examples from congressional races as well. Chapter 12 will specifically discuss the congressional election process.

Campaigns in American politics can be divided into two stages: first, nominations, and second, campaigns between the two nominees. The prize for a nomination campaign is garnering a party's nod as its candidate; the prize for an election campaign is winning an office. This chapter discusses what happens up to election day. Chapter 10 explores how people decide whether to vote and whom to vote for.

The Nomination Game

nomination

The official endorsement of a candidate for office by a **political party.** Generally, success in the nomination game requires momentum, money, and media attention.

campaign strategy

The master game plan candidates lay out to guide their electoral campaign.

A **nomination** is a party's official endorsement of a candidate for office. Anyone can play the nomination game, but few have any serious chance of victory. Generally, success in the nomination game requires money, media attention, and momentum. **Campaign strategy** is the way in which candidates attempt to manipulate each of these elements to achieve the nomination.

Deciding To Run

Believe it or not, not every politician wants to run for president. One reason why is that campaigns have become more physically and emotionally taxing than ever. As former Speaker of the House Thomas Foley once said, "I know of any number of people who I think would make good presidents, even great presidents, who are deterred from running by the torture candidates are obliged to put themselves through."[2] To run for president, a person needs what Walter Mondale once called a "fire in the belly." Remarking on his 1984 bid for the presidency, Mondale said, "For four years, that's all I did. I mean, all I did. That's all you think about. That's all you talk about. . . . That's your leisure. That's your luxury. . . . I told someone, 'The question is not whether I can get elected. The question is whether I can be elected and not be nuts when I get there.'"[3]

In most advanced industrialized countries, campaigns last no more than two months according to either custom and/or law. In contrast, American campaigns seem endless; a presidential candidacy needs to be either announced or an open secret for at least a year before the election. In the winter of 1999, it was already clear to most observers that George W. Bush, John McCain, Elizabeth Dole, Steve Forbes, Pat Buchanan, Dan Quayle, and others were laying the groundwork for a shot at the Republican presidential nomination for 2000.

Political scientists David Rohde and John Aldrich emphasize that presidential candidates need to be risk takers.[4] Presidential candidates need sufficient self-confidence to put everything on the line in hopes of reaching America's highest political office. In order to make it worthwhile to take such a risk, presidential aspirants typically need an electoral base from which to begin. Rarely in American history has a Democratic or Republican candidate for the presidency been taken seriously as a presidential contender without first holding a key political office; most of the exceptions have been famous generals, such as General Eisenhower after World War II or General Grant after the Civil War. Three offices—U.S. senator, U.S. representative, and state governor—have provided the electoral base for about 80 percent of the major candidates since 1972.[5]

Having an electoral base is a first step, but the road to the convention is long and full of stumbling blocks. From the convention, held in the summer of election years, only one candidate emerges as each party's nominee.

Why does it matter?

Today, any successful campaign for the presidency requires an intense commitment for at least 18 months prior to the election. What type of candidate benefits from such a long and arduous process? What sort of politician might be discouraged from running in such a campaign? Can you think of any ways to improve the campaign process?

When Elizabeth Dole announced her campaign for the Republican Party's presidential nomination in 2000 she became the first woman ever to be considered a serious presidential candidate. Her experience in two Cabinet posts gave her much credibility, as did the name recognition she had acquired while campaigning for her husband, Bob Dole.

Competing for Delegates

In some ways, the nomination game is tougher than the general election game; it whittles a large number of players down to two. The goal of the nomination game is to win the majority of delegates' support at the **national party convention**—the supreme power within each of the parties, which functions to select presidential and vice presidential candidates and to write a party platform.

national party convention

The supreme power within each of the parties. The convention meets every four years to nominate the party's presidential and vice-presidential candidates and to write the party's platform.

There are 50 different roads to the national convention, one through each state. From February through June of the election year, the individual state parties busily choose their delegates to the national convention via either caucuses or primaries. Candidates try to ensure that delegates committed to them are chosen.

The Caucus Road. Before primaries existed, all state parties selected their delegates to the national convention in a meeting of state party leaders called a **caucus.** Sometimes one or two party "bosses" ran the caucus show, such as Mayor Daley of Chicago or Governor Connally of Texas. Such state party leaders could control who went to the convention and how the state's delegates voted once they got there. They were the kingmakers of presidential politics who met in smoke-filled rooms at the convention to cut deals and form coalitions.

caucus (state party)

A meeting of all state party leaders for selecting delegates to the **national party convention.** Caucuses are usually organized as a pyramid.

Today's caucuses are different from those of the past. In the dozen states that still have them, caucuses are now open to all voters who are registered with the party. Caucuses are usually organized like a pyramid. Small, neighborhood, precinct-level caucuses are held initially—often meeting in a church, an American Legion hall, or even someone's home. At this level, delegates are chosen, on the basis of their preference for a certain candidate, to attend county caucuses and then congressional district caucuses, where delegates are again chosen to go to a higher level—a state convention. At the state convention, which usually occurs months after the precinct caucuses, delegates are finally chosen to go to the national convention.

Since 1972 the state of Iowa has held the nation's first caucuses. Because the Iowa caucuses are the first test of the candidates' vote-getting ability, they usually become a full-blown media extravaganza.[6] Well-known candidates like Phil Gramm in 1996 and

When the media reports a scandal, a presidential campaign can fall apart quickly. In 1987, Democratic front-runner Gary Hart vehemently denied charges of marital infidelity when they were raised by members of the press corps. But when this photo of Hart with model Donna Rice appeared on the newswires, his credibility was badly damaged, and so were his chances for the nomination.

John Glenn in 1984 have seen their campaigns virtually fall apart as a result of poor showings in Iowa. Most important, candidates who were not thought to be contenders have received tremendous boosts from unexpected strong showings in Iowa. An obscure former Georgia governor named Jimmy Carter took his first big presidential step by winning there in 1976. George Bush also made his first big step into the national scene with an upset victory over Ronald Reagan in Iowa in 1980. Pat Buchanan's strong second-place finish behind Bob Dole in 1996 catapulted him into the national spotlight. Iowa has become so important that citizens of the state can expect at least one presidential candidate to come through the state every week during the year preceding the caucus.

presidential primaries

Elections in which voters in a state vote for a candidate (or delegates pledged to him or her). Most delegates to the **national party conventions** are chosen this way.

The Primary Road. Today, most of the delegates to the Democratic and Republican national conventions are selected in **presidential primaries,** in which voters in a state go to the polls and vote for a candidate or delegates pledged to that candidate. The presidential primary was promoted around the turn of the century by reformers who wanted to take nominations out of the hands of the party bosses. The reformers wanted to let the people vote for the candidate of their choice and then bind the delegates to vote for that candidate at the national convention. In 1912, the first presidential primaries were held in 13 states.

Half a century later, when John Kennedy sought the presidency, primaries still played a rather small role in the process. In contrast to the primary marathon that Al Gore had to run in, only two primary contests drew any attention in 1960. All told, Kennedy's primary victories (mostly in uncontested races, such as in New Hampshire), produced just 18 percent of the delegates he needed for the nomination. Had the party leaders turned against him, Kennedy could clearly have been denied the party's nomination by someone who had bypassed the primaries. Indeed, Democratic Party leaders selected Hubert Humphrey as their candidate in 1968 even though he had not entered a single primary. Today, such a nomination would be unthinkable due to the fact that most delegates are now selected via primaries.

Televised debates have become a regular part of presidential primaries. Here, candidates for the 2000 Republican nomination are shown participating in a TV forum.

The increase in the number of presidential primaries occurred after the Democratic Party's disastrous 1968 national convention led many to rethink the delegate selection procedures then in place. As the war in Southeast Asia raged, another war of sorts took place in the streets of Chicago during the Democratic convention. Demonstrators against the war battled Mayor Richard Daley's Chicago police in what an official report later called a "police riot." Beaten up in the streets and defeated in the convention hall, the antiwar faction won one concession from the party regulars: a special committee to review the party's structure and delegate selection procedures, which they felt had discriminated against them. Minorities, women, youth, and other groups that had been poorly represented in the party leadership also demanded a more open process of convention delegate selection. The result was a committee of inquiry, which was chaired first by Senator George McGovern and later by Representative Donald Fraser, who took over when McGovern left the committee to run for president.

The **McGovern-Fraser Commission** had a mandate to try to make Democratic Party conventions more representative. As a result of their decisions, no longer could party leaders handpick the convention delegates virtually in secret. All delegate selection procedures were required to be open, so that party leaders had no more clout than college students or anyone else who wanted to participate. One of the unforeseen results of these new rules was that many states decided that the easiest way to comply was simply to hold primary elections to select convention delegates.[7] Because state laws instituting primaries typically apply to selection of both parties' selection of delegates, the Republican Party's nomination process was similarly transformed.

McGovern-Fraser Commission

A commission formed at the 1968 Democratic convention in response to demands for reform by minority groups and others who sought better representation.

Few developments have changed American politics as much as the proliferation of presidential primaries. Presidential election watcher Theodore White calls the primaries the "classic example of the triumph of goodwill over common sense." Says White,

> *delegates, who were supposed to be free to vote by their own common sense and conscience, have become for the most part anonymous faces, collected as background for the television cameras, sacks of potatoes packaged in primaries, divorced from party roots, and from the officials who rule states and nation.*[8]

Whereas once many of the delegates were experienced politicians who knew the candidates, today they are typically people who have worked on a candidate's campaign and who owe their position as a delegate strictly to that candidate's ability to pull in primary votes.

Riots at the 1968 Democratic national convention led to the creation of the McGovern-Fraser Commission, which established open procedures and affirmative action guidelines for delegate selection. These reforms have made party conventions more representative than they once were.

superdelegates

National party leaders who automatically get a delegate slot at the Democratic **national party convention.**

The Democratic Party became so concerned about the lack of a role for party leaders at their conventions that starting in 1984 they automatically set aside about 15 percent of their delegate slots for public officeholders and party officials. These politicians who are awarded convention seats on the basis of their position are known as **superdelegates.** The addition of these delegates to the Democratic national convention was designed to restore an element of "peer review" to the process, ensuring participation of the people most familiar with the candidates. However, to date the primaries have proved to be far more crucial than the superdelegates.

The primary season begins during the winter in New Hampshire, where license plates boldly state, "Live free or die." (One can only guess what the prison inmates of New Hampshire must think while making these plates.) Like the Iowa caucuses, the importance of New Hampshire is not the number of delegates or how representative the state is, but rather that it is traditionally the first primary.[9] At this early stage, the campaign is not for delegates, but for images—candidates want the rest of the country to see them as front-runners. The frenzy of political activity in this small state is given lavish attention in the national press. During the week of the primary, half the portable satellite dishes in the country can be found in Manchester, N. H., and the networks move their anchors and top reporters to the scene to broadcast the nightly news. In 1996, 22 percent of TV coverage of the nomination races was devoted to the New Hampshire primary.[10]

frontloading

The recent tendency of states to hold primaries early in the calendar in order to capitalize on media attention.

At one time, it was considered advantageous for a state to choose its delegates late in the primary season so that it could play a decisive role. However, in recent years states that have held late primaries, such as Pennsylvania and New Jersey, have found their primary results irrelevant given that one candidate had already sewn up the nomination by the time their primaries were held. With so much attention being paid to the early contests, more states have moved their primaries up in the calendar in order to capitalize on the media attention. This **frontloading** of the process resulted in two-thirds of both Democratic and Republican delegates being chosen within six weeks of the New Hampshire primary in 2000. The most obvious example of frontloading is California, which from 1948 through 1992 held its presidential primary during the first week of June. In an attempt to gain more clout, in 1996 the nation's most populous state moved its primary date to late March. Yet, by then Dole had already knocked out all his competitors and once again the California primary was inconsequential. In a move that ensured California's relevance in 2000, the state legislature moved its primary up to the first Tuesday in March.

State laws determine how the delegates are allocated, operating within the general guidelines set by the parties. Some are closed to only people who are registered with the party, whereas others are open. The Democrats require all states to use some form of proportional representation in which a candidate who gets 15 percent or more of a state's vote is awarded a roughly proportional share of the delegates. The Republicans practice what they preach, giving states a large degree of discretion. Some states like California allocate all Republican delegates to whoever wins the most votes, others like Texas award delegates according to who wins each congressional district, and yet others employ some form of proportional representation.

Week after week, the primaries serve as elimination contests, as the media continually monitor the count of delegates won. The politicians, the press, and the public all love a winner. Candidates who fail to score early wins get labeled as losers and typically drop out of the race. Usually they have little choice since losing quickly inhibits a candidate's ability to raise the money necessary to win in other states. As one veteran fundraiser put it, "People don't lose campaigns. They run out of money and can't get their planes in the air. That's the reality."[11]

In the 1980 delegate chase, a commonly used football term became established in the language of American politics. After George Bush scored a surprise victory over Ronald Reagan in Iowa, he proudly claimed to possess "the big mo"—momentum. Actually, Bush had only a little "mo" and quickly fell victim to a decisive Reagan victory in New Hampshire. But the term neatly describes what candidates for the nomination are after. Primaries and caucuses are more than an endurance contest, though they are certainly that; they are also proving grounds. Week after week, the challenge is to do better than expected. To get "mo" going, candidates have to beat people they were not expected to beat, collect margins above predictions, and—above all else—never lose to people they were expected to trounce. Momentum is good to have, but it is no guarantee of victory because candidates with a strong base sometimes bounce back. Political scientist Larry Bartels found that "substantive political appeal may overwhelm the impact of momentum."[12]

Why does it matter?

In baseball, no one would declare a team out of the pennant race after it lost the first two games of the season. But in the race for the presidential nomination, the results of Iowa caucus and New Hampshire primary frequently end the campaigns of many candidates after only a handful of national delegates have been selected. Why are these two early contests so crucial? How might the nomination process be altered if no small state were allowed to vote before at least one of the large states?

Evaluating the Primary and Caucus System. The primaries and the caucuses are here to stay. That reality does not mean, however, that political scientists or commentators are particularly happy with the system. Criticisms of this marathon campaign are numerous; here are a few of the most important:

- *Disproportionate attention goes to the early caucuses and primaries.* Take a look at Figure 9.1, which shows how critics think America's media-dominated campaigns are distorted by early primaries and caucuses. Neither New Hampshire nor Iowa is particularly representative of the national electorate. Both are rural, both have only small minority populations, and neither is at the center of the political mainstream. Whereas Iowa is more liberal than the nation as a whole, New Hampshire is the reverse. Although Iowa and New Hampshire are not always "make or break" contests, they play a key—and a disproportionate—role in building momentum, generating money, and generating media attention.
- *Prominent politicians find it difficult to take time out from their duties to run.* Running for the presidency has become a full-time job. The governor of a big state or a member of the congressional leadership is likely to find the task of balancing the demands of a presidential race and political office to be quite tricky. One 1988 candidate who did not let his official responsibilities keep him from running for president was Massachusetts Governor Michael Dukakis. In an extraordinary apology to the state, Dukakis said he underestimated the demands of running for the presidency and managing the state simultaneously. "Trying to do two jobs at the same time was more difficult and more grueling than I expected," he said.[13]
- *Money plays too big a role in the caucuses and primaries.* Momentum means money—getting more of it than your opponents do. Many people think that money plays too large a role in American presidential elections. (This topic will be discussed in detail shortly.) Candidates who drop out early in the process often lament that their inability to raise money left them without a chance to compete.
- *Participation in primaries and caucuses is low and unrepresentative.* Although about 50 percent of the population votes in the November presidential election, only about 20 percent casts ballots in presidential primaries. Participation in caucus states is much smaller because a person must usually devote several hours to attending a caucus. Except for Iowa, where the extraordinary media attention usually boosts the participation, only about 5 percent of registered voters typically show up for caucuses. Moreover, voters in primaries and caucuses are hardly rep-

Figure 9.1 The Inflated Importance of Iowa and New Hampshire

In 1996, 40 percent of all TV news stories about the nomination campaigns focused on Iowa and New Hampshire, even though these two small states selected only about 2 percent of the convention delegates. Here are the 50 states drawn to scale in terms of the media attention their primaries and caucuses received in 1996, according to a content analysis of the ABC, CBS, and NBC evening news by the Center for Media and Public Affairs.

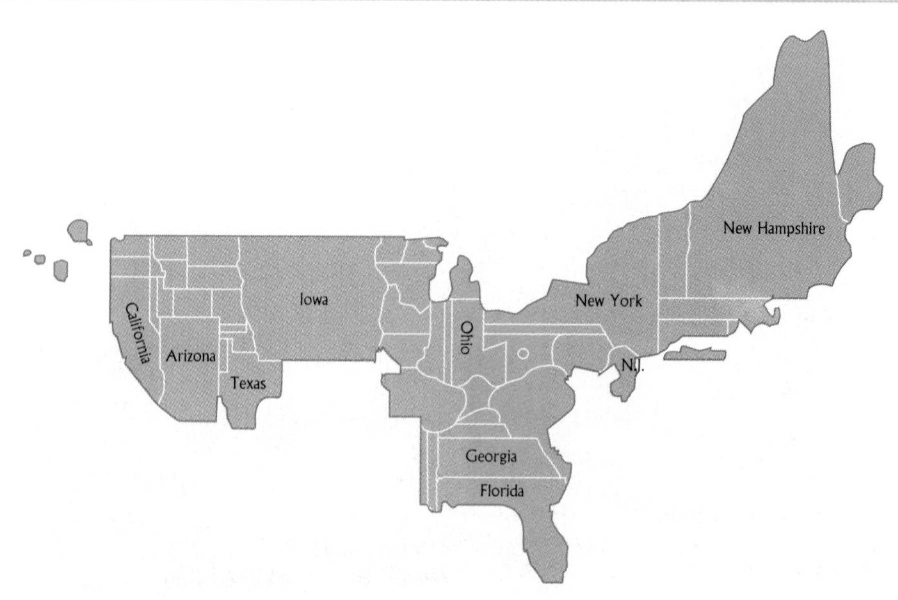

Source: Center for Media and Public Affairs, as reported in Harold W. Stanley and Richard G. Niemi, *Vital Statistics on American Politics*, 6th ed. (Washington, D.C.: Congressional Quarterly Press), 1998, 172–174.

resentative of voters at large; they tend to be older and more affluent than the typical citizen.

- *The system gives too much power to the media.* Critics contend that the media have replaced the party bosses as the new kingmakers. Deciding who has momentum at any given moment, the press readily labels candidates as winners and losers. The fact that the press accepted Bill Clinton's interpretation of his second place finish in New Hampshire as a great comeback may well have saved his campaign in 1992.

Is this the best way to pick a president? Critics think not and have come up with a number of reform proposals (see "You Are the Policymaker: National and Regional Presidential Primary Proposals".

Nevertheless, the current system has powerful defenders—most notably the candidates themselves. For example, on the eve of the 2000 New Hampshire primary President Clinton defended the current process, noting that presidential candidates "ought to have to go out and sit down with people . . . talk to them and be sized up."[14] Even candidates who finish well back in the pack usually support the process. Senator Paul Simon, who won only his home state in 1988, argues that it is best to start the race in small states where people can meet the candidates face to face and where "a candidate of limited means has a chance."[15] Former Interior Secretary Bruce Babbitt, who got great press coverage but few votes in 1988, defends the length of the nomination race. He argues that "it has to be long, to allow us to surface national leadership outside of a parliamentary system. Congress does not automatically produce national leadership."[16] It is important to enable new national leaders to emerge, says Babbitt, and the current American system facilitates this.

Obviously, some candidates would like to see changes, but as long as most candidates and citizens support the process in general, major reform is unlikely. For the foreseeable future, states will continue to select delegates in primaries and caucuses who will attend the national conventions, where the nominees are formally chosen.

visual literacy
American Electoral Rules: How Do They Influence Campaigns?

The Convention Send-off

At one time party conventions provided great drama. Great speeches were given, dark-horse candidates suddenly appeared, and numerous ballots were held as candidates jockeyed to win the nomination. It took the Democrats 46 ballots in 1912, 44 in 1920, and a record 103 in 1924 to nominate their presidential standard bearer. Multiballot conventions died out in 1952, however, with the advent of television.

Nevertheless, television did not immediately put an end to drama at the conventions. In fact, for a while it helped to create it. In 1964, NBC's John Chancellor was arrested for standing in the aisles while reporting from the floor of the Republican convention. His producers promised him bail, and as he was escorted off the floor, he signed off saying, "This is John Chancellor reporting under custody and now returning you to the anchor booth." Four years later it was protesters in the streets of Chicago who were being arrested at the Democratic convention. The networks shifted back and forth from scenes of violence in the streets to the bitter debate and occasional scuffles inside the convention hall. In 1972, the Democrats were at it again, this time extending their debates late into the night, causing nominee George McGovern to give his acceptance speech at 3 A.M.

Today, though, the drama has largely been drained from the conventions because the winner is a foregone conclusion. No longer can a powerful governor shift a whole block of votes at the last minute. Delegates selected in primaries and open caucuses have known preferences. The last time there was any doubt about who would win at the convention was in 1976, when Ford barely edged out Reagan for the Republican nomination. The parties have also learned that it is not in their best interest to provide high drama. The raucous conventions held by the

You Are the Policymaker

National and Regional Presidential Primary Proposals

The idea of holding a **national primary** to select party nominees has been discussed virtually ever since state primaries were introduced. In 1913, President Woodrow Wilson proposed it in his first message to Congress. Since then over 250 proposals for a national presidential primary have been introduced in Congress. These proposals do not lack public support; opinion polls have consistently shown that a substantial majority of Democrats, Republicans, and Independents alike favor such reform.

According to its proponents, a national primary would bring directness and simplicity to the process for the voters as well as the candidates. The length of the campaign would be shortened, and no longer would votes in one state have more political impact than votes in another. The concentration of media coverage on this one event, say its advocates, would increase not only political interest in the nomination decision but also public understanding of the issues involved.

A national primary would not be so simple, respond the critics. Because Americans would not want a candidate nominated with 25 percent of the vote from among a field of six candidates, in most primaries a runoff election between the top two finishers in each party would have to be held. So much for making the campaign simpler, national primary critics note. Each voter would have to vote three times for president—twice in the primaries and once in November.

Another common criticism of a national primary is that only well-established politicians would have a shot at breaking through in such a system. Big money and big attention from the national media would become more crucial than ever. Obscure candidates, such as Jimmy Carter in 1976, would never have a chance. Do Americans, however, really want politicians without an established reputation to become president?

Perhaps more feasible than a national primary is holding a series of **regional primaries** in which, say, states in the eastern time zone would vote one week, those in the central time zone the next, and so on. This would impose a more rational structure and cut down on candidate travel. A regional primary system would also put an end to the jockeying between states for an advantageous position in the primary season. Recently, the National Association of Secretaries of State—the organization of the leading election officials of the states—endorsed a plan to establish regional primaries for the 2004 campaign.

The major problem with the regional primary proposal, however, is the advantage gained by whichever region goes first. For example, if the western states were the first to vote, any candidate from California would have a clear edge in building momentum. Although most of the proposed plans call for the order of the regions to be determined by lottery, this would not erase the fact that regional advantages would surely be created from year to year.

Another prominent proposal is to have states vote in four stages according to their population size, with the least populous states leading off and the big states like California and Texas voting last. Such a proposal received serious consideration from the Republican National Committee in 2000 and was about to be voted on at the convention until George W. Bush let it be known that he did not favor it. Bush expressed concern that the plan would be unworkable because candidates would be asked to campaign all over the country in each stage.

Put yourself in the role of policymaker. Do the advantages of the reform proposals outweigh the disadvantages? Would any of them represent an improvement over the current system? Keep in mind that there are almost always unintended consequences associated with reforms.

national primary

A proposal by critics of the **caucuses** and **presidential primaries**, which who would replace these electoral methods with a nationwide **primary** held early in the election year.

regional primaries

A proposal by critics of the **caucuses** and **presidential primaries** to replace these electoral methods with a series of primaries held in each geographic region.

Republicans in 1964 and the Democrats in 1968 and 1972 captured the public's attention, but they also exposed such divisiveness that the parties were unable to unite for the fall campaign.

Without such drama, the networks have substantially scaled back the number of hours of coverage in recent years, as you can see in Figure 9.2. Even with the condensed TV coverage, the Nielsen ratings have fallen to abysmal levels.[17] The biggest convention audience in 2000 occurred when 22 million viewers tuned in to watch Al Gore's speech to the Democratic convention, which was covered by all the major broadcast networks as well as the cable news channels. By contrast, the next week CBS alone got 58 million viewers for its final episode of "Survivor."

Although conventions are no longer very interesting, they are a significant rallying point for the parties. As George W. Bush said prior to the Republican con-

Figure 9.2 The Declining Coverage of Conventions on Network TV

Believe it or not, Democratic and Republican conventions once got far more coverage on the major networks (CBS, NBC, and ABC) than the Summer Olympics. As the number of presidential primaries has increased, however, nominations have come to be decided in these contests. Thus, by the time the conventions are held, there is little element of political suspense. Hence, the networks have drastically cut back on their coverage of these events, as you can see in the data displayed below.

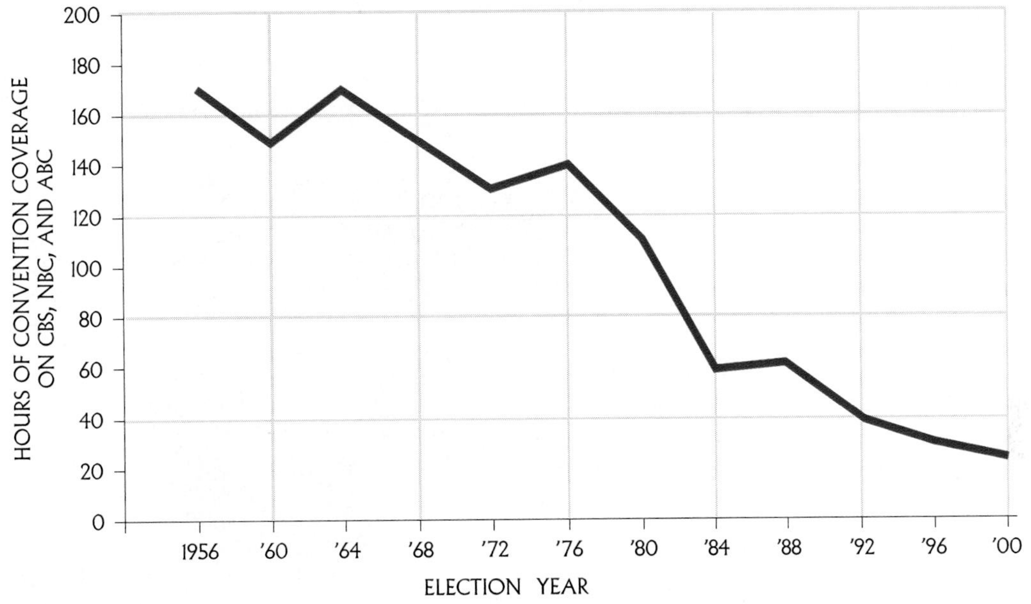

Source: For 1956-1984, calculated from data reported in Byron E. Schafer, *Bifurcated Politics: Evolution and Reform in the National Party Convention* (Cambridge, MA: Harvard University Press, 1988), 274; updated by the authors for 1988 through 2000.

vention in 2000, "The convention system provides a system of rewards for hard-working, grass-roots people who end up being delegates. I view it as an opportunity for these people to go back home, energized to help me get elected."[18] Modern conventions are carefully scripted to present the party in its best light. Delegates are no longer there to argue for their causes but merely to support their candidate. The parties carefully orchestrate a massive send-off for the presidential and vice-presidential candidates. The party's leaders are there in force, as are many of its most important followers—people whose input will be critical during the general election campaign.

The conventions are also important in developing the party's policy positions and in promoting political representation. In the past, conventions were essentially an assembly of party leaders, gathered together to bargain over the selection of the party's ticket. Almost all delegates were White, male, and over 40. Lately, party reformers, especially among the Democrats, have worked hard to make the conventions far more demographically representative. Meeting in an oversized, overstuffed convention hall in a major city, a national convention is a short-lived affair. The highlight of the first day is usually the keynote speech, in which a dynamic speaker recalls party heroes, condemns the opposition party, and touts the nominee apparent.

The second day centers on the **party platform**—the party's statement of its goals and policies for the next four years. The platform is drafted prior to the convention by a committee whose members are chosen in rough proportion to each candidate's strength. Any time over 20 percent of the delegates to the platform committee disagree with the majority, they can bring an alternative minority plank to the convention floor for debate. In former times, contests over the platform were key tests of candidates'

party platform

A political party's statement of its goals and policies for the next four years. The platform is drafted prior to the party convention by a committee whose members are chosen in rough proportion to each candidate's strength. It is the best formal statement of a party's beliefs.

In writing a party platform, disagreements between various factions of the party often become evident. In 1992 and 1996, Ann Stone led a movement of Republican women in favor of a pro-choice plank on abortion. Although Ann Stone drew a fair amount of media attention, she was unsuccessful in getting the Republican convention to consider changing its pro-life platform.

strength before the actual nomination. When a peace plank failed to be adopted by the 1968 Democratic national convention it was clear that Vice President Hubert Humphrey would defeat antiwar candidate Eugene McCarthy. In contrast, recent contests over the platform have served mostly as a way for the minority factions in the party to make sure that their voices are heard. Since 1992, pro-choice Republicans have tried in vain every four years to force a vote on the solidly antiabortion plank in the GOP platform. Fearing the negative publicity the party would incur by showing open disagreement on this emotionally charged issue, Republican leaders such as New Jersey's pro-choice Governor Christine Todd Whitman have dissuaded delegates from forcing such a confrontation.

The third day of the convention is devoted to formally nominating a candidate for president. One of each candidate's eminent supporters gives a speech extolling the candidate's virtues; a string of seconding speeches then follow. Demonstrations erupt as if spontaneous, though in reality they are carefully planned. Toward the end of the evening, balloting begins as states announce their votes ("Florida, the sunshine state, casts all its votes for . . ."). After all the votes are counted, the evening's last demonstration celebrates the long-anticipated nomination.

The vice-presidential nominee is chosen by roll call vote on the convention's final day, though custom dictates that delegates simply vote for whomever the presidential nominee recommends. The vice-presidential candidate then comes to the podium to

Technology has changed the way campaigns are run and the way candidates attempt to reach the people. Most serious candidates for a major office these days have their own official website. This provides an effective way to make their policy positions available for anyone interested. In addition, many candidates have found websites to be a great way to raise funds for their campaigns. Here, you can see the front page of Hillary Clinton's Senate campaign website not long after she won her race in 2000.

make a brief acceptance speech. This speech is followed by the grand finale—the presidential candidate's acceptance speech, in which the battle lines for the coming campaign are drawn. Afterward, all the party leaders come out to congratulate the party's ticket, raise their hands, and bid the delegates farewell.

The Campaign Game

Once nominated, candidates concentrate on campaigning for the general election. These days, the word *campaign* is part of the American political vocabulary, but it was not always so. The term was originally a military one: Generals mounted campaigns, using their scarce resources to achieve strategic objectives. Political campaigns proceed in a similar fashion, with candidates allocating their scarce resources of time, money, and energy to achieve their political objectives.

Campaigns involve more than organization and leadership. Artistry also enters the picture, for campaigns deal in images. The campaign is the canvas on which political strategists try to paint portraits of leadership, competence, caring, and other images Americans value in presidents. Campaigning today is an art and a science, heavily dependent—like much else in American politics—on technology.

Television has been the primary way that candidates for national office have gotten out their message since about 1960. Here, Vice President Richard Cheney is seen waiting to appear on "Face the Nation" during the 2000 campaign.

The High-Tech Media Campaign

The new machines of politics have changed the way campaigns are run. During the first half of the twentieth century, candidates and their entourage piled onto a campaign train and tried to speak to as many people as time, energy, and money would allow. Voters journeyed from miles around to see a presidential whistle-stop tour go by and to hear a few words in person from the candidate. Today, television is the most prevalent means used by candidates to reach voters. Thomas Patterson stresses that "today's presidential campaign is essentially a mass media campaign. . . . It is no exaggeration to say that, for the majority of voters, the campaign has little reality apart from its media version."[19] Technology has made it possible for candidates to speak directly to the American people in the comfort of their living rooms, or in front of their computer monitors. At the grass-roots level, some candidates now distribute 10-minute videotapes of themselves rather than the old-fashioned political pamphlet. During the 1992 New Hampshire primary, the Clinton campaign passed out over 25,000 videotapes detailing his economic plan.[20]

participation
The Net Election: Campaigning on the Internet

Things have certainly changed since President Dwight Eisenhower first struggled to use a TelePrompTer—a machine used to magnify a speech so that the speaker does not have to look down at his or her text—and found it totally confusing. He grumbled in front of a national television audience, "How does this damned thing work, anyway?" The computer revolution has also now overtaken political campaigns. At the end of the first presidential debate in 1996, Bob Dole encouraged viewers to go to his site on the World Wide Web for more information on his issue stands. So many people immediately tried to check it out that the server soon crashed. Following his stunning win in the 2000 New Hampshire primary, John McCain's campaign received millions of dollars in donations through its website. There is little doubt this form of communication will play an increasingly important role in the campaigns of the twenty-first century.

direct mail

A high-tech method of raising money for a political cause or candidate. It involves sending information and requests for money to people whose names appear on lists of those who have supported similar views or candidates in the past.

Perhaps the most important use of computer technology in campaigns thus far has been the use of targeted mailings to prospective supporters. The technique of **direct mail** involves locating potential supporters by sending information and a request for money to huge lists of people who have supported candidates of similar views in the past. Conservative fund-raiser Richard Viguerie pioneered the mass-mailing list, including in his computerized list the names and addresses of hundreds of thousands of individuals who contributed to conservative causes. The accumulation of mailing lists enables candidates to pick almost any issue, be it helping the homeless, opposing abortion, aiding Israel, or anything else, and write to a list of people concerned about that issue. Direct mail induces millions of people each year to contribute to various candidates and political causes, totaling over $1 billion.[21] The high-tech campaign is no longer a luxury. Candidates *must* use the media and computer technology just to stay competitive.

The most important goal of any media campaign is simply to get attention. Media coverage is determined by two factors: (1) how candidates use their advertising budget and (2) the "free" attention they get as newsmakers. The first, obviously, is relatively easy to control; the second is more difficult but not impossible. Almost every logistical decision in a campaign—where to eat breakfast, whom to include on the rostrum, when to announce a major policy proposal—is calculated according to its intended media impact. In the first half of the twentieth century, the biggest item in a campaign budget might have been renting a railroad train. Today the major item is unquestionably television advertising. About half the total budget for a presidential or senatorial campaign will be used for television advertising.

Many observers worry that we have entered a new era of politics in which the slick slogan and the image salesperson dominates—an era when Madison Avenue is more influential than Main Street. Most political scientists, however, are concluding that such fears are overblown. Research has shown that campaign advertising can be a source of information about issues as well as about images. Thomas Patterson and Robert McClure examined the information contained in TV advertising and found that viewers learned more about candidates' stands on the issues from watching their ads than from watching the nightly news. Most news coverage stresses where the candidates went, how big their crowds were, and other campaign details. Only rarely do the networks delve into where the candidates stand on the issues. In contrast, political ads typically address issues; a study of 230,000 candidate ads that ran in 1998 found that spots that emphasized policy outnumbered those that stressed personal image by a six to one ratio.[22] Most candidates apparently believe that their policy positions are a crucial part of their campaign, and they are willing to pay substantial sums to communicate them to voters.

Presidential Candidates and Their Television Ads

Candidates have much less control over the other aspect of the media, news coverage. To be sure, most campaigns have press aides who feed "canned" news releases to reporters. Still, the media largely determine for themselves what is happening in a campaign. Campaign coverage seems to be a constant interplay between hard news about what candidates say and do and the human interest angle, which most journalists think sells newspapers or interests television viewers.

Apparently, news organizations believe that policy issues are of less interest to voters than the campaign itself. The result is that news coverage is disproportionately devoted to campaign strategies, speculation about what will happen next, poll results, and other aspects of the campaign game. Patterson tabulated the amount of media attention to the campaign itself and the amount of attention to such substantive issues as the economy in the 1976 presidential race. Examining several newspapers and news magazines as well as television network news, he found that attention to the "game" far exceeded attention to substance, and subsequent research through the 1990s has found that this pattern continues to hold true.[23] Once a candidate has taken a policy position and it has been reported, it becomes old news. The latest poll showing Smith ahead of Jones is thus more newsworthy in the eyes of the media. Republican media consultant Roger Ailes calls this his "orchestra pit" theory of American politics: "If you have two guys on stage and one guy says, 'I have a solution to the Middle East problem,' and the other guy falls in the orchestra pit, who do you think is going to be on the evening news?"[24]

Organizing the Campaign

In every campaign, there is too much to do and too little time to do it. Every candidate must prepare for nightly banquets and endless handshaking. More important, to organize their campaigns effectively, candidates must do the following:

- *Get a campaign manager.* Some candidates try to run their own campaign, but they usually end up regretting it. A professional campaign manager can keep the candidate from getting bogged down in organizational details. This person also bears the day-to-day responsibility for keeping the campaign square on its message and setting its tone (see "Making a Difference: Lee Atwater and the Politics of Slash and Burn").

Making a Difference

Lee Atwater and the Politics of Slash and Burn

During his short turbulent life, Lee Atwater of South Carolina rose to political prominence at a young age and reshaped the role of a campaign manager. In a profile of Atwater, the *New York Times* wrote that he "may be the person most responsible" for how the role of a campaign manager is now practiced. He became the master of negative campaigning, using wedge issues that divide segments of the electorate sharply, such as crime, race, and religious values to skewer his opponents.

Having worked on numerous campaigns since the time he enrolled in college, Lee Atwater became a star campaign consultant at the age of 27 as a result of his instrumental role in the 1978 reelection of Senator Strom Thurmond. Atwater helped put together a negative campaign that painted Thurmond's opponent as more in touch with the Eastern liberal establishment than with the mainstream South Carolina voter. Two years later, Senator Thurmond helped Atwater land a job in the Reagan White House even though he was not yet 30 years old. By 1984 he was Reagan's deputy campaign manager, supervising the directors of each of the 50 state campaigns. Soon afterward, then Vice President Bush signed him up to be his campaign manager for 1988. Bush did so with some trepidation; Atwater was already known by many as "the Babe Ruth of negative politics."

In the 1988 campaign, Atwater had a negative campaigner's equivalent of a 60-homer season. When Michael Dukakis became the apparent Democratic nominee, he was quoted as saying "I'm going to scrape the bark off that little bastard." Atwater allocated $1.2 million of campaign money to opposition research against Dukakis. He instructed researchers not to worry much about major policies affecting the scope of government, but rather to find examples of Dukakis's cultural liberalism that would tap into voters' emotions and turn them irrevocably against him. Using examples of how Dukakis had signed off on furloughs for murderers and rapists while at the same time opposing the death penalty for even the worst offenses, Atwater painted Dukakis as soft on crime. Much attention was also given to Dukakis's veto of a state bill requiring teachers to lead students in the Pledge of Allegiance, which made him seem unpatriotic compared to Bush—who Atwater shamelessly had recite the pledge at every major speech, including one at a flag factory. Dukakis was also labeled as soft on national defense for his opposition to military strikes against terrorists and various weapons systems, as well as his one-time support for unilateral nuclear disarmament. Rather than being able to discuss their theme of "good jobs at good wages," the Democrats found themselves constantly on the defensive from these and other value-laden attacks.

After Bush won he appointed Lee Atwater to be chair of the Republican Party, the first professional political consultant to ever hold such a position. From this position, Atwater launched a permanent campaign to make the GOP the nation's majority party. A poll during his first year as head of the party found that 41 percent of the public knew who he was, a number far above the chief justice of the Supreme Court. But Atwater was to serve in this position for just over a year. One day he had a seizure while giving a speech and was rushed to the hospital. He was diagnosed with a brain tumor and given a year to live. As he lay dying at the age of 40, Atwater thought a lot about the role he had played in American politics and decided to write an article for *Life* magazine about his regrets. In it, he apologized to Michael Dukakis and stated that he was "sorry for the way I thought of other people. Like a good general, I had treated everyone who wasn't with me as against me." Atwater concluded that his illness had led him to believe that politics could use a lot more heart and brotherhood. In death, as in life, Lee Atwater set a powerful example for all future campaign managers to consider.

Source: John Brady, *Bad Boy: The Life and Politics of Lee Atwater* (Reading, MA: Addison Wesley, 1997).

- *Get a fund-raiser.* Money, as this chapter will soon discuss in detail, is an important key to election victory.
- *Get a campaign counsel.* With all the current federal regulation of campaign financing, legal assistance is essential to ensure compliance with the laws.
- *Hire media and campaign consultants.* Candidates have more important things to do with their time than plan ad campaigns, contract for buttons and bumper stickers, and buy TV time and newspaper space. Professionals can get them the most exposure for their money.
- *Assemble a campaign staff.* It is desirable to hire as many professionals as the campaign budget allows, but it is also important to get a coordinator of volunteers to ensure that envelopes are licked, doorbells rung, and other small but vital tasks addressed.
- *Plan the logistics.* A modern presidential campaign involves jetting around the country at an incredible pace. Good advance people handle the complicated details of candidate scheduling and see to it that events are well publicized and well attended.
- *Get a research staff and policy advisors.* Candidates have little time to master the complex issues reporters will ask about. Policy advisors—often distinguished academics—feed them the information they need to keep up with events.
- *Hire a pollster.* Dozens of professional polling firms conduct opinion research to tell candidates how the voters view them and what is on the voters' minds.
- *Get a good press secretary.* Candidates running for major office have reporters dogging them every step of the way. The reporters need news, and a good press secretary can help them make their deadlines with stories that the campaign would like to see reported.

You are a Professional Campaign Consultant

Most of these tasks cost money. Campaigns are not cheap, and the role of money in campaigns is a controversial one.

How You Can Make a Difference

Volunteering for Political Campaigns

In order to change how government operates or to maintain a desired policy in this country, you generally have to get involved. Personal involvement in politics and the political system is important.

One way to do this is to volunteer on a political campaign. You may wish to help out at a local level by helping a candidate in a race for school board, city council, or mayor. For most local elections you can call the candidate yourself and offer your services. You may wish to work on a race for the state legislature. If you are interested in assisting a candidate for a major office call the candidate's campaign headquarters and ask to talk with the volunteer coordinator. The campaigns for top tier political offices such as state governor, U.S. Senator, U.S. Congressperson, or President are generally huge operations that require the assistance of numerous volunteers. Candidates for these offices will usually have a big campaign organization somewhere in your state and maybe smaller campaign headquarters in regional cities. You can find these by calling the candidate's local party office and asking where the election headquarters is located and how to contact it. Then talk with the volunteer coordinator at headquarters.

All political campaigns need volunteers! And, campaign work is fun. You will meet all sorts of people from all over your city, your state, or the nation and make lots of new friends. You will do things like go door-to-door distributing campaign literature, put up yard signs, stuff envelopes, and answer telephones at campaign headquarters. You'll play an important role in helping elect someone who will work for your ideals. Many colleges and universities offer credit for campaign work. Ask at your school. You can be an intern on a campaign, do a useful bit for democracy, earn college credits, and maybe even get paid.

Money and Campaigning

There is no doubt that campaigns are expensive and, in America's high-tech political arena, growing more so. As the old saying goes, "Money is the mother's milk of politics." Candidates need money to build a campaign organization and to get their message out. Many people and groups who want certain things from the government are all too willing to give it; thus, there is the common perception that money buys votes and influence. The following sections examine the role of money in campaigns.

The Maze of Campaign Finance Reforms

As the costs of campaigning skyrocketed with the growth of television, and as the Watergate scandal exposed large, illegal campaign contributions, momentum developed for campaign finance reform in the early 1970s. Several public interest lobbies (see Chapter 11), notably Common Cause and the National Committee for an Effective Congress, led the drive. In 1974, Congress passed the **Federal Election Campaign Act.** It had two main goals: tightening reporting requirements for contributions and limiting overall expenditures. The 1974 act and its subsequent amendments:

Federal Election Campaign Act

A law passed in 1974 for reforming campaign finances. The act created the **Federal Election Commission (FEC)**, provided public financing for presidential primaries and general elections, limited presidential campaign spending, required disclosure, and attempted to limit contributions.

Federal Election Commission (FEC)

A six-member bipartisan agency created by the **Federal Election Campaign Act** of 1974. The FEC administers the campaign finance laws and enforces compliance with their requirements.

- *created the* ***Federal Election Commission (FEC).*** A bipartisan body, the six-member FEC administers the campaign finance laws and enforces compliance with their requirements.
- *provided public financing for presidential primaries and general elections.* Presidential candidates who raise $5,000 on their own in at least 20 states can get individual contributions of up to $250 matched by the federal treasury. For the general election, each major party nominee gets a fixed amount of money to cover all campaign expenses. All this money is raised via a $3 voluntary check-off box on income tax returns. By checking this box, taxpayers do not add to their tax bill but simply specify that they would like $3 of their taxes to go to this fund. As you can see in Figure 9.3, the percentage of taxpayers checking this box has declined dramatically since the early 1980s.
- *limited presidential campaign spending.* If presidential candidates accept federal support, they agree to limit their campaign expenditures to an amount prescribed by federal law. For 2000, this amounted to approximately $35 million in the primaries and $80 million in the general election. Although he decided not to accept federal support in the 2000 primaries, George W. Bush followed the practice of all previous major party nominees in taking federal money for the general election.
- *required disclosure.* Regardless of whether they accept any federal funding, all candidates for federal office must file periodic reports with the FEC, listing who contributed and how the money was spent. In the spirit of immediate disclosure, some 2000 presidential candidates regularly posted updated campaign contribution information on their websites.
- *limited contributions.* Scandalized to find out that wealthy individuals such as W. Clement Stone and J. Willard Marriott had contributed a million dollars to the 1972 Nixon campaign, Congress limited individual contributions to presidential and congressional candidates to $1,000. The $1,000 limit has been in place unchanged ever since, and many observers would like to see it indexed to rise along with inflation.

Although the campaign reforms were generally welcomed by both parties, the constitutionality of the act was challenged in the 1976 case of *Buckley v. Valeo.* In this case the Supreme Court struck down, as a violation of free speech, the portion of the act that had limited the amount individuals could contribute to their own campaigns. This aspect of the Court ruling made it possible for Ross Perot to spend over $60 million of his own fortune on his independent presidential candidacy in 1992, and for Wall Street tycoon John Corzine to spend over $60 million in pursuit of a New Jersey

Figure 9.3 The Decline in Income Tax Check-Off Participation for Federal Financing of Campaigns

This figure displays the percentage of income tax filers checking off the voluntary box to contribute to the federal financing of presidential campaigns. This amounted to $1 per taxpayer up until 1994, when the amount was increased to $3 due to an anticipated shortfall in the fund. Given the current low rate of participation, it is estimated there will not be adequate funds to finance the 2004 campaign. If this occurs, some candidates may choose to borrow the money from banks using the money owed to them by the federal government as collateral; others may well choose to forego federal funding under these circumstances.

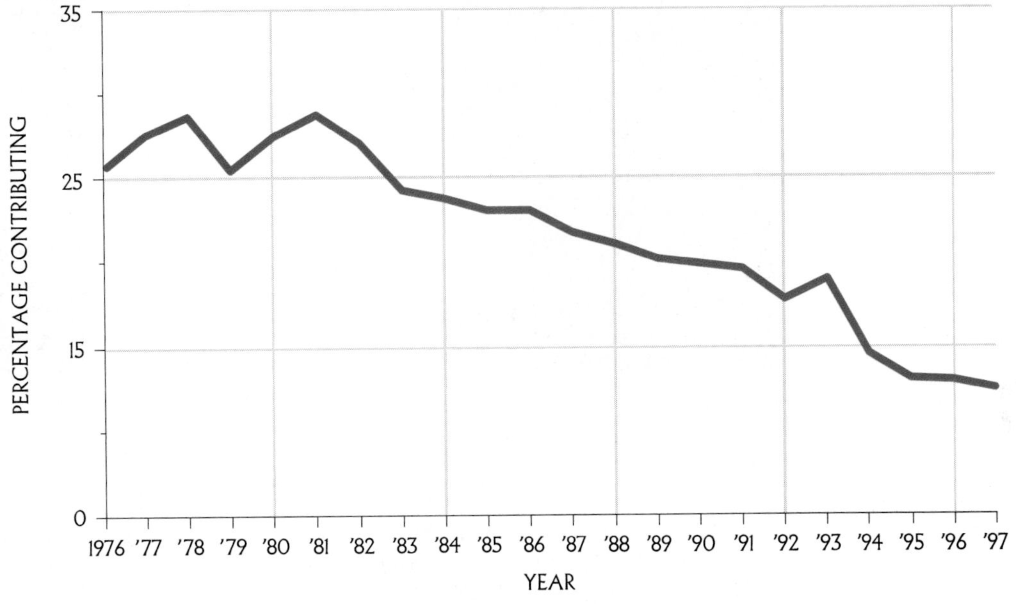

Source: Data from Federal Election Commission, as reported at http://www.opensecrets.org/2000elect/other/presfund/checkoff.htm

Senate seat in 2000. All told, congressional candidates threw in over $110 million of their personal funds to help out their campaigns in 2000.

Another loophole was opened in 1979 with an amendment to the original act that made it easier for political parties to raise money for voter registration drives and the distribution of campaign material at the grass-roots level or for generic party advertising. Money raised for such purposes is known as **soft money** and is not subject to any contribution limits. In 2000, an unprecedented amount of money flowed into the coffers of the national parties through this loophole. Republicans raised $211 million in soft money, and the Democrats were only a bit behind with $199 million. These totals were over 15 times those raised in 1980, when the soft money donations were first allowed. Critics of soft money, such as Republican Senator John McCain and Democratic Senator Russell Feingold, point to a number of instances in which individuals who have given more than $100,000 have been appointed as ambassadors. Furthermore, they emphasize that companies such as Philip Morris and Amway have had their policy concerns heard "loud and clear" by making multimillion-dollar soft money donations. Yet, the McCain-Feingold bill to eliminate soft money contributions has been repeatedly stymied in Congress.

soft money

Political contributions earmarked for party-building expenses at the grass-roots level or for generic party advertising. Unlike money that goes to the campaign of a particular candidate, such party donations are not subject to contribution limits.

Overall, there is little doubt that campaign spending reforms have made campaigns more open and honest. Small donors are encouraged, and the rich are restricted—at least in terms of the money they can give directly to a candidate. All contribution and expenditure records are now open for all to examine, and FEC auditors try to make sure that the regulations are enforced. As Frank Sorauf writes, the detailed FEC reports have "become a wonder of the democratic political world. Nowhere else do scholars and journalists find so much information about the funding of campaigns, and the openness of Americans about the flow of money stuns many other nationals accustomed to silence and secrecy about such traditionally private matters."[25]

President Clinton spent much time and energy on raising soft money for the 1996 campaign. Many people criticized his use of White House coffee meetings, shown here, to entertain wealthy donors, as well as offering some donors the chance to spend the night in the famous Lincoln bedroom.

The Proliferation of PACs

Political Action Committees (PACs)

Funding vehicles created by the 1974 campaign finance reforms. A corporation, union, or some other interest group can create a PAC and register it with the **Federal Election Commission (FEC)**, which will meticulously monitor the PAC's expenditures.

The campaign reforms also encouraged the spread of **political action committees**, generally known as **PACs.** Before the 1974 reforms, corporations were technically forbidden to donate money to political campaigns, but many wrote big checks anyway. Unions could make indirect contributions, although limits were set on how they could aid candidates and political parties. The 1974 reforms created a new, more open way for interest groups such as business and labor to contribute to campaigns. Any interest group, large or small, can now get into the act by forming its own PAC to directly channel contributions of up to $5,000 per candidate in both the primary and the general election.

Buckley v. Valeo extended the right of free speech to PACs, and they can now spend unlimited amounts indirectly, that is, if such activities are not coordinated with the campaign. For example, in 1988 it was a PAC that aired the infamous "Willie Horton" ad accusing Democratic candidate Michael Dukakis of allowing criminals such as Horton out on parole, during which time they committed other crimes. Because the ad showed a sinister looking photo of the African-American Horton, many thought it was a veiled attempt to stimulate racist feelings. The Bush campaign responded to such criticism by saying there was nothing they could do about the ad because it was sponsored by a PAC who had not coordinated it with them.

As of 2001, the FEC reported that there were 3,907 PACs. In the most recent congressional elections, PACs contributed over $212 million to House and Senate candidates. Many believe that this has led to a system of open graft.[26] Few developments since the Watergate crisis have generated so much cynicism about government as the explosive growth of PACs over the last three decades.

A PAC is formed when a business association, or some other interest group, decides to contribute to candidates whom it believes will be favorable toward its goals. The group registers as a PAC with the FEC and then puts money into the PAC coffers. The PAC can collect money from stockholders, members, and other interested parties. It then donates the money to candidates, often after careful research on their issue stands and past voting records. One very important ground rule prevails: All expenditures must be meticulously reported to the FEC. If PACs are corrupting democracy, at least they are doing so openly.

Candidates need PACs because high-tech campaigning is expensive. Tightly contested races for the House of Representatives can sometimes cost over $1 million; Senate races can easily cost $1 million for television alone. PACs play a major role in paying for expensive campaigns. Thus there emerges a symbiotic relationship between

the PACs and the candidates: Candidates need money, which they insist can be used without compromising their integrity; PACs want access to officeholders, which they insist can be gained without buying votes. Justin Dart of Dart Industries, a close friend of former President Reagan, remarks of his PAC that "talking to politicians is fine, but with a little money, they hear you better."[27]

There are an abundance of PACs willing to help out the candidates. There are big PACs, such as the Realtors Political Action Committee and the American Medical Association Political Action Committee. There are little ones, too, representing smaller industries or business associations: EggPAC, FishPAC, FurPAC, LardPAC, and—for the beer distributors, SixPAC.[28] Table 9.1 lists the business, labor, and ideological PACs that gave the most money to congressional candidates in 2000 and shows which party each favored.

Critics of the PAC system worry that all this money leads to PAC control over what the winners do once in office. Archibald Cox and Fred Wertheimer of Common Cause write that the role of PACs in campaign finance "is robbing our nation of its democratic ideals and giving us a government of leaders beholden to the monied interests who make their election possible."[29] On some issues, it seems clear that PAC money has made a difference. The Federal Trade Commission, for example, once passed a regulation requiring that car dealers list known mechanical defects on the window stickers of used cars. The National Association of Automobile Dealers quickly became one of the largest donors to congressional incumbents, contributing just over $1 million to candidates of both parties. Soon afterward, 216 representatives cosponsored a House resolution nullifying the FTC regulation. Of these House members, 186 had been aided by the auto dealers' PAC.[30]

It is questionable, however, whether such examples are the exception or the rule. Most PACs give money to candidates who agree with them in the first place. For instance, the antiabortion PACs will not waste their money supporting pro-choice candidates. Frank Sorauf's careful review of the subject concludes that "there simply are no data in the systematic studies that would support the popular assertions about the 'buying' of the Congress or about any other massive influence of money on the legislative process."[31]

Why does it matter?

In 1999 most pundits argued that any serious candidate for the presidency needed to raise $20 million by the end of the year in order to be a serious contender in 2000. Why is raising money so important in American presidential election campaigns? What influence does money have on the democratic process in America? Can you think of any practical ways to limit the influence of money in politics?

Table 9.1 The Big-Spending PACs

According to an analysis of Federal Election Commission data by the Center for Responsive Politics, here are the largest business, labor, and ideological/single-issue PAC contributors to congressional candidates for the 1999–2000 election cycle and the percentage that they gave to Republicans.

	AMOUNT CONTRIBUTED	PERCENTAGE GIVEN TO REPUBLICANS
Business		
Microsoft	$3,942,435	53
Goldman Sachs Group	3,546,432	32
AT&T	3,510,391	62
National Association of Retailers	3,298,100	58
Association of Trial Lawyers	2,951,500	12
United Parcel Service	2,919,584	74
Philip Morris	2,830,985	80
Labor		
American Federation of State/County/Municipal Employees	6,500,889	1
Service Employees International Union	4,724,664	4
Communication Workers of America	3,687,614	1
International Brotherhood of Electrical Workers	3,369,840	3
United Food and Commercial Workers Union	3,242,057	1
Ideological/Single-Issue		
National Rifle Association	2,884,127	92
Emily's List	1,979,829	0

Source: Center for Responsive Politics.

The impact of PAC money on presidents is even more doubtful. Presidential campaigns, of course, are partly subsidized by the public and so are less dependent upon PACs. Moreover, presidents have well-articulated positions on most important issues. A small contribution from any one PAC is not likely to turn a presidential candidate's head.

Money matters in campaigns and sometimes also during legislative votes. Although the influence of PACs may be exaggerated, the high cost of running for office ensures their continuing major role in the campaign process.

Are Campaigns Too Expensive?

Every four years, Americans spend over $2 billion on national, state, and local elections. This seems like a tremendous amount of money. Yet American elections cost, per person, about as much as an audio CD.

What bothers politicians most about the rising costs of high-tech campaigning is that fund-raising has come to take up so much of their time. Former Florida Governor Reuben Askew pulled out of a Senate race he was favored to win for this very reason. "Something is seriously wrong with our system when many candidates for the Senate need to spend 75 percent of their time raising money," Askew said.[32] Many American officeholders feel that the need for continuous fund-raising distracts them from their jobs as legislators. They look with envy at how politicians in other countries can win major office without worrying about raising huge sums of money (see "America in Perspective: Arlene McCarthy's Election to the European Parliament").

Public financing of congressional campaigns would take care of this problem. Some lawmakers support some sort of public financing reform; however, it will be very difficult to get Congress to consent to equal financing for the people who will challenge them for their seats. Incumbents will not readily give up the advantage they have in raising money.

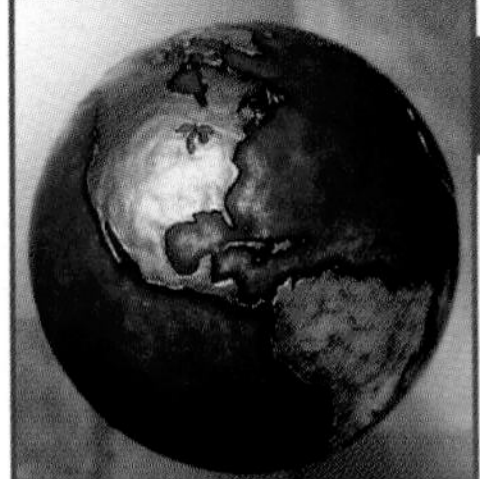

America in Perspective

Arlene McCarthy's Election to the European Parliament

Arlene McCarthy is one of Europe's up-and-coming young politicians. She was first elected to represent England's Peak District in the European Parliament at the age of 33, and in 1999 she was easily reelected. When asked if she could have won a similar election in the United States, she responds with a firm "No—I would never have been able to raise enough money."

A substantial bankroll, however, was not required for Ms. McCarthy to get her start in European politics. All told, she estimates that she spent about $1,600 to get the Labour Party's nomination in her district. Of this, roughly half was spent on new clothes, with the rest going for traveling costs, such as hotels, gasoline, and food. No one contributed any money to support her campaign for the nomination, and she never felt this was necessary. The party took charge of sending out information about her to the voters who would decide the nomination, and all candidates were forbidden from sending out anything else. Only 4,500 dues-paying members of the party could participate in the nomination process, thus making it possible for Ms. McCarthy to speak personally with many of the activists who ultimately gave her a start in politics. Her major appeal was that she had gained much knowledge about how the European Parliament worked during her service as a staff member there, and that she could effectively represent the interests of people back home in England.

About 1,800 voters returned their mail ballot, and Arlene McCarthy finished first among five candidates. The general election loomed only six weeks away when she became the Labour Party's nominee, but the party took charge of her campaign from this point on. The party provided her with about $40,000 in campaign funds, as well as staff and campaign literature. When Labour won a smashing victory across the country, Ms. McCarthy was swept into office, and had suddenly gone from being a young staff member to a member of the European Parliament.

The nomination and general election campaign of Arlene McCarthy illustrates several differences between European campaigns and those of the United States. Had she run a similar campaign in the United States she would have had to raise far more money, appeal to far more people to get her party's nomination, and run a much longer campaign. Which type of campaign do you think is best? Does the European-style campaign make it easier for young people and women to break into political office?

Source: Personal interview with Arlene McCarthy, December 12, 1998.

Does Money Buy Victory?

Important offices are rarely won these days by candidates who fail to raise a substantial amount of campaign funds. One of the last of the nonspending breed was Senator William Proxmire of Wisconsin, who recently retired. He was succeeded by wealthy businessman Herbert Kohl, who funded his multimillion-dollar campaign entirely out of his own pocket. As Kohl said, he was so rich that at least no one had to worry about him being bought by special interests.

Perhaps the most basic complaint about money and politics is that there may be a direct link between dollars spent and votes received. Few have done more to dispel this charge than political scientist Gary Jacobson. His research has shown that "the more incumbents spend, the worse they do."[33] This fact is not as odd as it sounds. It simply means that incumbents who face a tough opponent must raise more money to meet the challenge. When a challenger is not a serious threat, as they all too often are not, incumbents can afford to campaign cheaply. As you can see in Table 9.2, Democratic House incumbents who won with over 70 percent of the vote in 1994 had little to worry about because their Republican opponents were so poorly funded. In contrast, the Democrats who lost their seats raised great sums of money in their struggle to beat back a set of well-funded opponents.

More important than having "more" money is having "enough" money. Herbert Alexander calls this "the doctrine of sufficiency." As he writes, "Enough money must

Table 9.2 1994 Campaign Spending by Democratic House Incumbents and Republican Challengers

In 1994, an unusual number of House incumbents lost their reelection bids—35, all of them Democrats. Was it because these Democrats failed to raise enough money for their campaigns? In fact, this was not the case at all: The more money Democratic incumbents raised in 1994 the worse they did at the polls. The big-spending Democratic incumbents did poorly not because they spent so much money, but rather because they faced well-financed Republican challengers, as you can see in the following data.

	Average Campaign Spending By:	
	DEMOCRATIC INCUMBENT	REPUBLICAN CHALLENGER
Democrat won with over 70% of the vote	$373,524	$23,881
Democrat won with between 60 and 70% of the vote	$455,136	$109,542
Democrat won with less than 60% of the vote	$693,973	$268,203
Democrat lost	$943,588	$612,588

[a]by Democratic Vote Percentage

Source: Authors' analysis of 1994 election returns and Federal Election Commission Report of campaign spending.

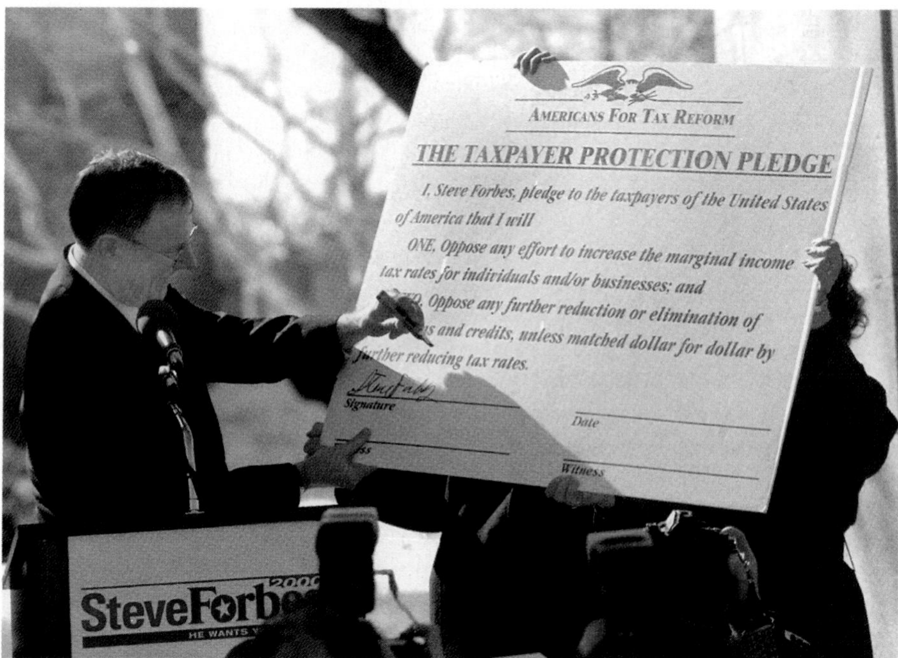

One candidate for president who didn't have to worry much about fundraising in 2000 was Steve Forbes, who relied on his own personal fortune to finance his campaign. Here, Forbes is shown in New Hampshire signing a pledge not to increase tax rates if he is elected president.

be spent to get a message across to compete effectively but outspending one's opponent is not always necessary—even an incumbent with a massive ratio of higher spending."[34] One case in point is that of Paul Wellstone, a previously obscure political science professor who beat an incumbent senator in 1990 despite being outspent by eight to one. Another example is the 1994 California Senate race, in which incumbent Democrat Dianne Feinstein prevailed even though she was outspent two to one by Republican challenger Michael Huffington.

The Impact of Campaigns

Almost all politicians figure that a good campaign is the key to victory. Many political scientists, however, question the importance of campaigns. Reviewing the evidence, Dan Nimmo concluded, "Political campaigns are less crucial in elections than most politicians believe."[35] For years, researchers studying campaigns have stressed that campaigns have three effects on voters: reinforcement, activation, and conversion.

Campaigns can reinforce voters' preferences for candidates; they can activate voters, getting them to contribute money or ring doorbells as opposed to merely voting; and they can convert, changing voters' minds.

Five decades of research on political campaigns lead to a single message: Campaigns mostly reinforce and activate; only rarely do they convert. The evidence on the impact of campaigns points clearly to the conclusion that the best-laid plans of campaign managers change very few votes. Given the millions of dollars spent on political campaigns, it may be surprising to find that they do not have a great effect. Several factors tend to weaken campaigns' impact on voters:

- Most people pay relatively little attention to campaigns in the first place. People have a remarkable capacity for **selective perception**—paying most attention to things they already agree with and interpreting events according to their own predispositions.
- Factors such as party identification—though less important than they used to be—still influence voting behavior regardless of what happens in the campaign.
- Incumbents start with a substantial advantage in terms of name recognition and an established track record.

selective perception

The phenomenon that people often pay the most attention to things they already agree with and interpret them according to their own predispositions.

Such findings do not mean, of course, that campaigns never change voters' minds or that converting a small percentage is unimportant. In tight races, a good campaign can make the difference between winning and losing.

Understanding Nominations and Campaigns

Throughout the history of American politics, election campaigns have become longer and longer as the system has become increasingly open to public participation. Reformers in the nineteenth and twentieth centuries held that the solution to democratic problems was more democracy—or as John Lennon sang, "Power to the people." In principle, more democracy always sounds better than less, but it is not such a simple issue in practice.

Are Nominations and Campaigns Too Democratic?

If American campaigns are judged solely by how open they are, then certainly the American system must be viewed favorably. In other countries, the process of leadership nomination occurs within a relatively small circle of party elites. Thus, politicians must work their way up through an apprenticeship system. In contrast, America has an entrepreneurial system in which the people play a crucial role at every stage from nomination to election. In this way, party outsiders can get elected in a way virtually unknown outside the United States. By appealing directly to the people, a candidate can emerge from obscurity to win the White House. For example, former one-term Governor Jimmy Carter was scarcely known outside of his home state a year before his election to the presidency. After serving a number of terms as governor of Arkansas, Bill Clinton was only in a slightly better position than Carter in terms of name recognition when he announced his first campaign for the presidency in 1991. In this sense, the chance to win high office is open to almost any highly skilled politician with even a small electoral base.

There is a price to be paid for all this openness, however. The process of selecting American leaders is a long and convoluted one that has little downtime before it revs up all over again. George W. Bush had scarcely been elected when potential candidates for 2004 started to schedule visits to Iowa and New Hampshire again. Some analysts have even called the American electoral process "the permanent campaign."[36] Many wonder whether people would pay more attention to politics if it did not ask so much of them. Given so much democratic opportunity, many citizens are simply overwhelmed

The American political system allows citizens a voice at almost every point of the election process, unlike many countries where a political elite controls the nomination process. Bill Clinton, for example, was little known outside the state of Arkansas at the beginning of the 1992 calendar year.

by the process and stay on the sidelines. Similarly, the burdens of the modern campaign can discourage good candidates from throwing their hats into the ring. One of the most worrisome burdens that candidates face is amassing a sufficient campaign treasury. The system may be open, but it requires a lot of fund-raising to be able to take one's case to the people.

Today's campaigns clearly promote individualism in American politics. The current system of running for office has been labeled by Wattenberg the "candidate-centered age."[37] It allows for politicians to decide on their own to run, to raise their own campaign funds, to build their own personal organizations, and to make promises about how they specifically will act in office. The American campaign game is one of individual candidates, by individual candidates, and for individual candidates.

Do Big Campaigns Lead to an Increased Scope of Government?

Today's big campaigns involve much more communication between candidates and voters than America's founders ever could have imagined. In their view, the presidency was to be an office responsible for seeing to the public interest as a whole. They wished to avoid "a contest in which the candidates would have to pose as 'friends' of the people or make specific policy commitments."[38] Thus, the founders would probably be horrified by the modern practice in which candidates make numerous promises during nomination and election campaigns.

States are the key battlegrounds of presidential campaigns, and candidates must tailor their appeals to the particular interests of each major state. When in Iowa, for instance, candidates typically promise to keep agricultural subsidies high; in New York, to help big cities with federal programs; in Texas, to help the oil and gas industry. To secure votes from each region of the country, candidates end up supporting a variety of local interests. Promises mount as the campaign goes on, and these promises usually add up to new government programs and money. The way modern campaigns are conducted is thus one of many reasons why politicians usually find it easier to promise, at least, that government will do more. Furthermore, with their finger constantly to the wind assessing all the different political crosscurrents, it is hard for politicians to promise that the scope of government will be limited through specific cuts.

Summary

In this age of high-tech politics, campaigns have become more media oriented and far more expensive. There are really two campaigns of importance in presidential (and other) contests: the campaign for nomination and the campaign for election.

There are two ways by which delegates are selected to the national party conventions: state caucuses and primaries. The first caucus is traditionally held in Iowa, the first primary in New Hampshire. These two small, atypical American states have disproportionate power in determining who will be nominated and thus become president. This influence stems from the massive media attention devoted to these early contests and the momentum generated by winning them.

Career Profile

Position: Associate Director of Advance, Gore 2000
Employer: Gore 2000, the presidential campaign of Vice President Al Gore
Starting Salary: $30,000 for work from June to November, 2000
Benefits: complete health and dental insurance
Qualifications: College graduate with knowledge of politics, excellent organizational skills, ability to work 14 hour days, seven days a week with no time off for five to six months straight

Real People on the Job: David Slade

David Slade had one of the few paid positions on the Gore 2000 campaign. As associate director of Advance, it was his job to ensure that every visit that Gore made during the campaign was well planned and well received by the public. David coordinated all logistical arrangements for the Gore campaign. Five days before Gore would visit a spot on the campaign trail, David would send his staffers to that location where they would work on crowd building, rally creation, signage, and logistics for the entire visit. If there were any problems with rental cars, hotel accommodations, or motorcade routes, it was David's responsibility to fix them.

Another important part of David's job was to make sure that local and national media covered each of Gore's campaign stops. The goal of his Advance department was to get two minutes of positive campaign coverage for Gore on each major network's nightly news broadcast and to be covered favorably in the newspapers.

Gore 2000, like most national campaigns, was staffed by college students and recent college graduates who had not yet settled into careers or family life and could still work the long, demanding hours required on a presidential campaign. David's work carried him all over the country and introduced him to many interesting people. Despite Gore's controversial loss, he said he felt very fortunate to be part of the campaign and part of history.

If you want to be a part of a campaign staff in the next election, you should contact the campaign directly. All major candidates will have their own websites. You can also get information about the campaign from your state or national political party offices. Call the campaign and volunteer your services as an intern (David got his start in politics as a White House intern). Once you are on the campaign, if you have the right qualifications and prove yourself to be a competent, hard worker, you may be asked to stay on in a paid position. If your candidate wins, you may even be offered a job in his or her administration.

Money matters in political campaigns. As the costs of campaigning have increased, it has become all the more essential to amass large campaign war chests. Although federal campaign finance reform in the 1970s lessened the impact of big contributors, it also allowed the proliferation of PACs. Some observers believe that PACs have created a system of legal graft in campaigning; others say that the evidence for this view is relatively weak.

In general, politicians tend to overestimate the impact of campaigns; political scientists have found that campaigning serves primarily to reinforce citizens' views rather than to convert them. American election campaigns are easily the most open and democratic in the world—some say too open. They are also extraordinarily long, leading politicians to make many promises that contribute to big government.

Key Terms

nomination
campaign strategy
national party convention
caucus
presidential primaries
McGovern-Fraser Commission
superdelegates
frontloading
national primary
regional primaries
party platform
direct mail
Federal Election Campaign Act
Federal Election Commission (FEC)
soft money
political action committees (PACs)
selective perception

For Further Reading

Bartels, Larry M. *Presidential Primaries and the Dynamics of Public Choice.* Princeton, NJ: Princeton University Press, 1988. An excellent analysis of voters' decision-making process in the nominating season.

Brown, Clifford W. Jr., Lynda W. Powell, and Clyde Wilcox. *Serious Money: Fundraising and Contributing in Presidential Nomination Campaigns.* New York: Cambridge University Press, 1995. A unique look into who contributes to presidential campaigns and why.

Fenno, Richard F. *The Presidential Odyssey of John Glenn.* Washington, D.C.: Congressional Quarterly Press, 1990. A marvelous case study of a failed presidential campaign.

King, Anthony. *Running Scared.* New York: Free Press, 1997. King argues that American politicians campaign too much and govern too little.

Mayer, William G., ed. *In Pursuit of the White House 2000: How We Choose Our Presidential Nominees.* Chatham, NJ: Chatham House, 2000. A good set of current readings on the presidential nomination process.

Orren, Gary R., and Nelson W. Polsby, eds. *Media and Momentum.* Chatham, NJ: Chatham House, 1987. The story of the exaggerated impact of New Hampshire on our presidential selection process.

Patterson, Thomas E. *Out of Order.* New York: Knopf, 1993. A good review of the role of the media in elections.

Shafer, Byron E. *Bifurcated Politics: Evolution and Reform in the National Party Convention.* Cambridge, MA: Harvard University Press, 1988. The story of how conventions have been transformed from important decision-making bodies to TV sideshows.

Sorauf, Frank J. *Inside Campaign Finance: Myths and Realities.* New Haven, CT: Yale University Press, 1992. A definitive work on the impact of money on elections—an impact that Sorauf thinks is often exaggerated.

The Institute of Politics, ed. *Campaign for President: The Managers Look at '96.* Hollis, NH: Hollis Publishing Co., 1997. The campaign managers for all the 1996 presidential candidates gather at Harvard to discuss their experiences in the primaries and the general election.

Winebrenner, Hugh. *The Iowa Precinct Caucuses: The Making of a Media Event,* 2nd ed. Ames: Iowa State University Press, 1998. A highly critical view of the Iowa caucuses from one of the state's leading political analysts.

Internet Resources

www.fec.gov
The Federal Election Commission's reports on campaign spending can be found at this site.

www.opensecrets.org
The Center for Responsive Politics posts a wealth of analysis about PAC contributions at its site.

www.camelect.com
Campaigns and Elections magazine posts some of its articles here.

www.klipsan.com/elecnews.htm
This site for Klipsan Election notes contains links to daily stories about elections around the country, as well as around the world.

Notes

1. Anthony King, *Running Scared* (New York: Free Press, 1997).
2. R. W. Apple, Jr., "Foley Assesses Presidential Elections and Tells Why He Wouldn't Run," the *New York Times*, November 4, 1998, A12.
3. Paul Taylor, "Is This Any Way To Pick a President?" *Washington Post National Weekly Edition*, April 13, 1987, 6.
4. The Rohde theory is explained in "Risk-Bearing and Progressive Ambition: The Case of the U.S. House of Representatives," *American Journal of Political Science* 23 (February 1979): 1–26. The Aldrich adaptation of the theory to the presidency appears in *Before the Convention* (Chicago: University of Chicago Press, 1980), chap. 2.
5. Paul R. Abramson, John H. Aldrich, and David W. Rohde, *Change and Continuity in the 1992 Elections* (Washington, D.C.: Congressional Quarterly Press, 1994), 20.
6. See Hugh Winebrenner, *The Iowa Precinct Caucuses: The Making of a Media Event* (Ames: Iowa State University Press, 1987).
7. See Byron Shafer, *Quiet Revolution: The Struggle for the Democratic Party and the Shaping of Post-Reform Politics* (New York: Russell Sage, 1983).
8. Theodore White, *America in Search of Itself: The Making of the President 1956–1980* (New York: Harper & Row, 1982), 285.
9. This tradition extends back to 1916. The early primary date was chosen then to coincide with the already existing town meetings. Town meetings were held in February prior to the thawing of the snow, which in the days of unpaved roads made traveling extremely difficult in the spring. In 1916 no one could have dreamed that by holding the state's primary so early they were creating a mass media extravaganza for New Hampshire.
10. Harold W. Stanley and Richard G. Niemi, *Vital Statistics on American Politics*, 6th ed. (Washington, D.C.: Congressional Quarterly Press, 1998), 173. The same research also showed that New Hampshire received just 3 percent of the TV coverage during the general election—a figure far more in line with its small population size.
11. Robert Farmer, quoted in Clifford W. Brown, Jr., Lynda W. Powell, and Clyde Wilcox, *Serious Money: Fundraising and Contributing in Presidential Nomination Campaigns* (New York: Cambridge University Press, 1995), 1.
12. Larry M. Bartels, *Presidential Primaries and the Dynamics of Public Choice* (Princeton, NJ: Princeton University Press, 1988), 269.
13. "Dukakis Says Campaign Damage a Surprise," the *New York Times*, January 18, 1990, A15.
14. "Clinton Says N.H. Is Unpredictable," Associated Press, February 1, 2000.
15. Paul Simon, *Winners and Losers: The 1988 Race for the Presidency—One Candidate's Perspective* (New York: Continuum, 1989), 112.
16. Bruce Babbitt, "Bruce Babbitt's View from the Wayside," *Washington Post National Weekly Edition*, February 29, 1988, 24.
17. See Martin P. Wattenberg, "When You Can't Beat Them, Join Them: Shaping the Presidential Nominating Process to the Television Age," *Polity* 21 (Spring 1989): 587–597.
18. R. W. Apple, "No Decisions, No Drama," the *New York Times*, August 1, 2000, A14.
19. Thomas E. Patterson, *The Mass Media Election* (New York: Praeger, 1980), 3.
20. Charles T. Royer, *Campaign for President: The Managers Look at '92* (Hollis, NH: Hollis Publishing Co., 1994), 77.
21. See R. Kenneth Godwin, *One Billion Dollars of Influence: The Direct Marketing of Politics* (Chatham, NJ: Chatham House, 1988).
22. Jonathan S. Krason and Daniel E. Seltz, "Buying Time: Television Advertising in the 1998 Congressional Elections." Posted on Internet at: www.brennancenter.org/programs/cmag_temp/download.html.
23. Patterson, *Mass Media Election*, 22–25. For a more recent study that shows similar results, see S. Robert Lichter and Richard E. Noyes, *Good Intentions Make Bad News*, 2nd ed. (Lanham, MD: Rowman & Littlefield, 1996).
24. David R. Runkel, ed., *Campaign for President: The Managers Look at '88* (Dover, MA: Auburn, 1989), 136.
25. Frank J. Sorauf, *Inside Campaign Finance: Myths and Realities* (New Haven, CT: Yale University Press, 1992), 229.
26. See, for example, Brooks Jackson, *Honest Graft: Big Money and the American Political Process* (New York: Knopf, 1988).
27. Quoted in Jeffrey Berry, *The Interest Group Society* (Boston: Little, Brown, 1984), 162.
28. *Ibid.*, 162–163.
29. Archibald Cox and Fred Wertheimer, "The Choice Is Clear: It's People vs. the PACs," in Peter Woll, ed., *Debating American Government*, 2nd ed. (Glenview, IL: Scott, Foresman, 1988), 125.
30. This is discussed in Berry, *The Interest Group Society*, 172.
31. Frank J. Sorauf, *Money in American Elections* (Glenview, IL: Scott, Foresman, 1988), 312.
32. Dexter Filkins, "The Only Issue Is Money," *Washington Post National Weekly Edition*, June 13, 1988, 28.
33. Gary C. Jacobson, "The Effects of Campaign Spending in Congressional Elections," *American Political Science Review* 72 (June 1978): 469. For an updated analysis of this argument, see Gary C. Jacobson, "The Effects of Campaign Spending in House Elections: New Evidence for Old Arguments," *American Journal of Political Science* 34 (May 1990): 334–362.
34. Herbert E. Alexander, *Financing Politics: Money, Elections, and Political Reform*, 4th ed. (Washington, D.C.: Congressional Quarterly Press, 1992), 96.
35. Nimmo, Dan, *The Political Persuaders* (Englewood Cliffs, NJ: Prentice-Hall, 1970), 5.
36. Sidney Blumenthal, *The Permanent Campaign* (New York: Simon & Schuster, 1982).
37. See Martin P. Wattenberg, *The Rise of Candidate-Centered Politics: Presidential Elections of the 1980s* (Cambridge, MA: Harvard University Press, 1991).
38. James W. Ceaser, *Presidential Selection: Theory and Development* (Princeton, NJ: Princeton University Press, 1979), 83.

10 Elections and Voting Behavior

Chapter Outline

One of the most memorable images of the 2000 presidential election was the regularly repeated scene of Florida election officials holding up a ballot to the light to try to determine whether a punch was present or not. When Joseph Harris, professor of political science at the University of California at Berkeley, invented the first punch-card voting system in the early 1960s it was hailed as a great technological innovation, enabling unprecedented speed in vote counting. But although also reputed to be more accurate than previous methods of voting, by 2000 the punch cards had become an antiquated technology compared to modern scantron and touch-screen methods. Embarrassed election officials were quick to admit that they had long been aware of the problems with punch-card voting systems. Such systems theoretically worked fine, as long as people followed the directions—placing the cards in the machines properly, and punching the chads through the card completely. But as we saw

in Florida in 2000, many people did not follow the instructions. With the election coming down to just hundreds of votes, the question became whether election officials could accurately and fairly ascertain the intent of voters whose ballots had not been properly punched. Should a vote be counted if one, two, or three of the four corners of the chad had been perforated? How about if only a dimple was visible on the chad, indicating that the voter had at least touched the stylus to the ballot at that point? Election officials struggled to do the best they could by holding them up to the light and examining them carefully. Some applauded the process as a valiant attempt to make sure every vote was counted, whereas others criticized them for trying to "divine the intent of the voter."

Scholars who analyze elections have a seemingly easier job—figuring out the meaning of the vote totals once they have been counted. But as Walter Lippman, one of the most astute observers of American politics, once remarked:

> *We call an election an expression of the popular will. But is it? We go into a polling booth and mark a cross on a piece of paper for one of two, or perhaps three or four names. Have we expressed our thoughts on the public policy of the United States? Presumably we have a number of thoughts on this and that with many buts and ifs and ors. Surely the cross on a piece of paper does not express them.*[1]

This chapter will discuss why it is difficult for elections to be a faithful mechanism for expressing the public's desires concerning what government should do. The fact that only about half the eligible electorate participates is one such factor. And those who do go to the polls often have to choose from candidates who obscure the issues. Even on an issue as fundamental as the scope of government, it has not always been crystal clear regarding what the candidates would do if they were elected. As you read this chapter, the crucial question to consider is: Are the people represented by elections in America?

Elections serve a critical function in American society. They *institutionalize* political activity, making it possible for most political participation to be channeled through the electoral process rather than bubbling up through demonstrations, riots, or revolutions. Elections provide *regular access to political power,* so that leaders can be replaced without being overthrown. As you will see shortly, the presidential election of 1800 was the first transition of power between parties accomplished by voters' ballots in the history of the world. One set of leaders left office and another set assumed control peacefully—all because of an election. This was possible because the election had **legitimacy** in the eyes of the American people; that is, the election was almost universally accepted as a fair and free method of selecting political leaders. Furthermore, by choosing who is to lead the country, the people—if they make their choices carefully—can also guide the policy direction of the government.

legitimacy

A characterization of elections by political scientists meaning that they are almost universally accepted as a fair and free method of selecting political leaders. When legitimacy is high, as in the United States, even the losers accept the results peacefully.

This chapter will give you a perspective on how elections function in the American system, as well as how voters generally behave—both in terms of their decisions on whether to vote and how those who do vote make their choices. The focus here is primarily on presidential elections; Chapter 12 on the Congress will examine congressional elections in detail.

How American Elections Work

The United States has three general kinds of elections: primary elections in which voters select party nominees, general elections that are contested between the nominees of the parties, and elections on specific policy questions in which voters engage in making or ratifying legislation. Primary elections were covered in the previous chapter, and general elections will be the main topic of this chapter. But before turning to this subject, we briefly examine elections that decide policy questions, because such contests are becoming increasingly important in many states.

At present, there is no constitutional provision for specific policy questions to be decided by a nationwide vote. It is certainly conceivable that this may come to pass sometime in the twenty-first century,[2] as a number of European democracies have recently started to put questions of great importance—such as joining the European Monetary Union—to a national vote. Procedures allowing the public to pass legislation directly have been in effect for quite some time in many American states. There are two methods for getting items on a state ballot. The first is via a **referendum,** whereby voters are given the chance to approve or disapprove some legislative act, bond issue, or constitutional amendment proposed by the legislature. The second method is through an **initiative petition,** which typically requires gaining signatures on a proposed law equal to 10 percent of the number of voters in the previous election.

referendum

A state-level method of direct legislation that gives voters a chance to approve or disapprove proposed legislation or a proposed constitutional amendment.

initiative petition

A process permitted in some states whereby voters may put proposed changes in the state constitution to a vote if sufficient signatures are obtained on petitions calling for such a referendum.

Initiative petitions are often portrayed as lawmaking from the ground up, with the people taking charge of the political agenda. In this way, citizens can force a decision on an issue upon which state legislatures have failed to act. Twenty-four states, mostly in the West, currently enable voters to propose and decide legislation through the route of an initiative petition. The most famous example is California's Proposition 13, which in 1978 put a limit on the rise in property taxes in California. Eighteen years and 196 propositions later, California voters passed Proposition 209, a measure intended to end affirmative action programs in the state. In 2000, many initiatives were passed around the country. Colorado legalized marijuana for medical use. Oregon voters passed a measure requiring background checks at gun shows. South Dakota prohibited the imposition of any state taxes on inheritances.

Although such initiatives require the support of a majority of voters, Daniel Smith argues that they often stem from the actions of a dedicated political entrepreneur more than anything.[3] For example, in 1998 actor and director Rob Reiner spearheaded a California initiative to raise cigarette taxes to discourage teenage smoking and in order to pay for additional educational programs for children. Reiner not only was the point-

One recent referendum that has drawn national attention is California's vote on Proposition 209, which ended affirmative action programs in the state. Here, opponents make their point of view clear.

man for the initiative in TV commercials, but also paid for much of the cost of getting the initiative on the ballot in the first place. Yet, Smith's examples of policy entrepreneurs who successfully used the initiative process all lacked public notoriety and personal wealth. These case studies of people who have spearheaded major initiative campaigns demonstrate how ordinary individuals can sometimes change the course of public policy, as you can see in "Making a Difference: Barbara Anderson and the Politics of Tax Relief in Massachusetts."

A Tale of Three Elections

Times change, and so do elections. Modern campaigns are slick, high-tech affairs. Imagine John Adams and Thomas Jefferson standing under bright TV lights, adjusting their wigs, and waiting for the "Presidential Debate of 1800" to begin. Or think of Abraham Lincoln securing the nomination and then lining up an ad agency and a professional pollster. Early twentieth-century candidates like Woodrow Wilson and Franklin Roosevelt did not have network exit polls to report their victories before the polls closed in the West; they had to wait for the returns to come in slowly. A glance at three American elections—1800, 1896, and 2000—should give you a good idea of how elections have changed over nearly two centuries.

1800: The First Electoral Transition of Power

By current standards, the 1800 election was not much of an election at all. There were no primaries, no nominating conventions, no candidate speeches, and no entourage of reporters. Both incumbent President John Adams and challenger Thomas Jefferson were nominated by their parties' elected representatives in Congress—Federalists for Adams and Democratic-Republicans for Jefferson. Once nominated, the candidates sat back and let their state and local organizations promote their cause. Communication and travel were too slow for candidates to get their message across themselves. Besides, campaigning was considered below the dignity of the presidential office.

At that time, however, newspapers were little concerned with dignity, or for that matter honesty. Most were rabidly partisan and did all they could to run down the opposition's candidate. Jefferson was regularly denounced as a bible-burning atheist, the father of mulatto children (much later shown to be probably true based on DNA

Making a Difference

Barbara Anderson and the Politics of Tax Relief in Massachusetts

Barbara Anderson first became interested in the politics of tax relief when she moved back to Massachusetts in the mid-1970s. Critics of the state's high level of taxes had labeled the state "Taxachusetts" by then, and Ms. Anderson felt the impact right away upon her return. In 1976, she began working as a volunteer for a group called Citizens for Limited Taxation (CLT) in her spare time while making a meager living as a swimming instructor at a local YMCA. After a few years as a dedicated volunteer whose primary task was to gather signatures for initiative petitions to reduce taxes, she was given a part-time job as a secretary for the organization. In the summer of 1980 the executive director of the CLT resigned and Anderson was suddenly asked to assume the leadership post of this small group. She had just been through a divorce, and needed another job to help support herself and her young son. She quite modestly described her credentials as having "a degree in water safety instructorship from the Red Cross," while at the same time arguing that as an average citizen she could be a true voice of the people.

At the time Barbara Anderson took over the reins of Citizens for Limited Taxation, the organization could claim credit for helping to place an initiative on the 1980 Massachusetts ballot to limit property taxes. This was known as Proposition 2 1/2, as it would limit taxes on property to 2 1/2 percent per year of their cash value. Few pundits thought such a tax reduction package could pass in liberal Massachusetts, but such was Anderson's task. She carefully studied the details of the proposition line by line in order to be able to answer any questions from reporters and practiced pithy soundbites they could hardly resist putting into print. As the campaign started to receive press attention, she then turned to raising money from the small business community—particularly car dealers, whose sales would be increased if the tax cuts mandated by Proposition 2 1/2 were approved. A sufficient amount of money came in for CLT to run its first TV ads ever. Anderson hired Dick Morris (who went on to fame as the guru behind President Clinton's 1996 campaign) to produce a barrage of ads. He came up with a classic known as the "Alka Seltzer spot," showing increases in taxation over the years in a series of bar graphs, and how Proposition 2 1/2 could turn reactions of "oooh" from high taxes into "ahhhs" of relief. On election day, Anderson's forces won a stunning 59 to 41 victory, which years later is still considered one of the most significant tax-cutting propositions enacted in any state.

Today, Barbara Anderson continues to make a difference serving as codirector of Citizens for Limited Taxation and Government (http://www.cltg.org), which seeks to limit the size, growth, power, and reach of government at all levels. She has been periodically involved in statewide initiative campaigns regarding taxation since 1980, and writes a regular newspaper column. After the 1998 elections, she was named to Massachusetts Governor Cellucci's Economic and Fiscal Policy Working Group.

Sources: Daniel A. Smith, *Tax Crusaders and the Politics of Direct Democracy* (New York: Routledge, 1998), chap. 5 and http://www.cltg.org.

tests), and a mad scientist. Adams, on the other hand, was said to be a monarchist "whose grand object was to destroy every man who differed from his opinions."[4]

The focus of the campaign was not on voters, but rather on the state legislatures, which had the responsibility for choosing members of the electoral college. When the dust settled, the Jeffersonians had won a slim victory in terms of electoral votes; however, they had also committed a troubling error. In the original constitutional system each elector cast two ballots, and the top vote getter was named president and the runner-up became vice president.[5] In 1796 Jefferson had become Adams' vice president by virtue of finishing second. Not wanting Adams to be his vice president, Jefferson made sure that all his electors also voted for his vice-presidential choice—Aaron Burr of New York. The problem was that when each and every one of them did so, Jefferson and Burr ended up tied for first. This meant that the Federalist-controlled House of Representatives would have to decide between the two Democratic-Republican candidates. Burr saw the chance to steal the presidency from Jefferson by cutting a deal with the Federalists, but his efforts failed. After 35 indecisive ballots in the House, the

William Jennings Bryan was the Democratic Party's standard bearer at the turn of the century. Eastern industrialists, fearing Bryan's powerful speeches and populist politics, used their financial clout to help William McKinley defeat "The Boy Orator of the Platte" (thus named after a river in his native Nebraska) in the 1896 and 1900 presidential elections.

Federalists finally threw their support to Jefferson. On March 4, 1801, the transition from Adams to Jefferson marked the first peaceful transfer of power between parties via the electoral process in history.

1896: A Bitter Fight over Economic Interests

Nearly a century later the election of 1896 was largely fought over economics. By then national nominating conventions had become well established, and Republicans, meeting in St. Louis for their convention, had a clear front-runner—former Congressman William McKinley. The Republicans' major issues were support for the gold standard and high tariffs. The gold standard linked money to this scarce precious metal so that debtors never got a break from inflation. Tariffs protected capitalists and their workers from foreign competition. After piling up a commanding majority on the first ballot at St. Louis, McKinley sat back to see what the upcoming Democratic convention would do.

The Democrats met in Chicago's sticky July heat. They had an issue—unlimited coinage of silver—but no clear front-runner. Their incumbent president, Grover Cleveland, was blamed for the 1893 depression. The high point of the Chicago convention was a speech by 36-year-old William Jennings Bryan of Nebraska, who proclaimed the virtues of the silver rather than the gold standard. Bryan went on to win the nomination on the fifth ballot and become the youngest nominee of a major party in American history.

The flamboyant Bryan broke with tradition and took to the stump in person. He gave 600 speeches as his campaign train traveled through 26 states, logging 18,000 miles. Debtors and silver miners were especially attracted to Bryan's pitch for cheap silver money. In contrast, the serene McKinley was advised to sit home in Ohio and run a front-porch campaign. He did, and managed to label the Democrats as the party of depression ("In God We Trust, With Bryan We Bust").

Bryan won the oratory, but McKinley won the election. Eastern manufacturers contributed a small fortune to the Republicans. Only white Southerners, Westerners in the silver-producing states, and rural debtors lined up behind the Democrats. The Republicans won overwhelmingly in the industrial Northeast and Midwest, and became firmly entrenched as the nation's majority party for the next several decades. McKinley triumphed by a margin of 271 to 176 in the electoral college. Nearly 80 percent of the eligible electorate voted in one of the highest turnouts ever.

2000: What a Mess!

The 2000 presidential election will no doubt go into the history books as one of the most memorable finishes in the history of democracy. The election coverage on television provided a wild night of entertainment, full of ups and downs for everyone. The networks first reported that Gore had won the crucial state of Florida while the polls were still open in the Florida panhandle (which is on Central Time), but within an hour they rescinded their call. Early in the morning, with virtually all the votes counted, they at last called Florida for Bush and declared him the president-elect. But just as Gore was ready to give his concession speech, the word broke that the networks were again rescinding their call, saying that it was so close that a recount would be necessary to determine the winner.

Because Bush's lead over Gore in the initial count was less than one-tenth of one percent, Florida law mandated an automatic recount. How common are such narrow margins? In the three other close national elections in the last four decades—1960 (Kennedy vs. Nixon), 1968 (Nixon vs. Humphrey), and 1976 (Carter vs. Ford)—only once did any state result meet this criteria for closeness. This was the tiny state of Hawaii in 1960, whose four electoral votes were never considered crucial to the outcome. Thus, few novelists would have dared imagine the scene of a nation watching transfixed as county by county recount figures came in from a state where 6 million people voted. Adding to the surrealistic atmosphere was the national firestorm over Democratic complaints about the confusing butterfly ballot used in Palm Beach County.

Ultimately, with the margin between Bush and Gore down to 537 votes, the election hinged on whether or not the undervotes (ballots that showed no vote for president) would be examined by hand or not. The Gore campaign pointed out that in counties that used punch-card systems (such as Palm Beach, Miami-Dade, and Broward), that 1.5 percent of the ballots showed no presidential vote whereas only 0.3 percent of the ballots in counties that used scantrons were recorded as blank. The reason offered for this difference was that some people do not punch holes all the way through the card, thereby not fully removing the indentation—the now-famous "chad." It just so happened that the counties that used punch cards favored Gore, so any manual recount would likely have found more additional votes for Gore than Bush. Naturally, the Bush campaign realized this and opposed any manual recount. They argued that such a review of the ballots was inherently arbitrary, and subject to manipulation and differing standards.

As with any legal dispute, this one ended up in the courts, which played a pivotal role in a presidential election for the first time ever. There was constant litigation in Florida over whether there would be hand recounts of ballots, the standards to be used in evaluating ballots, the time allowed for recounts, the acceptability of the design of the butterfly ballot, and a host of related questions. The Florida Supreme Court ultimately ruled in favor of Gore's request to have any ballots that did not register a vote for president recounted by hand. It also ordered counties to apply the vague standard of "the clear intention of the voter" in evaluating ballots, the standard established by the Florida legislature. However, the U.S. Supreme Court in *Bush v. Gore* (2000) overruled the Florida Supreme Court and held that although a recount was legal, the same (and more precise) standards for evaluating ballots would have to be applied in all counties. Most importantly, they ruled that there was not enough time to recount all the ballots in an orderly fashion by the time the electors were to vote on December 12. Thus, the U.S. Supreme Court ultimately determined that George W. Bush would emerge the winner.

For academic voting behavior specialists, Bush's election came as quite a surprise. At the annual convention of the American Political Science Association in September 2000, a set of scholars presented a variety of models to predict the election, all of which had been accurate in previous years. Although some of these scholars were Democrats and others were Republicans, they unanimously predicted a margin of victory for Gore of about 10 percent. These models used economic indicators and the public's approval of the incumbent president to project the outcome. With the economy rolling along, and with Bill Clinton's job approval rating hovering around 60 percent, it seemed like a no-brainer for them to project that the Democrats would retain the White House.

The 2000 election, however, showed that how candidates present themselves to the American people really matters. Had Gore been able to keep the focus on past performance he no doubt would have done better. Instead, at the Democratic Convention he proudly announced that he was running as his own man. Throughout the campaign, he primarily looked forward to the future with new programs and initiatives rather than discussing the last four years. When President Clinton volunteered to help out to make the case for staying the course, the Gore campaign told him to lay low.

George W. Bush sought to take advantage of concerns over presidential character raised during the Clinton Administration by repeatedly promising to "restore dignity and honor to the White House." He also gave a great deal of emphasis to the issue of the scope of government. Portraying Gore's proposals as big government, he regularly

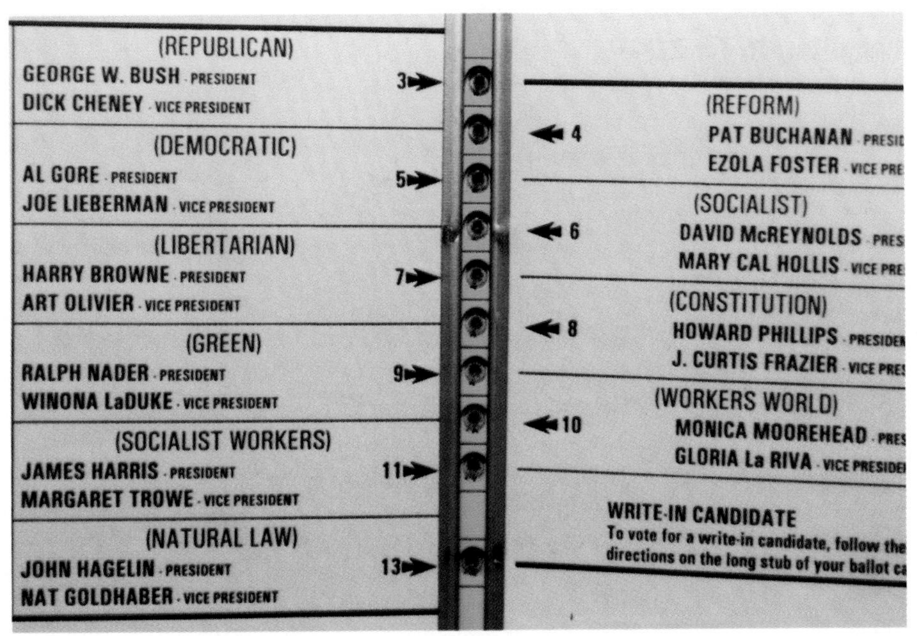

With the margin of victory in the 2000 presidential race coming down to Florida, and with the margin in Florida being razor thin, national attention was focused on the ballot format shown here from Palm Beach County. Many people argued that as a result of the confusing format that thousands of voters mistakenly voted for Buchanan rather than Gore. It was also argued that thousands of confused voters punched the holes for both Buchanan and Gore, thereby invalidating votes that were intended for Gore. These thousands of votes drew international attention when it became clear that they may have been crucial to the presidential outcome in 2000.

stated that while Vice President Gore trusted government, he trusted the people. In this first election in decades held during a time of federal budget surpluses, he argued that government was taking in more than it needs. Rather than new government spending initiatives proposed by Gore, Bush called for a big tax cut that would benefit everyone.

While Bush and Gore debated the crucial theme of the scope of government, Green Party candidate Ralph Nader raised issues neglected by the major parties. Nader argued that both parties were dominated by corporate interests and called for fundamental campaign finance reform and policies that place the protection of jobs for working Americans above the interests of big corporations. As it became clear that the race would be close, many liberal publications and political leaders tried to convince Nader to pull out of the race. Although Nader's support dropped from 5 percent in some preelection polls to about 2.7 percent on election day, it seems likely that he cost Gore the election in some states. In Florida, Nader received over 97,000 votes—or nearly 200 times the 537 vote margin between Bush and Gore.

As shown in the Electoral College results displayed in Figure 10.1, there were sharp regional divisions in the vote in 2000. Bush ran strong in the South and Mountain West, whereas Gore turned in a good showing in the Northeast and the Pacific Coast states. Although Bush won in the Electoral College by 271 to 266 (one elector from Washington, D.C. abstained in protest), Gore narrowly won the popular vote by 48.4 to 47.9 percent. This marked the first time since 1888 that the winner of the popular vote lost the decisive electoral college count. As a result, serious discussion is now being given to changing the electoral college system. Senator Hillary Clinton of New York announced soon after her election that she would seek a constitutional amendment to provide for direct election of the president. But as with past proposals to reform this aspect of our elections, it is likely that reform proposals will encounter strong opposition from senators who represent small states. Getting such a constitutional amendment ratified by the required 38 out of the 50 states will present an even steeper difficulty given that well over a dozen states receive extra power as a result of the Electoral College formula. As the framers intended, anything other than an overwhelming majority is not likely to result in any constitutional change, and given the current state of divided opinion this is not likely.

In 2000, as in all election years, voters faced two key choices: whether to vote and, if they chose to do so, how to vote. The following sections will investigate how voters make these choices.

Figure 10.1 The Electoral College Results for 2000

The following map shows the number of delegates each state has in the electoral college and which states were carried by Al Gore (green) and George W. Bush (rose) in 2000.

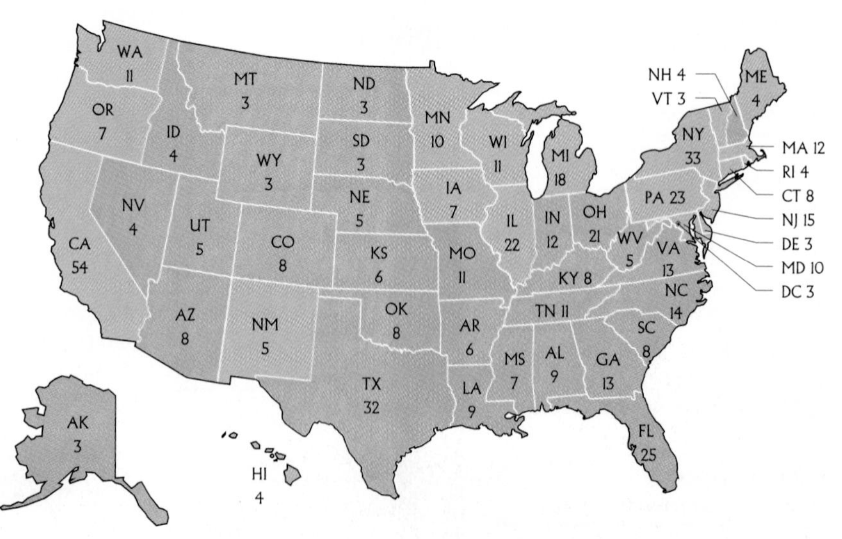

Whether to Vote: A Citizen's First Choice

Over two centuries of American electoral history include greatly expanded **suffrage**—the right to vote. In the election of 1800, only property-owning white males over the age of 21 were typically allowed to vote. Now virtually everyone over the age of 18—male or female, White or non-White, rich or poor—has the right to vote. (For these developments, particularly as they affect women and minorities, see Chapter 5.) The two major exceptions concern noncitizens and convicted criminals. There is no federal requirement stating that voters must be citizens, and indeed it was quite common in the nineteenth century for immigrants to vote prior to attaining citizenship. However, no state currently permits residents who are not citizens to vote. In contrast, state law varies widely when it comes to crime and voting: 46 states deny prisoners the right to vote, 32 states extend the ban to people on parole, and 10 states impose a lifetime ban on convicted felons.

suffrage

The legal right to vote, extended to African Americans by the **Fifteenth Amendment**, to women by the **Nineteenth Amendment**, and to people over the age of 18 by the **Twenty-sixth Amendment.**

Interestingly, as the right to vote has been extended, proportionately fewer of those eligible have chosen to exercise that right. In the past 100 years, the 80 percent turnout in the 1896 election was the high point of electoral participation. In 2000, only 51 percent of the adult population voted in the presidential election, and in the 1998 congressional elections only 33 percent took part (see Figure 10.2).

Deciding Whether To Vote

Realistically, when over 100 million people vote in a presidential election, as they did in 2000, the chance of one vote affecting the outcome is very, very slight. Once in a while, of course, an election is decided by a small number of votes, as occurred in Florida in 2000. It is more likely, however, that you will be struck by lightning during your lifetime than participate in an election decided by a single vote.

Not only does your vote probably not make much difference to the outcome, but voting is somewhat costly. You have to spend some of your valuable time becoming

Figure 10.2 The Decline of Turnout: 1892–2000

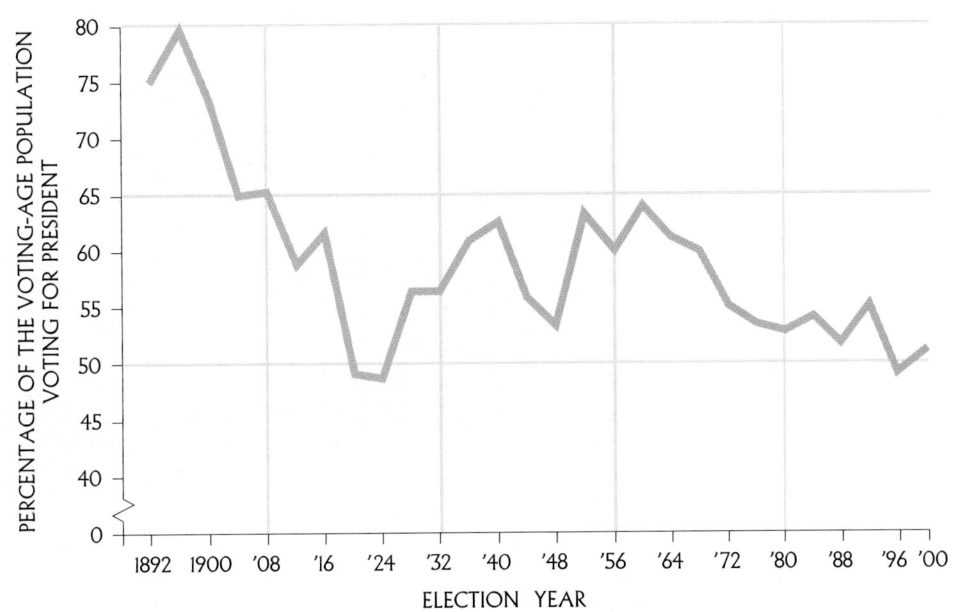

Sources: For data up to 1968, Historical Statistics of the United States (Washington, D.C.: Government Printing Office, 1975), part 2, 1071. For 1972–1988, *Statistical Abstract of the United States,* 1990 (Washington, D.C.: Government Printing Office, 1990), 264. Subsequent years from Census reports and authors' calculations.

informed, making up your mind, and getting to the polls. If you carefully calculate your time and energy, you might rationally decide that the costs of voting outweigh the benefits. Indeed, the most frequent response given by nonvoters in the 1996 Census Bureau survey on turnout was that they could not take time off from work or school that day.[6] Some scholars have therefore proposed that one of the easiest ways to increase American turnout levels would be to move election day to Saturday or make it a holiday.[7]

Economist Anthony Downs, in his model of democracy, tries to explain why a rational person would ever bother to vote. He argues that rational people vote if they believe that the policies of one party will bring more benefits than the policies of the other party.[8] Thus people who see policy differences between the parties are more likely to join the ranks of voters. If you are an environmentalist and you expect the Democrats to pass more environmental legislation than the Republicans, then you have an additional incentive to go to the polls. On the other hand, if you are truly indifferent—that is, if you see no difference whatsoever between the two parties—you may rationally decide to abstain.

political efficacy

The belief that one's **political participation** really matters—that one's vote can actually make a difference.

civic duty

The belief that in order to support democratic government, a citizen should always vote.

Another reason why many people vote is that they have a high sense of **political efficacy**—the belief that ordinary people can influence the government. Efficacy is measured by asking people to agree or disagree with statements such as "I don't think public officials care much what people like me think." Those who lack strong feelings of efficacy are being quite rational in staying home on election day because they don't think they can make a difference. Yet even some of these people will vote anyway, simply to support democratic government. In this case, people are impelled to vote by a sense of civic duty. The benefit from doing one's **civic duty** is the long-term contribution made toward preserving democracy.

Young people have one of the lowest rates of election turnout. Groups such as Rock the Vote have tried to change this by enlisting rock stars and other celebrities to try to convince people of the importance of voting. Here, Rosie O'Donnell appears on behalf of Rock the Vote in 2000.

Registering To Vote

A century ago politicians used to say, "Vote early and often." Cases such as West Virginia's 159,000 votes being cast by 147,000 eligible voters in 1888 were not that unusual. Largely to prevent corruption associated with stuffing ballot boxes, states adopted **voter registration** laws around the turn of the century, which require individuals to first place their name on an electoral roll in order to be allowed to vote. Although these laws have made it more difficult to vote more than once, they have also discouraged some people from voting at all. America's unique registration system is, in part, to blame for why Americans are significantly less likely to go to the polls than citizens of other democratic nations (see "America in Perspective: Why Turnout in the United States Is So Low Compared to Other Countries").

voter registration

A system adopted by the states that requires voters to register well in advance of election day. A few states permit election day registration.

Registration procedures currently differ from state to state. In sparsely populated North Dakota there is no registration at all, and in Minnesota, Wisconsin, Wyoming, Idaho, New Hampshire, and Maine voters can register on election day. It is probably no coincidence that these states all ranked near the top in voter turnout in 2000 (see Table 10.1). Prior to 1996, some states—particularly in the South—had burdensome

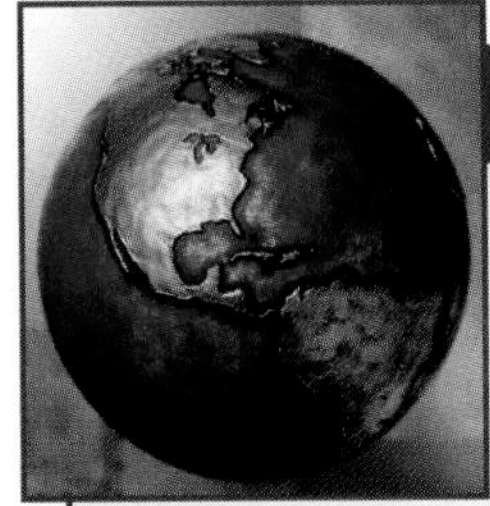

America in Perspective

Why Turnout in the United States Is So Low Compared to Other Countries

Despite living in a culture that encourages participation, Americans have a woefully low turnout rate compared to other democracies. Here are some figures on voting rates in the United States and other industrial nations:

Italy, 1996	87
Denmark, 1998	83
Belgium, 1999	83
Greece, 2000	82
Australia, 1998	82
Spain, 1996	81
Finland, 2000	79
Sweden, 1998	78
Brazil, 1998	77
Norway, 1997	77
New Zealand, 1999	76
Germany, 1998	75
Austria, 1999	73
France, 1995	72
United Kingdom, 1997	69
Russia, 1996	68
Ireland, 1997	67
Israel, 2001	62
Japan, 2000	62
Mexico, 2000	60
India, 1999	60
Canada, 2000	53
United States, 2000	**51**
Switzerland, 1999	35
United States, 1998	**33**

There are several reasons given for Americans' abysmally low turnout rate. Probably the reason most often cited is the unique American requirement of voter registration. The governments of other democracies take the responsibility of seeing to it that all their eligible citizens are on the voting lists. In America, the responsibility for registration lies solely with the individual.

A second difference between the United States and other countries is that the American government asks citizens to vote far more often. Whereas the typical European voter may be called upon to cast two or three ballots in a four-year period, many Americans are faced with a dozen or more separate elections in the space of four years. Furthermore, Americans are expected to vote for a much wider range of political offices. With 1 elected official for every 442 citizens and elections held somewhere virtually every week, it is no wonder that it is so difficult to get Americans to the polls. It is probably no coincidence that the one European country that has a comparable turnout rate—Switzerland—has also overwhelmed its citizens with voting opportunities, typically asking people to vote three times every year.

Finally, the stimulus to vote is low in the United States because the choices offered Americans are not as stark as in other countries. This is because the United States stands virtually alone in the democratic world in lacking a major left-wing socialist party. When European voters go to the polls, they are deciding on whether their country will be run by parties with socialist goals or by conservative (and in some cases religious) parties. The consequences of their vote for redistribution of income and the scope of government are far greater than the ordinary American voter can imagine.

Source: http://www.idea.int/voter_turnout/index.html. Turnout rates for all countries are calculated based on the percentage of the voting-age population casting ballots.

Table 10.1 Turnout in 2000: State by State (in percents)

State	%	State	%
Minnesota	69	Illinois	53
Maine	67	Utah	53
Alaska	66	Virginia	52
Wisconsin	66	Kentucky	52
Vermont	64	Maryland	52
New Hampshire	62	New Jersey	51
Montana	62	Florida	51
Wyoming	61	North Carolina	50
Iowa	61	Alabama	50
Oregon	61	Indiana	49
North Dakota	60	New York	49
Connecticut	58	Tennessee	49
South Dakota	58	District of Columbia	49
Michigan	57	Oklahoma	49
Washington	57	Mississippi	49
Massachusetts	57	Arkansas	48
Colorado	57	New Mexico	47
Nebraska	56	South Carolina	47
Delaware	56	West Virginia	46
Ohio	56	California	44
Louisiana	55	Georgia	44
Idaho	54	Nevada	44
Rhode Island	54	Texas	43
Kansas	54	Arizona	42
Pennsylvania	54	Hawaii	40

Source: Calculated by the authors on the basis of election results and U.S. Census estimates of the voting-age population in each state.

Motor Voter Act

Passed in 1993, this Act went into effect for the 1996 election. It requires states to permit people to register to vote at the same time they apply for their driver's license.

registration procedures, such as requiring people to make a trip to their county courthouse during normal business hours. As a result of the 1993 **Motor Voter Act,** this is no longer the case. The Motor Voter Act made voter registration easier by requiring states to allow eligible voters to register by simply checking a box on their driver's license application or renewal form. Nevertheless, its impact on turnout has thus far been disappointing. The percentage of the population that was registered increased, but turnout in 1996 and 2000 was still significantly lower than in 1992.

Ruy Teixeira notes that turnout has steadily declined in the United States since 1960, even though registration procedures have actually been made easier. Thus, in recent decades, those who have been registered have shown less propensity to actually vote. Teixeira traces the drop in turnout to a decline in Americans' social and political connectedness. A younger, single, and less church-going electorate has resulted in voters who are less socially tied to their political communities. Furthermore, political withdrawal has resulted from declines in partisanship, political interest, and the belief that government is responsive, according to Teixeira's research.[9]

Who Votes?

When just over half the population votes, the necessity of studying nonvoters takes on added importance. Table 10.2 displays data regarding the turnout rates of various groups in the 2000 presidential election. This information reveals numerous demographic factors that are related to turnout:

- *Education.* People with higher than average educational levels have a higher rate of voting than people with less education. Among all factors affecting turnout, this one is

How You Can Make a Difference

Voter Registration and Voting

The close presidential election of 2000 was notable not only for the post-election struggle in Florida but also for efforts to bring new voters to the polls—especially African-American citizens. The NAACP, through its National Voter Fund, spent over $10 million to register and bring people to the polls. Though the money is necessary in some efforts, the individual volunteers and staffers must always perform the hard work. This is where you can make a difference.

How can you improve voter turnout? Start by initiating a voter registration drive on campus and throughout your community. While the impetus to register is highest around presidential elections, organizing voters for local elections usually has a far greater impact on politics than in presidential elections. Working through existing political organizations (Democratic, Republican, Green, Reform, League of Women Voters) both on campus and in the community can help you overcome potential financial and administrative difficulties. You should remain nonpartisan in this effort and clearly post a sign that your voter registration service is available to all voters without reference to their political preferences. Do not campaign for a particular candidate or tell a person how they should vote while taking part in a registration campaign. You must also take care to educate newly registered voters in the correct voting procedure to avoid the problems faced by confused voters in Florida during the 2000 election.

Finally, of course, you need to remind people to actually vote. Getting people registered is only half the battle. You may need to provide transportation if necessary or try to ensure convenient polling places on campus. You can also distribute straightforward, nonpartisan voting guides (League of Women Voters) on candidates and their stances on issues. At some colleges, many of your friends may already be registered in their hometowns and do not want to switch their place of residence for a variety of reasons. This should not hinder your efforts. Instead, your turnout drive should also include an educational component that continually reminds students to request absentee ballots. Using all of these strategies along with e-mail, bulletin boards, and campus newspapers, you can boost voter participation at little or no cost.

Table 10.2 Reported Turnout Rate in 2000 by Social Groups (in percents)

Group	Percent
18–20	29
21–24	35
25–44	50
45–64	65
65 and over	68
No HS Diploma	31
High School	49
Some College	60
College	72
White	56
African American	44
Hispanic citizens	45
Asian American	43
Men	53
Women	56
Married	61
Single	45
Union member	65
Not union member	53

Source: Authors' analysis of 1998 U.S. Census Bureau survey through FERRETT (http://ferrett.bls.census.gov/)

the most important. Highly educated people are more capable of discerning the major differences between the candidates. In addition, their educational training comes in handy in clearing the bureaucratic hurdles imposed by registration requirements.

- *Age.* Older people are far more likely to vote than younger people. In 1998, the Census Bureau found that only 14 percent of people between 18 and 20 voted, as opposed to 60 percent among those over 65 years of age.
- *Race.* African Americans and Hispanics are underrepresented among voters relative to their share of the population. This finding can largely be explained by their generally low levels of education. African Americans and Hispanics with high levels of education have a higher turnout rate than Whites with comparable educational achievement.
- *Gender.* In an earlier period many women were discouraged from voting, but today women actually participate in elections at a slightly higher rate than men.
- *Marital status.* People who are married are more likely to vote than those who are not. This pattern is true among all age categories and generally reflects the fact that married people are more tied into their community.
- *Mobility.* People who have lived at the same address for a while also are more tied into their community, and hence more likely to vote. Those who have moved recently have to deal with the task of registering to vote at their new address, which, although easier due to the Motor Voter Act, still requires some effort.
- *Union membership.* Unions have long been active in the political process and often devote considerable resources to encouraging their members to vote. People who live in a household with a union member do indeed have higher than average turnout levels.

These differences in turnout rates are cumulative. Possessing several of these traits (say, being elderly, well educated, and married) adds significantly to one's likelihood of voting. Conversely, being young, poorly educated, and single is likely to add up to a very low probability of voting. If you possess many of the demographic traits of nonvoters, then the interests of people like you are probably not drawing a great deal of attention from politicians—regardless of whether you personally vote or not. Politicians listen far more carefully to groups with high turnout rates, as they know their fate may well be in their hands. Who votes does matter.

visual literacy
Voter Turnout: Who Votes? Do Americans Vote as Much as Other Citizens?

The Political Consequences of Turnout Bias

Scholars have long debated whether who votes influences election outcomes, and whether low turnout rates benefit the Republicans or the Democrats. The consensus seems to be that election outcomes are not likely to be affected unless they are very close. No doubt the presidential election of 2000 was one of these cases.

In all the congressional elections between 1994 and 2000 the struggle for control of the House of Representatives was decided by the outcome of roughly a dozen close races. Thus, a slight shift to the Democrats could have easily kept the Republicans from winning the majority of the 435 House seats. After the historic GOP takeover of the Congress in 1994 led by Newt Gingrich, a popular bumper sticker in Democratic areas read "Newt happens when only 37 percent of Americans vote." Besides expressing the popularly held perception that turnout matters, this slogan poses an important research question: Would Gingrich and the Republicans have won the majority of House seats if turnout had been greater?

A simple way to address this question is to assess the difference it would have made if voters had mirrored the adult population in terms of education, which, as noted, is the best demographic predictor of turnout. Martin Wattenberg's analysis of national survey data found that 30 percent of 1994 voters who lacked a high school diploma voted for GOP House candidates compared with 62 percent of voters with college degrees. Therefore, just increasing the turnout rate of the least educated citizens would

Why does it matter?

Voter turnout rates in the United States have been declining for quite some time. The very low participation rate of young people has been one of the biggest reasons for this decline. What difference would it make if more young people voted? Can you think of any ways to interest more young people in voting?

You mean, like, wow, we can actually get rid of, you know, incumbents with this whatchamacallit?"

surely have made some difference. Overall, Wattenberg calculates that if turnout rates had been equal among all education categories the Republican share of the vote would have fallen from 52.0 to 49.2 percent. Applying this loss uniformly to all districts yielded an estimate of only 206 seats won by the Republicans, which is 24 less than they actually won and 12 short of a majority. Thus, Wattenberg concludes that Newt Gingrich probably would not have become Speaker of the House if turnout had been equal among all educational groups in 1994.[10]

Such findings may well decrease the chances that anything will be done to increase turnout rates in America. Few Republicans want to correct a situation that has benefited them in the past. Nevertheless, one clear possibility for the twenty-first century is to conduct elections through e-mail (see "You Are the Policymaker: Registering and Voting by E-mail?"). In the meantime, it is likely that American presidential elections will continue to be decided by only about half of the eligible voters. The following sections will discuss how those who do make it to the polls make their decisions.

How Americans Vote: Explaining Citizens' Decisions

A common explanation of how Americans vote—one favored by journalists and politicians—is that people vote because they agree more with the policy views of Candidate A than with those of Candidate B. Of course, the candidates have invested a lot of time and money to get those views implanted in the public mind. Because citizens vote for the candidate whose policy promises they favor, many journalists and politicians say that the election winner has a mandate from the people to carry out the promised policies. This idea is sometimes called the **mandate theory of elections.**

mandate theory of elections

The idea that the winning candidate has a mandate from the people to carry out his or her platforms and politics. Politicians like the theory better than political scientists do.

You Are the Policymaker

Registering and Voting by E-Mail?

Although modern technology is widely available, Americans have not harnessed much of it to improve democracy. Though many precincts now use computer punch cards to record votes, the high-tech age has not yet made much of an impact on the voting process. There is good reason to expect that this will change in the twenty-first century.

The development of the personal computer and the World Wide Web is likely to facilitate the process of voter registration. Already, one can go to the website of the Federal Election Commission (http://www.fec.gov/votregis/vr.htm) and download the "National Mail Voter Registration Form." Twenty-two states currently accept copies of this application printed from the computer image, signed by the applicant, and mailed in the old-fashioned way. As e-mail becomes ever more popular and "snail mail" fades into a method reserved for packages, the entire voter registration process may someday be conducted mostly through electronic means. In an age where personal computers in the home will be as common as television sets are today, this technology would clearly make registering to vote more user-friendly.

If people can register by computer, the next step is naturally voting by e-mail. A growing trend in the Pacific Coast states has been voting by mail. In 1998, Oregon voters approved a referendum to eliminate traditional polling places and conduct all future elections by mail. In California, approximately 25 percent of the votes cast currently come in via the post office. Again, as e-mail takes the place of regular mail, why not have people cast their votes through cyberspace? In the Arizona Democratic presidential primary in 2000, PC (but not Mac) users had a chance to vote through the Internet and 45 percent of all votes cast came in via this means (though many voters reported problems in getting through to the website).

Voting through the Internet would be less costly for the state, as well as easier for the average citizen—assuming that computer literacy reaches near-universal proportions sometime in the future. The major concerns, of course, would be ensuring that no one votes more than once and preserving the confidentiality of the vote. These security concerns are currently being addressed by some of the world's top computer programmers, as commercial enterprises look toward using the Internet to conduct business. If the technology can be perfected to allow trillions of dollars of business to be conducted via the Internet, then it seems reasonable that similar problems can be overcome with regard to the voting process.

Whether these possible developments will improve democracy in America is debatable. Making voting more user-friendly should encourage turnout, but people will still have to be interested enough in the elections of the future to send in their e-mail ballots. If old-style polling places are relegated to the history books and everyone votes electronically in the convenience of their own homes, the sense of community on election day may be lost. This loss could lead to even lower turnout. You be the policymaker: Do the benefits of voting by e-mail outweigh the potential costs?

Politicians, of course, are attracted to the mandate theory. It lets them justify what they want to do by claiming public support for their policies. As President Clinton said during the final presidential debate in 1992: "That's why I am trying to be so specific in this campaign—to have a mandate, if elected, so the Congress will know what the American people have voted for."

Political scientists, however, think little of the mandate theory of elections.[11] Whereas victorious politicians are eager to proclaim "the people have spoken," political scientists know that the people rarely vote a certain way for the same reasons. Instead, political scientists focus on three major elements of voters' decisions: (1) voters' party identification; (2) voters' evaluation of the candidates; and (3) the match between voters' policy positions and those of the candidates and parties—a factor termed "policy voting."

Party Identification

Party identifications are crucial for many voters because they provide a regular perspective through which voters can view the political world. "Presumably," say Niemi and Weisberg, "people choose to identify with a party with which they generally agree. . . . As

Table 10.3 Changing Patterns in Voting Behavior: 1960 and 2000 Compared

Some of the demographic characteristics that most distinguished Kennedy voters from Nixon voters in 1960 are of far less relevance to voting behavior now. In particular, the divide between Protestants and Catholics has dwindled dramatically, and union membership is slightly less associated with voting Democratic than it once was. On the other hand, race and income were more closely related to voting behavior in 2000 than in 1960. Gore clearly drew more support from African Americans and lower-income voters than did Kennedy. Another major advantage that Democrats now enjoy is with female voters, who preferred Gore by 10 percent more than men. Interestingly, women were actually slightly less likely than men to have supported the handsome JFK in 1960.

	KENNEDY	NIXON	GORE	BUSH	NADER
Protestant	36	63	47	50	2
Catholic	83	17	48	49	2
Jewish	89	11	90	10	0
White	48	52	44	53	3
African American	71	29	89	8	2
Hispanic	NA	NA	57	34	9
Male	52	48	44	51	4
Female	47	53	54	42	3
18–34	52	48	50	43	6
35–64	50	49	49	48	2
65+	39	60	52	46	1
Lowest income third	45	54	63	34	2
Middle income third	55	45	48	47	4
Upper income third	48	52	46	50	4
Union	63	37	58	36	6
Not union member	44	56	48	48	3

Source: 1960 and 2000 National Election Surveys.
Note: The 2000 survey slightly overrepresents Gore voters, giving him a margin in the national popular vote of 3.7%, as compared to the actual margin of 0.5%.

a result they need not concern themselves with every issue that comes along, but can generally rely on their party identification to guide them."[12] Parties tend to rely on groups that lean heavily in their favor to form their basic coalition. Even before an election campaign begins, Republicans usually assume they will not receive much support from African Americans, Jews, and Hispanic Americans. Democrats have an uphill struggle attracting groups that are staunchly Republican in their leanings, such as conservative evangelical Christians or upper-income voters. As you can see in Table 10.3, there have been substantial changes in how various groups have voted for president since 1960.

With the emergence of television and candidate-centered politics, the parties' hold on voters eroded substantially during the 1960s and 1970s, and then stabilized at a new and lower level.[13] In the 1950s, scholars singled out party affiliation as the best single predictor of a voter's decision. It was said that many Southern Democrats would vote for a yellow dog if their party nominated one. "My party—right or wrong" was the motto that typified strong party identifiers. Voting along party lines is less common, particularly in elections for the House of Representatives, where incumbency is now paramount (see Chapter 12). Many voters now feel that they no longer need the parties to guide their choices, given that modern technology makes it possible for them to evaluate and make their own decisions about the candidates. Thus, American voters have become increasingly individualistic. Voting choices have become largely a matter of individual choice, and many voters are up for grabs in each election (the so-called "floating voters"). In such an individualistic political environment, the characteristics of each candidate for office play an important role.

Candidate Evaluations: How Americans See the Candidates

All candidates try to present a favorable personal image. Using laboratory experiments, political psychologists Shawn Rosenberg and Patrick McCafferty showed that it is possible to manipulate a candidate's appearance in a way that affects voters' choices. Holding a candidate's policy views and party identification constant, they found that when good pictures are substituted for bad ones, a candidate's vote-getting ability is significantly increased. Although a laboratory setting may not be representative of the real world, Rosenberg and McCafferty conclude that "with appropriate pretesting and adequate control over a candidate's public appearance, a campaign consultant should be able to significantly manipulate the image projected to the voting public."[14]

To do so, a consultant would need to know what sort of candidate images voters are most attuned to. Research by Miller, Wattenberg, and Malanchuk shows that the three most important dimensions of candidate image are integrity, reliability, and competence.[15] In 1976, Jimmy Carter told Americans, "I will never lie to you." Even going down to defeat in 1980, Carter was still seen as a man with great integrity. Therefore, it obviously takes more than honesty to win. A candidate must also be seen as dependable and decisive—traits that Miller, Wattenberg, and Malanchuk label as "reliability." When George Bush broke his "no new taxes" pledge prior to the 1992 campaign, his image of reliability clearly suffered. The personal traits most often mentioned by voters, though, involve competence. In 1988, Michael Dukakis proudly proclaimed that the major election issue was not ideology but competence. Ironically, the majority of voters were more impressed with Bush's wide experience in office than with Dukakis's lawyer-like precision.

Such evaluations of candidate personality are sometimes seen as superficial and irrational judgments. Miller and his colleagues disagree with this interpretation, arguing that voters rely on their assessments of candidates' personalities to predict how they would perform in office. If a candidate is too incompetent to carry out policy promises, or too dishonest for those promises to be trusted, it makes perfect sense for a voter to pay more attention to personality than policies. Interestingly, Miller and his colleagues find that college-educated voters are actually the most likely to view the candidates in terms of their personal attributes. They argue that better educated voters are able to make important issue-oriented inferences from these attributes (for example, that a candidate who is unreliable may not be the right person to be the commander in chief of the armed forces).

Policy Voting

policy voting

Electoral choices that are made on the basis of the voters' policy preferences and on the basis of where the candidates stand on policy issues.

Policy voting occurs when people base their choices in an election on their own issue preferences. True policy voting can only take place when four conditions are met. First, voters must have a clear view of their own policy positions. Second, voters must know where the candidates stand on policy issues. Third, they must see differences between the candidates on these issues. And finally, they must actually cast a vote for the candidate whose policy positions coincide with their own.

Given these conditions, policy voting is not always easy—even for the educated voter. Abramson, Aldrich, and Rohde analyzed responses to nine questions about policy issues in the 1996 National Election Study. They found that 65 percent of the respondents met the first three informational criteria for policy voting on the average issue. About 70 percent of the time, when someone knew the candidates' stances and saw differences between them, they voted for the candidate closest to their own position.[16] Of course, we should never expect all votes to be consistent with policy views, as many people will prefer one candidate on some policies and another candidate on other policies.

One regular obstacle to policy voting is that candidates often decide that the best way to handle a controversial issue is to cloud their positions in rhetoric. For example, in 1968 both major party candidates—Nixon and Humphrey—were deliberately ambiguous about what they would do to end the Vietnam War. This made it extremely difficult for voters to cast their ballots according to how they felt about the war. The media may not be much help, either, as they typically focus more on the "horse race" aspects of the campaign than on the policy stands of the candidates, as discussed in Chapter 7. Voters thus often have to work fairly hard just to be well informed enough to potentially engage in policy voting.

simulation
You Are a Presidential Campaign Consultant

In the early days of voting research, the evidence seemed clear—voters rarely voted on policies, preferring to rely on party identification or candidate evaluations to make up their minds. In the 1950s, the authors of *The American Voter* stressed that only a small percentage of the American electorate relied on issues to decide their votes.[17] *The Changing American Voter* challenged this claim, however, arguing that voters had become more sophisticated about issues and better able to use policy positions to gauge candidates.[18]

Why does it matter?

The mandate theory of elections asserts that voters send a policy message when they elect one candidate over another. How accurate do you think this theory is? What informs your own voting decisions most strongly: party, policies, or personality?

Although it is questionable whether today's voters are more sophisticated about issues (see Chapter 6), policy voting has become somewhat easier than in the past; today's candidates are regularly forced to take clear stands to appeal to their own party's primary voters. As late as 1968, it was still possible to win a nomination by dealing with the party bosses; now candidates must appeal first to the issue-oriented activists in the primaries. Whatever the major issues are in the next presidential election, it is quite likely that the major contenders for the Democratic and Republican nominations will be taking stands on them in order to gain the support of these activists. Thus, what has changed is not the voters, but the electoral process that now provides much more incentive for candidates to draw clear policy distinctions between one another.

Party voting, candidate evaluation, and policy voting all play a role in elections. Their impact is not equal from one election to another, but they are the main factors affecting voter decisions. Once voters make their decisions in presidential elections, it is not just a simple matter of counting the ballots to see who has won the most support nationwide. Rather, the complicated process of determining electoral college votes begins.

The Last Battle: The Electoral College

electoral college

A unique American institution, created by the Constitution, providing for the selection of the president by electors chosen by the state parties. Although the electoral college vote usually reflects a popular majority, the winner-take-all rule gives clout to big states.

It is the members of the **electoral college,** not the people at large, who actually cast the determining votes for president and vice president of the United States. The electoral college is a unique American institution, created by the Constitution. The American Bar Association once called it, "archaic, undemocratic, complex, ambiguous, indirect, and dangerous."[19] Many, but certainly not all, political scientists oppose its continued use, as do most voters.

The Founders wanted the president to be selected by the nation's elite, not directly by the people. They created the electoral college for this purpose, and left the decision as to how the electors are chosen to each state. Since 1828, though, political practice has been for electors to vote for the candidate who won their state's popular vote. Occasionally, electors will exercise the right to vote their conscience, as did one West Virginia elector in 1988 who reversed the Democratic ticket by voting for Lloyd Bentsen for president and Michael Dukakis for vice president. This is how the electoral college system works today:

- Each state, according to the Constitution, has as many electoral votes as it has U.S. senators and representatives.[20] The state parties select slates of electors, positions they use as a reward for faithful service to the party.
- Aside from Maine and Nebraska, each state has a winner-take-all system.[21] Electors vote as a bloc for the winner, whether the winner got 35 percent or 95 percent of the popular vote in their state.
- Electors meet in their states in December, following the November election, and then mail their votes to the vice president (who is also president of the Senate). The vote is counted when the new congressional session opens in January, and reported by the vice president. Thus, Al Gore had the duty of announcing the election of George W. Bush in January of 2001.
- If no candidate receives an electoral college majority, then the election is thrown into the House of Representatives, which must choose from among the top three electoral vote winners. A significant aspect of the balloting in the House is that each state delegation has one vote, thus giving the 1 representative from Wyoming an equal say with the 52 representatives from California.

visual literacy
American Electoral Rules: How Do They Influence Campaigns?

The electoral college is important to the presidential election for two reasons. First, it introduces a bias into the campaign and electoral process. Providing the election is not thrown into the House, it gives extra clout to big states, especially those where the race is thought to be close. The winner-take-all rule means that winning big states like California, New York, Texas, and Ohio is more important than piling up big leads in small states (see Figure 10.1). Furthermore, big states are likely to have big cities (New York has New York City, Texas has Houston, California has Los Angeles, Illinois has Chicago, and so on). Thus, the big-state bias produces an urban bias in the electoral college.

Understanding Elections and Voting Behavior

Elections accomplish two tasks according to democratic theory. First, and most obviously, they *select the policymakers*. Second, elections are supposed to help *shape public policy*. Whether elections in fact make the government pay attention to what the

The final chapter of any presidential campaign is the swearing in of the winner at noon on the following January 20. Here, Chief Justice Rehnquist administers the oath to George W. Bush as Laura Bush holds the Bible.

people think is at the center of debate concerning how well democracy works in America. In the hypothetical world of rational choice theory and the Downs model (see Chapter 8), elections do in fact guide public policy; however, over a generation of social science research on this question has produced mixed findings. It is more accurate to describe the connection between elections and public policy as a two-way street: Elections, to some degree, affect public policy, and public policy decisions partly affect electoral outcomes.

Democracy and Elections

There will probably never be a definitive answer to the question of how much elections affect public policy—for it is a somewhat subjective matter. The broad contours of the answer, however, seem reasonably clear: *The greater the policy differences between the candidates, the more likely voters will be able to steer government policies by their choices.*

Why does it matter?

The electoral college has survived the test of time, but not without many critics who consider the process antiquated. Reform proposals typically call for direct election of the president by popular vote. What might be some of the consequences of such a change?

Of course, the candidates do not always help to clarify the issues. One result is that the policy stands are often shaped by what Benjamin Page once called "the art of ambiguity," in which "presidential candidates are skilled at appearing to say much while actually saying little."[22] Learning how to sidestep controversial questions and hedge answers is indeed part of becoming a professional politician, as you can observe at almost every presidential press conference. So long as politicians can take refuge in ambiguity (and the skimpy coverage of issues in the media does little to make them clarify their policy stands), the possibility of democratic control of policy is lessened. As with policy voting, if citizens cannot see the policy differences between candidates, they can hardly express their own beliefs by voting for one candidate over the other.

When individual candidates do offer a plain choice to the voters (what 1964 Republican nominee Barry Goldwater once called "a choice, not an echo"), voters are better able to guide the government's policy direction. Ronald Reagan followed in Goldwater's footsteps in the 1980s by making clear his intention to cut the growth of domestic spending, reduce taxes, and build up American military capability. Once elected, he proceeded to do much of what he said he would—demonstrating that elections can sometimes dramatically affect public policy.

If elections affect policies, then policies can also affect elections. Most policies have consequences for the well-being of certain groups or the society as a whole. Those who feel better off as a result of certain policies are likely to support candidates who pledge to continue those policies, whereas those who feel worse off are inclined to support opposition candidates. This is known as the theory of **retrospective voting**,[23] in which voters essentially ask the simple question, "What have you done for me lately?"

retrospective voting

A theory of voting in which voters essentially ask this simple question: "What have you done for me lately?"

Incumbents who provide desired results are rewarded; those who fail to do so are not reelected.

Nothing makes incumbent politicians more nervous than the state of the economy. When the economy takes a downturn, the call to "throw the rascals out" usually sweeps the nation. In presidential elections, people unhappy with the state of the economy tend to blame the incumbent. Republican Herbert Hoover was in office when the stock market crash of 1929 sparked the Great Depression. Hoover became so unpopular that the shantytowns occupied by unemployed people were called "Hoovervilles" and the apples they sold were called "Hoover apples." Hoover and his fellow Republicans were crushed by Franklin Roosevelt in the 1932 elections. Sixty years later, Democrats were still hitting the Republicans with the memory of Hoover—calling George Bush a modern-day Hoover who had spent all his energy on foreign policy while the American economy was sinking.

Clearly, elections affect policy, and public policy—especially the perception of economic policy impacts—can affect elections. Once in office, politicians use fiscal policy to keep the American economy running on an even keel. (How they try to do this is considered in Chapter 17.) If economic troubles mount, voters point their fingers at incumbent policymakers, and those fingers are more likely to pull the lever for the challengers on election day. In recent elections people who felt the national economy had improved voted strongly for the incumbent whereas those who thought the economy had gotten worse strongly favored the major challenger. As V. O. Key once wrote, "The only really effective weapon of popular control in a democratic regime is the capacity of the electorate to throw a party from power."[24]

Economic conditions can have a profound effect on election outcomes. In 1932, voters expressed their despair over the Great Depression by electing Franklin Roosevelt in a landslide over Herbert Hoover. Here, an unemployed man sells "Hoover apples" in front of the capitol.

Elections and the Scope of Government

While the threat of electoral punishment constrains policymakers, it also helps to increase generalized support for government and its powers. Voters know that the government can be replaced at the next election, so they are much more likely to feel that it will be responsive to their needs. Furthermore, when people have the power to dole out electoral reward and punishment, they are more likely to see government as their servant instead of their master. As Benjamin Ginsberg writes, "Democratic elections help to persuade citizens that expansion of the state's powers represents an increase in the state's capacity to serve them."[25]

Therefore, rather than wishing to be protected from the state, citizens in a democracy often seek to benefit from it. It is no coincidence that "individuals who believe they can influence the government's actions are also more likely to believe, in turn, that the government should have more power."[26] Voters like to feel that they are sending a message to the government to accomplish something. It should thus be no surprise that as democracy has spread government has come to do more and more, and its scope has grown.

Summary

This chapter has examined the final act in the electoral drama. Once the parties have made their nominations and the campaign has concluded, voters take center stage. Elections have changed dramatically since 1800 when Adams ran against Jefferson. By 1896, it was acceptable for candidates to campaign in person, and William Jennings Bryan did so with a vengeance. At that time suffrage—the right to vote—was still limited mostly to white males. Now the democratization of elections has made suffrage available to all American citizens over the age of 18.

Voters make two basic decisions at election time. The first is whether to vote. Americans' right to vote is well established, but in order to do so citizens must go through the registration process. America's unique registration system is one major reason why turnout in American elections is much lower than in most other democracies. The 2000 election was another in a long string of low-turnout elections. Second, those who choose to vote must decide for whom to cast their ballots. Over a generation of research on voting behavior has helped political scientists understand the dominant role played by three factors in voters' choices: party identification, candidate evaluations, and policy positions.

Elections are the centerpiece of democracy. Few questions are more important in understanding American government than this: Do elections matter? Under the right conditions, elections can influence public policy, and policy outcomes can influence elections. Elections also legitimize the power of the state, thereby making it easier to expand the scope of the government.

Key Terms

legitimacy
referendum
initiative petition
suffrage
political efficacy
civic duty
voter registration
Motor Voter Act
mandate theory of elections
policy voting
electoral college
retrospective voting

For Further Reading

Abramson, Paul R., John H. Aldrich, and David W. Rohde. *Change and Continuity in the 1996 Elections.* Washington, D.C.: Congressional Quarterly Press, 1998. A good overview of voting behavior in the 1996 elections, which also focuses on recent historical trends.

Campbell, Angus, et al. *The American Voter.* New York: John Wiley, 1960. The classic study of the American electorate in the 1950s, which has shaped scholarly approaches to the subject ever since.

Career Profile

Position: Administrator of Elections, Davidson County, Tenn.
Salary Range: $55,000-$72,000
Benefits: full benefit package as provided to all county employees, including health, life, and dental insurance, vacation days, sick and parental leaves, and retirement plan
Qualifications: The successful candidate for this position must be firmly nonpartisan and cannot participate in political campaigns. A high school degree or equivalent is required, although a college degree is recommended. The candidate must also possess management skills and some legal knowledge

Real People on the Job: Michael McDonald

Michael McDonald is the administrator of elections for Davidson County, Tenn., an area of over a half million people that includes the state capital, Nashville. His duties include overseeing all voter registration in the county, certifying candidates to run for office, election law enforcement, campaign finance law enforcement, redistricting, and ensuring that all elections (local, state, and federal) are held in a lawful manner. He generally has 27 full-time employees, but around Election Day that number jumps to 1,300.

Michael takes great satisfaction from the part he plays in protecting democracy in the United States. As an African American, he remembers his parents being denied the right to vote due to poll taxes and literacy tests. He grew up listening to stories about his aunts and uncles struggling to secure voting rights for black Americans. He clearly recalls entering the voting booth with his parents the first time they were allowed to vote. As administrator of elections, Michael takes great pride in ensuring that no one in Davidson County is disenfranchised.

Every city or county has an administrator of elections. In some places they call the position the county registrar. It is an appointed position, made by the county election commission, usually a body of five to seven members often chosen by the state legislature. If you are interested in becoming an administrator of elections, keep in mind that each state has different procedures for selecting candidates for the position. For details, call your local county election commission (in the phone book under your county government offices).

Kelley, Stanley G., Jr. *Interpreting Elections.* Princeton, NJ: Princeton University Press, 1983. Presents a theory of "the simple act of voting."

McCormick, Richard P. *The Presidential Game.* New York: Oxford University Press, 1982. An interesting historical look at the origins of presidential politics.

Nie, Norman H., Sidney Verba, and John R. Petrocik. *The Changing American Voter.* Cambridge, MA: Harvard University Press, 1976. Challenges some of the assumptions of Campbell et al.'s *The American Voter.*

Niemi, Richard G., and Herbert F. Weisberg, eds. *Controversies in Voting Behavior,* 4th ed. Washington, D.C.: Congressional Quarterly Press, 2001. An excellent set of readings on some of the most hotly debated facets of voting.

Polsby, Nelson W., and Aaron Wildavsky. *Presidential Elections,* 10th ed. Chatham, NJ: Chatham House, 2000. The classic text on the subject.

Pomper, Gerald M., et al. *The Election of 2000: Reports and Interpretations.* Chatham, NJ: Chatham House, 2001. A good collection of readings on a variety of aspects of the 2000 campaign.

Smith, Daniel A. *Tax Crusaders and the Politics of Direct Democracy.* New York: Routledge, 1998. A collection of interesting essays about activists who have made a difference through their advocacy of tax cut initiatives.

Teixeira, Ruy A. *The Disappearing American Voter.* Washington, D.C.: Brookings Institution, 1992. A good review of the reasons for declining voter turnout, as well as what can be done about it.

Wolfinger, Raymond E., and Steven J. Rosenstone. *Who Votes?* New Haven, CT: Yale University Press, 1980. A classic quantitative study of who turns out and why.

Internet Resources

www.umich.edu/~nes
The National Election Studies are a standard source of survey data about voting behavior. You can find information about these studies, as well as some of the results from them, at this site.

www.census.gov/population/www/socdemo/voting.html
The Census Bureau's studies of registration and turnout can be found at this address.

www.geocities.com/CapitolHill/6228/
A good collection of election news and results.

Notes

1. Quoted in Stanley G. Kelley, Jr., *Interpreting Elections* (Princeton, NJ: Princeton University Press, 1983), 3–4.
2. See Thomas E. Cronin, *Direct Democracy* (Cambridge, MA: Harvard University Press, 1989), chap. 7.
3. Daniel A. Smith, *Tax Crusaders and the Politics of Direct Democracy* (New York: Routledge, 1998).
4. Morton Grodzins, "Political Parties and the Crisis of Succession in the United States: The Case of 1800," in Joseph LaPalombara and Myron Weiner, eds., *Political Parties and Political Development* (Princeton, NJ: Princeton University Press, 1966), 319.
5. In 1804, the Twelfth Amendment to the Constitution changed the procedure to the one we know today, in which each elector votes separately for president and vice president.
6. Martin P. Wattenberg, "Turnout Decline in the U.S. and Other Advanced Industrialized Democracies." This paper is available at http://www.hypatia.ss.uci.edu/democ//papers/marty.html.
7. See Martin P. Wattenberg, "Should Election Day Be a Holiday?" *The Atlantic Monthly*, October 1998, 42–46.
8. Anthony Downs, *An Economic Theory of Democracy* (New York: Harper & Row, 1957), chap. 14.
9. Ruy A. Teixeira, *The Disappearing American Voter* (Washington, D.C.: Brookings Institution, 1992), chap. 2.
10. See Wattenberg, "Turnout Decline."
11. See George C. Edwards III, *At the Margins* (New Haven, CT: Yale University Press, 1989), chap. 8.
12. Richard G. Niemi and Herbert F. Weisberg, eds., *Controversies in Voting Behavior*, 2nd ed. (Washington, D.C.: Congressional Quarterly Press, 1984), 164–165.
13. See Martin P. Wattenberg, *The Decline of American Political Parties, 1952–1996* (Cambridge, MA: Harvard University Press, 1998).
14. Shawn W. Rosenberg with Patrick McCafferty, "Image and Voter Preference," *Public Opinion Quarterly* 51 (Spring 1987): 44.
15. Arthur H. Miller, Martin P. Wattenberg, and Oksana Malanchuk, "Schematic Assessments of Presidential Candidates," *American Political Science Review* 80 (1986): 521–540.
16. Paul R. Abramson, John H. Aldrich, and David W. Rohde, *Change and Continuity in the 1996 Elections* (Washington, D.C.: Congressional Quarterly Press, 1998), chap. 6.
17. Angus Campbell et al., *The American Voter* (New York: John Wiley, 1960) chap. 6.
18. Norman H. Nie, Sidney Verba, and John R. Petrocik, *The Changing American Voter* (Cambridge, MA: Harvard University Press, 1976).
19. American Bar Association, *Electing the President* (Chicago: ABA, 1967), 3.
20. The Twenty-third Amendment (1961) permits the District of Columbia to have three electors, even though it has no representatives in Congress.
21. In both Maine and Nebraska, an elector is allocated for every congressional district won, and whoever wins the state as a whole wins the two electors allotted to the state for its senators.
22. Benjamin Page, *Choices and Echoes in American Presidential Elections* (Chicago: University of Chicago Press, 1978), 153.
23. See Morris P. Fiorina, *Retrospective Voting in American National Elections* (New Haven, CT: Yale University Press, 1981).
24. V. O. Key, *The Responsible Electorate* (New York: Random House, 1966), 76.
25. Benjamin Ginsberg, *Consequences of Consent* (Reading, MA: Addison-Wesley, 1982), 194.
26. *Ibid.*, 198.

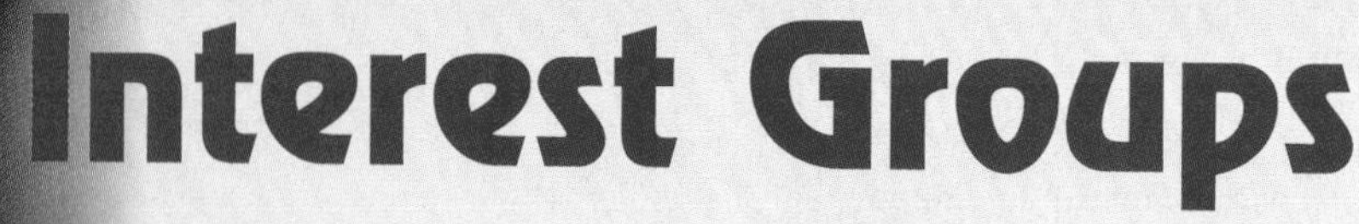

Interest Groups

11

Chapter Outline

One of the most successful lobbies in Washington during the 1980s was that of the savings and loan industry. The members of this industry wanted more freedom from federal regulators to run their business and make investments as they saw fit. Because President Reagan made the deregulation of business a high priority, they were quite successful. The result was that while some S & Ls profited, many others undertook risky investments that ultimately lost money. The government had to take over many failed savings and loans and use billions of taxpayer dollars to pay back depositors.

Probably the most famous case of S & L failure is that of Lincoln Savings and Loan, headed by Charles Keating. When federal regulators threatened to take over Lincoln, Keating turned to five U.S. senators to intervene on his behalf. Not surprisingly, the five politicians he called upon for help (John McCain, John Glenn, Alan Cranston, Donald Riegle, and Dennis DeConcini) had all been recipients of very large political

contributions from Keating. The five senators met twice as a group for over two hours with the head of the Federal Home Loan Bank Board, pressuring him to drop his plan to shut down the financially ailing business. When five senators get together, bureaucrats usually listen. Lincoln was allowed to stay in business for two more years, accumulating more and more debt until it was finally closed with a staggering $2.5 billion deficit.

When the story of the senators' involvement broke, all five contended that whatever they did on Keating's behalf was no different from inquiries that members of Congress routinely make on behalf of constituents. Senator McCain, who in the 2000 campaign frankly admitted that his involvement in this scandal had been the biggest mistake of his political life, initially compared his actions to helping a little old lady who did not get her Social Security check. Other senators involved noted that they were concerned by the possibility that thousands of their constituents could lose their jobs if Lincoln were closed.

Many critics took a more cynical view of the senators' actions, however, calling the case a prime example of how special interests' campaign contributions taint congressional action. They argued that Keating's situation was a regulatory matter in which the goal should have been the integrity of the savings and loan system, not the protection of constituents. They viewed the fact that Keating had made such large contributions to the senators as clear evidence that influence had been bought and sold. It is doubtful that the senators would have gone to such lengths for Keating—perhaps even given him the time of day—without the contributions.

The worst and oldest stereotype of a lobbyist is of someone who bribes a lawmaker to get a favorable policy decision. In contrast, Charles Keating's leverage with the five senators was obtained by open and legal means. Indeed, as this chapter will show, the problems of honest lobbying now appear to outweigh the traditional problems of dishonest lobbying.

By making the system so openly democratic, the means have been created for an incredible array of interests to be heard loud and clear in Washington. Some critics believe that the basic problem is that there are too many interest groups making demands on the government; others say the real problem is that the moneyed interests get a disproportionate share of access and influence. Those who are concerned that the system is too democratic often argue that the result is the frustration of any proposals for changing the existing scope of government. For those most concerned with the domination of well-off interest groups, the scope of government that results is inevitably seen as helping the rich get richer. Nevertheless, there are scholars who believe that the interest group system is working pretty much as the founders intended. James Madison argued in *Federalist Paper No.10* that the sphere of influence must be extended in order to prevent any one group from having too much power. Whether we are far along in reaching this goal is a crucial question for you to consider when reading this chapter.

Our nation's capital has become a hub of interest group activity. On any given day, it is possible to observe pressure groups in action in many forums. In the morning, you could attend congressional hearings in which you are sure to see interest groups testifying for and against proposed legislation. At the Supreme Court, you might stop in to watch a public interest lawyer arguing for strict enforcement of environmental regulations. Take a break for lunch at a nice Washington restaurant, and you may see a lobbyist entertaining a member of Congress.

You could spend the afternoon in any department of the executive branch (such as commerce, labor, or the interior), where you might catch bureaucrats working out rules and regulations with friendly—or sometimes unfriendly—representatives of the interests they are charged with overseeing. You could stroll past the impressive headquarters of the National Rifle Association, the AFL-CIO, or the American Association of Retired Persons to get a sense of the size of some of the major lobbying organizations. To see some lobbying done on college students' behalf, you might drop by One Dupont Circle, where all the higher education groups have their offices. These groups lobby for student loans and scholarships, as well as for aid to educational institutions. At dinner time, if you are able to finagle an invitation to a Georgetown cocktail party, you may see lobbyists trying to get the ear of government officials—both elected and unelected.

All of this lobbying activity poses an interesting paradox: Although turnout in elections has declined since 1960, participation in interest groups has mushroomed. As Kay Schlozman and John Tierney write, "Recent decades have witnessed an expansion of astonishing proportions in the involvement of private organizations in Washington politics."[1] This chapter will explore the factors behind the interest group explosion, how these groups enter the policymaking process, and what they get out of it.

The Role and Reputation of Interest Groups

All Americans have some interests they want represented. Organizing to promote these interests is an essential part of democracy. The right to organize groups is protected by the Constitution, which guarantees people the right "peaceably to assemble, and to petition the Government for a redress of grievances." This important First Amendment right has been carefully defended by the Supreme Court. The freedom to organize is as fundamental to democratic government as freedom of speech and freedom of the press.

All candidates for public office seek to obtain the votes of various interest groups. Here, George W. Bush appears with leaders of a Veterans' group. Military veterans have long leaned toward Republican candidates.

Defining Interest Groups

interest group
An organization of people with shared policy goals entering the policy process at several points to try to achieve those goals. Interest groups pursue their goals in many arenas.

The term *interest group* seems simple enough to define. Interest refers to a policy goal; a group is a combination of people. An **interest group,** therefore, is an organization of people with similar policy goals who enter the political process to try to achieve those aims. Whatever their goals—outlawing abortion or ensuring the right to one, regulating tax loopholes or creating new ones—interest groups pursue them in many arenas. Every branch of government is fair game; every level of government, local to federal, is a possible target. A policy battle lost in Congress may be turned around when it comes to bureaucratic implementation or to the judicial process.

This multiplicity of policy arenas helps distinguish interest groups from political parties. Parties fight their battles through the electoral process; they run candidates for public office. Interest groups may support candidates for office, but American interest groups do not run their own slate of candidates, as in some other countries (see "America in Perspective: Interest Groups as Parties in Other Democracies"). In other words, no serious candidate is ever listed on the ballot as a candidate of the National Rifle Association or Common Cause. It may be well known that a candidate is actively supported by a particular group, but that candidate faces the voters as a Democrat, a Republican, or perhaps, a third-party candidate.

Another key difference between parties and interest groups is that interest groups are often policy specialists, whereas parties are policy generalists. Most interest groups have a handful of key policies to push: A farm group cares little about the status of urban transit; an environmental group has its hands full bringing polluters into court without worrying about the minimum wage. Unlike political parties, these groups do not face the constraints imposed by trying to appeal to everyone.

Why Interest Groups Get Bad Press

Despite their importance to democratic government, interest groups traditionally have received bad press in America. The authors of the *Federalist Papers* thought interest groups were no better than political parties, which they also disliked. Madison's derogatory term *faction* was general enough to include both parties and interest groups.

Today, Americans' image of interest groups is no more favorable. As one lobbyist writes, "My mother has never introduced me to her friends as 'My son, the lobbyist. . . .' I can't say I blame her. Being a lobbyist has long been synonymous in the

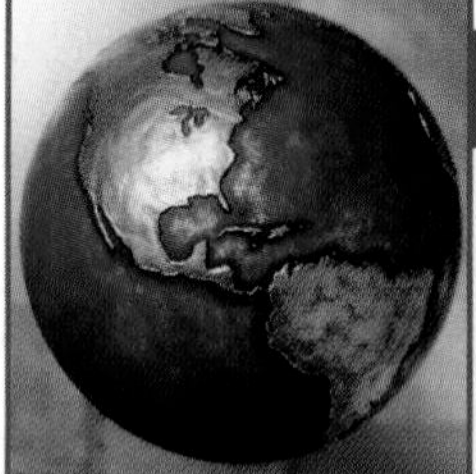

America in Perspective

Interest Groups as Parties in Other Democracies

In many countries with multiparty systems, interest groups form their own political parties to push for their demands. With proportional representation systems (see Chapter 8), all it takes is between 1 and 5 percent of the vote, depending on the country, for a narrowly based party to win seats in the national legislature. Although special interest groups usually cannot win very many seats, their impact can be large if their votes are crucial in obtaining a majority in the Parliament.

In many of the Scandinavian countries, for example, farmers' parties have long been in existence. Typically, the farmers' party has received between 10 and 20 percent of the vote in nations such as Sweden and Finland. For a conservative, nonsocialist government to be formed, their support is often critical. Therefore, any conservative government in these countries will be quite responsive to agrarian interests. If you are troubled by the fact that American agricultural policy is heavily influenced by congressional representatives from farm states, imagine a situation where key officeholders owe their election exclusively to this single economic interest.

Many new interest groups in Europe have formed parties not on the basis of shared economic interests, such as labor or agriculture, but rather on the basis of shared values. In particular, Green parties have sprung up throughout Western Europe to represent the concerns of environmentalists. Imagine having two dozen members of the American Congress insist on discussing the environmental impact of every decision. These members might not often win, but they would certainly draw more attention to the issue of environmental protection. This is the situation in countries such as Germany where the Greens have won enough votes to enter the national legislature and are currently part of the governing coalition.

minds of many Americans with being a glorified pimp."[2] On a slow news day, editorial cartoonists can always depict lobbyists skulking around in the congressional hallways, their pockets stuffed with money, just waiting to funnel it to a legislator's wallet. Comedians often reinforce the stereotype: Jay Leno once suggested that the Home Shopping Network should merge with C-SPAN for those who want the convenience of buying a politician in the privacy of their own home.

Defenders of the interest group system counter that the relationship between public officials and lobbyists is probably more free of out-and-out bribery than ever before in American history. The principal method of controlling dishonest lobbying has been through disclosure laws, which have been tightened substantially over the past several decades. Lobbyists are required to identify themselves, whom they represent, and their legislative interests. PACs must keep complete records of where they get their money and how they spend it. Members of Congress are required to file regular, detailed financial statements, which makes it difficult to hide ill-gotten income.

For every scandal that makes the headlines, hundreds of basically honest transactions between Congress and interest groups take place. There is little doubt that honest lobbying outpaces dishonest lobbying by a wide margin. However, many political scientists now believe that open and legal lobbying (such as the Lincoln Savings case) poses greater problems for democracy than illegal lobbying activities.

pluralist theory

A theory of government and politics emphasizing that politics is mainly a competition among groups, each one pressing for its own preferred policies.

elite theory

A theory of government and politics contending that societies are divided along class lines and that an upper-class elite will rule, regardless of the formal niceties of governmental organization.

hyperpluralist theory

A theory of government and politics contending that groups are so strong that government is weakened. Hyperpluralism is an extreme, exaggerated, or perverted form of **pluralism**.

Theories of Interest Group Politics

Understanding the debate over whether honest lobbying—and interest groups in general—create problems for government in America requires an examination of three important theories, which were introduced in Chapter 1. **Pluralist theory** argues that interest group activity brings representation to all. According to pluralists, groups compete and counterbalance one another in the political marketplace. In contrast, **elite theory** argues that a few groups (primarily the wealthy) have most of the power. Finally, **hyperpluralist theory** asserts that too many groups are getting too much of what they want, resulting in government policy that is often contradictory and lacking in direction. The following sections will examine each of these three theories with respect to interest groups.

Pluralism and Group Theory

Pluralist theory rests its case on the many centers of power in the American political system. Pluralists consider the extensive organization of competing groups evidence that influence is widely dispersed among them. They believe that groups win some and lose some but that no group wins or loses all the time. Pluralist theorists offer a *group theory of politics*, which contains several essential arguments.[3]

- *Groups provide a key link between people and government.* All legitimate interests in the political system can get a hearing from government once they are organized.
- *Groups compete.* Labor, business, farmers, consumers, environmentalists, and other interests constantly make competing claims on the government.
- *No one group is likely to become too dominant.* When one group throws its weight around too much, its opponents are likely to intensify their organization and thus restore balance to the system. For every action, there is a reaction.
- *Groups usually play by the "rules of the game."* In the United States group politics is a fair fight, with few groups lying, cheating, stealing, or engaging in violence to get their way.
- *Groups weak in one resource can use another.* Big business may have money on its side, but labor has numbers. All legitimate groups are able to affect public policy by one means or another.

Pluralists would never deny that some groups are stronger than others or that competing interests do not always get an equal hearing. Still, they can point to many cases in which a potential group organized itself and, once organized, affected policy decisions. African Americans, women, and consumers are all groups who were long ignored by government officials but who, once organized, redirected the course of public policy. In sum, pluralists argue that lobbying is open to all and is therefore not to be regarded as a problem.

Elites and the Denial of Pluralism

Whereas pluralists are impressed by the vast number of organized interests, elitists are impressed by how insignificant most of them are. Real power, elitists say, is held by relatively few people, key groups, and institutions. They maintain that the government is run by a few big interests looking out for themselves—a view that the majority of the public has agreed with in recent decades, as you can see in Figure 11.1.

Elitists critique pluralist theory by pointing to the concentration of power in a few hands. Where pluralists find dispersion of power, elitists find interlocking and concentrated power centers. About one-third of top institutional positions—corporate boards, foundation boards, university trusteeships, and so on—are occupied by people who hold more than one such position.[4] Elitists see the rise of mighty multinational corporations as further tightening the control of corporate elites. A prime example is America's giant oil companies. Robert Engler has tried to show that government has always bent over backward to maintain high profits for the oil industry.[5] When they come up against the power of these multinational corporations, consumer interests are readily pushed aside, according to elitists.

In sum, the elitist view of the interest group system makes the following assertions:

- The fact that there are numerous groups proves nothing because groups are extremely unequal in power.

Figure 11.1 Perceptions of the Dominance of Big Interests

Would you say the government is pretty much run by a few big interests looking out for themselves or that it is run for the benefit of all the people?

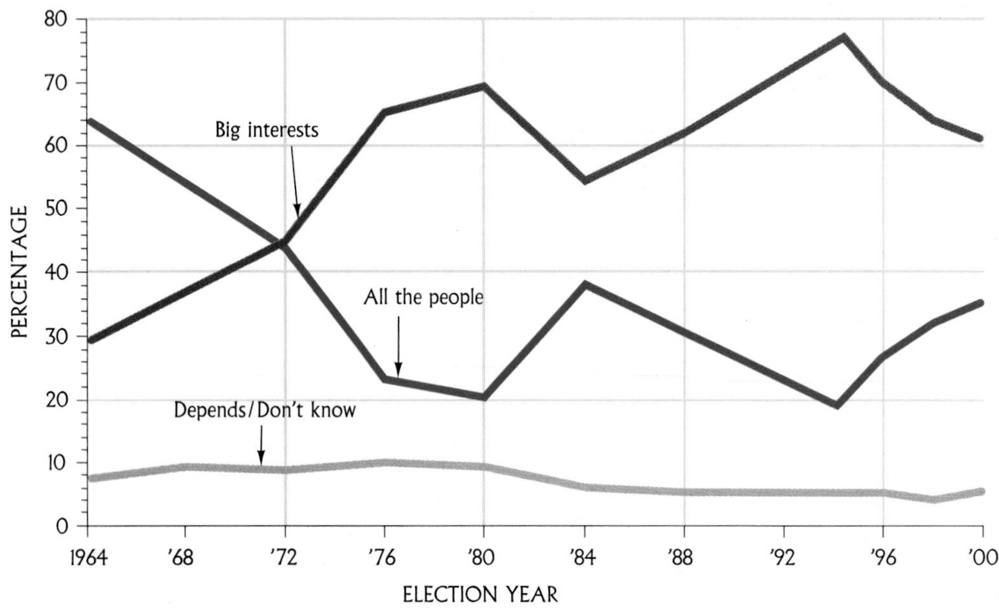

Source: The question as worded is taken directly from National Election Studies conducted by the University of Michigan, Center for Political Studies.

- Awesome power is held by the largest corporations.
- The power of a few is fortified by an extensive system of interlocking directorates.
- Other groups may win many minor policy battles, but the corporate elites prevail when it comes to the big decisions.

Thus, even honest lobbying is a problem, say elite theorists, because it benefits few at the expense of many.

Hyperpluralism and Interest Group Liberalism

Hyperpluralists, also critical of pluralism, argue that the pluralist system is out of control. Theodore Lowi coined the phrase *interest group liberalism* to refer to the government's excessive deference to groups. Interest group liberalism holds that virtually all pressure group demands are legitimate and that the job of the government is to advance them all.[6]

In an effort to please and appease every interest, agencies proliferate, conflicting regulations expand, programs multiply, and of course, the budget skyrockets. If environmentalists want clean air, government imposes clean-air rules; if businesses complain that cleaning up pollution is expensive, government gives them a tax write-off for pollution control equipment. If the direct-mail industry wants cheap rates, government gives it to them; if people complain about junk mail, the postal service gives them a way to take their names off mailing lists. If cancer researchers convince the government to launch an antismoking campaign, tobacco sales may drop; if they do, government will subsidize tobacco farmers to ease their loss.[7]

subgovernments

A network of groups within the American political system that exercise a great deal of control over specific policy areas. Also known as iron triangles, subgovernments are composed of interest group leaders interested in a particular policy, the government agency in charge of administering that policy, and the members of congressional committees and subcommittees handling that policy.

Interest group liberalism is promoted by the network of **subgovernments** in the American political system that exercise a great deal of control over specific policy areas. These subgovernments, which are also known as iron triangles, are composed of key interest group leaders interested in policy X, the government agency in charge of

Hyperpluralist theorists often point to the government's contradictory tobacco-related policies as an example of interest group liberalism. Former Surgeon General C. Everett Koop (left), for example, led a high-profile government campaign against smoking, whereas North Carolina Senator Jesse Helms (below) has long worked to keep subsidies to tobacco farmers high.

administering policy X, and the members of congressional committees and subcommittees handling policy X.

All the elements composing subgovernments have the same goal: protecting their self-interest. The network of subgovernments in the agricultural policy area of tobacco is an excellent example. Tobacco interest groups include the Tobacco Institute, the Retail Tobacco Distributors of America, and the tobacco growers. Various agencies in the Department of Agriculture administer tobacco programs, and they depend on the tobacco industry's clout in Congress to help keep their agency budgets safe from cuts. Finally, most of the members of the House Tobacco Subcommittee are from tobacco-growing regions. All these elements want to protect the interests of tobacco farmers. Similar subgovernments of group-agency-committee ties exist in scores of other policy areas.

Hyperpluralists' major criticism of the interest group system is that relations between groups and the government have become too cozy. Hard choices about national policy are rarely made. Instead of making choices between X and Y, the government pretends there is no need to choose and instead tries to favor both policies. It is a perfect script for policy gridlock. In short, the hyperpluralist position on group politics is that:

- Groups have become too powerful in the political process as government tries to appease every conceivable interest.
- Interest group liberalism is aggravated by numerous subgovernments—comfortable relationships among a government agency, the interest group it deals with, and congressional subcommittees.
- Trying to please every group results in contradictory and confusing policy.

Why does it matter?

Suppose James Madison's descendants were studying American government in order to assess how well the system he devised controls the power of special interests. What different conclusions might they draw depending on whether they assessed the current system using pluralist, elitist, or hyperpluralist interpretations?

Ironically, the recent interest group explosion is seen by some scholars as weakening the power of subgovernments. As Morris Fiorina writes, "A world of active public interest groups, jealous business competitors, and packs of budding investigative reporters is less hospitable to subgovernment politics than a world lacking in them."[8] With so many more interest groups to satisfy, and with many of them competing against one another, a cozy relationship between groups and the government is plainly more difficult to sustain.

What Makes an Interest Group Successful?

In recent years, *Fortune* magazine has issued a yearly list of the 25 most powerful interest groups in politics. Table 11.1 displays one of their recent lists. A quick look through it will probably reveal some surprises. Whereas some of these powerful lobbying groups are well known, others are not.

Many factors affect the success of an interest group, as indicated by the diversity of groups in *Fortune's* "Power 25." Among these factors are the size of the group, its intensity, and its financial resources. While greater intensity and more financial resources work to a group's advantage, surprisingly, smaller groups are more likely to achieve their goals than larger groups.

The Surprising Ineffectiveness of Large Groups

In one of the most oft-quoted statements concerning interest groups, E. E. Schattschneider wrote that "pressure politics is essentially the politics of small groups. . . . Pressure tactics are not remarkably successful in mobilizing general interests."[9] There are perfectly good reasons why consumer groups are less effective than producer groups, patients are less effective than doctors, and energy conservationists are less effective than oil companies: Small groups have organizational advantages over large groups.

To shed light on this point, it is important to distinguish between a potential and an actual group. A **potential group** is composed of all people who might be group members because they share some common interest.[10] In contrast, an **actual group** is composed of those in the potential group who choose to join. Groups vary enormously in the degree to which they enroll their potential membership. Consumer organizations are minuscule when compared with the total number of consumers, which is almost every American. Some organizations, however, do very well in organizing virtually all their potential members. The National Beer Wholesalers Association (ranked #20 in Table 11.1), the Tobacco Institute, and the Air Transport Association include a good portion of their potential members. Compared with consumers, these groups are tightly organized.

potential group

All the people who might be **interest group** members because they share some common interest. A potential group is almost always larger than an actual group.

actual group

That part of the **potential group** consisting of members who actually join.

Table 11.1 The Power 25

Fortune magazine has long been famous for its lists of the richest companies and individuals in the country. Lately, editors have expanded their analysis to ranking the most powerful lobbying associations. Members of Congress, prominent congressional staffers, senior White House aides, and top-ranking officers of the largest lobbying groups in Washington were asked to assess, on a scale of 0 to 100, the political clout of 114 major trade associations, labor unions, and interest groups. Here is the list of the groups that finished in the top 25 in terms of political clout:

1. American Association of Retired Persons
2. National Rifle Association
3. National Federation of Independent Business
4. American Israel Public Affairs Committee
5. AFL-CIO
6. Association of Trial Lawyers of America
7. Chamber of Commerce
8. National Right to Life Committee
9. National Education Association
10. National Restaurant Association
11. American Bankers Association
12. National Governors' Association
13. American Medical Association
14. National Association of Manufacturers
15. National Association of Realtors
16. National Association of Homebuilders
17. Motion Picture Association of America
18. Credit Union National Association
19. National Beer Wholesalers Association
20. National Association of Broadcasters
21. American Farm Bureau Federation
22. American Federation of State, County, and Municipal Employees
23. International Brotherhood of Teamsters
24. United Auto Workers
25. Health Insurance Association of America

Source: Fortune, December 6, 1999.

Economist Mancur Olson explains this phenomenon in *The Logic of Collective Action.*[11] Olson points out that all groups, unlike individuals, are in the business of providing collective goods. A **collective good** is something of value, such as clean air, that cannot be withheld from a potential group member. When the AFL-CIO wins a higher minimum wage, all low-paid workers benefit, regardless of whether they are members of the union. In other words, members of the potential group share in benefits that members of the actual group work to secure. If this is the case, an obvious and difficult problem results: Why should potential members work for something if they can get it free? Why join the group, pay dues, and work hard for a goal when a person can benefit from the group's activity without doing anything at all? A perfectly rational response is thus to sit back and let other people do the work. This is commonly known as the **free-rider problem.**

The bigger the group, the more serious the free-rider problem. That is the gist of **Olson's law of large groups:** "The larger the group, the further it will fall short of providing an optimal amount of a collective good."[12] Small groups thus have an organizational advantage over large ones. In a small group, members' shares of the collective good may be great enough that they will try to secure it. The old saying that "everyone can make a difference" is much more credible in the case of a relatively small group. In the largest groups, however, each member can expect to get only a

collective good

Something of value (money, a tax write-off, prestige, clean air, and so on) that cannot be withheld from a group member.

free-rider problem

The problem faced by unions and other groups when people do not join because they can benefit from the group's activities without officially joining. The bigger the group, the more serious the free-rider problem.

Olson's law of large groups

Advanced by Mancur Olson, a principle stating that "the larger the group, the further it will fall short of providing an optimal amount of a collective good."

tiny share of the policy gains. Weighing the costs of participation against the relatively small benefits, the temptation is always to "let somebody else do it." Therefore, as Olson argues, the larger the potential group, the less likely potential members are to contribute.

This distinct advantage of small groups helps explain why consumer groups have a hard time making ends meet. Such groups claim to seek "public interest" goals, but the gains they win are usually spread thin over millions of people. In contrast, the lobbying costs and benefits for business are concentrated. Suppose, for example, that consumer advocates take the airlines to court over charges of price fixing and force the airlines to return $10 million to consumers in the form of lower prices. This $10 million settlement is spread over 280 million Americans—about four cents per person (actually, the benefit is a little higher if one divides only by the number of people who use airlines). The $10 million airline loss is shared by 60 carriers at over $165,000 apiece. One can quickly see which side will be better organized in such a struggle.

In sum, Olson's law of large groups explains why interest groups with relatively few members are often so effective. The power of business in the American political system is thus due to more than just money, as proponents of elite theory would have us believe. Besides their financial strength, wealthy corporations also enjoy an inherent size advantage. Because there are a limited number of multinational corporations, these businesses have an easier time organizing themselves for political action than larger potential groups, such as consumers. Once well organized, large groups may be very effective, but it is much harder for them to get together in the first place.

selective benefits

Goods (such as information publications, travel discounts, and group insurance rates) that a group can restrict to those who pay their annual dues.

The primary way for large potential groups to overcome Olson's law is to provide attractive benefits for only those who join the organization. **Selective benefits** are goods that a group can restrict to those who pay their yearly dues, such as information publications, travel discounts, and group insurance rates. The top rated group in *Fortune's* "Power 25"—the American Association of Retired Persons (AARP)—has built up a membership list of 33 million senior citizens by offering a variety of selective benefits (see Figure 11.2). Similarly, Consumers Union gains most of its members not because of its efforts on behalf of product safety but by offering the selective benefit of receiving *Consumer Reports*, a monthly magazine that rates the reliability, safety, and cost-effectiveness of products.

Intensity

Another way a large potential group may be mobilized is through an issue that people feel intensely about. Intensity is a psychological advantage that can be enjoyed by small and large groups alike. When a group shows that it cares deeply about an issue, politicians are more likely to listen; many votes may be won or lost on a single issue. The rise of single-issue groups (discussed in Chapter 1) has been one of the most dramatic political developments in recent years.

single-issue groups

Groups that have a narrow interest, tend to dislike compromise, and often draw membership from people new to politics. These features distinguish them from traditional **interest groups**.

A **single-issue group** can be defined as a group that has a narrow interest, dislikes compromise, and single-mindedly pursues its goal. Anti-Vietnam War activists may have formed the first modern single-issue group. Opponents of nuclear power plants, gun control (ranked #2 in "The Power 25"), and abortion are some of the many such groups that exist today. All these groups deal with issues that evoke the strong emotions characteristic of single-interest groups.

Perhaps the most emotional issue of recent times has been that of abortion. As befits the intensity of the issue, activities have not been limited to conventional means of political participation. Protesting—often in the form of blocking entrances to abortion clinics—has now become a common practice for anti-abortion activists. Pro-choice activists have organized as well, especially in the wake of the 1989 *Webster v.*

Figure 11.2 The Benefits of Membership in the AARP

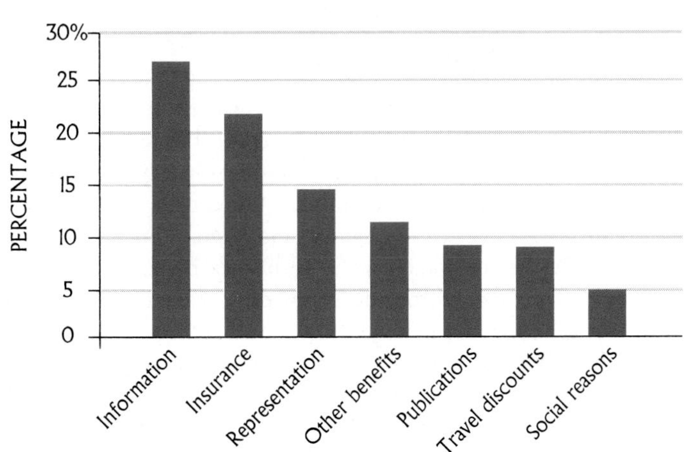

This chart illustrates the answers given by a sample of AARP members when they were asked why they had joined the organization.

Source: American Association for Retired Persons.

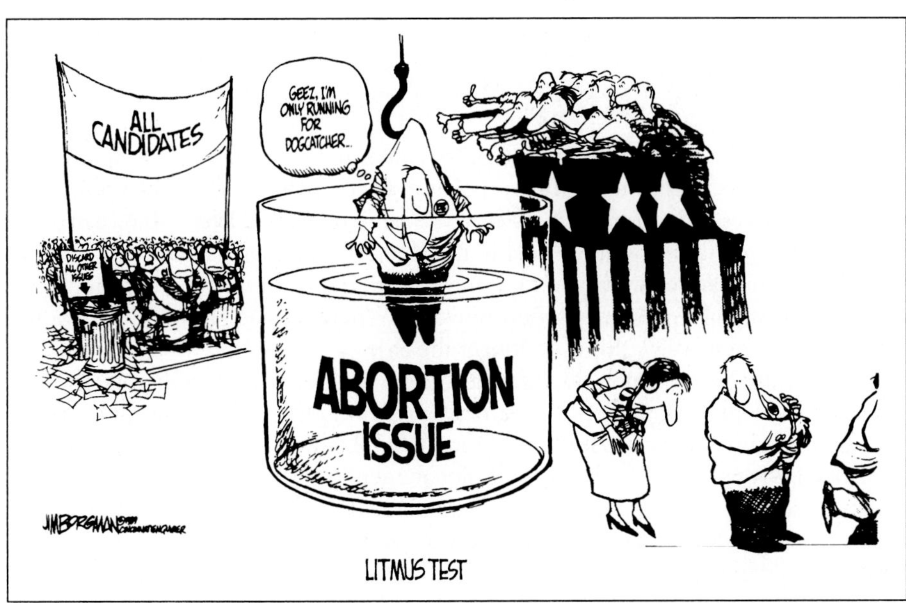

Reproductive Health Services case, which allowed states greater freedom to restrict abortions. Both groups' positions are clear, not subject to compromise, and influence their vote. Regardless of which side candidates for political office are on, they will be taking heat on the abortion issue for years to come.

Financial Resources

One of the major indictments of the American interest group system is that it is biased toward the wealthy. When he was the majority leader in the Senate, Bob Dole once remarked that he had never been approached by a Poor People's PAC. There is no doubt that money talks in the American political system, and those who have it get heard. All groups listed in Table 11.1 spend over a million dollars a year on lobbying and campaign contributions. A big campaign contribution may ensure a phone call, a meeting, or even a favorable vote or action on a particular policy. When Lincoln Savings and Loan Chair Charles Keating was asked whether the \$1.3 million he had funneled into the campaigns of five U.S. senators had anything to do with these senators later meeting with federal regulators on his behalf, he candidly responded, "I certainly hope so."

It is important to emphasize, however, that even on some of the most important issues, the big interests do not always win. An excellent example of this is the Tax Reform Act of 1986. In *Showdown at Gucci Gulch,* two reporters from the *Wall Street Journal* chronicle the improbable victory of sweeping tax reform.[13] In this case, a large group of well-organized, highly paid (and Gucci-clad) lobbyists were unable to preserve many of their most prized tax loopholes. One of the heroes of the book, former Senator Robert Packwood of Oregon, was Congress's top PAC recipient during the tax reform struggle; he had raked in $992,000 for his reelection campaign. As chair of the Senate Finance Committee, however, Packwood ultimately turned against the hordes of lobbyists trying to get his ear on behalf of various loopholes. The only way to deal with the tax loophole problem, he concluded, was to go virtually cold turkey by eliminating all but a very few. "There is special interest after special interest that is hit in this bill," Packwood gloated, pointing out that many of them contributed to his campaign. In the end, passage of the reform bill offered "encouraging proof that moneyed interests could not always buy their way to success in Congress."[14]

The Interest Group Explosion

timeline
Interest Groups in America

The number of interest groups in the United States has been increasing rapidly over the last several decades. Although no one has ever compiled a *Who's Who* of interest groups, the closest thing is the annual *Encyclopedia of Associations.*[15] Between 1959 and 1995, the number of groups listed in the *Encyclopedia* skyrocketed from 5,843 to 23,298.[16] As you can see in Figure 11.3, the growth in the number of groups reflects a growing diversity in the interest group universe. Whereas trade groups clearly dominated the picture in 1959, this is no longer the case.

It seems that there is now an organized group for every conceivable interest. Jack Walker studied 564 groups listed in the *Washington Information Directory* and tried to trace their origins and expansion.[17] He found that 80 percent of the groups originated from occupational, industrial, or professional memberships. Interestingly, half the groups he studied were established after World War II. Walker also found a gravitation of groups to Washington, D.C. In 1960, only 66 percent of the groups in his study were headquartered in the nation's capital; today, over 90 percent are located there. Very few occupations or industries now go without an organized group to represent them in Washington. Even lobbyists themselves now have lobbies to represent their profession, such as the American League of Lobbyists.

There are many reasons for this explosion in the number of interest groups. Certainly one of the major factors has been the development of sophisticated technology. Andrew McFarland observes that

> *Technological innovations have made the coordination of constituents' activities and efforts of lobbyists much easier. Many lobbyists, for example, have available computerized lists of names and phone numbers of group members that can be easily arranged by congressional district or state. Address labels can be printed automatically or members can be called by WATS line from a group's headquarters.*[18]

Technology has also made it easier for groups back on Main Street to make their voices immediately heard in Washington. A well-organized interest group can deluge members of Congress with tens of thousands of faxes and e-mail messages in a matter of hours. Technology did not create interest group politics, but it has surely made the process much easier.

Figure 11.3 Associations by Type

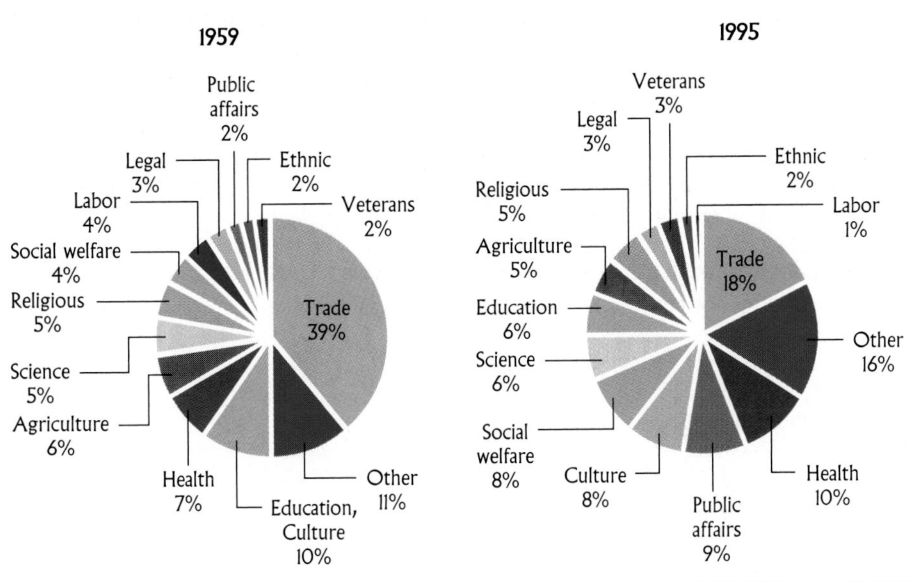

The following two pie charts illustrate how the interest group world has become more diverse since the late 1950s.

Source: Data from Frank R. Baumgartner and Beth L. Leech, *Basic Interests: The Importance of Groups in Politics and in Political Science* (Princeton, NJ: Princeton University Press, 1998), 109.

How Groups Try to Shape Policy

No interest group has enough staff, money, or time to do everything possible to achieve its policy goals. Interest groups must therefore choose from a variety of tactics. Table 11.2 illustrates the range and frequency of tactics employed by a sample of interest groups. The four basic strategies are lobbying, electioneering, litigation, and appealing to the public.

Lobbying

The term **lobbying** comes from the place where petitioners used to collar legislators. In the early years of politics in Washington, members of Congress had no offices and typically stayed in boarding houses or hotels while Congress was in session. A person could not call them up on the phone or make an appointment with their secretary; the only sure way of getting in touch with a member of Congress was to wait in the lobby where he was staying to catch him either coming in or going out. These people were dubbed *lobbyists* because they spent so much of their time waiting in lobbies.

lobbying

According to Lester Milbrath, a "communication, by someone other than a citizen acting on his own behalf, directed to a governmental decisionmaker with the hope of influencing his decision."

Of course, merely loitering in a lobby does not make one a lobbyist; there must be a particular reason for such action. Lester Milbrath has offered a more precise definition of the practice. He writes that lobbying is a "communication, by someone other than a citizen acting on his or her own behalf, directed to a governmental decision maker with the hope of influencing his or her decision."[19] Lobbyists, in other words, are political persuaders who represent organized groups. They usually work in Washington, handling groups' legislative business. They are often former legislators themselves.

There are two basic types of lobbyists. Members of the first type are regular, paid employees of a corporation, union, or association. They may hold a title such as vice president for government relations, but everyone knows that their office is in Washington for a reason, even if the company headquarters is in Houston. Members of the second type are available for hire on a temporary basis. One group may be too

Table 11.2 Percentage of Groups Using Various Lobbying Techniques

Schlozman and Tierney surveyed a variety of interest groups and found the following lobbying techniques were used most often.

TECHNIQUE	% USING
Testifying at hearings	99
Contacting government officials directly to present a point of view	98
Engaging in informal contacts with officials—at conventions, over lunch, etc.	95
Presenting research results or technical information	92
Sending letters to members of an organization to inform them about its activities	92
Entering into coalitions with other organizations	90
Attempting to shape the implementation of policies	89
Talking with people from the press and the media	86
Consulting with government officials to plan legislative strategy	85
Helping to draft legislation	85
Inspiring letter-writing or telegram campaigns	84
Shaping the government's agenda by raising new issues and calling attention to previously ignored problems	84
Mounting grass-roots lobbying efforts	80
Having influential constituents contact their congressperson's office	80
Helping to draft regulations, rules, or guidelines	78
Serving on advisory commissions and boards	76
Alerting members of Congress to the effects of a bill on their districts	75
Filing lawsuits or otherwise engaging in litigation	72
Making financial contributions to electoral campaigns	58
Doing favors for officials who need assistance	56
Attempting to influence appointments to public office	53
Publicizing candidates' voting records	44
Engaging in direct-mail fund-raising	44
Running advertisements in the media about issues	31
Contributing work or personnel to electoral campaigns	24
Making public endorsements of candidates for office	22
Engaging in protests or demonstrations	20

Source: From Kay L. Schlozman and John T. Tierney, *Organized Interests and American Democracy*, 1986. Reprinted by permission of Addison Wesley Educational Publishing.

small to afford a full-time lobbyist; another may have a unique, but temporary, need for access to Congress or the executive branch. Several thousand Washingtonians are available as "lobbyists for hire."

Although lobbyists are primarily out to influence members of Congress, it is important to remember that they can be of help to them as well. Ornstein and Elder list four important ways in which lobbyists can help a member of Congress.[20]

- *They are an important source of information.* Members of Congress have to concern themselves with many policy areas; lobbyists can confine themselves to only one area and can thus provide specialized expertise. If information is power, then lobbyists can often be potent allies.
- *They can help politicians with political strategy for getting legislation through.* Lobbyists are politically savvy people, and they can be useful consultants. When he served as White House Chief of Staff, Leon Panetta regularly convened a small group of Washington lobbyists to discuss how the administration should present its proposals.[21]

For years, the National Rifle Association has successfully lobbied against gun control measures, arguing that the Second Amendment to the Constitution guarantees all citizens the right to bear arms. Its current president is Charlton Heston, who has long been a prominent member of the group.

- *They can help formulate campaign strategy and get the group's members behind a politician's reelection campaign.* Labor union leaders, for example, often provide help in how to appeal to typical working people, and they often provide volunteers to help out in campaigns as well.
- *They are a source of ideas and innovations.* Lobbyists cannot introduce bills, but they can peddle their ideas to politicians eager to attach their name to an idea that will bring them political credit.

Like anything else, lobbying can be done crudely or gracefully. Lobbyists can sometimes be heavy handed. They can threaten or cajole a legislator, implying that electoral defeat is a certain result of not "going along." They can even make it clear that money flows to the reelection coffers of those who cooperate. It is often difficult to tell the difference between lobbying as a shady business and lobbying as a strictly professional representation of legitimate interests.

simulation
You are a Lobbyist

Political scientists disagree about the effectiveness of lobbying. Much evidence suggests that lobbyists' power over policy is often exaggerated. A classic 1950s study of the influence of groups on foreign trade policy started with the hypothesis that when major business lobbies spoke, Congress listened—and acted accordingly.[22] Instead, the study found groups involved in trade policy to be ineffective, understaffed, and underfinanced. Usually the lobbyists were too disorganized to be effective. Members of Congress often had to pressure the interest groups to actively support legislation that would be in their own interest. Similarly, Milbrath concluded his own analysis of lobbying by arguing that "there is relatively little influence or power in lobbying per se."[23] Lobbyists are most effective as information sources, he claims, and are relatively ineffectual in winning over legislators.

Plenty of other evidence, however, suggests that sometimes lobbying can persuade legislators to support a certain policy.[24] The National Rifle Association, which for years kept major gun control policies off the congressional agenda, has long been one of Washington's most effective lobbying groups.[25] In a more specific example, intensive lobbying by the nation's most wealthy senior citizens—enraged by the tax burden imposed upon them by the Catastrophic Health Care Act—led Congress to repeal the act only a year after it was passed in the late 1980s.

Nailing down the specific effects of lobbying is difficult, partly because it is difficult to isolate its effects from other influences. Lobbying clearly works best on people already committed to the lobbyist's policy position. Thus, like campaigning, lobbying is directed primarily toward activating and reinforcing supporters. For example, antiabortion lobbyists would not think of approaching California's Barbara Boxer to attempt to convert her to their position, because Boxer clearly supports the pro-choice movement. If Senator Boxer is lobbied by anyone on the abortion issue, it will be by the pro-choice faction, urging her not to compromise with the opposition.

Electioneering

electioneering

Direct group involvement in the electoral process. Groups can help fund campaigns, provide testimony, and get members to work for candidates, and some form **political action committees (PACs).**

political action committees (PACs)

Political funding vehicles created by the 1974 campaign finance reforms. A corporation, union, or some other interest group can create a PAC and register it with the **Federal Election Commission (FEC)**, which will meticulously monitor the PAC's expenditures.

Because lobbying works best with those already on the same side, getting the right people into office and keeping them there is also a key strategy of interest groups. Many groups therefore get involved in **electioneering**—aiding candidates financially and getting group members out to support them. Pressure group involvement in campaigns is nothing new. In the election of 1896 (see Chapter 10) silver-mining interests poured millions into the losing presidential campaign of William Jennings Bryan, who advocated unlimited coinage of silver.

Political action committees (PACs) provide a means for groups to participate in electioneering. The number of PACs has exploded from 608 in 1974 to 3,835 in 2000, according to the Federal Election Commission. No major interest group seeking to exert influence on the electoral process these days can pass up the opportunity to funnel money honestly and openly into the campaign coffers of its supporters. As campaign costs have risen, PACs have come along to help pay the bill. In recent years, nearly half the candidates running for reelection to the House of Representatives have received the majority of their campaign funds from PACs. Furthermore, their challengers did not enjoy this advantage. PACs gave a whopping $134 million to House incumbents during the 1999–2000 election cycle, compared to a mere $17 million to the challengers. Why does PAC money go so overwhelmingly to incumbents? The answer is that PAC contributions are basically investments for the future, and incumbents are the most likely to return the investment.

Why does it matter?

The great increase in the number of PACs over the last quarter of a century has enabled far more groups to become involved in electioneering. Why do you think most every organized interest has a PAC these days? How might a group have influence on the political scene if it did not have a PAC?

Only a handful of serious congressional candidates have resisted the lure of PAC money in recent years. One candidate described his experiences trying to get on the PAC bandwagon. When Democrat Steve Sovern ran for the House from Iowa's Second District, he made the now common pilgrimage to Washington to meet with potential contributors. "I found myself in line with candidates from all over," he reported. Each PAC had eager candidates fill out a multiple-choice questionnaire on issues important to the PAC. Candidates who shared the same concerns and views and who looked like winners got the money. Sovern later reported that "the process made me sick." After his defeat, he organized his own PAC called LASTPAC (for Let the American System Triumph), which urged candidates to shun PAC campaign contri-

You Are the Policymaker

Should PACs Be Eliminated?

The effect of PAC campaign contributions on congressional votes has become a perennial issue in American politics. Critics of PACs are convinced that they are distorting the democratic process and corrupting our political system in favor of those who can raise the most money. Many politicians freely admit — once they are out of office — that it is a myth to think that the PACs don't want something in return. They may only want to be remembered on one or two crucial votes or with an occasional intervention with government agencies, but multiply this by the thousands of special interests that are organized today and the worst fears of the hyperpluralists could be realized—a government that constantly yields to every special interest.

Common Cause (www.commoncause.org) has made it their primary mission to expose what they see as the evils of the PAC system. They argue that the influence of corporate PACs on Capitol Hill has led to "corporate welfare" and costs taxpayers billions of dollars. For example, Common Cause maintains that the timber industry prevailed against a Clinton Administration proposal in 1997 to eliminate logging subsidies because of their $8 million in recent PAC contributions. Similarly, they argue that $5 million in PAC contributions from the broadcast industry led to a massive government giveaway of free digital TV licenses worth as much as $70 billion. And Common Cause and others have attributed the failure of Congress to further regulate tobacco and cigarette advertising to the more than $30 million of PAC contributions from the tobacco companies over the past decade.

However, others argue that connection is not causation. They believe that most members of congress are not affected by PAC contributions, which largely come from groups they already agree with anyway. Defenders of the PAC system also point out that the PAC system further increases participation in the political process. As opposed to individual donations, PACs—which represent groups of people—allow better representation of occupational groups. The PAC system allows people with common professional interests, such as farmers, lawyers, dentists, and college professors, to express their support of candidates jointly through political contributions.

Similarly, corporation PACs represent the interests of many stockholders and employees with common political interests. If James Madison's notion that the key to controlling the power of interest groups is to expand their sphere of participation, then PACs certainly do this according to their defenders. Beyond this, the money for today's expensive media campaigns has to come from somewhere. Those who wish to maintain the PAC system typically point to the alternative of public financing of campaigns as impractical and unpopular given the low rate of participation on the voluntary income tax check-off box (see Chapter 9).

You be the policymaker: What would you do? Would you consider eliminating PACs? Or, as a middle course, would you favor further limits on the amount of money they can donate?

butions.[26] There have been serious calls to do away with PACs altogether, as discussed in "You Are the Policymaker: Should PACs Be Eliminated?"

visual literacy
PACs and the Money Trail

Litigation

If interest groups fail in Congress or get only a vague piece of legislation, the next step is to go to court in the hope of getting specific rulings. Karen Orren has linked much of the success of environmental interest groups to their use of lawsuits. "Frustrated in Congress," she wrote, "they have made an end run to the courts, where they have skillfully exploited and magnified limited legislative gains."[27] Environmental legislation, such as the Clean Air Act, typically includes written provisions allowing ordinary citizens to sue for enforcement. As a result, every federal agency involved in environmental regulation now has hundreds of suits pending against it at any given time. These suits may not halt environmentally troublesome practices, but the constant threat of a lawsuit increases the likelihood that businesses will consider the environmental impact of what they do.

Perhaps the most famous interest group victories in court were by civil rights groups in the 1950s. While civil rights bills remained stalled in Congress, these groups won major victories in court cases concerning school desegregation, equal housing, and labor market equality. More recently, consumer groups have used suits against businesses and federal agencies as a means of enforcing consumer regulations. As long as law schools keep producing lawyers, groups will fight for their interests in court. Indeed, the increase in the number of lawyers licensed to practice in Washington has been phenomenal—from 11,000 in 1972 to 63,000 in 1994.[28]

amicus curiae briefs

Legal briefs submitted by a "friend of the court" for the purpose of raising additional points of view and presenting information not contained in the briefs of the formal parties. These briefs attempt to influence a court's decision.

One tactic that lawyers employ to make the views of interest groups heard by the judiciary is the filing of ***amicus curiae*** ("friend of the court") **briefs.** *Amicus* briefs consist of written arguments submitted to the courts in support of one side of a case. Through these written depositions, a group states its collective position as well as how its own welfare will be affected by the outcome of the case. Numerous groups may file *amicus* briefs in highly publicized and emotionally charged cases. For example, in the case of *Regents of the University of California v. Bakke* (see Chapter 5), which challenged affirmative action programs as reverse discrimination, over 100 different groups filed *amicus* briefs. A study of participation in *amicus* briefs by Caldeira and Wright found that the Supreme Court has been accessible to a wide array of organized interests, in terms of deciding both which cases to hear and how to rule.[29]

class action suits

Lawsuits permitting a small number of people to sue on behalf of all other people similarly situated.

A more direct judicial strategy employed by interest groups is the filing of **class action lawsuits,** which enable a group of people in a similar situation to combine their common grievances into a single suit. For instance, flight attendants won a class action suit against the airline industry's regulation that all stewardesses be unmarried. As one lawyer who specializes in such cases states, "The class action is the greatest, most effective legal engine to remedy mass wrongs."[30]

Going Public

Groups are also interested in the opinions of the public. Because public opinion ultimately makes its way to policymakers, interest groups carefully cultivate their public image and use public opinion to their advantage when they can. As Ken Kollman finds, even the wealthiest and most powerful groups in America appeal to public opinion to help their cause. For example, when the government instituted a requirement for tax-withholding on savings accounts, the American Bankers Association appealed to their customers to protest this to their congressional representatives. After 22 million postcards flooded into Congress, lawmakers quickly reversed the policy.[31]

Interest groups market not only their stand on issues but also their reputations. Business interests want people to see them as "what made America great," not as wealthy Americans trying to ensure large profits. The Teamsters Union likes to be known as a united organization of hard-working men and women, not as an organization often influenced by organized crime. Farmers promote the image of a sturdy family working to put bread on the table, not the huge agribusinesses that have largely replaced family farms. In this way, many groups try to create a reservoir of goodwill with the public.

Interest groups' appeals to the public for support have a long tradition in American politics. In 1908, AT&T launched a major magazine advertising campaign to convince people of the need for a telephone monopoly. Similarly, after President Truman proposed a system of national health insurance in 1948, the American Medical Association spent millions of dollars on ads attacking "socialized medicine." In 1994, the Health Insurance Association of America ran a $15 million nationally televised ad campaign criticizing President Clinton's health care package, which many analysts believe lessened public support for the reform bill. So many groups placed advertisements regarding the Clinton health care reform package and so much money was spent (over $100 million), that many observers compared this activity to a national electoral campaign.

Paid for by the Coalition to Scare Your Pants Off

Interest groups spent over $50 million appealing to public opinion during the debate over health care in 1994. In a counter-ad produced by the Democratic National Commitee, the argument was made that opponents of the Clinton health care plan were using scare tactics. You can see the tag end of the ad in this photo.

Lately, more and more organizations have undertaken expensive public relations (PR) efforts. Soft sell and reasoned analysis—presenting both sides of the issues equally—are the hallmark of this new era of public relations. Caterpillar, the manufacturer of massive earth-moving and strip-mining machinery, inundated *National Geographic* and other magazines with balanced ads presenting both sides of environmental issues, such as strip-mining. Mobil Oil runs the most visible corporate PR effort to influence the public with its regular op-ed style ads in the *New York Times* and other major publications. These ads typically address issues that affect the oil industry and big business in general. Once Mobil even ran an ad entitled "Why Do We Buy This Space?" It answered "that business needs voices in the media, the same way labor unions, consumers, and other groups in our society do."[32] No one knows just how effective these image-molding efforts are, but many groups seem to believe firmly that advertising pays off.

Types of Interest Groups

Whether they are lobbying, electioneering, litigating, or appealing to the public, interest groups are omnipresent in the American political system. As with other aspects of American politics and policymaking, political scientists loosely categorize interest groups into clusters. Among the most important clusters are those that deal with: (1) economic issues, (2) environmental concerns, (3) equality issues, and (4) the interests of all consumers. An examination of these four distinct types of interest groups will give you a good picture of much of the American interest group system.

Economic Interests

All economic interests are ultimately concerned with wages, prices, and profits. In the American economy, government does not determine these directly. Only on rare occasions has the government imposed wage and price controls. This has usually been during wartime, although the Nixon Administration briefly used wage and price controls to combat inflation. More commonly, public policy in America has economic effects through regulations, tax advantages, subsidies and contracts, and international trade policy.

Business, labor, and farmers all fret over the impact of government regulations. Even a minor change in government regulatory policy can cost industries a great deal or bring increased profits. Tax policies also affect the livelihood of individuals and firms. How the tax code is written determines whether people and producers pay a lot or a little of their incomes to the government. Because government often provides subsidies to farmers, small businesses, railroads, minority businesses, and others, every economic group wants to get its share of direct aid and government contracts. In this era of economic global interdependence, all groups worry about import quotas, tariffs (fees imposed on imports), and the soundness of the American dollar. In short, business executives, factory workers, and farmers seek to influence government because regulations, taxes, subsidies, and international economic policy all affect their economic livelihoods. The following sections discuss some of the major organized interests and their impact on economic policy.

Labor. Labor has more affiliated members than any other interest group except the American Association for Retired Persons. Fourteen million workers are members of unions belonging to the AFL-CIO—itself a union of unions. Several million others are members of non-AFL-CIO unions, such as the National Education Association, which represents schoolteachers.

Like labor unions everywhere, American unions press for policies to ensure better working conditions and higher wages. Recognizing that many workers would like to enjoy union benefits without actually joining a union and paying dues, unions have fought hard to establish the **union shop**, which requires new employees to join the union representing them. In contrast, business groups have supported **right-to-work laws,** which outlaw union membership as a condition of employment. They argue that such laws deny a basic freedom—namely, the right not to belong to a group. In 1947, the biggest blow ever to the American labor movement occurred when Congress passed the Taft-Hartley Act, permitting states to adopt right-to-work laws (known as "slave labor laws" within the AFL-CIO). Most of the states that have right-to-work laws are in the South, which traditionally has had the lowest percentage of unionized workers.

union shop

A provision found in some collective bargaining agreements requiring all employees of a business to join the union within a short period, usually 30 days, and to remain members as a condition of employment.

right-to-work law

A state law forbidding requirements that workers must join a union to hold their jobs. State right-to-work laws were specifically permitted by the Taft-Hartley Act of 1947.

The American labor movement reached its peak in 1956, when 33 percent of the nonagricultural workforce belonged to a union; since then, the percentage has declined to about 16 percent. One factor behind this decline is that low wages in other countries have diminished the American job market in a number of key manufacturing areas. Steel, once made by American workers, is now made more cheaply in Korea and imported to the United States. The United Auto Workers has found its clout greatly reduced as Detroit has faced heavy competition from Japanese automakers. Some political scientists, however, believe labor's problems result from more than the decline of blue-collar industries. Paul Johnson argues that the biggest factor causing the decline in union membership is the problems unions have had in convincing today's workers that they will benefit from unionization. In particular, Johnson argues that this task has become more difficult in recent years because of employers' efforts to make nonunion jobs satisfying.[33]

Whatever the reason, it is clear that labor unions' ability to shape public policy has decreased. Labor is still a major Democratic constituency, and it surely preferred Bill Clinton to George W. Bush on many issues, such as raising the minimum wage. But the Clinton agenda and labor's agenda were hardly one and the same. Organized labor can no longer expect to be protected from policies that may cost their members jobs when the Democrats are in office. In particular, labor recently found themselves battling in vain to stop trade agreements negotiated by Bill Clinton.

Agriculture. Though it once was the occupation of the majority of Americans, only 3 percent now make their living in farming. The family farm has given way to massive agribusinesses, often heavily involved with exports. To the vast majority who have never lived on a farm, the tangled policies of acreage controls, price supports, and import quotas are mysterious and confusing. To agribusinesses and the few family farmers still around, however, government policies are often more important than the whims of nature.

There are several broad-based agricultural groups, such as the American Farm Bureau Federation. But equally important are the commodity associations formed of

Strikes are among labor unions' most powerful weapons. This strike by United Parcel Service workers attracted a great deal of public attention and affected people all over the country who were expecting packages. The workers got much of what they asked for.

peanut farmers, potato growers, dairy farmers, and other producers. The U.S. Department of Agriculture and the agricultural subcommittees in Congress are organized along commodity lines, such as dairy or wheat. As mentioned earlier in this chapter, this organizational system leads to very cordial relations between the policymakers, the bureaucrats, and the interest groups—promoting classic examples of what hyperpluralists call subgovernments.

Business. If the elite theorists are correct, however, and there is an American power elite, it certainly must be dominated by leaders of the biggest banks, insurance companies, and multinational corporations. Elitists' views may or may not be exaggerated, but business is certainly well organized for political action. Most large firms, such as AT&T and Ford, now have offices in Washington that monitor legislative activity. Schlozman and Tierney report that 70 percent of all interest group organizations that have a Washington presence represent business.[34] Furthermore, business PACs have increased more dramatically than any other category of PACs over the last several decades. Two umbrella organizations, the National Association of Manufacturers (NAM) and the Chamber of Commerce, include most corporations and businesses and speak for them when general business interests are at stake.

Different business interests compete on many specific issues, however. Microsoft and Netscape both have their lobbyists on Capitol Hill pressing their competing interests. Trucking and construction companies want more highways, but railroads do not. An increase in international trade will help some businesses expand their markets, but others may be hurt by foreign competition. Business interests are generally unified when it comes to promoting greater profits, but are often fragmented when policy choices have to be made.

The hundreds of trade and product associations are far less visible than the NAM and the Chamber of Commerce, but they are at least as important in pursuing policy goals for their members. These associations fight regulations that would reduce their profits and seek preferential tax treatment as well as government subsidies and contracts. America's complex schedules of tariffs are monuments to the activities of the trade associations. Although they are the least visible of Washington lobbies, their successes are measured in amendments won, regulations rewritten, and exceptions made. It is not only American trade associations that are concerned with these policies, but foreign corporations and governments as well. The practice of foreign economic interests hiring influential former governmental officials to lobby on their behalf has recently led to a number of reform proposals.[35]

Earth Day was first held in 1970. Its mood was one of protest, as speakers demanded that the government take stronger action to protect the environment. Today, Earth Day is more of an occasion for people to conduct local cleanup efforts and to publicize things that everyone can do to protect the enviornment. Here, a University of Maine student displays some ideas at an Earth Day awareness ceremony.

Environmental Interests

Among the newest political interest groups are the environmentalists. A handful, such as the Sierra Club and the Audubon Society, have been around since the nineteenth century, but many others trace their origins to the first Earth Day, April 22, 1970. On that day, ecology-minded people marched on Washington and other places to symbolize their support for environmental protection. Twenty years later, one estimate pegged the number of environmental groups at over 10,000 and their combined revenues at $2.9 billion—demonstrating "how widely and deeply green values had permeated the society."[36] Environmental groups continue to be formed all the time—for example, Earth 2000 was founded by an enterprising 12-year-old in order to provide an outlet for teenagers to participate in environmental protection (see "Making a Difference: Danny Seo").

Environmental groups have promoted pollution-control policies, wilderness protection, and population control. Perhaps more significant, however, is what they have opposed. Their hit list has included strip-mining, supersonic aircraft, the Alaskan oil pipeline, offshore oil drilling, and nuclear power plants. On these and other issues, environmentalists have exerted a great deal of influence on Congress and state legislatures.

The concerns of environmentalists often come into direct conflict with energy goals. Environmentalists insist that, in the long run, energy supplies can be ensured without harming the environment or risking radiation exposure from nuclear power plants. On the issue of nuclear power plants, their arguments have had a profound impact on public policy. No new nuclear power plants have been approved since 1977, and many that had been in the works were canceled.[37] Short-term energy needs, however, have won out over environmental concerns in many other cases. Energy producers argue that environmentalists oppose nearly every new energy project. Given that there is no sign of a major drop in energy demands, they argue that some limited risks have to be taken. What is worse, they ask, an occasional oil spill off the shore of Alaska or long lines every day at the gas pumps? Thus, despite the opposition of environmentalists, Congress subsidized the massive trans-Alaskan pipeline, which a consortium of companies use to transport oil from Alaska's North Slope. Similarly, the strip-mining of coal continues despite constant objections from environmentalists. Group politics intensifies with the clash of two public interests, such as environmental protection and an ensured supply of energy.

Making a Difference

Danny Seo

Danny Seo was born on Earth Day in 1977. On his twelfth birthday, he devoted his birthday party to forming an environmental group with his friends. The first project of his Earth 2000 group (named to reflect its goal of saving the Earth by the year 2000) was to promote recycling. The next year the group took on the cause of protecting 66 acres of forest and wetlands near their Redding, Penns., home from development. While Danny Seo was walking around the wilderness he was trying to save, he came across some nineteenth-century artifacts. With the help of the media he publicized his find, and suddenly lawyers volunteered to help the group's effort. In the end 70 percent of the land was protected from any future development; a bunch of kids had triumphed over a wealthy land development firm.

As he grew older, Danny Seo expanded the scope of his group's activities to protect animal rights as well. When he was told that he had to dissect a frog in biology class, he mobilized Earth 2000 to successfully pressure the Pennsylvania legislature to pass a bill giving students the right to refuse to dissect animals. At the age of 16, Seo set his organization's sights on stopping the killing of pilot whales off the coast of Denmark. They traveled to Washington, D.C. where they set up a protest in front of the Danish embassy. The sight of teenagers causing a stir in front of an embassy drew international press attention. An environmental group in the United Kingdom heard about the protest and decided to start a boycott of Danish seafood, which had a substantial impact on the Danish fishing industry.

Seo's current focus is to utilize kids' economic power to influence environmental decisions. The group has already persuaded 4,000 retailers to sign an agreement not to sell fur products. Danny Seo has his own website (www.dannyseo.com) and a book called *Generation React,* which presents his ideas for political activism among young people. In 1998, he was named one of the "50 most beautiful people in the world" by *People* magazine.

A few interest groups use unconventional methods to get attention for their views and demands. The enviornmental activist group Greenpeace is well-known for coming up with activities that the media can hardly ignore. Here, group members can be seen protesting the Bush administration's policies by placing a huge banner in front of the main entrance of the Department of the Interior early in the morning.

Equality Interests

The Fourteenth Amendment guarantees equal protection under the law. American history, though, shows that this is easier said than done. Two sets of interest groups, representing minorities and women, have made equal rights their main policy goal.

Chapter 5 reviewed the long history of the civil rights movement; this section is concerned with its policy goals and organizational base.

Equality at the polls, in housing, on the job, in education, and in all other facets of American life has long been the dominant goal of African-American groups. The oldest and largest of these groups is the National Association for the Advancement of Colored People (NAACP). It argued and won the monumental *Brown v. Board of Education* case in 1954, in which the Supreme Court held that segregated schools were unconstitutional. Although the NAACP has won many victories in principle, equality in practice has been much slower in coming. Today, civil rights groups continue to push for more effective affirmative action programs to ensure that minority groups are given educational and employment opportunities. In recent years, the NAACP's main vehicle has been the Fair Share program, which negotiates agreements with national and regional businesses to increase minority hiring and the use of minority contractors. As an issue, affirmative action is not as emotionally charged as was desegregation, but it too has been controversial.

Although the work of civil rights interest groups in fighting segregation and discrimination is well known, Dona and Charles Hamilton argue that "much less is known about the 'social welfare agenda,'—the fight for social welfare policies to help the poor."[38] They argue that since the 1930s, civil rights groups have been concerned with larger and more universal economic problems in American society.

When the NAACP was just beginning, suffragists were in the streets and legislative lobbies were demanding women's right to vote. The Nineteenth Amendment, ratified in 1920, guaranteed women the vote, but other guarantees of equal protection remained absent from the Constitution. More recently, women's rights groups, such as the National Organization for Women (NOW), have lobbied for an end to gender discrimination. Their primary goal has been the passage of the Equal Rights Amendment (ERA), which states that "equality of rights under the law shall not be abridged on account of sex."

In the first month after the ERA was approved by Congress in 1972, it was overwhelmingly ratified by 15 states. Even Texas and Kansas, fairly conservative states, voted decisively for the ERA in the first year. The quiet consensual politics of the ERA ratification process soon came to a boisterous end, however, when Phyllis Schlafly, a conservative activist from Alton, Ill., began a highly visible STOP ERA movement. She and her followers argued the ERA would destroy the integrity of the family, require communal bathrooms, lead to women in combat, and eliminate legal protections that women already had. Their emotional appeal was just enough to stop the ERA 3 states short of the 38 necessary for ratification.

Though the ERA seems dead for the moment, NOW remains committed to enacting the protection that the amendment would have constitutionally guaranteed by advocating the enactment of many individual statutes. As is often the case with interest group politics, issues are rarely settled once and for all; rather, they shift to different policy arenas.

Consumers and Public Interest Lobbies

Pluralist theory holds that for virtually every interest in society, there is an organized group. But what about the interests of all of us—the buying public? Today over 2,000 organized groups are championing various causes or ideas "in the public interest."[39] These **public interest lobbies** are organizations that seek "a collective good, the achievement of which will not selectively and materially benefit the membership or activists of the organization."[40] If products are made safer by the lobbying of consumer protection groups, it is not the members of such groups alone that benefit. Rather, everyone should be better off, regardless of whether they joined in the lobbying.

public interest lobbies

According to Jeffrey Berry, organizations that seek "a collective good, the achievement of which will not selectively and materially benefit the membership or activities of the organization."

If ever a lobbying effort was spurred by a single person, it was the consumer movement. At first, Ralph Nader took on American business almost single-handedly in the

Interest groups often clash on issues, as when Phyllis Schlafly's Eagle Forum battled NOW and other women's groups over ratification of the ERA. Here, Schlafly addresses a STOP ERA rally in the rotunda of the Illinois state capitol; her well-publicized efforts helped defeat pro-ERA forces in her home state.

Like other public interest groups, the Children's Defense Fund works against Olson's law of large groups; that is, it is easier to organize a small group with clear economic goals than it is to organize a large group with broader goals.

name of consumerism. He was propelled to national prominence by his book, *Unsafe at Any Speed* which attacked General Motors' Corvair as a mechanically deficient and dangerous automobile. General Motors made the mistake of hiring a private detective to dig into Nader's background and follow him around, hoping that there might be some dirt they could uncover that would discredit him. Nader eventually learned about the investigation, sued General Motors for invasion of privacy, and won a hefty damage settlement in court. He used the proceeds to launch the first major consumer group in Washington.

Consumer groups have won many legislative victories. In 1973, Congress responded to consumer advocacy by creating the Consumer Product Safety Commission. Congress authorized it to regulate all consumer products and even gave it the power to ban particularly dangerous ones, bearing in mind that household products are responsible for 30,000 deaths annually. Among the products the commission has investigated are children's sleepwear (some of which contained a carcinogen), hot tubs, and lawn mowers.

Consumer groups are not the only ones that claim to be public interest groups. Groups speaking for those who cannot speak for themselves seek to protect children, animals, and the mentally ill; good-government groups such as Common Cause push for openness and fairness in government; and religious groups like the Christian Coalition crusade for the protection of ethical and moral standards in American society.

Why does it matter?

Consumer groups fight for the interests of us all. Yet, they face an organizational disadvantage inherent in Olson's law of large groups. How have consumer groups managed to accomplish anything at all in the political arena? How might they become more effective? How might this affect you?

How You Can Make A Difference

Interest Groups

Student activism for political causes has a long and proud history in the United States. You can be part of this—and help make a difference! Is there an issue or cause that is dear to you? Something about the country that you would like to protect or to change? If so, get involved. There are groups representing just about every conceivable viewpoint. Find the one that matches your views. Join, go to meetings, and volunteer. Give your time and money to a group that fights for what you believe in. Know your legislators (local, state, and national) and how to contact them. Learn how legislation is made and how it can be blocked or overturned. If conventional political tactics don't produce the result you want, consider adopting unconventional tactics to attract media attention.

One way to find interest groups that reflect your own views is through the Internet. Just about all interest groups have their own websites. You can also use the resources and directories listed here to locate specific interest groups:

Political science resources: links to political parties, interest groups, and other political groups around the world www.psr.keele.ac.uk/parties.htm

Activist groups directory: www.goodmoney.com/directory_active.htm

Environmental action groups:
www.mamagaia.com/ecogroupsa-l.htm
www.mamagaia.com/ecogroupsm-z.htm

Links to activist groups on affirmative action, civil liberties, free speech, disability rights, and ethnic and minority rights: http://ncec.org/links/issues.htm

Index of activist groups:
www.politicalindex.com/sect10.htm

Youth activist groups:
www.politicalusa.com/youth1.htm

Other activist groups: http://crash.ihug.co.nz/~bwmm/groups.htm

Understanding Interest Groups

The problem of interest groups in America today remains much the same as Madison defined it over 200 years ago. A free society must allow for the representation of all groups that seek to influence political decision making. Yet groups are usually more concerned with their own self-interest than with the needs of society as a whole, and for democracy to work well, it is important that they not be allowed to assume a dominant position.

Interest Groups and Democracy

James Madison's solution to the problems posed by interest groups was to create a wide-open system in which many groups would be able to participate. In such an extended sphere of influence, according to Madison, groups with opposing interests would counterbalance one another. Pluralist theorists believe that a rough approximation of the public interest emerges from this competition.

With the tremendous growth of interest group politics in recent years, some observers say that Madison may at last have gotten his wish. For every group with an interest, there now seems to be a competing group to watch over it—not to mention public interest lobbies to watch over them all. Robert Salisbury argues that "the growth in the number, variety, and sophistication of interest groups represented in Washington" has transformed policymaking such that it "is not dominated so often by a relatively small number of powerful interest groups as it may once have been."[41] Paradoxically, Salisbury concludes that the increase in lobbying activity has resulted in less clout overall for interest groups—and better democracy.

Elite theorists clearly disagree with this conclusion and point to the proliferation of business PACs as evidence of more interest group corruption in American politics than ever. A democratic process requires a free and open exchange of ideas in which candidates and voters should be able to hear one another out, but PACs—the source of so much money in elections—distort the process. Elite theorists particularly note that wealthier interests are greatly advantaged by the PAC system. Business PACs have become the dominant force in the fund-raising game. Furthermore, the richest 3 percent of PACs account for over half the campaign contributions from such groups.[42]

PACs can sometimes link money to politics at the highest levels. The old party machines may have bought votes in the voting booth; the new PACs are accused of buying votes in legislatures. Technology, especially television, makes American elections expensive; candidates need money to pay for high-tech campaigns, and PACs are able to supply that money. In return, they ask only to be remembered when their interests are clearly at stake.

Hyperpluralist theorists maintain that whenever a major interest group objects strongly to proposed legislation, policymakers will bend over backward to try to accommodate it. With the formation of so many groups in recent years, and with so many of them having influence in Washington, hyperpluralists argue that it has been increasingly difficult to accomplish major policy change in Washington. Thus hyperpluralist theory offers a powerful explanation for the policy gridlock evident in American politics today.

Interest Groups and the Scope of Government

Though individualistic, Americans are also very associational. As Alexis de Tocqueville wrote in the 1830s, "Americans of all ages, all conditions, and all dispositions constantly form associations."[43] This is not at all contradictory. By joining a number of political associations, Americans are able to politicize a variety of aspects of their own individualism. The multiplicity of the American interest group structure and the openness of American politics to inputs from interest groups allow individuals many channels for political participation and thus facilitate representation of individual interests.

Though individualism is most often treated in this book as being responsible for the relatively small scope of American government, when it works its way through interest group politics, the result is just the opposite. Individual interest groups fight to sustain government programs that are important to them, thereby making it hard for politicians ever to reduce the scope of government. Both President Carter and President Reagan remarked at the end of their time in office that their attempts to cut waste in federal spending had been frustrated by interest groups. In his farewell address, Carter "suggested that the reason he had so much difficulty in dealing with Congress was the fragmentation of power and decision making that was exploited by interest groups."[44] Similarly, Reagan remarked a month before leaving office that "special interest groups, bolstered by campaign contributions, pressure lawmakers into creating and defending spending programs."[45] Above all, most special interest groups strive to maintain established programs that benefit them.

However, one can also argue that the growth in the scope of government in recent decades accounts for a good portion of the proliferation of interest groups. The more areas in which the federal government has become involved, the more interest groups have developed to attempt to influence policy. As William Lunch notes, "a great part of the increase was occasioned by the new government responsibility for civil rights, environmental protection, and greater public health and safety."[46] For example, once the government got actively involved in protecting the environment, many groups sprung up to lobby for strong standards and enforcement. Given the tremendous effects of environmental regulations on many industries, it should come as no surprise that these industries also organized to ensure that their interests were taken into account. As Salisbury writes, many groups have "come to Washington out of need and dependence rather than because they have influence."[47] He argues that interest groups spend much of their time merely monitoring policy developments in order to alert their membership and develop reactive strategies.

Career Profile

Position: Director of Public Policy
Employer: Electronic Frontier Foundation, a nonprofit interest group
Starting Salary: $40,000
Benefits: Health and life insurance, retirement plan
Qualifications: Master's degree and some law knowledge, good public speaking skills, ability to think "outside the box"

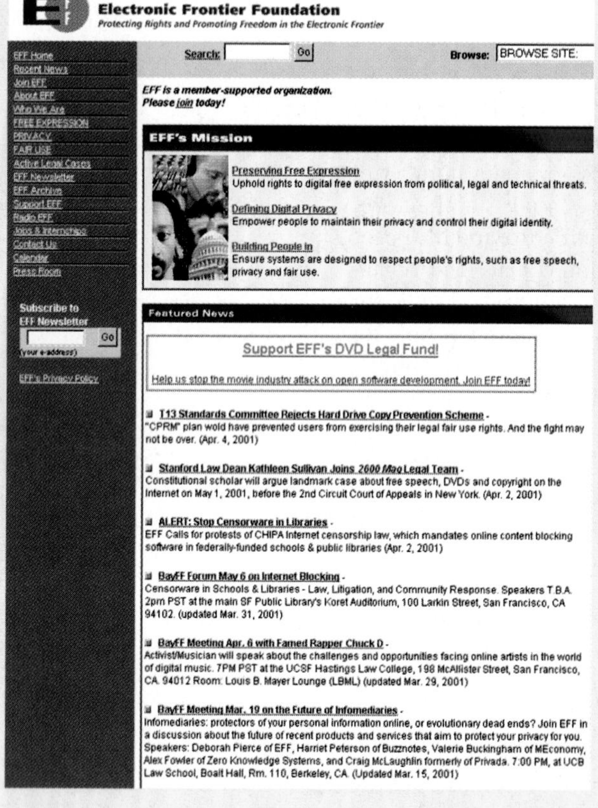

Real People on the Job: Lauren Gelman

Lauren Gelman works at the Electronic Frontier Foundation, a nonprofit interest group in Washington, D.C. The foundation is essentially a civil liberties organization. It fights to protect privacy and freedom of expression on the Internet and other new technologies by lobbying Congress and, when necessary, engaging in litigation.

As the director of public policy, Lauren plays a big part in establishing the foundation's policy. To do her job effectively, she must closely follow what's going on in Congress and in regulatory agencies that might affect online rights of citizens. When Congress debates the merits of a bill regulating the Internet, she will testify before them. When Congress passes a bill that the foundation deems to be a threat to individual rights, she will speak before various groups and explain why the law is bad. Lauren also writes press briefings, talks to the press, testifies before the FCC, engages in coalition building efforts with similar civil liberties groups, and writes opinion pieces for newspapers. In all, it is a job that requires a great deal of energy and creative thinking.

When the Communications Decency Act was before Congress in 1999, Lauren had to get busy. The EFF believed this proposed law was written to severely restrict free speech on the Internet, including the distribution of pornography. The EFF felt that if the law were to be passed, it would violate the first amendment's protection of free speech, so they fought its passage in Congress. To do this, Lauren testified before Congress arguing that the government cannot create a world that is safe only for kids at the expense of everyone's right to express themselves. The law passed despite Lauren's testimony and the EFF entered a court challenge to the new law.

Lauren said the knowledge that she's making a difference is the most satisfying part of the job. Laws and rules created to regulate the Internet today will have a lasting impact on our country for many years to come. Because her efforts to protect civil liberties are likely to endure for some time, Lauren feels that she is making a positive contribution to the future. Another great part of the job is the people she works with, a group of young, smart people who care passionately about the cause.

If you want to work for an interest group in Washington, you will need the same drive and commitment to a cause that Lauren and her peers have. This is not a standard 9 to 5 sort of job where you know exactly what you'll be doing every day or what time you'll be going home. If you really care about an issue, however, it's a great way to get involved and make a difference. For more information, contact the interest group(s) you are interested in working for. Discuss your ideas and your résumé with them. Show them how you can be an asset to their team!

Summary

This chapter discusses the vast array of interest groups in American politics—all vying for policies they prefer. Pluralists see groups as the most important way people can have their policy preferences represented in government. Hyperpluralists, though, fear that too many groups are getting too much of what they want, skillfully working the many subgovernments in the American system. Elitist theorists believe that a few wealthy individuals and multinational corporations exert control over the major decisions regarding distribution of goods and services.

A number of factors influence a group's success in achieving its policy goals. Most surprising is that small groups have an organizational advantage over large groups. Large groups often fall victim to the free-rider problem, which is explained by Olson's law of large groups. Both large and small groups can benefit from the intensity of their members' beliefs. Money always helps lubricate the wheels of power, though it is hardly a surefire guarantee of success.

Interest groups use four basic strategies to maximize their effectiveness. Lobbying is one well-known group strategy. Although the evidence on its influence is mixed, it is clear that lobbyists are most effective with those legislators already sympathetic to their side. Thus electioneering becomes critical because it helps put supportive people in office. Often today, groups operate in the judicial as well as the legislative process, using litigation in the courts when lobbying fails or is not enough. Many also find it important to project a good image, employing public relations techniques to present themselves in the most favorable light.

This chapter also examined some of the major kinds of interest groups, particularly those concerned with economic, environmental, and equality policy. Public interest lobbies claim to be different from other interest groups, representing, they say, an important aspect of the public interest. Recently there has been a rapid growth of single-interest groups, which focus narrowly on one issue and are not inclined to compromise.

The issue of controlling interest groups remains as crucial to democracy today as it was in Madison's time. Some scholars believe that the growth of interest groups has worked to divide political influence just as Madison hoped it would. Other scholars point to the PAC system as the new way in which special interests corrupt American democracy.

Key Terms

interest group
pluralist theory
elite theory
hyperpluralist theory
subgovernments
potential group
actual group
collective good
free-rider problem
Olson's law of large groups
selective benefits
single-issue group
lobbying
electioneering
political action committees (PACs)
amicus curiae briefs
class action lawsuits
union shop
right-to-work laws
public interest lobbies

For Further Reading

Baumgartner, Frank R., and Beth L. Leech. *Basic Interests: The Importance of Groups in Politics and in Political Science.* Princeton, NJ: Princeton University Press, 1998. An excellent review and analysis of the academic literature on interest groups.

Berry, Jeffrey M. *The Interest Group Society*, 3rd ed. New York: Longman, 1997. One of the best contemporary textbooks on interest groups.

Berry, Jeffrey M. *The New Liberalism: The Rising Power of Citizen Groups.* Washington, D.C.: Brookings, 1999. Berry argues that citizen groups have been strikingly successful in influencing the policy agenda in recent decades.

Birnbaum, Jeffrey H., and Alan S. Murray. *Showdown at Gucci Gulch: Lawmakers, Lobbyists, and the Unlikely Triumph of Tax Reform.* New York: Vintage, 1987. A fascinating account of how the 1986 tax reform bill passed over the objections of the Gucci-clad lobbyists.

Cigler, Allan J., and Burdett A. Loomis, eds. *Interest Group Politics*, 5th ed. Washington, D.C.: Congressional Quarterly Press, 1998. An excellent collection of original articles on the modern interest group system.

Day, Christine. *What Older Americans Think: Interest Groups and Aging Policy.* Princeton, NJ: Princeton University Press, 1990. A good study of lobbying on behalf of the elderly.

Dye, Thomas R. *Who's Running America?*, 6th ed. Englewood Cliffs, NJ: Prentice-Hall, 1995. A good summary of the elitist view of interest groups.

Herrnson, Paul S., Ronald G. Shaiko, and Clyde Wilcox, eds. *The Interest Group Connection.* Chatham, NJ: Chatham House, 1998. A collection of up-to-date essays on interest groups with the added bonus of commentaries from major lobbyists themselves.

Godwin, R. Kenneth. *One Billion Dollars of Influence.* Chatham, NJ: Chatham House, 1988. An interesting look at the direct marketing of politics via direct mail.

Kollman, Ken. *Outside Lobbying: Public Opinion and Interest Group Strategies.* Princeton, NJ: Princeton University Press, 1998. An insightful study of how many interest groups use public opinion in the lobbying process.

Lowi, Theodore J. *The End of Liberalism*, 2nd ed. New York: Norton, 1979. A critique of the role of subgovernments and the excessive deference to interest groups in the American political system.

Olson, Mancur. *The Logic of Collective Action.* Cambridge, MA: Harvard University Press, 1965. Develops an economic theory of groups, showing how the cards are stacked against larger groups.

Rauch, Jonathan. *Demosclerosis: The Silent Killer of American Government.* New York: Random House, 1994. A good recent treatment of hyperpluralism in American politics.

Rozell, Mark J., and Clyde Wilcox. *Interest Groups in American Campaigns.* Washington, D.C.: Congressional Quarterly Press, 1999. A good review of how interest groups are playing an increasingly important role in electioneering.

Schlozman, Kay L., and John T. Tierney. *Organized Interests and American Democracy.* New York: Harper & Row, 1986. Survey results from a sample of Washington lobbyists are used to draw a portrait of the interest group system.

Walker, Jack L. *Mobilizing Interest Groups in America: Patrons, Professions and Social Movements.* Ann Arbor: University of Michigan Press, 1991. An important collection of essays on the formation and activities of interest groups.

Internet Resources

www.aarp.org
The official site of the American Association of Retired Persons.

www.aflcio.org
The nation's largest labor association, the AFL-CIO, posts material at this site.

www.nea.org
The site of the National Education Association.

www.greenpeaceusa.org
The place to go to learn more about the activities of this environmental protection group.

www.commoncause.org
The official site of Common Cause, one of the nation's oldest and largest public affairs interest groups.

www.freespeech.org/x-pac/
A site for an interest group that represents young people, particularly on Social Security issues.

Notes

1. Kay L. Schlozman and John T. Tierney, *Organized Interests and American Democracy* (New York: Harper & Row, 1986), 1.
2. Quoted in Schlozman and Tierney, *Organized Interests*, 261–262.
3. The classic work is David B. Truman, *The Governmental Process*, 2nd ed. (New York: Knopf, 1971).
4. Thomas R. Dye, *Who's Running America?*, 5th ed. (Englewood Cliffs, NJ: Prentice-Hall, 1990), 170.
5. Robert Engler, *The Brotherhood of Oil* (Chicago: University of Chicago Press, 1977).
6. Theodore J. Lowi, *The End of Liberalism*, 2nd ed. (New York: Norton, 1979).
7. See Lee Fritschler, *Smoking and Politics: Policy Making and the Federal Bureaucracy* (Englewood Cliffs, NJ: Prentice-Hall, 1983).
8. Morris P. Fiorina, *Congress: Keystone of the Washington Establishment*, 2nd ed. (New Haven, CT: Yale University Press, 1989), 122.
9. E. E. Schattschneider, *The Semisovereign People* (New York: Holt, Rinehart & Winston, 1960), 35.
10. Truman, *The Governmental Process*, 511.
11. Mancur Olson, *The Logic of Collective Action* (Cambridge, MA: Harvard University Press, 1965), especially 9–36.
12. *Ibid.*, 35.
13. Jeffrey H. Birnbaum and Alan S. Murray, *Showdown at Gucci Gulch: Lawmakers, Lobbyists, and the Unlikely Triumph of Tax Reform* (New York: Vintage, 1987).
14. *Ibid.*, 235.
15. Christine Mauer and Tara E. Sheets, eds., *Encyclopedia of Associations*, 33rd ed. (Detroit: Gale Research Company, 1998).
16. Frank R. Baumgartner and Beth L. Leech, *Basic Interests: The Importance of Groups in Politics and in Political Science* (Princeton, NJ: Princeton University Press, 1998), 109.
17. Jack L. Walker, "The Origins and Maintenance of Interest Groups in America," *American Political Science Review* 77 (June 1983): 390–406.
18. Andrew S. McFarland, *Common Cause: Lobbying in the Public Interest* (Chatham, NJ: Chatham House, 1984), 1.
19. Lester W. Milbrath, *The Washington Lobbyists* (Chicago: Rand McNally, 1963), 8.
20. Norman Ornstein and Shirley Elder, *Interest Groups, Lobbying, and Policymaking* (Washington, D.C.: Congressional Quarterly Press, 1978), 59–60.
21. Peter H. Stone, "Friends, After All," *National Journal*, October 22, 1994, 2,440.

22. Raymond A. Bauer, Ithiel de Sola Pool, and Lewis A. Dexter, *American Business and Public Policy* (New York: Atherton, 1963).
23. Milbrath, *The Washington Lobbyists*, 354.
24. For a summary of recent studies on the influence of lobbying, see Baumgartner and Leech, *Basic Interests*, 130.
25. See Laura Langbein and Mark Lotwis, "The Political Efficacy of Lobbying and Money: Gun Control in the U.S. House, 1986," *Legislative Studies Quarterly* 15 (Fall 1990): 413–440.
26. The Sovern story is told in "Taking an Ax to PACs," *Time*, August 20, 1984, 27.
27. Karen Orren, "Standing To Sue: Interest Group Conflict in Federal Courts," *American Political Science Review* 70 (September 1976): 724.
28. Jeffrey M. Berry, *The Interest Group Society*, 3rd ed. (New York: Longman, 1997), 25.
29. Gregory A. Caldeira and John R. Wright, "*Amici Curiae* Before the Supreme Court: Who Participates, When, and How Much," *Journal of Politics* 52 (August 1990): 782–804.
30. Ronald J. Hrebenar and Ruth K. Scott, *Interest Group Politics in America*, 2nd ed. (Englewood Cliffs, NJ: Prentice-Hall, 1990), 201.
31. Ken Kollman, *Outside Lobbying: Public Opinion and Interest Group Strategies* (Princeton, NJ: Princeton University Press, 1998), 33.
32. Quoted in Jeffrey M. Berry, *The Interest Group Society*, 2nd ed. (Glenview, IL: Scott, Foresman, 1989), 103.
33. Paul Edward Johnson, "Organized Labor in an Era of Blue-Collar Decline," in Allan J. Cigler and Burdett A. Loomis, eds., *Interest Group Politics*, 3rd ed. (Washington, D.C.: Congressional Quarterly Press, 1991), 33–62.
34. Schlozman and Tierney, *Organized Interests*, 68.
35. See Pat Choate, *Agents of Influence: How Japan Manipulates America's Political and Economic System* (New York: Simon & Schuster, 1990).
36. Christopher J. Bosso, "The Color of Money: Environmental Groups and the Pathologies of Fund Raising," in Allan J. Cigler and Burdett A. Loomis, *Interest Group Politics*, 4th ed. (Washington, D.C.: Congressional Quarterly Press, 1995), 102.
37. For an interesting analysis of how changes in the regulatory environment, congressional oversight, and public opinion altered the debate on nuclear power, see Frank R. Baumgartner and Bryan D. Jones, *Agendas and Instability in American Politics* (Chicago: University of Chicago Press, 1993).
38. Dona C. Hamilton and Charles V. Hamilton, *The Dual Agenda: Race and Social Welfare Policies of Civil Rights Organizations* (New York: Columbia University Press, 1997), 2.
39. H. R. Mahood, *Interest Group Politics in America: A New Intensity* (Englewood Cliffs, NJ: Prentice-Hall, 1990), 162.
40. Jeffrey M. Berry, *Lobbying for the People* (Princeton, NJ: Princeton University Press, 1977), 7.
41. Robert H. Salisbury, "The Paradox of Interest Groups in Washington—More Groups, Less Clout," in Anthony King, ed., *The New American Political System*, 2nd ed. (Washington, D.C.: American Enterprise Institute, 1990), 204.
42. Paul S. Herrnson, *Congressional Elections: Campaigning at Home and in Washington* (Washington, D.C.: Congressional Quarterly Press, 1995), 108.
43. Alexis de Tocqueville, *Democracy in America*, vol. 2 (New York: Vintage, 1945), 114.
44. Hrebenar and Scott, *Interest Group Politics in America*, 2nd ed., 234.
45. Steven V. Roberts, "Angered President Blames Others for the Huge Deficit," the *New York Times*, December 14, 1988, A16.
46. William M. Lunch, *The Nationalization of American Politics* (Berkeley: University of California Press, 1987), 206.
47. Salisbury, "The Paradox of Interest Groups," 229.

12

Chapter Outline

- The Representatives and Senators
- Congressional Elections
- How Congress Is Organized to Make Policy
- The Congressional Process
- Understanding Congress
- Summary

David Boren of Oklahoma decided to quit. He was a senior U.S. senator in good health and could look forward to years of prominence in making public policy. Yet he chose to leave office midterm to become president of the University of Oklahoma. The same year, a record number of Boren's colleagues decided to voluntarily retire from the Senate. They had had enough.

To many Americans, being a U.S. senator may seem rather glamorous. What citizens do not see is the 14-hour days spent dashing from one meeting to the next, the continuous travel between Washington and constituencies, the lack of time for reflection or exchange of ideas, the constant fund-raising, the partisan rancor that permeates Congress, and—perhaps most important of all—the feeling that Congress is making little headway in solving the country's problems.

It is ironic that such frustrations exist in an organization whose members put so much blood, sweat, and tears into joining. Yet it

is difficult to get anything done. The movement of legislation through the congressional labyrinth has never been more complicated. Power is fragmented within Congress, and members of Congress are often fiercely independent. Former Senate Majority Leader Howard Baker declared that moving the Senate is like "trying to push a wet noodle."

And then there is the president. Often the majority in Congress and the chief executive are of different political parties. Even if a bill passes Congress, it may be vetoed at the other end of Pennsylvania Avenue. Lack of agreement between the two branches may even lead to a shutdown of the government, as happened during the battle over the 1996 budget.

"So," many senators and representatives ask themselves, "what is the point of serving? The public holds us in low regard, the pundits criticize us continuously, and we get little done. Isn't it better to be doing something else?"

The discontent with Congress among its own members is also ironic. The framers of the Constitution conceived of the legislature as the center of policymaking in America. The great disputes over public policy were to be resolved there, not in the White House or the Supreme Court. Although the prominence of Congress has ebbed and flowed over the course of American history, in recent years Congress has been the true center of power in Washington.

Congress is not only our central policymaking branch, but is also our principal *representative* branch. As such, it lies at the heart of American democracy. How does Congress combine its roles of representing constituents *and* making effective public policy? Not very well, according to many critics. Some argue that Congress is too responsive to constituents and, especially, to organized interests and is thus unable to make difficult choices regarding public policy. Conversely, others argue that Congress is too insulated from ordinary citizens. Many critics even support efforts to force members of Congress to retire after serving just a few terms.

Other critics focus on Congress as the source of government expansion. If Congress is responsive to a multitude of interests and those interests want government policies to aid them in some way, the logical result is an increase in the size of the public sector. In addition, do the benefits of servicing constituents provide an incentive for members of Congress to tolerate—even to expand—an already big government?

Congress's tasks become more difficult each year. On any day a representative or senator can be required to make a sensible judgment about nuclear missiles, nuclear waste dumps, abortion, trade competition with Japan, income tax rates, the soaring costs of Social Security and Medicare, and countless other issues. President Clinton's 1993 health care reform proposal was 1,342 pages long and weighed six pounds. Just finding time to think about these issues—much less debate them—has become increasingly difficult.

Despite the many demands of the job, there is no shortage of men and women running for congressional office. The following sections will introduce you to these people.

The Representatives and Senators

Being a member of Congress is a difficult and unusual job. A person must be willing to spend considerable time, trouble, and money to obtain a crowded office on Capitol Hill. To nineteenth-century humorist Artemus Ward, such a quest was inexplicable: "It's easy to see why a man goes to the poorhouse or the penitentiary. It's because he can't help it. But why he should voluntarily go live in Washington is beyond my comprehension."

The Job

Hard work is perhaps the most prominent characteristic of a congressperson's job. Representatives and senators deeply resent common beliefs that they are overpaid, underworked, corrupt, and ineffective. Members have even commissioned their own time and motion studies of their efficiency to demonstrate that they do work hard (see Table 12.1). For example, the typical representative is a member of about six committees and subcommittees; a senator is a member of about ten. Members are often scheduled to be in two places at the same time.

There are attractions to the job, however. First and foremost is power. Members of Congress make key decisions about important matters of public policy. In addition, the salary and the perks that go with the job help make it tolerable. Members of Congress receive the following:

- A salary of $145,100, about four times the income of the typical American family, but well below that of hundreds of corporate presidents who earn several times as much
- Generous retirement benefits
- Office space in Washington and in their constituencies
- A substantial congressional staff who serve individual members, committees, and party leaders
- Handsome travel allowances to see their constituents each year, plus opportunities to travel at low fares or even free to foreign nations on congressional inquiries (what critics call "junkets")
- Franking privileges—the free use of the mail system to communicate with constituents, and machines that duplicate a member's signature in real ink
- Plenty of small privileges, such as free flowers from the National Botanical Gardens, research services from the Library of Congress, and access to exercise rooms and pools

Despite the salaries, the perquisites, and the thousands of staff members, Congress is relatively inexpensive. Per citizen, it costs Americans about the same amount to run the nation's legislature for a year or to buy a hamburger, fries, and cola at a favorite fast food franchise.

Table 12.1 A Day in the Life of a Member of Congress

TYPICAL SCHEDULE IN WASHINGTON		TYPICAL SCHEDULE IN CONSTITUENCY	
8:00 A.M.	Budget Study Group:—Chair Leon Panetta, Budget Committee	7:30 A.M.	Business group breakfast: 20 leaders of the business community
8:45 A.M.	Mainstream Forum meeting	8:45 A.M.	Hoover Elementary School: 6th grade class assembly
9:15 A.M.	Meeting with Consulting Engineers Council from constituency about various issues of concern	9:45 A.M.	National Agriculture Day: speech
9:45 A.M.	Meet with Soybean Association representatives regarding agriculture appropriations projects	10:45 A.M.	Supplemental Food Shelf: pass foodstuffs to needy families
10:15 A.M.	WCHL radio interview (by phone)	12:00 NOON	Community college: student/faculty lunch, speech and Q & A
10:30 A.M.	Tape weekly radio show—budget	1:00 P.M.	Sunset Terrace Elementary School: assembly 4,5,6 grades, remarks/Q & A
11:00 A.M.	Meet with former student, now an author, about intellectual property issue	(Travel Time: 1:45 P.M.–2:45 P.M.)	
1:00 P.M.	Agriculture Subcommittee Hearing—Budget Overview and General Agriculture Outlook	2:45 P.M.	Plainview Day Care Facility: discuss changes in federal law with owner
2:30 P.M.	Meeting with Chair Bill Ford and Southern Democrats regarding HR–5, Striker Replacement Bill, possible amendments	4:00 P.M.	Town Hall meeting: American Legion
3:15 P.M.	Meet with Close-up students from district on steps of Capitol for photo and discussions	(Travel Time: 5:00 P.M.–5:45 P.M.)	
3:45 P.M.	Meet with professor regarding energy research programs	5:45 P.M.	PTA meeting: speech on education issues before Congress (also citizen involvement with national associations)
4:30 P.M.	Meet with constituent of Kurdish background regarding situation in Iraq	6:30 P.M.	Annual Dinner: St. John's Lutheran Church Development Activity Center
5:30–7:00 P.M.	Reception—Sponsored by National Association of Home Builders, honoring new president Mark Tipton from constituency	7:15 P.M.	Association for Children for Enforcement of Support meeting: discuss problems of enforcing child support payments
6:00–8:00 P.M.	Reception—Honoring retiring Rep. Bill Gray	(Travel Time 8:00 P.M.–8:30 P.M.)	
6:00–8:00 P.M.	Reception—Sponsored by Firefighters Association	8:30 P.M.	Students Against Drunk Driving (SADD) meeting: speech on drinking age, drunk driving, uniform federal penalties
6:00–8:00 P.M.	Reception—Sponsored by American Financial Services Association	9:30 P.M.	State university class: discuss business issues before Congress

Sources: Adapted by permission from Craig Schultz, ed., *Setting Course: A Congressional Management Guide.* Copyright © 1994 Congressional Management Foundation, Washington, D.C. and from David E. Price, *The Congressional Experience: A View from the Hill.* Copyright © 1999 Westview Press, a division of HarperCollins Publishers. Reprinted by permission of Westview Press, a member of Perseus Books, L.L.C.

The Members

There are 535 members of Congress. An even hundred, two from each state, are members of the Senate. The other 435 are members of the House of Representatives. The Constitution specifies only that members of the House must be at least 25 years old and American citizens for seven years; senators must be at least 30 and American citizens for nine years. In addition, all members of Congress must be residents of the states from which they are elected.

Members of Congress are not typical or average Americans, however, as the figures in Table 12.2 reveal. Elite theorists are quick to point out that members come largely from occupations with high status and usually have substantial incomes. Although calling the Senate a "millionaires' club" is an exaggeration, the proportion of millionaires and near-millionaires is much higher in Congress than in an average

Table 12.2 A Portrait of the 107th Congress: Some Statistics

CHARACTERISTIC	HOUSE (435 TOTAL)	SENATE (100 TOTAL)
Party		
Democrat	212	50
Republican	221	49
Independent	2	1
Gender		
Men	376	87
Women	59	13
Race		
Asian	4	2
African American	36	0
Hispanic	19	0
White and other	376	98
Average Age	54 years	60 years
Religion		
Protestant	271	63
Roman Catholic	125	24
Jewish	27	10
Other and unspecified	11	3
Prior Occupation[a]		
Law	156	53
Business	159	24
Education	92	16
Public service/politics	126	28
Agriculture	25	6
Journalism	9	7
Real estate	24	4
Medicine	14	3
Other	49	7

[a]Some members specify more than one occupation.
Source: "Congress of Relative Newcomers Poses Challenges to Bush, Leadership, "*Congressional Quarterly Weekly Report,* January 20, 2001, 178–182.

crowd of 535 people. Business and law are the dominant prior occupations; other elite occupations such as academia are also well represented.

Law especially attracts persons interested in politics and provides the flexibility (and often the financial support of a law firm) to wage election campaigns. In addition, many government positions in which aspiring members of Congress can make their marks, such as district attorney, are reserved for lawyers.

Less than 10 percent of the House are African American (compared with about 12 percent of the total population), and most (but not all) of these representatives have been elected from overwhelmingly African-American constituencies. No state is predominantly African American, and there are no African Americans in the Senate. There are fewer than 20 Hispanics in the House and none in the Senate. Asian and Native Americans are also underrepresented. In terms of numbers, however, women are the most underrepresented group; more than half the population is female, but only 13 senators and 59 voting representatives are female (the representative from Washington, D.C. does not vote).

How important are the personal characteristics of members of Congress? Can a group of predominantly white, upper-middle-class, middle-aged Protestant males ade-

Despite their gains in recent congressional elections, women are the most underrepresented demographic group in Congress. Here a group of female representatives gather to advocate legislation that would require federal employees' health insurance plans to cover the cost of prescription contraceptives.

quately represent a much more diverse population? Would a group of more typical citizens be more effective in making major policy decisions? Because power in Congress is highly decentralized, the backgrounds of representatives and senators can be important if they influence how issues are prioritized and how officials vote on these issues. There is evidence that African-American members are more active than white members in serving African-American constituents.[1] Similarly, on the average, women legislators seem to be more active than men in pursuing the interests of women.[2]

Obviously, members of Congress cannot claim *descriptive* representation—that is, representing constituents by mirroring their personal, politically relevant characteristics. They may, however, engage in *substantive* representation—representing the interests of groups.[3] For example, members of Congress with a background of wealth and privilege, such as Senator Edward Kennedy, can be champions for the interests of the poor. Moreover, most members of Congress have lived in the constituencies they represent for many years, and share the beliefs and attitudes of at least a large proportion of their constituents. If they do not share such perspectives, they may find it difficult to keep their seats come election time. At the same time, females and African Americans who are in Congress are achieving important positions on committees, increasing the chances of making descriptive representation effective.[4]

Congressional Elections

Congressional elections are demanding, expensive,[5] and, as you will see, generally foregone conclusions—yet the role of politician is the most universal one in Congress. Men and women may run for Congress to forge new policy initiatives, but they also run because they are politicians, they enjoy politics, and they consider a position in Congress near the top of their chosen profession. Even if they dislike politics, without reelection they will not be around long enough to shape policy.

Members of Congress who do not share their constituents' economic and social backgrounds can nonetheless represent their concerns. Senator Edward Kennedy, for example, born into one of America's wealthiest families, has championed the poor and underprivileged throughout his career. Here, Kennedy speaks to workers concerned over proposed cuts in their pay and benefits.

Who Wins Elections?

Everyone in Congress is a politician, and politicians continually have their eyes on the next election. The players in the congressional election game are the incumbents and the challengers.

incumbents

Those already holding office. In congressional elections, incumbents usually win.

Incumbents are individuals who already hold office. Sometime during each term, the incumbent must decide whether to run again or to retire voluntarily. Most decide to run for reelection. They enter their party's primary, almost always emerge victorious, and typically win in the November general election, too. Indeed, the most important fact about congressional elections is this: *Incumbents usually win.*

Thus, the key to ensuring an opponent's defeat is not having more money than the opponent, although that helps. It is not being more photogenic, although that helps, too. The best thing a candidate can have going for him or her is simply to be the incumbent (see Figure 12.1). Even in a year of great political upheaval such as 1994, in which the Republicans gained 8 seats in the Senate and 53 seats in the House, 92 percent of incumbent senators and 89 percent of incumbent representatives won their bids for reelection.

Not only do more than 90 percent of the incumbents seeking reelection win, but most of them win with more than 60 percent of the vote. Perhaps most astonishing is the fact that even when challengers' positions on the issues are closer to the voters' positions, incumbents still tend to win.[6]

The picture for the Senate is a little different. Even though senators still have a good chance of beating back a challenge, the odds of reelection are often not as handsome as for House incumbents; senators typically win by narrower margins.

One reason for the greater competition in the Senate is that an entire state is almost always more diverse than a congressional district and thus provides a larger base for opposition to an incumbent. At the same time, senators have less personal contact with their constituencies, which on average are nearly 10 times larger than those of members of the House of Representatives. Senators also receive more coverage in the media than representatives do and are more likely to be held accountable on controversial issues. Moreover, senators tend to draw more visible challengers, such as governors or members

Figure 12.1 The Incumbency Factor in Congressional Elections

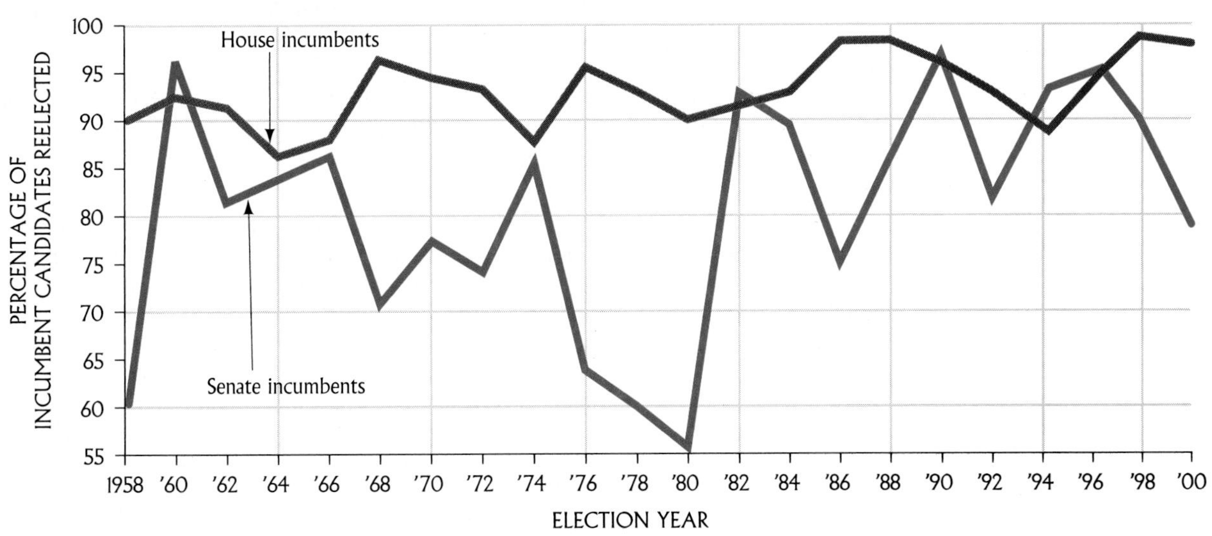

Source: Norman J. Ornstein, Thomas E. Mann, and Michael J. Malbin, *Vital Statistics on Congress, 1997–1998* (Washington, D.C.: Congressional Quarterly Press, 1998). Data for 1998 and 2000 compiled by the authors. Figures reflect incumbents running in both primary and general elections.

of the House, whom voters already know and who have substantial financial backing—a factor that lessens the advantages of incumbency. Many of these challengers know that the Senate is a stepping stone to national prominence and sometimes even the presidency.

Despite their success at reelection, incumbents often feel quite vulnerable. As Thomas Mann put it, members of Congress perceive themselves as "unsafe at any margin."[7] Thus, they have been raising and spending more campaign funds, sending more mail to their constituents, visiting their states and districts more often, and staffing more local offices than ever before.[8] They realize that with the decline of partisan loyalty in the electorate, they bear more of the burden of obtaining votes.

The Advantages of Incumbents

There are several possible explanations for the success of incumbents. One is that voters know how their elected representatives vote on important policy issues and agree with their stands, sending them back to Washington to keep up the good work. This, however, is usually not the case. In fact, voters are rather oblivious to how their senators and representatives actually vote. One study found that only about one-fifth of Americans can make an accurate guess about how their representatives have voted on any issue in Congress.[9] As one expert put it, "Mass public knowledge of congressional candidates declines precipitously once we move beyond simple recognition, generalized feelings, and incumbent job ratings."[10]

Another possibility is that voter assessments of presidential candidates influence their voting for Congress. Most stories of presidential "coattails" (when voters support congressional candidates because of their support for the president), however, seem to be just stories.[11] Bill Clinton received a *smaller* percentage of the vote than did almost every winning Democrat in Congress in both 1992 and 1996. The same was true for George W. Bush and Republicans in 2000. He had little in the way of coattails.

Journalists often claim that voters are motivated primarily by their pocketbooks. Yet members of Congress do not gain or lose many votes as a result of the ups and downs of the economy.[12]

What accounts for the success of congressional incumbents? Members of Congress engage in three primary activities that increase the probability of their reelection: advertising, credit claiming, and position taking.[13] In addition, the lack of strong opponents further ensures their success.

Advertising. For members of Congress, advertising means much more than placing ads in the newspapers and on television. Most congressional advertising takes place between elections in the form of contact with constituents. The goal is *visibility*.

Members of Congress work hard to get themselves known in their constituencies. As Figure 12.2 demonstrates, they usually succeed. Not surprisingly, members concentrate on staying visible. Trips home are frequent. In a typical week, members spend some time in their home districts,[14] even though their districts may be hundreds of miles from Washington. Similarly, members use the franking privilege to mail newsletters to every household in their constituency.

Credit Claiming. Congresspersons also engage in credit claiming, which involves enhancing their standing with constituents through service to individuals and the district. One member told Richard Fenno about the image he tried to cultivate in his constituency:

> *[I have] a very high recognition factor. And of all the things said about me, none of them said, "He's a conservative or a liberal," or "He votes this way on such and such an issue." None of that at all. There were two things said. One, "He works hard." Two, "He works for us." Nothing more than that. So we made it our theme, "O'Connor gets things done"; and we emphasized the dams, the highways, the buildings, the casework.*[15]

Morris Fiorina has emphasized this close link between service and success.[16] Members of Congress, he says, *can* go to the voters and stress their policymaking record and their stands on new policy issues on the agenda. The problem with facing the voters on one's record—past, present, and future—is that policy positions make enemies as well as friends. A member of Congress's vote for reducing government spending may win some friends, but it will make enemies of voters who happen to link that vote with service cutbacks. Besides, a congressperson can almost never show that he or she alone was responsible for a major policy. Being only 1 of 435 members of the House or 1 of 100 senators, a person can hardly promise to end inflation, cut taxes, or achieve equal rights for women single handedly.

Figure 12.2 Contact With Members of the House of Representatives

Members of Congress have high levels of contact with their constituents, giving them a substantial advantage in visibility relative to their election challengers. This contact is the result of a sustained effort and not simply a product of advertisements during an election campaign. Continuous attention to constituents brings visibility.

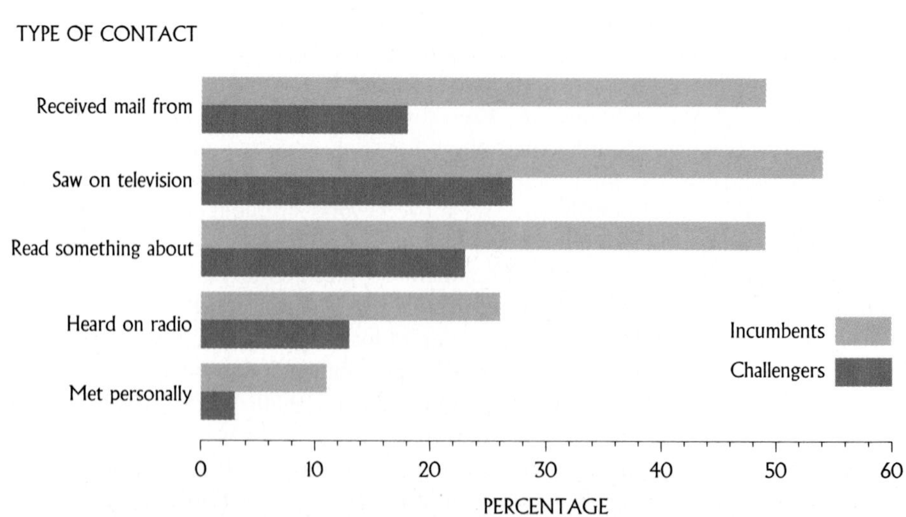

Source: From the National Election Studies conducted by the University of Michigan, Center for Political Studies, 1994.

Representative Silivo Conte used a pig nose and ears to protest pork barrel spending—until he wanted multimillion-dollar federal grants for his Massachusetts district. Because credit claiming is so important to reelection, members of Congress rarely pass up the opportunity to increase federal spending in their state or district.

One thing, though, always wins friends and almost never makes enemies: *servicing the constituency.* There are two ways in which members of Congress can do so: through casework and through the pork barrel. **Casework** is helping constituents as individuals—cutting through some bureaucratic red tape to give people what they think they have a right to get. The **pork barrel** is the mighty list of federal projects, grants, and contracts available to cities, businesses, colleges, and institutions.

casework

Activities of members of Congress that help constituents as individuals; cutting through bureaucratic red tape to get people what they think they have a right to get.

pork barrel

The mighty list of federal projects, grants, and contracts available to cities, businesses, colleges, and institutions available in a congressional district.

Do you have trouble getting your check from the Social Security Administration on time? Call your congressperson; he or she can cut red tape. Does your town have trouble getting federal bureaucrats to respond to its request for federal construction money? Call your congressperson. Representatives and senators can single-handedly take credit for each of these favors. Fiorina puts it like this:

> *Even committee chairmen have a difficult time claiming credit for a piece of major legislation, let alone a rank-and-file congressman. Ah, but casework, and the pork barrel. In dealing with the bureaucracy, the congressman is not merely 1 vote in 435. Rather he is a nonpartisan power, someone whose phone calls snap an office to attention. He is not kept on hold. The constituent who receives aid believes that his congressman and his congressman alone got results. Similarly, congressmen find it easy to claim credit for federal projects awarded in their districts. The congressman may have instigated the project in the first place, issued regular progress reports, and ultimately announced the award through his office. Maybe he can't claim credit for the 1965 Voting Rights Act, but he can take credit for Littletown's spanking new sewage treatment plant.*[17]

Getting things done for the folks back home often gets an incumbent the chance to serve them again.

As a result of the advantages of incumbency in advertising and credit claiming, incumbents, especially in the House, are usually much better known and have a more favorable public image than do their opponents.[18] Shrewd use of the resources available to incumbents may give them an advantage, but by themselves, casework and pork barrel do not determine congressional elections.[19]

Position Taking. Members of Congress must also engage in position taking on issues when they vote and when they respond to constituents' questions. In establishing their public images, members of Congress emphasize their personal qualities as experienced, hard-working, trustworthy representatives who have served their constituencies—an image often devoid of partisan or programmatic content.

Nevertheless, all members must take policy stands, and the positions they take may affect the outcome of an election, especially if the issues are on matters salient to voters and the candidates' stands differ from those of a majority of their constituents. This is especially true in elections for the Senate, in which issues are likely to play a greater role than in House elections.

Weak Opponents. Another advantage for incumbents is that they are likely to face weak opponents. Confronted with the advantages of incumbency, potentially effective opponents are often unlikely to risk challenging members of the House.[20] Those individuals who do run are usually not well known or well qualified and lack experience and organizational and financial backing.[21] The lack of adequate campaign funds is a special burden because challengers need money to compensate for the "free" recognition incumbents receive from their advertising and credit claiming.[22]

The Role of Party Identification

At the base of every electoral coalition are the members of the candidate's party in the constituency. Although party loyalty at the voting booth is not as strong as it was a generation ago, it is still a good predictor of voting behavior. In the 1998 congressional elections, for example, nearly 90 percent of voters who identified with a party voted for the House candidates of their party.[23] Most members of Congress represent constituencies in which their party is in the majority.

Defeating Incumbents

In light of the advantages of incumbents, it is reasonable to ask why anyone challenges them at all. One of the main reasons is simply that challengers are often naïve about their chances of winning. Because few have money for expensive polls, they rely on friends and local party leaders, who often tell them what they want to hear. Sometimes they do get some unexpected help; incumbents almost have to beat themselves, and some do.

An incumbent tarnished by scandal or corruption becomes instantly vulnerable. Clearly, voters do take out their anger at the polls. For example, representatives who bounced large numbers of checks at the House bank were much more likely to lose their seats in the 1992 elections than their more fiscally responsible colleagues.[24] In a close election, negative publicity can turn victory into defeat.[25]

visual literacy
Why is it so Hard to Defeat an Incumbent?

Incumbents may also be redistricted out of their familiar turfs. After each federal census, Congress reapportions its membership. States that have gained significantly in population will be given more House seats; states that have lost substantial population will lose one or more of their seats. The state legislatures must then redraw their states' district lines; one incumbent may be moved into another's district, where the two must battle for one seat. A state party majority is more likely to move two of the opposition party's representatives into a single district than two of its own.

Finally, major political tidal waves occasionally roll across the country, leaving defeated incumbents in their wake. One such wave occurred in 1994, when the public mood turned especially sour and voters took out their frustration on Democratic incumbents, defeating 35 in the House and 2 in the Senate.

Money in Congressional Elections

When an incumbent is not running for reelection and the seat is open, there is greater likelihood of competition. If the party balance in a constituency is such that either party has a chance of winning, each side may offer a strong candidate—each with enough money to establish name recognition among the voters. Most of the turnover in the membership of Congress results from vacated seats, particularly in the House.

Figure 12.3 Spending in Congressional Elections, 1998

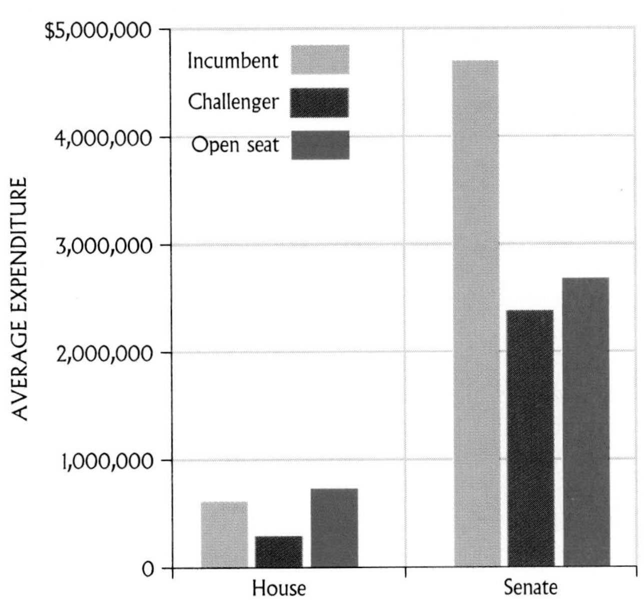

A typical major-party candidate who won the general election for a House seat in 1998 spent more than $740,000 on the campaign; Senate candidates spent more than six times as much. The costs of congressional elections escalated in the 2000 elections. Incumbents, especially in House elections, have a considerable advantage over their opponents, which, of course, is one reason why incumbents do so well. The real spending contest, though, is in districts where the seat is open. When there is no incumbent and each party has a chance to win, the spending is much greater than for a challenger facing an incumbent.

Source: Federal Election Commission, 1998, 1999.

It costs a great deal more money to elect a Congress than to elect a president. In 2000 George W. Bush, Al Gore, Patrick Buchanan, and Ralph Nader together spent about $200 million on their general election campaigns. The 2000 general election Senate races alone cost at least $350 million (with the average winner spending over $6 million), and House candidates spent another $500 million (with the average winner spending over $800,000). In addition, the two political parties spent millions more in coordinated expenditures on behalf of their candidates. The cost of congressional elections in the 1999–2000 election cycle—for those who made it to the general election—was over $850 million! Candidates who lost in primary elections spent an additional $100 million. Data on spending in congressional elections can be found in Figure 12.3.

Where does all this campaign money come from? And, more important, what does it buy? Although most of the money spent in congressional elections comes from individuals, nearly 30 percent (about $225 million) of the funds raised by candidates for Congress in 2000 came from the nearly 4,000 political action committees (PACs) (see Chapters 9 and 11). Critics of PACs offer plenty of complaints about the present system of campaign finance. Why, they ask, is money spent to pay the campaign costs of a candidate who is already heavily favored to win? In 1997–1998, House incumbents received $157 million from PACs, compared to only $21 million for challengers. Even more interesting is that PACs often make contributions *after* the election. Congressional candidates elected in 1994, for example, received nearly $600,000 from just business-related PACs in the two months following the election. Much of this money came from groups that had supported the representatives' opponents during the election.[26]

There is a continuous debate in America today on whether PACs "buy" votes in Congress (see "You Are the Policymaker: Should We Do Away With PACs?" in Chapter 11). Although this question remains unresolved, everyone agrees that at the very least, PACs seek *access* to policymakers. Thus they give most of their money to incumbents, who are likely to win anyway. When they support someone who loses, they quickly make amends and contribute to the winner. PACs want to keep the lines of communication open and create a receptive atmosphere in which to be heard. Because each PAC is limited to an expenditure of $5,000 per candidate (most give less), a single PAC can at most account for only a small percentage of a winner's total spending. If one PAC does not contribute to a candidate, there are always other PACs from which to seek funds.

Some organized interests circumvent the limitations on contributions, however, and create or contribute to several PACs. This tactic may increase their leverage with the recipients of these funds. As we saw in Chapter 11, in the late 1980s one tycoon, Charles Keating, managed to contribute $1.3 million to the campaigns of five senators. These senators then interceded with the Federal Home Loan Bank Board to avoid (for a while, at least) enforcement of banking regulations on Keating's savings and loan. Many people saw a connection between the campaign contributions and the senators' actions.

Aside from the question of whether money buys influence, what does it buy the candidates who spend it? In 1998, Alfonse D'Amato spent more than $23 million to retain his Senate seat in New York—and lost. In 1994, Californian Michael Huffington spent nearly $30 million—most of it his own money—about twice the expenditures of his rival, Senator Dianne Feinstein, and still lost. Oliver North spent about $20 million in the much smaller state of Virginia, and he lost as well. Obviously, prolific spending in a campaign is no guarantee of success.

Money is important for challengers, however. The more they spend, the more votes they receive. Money buys them name recognition and a chance to be heard. Incumbents, by contrast, already have high levels of recognition among their constituents and benefit less (but still benefit) from campaign spending; what matters most is how much their opponents spend. Challengers have to raise large sums if they hope to defeat an incumbent, but they usually are substantially outspent by incumbents.[27] In contests for open seats, the candidate who spends the most usually wins.

Stability and Change

Because incumbents usually win reelection, there is some stability in the membership of Congress. This provides the opportunity for representatives and senators to gain some expertise in dealing with complex questions of public policy. At the same time, it also may insulate them from the winds of political change. Safe seats make it more difficult for citizens to "send a message to Washington" with their votes. Particularly in the House, it takes a large shift in votes to affect the outcomes of most elections. To increase turnover in the membership of Congress, some reformers have proposed *term limitations* for representatives and senators[28] (see "You Are the Policymaker: Should We Impose Term Limits on Members of Congress?").

How Congress Is Organized to Make Policy

Of all the senators' and representatives' roles, making policy is the toughest. Congress is a collection of generalists trying to make policy on specialized topics. Members are short of time and expertise. As amateurs in almost every subject, they are surrounded by people who know (or claim to know) more than they do—lobbyists, agency administrators, even their own staffs. Even if they had time to study all the issues thoroughly, making wise national policy would be difficult. If economists disagree about policies to fight unemployment, how are legislators to know which policies may work better than others?

When ringing bells announce a roll-call vote, representatives or senators rush into the chamber from their offices or from a hearing—often unsure of what is being voted on. Frequently, "uncertain of their position, members of Congress will seek out one or two people who serve on the committee which considered and reported the bill, in whose judgment they have confidence."[29]

The founders gave Congress's organization just a hint of specialization when they split it into the House and the Senate. The complexity of today's issues, however, requires much more specialization. Congress tries to cope with policymaking demands through its elaborate committee system.

You Are the Policymaker

Should We Impose Term Limits on Members of Congress?

In the late 1980s many reformers were concerned that the incumbency advantage enjoyed by legislators created, in effect, lifetime tenure, which served as a roadblock to change and encouraged ethics abuses. To increase turnover among legislators, these reformers proposed term limitations, generally restricting representatives to 6 or 12 consecutive years in office.

The movement to limit the terms of legislators spread rapidly across the country. Within a few years, 23 states enacted term limitations for members of their state legislatures. The House Republicans made terms limits for Congress part of their Contract With America in the 1994 election. Yet changing the terms of members of Congress requires changing the Constitution, which is difficult to do, and many members of Congress have fought term limitations fiercely.

Opponents of term limitations object to the loss of experienced legislators and of the American people's ability to vote for whomever they please. In addition, they add, there is plenty of new blood in the legislature: At the beginning of the 105th Congress (1997), more than half the members of House and 40 percent of the senators had no more than four years of experience in their chambers. Moreover, recent research indicates that the movement of party fortunes in the House follows the movement of citizen preferences for public policy.*

Proponents of term limits suffered two setbacks in 1995 when Congress failed to pass a constitutional amendment on term limitations (it also failed in 1997), and when the Supreme Court, in *U.S. Term Limits, Inc. et al. v. Thornton et al.*, decided that state-imposed term limits on members of Congress were unconstitutional. In the meantime, most people seem comfortable with their own representatives and senators and appear content to reelect them again and again.

Nevertheless, many Americans support a constitutional amendment to impose term limitations on members of Congress. You be the policymaker: What would *you* do?

*Suzanna De Boef and James A. Stimson, "The Dynamic Structure of Congressional Elections," *Journal of Politics* 57 (August 1995): 630–648.

American Bicameralism

A **bicameral legislature** is a legislature divided into two houses. The U.S. Congress is bicameral, as is every American state legislature except Nebraska's, which has one house (unicameral). As we learned in Chapter 2, the Connecticut Compromise at the Constitutional Convention created a bicameral Congress. Each state is guaranteed 2 senators, and its number of representatives is determined by the population of the state (California has 52 representatives; Alaska, Delaware, Montana, North Dakota, South Dakota, Vermont, and Wyoming have just 1 each). By creating a bicameral Congress, the Constitution set up yet another check and balance. No bill can be passed unless both House and Senate agree on it; each body can thus veto the policies of the other. Some of the basic differences between the two houses are shown in Table 12.3.

bicameral legislature

A legislature divided into two houses. The U.S. Congress and every American state legislature except Nebraska's are bicameral.

The House. More than four times larger than the Senate, the House is also more institutionalized—that is, more centralized, more hierarchical, and less anarchic.[30] Party loyalty to leadership and party-line voting are more common in the House than in the Senate. Partly because there are more members, leaders in the House do more leading than do leaders in the Senate. First-term House members are more likely to be seen and not heard, and they have less power than senior representatives.[31]

Both the House and the Senate set their own agendas. Both use committees, which we will examine shortly, to winnow down the thousands of bills introduced. One institution unique to the House, however, plays a key role in agenda setting: the **House Rules Committee.** This committee reviews most bills coming from a House committee before they go to the full House. Performing a traffic cop function, the Rules Committee gives each bill a "rule," which schedules the bill on the calendar,

House Rules Committee

An institution unique to the House of Representatives that reviews all bills (except revenue, budget, and appropriations bills) coming from a House committee before they go to the full House.

Table 12.3 House Versus Senate: Some Key Differences

CHARACTERISTIC	HOUSE OF REPRESENTATIVES	SENATE
Constitutional powers	Must initiate all revenue bills; must pass all articles of impeachment	Must give "advice and consent" to many presidential nominations; must approve treaties; tries impeached officials
Membership	435 members	100 members
Term of office	2 years	6 years
Constituencies	Smaller	Larger
Centralization of power	More centralized; stronger leadership	Less centralized; weaker leadership
Political prestige	Less prestige	More prestige
Role in policymaking	More influential on budget; more specialized	More influential on foreign affairs; less specialized
Turnover	Small	Moderate
Role of seniority	More important in determining power	Less important in determining power
Procedures	Limited debate; limits on floor amendments allowed	Unlimited debate

allots time for debate, and sometimes even specifies what kind of amendments may be offered. The Rules Committee is generally responsive to the House leadership, in part because the Speaker of the House now appoints the committee's members.

The Senate. The Constitution's framers thought the Senate would protect elite interests to counteract the tendencies of the House to protect the masses. They gave the House power to initiate all revenue bills and to impeach officials; they gave the Senate the responsibility to ratify all treaties, to confirm important presidential nominations (including nominations to the Supreme Court), and to try impeached officials. History shows that when the same party controls each chamber, the Senate is just as liberal as, and perhaps more liberal than, the House.[32] The real differences between the bodies lie in the Senate's organization and decentralized power.

Smaller than the House, the Senate is also less disciplined and less centralized. Today's senators are more nearly equal in power than representatives are. They are also more nearly equal in power than senators have been in the past. Even incoming senators sometimes get top committee assignments; they may even become chairs of key subcommittees. In 1981, the Senate had 16 newcomers, none of them eager to take a backseat to old-timers. For example, in 1981 Dan Quayle, who would become vice president eight years later, was elected to the Senate from Indiana and made his mark chairing a subcommittee handling a key bill on job training.

Committees and the party leadership are important in determining the Senate's legislative agenda, just as they are in the House. Party leaders do for Senate scheduling what the Rules Committee does in the House.

filibuster

A strategy unique to the Senate whereby opponents of a piece of legislation try to talk it to death, based on the tradition of unlimited debate. Today, 60 members present and voting can halt a filibuster.

One activity unique to the Senate is the **filibuster.** This is a tactic by which opponents of a bill use their right to unlimited debate as a way to prevent the Senate from ever voting on a bill. Unlike their fellow legislators in the House, once senators have the floor in a debate, tradition holds that they can talk as long as they wish. Strom Thurmond of South Carolina once held forth for a full 24 hours. Working together, then, like-minded senators can practically debate forever, tying up the legislative agenda until the proponents of a bill finally give up their battle. In essence, they literally talk the bill to death.

The power of the filibuster is not absolute, however. Sixty members present and voting can halt a filibuster by voting for *cloture* on debate, but many senators are reluctant to vote for cloture for fear of setting a precedent to be used against them when *they* want to filibuster.

At its core the filibuster raises profound questions about American democracy because it is used by a minority, sometimes a minority of one, to defeat a majority. Southern senators once used filibusters to prevent civil rights legislation.[33] More recently, the opponents of all types of legislation have used them. Indeed, during Bill Clinton's presidency, filibusters became the weapon of first resort for even the most trivial matters. Each senator knows that he or she has at least six opportunities to filibuster a single bill and that these opportunities can be used one after another. In addition, the tactical uses of a filibuster have expanded. A senator might threaten to filibuster an unrelated measure in order to gain concessions on a bill he or she opposes.

If the minority is blocking the majority, why doesn't the majority change the rules to prevent filibuster? The answer is twofold. First, changing the rules requires 67 votes. It is always difficult to obtain the agreement of two-thirds of the Senate on a controversial matter. Second, every senator knows that he or she might be in the minority on an issue at some time. A filibuster gives senators who are in the minority a powerful weapon for defending their (or their constituents') interests.

In the meantime, Americans complain about gridlock in Congress. Nevertheless, senators have decided that they are more concerned with allowing senators to block legislation they oppose than with expediting the passage of legislation a majority favors.

Congressional Leadership

Leading 100 senators or 435 representatives in Congress—each jealous of his or her own power and responsible to no higher power than the constituency—is no easy task. "Few members of the House, fewer still in the Senate," Robert Peabody once wrote, "consider themselves followers."[34] Chapter 8 discussed the party in government. Much of the leadership in Congress is really party leadership. There are a few formal posts whose occupants are chosen by nonparty procedures, but those who have the real power in the congressional hierarchy are those whose party put them there.

The House. Chief among leadership positions in the House of Representatives is the **Speaker of the House.** This is the only legislative office mandated by the Constitution. In practice, the majority party selects the Speaker. Before each Congress begins, the majority party presents its candidate for Speaker, who—because this person attracts the unanimous support of the majority party—turns out to be a shoo-in. Typically, the Speaker is a senior member of the party. J. Dennis Hastert of Illinois, who has served in Congress since 1987, was elected Speaker in 1999. The Speaker is also two heartbeats away from the presidency, being second in line (after the vice president) to succeed a president who resigns, dies in office, or is convicted after impeachment.

Speaker of the House

An office mandated by the Constitution. The Speaker is chosen in practice by the majority party, has both formal and informal powers, and is second in line to succeed to the presidency should that office become vacant.

Years ago, the Speaker was king of the congressional mountain. Autocrats such as "Uncle Joe Cannon" and "Czar Reed" ran the House like a fiefdom. A great revolt in 1910 whittled down the Speaker's powers and gave some of them to committees, but six decades later, members of the House restored some of the Speaker's powers. Today the Speaker

- presides over the House when it is in session
- plays a major role in making committee assignments, which are coveted by all members to ensure their electoral advantage
- appoints or plays a key role in appointing the party's legislative leaders and the party leadership staff

timeline
The Speaker of the House

Dennis Hastert of Illinois was elected Speaker of the House in 1999. Minority Leader Richard Gephardt leads the Democrats in the House. Thomas Daschle of South Dakota is the Senate Majority Leader, which makes him the most powerful member of that body. Nevertheless, in the decentralized power structure in the upper chamber, even he must work for support.

majority leader

The principal partisan ally of the Speaker of the House or the party's wheel horse in the Senate. The majority leader is responsible for scheduling bills, influencing committee assignments, and rounding up votes in behalf of the party's legislative positions.

whips

Party leaders who work with the **majority leader** or **minority leader** to count votes beforehand and lean on waverers whose votes are crucial to a bill favored by the party.

minority leader

The principal leader of the minority party in the House of Representatives or in the Senate.

- exercises substantial control over which bills get assigned to which committees

In addition to these formal powers, the Speaker has a great deal of informal clout inside and outside Congress. When the Speaker's party differs from the president's party, as it frequently does, the Speaker is often a national spokesperson for the party. The bank of microphones in front of the Speaker of the House is a commonplace feature of the evening news. A good Speaker also knows the members well—including their past improprieties, the ambitions they harbor, and the pressures they feel.

Leadership in the House, however, is not a one-person show. The Speaker's principal partisan ally is the **majority leader**—a job that has been the main stepping stone to the Speaker's role. The majority leader is responsible for scheduling bills in the House. More important, the majority leader is responsible for rounding up votes on behalf of the party's position on legislation. Working with the majority leader are the party's **whips**, who carry the word to party troops, counting votes before they are cast and leaning on waverers whose votes are crucial to a bill. Party whips also report the views and complaints of the party rank and file back to the leadership.

The minority party is also organized, poised to take over the Speakership and other key posts if it should win a majority in the House. The Republicans had been the minority party in the House for 40 years before 1995, although they had a president to look to for leadership for much of that period. Now the Democrats are experiencing minority status, led by the **minority leader,** Richard Gephardt of Missouri.

The Senate. The Constitution makes the vice president of the United States the president of the Senate; this is the vice president's only constitutionally defined job. But even the mighty Lyndon Johnson, who had been the Senate majority leader before becoming vice president, found himself an outsider when he returned as the Senate's president. Vice presidents usually slight their senatorial chores, leaving power in the Senate to party leaders. Senators typically return the favor, ignoring vice presidents except in the rare case when their vote can break a tie.

Thus the Senate majority leader (currently, South Dakota Senator Thomas Daschle)—aided by the majority whips—is a party's workhorse, corralling votes, scheduling the floor action, and influencing committee assignments. The majority leader's counterpart in the opposition, the minority leader (currently Trent Lott of Mississippi), has similar responsibilities. Power is widely dispersed in the contemporary Senate; it no longer lies in the hands of a few key members of Congress who are insulated from the public. Therefore party leaders must appeal broadly for support, often speaking to the country directly or indirectly over television.

Congressional Leadership in Perspective. Despite their stature and power, congressional leaders are not in strong positions to move their troops. Both houses of Congress are highly decentralized and rarely show an inclination for major changes in the way they operate. Leaders are elected by their party members and must remain responsive to them. Except in the most egregious cases (which rarely arise), leaders cannot punish those who do not support the party's stand, and no one expects members to vote against their constituents' interests. Senator Robert Dole nicely summed up the leader's situation when he once dubbed himself the "Majority Pleader."

Nevertheless, party leadership, at least in the House, has been more effective in recent years. As the party contingents have become more homogeneous, there has been more policy agreement within the parties and thus more party unity in voting on the floor. Increased agreement has made it easier for the Speaker to exercise his prerogatives regarding the assignment of bills and members to committees, the rules by which legislation is brought to the floor, and the use of an expanded whip system—all developments that have enabled the parties to advance an agenda that reflects party preferences.[35] Following the Republican takeover of Congress in 1995, Speaker Newt Gingrich began centralizing power and exercising vigorous legislative leadership.

Why does it matter?

Parties organize Congress, but they are relatively weak. If the parties enforced strict party loyalty on their members in Congress, would each party be more likely to keep its promises to voters like you? Or would strict party loyalty make it more difficult for members of Congress to effectively represent your special needs and interests?

The Committees and Subcommittees

Will Rogers, the famous Oklahoma humorist, once remarked that "outside of traffic, there is nothing that has held this country back as much as committees." Members of the Senate and the House would apparently disagree. Most of the real work of Congress goes on in committees, and committees dominate congressional policymaking in all its stages.

Committees regularly hold hearings to investigate problems and possible wrongdoing and to oversee the executive branch. Most of all, *they control the congressional agenda and guide legislation* from its introduction to its send-off to the president for his signature. Committees can be grouped into four types, the first of which is by far the most important.

1. **Standing committees** are formed to handle bills in different policy areas (see Table 12.4). Each house of Congress has its own standing committees; members do not belong to a committee in the other house. In the 107th Congress, the typical representative served on two committees and four subcommittees; senators averaged three committees and seven subcommittees each. Subcommittees are smaller units of a committee created out of the committee membership.
2. **Joint committees** exist in a few policy areas, such as the economy and taxation; their membership is drawn from both the Senate and the House.
3. **Conference committees** are formed when the Senate and the House pass a particular bill in different forms. Appointed by the party leadership, a conference committee consists of members of each house chosen to iron out Senate and House differences and to report back a compromise bill.
4. **Select committees** are appointed for a specific purpose. The Senate select committee that investigated Watergate is a well-known example.

standing committees
Separate subject-matter committees in each house of Congress that handle **bills** in different policy areas.

joint committees
Congressional committees on a few subject-matter areas with membership drawn from both houses.

conference committees
Congressional committees formed when the Senate and the House pass a particular **bill** in different forms. Party leadership appoints members from each house to iron out the differences and bring back a single bill.

select committees
Congressional committees appointed for a specific purpose, such as the Watergate investigation.

The Committees at Work: Legislation and Oversight. With more than 11,000 bills submitted by members every two years, some winnowing is essential. Every bill goes to a committee, which has virtually the power of life and death over it. The whole House or Senate usually considers only bills that obtain a favorable committee report.

New bills sent to a committee typically go directly to a subcommittee, which can hold hearings on the bill. Sizable committee and subcommittee staffs conduct research, line up witnesses for hearings, and write and rewrite bills. Committees and their subcommittees report on proposed legislation; these reports are typically bound

Table 12.4 Standing Committees in the Senate and in the House

SENATE COMMITTEES	HOUSE COMMITTEES
Agriculture, Nutrition, and Forestry	Agriculture
Appropriations	Appropriations
Armed Services	Armed Services
Banking, Housing, and Urban Affairs	Financial Services
Budget	Budget
Commerce, Science, and Transportation	Energy and Commerce
Energy and Natural Resources	Education and the Workforce
Environment and Public Works	Government Reform
Finance	House Administration
Foreign Relations	International Relations
Governmental Affairs	Judiciary
Judiciary	Resources
Labor and Human Resources	Rules
Rules and Administration	Science
Small Business	Small Business
Veterans' Affairs	Standards of Official Conduct
	Transportation and Infrastructure
	Veterans' Affairs
	Ways and Means

in beige or green covers and are available from the Government Printing Office. A committee's most important output, however, is the "marked up" (rewritten) bill itself, submitted to the full House or Senate for debate and voting.

The work of committees does not stop when the bill leaves the committee room. Members of the committee usually serve as "floor managers" of the bill, helping party leaders hustle votes for it. They are also the "cue givers" to whom other members turn for advice. When the Senate and House pass different versions of the same bill, some committee members serve on the conference committee.

legislative oversight

Congress's monitoring of the bureaucracy and its administration of policy, performed mainly through hearings.

The committees and subcommittees do not leave the scene even after legislation is passed. They stay busy in **legislative oversight,** the process of monitoring the bureaucracy and its administration of policy. Oversight is handled mainly through hearings. When an agency wants a bigger budget, the use of its present budget is reviewed. Even if no budgetary issues are involved, members of committees constantly monitor how a law is being implemented. Agency heads and even cabinet secretaries testify, bringing graphs, charts, and data on the progress they have made and the problems they face. Committee staffs and committee members grill agency heads about particular problems. For example, a member may ask a Small Business Administration official why constituents who are applying for loans get the runaround. On another committee, officials charged with listing endangered species might defend the gray wolf against a member of Congress whose sheep-ranching constituents are not fond of wolves. Oversight, one of the checks Congress can exercise on the executive branch, gives Congress the power to pressure agencies and, in extreme cases, cut their budgets in order to secure compliance with congressional wishes and even congressional whims.[36]

Occasionally, congressional oversight rivets the nation's attention. In 1973 the Senate established the Select Committee on Campaign Activities to investigate the misdeeds and duplicity of the 1972 presidential campaign, otherwise known as the Watergate scandal. This action was followed the next year by the House Judiciary Committee's hearings on the impeachment of President Nixon for his conduct in attempting to cover up the scandal. Shortly after the Judiciary Committee recommended three articles of impeachment, the president resigned.

Most of Congress's work takes place—and most of its members' power is wielded—in the standing committees and their numerous subcommittees. Here, the Senate Armed Services Committee is holding hearings on the issue of gays in the military.

More recently, a special joint committee was established in 1987 to investigate what became known as the Iran-Contra affair, a term that refers to the secret sale of arms to Iran (for which President Reagan hoped to obtain the release of American hostages held in the Middle East) and the diversion of some of the funds from these sales to the Contras fighting the Sandinista government in Nicaragua (in the face of congressional prohibition of such aid). Many people thought the hearings, especially the testimony of Lieutenant Colonel Oliver North, made for great spy novel entertainment but did little to illuminate the issues involved in the matter.

Congress keeps tabs on more routine activities of the executive branch through its committee staff members. These members have specialized expertise in the fields and agencies that their committees oversee and maintain an extensive network of formal and informal contacts with the bureaucracy. By reading the voluminous reports that Congress requires of the executive and by receiving information from numerous sources—agencies, complaining citizens, members of Congress and their personal staff, state and local officials, interest groups, and professional organizations—staff members can keep track of the implementation of public policy.[37]

Nevertheless, members of Congress have many competing responsibilities, and there are few political payoffs for carefully watching a government agency to see whether it is implementing policy properly. It is difficult to go to voters and say, "Vote for me. I oversaw the routine handling of road building." Because of this lack of incentives, problems may be overlooked until it is too late to do much about them. A major scandal involving the Department of Housing and Urban Development's administration of housing programs during the Reagan presidency was not uncovered until 1989, after Reagan had left office. Similarly, taxpayers could have saved well over $100 billion if Congress had insisted that the agencies regulating the savings and loan industry enforce their regulations more rigorously.

Nevertheless, Congress *did* substantially increase its oversight activities in the 1970s and 1980s. As the size and complexity of the national government grew in the 1960s, and after numerous charges that the executive branch had become too powerful (especially in response to the widespread belief that Presidents Johnson and Nixon had abused their power), Congress responded with more oversight. The tight budgets of recent years have provided additional incentives for oversight, as members of Congress have sought to protect programs they favor from budget cuts and to get more value for the tax dollars spent on them. As the publicity value of receiving credit for controlling governmental spending has increased, so has the number of representatives and senators interested in oversight.[38]

Getting on a Committee. One of the first worries for an incoming member of Congress (after paying off campaign debts) is getting on the right committee. Although it is not always easy to figure out what the right committee is, it is fairly easy to recognize some wrong committees. The Iowa newcomer does not want to get stuck on the Banking, Housing, and Urban Affairs Committee; the Brooklyn freshman would like to avoid Agriculture. Members seek committees that will help them achieve three goals: reelection, influence in Congress, and the opportunity to make policy in areas they think are important.[39]

Just after their election, new members write to the party's congressional leaders and members of their state delegation, indicating their committee preferences. Every committee includes members from both parties, but a majority of each committee's members, as well as its chair, come from the majority party. Each party in each house has a slightly different way of picking its committee members. Party leaders almost always play a key role.

Those who have supported the leadership are favored in the committee selection process, but generally the parties try to grant members' requests for committee assignments whenever possible. They want their members to please their constituents (being on the right committee should help them represent their constituency more effectively and reinforce their ability to engage in credit claiming) and to develop expertise in an area of policy. The parties also try to apportion the influence that comes with committee membership among the state delegations, in order to accord representation to diverse components of the party.[40]

committee chairs

The most important influencers of the congressional agenda. They play dominant roles in scheduling hearings, hiring staff, appointing subcommittees, and managing committee bills when they are brought before the full house.

seniority system

A simple rule for picking **committee chairs,** in effect until the 1970s. The member who had served on the committee the longest and whose party controlled Congress became chair, regardless of party loyalty, mental state, or competence.

Getting Ahead on the Committee: Chairs and the Seniority System. If committees are the most important influencers of the congressional agenda, **committee chairs** are the most important influencers of the committee agenda. Committee chairs play dominant—though no longer monopolistic—roles in scheduling hearings, hiring staff, appointing subcommittees, and managing committee bills when they are brought before the full house.

Until the 1970s, there was a simple way of picking committee chairs: the **seniority system.** If committee members had served on their committee longest and their party controlled the chamber, they got to be chairs—regardless of their party loyalty, mental state, or competence. This system gave a decisive edge to members from "safe" districts. They were least likely to be challenged for reelection and most likely to achieve seniority. In the Democratic Party, most safe districts were in the South; as a result, Southern politicians exercised power beyond their numbers. They chaired many committees, often dominating them. The South has become a two-party region, however, and electoral losses, aging, and mortality have taken their toll on Southern committee chairs.

Why does it matter?

The committee system in Congress is highly decentralized. As a result, it is open to the appeals of a large range of interests, especially those represented by highly paid lobbyists. What if Congress were highly *centralized?* What if only those interests cleared by the elected leadership could receive a serious hearing? Would special interests be restrained and the national interest be better served? Or would legitimate interests, such as yours, be shut out of the process?

Woodrow Wilson, a political scientist before he became a politician, once said that the government of the United States was really government by the chairs of the standing committees of Congress. The chairs were so powerful for most of the twentieth century that they could bully members or bottle up legislation at any time—and with almost certain knowledge that they would be chairs for the rest of their electoral life. But in the 1970s, Congress faced a revolt of its younger members. Both parties in both branches permitted members to vote on committee chairs; in 1975, the House Democrats dumped four chairs with 154 years of seniority among them.

Today seniority remains the *general rule* for selecting chairs, but there are exceptions. For example, ailing Jamie Whitten of Mississippi was stripped of his Appropriations Committee gavel in 1992. When his successor, William Natcher of Kentucky, died in 1994, David Obey of Wisconsin became chair, although he was not the most senior Democrat on the committee. The Republicans skipped over several senior representatives when they named the House committee chairs in 1995 and have continued to do so in subsequent Congresses.

These and other reforms discussed later in this chapter have somewhat reduced the clout of the chairs from that of a generation ago. Chairs are far less able to mold the decision-making processes of their committees.[41] Yet there are disadvantages to decentralizing committee power. Richard Fenno, a veteran congressional observer, once remarked that the "performance of Congress as an institution is very largely the performance of its committees" but that the committee system is the "epitome of fragmentation and decentralization."[42] The more that power is dispersed, the more difficult it is to make coherent policy.

Caucuses: The Informal Organization of Congress

Although the formal organization of Congress consists of its party leadership and its committee structures, the informal organization of the House and Senate is also important. The informal networks of trust and mutual interest can spring from numerous sources. Friendship, ideology, and geography are long-standing sources of informal organization.

Lately, these traditional informal groupings have been dominated by a growing number of caucuses. In this context, a **caucus** is a group of members of Congress who share some interest or characteristic. In the 107th Congress, there are more than 100 of these caucuses, most of them containing members from both parties, and some containing members from both the House and the Senate. The goal of all caucuses is to promote the interests around which they are formed. Within Congress they press for committees to hold hearings, they push particular legislation, and they pull together votes on bills they favor. They are somewhat like interest groups, but with a difference: Their members are members of Congress, not petitioners to Congress on the outside looking in. Thus caucuses—interest groups within Congress—are nicely situated to pack more punch than interest groups outside Congress.[43]

caucus (congressional)

A group of members of Congress sharing some interest or characteristic. Most are composed of members from both parties and from both houses.

Some, such as the Black Caucus, the Congresswomen's Caucus, and the Hispanic Caucus, are based on the characteristics of their members. Others, such as the Sunbelt Caucus and the Northeast-Midwest Congressional Coalition, are based on regional groupings. Still others, such as the Moderate/Conservative Democrats, are ideological

The proliferation of congressional caucuses gives members of Congress an informal, yet powerful, means of shaping the policy agenda. Composed of legislative insiders who share similar concerns, the caucuses—such as the Black Caucus pictured here—exert a much greater influence on policymaking than most citizen-based interest groups can.

groupings. And still others, such as the Steel, Travel and Tourism, Coal, and Mushroom caucuses, are based on some economic interest that is important to a set of constituencies (yes, there really is a Mushroom Caucus; it is composed of members interested in protecting the interests of mushroom growers).

This explosion of informal groups in Congress has made the representation of interests in Congress a more direct process. The caucuses proceed on the assumption that no one is a more effective lobbyist than a senator or representative.

Congressional Staff

As we discussed earlier, members of Congress are overwhelmed with responsibilities. It is virtually impossible to master the details of the hundreds of bills on which they must make decisions each year or to prepare their own legislation. They need help to meet their obligations, so they turn to their staff.

Personal Staff. Most staff members work in the personal offices of individual members. The average representative has 17 assistants and the average senator has 44. In total, about 11,500 individuals serve on the personal staffs of members of Congress.[44] Most of these staffers spend their time providing services to constituents, the casework we discussed earlier regarding congressional elections. They answer mail, communicate the member's views to voters, and help constituents solve problems. Nearly one-half of these House staffers and nearly one-third of the Senate personal staff work in members' offices in their constituencies, not in Washington. This makes it easier for people to make contact with the staff. Other personal staff help members of Congress with legislative functions, including drafting legislation, meeting with lobbyists and administrators, negotiating agreements on behalf of their bosses, writing questions to ask witnesses at committee hearings, summarizing bills, and briefing legislators. Senators, who must cover a wider range of committee assignments than members of the House, are especially dependent on staff. Indeed, members of both houses are now more likely to deal with each other through staff intermediaries than through personal interactions.

Committee Staff. The committees of the House and Senate employ another 2,500 staff members.[45] These staff members organize hearings, research legislative options, draft committee reports on bills, write legislation, and, as we have seen, keep tabs on the activities of the executive branch. Committee staff members often possess high levels of expertise and can become very influential in policymaking (see "Making a Difference: Tony Battista"). As a result, lobbyists spend a lot of time cultivating these staffers both to obtain information about likely legislative actions and to plant ideas for legislation.

Staff Agencies. Finally, Congress has three important staff agencies that aid it in its work. The first is the *Congressional Research Service (CRS)*, administered by the Library of Congress. The CRS employs nearly 750 researchers, many with advanced degrees and highly developed expertise. Each year it responds to more than 250,000 congressional requests for information and provides members with nonpartisan studies. CRS also tracks the progress of major bills, prepares summaries of bills, and makes this information available electronically.

The *General Accounting Office (GAO)*, with more than 3,500 employees, helps Congress perform its oversight functions by reviewing the activities of the executive branch to see if it is following the congressional intent of laws and by investigating the efficiency and effectiveness of policy implementation. The GAO also sets government standards for accounting, provides legal opinions, and settles claims against the government.

The *Congressional Budget Office (CBO)* (discussed in more detail in Chapter 14) employs more than 230 people. Its principal focus is on analyzing the president's budget

Making a Difference

Tony Battista

Blunt-talking, heavily accented, unknown to the public, but respected and feared by the Pentagon, Tony Battista was a legendary staffer for the Research and Development Subcommittee of the House Armed Services Committee. A weapons expert and antique car buff who liked to spend his weekends restoring vintage cars, his frequent reaction to the outrageous prices of military parts was to tell the Pentagon that he could make them for less in his own garage. More than once, he actually did so.

A tireless foe of duplication and inefficiency, Battista would grill generals mercilessly and often succeed against highly paid lobbyists for defense contractors. In one hearing he went toe-to-toe with the deputy secretary of defense, the undersecretary of defense, and three generals—and won. The subcommittee heeded his recommendation to kill funding for a new cargo plane.

What was the secret to his success? Technical expertise, intelligence, thorough homework, fearlessness, and tenacity were at the core. Members from both sides of the aisle trusted him to provide a bipartisan assessment of weapons systems. As a result, he set the subcommittee's agenda with his personal report on the Pentagon's research and development budget. He also saved taxpayers millions of dollars in defense expenditures. In other words, Tony Battista made a difference.

Source: Hedrick Smith, *The Power Game* (New York: Random House, 1988), 292–297.

and making economic projections about the performance of the economy, the costs of proposed policies, and the economic effects of taxing and spending alternatives.

Committees, caucuses, and individual legislators follow bills from their introduction to their approval. The next sections will discuss this process, which is often termed "labyrinthine" to reflect the fact that getting a bill through Congress is very much like navigating a difficult, intricate maze.

The Congressional Process

Congress's agenda is, of course, a crowded one—about 11,000 bills are introduced in each Congress. A **bill** is a proposed law, drafted in precise, legal language. Anyone—even you or I—can draft a bill. The White House and interest groups are common sources of polished bills. However, only members of the House or the Senate can formally submit a bill for consideration. The traditional route for a bill as it works its way through the legislative labyrinth is depicted in Figure 12.4. Most bills are quietly killed off early in the process. Some are introduced mostly as a favor to a group or a constituent; others are private bills, granting citizenship to a constituent or paying a settlement to a person whose car was demolished by a postal service truck. Still other bills may alter the course of the nation.

bill

A proposed law, drafted in precise, legal language. Anyone can draft a bill, but only a member of the House of Representatives or the Senate can formally submit a bill for consideration.

Congress is typically a reactive and cumbersome decision-making body. Rules are piled upon rules, and procedures upon procedures.[46] Moreover, reforms in the 1970s (which we discuss later in the chapter) decentralized the internal distribution of power in Congress, making legislating more difficult. The polarized political climate of the 1980s also exacerbated the problems of legislating. Party leaders sought ways to cope with these problems, and what Barbara Sinclair has termed *unorthodox lawmaking* has become common in the congressional process, especially for the most significant legislation.[47]

In both chambers party leaders involve themselves in the legislative process on major legislation earlier and more deeply, using special procedures to aid the passage of legislation. Bills are often referred to several committees at the same time, bringing more interests to bear on an issue but complicating the process of passing legislation.

simulation
You are a Member of Congress

Figure 12.4 How a Bill Becomes a Law

Many bills travel full circle, coming first from the White House as part of the presidential agenda, then returning to the president at the end of the process. In the interim, there are two parallel processes in the Senate and House, starting with committee action. If a committee gives a bill a favorable report, the whole chamber considers it. When it is passed in different versions by the two chambers, a conference committee drafts a single compromise bill.

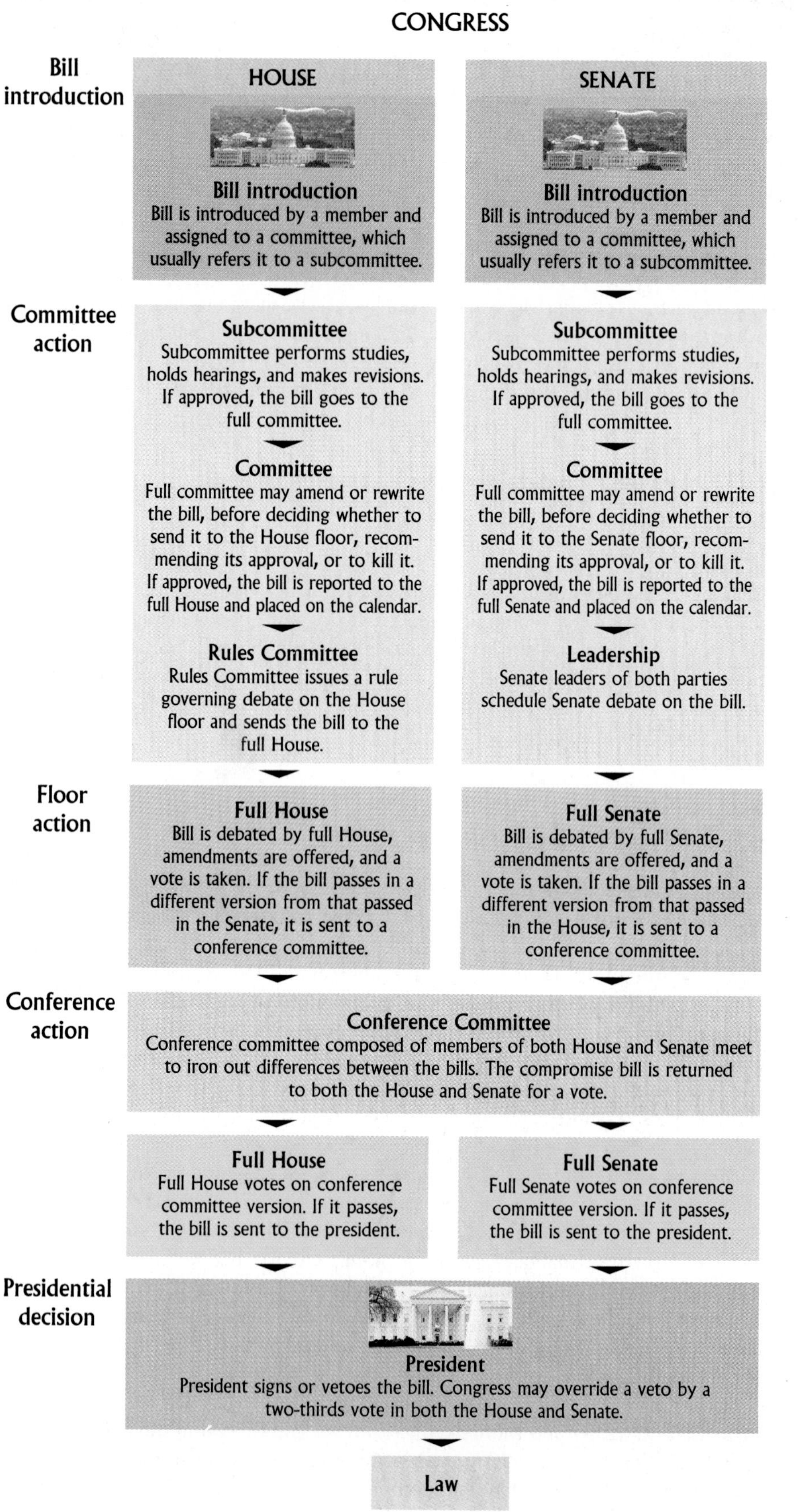

CONGRESS

Bill introduction

HOUSE

Bill introduction
Bill is introduced by a member and assigned to a committee, which usually refers it to a subcommittee.

SENATE

Bill introduction
Bill is introduced by a member and assigned to a committee, which usually refers it to a subcommittee.

Committee action

House:

Subcommittee
Subcommittee performs studies, holds hearings, and makes revisions. If approved, the bill goes to the full committee.

Committee
Full committee may amend or rewrite the bill, before deciding whether to send it to the House floor, recommending its approval, or to kill it. If approved, the bill is reported to the full House and placed on the calendar.

Rules Committee
Rules Committee issues a rule governing debate on the House floor and sends the bill to the full House.

Senate:

Subcommittee
Subcommittee performs studies, holds hearings, and makes revisions. If approved, the bill goes to the full committee.

Committee
Full committee may amend or rewrite the bill, before deciding whether to send it to the Senate floor, recommending its approval, or to kill it. If approved, the bill is reported to the full Senate and placed on the calendar.

Leadership
Senate leaders of both parties schedule Senate debate on the bill.

Floor action

Full House
Bill is debated by full House, amendments are offered, and a vote is taken. If the bill passes in a different version from that passed in the Senate, it is sent to a conference committee.

Full Senate
Bill is debated by full Senate, amendments are offered, and a vote is taken. If the bill passes in a different version from that passed in the House, it is sent to a conference committee.

Conference action

Conference Committee
Conference committee composed of members of both House and Senate meet to iron out differences between the bills. The compromise bill is returned to both the House and Senate for a vote.

Full House
Full House votes on conference committee version. If it passes, the bill is sent to the president.

Full Senate
Full Senate votes on conference committee version. If it passes, the bill is sent to the president.

Presidential decision

President
President signs or vetoes the bill. Congress may override a veto by a two-thirds vote in both the House and Senate.

Law

Since committee leaders cannot always negotiate compromises *among* committees, party leaders have accepted this responsibility, often negotiating compromises and making adjustments to bills after a committee or committees report legislation. On the other hand, committees may be bypassed altogether when party leaders form special task forces for high-priority legislation.

In the House, special rules from the Rules Committee have become powerful tools for controlling floor consideration of bills and sometimes for shaping the outcomes of votes. Often party leaders from each chamber negotiate among themselves instead of creating conference committees. Sometimes, special "summits" between the legislative and executive branches are employed to obtain agreement on the passage of legislation. Party leaders also use *omnibus* legislation that addresses numerous and perhaps unrelated subjects, issues, and programs to create winning coalitions.

These new procedures are generally under the control of party leaders in the House, but in the Senate, leaders have less leverage and *individual* senators have retained great opportunities for influence (such as using the filibuster). As a result, it is often more difficult to pass legislation in the Senate.

There are, of course, countless influences on this legislative process. Presidents, parties, constituents, interest groups, the congressional and committee leadership structure—these and other influences offer members cues for their decision making.

Presidents and Congress: Partners and Protagonists

Political scientists sometimes call the president the *chief legislator,* a phrase that might have appalled the Constitution writers, with their insistence on separation of powers. Presidents do, however, help create the congressional agenda. They are also their own best lobbyists.

Presidents have their own legislative agenda, based in part on their party's platform and their electoral coalition. Their task is to persuade Congress that their agenda should also be Congress's agenda. Lyndon Johnson once claimed (with perhaps a touch of overstatement), "If an issue is not included on the presidential agenda, it is almost impossible—short of crisis—to get the Congress to focus on it."[48]

Presidents have many resources with which to influence Congress. (The next chapter will examine presidential leadership.) They may try to influence members directly—calling up wavering members and telling them that the country's future hinges on their votes, for example—but they do not do this often. If presidents were to pick just one key bill and spend 10 minutes on the telephone with each of the 535 members of Congress, they would spend 89 hours chatting with them. Instead, presidents wisely leave most White House lobbying to the congressional liaison office and work mainly through regular meetings with the party's leaders in the House and Senate.

It seems a wonder that presidents, even with all their power and prestige, can push and wheedle anything through the labyrinthine congressional process. The president must usually win at least 10 times to hope for final passage:

1. in one House subcommittee
2. in the full House committee
3. in the House Rules Committee to move to the floor
4. on the House floor
5. in one Senate subcommittee
6. in the full Senate committee
7. on the Senate floor
8. in the House-Senate conference committee to work out the differences between the two bills
9. back to the House floor for final passage
10. back to the Senate floor for final passage.

As one scholar put it, presidential leadership of Congress is *at the margins*.[49] In general, successful presidential leadership of Congress has not been the result of the dominant chief executive of political folklore who reshapes the contours of the political landscape to pave the way for change. Rather than creating the conditions for important shifts in public policy, the effective American leader is the less heroic *facilitator* who works at the margins of coalition building to recognize and exploit opportunities presented by a favorable configuration of political forces. Of course, presidents can exercise their veto to *stop* legislation they oppose.

Presidents are only one of many claimants for the attention of Congress, especially on domestic policy. As we will show in the next chapter, popular presidents and presidents with a large majority of their party in each house of Congress have a good chance of getting their way. Yet, as Figure 12.5 shows, presidents often lose. Ronald Reagan was considered a strong chief executive, and budgeting was one of his principal tools for affecting public policy. Yet the budgets he proposed to Congress were typically pronounced DOA, dead on arrival. Members of Congress truly compose an independent branch.

Party, Constituency, and Ideology

Presidents come and go; the parties linger on. Presidents do not determine a congressional member's electoral fortunes; constituents do. Where presidents are less influential, on domestic policies especially, party, personal ideology, and constituency are more important.

Figure 12.5 Presidential Success on Votes in Congress

Presidential success rates for influencing congressional votes vary widely among presidents and within a president's tenure in office. Presidents are usually most successful early in their tenures and when their party has a majority in one or both houses of Congress. Regardless, in almost any year the president will lose on many issues. Congress considers the president's views when it makes decisions, but when it disagrees with the White House, which it often does, it does not hesitate to go in its own direction.

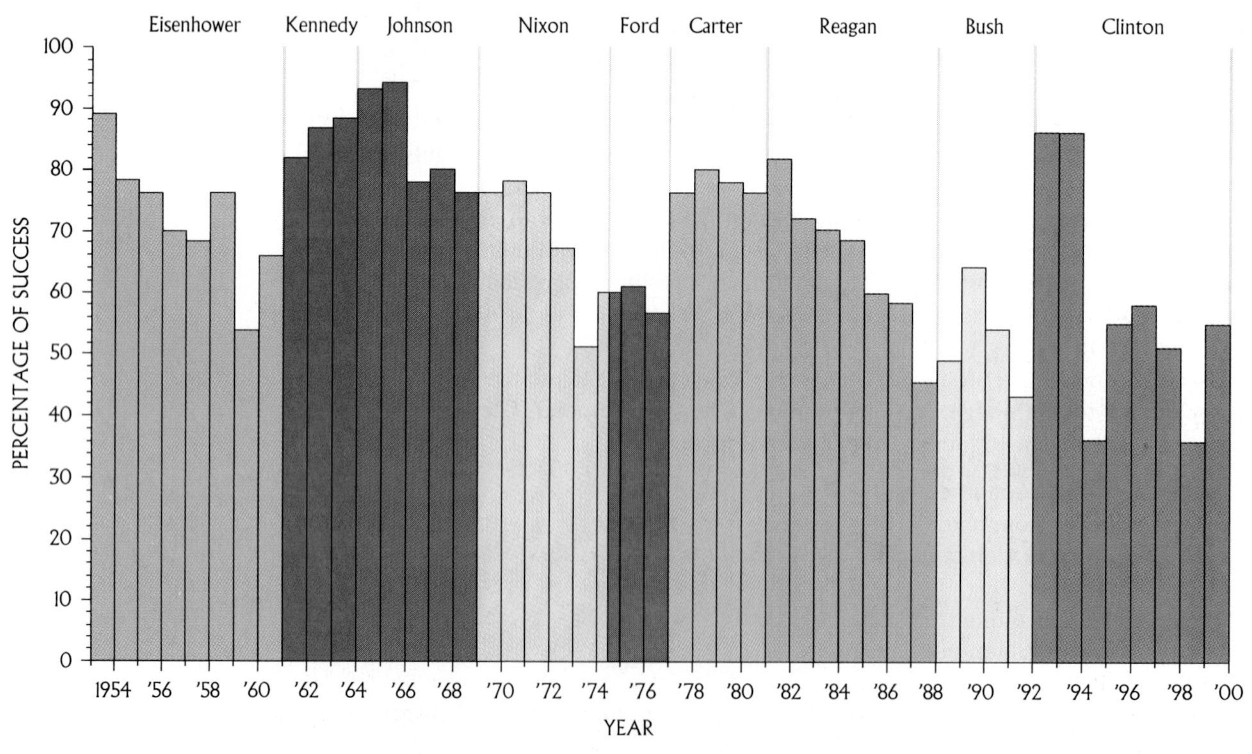

Source: Independent calculation of *Congressional Quarterly* data. See George C. Edwards III, *At the Margins: Presidential Leadership of Congress* (New Haven, CT: Yale University Press, 1989), Table 2.1.

Party Influence. On some issues, members of the parties stick together like a marching band. They are most cohesive when Congress is electing its official leaders. A vote for Speaker of the House is a straight party-line vote, with every Democrat on one side and every Republican on the other. On other issues, however, the party coalition may come unglued. Votes on civil rights policies, for example, have revealed deep divisions within each party. Figure 12.6 shows the percentage of times a majority of Democrats were opposed by a majority of Republicans.

Differences between the parties are sharpest on questions of social welfare and economic policy.[50] When voting on labor issues, Democrats traditionally cling together, leaning toward the side of the unions, whereas Republicans almost always vote with business. On social welfare issues—poverty, unemployment aid, help to the cities—Democrats are more generous than Republicans are. This split between the parties should not be too surprising if you recall the party coalitions described in Chapter 8. Once in office, party members favor their electoral coalitions.

Party leaders in Congress help "whip" their members into line. Their power to do so is limited, of course. They cannot drum a recalcitrant member out of the party. Leaders have plenty of influence, however, including some say about committee posts, the power to boost a member's pet projects, and the subtle but significant influence of information to which a member is not privy.

Figure 12.6 Party Unity Votes in Congress[a]

In democracies with parliamentary systems such as Great Britain, almost all votes are party-line votes. Parties, as Chapter 8 showed, are considerably weaker in the United States. Party affiliation is a rallying point for representatives and senators and does influence their votes, yet in a typical year, a majority of Democrats and Republicans oppose each other only half the time. Members of both parties often end up deserting their colleagues and voting against the party line. In recent years, partisanship has been stronger in the House than in the Senate.

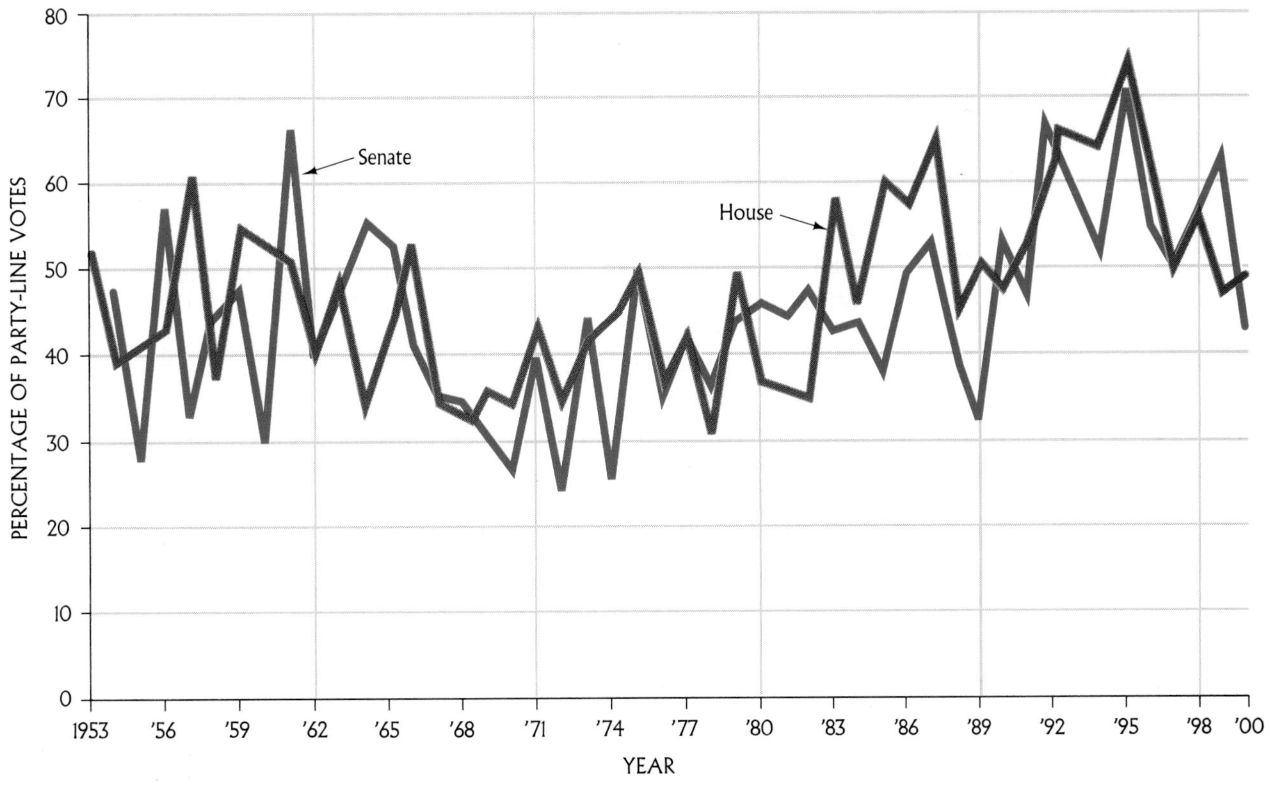

[a]Data indicate the percentage of all recorded votes on which a majority of voting Democrats opposed a majority of voting Republicans.

Source: Independent calculation of *Congressional Quarterly* data.

Recently the parties, especially the Republicans, have been a growing source of money for congressional campaigns. The congressional campaign committees have energized both parties, helping to recruit candidates, running seminars in campaign skills, and conducting polls. Equally important, the congressional campaign committees today have money to hand out to promising candidates. The parties can thus impact the kinds of people who sit in Congress on either side of the aisle.

Constituency versus Ideology. Members of Congress are representatives; their constituents expect them to represent their interests in Washington. In 1714, Anthony Henry, a member of the British Parliament, received a letter from some of his constituents asking him to vote against an excise tax. He is reputed to have replied in part:

> *Gentlemen: I have received your letter about the excise, and I am surprised at your insolence in writing to me at all . . . may God's curse light upon you all, and may it make your homes as open and as free to the excise officers as your wives and daughters have always been to me while I have represented your rascally constituency.*[51]

Needless to say, notions of representation have changed since Henry's time.

Sometimes representation requires a balancing act. If some representatives favor more defense spending but suspect that their constituents do not, what are they to do? The English politician and philosopher Edmund Burke favored the concept of legislators as *trustees*, using their best judgment to make policy in the interests of the people. Others prefer the concept of representatives as *instructed delegates*, mirroring the preferences of their constituents. Actually, members of Congress are *politicos*, adopting both trustee and instructed delegate roles as they strive to be both representatives and policymakers.[52]

The best way constituents can influence congressional voting is also simple: Elect a representative or senator who agrees with their views. John Sullivan and Robert O'Connor discovered that congressional candidates tend to take policy positions different from their opponent's. Moreover, the winners generally vote on roll calls as they said they would during their campaigns.[53] If voters use their good sense to elect candidates who share their policy positions, then constituents *can* influence congressional policy.

If voters miss their chance and elect someone out of step with their thinking, it may be difficult to influence that person's votes. It is difficult even for well-intentioned legislators to know what people want. Some legislators pay careful attention to their mail, but the mail is a notoriously unreliable indicator of people's thinking; individuals with extreme opinions on an issue are more likely to write than those with moderate views. Some members send questionnaires to constituents, but the answers they receive are unreliable because few people respond. Some try public opinion polling, but it is expensive if professionally done and unreliable if not.

Defeating an incumbent is no easy task. Even legislators whose votes conflict with the views of their constituents tend to be reelected. Most citizens have trouble recalling the names of their congressional representatives (one study found that only 28 percent of the public could name their representatives in the House),[54] let alone keeping up with their representatives' voting records. According to one expert, "Probably less than a third of all constituents can recognize who their representatives are and what policy positions they have generally taken—and even that third tends not to evaluate incumbents on the basis of policy."[55] A National Election Study found that only 11 percent of the people even claimed to remember how their congressperson voted on a particular issue.

On some controversial issues, however, legislators ignore constituent opinion at great peril. For years, Southern members of Congress would not have dared to vote for a civil rights law. Lately, representatives and senators have been concerned about the many new single-issue groups. Such groups care little about a member's overall record; to them, a vote on one issue—gun control, abortion, the ERA—is all that counts.

Ready to pounce on one wrong vote and pour money into an opponent's campaign, these new forces in constituency politics make every legislator nervous.

Nevertheless, most issues remain obscure. On such issues legislators can safely ignore constituency opinion. On a typical issue, the prime determinant of a congressional member's vote is personal ideology. On issues where ideological divisions are sharp and constituency preferences and knowledge are likely to be weak, such as defense and foreign policy, ideology is virtually the only determinant of voting.[56] As ideological divisions weaken and constituency preferences strengthen, members are more likely to deviate from their own position and adopt those of their constituencies.[57] Thus, when they have differences of opinion with their constituencies, members of Congress consider constituency preferences but are not controlled by them.[58]

Lobbyists and Interest Groups

The nation's capital is crawling with lawyers, lobbyists, registered foreign agents, public relations consultants, and others—more than 14,000 individuals representing nearly 12,000 organizations at last count—all seeking to influence Congress.[59] Several dozen groups are concerned with the single issue of protecting Alaska's environment; the bigger the issue, the more lobbyists are involved in it. Any group interested in influencing national policymaking—and that includes almost everyone—either hires Washington lobbyists or sends its own. Washington lobbyists can be a formidable group.

Lobbyists have a dismal image, one worsened by periodic scandals in which someone seeking to influence Congress presents huge amounts of cash to senators and representatives. In 1997, lobbyists spent $1.17 billion on lobbying Congress—plus millions more in campaign contributions and attempts to try to persuade members' constituents to send messages to Washington.[60] Such spending gives lobbyists a bad name, no doubt often deserved. But lobbyists have a job to do—namely, to represent the interests of their organizations. Lobbyists, some of them former members of Congress, can provide legislators with crucial information and often with assurances of financial aid in the next campaign.

Lobbyists have never been held in high esteem by the public, and they have come under especially harsh criticism in recent years. Nevertheless, lobbyists play an important role in the legislative process.

How You Can Make A Difference

Gun Control

Besides abortion, perhaps no other issue under consideration by Congress evokes more emotion and public attention than gun control. On both sides of this issue, advocate organizations constantly press members of Congress to either pass or defeat legislation favorable to their position. Like abortion, the gun control debate involves not only matters of life and death but also constitutional concerns and interpretations. This issue remains contentious not only because of strong emotions of those involved but also because of convincing arguments and impressive organizations on both sides of the debate.

Organizations in favor of gun control tend to emphasize grass-roots organization and local visibility. While most gun control organizations agree upon the key issues, a smorgasbord of organizations allow individuals favorable to gun control legislation to find a group with agreeable tactics and positions. The Educational Fund to End Handgun Violence (www.endhandgunviolence.org) provides a good entry point to antigun organizations on the Internet including the Children's Defense Fund, Coalition To Stop Gun Violence, Handgun Control, Inc., Mothers Against Violence in America, and many others.

Opponents of gun control rally to the NRA (www.nra.org). With a single dominant organization, gun supporters can mount a more organized, better funded, more centralized campaign. This advantage is clear in the NRA's influence on Capitol Hill on issues of gun control. On the downside, a single organization makes it easier for opponents to target the entire issue by identifying it with one organization. Another drawback of such a strong, nearly monolithic organization as the NRA is that it cannot easily accommodate diverse opinions about the issue of gun control.

If you examine the websites of these organizations, you'll find that nearly all ask for money to support their causes. Being a college student and, most likely, short on cash, you would likely make a far greater impact by writing your congressional representatives a personal, handwritten letter. Even better, you could organize a letter-writing campaign on campus in your dorm or fraternity/sorority, at church, or in your neighborhood. Be sure to insist on handwritten letters because they convey a personal interest that mass-produced form letters, e-mails, and petitions cannot hope to duplicate. Tell your fellow letter writers to be short, include a name, address, and phone number, and, if possible, incorporate a memorable personal story. You can also make a personal phone call to your legislators by dialing the congressional switchboard at 202–224–3121. Though you'll only get to talk to a legislative aide, these assistants are influential in bringing information and legislation to the attention of their boss. Involvement in high profile marches, protests, and rallies also can also influence how members of Congress, especially in swing districts, eventually vote on gun control issues.

These inexpensive, low-tech approaches are effective precisely because they demonstrate to members of Congress a high level of concern representative of a far higher percentage among their constituents.

Lobbyists do not hold all the high cards in their dealings with Congress; congressional representatives hold some trump cards of their own. The easiest way to frustrate lobbyists is to ignore them. Lobbyists usually make little headway with their opponents anyway: The lobbyist for General Motors arguing against automobile pollution controls would not have much influence with a legislator concerned about air pollution. Members of Congress can also make life uncomfortable for lobbyists. They can embarrass them, expose heavy-handed tactics, and spread the word among an organization's members that it is being poorly represented in Washington. Last but not least, Congress *can* regulate lobbyists.

In 1995, Congress passed a law requiring anyone hired to lobby members of Congress, congressional staff members, White House officials, and federal agencies to report what issues they were seeking to influence, how much they were spending on the effort, and the identities of their clients. This law was designed to close loopholes in a 1946 law that allowed most lobbyists to avoid registering and had permitted those who did to disclose only limited information about their activities. Congress also placed severe restrictions on the gifts, meals, and expense-paid travel that public officials may accept from lobbyists. In theory, these reporting requirements and restrictions not only prevent shady deals between lobbyists and members of Congress but also curb the influence of special interests. Nevertheless, interest groups are thriving; indi-

"Mr. Speaker, will the gentleman from Small Firearms yield the floor to the gentleman from Big Tobacco?"

rect, grass-roots lobbying—such as computerized mailings to encourage citizens to pressure their representatives on an issue—has grown also.

There are many forces that affect senators and representatives as they decide how to vote on a bill. After his exhaustive study of influences on congressional decision making, John Kingdon concluded that none was important enough to suggest that congresspeople vote as they do because of one influence.[61] The process is as complex for individual legislators as it is for those who want to influence their votes.

Understanding Congress

Congress is a complex institution. Its members want to make sound national policy, but they also want to return to Washington after the next election. How do these sometimes conflicting desires affect American democracy and the scope of American government?

Congress and Democracy

In a large nation, the success of democratic government depends on the quality of representation. Americans could hardly hold a national referendum on every policy issue on the government agenda; instead, they delegate decision-making power to representatives. If Congress is a successful democratic institution, it must be a successful representative institution.

Certainly, some aspects of Congress make it very *un*representative. Its members are an American elite (see "America in Perspective: The Russian Duma: A Reformer's Paradise"). Its leadership is chosen by its own members, not by any vote of the American people. Voters have little direct influence over the individuals who chair key committees or lead congressional parties. Voters in just a single constituency control

comparative
Comparing Legislatures

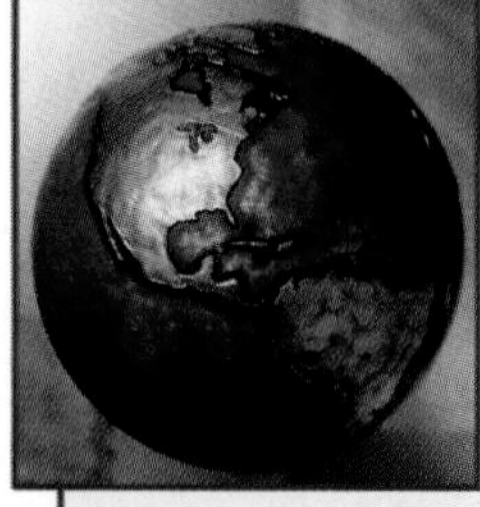

America in Perspective

The Russian Duma: A Reformer's Paradise

The next time you grow exasperated at Congress, just remember the Russian Duma, the 450-member lower house of Parliament. In the anything-goes world of the Duma, there are no rules of sexual conduct, no sensitivities about political correctness, and no ethics investigations. Sergie Semyonov is the deputy chair of the committee on women, families, and youth. His expertise in the area seems to be a result of living with three women. Recently, he proposed a bill to legalize polygamy, arguing that he had "the money and energy to keep all my women fully satisfied."

But Mr. Semyonov appears positively chivalrous compared to the ultranationalist leader of his party, Vladimir V. Zhirinovsky. Mr. Zhirinovsky got into a fistfight on the floor of the Duma and punched another deputy—a woman—in the face. He later claimed he was fending off her sexual advances!

Parliamentary immunity attracts candidates who face criminal charges and want to escape prosecution by becoming legislators. They should feel right at home. There are no financial scandals in the Duma because no one even tries to hide their conflicts of interest. Graft and corruption are blatant, and there is no way to trace illicit money, no oversight committees, no paper trail for prosecutors to follow, and no watchdog press to hold lawmakers accountable.

Such ethical improprieties seem to have replaced the work ethic as a norm of behavior. Often the deputies simply do not show up at all, even for key votes. In several instances, all the leaders were absent, leaving Communist Party leader Anatoly Lukyanov, who supported the 1991 coup against Mikhail Gorbachev, in charge. There is one saving grace for the Russian people, however. The newest Russian constitution has stripped the Duma of most of its power.

Source: Alesandra Stanley. "Russia's Gross National Legislature," in the *New York Times*, January 19, 1997, D3.

the fate of committee chairs and party leaders. Voters in the other 434 House districts and the other 49 states have no real say, for example, about who chairs a committee considering new forms of energy, a committee considering defense buildups, or a committee making economic policy.

Nevertheless, the evidence in this chapter demonstrates that Congress *does* try to listen to the American people. Whom voters elect makes a difference in how congressional votes turn out; which party is in power affects policies. Linkage institutions actually link voters to policymakers. Perhaps Congress could do a better job at representation than it does, but there are many obstacles to improved representation. Legislators find it hard to know what constituents want. Groups may keep important issues off the legislative agenda. Members may spend so much time servicing their constituencies that they have little time left to represent those constituencies in the policymaking process.

participation
Write to your Congressperson

Members of Congress are responsive to the people, if the people make clear what they want. For example, in response to popular demands, Congress established a program in 1988 to shield the elderly against the catastrophic costs associated with acute illness. In 1989, in response to complaints from the elderly about higher Medicare premiums, Congress abolished most of what it had created the previous year.

Reforming Congress

Reformers have tried to promote a more open, democratic Congress. To a large degree, they have succeeded. Looking at Congress in the 1950s, one could say that it was like a stepladder. The members advanced one rung at a time toward the heights of power with each reelection. At the top was real power in Congress. Committee chairs were automatically selected by seniority. Their power on the committee was unquestioned. Bills disappeared forever into chairs' "vest pockets" if those chairs did not like them. The chairs alone created subcommittees, picked their members, and routed bills to them. If committees controlled bills from the cradle to the grave, the chairs were both midwives and undertakers. At the bottom of the ladder, the norm of apprenticeship—"be seen and not heard"—prevailed. The standing Washington line about seniority was this: "Son, the longer you're here, the more you'll come to appreciate the seniority system." The system was democratic—one person, one vote—when the roll call came, but it was not democratic when the bill itself was shaped, shelved, or sunk.

Democratization. The waves of congressional reform in the 1960s and especially the 1970s changed this political atmosphere. Lyndon Johnson started the reform ball rolling during his majority leadership with the "Johnson rule," which gave each senator a seat on at least one key committee. This reform allowed junior members more room at the top.

By the 1970s the reform movement picked up speed.[62] Reformers tried to create more democracy by spreading power around. First to go was the automatic and often autocratic dominance of the most senior members as committee chairs. Instead, the majority party elected chairs, and some of the most objectionable chairs were dropped. The chairs' power was also reduced by the proliferation of subcommittees, which widened the distribution of authority, visibility, and resources in both chambers. Subcommittees became the new centers of power in Congress.

Not only the formal reforms of Congress but also the proliferation of informal caucuses tended to decentralize power in Congress. Burdett Loomis remarks that "the proliferation of caucuses illustrates the shoring up of particularistic forces in Congress. . . . And while members decry the increase in single-issue politics, they have only to consider their own behavior."[63]

Partially in response to the problems of decentralized power in the House, the Republicans passed prominent reforms when they took control in 1995. Committee chairs were allowed to choose the chairs of subcommittees on their committees and to hire all the committee and subcommittee staff. Some subcommittees were simply eliminated. At the same time, both committee and subcommittee chairs were limited to three consecutive two-year terms as chair (Senate Republicans also adopted this rule), and committee chairs lost the power to cast proxy votes for those committee members not in attendance. Members were prohibited from using appropriations for their office allowances to fund the various caucuses. The Speaker also put the committees on short leashes, giving them instructions regarding the legislation they were to report and a timetable for reporting it. In a few instances, the leadership bypassed committees by setting up separate task forces to prepare legislation.

Cable television's live coverage of Congress has further democratized the legislative process by letting Americans see their representatives at work. Here, the U.S. House of Representatives is shown discussing security at U.S. embassies.

Why does it matter?

The Speaker of the House is the highest ranking member in Congress, yet the Speaker has to be responsive to the wishes of party members. What would happen if the Speaker were able to impose his views on the House? Would the House operate more efficiently? Would stronger leadership result in better public policy? Would your interests be better served by a more powerful Speaker?

By 1997, however, the leadership backed off. Weakened by his low ratings in the polls, Speaker Newt Gingrich gave committee chairs greater leeway to set their committee's agenda and promised to allow legislation to be first fashioned by committees. For now, both the Speaker and the committee chairs are stronger than they were in the 1980s. How this will affect the quality of public policy remains to be seen.

Representativeness versus Effectiveness. The central legislative dilemma for Congress is combining the faithful representation of constituents with making effective public policy. Supporters see Congress as a forum in which many interests compete for a spot on the policy agenda and over the form of a particular policy—which is just as the founders intended it to be.

Critics charge that Congress is responsive to so many interests that policy is as uncoordinated, fragmented, and decentralized as Congress itself. Interest groups grow on committees and subcommittees like barnacles on a boat. After a while, these groups develop intimacy and influence with "their" committee. Committee decisions usually carry over to the roll-call vote. Thus the committee system links congressional policymaking to a multiplicity of interests, rather than to a majority's preferences.

In addition, some observers believe Congress is too representative—so much so that it is incapable of taking decisive action to deal with difficult problems. The agricultural committees busily tend to the interests of tobacco farmers, while committees on health and welfare spend millions for lung cancer research. One committee wrestles with domestic unemployment while another makes tax policy that encourages businesses to open new plants out of the country. One reason why government spends too much, critics say, is that Congress is protecting the interests of too many people. As long as each interest tries to preserve the status quo, bold reforms cannot be enacted.

"Listen , pal! I didn't spend seven million bucks to get here so I could yield the floor to you."

Drawing by Dana Fardon: ©1987 *The New Yorker* magazine.

On the other hand, defenders of Congress point out that, thanks to its being decentralized, there is no oligarchy in control to prevent the legislature from taking comprehensive action. In fact, Congress has enacted the huge tax cut of 1981, the comprehensive (and complicated) tax reform of 1986, and various bills structuring the budgetary process designed to balance the budget.[64]

There is no simple solution to Congress's dilemma. It tries to be both a representative and an objective policymaking institution. As long as this is true, it is unlikely that Congress will please all its critics.

Congress and the Scope of Government

If Congress is responsive to a multitude of interests and those interests desire government policies to aid them in some way, does the nature of Congress predispose it to continually increasing the scope of the public sector? Do the benefits of servicing constituents provide an incentive for members of Congress to tolerate, even to expand, an already big government? The more policies there are, the more potential ways members can help their constituencies. The more bureaucracies there are, the more red tape members can help cut. Big government helps members of Congress get reelected and even gives them good reason to support making it bigger.

Members of Congress vigorously protect the interests of their constituents. At the same time, there are many members who agree with Ronald Reagan that government is not the answer to problems but rather *is* the problem. These individuals make careers out of fighting against government programs (although these same senators and representatives typically support programs aimed at aiding *their* constituents).

Americans have contradictory preferences regarding public policy. As we have noted in previous chapters, they want to balance the budget and pay low taxes, but they also support most government programs. Congress does not impose programs on a reluctant public; instead, it responds to the public's demands for them.

Summary

According to the Constitution, members of Congress are the government's policymakers, but legislative policymaker is only one of the roles of members of Congress. They are also politicians, and politicians always keep one eye on the next election. Success in congressional elections may be determined as much by constituency service—casework and the pork barrel—as by policymaking. Senators and representatives have become so skilled at constituency service that incumbents have a big edge over challengers, making it more difficult to bring about major changes in the makeup, and thus the policies, of Congress.

The structure of Congress is so complex that it seems remarkable that legislation gets passed at all. Its bicameral division means that bills have two sets of committee hurdles to clear. Because recent reforms have decentralized power, the job of leading Congress is more difficult than ever.

Presidents try hard to influence Congress, and parties and elections can also shape legislators' choices. The impact of these factors clearly differs from one policy area to another. Party impacts are clearest on issues for which the party's coalitions are clearest, especially social welfare and economic issues. Constituencies influence policy mostly by the initial choice of a representative. Members of Congress do pay attention to voters, particularly on visible issues, but most issues do not interest voters. On these less visible issues other factors, such as lobbyists and members' individual ideologies, influence policy decisions.

Congress clearly has some undemocratic and unrepresentative features. Its members are hardly average Americans. Even so, members pay attention to popular preferences, when they can figure out what they are. People inside and outside the institution, however, think that Congress is ineffective. Its objective policymaking decisions and representative functions sometimes conflict, yet from time to time Congress does show that it can deal with major issues in a comprehensive fashion. Many members of Congress have incentives to increase the scope of the federal government, but the people who put those representatives in office provide these incentives.

Career Profile

Position: Legislative Aide and Correspondent for Rep. Steve Largent (R-OK)
Salary: $28,000–$35,000
Benefits: Health, life, and retirement benefits
Qualifications: A bachelor's degree is usually required. Any field is fine, but some experience with political systems and political philosophy is helpful. Ideological and policy compatibility with congressperson is a must. Writing and analytical skills are mandatory

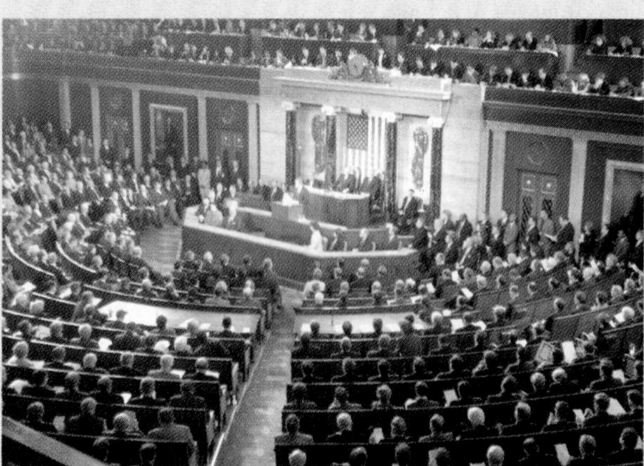

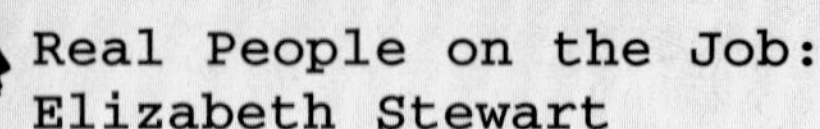

Real People on the Job: Elizabeth Stewart

Not old enough or rich enough to run for Congress yourself but still want to work in the Capitol Building after graduating college? Well, if there is a job in the federal government perfectly suited for a recent college graduate, then a legislative aide is probably it. Elizabeth Stewart would certainly agree. Using her connections from a semester-long internship in Washington, D.C., Elizabeth landed a job as legislative correspondent and aide for Representative Steve Largent (R-OK).

Elizabeth is Rep. Largent's primary contact person for seven legislative areas: agriculture, census, housing, Indian affairs, labor, science, and tort reform. Whenever bills are introduced in these areas, Elizabeth knows about it. She'll find out who is sponsoring the bill (Democrat or Republican) and ask for more information from the sponsor's office. In addition to her own investigative work, Elizabeth often relies on outside sources to uncover the history of legislation in her policy areas. The Congressional Research Service (CRS), a group of non-partisan researchers, produces in-depth background briefs on legislation and policy issues. Legislative aides also rely on think tanks like the Cato Institute and the Brookings Institute to get information about legislation.

Rep. Largent is often one of the lead legislators on tax reform bills. Elizabeth must round up support for these bill from other members of Congress and compile the necessary arguments and information to help get the bill passed in the full House. As such, she must sift through testimony and information that will be introduced as evidence in committee and on the House floor. She must also coordinate press coverage for the legislation with the aim of generating public pressure to pass this legislation.

One of the most important aspects of the job is the dialogue Elizabeth must maintain with her boss. She must know his thinking on various issues in order to do her job well. When Rep. Largent is in Washington, D.C. (usually Tuesday through Thursday when Congress is in session), Elizabeth must put in long hours to make the best use of his time. On Mondays and Fridays, though, when Rep. Largent returns to his home district, hours become more regular and the pace slightly less hectic.

Work as a legislative aide is not for everyone. Jobs offering relatively low pay with long hours are usually unappealing to most established job seekers. However, recent college graduates are ideal candidates for this position and the long-term rewards can be great. Many former legislative aides parlay their hard-earned expertise into a stepping-stone for high-paying private sector jobs. Many companies need lobbyists, spokespeople, and liaison officers to deal with legislative issues favorable to their industry. There is no better way to gain the required experience than on the Hill itself and working in the trenches. If work as an aide seems interesting to you, call your congressman's office to intern while you are still in school. An internship will help pave the way to a full-time job after graduation.

Key Terms

incumbents
casework
pork barrel
bicameral legislature
House Rules Committee
filibuster
Speaker of the House
majority leader
whips
minority leader
standing committees
joint committees
conference committees
select committees
legislative oversight
committee chairs
seniority system
caucus
bill

For Further Reading

Aberbach, Joel D. *Keeping a Watchful Eye: The Politics of Congressional Oversight.* Washington, D.C.: Brookings Institution, 1990. A thorough study of congressional oversight of the executive branch.

Bernstein, Robert A. *Elections, Representation, and Congressional Voting Behavior.* Englewood Cliffs, NJ: Prentice-Hall, 1989. Examines the issue of constituency control over members of Congress.

Deering, Christopher J., and Steven S. Smith. *Committees in Congress*, 3rd ed. Washington, D.C.: Congressional Quarterly Press, 1997. A thorough overview of the complex committee structure in the House and Senate.

Dodd, Lawrence C., and Bruce I. Oppenheimer. *Congress Reconsidered*, 7th ed. Washington, D.C.: Congressional Quarterly, 2001. Excellent essays covering many aspects of Congress.

Fenno, Richard F., Jr. *Home Style.* Boston: Little, Brown, 1978. How members of Congress mend fences and stay in political touch with the folks back home.

Fiorina, Morris P. *Congress: Keystone of the Washington Establishment*, 2nd ed. New Haven, CT: Yale University Press, 1989. Argues that members of Congress are self-serving in representing their constituents, ensuring their reelection but harming the national interest.

Jacobson, Gary C. *The Politics of Congressional Elections*, 5th ed. New York: Addison-Wesley Longman, 2001. An excellent review of congressional elections.

Kingdon, John W. *Congressmen's Voting Decisions*, 3rd ed. Ann Arbor: University of Michigan Press, 1989. A thorough and insightful study of congressional voting decisions.

Lee, Frances E., and Bruce I. Oppenheimer. *Sizing Up the Senate: The Unequal Consequences of Equal Representation.* Chicago: University of Chicago Press, 1999. How representation in the Senate affects how people are represented, the distribution of government benefits, and the nature of election campaigns.

Loomis, Burdett. *The New American Politician.* New York: Basic Books, 1988. Focuses on how a new generation of political entrepreneurs has come to dominate Congress.

Mayhew, David R. *Congress: The Electoral Connection.* New Haven, CT: Yale University Press, 1974. An analysis of Congress based on the premise that the principal motivation of congressional behavior is reelection.

Internet Resources

www.house.gov/
The official House website contains information on the organization, operations, schedule, and activities of the House and its committees. The site also contains links to the offices of members and committees and enables you to contact your representative directly.

www.senate.gov/
The official Senate website contains information and links similar to those for the House.

Thomas.loc.gov/
Information on the activities of Congress, the status and text of legislation, the *Congressional Record*, committee reports, and historical documents.

www.rollcall.com/
Roll Call, the online version of the Capitol Hill newspaper.

www.fec.gov/
Federal Election Commission data on campaign expenditures.

www.opensecrets.org
The Center for Responsive Politics website with data on the role of money in politics.

www.c-span.org
Video coverage of Congress in action.

Notes

1. David T. Canon, *Race, Redistricting, and Representation: The Unintended Consequences of Black Majority Districts* (Chicago: University of Chicago Press, 1999).
2. There is some evidence that women state legislators in states with the highest percentage of female representatives are more likely than men to introduce and pass legislation dealing with women, children, and families. See Sue Thomas, "The Impact of Women on State Legislative Policies," *Journal of Politics* 53 (November 1991): 958–976. See also Arturo Vega and Juanita M. Firestone, "The Effects of Gender on Congressional Behavior and the Substantive Representation of Women," *Legislative Studies Quarterly* 20 (May 1995): 213–222.

3. On various views of representation, see Hanna Pitkin, *The Concept of Representation* (Berkeley: University of California Press, 1967).
4. Sally Friedman, "House Committee Assignments of Women and Minority Newcomers, 1965–1994," *Legislative Studies Quarterly* 21 (February 1996): 73–81; Alan Gerber, "African Americans' Congressional Careers and the Democratic House Delegation," *Journal of Politics* 58 (August 1996): 831–845.
5. An excellent review of congressional campaign costs and spending is Edie N. Goldenberg and Michael W. Traugott, *Campaigning for Congress* (Washington, D.C.: Congressional Quarterly Press, 1984). Another is Paul S. Herrnson, *Congressional Elections: Campaigning at Home and in Washington* (Washington, D.C.: Congressional Quarterly Press, 1995).
6. John L. Sullivan and Eric Uslaner, "Congressional Behavior and Electoral Marginality," *American Journal of Political Science* 22 (August 1978): 536–553.
7. Thomas Mann, *Unsafe at Any Margin* (Washington, D.C.: American Enterprise Institute, 1978).
8. Glenn R. Parker, *Homeward Bound* (Pittsburgh: University of Pittsburgh Press, 1986); and John R. Johannes, *To Serve the People* (Lincoln: University of Nebraska Press, 1984).
9. Patricia Hurley and Kim Q. Hill, "The Prospects for Issue Voting in Contemporary Congressional Elections," *American Politics Quarterly* 8 (October 1980): 446.
10. Mann, *Unsafe at Any Margin*, 37.
11. That presidential elections and congressional elections are not closely related is an argument made in Lyn Ragsdale, "The Fiction of Congressional Elections as Presidential Events," *American Politics Quarterly* 8 (October 1980): 375–398. For evidence that voters' views of the president affect their voting for senators, see Lonna Rae Atkeson and Randall W. Partin, "Economic and Referendum Voting: A Comparison of Gubernatorial and Senatorial Elections," *American Political Science Review* 89 (March 1995): 99–107.
12. John R. Owens and Edward C. Olson, "Economic Fluctuations and Congressional Elections," *American Journal of Political Science* 24 (August 1980): 469–493; Benjamin Radcliff, "Solving a Puzzle: Aggregate Analysis and Economic Voting Revisited," *Journal of Politics* 50 (May 1988): 440–458; Robert S. Erikson, "Economic Conditions and the Congressional Vote: A Review of the Macrolevel Evidence," *American Journal of Political Science* 34 (May 1990): 373–399; James E. Campbell, *The Presidential Pulse of Congressional Elections* (Lexington: University Press of Kentucky, 1993), 119; and Gary C. Jacobson, "Does the Economy Matter in Midterm Elections?" *American Journal of Political Science* 34 (May 1990): 400–404.
13. David R. Mayhew, *Congress: The Electoral Connection* (New Haven, CT: Yale University Press, 1974).
14. Richard F. Fenno, Jr., *Home Style* (Boston: Little, Brown, 1978), 32.
15. *Ibid.*, 106–107.
16. The "service spells success" argument is made in Morris P. Fiorina, *Congress: Keystone of the Washington Establishment*, 2nd ed. (New Haven, CT: Yale University Press, 1989); and, with a slightly different emphasis, in Glenn R. Parker, "The Advantages of Incumbency in Congressional Elections," *American Politics Quarterly* 8 (October 1980): 449–461.
17. Fiorina, *Congress: Keystone of the Washington Establishment*, 43.
18. Gary C. Jacobson, *The Politics of Congressional Elections*, 4th ed. (New York: Longman, 1997), 108–116; Stephen Ansolabehere, James M. Snyder, Jr., and Charles Stewart, III, "Old Voters, New Voters, and the Personal Vote; Using Redistricting To Measure the Incumbency Advantage," *American Journal of Political Science* 44 (January 2000): 17–34.
19. See, for example, Paul Feldman and James Jondrow, "Congressional Elections and Local Federal Spending," *American Journal of Political Science* 28 (February 1984): 147–163; Glenn R. Parker and Suzanne L. Parker, "The Correlates and Effects of Attention to District by U.S. House Members," *Legislative Studies Quarterly* 10 (May 1985): 223–242; and John C. McAdams and John R. Johannes, "Congressmen, Perquisites, and Elections," *Journal of Politics* 50 (May 1988): 412–439.
20. On strategies of challengers, see Gary C. Jacobson and Samuel Kernell, *Strategy and Choice in Congressional Elections*, 2nd ed. (New Haven, CT: Yale University Press, 1983); and Gary C. Jacobson, "Strategic Politicians and the Dynamics of U.S. House Elections, 1946–1986," *American Political Science Review* 83 (September 1989): 773–794. See also Steven D. Levitt and Catherine D. Wolfram, "Decomposing the Sources of Incumbency Advantage in the U.S. House," *Legislative Studies Quarterly* 22 (February 1997): 45–60.
21. See Gary C. Jacobson, *Money in Congressional Elections* (New Haven, CT: Yale University Press, 1980).
22. On the importance of challenger quality and financing, see Alan I. Abramowitz, "Explaining Senate Election Outcomes," *American Political Science Review* 82 (June 1988): 385–403; and Donald Philip Green and Jonathan S. Krasno, "Salvation for the Spendthrift Incumbent," *American Journal of Political Science* 32 (November 1988): 884–907.
23. Voter News Service exit polls, 1998.
24. Gary C. Jacobson and Michael A. Dimock, "Checking Out: The Effects of Bank Overdrafts on the 1992 House Elections," *American Journal of Political Science* 38 (August 1994): 601–624. See also "Checks and Choices: The House Bank Scandal's Impact on Voters in 1992," *Journal of Politics* 57 (November 1995): 1,143–1,159; and Carl McCurley and Jeffrey J. Mondak, "Inspected by #1184063113: The Influence of Incumbents' Competence and Integrity in U.S. House Elections," *American Journal of Political Science* 39 (November 1995): 864–885.
25. John G. Peters and Susan Welch, "The Effects of Corruption on Voting Behavior in Congressional Elections," *American Political Science Review* 74 (September 1980): 697–708; and Susan Welch and John R. Hibbing, "The Effects of Charges of Corruption on Voting Behavior in Congressional Elections, 1982–1990," *Journal of Politics* 59 (February 1997): 226–239.
26. Federal Election Commission, 1995.
27. Jacobson, *The Politics of Congressional Elections*, 38–43, 104–106. See also Gary C. Jacobson, "The Effects of Campaign Spending in House Elections: New Evidence for Old Arguments," *American Journal of Political Science* 34 (May 1990): 334–362; Christopher Kenny and Michael McBurnett, "An Individual-Level Multiequation Model of Expenditure Effects in Contested House Elections," *American Political Science Review* 88 (September 1994): 699–707; Robert S. Erikson and Thomas R. Palfrey, "Campaign Spending and Incumbency: An Alternative Simultaneous Equation Approach," *Journal of Politics* 60

(May 1998): 355–373; and Alan Gerber, "Estimating the Effect of Campaign Spending on Senate Election Outcomes Using Instrumental Variables," *American Political Science Review* 92 (June 1998): 401–412.

28. On term limits, see Gerald Benjamin and Michael J. Malbin, eds., *Limiting our Legislative Terms* (Washington, D.C.: Congressional Quarterly Press, 1992).
29. Said former House Speaker Jim Wright in *You and Your Congressman* (New York: Putnam, 1976), 190. See also Donald R. Matthews and James Stimson, *Yeas and Nays: Normal Decision-Making in the House of Representatives* (New York: Wiley, 1975); and John L. Sullivan et al., "The Dimensions of Cue-Taking in the House of Representatives: Variations by Issue Area," *Journal of Politics* 55 (November 1993): 975–997.
30. Nelson W. Polsby et al., "Institutionalization of the House of Representatives," *American Political Science Review* 62 (1968): 144–168.
31. John R. Hibbing, "Contours of the Modern Congressional Career," *American Political Science Review* 85 (June 1991): 405–428.
32. See Bernard Grofman, Robert Griffin, and Amihai Glazer, "Is the Senate More Liberal than the House? Another Look," *Legislative Studies Quarterly* 16 (May 1991): 281–296.
33. See Sarah A. Binder and Steven S. Smith, *Politics or Principle? Filibustering in the United States Senate* (Washington, D.C.: Brookings Institution, 1997).
34. Robert L. Peabody, *Leadership in Congress* (Boston: Little, Brown, 1976), 4.
35. On the increasing importance of party leadership in the House, see David W. Rohde, *Parties and Leaders in the Postreform House* (Chicago: University of Chicago Press, 1991); Barbara Sinclair, "The Emergence of Strong Leadership in the 1980s House of Representatives," *Journal of Politics* 54 (August 1992): 657–684; and Gary W. Cox and Matthew D. McCubbins, *Legislative Leviathan* (Berkley: University of California Press, 1993).
36. For more on congressional oversight, see Christopher H. Foreman, Jr., *Signals from the Hill* (New Haven, CT: Yale University Press, 1988); and Diana Evans, "Congressional Oversight and the Diversity of Members' Goals,"*Political Science Quarterly* 109 (No. 4, 1994): 669–687.
37. Joel D. Aberbach, *Keeping a Watchful Eye: The Politics of Congressional Oversight* (Washington, D.C.: Brookings Institution, 1990).
38. Aberbach, *Keeping a Watchful Eye.*
39. Richard F. Fenno, Jr., *Congressmen in Committees* (Boston: Little, Brown, 1973), 1.
40. Useful studies of committee assignments include Kenneth Shepsle, *The Giant Jigsaw Puzzle* (Chicago: University of Chicago Press, 1978); and Cox and McCubbins, *Legislative Leviathan,* chaps. 1, 7, and 8.
41. See Christopher J. Deering and Steven S. Smith, *Committees in Congress,* 3rd ed. (Washington, D.C.: Congressional Quarterly Press, 1997).
42. Richard F. Fenno, Jr., "If, as Ralph Nader Says, Congress Is the 'Broken Branch,' How Come We Love Our Congressmen So Much?" in Norman Ornstein, ed., *Congress in Change* (New York: Praeger, 1975), 282.
43. See Susan Webb Hammond, *Congressional Caucuses in National Policy Making* (Baltimore: Johns Hopkins University Press, 1998).
44. Norman J. Ornstein, Thomas E. Mann, and Michael J. Malbin, *Vital Statistics on Congress, 1999–2000* (Washington D.C.: Congressional Quarterly Press, 2000), chap. 5.
45. *Ibid.*
46. For a thorough discussion of recent rule changes and the impact of procedures, see Steven S. Smith, *Call to Order: Floor Politics in the House and Senate* (Washington, D.C.: Brookings Institution, 1989).
47. Barbara Sinclair, *Unorthodox Lawmaking* (Washington, D.C.: Congressional Quarterly Press, 1997).
48. Quoted in Doris Kearns, *Lyndon Johnson and the American Dream* (New York: New American Liberty, 1976), 146.
49. George C. Edwards III, *At the Margins: Presidential Leadership of Congress* (New Haven, CT: Yale University Press, 1989).
50. James M. Snyder, Jr. and Tim Groseclose, "Estimating Party Influence in Congressional Roll-Call Voting," *American Journal of Political Science* 44 (April 2000): 187–205; Aage Clausen, *How Congressmen Decide: A Policy Focus* (New York: St. Martin's, 1973).
51. Quoted in Peter G. Richards, *Honourable Members* (London: Faber and Faber, 1959), 157.
52. See Roger H. Davidson, *The Role of the Congressman* (New York: Pegasus, 1969); and Thomas E. Cavanaugh, "Role Orientations of House Members: The Process of Representation" (paper delivered at the annual meeting of the American Political Science Association, Washington, D.C., August 1979).
53. John L. Sullivan and Robert E. O'Connor, "Electoral Choice and Popular Control of Public Policy: The Case of the 1966 House Elections," *American Political Science Review* 66 (December 1972): 1,256–1,268.
54. The *New York Times*/CBS News Poll cited in "Voters Disgusted With Politicians as Election Nears," the *New York Times,* November 13, 1994, A10.
55. Robert A. Bernstein, *Elections, Representation, and Congressional Voting Behavior* (Englewood Cliffs, NJ: Prentice-Hall, 1989), 99.
56. Larry M. Bartels, however, found that members of Congress were responsive to constituency opinion in supporting the Reagan defense buildup. See "Constituency Opinion and Congressional Policy Making: The Reagan Defense Buildup," *American Political Science Review* 85 (June 1991): 457–474.
57. Kim Quaile Hill and Patricia A. Hurley, "Dyadic Representation Reappraised," *American Journal of Political Science* 43 (January 1999): 109–137.
58. On the importance of ideology, see Bernstein, *Elections, Representation, and Congressional Voting Behavior.*
59. *Washington Representatives 1998* (Washington, D.C.: Columbia Books, 1998).
60. Center for Responsive Politics.
61. John W. Kingdon, *Congressmen's Voting Decisions,* 3rd ed. (Ann Arbor: University of Michigan Press, 1989), 242.
62. For more on congressional reform, see Leroy N. Rieselbach, *Congressional Reform* (Washington, D.C.: Congressional Quarterly Press, 1986).
63. Burdett Loomis, "Congressional Caucuses and the Politics of Representation," in *Congress Reconsidered,* 2nd ed., Lawrence C. Dodd and Bruce I. Oppenheimer, eds. (Washington, D.C.: Congressional Quarterly Press, 1981).
64. See M. Darrell West, *Congress and Economic Policymaking* (Pittsburgh: University of Pittsburgh Press, 1987).

13 The Presidency

Chapter Outline

As George W. Bush stood before a joint session of Congress in early 2001, he was reminded of the experiences of his predecessor, Bill Clinton. During his first three years as president, Clinton struggled in the public opinion polls, never averaging even 50 percent approval. Congress had failed to pass many of his major initiatives, including health care reform, and both houses of Congress had been in the hands of the opposition party since the 1994 elections. Winning a contested vote on an important issue before Congress was always difficult. He had faced a critical press almost from the beginning of his tenure and had run up millions of dollars in legal bills defending himself against a series of investigations, some extending back to his days as governor of Arkansas. In 1998, the House of Representatives impeached him. Although he had survived politically, he was frustrated in his efforts to forge a notable legacy for his presidency.

Powerful, strong, leader of the free world, commander in chief—

these are common images of the American president. The president epitomizes American government. The only place in the world where television networks assign a permanent camera crew is the White House. The presidency is power—at least according to popular myth.

In this presidency-as-powerhouse myth, presidents are the government's command center. Problems are brought to their desk, they decide on the right courses of action, they issue orders, and an army of aides and bureaucrats carry out their commands.

As George W. Bush and all other presidents soon discover, nothing could be further from the truth. The main reason why presidents have trouble getting things done is that other policymakers with whom they deal have their own agendas, their own interests, and their own sources of power. Presidents operate in an environment filled with checks and balances and competing centers of power. As one presidential aide put it, "Every time you turn around people resist you."[1] Congress is beholden not to the president but to the individual constituencies of its members. Cabinet members often push their departmental interests and their constituencies (the Department of Agriculture has farmers as its constituency, for example). Rarely can presidents rely on unwavering support from their party, the public, or even their own appointees.

As the pivotal leader in American politics, the president is the subject of unending political analysis and speculation. A perennial question focuses on presidential power. World history is replete with examples of leaders who have exceeded the prescribed boundaries of their power. Can the presidency become too powerful and thus pose a threat to democracy? Or is the Madisonian system strong enough to check any such tendencies? On the other hand, is the president *strong enough* to stand up to the diverse interests in the United States? Does the president have enough power to govern on behalf of the majority?

A second fundamental question regarding democratic leaders is the nature of their relationship with the public and its consequences for public policy. The president and vice president are the only officials elected by the entire nation. In their efforts to obtain public support from the broad spectrum of interests in the public, are presidents natural advocates of an expansion of government? Do they promise more than they should in order to please the voters? As they face the frustrations of governing, do presidents seek to centralize authority in the federal government, where they have greater influence, while reducing that of the states? Does the chief executive seek more power through increasing the role of government?

Since not everyone bends easily to even the most persuasive president, the president must be a *leader.* As Richard Neustadt has argued, presidential power is the power to *persuade,* not to command.[2] To accomplish policy goals, the president must get other people—important people—to do things they otherwise would not do. To be effective, the president must have highly developed *political skills* to mobilize influence, manage conflict, negotiate, and fashion compromises. Presidential leadership has varied over the years, depending in large part on the individual who holds our nation's highest office.

The Presidents

The presidency is an institution composed of the roles presidents must play, the powers at their disposal, and the large bureaucracy at their command. It is also a highly personal office. The personality of the individual serving as president makes a difference.

Great Expectations

When a new president takes the oath of office, he faces many daunting tasks. Perhaps the most difficult is living up to the expectations of the American people. Americans expect the chief executive to ensure peace, prosperity, and security.[3] As President Carter remarked, "The President is . . . held to be responsible for the state of the economy . . . and for the inconveniences, or disappointments, or the concerns of the American people."[4] Americans want a good life, and they look to the president to provide it.

Americans are of two minds about the presidency. On the one hand, they want to believe in a powerful president, one who can do good. They look back longingly on the great presidents of the first American century—Washington, Jefferson, Lincoln—and some in the second century as well, especially Franklin D. Roosevelt and John F. Kennedy.

On the other hand, Americans dislike a concentration of power. Although presidential responsibilities have increased substantially in the past few decades, there has been no corresponding increase in presidential authority or administrative resources to meet these new expectations. Americans are basically individualistic and skeptical of authority. According to Samuel Huntington, "The distinctive aspect of the American Creed is its antigovernment character. Opposition to power, and suspicion of government as the most dangerous embodiment of power, are the central themes of American political thought."[5] The American political culture's tenets of limited government, liberty, individualism, equality, and democracy generate a distrust of strong leadership, authority, and the public sector in general.

Because Americans' expectations of the presidency are so high, who serves as president is especially important. Just who are the people who have occupied the Oval Office?

Who They Are

When Warren G. Harding, one of the least illustrious American presidents, was in office, attorney Clarence Darrow remarked, "When I was a boy, I was told that anybody could become president. Now I'm beginning to believe it." The Constitution simply states that the president must be a natural-born citizen at least 35 years old and must have resided in the United States for at least 14 years. In fact, all American presidents have been White, male, and (except for John Kennedy) Protestant. In other ways, however, the recent collection of presidents suggests considerable variety. Since World War II, the White House has been home to a Missouri haberdasher, a war hero, a Boston Irish politician, a small-town Texas boy who grew up to become the biggest wheeler-dealer in the Senate, a California lawyer described by his enemies as "Tricky Dick" and by his friends as a misunderstood master of national leadership, a former Rose Bowl player who had spent his entire political career in the House of Representatives, a former governor who had been a Georgia peanut wholesaler, an actor who was also a former gov-

'Okay, bring in the new guy . . .'

ernor of California, a CIA chief and ambassador who was the son of a U.S. senator, an ambitious governor from a small state and a former managing director of a major league baseball team who won his first election only six years before becoming president (see Table 13.1).

All manner of men have occupied the Oval Office. Thomas Jefferson was a scientist and scholar who assembled dinosaur bones when presidential business was slack. Woodrow Wilson, the only political scientist ever to become president, combined a Presbyterian moral fervor and righteousness with a professor's intimidating style of leadership and speech making. His successor, Warren G. Harding, became president because Republican leaders thought he looked like one. Poker was his pastime. Out of his element in the job, Harding is almost everyone's choice as the worst American president. His speech making, said opponent William G. McAdoo, sounded "like an army of pompous phrases marching across the landscape in search of an idea." Harding's friends stole the government blind, prompting his brief assessment of the presidency: "God, what a job!"

How They Got There

No one is born to be the future president of the United States solely because of royal lineage like the future kings or queens of England. Regardless of their background or character, all presidents must come to the job through one of two basic routes.

Elections: The Normal Road to the White House. Most presidents take a familiar journey to 1600 Pennsylvania Avenue: They run for president through the electoral process, which is described in Chapters 9 and 10. Once in office, presidents are guaranteed a four-year term by the Constitution, but the **Twenty-second Amendment,** passed in 1951, limits them to two such terms.

Twenty-second Amendment

Passed in 1951, the amendment that limits presidents to two terms of office.

Only 12 of the 42 presidents before George W. Bush have actually served two or more full terms in the White House: Washington, Jefferson, Madison, Monroe, Jackson, Grant, Cleveland (whose terms were not consecutive), Wilson, Franklin Roosevelt, Eisenhower, Reagan, and Clinton. A few decided against a second term ("Silent Cal" Coolidge said simply, "I do not choose to run"). Five other presidents (Polk, Pierce, Buchanan, Hayes, and Lyndon Johnson) also threw in the towel at the end of one full term. Seven others (both of the Adamses, Van Buren, Taft, Hoover, Carter, and Bush) thought they had earned a second term, but the voters disagreed.

Table 13.1 Recent Presidents

PRESIDENT	TERM	PARTY	BACKGROUND	SIGNIFICANT EVENTS
Harry S Truman	1945–1953	Democrat	• U.S. senator from Missouri • chosen as FDR's running mate in 1944 • became president when FDR died	• made decision to drop atomic bombs on Japan to end World War II • presided over postwar recovery • laid foundation for Cold War policy • relatively unpopular during term
Dwight D. Eisenhower	1953–1961	Republican	• commander of Allied forces in Europe in World War II • never voted until he ran for president	• presided over relatively tranquil 1950s • conservative domestic policies • cool crisis management • enjoyed strong public approval
John F. Kennedy	1961–1963	Democrat	• U.S. senator from Massachusetts • from very wealthy family	• known for personal style • presided over Cuban missile crisis • ushered in era of liberal domestic policies • assassinated in 1963
Lyndon B. Johnson	1963–1969	Democrat	• Senate majority leader • chosen as Kennedy's running mate; succeeded him after the assassination	• skilled legislative leader with a coarse public image • launched the Great Society • escalated the Vietnam War • war policies proved unpopular; did not seek reelection
Richard M. Nixon	1969–1974	Republican	• U.S. senator from California • served two terms as Eisenhower's vice president • lost presidential election of 1960 to John F. Kennedy	• presided over period of legislative innovation • renewed relations with China • ended Vietnam War • resigned as a result of Watergate scandal
Gerald R. Ford	1974–1977	Republican	• House minority leader • only person ever nominated as vice president under twenty-fifth Amendment	• pardoned Richard Nixon • helped heal the nation's wounds • lost election in 1976 to Jimmy Carter
Jimmy Carter	1977–1981	Democrat	• governor of Georgia • peanut farmer	• viewed as honest, but politically unskilled • hurt by economic downturn • managed Iranian hostage crisis • lost bid for reelection 1980
Ronald W. Reagan	1981–1989	Republican	• governor of California • well-known actor	• brought about substantial tax cuts • led fight for a large increase in defense spending • advocated conservative politics • known as the Great Communicator
George Bush	1989–1993	Republican	• U.S. representative from Texas • director of CIA • ambassador to UN • served two terms as Reagan's vice president	• led international coalition to victory in Gulf War • presided over end of Cold War • popular until economy stagnated • lost reelection bid in 1992

(continued)

Table 13.1 Recent Presidents (*continued*)

PRESIDENT	TERM	PARTY	BACKGROUND	SIGNIFICANT EVENTS
William J. Clinton	1993–2001	Democrat	• governor of Arkansas • Rhodes Scholar	• moved Democrats to center • presided over balanced budget • benefited from strong economy • tenure marred by Monica Lewinsky scandal • impeached
George W. Bush	2001–	Republican	• governor of Texas • son of President George Bush • elected without plurality of the vote	

Succession and Impeachment. For more than 10 percent of American history, the presidency has actually been occupied by an individual who was not elected to the office. About one in five presidents got the job because they were vice president when the incumbent president either died or (in Nixon's case) resigned (see Table 13.2). In the twentieth century, almost one-third (5 of 16) of those who occupied the office were "accidental presidents." The most accidental of all was Gerald Ford, who did not run for either the vice presidency or the presidency before taking office. Ford was nominated vice president by President Nixon when Vice President Spiro Agnew resigned; Ford then assumed the presidency when Nixon himself resigned.

Removing a discredited president before the end of a term is not easy. The Constitution prescribes the process through **impeachment,** which is roughly the political equivalent of an indictment in criminal law. The House of Representatives may, by majority vote, impeach the president for "Treason, Bribery, or other high Crimes and Misdemeanors." Once the House votes for impeachment, the case goes to the Senate, which tries the accused president, with the Chief Justice of the Supreme Court presiding. By a two-thirds vote, the Senate may convict and remove the president from office.

impeachment

The political equivalent of an indictment in criminal law, prescribed by the Constitution. The House of Representatives may impeach the president by a majority vote for "Treason, Bribery, or other high Crimes and Misdemeanors."

Only two presidents have been impeached. The House impeached Andrew Johnson, Lincoln's successor, in 1868 on charges stemming from his disagreement with radical Republicans. He narrowly escaped conviction. Richard Nixon came as close to impeachment as anyone since. On July 31, 1974, the House Judiciary

Table 13.2 Incomplete Presidential Terms

PRESIDENT	TERM	SUCCEEDED BY
William Henry Harrison	March 4, 1841–April 4, 1841	John Tyler
Zachary Taylor	March 5, 1849–July 9, 1850	Millard Fillmore
Abraham Lincoln	March 4, 1865–April 15, 1865[a]	Andrew Johnson
James A. Garfield	March 4, 1881–September 19, 1881	Chester A. Arthur
William McKinley	March 4, 1901–September 14, 1901[a]	Theodore Roosevelt
Warren G. Harding	March 4, 1921–August 2, 1923	Calvin Coolidge
Franklin D. Roosevelt	January 20, 1945–April 12, 1945[b]	Harry S Truman
John F. Kennedy	January 20, 1961–November 22, 1963	Lyndon B. Johnson
Richard M. Nixon	January 20, 1973–August 9, 1974[a]	Gerald R. Ford

[a]Second term.
[b]Fourth term.

Watergate

The events and scandal surrounding a break-in at the Democratic National Committee headquarters in 1972 and the subsequent cover-up of White House involvement, leading to the eventual resignation of President Nixon under the threat of **impeachment.**

Twenty-fifth Amendment

Passed in 1951, this amendment permits the vice president to become acting president if both the vice president and the president's cabinet determine that the president is disabled. The amendment also outlines how a recuperated president can reclaim the job.

Committee voted to recommend his impeachment to the full House as a result of the **Watergate** scandal. Nixon escaped a certain vote for impeachment by resigning. In 1998, the House voted two articles of impeachment against President Clinton on party-line votes. The public clearly opposed the idea, however, and the Senate voted to acquit the president on both counts in 1999 (see "You Are the Policymaker: Should President Clinton Have Been Convicted?").

Constitutional amendments cover one other important problem concerning the presidential term: presidential disability and succession. Several times a president has become disabled, incapable of carrying out the job for weeks or even months at a time. After Woodrow Wilson suffered a stroke, his wife, Edith Wilson, became virtual acting president. The **Twenty-fifth Amendment** (1967) clarifies some of the Constitution's vagueness about disability. The amendment permits the vice president to become acting president if the vice president and the president's cabinet determine that the president is disabled or if the president declares his own disability, and it outlines how a recuperated president can reclaim the Oval Office. Other laws specify the order of presidential succession—from the vice president, to the Speaker of the House, to the president *pro tempore* of the Senate and down through the cabinet members in the order their departments were created.

The Twenty-fifth Amendment also created a means for selecting a new vice president when the office becomes vacant (a frequent occurrence). The president nominates a new vice president, who assumes the office when both houses of Congress approve the nomination.

Presidential Powers

comparative
Comparing Chief Executives

The contemporary presidency hardly resembles the one the Constitution framers designed in 1787. The executive office they conceived had more limited authority, fewer responsibilities, and much less organizational structure than today's presidency. The founders feared both anarchy and monarchy. They wanted an independent executive but disagreed about both the form the office should take and the powers it should exercise. In the end, they created an executive unlike any the world had ever seen[6] (see "America in Perspective: President or Prime Minister?").

Richard Nixon was the only American president ever to resign his office. Nixon decided to resign rather than face impeachment for his role in the Watergate scandal, a series of illegal wiretaps, break-ins, and cover-ups.

You Are the Policymaker

Should President Clinton Have Been Convicted?

Monica Lewinsky became a household name in January 1998. By the end of the year, the most intimate details of her two-year affair with President Bill Clinton were known to almost everyone in the country. The nation had to do more than live through a new soap opera of sex and politics, however. The question became whether the president should be removed from office.

In September, Independent Counsel Kenneth Starr issued a report to Congress accusing President Clinton of 11 counts of possible impeachable offenses, including perjury, obstruction of justice, witness tampering, and abuse of power. The president's detractors used the report as a basis for charging that he had broken the law, failed in his primary constitutional duty to take care that the laws be faithfully executed, betrayed the public's trust, and dishonored the nation's highest office. As a result, they argued, the president should be removed from office through the process of impeachment. They also argued that other public officials would be removed from office for having an affair with a young intern. Why, they asked, should the president be held to lower standards?

The White House fought back. First, the president apologized to the nation—sort of. Then he engaged in a round of expressions of remorse before a variety of audiences. At the same time, the White House accused Starr of engaging an intrusive investigation motivated by a political vendetta against the president. The White House argued that the president made a mistake in his private behavior, apologized for it, and should continue to do the job he was elected to do. Impeachment, the president's defenders said, was grossly disproportionate to the president's offense.

The Constitution provides only the most general guidelines as to the grounds for impeachment. Article II, Section 4, says "The President, Vice President and all civil Officers of the United States, shall be removed from Office on Impeachment for, and Conviction of, Treason, Bribery, or other high Crimes and Misdemeanors."

There is agreement on at least four points regarding impeachable offenses.

1. Impeachable behavior does not have to be a crime. If the president refused to work or chose to invade a country solely to increase his public support, his actions could be grounds for impeachment, even though they would not violate the law.
2. The offense should be grave for it to be impeachable. A poker game in the White House, even though it may violate the law, would not constitute an impeachable offense.
3. A matter of policy disagreement is not grounds for impeachment. The only president who had been impeached before Clinton was Andrew Johnson, who was tried in 1868. He survived by one vote. The real issue was disagreement between the president and Congress over the policy of Reconstruction following the Civil War. Johnson's impeachment and trial are widely viewed as an abuse of impeachment power.
4. Impeachment is an inherently political process and the grounds for impeachment are ultimately whatever Congress decides they are because the Constitution assigns these calibrations to members' political judgment.

Beyond these points of agreement, we enter speculative territory. In 1974, the House Judiciary Committee passed three articles of impeachment against President Richard Nixon, but the president resigned before the House took up the charges. The three articles charged that Nixon had (1) obstructed justice, (2) abused his power, and (3) failed to comply with congressional subpoenas. The Democrats overwhelmingly supported all three articles, and the Republicans generally opposed them. In 1998 and 1999, the tables were turned, as the Republicans supported a lower threshold for an impeachable offense while the Democrats argued for a higher one.

In December 1998, the House voted two articles of impeachment against President Clinton on nearly straight party-line votes. The articles charged him with lying to a grand jury and obstructing justice.

Most Americans felt that the president had behaved improperly, but they also felt he was doing a good job as president. Thus, most opposed impeaching Clinton. Opinion among officeholders and journalists was more negative toward the president, however. After a Senate trial, senators voted to acquit the president. If *you* were a member of the Senate, would you have voted to convict the president?

At first some delegates proposed a plural executive—dividing responsibility for various areas of power or else functioning as a committee. Others thought that governing a large nation required a single president with significant powers. James Wilson, a delegate from Pennsylvania, argued that only a single individual could combine the necessary characteristics of "energy, dispatch, and responsibility." Critics immediately

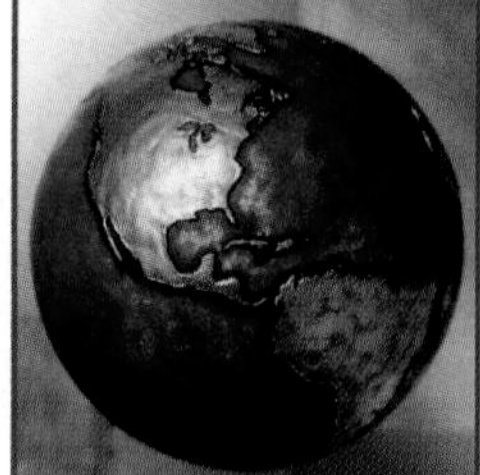

America in Perspective

President or Prime Minister?

The founders selected a presidential system of government for the United States. Most democracies in developed countries, however, have chosen a parliamentary system. In such a system the chief executive, the prime minister, is selected by the legislature, not the voters. The prime minister is a member of the legislature, elected from one district as a member of parliament. The majority party, or the largest bloc of votes in the legislature if there is no majority party, votes its party leader to be prime minister. The prime minister may remain in power for a long time—as long as his or her party or coalition has a majority of the seats and supports the leader.

Presidents and prime ministers govern quite differently. Prime ministers never face divided government, for example. Since they represent the majority party or coalition, they can almost always depend on winning on votes. In addition, party discipline is better in parliamentary systems than in the United States. Parties know that if the prime minister should lose on an important vote, the government might have to call elections under circumstances unfavorable to the majority. As a result, members of parliament almost always support their leaders.

Prime ministers generally differ in background from presidents as well. They must be party leaders, as we have seen, and they are usually very effective communicators with skills honed in the rough and tumble of parliamentary debate. In addition, they have had substantial experience dealing with national issues, unlike American governors who may move directly into the presidency. Cabinet members, who are usually senior members of parliament, have similar advantages.

So why does the United States maintain a presidential system? The founders were concerned about the concentration of power, such as that found in the prime minister. Instead, they wanted to separate power so that the different branches could check each other. More concerned with the abuse of power than its effective use, they chose a presidential system—the first the world had ever known.

responded that such an executive would be dangerous—"the fetus of monarchy," claimed Edmund Randolph. Wilson carried the day, aided by the fact that virtually everyone assumed that the first president would be George Washington, the person the delegates most trusted not to abuse power.

Constitutional Powers

When it came to detailing the executive's power, the delegates to the Constitutional Convention turned for inspiration to the constitutions of New York and New Jersey, states with strong governors. Couching the description of presidential powers in the language of two state constitutions with which they were familiar and comfortable made it more palatable to the delegates, who adopted most of it with little debate.

The Constitution says remarkably little about presidential power. The discussion of the presidency begins with these general words: "The executive power shall be vested in a president of the United States of America." It goes on to list just a few powers (see Table 13.3). The framers' invention fit nicely within the Madisonian system of shared power and checks and balances. There is little that presidents can do on their own, and they share executive, legislative, and judicial power with the other branches of government.

Institutional balance was essential to the convention delegates, who had in mind the abuses of past executives (including both the king and colonial governors) combined with the excesses of state legislatures (discussed in Chapter 2). The problem was how to preserve the balance without jeopardizing the independence of the separate branches or impeding the lawful exercise of their authority. The framers resolved this problem by checking those powers that they believed to be most dangerous, the ones that historically had been subject to the greatest abuse (for example, they gave Congress the power to declare war and the Senate the power to approve treaties and presidential appointments), while protecting the general spheres of authority from encroachment (the executive, for instance, was given a qualified veto).

Why does it matter?

It is not easy to impeach a president; the threshold for an impeachable offense is a high one. Since there is no other way for citizens to remove a president who they feel is performing poorly, would it be better if it were easier to change presidents *between* elections? Would this increase the likelihood of the president having the public's support? Or would it turn the United States into a parliamentary system in which the chief executive can be changed at any time?

Table 13.3 Constitutional Powers of the President

National Security Powers
Serve as commander in chief of the armed forces
Make treaties with other nations, subject to the agreement of two-thirds of the Senate
Nominate ambassadors, with the agreement of a majority of the Senate
Receive ambassadors of other nations, thereby conferring diplomatic recognition on other governments

Legislative Powers
Present information on the state of the union to Congress
Recommend legislation to Congress
Convene both houses of Congress on extraordinary occasions
Adjourn Congress if the House and Senate cannot agree on adjournment
Veto legislation (Congress may overrule with two-thirds vote of each house)

Administrative Powers
"Take care that the laws be faithfully executed"
Nominate officials as provided for by Congress and with the agreement of a majority of the Senate
Request written opinions of administrative officials
Fill administrative vacancies during congressional recesses

Judicial Powers
Grant reprieves and pardons for federal offenses (except impeachment)
Nominate federal judges, who are confirmed by a majority of the Senate

Provisions for reelection and a short term of office also encouraged presidential responsibility. For those executives who flagrantly abused their authority, impeachment was the ultimate recourse.

The Expansion of Power

Today there is more to presidential power than the Constitution alone suggests, and that power is derived from many sources. The role of the president has changed as America has increased in prominence on the world stage; technology has also reshaped the presidency. George Washington's ragtag militias (mostly disbanded by the time the first commander in chief took command) were much different from the mighty nuclear arsenal that today's president commands.

Presidents themselves have taken the initiative to develop new roles for the office. In fact, many presidents have enlarged the power of the presidency by expanding the president's responsibilities and political resources. Thomas Jefferson was the first leader of a mass political party. Andrew Jackson presented himself as the direct representative of the people. Abraham Lincoln mobilized the country for war. Theodore Roosevelt mobilized the public behind his policies. He and Woodrow Wilson set precedents for presidents to serve as world leaders; Wilson and Franklin D. Roosevelt developed the role of the president as manager of the economy.

Perspectives on Presidential Power

During the 1950s and 1960s it was fashionable for political scientists, historians, and commentators to favor a powerful presidency. Historians rated presidents from strong to weak—and there was no question that "strong" meant good and "weak" meant bad. Political scientists waxed eloquent about the presidency as the epitome of democratic governments.[7]

By the 1970s, many felt differently. The Vietnam War was unpopular. Lyndon Johnson and the war made people reassess the role of presidential power, and Richard

Nixon and the Watergate scandal heightened public distrust. Presidential duplicity was revealed in the Pentagon papers, a series of secret documents slipped to the press by Daniel Ellsberg. Nixon's "enemies list" and his avowed goal to "screw our enemies" by illegally auditing their taxes, tapping their phones, and using "surreptitious entry" (a euphemism for burglary) asserted that presidents considered themselves above the law. Nixon's lawyers argued solemnly to the Supreme Court and Congress that the presidency has "inherent powers" permitting presidents to order acts that otherwise would be illegal. Nixon protected himself with an umbrella defense of executive privilege, claiming that he did not need to provide evidence to Congress or the courts.

Early defenders of a strong presidency made sharp turnabouts in their position. In his book *The Imperial Presidency*, historian Arthur Schlesinger, an aide of John Kennedy's, argued that the presidency had become too powerful for the nation's own good.[8] (Critics pointed out that Schlesinger did not seem to feel that way when he worked in the White House.) Whereas an older generation of scholars had written glowing accounts of the presidency, a newer generation wrote about "The Swelling of the Presidency" and "Making the Presidency Safe for Democracy."[9]

The Nixon era was followed by the presidencies of Gerald Ford and Jimmy Carter, whom many critics saw as weak leaders and failures. Ford himself spoke out in 1980, claiming that Carter's weakness had created an "imperiled" presidency. In the 1980s, Ronald Reagan experienced short periods of great influence and longer periods of frustration as the American political system settled back into its characteristic mode of stalemate and incremental policymaking. The Iran-Contra affair kept concern about a tyrannical presidency alive, while, in most instances, Reagan's inability to sway Congress evoked a desire on the part of some (mostly conservatives) for a stronger presidency. Reagan's immediate successors, George Bush and Bill Clinton, found it difficult to get things done.

The following sections will explore the relationship between the president's responsibilities and resources by examining how contemporary presidents try to lead the nation.

Running the Government: The Chief Executive

Although the president is often called the "chief executive," it is easy to forget that one of the president's most important roles is presiding over the administration of government. This role does not receive the same publicity as other functions do, such as appealing to the public for support for policy initiatives, dealing with Congress, or negotiating with foreign powers, but it is of great importance nevertheless.

The Constitution exhorts the president to "take care that the laws be faithfully executed." In the early days of the republic, this clerical-sounding function was fairly easy. Today, the sprawling federal bureaucracy spends nearly $2 trillion a year and numbers about 4.1 million civilian and military employees. Running such a large organization would be a full-time job for even the most talented of executives, yet it is only one of the president's many jobs.

One of the resources for controlling this bureaucracy is the presidential power to appoint top-level administrators. New presidents have about 500 high-level positions available for appointment—cabinet and subcabinet jobs, agency heads, and other noncivil service posts—plus 2,500 lesser jobs. Since passage of the Budgeting and Accounting Act of 1921, presidents have had one other important executive tool: the power to recommend agency budgets to Congress.

timeline
The Executive Order over Time

The vastness of the executive branch, the complexity of public policy, and the desire to accomplish their policy goals have led presidents in recent years to pay even closer attention to appointing officials who will be responsive to the president's policies. Presidents have also taken more interest in the regulations issued by agencies. This trend toward centralizing decision making in the White House pleases those who think the bureaucracy should be more responsive to elected officials. On the other hand, it dismays those who believe that increased presidential involvement in policymaking will undermine the "neutral competence" of professional bureaucrats by encouraging them to follow the president's policy preferences rather than the intent of laws as passed by Congress.

Chapter 15 on the bureaucracy explores the president's role as chief executive further. This chapter will focus on how presidents go about organizing and using the parts of the executive branch most under their control—the vice president, the cabinet, the Executive Office of the President, and the White House staff.

The Vice President

Neither politicians nor political scientists have paid much attention to the vice presidency. Once the choice of a party's "second team" was an afterthought; now it is often an effort to placate some important symbolic constituency. Southerner Jimmy Carter selected a well-known liberal, Walter Mondale, as his running mate, and Ronald Reagan chose his chief rival, George Bush, in part to please Republican moderates.[10]

Vice presidents have rarely enjoyed the job. John Nance Garner of Texas, one of Franklin Roosevelt's vice presidents, declared that the job was "not worth a warm bucket of spit." Some have performed so poorly that they were deemed an embarrassment to the president. After Woodrow Wilson's debilitating stroke, almost everyone agreed that Vice President Thomas Marshall—a man who shirked all responsibility, including cabinet meetings—would be a disaster as acting president. Spiro Agnew, Richard Nixon's first vice president, had to resign and was convicted of evading taxes (on bribes he had accepted).

Once in office, vice presidents find that their main job is waiting. Constitutionally, they are assigned the minor tasks of presiding over the Senate and voting in case of a tie among the senators. As George Bush put it when he was vice president, "the buck doesn't stop here." Recent presidents, though, have taken their vice presidents more seriously, involving them in policy discussions and important diplomacy.[11]

Jimmy Carter and Ronald Reagan, both Washington outsiders, chose vice presidents who had substantial Washington experience: Walter Mondale and George Bush. To become intimates of the president, both had to be completely loyal, losing their political independence in the process. Vice President Bush, for example, was accused of knowing more about the Iran-Contra affair than he admitted, but he steadfastly refused to reveal his discussions with President Reagan on the matter.

When his turn came to choose a vice president, Bush selected Senator Dan Quayle of Indiana, considered by many a political lightweight. Quayle met regularly with the president, represented him in discussions with the leaders of numerous countries, chaired a prominent effort to decrease government regulation, and raised funds for Republican candidates. Albert Gore, Bill Clinton's vice president, was a Washington insider and played a prominent role in the administration. Similarly, George W. Bush chose Richard Cheney, who had extensive experience in high-level positions in the national government, as his vice president and assigned him a central role in his administration.

The Cabinet

Although the Constitution does not mention the group of presidential advisors known as the **cabinet**, every president has had one. The cabinet is too large and too diverse, and its members are too concerned with representing the interests of their departments, for it to serve as a collective board of directors, however. The major decisions remain in the president's hands. Legend has it that Abraham Lincoln asked his cabinet to vote on an issue, and the result was unanimity in opposition to his view. He announced the decision as "seven nays and one aye, the ayes have it."

cabinet

A group of presidential advisors not mentioned in the Constitution, although every president has had one. Today the cabinet is composed of 13 secretaries and the attorney general.

George Washington's cabinet was small, consisting of just three secretaries (state, treasury, and war) and the attorney general. Presidents since Washington have increased the size of the cabinet by requesting that new executive departments

Members of the president's cabinet are important for both the power they exercise and the status they symbolize. President George W. Bush formed a cabinet that was representative of America's diversity. Pictured here is Secretary of Housing and Urban Development Mel Martinez, an Hispanic.

be established. These requests must be approved by Congress, which creates the department. Today 13 secretaries and the attorney general head executive departments and constitute the cabinet (see Table 13.4). In addition, presidents may designate other officials (the ambassador to the United Nations is a common choice) as cabinet members.[12]

Even in making his highest level appointments, the president is subject to the constitutional system of checks and balances. President Bush met resistance when he nominated John Tower, a former senator, to be secretary of defense. After a bitter debate (which focused on the nominee's use of alcohol and relations with women), the Senate handed the president a serious defeat by rejecting Tower. President Clinton's first nominee to serve as attorney general, Zoe Baird, withdrew from consideration

The president must sometimes fight for his nominees, even to his cabinet. President George W. Bush met resistance to his nomination of John Ashcroft, shown here being sworn in during his Senate confirmation hearing, to be Attourney General. Ultimately, Ashcroft was confirmed.

Table 13.4 The Cabinet Departments

DEPARTMENT	YEAR CREATED	FUNCTION
State	1789	Makes foreign policy, including treaty negotiations
Treasury	1789	Serves as the government's banker
Defense	1947	Formed by the consolidation of the former Departments of the Army and the Navy
Justice	1870	Serves as the government's attorney; headed by the attorney general
Interior	1849	Manages the nation's natural resources, including wildlife and public lands
Agriculture	1862	Administers farm and food stamp programs and aids farmers
Commerce	1903	Aids businesses and conducts the U.S. census
Labor	1913	Formed through separation from the Department of Commerce; runs programs and aids labor in various ways
Health and Human Services	1953	Originally created as the Department of Health, Education, and Welfare, it lost its education function in 1979 and Social Security in 1995
Housing and Urban Development	1966	Responsible for urban and housing programs
Transportation	1966	Responsible for mass transportation and highway programs
Energy	1977	Responsible for energy policy and research, including atomic energy
Education	1979	Responsible for the federal government's education programs
Veterans Affairs	1988	Responsible for programs aiding veterans

after she came under fire from senators of both parties for hiring an illegal alien as her baby-sitter and for failing to pay Social Security taxes for her employee.

The Executive Office

Next to the White House sits an ornate building called the EEOB, or Eisenhower Executive Office Building. It houses a collection of offices and organizations loosely grouped into the Executive Office of the President.[13] Some of these offices (such as the Council of Economic Advisors) are created by legislation, and some are organized essentially by the president. The Executive Office started small in 1939 when President Roosevelt established it, but has grown with the rest of government. In the Executive Office are housed three major policymaking bodies—the National Security Council, the Council of Economic Advisors, and the Office of Management and Budget—along with several other units that serve the president (see Figure 13.1).

The **National Security Council (NSC)** is the committee that links the president's key foreign and military policy advisors. Its formal members include the president, vice president, and secretaries of state and defense, but its informal membership is broader. The president's special assistant for national security affairs plays a major role in the NSC. The occupant of this post has responsibility for running the council's staff; together they provide the president with information and policy recommendations on national security, aid the president in national security crisis management, coordinate agency and departmental activities bearing on national security, and monitor the implementation of national security policy.

The **Council of Economic Advisors (CEA)** has three members, each appointed by the president, who advise him on economic policy. They prepare the annual *Economic Report of the President*, which includes data and analysis on the current state and future trends of the economy, and help the president make policy on inflation, unemployment, and other economic matters.

National Security Council

An office created in 1947 to coordinate the president's foreign and military policy advisors. Its formal members are the president, vice president, **secretary of state**, and **secretary of defense**, and it is managed by the president's national security advisor.

Council of Economic Advisors (CEA)

A three-member body appointed by the president to advise the president on economic policy.

Figure 13.1 Executive Office of the President

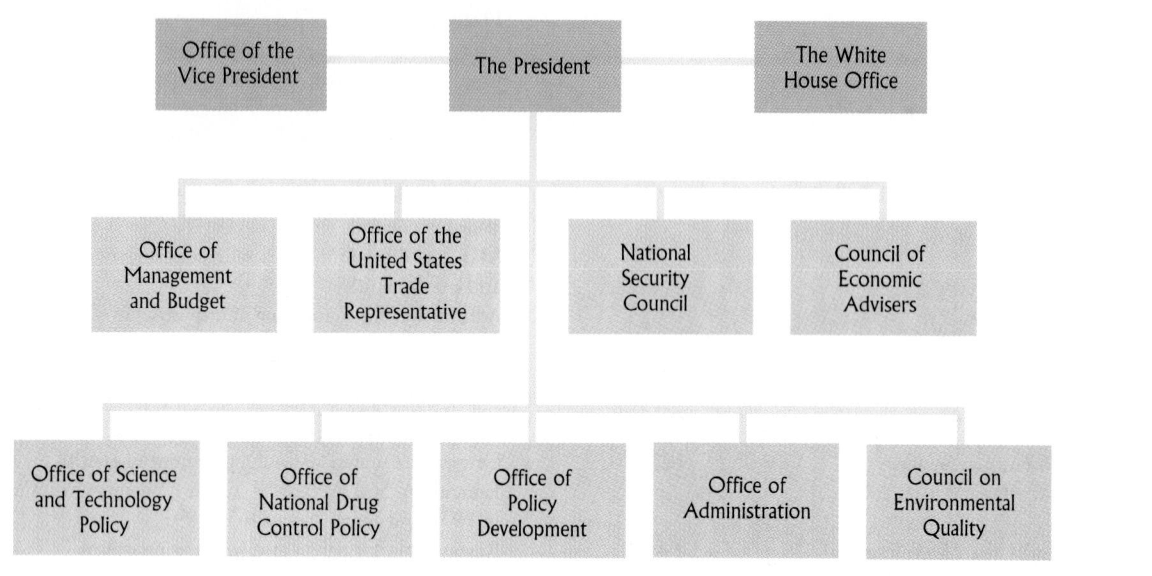

Source: Office of the Federal Register, *The United States Government Manual,* 2000/01 (Washington, D.C.: U.S. Government Printing Office, 2000).

Office of Management and Budget (OMB)

An office that grew out of the Bureau of the Budget, created in 1921, consisting of a handful of political appointees and hundreds of skilled professionals. The OMB performs both managerial and budgetary functions. See also **Congressional Budget Office.**

The **Office of Management and Budget (OMB)** grew out of the Bureau of the Budget (BOB) created in 1921. The OMB is composed of a handful of political appointees and more than 600 career officials, many of whom are highly skilled professionals. Its major responsibility is to prepare the president's budget (discussed in Chapter 14). President Nixon revamped the BOB in 1970 in an attempt to make it a managerial as well as a budgetary agency, changing its name in the process to stress its managerial functions.

Because each presidential appointee and department have their own agenda, presidents need a clearinghouse—the OMB. Presidents use the OMB to review legislative proposals from the cabinet and other executive agencies so that they can determine whether they want an agency to propose these initiatives to Congress. The OMB assesses the proposals' budgetary implications and advises presidents on the proposals' consistency with their overall program. The OMB also plays an important role in reviewing regulations proposed by departments and agencies.

Though presidents find that the Executive Office is smaller and more manageable than the cabinet departments, it is still filled with people performing jobs required by law and whose primary allegiance is to their office, rather than to the president. There is, however, one part of the presidential system that presidents can truly call their own: the White House staff.

The White House Staff

Before Franklin D. Roosevelt, the president's personal staff resources were minimal. Only one messenger and one secretary served Thomas Jefferson. One hundred years later the president's staff had grown only to 13, including clerks and secretaries. Woodrow Wilson was in the habit of typing his own letters. As recently as the 1920s, the entire budget for the White House staff was no more than $80,000 per year.

The White House staff consists of the key aides the president sees daily: the chief of staff, congressional liaison people, a press secretary, a national security assistant, and a few other administrative and political assistants. Today, there are about 600 people at work on the White House staff—many of whom the president

eled and advocated New Deal policies. She became her crippled husband's eyes and ears around the country and urged him to adopt liberal social welfare policies. Lady Bird Johnson chose to focus on one issue, beautification, and most of her successors followed this single-issue pattern. Rosalyn Carter chose mental health, Nancy Reagan selected drugs, and Barbara Bush advocated literacy. Laura Bush, a former librarian, has also chosen to focus on increasing literacy.

In what was perhaps a natural evolution in a society where women have moved into positions formerly held only by males, Hillary Rodham Clinton attained the most responsible and visible leadership position ever held by a First Lady. She was an influential advisor to the president, playing an active role in the selection of nominees for cabinet and judicial posts, for example. Most publicly, she headed the planning for the president's massive health care reform plan in 1993 and became, along with her husband, its primary advocate.

Although many have hailed her as a model for our times, successfully combining career and family, others have criticized her as a political liability. The health plan failed to pass Congress and was seen by many observers as a leading cause of the Democrats' crushing defeat in the 1994 congressional elections. As a result, she retreated to a more traditional role, focusing on representing the United States abroad and on advocating policies to help children and women in developing countries. In 2000, however, she was elected to the U.S. Senate.

Presidents not only have responsibility for running the executive branch, they must also deal intensively with the legislative branch. These dealings are the topic of the following section.

Presidential Leadership of Congress: The Politics of Shared Powers

Near the top of any presidential job description would be "working with Congress." Because the American system of separation of powers is actually one of *shared* powers, presidents can rarely operate independently of Congress. If presidents are to succeed in leaving their stamp on public policy, much of their time in office must be devoted to leading the legislature to support presidential initiatives.

Chief Legislator

Nowhere does the Constitution use the phrase *chief legislator*; it is strictly a phrase invented to emphasize the executive's importance in the legislative process. The Constitution does require that the president give a State of the Union address to Congress and instructs the president to bring other matters to Congress's attention "from time to time." In fact, as noted in Chapter 12, the president plays a major role in shaping the congressional agenda.

The Constitution also gives the president power to **veto** congressional legislation. Once Congress passes a bill, the president may (1) sign it, making it law; (2) veto it, sending it back to Congress with the reasons for rejecting it; or (3) let it become law after 10 working days by not doing anything. Congress can pass a vetoed law, however, if two-thirds of each house vote to override the president. At one point in the lawmaking process the president has the last word, however: If Congress adjourns within 10 days after submitting a bill, the president can simply let it die by neither signing nor vetoing it. This process is called a **pocket veto.** Table 13.5 shows how frequently recent presidents have used the veto.

veto

The constitutional power of the president to send a bill back to Congress with reasons for rejecting it. A two-thirds vote in each house can override a veto.

pocket veto

A veto taking place when Congress adjourns within 10 days of submitting a bill to the president, who simply lets it die by neither signing nor vetoing it.

The presidential veto is usually effective; only about 4 percent of all vetoed bills have been overridden by Congress since the nation's founding. Thus, even the threat of a presidential veto can be an effective tool for persuading Congress to give more weight to the president's views. On the other hand, the veto is a blunt instrument. Presidents must accept or reject bills in their entirety; they cannot veto only the parts they do not like (most

Table 13.5 Presidential Vetoes

PRESIDENT	REGULAR VETOES	VETOES OVERRIDDEN	PERCENTAGE OF VETOES OVERRIDDEN	POCKET VETOES	TOTAL VETOES
Eisenhower	73	2	3	108	181
Kennedy	12	0	0	9	21
Johnson	16	0	0	14	30
Nixon	26	7	27	17	43
Ford	48	12	25	18	66
Carter	13	2	15	18	31
Reagan	39	9	23	39	78
Bush	31	1	3	15	46
Clinton	36	2	5	1	37

governors have a *line item veto* that allows them to veto particular portions of a bill). As a result, the White House often must accept provisions of a bill it opposes in order to obtain provisions that it desires. For example, in 1987, Congress passed the entire discretionary budget of the federal government in one bill (called an "omnibus" bill). President Reagan had to accept the whole package or lose appropriations for the entire government.

In 1996, Congress passed a law granting the president authority to propose rescinding funds in appropriations bills and tax provisions that apply to only a few people. Once the president signed tax or spending bills, he had five days to propose rescissions; such provisions could become law only if Congress passed them as separate bills—which would then be subject to a presidential veto. The 1996 law was immediately challenged in the courts as being an unconstitutional grant of power to the president. In 1998 the Supreme Court agreed in *Clinton v. City of New York*, and voided the law.

The presidential veto is an inherently negative resource. It is most useful for preventing legislation. Much of the time, however, presidents are more interested in passing their own legislation. To do so, they must marshal their political resources to obtain positive support for their programs. Presidents' three most useful resources are their party leadership, public support, and their own legislative skills.

Why does it matter?

Unlike most governors, the president does not have the power to veto parts of a bill. Would the country be better off if the president possessed a-line-item veto? Would less money be wasted? Or would such a veto upset the delicate balance of separate institutions sharing powers?

Party Leadership

No matter what other resources presidents may have at their disposal, they remain highly dependent on their party to move their legislative programs. Representatives and senators of the president's party usually form the nucleus of coalitions supporting presidential proposals and provide considerably more support than do members of the opposition party. Thus, party leadership in Congress is every president's principal task when countering the natural tendency toward conflict between the executive and legislative branches that is inherent in the government's system of checks and balances.[15]

The Bonds of Party. For most senators and representatives, being in the same political party as the president creates a psychological bond. Personal loyalties or emotional commitments to their party and their party leader, a desire to avoid embarrassing "their" administration and thus hurting their chances for reelection, and a basic distrust of the opposition party are inclinations that produce support for the White House. Members of the same party also agree on many matters of public policy, and they are often supported by similar electoral coalitions, reinforcing the pull of party ties.

If presidents could rely on their party members to vote for whatever the White House sent up to Capitol Hill, presidential leadership of Congress would be rather easy. All presidents would have to do is make sure members of their party showed up to vote. If their party had the majority, presidents would always win. If their party was in the minority, presidents would only have to concentrate on converting a few members of the other party.

Presidents frequently face opposition party majorities in Congress and must seek the opposition's support to pass their policies. Here, President George W. Bush, a Republican, meets with Senate Minority Leader Trent Lott, and Speaker Dennis Hastert, Republicans, *and* House Minority Leader Richard Gephardt and Senate Majority Leader Thomas Daschle, both Democrats.

Slippage in Party Support. Things are not so simple, however. Despite the pull of party ties, all presidents experience substantial slippage in the support of their party in Congress. Presidents can count on their own party members for support no more than two-thirds of the time, even on key votes. Presidents are thus forced to be active in party leadership and to devote their efforts to conversion as much as to mobilization of members of their party.

The primary obstacle to party unity is the lack of consensus on policies among party members, especially in the Democratic Party. Jimmy Carter, a Democrat, remarked, "I learned the hard way that there was no party loyalty or discipline when a complicated or controversial issue was at stake—none."[16]

This diversity of views often reflects the diversity of constituencies represented by party members. The frequent defection of Southern Democrats from Democratic presidents (such defectors are called "boll weevils") has been one of the most prominent features of American politics. When constituency opinion and the president's proposals conflict, members of Congress are more likely to vote with their constituents, whom they rely on for reelection. If the president is not popular with their constituencies, congressional party members may avoid identifying too closely with the White House.

Leading the Party. The president has some assets as party leader, including congressional party leaders, services and amenities for party members, and campaign aid. Each asset is of limited utility, however.

The president's relationship with party leaders in Congress is a delicate one. Although the leaders are predisposed to support presidential policies and typically work closely with the White House, they are free to oppose the president or lend only symbolic support; some party leaders may be ineffective themselves. Moreover, party leaders are not in a position to reward or discipline members of Congress on the basis of presidential support.

To create goodwill with congressional party members, the White House provides them with many amenities, ranging from photographs with the president to rides on Air Force One. Although this arrangement is to the president's advantage and may earn the benefit of the doubt on some policy initiatives, party members consider it their right to receive benefits from the White House and as a result are unlikely to be especially responsive to the president.

Just as the president can offer a carrot, so too can the president wield a stick in the form of withholding favors, although this is rarely done. Despite the resources available to the president, if party members wish to oppose the White House, there is little the president can do to stop them. The parties are highly decentralized, as we saw in Chapter 8. National party leaders do not control those aspects of politics that are of vital concern to members of Congress—nominations and elections. Members of Congress are largely self-recruited, gain their party's nomination by their own efforts and not the party's, and provide most of the money and organizational support needed for their elections. Presidents can do little to influence the results of these activities.

One way for the president to improve the chances of obtaining support in Congress is to increase the number of fellow party members in the legislature. The phenomenon of **presidential coattails** occurs when voters cast their ballots for congressional candidates of the president's party because those candidates support the president. Most recent studies show a diminishing connection between presidential and congressional voting, however, and few races are determined by presidential coattails.[17] The change in party balance that usually emerges when the electoral dust has settled is strikingly small. In the 13 presidential elections between 1952 and 2000, the party of the winning presidential candidate gained an average of 7 seats (out of 435) per election in the House. In the Senate the opposition party actually gained seats in seven of the elections (1956, 1960, 1972, 1984, 1988, 1996, and 2000), and there was no change in 1976 and 1992. The net gain for the president's party in the Senate averaged less than one seat per election (see Table 13.6).

presidential coattails

These occur when voters cast their ballots for congressional candidates of the president's party because they support the president. Recent studies show that few races are won this way.

What about midterm elections—those held between presidential elections? Can the president depend on increasing the number of fellow party members in Congress then? Actually, the picture is even bleaker than during presidential elections. As you can see in Table 13.7, the president's party typically *loses* seats in these elections. In 1986, the Republicans lost 8 seats in the Senate, depriving President Reagan of a majority. In 1994, the Democrats lost 8 Senate seats and 52 House seats, losing control of both houses in the process.[18] The 1998 election was an exception: the Democrats gained 5 seats in the House.

Table 13.6 Congressional Gains or Losses for the President's Party in Presidential Election Years

Presidents cannot rely on their coattails to carry their party's legislators into office to help pass White House legislative programs. The president's party typically gains few, if any, seats when the president wins election. For instance, the Republicans lost seats in both houses when President Bush was elected in 2000.

YEAR	PRESIDENT	HOUSE	SENATE
1952	Eisenhower (R)	+22	+1
1956	Eisenhower (R)	−2	−1
1960	Kennedy (D)	−22	−2
1964	Johnson (D)	+37	+1
1968	Nixon (R)	+5	+6
1972	Nixon (R)	+12	−2
1976	Carter (D)	+1	0
1980	Reagan (R)	+34	+12
1984	Reagan (R)	+14	−2
1988	Bush (R)	−3	−1
1992	Clinton (D)	−10	0
1996	Clinton (D)	+9	−2
2000	Bush (R)	−2	−4
	Average	+7	+.4

Table 13.7 Congressional Gains or Losses for the President's Party in Midterm Election Years

The president's party typically *loses* seats in midterm elections. Thus, presidents cannot be certain of helping to elect members of their party once in office.

YEAR	PRESIDENT	HOUSE	SENATE
1954	Eisenhower (R)	−18	−1
1958	Eisenhower (R)	−47	−13
1962	Kennedy (D)	−4	+3
1966	Johnson (D)	−47	−4
1970	Nixon (R)	−12	+2
1974	Ford (R)	−47	−5
1978	Carter (D)	−15	−3
1982	Reagan (R)	−26	0
1986	Reagan (R)	−5	−8
1990	Bush (R)	−9	−1
1994	Clinton (D)	−52	−8
1998	Clinton (D)	+5	0
	Average	−23	−2

To add to these party leadership burdens, the president's party often lacks a majority in one or both houses of Congress. Since 1953 there have been 28 years in which Republican presidents faced a Democratic House of Representatives and 20 years in which they encountered a Democratic Senate. President Clinton faced both a House and a Senate with Republican majorities from 1995 through 2000. Beginning in May 2001, George W. Bush faced a Democratic Senate.

As a result of election returns and the lack of dependable party support, the president usually has to solicit help from the opposition party. This is often a futile endeavor, however, since the opposition is generally not fertile ground for seeking support. Nevertheless, even a few votes may be enough to give the president the required majority.

Public Support

One of the president's most important resources for leading Congress is public support. Presidents who enjoy the backing of the public have an easier time influencing Congress. Said one top aide to Ronald Reagan, "Everything here is built on the idea that the president's success depends on grassroots support."[19] Presidents with low approval ratings in the polls find it difficult to influence Congress. As one of President Carter's aides put it, "No president whose popularity is as low as this president's has much clout on the Hill."[20] Members of Congress and others in Washington closely watch two indicators of public support for the president: approval in the polls and mandates in presidential elections.

Public Approval. Members of Congress anticipate the public's reactions to their support for or opposition to presidents and their policies. They may choose to be close to or independent of the White House—depending on the president's standing with the public—to increase their chances for reelection. Representatives and senators may also use the president's standing in the polls as an indicator of presidential ability to mobilize public opinion against presidential opponents.

Public approval also makes other leadership resources more efficacious. If the president is high in the public's esteem, the president's party is more likely to be responsive, the public is more easily moved, and legislative skills become more effective. Thus public approval is the political resource that has the most potential to turn a stalemate between the president and Congress into a situation supportive of the president's legislative proposals.

Public approval operates mostly in the background and sets the limits of what Congress will do for or to the president. Widespread support gives the president leeway and weakens resistance to presidential policies. It provides a cover for members of Congress to cast votes to which their constituents might otherwise object. They can defend their votes as support for the president rather than support for a certain policy alone.

Lack of public support strengthens the resolve of the president's opponents and narrows the range in which presidential policies receive the benefit of the doubt. In addition, low ratings in the polls may create incentives to attack the president, further eroding an already weakened position. For example, after the arms sales to Iran and the diversion of funds to the Contras made the headlines in late 1986, it became more acceptable in Congress and in the press to raise questions about Ronald Reagan's capacities as president. Disillusionment is a difficult force for the White House to combat.

The impact of public approval or disapproval on the support the president receives in Congress is important, but it occurs at the margins of the effort to build coalitions behind proposed policies. No matter how low presidential standing dips, the president still receives support from a substantial number of senators and representatives. Similarly, no matter how high approval levels climb, a significant portion of Congress will still oppose certain presidential policies. Members of Congress are unlikely to vote against the clear interests of their constituencies or the firm tenets of their ideology out of deference to a widely supported chief executive. Public approval gives the president leverage, not command.[21]

In addition, presidents cannot depend on having the approval of the public, and it is not a resource over which they have much control, as we will see later. Once again, it is clear that presidents' leadership resources do not allow them to dominate Congress.

Mandates. The results of presidential elections are another indicator of public opinion regarding presidents. An electoral mandate—the perception that the voters strongly support the president's character and policies—can be a powerful symbol in American politics. It accords added legitimacy and credibility to the newly elected president's proposals. Moreover, concerns for both representation and political survival encourage members of Congress to support new presidents if they feel the people have spoken.

More important, mandates change the premises of decisions. Following Roosevelt's decisive win in the 1932 election, the essential question became *how* government should act to fight the Depression rather than *whether* it should act. Similarly, following Johnson's overwhelming win in the 1964 election, the dominant question in Congress was not whether to pass new social programs but how many social programs to pass and how much to increase spending. In 1981, the tables were turned; Ronald Reagan's victory placed a stigma on big government and exalted the unregulated marketplace and large defense efforts. Reagan had won a major victory even before the first congressional vote.

Although presidential elections can structure choices for Congress, merely winning an election does not provide presidents with a mandate. Every election produces a winner, but mandates are much less common. Even large electoral victories, such as Richard Nixon's in 1972 and Ronald Reagan's in 1984, carry no guarantee that Congress will interpret the results as mandates from the people to support the president's programs. Perceptions of a mandate are weak if the winning candidate did not stress his policy plans in the campaign or if the voters also elected majorities in Congress from the other party (of course, the winner may *claim* a mandate anyway).[22]

Legislative Skills

Presidential legislative skills come in a variety of forms, including bargaining, making personal appeals, consulting with Congress, setting priorities, exploiting "honeymoon" periods, and structuring congressional votes. Of these skills, bargaining receives perhaps the most attention from commentators on the presidency, and by examining it, one can learn much about the role that a president's legislative skills play in leading Congress.

Bargains occur in numerous forms. Reagan's budget director David Stockman recalled that "the last 10 or 20 percent of the votes needed for a majority of both houses on the 1981 tax cut had to be bought, period." The concessions for members of Congress included special breaks for oil-lease holders, real estate tax shelters, and generous loopholes that virtually eliminated the corporate income tax. "The hogs were really feeding," declared Stockman. "The greed level, the level of opportunities, just got out of control."[23]

Nevertheless, bargaining, in the form of trading support on two or more policies or providing specific benefits for representatives and senators, occurs less often and plays a less critical role in the creation of presidential coalitions in Congress than one might think. For obvious reasons, the White House does not want to encourage the type of bargaining Stockman describes, and there is a scarcity of resources with which to bargain, especially in an era where balancing the budget is a prominent goal for policymakers (discussed in Chapter 14).

Moreover, the president does not have to bargain with every member of Congress to receive support. On controversial issues on which bargaining may be useful, the president usually starts with a sizable core of party supporters and may add to this group those of the opposition party who provide support on ideological or policy grounds. Others may support the president because of relevant constituency interests or strong public approval. The president needs to bargain only if this coalition does not provide a majority (or two-thirds on treaties and one-third on veto overrides).

Presidents may improve their chances of success in Congress by making certain strategic moves. It is wise, for example, for a new president to be ready to send legislation to the Hill early during the first year in office in order to exploit the "honeymoon" atmosphere that typically characterizes this period. Obviously, this is a one-shot opportunity.

Presidents influence the legislative agenda more than any other political figure. One of Ronald Reagan's chief legislative skills was the ability to communicate his policy priorities effectively to Congress and the public. No matter what a president's skills are, however, the "chief legislator," as the president is often called, can rarely exercise complete control over the agenda.

An important aspect of presidential legislative strategy can be establishing priorities among legislative proposals. The goal of this effort is to set Congress's agenda. If presidents are unable to focus the attention of Congress on their priority programs, these programs may become lost in the complex and overloaded legislative process. Setting priorities is also important because presidents and their staffs can lobby effectively for only a few bills at a time. Moreover, each president's political capital is inevitably limited, and it is sensible to focus on a limited range of personally important issues; otherwise, this precious resource might be wasted.

In 1981 Ronald Reagan followed both of these strategies, moving fast and setting priorities. He had great success—obtaining passage of a large tax cut, a substantial increase in defense expenditures, and sizable decreases in the rate of spending for domestic policies. George Bush, in contrast, did not enter the White House geared for legislative action and did little to articulate his priorities. With a large budget deficit, few legislative goals, and the opposition in the majority in both the House and Senate, he did not feel it necessary or useful to focus his energies on Congress. From the outset Bush seemed destined to make his mark on foreign policy, where the president has more latitude to maneuver.

Within a month after taking office, President Clinton presented Congress with an ambitious agenda, including tax increases and both spending cuts and increases. He proposed a major health care reform bill and the North American Free Trade Agreement later in the year. The president lacked the political capital to pass much of his agenda, however, and some of the most important proposals fell prey to Republican opposition. By failing to focus on his priorities, Clinton spent his political capital on matters of less importance. Although he engaged in an endless campaign of public appearances and congressional meetings to build support for his legislation, in the end he met with substantial disappointment and was rebuffed by the voters in the 1994 midterm elections as the Republicans captured both houses of Congress. In his early months in office, George W. Bush followed Reagan's example of moving rapidly and focusing on his priority legislation.

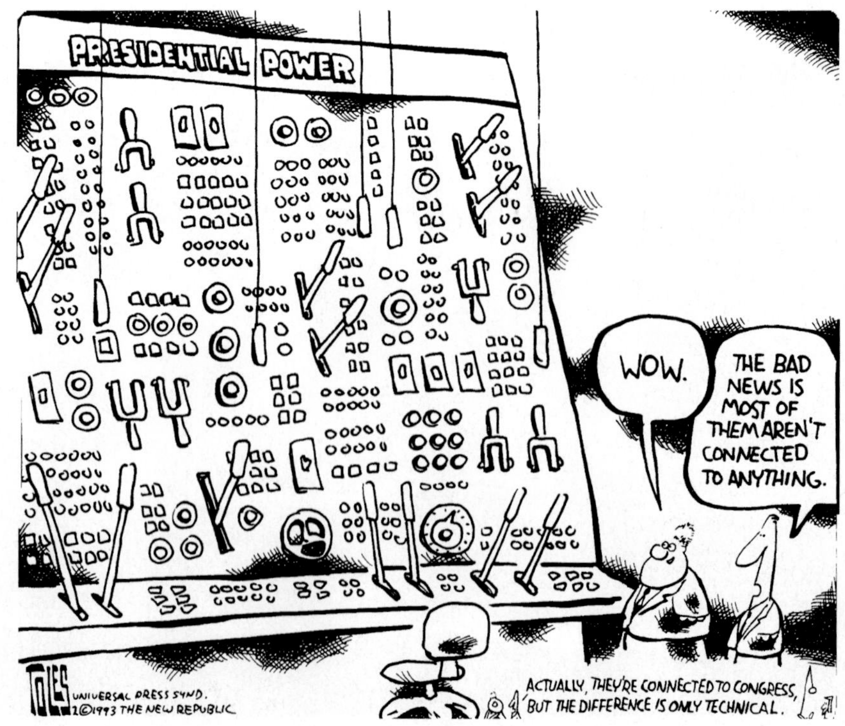

The president is the nation's key agenda builder; what the administration wants strongly influences the parameters of Washington debate.[24] John Kingdon's careful study of the Washington agenda found that "no other single actor in the political system has quite the capability of the president to set agendas."[25] There are limits to what the president can do, however.

By his second year in office, Ronald Reagan's honeymoon with Congress was over, and he had lost control of the legislative agenda. Although the White House can put off dealing with many national issues at the beginning of a new president's term in order to focus on its highest priority legislation, it cannot do so indefinitely. Eventually it must make decisions about a wide range of matters. Soon the legislative agenda is full and more policies are in the pipeline, as the administration attempts to satisfy its constituents and responds to unanticipated or simply overlooked problems. Moreover, Congress is quite capable of setting its own agenda, providing competition for the president's proposals.

In general, presidential legislative skills must compete—as presidential public support does—with other, more stable factors that affect voting in Congress: party, ideology, personal views and commitments on specific policies, constituency interests, and so on. By the time a president tries to exercise influence on a vote, most members of Congress have made up their minds on the basis of these other factors.

After accounting for the status of the president's party in Congress and standing with the public, systematic studies have found that presidents known for their legislative skills (such as Lyndon Johnson) are no more successful in winning votes, even close ones, or obtaining congressional support than those considered less adept at dealing with Congress (such as Jimmy Carter).[26] The president's legislative skills are not at the core of presidential leadership of Congress. Even skilled presidents cannot reshape the contours of the political landscape and *create* opportunities for change. They can, however, recognize favorable configurations of political forces—such as existed in 1933, 1965, and 1981—and effectively exploit them to embark on major shifts in public policy.

Perhaps the most important role of presidents—and their heaviest burden—is their responsibility for national security. Dealing with Congress is only one of the many challenges presidents face in the realm of defense and foreign policy.

visual literacy
Presidential Success in Congress

Presidents find the role of legislative leader a challenging one. Often they must compromise with opponents in Congress, as President Bill Clinton did in 1996 when he signed the welfare reform bill.

The President and National Security Policy

Constitutionally, the president has the leading role in American defense and foreign policy (often termed *national security* policy). Such matters, ranging from foreign trade to war and peace, occupy much of the president's time. There are several dimensions to the president's national security responsibilities, including negotiating with other nations, commanding the armed forces, waging war, managing crises, and obtaining the necessary support in Congress.

Chief Diplomat

The Constitution allocates certain powers in the realm of national security exclusively to the executive. The president alone extends diplomatic recognition to foreign governments—as Jimmy Carter did on December 14, 1978, when he announced the exchange of ambassadors with the People's Republic of China and the downgrading of the U.S. Embassy in Taiwan. The president can also terminate relations with other nations, as Carter did with Iran after Americans were taken hostage in Tehran.

The president also has the sole power to negotiate treaties with other nations, although the Constitution requires the Senate to approve them by a two-thirds vote. Sometimes presidents win and sometimes they lose when presenting a treaty to the Senate. After extensive lobbying, Jimmy Carter persuaded the Senate to approve a treaty returning the Panama Canal to Panama (over objections such as those of one senator who declared, "We stole it fair and square"). Carter was not so lucky when he presented the SALT II treaty on arms control; it never even made it to a vote on the Senate floor.

In addition to treaties, presidents also negotiate *executive agreements* with the heads of foreign governments. However, executive agreements do not require Senate ratification (although they are supposed to be reported to Congress and may require implementing legislation passed by majorities of each house). Most executive agreements are routine and deal with noncontroversial subjects such as food deliveries or customs enforcement, but some, such as the Vietnam peace agreement and the SALT I agreement limiting offensive nuclear weapons, implement important and controversial policies.

Occasionally presidential diplomacy involves more than negotiating on behalf of the United States. Theodore Roosevelt won the Nobel Peace Prize for his role in settling the war between Japan and Russia. One of Jimmy Carter's greatest achievements

Presidents usually conduct diplomatic relations through envoys, but occasionally they engage in personal diplomacy. Here, President Carter celebrates a peace agreement he brokered between Israeli Prime Minister Menachem Begin and Egyptian President Anwar Sadat.

In 1950, President Harry Truman fulfilled his role as commander in chief by pinning a distinguished service medal on the shirt of General Douglas MacArthur, who was commanding American troops in Korea. The following year, Truman exercised his powers by dismissing MacArthur for disobeying orders—an unpopular decision given MacArthur's fame as a World War II hero.

was forging a peace treaty between Egypt and Israel. For 13 days he mediated negotiations between the leaders of both countries at his presidential retreat, Camp David.

As the leader of the Western world, the president must try to lead America's allies on matters of both economics and defense. This is not an easy task, given the natural independence of sovereign nations; the reduced status of the United States as an economic power relative to other countries, such as Japan and Germany; and the many competing influences on policymaking in other nations. As in domestic policymaking, the president must rely principally on persuasion to lead.

Commander in Chief

Because the Constitution's framers wanted civilian control of the military, they made the president the commander in chief of the armed forces. President George Washington actually led troops to crush the Whiskey Rebellion in 1794. Today, presidents do not take the task quite so literally, but their military decisions have changed the course of history. Harry Truman personally selected the target and the date for dropping atomic bombs on Japan to end World War II. Two decades later, Lyndon Johnson selected targets for bombing missions in North Vietnam. Richard Nixon made the decision to invade Cambodia in 1970. Bill Clinton joined the ranks of presidents exerting their prerogatives as commander in chief when he sent American troops to occupy Haiti, keep the peace in Bosnia, restore order in Somalia, prevent an invasion of Kuwait, and bomb Yugoslavia, Iraq, Afghanistan, and the Sudan.

When the Constitution was written, the United States did not have—nor did anyone expect it to have—a large standing or permanent army. Today the president is commander in chief of about 1.4 million uniformed men and women. In his farewell address, George Washington warned against "entangling alliances," but today America has commitments to defend nations across the globe. Even more important, the president commands a vast nuclear arsenal. Never more than a few steps from the president is "the football," a briefcase with the codes needed to unleash nuclear war. The Constitution, of course, states that only Congress has the power to declare war, but it is unreasonable to believe that Congress can convene, debate, and vote on a declaration of war in the case of a nuclear attack. The House and Senate chambers would be gone—*literally* gone—before the conclusion of a debate.

War Powers

Perhaps no issue of executive-legislative relations generates more controversy than the continuing dispute over war powers. Though charged by the Constitution with declaring war and voting on the military budget, Congress long ago accepted that presidents make short-term military commitments of troops or naval vessels. In recent decades, however, presidents have paid even less attention to constitutional details; for example, Congress never declared war during the conflicts in either Korea or Vietnam.

War Powers Resolution

A law, passed in 1973 in reaction to American fighting in Vietnam and Cambodia, requiring presidents to consult with Congress whenever possible prior to using military force and to withdraw forces after 60 days unless Congress declares war or grants an extension. Presidents view the resolution as unconstitutional.

legislative veto

The ability of Congress to override a presidential decision. Although the **War Powers Resolution** asserts this authority, there is reason to believe that, if challenged, the Supreme Court would find the legislative veto in violation of the doctrine of separation of powers.

In 1973 Congress passed the **War Powers Resolution** (over President Nixon's veto). As a reaction to disillusionment about American fighting in Vietnam and Cambodia, the law was intended to give Congress a greater voice in the introduction of American troops into hostilities. It required presidents to consult with Congress, whenever possible, before using military force, and it mandated the withdrawal of forces after 60 days unless Congress declared war or granted an extension. Congress could at any time pass a concurrent resolution (which could not be vetoed) ending American participation in hostilities.

The War Powers Resolution cannot be regarded as a success for Congress, however. All presidents serving since 1973 have deemed the law an unconstitutional infringement on their powers, and there is reason to believe the Supreme Court would consider the law's use of the **legislative veto** (the ability of Congress to pass a resolution to override a presidential decision) to be a violation of the doctrine of separation of powers. Presidents have largely ignored the law and sent troops into hostilities, sometimes with heavy loss of life, without effectual consulting with Congress. The legislature has found it difficult to challenge the president, especially when American troops were endangered, and the courts have been reluctant to hear a congressional challenge on what would be construed as a political, rather than a legal, issue.[27]

Following numerous precedents, George Bush took an expansive view of his powers as commander in chief. On his own authority, he ordered the invasion of Panama in 1989 and moved half a million troops to Saudi Arabia to liberate Kuwait after its invasion by Iraq in 1990.

Matters came to a head in January 1991. President Bush had given President Saddam Hussein of Iraq until January 15 to pull out of Kuwait. At that point, President Bush threatened to move the Iraqis out by force. Debate raged over the president's power to act unilaterally to engage in war. A constitutional crisis was averted when Congress passed (on a divided vote) a resolution on January 12 authorizing the president to use force against Iraq.

Why does it matter?

The question as to the president's war powers has never been fully resolved. How would our foreign policy be affected if the president could only send troops into combat after a congressional resolution authorizing the use of force? Would this restriction be more likely to keep us out of war? Or would it unduly hamper the president's ability to conduct an effective foreign policy? Would you feel better about fighting in a war if Congress were involved?

In a sweeping assertion of presidential authority, Bill Clinton moved toward military intervention in Haiti in 1994 and essentially dared Congress to try to stop him. Congress did nothing but complain to block military action, even though a majority of members of both parties clearly opposed an invasion. In the end, an invasion (as opposed to a more peaceful "intervention") was avoided, but Congress was unlikely to have cut off funds for such an operation had it occurred. In 1999, the president authorized the United States to take the leading role in a sustained air attack against Serbia, but Congress could not agree on a resolution supporting the use of force.

Questions continue to be raised about the relevance of America's 200-year-old constitutional mechanisms for engaging in war. Some observers worry that the rapid response capabilities afforded the president by modern technology allow him to bypass congressional opposition, thus undermining the separation of powers. Others stress the importance of the commander in chief's having the flexibility to meet America's global responsibilities and combat international terrorism without the hindrance of congressional checks and balances. All agree that the change in the nature of warfare brought about by nuclear weapons inevitably delegates to the president the ultimate decision to use such weapons.

Crisis Manager

The president's roles as chief diplomat and commander in chief are related to another presidential responsibility: crisis management. A **crisis** is a sudden, unpredictable, and potentially dangerous event. Most crises occur in the realm of foreign policy. They often involve hot tempers and high risks; quick judgments must be made on the basis of sketchy information. Be it American hostages held in Iran or the discovery of Soviet missiles in Cuba, a crisis challenges the president to make difficult decisions. Crises are rarely the president's doing, but handled incorrectly, they can be the president's undoing.

crisis

A sudden, unpredictable, and potentially dangerous event requiring the president to play the role of crisis manager.

Early in American history there were fewer immediate crises. By the time officials were aware of a problem, it often had resolved itself. Communications could take weeks or even months to reach Washington. Similarly, officials' decisions often took weeks or months to reach those who were to implement them. The most famous land battle of the War of 1812, the Battle of New Orleans, was fought *after* the United States had signed a peace treaty with Great Britain. Word of the treaty did not reach the battlefield; thus, General Andrew Jackson won a victory for the United States that contributed nothing toward ending the war, although it did help put him in the White House as the seventh president.

With modern communications, the president can instantly monitor events almost anywhere. Moreover, because situations develop more rapidly today, there is a premium on rapid action, secrecy, constant management, consistent judgment, and expert advice. Congress usually moves slowly (one might say deliberately), and it is large (making it difficult to keep secrets), decentralized (requiring continual compromising), and composed of generalists. As a result, the president—who can come to quick and consistent decisions, confine information to a small group, carefully oversee developments, and call upon experts in the executive branch—has become more prominent in handling crises.

Working With Congress

As America moves through its third century under the Constitution, presidents might wish the framers had been less concerned with checks and balances in the area of national security. In recent years, Congress has challenged presidents on all fronts, including foreign aid; arms sales; the development, procurement, and deployment of weapons systems; the negotiation and interpretation of treaties; the selection of diplomats; and the continuation of nuclear testing.

Congress has a central constitutional role in making national security policy, although this role is often misunderstood. The allocation of responsibilities for such matters is based on the founders' apprehensions about the concentration of power and the subsequent potential for its abuse. They divided the powers of supply and command, for example, in order to thwart adventurism in national security affairs. Congress can thus refuse to provide the necessary authorizations and appropriations for presidential actions, whereas the chief executive can refuse to act (for example, by not sending troops into battle at the behest of the legislature).

Despite the constitutional role of Congress, the president is the driving force behind national security policy, providing energy and direction. Congress is well organized to deliberate openly on the discrete components of policy, but it is not well designed to take the lead on national security matters. Its role has typically been overseeing the executive rather than initiating policy. Congress frequently originates proposals for domestic policy, but it is less involved in national security policy.[28]

The president has a more prominent role in foreign affairs as the country's sole representative in dealing with other nations and as commander in chief of the armed forces (functions that effectively preclude a wide range of congressional diplomatic and military initiatives). In addition, the nature of national security issues may make the failure to integrate the elements of policy more costly than in domestic policy. Thus, members of Congress typically prefer to encourage, criticize, or support the president rather than to initiate their own national security policy. If leadership occurs, it is usually centered in the White House.

Commentators on the presidency often refer to the "two presidencies"—one for domestic policy and the other for national security policy.[29] By this phrase they mean that the president has more success in leading Congress on matters of national security than on matters of domestic policy. The typical member of Congress, however, supports the president on roll-call votes about national security only slightly more than half the time. There is a significant gap between what the president requests and what members of Congress are willing to give. Certainly the legislature does not accord the president automatic support on national security policy.[30]

Nevertheless, presidents do end up obtaining much, often most, of what they request from Congress on national security issues. Some of the support they receive is the result of agreement on policy, but presidential leadership also plays an important role. That role is not one in which presidents simply bend the legislature to their will, however; rather, they lead by persuasion.

Presidents need resources to persuade others to support their policies. One important presidential asset can be the support of the American people. The following sections will take a closer look at how the White House tries to increase and use public support.

Power from the People: The Public Presidency

"Public sentiment is everything. With public sentiment nothing can fail; without it nothing can succeed." These words, spoken by Abraham Lincoln, pose what is perhaps the greatest challenge to any president—to obtain and maintain the public's support. Because presidents are rarely in a position to command others to comply with their wishes, they must rely on persuasion. *Public support is perhaps the greatest source of influence a president has,* for it is difficult for other power holders in a democracy to deny the legitimate demands of a president who has popular backing.

Going Public

Presidents are not passive followers of public opinion. The White House is a virtual whirlwind of public relations activity.[31] John Kennedy, the first "television president," held considerably more public appearances than did his predecessors. Kennedy's successors, with the notable exception of Richard Nixon, have been even more active in making public appearances. Indeed, they have averaged more than one appearance every weekday of the year. Bill Clinton invested enormous time and energy in attempting to sell his programs to the public. George W. Bush has followed the same pattern.

Often the president's appearances are staged purely to get the public's attention. When George Bush introduced his clean air bill in 1989, he traveled to Wyoming to use the eye-catching Grand Tetons as a backdrop. He announced his support for a constitutional amendment to prohibit flag burning in front of the Iwo Jima Memorial in Arlington National Cemetery. In cases such as these, the president could have simply made an announcement, but the need for public support drives the White House to employ public relations techniques similar to those used to publicize commercial products.

In many democracies, different people occupy the jobs of head of state and head of government. For example, the queen is head of state in England, but she holds little power in government and politics. In America, these roles are fused. As head of state, the president is America's ceremonial leader and symbol of government. Trivial but time-consuming activities—tossing out the first baseball of the season, lighting the White House Christmas tree, meeting an extraordinary Boy or Girl Scout—are part of the ceremonial function of the presidency. Meeting foreign heads of state, receiving ambassadors' credentials, and making global goodwill tours represent the international side of this role. Presidents rarely shirk these duties, even when they are not inherently

Presidents often use commercial public relations techniques to win support for their policy initiatives. President Bush, for example, used the spectacular backdrop of the Grand Tetons to gain public approval for renewal and strengthening of the Clean Air Act.

important. Ceremonial activities give them an important symbolic aura and a great deal of favorable press coverage, contributing to their efforts to build public support.

Presidential Approval

Much of the energy the White House devotes to public relations is aimed at increasing the president's public approval. The reason is simple: The higher the president stands in the polls, the easier it is to persuade others to support presidential initiatives.

Because of the connection between public support and presidential influence, the president's standing in the polls is monitored closely by the press, members of Congress, and others in the Washington political community. "President watching" is a favorite American pastime. For years, the Gallup Poll has asked Americans this question: "Do you approve or disapprove of the way John Kennedy, George W. Bush, or whoever is handling his job as president?" You can see the results in Figure 13.3.

Presidents frequently do not have widespread public support, often failing to win even majority approval. Figure 13.4 shows the average approval levels of recent presidents. Presidents Nixon, Ford, and Carter did not even receive approval from 50 percent of the public on the average. Ronald Reagan, a "popular" president, had only a 52 percent approval level. For three years, George Bush enjoyed much higher levels of approval on the average than his predecessors did. In his fourth year, however, his ratings dropped below the 40 percent mark. For much of his tenure in office, President Clinton struggled to rise above the 50 percent mark.

Presidential approval is the product of many factors.[32] At the base of presidential evaluations is the predisposition of many people to support the president. Political party identification provides the basic underpinning of approval or disapproval and mediates the impact of other factors. On average, those who identify with the president's party give approval nearly 40 percentage points higher than that

Figure 13.3 Average Yearly Presidential Approval

For years the Gallup Poll has asked Americans, "Do you approve or disapprove of the way ____ is handling his job as president?" Here you can track the percentage approving of presidential performance from Eisenhower to George W. Bush. Notice that most presidents seem to be most popular when they first enter office; later on, their popularity often erodes. Bill Clinton was an exception.

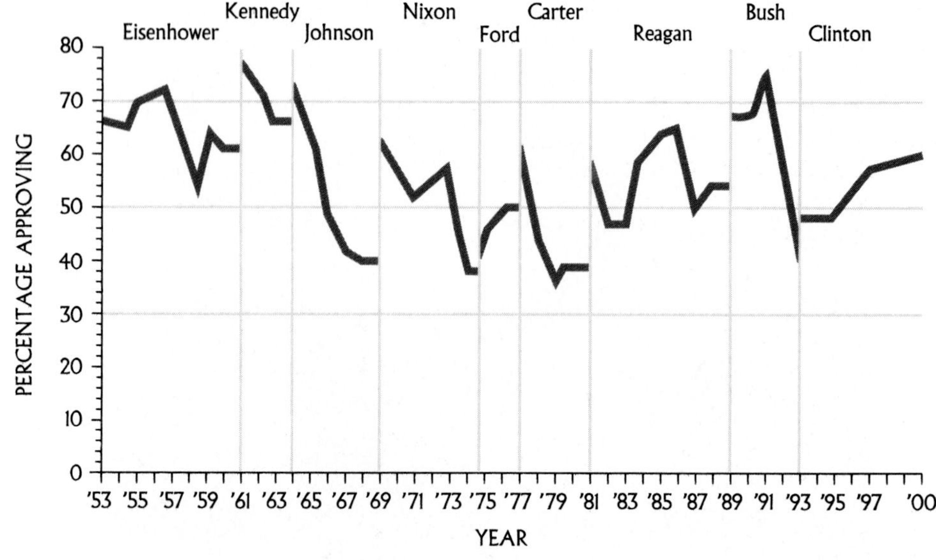

Source: George C. Edwards III, *Presidential Approval* (Baltimore, MD: Johns Hopkins University Press, 1990); updated by the authors.

expressed by those who identify with the opposition party. In other words, Democrats love Democratic presidents, and Republicans are equally fond of GOP chief executives. Moreover, partisans are not inclined to approve presidents of the other party. Predispositions provide the foundations of presidential approval and furnish it with a basic stability.

Presidents also usually benefit from a "honeymoon" with the American people after taking office. Some observers believe that "honeymoons" are fleeting phenomena in which the public affords new occupants of the White House only a short grace period before they begin their inevitable descent in the polls. You can see in Figure 13.3 that declines do take place, but they are neither inevitable nor swift. Throughout his two terms in office, Ronald Reagan experienced considerable volatility in his relations with

Figure 13.4 Average Presidential Approval for Entire Terms in Office

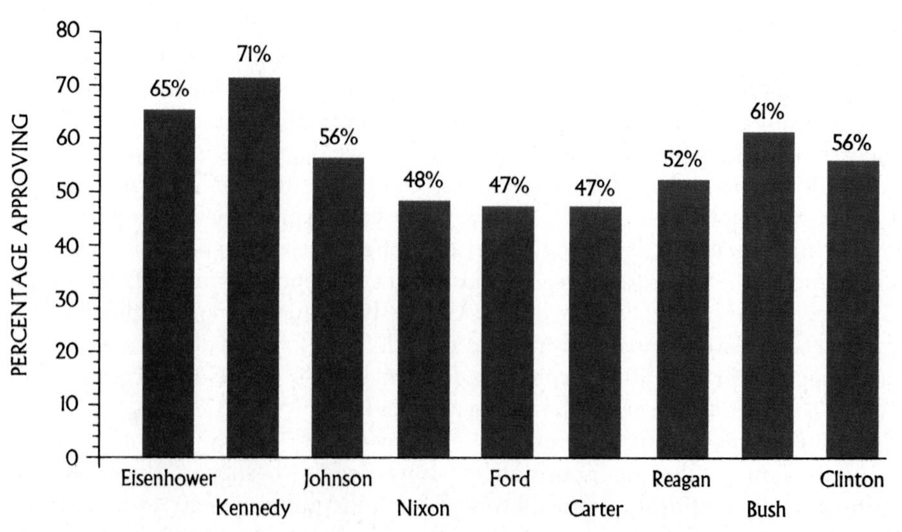

Source: George C. Edwards III, *Presidential Approval* (Baltimore, MD: Johns Hopkins University Press, 1990); updated by the authors.

the public, but his record certainly does not indicate that the loss of public support is inexorable or that support cannot be revived and maintained. George Bush obtained more public support in his third year in office than in his first two years, and Bill Clinton enjoyed more approval in his second term in office than in his first.

Changes in approval levels appear to reflect the public's evaluation of how the president is handling policy areas such as the economy, war, and foreign affairs. Different policies are salient to the public at different times. For example, if communism is collapsing, then foreign policy is likely to dominate the news and to be on the minds of Americans. If the economy turns sour, then people are going to be concerned about unemployment.

Contrary to the conventional wisdom, citizens seem to focus on the president's efforts and stands on issues rather than on personality ("popularity") or simply how presidential policies affect them (the "pocketbook"). Job-related personal characteristics of the president, such as integrity and leadership skills, also play an important role in influencing presidential approval.

Sometimes public approval of the president takes sudden jumps. One popular explanation for these surges of support is "rally events," which John Mueller defined as events that are related to international relations, directly involve the United States and particularly the president, and are specific, dramatic, and sharply focused.[33] A classic example is the 18-percentage-point rise in President Bush's approval ratings immediately after the fighting began in the Gulf War in 1991. Such occurrences are unusual and isolated events, however; they have little enduring impact on a president's public approval. President Bush, for example, dropped precipitously in the polls and lost his bid for reelection in 1992.

The criteria on which the public evaluates presidents—such as the way they are handling the economy, where they stand on complex issues, and whether they are "strong" leaders—are open to many interpretations. The modern White House makes extraordinary efforts to control the context in which presidents appear in public and the way they are portrayed by the press, to try to influence how the public views them. The fact that presidents are frequently low in the polls anyway is persuasive testimony to the limits of presidential leadership of the public. As one student of the public presidency put it, "The supply of popular support rests on opinion dynamics over which the president may exert little direct control."[34]

participation
Rate the Presidents

Policy Support

Commentators on the presidency often refer to it as a "bully pulpit" (as Theodore Roosevelt termed it), implying that presidents can persuade or even mobilize the public to support their policies if they are skilled communicators. Certainly presidents frequently do attempt to obtain public support for their policies with television or radio appearances and speeches to large groups.[35] All presidents since Truman have had media advice from experts on lighting, makeup, stage settings, camera angles, clothing, pacing of delivery, and other facets of making speeches.

Despite this aid and despite the experience that politicians have in speaking, presidential speeches designed to lead public opinion have typically been rather unimpressive. In the modern era only Franklin D. Roosevelt, John Kennedy, Ronald Reagan, and Bill Clinton could be considered especially effective speakers. The rest were not, and they appeared unimpressive under the glare of hot lights and the unflattering gaze of television cameras. Partly because of his limitations as a public speaker, President Bush waited until he had been in office for over seven months before making his first nationally televised address in 1989.

Moreover, the public is not always receptive to the president's message. Chapter 6 showed that Americans are not especially interested in politics and government; thus, it is not easy to get their attention. Citizens also have predispositions about public policy (however ill-informed) that act as screens for presidential messages. In the absence of national crises, most people are unreceptive to political appeals.[36]

The public may misperceive or ignore even the most basic facts regarding presidential policy. For example, at the end of October 1994, 59 percent of the public thought the economy was still in recession (although it was growing so fast that the Federal Reserve Board was taking strong action to cool it off), only 34 percent knew the deficit had decreased since Clinton became president (it had decreased substan-

John Kennedy was the first president to use public appearances regularly to seek popular backing for his policies. Despite his popularity and skills as a communicator, Kennedy was often frustrated in his attempts to win widespread support for his administration's "New Frontier" policies.

tially), and 65 percent thought taxes on the middle class had increased during that period (income taxes had been raised for less than 2 percent of the public).[37] Partly as a consequence of these misconceptions, Clinton was frustrated repeatedly in his efforts to obtain public support for his policy initiatives.[38]

Ronald Reagan, sometimes called the "Great Communicator," was certainly interested in policy change and went to unprecedented lengths to influence public opinion on behalf of such policies as deregulation, decreases in spending on domestic policy, and increases in the defense budget. Nevertheless, support for regulatory programs and spending on health care, welfare, urban problems, education, environmental protection, and aid to minorities increased, not decreased, during Reagan's tenure. Support for increased defense expenditures was decidedly lower when he left office than when he was inaugurated.[39]

Mobilizing the Public

Sometimes merely changing public opinion is not sufficient, and the president wants the public to communicate its views directly to Congress. Mobilization of the public may be the ultimate weapon in the president's arsenal of resources with which to influence Congress. When the people speak, especially when they speak clearly, Congress listens.

Mobilizing the public involves overcoming formidable barriers and accepting substantial risks. It entails the double burden of obtaining both opinion support and political action from a generally inattentive and apathetic public. If the president tries to mobilize the public and fails, the lack of response speaks clearly to members of Congress.

Perhaps the most notable recent example of the president's mobilization of public opinion to pressure Congress is Ronald Reagan's effort to obtain passage of his tax-cut bill in 1981. Shortly before the crucial vote in the House, the president made a televised plea for support of his tax-cut proposals and asked the people to let their representatives in Congress know how they felt. Evidently Reagan's plea worked; thousands of phone calls, letters, and telegrams poured into congressional offices. On the morning of the vote, Speaker Tip O'Neill declared, "We are experiencing a telephone blitz like this nation has never seen. It's had a devastating effect."[40] The president easily carried the day.

The Reagan administration's effort to mobilize the public on behalf of the 1981 tax cut is significant not only because of the success of presidential leadership but also because it appears to be an anomaly. In the remainder of Reagan's tenure, the president went repeatedly to the people regarding a wide range of policies, including the budget, aid to the Contras in Nicaragua, and defense expenditures. Despite high levels of approval for much of that time, Reagan was never again able to arouse many in his audience to communicate their support of his policies to Congress. Substantial tax cuts hold more appeal to the public than most other issues.

The President and the Press

Despite all their efforts to lead public opinion, presidents do not directly reach the American people on a day-to-day basis. The mass media provide people with most of what they know about chief executives and their policies. The media also interpret and analyze presidential activities, even the president's direct appeals to the public. The press is thus the principal intermediary between the president and the public, and relations with the press are an important aspect of the president's efforts to lead public opinion.

No matter who is in the White House or who reports on presidential activities, presidents and the press tend to be in conflict. George Washington complained that the "calumnies" against his administration were "outrages of common decency." Thomas Jefferson once declared that "nothing in a newspaper is to be believed." Presidents are inherently policy advocates. They want to control the amount and timing of information about their administration, whereas the press wants all the information that exists without delay. As long as their goals are different, presidents and the media are likely to be adversaries (see "Making a Difference: Helen Thomas").

Making a Difference

Helen Thomas

There is no one quite like her. She turned 80 in the year 2000 and has been covering the White House since the Kennedy administration. For most of that time she worked for a news agency, United Press International (UPI), that was in serious financial trouble and that paid her the salary of a cub reporter. She often arrives at 5:30 A.M., where her office is a tiny cubicle the size of a phone booth. Yet she is always there.

This is Helen Thomas, dean of the White House press and perhaps the most remarkable reporter in the country. Although a naturally kind and caring person (and a lover of good rum cake), she has been terrorizing presidents and their press secretaries for decades. With a legendary nose for news that can anticipate a story days before it breaks, there is no more tenacious questioner in the press corps.

Each weekday she and a small group of other reporters meet with the president's press secretary to begin the process of ferreting out the day's news. Later in the morning is the daily briefing, where Helen asks the first, and often also last, question. The briefing does not end until she tells the press secretary "thank you very much"—which she is reluctant to do. The rest of her day is spent watching official White House activities and bombarding the president and his staff with more questions.

Helen believes, even at her age, in taking no shortcuts, in receiving no information secondhand. She has to "be there." That meant going to Saudi Arabia and riding in the back of a military truck in 110-degree heat at the age of 70 to see what the president was doing while visiting U.S. troops fighting in the Gulf War.

Helen Thomas is not rich. She has little organizational power. She receives few perks. Yet more than anyone else, she sets the tone for White House coverage and ensures that Americans know as much as possible about the presidency.

Because of the importance of the press to the president, the White House monitors the media closely. Some presidents have installed special televisions so that they can watch the news on all the networks at once; Lyndon Johnson even had news tickers from AP, UPI, and Reuters in the Oval Office. The White House also goes to great lengths to encourage the media to project a positive image of the president's activities and policies. About one-third of the high-level White House staff members are directly involved in media relations and policy of one type or another, and most staff members are involved at some time in trying to influence the media's portrayal of the president.

The person who most often deals directly with the press is the president's *press secretary*, who serves as a conduit of information from the White House to the press. Press secretaries conduct daily press briefings, giving prepared announcements and answering questions. They and their staff also arrange private interviews with White House officials (often done on a background basis, in which the reporter may not attribute remarks to the person being interviewed), photo opportunities, and travel arrangements for reporters when the president leaves Washington.

The best known direct interaction between the president and the press is the formal presidential press conference. Since the presidency of George Bush, however, prime time, televised press conferences have become rare events. Bill Clinton took office with an antagonistic attitude toward the national media and planned to bypass it rather than use it as part of his political strategy. After a rocky start in his press relations, the president made himself somewhat more accessible to the national press. Like Clinton, George W. Bush has relied more on travel around the country to gain television time to spread his message than on formal press conferences.

Despite their visibility, press conferences are not very useful means of eliciting information. Presidents and their staffs can anticipate most of the questions that will be asked and prepare answers to them ahead of time, reducing the spontaneity of the sessions. Moreover, the large size and public nature of press conferences reduce the candor with which the president responds to questions.

Most of the news coverage of the White House comes under the heading "body watch." In other words, reporters focus on the most visible layer of the president's per-

The press secretary is the primary channel through which the White House communicates with the media. Here, President George W. Bush's press secretary, Ari Fleischer, responds to reporters' questions.

sonal and official activities and provide the public with step-by-step accounts. They are interested in what presidents are going to do, how their actions will affect others, how they view policies and individuals, and how they present themselves, rather than in the substance of policies or the fundamental processes operating in the executive branch. Former ABC White House correspondent Sam Donaldson tells of covering a meeting of Western leaders on the island of Guadeloupe. It was a slow news day, so Donaldson did a story on the roasting of the pig the leaders would be eating that night, including "an exclusive look at the oven in which the pig would be roasted."[41] Because there are daily deadlines to meet and television reporters must squeeze their stories into sound bites measured in seconds, not minutes, there is little time for reflection, analysis, or comprehensive coverage.

Bias is the most politically charged issue in relations between the president and the press. A large number of studies have concluded that the news media, including the television networks and major newspapers, are not biased *systematically* toward a particular person, party, or ideology, as measured in the amount or favorability of coverage.[42]

To conclude that the news contains little explicitly partisan or ideological bias is not to argue that the news does not distort reality in its coverage of the president. As the following excerpt from Jimmy Carter's diary regarding a visit to a U.S. Army base in Panama in 1978 illustrates, "objective" reporting can be misleading.

> *I told the Army troops that I was in the Navy for 11 years, and they booed. I told them that we depended on the Army to keep the Canal open, and they cheered. Later, the news reports said that there were boos and cheers during my speech.*[43]

We learned in Chapter 7 that the news is fundamentally superficial, oversimplified, and often overblown, all of which provides the public with a distorted view of, among other things, presidential activities, statements, policies, and options. We have also seen that the press prefers to frame the news in themes, which both simplifies complex issues and events and provides continuity of persons, institutions, and issues. Once these themes are established, the press tend to maintain them in subsequent stories. Of necessity, themes emphasize some information at the expense of other data, often determining what information is most relevant to news coverage and the context in which it is presented.

Once a stereotype of President Ford as a "bumbler" was established, every stumble was magnified as the press emphasized behavior that fit the mold. He was repeatedly forced to defend his intelligence, and many of his acts and statements were reported as efforts to "act" presidential. Once Ford was typecast, his image was repeatedly reinforced and was very difficult to overcome.[44]

News coverage of the presidency often tends to emphasize the negative (even if the negative stories are presented in a seemingly neutral manner),[45] a trend that has increased over the past 20 years.[46] In the 1980 election campaign, the press portrayed President Carter as mean and Ronald Reagan as imprecise rather than Carter as precise and Reagan as pleasant. The emphasis, in other words, was on the candidates' negative qualities. George Bush received extraordinarily negative press coverage during the 1992 election campaign, and the television networks' portrayal of the economy, for which Bush was blamed, got worse as the economy actually improved to a robust rate of growth![47]

President Clinton received mostly negative coverage during his tenure in office, with a ratio of negative to positive comments on network television of about 2 to 1.[48] When the story broke regarding his affair with Monica Lewinsky, the press engaged in a feeding frenzy, providing an extraordinary amount of information on both the affair and the president's attempts to cover it up. Little of this coverage was favorable to the president.

White House reporters are always looking to expose conflicts of interest and other shady behavior of public officials. In addition, many of their inquiries revolve around the question "Is the president up to the job?" Reporters who are confined in the White House all day may attempt to make up for their lack of investigative reporting with sarcastic and accusatory questioning. Moreover, the desire to keep the public interested and the need for continuous coverage may create in the press a subconscious bias against the presidency that leads to negative stories.

On the other hand, the president has certain advantages in dealing with the press. He is typically portrayed with an aura of dignity and treated with deference.[49] According to Sam Donaldson, who was generally considered an aggressive White House reporter, "For every truly tough question I've put to officials, I've asked a dozen that were about as tough as Grandma's apple dumplings."[50] Thus, when he left after serving as President Reagan's press secretary for six years, Larry Speakes told reporters they had given the Reagan administration "a fair shake."[51]

Remember that the White House can largely control the environment in which the president meets the press—even going so far as to have the Marine helicopters revved as Ronald Reagan approached them so that he could not hear reporters' questions and give unrehearsed responses.

Understanding the American Presidency

Because the presidency is the single most important office in American politics, there has always been concern about whether the president is a threat to democracy. The importance of the president has raised similar concerns for the scope of government in America.

The Presidency and Democracy

From the time the Constitution was written, there has been a fear that the presidency would degenerate into a monarchy or a dictatorship. Even America's greatest presidents have heightened these fears at times. Despite George Washington's well-deserved reputation for peacefully relinquishing power, he also had certain regal tendencies that fanned the suspicions of the Jeffersonians. Abraham Lincoln, for all his humility, exercised extraordinary powers at the outbreak of the Civil War. Since that time, political commentators have alternated between extolling and fearing a strong presidency.

Concerns over presidential power are generally closely related to policy views. Those who oppose the president's policies are the most likely to be concerned about *too much* presidential power. As you have seen, however, aside from acting outside the

How You Can Make A Difference

The Fast Track to the White House

Since the scandal involving President Clinton and Monica Lewinsky, presidential interns have become the butt of late night comedians' jokes. However, this bad publicity should not discourage you from investigating one of the best opportunities available to college students eager to get a taste of politics at the top. This prestigious and highly competitive program allows you to actively participate in the federal government's policy decisions from inside the White House.

The White House Internship Program allows select college students to work within over 30 different offices under the control of the Executive Office of the President. Interns work in the more familiar offices of the Chief of Staff, Communications, and Press Secretary's Office as well as the lesser known offices of the Counsel to the President, Executive Clerk's Office and National Economic Council. Most of these internships are not located within the West Wing (where the president works) but at other buildings, especially the Eisenhower Executive Office Building, within the White House complex. In fact, fewer than a third of the over 500 interns at any one time ever secure valid passes granting them access to the West Wing. Because the purpose of this program is primarily educational, interns learn skills and information that prove extremely valuable after graduation whether one pursues a career in public office or the private sector. The work, though, is grinding and seldom glamorous. Long hours and hard work can gain an intern the reputation as a "trooper," a long sought-after title. Intense competition between in-terns for recognition is normal. Many interns hope to translate their internship into a paid position within the White House or another government agency after graduation.

How do you become a White House intern? There are two routes. First, according to Mike McCurry, former White House spokesman, it helps to have connections. "Many of [the interns] are sons and daughters of supporters," notes McCurry. Most college students, however, will compete purely on merit with the other applicants. To learn more, go to the White House homepage (www.whitehouse.gov/internship) to download an application. Along with the application, you must submit a résumé, a personal statement, a writing sample, two letters of recommendation, and a transcript. Although one is only required to be 18 years or older, most interns are either juniors or seniors in college. Among the criteria considered in the selection process are community service, leadership, academic achievement, extracurricular activity, and writing skills. Also, be aware that you must pass a background investigation to be admitted to the White House complex. Remember, in a few years, those late night comedy skits will be ancient history, but the opportunity to serve as a White House intern will remain with you (and your résumé) for a lifetime!

Source: Duncan Moon, "Washington Interns: Lots of Gofer Work, Little Glamour," *Christian Science Monitor,* 90 (January 29, 1998), 44: 12.

law and the Constitution, there is little prospect that the presidency will be a threat to democracy. The Madisonian system of checks and balances remains intact.

This system is especially evident in an era characterized by divided government—government in which the president is of one party and a majority in each house of Congress is of the other party. Some observers are concerned that there is too much checking and balancing and too little capacity to act on pressing national challenges. More potentially important legislation fails to pass under divided government than when one party controls both the presidency and Congress.[52] However, major policy change *is* possible under a divided government. One author found that major change is just as likely to occur when the parties share control as when one party holds both the presidency and a majority in each house of Congress.[53]

The Presidency and the Scope of Government

Some of the most noteworthy presidents in the twentieth century (including Theodore Roosevelt, Woodrow Wilson, and Franklin Roosevelt) have successfully advocated substantial increases in the role of the national government. Supporting an increased role for government is not inherent in the presidency, however; leadership can move in many directions.

All seven presidents since Lyndon Johnson have championed constraints on government and limits on spending, especially in domestic policy. It is often said that the American people are ideologically conservative and operationally liberal. For most of the past generation, it has been their will to choose presidents who reflected their ideology and a Congress that represented their appetite for public service. It has been the president more often than Congress who has said "no" to government growth.

Career Profile

Position: Executive Assistant for the Assistant to the President of the United States
Salary Range: $28,000-32,000
Benefits: Health, life, and dental insurance; prestige and honor of serving the president of the United States
Qualifications: Superior communication and interpersonal skills, organizational proficiency, and analytical capabilities required. Willingness to work long hours at low pay in city with a high cost of living. A proven track record within a political campaign or a government office

Real People on the Job: Karen Ewing

Working in the White House can be an exciting and rewarding experience. The television show *West Wing* has recently captured the American public's imagination and made government work cool again. One of the show's popular characters, Donna (the executive assistant to Josh, the Deputy White House Chief of Staff) illustrates the vital importance of the oft-overlooked staff members in the Executive Office of the President. In real life, Karen Ewing worked as a White House staffer during the Clinton Administration in a position very similar to that of *West Wing's* Donna.

Karen began her career at the White House by serving directly under Assistant to the President for National Service, Eli Segal. She helped research and write the legislation that created Americorp, a Peace Corps-like program for rural and urban America. Working out of an office in the Executive Office Building next to the West Wing, Karen coordinated congressional contacts and media relations for Segal. In order to show congressional leaders that this National Service Project could work on a larger scale, Karen helped create a "Summer of Service" as a scaled down version of Americorp in targeted cities and localities. Karen worked to enlist the aid of celebrities to volunteer for these projects and gain greater visibility for the endeavor. Soon after Americorp became a reality, Karen moved into a West Wing office across from the Navy mess hall and served as special assistant to White House chief of staff.

In both jobs, Karen's hours usually lasted from 7 A.M. to 7:30 P.M. or longer, depending upon the situation. Though the work was demanding, the best part of both jobs was being part of history and getting to know the inner workings of the White House. The knowledge that her memos and e-mails were destined to join the archives of a future Clinton Presidential Library guided nearly all her actions during her tenure.

But how can you make the career leap into the White House, especially if you haven't met the constitutional age requirement for the top job? According to Karen, you should start out like she did by getting involved in political campaigns as a volunteer stuffing envelopes and making phone calls, especially early in a campaign. Call your representative or even the White House directly at 202-456-1414 and ask if you can volunteer as part of an advance team on future trips that the president takes outside Washington, D.C.

Summary

Americans expect a lot from presidents—perhaps too much. The myth of the president as a powerhouse clouds Americans' image of presidential reality. Presidents mainly have the power to persuade, not to impose their will.

Presidents do not work alone. Gone are the days when the presidency meant the president plus a few aides and advisors. The cabinet, the Executive Office of the President, and the White House staff all assist today's presidents. These services come at a price, however, and presidents must organize their subordinates effectively for decision making and policy execution.

Although presidential leadership of Congress is central to all administrations, it often proves frustrating. Presidents rely on their party, the public, and their own legislative skills to persuade Congress to support their policies, but most of the time their efforts are at the margins of coalition building. Rarely are presidents in a position to create—through their own leadership—opportunities for major changes in public policy. They may, however, use their skills to exploit favorable political conditions to bring about policy change.

Some of the president's most important responsibilities fall in the area of national security. As chief diplomat and commander in chief of the armed forces, the president is the country's crisis manager. Still, disputes with Congress over war powers and presidential discretion in foreign affairs demonstrate that even in regard to national security, the president operates within the Madisonian system of checks and balances.

Because presidents are dependent on others to accomplish their goals, their greatest challenge is to obtain support. Public opinion can be an important resource for presidential persuasion, and the White House works hard to influence the public. Public approval of presidents and their policies is often elusive, however; the public does not reliably respond to presidential leadership. The press is the principal intermediary between the president and the public, and relations with the press present yet another challenge to the White House's efforts to lead public opinion.

Key Terms

Twenty-second Amendment
impeachment
Watergate
Twenty-fifth Amendment
cabinet
National Security Council (NSC)
Council of Economic Advisors (CEA)
Office of Management and Budget (OMB)
veto
pocket veto
presidential coattails
War Powers Resolution
legislative veto
crisis

For Further Reading

Barber, James David. *The Presidential Character,* 4th ed. Englewood Cliffs, NJ: Prentice-Hall, 1992. Provocative work predicting performance in the White House.

Burke, John P. *The Institutional Presidency,* 2nd ed. Baltimore: Johns Hopkins University Press, 2000. Examines White House organization and presidential advising.

Burke, John P., and Fred I. Greenstein. *How Presidents Test Reality.* New York: Russell Sage Foundation, 1989. Excellent work on presidential decision making.

Edwards, George C., III. *At the Margins: Presidential Leadership of Congress.* New Haven, CT: Yale University Press, 1989. Examines the presidents' efforts to lead Congress and explains their limitations.

Edwards, George C., III. *Presidential Approval.* Baltimore: Johns Hopkins University Press, 1990. The relationship between the president and public opinion in the White House's pursuit of popular support.

Fisher, Louis. *Constitutional Conflicts Between Congress and the President,* 4th ed. rev. Lawrence: University Press of Kansas, 1997. Presents the constitutional dimensions of the separation of powers.

Grossman, Michael Baruch, and Martha Joynt Kumar. *Portraying the President: The White House and the News Media.* Baltimore: Johns Hopkins University Press, 1981. A comprehensive study of presidential relations with the press.

Hart, John. *The Presidential Branch,* 2nd ed. Chatham, NJ: Chatham House, 1995. Discusses the Executive Office of the President and the White House staff.

Nathan, Richard P. *The Administrative Presidency.* New York: Wiley, 1983. The president's role in managing the bureaucracy.

Neustadt, Richard E. *Presidential Power and the Modern Presidents.* New York: Free Press, 1990. The most influential book on the American presidency; argues that presidential power is the power to persuade.

Pfiffner, James P. *The Strategic Presidency,* 2nd ed. Lawrence: University Press of Kansas, 1996. Organizing the presidency.

Internet Resources

www.whitehouse.gov/
Links to presidential speeches, documents, schedules, radio addresses, federal statistics, and White House press releases and briefings.

www.whitehouse.gov/WH/EOP/html/EOP_org.html
Information about the Executive Office of the President.

www.ibiblio.org/lia/president/
Links to presidents and presidential libraries.

www.nara.gov/fedreg/elctcoll/index.html
Information about the Electoral College.

www.ipl.org/ref/POTUS/
Background on presidents and their administrations.

www.lib.umich.edu/libhome/documents.center.fedprs.html
Wide range of documents regarding the president's activities.

www.nara.gov/education/teaching/watergate/
Contains background and details of the Watergate scandal.

Notes

1. Quoted in Thomas E. Cronin, *The State of the Presidency,* 2nd ed. (Boston: Little, Brown, 1980), 223.
2. Richard E. Neustadt, *Presidential Power and the Modern Presidents* (New York: Free Press, 1990).
3. On the public's expectations of the president, see George C. Edwards III, *The Public Presidency* (New York: St. Martin's Press, 1983), chap. 5.
4. Office of the White House Press Secretary, Remarks of the President at a Meeting With Non-Washington Editors and Broadcasters, September 21, 1979, 12.
5. Samuel P. Huntington, *American Politics: The Promises of Disharmony* (Cambridge, MA: Belknap, 1981), 33.
6. On the creation of the presidency, see Donald L. Robertson, *"To the Best of My Ability"* (New York: Norton, 1987); and Thomas E. Cronin, ed., *Inventing the American Presidency* (Lawrence: University Press of Kansas, 1989).
7. A good example is Clinton Rossiter, *The American Presidency,* rev. ed. (New York: Harcourt, 1960).
8. Arthur Schlesinger, *The Imperial Presidency* (Boston: Houghton Mifflin, 1973).
9. The titles of chaps. 5 and 11 in Thomas E. Cronin, *The State of the Presidency,* 2nd ed. (Boston: Little, Brown, 1980).
10. On the factors important in the presidential nominee's choice of a running mate, see Lee Sigelman and Paul J. Wahlbeck, "The 'Veepstakes': Strategic Choice in Presidential Running Mate Selection," *American Political Science Review* 91 (December 1997): 855–864.
11. See Paul C. Light, *Vice Presidential Power* (Baltimore: Johns Hopkins University Press, 1984).
12. For a study of the backgrounds of cabinet members, see Jeffrey E. Cohen, *The Politics of the U.S. Cabinet* (Pittsburgh: University of Pittsburgh Press, 1988).
13. For background on the Executive Office, see John Hart, *The Presidential Branch,* 2nd ed. (Chatham, NJ: Chatham House, 1995).
14. Two useful books on the history and functions of the White House staff are Hart, *The Presidential Branch*; and Bradley H. Patterson, Jr., *The Ring of Power* (New York: Basic Books, 1988).
15. For a discussion of presidential party leadership in Congress, see George C. Edwards III, *At the Margins: Presidential Leadership of Congress* (New Haven, CT: Yale University Press, 1989), chaps. 3–5.
16. Jimmy Carter, *Keeping Faith* (New York: Bantam, 1982), 80.
17. For a review of these studies and an analysis showing the limited impact of presidential coattails on congressional election outcomes, see Edwards, *The Public Presidency,* 83–93.
18. For evidence of the impact of the president's campaigning in midterm elections, see Jeffrey E. Cohen, Michael A. Krassa, and John A. Hamman, "The Impact of Presidential Campaigning on Midterm U.S. Senate Elections," *American Political Science Review* 85 (March 1991): 165–178. On the president's effect on congressional elections more broadly, see James E. Campbell, *The Presidential Pulse of Congressional Elections* (Lexington: University Press of Kentucky, 1993).
19. Quoted in Sidney Blumenthal, "Marketing the President," *New York Times Magazine,* September 13, 1981, 110.
20. Quoted in "Slings and Arrows," *Newsweek,* July 31, 1978, 20.
21. Edwards, *At the Margins,* chaps. 6–7.
22. For an analysis of the factors that affect perceptions of mandates, see Edwards, *At the Margins,* chap. 8.
23. David Stockman, *The Triumph of Politics* (New York: Harper & Row, 1986), 251–265; and William Greider, "The Education of David Stockman," *Atlantic,* December 1981, 51.
24. George C. Edwards III and Andrew Barrett, "Presidential Agenda Setting in Congress," in Jon R. Bond and Richard Fleisher, eds., *Polarized Politics* (Washington, DC: Congressional Quarterly Press, 2000).
25. John Kingdon, *Agendas, Alternatives, and Public Policies* (Boston: Little, Brown, 1984), 25. On presidential agenda setting, see Paul C. Light, *The President's Agenda* (Baltimore: Johns Hopkins University Press, 1991); and George C. Edwards III and B. Dan Wood, "Who Influences

Whom?" *American Political Science Review* 93 (June 1999): 327–344.

26. Edwards, *At the Margins*, chaps. 9–10; and Jon R. Bond and Richard Fleisher, *The President in the Legislative Arena* (Chicago: University of Chicago Press, 1990), chap. 8.
27. For an analysis of war powers and other issues related to separation of powers, see Louis Fisher, *Constitutional Conflicts Between Congress and the President*, 4th ed. rev. (Lawrence: University Press of Kansas, 1997); and Louis Fisher, *Presidential War Power* (Lawrence: University Press of Kansas, 1995).
28. See Barbara Hinckley, *Less than Meets the Eye* (Chicago: University of Chicago Press, 1994).
29. The phrase was originated by Aaron Wildavsky in "The Two Presidencies," *TransAction* 4 (December 1966): 7–14. He later determined that the two presidencies applied mostly to the 1950s. See Duane M. Oldfield and Aaron Wildavsky, "Reconsidering the Two Presidencies," in Steven A. Shull, ed., *The Two Presidencies: A Quarter Century Assessment* (Chicago: Nelson-Hall, 1991), 181–190.
30. Edwards, *At the Margins*, chap. 4.
31. See William W. Lammers, "Presidential Attention-Focusing Activities," in Doris A. Graber, ed., in *The President and the Public* (Philadelphia: ISHI, 1982), 145–171; and Samuel Kernell, *Going Public*, 3rd ed. (Washington, D.C.: Congressional Quarterly Press, 1997), chap. 4.
32. Edwards, *The Public Presidency*, chap. 6; and George C. Edwards III, *Presidential Approval* (Baltimore: Johns Hopkins University Press, 1990).
33. Mueller also included the inaugural period of a president's term as a rally event. See John E. Mueller, *War, Presidents and Public Opinion* (New York: Wiley, 1973), 208–213.
34. Kernell, *Going Public*, 169.
35. See Jeffrey K. Tulis, *The Rhetorical Presidency* (Princeton, NJ: Princeton University Press, 1987), on presidents' efforts to build policy support.
36. For a discussion of the social flow of information, see Robert Huckfeldt and John Sprague, "Networks in Context: The Social Flow of Political Information," *American Political Science Review* 81 (December 1987): 1,197–1,216.
37. *Newsweek* Poll, October 28–30, 1994, cited in "The Problem With the President," *Newsweek*, November 7, 1994, 42.
38. George C. Edwards III, "Frustration and Folly: Bill Clinton and the Public Presidency," in Colin Campbell and Bert A. Rockman, eds., *The Clinton Presidency: First Appraisals* (Chatham, NJ: Chatham House, 1995).
39. Useful comparisons over Reagan's tenure can be found in William G. Mayer, *The Changing American Mind* (Ann Arbor: University of Michigan Press, 1992); Benjamin I. Page and Robert Y. Shapiro, *The Rational Public* (Chicago: University of Chicago Press, 1992); and James A. Stimson, *Public Opinion in America: Moods, Cycles, and Swings* (Boulder, CO: Westview, 1991).
40. Quoted in "Tax Cut Passed by Solid Margin in House, Senate," *Congressional Quarterly Weekly Report*, August 1, 1981, 1,374.
41. Sam Donaldson, *Hold On, Mr. President!* (New York: Random House, 1987), 196–197.
42. Two of the leading studies are found in Michael J. Robinson and Margaret A. Sheehan, *Over the Wire and on TV* (New York: Russell Sage Foundation, 1983); and Daniel C. Hallin, "The Media, the War in Vietnam, and Political Support," *Journal of Politics* 46 (February 1984): 2–24.
43. Carter, *Keeping Faith*, 179–180.
44. See Mark J. Rozell, *The Press and the Ford Presidency* (Ann Arbor: University of Michigan Press, 1992).
45. Doris A. Graber, *Mass Media and American Politics*, 5th ed. (Washington, D.C.: Congressional Quarterly Press, 1997), 277. On the 1992 presidential campaign, see "Clinton's the One," *Media Monitor* 6 (November 1992): 3–5.
46. Thomas E. Patterson, *Out of Order* (New York: Knopf, 1993), chap. 3.
47. *Ibid.*, 113.
48. *Media Monitor*, May/June 1995, pp. 2–5; Thomas E. Patterson, "Legitimate Beef: The Presidency and a Carnivorous Press," *Media Studies Journal* (Spring 1994): 21–26; "Sex, Lies, and TV News," *Media Monitor* 12 (September/October 1998); "TV News Coverage of the 1998 Midterm Elections," Media Monitor 12 (November/December 1998). But see Andras Szanto, "In Our Opinion . . . : Editorial Page Views of Clinton's First Year," *Media Studies Journal* (Spring 1994): 97–105.
49. Michael Baruch Grossman and Martha Joynt Kumar, *Portraying the President: The White House and the News Media* (Baltimore: Johns Hopkins University Press, 1981), chaps. 10–11.
50. Donaldson, *Hold On, Mr. President!*, 237–238.
51. Quoted in Eleanor Randolph, "Speakes Aims Final Salvo at White House Practices," *Washington Post*, January 31, 1987, A3.
52. George C. Edwards III, Andrew Barrett, and Jeffrey S. Peake, "The Legislative Impact of Divided Government," *American Journal of Political Science* 41 (April 1997): 545–563.
53. David R. Mayhew, *Divided We Govern* (New Haven, CT: Yale University Press, 1991).

14 The Congress, the President, and the Budget: The Politics of Taxing and Spending

Chapter Outline

Sources of Federal Revenue

Federal Expenditures

The Budgetary Process

Understanding Budgeting

Summary

In 1776 the cry of "no taxation without representation" was enough to spark a revolution. Today issues of taxes and budgetary measures continue to dominate national public policy: How much should we spend to feed the poor, provide health care for the elderly, subsidize student loans, or clean up the environment? And how should we pay for these programs?

In the presidential election of 2000, for example, George W. Bush argued that the budget surplus should be used for a substantial cut in taxes. Al Gore, on the other hand, advocated a more modest tax so we could use the surplus to pay down the national debt and to invest in new or expanded programs.

Politicians who attempt to make tough decisions about the budget risk incurring voters' wrath. In 1985, Republican senators took the lead with a reform that was designed to balance the budget. In the 1986 congressional elections, Republicans lost control of the Senate. In 1990, President George Bush bit the bullet and reversed his pledge not to raise taxes. He

agreed to a budget deal with the congressional Democrats that succeeded in reducing the deficit and limiting spending. In 1992, he lost his bid for reelection.

In 1993, President Clinton followed Bush's precedent and reversed his promise to lower taxes with a program of higher taxes and spending constraints. In the 1994 elections, Republicans won majorities in both houses of Congress for the first time since 1952. They pledged to cut taxes, balance the budget, and reduce expenditures for important social welfare programs. A two-year political battle ensued between congressional Republicans and President Clinton, who vigorously opposed the scope of their proposals. In the end, little changed, and each side vowed to take its case to the American people in the 1996 elections.

The public—which typically seeks a balanced budget, little or no cut in government programs, and tax relief—split its decision. The Democrats won the presidency, but Republicans won both houses of Congress—the only time that had *ever* happened. In the 1998 elections, little changed. It is not surprising, then, that the battle of the budget remains at the center of American politics.

Two questions are central to public policy: *Who bears the burdens of paying for government? Who receives the benefits?* Some observers are concerned that democracy poses a danger to budgeting. Do politicians seek to "buy" votes by spending public funds on things voters will like—and will remember on election day? Or is spending the result of demands made on government services by the many segments of American society? In addition, does the public choose to "soak the rich" with taxes that redistribute income?

Budgets are central to our theme of the scope of government. Indeed, for many programs, budgeting *is* policy. The amount of money spent on a program determines how many people are served, how well they are served, or how much of something (weapons, vaccines, and so on) the government can purchase. The bigger the budget, the bigger the government. But is the growth of the government's budget inevitable? Or are the battles over the allocation of scarce public resources actually a *constraint* on government?

The Constitution allocates various tasks to both the president and Congress, but it generally leaves to each branch the decision of whether to exercise its power to perform a certain task. There is an exception, however. Every year the president and Congress must appropriate funds. If they fail to do so, the government will come to a standstill. The army will be idled, Social Security offices will close, and food stamps will not be distributed to the poor.

Everyone has a basic understanding of budgeting. Public budgets are superficially like personal budgets. Aaron Wildavsky has remarked that a budget is a document that "contains words and figures that propose expenditures for certain objects and purposes." There is more to public budgets than bookkeeping, however, because such a **budget** is a policy document allocating burdens (taxes) and benefits (expenditures). Thus, "budgeting is concerned with translating financial resources into human purposes. A budget therefore may also be characterized as a series of goals with price tags attached."[1]

budget

A policy document allocating burdens (taxes) and benefits (expenditures).

deficit

An excess of federal **expenditures** over federal **revenues.**

expenditures

Federal spending of **revenues.** Major areas of such spending are social services and the military.

revenues

The financial resources of **the federal government.** The individual income tax and Social Security tax are two major sources of revenue.

During the 1980s and 1990s, the national government ran up large annual budget deficits. A budget **deficit** occurs when **expenditures** exceed **revenues** in a fiscal year. In other words, the national government spends more money than it receives in taxes. As a result, the total national debt rose sharply during the 1980s, increasing from less than $1 trillion to about $5.6 trillion by the year 2000. About 10 percent of all current budget expenditures go to paying just the *interest* on this debt.

The president and Congress have often been caught in a budgetary squeeze: Americans want them to balance the budget, maintain or increase the level of government spending on most policies, and keep taxes low. As a result, the president and Congress are preoccupied with budgeting, trying to cope with these contradictory demands.

In this chapter you will learn how the president and Congress produce a budget, making decisions on both taxes and expenditures. In short, you will look at how government manages its money—which is, of course, really *your* money.

Sources of Federal Revenue

"Taxes," said the late Supreme Court Justice Oliver Wendell Holmes, Jr., "are what we pay for civilization." Despite his assertion that "I like to pay taxes," most taxpayers throughout history do not agree. The art of taxation, said Jean-Baptiste Colbert, Louis XIV's finance minister, is in "so plucking the goose as to procure the largest quantity of feathers with the least possible amount of squealing."[2] In Figure 14.1, you can see where the federal government has been getting its feathers. Only a small share comes from excise taxes (a tax levied upon the manufacture, transportation, sale, or consumption of a good—for example, those on gasoline) and other sources; the three major sources of federal revenues are the personal and corporate income tax, social insurance taxes, and borrowing.

Income Tax

Millions of bleary-eyed American taxpayers struggle to the post office before midnight every April 15th to mail their income tax forms. Individuals are required to pay the government a portion of the money they earn; this portion is an **income tax.** Although the government briefly adopted an income tax during the Civil War, the first peacetime income tax was enacted in 1894. Even though the tax was only 2 percent of income earned beyond the then magnificent sum of $4,000, a lawyer opposing it called the tax the first step of a "communist march." The Supreme Court wasted little time in declaring the tax unconstitutional in *Pollock* v. *Farmer's Loan and Trust Co.* (1895).

income tax

Shares of individual wages and corporate revenues collected by the government. The **Sixteenth Amendment** explicitly authorized Congress to levy a tax on income. See also **Internal Revenue Service.**

Sixteenth Amendment

The constitutional amendment adopted in 1915 that explicitly permitted Congress to levy an **income tax.**

In 1913, the **Sixteenth Amendment** was added to the Constitution, explicitly permitting Congress to levy an income tax. Congress was already receiving income tax revenue before the amendment was ratified, however, and the *Internal Revenue*

Figure 14.1 Federal Revenues

About one-half of federal revenues come from individual income taxes. Another third comes from social insurance taxes.

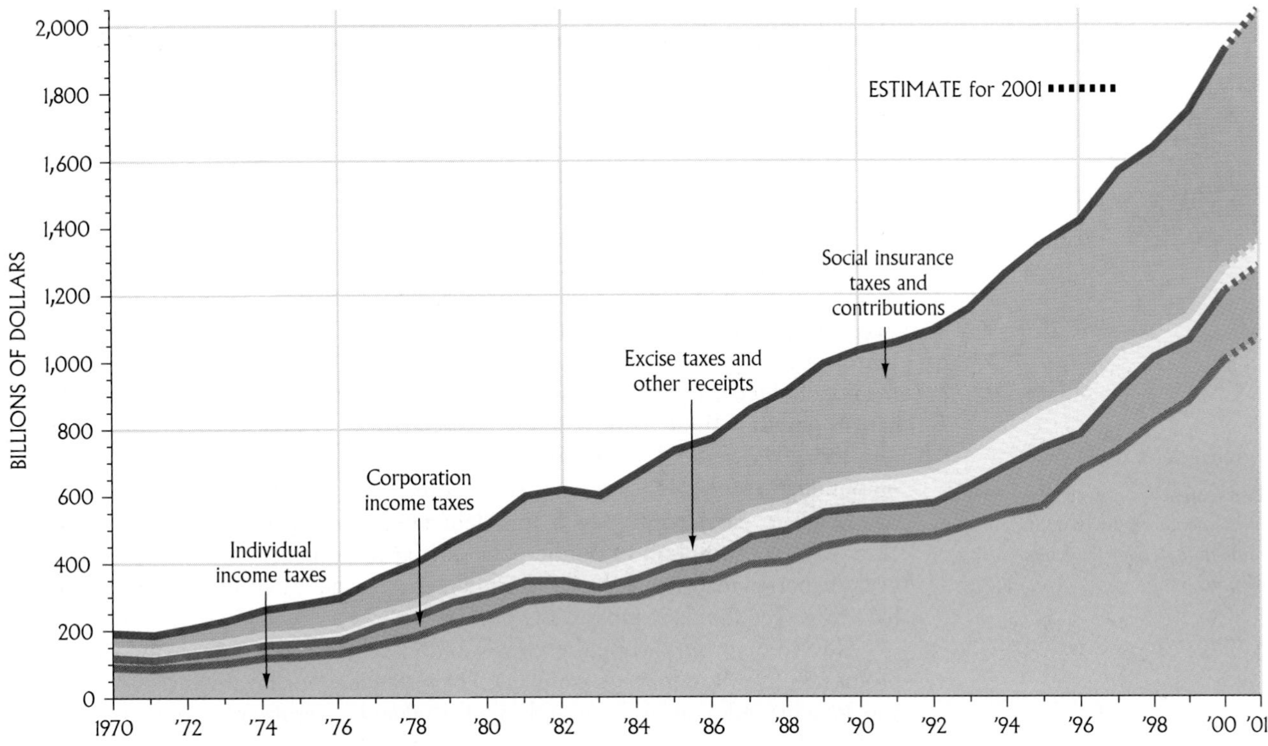

Source: Budget of the United States Government, Fiscal Year 2002: Historical Tables (Washington, D.C.: U.S. Government Printing Office, 2001), Table 2.1.

Service was established to collect it. Today the IRS receives more than 120 million individual tax returns each year. People or computers scrutinize each return. In addition, the IRS audits in greater detail more than a million tax returns, investigates thousands of suspected criminal violations of the tax laws, and annually prosecutes and secures the conviction of thousands of errant taxpayers or nonpayers.[3] Never a popular agency, in recent years the IRS has received substantial criticism for abusing taxpayers with its aggressive efforts to enforce the tax code. In 1998 Congress passed a law designed to rein in the IRS and make it a more consumer-oriented agency.

Corporations, like individuals, pay income taxes. Although corporate taxes once yielded more revenues than individual income taxes, this is no longer true. Today corporate taxes yield about 10 cents of every federal revenue dollar, compared with 50 cents from individual income taxes.

The income tax is generally *progressive*, meaning that those with more income pay higher *rates* of tax on their income. Some people feel that a progressive tax is the fairest type of taxation because those who have the most pay higher rates. Others see things differently and propose a "flat" tax, with everyone taxed at the same rate. Still others suggest that we abandon the income tax altogether and rely on a national sales tax, much like the sales taxes in most states. As you can see, it is easy to criticize the income tax but difficult to obtain agreement on a replacement.

Why does it matter?

The principal source of revenue for the federal government is the income tax, which is progressive in that those with higher incomes typically pay a higher rate of taxes. What if everyone paid the same rate? Would you find it fair to pay taxes at the same rate as a millionaire? If the rate were set at a level you could afford to pay, would there be sufficient revenues to fund critical government programs?

Social Insurance Taxes

Both employers and employees pay Social Security taxes. Money is deducted from employees' paychecks and matched by their employers. Unlike other taxes, these payments do not go into the government's general money fund but are earmarked for a specific purpose: the Social Security Trust Fund that pays benefits to the elderly, the disabled, the widowed, and the unemployed.

Social Security taxes have grown faster than any other source of federal revenue, and they will continue to grow as the population ages. In 1957, these taxes made up a mere 12 percent of federal revenues; today they account for about one-third. In 2001, employees and employers each paid a Social Security tax equal to 6.2 percent of the first $80,400 of earnings, and for Medicare they paid another 1.45 percent on all earnings.

Borrowing

Like families and firms, the federal government may borrow money to make ends meet. When families and firms need money, they go to their neighborhood bank, savings and loan association, or moneylender. When the federal government wants to borrow money, the Treasury Department sells bonds, guaranteeing to pay interest to the bondholder. Citizens, corporations, mutual funds, and other financial institutions can all purchase these bonds; there is always a lively market for government bonds.

federal debt

All the money borrowed by the federal government over the years and still outstanding. Today the federal debt is about $5.6 trillion.

Today the **federal debt**—all the money borrowed over the years that is still outstanding—exceeds $5.6 *trillion* (see Figure 14.2). Ten percent of all federal expenditures go to paying interest on this debt rather than paying for current policies. Yesterday's consumption of public policies is at the expense of tomorrow's taxpayers because borrowing money shifts the burden of repayment to future taxpayers who will have to service the debt and pay the principal.

Government borrowing also crowds out private borrowers, both individuals and businesses, from the loan marketplace. For instance, your local bank may know that you are a low-risk borrower, but it thinks the federal government is an even lower risk.

Figure 14.2 Total National Debt

The national debt climbed steadily throughout the 1980s but leveled off by 2000.

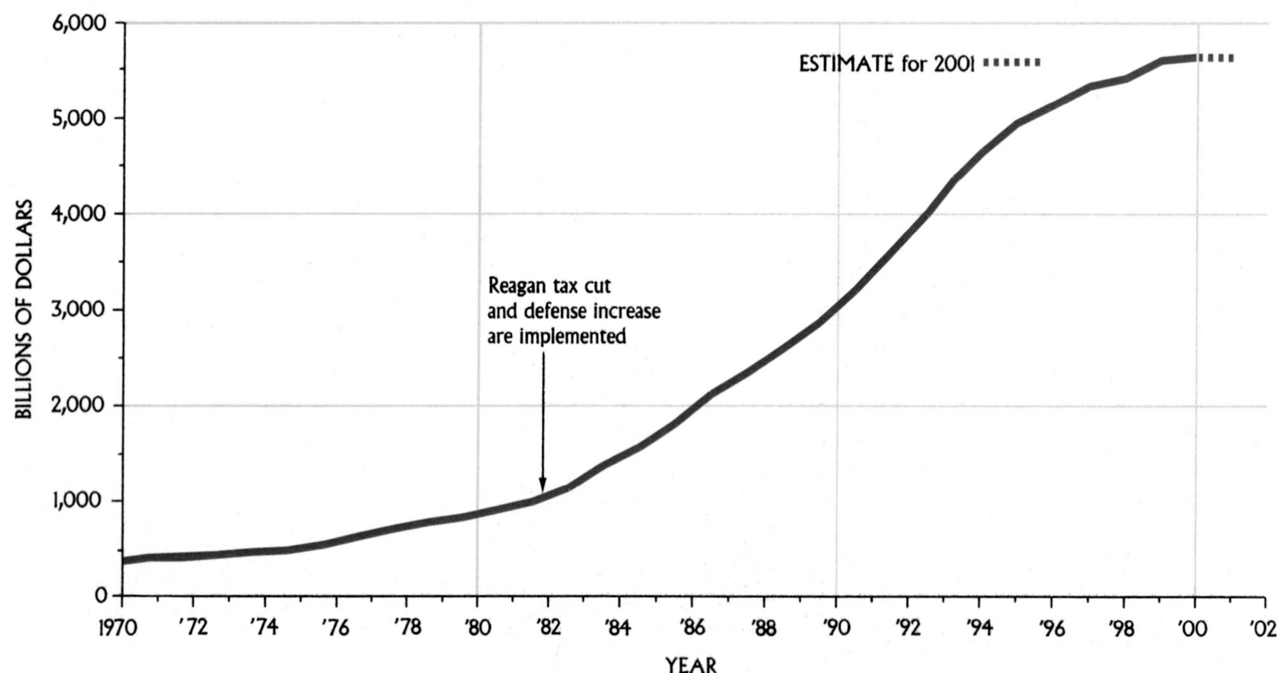

Source: Budget of the United States Government, Fiscal Year 2002: Historical Tables (Washington, D.C.: U.S. Government Printing Office, 2001), Table 7.1.

Over the past 70 years substantial percentage of all the net private savings in the country have gone to the federal government. Large deficits also make the American government dependent on foreign investors, including other governments, to fund its debt—not a favorable position for a superpower. Most economists believe that this competition to borrow money increases interest rates and makes it more difficult for businesses to invest in capital expenditures (such as new plants and equipment) that produce economic growth.

Aside from its impact on private borrowing, federal debt raises additional concerns. Every dollar that the government borrows today will cost taxpayers many more dollars in interest over the next 30 years. Most government borrowing is not for its capital needs (such as a house or a factory) but for its day-to-day expenses. Most families wisely do not borrow money for their food and clothing, yet the government has largely borrowed money for its farm subsidies, its military pensions, and its aid to states and cities.

Most economists and policymakers are concerned about the national debt.[4] The perceived perils of the gigantic deficits of the 1980s and early 1990s led to calls for a *balanced budget amendment.* This proposed amendment to the Constitution would require Congress to balance peacetime federal budgets. Only a supermajority (larger than a simple majority) vote in both houses of Congress could authorize a specific expenditure beyond the government's expected revenues.[5]

Opponents argue that it is difficult to estimate both expenditures and revenues more than a year ahead (if the economy performs worse than expected, for example, revenues go down and expenditures go up). In addition, both Congress and the president could circumvent the intent of the amendment by adjusting economic assumptions or even changing the dates of the fiscal year.

Sometimes we hear politicians complain that because families and businesses and even state and local governments balance their budgets, the federal government ought to be able to do the same. Such statements reflect a fundamental misunderstanding of budgeting, however. Most families do *not* balance their budgets. They use credit cards to give themselves instant loans, and they go to the bank to borrow money to purchase automobiles, boats, and, most important, homes. The mortgages on their homes are debts they owe for most of their lives.

Unlike state and local governments and private businesses, the federal government does not have a *capital budget,* a budget for expenditures on items that will serve for the long term, such as equipment, roads, and buildings. Thus, for example, when airlines purchase new airplanes or when school districts build new schools, they do not pay for them out of current income. Instead, they borrow money, often through

Why does it matter?

The federal government can run a deficit and borrow money to pay its current expenses. States and cities do not have the power to do this. What might be the consequences of amending the Constitution to require a balanced budget? Would your federal tax dollars be spent more efficiently? Or would essential federal policies such as student loans be underfunded? Would your taxes have to be raised as a result?

Because budgetary policy is so important, decision makers may be reluctant to compromise. In 1995–1996, the inability of the president and Congress to reach agreement led to the shutdown of the federal government.

issuing bonds. These debts do not count against the operating budget. When the federal government purchases new jets for the air force or new buildings for medical research, however, these purchases are counted as current expenditures and run up the deficit.

Despite its borrowing habits, most of the government's income still comes from taxes. Few government policies provoke more heated discussion than taxation.

Taxes and Public Policy

No government policy affects as many Americans as tax policy. In addition to raising revenues to finance its services, the government can use taxes to make citizens' incomes more nearly or less nearly equal, to encourage or discourage growth in the economy, and to promote specific interests. Whereas Chapters 17 and 18 discuss how taxes affect economic and equality issues, the following sections focus on how tax policies can promote the interests of particular groups or encourage specific activities.

Tax Loopholes. No discussion of taxes goes very far before the subject of tax loopholes comes up. Difficult to define, a *tax loophole* is presumably a tax break or tax benefit. The IRS Code, which specifies what income is subject to taxation, contains many legal exemptions, deductions, and special cases. Of course, some taxpayers benefit more from these loopholes than others. Jimmy Carter, campaigning for the presidency, called the American tax system a "national disgrace" because of its special treatment of favored taxpayers. Businesspeople, he complained, could deduct costly "three-martini lunches" as business expenses, whereas ordinary workers, carrying coffee in a Thermos and a sandwich to work, cannot write off their lunch expenses.

In 1975, Texas computer magnate and 1992 and 1996 presidential candidate H. Ross Perot hired a former Internal Revenue Service commissioner to lobby for a change in the tax code. The proposed change would have saved Perot $15 million in taxes. The amendment passed through the House Ways and Means Committee (billionaire Perot was reported to be a generous contributor to the campaign chests of several members) but was killed on the House floor when the press reported that only Perot would benefit from the proposed provision.[6]

Tax loopholes may offend Americans' sense of fair play, but they cost the treasury relatively little because they apply to only a few people. Loopholes are actually only one type of tax expenditure.

tax expenditures

Revenue losses that result from special exemptions, exclusions, or deductions on federal tax law.

Tax Expenditures. What does cost the federal budget a substantial sum is the system of **tax expenditures,** defined by the 1974 Budget Act as "revenue losses attributable to provisions of the federal tax laws which allow a special exemption, exclusion, or deduction." These expenditures represent the difference between what the government actually collects in taxes and what it would have collected without special exemptions. Thus tax expenditures amount to subsidies for different activities. For example,

- The government *could* send checks for billions of dollars to charities. Instead, it permits some taxpayers to deduct their contributions to charities from their income, thus the government encourages charitable contributions.
- The government *could* give cash to families with the desire and financial means to buy a home. Instead, it permits homeowners to deduct from their income the billions of dollars they colletively pay each year in mortgage interest.
- The government *could* write a check to all businesses that invest in new plants and equipment. Instead, it allows such businesses to deduct these expenses from their taxes at a more rapid rate than they decuct other expenses. In effect, the owners of these businesses, including stockholders, get a subsidy that is unavailable to owners of other businesses.

Table 14.1 Tax Expenditures: The Money Government Does Not Collect

Tax expenditures are essentially monies that government could collect but does not because they are exempted from taxation. The Office of Management and Budget estimated that the total tax expenditures in 2001 would be nearly $700 billion—about a third of the total federal receipts. Individuals receive most of the tax expenditures, and corporations get the rest. Here are some of the largest tax expenditures and their cost to the treasury:

TAX EXPENDITURE	MAIN BENEFICIARY	COST
Exclusion of company contributions to pension funds	Families	$93 billion
Exclusion of company-paid benefits	Families	$84 billion
Capital gains	Families	$70 billion
Deductions for state and local taxes	Families	$70 billion
Deduction of mortgage interest on owner-occupied houses	Families	$63 billion
Accelerated depreciation	Corporations	$33 billion
Deductions for charitable contributions	Families and corporations	$27 billion
Exclusion for interest earned on state and local government bonds	Families	$23 billion
Exclusion of Social Security benefits	Families	$19 billion
Deferral of capital gains on home sales	Families	$19 billion
Child credit	Families	$19 billion
Exclusion of interest on life insurance savings	Families	$15 billion
Exclusion of Individual Retirement Account contributions and earnings	Families	$16 billion

Government could lower overall tax rates by taxing things it does not currently tax, such as Social Security benefits, pension fund contributions, charitable contributions, and the like. You can easily figure out, though, that these are not popular items to tax, and doing so would evoke strong opposition from powerful interest groups.

Source: Budget of the United States Government, Fiscal Year 2002: Analytical Perspectives (Washington, D.C.: U.S. Government Printing Office, 2001), Table 5-1.

Tax expenditures are among the most obscure aspects of a generally obscure budgetary process, partly because they receive no regular review by Congress—a great advantage for those who benefit from a tax expenditure. Few ordinary citizens seem to realize their scope; you can see the magnitude of tax expenditures in Table 14.1.

On the whole, tax expenditures benefit middle- and upper-income taxpayers and corporations. Poorer people, who tend not to own homes, can take little advantage of provisions that permit homeowners to deduct mortgage interest payments. Likewise, poorer people in general can take less advantage of a deduction for charitable expenses.

To some, tax expenditures such as business-related deductions, tuition tax credits, and capital gains tax rates are loopholes. To others, they are public policy choices that support a social activity worth subsidizing. Either way, they amount to the same thing: revenues that the government loses because certain items are exempted from normal taxation or are taxed at lower rates. The Office of Management and Budget (OMB) estimates that the total tax expenditures equal about one-third of the federal government's total receipts.

Tax Reduction. The annual rite of spring—the preparation of individual tax returns—is invariably accompanied by calls for tax reform and, frequently, tax reduction. Early in his administration, President Reagan proposed a massive tax-cut bill. Standing in the way of tax cuts is never popular, and in July 1981, Congress passed

Reagan's tax-cutting proposal. Over a three-year period, the federal tax bills of Americans were reduced 25 percent, corporate income taxes were also reduced, new tax incentives were provided for personal savings and corporate investment, and taxes were *indexed* to the cost of living. Indexing taxes meant that beginning in 1985, government no longer received a larger share of income when inflation pushed incomes into higher brackets while the tax rates stayed the same. (This point is important because people with high incomes also pay a higher *percentage* of their incomes in taxes.)

Families with high incomes saved many thousands of dollars on taxes, but those at the lower end of the income ladder saw little change in their tax burden because social insurance and excise taxes (which fall disproportionately on these people) rose during the same period. Many blamed the massive deficits of the 1980s and 1990s at least partially on the 1981 tax cuts, as government continued to spend but at the same time reduced its revenues. The appropriate level of taxation remains one of the most vexing problems in American politics (see "America in Perspective: How Much Is Too Much?").

Tax Reform. Gripes about taxes are at least as old in America as the Boston Tea Party. When President Reagan first revealed his massive tax simplification plan in 1985—with its proposals to eliminate many tax deductions and tax expenditures—it was met with howls of protest. The insurance industry, for example, launched a $6 million advertising campaign to save the tax deductions for fringe benefits (much of which are in the form of life and health insurance) that employers set aside for employees. A pitched battle raged between tax reformers and interest groups determined to hold on to their tax benefits.

For once, however, a tax reform plan was not derailed. Democrats, including the powerful chair of the House Ways and Means Committee, Dan Rostenkowski, were enthusiastic about tax reform. They also did not want the Republicans to get all the credit for it. In fact, the president actually had more problems obtaining the support of those in his own party and had to make an unusual trip to Capitol Hill to plead with House Republicans to support the tax bill after its initial defeat when it came to the floor.

The Senate posed an even bigger problem because the bill was loaded with special tax treatments for a wide variety of groups. While the president was on a trip abroad, the Finance Committee met behind closed doors and emerged with a bill similar in spirit to the bill supported by the president and the House. The *Tax Reform Act of 1986* was one of the most sweeping alterations in federal tax policy history. It eliminated or reduced the value of many tax deductions, removed several million low-income individuals from the tax rolls, and reduced the 15 separate tax brackets (categories of income that are taxed at different rates) to just two generally lower rates

simulation
You are Changing Tax Policy

President Reagan signs the Tax Reform Act of 1986, passed with the backing of congressional leaders and administration officials. The legislation—the most wide-ranging reform of federal tax policy since the Sixteenth Amendment legalized income taxes in 1913—was implemented despite protests from numerous interest groups that did not want to lose their tax deductions.

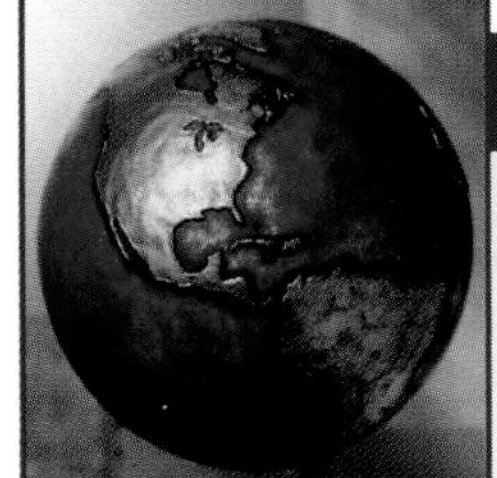

America in Perspective

How Much Is Too Much?

No one likes to pay taxes, and it is common for Americans—and citizens all over the world—to complain that taxes are too high. The figures in the accompanying graph show that the national, state, and local governments in the United States tax a smaller percentage of the resources of the country than do those in almost all other democracies with developed economies. The Scandinavian countries of Sweden, Finland, and Denmark take about half of the wealth of the country in taxes each year.

Comparatively, citizens in the United States have a rather light tax burden. Naturally, tax levels are related to the level of public services that governments provide. If you compare this graph with "America in Perspective: How Big Is Too Big?" (page 448), you will see that the big taxers are also the big spenders.

Source: Organization for Economic Cooperation and Development, 2000.

TOTAL GOVERNMENT TAX REVENUES AS A PERCENTAGE OF THE GROSS DOMESTIC PRODUCT

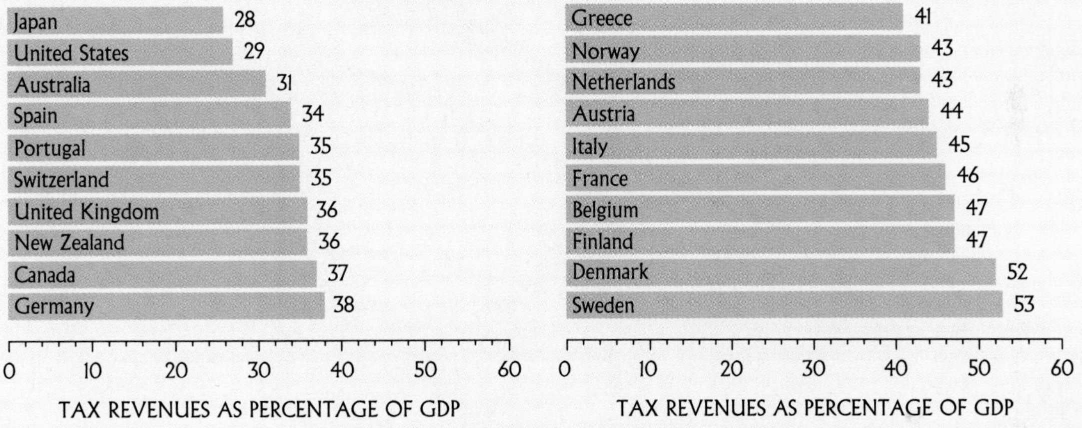

(28 percent and 15 percent). In 1990, a third bracket of 31 percent was added for those with high incomes.

In 1993, Congress agreed to President Clinton's proposal to raise the income tax rate to 36 percent for families with incomes over $140,000 and to add an additional surcharge of 3.6 percent to those families with incomes over $250,000. Congress also increased the top corporate income tax and an energy tax that would be paid by all but those with low incomes.

Federal Expenditures

In 1932, when President Franklin D. Roosevelt took office in the midst of the Great Depression, the federal government was spending just over $3 billion a year. Today, that sum would get the federal government through less than a day. Program costs once measured in the millions are now measured in billions. Comparisons over time are a little misleading, of course, because they do not account for changes in the value of the dollar. You can see in Figure 14.3 how the federal budget has grown in actual dollars (controlling for changes in the value of the dollar).

Figure 14.3 makes two interesting points. First, the policies and programs on which the government spends money change over time. Second, expenditures keep rising. The following sections explore three important questions: Why are government budgets so big? Where does the money go? Why is it difficult to control federal expenditures?

Growth of the Budget and Federal Spending

Figure 14.3 Federal Expenditures

The biggest category of federal expenditures is payments to individuals. National defense accounts for about one-sixth of the budget.

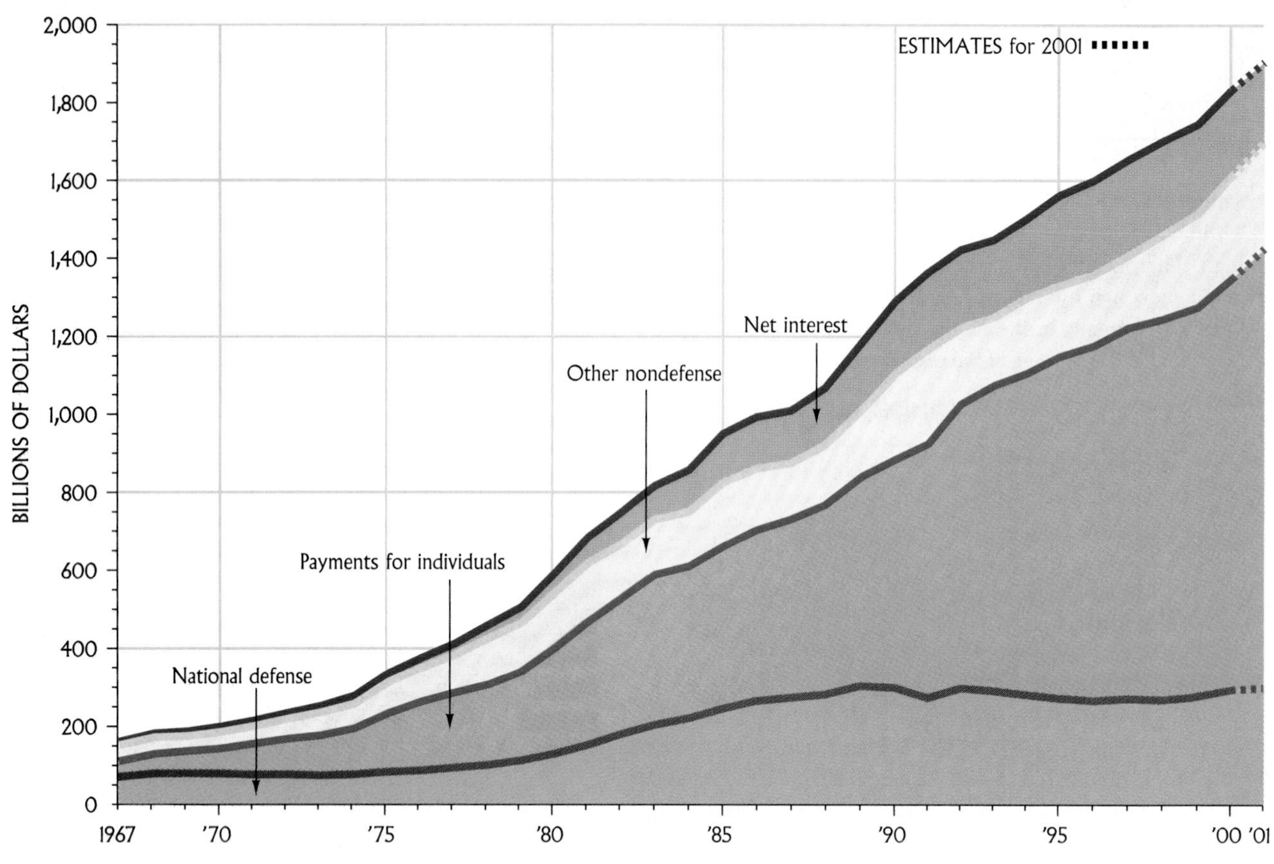

Source: Budget of the United States Government, Fiscal Year 2002: Historical Tables (Washington, D.C.: U.S. Government Printing Office, 2001), Table 6.1.

Big Governments, Big Budgets

One answer to the question of why budgets are so large is simple: Big budgets are necessary to pay for big governments. Among the most important changes of the twentieth century is the rise of large governments.[7] Actually, as you can see in "America in Perspective: How Big Is Too Big?" among Western nations, America has one of the *smallest* public sectors relative to the size of the economy, which is measured as the gross domestic product (GDP). Nevertheless, it is difficult to characterize the national government, with a budget of about $2 trillion per year, as anything but large—some critics would say enormous.

As with other Western nations, the growth of government in the United States has been dramatic. Political scientist E. E. Schattschneider described the small beginnings of American government:

> *President Washington made his budget on a single sheet of paper. Jefferson ran his Department of Foreign Affairs with a staff of six writing clerks. . . . As late as 1822 the government spent $1,000 for the improvement of rivers and harbors and President Monroe vetoed a $9,000 appropriation for the repair of the Cumberland Road.*[8]

This relatively tiny government was, said Schattschneider, the "grain of mustard seed" from which today's huge government has grown. American governments—national, state, and local—spend an amount equal to one-third of the gross domestic product. The national government's expenditures alone equal about 20 percent of the GDP.

Making a Difference

Robert McIntyre

Not long after graduating from law school, Robert McIntyre joined Citizens for Tax Justice (CTJ), a nonpartisan research and advocacy group formed in 1979 to give ordinary people a greater voice in the development of tax laws and to fight against the armies of special interest lobbyists for corporations and the wealthy. It wasn't long before he began to make a difference.

McIntyre spent the summer of 1984 extracting tax data from the annual reports of the nation's largest businesses. He found that 128 large corporations avoided paying federal income taxes in at least one of the three previous years despite earning billions of dollars in profits. Then he named names. CTJ issued a report entitled "The Top Ten Corporate Freeloaders," which was an instant media sensation. Newspapers across the country highlighted stories about freeloaders like General Electric and Anheuser-Busch. The report raised public ire against corporate tax evaders and was a key turning point in the debate over tax reform that led to the Tax Reform Act of 1986.

As Alan Murray of the *Wall Street Journal* put it, unlike corporate tax lobbyists, McIntyre "had no budget to wine and dine anyone. He just kept churning out press releases and lists. He's shown what you can do with a good head, public information, and a personal computer."

McIntyre now is the director of CTJ and frequently testifies before Congress, appears on television, and writes articles for major newspapers and magazines. He continues to raise important questions about tax policies and keeps public officials and private corporations on their toes. Robert McIntyre is making a difference.

Source: Rita McWilliams, "The Best and Worst of Public Interest Groups: From Lifting Up the Poor to Shaking Down the Elderly," *Washington Monthly*, March 1998, 19.

Of course, no one knows for sure exactly why government has grown so rapidly in all the Western democracies. William Berry and David Lowery launched a major investigation into the question, but their findings were mixed. Overall, however, they found that the public sector expands principally in response to the public's preferences and changes in economic and social conditions that affect the public's level of demand for government activity.[9] This is why the rise of big government has been strongly resistant to reversal: Citizens like government services. Even Ronald Reagan, a strong leader with an antigovernment orientation, succeeded only in slowing the growth of government, not in actually trimming its size. When he left office, the federal government employed more people and spent more money than when he was inaugurated.

Two conditions associated with government growth in America are the rise of the national security state and the rise of the social service state.

The Rise and Decline of the National Security State

A generation ago, the most expensive part of the federal budget was not its social services but its military budget. Before World War II, the United States customarily disbanded a large part of its military forces at the end of a war. After World War II, however, the "Cold War" with the Soviet Union resulted in a permanent military establishment and expensive military technology. Fueling the military machine greatly increased the cost of government. It was President Eisenhower—not some liberal antimilitary activist—who coined the phrase *military industrial complex* to characterize the close relationship between the military hierarchy and the defense industry that supplies its hardware needs.

In the 1950s and early 1960s, spending for past and present wars amounted to more than half the federal budget. The Department of Defense received the majority of federal dollars. Liberals complained that government was shortchanging the poor

America in Perspective

How Big Is Too Big?

When one hears about trillion-dollar federal budgets and budget deficits that may run $200 billion in a single year, it's easy to think of "big government." The figures in the accompanying graph, however, show that the national, state, and local governments in the United States actually spend a smaller percentage of their country's resources than those in most other democracies with developed economies. All the major Western democracies devote a considerably larger share of their wealth to government services, with Sweden spending two out of every three dollars in the economy on government programs. Compared with these countries, the United States has a rather modest public sector.

Source: Organization for Economic Cooperation and Development, *National Accounts,* 44–47, Paris, 1998.

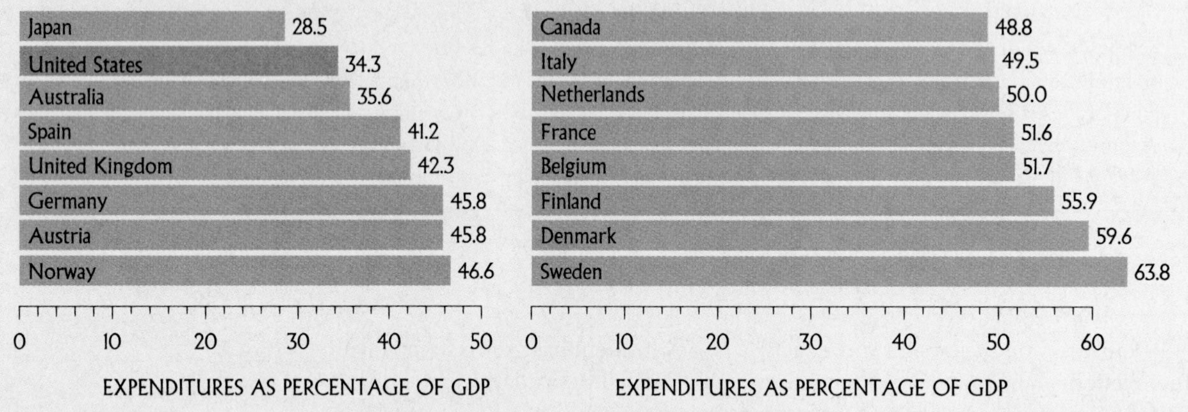

while lining the pockets of defense contractors. Things soon changed, however. Over 15 years, from the mid-1960s to the early 1980s, defense expenditures crept downward in real dollars while social welfare expenditures more than doubled.

Although President Reagan proposed eliminating scores of domestic programs in his annual budget requests, he also urged Congress to increase the defense budget substantially. Throughout his entire second term, Congress balked, however, and in the 1990s defense expenditures decreased in response to the lessening tensions in Europe (discussed in Chapter 20). The budget of the Department of Defense, once the driving force in the expansion of the federal budget, now constitutes only about one-sixth of all federal expenditures (see Figure 14.4).

Payrolls and pensions for the 2.1 million Pentagon employees, the 865,000 reservists, the 1.7 million people who receive military retirement pay, and the 3.3 million veterans who receive pensions and disability compensation constitute a large component of the defense budget. So do the research, development, and *procurement* (purchasing) of military hardware. The costs of procurement are high, even though total military expenditures have declined as a percentage of American GDP since the end of World War II. The cost of advanced technology makes any weapon, fighter plane, or component more expensive than its predecessors. Moreover, cost overruns are common. The American fleet of Stealth bombers will cost several times the original estimate—over a *billion* dollars each. According to former Secretary of the Air Force Edward C. Aldridge, "Whatever it costs, it's worth it."[10] Many critics of such expensive military hardware disagree.

Figure 14.4 Trends in National Defense Spending

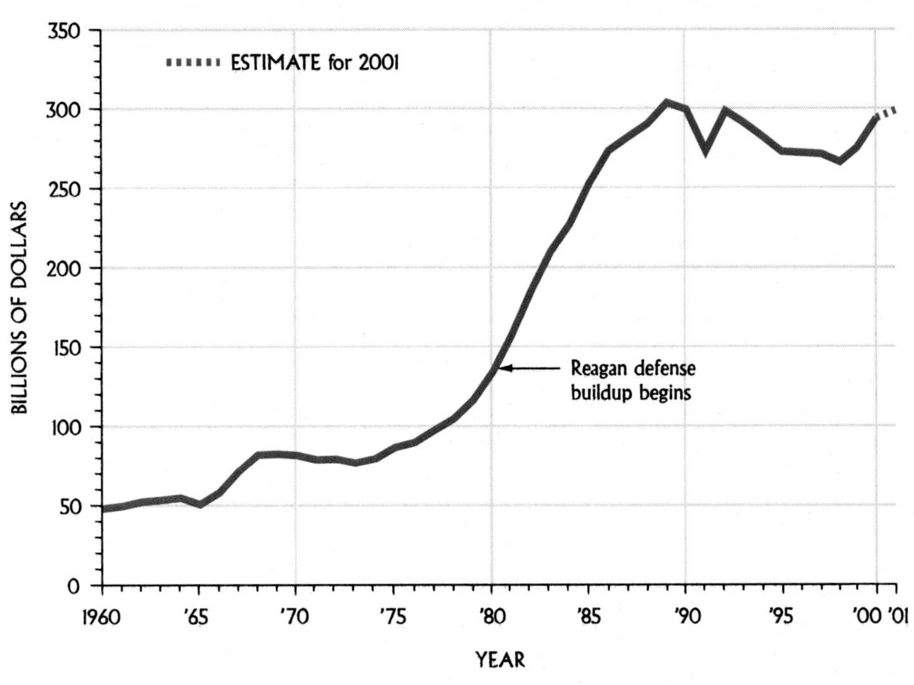

Defense expenditures increased rapidly during the Reagan administration, but they declined with the end of the Cold War.

Source: Budget of the United States Government, Fiscal Year 2002: Historical Tables (Washington, D.C.: U.S. Government Printing Office, 2001), Table 3.1.

The Rise of the Social Service State

The biggest slice of the budget pie, once reserved for defense, now belongs to *income security* expenditures, a bundle of policies extending direct and indirect aid to the elderly, the poor, and the needy. In 1935, during the Great Depression and the administration of President Franklin D. Roosevelt, Congress passed the **Social Security Act.** The act was intended to provide a minimal level of sustenance to older Americans, saving them from poverty.

Social Security Act

A 1935 law passed during the Great Depression that was intended to provide a minimal level of sustenance to older Americans and thus save them from poverty.

The U.S. Air Force unveiled its new Stealth Bomber in 1989. The plane's unusual shape allows it to fly undetected by enemy radar, but such technology costs money—over $1 billion per plane. These huge expenditures contributed to substantial increases in the defense budget in the 1980's.

In January 1940, the treasurer of the United States sent the nation's first Social Security check to Ida Fuller of Brattleboro, Vt. in the amount of $22.54. An early entrant into the fledgling Social Security program, Fuller had contributed less than the amount of her first check to the system. By the time she died in December 1974 at the age of 100, she had collected $20,944.42 from the Social Security Administration. These days, nearly 45 million Americans receive payments from the Social Security system each month. The typical retired worker received about $825 a month in 2001.

In the 1950s, disability insurance became a part of the Social Security program; thus, workers who had not retired but who were disabled could also collect benefits. In 1965, **Medicare,** which provides both hospital and physician coverage to the elderly, was added to the system. Although most Social Security checks go to retired workers, many also go to the disabled, to Medicare patients, and to widows and widowers of workers.

Medicare

A program added to the Social Security system in 1965 that provides hospitalization insurance for the elderly and permits older Americans to purchase inexpensive coverage for doctor fees and other health expenses.

Social Security is less an insurance program than a kind of intergenerational contract. Essentially, money is taken from the working members of the population and spent on the retired members. Today, however, demographic and economic realities threaten to dilute this intergenerational relationship. In 1940, the entire Social Security system was financed with a 3 percent tax on payrolls; by 1990, the tax exceeded 15 percent. In 1945, 50 workers paid taxes to support each Social Security beneficiary. In 1990, about three workers supported each beneficiary. By the year 2040, when today's young college students will be getting their Social Security checks, only two workers will be supporting each beneficiary.

Not surprisingly, by the early 1980s the Social Security program faced a problem. As Paul Light candidly described the problem: "It was going broke fast. More money was going out in benefits than was coming in. . . . At the height of the crisis, social security was spending about $3,000 more per minute than it was taking in."[11] And that was only the short-term problem. The aging population has added more people to the Social Security rolls annually; once there, people tend to stay on the rolls because life expectancies are increasing. Congress responded by increasing social insurance taxes so that more was coming in to the Social Security Trust Fund than was being spent. The goal was to create a surplus to help finance payments when the baby boomers retire.

In 1999, President Clinton made financing Social Security his highest priority. He proposed allocating much of the new budget surplus to Social Security and investing some of it in the stock market. Everyone agreed that saving Social Security was a high

Lyndon Johnson's "Great Society" initiatives in the mid-1960s greatly expanded America's social services network, adding Medicare and Medicaid to the Social Security system and creating many new programs designed to aid the poor. Here, LBJ campaigns during the 1964 presidential election.

Figure 14.5 Trends in Social Service Spending

Social Service spending has increased rapidly since the 1960s.

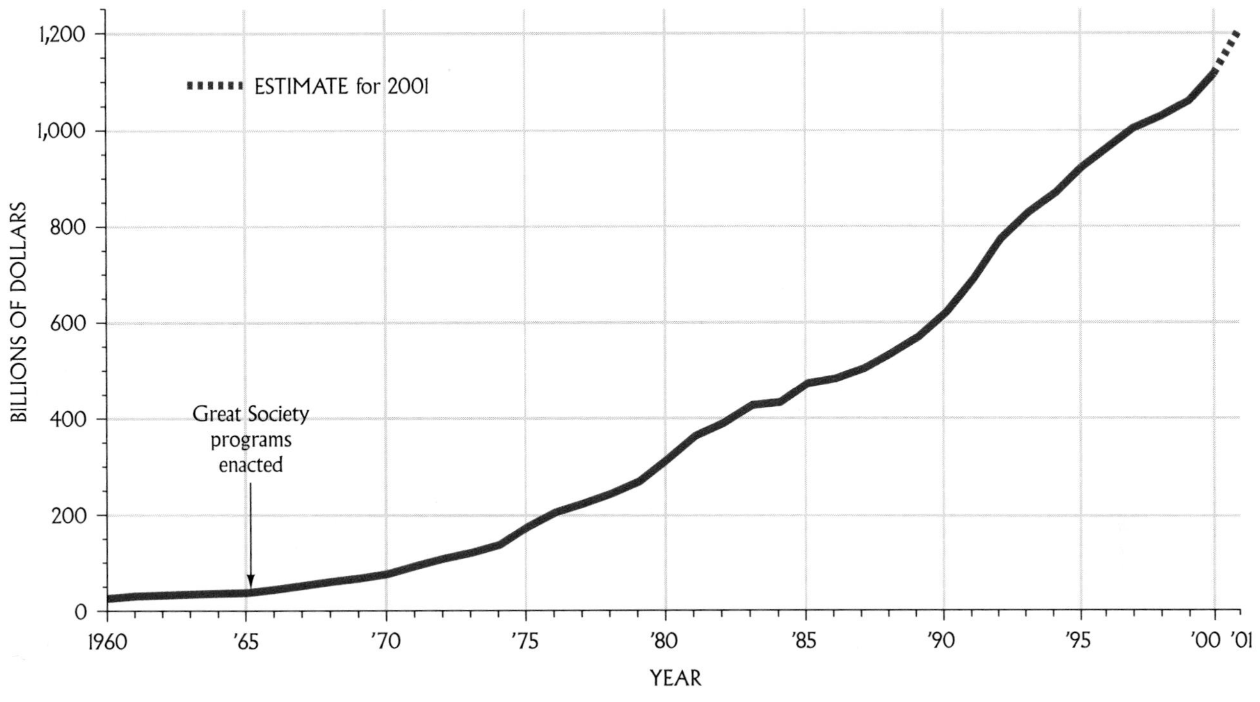

Source: Budget of the United States Government, Fiscal Year 2002: Historical Tables (Washington, D.C.: U.S. Government Printing Office, 2001), Table 3.1

priority, but not everyone agreed with the president's solutions. As a result, no major changes occurred.

Social Security is the largest social policy of the federal government (Social Security and Medicare account for about one-third of the federal budget). However, other social service expenditures have paralleled the upward growth of income security. In health, education, job training, and many other areas, the rise of the social service state has also contributed to America's growing budget. No brief list can do justice to the range of government social programs, which provide funds for the elderly, businesses run by minority entrepreneurs, consumer education, drug rehabilitation, environmental education, food subsidies for the poor, guaranteed loans to college students, housing allowances for the poor, inspections of hospitals, and so on. Liberals often favor these programs to assist individuals and groups in society; conservatives see them as a drain on the federal treasury. In any event, they cost money—a lot of it (see Figure 14.5).

visual literacy
Evaluating Federal Spending and Economic Policy

The rise of the social service state and the national security state are linked with much of American governmental growth since the end of World War II. Although American social services expanded less than similar services in Western European nations, for most of the postwar period American military expenditures expanded more rapidly. Together, these factors help explain why the budget is the center of attention in American governmnt today. Why is it so difficult to bring this increasing federal budget under control?

Incrementalism

Sometimes political scientists use the term *incrementalism* to describe the spending and appropriations process. **Incrementalism** means simply that the best predictor of this year's budget is last year's budget plus a little bit more (an increment). According to Wildavsky and Caiden, "The largest determining factor of the size and content of

incrementalism

The belief that the best predictor of this year's **budget** is last year's budget, plus a little bit more (an increment). According to Aaron Wildavsky, "Most of the budget is a product of previous decisions."

this year's budget is last year's. Most of each budget is a product of previous decisions."[12] Incremental budgeting has several features:

- Very little attention is focused on the budgetary base—the amounts agencies have had over the previous years.
- Usually, agencies can safely assume they will get at least the budget they had the previous year.
- Most of the debate and most of the attention of the budgetary process are focused on the proposed increment.
- The budget for any given agency tends to grow by a little bit every year.

This picture of the federal budget is one of constant growth. Expenditures mandated by an existing law or obligation (such as Social Security) are particularly likely to follow a neat pattern of increase.[13] There are exceptions, however. Paul Schulman observed that budgets for the National Aeronautics and Space Administration (NASA) were hardly incremental; they initially rose as fast as a NASA rocket but later plummeted to a fraction of their former size.[14] Incrementalism may be a general tendency of the budget, but it does not fully describe all budgetary politics.

Because so much of the budgetary process looks incremental, there is a never-ending call for budgetary reform. The idea is always to make it easier to compare programs so that the "most deserving" ones can be supported and the "wasteful" ones cut. Nevertheless, the budgetary process, like all aspects of government, is affected by groups with interests in taxes and expenditures. These interests make it difficult to pare the budget. In addition, the budget is too big to review from scratch each year, even for the most systematic and conscientious members of Congress. The federal budget is a massive document, detailing annual outlays larger than the entire economies of individual countries except those of the United States, Japan, and Russia. Although efforts to check incrementalism have failed, so have attempts to reduce more rapidly rising expenses. Much of the federal budget has become "uncontrollable."

"Uncontrollable" Expenditures

At first glance, it is hard to see how one could call the federal budget uncontrollable. After all, Congress has the constitutional authority to budget—to add or subtract money from an agency. Indeed, Presidents Reagan, Bush, and Clinton proposed and Congress adopted some proposals to cut the growth of government spending. How, then, can one speak of an uncontrollable budget?

Consider for a moment what we might call the "allowance theory" of the budget. Using this theory, a government budget works like an allowance. Mom and Dad hand over to Mary Jean and Tommy a monthly allowance, say $10 each, with the stern admonition, "Make that last to the end of the month because that's all we're giving you until then." In the allowance model of the budget, Congress plays this parental role; the agencies play the roles of Mary Jean and Tommy. Congress thus allocates a lump sum—say, $5.2 billion—and instructs agencies to meet their payrolls and other expenses throughout the fiscal year. When most Americans think of the government's budget, they envision the budget as a kind of allowance to the agencies.

uncontrollable expenditures

Expenditures that are determined not by a fixed amount of money appropriated by Congress but by how many eligible beneficiaries there are for a program or by previous obligations of the government.

entitlements

Policies for which Congress has obligated itself to pay X level of benefits to Y number of recipients. Social Security benefits are an example.

About two-thirds of the government's budget, however, does not work this way at all. **Uncontrollable expenditures** result from policies that make some group automatically eligible for some benefit or by previous obligations of the government, such as pensions and interest on the national debt. The government does not decide each year, for example, whether it will pay the interest on the federal debt, or that it will chop the pensions earned by former military personnel in half.

Many expenditures are uncontrollable because Congress has in effect obligated itself to pay X level of benefits to Y number of recipients. Congress writes the eligibility rules; the number of people eligible and their level of guaranteed benefits determine how much Congress must spend. Such policies are called **entitlements,** and they range from agricultural subsidies to veterans' aid. Each year, Congress's bill is a straightforward function of the X level of benefits times the Y beneficiaries. The biggest uncontrollable expenditure of all is the Social Security system, including Medicare, which costs more than $600 billion per year. The Social Security Administration does not merely provide benefits on a first-come, first-served basis until the money runs out. Instead, eligible individuals automatically receive Social Security payments. Of course, Congress can, if it desires, cut the benefits or tighten eligibility restrictions. Doing so, however, would provoke a monumental outcry from millions of elderly voters.

Why does it matter?

Much of the federal budget is "uncontrollable" in the sense that it does not come up for reauthorization on a regular basis. What if entitlement programs were subject to annual authorizations as most other programs are? Would they be endangered? Would we spend less money on them and more on other services? How would you feel about annual authorizations if you were receiving Social Security benefits?

The Budgetary Process

Budgets are produced through a long and complex process that starts and ends with the president and has the Congress squarely in the middle. Because budgets are so important to almost all other policies, the budgetary process is the center of political battles in Washington and involves nearly everyone in government.

Figure 14.6 gives a quick overview of the federal budget. It offers a simplified picture of the two sides of the budgetary coin, revenues and expenditures. The distribution of the government's budget is the outcome of a very complex budgetary process. Nestled inside the tax and expenditures figures are thousands of policy choices, each prompting plenty of politics.

Budgetary Politics

Public budgets are the supreme example of Harold Lasswell's definition of politics as "who gets what, when, and how." Budget battles are fought over contending interests, ideologies, programs, and agencies.

Stakes and Strategies. Every political actor has a stake in the budget. Mayors want to keep federal grants-in-aid flowing in; defense contractors like a big defense budget; scientists push for a large budget for the National Science Foundation. Agencies within the government also work to protect their interests. Individual members of Congress act as policy entrepreneurs for new ideas and support constituent benefits, both of which cost money. Presidents try to use budgets to manage the economy and leave their imprint on Congress's policy agenda.

Think of budgetary politics as resembling a game in which players choose among strategies.[15] Agencies pushing their budgetary needs to the president and Congress, for instance, try to link the benefits of their program to a senator's or representative's electoral needs.[16] Almost invariably, agencies pad their requests a bit, hoping that the almost inevitable cuts will be bearable. President John Adams justified this now common

Figure 14.6 The Federal Government Dollar (Fiscal Year 2002 Estimate)

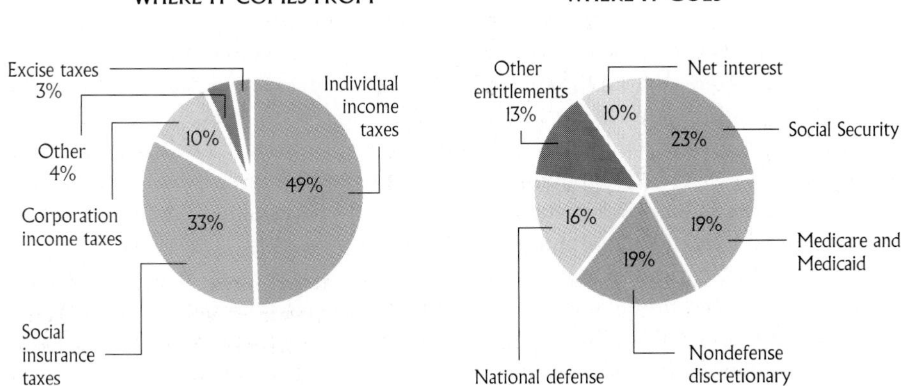

Source: Budget of the United States Government, Fiscal Year 2002: A Citizen's Guide to the Federal Budget (Washington, D.C.: U.S. Government Printing Office, 2001), 5,9.

budgetary gambit by saying to his cabinet, "If some superfluity not be given Congress to lop off, they will cut into the very flesh of the public necessities." Interest groups try to identify their favorite programs with the national interest. Mayors tell Congress not how much they like to receive federal aid but how crucial cities are to national survival. Farmers stress not that they like federal aid but that feeding a hungry nation and world is the main task of American agriculture. In the game of budgetary politics, there are plenty of players, each with their own strategies.

The Players. Deciding how to carve up more than one-fifth of the GDP is a process likely to attract plenty of interest—from those formally required to participate in the budgeting process as well as those whose stakes are too big to ignore it. Here are the main actors in the budgetary process:

- *The interest groups.* No lobbyist worth his or her pay would ignore the budget. Lobbying for a group's needs takes place in the agencies, with presidents (if the lobbyist has access to them), and before congressional committees. A smart agency head will be sure to involve interest groups in defending the agency's budget request.
- *The agencies.* Convinced of the importance of their mission, the heads of agencies almost always push for higher budget requests. They send their requests to the Office of Management and Budget and later get a chance to present themselves before congressional committees as well.[17]
- *The Office of Management and Budget (OMB).* The OMB is responsible to the president, its boss, but no president has the time to understand and make decisions about the billions of dollars in the budget—parceled out to hundreds of agencies, some of which the chief executive knows little or nothing about. The director and staff of the OMB have considerable independence from the president, which makes them major actors in the annual budget process.
- *The president.* The president makes the final decisions on what to propose to Congress. In early February, the president unveils the proposed budget; the president then spends many a day trying to ensure that Congress will stick close to the recommendations.
- *The Tax Committees in Congress.* The government cannot spend money it does not have. The **House Ways and Means Committee** and the **Senate Finance Committee** write the tax codes, subject to the approval of Congress as a whole.
- *The Budget Committees and the Congressional Budget Office (CBO).* The CBO—which is the congressional equivalent of the OMB—and its parent committees, the Senate and House Budget Committees, set the parameters of the congressional budget process through examining revenues and expenditures in the aggregate and proposing resolutions to bind Congress within certain limits.
- *The subject-matter committees.* Committees of Congress, ranging from Agriculture to Veterans' Affairs, write new laws, which require new expenditures. Committee members may use hearings either to publicize the accomplishments of their pet agencies, thus supporting larger budgets for them, or to question agency heads about waste or overspending.
- *The Appropriations Committees and their subcommittees.* The Appropriations Committee in each house decides who gets what. These committees take new or old policies coming from the subject-matter committees and decide how much to spend. Appropriations subcommittees hold hearings on specific agency requests.
- *The Congress as a whole.* The Constitution requires that Congress as a whole approve taxes and appropriations, and senators and representatives alike have a strong interest in delivering federal dollars to their constituents. A dam here, a military base there, and a job-training program somewhere else—these are items that members look for in the budget.
- *The General Accounting Office (GAO).* Congress's role does not end when it has passed the budget. The GAO works as Congress's eyes and ears, auditing, monitoring, and evaluating what agencies are doing with their budgets.

House Ways and Means Committee

The House of Representatives committee that, along with the **Senate Finance Committee**, writes the tax codes, subject to the approval of Congress as a whole.

Senate Finance Committee

The Senate committee that, along with the **House Ways and Means Committee**, writes the tax codes, subject to the approval of Congress as a whole.

Budgeting involves a cast of thousands. However, their roles are carefully scripted and their time on stage is limited because budget making is both repetitive (the same things must be done each year) and sequential (actions must occur in the proper order and more or less on time). The budget cycle begins in the executive branch a full 19 months before the fiscal year begins.

The President's Budget

Until 1921, the various agencies of the executive branch sent their budget requests to the secretary of the treasury, who in turn forwarded them to the Congress. Presidents played a limited role in proposing the budget; sometimes they played no role at all. Agencies basically peddled their own budget requests to Congress. In 1921 Congress, concerned about retiring the debt the country had accumulated during World War I, passed the Budget and Accounting Act, which required presidents to propose an executive budget to Congress, and created the Bureau of the Budget to help them. In the 1970s, President Nixon reorganized the Bureau of the Budget and gave it a new name, the Office of Management and Budget (OMB). The OMB, whose director is a presidential appointee requiring Senate approval, now supervises preparation of the federal budget and advises the president on budgetary matters.

It takes a long time to prepare a presidential budget.[18] By law, the president must submit a budget by the first Monday in February. The process begins almost a year before (see Table 14.2), when the OMB communicates with each agency, sounding out its requests and tentatively issuing guidelines. By the summer, the president has decided on overall policies and priorities and has established general targets for the budget. These are then communicated to the agencies.

The budget makers now get down to details. During the fall, the agencies submit formal, detailed estimates for their budgets, zealously pushing their needs to the OMB. Budget analysts at the OMB pare, investigate, weigh, and meet on agency requests.

Table 14.2 The President's Budget: An Approximate Schedule

Spring Budget policy developed	The OMB presents the president with an analysis of the economic situation, and they discuss the budgetary outlook and policies. The OMB then gives guidelines to the agencies, which in turn review current programs and submit to the OMB their projections of budgetary needs for the coming year. The OMB reviews these projections and prepares recommendations to the president on final policy, programs, and budget levels. The president establishes guidelines and targets.
Summer Agency estimates submitted	The OMB conveys the president's decisions to the agencies and advises and assists them in preparing their budgets.
Fall Estimates reviewed	The agencies submit to the OMB formal budget estimates for the coming fiscal year, along with projections for future years. The OMB holds hearings, reviews its assessment of the economy, and prepares budget recommendations for the president. The president reviews these recommendations and decides on the agencies' budgets and overall budgetary policy. The OMB advises the agencies of these decisions.
Winter President's budget determined and submitted	The agencies revise their estimates to conform with the president's submitted decisions. The OMB once again reviews the economy and then drafts the president's budget message and prepares the budget document. The president revises and approves the budget message and transmits the budget document to Congress.

Typically, the agency heads ask for hefty increases; sometimes they threaten to go directly to the president if their priorities are not met by the OMB. As the Washington winter sets in, the budget document is readied for final presidential approval. There is usually some last-minute juggling—agencies may be asked to change their estimates to conform with the president's decisions, or cabinet members may make a last-ditch effort to bypass the OMB and convince the president to increase their funds. With only days—or hours—left before the submission deadline, the budget document is rushed to the printers. Then the president sends it to Capitol Hill. The next steps are up to Congress.

Congress and the Budget

According to the Constitution, Congress must authorize all federal appropriations. Thus, Congress always holds one extremely powerful trump card in national policymaking: the power of the purse.[19] Congress decides how to spend nearly $2 trillion each year.

Reforming the Process. For years Congress budgeted in a piecemeal fashion. A subcommittee of the House and Senate Appropriations Committees handled each agency request; then all these appropriations were added to produce a total budget. People never quite knew what the budget's bottom line would be until all the individual bills were totaled up. What Congress spent had little to do with any overall judgment of how much it should spend.

Congressional Budget and Impoundment Control Act of 1974

An act designed to reform the congressional budgetary process. Its supporters hoped that it would also make Congress less dependent on the president's budget and better able to set and meet its own budgetary goals.

The **Congressional Budget and Impoundment Control Act of 1974** was designed to reform the congressional budgetary process. Its supporters hoped that it would also make Congress less dependent on the president's budget and more able to set and meet its own budgetary goals. The act established:

- A *fixed budget calendar.* Each step in the budgetary process has an established completion date. In the past, Congress sometimes failed to appropriate money to agencies until after the fiscal year was over, leaving agencies drifting for months with no firm budget. Now there is a timetable mandated by law, which has been amended several times (see Table 14.3).
- A *budget committee in each house.* These two committees are supposed to recommend target figures to Congress for the total budget size by April 1 of each year. By April 15, Congress is to agree on the *total* size of the budget, which guides the Appropriations Committee to juggling figures for individual agencies.
- A *Congressional Budget Office.* **The Congressional Budget Office (CBO)** advises Congress on the probable consequences of its budget decisions, forecasts revenues, and is a counterweight to the president's OMB.

One purpose of the new budgeting system was to force Congress to consider the budget (both projected expenditures and projected revenues) as a whole, rather than in bits and pieces as it had done before. An important part of the process of establishing a budget is to set limits on expenditures on the basis of revenue projections—a step that is supposed to be done through a **budget resolution.** Thus, in April of each year, both houses are expected to agree on a budget resolution—thereby binding Congress to a total expenditure level that should form the bottom line of all federal spending for all programs. Only then is Congress supposed to begin acting on the individual appropriations.

budget resolution

A resolution binding Congress to a total expenditure level, supposedly the bottom line of all federal spending for all programs.

In terms of a family budget, Family A might decide to budget by adding up all its needs and wants and calling that its budget. Such a strategy almost guarantees overspending the family income. Family B, though, might begin by looking first at its revenue and then trying to bring its total expenditures into line with its revenue before dealing with its individual expenditure decisions. With its 1974 reforms, Congress was trying to force itself to behave more like Family B than Family A.

Table 14.3 The Congressional Budget Process: Targets and Timetables

DATE	ACTION TO BE COMPLETED
First Monday in February	Congress receives the president's budget.
February 15	The CBO submits a budget report to the House and Senate Budget Committees, including an analysis of the president's budget.
February 25	Other committees submit reports on outlays and revenues to Budget Committees in each house.
April 1	Budget Committees report concurrent resolution on the budget, which sets a total for budget outlays, an estimate of expenditures for major budget categories, and the recommended level of revenues. This resolution acts as an agenda for the remainder of the budgetary process.
April 15	Congress completes action on concurrent resolution on the budget.
May 15	Annual appropriations bills may be considered in the House.
June 10	House Appropriations Committee reports last annual appropriations bill.
June 15	Congress completes action on reconciliation legislation, bringing budget totals into conformity with established ceilings.
June 30	House completes action on annual appropriation bills.
October 1	The new fiscal year begins.

Source: From Howard E. Shuman, *Politics and the Budget*, 3rd ed. (Englewood Cliffs, NJ: Prentice-Hall, 1992), 67.

Like the president's budget proposal, the congressional budget resolution often requests that certain changes be made in law, primarily to achieve savings incorporated into the spending totals and thus meet the budget resolution. These changes are legislated in two separate ways.

First is budget **reconciliation,** a process by which program authorizations are revised to achieve required savings; it frequently also includes tax or other revenue adjustments. Usually reconciliation comes near the end of the budgetary process. However, in an attempt to strike while his political standing was high and to overcome the opposition of special interests and the parochialism and power of congressional committees, President Reagan in 1981 successfully proposed using an extremely complex reconciliation bill to reduce the budget by approximately $40 billion. Reagan thought that he could obtain substantial cuts only if he lumped them all together in one bill in which everyone lost something. The preparation of the bill was so hurried that few members of Congress could give it serious consideration.

reconciliation

A congressional process through which program authorizations are revised to achieve required savings. It usually also includes tax or other revenue adjustments.

The second way that laws are changed to meet the budget resolution (or to create or change programs for other reasons) involves more narrowly drawn legislation. An **authorization bill** is an act of Congress that establishes a discretionary government program or an entitlement, or that continues or changes such programs. Authorizations specify program goals and, for discretionary programs, set the maximum amount that they may spend. For entitlement programs, an authorization sets or changes eligibility standards and benefits that must be provided by the program. Authorizations may be for one year, or they may run for a specified or indefinite number of years.

authorization bill

An act of Congress that establishes, continues, or changes a discretionary government program or an entitlement. It specifies program goals and maximum expenditures for discretionary programs.

An additional measure, termed an **appropriations bill,** must be passed to fund programs established by authorization bills. Appropriations bills usually fund programs for one year and cannot exceed the amount of money authorized for a program; in fact, they may appropriate *less* than was authorized.

appropriations bill

An act of Congress that actually funds programs within limits established by authorization bills. Appropriations usually cover one year.

The Success of the 1974 Reforms. Have these reforms worked? If *worked* means that Congress has brought its spending into line with its revenues, then the reforms have been almost a total failure. Congressional budgets were in the red every year between the 1974 amendments and 1998. In fact, the red ink grew from a puddle to an ocean (see Figure 14.7). Presidents made matters worse, submitting budget proposals that contained large deficits.

In addition, Congress has often failed to meet its own budgetary timetable. There has been too much conflict over the budget for the system to work according to design. Moreover, in many instances Congress has not been able to reach agreement and pass appropriations bills at all and has instead resorted to **continuing resolutions**—laws that allow agencies to spend at the previous year's level. Sometimes, as in 1986 and 1987, appropriations bills have been lumped together in one enormous and complex bill (rather than in the 13 separate appropriations bills that are supposed to pass), precluding adequate review by individual members of Congress and forcing the president either to accept unwanted provisions or to veto the funding for the entire government. These omnibus bills in 1986 and 1987 also became magnets for unrelated and controversial pieces of legislation that could not pass on their own.

continuing resolutions

When Congress cannot reach agreement and pass appropriations bills, these resolutions allow agencies to spend at the level of the previous year.

On the other hand, the 1974 reforms have helped Congress view the entire budget early in the process; now Congress can at least see the forest as well as the trees. The problem is not so much the procedure as disagreement over how scarce resources should be spent—or whether they should be spent at all.

More Reforms. By 1985 Congress was desperate. President Reagan refused to consider tax increases to pay for federal spending and continued to submit budgets that contained huge deficits. In response to growing frustration at its inability to reduce annual budget deficits substantially, Congress enacted the Balanced Budget and

Figure 14.7 Annual Federal Deficits

Yearly deficits mushroomed during the Reagan Administration (1981–1988), despite the president's oft-repeated commitment to a balanced budget. The deficit disappeared during the Clinton Administration, and the nation began running a surplus in fiscal year 1998.

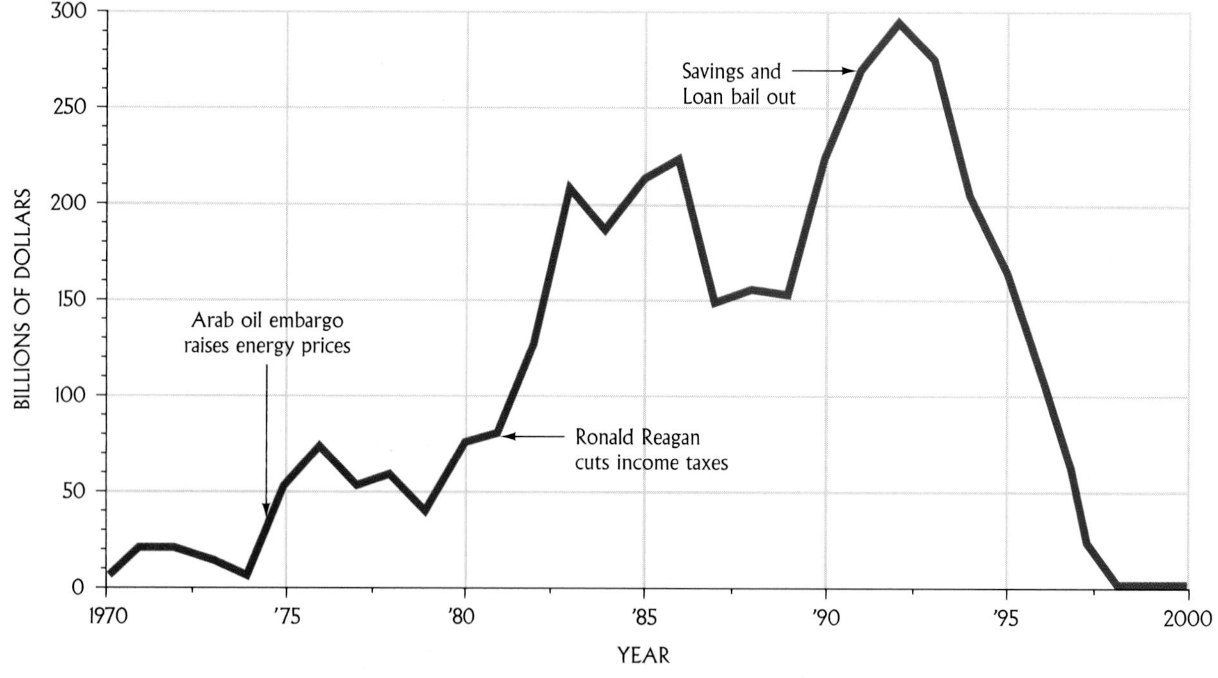

Source: Budget of the United States Government, Fiscal Year 2002: Historical Tables (Washington, D.C.: U.S. Government Printing Office, 2001), Table 1.1.

Emergency Deficit Control Act, better known as Gramm-Rudman-Hollings after its cosponsors, Senators Phil Gramm (R) of Texas, Warren Rudman (R) of New Hampshire, and Ernest Hollings (D) of South Carolina.

This legislation, as it was amended in 1987, mandated maximum allowable deficit levels for each year until 1993, when the budget was supposed to be in balance. If Congress failed to meet the deficit goals, automatic across-the-board spending cuts, called *sequestrations*, were to be ordered by the president (a number of programs, including Social Security and interest on the national debt, were exempt from this process).

Gramm-Rudman-Hollings was clearly an indelicate, unthinking approach to budgeting; no one liked the arbitrary nature of the automatic budget cuts, half of which were to come from defense and half from domestic programs. Even Senator Rudman described it as "a bad idea whose time has come." In the absence of consensus on spending priorities, Congress believed it had no other way to force itself to reduce the deficit. Success was elusive, however, as you can see in Figure 14.7.

Near the end of 1990, Congress abandoned Gramm-Rudman-Hollings and approved a major change in budgeting policy. It decided to shift its focus from controlling the size of the deficit to controlling increases in spending. Discretionary spending was divided into three categories: domestic, defense, and international. Any new spending in any of these categories had to be offset by decreases elsewhere within the category. Violations of these strictures would lead to across-the-board sequestration within the affected category. Spending for entitlement programs such as Medicare was placed on a "pay-as-you-go" basis, requiring that any expansion be paid for by a corresponding entitlement cut or revenue increase. Similarly, any tax cut was to be paid for by a compensating tax increase or entitlement cut.

President Clinton presented his first budget to Congress in 1993. After the dust cleared following a highly partisan legislative battle, the president and Congress had made a significant decrease in the deficit. There was a single cap for all discretionary spending (rather than one for each of the three components), imposing a hard freeze on appropriations, yet there was little prospect of balancing the budget in the foreseeable future.

The results of the 1994 congressional elections once again altered the budgetary game. In 1995, the new Republican majorities in each house, determined to balance the budget within seven years, argued for substantial cuts in the rate of growth of popular entitlement programs such as Medicaid and for the outright elimination of many other programs. Most Democrats strongly opposed these proposals. The president agreed with the goal of balancing the budget—but on his terms—and took his case to the voters in 1996. The outcome, as we have seen, was divided government.

In 1997, the president and Congress agreed to a budget that was to be in balance—by 2002. Each political party claimed victory, but the path to a balanced budget was eased by the booming economy, which produced more tax revenues than either side had anticipated. Indeed, the economy was so strong that the government began running surpluses beginning in fiscal year 1999. Whether the budget can remain in balance in the face of an economic downturn (in which tax revenues would decrease and expenditures would increase) remains to be seen. In the meantime, the budget surplus has given policymakers a new source of conflict (see "You Are the Policymaker: Spending the Budget Surplus").

participation
Dealing With the Surplus: Having a say

Understanding Budgeting

Citizens and politicians alike fret about whether government is too big. In 1988 President Bush was elected by claiming that government has too many hands in Americans' pockets. He promised not to raise taxes to pay for more government spending. Of course, not everyone agrees that the national government is too large—even Bush backtracked on his "no new taxes" pledge by 1990 and was defeated by the more activist Bill Clinton in 1992. There is agreement on the centrality of budgeting to modern government and politics, however.

Long a goal of many elected officials, balancing the budget was aided by the booming economy that produced more tax revenues than anticipated and the budget agreements of the 1990s that constrained spending. Here President Clinton shows how the deficit fell during his tenure.

Democracy and Budgeting

Almost all democracies have seen a substantial growth in government in the twentieth century. One explanation for this growth is that politicians spend money to "buy" votes. They do not buy votes in the sense that a corrupt political machine pays voters to vote for its candidates; rather, policymakers spend public money on things voters will like—and will remember on election day. As you saw in Chapter 12, members of Congress have incentives to make government grow; they use both constituency services and pork barrel policies to deliver benefits to the folks back home, and government grows as a result.

You Are the Policymaker

Spending the Budget Surplus

Something dramatic happened in the late 1990s: The budget, instead of being in the red, began to run a *surplus*. In 1999 President Clinton called for a great national debate about how to spend the growing surplus. Because the surplus is projected to amount to more than five trillion dollars over the next decade, the stakes are high for the decision that now confronts the nation.

The biggest federal programs affect the elderly. The aging population is increasingly straining both the Medicare and Social Security systems. President Clinton wanted to use most of the surplus to shore up Social Security and Medicare. He also proposed to spend most of the remainder of the funds on a variety of programs, ranging from defense to education.

The Republicans have a different view. Although they agree that Social Security must be properly financed, their priority was on a substantial income tax cut. They argue that the best use of a tax surplus is to give much of it back to the taxpayers who paid for it.

There are many other options for spending this money. We could give grants to parents with small children to pay for day care or scholarships to all college students. We could spend substantially more on medical research or on cleaning up toxic wastes. Or we could give it *all* back to the taxpayers and worry about Social Security and Medicare later. You be the policymaker: What would *you* do?

How You Can Make a Difference

The Federal Government and Student Loans

Since 1965, the Federal Family Education Program (FFEL) has provided federally guaranteed student loans worth nearly $200 billion. Under this system, private banks issue the loans and profit from them while the federal government subsidizes the interest rate and guarantees the loans. The Clinton administration, however, advocated that the federal government provide direct lending to the students and bypass private banks. If the pilot program were adopted on a permanent basis, the government's partnership with the private banking sector would likely end.

Is direct lending better than the traditional public/private venture used for the last 35 years? According to the proponents of direct lending, college students would likely pay lower interest rates on their students loans under a direct lending plan. Likewise, critics of the traditional system point out that even the Congressional Budget Office notes that because these loans have been subsidized and guaranteed by the federal government, private banks take on less risk and reap hefty profits from student loan programs. In short, many college and student interest groups claim that the only reason to continue the present system is to guarantee larger profits to private banks.

The Alliance To Save Student Aid is a coalition of 50 educational organizations. By calling them at 1-800-574-4243 you can get information about the current status of government funding for student loans. Give them your zip code, and the Alliance will directly connect you to your congressional representatives' office to voice your educated opinion.

Many citizens, especially libertarians and fiscal conservatives, strongly oppose the expansion of the direct lending program. The Heritage Foundation (www.heritage.org) argues that the direct lending plan costs the government more money in administrative costs but also adds to the national debt. In fact, a similar program in the 1970s failed because of poor government management and soaring default rates due to poor loan collection. In short, the argument against direct lending remains both ideological (in favor of limited government) and practical (direct lending did not work the last time around).

However you view this debate, do not let your short tenure as a college student keep you from participating in it. Although nothing may get done while you are still an undergraduate student, your involvement in this debate may impact your graduate education funding. For a more detailed list of student aid lobbying and advocacy groups and their websites from both sides of the political spectrum, see www.finaid.org/questions/advocacy.

Economists Allen Meltzer and Scott Richard have argued that government grows in a democracy because of the equality of suffrage. They maintain that in the private sector people's incomes are unequal, whereas in the political arena power is much more equally distributed. Each voter has one vote. Parties must appeal to a majority of the voters. Hence, claim Meltzer and Richard, poorer voters will always use their votes to support public policies that redistribute benefits from the rich to the poor. Even if such voters cannot win in the marketplace, they can use the electoral process to their advantage.[20] Many politicians willingly cooperate with the desire of the working-class voters to expand their benefits because voters return the favor at election time. Not surprisingly, the most rapidly growing areas of expenditures are Social Security, Medicaid, Medicare, and social welfare programs, which benefit the poor more than the rich.

Many believe that elites, particularly corporate elites, oppose big government. However, Lockheed and Chrysler Corporation appealed to the government for large bailouts when times got rough. Corporations support a big government that offers them contracts, subsidies, and other benefits. A $100 billion procurement budget at the Department of Defense benefits defense contractors, their workers, and their shareholders.

Low-income and wealthy voters alike have voted for parties and politicians who promised them benefits. When the air is foul, Americans expect government to help clean it up. When Americans get old, they expect a Social Security check. In a democracy, what people want affects what government does. Citizens are not helpless victims of big government and its big taxes; they are at least coconspirators.

Government also grows by responding to groups and their demands. The parade of PACs is one example of groups asking government for assistance. From agricultural lobbies supporting loans to zoologists pressing for aid from the National Science Foundation, groups seek to expand their favorite part of the budget. They are aided by committees and government agencies that work to fund projects favored by supportive groups (see the discussion on iron triangles in Chapter 15).

You have also seen, however, that some politicians compete for votes by promising not to spend money. After all, Ronald Reagan did not win election to the presidency twice by promising to raise taxes and provide more services, nor did the Republicans who took control of Congress in 1995. No country has a more open political system than the United States, but as the "America in Perspective" features in this chapter demonstrate, Americans have chosen to tax less and spend less on public services than almost all other democracies with developed economies. The size of government budgets varies widely among democratic nations. Democracy may encourage government spending, but it does not compel it.

One of the most common criticisms of government is its failure to balance the budget. Public officials are often criticized for lacking the will to deal with the problem, yet it was not lack of resolve that prevented a solution to enormous budget deficits. Instead, it was a lack of consensus on policy. Americans wanted to spend but not pay taxes and, being a democracy, this is exactly what the government did. The inevitable result was red ink. By 1998, however, the president was able to propose a balanced budget.

The Budget and the Scope of Government

Issues regarding the scope of government have pervaded this chapter. The reason is obvious—in many ways, the budget *is* the scope of government. The bigger the budget, the bigger the government.

The budgetary process can also limit government. One could accurately characterize policymaking in the American government since 1980 as the "politics of scarcity"—scarcity of funds, that is. Thus, the budget can be a force for reining in the government as well as for expanding its role.[21] President Clinton came into office hoping to make new investments in education, worker training, and the country's physical infrastructure, such as roads and bridges. He soon found, however, that there was no money to fund new programs.

Public opinion is a key element in the budgeting process. Occasionally, the public has a direct role in budget making, as when the citizens of California voted on Proposition 13, a referendum proposing strict limits to local property taxes. Despite protests against the proposed legislation—many citizens argued that tax limits would restrict many government services—the proposition was passed.

Career Profile

Position: Associate Director of Communications for Office of Management and Budget (OMB)
Salary Range: $106,000-$130,000 (Senior Executive Service Rank)
Benefits: Health and life insurance, retirement pension plan, and sick leave.
Qualifications: Background in public relations/press recommended. Ability to explain and advocate ideas in a convincing manner. Strong interpersonal skills are mandatory

Real People on the Job: Linda Ricci

As associate director of communications for the Office of Management and Budget (OMB), Linda Ricci served as one of OMBs key spokespersons and press during the Clinton administration. As this chapter explains, the OMB serves as the executive branch's eyes and ears on all matters related to the national budget. The OMB's scope encompasses every part of the federal government that involves funding issues. Thus, it's the OMB the president consults when he proposes a budget each year. Linda's job was to serve as an advocate for the president's policies and programs. In order to perform her job, however, Linda had to fully understand President Clinton's various policy proposals and how they might be funded.

One of Linda's key duties involved writing and editing the president's proposed budget every year. For example, when the president proposed new policies for the Social Security Agency, Linda had to explain the policy implications of his proposal to Congress, the press, and the American public. While the detailed budget might be impenetrable to the average citizen, Linda's explanations aimed to get rid of the jargon so that an average person could comprehend the issues. By trying to anticipate many of the potential questions and comments regarding the president's plan, Linda sought to convey clearly and simply the rationale behind the president's funding requests.

As you might have noticed, Linda's job paid very well compared to most of the other jobs examined in this book. Linda, along with nearly 7,000 federal employees, was a member of Senior Executive Service (SES). The SES was created in 1978 to provide a corps of highly qualified executives to serve in key positions that fall just below the rank of presidential appointees who require Senate confirmation. To prevent losing key executives to the private sector, the SES provides an avenue of advancement and monetary rewards to keep effective leaders working for the federal government. Although Linda was appointed by President Clinton as a noncareer position, nearly all of the SES members are career appointees working in the Washington, D.C. area. Whereas most government jobs are covered by the General Schedule Pay plan (e.g. GS-1, GS-8), SES members earn at an ES or Executive Scale range that begins at 120% of the highest GS salary ($106,200). So the next time you think that getting a government job means low pay and poor benefits, remember the Senior Executive Service. To find out more about the OMB, go to http://www.whitehouse.gov/omb. To find out more about the SES, go to www.opm.gov/ses.

The president was reduced to speaking loudly and carrying a small budgetary stick in other policy areas as well. Because there was not enough money in the budget to pay for health care reform, he had to accept a reduced benefits package and advocate the politically difficult option of forcing employers to pay for their employees' health insurance. Welfare reform faced a similar obstacle. America's large budget deficits have been as much a constraint on government as they have been evidence of a burgeoning public sector.

Summary

When the federal government's budget consumes one-fifth of America's gross domestic product, it demands close attention. The government's biggest revenue source remains the income tax, but the Social Security tax is becoming increasingly important. Lately, much of the government's budget has been financed through borrowing. Annual deficits exceeding $100 billion—and sometimes reaching nearly $300 billion—boosted the federal debt to about $5.6 trillion by 2000.

In all Western democracies, government budgets grew during the twentieth century. In the United States, government spending also experienced significant change. Defense spending dominated the 1950s; social services spending dominated the 1990s. President Reagan, for one, wanted to reverse this trend by increasing military expenditures and cutting domestic ones. Nonetheless, much of the American budget consists of "uncontrollable" expenditures that are extremely difficult to pare. Many of these expenditures are associated with Social Security payments and with grants-in-aid.

Budget making is complex, with many actors playing many roles. The president sets the budgetary agenda, whereas Congress and its committees approve the budget itself.

Some critics believe that democracy turns politics into a bidding war for votes, increasing the size of the budget in the process. In the United States, however, many candidates campaign on *not* spending money or increasing taxes. Although larger budgets mean larger government, the budget, at least in times of substantial deficits such as those the United States experienced in the previous decade, can also serve as a constraint on further government growth.

Key Terms

budget
deficit
expenditures
revenues
income tax
Sixteenth Amendment
federal debt
tax expenditures
Social Security Act
Medicare
incrementalism
uncontrollable expenditures
entitlements
House Ways and Means Committee
Senate Finance Committee
Congressional Budget and Impoundment Control Act of 1974
Congressional Budget Office (CBO)
budget resolution
reconciliation
authorization bill
appropriations bill
continuing resolutions

For Further Reading

Bennett, Linda L. M., and Stephen Earl Bennett. *Living with Leviathan.* Lawrence: University Press of Kansas, 1990. Examines Americans' coming to terms with big government and their expectations of government largesse.

Berry, William D., and David Lowery. *Understanding United States Government Growth.* New York: Praeger, 1987. An empirical analysis of the causes of the growth of government in the period since World War II.

King, Ronald F. *Money, Taxes, and Politics*. New Haven, CT: Yale University Press, 1993. Explains why democratically elected officials approve tax policies that make rich people richer.

Light, Paul. *Artful Work: The Politics of Social Security Reform*. New York: Random House, 1985. A case study of the perennial crisis of Social Security and what has been done about it.

Schick, Allen. *The Federal Budget, rev. ed.* Washington, D.C.: Brookings Institution, 2000. A useful "hands-on" view of federal budgeting.

Schuman, Howard E. *Politics and the Budget*, 3rd ed. Englewood Cliffs, NJ: Prentice-Hall, 1992. An excellent primer on the entire budgetary process.

Wildavsky, Aaron, and Naomi Caiden. *The New Politics of the Budgetary Process*, 4th ed. New York: Longman, 2001. The standard work on the budgetary process.

Internet Resources

w3.access.gpo.gov/usbudget/index.html
The *Economic Report of the President* and the budget for the federal government.

www.irs.ustreas.gov
The Internal Revenue Service homepage, containing a wealth of information about taxes.

www.whitehouse.gov/omb
The Office of Management and Budget homepage.

www.washingtonpost.com/wp-srv/politics/special/budget/budget.htm
Washington Post series on the budget, including a glossary of terms, budget "games," and links to current news on the budget and the economy.

www.cbo.gov/
Congressional Budget Office homepage, containing budgetary analyses and data.

Notes

1. Aaron Wildavsky and Naomi Caiden, *The New Politics of the Budgetary Process*, 4th ed. (New York: Longman, 2001), 2.
2. Quoted in Gerald Carson, *The Golden Egg: The Personal Income Tax, Where It Came From, How It Grew* (Boston: Houghton Mifflin, 1977), 12.
3. Statistics on the number of returns and audits come from the U.S. Department of Commerce, *Statistical Abstract of the United States, 2000* (Washington, D.C.: U.S. Government Printing Office, 2001), 349.
4. An exception is Robert Eisner, who argues that if the government counted its debt as families and business firms do—that is, by balancing assets against liabilities—the government would be in pretty good shape. See *How Real Is the Federal Deficit?* (New York: Free Press, 1986).
5. On the balanced budget amendment, see Aaron Wildavsky, *How To Limit Government Spending* (Berkeley: University of California Press, 1980).
6. Carson, *The Golden Egg*, 181–182.
7. For some perspectives on the rise of government expenditures, see David Cameron, "The Expansion of the Public Economy: A Comparative Analysis," *American Political Science Review* 72 (December 1978): 1,243–1,261; and William D. Berry and David Lowery, *Understanding United States Government Growth* (New York: Praeger, 1987).
8. E. E. Schattschneider, *Two Hundred Million Americans in Search of a Government* (New York: Holt, Rinehart and Winston, 1969), 29–30.
9. Berry and Lowery, *Understanding United States Government Growth*.
10. Richard Halloran, "Cost Estimate of Stealth Bombers Increased 16% by the Air Force," the *New York Times*, December 17, 1988, 10.
11. Paul Light, *Artful Work: The Politics of Social Security Reform* (New York: HarperCollins, 1992), 82.
12. Aaron Wildavsky and Naomi Caiden, *The New Politics of the Budgetary Process*, 3rd ed. (New York: Longman, 1997), 45.
13. John R. Gist, *Mandatory Expenditures and the Defense Sector* (Beverly Hills, CA: Russell Sage Foundation, 1974).
14. Paul R. Schulman, "Nonincremental Policymaking: Notes Toward an Alternative Paradigm," *American Political Science Review* 69 (December 1975): 1,354–1,370.
15. A good description of budgetary strategies is in Wildavsky and Caiden, *The New Politics of the Budgetary Process*, chap. 3.
16. *Ibid.*, 2.
17. For a discussion of the ways in which bureaucracies manipulate benefits to gain advantage with members of Congress, see Douglas Arnold, *Congress and the Bureaucracy* (New Haven, CT: Yale University Press, 1979); and the articles in Barry S. Rundquist, ed., *Political Benefits* (Lexington, MA: D.C. Heath, 1980).
18. A good review of the formation of the executive budget is Howard E. Schuman, *Politics and the Budget*, 3rd ed. (Englewood Cliffs, NJ: Prentice-Hall, 1992), chap. 2.
19. An important work on congressional budget making is Wildavsky and Caiden, *The New Politics of the Budgetary Process*.
20. Allen Meltzer and Scott F. Richard, "Why the Government Grows (and Grows) in a Democracy," *The Public Interest* 52 (Summer 1978): 117.
21. See James D. Savage, *Balanced Budgets and American Politics* (Ithaca, NY: Cornell University Press, 1988) for a study of the influence the principle of budget balancing has had on politics and public policy from the earliest days of U.S. history.

15 The Federal Bureaucracy

Chapter Outline

Americans do not want to worry about the safety of the food we eat. Indeed, food safety is something we take for granted. But who assures this safety? Bureaucrats. It is their job to keep our food safe from contamination. Although we rarely think about food inspections, they represent one of the most important regulatory functions of government. The fact that we rarely think about food safety is testimony to the success of bureaucrats in carrying out their tasks.[1]

Policing the food supply is not a straightforward task, however. It involves a complex web of federal agencies with overlapping jurisdictions. Twelve agencies and 35 statutes regulate food safety. Eggs in the shell fall under the purview of the Food and Drug Administration (FDA), but once cracked and processed, they come under the jurisdiction of the U.S. Department of Agriculture (USDA). The USDA is responsible for regulating meat and poultry, while the FDA handles most other food products, including seafood and produce. Cheese pizzas

are the FDA's responsibility, but if they have pepperoni on top, Agriculture inspectors step in. Other parts of the government also play a prominent role in enforcing food safety laws. For example, the Environmental Protection Agency oversees pesticides applied to crops, and the Centers for Disease Control and Prevention track food-related illnesses.

Is this complex system the result of bureaucratic maneuvering? No, the system was created by Congress layer on top of layer, with little regard to how it should work as a whole. Critics argue that the system is outdated and it would be better to create a single food safety agency that could target inspections, streamline safety programs, and use resources more efficiently. Such proposals have generated little enthusiasm in Congress, however, where committees are sensitive about losing jurisdiction over agencies. For example, in the House the Commerce Committee has oversight over the FDA while the Agriculture Committee has responsibility for the USDA. Growers and manufacturers fear a single agency would impose onerous new regulations, product recalls, and fines, and could be used by empire-building bureaucrats to expand their budget and regulatory authority. So little change occurs.

Bureaucrats face other challenges in insuring safe food. The FDA has only about 430 inspectors to keep tabs on more than 53,000 establishments that produce, process, or store food other than meat and poultry. The agency carries out about 5,000 inspections per year, so the average company is subject to an FDA inspection just once every 10 years.

Bureaucrats are central to our lives. They provide essential public services. They possess crucial information and expertise that make them partners with the president and Congress in decision making about public policy. Who knows more than bureaucrats about Social Security recipients or the military capabilities of China? Bureaucrats are also central to politics. They do much more than simply follow orders. Because of their expertise, bureaucrats inevitably have discretion in carrying out policy decisions, which is why congressional committees and interest groups take so much interest in what they do.

Bureaucratic power extends to every corner of American economic and social life, yet bureaucracies are scarcely hinted at in the Constitution. Each bureaucratic agency is created by Congress, which sets its budget and writes the policies it administers. Most agencies are responsible to the president, whose constitutional responsibility to "take care that the laws shall be faithfully executed" sheds only a dim light on the problems of managing so large a government. How to manage and control bureaucracies is a central problem of democratic government.

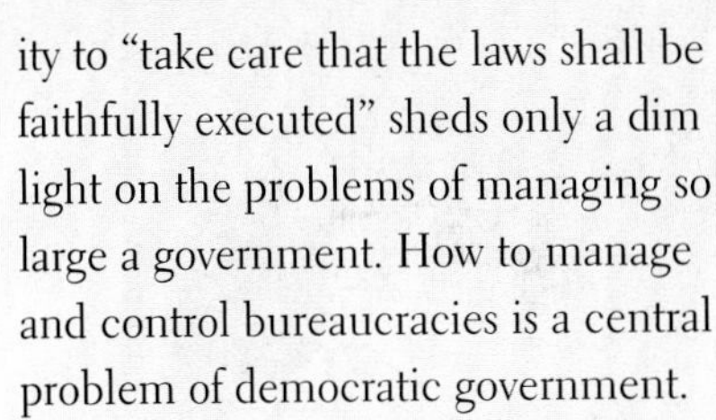

Reining in the power of bureaucracies is also a common theme in debates over the scope of government in America. Some political commentators see the bureaucracy as the prime example of a federal government growing out of control. They view the bureaucracy as acquisitive, constantly seeking to expand its size, budgets, and authority while being entwined in red tape and spewing forth senseless regulations. Others see the bureaucracy as laboring valiantly against great odds to fulfill the missions elected officials have assigned it. Where does the truth lie? The answer is less obvious than you may think. Clearly, bureaucracies require closer examination.

The Bureaucrats

Bureaucrats are typically much less visible than the president or members of Congress. As a result, Americans usually know little about them. This section will examine some myths about bureaucrats and explain who they are and how they got their jobs.

Some Bureaucratic Myths and Realities

Bureaucrat baiting is a popular American pastime. George Wallace, former Alabama governor and frequent presidential hopeful, warmed up his crowds with a line about "pointy-headed Washington bureaucrats who can't even park their bicycles straight." Even successful presidential candidates climbed aboard the antibureaucracy bandwagon. Jimmy Carter complained about America's "complicated and confused and overlapping and wasteful" bureaucracies; Gerald Ford complained about the "dead weight" of bureaucracies; and Ronald Reagan insisted that bureaucrats "overregulated" the American economy, causing a decline in productivity.

Any object of such unpopularity will spawn plenty of myths. The following are some of the most prevalent myths about bureaucracy:

- *Americans dislike bureaucrats.* Despite the rhetoric about bureaucracies, Americans are generally satisfied with bureaucrats and the treatment they get from them. Americans may dislike bureaucracies, but they like individual bureaucrats. Surveys have found that two-thirds or more of those who have had encounters with a bureaucrat evaluate these encounters positively. In most instances, bureaucrats are described as helpful, efficient, fair, courteous, and working to serve their clients' interests.[2]
- *Bureaucracies are growing bigger each year.* This myth is half true and half false. The number of government employees has been expanding, but not the number of *federal* employees. Almost all the growth in the number of public employees has occurred in state and local governments. The 18 million state and local public employees far outnumber the fewer than 4.1 million civilian and military federal government employees (see Figure 15.1). As a percentage of America's total work force, *federal* government employment has been shrinking, not growing; it now accounts for about 3 percent of all civilian jobs. Of course, many state and local employees work on programs that are federally funded, and the federal government hires many private contractors to provide goods and services ranging from hot meals to weapons systems.[3]

visual literacy
The Changing Face of the Federal Bureaucracy

- *Most federal bureaucrats work in Washington, D.C.* Only about 16 percent of federal civilian employees work in the Washington, D.C. metropolitan area. California leads the nation in federal employees, with 265,000. Texas has 175,000, New York 139,000. About 100,000 federal employees work in foreign countries and American territories.[4] You can see where federal bureaucrats work by looking in your local phone book under "U.S. Government." You will probably find listings for the local offices of the Postal Service, the Social Security Administration, the FBI, the Department of Agriculture's county agents, recruiters for the armed services, air traffic controllers, the Internal Revenue Service, and many others.
- *Bureaucracies are ineffective, inefficient, and always mired in red tape.* No words describing bureaucratic behavior are better known than "red tape."[5] Bureaucracy, however, is simply a way of organizing people to perform work. General Motors, a college or university, the U.S. Army, the Department of Health and Human Services, and the Roman Catholic Church are all bureaucracies. Bureaucracies are a little like referees: When they work well, no one gives them much credit, but when they work poorly, everyone calls them unfair, incompetent, or inefficient. Bureaucracies may be inefficient at times, but no one has found a substitute for them; and no one has yet demonstrated that government bureaucracies are more or less inefficient, ineffective, or mired in red tape than private bureaucracies.[6]

Figure 15.1 Growth in Government Employees

The number of government employees has grown since 1965. The real growth, however, has been in the state and local sector, with its millions of teachers, police officers, and other service deliverers. Many state and local employees and programs, though, are supported by federal grants-in-aid. (Note that the figures for federal employment do not include military personnel.)

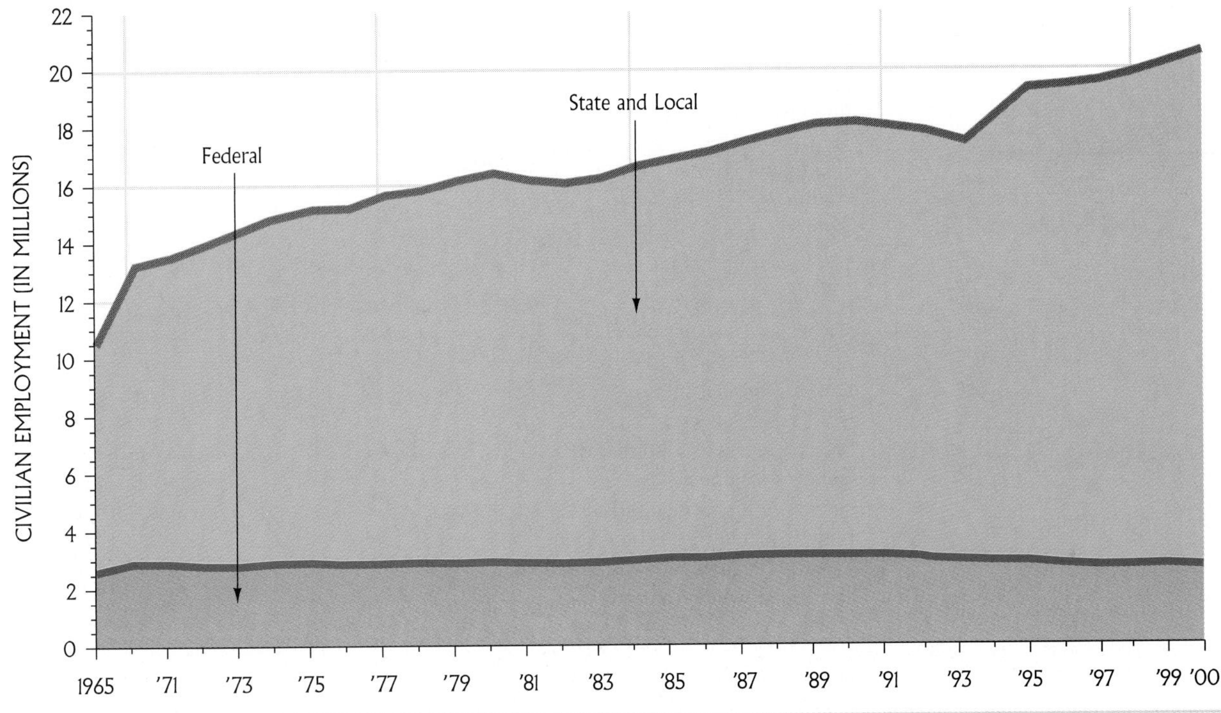

Source: Budget of the United States Government, Fiscal Year 2002: Historical Tables (Washington, D.C.: U.S. Government Printing Office, 2001), Table 17-5.

Anyone who looks with disdain on American bureaucracies should contemplate life without them. Despite all the complaining about bureaucracies, the vast majority of tasks carried out by governments at all levels are noncontroversial. Bureaucrats deliver mail, test milk, clean streets, issue Social Security and student loan checks, run national parks, and perform other routine governmental tasks in a perfectly acceptable manner. Most of the people who work for cities, states, and the national government are typical Americans, the type who are likely to be your neighbors.

Most federal civilian employees work for just a few of the agencies (see Table 15.1). The Department of Defense (DOD) employs about one-fourth of federal *civilian* workers in addition to the 1.4 million men and women in uniform. Altogether, the DOD makes up more than half of the federal bureaucracy. The postal service accounts for an additional quarter of the federal civilian employees, and the various health professions constitute nearly 10 percent (one in three doctors, for example, works for the government). The Department of Veterans Affairs, clearly related to national defense, has more than 205,000 employees. All other functions of government are handled by the remaining 20 percent of federal employees.

Who They Are and How They Got There

Because there are nearly 3 million civilian bureaucrats (20 million if we include state and local public employees), it is hard to imagine a statistically typical bureaucrat. Bureaucrats are male and female, all races and religions, well paid and not so well paid. Like other institutions, the federal government has been under pressure to expand its hiring of women and minorities. Congress has ordered federal agencies to make special

participation
Who Wants to be a Bureaucrat

Table 15.1 Federal Civilian Employment

EXECUTIVE DEPARTMENTS	NUMBER OF EMPLOYEES[a]
Defense (military functions)	641,100
Veterans Affairs	205,900
Treasury	148,400
Justice	129,100
Agriculture	97,900
Interior	69,900
Transportation	65,000
Health and Human Services	63,500
Commerce	39,700
State	27,700
Labor	17,700
Energy	16,400
Housing and Urban Development	10,300
Education	4,700
Larger Non-Cabinet Agencies	
U.S. Postal Service	841,002
Social Security Administration	63,200
Corps of Engineers	24,800
National Aeronautics and Space Administration	19,000
Environmental Protection Agency	18,000
General Services Administration	14,000
Tennessee Valley Authority	13,200

[a]Figures are for 2001.
Source: Budget of the United States Government, Fiscal Year 2002: Analytical Perspectives (Washington, D.C.: U.S. Government Printing Office, 2001), Tables 10-1, 10-3.

efforts to recruit and promote previously disadvantaged groups, but women and non-Whites still cluster at the lower ranks. As a whole, however, the permanent bureaucracy is more broadly representative of the American people than are legislators, judges, or presidential appointees in the executive branch[7] (see Figure 15.2).

Figure 15.2 Characteristics of Federal Civilian Employees[a]

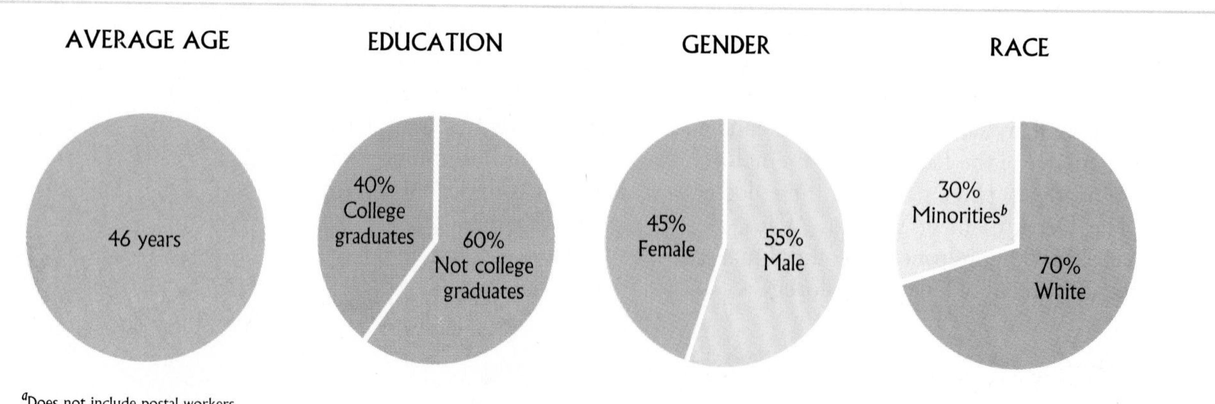

[a]Does not include postal workers.
[b]Includes African Americans, Asian Americans, Native Americans, and Hispanics.

Source: Data from United States Office of Personnel Management, The Factbook, 2000 Ed. (Washington, D.C.: U.S. Government Printing Office, 2000), 10–13.

The diversity of bureaucratic jobs mirrors the diversity of private-sector jobs, including occupations literally ranging from A to Z. Accountants, bakers, census analysts, defense procurement specialists, electricians, foreign service officers, guards in federal prisons, home economists, Indian Affairs agents, judges, kitchen workers, lawyers, missile technologists, narcotics agents, ophthalmologists, postal carriers, quarantine specialists, radiologists, stenographers, truck drivers, underwater demolition experts, virologists, wardens, X-ray technicians, youth counselors, and zoologists all work for the government (see Table 15.2).

Civil Service: From Patronage to Protection. Until roughly 100 years ago, a person got a job with the government through the patronage system. **Patronage** is a hiring and promotion system based on political reasons rather than on merit or competence. Working in a congressional campaign, making large donations, and having the right connections helped people secure jobs with the government. Nineteenth-century presidents staffed the government with their friends and allies, following the view of Andrew Jackson that "to the victors belong the spoils." Scores of office seekers would swarm the White House after Inauguration Day. It is said that during a bout with malaria, Lincoln told an aide to "send in the office seekers" because he finally had something to give them.

A disappointed office seeker named Charles Guiteau helped end this "spoils system" of federal appointments in 1881. Frustrated because President James A. Garfield would not give him a job, Guiteau shot and killed Garfield. The so-called Prince of Patronage himself, Vice President Chester A. Arthur, then became president. Arthur, who had been collector of the customs for New York—a patronage-rich post—surprised his critics by encouraging passage of the **Pendleton Civil Service Act** (1883), which created the federal Civil Service. Today, most federal agencies are covered by some sort of civil service system.

patronage

One of the key inducements used by machines. A patronage job, promotion, or contract is one that is given for political reasons rather than for merit or competence alone. Compare **civil service** and the **merit principle**.

timeline
Evolution of the Federal Bureaucracy

Pendleton Civil Service Act

Passed in 1883, an Act that created a federal **civil service** so that hiring and promotion would be based on merit rather than **patronage**.

Table 15.2 Full-Time Civilian White-Collar Employees of the Federal Government

SELECTED OCCUPATIONAL CATEGORIES	NUMBER OF EMPLOYEES
General administrative, clerical, and office services	369,009
Medical, dental, and public health	141,555
Engineering and architecture	132,466
Accounting and budget	128,142
Business and industry	92,231
Investigation	88,415
Legal and kindred	78,755
Social science, psychology, and welfare	65,740
Biological sciences	58,003
Transportation	45,265
Personnel management and industrial relations	41,895
Supply	34,402
Physical sciences	34,272
Education	33,127
Information and the arts	18,639
Equipment, facilities, and services	13,646
Mathematics and statistics	13,337
Quality assurance, inspection, and grading	11,009
Library and archives	8,412
Copyright, patent, and trademark	2,961
Veterinary medical science	2,188

Source: U.S. Office of Personnel Management, *Occupations of Federal White-Collar and Blue-Collar Workers, Federal Civilian Workforce Statistics, as of September 30, 1997* (Washington, D.C.: U.S. Government Printing Office, 1998), Table W-2.

civil service

A system of hiring and promotion based on the **merit principle** and the desire to create a nonpartisan government service.

merit principle

The idea that hiring should be based on entrance exams and promotion ratings to produce administration by people with talent and skill.

Hatch Act

A federal law prohibiting government employees from active participation in partisan politics.

Office of Personnel Management (OPM)

The office in charge of hiring for most agencies of the federal government, using elaborate rules in the process.

GS (General Schedule) rating

A schedule for federal employees, ranging from GS 1 to GS 18, by which salaries can be keyed to rating and experience.

Senior Executive Service (SES)

An elite cadre of about 9,000 federal government managers, established by the Civil Service Reform Act of 1978, who are mostly career officials but include some political appointees who do not require Senate confirmation.

All **civil service** systems are designed to hire and promote members of the bureaucracy on the basis of merit and to create a nonpartisan government service. The **merit principle**—using entrance exams and promotion ratings to reward qualified individuals—is intended to produce an administration of people with talent and skill. Creating a nonpartisan civil service means insulating government workers from the risk of being fired when a new party comes to power. At the same time, the **Hatch Act,** originally passed in 1939 and amended most recently in 1993, prohibits civil service employees from actively participating in partisan politics while on duty. While off duty they may engage in political activities, but they cannot run for partisan elective offices or solicit contributions from the public. Employees with sensitive positions, such as those in the national security area, may not engage in political activities even while off duty.

The **Office of Personnel Management (OPM)** is in charge of hiring for most federal agencies. Its director is appointed by the president and confirmed by the Senate. The OPM has elaborate rules about hiring, promotion, working conditions, and firing. To get a civil service job, usually candidates must first take a test. If they pass, their names are sent to agencies when jobs requiring their particular skills become available. For each position open, the OPM will send three names to the agency. Except under unusual circumstances, the agency must hire one of these three individuals. (This process is called the "rule of three.") Each job is assigned a **GS (General Schedule) rating** ranging from GS 1 to GS 18. Salaries are keyed to rating and experience. At the very top of the civil service system are about 9,000 members of the **Senior Executive Service,** the "cream of the crop" of the federal employees. These executives earn high salaries and may be moved from one agency to another as leadership needs change.

Once hired, and after a probationary period, civil servants are protected—overprotected, critics claim—by the civil service system. Ensuring a nonpartisan civil service requires that workers have protection from dismissals that are politically motivated. Protecting all workers against political firings may also protect a few from dismissal for good cause. Firing incompetents is hard work. Recently, the government managed to fire only 314 employees for poor performance and another 2,700 for misconduct, about 0.001 percent of civilian federal workers. According to Civil Service regulations, the right of appeal must be exhausted before one's paycheck stops. Appeals can consume weeks, months, or even years. More than one agency has decided to tolerate incompetents, assigning them trivial or no duties, rather than invest its resources in the nearly hopeless task of discharging them. Firing incompetent female, minority, or older workers may be even more difficult than dislodging incompetent young or middle-aged white males. These groups not only have the usual Civil Service protections but also can resort to antidiscrimination statutes to appeal their dismissals.

comparative
Comparing Bureaucracies

The Other Route to Federal Jobs: Recruiting from the Plum Book. As an incoming administration celebrates its victory and prepares to take control of the government, Congress publishes the *plum book,* which lists top federal jobs (that is, "plums") available for direct presidential appointment, often with Senate confirmation. There are about 400 of these top policymaking posts (mostly cabinet secretaries, undersecretaries, assistant secretaries, and bureau chiefs) and about 2,500 lesser positions.

All incoming presidents launch a nationwide talent search for qualified personnel. Presidents seek individuals who combine executive talent, political skills, and sympathy for policy positions similar to those of the administration. Often, the president tries to include men and women, Whites and non-Whites, people from different regions, and party members who represent different interests (although few recent presidents have appointed as high a percentage of middle-aged white males as did Ronald Reagan). Some positions, especially ambassadorships, go to large campaign contributors. A few of these appointees will be civil servants, temporarily elevated to a "political" status; most, though, will be political appointees, "in-and-outers" who stay for a while and then leave.[8]

Once in office, these administrative policymakers constitute what Heclo has called a "government of strangers."[9] Their most important trait is their transience. The average

assistant secretary or undersecretary lasts about 22 months.[10] Few top officials stay long enough to know their own subordinates well, much less people in other agencies. Administrative routines, budget cycles, and legal complexities are often new to them. To these new political executives, the possibilities of power may seem endless. Nevertheless, although plum book appointees may have the outward signs of power, many of them find it challenging to exercise real control over much of what their subordinates do and have difficulty leaving their mark on policy. They soon learn that they are dependent on senior civil servants, who know more, have been there longer, and will outlast them.

Why does it matter?

People obtain positions in the federal bureaucracy through a merit system and are protected against losing their jobs because of their political views. What if the president could appoint a substantial percentage of bureaucrats? Would bureaucracies serve the public better? Would they be more responsive to the president?

What They Do: Some Theories of Bureaucracy

Governmental bureaucracies are not the only type of bureaucracy. Perhaps the oldest is the hierarchical governance of the Roman Catholic Church. Bureaucracies also run American armies, corporations, schools, and almost every other social, political, and economic institution. Social scientists have studied these organizations and formulated numerous theories about how bureaucracies work (or don't work). Three of the most prominent theories are described here.

The Weberian Model. Most people have confronted a bureaucracy only to be told, "Perhaps Mrs. Smith could help you; your problem is really under her jurisdiction," or "You'll have to talk to the supervisor because I am only enforcing our rules."

The classic conception of bureaucracy was advanced by the German sociologist Max Weber, who stressed that the bureaucracy was a "rational" way for a modern society to conduct its business.[11] According to Weber, a **bureaucracy** depends on certain elements: It has a *hierarchical authority structure,* in which power flows from the top down and responsibility flows from the bottom up; it uses *task specialization* so that experts instead of amateurs perform technical jobs; and it develops extensive *rules,* which may seem extreme at times, but which allow similar cases to be handled similarly instead of capriciously. Bureaucracies operate on the *merit principle,* in which entrance and promotion are awarded on the basis of demonstrated abilities rather than on "who you know." Bureaucracies behave with *impersonality* so that all their clients are treated impartially. Weber's classic prototype of the bureaucratic organization depicts the bureaucracy as a well-organized machine with plenty of working, but hierarchical, parts.

bureaucracy
According to Max Weber, a hierarchical authority structure that uses task specialization, operates on the merit principle, and behaves with impersonality. Bureaucracies govern modern states.

The Acquisitive, Monopolistic Bureaucracy. The neat, Weberian model is only one way of thinking about bureaucracies. Other, more contemporary writers have seen bureaucracies as essentially "acquisitive," busily maximizing their budgets and expanding their powers.[12] Conservative economist William Niskanen, once a member of President Reagan's Council of Economic Advisors, believes that bureaucracies are like private corporations in seeking goals,[13] except that private corporations seek to maximize their *profits* whereas governmental bureaucracies seek to maximize their *budgets*. Bureaucratic administrators are committed to the "products" they "sell"—national security, schooling, public health, higher education, police protection—and their piece of the government's total budget pie is a good measure of how highly their product is valued. Moreover, all administrators take more professional pride in running a large, well-staffed agency than a puny one. For these reasons, insists Niskanen, bureaucracies are themselves largely responsible for the growth of modern governments.[14] Bureaucracies may even couple with Congress in an unholy alliance to expand big government (see Table 15.3 and the discussion of Fiorina's theory in Chapter 12).

Not only can bureaucracies be acquisitive, they also can be monopolistic. In the private sector, a monopoly, the sole supplier of some key good, is free from competition. It can afford to exact high prices and behave inefficiently. Public bureaucracies are typically monopolies, too. As a general rule, there is no alternative to the local fire department or water supply system; there is certainly no alternative to the national defense system. Only wealthy people really have an alternative to the local school system, the Social Security system, or government-run Medicare for the elderly. Some of Americans' complaints about bureaucracies are really complaints about bureaucratic monopoly. No matter how the bureaucracies behave, they will not lose their clients. There is no competitive pressure to force them to improve service or provide services more efficiently.[15]

Many conservative—and even liberal—critics of bureaucracy have favored *privatizing* some bureaucratic services to cut back on their monolithic and monopolistic power.[16] Local garbage collection or fire protection, for example, could be (and sometimes is) contracted out to private companies. Governments might thus accept the best service at the lowest price.[17]

Garbage Cans and Bureaucracies. One Washington official, lobbying for some policy changes in the nation's capital, told John Kingdon, "I can trace the path of ideas. But my personal theory is that people plant seeds every day. There are a lot of ideas around. . . . The real question is, which of these ideas will catch hold? When you plant a seed, you need rain, soil, and luck."[18]

Both the Weberian model and the model of the acquisitive, monopolistic bureaucracy make bureaucracies sound calculating and purposive. Another view of bureaucracy, though, makes them sound ambling and groping, affected by chance. Cohen, March, and Olsen suggest that the typical organization is a "loose collection of ideas, rather than a coherent structure."[19] As likely as not, they say, organizations operate by trial and error. Far from being tightly controlled, they are typically loosely run. For most organizations, it is rarely clear that one policy will work and another fail. Lots of ideas may be floating around any organization. Faced with a particular problem, members of the organization may pull one of these ideas from the "garbage can" of ideas and latch onto it. Organizations are not necessarily trying to find solutions to problems;

Table 15.3 Bureaucracy and Governmental Waste

Do you think people in the government waste a lot of the money we pay in taxes, waste some of it, or don't waste very much of it?

	1964	1968	1972	1984	1988	1992	1996
A lot	47%	59%	66%	65%	64%	68%	60%
Some	44%	34%	30%	29%	34%	30%	38%
Not very much	6%	4%	2%	4%	3%	2%	2%

Source: The question as worded is taken directly from National Election Studies.

just as often, solutions are in search of problems. The police department gets a new computer and then discovers how many tasks it has that need computerizing. Kingdon's careful study of governmental agenda building found much to recommend the "garbage can" model of policymaking.[20]

Each of these perspectives offers a different view of the American bureaucracy. None of them is completely right. Consider each of them as you examine the organization and functions of bureaucracies in modern America.

How Bureaucracies Are Organized

A complete organizational chart of the American federal government would be big enough to occupy a large wall. You could pore over this chart, trace the lines of responsibility and authority, and see how government is organized—at least on paper. A very simplified organizational chart of the executive branch appears in Figure 15.3. A much easier way to look at how the federal executive branch is organized is to group agencies into four basic types: cabinet departments, regulatory agencies, government corporations, and independent executive agencies.

The Cabinet Departments

Each of the 14 cabinet departments is headed by a secretary (except the Department of Justice, which is headed by the attorney general), chosen by the president, and approved by the Senate. Undersecretaries, deputy undersecretaries, and assistant secretaries report to the secretary . Each department manages specific policy areas (see the list in Table 13.4, page 405), and each has its own budget and its own staff.

Each department has a unique mission and is organized somewhat differently. The Department of the Interior, charged with overseeing the nation's natural resources and administering policies that affect Native Americans, is a well-established and traditional department (see Figure 15.4). The real work of a department is done in the bureaus, which divide the work into more specialized areas (a bureau is sometimes called a *service, office, administration*, or other name).

Until the 1970s, the largest cabinet department was the Department of Defense. From then until 1995, the Department of Health and Human Services (HHS) was the largest federal department in dollars spent (although the Department of Defense still had more employees). The Social Security Administration split from HHS and became an independent agency in 1995, spending one-third of the federal budget on the massive programs of Social Security and Medicare.

Sometimes status as a cabinet department can be controversial. For several years, Republicans have been trying to disband the Departments of Education, Energy, and Commerce, arguing that they waste tax dollars and implement policies that should be terminated.

The Regulatory Agencies

Each **independent regulatory agency** has responsibility for some sector of the economy, making and enforcing rules designed to protect the public interest. The independent regulatory agencies also judge disputes over these rules.[21] They are also sometimes called the alphabet soup of American government, because most such agencies are known in Washington by their initials. For example:

- *FRB (the Federal Reserve Board)*, charged with governing banks and, even more important, regulating the supply of money and thus interest rates
- *NLRB (the National Labor Relations Board)*, created to regulate labor-management relations

independent regulatory agency

A government agency responsible for some sector of the economy, making and enforcing rules to protect the public interest. It also judges disputes over these rules. The Interstate Commerce Commission is an example.

Figure 15.3 Organization of the Executive Branch

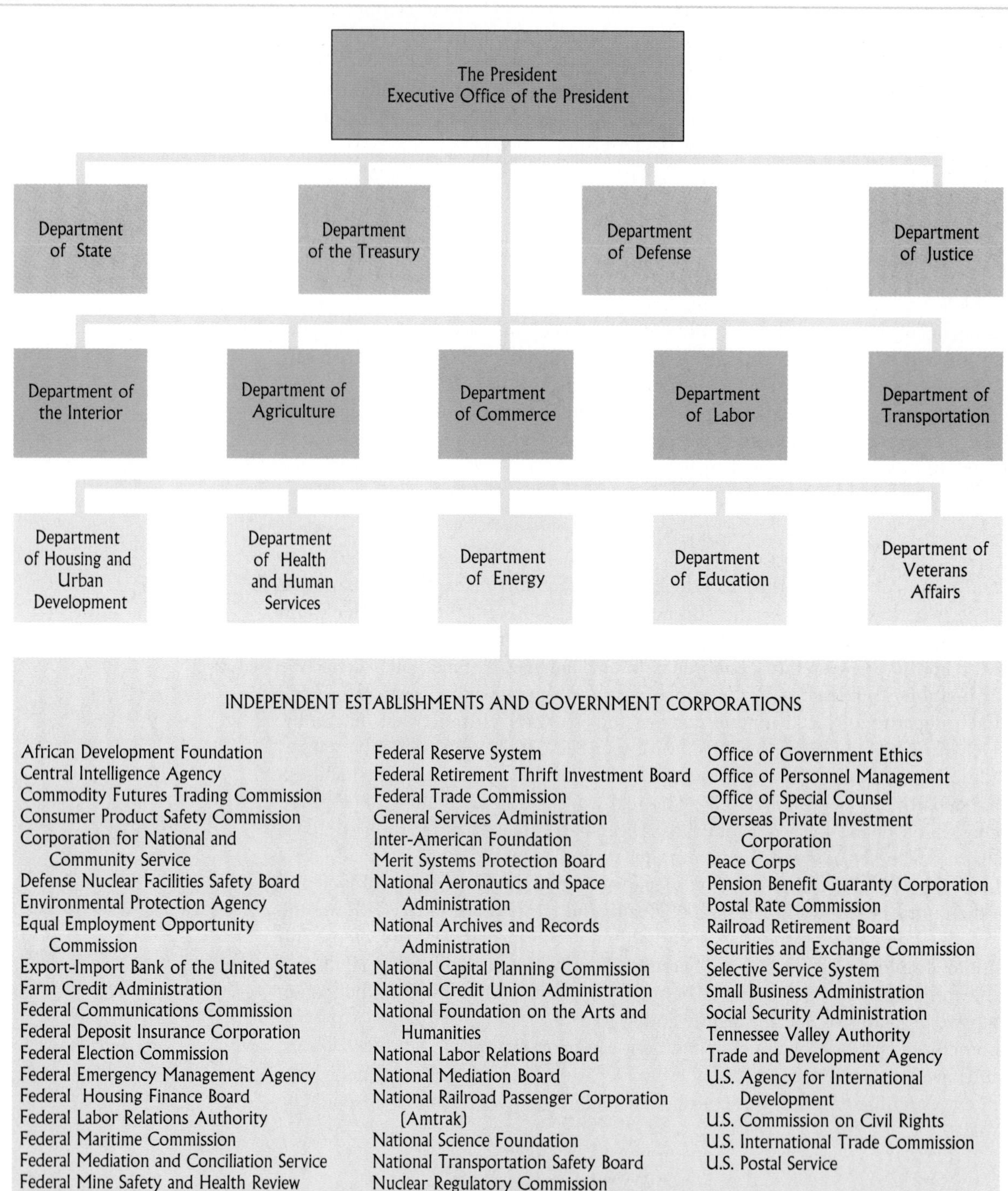

Source: Office of the Federal Register, *United States Government Manual 2000–2001* (Washington, D.C.: U.S. Government Printing Office, 2000), 22.

- *FCC (the Federal Communications Commission)*, charged with licensing radio and TV stations and regulating their programming in the public interest, as well as with regulating interstate long-distance telephone rates, cable television, and the Internet

Figure 15.4 Organization of the Department of the Interior

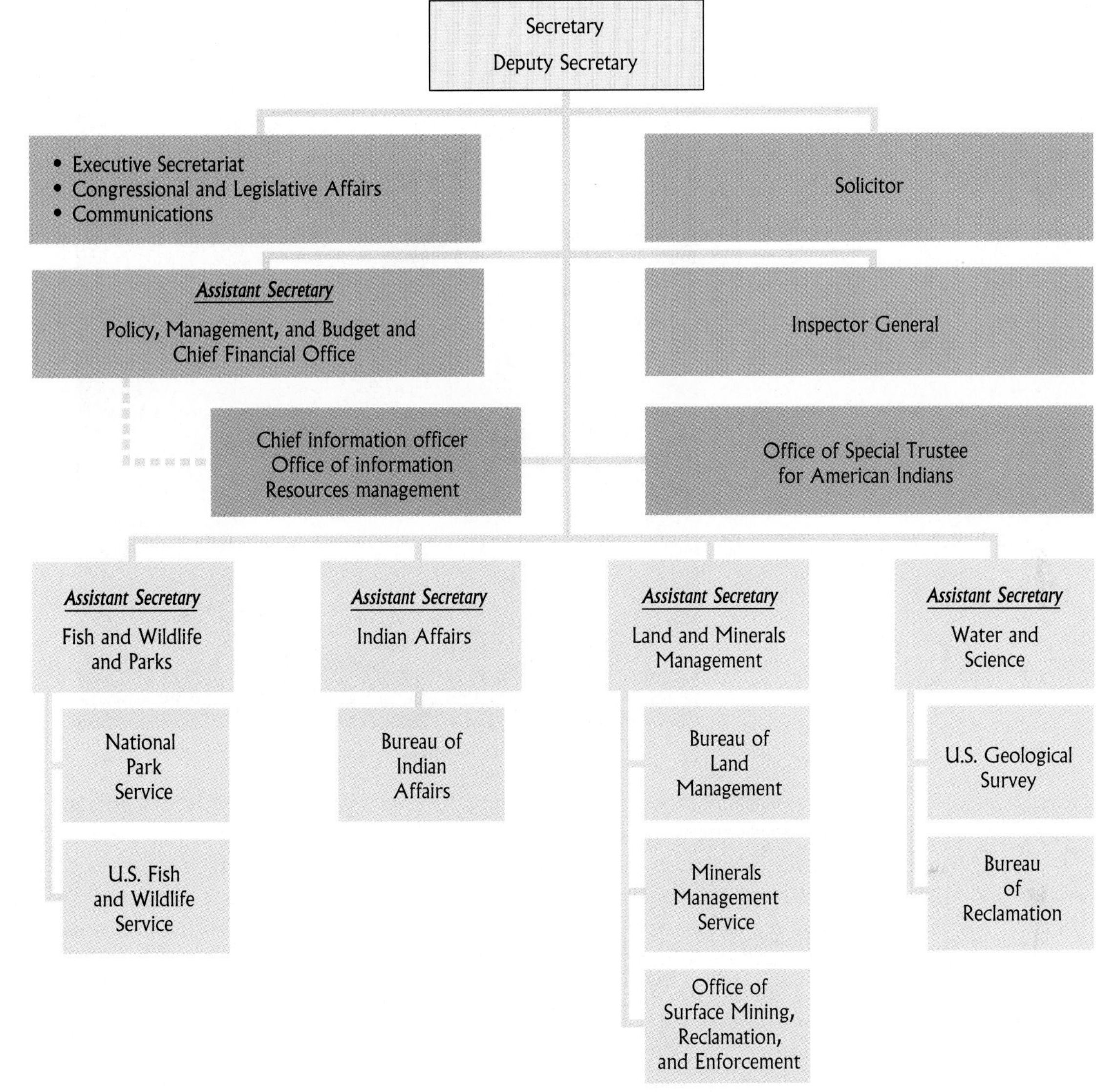

Source: Office of the Federal Register, *United States Government Manual 2000–2001* (Washington, D.C.: U.S. Government Printing Office, 2000), 253.

- *FTC (the Federal Trade Commission)*, responsible for regulating business practices and controlling monopolistic behavior, and now involved in policing the accuracy of advertising
- *SEC (the Securities and Exchange Commission)*, created to police the stock market

Each of these independent regulatory agencies is governed by a small commission, usually with 5 to 10 members appointed by the president and confirmed by the Senate for fixed terms. Unlike cabinet officers and members of the president's staff, regulatory commission members cannot be fired easily by the president. The Supreme Court made this ruling after President Franklin Roosevelt fired a man named Humphrey from the Federal Trade Commission. Humphrey died shortly afterward, but the angry executors of his estate sued for back pay, and the Court held that presidents could not fire members of regulatory agencies without just cause (*Humphrey's Executor v. United States*, 1935). "Just cause" has never been defined clearly, and no member of a regulatory commission has been fired since Humphrey.

The Environmental Protection Agency is the federal government's largest independent regulatory agency, overseeing the administration of all environmental legislation. Here, EPA workers clean up hazardous waste.

Interest groups consider the rule making by independent regulatory agencies (and, of course, their membership) very important. The FCC can deny a multimillion-dollar TV station a license renewal—a power that certainly sparks the interest of the National Association of Broadcasters. The FTC regulates business practices—a power that prompts both business and consumers to pay careful attention to its activities and membership.

Why does it matter?

Independent regulatory agencies, such as the Federal Reserve Board, are designed to be somewhat insulated from the influence of politics. Would you be more comfortable if the president and Congress had more direct influence on these agencies?

Interest groups are so concerned with these regulatory bodies that some critics point to the "capture" of the regulators by the regulatees.[22] It is common for members of commissions to be recruited from the ranks of the regulated. Sometimes, too, members of commissions or staffs of these agencies move on to jobs in the very industries they were regulating. Some lawyers among them use contacts and information gleaned at the agency when they represent clients before their former employers at the agency. A later section of this chapter will discuss the bureaucracy's relationship with interest groups.

The Government Corporations

The federal government also has a handful of **government corporations.** These are not exactly like private corporations in which you can buy stock and collect dividends, but they *are* like private corporations—and different from other parts of the government—in two ways. First, they provide a service that *could be* handled by the private sector. Second, they typically charge for their services, though often at rates cheaper than those the consumer would pay to a private-sector producer.

government corporation

A government organization that, like business corporations, provides a service that could be provided by the private sector and typically charges for its services. The U.S. Postal Service is an example. Compare **independent regulatory agency** and **independent executive agency.**

The granddaddy of the government corporations is the Tennessee Valley Authority (TVA). Established in 1933 as part of the New Deal, it has controlled floods, improved navigation, protected the soil against erosion, and provided inexpensive electricity to millions of Americans in Tennessee, Kentucky, Alabama, and neighboring states. Through Comsat—a modern-day government corporation that sells time-sharing on NASA

In an effort to make the agency financially independent as well as more responsive to consumers, in 1970, Congress transformed the Post Office Department into the U.S. Postal Service, the government's largest corporation. The agency has improved its fiscal performance (partly as a result of increased postal rates), although it is now subject to direct competition from private businesses that offer parcel and overnight mail services.

satellites—you can rent time on a space satellite for radio communications. The post office, one of the original cabinet departments (first headed by Benjamin Franklin), has become the government's largest corporation: the U.S. Postal Service.

Occasionally the government has taken over a "sick industry" and turned it into a government corporation. Amtrak, the railroad passenger service, is one example. Congress grumbles about Amtrak's multibillion-dollar subsidy (although some critics point out that billions of dollars in federal highway funds also constitute something of a subsidy for the auto industry), but members of Congress have only reluctantly agreed to let Amtrak shed its most unprofitable runs.

The Independent Executive Agencies

The **independent executive agencies** are essentially all the rest of the government—not cabinet departments, not regulatory commissions, and not government corporations. Their administrators typically are appointed by the president and serve at his will. These scores of bureaus are listed in the current issue of the *United States Government Manual.* A few of the biggest independent executive agencies (in size of budget) are:

- *General Services Administration (GSA),* the government's landlord, which handles buildings, supplies, and purchasing
- *National Science Foundation (NSF),* the agency supporting scientific research
- *National Aeronautics and Space Administration (NASA),* the agency that takes Americans to the moon and points beyond

independent executive agency

The government not accounted for by **cabinet** departments, **independent regulatory agencies,** and **government corporations.** Its administrators are typically appointed by the president and serve at the president's pleasure. NASA is an example.

Bureaucracies as Implementors

Today, bureaucracies are essentially *implementors* of policy. They take congressional, presidential, and sometimes even judicial pronouncements and develop procedures and rules for implementing policy goals. They also manage the routines of government, from delivering mail to collecting taxes to training troops.

What Implementation Means

Public policies are rarely self-executing. One of the few policies that administers itself is the president's decision to "recognize" a foreign government. It is entirely the chief executive's prerogative to do so, and once it is done, diplomatic relations with the country are thereby established.

Most policies, however, are not self-executing. Congress typically announces the goals of a policy in broad terms, sets up an administrative apparatus, and leaves the bureaucracy the task of working out the details of the program. In other words, the bureaucracy is left to implement the program. **Policy implementation** is the stage of policymaking between the establishment of a policy (such as the passage of a legislative act, the issuing of an executive order, the handing down of a judicial decision, or the promulgation of a regulatory rule) and the results of the policy for individuals.[23] To paraphrase loosely a famous line about war from German General Karl von Clausewitz: "Implementation is the continuation of policymaking by other means."[24] At a minimum, implementation includes three elements:

policy implementation

The stage of policymaking between the establishment of a policy and the consequences of the policy for the people whom it affects. Implementation involves translating the goals and objectives of a policy into an operating, ongoing program. See also **judicial implementation.**

1. Creation of a new agency or assignment of a new responsibility to an old agency
2. Translation of policy goals into operational rules and development of guidelines for the program
3. Coordination of resources and personnel to achieve the intended goals[25]

Why the Best-Laid Plans Sometimes Flunk the Implementation Test

The Scottish poet Robert Burns once wrote: "The best laid schemes o'mice and men/Gang aft a-gley [often go awry]." So, too, with the best intended public policies. Policies that people expect to work often fail. In 1996, Congress overwhelmingly passed a bill to guarantee health insurance to millions of Americans when they change or lose their jobs or lose coverage. Yet the law has been ineffective because insurance companies often charge these individuals premiums far higher than standard rates.[26] High expectations followed by dashed hopes are the frequent fate of well-intended public policies.

Program Design. Implementation can break down for several reasons. One is faulty program design. "It is impossible," said Eugene Bardach, "to implement well a policy or program that is defective in its basic theoretical conception." Consider, he suggested, the following hypothetical example:

> *If Congress were to establish an agency charged with squaring the circle with compass and straight edge—a task mathematicians have long ago shown is impossible—we could envision an agency coming into being, hiring a vast number of consultants, commissioning studies, reporting that progress was being made, while at the same time urging in their appropriations request for the coming year that the Congress augment the agency's budget.*[27]

And the circle would remain round.[28]

Lack of Clarity. Congress is fond of stating a broad policy goal in legislation and then leaving implementation up to the bureaucracies. Members of Congress can thus escape messy details, and place blame for the implementation decisions elsewhere.

Such was the case with the controversial Title IX of the Education Act of 1972,[29] which said: "No person in the United States shall, on the basis of sex, be excluded from participation in, be denied the benefits of, or be subjected to discrimination under any education program or activity receiving federal financial assistance." Because almost every college and university receives some federal financial assistance, almost all were thereby forbidden to discriminate on the basis of gender. Interest groups supporting women's athletics convinced Congress to include a provision about college athletics as well. Thus Section 844 reads,

> *The Secretary of [Health, Education, and Welfare (HEW) then, today of Education] shall prepare and publish . . . proposed regulations implementing the provisions of Title IX relating to prohibition of sex discrimination in Federally assisted education programs which shall include with respect to intercollegiate athletic activities reasonable provisions considering the nature of the particular sports [italics added].*

Just what does this section mean? Proponents of women's athletics thought it meant that discrimination against women's sports was also prohibited. Some, with good reason, looked forward to seeing women's sports on an equal footing with men's. One member of the House-Senate Conference Committee proposed language specifically exempting "revenue-producing athletics" (meaning men's football and basketball) from the prohibition. The committee rejected this suggestion, but to colleges and universities with big-time athletic programs, and to some alumni, the vague Section 844 called for equality in golf and swimming, not men's football and basketball programs, which could continue to have the lion's share of athletic budgets.

Joseph Califano, President Carter's secretary of HEW, was the man in the middle on this tricky problem. His staff developed a "policy interpretation" of the legislation, which he announced in December 1978. HEW's interpretation of the 100 or so words of Section 844 of Title IX numbered 30 pages. The interpretation recognized that football was "unique" among college sports. If football was unique, then the interpretation implied (but did not directly say) that male-dominated football programs could continue to outspend women's athletic programs.

Supporters of equal budgets for male and female athletics were outraged. Charlotte West of the Association for Intercollegiate Athletics for Women called HEW's interpretation

Bureaucracies are often asked to implement unclear laws. When Congress decided to prohibit gender discrimination in college athletics, for example, it left to bureaucrats the task of creating guidelines that would end discrimination while addressing the diverse needs of different sports. It took years—and several lawsuits—to establish the law's meaning.

"a multitude of imprecise and confusing explanations, exceptions, and caveats." Even the football-oriented National Collegiate Athletic Association was wary of the interpretation. One of its lawyers allowed, "They are trying to be fair. The question is how successful they are." A 100-word section in a congressional statute, which prompted a 30-page interpretation by the bureaucracy, in turn prompted scores of court cases. The courts have had to rule on such matters as whether Title IX requires that exactly equivalent dollar amounts be spent on women's and men's athletics. Litigation continues to this day.

The complex case of implementing Title IX for intercollegiate athletics contains an important lesson: Policy problems that Congress cannot resolve are not likely to be easily resolved by bureaucracies.

Bureaucrats receive not only unclear orders but also contradictory ones. James Q. Wilson points out that the Immigration and Naturalization Service is supposed to keep out illegal immigrants but let in necessary agricultural workers; to carefully screen foreigners seeking to enter the country but facilitate the entry of foreign tourists; and to find and expel illegal aliens but not break up families, impose hardships, violate civil rights, or deprive employers of low-paid workers. "No organization can accomplish all of these goals well, especially when advocates of each have the power to mount newspaper and congressional investigations of the agency's 'failures.'"[30] Similarly, the National Park Service is ordered to preserve the environmental quality of national parks; it is also obliged to keep them accessible to tourists at the same time. The Forest Service is supposed to help timber companies exploit the lumber potential in the national forests *and* preserve the natural environment.

Lack of Resources. As noted earlier, bureaucracies are often perceived as bloated. The important issue, however, is not the size of the bureaucracy in the abstract but whether it is the appropriate size to do the job it has been assigned to do. As big as a bureaucracy may seem in the aggregate, it frequently lacks the staff—along with the necessary training, funding, supplies, and equipment—to carry out the tasks it has been assigned. Recently, for example, the news has been filled with complaints such as the following:

- A shortage of staff causes delays in testing new drugs to combat AIDS.
- Because of lack of funding, the popular Head Start program serves fewer than half the children who are theoretically eligible to participate.
- The Immigration and Naturalization Service lacks the resources even to identify, much less deport, more than 10 percent of the 200,000 convicted criminal aliens in the United States. It also lacks the personnel to open letters containing checks for application fees.
- The Department of Education's lack of sufficient auditors prevents it from detecting fraud in the federal government's student aid programs.
- In their inspections of facilities handling and storing hazardous wastes, inadequately trained inspectors for the Environmental Protection Agency overlooked more than half the serious violations.
- Some observers fear that the lack of financing to maintain national parks will lead to permanent deterioration of such treasured American vacation spots as Yosemite and Yellowstone.
- The Federal Aviation Agency lacks the proper personnel and equipment to direct the nation's air traffic safely.
- Drug runners have more and faster ships and planes for smuggling drugs into the country than government agents who are trying to catch them.
- The Internal Revenue Service lacks the appropriate computer systems to integrate the dozens of databases that contain the information necessary to collect the nearly $2 trillion in taxes that finance the federal government.

Why does it matter?

A case can be made that some bureaucracies are too small. What if we substantially increased the resources available to those who implement policies? Would you receive better service from programs that affect you?

Agencies may also lack the *authority* necessary to meet their responsibilities. For example, many observers believe that the Food and Drug Administration (FDA) lacks adequate powers to protect the public from dangerous drugs such as the sleeping pill Halcion and the sedative Versed. The FDA does no testing of its own and must rely entirely on the test results submitted by manufacturers. Yet it lacks the subpoena power to obtain documents when it suspects that drug companies are withholding data about adverse drug reactions or misrepresenting test results. It often lacks access to potentially damaging company documents that have been involved in private product-liability cases.

Administrative Routine. For most bureaucrats, administration is a routine matter most of the time. They follow **standard operating procedures,** better known as SOPs, to help them make numerous everyday decisions. Standard rules save time. If a Social Security caseworker had to invent a new rule for every potential client and then have it cleared at higher levels, few clients would be served. Thus detailed manuals are written to cover as many particular situations as officials can anticipate. The regulations elaborating the Internal Revenue Code compose an IRS agent's bible. Similarly, a customs agent has binders filled with rules and regulations about what can and cannot be brought into the United States duty free.

standard operating procedures

Better known as SOPs, these procedures are used by bureaucrats to bring uniformity to complex organizations. Uniformity improves fairness and makes personnel interchangeable. See also **administrative discretion.**

SOPs also bring uniformity to complex organizations. Justice is better served when rules are applied uniformly, as in the implementation of welfare policies that distribute benefits to the needy or in the levying of fines for underpayment of taxes. Uniformity also makes personnel interchangeable. Soldiers, for example, can be transferred to any spot in the world and still find out how to do their job by referring to the appropriate manual.

Routines are essential to bureaucracy. Yet they sometimes become frustrating to citizens, who term them "red tape" when they do not seem appropriate to a situation. SOPs then become obstacles to action. In an October 1983 terrorist attack on their barracks outside Beirut, Lebanon, 241 Marines were killed while they slept. A presidential commission appointed to examine the causes of the tragedy concluded that, among other factors contributing to the disaster, the Marines in the peacekeeping force were "not trained, organized, staffed, or supported to deal effectively with the terrorist threat."[31] In other words, they had not altered their SOPs regarding security, which is basic to any military unit, to meet the unique challenges of a terrorist attack.

simulation
You Are the Administrator

Sometimes an agency simply fails to establish routines that are necessary to complete its tasks. For example, in late 1997, the General Accounting Office found that the Federal Aviation Agency (FAA) failed to determine whether the violations its inspectors uncovered at aircraft repair stations were ever corrected. The FAA did not keep the proper paperwork for adequate follow-up activities.

Problems with SOPs are nothing new. They certainly frustrated Franklin D. Roosevelt:

> *The Treasury is so . . . ingrained in its practices that I find it impossible to get the action and results I want. . . . But the Treasury is not to be compared with the State Department. You should go through the experience of trying to get any changes in the thinking, policy, and action of the career diplomats . . . But both put together are nothing as compared to the Na-a-vy. . . . To change anything in the Na-a-vy is like punching a feather bed. You punch it with your right and you punch it with your left until you are finally exhausted, and then you find the damn bed just as it was before you started punching.*[32]

Sometimes routines seem impenetrable to the average citizen, who must understand them in order to make use of the service bureaucracies offer. The Clinton administration has made an effort to simplify government regulations. You can see an example of one success in "Making a Difference: Harry Carey and Sara Pratt."

Administrators' Dispositions. Paradoxically, bureaucrats operate not only within the confines of routines, but often with considerable discretion to behave independently. **Administrative discretion** is the authority of administrative actors to select among various responses to a given problem.[33] Discretion is greatest when rules do not fit a particular case, and this is often the case—even in agencies with elaborate rules and regulations.

administrative discretion

The authority of administrative actors to select among various responses to a given problem. Discretion is greatest when routines, or **standard operating procedures,** do not fit a case.

Although the income tax code is massive and detailed, the IRS wields vast discretion because of the complexity of the U.S. economy and the multitude of tax situations it produces. Here are a few examples:[34]

Making a Difference

Harry Carey and Sara Pratt

As part of its work to revitalize communities, create jobs, produce affordable housing, and expand home ownership, the Department of Housing and Urban Development (HUD) enforces the Fair Housing Act, which outlaws housing discrimination. Filing a complaint starts the enforcement process, but for many people this has been more easily said than done.

As Vice President Gore put it, "There are few things more damaging than housing discrimination because when you deny people a home, you deny them the school they want, the neighborhood they want, and often the job they need . . . But . . . if you look at what it took to file a complaint, you found a 600-word form that raised more questions than it answered."

In the fall of 1998, Vice President Al Gore presented Harry Carey, assistant general counsel for Fair Housing Enforcement, and Sara Pratt, director of the Office for Fair Housing Enforcement, with the "No Gobbledygook Award" for putting into plain language a regulation on how to file a housing discrimination complaint, making it much easier for average Americans to file such complaints.

You can see what Harry Carey and Sara Pratt accomplished by comparing the old and new versions of the regulation.

Before

Sec. 103.40 Date of filing of complaint.

(a) Except as provided in paragraph (b) of this section, a complaint is filed when it is received by HUD, or dual filed with HUD through a substantially equivalent State or local agency, in a form that reasonably meets the standards of Sec. 103.30.

(b) The Assistant Secretary may determine that a complaint is filed for the purposes of the one-year period for the filing of complaints, upon the submission of written information (including information provided by telephone and reduced to writing by an employee of HUD) identifying the parties and describing generally the alleged discriminatory housing practice.

Where a complaint alleges a discriminatory housing practice that is continuing, as manifested in a number of incidents of such conduct, the complaint will be timely if filed within one year of the last alleged occurrence of that practice.

After

Sec. 103.18 Is there a time limit on when I can file?

Yes. You must notify us within one year that you are a victim of discrimination. If you indicate there is more than one act of discrimination, or that it is continuing, we must receive your information within one year of the last incident.

Source: Press release from the White House, "Vice-President Gore Lauds HUD Employees for Using 'Plain Language.'" Taken from http://www.npr.gov/library/news/102898.html.

- Congress and the IRS code say that medical expenses above a certain percentage of income are deductible, but how about the expenses of a vasectomy? (The IRS said yes.)
- A girl who had been ordered to take strenuous exercise under the supervision of a doctor was enrolled by her father in $8,436 worth of ballet lessons. Was it deductible? (The IRS said no.)
- Congress and the IRS code say that business expenses are deductible, but can an airline flight attendant deduct the cost of uniforms? (The IRS said yes.)
- Are taxi expenses incurred in visiting your stockbroker a deductible expense? (The IRS said yes.)

street-level bureaucrats

A phrase coined by Michael Lipsky, referring to those bureaucrats who are in constant contact with the public and have considerable **administrative discretion.**

Some administrators exercise more discretion than others. Michael Lipsky coined the phrase **street-level bureaucrats** to refer to those bureaucrats who are in constant contact with the public (often a hostile one) and have considerable discretion; they include police officers, welfare workers, and lower-court judges.[35] No amount of rules, not even the thousands of pages of IRS rules, will eliminate the need for bureaucratic discretion on some policies. The highway patrol officer who stops you can choose to issue you a warning or a ticket.

Because bureaucrats will inevitably exercise discretion, it is important to understand how they use it. Ultimately, how they use discretion depends on their dispositions about the policies and rules they administer. Although bureaucrats may be indifferent to the implementation of many policies, other policies may conflict with their views or their personal or organizational interests. When people are asked to execute orders

Bureaucrats typically apply thousands of pages of rules in the performance of routine tasks, but many bureaucrats—especially street-level bureaucrats—must use administrative discretion as well. This border patrol officer, shown arresting an illegal immigrant on the U.S.-Mexican border, must decide whom he will search carefully and whom he will let pass with a quick check.

with which they do not agree, slippage is likely to occur between policy decisions and performance. A great deal of mischief may occur as well.

On one occasion, President Nixon ordered Secretary of Defense Melvin Laird to bomb a Palestine Liberation Organization hideaway, a move Laird opposed. According to the secretary, "We had bad weather for forty-eight hours. The Secretary of Defense can always find a reason not to do something."[36] The president's order was stalled for days and eventually rescinded.

Controlling the exercise of discretion is a difficult task. It is not easy to fire bureaucrats in the civil service, and removing appointed officials may be politically embarrassing to the president, especially if those officials have strong support in Congress and among interest groups. In the private sector, leaders of organizations provide incentives such as pay raises to encourage employees to perform their tasks in a certain way. In the public sector, however, special bonuses are rare, and pay raises tend to be small and across the board. Moreover, there is not necessarily room at the top for qualified bureaucrats. Unlike a typical private business, a government agency cannot expand just because it is performing a service effectively and efficiently.

In the absence of positive and negative incentives, the government relies heavily on rules to limit the discretion of implementors. As Vice President Al Gore put it in a report issued by the National Performance Review,

> *Because we don't want politicians' families, friends, and supporters placed in "no-show" jobs, we have more than 100,000 pages of personnel rules and regulations defining in exquisite detail how to hire, promote, or fire federal employees. Because we don't want employees or private companies profiteering from federal contracts, we create procurement processes that require endless signatures and long months to buy almost anything. Because we don't want agencies using tax dollars for any unapproved purpose, we dictate precisely how much they can spend on everything from telephones to travel.*[37]

Often these rules end up creating new obstacles to effective and efficient governing, however. As U.S. forces were streaming toward the Persian Gulf in the fall of 1990 to liberate Kuwait from Iraq, the air force placed an emergency order for 6,000 Motorola commercial radio receivers. But Motorola refused to do business with the air force because of a government requirement that the company set up separate accounting and cost-control systems to fill the order. The only way the U.S. Air Force could acquire the much-needed receivers was for Japan to buy them and donate them to the United States!

Fragmentation. Sometimes responsibility for a policy is dispersed among several units within the bureaucracy. The federal government has more than 150 training and employment programs spread across 14 departments, agencies, and commissions. In the field of welfare, 10 different departments and agencies administer more than 100 federal human services programs. The Department of Health and Human Services has responsibility for basic welfare grants to families, the Department of Housing and Urban Development provides housing assistance, the Department of Agriculture runs the food stamp program, and the Department of Labor administers training programs and provides assistance in obtaining employment.

This diffusion of responsibility makes the coordination of policies both time consuming and difficult. For years, efforts to control the flow of illicit drugs into the country have been hindered by lack of cooperation among the Drug Enforcement Administration in the Department of Justice, the Customs Service in the Treasury Department, the State Department, and other relevant agencies.

Sometimes different agencies send contradictory signals to those who are supposed to comply with a law. The regulation of hazardous wastes, such as the radioactive waste produced by the nuclear power industry, is one of the major concerns of the Environmental Protection Agency and a matter of paramount importance to the public. The Department of Energy, however, has routinely paid all the fines its contractors have received for violating laws designed to protect the environment, and it has even paid the legal fees the contractors incurred while defending themselves against the fines. The Department of Energy has also given generous bonuses to its contractors even while the EPA was fining them. Such contradictory policies obviously undermine efforts to limit pollution of the environment.

If fragmentation is a problem, why not reorganize the government? The answer lies in hyperpluralism and the decentralization of power. Congressional committees recognize that they would lose jurisdiction over agencies if these agencies were merged with others. Interest groups (such as the nuclear power industry) do not want to give up the close relationships they have developed with "their" agencies. Agencies themselves do not want to be submerged within a broader bureaucratic unit. All these forces fight reorganization, and they usually win.[38] President Clinton's proposal to merge the Drug Enforcement Administration and the Customs Service met with immediate opposition from the agencies and their congressional allies. Pursuing the merger became too costly for the president, who had to focus on higher-priority issues.

A Case Study: The Voting Rights Act of 1965

Even when a policy is controversial, however, implementation can be effective if goals are clear and there are adequate means to achieve them. In 1965, Congress, responding to generations of discrimination against prospective African-American voters in the South, passed the Voting Rights Act. The act singled out six states in the Deep South in which the number of registered African-American voters was minuscule. Congress ordered the Justice Department to send federal registrars to each county in those states to register qualified voters. Congress outlawed literacy tests and other tests previously used to discriminate against African-American registrants. The government promised stiff penalties for those who interfered with the work of federal registrars.

Congress charged the attorney general with implementing the Voting Rights Act. He acted quickly and dispatched hundreds of registrars—some protected by U.S. marshals—to Southern counties. Within seven-and-a-half months after the act's passage, more than 300,000 new African-American voters were on the rolls. The proportion of the Southern African-American population registered to vote increased

How You Can Make a Difference

The Federal Bureaucracy

From the beginning of this book, you've seen how government affects nearly every part of our daily lives. On the whole, government can seem monolithic, and the many different bureaucratic agencies impervious to change. Bureaucracy can reinvent itself, however, as the example of Harry Carey and Sara Pratt illustrates in "Making a Difference." In fact, all citizens—including college students—have an opportunity to effect change at even the highest levels of the federal government. Rather than focus on a specific issue or agency, it might be useful to highlight the various strategies and tactics available to people determined to bring about change within a federal agency. Many of the following ideas and information are borrowed from a variety of activist groups from the liberal *For Mother Earth* organization (www. motherearth.org) and the progressive *20/20 Vision* (www.2020vision.org) to the conservative Citizen Lobbying Kit from the *Conservative Caucus* (www. conservativeusa.org). Whether you are a liberal, a conservative, or something in between, these methods work.

Lobbying to change agencies and organizations, especially those falling within presidential purview, is different from lobbying and influencing Congress. Many officials working for federal agencies, especially those whose upper-level executives change constantly, can be difficult to pin down. Furthermore, while a member of Congress may be directly responsible to you—his or her constituent, the director of the EPA is directly responsible to no one but the president. As such, it is much harder to use political pressure techniques on agency staff members than it is on elected officials. This is important to remember when contacting the different bureaucracies. Unlike Congress, many agencies are unable to handle large amounts of public correspondence and do not tally and track the different contacts made by the public.

So, how to influence the federal agencies, then? If federal bureaucracies are not always responsive to the general public, they tend to be far more sympathetic to phone calls from members of Congress who control their budgets—especially those who are members on committees related to that agency and those who have seniority. If possible, try to work through any regional offices that the agency may have in your area. Many of the regional offices are concerned with community outreach and are likely to be far more responsive and accessible than a staffer located in Washington, D.C. Check on the internet sites for the individual agency under consideration. If possible, use the media to capture the attention of both bureaucrats and politicians. For example, agencies often clip news items from around the country dealing with their agency—even those articles solely directed at regional offices. By writing letters to the editor, an op-ed piece, or by staging a public event worthy of press coverage, your issue will come to the attention of the agency involved very forcefully. Remember to avoid mass-generated form letters. A personal, handwritten letter will garner a much better response. A well-known individual or organization as a spokesman for your issue further increases your chances of wider coverage. Following these simple guidelines can result in amazing results.

from 43 percent in 1964 to 66 percent in 1970, partly (though not entirely) because of the Voting Rights Act.[39]

The Voting Rights Act was a successful case of implementation by any standard, but not because it was popular with everyone. Southern representatives and senators were outraged by it, and a filibuster delayed its passage in the Senate. It was successful because its goal was clear (to register large numbers of African-American voters), its implementation was straightforward (sending out people to register them), and the authority of the implementors was clear (they had the support of the attorney general and even U.S. marshals) and concentrated in the Justice Department, which was disposed to implementing the law vigorously.

Bureaucracies as Regulators

regulation
The use of governmental authority to control or change some practice in the private sector. Regulations pervade the daily lives of people and institutions.

Government **regulation** is the use of governmental authority to control or change some practice in the private sector. Regulations by government pervade Americans' everyday lives and the lives of businesses, universities, hospitals, and other institutions. Federal regulations now fill more than 200 volumes. Regulation is the most controversial role of the

The Voting Rights Act of 1965 was successfully implemented because its goal was clear: to register African Americans to vote in Southern counties where their voting rights had been denied for years. This federal registrar, like hundreds of others working for the Department of Justice, helped bring the vote to some 300,000 African Americans in less than a year.

bureaucracies, yet Congress gives bureaucrats broad mandates to regulate activities as diverse as interest rates, the location of nuclear power plants, and food additives.

Regulation in the Economy and in Everyday Life

The notion that the American economy is largely a "free enterprise" system, unfettered by government intervention, is about as up to date as a Model T Ford. You can begin to understand the sweeping scope of governmental regulation by examining how the automobile industry is regulated.

- The Securities and Exchange Commission regulates buying and selling stock in an automobile corporation.
- Relations between the workers and managers of the company come under the scrutiny of the National Labor Relations Board.
- Affirmative action in hiring workers is mandated and administered by the Department of Labor and the Equal Employment Opportunity Commission because automakers are major government contractors.
- The Environmental Protection Agency, the National Highway Traffic Safety Administration, and the Department of Transportation require pollution-control, energy-saving, and safety devices.
- Unfair advertising and deceptive consumer practices in marketing cars come under the watchful eye of the Federal Trade Commission.

A Full Day of Regulation. Everyday life itself is the subject of bureaucratic regulation. Almost all bureaucratic agencies—not merely the ones called independent regulatory agencies—are in the regulatory business. Consider a typical factory worker (we'll name him John Smith) who works in the city of Chicago and lives with his wife, Joan Smith, and their three young children in suburban Mount Prospect, Ill. Both at work and at home, federal regulations affect John's life. At 5:30 A.M. he is awakened by his clock radio, which is set to a country music station licensed to operate by the Federal Communications Commission. For breakfast he has cereal, which has passed inspection by the Food and Drug Administration, as has the lunch Joan packs for him.

The processed meat in his sandwich is packed under the supervision of the Food Safety and Quality Service of the U.S. Department of Agriculture.

John takes the train to work and buys a quick cup of coffee before the journey. The caffeine in his coffee, the FDA has warned, has caused birth defects in laboratory animals, and there is discussion in Washington about regulating it. After paying his fare (regulated by the state government), he hops aboard and shortly arrives at work, a small firm that makes equipment for the food industry.

At home, Joan Smith is preparing breakfast for the children. The price of the milk she serves is affected by the dairy price supports regulated by the Agricultural Stabilization and Conservation Service. As the children play, she evaluates the toys they use, wanting to avoid any that could be dangerous. A Washington agency, the Consumer Product Safety Commission, also takes note of children's toys, regulating their manufacture and sale. The Consumer Product Safety Commission also regulates the lawn mower, the appliances, the microwave oven, and numerous other items around the Smith house.

Setting out for the grocery store and the bank, Joan encounters even more government regulations. The car has seat belts mandated by the National Highway Traffic Safety Administration, and the Department of Transportation certifies its gas mileage. The car's pollution-control devices are now in need of service because they do not meet the requirements of the Environmental Protection Agency. The bank where Joan deposits money and writes a check is among the most heavily regulated institutions she encounters in her daily life. Her passbook savings rate is regulated by the Depository Institutions Deregulation Committee, and her account is insured by the Federal Deposit Insurance Commission.

Meanwhile, John Smith is at work assembling food-processing machinery. He and the other workers are members of the International Association of Machinists. Their negotiations with the firm are held under rules laid down by the National Labor Relations Board. Not long ago, the firm was visited by inspectors from the Occupational Safety and Health Administration (OSHA), a federal agency charged with ensuring worker safety. OSHA inspectors noted several violations and forwarded a letter recommending safety changes to the head of the firm.

Most government regulation is clearly in the public interest. For example, the U.S. Department of Agriculture is charged with regulating the quality of meat products, a task it was given after novelist Upton Sinclair exposed the meat-packaging industry's unsanitary conditions at the turn of the century.

Back at home, John has a beer before dinner. It was made in a brewery carefully supervised by the Bureau of Alcohol, Tobacco, and Firearms, and federal and state taxes were collected when it was sold. After dinner (almost all the food served has been transported by the regulated trucking industry), the children are sent to bed. An hour or so of television, broadcast on regulated airwaves, is followed by bedtime. A switch will turn off the electric lights, whose rates are regulated by the Illinois Commerce Commission and the Federal Energy Regulatory Commission.[40]

Regulation: How It Grew, How It Works

From the beginnings of the American republic until 1887, the federal government made almost no regulatory policies; the little regulation produced was handled by state and local authorities. Even the minimal regulatory powers of state and local governments were much disputed. In 1877, the Supreme Court upheld the right of government to regulate the business operations of a firm. The case, *Munn v. Illinois,* involved the right of the state of Illinois to regulate the charges and services of a Chicago warehouse. During this time, farmers were seething about alleged overcharging by railroads, grain elevator companies, and other business firms. In 1887—a decade after *Munn*—Congress created the first regulatory agency, the Interstate Commerce Commission (ICC), and charged it with regulating the railroads, their prices, and their services to farmers; the ICC thus set the precedent for regulatory policymaking.

As regulators, bureaucratic agencies typically operate with a large grant of power from Congress, which may detail goals to be achieved but may also permit the agencies to sketch out the regulatory means. In 1935, for example, Congress created the National Labor Relations Board to control "unfair labor practices," but the NLRB had to play a major role in defining "fair" and "unfair." Most agencies charged with regulation must first develop a set of rules, often called *guidelines.* The appropriate agency may specify how much food coloring it will permit in a hot dog, how many contaminants it will allow an industry to dump into a stream, how much radiation from a nuclear reactor is too much, and so forth. Guidelines are developed in consultation with, and sometimes with the agreement of, the people or industries being regulated.

Next, the agency must apply and enforce its rules and guidelines, either in court or through its own administrative procedures. Sometimes it waits for complaints to

Opponents of government regulation contend that the rapid increase in the number and scope of environmental regulations during the past two decades has stifled economic growth. Others argue that such regulations are essential to protect the nation's air, land, and water—and the people who use them.

You Are the Policymaker

How Should We Regulate?

Almost every regulatory policy was created to achieve some desirable social goal. When more than 10,000 people are killed annually in industrial accidents, who would disagree with the goal of a safer workplace? Who would dissent from greater highway safety, when more than 50,000 die each year in automobile accidents? Who would disagree with policies to promote equality in hiring, when the history of opportunities for women and minorities is one of discrimination? Who would disagree with policies to reduce industrial pollution, when pollution threatens health and lives? However, there may be more than one way to achieve these—and many other—desirable social goals.

Charles L. Schultze, chair of President Carter's Council of Economic Advisors, is—like Murray L. Weidenbaum, who held the same position under President Reagan—a critic of the current state of federal regulation. Schultze reviewed the regulatory activities of the Environmental Protection Agency (EPA) and the Occupational Safety and Health Administration (OSHA). Neither agency's policies, he concluded, had worked very well. He described the existing system as **command-and-control policy:** The government tells business how to reach certain goals, checks that these commands are followed, and punishes offenders.

Schultze advocates an **incentive system.** He argues that instead of telling construction businesses how their ladders must be constructed, measuring the ladders, and charging a small fine for violators, it would be more efficient and effective to levy a high tax on firms with excessive worker injuries. Instead of trying to develop standards for 62,000 pollution sources, as the EPA now does, it would be easier and more effective to levy a high tax on those who cause pollution. The government could even provide incentives in the form of rewards for such socially valuable behavior as developing technology to reduce pollution. Incentives, Schultze argues, use marketlike strategies to regulate industry. They are, he claims, more effective and efficient than command-and-control regulation.

Not everyone is as keen on the use of incentives as Schultze. Defenders of the command-and-control system of regulation compare the present system to preventive medicine—it is designed to minimize pollution or workplace accidents before they become too severe. Defenders of the system argue, too, that penalties for excessive pollution or excessive workplace accidents would be imposed only after substantial damage had been done. They also add that if taxes on pollution or unsafe work environments were merely externalized (that is, passed along to the consumer as higher prices), they would not be much of a deterrent. Moreover, it would take a large bureaucracy to monitor carefully the level of pollution discharged, and it would require a complex calculation to determine the level of tax necessary to encourage businesses not to pollute.

The issue of the manner of regulation is a complex one. What would *you* do?

Sources: Charles L. Schultze, *The Public Use of the Private Interest* (Washington, D.C.: Brookings Institution, 1977); and Steven Kelman, *What Price Incentives? Economists and the Environment* (Boston: Auburn House, 1981).

come to it, as the Equal Employment Opportunity Commission does; sometimes it sends inspectors into the field, as the Occupational Safety and Health Administration does; and sometimes it requires application for a permit or license to demonstrate performance consistent with congressional goals and agency rules, as the Federal Communications Commission does. Often government agencies take violators to court, hoping to secure a judgment and fine against an offender (see "You Are the Policymaker: How Should We Regulate?"). Whatever strategy Congress permits a regulating agency to use, all regulation contains these elements: (1) *a grant of power and set of directions from Congress,* (2) *a set of rules and guidelines* by the regulatory agency itself, and (3) *some means of enforcing compliance* with congressional goals and agency regulations.

Government regulation of the American economy and society has, of course, grown in recent decades. The budgets of regulatory agencies, their level of employment, and the number of rules they issue are all increasing—and did so even during the conservative Reagan Administration. As we have seen, few niches in American society are *not* affected by regulation. Not surprisingly, this situation has led to charges that government is overdoing it.

command-and-control policy

According to Charles Schultze, the existing sysetm of **regulation** whereby government tells business how to reach certain goals, checks that these commands are followed, and punishes offenders. Compare **incentive system.**

incentive system

According to Charles Schultze, a more effective and efficient policy than **command-and-control;** in the incentive system, marketlike strategies are used to manage public policy.

Toward Deregulation

deregulation

The lifting of restrictions on business, industry, and professional activities for which government rules had been established and that bureaucracies had been created to administer.

Deregulation—the lifting of government restrictions on business, industry, and professional activities—is currently a fashionable term.[41] The idea behind deregulation is that the number and complexity of regulatory policies have made regulation too complicated and burdensome. To critics, the problem with regulation is that it raises prices, distorts market forces, and—worst of all—does not work. They claim that the regulatory system:

- *Raises prices.* If the producer is faced with expensive regulations, the cost will inevitably be passed on to the consumer in the form of higher prices.
- *Hurts America's competitive position abroad.* Other nations may have fewer regulations on pollution, worker safety, and other business practices than the United States. Thus American products may cost more in the international marketplace, undermining sales in other countries.
- *Does not always work well.* Tales of failed regulatory policies are numerous. Regulations may be difficult or cumbersome to enforce. Critics charge that regulations sometimes do not achieve the results that Congress intended and maintain that they simply create massive regulatory bureaucracies.

President Reagan's conservative political philosophy was opposed to much government regulation, but even before the Reagan administration, sentiment favoring deregulation was building in the Washington community. Even liberals sometimes joined the antiregulation chorus; for example, Senator Edward Kennedy of Massachusetts pushed for airline deregulation. The airline industry also pressed for deregulation and in 1978 the Civil Aeronautics Board (CAB) began to deregulate airline prices and airline routes. In 1984, the CAB formally disbanded; it even brought in a military bugler to play taps at its last meeting.

Not everyone, however, believes that deregulation is in the nation's best interest.[42] For example, critics point to severe environmental damage resulting from lax enforcement of environmental protection standards during the Reagan administration. Similarly, many observers attribute at least a substantial portion of the blame for the enormously expensive bailout of the savings and loan industry to deregulation in the 1980s. Many people now argue for more regulation of savings and loan institutions. Californians found that deregulation led to severe power shortages in 2001.

In addition, many regulations have proved beneficial to Americans. As a result of government regulations, we breathe cleaner air,[43] we have lower levels of lead in our blood, miners are safer at work,[44] seacoasts have been preserved,[45] and children are more likely to survive infancy.[46]

Understanding Bureaucracies

As both implementors and regulators, bureaucracies are making public policy, not just administering someone else's decisions. The fact that bureaucrats, who are not elected, compose most of the government raises fundamental issues about who controls governing and what the bureaucracy's role should be.

Bureaucracy and Democracy

Bureaucracies constitute one of America's two unelected policymaking institutions (courts are the other). In democratic theory, popular control of government depends on elections, but we could not possibly elect the 4.1 million federal civilian and military employees, or even the few thousand top men and women, though they spend more than nearly $2 trillion of the American GDP. Furthermore, the fact that voters do not elect civil servants does not mean that bureaucracies cannot respond to and represent

Former FBI Director J. Edgar Hoover is an example of a powerful bureaucrat who worked outside the law. Hoover took over the new agency in 1924 and, after consolidating his power following World War II, began collecting information on presidents, members of Congress, and later, liberal groups and civil rights leaders. Partly because they were afraid of what he might have in his files, elected officials were unwilling to control Hoover, who did not relinquish power until his death in 1972.

the public's interests. When we compare the backgrounds of bureaucrats with those of members of Congress or presidents, we find that bureaucrats are more representative than elected officials. Much depends on whether bureaucracies are effectively controlled by the policymakers citizens do elect—the president and Congress.[47]

Presidents Try to Control the Bureaucracy. Chapter 13 looked at some of the frustrations presidents endure in trying to control the government they are elected to run. Presidents try hard—not always with success—to impose their policy preferences on agencies (see "America in Perspective: Influencing Independent Agencies"). Following are some presidential methods of exercising control over bureaucracies:

- *Appoint the right people to head the agency.* Normally, presidents control the appointments of agency heads and subheads. Putting their people in charge is one good way for presidents to influence agency policy,[48] yet even this has its problems. President Reagan's efforts to whittle the powers of the Environmental Protection Agency led to his appointment of controversial Anne Gorsuch to head the agency. Gorsuch had previously supported policies contrary to the goals of the EPA. When Gorsuch attempted to implement her policies, legal squabbles with Congress and political controversy ensued, ultimately leading to her resignation. To patch up the damage Gorsuch had done to his reputation, Reagan named a moderate and seasoned administrator, William Ruckelshaus, to run the agency. Ironically, Ruckelshaus demanded, and got, more freedom from the White House than Gorsuch had sought.
- *Issue orders.* Presidents can issue **executive orders** to agencies. These orders carry the force of law and are used to implement statutes, treaties, and provisions of the Constitution. Sometimes presidential aides simply pass the word that "the President was wondering if . . ." These messages usually suffice, although agency heads are reluctant to run afoul of Congress or the press on the basis of a broad presidential hint.
- *Tinker with an agency's budget.* The Office of Management and Budget is the president's own final authority on any agency's budget. The OMB's threats to cut here or add there will usually get an agency's attention. Each agency, however, has its constituents within and outside of Congress, and Congress, not the president, does the appropriating.
- *Reorganize an agency.* Although President Reagan promised, proposed, and pressured to abolish the Department of Energy and the Department of Education, he

executive orders

Regulations originating from the executive branch. Executive orders are one method presidents can use to control the bureaucracy.

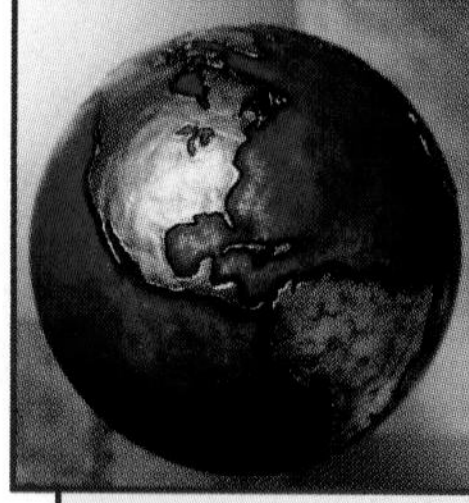

America in Perspective

Influencing Independent Agencies

We often think of the president as head of the executive branch, but there are agencies, such as the Federal Reserve Board, that are very powerful and are generally free from the chief executive's direction. This often leaves presidents frustrated, as when they wish the Federal Reserve Board to lower interest rates to stimulate the economy. There are even more autonomous agencies in Latin America, however—agencies removed from the direct control of the president and the legislature.

Why would Latin American governments create agencies they cannot control? The primary reason is to protect a new agency providing a new service from changes in policy made by future decision makers. Those who create an agency fear that its policies will be undone by a new administration or legislature, so they make it autonomous.

These agencies often have their own sources of revenue and thus can increase their budgets without going through the public and controversial process of government budget debates. They are also freer from legislative oversight and formal presidential controls than are regular agencies, and conflict over their programs is less visible. Expenditures for autonomous agencies also allow the government to engage in creative financing because when these agencies contract debt, it does not count against the central government's debt (which is substantial in Latin America).

Autonomy is decidedly a mixed blessing, however. Creative financing is not necessarily good for a nation, nor is the difficulty policymakers have in consolidating bureaucracies and increasing their efficiency. The lack of traditional means of influence also makes it difficult to alter the priorities of agencies, such as shifting the emphasis from building roads to building apartments.

Sources: Michelle M. Taylor, "When Are Juridicially Autonomous Agencies Responsive to Elected Officials? A Simulation Based on the Costa Rican Case," *Journal of Politics* 57 (November 1995): 1,070–1,092; and Gene E. Bigler and Enrique Viloria, "State Enterprises and the Decentralized Public Administration," in John D. Martz and David J. Myers, eds., *Venezuela, the Democratic Experience*, rev. ed. (New York: Praeger, 1986).

never succeeded—largely because each department was in the hands of an entrenched bureaucracy backed by elements in Congress and strong constituent groups. Reorganizing an agency is hard to do if it is a large and strong agency; reorganizing a small and weak agency is often not worth the trouble.

Congress Tries To Control the Bureaucracy. Congress exhibits a paradoxical relationship with the bureaucracies. On the one hand (as we have seen), members of Congress may find a big bureaucracy congenial.[49] Big government provides services to constituents, who may show their appreciation at the polls. Moreover, when Congress lacks the answers to policy problems, it hopes the bureaucracies will find them. Unable itself, for example, to resolve the touchy issue of equality in intercollegiate athletics, Congress passed the ball to the Department of Health, Education, and Welfare. Unable to decide how to make workplaces safer, Congress produced the Occupational Safety and Health Administration (OSHA). As you saw in Chapter 12, Congress is increasingly the problem-identifying branch of government, setting the bureaucratic agenda but letting the agencies decide how to implement the goals it sets.

On the other hand, Congress has found it hard to control the government it helped create. There are several measures Congress can take to oversee the bureaucracy:

- *Influence the appointment of agency heads.* Even when senatorial approval of a presidential appointment is not required, members of Congress are not shy in offering their opinions about who should and should not be running the agencies. When congressional approval is required, members are doubly influential. Committee hearings on proposed appointments are almost guaranteed to produce lively debates if some members find the nominee's probable orientations objectionable.
- *Tinker with an agency's budget.* With the congressional power of the purse comes a mighty weapon for controlling bureaucratic behavior. At the same time,

Congress knows that agencies perform services that its constituents demand. Too much budget cutting may make an agency more responsive—at the price of losing an interest group's support for a reelection campaign.

- *Hold hearings.* Committees and subcommittees can hold periodic hearings as part of their oversight job. Flagrant agency abuses of congressional intent can be paraded in front of the press, but responsibility for oversight typically goes to the very committee that created a program; the committee thus has some stake in showing the agency in a favorable light.
- *Rewrite the legislation or make it more detailed.* Every statute is filled with instructions to its administrators. To limit bureaucratic discretion and make its instructions clearer, Congress can write new or more detailed legislation. Still, even voluminous detail (as in the case of the IRS) can never eliminate discretion.

Through these and other devices, Congress tries to keep bureaucracies under its control. Never entirely successful, Congress faces a constant battle to limit and channel the vast powers that it delegated to the bureaucracy in the first place.

Sometimes these efforts are detrimental to bureaucratic performance. The explosion of legislative subcommittees has greatly increased Congress's oversight activities. Numerous subcommittees may review the actions of a single agency. A half-dozen or more subcommittees may review the activities of the Department of Energy, the Department of Agriculture, or the Department of Commerce. Different committees may send different signals to the same agency. One may press for stricter enforcement, another for more exemptions. As the oversight process has become more vigorous, it has also become more fragmented, thus limiting the effectiveness of the bureaucracies.

Iron Triangles and Issue Networks. Agencies' strong ties to interest groups on the one hand and to congressional committees and subcommittees on the other further complicate efforts to control the bureaucracy. Chapter 11 illustrated that bureaucracies often enjoy cozy relationships with interest groups and with committees or subcommittees of Congress. When agencies, groups, and committees all depend on one another and are in close, frequent contact, they form what are sometimes called ***iron triangles*** or *subgovernments.* These triads have advantages on all sides (see Figure 15.5).

iron triangles

A mutually dependent relationship between bureaucratic agencies, interest groups, and congressional committees or subcommittees. Iron triangles dominate some areas of domestic policymaking.

There are plenty of examples of subgovernments at work. A subcommittee on aging, senior citizens' interest groups, and the Social Security Administration are likely to agree on the need for more Social Security benefits. Richard Rettig has recounted how an alliance slowly jelled around the issue of fighting cancer. It rested on three pillars: cancer researchers, agencies within the National Institutes of Health, and members of congressional health subcommittees.[50]

When these iron triangles shape policies for senior citizens, cancer, tobacco, or any other interest, each policy is made independently of the others, sometimes even in contradiction to other policies. For example, for years the government has supported tobacco farmers in one way or another while encouraging people not to smoke. Moreover, the iron triangles' decisions tend to bind larger institutions, such as Congress and the White House. Congress often defers to the decisions of committees and subcommittees, especially on less visible issues. The White House may be too busy wrestling with global concerns to fret over agricultural issues or cancer. Emboldened by this lack of involvement, subgovernments flourish and add a strong decentralizing and fragmenting element to the policymaking process.

Hugh Heclo points out that the system of subgovernments is now overlaid with an amorphous system of *issue networks.* There is more widespread participation in bureaucratic policymaking, and many of the participants have technical policy expertise and are drawn to issues because of intellectual or emotional commitments rather than material interests. Those concerned with environmental protection, for example, have challenged formerly closed subgovernments on numerous fronts (see Chapter 19). This opening of the policymaking process complicates the calculations and decreases

Figure 15.5 Iron Triangles: One Example

Iron triangles—composed of bureaucratic agencies, interest groups, and congressional committees or subcommittees—have dominated some areas of domestic policymaking by combining internal consensus with a virtual monopoly on information in their area. The tobacco triangle is one example; there are dozens more. Iron triangles are characterized by mutual dependency, in which each element provides key services, information, or policy for the others. The arrows indicate some of these mutually helpful relationships. In recent years, a number of well-established iron triangles, including the tobacco triangle, have been broken up.

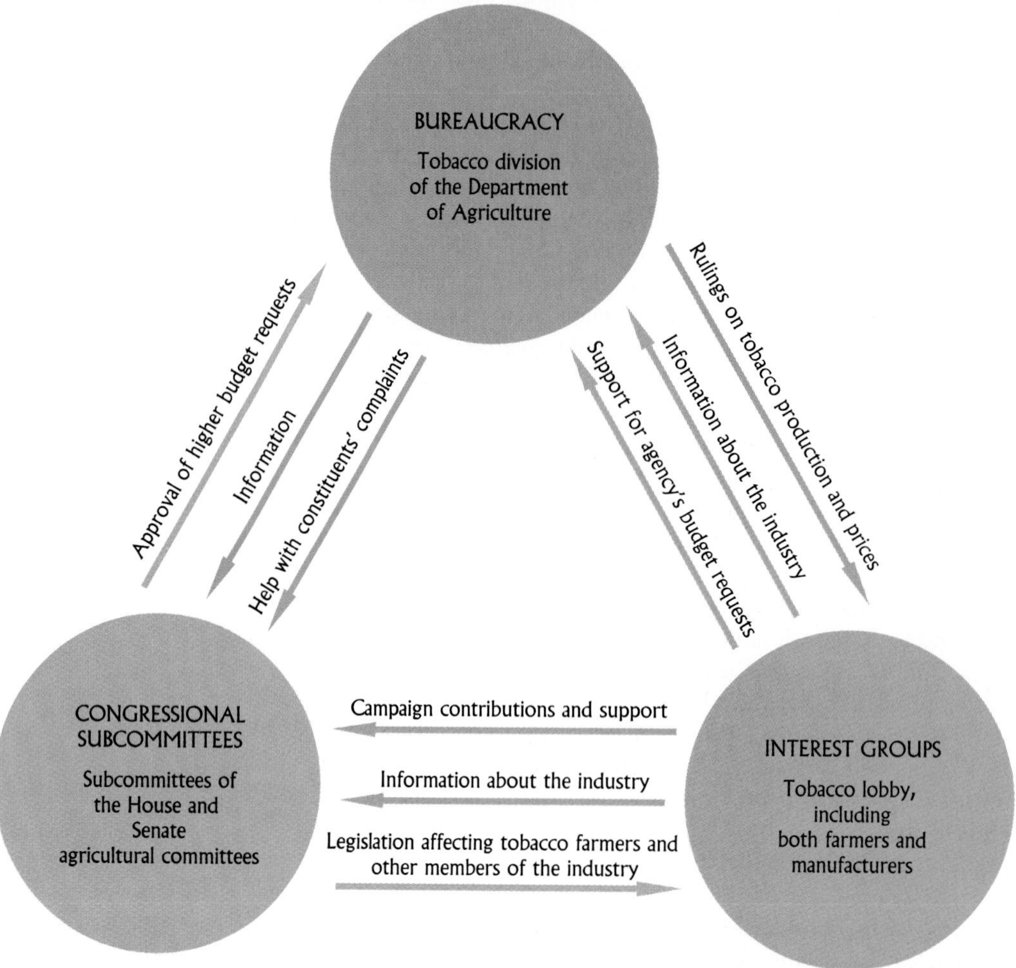

the predictability of those involved in the stable and relatively narrow relationships of subgovernments.[51]

Although subgovernments are often able to dominate policymaking for decades, they are not indestructible.[52] For example, the subgovernment pictured in Figure 15.5 long dominated smoking and tobacco policy, focusing on crop subsidies to tobacco farmers. But increasingly, these policies have come under fire from health authorities, who were not involved in tobacco policymaking in earlier years. Similarly, pesticide policy, once dominated by chemical companies and agricultural interests, is no longer considered separately from environmental and health concerns.

An especially vivid example of the death of an iron triangle is the case of nuclear power.[53] During the 1940s and 1950s, Americans were convinced that the technology that had ended World War II could also serve peaceful purposes. Nuclear scientists spoke enthusiastically about harnessing the atom to achieve all sorts of goals, eventually making electricity so inexpensive that it would be "too cheap to meter." Optimism in progress through science was the rule, and the federal government encouraged the development of nuclear power through a powerful iron triangle.

A special congressional joint committee, the Joint Committee on Atomic Energy, was established and given complete control over questions of nuclear power in Congress. A new executive agency, the Atomic Energy Commission (AEC), was created, and together with the private companies that built the nuclear power plants and the electrical utilities that wanted to operate them, they formed a powerful subgovernment. America built more nuclear power plants than any other country in the world, and American technology was exported overseas to dozens of nations.

Nuclear power today—after the accidents at Three Mile Island and Chernobyl and the various cost overruns associated with the industry—bears almost no resemblance to that of the early 1960s when the iron triangle was at its peak. What happened? The experts lost control. When questions arose concerning the safety of the plants and when opponents were able to get local officials to question the policies publicly, the issue grew into a major political debate of the late 1960s, associated with the growth of environmentalism. Two of the most powerful legs of the iron triangle were destroyed. The Joint Committee on Atomic Energy was disbanded; a variety of congressional committees now claim some jurisdiction over nuclear power questions. Similarly, the AEC was replaced by two new agencies: the Nuclear Regulatory Commission and the Department of Energy.

The nuclear power industry has been devastated: No new nuclear power plants have been built in the United States since 1978, and almost all those under construction at that time have been abandoned at huge financial loss. In sum, the wave of environmental concern that developed in the late 1960s swept away one of the most powerful iron triangles in recent American history.

Bureaucracy and the Scope of Government

To many, the huge American bureaucracy is the prime example of the federal government growing out of control. As this chapter discussed earlier, some observers view the bureaucracy as acquisitive, constantly seeking to expand its size, budgets, and authority. Much of the political rhetoric against big government also adopts this line of argument, along with complaints about red tape, senseless regulations, and the like. It is easy to take pot shots at a faceless bureaucracy that usually cannot respond.

One should keep in mind, however, that the federal bureaucracy has not grown over the past two generations, as Figure 15.1 illustrates. If one considers the fact that the population of the country has grown significantly over this period, then the federal bureaucracy has actually *shrunk* in size relative to the population it serves.

Originally, the federal bureaucracy had the modest role of promoting the economy, defending the country, managing foreign affairs, providing justice, and delivering the mail. Its role gradually expanded to include providing services to farmers, businesses, and workers. The discussion of federalism in Chapter 3 showed that as the economy and the society of the United States changed, additional demands were made on government. Government—and the bureaucracy—are now expected to play an active role in dealing with social and economic problems. A good case can be made that the bureaucracy is actually too *small* for many of the tasks currently assigned to it—tasks ranging from the control of illicit drugs to protection of the environment.

In addition, it is important to remember that when the president and Congress have chosen to deregulate certain areas of the economy or cut taxes, the bureaucracy could not and did not prevent them from doing so. The question of what and how much the federal government should do—and thus how big the bureaucracy should be—is answered primarily at the polls and in Congress, the White House, and the courts—not by faceless bureaucrats.

Summary

Americans rarely congratulate someone for being a good bureaucrat. Unsung, taunted by cartoonists, and maligned by columnists, bureaucrats are the scapegoats of American politics. Americans may call presidents great and reelect members of Congress, but almost no one praises bureaucrats. Those who compose the bureaucracy, however, perform most of the vital services provided by the federal government.

Bureaucrats shape policy as administrators, as implementors, and as regulators. In this chapter we examined who bureaucrats are, how they got their positions, and what they do.

Career Profile

Position: Aerospace Technology Human Performance Research Psychologist

Salary Range: $67,000-68,000

Benefits: Health, life and retirement benefits. Relatively high level of freedom and autonomy on the job. Unlimited access to cutting edge technology and developments within NASA.

Qualifications: Ph.D. in field of expertise. Usually requires a national reputation in some field deemed important in NASA's future. Applicants should be self-motivated and work well under pressure

Real People on the Job: Yvonne Clearwater

Many kids dream about growing up to become an astronaut. No one dreams of growing up to be a bureaucrat. Unfortunately, becoming an astronaut still remains a long shot at best. Becoming part of the NASA team here on earth—in essence, a "bureaucrat"—however, is a much easier goal to achieve. As an Aerospace Technology Human Performance Research Psychologist, Yvonne Clearwater is one such bureaucrat at NASA's Ames Research Center in the San Francisco Bay area.

With a graduate degree in psychology, Yvonne started at NASA as a design researcher for the International Space Station. During her first seven years at the agency, she ran a research project that focused on the interior design of the space station's habitat modules. It was her job to advise engineers about the environmental and behavioral impact their designs would have on astronauts. Working with engineers, Yvonne helped design the shape and size of the crew quarters, eating facilities, lighting, and spatial orientation.

More recently, Yvonne has worked as a Media Producer and Writer for NASA. The primary purpose of her new job is to better inform the public about what NASA does with the tax dollars it receives. Yvonne now spends most of her time studying the cutting edge technology developed at Ames Research Center and working with the media to convey the benefits of these technological advances to the public. In particular, Yvonne focuses on earth-based applications of technology originally developed by NASA for use in space. For example, she recently completed working on a new PBS special "Unlocking the Grid," which documents the problem with flight delays in America and possible technological solutions being developed at NASA.

Yvonne's story is an example of putting your principles before your pocketbook. After earning her Ph.D., Yvonne landed a high-paying job for a large international company. But she turned her back on the private office and the big paycheck and decided instead to join NASA. Why? The way Yvonne sees it, her work in the private sector was a just means of making money for herself and her company. By contrast, her work at NASA has the potential to benefit all of society. The choice was an easy one for Yvonne.

If you want to learn more about the Ames Research Center, go to http://www.arc.nasa.gov. For those of you interested in pursuing a possible career within NASA, look at some of jobs available right now at www.usajobs.opm.gov/a9nasa.htm.

Today, most bureaucrats working for the federal government get their jobs through the civil service system, although a few at the very top are appointed by the president.

In general, there are four types of bureaucracies: the cabinet departments, the regulatory agencies, the government corporations, and the independent executive agencies.

As policymakers, bureaucrats play three key roles. First, they are policy implementors, translating legislative policy goals into programs. Policy implementation does not always work well, and when it does not, bureaucrats usually take the blame, whether they deserve it or not. Second, bureaucrats administer public policy. Much of administration involves a prescribed routine, but nearly all bureaucrats still have some discretion. Third, bureaucrats are regulators. Congress increasingly delegates large amounts of power to bureaucratic agencies and expects them to develop rules and regulations. Scarcely a nook or cranny of American society or the American economy escapes the long reach of bureaucratic regulation.

Although bureaucrats are not elected, bureaucracies are not necessarily undemocratic. Bureaucracies must be controlled by elected decision makers, but presidential or congressional control over bureaucracies is difficult. Bureaus have strong support from interest groups—a factor that contributes to pluralism because interest groups try to forge common links with bureaucracies and congressional committees. These subgovernments tend to decentralize policymaking, thereby contributing to hyperpluralism.

Although there are many critics of the increasing size of government, the federal bureaucracy has not grown over the past two generations. Instead, it has shrunk, even as the country has grown and the public has made additional demands on government.

Key Terms

patronage
Pendleton Civil Service Act
civil service
merit principle
Hatch Act
Office of Personnel Management (OPM)
GS (General Schedule) rating
Senior Executive Service
bureaucracy
independent regulatory agency
governmental corporations
independent executive agencies
policy implementation
standard operating proceedures
administrative discretion
street-level bureaucrats
regulation
deregulation
command-and-control policy
incentive system
executive orders
iron triangles

For Further Reading

Aberbach, Joel D., and Bert A. Rockman. *In the Web of Politics.* Washington, D.C.: Brookings Institution, 2000. Examines federal executives and the degree to which they are representative of the country and responsive to elected officials.

Arnold, Peri E. *Making the Managerial Presidency*, 2nd ed. Princeton, NJ: Princeton University Press, 1996. A careful examination of efforts to reorganize the federal bureaucracy.

Derthick, Martha, and Paul J. Quirk. *The Politics of Deregulation.* Washington, D.C.: Brookings Institution, 1985. Explains why advocates of deregulation prevailed over the special interests that benefited from regulation.

Edwards, George C., III. *Implementing Public Policy.* Washington, D.C.: Congressional Quarterly Press, 1980. A good review of the issues involved in implementation.

Goodsell, Charles T. *The Case for Bureaucracy*, 3rd ed. Chatham, NJ: Chatham House, 1993. A strong case on behalf of the effectiveness of bureaucracy.

Gormley, William T., Jr. *Taming the Bureaucracy.* Princeton, NJ: Princeton University Press, 1989. Examines remedies for controlling bureaucracies.

Heclo, Hugh M. *Government of Strangers: Executive Politics in Washington.* Washington, D.C.: Brookings Institution, 1977. A study of the top executives of the federal government, who constitute (says the author) a "government of strangers."

Kerwin, Cornelius M. *Rulemaking: How Government Agencies Write Law and Make Policy.* Washington, D.C.: Congressional Quarterly Press, 1994. Explains how agencies write regulations to implement laws.

Osborne, David, and Ted Gaebler. *Reinventing Government.* Reading, MA: Addison-Wesley, 1992. Simplistic but important view of making government more entrepreneurial and responsive to citizens.

Peterson, Paul, Barry G. Rabe, and Kenneth K. Wong. *When Federalism Works.* Washington, D.C.: Brookings Institution, 1986.

Examines federal grant-in-aid programs and explains why they are implemented better in some areas than in others.

Pressman, Jeffrey, and Aaron Wildavsky. *Implementation*, 3rd ed. Berkeley: University of California Press, 1984. The classic—and often witty—study of implementation.

Rourke, Francis E. *Bureaucratic Power in National Policymaking*, 4th ed. Boston: Little, Brown, 1986. Classic work on bureaucratic politics.

Savas, E. S. *Privatization: The Key to Better Government*. Chatham, NJ: Chatham House, 1987. A conservative economist's argument that many public services performed by bureaucracies would be better handled by the private sector.

Wilson, James Q. *Bureaucracy*. New York: Basic Books, 1989. Presents a "bottom up" approach to understanding how bureaucrats, managers, and executives decide what to do.

Internet Resources

www.npr.gov/
National Performance Review, the ongoing presidential task force to "reinvent government."

www.access.gpo.gov/su_docs/aces/aces140.html
U.S. Government Manual which provides information on the organization of the U.S. government.

www.access.gpo.gov/nara/
The Federal Register, which provides information on U.S. laws and regulations.

www.whitehouse.gov/WH/Cabinet/html/cabinet_links.html
Information on federal cabinet departments.

www.whitehouse.gov/WH/Independent_Agencies/html/independent_links.html
Information on federal independent agencies and commissions.

www.opm.gov
Office of Personnel Management website with information on federal jobs and personnel issues.

www.govexec.com/
The web site for *Government Executive* magazine.

Notes

1. This example is based on Allan Freedman, "Battles Over Jurisdiction Likely To Block Merger of Agencies," *Congressional Quarterly Weekly Report*, May 30, 1998, 1,440.
2. See Charles T. Goodsell, *The Case for Bureaucracy*, 3rd ed. (Chatham, NJ: Chatham House, 1993), chap. 2. See also Daniel Katz et al., *Bureaucratic Encounters* (Ann Arbor: Institute for Social Research, University of Michigan, 1975).
3. See Paul C. Light, *The True Size of Government* (Washington, D.C.: Brookings Institution, 1999), 1, 44.
4. U.S. Department of Commerce, *Statistical Abstract of the United States, 2000* (Washington, D.C.: U.S. Government Printing Office, *2001*), 357; Office of Personnel Management, *The Factbook, 2000 Edition* (Washington, D.C.: U.S. Government Printing Office, *2000*), 8,16.
5. See Herbert Kaufman, *Red Tape* (Washington, D.C.: Brookings Institution, 1977).
6. See Goodsell, *The Case for Bureaucracy*, 61–69.
7. *Ibid.*, chap. 5.
8. Hugh M. Heclo, *A Government of Strangers: Executive Politics in Washington* (Washington, D.C.: Brookings Institution, 1977).
9. On the transient nature of presidential appointees, see G. Calvin Mackenzie, ed., *The In-and-Outers* (Baltimore: Johns Hopkins University Press, 1987).
10. *Ibid.*, 103.
11. H. H. Gerth and C. Wright Mills, *From Max Weber: Essays in Sociology* (New York: Oxford University Press, 1958), chap. 8.
12. See Anthony Downs, *Inside Bureaucracy* (Boston: Little, Brown, 1967).
13. William Niskanen, *Bureaucracy and Representative Government* (Chicago: Aldine-Atherton, 1971).
14. For critiques of the Niskanen perspective, see Gary J. Miller and Terry M. Moe, "Bureaucrats, Legislators, and the Size of Government," *American Political Science Review* 77 (June 1983): 297–322; William D. Berry and David Lowery, *Understanding United States Government Growth* (New York: Praeger, 1987); Patrick Dunleavy, *Democracy, Bureaucracy and Public Choice: Economic Explanations in Political Science* (Englewood Cliffs, NJ: Prentice-Hall, 1991); and Andre Blais and Stephane Dion, eds., *The Budget-Maximizing Bureaucrat: Appraisals and Evidence* (Pittsburgh: University of Pittsburgh Press, 1991).
15. See Vincent Ostrom, *The Intellectual Crisis in American Public Administration* (University: University of Alabama Press, 1973).
16. See, for example, E. S. Savas, *Privatization: The Key to Better Government* (Chatham, NJ: Chatham House, 1987).
17. See Donald F. Kettl, *Sharing Power: Public Governance and Private Markets* (Washington, D.C.: Brookings Institution, 1993) on contracting with private firms to provide public services. Kettl and others fear that privatizing public services separates public officials from citizens and places discretionary authority in the operation of public programs in the hands of third-party, private implementors. Critics also are skeptical that there will be sufficient competition among contractors to furnish efficiently most of the services provided by the federal government.
18. John Kingdon, *Agendas, Alternatives, and Public Policies* (Boston: Little, Brown, 1984), 81.
19. Michael Cohen, James March, and Johan Olsen, "A Garbage Can Model of Organizational Choice," *Administrative Science Quarterly* 17 (March 1972): 1.
20. Kingdon, *Agendas, Alternatives, and Public Policies*, 88–94.

21. On the independent regulatory agencies, see the classic work by Marver Bernstein, *Regulating Business by Independent Commission* (Princeton, NJ: Princeton University Press, 1955). See also, on regulation, James Q. Wilson, ed., *The Politics of Regulation* (New York: Basic Books, 1980); and A. Lee Fritschler and Bernard H. Ross, *Business Regulation and Government Decision-Making* (Cambridge, MA: Winthrop, 1980).
22. Bernstein, *Regulating Business*, 90. For a partial test of the capture theory that finds the theory not altogether accurate, see John P. Plumlee and Kenneth J. Meier, "Capture and Rigidity in Regulatory Administration," in *The Policy Cycle*, Judith May and Aaron Wildavsky, eds. (Beverly Hills, CA: Russell Sage Foundation, 1978). Another critique of the capture theory is Paul J. Quirk, *Industry Influence in Federal Regulatory Agencies* (Princeton, NJ: Princeton University Press, 1981).
23. George C. Edwards III, *Implementing Public Policy* (Washington, D.C.: Congressional Quarterly Press, 1980), 1.
24. Eugene Bardach, *The Implementation Game* (Cambridge, MA: The M.I.T. Press, 1977), 85; and Robert L. Lineberry, *American Public Policy: What Government Does and What Difference It Makes* (New York: Harper & Row, 1977), 71. Clausewitz called war "the continuation of politics by other means."
25. Lineberry, *American Public Policy*, 70–71.
26. For another dramatic example, see Martha Derthick, *New Towns In-Town* (Washington, D.C.: The Urban Institute Press, 1972).
27. Bardach, *The Implementation Game*, 250–251.
28. A good discussion of how policymakers ignored the administrative capacity of one important agency when assigning it new responsibilities can be found in Martha Derthick, *Agency Under Stress* (Washington, D.C.: Brookings Institution, 1990).
29. The implementation of the athletics policy is well documented in two articles by Cheryl M. Fields in the *Chronicle of Higher Education*, December 11 and 18, 1978, on which this account relies.
30. James Q. Wilson, *Bureaucracy* (New York: Basic Books, 1989), 158.
31. *Report of the DOD Commission on Beirut International Airport Terrorist Act, October* 23, 1983, December 20, 1983, 133.
32. Quoted in M. S. Eccles, *Beckoning Frontiers* (New York: Knopf, 1951), 336.
33. On administrative discretion, see Gary S. Bryner, *Bureaucratic Discretion* (New York: Pergamon Press, 1987).
34. Gerald Carson, *The Golden Egg* (Boston: Houghton Mifflin, 1977), 10. The examples given in this paragraph are from Carson.
35. Michael Lipsky, *Street-Level Bureaucracy* (New York: Russell Sage Foundation, 1980).
36. Quoted in Seymour Hersh, *The Price of Power: Kissinger in the Nixon White House* (New York: Summit, 1983), 235–236.
37. Albert Gore, *From Red Tape to Results: Creating a Government That Works Better and Costs Less* (New York: Times Books, 1993), 11.
38. For a careful analysis of efforts to reorganize the federal bureaucracy, see Peri E. Arnold, *Making the Managerial Presidency*, 2nd ed. (Princeton, NJ: Princeton University Press, 1996).
39. On the implementation and impact of the Voting Rights Act, see Charles S. Bullock III and Harrell R. Rodgers, Jr., *Law and Social Change: Civil Rights Laws and Their Consequences* (New York: McGraw-Hill, 1972), chap. 2; Richard Scher and James Button, "Voting Rights Act: Implementation and Impact," in *Implementation of Civil Rights Policy*, ed. C. S. Bullock and C. M. Lamb (Monterey, CA: Brooks/Cole, 1984), chap. 2; and Abigail M. Thernstrom, *Whose Votes Count?* (Cambridge, MA: Harvard University Press, 1987).
40. Based on a more elaborate account by James Worsham, "A Typical Day Is Full of Rules," *Chicago Tribune*, July 12, 1981, 1ff, with updating by the authors.
41. See Martha Derthick and Paul J. Quirk, *The Politics of Deregulation* (Washington, D.C.: Brookings Institution, 1985).
42. See, for example, Susan J. Tolchin and Martin J. Tolchin, *Dismantling America: The Rush To Deregulate* (New York: Oxford University Press, 1983).
43. Evan J. Ringquist, "Does Regulation Matter? Evaluating the Effects of State Air Pollution Control Programs," *Journal of Politics* 55 (November 1993): 1,022–1,045.
44. Michael Lewis-Beck and John Alford, "Can Government Regulate Safety? The Coal Mine Example," *American Political Science Review* 74 (September 1980): 745–756.
45. Paul Sabatier and Dan Mazmanian, *Can Regulation Work? Implementation of the 1972 California Coastal Initiative* (New York: Plenum, 1983).
46. Gary Copeland and Kenneth J. Meier, "Gaining Ground: The Impact of Medicaid and WIC on Infant Mortality," *American Politics Quarterly* 15 (April 1987): 254–273.
47. See B. Dan Wood and Richard W. Waterman, *Bureaucratic Dynamics: The Role of Bureaucracy in a Democracy* (Boulder, CO: Westview, 1994).
48. A good work on this point is Richard P. Nathan, *The Administrative Presidency* (New York: Wiley, 1983).
49. Morris Fiorina, *Congress: Keystone of the Washington Establishment*, 2nd ed. (New Haven, CT: Yale University Press, 1989).
50. Richard A. Rettig, *Cancer Crusade* (Princeton, NJ: Princeton University Press, 1977).
51. Hugh M. Heclo, "Issue Networks and the Executive Establishment," in *The New American Political System*, Anthony King, ed. (Washington, D.C.: American Enterprise Institute, 1978), 87–124. See also William P. Browne and Won K. Paik, "Beyond the Domain: Recasting Network Politics in the Postreform Congress," *American Journal of Political Science* 37 (November 1993): 1,054–1,078; and John P. Heinz, Edward O. Laumann, Robert L. Nelson, and Robert L. Salisbury, *The Hollow Core: Private Interests in National Policy Making* (Cambridge, MA: Harvard University Press, 1993).
52. Frank R. Baumgartner and Bryan D. Jones, *Agendas and Instability in American Politics* (Chicago: University of Chicago Press, 1993).
53. *Ibid.*

The Federal Courts

16

Chapter Outline

Let us say that you are involved in a lawsuit regarding the application of an affirmative action policy in your college or university. A trial is held in a federal district court. After the trial, a verdict is rendered and you lose. Not content to accept this decision, you appeal to the court of appeals. Once again, you lose. Now you have only two options left: accept the decision or appeal to the U.S. Supreme Court. You decide to appeal, and of the thousands of petitions for hearings presented to the Court each year, yours is one of a few dozen the Court selects.

On the day of the oral argument (there are no trials in the Supreme Court), you walk up the steep steps of the Supreme Court building, the impressive "Marble Palace" with the motto "Equal Justice under Law" engraved over its imposing columns. The Court's surroundings and procedures suggest the nineteenth century. The justices, clothed in black robes, take their seats at the bench in front of a red velvet curtain. Behind the bench there are still spittoons, one for each justice. (Today, the spittoons are used as wastebaskets.)

Your case, like most of the cases the Court selects for oral arguments, is scheduled for about an hour. Lawyers arguing before the Court often wear frock coats and striped trousers. They find a goose quill pen on their desk, purchased by the Court from a Virginia supplier. (Lawyers may take the pen with them as a memento of their day in court.) As is the norm, each side is allotted 30 minutes to present its case. The justices may, and do, interrupt the lawyers with questions. When the time is up, a discreet red light goes on at your lawyer's lectern, and he immediately stops talking.

That is the end of the hearing, but not the end of the process. You have asked the Court to overrule a policy established by your state legislature. As the Court considers doing so, it recognizes that its decision will become precedent for all such policies across the nation. Months will go by, as the justices deliberate and negotiate an opinion, before the Court announces its decision. If you win, it will take many more months for your university, aided by lower courts, to interpret the decision and implement it.

The scope of the Supreme Court's power is great, extending even to overruling the decisions of elected officials. Despite the trappings of tradition and majesty, however, the Court does not reach its decisions in a political vacuum. Instead, it works in a context of political influences and considerations, a circumstance that raises important questions about the role of the judiciary in the U.S. political system.

The federal courts pose a special challenge to American democracy. Although it is common for state judges to be elected in one fashion or another, federal judges are *appointed* to their positions—for life. The framers of the Constitution purposefully insulated federal judges from the influence of public opinion. How can we reconcile powerful courts populated by unelected judges with American democracy? Do they pose a threat to majority rule? Or do the federal courts actually function to protect the rights of minorities and thus maintain the type of open system necessary for democracy to flourish?

The power of the federal courts also raises the issue of the appropriate scope of judicial power in our society. Federal courts are frequently in the thick of policymaking on issues ranging from affirmative action and abortion to physician-assisted suicide and the financing of public schools. Numerous critics argue that judges should not be actively involved in determining public policy. Instead, the critics say, judges should focus on settlement of routine disputes and leave the determination of policy to elected officials. On the other hand, advocates of a more aggressive role for the courts emphasize that judicial decisions have often met pressing needs—especially needs of those who are politically or economically weak—left unmet by the normal processes of policymaking. For example, we have already seen the leading role that the federal courts played in ending legally supported racial segregation in the United States. To determine the appropriate role of the courts in our democracy, we must first understand the nature of our judicial system.

However impressive the Supreme Court may be, only the tiniest fraction of American judicial policy is made there. To be sure, the Court decides a handful of key issues each year. Some will shape people's lives, perhaps even decide issues of life and death. In addition to the Supreme Court, there are 12 federal courts of appeal, a Court of Appeals for the Federal Circuit, 91 federal district courts, and thousands of state and local courts (the latter will be discussed in Chapter 21). It is in these less august courts that most of America's legal business is transacted. This chapter will focus on federal courts and the judges who serve on them—the men and women in black robes who are important policymakers in the American political system.

The Nature of the Judicial System

The judicial system in the United States is, at least in principle, an adversarial one in which the courts provide an arena for two parties to bring their conflict before an impartial arbiter (a judge). The system is based on the theory that justice will emerge out of the struggle between two contending points of view. The task of the judge is to apply the law to the case, determining which party is legally correct. In reality, most cases never go to trial because they are settled by agreements reached out of court.

There are two basic kinds of cases: criminal law cases and civil law cases. In a *criminal law* case, the government charges an individual who violated specific laws, such as those prohibiting robbery. The offense may be harmful to an individual or to society as a whole, but in either case it warrants punishment, such as imprisonment or a fine. In a *civil law* case, there is no charge of criminality—no charge that a law has been violated. Such a case involves a dispute between two parties (one of whom may be the government itself) and defines relationships between them. Civil law cases range from divorce proceedings to mergers of multinational companies. Civil law consists of both statutes (laws passed by legislatures) and common law (the accumulation of judicial decisions).

Just as it is important not to confuse criminal and civil law, it is important not to confuse state and federal courts. The vast majority of all criminal and civil cases involve state law and are tried in state courts. Criminal cases such as burglary and civil cases such as divorce normally begin and end in the state, not the federal, courts.

Participants in the Judicial System

The serenity and majesty of the U.S. Supreme Court are a far cry from the grimy urban courts where strings of defendants are bused from the local jails for their day—often only a few minutes—in court. Yet every case has certain components in common, including litigants, attorneys, and judges. Sometimes organized groups are also directly

Most criminal and civil cases involve state law and are tried in state courts, not the federal courts.

involved. Judges are the policymakers of the American judicial system, and we examine them extensively in later sections of this chapter. Here we will discuss the other regular participants in the judicial process.

Litigants. Federal judges are restricted by the Constitution to deciding *"cases or controversies"*—that is, actual disputes rather than hypothetical ones. Judges do not issue advisory opinions on what they think (in the abstract) may be the meaning or constitutionality of a law. The judiciary is essentially passive, dependent on others to take the initiative.

Thus two parties must bring a case to the court before it may be heard. Every case is a dispute between a *plaintiff* and a *defendant* in which the former brings some charge against the latter. Sometimes the plaintiff is the government, which may bring a charge against an individual or a corporation. The government may charge the defendant with the brutal murder of Jones or charge the XYZ Corporation with illegal trade practices. All cases are identified with the name of the plaintiff first and the defendant second, for example, *State v. Smith* or *Anderson v. Baker.* In many (but not all) cases, a *jury*, a group of citizens (usually 12), is responsible for determining the outcome of a lawsuit.

Litigants end up in court for a variety of reasons. Some are reluctant participants—the defendant in a criminal case, for example. Others are eager for their day in court. For some, the courts can be a potent weapon in the search for a preferred policy. For example, in the 1960s, atheist Madelyn Murray O'Hair was an enthusiastic litigant, always ready to take the government to court for promoting religion.

Not everyone can challenge a law, however. Plaintiffs must have what is called **standing to sue**; that is, they must have serious interest in a case, which is typically determined by whether they have sustained or are in immediate danger of sustaining a direct and substantial injury from another party or an action of government. Except in cases pertaining to governmental support for religion, merely being a taxpayer and being opposed to a law do not provide the standing necessary to challenge that law in court. Nevertheless, Congress and the Supreme Court have liberalized the rules for standing, making it somewhat easier for citizens to challenge governmental and corporate actions in court.

standing to sue
The requirement that **plaintiffs** have a serious interest in a **case**, which depends on whether they have sustained or are likely to sustain a direct and substantial injury from a party or an action of government.

In recent years, the concept of standing to sue has been broadened. **Class action suits** permit a small number of people to sue on behalf of all other people in similar circumstances. These suits may be useful in cases as varied as civil rights, in which a few persons seek an end to discriminatory practices on behalf of all who might be discriminated against, and environmental protection, in which a few persons may sue a

class action suits
Lawsuits permitting a small number of people to sue on behalf of all other people similarly situated.

Sometimes people find themselves involved in extraordinary court decisions. Linda Brown was a plaintiff in *Brown v. Board of Education,* a key civil rights case in which the Supreme Court overturned its earlier *Plessy v. Ferguson* ruling that legalized segregation.

polluting industry on behalf of all who are affected by the air or water the industry pollutes. Following an explosion of such cases, in 1974 the Supreme Court began making it more difficult to file class action suits.

justiciable disputes

A requirement that to be heard a case must be capable of being settled as a matter of law rather than on other grounds as is commonly the case in legislative bodies.

Conflicts must not only arise from actual cases between litigants with standing in court, but they must also be **justiciable disputes**—issues that are capable of being settled by legal methods. One would not go to court to determine whether Congress should fund the Strategic Defense Initiative (SDI), for the matter could not be resolved through legal methods or knowledge.

Groups. Because they recognize the courts' ability to shape policy, interest groups often seek out litigants whose cases seem particularly strong. Few groups have been more successful in finding good cases and good litigants than the National Association for the Advancement of Colored People, which selected the school board of Topeka, Kans., and a young schoolgirl named Linda Brown as the litigants in *Brown v. Board of Education* (1954). NAACP legal counsel Thurgood Marshall (see "Making a Difference: Thurgood Marshall") believed that Topeka represented a stronger case than other school districts in the United States in the effort to end the policy of "separate but equal"—meaning racially segregated—public education because the city provided segregated facilities that were otherwise genuinely equal. The courts could not resolve the case simply by insisting that expenditures for schools for white and African-American children be equalized.

The American Civil Liberties Union is another interest group that is always seeking cases and litigants to support in its defense of civil liberties. One ACLU attorney, stressing that principle took priority over a particular client, even admitted that the ACLU's clients are often "pretty scurvy little creatures. . . . It's the principle that we're going to be able to use these people for that's important."[1] (For an example, review the case in Chapter 4 of the Nazis who tried to march in Skokie, Ill.)

***amicus curiae* briefs**

Legal briefs submitted by a "friend of the court" for the purpose of raising additional points of view and presenting information not contained in the briefs of the formal parties. These briefs attempt to influence a court's decision.

At other times groups do not directly argue the case for litigants, but support them instead with ***amicus curiae*** ("friend of the court") **briefs** that attempt to influence the Court's decision, raise additional points of view, and present information not contained in the briefs of the attorneys for the official parties to the case. In controversial cases, there may be many such briefs submitted to the Court; 58 were presented in the landmark *Bakke* case on affirmative action (discussed in Chapter 5).

Attorneys. Lawyers are indispensable actors in the judicial system. Law is one of the nation's fastest growing professions. The United States counted about 100,000 lawyers in 1960 but has about 750,000 today—1 for every 360 Americans. Lawyers busily translate policies into legal language and then enforce or challenge them.

Once lawyers were primarily available to the rich. Today, public interest law firms can sometimes handle legal problems of the poor and middle classes. The federally funded Legal Services Corporation employs lawyers to serve the legal needs of the poor, although the Reagan administration made drastic cuts in legal aid. State and local governments provide public defenders for poor people accused of crimes. Some employers and unions now provide legal insurance, which works like medical insurance. Members with legal needs—for a divorce, a consumer complaint, or whatever—can secure legal aid through prepaid plans. As a result, more people than ever before can take their problems to the courts. Equality of access, of course, does not mean equality of representation. The wealthy can afford high-powered attorneys who can invest many hours in their cases and arrange for testimony by expert witnesses. The poor are often served by overworked attorneys with few resources to devote to an individual case.

simulation
You are A Young Lawyer

The audience for the judicial drama is a large and attentive one that includes interest groups, the press (a close observer of the judicial process, especially of its more sensational aspects), and the public, who often have very strong opinions about how the process works. All these participants—plaintiffs, defendants, lawyers, interest groups, and others—play a role in the judicial drama, even though many of their activ-

Making a Difference

Thurgood Marshall

Thurgood Marshall was a rebel. He led a civil rights revolution in the twentieth century that forever changed the landscape of American society. Yet he is less well known than Martin Luther King Jr., with his message of nonviolent resistance, and Malcolm X, the fiery street preacher who advocated a bloody overthrow of the system. Marshall rejected King's peaceful protest as rhetorical fluff and Malcolm X's talk of violent revolution and a separate black nation as racist nonsense in a multiracial society. Instead, Marshall turned to the courts to eradicate the legacy of slavery and to destroy the Jim Crow system of racial segregation.

The key to Marshall's work was his conviction that integration—and only integration—would allow equal rights under the law to take hold. He argued that once individual rights were accepted, African Americans and Whites could rise or fall based on their own ability. Marshall's deep faith in the power of racial integration came out of a middle class African-American perspective in turn-of-the- century Baltimore. He was a child of an activist African-American community that had established its own schools and fought for equal rights from the time of the Civil War. His own family, of an interracial background, had been at the forefront of demands by Baltimore African Americans for equal treatment. Thurgood Marshall was born out of that unique family and city in 1908.

After graduating first in his class from Howard University Law School in Washington, D.C. in 1933, Marshall began his legal career as counsel to the Baltimore branch of the National Association for the Advancement of Colored People (NAACP). He joined the national legal staff in 1936 and in 1938 became chief legal officer. In 1940, the NAACP created the Legal Defense and Education Fund, with Marshall as its director and counsel. For more than 20 years, Marshall coordinated the NAACP effort to end racial segregation.

During that time he won an astonishing 29 of 32 cases he argued before the Supreme Court, including cases in which the Court declared unconstitutional exclusion of African-American voters from primary elections (*Smith v. Allwright*, 1944), state judicial enforcement of racial "restrictive covenants" in housing (*Shelley v. Kraemer*, 1948), and "separate but equal" facilities for African-American professionals and graduate students in state universities (*Sweatt v. Painter* and *McLaurin v. Oklahoma State Regents*, both 1950). The culmination of his efforts to end segregation occurred in 1954, when he argued the case of *Brown v. Board of Education of Topeka* before the Supreme Court. Considered by many to be the most important legal case of the century, the decision in *Brown* ended the legal separation of African-American and White children in public schools.

The success of the *Brown* case sparked the 1960s civil rights movement and led to an increased number of African-American high school and college graduates and the rapid rise of the African-American middle class in both numbers and political power in the second half of the century.

President John F. Kennedy nominated Marshall to the United States Court of Appeals in 1961. It was not an easy confirmation: a group of Southern senators held up the confirmation for months, and he served initially under a special appointment made during a congressional recess. Still, from 1961 to 1965, he wrote 112 opinions on that court, none of which were overturned on appeal. In fact, several of his dissenting opinions were eventually adopted as majority opinions by the Supreme Court. From 1965 to 1967, he served as solicitor general under President Johnson, and in 1967 Johnson nominated Marshall to the Supreme Court, the first African-American justice to sit on the Court.

Marshall served 23 years on the Court. Although he can properly be called the architect of American race relations in the twentieth century, on the Court he was also a vigorous advocate for protections under law for women, children, prisoners, and the homeless. Upon his retirement at the age of 82 in 1991, Marshall could look back on a career of remarkable accomplishment. Truly, he had made a difference.

ities take place outside the courtroom. How these participants arrive in the courtroom and which court they go to reflect the structure of the court system.

The Structure of the Federal Judicial System

The Constitution is vague about the structure of the federal court system. Aside from specifying that there will be a Supreme Court, the Constitution left it to Congress's discretion to establish lower federal courts of general jurisdiction. In the Judiciary Act of

Figure 16.1 Organization of the Federal Court System

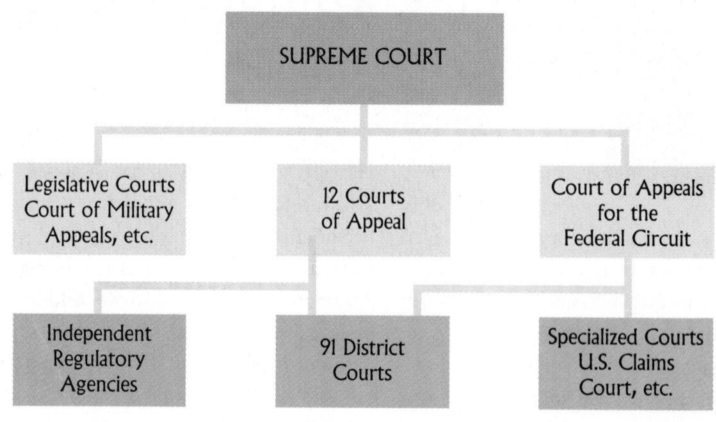

1789, Congress created these *constitutional courts,* and although the system has been altered over the years, America has never been without them. The current organization of the federal court system is displayed in Figure 16.1.

Congress has also established *legislative courts* for specialized purposes. These courts include the Court of Military Appeals, the Court of Claims, the Court of International Trade, and the Tax Court. These legislative courts are staffed by judges who have fixed terms of office and who lack the protections against removal or salary reductions that judges on constitutional courts enjoy. The following sections, however, will focus on the courts of general jurisdiction.

First, we must understand another difference among courts. Courts with **original jurisdiction** are those in which a case is heard first, usually in a trial. These are the courts that determine the facts about a case, whether it is a criminal charge or a civil suit. More than 90 percent of court cases begin and end in the court of original jurisdiction.

original jurisdiction

The jurisdiction of courts that hear a case first, usually in a trial. These are the courts that determine the facts about a case.

Lawyers can sometimes appeal an adverse decision to a higher court for another decision. Courts with **appellate jurisdiction** hear cases brought to them on appeal from a lower court. Appellate courts do not review the factual record, only the legal issues involved. At the state level, the appellate process normally ends with the state's highest court of appeal, which is usually called the state supreme court. Appeals from a state high court can be taken only to the U.S. Supreme Court.

appellate jurisdiction

The jurisdiction of courts that hear cases brought to them on appeal from lower courts. These courts do not review the factual record, only the legal issues involved.

District Courts

The entry point for most litigation in the federal courts is one of the 91 **district courts,** at least one of which is located in each state, in addition to one in Washington, D.C., and one in Puerto Rico (there are also three somewhat different territorial courts for Guam, the Virgin Islands, and the Northern Mariana Islands). The district courts are courts of original jurisdiction; they hear no appeals. They are the only federal courts in which trials are held and in which juries may be impaneled. The 675 district court judges usually preside over cases alone, but certain rare cases require that three judges constitute the court. Each district court has between 2 and 28 judges, depending on the amount of judicial work within its territory.

district courts

The 91 federal courts of original jurisdiction. They are the only federal courts in which trials are held and in which juries may be impaneled.

The jurisdiction of the district courts extends to

- Federal crimes
- Civil suits under federal law
- Civil suits between citizens of different states where the amount in question exceeds $50,000

- Supervision of bankruptcy proceedings
- Review of the actions of some federal administrative agencies
- Admiralty and maritime law cases
- Supervision of the naturalization of aliens

It is important to remember that about 98 percent of all the criminal cases in the United States are heard in state and local court systems, not in the federal courts. Moreover, only a small percentage of the persons convicted of federal crimes in the federal district courts actually have a trial. Most enter guilty pleas as part of a bargain to receive lighter punishment.

Most civil suits in the United States are also handled in state and local courts. The vast majority of civil cases that commence in the federal courts are settled out of court. Only about 3 percent of the more than 220,000 civil cases resolved each year are decided by trials.

Diversity of citizenship cases involve civil suits between citizens of different states (such as a citizen of California suing a citizen of Texas) or suits in which one of the parties is a citizen of a foreign nation and the matter in question exceeds $50,000. Congress established this jurisdiction to protect against the possible bias of a state court in favor of a citizen from that state. In these cases, federal judges are to apply the appropriate state laws.

An elaborate supporting cast assists district judges. In addition to clerks, bailiffs, law clerks, stenographers, court reporters, and probation officers, U.S. marshals are assigned to each district to protect the judicial process and to serve the writs that the judges issue. Federal magistrates, appointed to eight-year terms, issue warrants for arrest, determine whether to hold arrested persons for action by a grand jury, and set bail. They also hear motions subject to review by their district judge and, with the consent of both parties in civil cases and of defendants in petty criminal cases, preside over some trials. As the workload for district judges increases (there were more than 325,000 cases in 1997, an increase of nearly 50,000 cases over 1993),[2] magistrates are becoming essential components of the federal judicial system.

Another important player at the district court level is the U.S. attorney. Each of the 91 regular districts has a U.S. attorney who is nominated by the president and confirmed by the Senate and who serves at the discretion of the president (U.S. attorneys do not have lifetime appointments). These attorneys and their staffs prosecute violations of federal law and represent the U.S. government in civil cases.

Most of the cases handled in the district courts are routine, and few result in policy innovations. Usually district court judges do not even publish their decisions. Although most federal litigation ends at this level, a large percentage of these cases that district court judges actually decide (as opposed to those settled out of court or by guilty pleas in criminal matters) are appealed by the losers. A distinguishing feature of the American legal system is the relative ease of appeals. U.S. law gives everyone a right to an appeal to a higher court. So, the loser in a case only has to request an appeal to be granted one. Of course, the loser must pay a substantial legal bill to exercise this right.

Courts of Appeal

The U.S. **courts of appeal** are courts empowered to review all final decisions of district courts, except in rare instances in which the law provides for direct review by the Supreme Court (injunctive orders of special three-judge district courts and certain decisions holding acts of Congress unconstitutional). Courts of appeal also have authority to review and enforce orders of many federal regulatory agencies, such as the Securities and Exchange Commission and the National Labor Relations Board. About 90 percent of the more than 50,000 cases heard in the courts of appeal each year come from the district courts.

courts of appeal

Appellate courts empowered to review all final decisions of district courts, except in rare cases. In addition, they also hear appeals to orders of many federal regulatory agencies. Compare **district courts.**

Figure 16.2 The Federal Judicial Circuits

Not shown are Puerto Rico (First Circuit), Virgin Islands (Third Circuit), and Guam and the Northern Mariana Islands (Ninth Circuit).

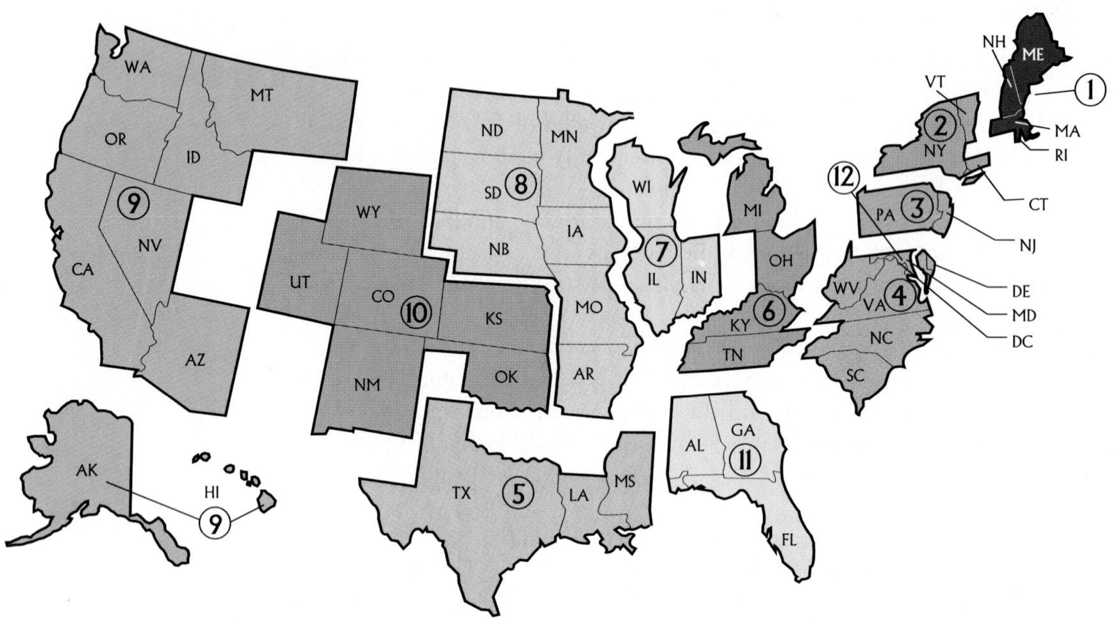

The United States is divided into 12 judicial circuits, including one for the District of Columbia (see Figure 16.2). Each circuit serves at least two states and has between 6 and 28 permanent circuit judgeships (179 in all), depending on the amount of judicial work in the circuit. Each court of appeal normally hears cases in panels consisting of three judges, but each may sit *en banc* (with all judges present) in particularly important cases. Decisions in either arrangement are made by majority vote of the participating judges.

There is also a special appeals court called the U.S. Court of Appeals for the Federal Circuit. Composed of 12 judges, it was established by Congress in 1982 to hear appeals in specialized cases, such as those regarding patents, claims against the United States, and international trade.

The courts of appeal focus on correcting errors of procedure and law that occurred in the original proceedings of legal cases, such as when a district court judge gave improper instructions to a jury or misinterpreted the rights provided under a law. These courts are appellate courts and hold no trials and hear no testimony. Their decisions set precedent for all the courts and agencies within their jurisdictions.

The Supreme Court

Supreme Court

The pinnacle of the American judicial system. The Court ensures uniformity in interpreting national laws, resolves conflicts among states, and maintains national supremacy in law. It has both **original jurisdiction** and **appellate jurisdiction,** but unlike other federal courts, it controls its own agenda.

Sitting at the pinnacle of the American judicial system is the U.S. **Supreme Court.** The Court does much more for the American political system than decide individual cases. Among its most important functions are resolving conflicts among the states and maintaining national supremacy in the law. The Supreme Court also plays an important role in ensuring uniformity in the interpretation of national laws. For example, in 1984 Congress created a federal sentencing commission to write guidelines aimed at reducing the wide disparities in punishment for similar crimes tried in federal courts. By 1989, more than 150 federal district judges had declared the law unconstitutional, and another 115 had ruled it valid. Only the Supreme Court could resolve this inconsistency in the administration of justice, which it did when it upheld the law.

There are nine justices on the Supreme Court: eight associates and one Chief Justice (only members of the Supreme Court are called justices; all others are called judges). The Constitution does not require this number, however, and there have been as few as 6 justices and as many as 10. The size of the Supreme Court was altered many times between 1801 and 1869. In 1866, Congress reduced the size of the Court from 10 to 8 members so that President Andrew Johnson could not nominate new justices to fill two vacancies. When Ulysses S. Grant took office, Congress increased the number of justices to 9 because it had confidence that he would nominate members to its liking. Since then, the number of justices has remained stable.

All nine justices sit together to hear cases and make decisions. But they must first decide which cases to hear. A familiar battle cry for losers in litigation in lower courts is "I'll appeal this all the way to the Supreme Court!" In reality, this is unlikely to happen. Unlike other federal courts, the Supreme Court decides which cases it will hear.

You can see in Figure 16.3 that the Court does have an original jurisdiction, yet very few cases arise under it, as Table 16.1 illustrates. Almost all the business of the Court comes from the appellate process, and cases may be appealed from both federal and state courts. In the latter instance, however, a "substantial federal question" must be involved. In deference to the states, the Supreme Court hears cases from state courts only if they involve federal law, and then only after the petitioner has exhausted all the potential remedies in the state court system. Cases from state courts cannot be appealed to any other federal court.

The Court will not try to settle matters of state law or determine guilt or innocence in state criminal proceedings. To obtain a hearing in the Supreme Court, a defendant convicted in a state court might demonstrate, for example, that the trial was not fair as required by the Bill of Rights, which was extended to cover state court proceedings by the due process clause of the Fourteenth Amendment. The majority of cases heard by the Supreme Court come from the lower federal courts.

Figure 16.3 The Organization and Jurisdiction of the Courts

UNITED STATES SUPREME COURT

Original jurisdiction of the Supreme Court	Appellate jurisdiction of the Supreme Court (federal route)	Appellate jurisdiction of the Supreme Court (state route)
Cases involving foreign diplomats Cases involving a state: • Between the United States and a state • Between two or more states • Between one state and citizens of another state • Between a state and a foreign country	U.S. Courts of Appeal Court of Appeals for the Federal Circuit Legislative Courts	State Courts of Last Resort

Table 16.1 Full Opinions in the Supreme Court's 1999–2000 Term

TYPE OF CASE	NUMBER OF CASES
Original jurisdiction	1
Civil actions from lower federal courts	57
Federal criminal and *habeus corpus* cases	25
Civil actions from state courts	7
State criminal cases	3
TOTAL	93

Source: "The Supreme Court, 1999 Term: The Statistics," *Harvard Law Review* 113 (November 2000).

The central participants in the judicial system are, of course, the judges. Once on the bench, they must draw on their backgrounds and beliefs to guide their decision making. Some, for example, will be more supportive of abortion or of prayer in the public schools than others. Because presidents and others involved in the appointment process know perfectly well that judges are not neutral automatons who methodically and literally interpret the law, they work diligently to place candidates sympathetic to presidential policies on the bench. Who are the men and women who serve as federal judges and justices, and how did they obtain their positions?

The Politics of Judicial Selection

Appointing a federal judge or a Supreme Court justice is a president's chance to leave an enduring mark on the American legal system. Guaranteed by the Constitution the right to serve "during good behavior," federal judges and justices enjoy, for all practical purposes, lifetime positions. They may be removed only by conviction of impeachment, which has occurred a mere seven times in two centuries under the Constitution. No Supreme Court justice has ever been removed from office, although one, Samuel Chase, was tried but not convicted by the Senate in 1805. Nor can members of the federal judiciary have their salaries reduced, a stipulation that further insulates them from political pressures.

Although the president nominates persons to fill judicial slots, the Senate must confirm each nomination by majority vote. Because the judiciary is a coequal branch, the upper house of the legislature sees no reason to be especially deferential to the executive's recommendations. Because of the Senate's role, the president's discretion is actually less important than it appears.

The Lower Courts

senatorial courtesy

An unwritten tradition whereby nominations for state-level federal judicial posts are not confirmed if they are opposed by a senator from the state in which the nominee will serve. The tradition also applies to courts of appeal when there is opposition from the nominee's state senator.

The customary manner in which the Senate handles state-level federal judicial nominations is through **senatorial courtesy.** Under this unwritten tradition (which began under George Washington in 1789), nominations for lower-court positions are not confirmed when opposed by a senator from the state in which the nominee is to serve. In the case of judges for courts of appeal, nominees are not confirmed if opposed by a senator of the president's party from the state of the nominee's residence.

To invoke the right of senatorial courtesy, the relevant senator usually simply states a general reason for opposition. Other senators then honor their colleague's views and oppose the nomination, regardless of their personal evaluations of the candidate's merits.

Because of the strength of this informal practice, presidents usually check carefully with the relevant senator or senators ahead of time to avoid making a nomination that will fail to be confirmed. In many instances, this is tantamount to giving the power of nomination to these senators. Typically, when there is a vacancy for a federal district judgeship, the one or two senators from the state where the judge will serve suggest one or more names to the attorney general and the president. If neither senator is of the president's party, then the party's state congresspersons or other state party leaders may make suggestions.

Once several names have been submitted to the president, the Department of Justice and the Federal Bureau of Investigation conduct competency and background checks on these persons, and the president usually selects a nominee from those who survive the screening process. It is difficult for the president to reject the recommendation of the party's senator in favor of someone else if the person recommended clears the hurdles of professional standing and integrity. Thus the Constitution is often turned on its head, and the Senate ends up making nominations, which the president then approves.

Others have input in judicial selection as well. The Department of Justice may ask sitting judges, usually federal judges, to evaluate prospective nominees. Sitting judges may also initiate recommendations to advance or retard someone's chances of being nominated. In addition, candidates for the nomination are often active on their own behalf. They have to alert the relevant parties that they desire the position and may orchestrate a campaign of support. As one appellate judge observed, "People don't just get judgeships without seeking them."[3]

The president usually has more influence in the selection of judges to the federal courts of appeal than to federal district courts. The decisions of appellate courts are generally more significant than those of lower courts, so the president naturally takes a greater interest in appointing people to these courts. At the same time, individual senators are in a weaker position to determine who the nominee will be because the jurisdiction of an appeals court encompasses several states. Although custom and pragmatic politics require that these judgeships be apportioned among the states in a circuit, the president has some discretion in doing this and therefore has a greater role in recruiting appellate judges than in recruiting district court judges. Even here, however, senators of the president's party from the state in which the candidate resides may be able to veto a nomination.

Why does it matter?

Because of the practice of senatorial courtesy, senators actually end up nominating persons to be district court judges. What if the Senate did away with this practice, allowing the president greater freedom in making nominations? Would the persons chosen to serve on the bench be better judges?

The Supreme Court

The president is vitally interested in the Supreme Court because of the importance of its work and will generally be intimately involved in recruiting potential justices. Nominations to the Court may be a president's most important legacy to the nation.

A president cannot have much impact on the Court unless there are vacancies to fill. Although on the average there has been an opening on the Supreme Court every two years, there is a substantial variance around this mean.[4] Franklin D. Roosevelt had to wait five years before he could nominate a justice; in the meantime, he was faced with a Court that found much of his New Deal legislation unconstitutional. More recently, Jimmy Carter was never able to nominate a justice. Between 1972 and 1984, there were only two vacancies on the Court. Nevertheless, Richard Nixon was able to nominate four justices in his first three years in office, and Ronald Reagan had the opportunity to add three new members.

When the Chief Justice's position is vacant, the president may nominate either someone already on the Court or someone from outside to fill the position. Usually presidents choose the latter course to widen their range of options, but if they decide to elevate a sitting associate justice—as President Reagan did with William Rehnquist in 1986—the nominee must go through a new confirmation hearing by the Senate Judiciary Committee.

The president operates under fewer constraints in nominating persons to serve on the Supreme Court than in naming persons to be judges in the lower courts. Although many of the same actors are present in the case of Supreme Court nominations, their influence is typically quite different. The president usually relies on the attorney general and the Department of Justice to identify and screen candidates for the Court. Sitting justices often try to influence the nominations of their future colleagues, but presidents feel little obligation to follow their advice.

Why does it matter?

The public directly elects most state and local judges. All federal judges and justices are nominated by the president and confirmed by the Senate. Would federal judges decide cases differently if they were subject to reelection? Would you prefer to vote for federal judges?

Senators also play a lesser role in the recruitment of Supreme Court justices than in the selection of lower-court judges. No senator can claim that the jurisdiction of the Court falls within the realm of his or her special expertise, interest, or sphere of influence. Thus presidents typically consult with senators from the state of residence of a nominee after they have decided whom to select. At this point, senators are unlikely to oppose a nomination because they like having their state receive the honor and are well aware that the president can simply select someone from another state.

Candidates for nomination usually keep a low profile. Little can be accomplished through aggressive politicking, and because of the Court's standing, actively pursuing the position might offend those who play important roles in selecting nominees. The American Bar Association's Standing Committee on the Federal Judiciary has played a varied but typically modest role at the Supreme Court level. Presidents have not generally been willing to allow the committee to prescreen candidates before their nominations are announced. George W. Bush chose not to seek its advice at all.

Through 2000, there have been 148 nominations to the Supreme Court, and 108 persons have served on the Court. Four people were nominated and confirmed twice, eight declined appointment or died before beginning service on the Court, and 28 failed to secure Senate confirmation. Presidents have failed 20 percent of the time to appoint the nominees of their choice to the Court—a percentage much higher than that for any other federal position.

Although home-state senators do not play prominent roles in the selection process for the Court, the Senate as a whole does. Through its Judiciary Committee, it may probe a nominee's judicial philosophy in great detail.

For most of the twentieth century, Supreme Court nominations were routine affairs. Only one nominee failed to win confirmation in the first two-thirds of the century (see Table 16.2). But the 1960s were tumultuous times and bred ideological conflict. Although John F. Kennedy had no trouble with his two nominations to the Court—Byron White and Arthur Goldberg—his successor, Lyndon Johnson, was not so fortunate. Johnson had to withdraw his nomination of Abe Fortas (already serving on the Court) to serve as Chief Justice in the face of strong opposition; therefore, the Senate never voted on Homer Thornberry, Johnson's nominee to replace Fortas as an associate justice. Richard Nixon, the next president, had two nominees rejected in a row after bruising battles in the Senate.

The most recent failed nominations occurred in 1987. President Reagan nominated Robert H. Bork to fill the vacancy created by the resignation of Justice Lewis Powell. Bork testified before the Senate Judiciary Committee for 23 hours. A wide range of interest groups entered the fray, mostly in opposition to the nominee, whose views they claimed were extremist. In the end, following a bitter floor debate, the Senate rejected the president's nomination by a vote of 42 to 58.

Table 16.2 Twentieth-Century Senate Rejections of Supreme Court Nominees

NOMINEE	YEAR	PRESIDENT
John J. Parker	1930	Hoover
Abe Fortas[a]	1968	Johnson
Homer Thornberry[b]	1968	Johnson
Clement F. Haynesworth, Jr.	1969	Nixon
G. Harrold Carswell	1970	Nixon
Robert H. Bork	1987	Reagan
Douglas H. Ginsburg[a]	1987	Reagan

[a]Nomination withdrawn. Fortas was serving on the Court as an associate justice and was nominated to be Chief Justice.

[b]The Senate took no action on Thornberry's nomination.

Six days after the Senate vote on Bork, the president nominated Judge Douglas H. Ginsburg to the high court. Just nine days later, however, Ginsburg withdrew his nomination after disclosures that he had used marijuana while a law professor at Harvard.

In June 1991, at the end of the Supreme Court's term, Associate Justice Thurgood Marshall announced his retirement from the Court. Shortly thereafter, President Bush announced his nomination of another African American, federal appeals judge Clarence Thomas, to replace Marshall on the Court. Thomas was a conservative, so this decision was consistent with the Bush administration's emphasis on placing conservative judges on the federal bench.

The president claimed that he was not employing quotas when he chose another African American to replace the only African American ever to sit on the Supreme Court. Not everyone believed him, but liberals were placed in a dilemma. On the one hand, they favored a minority group member serving on the nation's highest court. On the other hand, Thomas was unlikely to vote the same way as Thurgood Marshall had voted. Instead, Thomas presented the prospect of strengthening the conservative trend in the Court's decisions. In the end, this ambivalence inhibited spirited opposition to Thomas, who was circumspect about his judicial philosophy in his appearances before the Senate Judiciary Committee. The committee sent his nomination to the Senate floor on a split vote.

Just as the Senate was about to vote on the nomination, however, charges of sexual harassment leveled against Thomas by University of Oklahoma law professor Anita Hill were made public. Hearings were reopened on the charges in response to criticism that the Senate was sexist for not seriously considering them in the first place. For several days, citizens sat transfixed before their television sets as Professor Hill calmly and graphically described her recollections of Thomas's behavior. Thomas then emphatically denied any such behavior and charged the Senate with racism for raising the issue. Ultimately, public opinion polls showed that most people believed Thomas, and he was confirmed in a 52–48 vote—the closest vote on a Supreme Court nomination in more than a century.

The Senate's treatment of President Clinton's two nominees harks back to the Kennedy era. Neither Ruth Bader Ginsburg nor Stephen Breyer caused much controversy. Whether the days of deference to the president have returned, however, remains to be seen.

Nominations are most likely to run into trouble under certain conditions. Presidents whose parties are in the minority in the Senate or who make a nomination at the end of their terms face a greatly increased probability of substantial opposition. Equally important, opponents of a nomination usually must be able to question a nominee's competence or ethics in order to defeat a nomination. Opposition based on a nominee's ideology is generally not considered a valid reason to vote against confirmation. For example, liberals disagreed strongly with the views of William Rehnquist,

In 1991, after two weeks of riveting hearings in which Clarence Thomas was charged with sexual harassment, the Senate narrowly confirmed his nomination to the Supreme Court. Historically, about one-fifth of those nominated to the Court have failed to obtain confirmation.

but he was easily confirmed as Chief Justice. Questions of the legal competence and ethics of nominees must usually be raised by their opponents in order to attract moderate senators to their side and to make ideological protests seem less partisan.

The Backgrounds of Judges and Justices

The Constitution sets no special requirements for judges or justices, but most observers conclude that the federal judiciary is composed of a distinguished group of men and women. Competence and ethical behavior are important to presidents for reasons beyond merely obtaining Senate confirmation of their judicial nominees. Skilled and honorable judges and justices reflect well on the president and are likely to do so for many years. Moreover, these individuals are more effective representatives of the president's views.

Although the criteria of competence and character screen out some possible candidates, there is still a wide field from which to choose. Other characteristics then play prominent roles.

The judges serving on the federal district and circuit courts are not a representative sample of the American people (see Table 16.3). They are all lawyers (although this is not a constitutional requirement), and they are overwhelmingly White males. Jimmy Carter appointed 40 women, 37 African Americans, and 16 Hispanics to the federal bench, more than all previous presidents combined. Ronald Reagan did not continue this trend, although he was the first to appoint a woman to the Supreme Court. His administration placed a higher priority on screening candidates on the basis of ideology than on screening them in terms of ascriptive characteristics. From 1989 to1992 George Bush continued to place conservatives on the bench, but he was much more likely to appoint women and minorities than was Reagan. Bill Clinton nominated Democrats, who are more liberal than the nominees of Reagan and Bush, and a large percentage of them were women and minorities.

Federal judges have typically held office as a judge or prosecutor, and often they have been involved in partisan politics. This involvement is generally what brings them to the attention of senators and the Department of Justice when they seek nominees for judgeships. As former U.S. Attorney General and Circuit Court Judge Griffin Bell once remarked, "For me, becoming a federal judge wasn't very difficult. I man-

Most members of the federal judiciary have backgrounds atypical of most Americans. Sandra Day O'Connor, nominated in 1981, is the first woman to sit on the Supreme Court.

aged John F. Kennedy's presidential campaign in Georgia. Two of my oldest and closest friends were senators from Georgia. And I was campaign manager and special unpaid counsel for the governor."[5]

Like their colleagues on the lower federal courts, Supreme Court justices share characteristics that qualify them as an elite group. All have been lawyers, and all but four (Thurgood Marshall, nominated in 1967; Sandra Day O'Connor, nominated in 1981; Clarence Thomas, nominated in 1991; and Ruth Bader Ginsburg, nominated in 1993) have been white males. Most have been in their fifties and sixties when they took office, from the upper-middle or upper class, and Protestants.[6]

Race and gender have become more salient criteria in recent years. In the 1980 presidential campaign, Ronald Reagan promised to appoint a woman to the first vacancy on the Court if he were elected. In 1991, President Bush chose to replace the first African-American justice, Thurgood Marshall, with another African American, Clarence Thomas. Women and minorities may serve on all federal courts more frequently in the future because of increased opportunity for legal education and decreased prejudice against their judicial activity, as well as because of their increasing political clout.

Table 16.3 Backgrounds of Recent Federal District and Appeals Court Judges

Characteristic	Appeals Court				District Court			
	CLINTON[a]	BUSH	REAGAN	CARTER	CLINTON[a]	BUSH	REAGAN	CARTER
Total number of nominees	48	37	78	56	248	148	290	202
Occupation (%)								
Politics/government	4	11	6	5	11	11	13	4
Judiciary	56	60	55	47	47	42	37	40
Large law firm	19	16	13	11	16	26	18	14
Moderate-size firm	13	11	10	16	15	15	19	20
Solo or small firm	—	—	1	5	8	5	10	14
Professor of law	8	3	13	14	2	1	2	3
Other	—	—	1	2	1	1	1	1
Experience (%)								
Judicial	63	62	60	54	51	47	47	55
Prosecutorial	35	30	28	32	41	39	44	39
Neither one	27	32	35	38	30	32	28	28
Party (%)								
Democrat	85	5	—	82	89	5	5	93
Republican	6	89	97	7	5	89	93	4
Independent	8	5	1	11	6	6	2	3
Past party activism (%)	56	70	69	73	52	61	59	61
Ethnicity or race (%)								
White	77	89	97	79	74	90	92	79
African American	10	5	1	16	19	7	2	14
Hispanic	10	5	1	4	5	4	5	7
Asian	2	—	—	2	2	—	1	1
Gender (%)								
Male	67	81	95	80	72	80	92	86
Female	33	19	5	20	28	20	8	14
Average age	51	49	50	52	49	48	49	50

[a]Through 1998.
Source: From Sheldon Goldman and Elliot Slotnick, "Clinton's Second Term Judiciary: Picking Judges Under Fire," in *Judicature* 82 (No. 6, 1999), 275, 280. Reprinted by permission.

Geography was once a prominent criterion for selection to the Court, but it is no longer very important. Presidents do like to spread the slots around, however, as when Richard Nixon decided that he wanted to nominate a Southerner. At various times there have been what some have termed a "Jewish seat" and a "Catholic seat" on the Court, but these guidelines are not binding on the president. For example, after a half-century of having a Jewish justice, the Court did not have one from 1969 to 1993.

Typically, justices have held high administrative or judicial positions before moving to the Supreme Court (see Table 16.4). Most have had some experience as a judge, often at the appellate level, and many have worked for the Department of Justice. Some have held elective office, and a few have had no government service but have been distinguished attorneys. The fact that many justices, including some of the most distinguished ones, have not had previous judicial experience may seem surprising, but the unique work of the Court renders this background much less important than it might be for other appellate courts.

Partisanship is another important influence on the selection of judges and justices. Only 13 of 108 members of the Supreme Court have been nominated by presidents of a different party. Moreover, many of the 13 exceptions were actually close to the president in ideology, as was the case in Richard Nixon's appointment of Lewis Powell. Herbert Hoover's nomination of Benjamin Cardozo seems to be one of the few cases in which partisanship was completely dominated by merit as a criterion for selection. Usually more than 90 percent of presidents' judicial nominations are of members of their own parties.

The role of partisanship is really not surprising. Most of a president's acquaintances are made through the party, and there is usually a certain congruity between

Table 16.4 Supreme Court Justices, 2001

NAME	YEAR OF BIRTH	PREVIOUS POSITION	NOMINATING PRESIDENT	YEAR OF APPOINTMENT
William H. Rehnquist[a]	1924	Assistant U.S. Attorney General	Nixon	1971
John Paul Stevens	1920	U.S. Court of Appeals	Ford	1975
Sandra Day O'Connor	1930	State Court of Appeals	Reagan	1981
Antonin Scalia	1936	U.S. Court of Appeals	Reagan	1986
Anthony M. Kennedy	1936	U.S. Court of Appeals	Reagan	1988
David H. Souter	1939	U.S. Court of Appeals	Bush	1990
Clarence Thomas	1948	U.S. Court of Appeals	Bush	1991
Ruth Bader Ginsburg	1933	U.S. Court of Appeals	Clinton	1993
Stephen G. Breyer	1938	U.S. Court of Appeals	Clinton	1994

[a]William Rehnquist was promoted from associate justice to Chief Justice by President Reagan in 1986.

party and political views. Most judges and justices have at one time been active partisans—an experience that gave them visibility and helped them obtain the positions from which they moved to the courts.

Judgeships are also considered very prestigious patronage plums. Indeed, the decisions of Congress to create new judgeships, and thus new positions for party members, are closely related to whether the majority party in Congress is the same as the party of the president. Members of the majority party in the legislature want to avoid providing an opposition party president with new positions to fill with their opponents.

Ideology is as important as partisanship in the selection of judges and justices. Presidents want to appoint people who share their views to the federal bench. In effect, all presidents try to "pack" the courts. They want more than "justice"; they want policies with which they agree. Presidential aides survey candidates' decisions (if they have served on a lower court),[7] speeches, political stands, writings, and other expressions of opinion. They also glean information from people who know the candidates well. Although it is considered improper to question judicial candidates about upcoming court cases, it is appropriate to discuss broader questions of political and judicial philosophy. The Reagan administration was especially concerned about such matters and had each potential nominee fill out a lengthy questionnaire and be interviewed by a special committee in the Department of Justice. Like its predecessor, the Bush administration was attentive to appointing conservative judges. Bill Clinton was less concerned with the ideology of his nominees, at least partly to avoid costly confirmation fights. Instead, he focused on identifying persons with strong legal credentials, especially women and minorities.

Members of the federal bench also play the game of politics, of course, and may try to time their retirements so that a president with compatible views will choose their successor. This is one reason why justices remain on the Supreme Court for so long, even when they are clearly infirm. William Howard Taft, a rigid conservative, even feared that a successor would be named by Herbert Hoover, a more moderate conservative.[8]

Presidents are typically pleased with the performance of their nominees to the Supreme Court and through them have slowed or reversed trends in the Court's decisions. Franklin D. Roosevelt's nominees substantially liberalized the Court, whereas Richard Nixon's turned it in a conservative direction.

Nevertheless, it is not always easy to predict the policy inclinations of candidates, and presidents have been disappointed in their nominees about one-fourth of the time. President Eisenhower, for example, was displeased with the liberal decisions of both Earl Warren and William Brennan. Once, when asked whether he had made any mistakes as president, he replied, "Yes, two, and they are both sitting on the Supreme Court."[9] Richard Nixon was certainly disappointed when Warren Burger, whom he had nominated as Chief Justice, wrote the Court's decision calling for immediate desegregation of the nation's schools shortly after his confirmation. This turn of events did little for the president's "Southern strategy." Burger also wrote the Court's opinion in *United States v. Nixon*, which forced the president to release the Watergate tapes. Nixon's resignation soon followed.

Presidents influence policy through the values of their judicial nominees, but this impact is limited by numerous legal and "extra-legal" factors beyond the chief executive's control. As Harry Truman put it, "Packing the Supreme Court can't be done . . . I've tried it and it won't work. . . . Whenever you put a man on the Supreme Court, he ceases to be your friend. I'm sure of that."[10]

There is no doubt that various women's, racial, ethnic, and religious groups desire to have their members appointed to the federal bench. At the very least, judgeships have symbolic importance for them.[11] Presidents face many of the same pressures for representativeness in selecting judges that they experience in naming their cabinet.

What is less clear is what policy differences result when presidents nominate persons with different backgrounds to the bench. The number of female and minority group judges is too few and their service too recent to serve as a sound basis for generalizations about their decisions. Many members of each party have been appointed, of course, and it appears that Republican judges in general are somewhat more conservative

You are Appointing a Supreme Court Justice

than Democratic judges. Former prosecutors serving on the Supreme Court have tended to be less sympathetic toward defendants' rights than other justices. It seems that background does make some difference,[12] yet for reasons that we will examine in the following sections, on many issues, party affiliation and other characteristics bring no more predictability to the courts than they do to Congress.

The Courts as Policymakers

"Judicial decision making," a former Supreme Court law clerk wrote in the *Harvard Law Review*, "involves, at bottom, a choice between competing values by fallible, pragmatic, and at times nonrational men and women in a highly complex process in a very human setting."[13] This is an apt description of policymaking in the Supreme Court and in other courts, too. The next sections will look at how courts make policy, paying particular attention to the role of the U.S. Supreme Court. Although it is not the only court involved in policymaking and policy interpretation, its decisions have the widest implications for policy.

Accepting Cases

Deciding what to decide about is the first step in all policymaking. Courts of original jurisdiction cannot very easily refuse to consider a case; appeals courts, including the U.S. Supreme Court, have much more control over their agendas. The approximately 7,500 cases submitted annually to the U.S. Supreme Court must be read, culled, and sifted. Figure 16.4 shows the stages of this process. Every Wednesday afternoon and every Friday morning, the nine justices meet in conference. With them in the conference room sit some 25 carts, each wheeled in from the office of one of the nine justices, and each filled with petitions, briefs, memoranda, and every item the justices are likely to need during their discussions. These meetings operate under the strictest secrecy; only the justices themselves attend.

visual literacy
Case Overload

At these weekly conferences two important matters are hammered out. First is an agenda: The justices consider the Chief Justice's "discuss list" and decide which cases they want to discuss. Because few of the justices can take the time to read materials on every case submitted to the Court, most rely heavily on their law clerks (each justice has up to four to assist them in considering cases and writing opinions) to screen each case. If four justices agree to grant review of a case (the "rule of four"), it can be scheduled for oral argument or decided on the basis of the written record already on file with the Court.

Figure 16.4 Obtaining Space on the Supreme Court's Docket

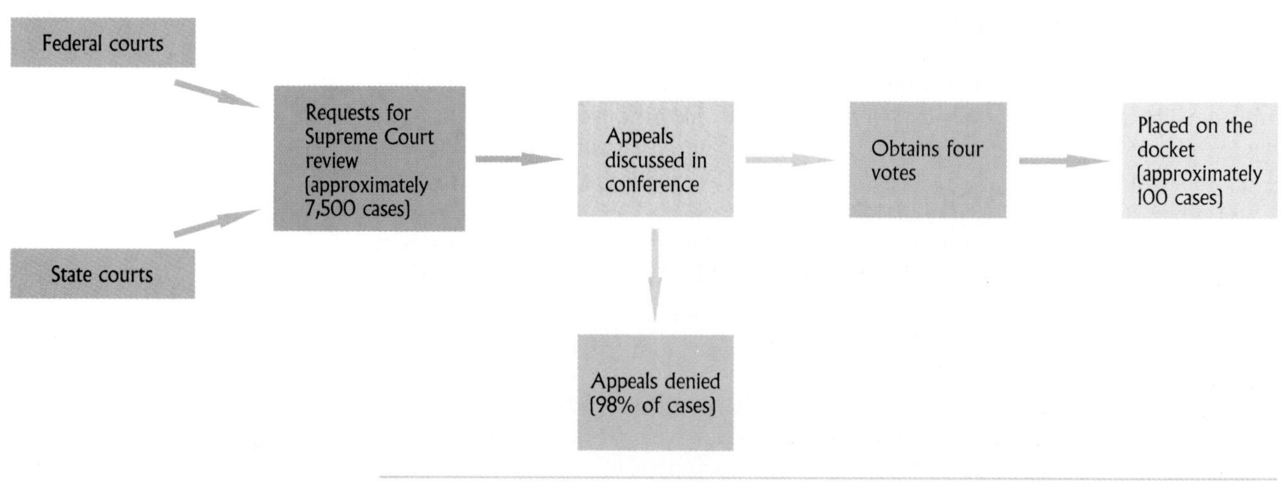

The most common way for the Court to put a case on its docket is by issuing to a lower federal or state court a *writ of certiorari*, a formal document that calls up a case. Until 1988, some cases—principally those in which federal laws had been found unconstitutional, in which federal courts had concluded that state laws violated the federal Constitution, or in which state laws had been upheld in state courts despite claims that they violated federal law or the Constitution—were technically supposed to be heard by the Court "on appeal." In reality, however, the Court always exercised broad discretion over hearing these and other cases.

Cases that involve major issues—especially civil liberties, conflict between different lower courts on the interpretation of federal law, or disagreement between a majority of the Supreme Court and lower-court decisions—are likely to be selected by the Court.[14]

Because getting into the Supreme Court is half the battle, it is important to remember this chapter's earlier discussion of standing to sue (litigants must have serious interest in a case, having sustained or being in immediate danger of sustaining a direct and substantial injury from another party or an action of government)—a criterion the Court often uses to decide whether to hear a case. In addition, the Court has used other means to avoid deciding cases that are too politically "hot" to handle or that divide the Court too sharply,[15] as we will discuss later in this chapter.

Another important influence on the Supreme Court is the **solicitor general.** As a presidential appointee and the third-ranking official in the Department of Justice, the solicitor general is in charge of the appellate court litigation of the federal government. The solicitor general and a staff of about two dozen experienced attorneys have four key functions: (1) to decide whether to appeal cases the government has lost in the lower courts, (2) to review and modify the briefs presented in government appeals, (3) to represent the government before the Supreme Court, and (4) to submit a brief on behalf of a litigant in a case in which the government is not directly involved. Unlike attorneys for private parties, the solicitors general are careful to seek Court review only of important cases. By avoiding frivolous appeals and displaying a high degree of competence, they typically earn the confidence of the Court, which in turn grants review of a large percentage of the cases they submit.

solicitor general

A presidential appointee and the third-ranking office in the Department of Justice. The solicitor general is in charge of the appellate court litigation of the federal government.

Ultimately, the Supreme Court decides very few cases. In recent years, the Court has made fewer than 100 formal written decisions per year in which their opinions could serve as precedent and thus as the basis of guidance for lower courts. In a few dozen additional cases, the Court reaches a *per curiam decision*—that is, a decision without explanation. Such decisions resolve the immediate case but have no value as precedent because the Court does not offer reasoning that would guide lower courts in future decisions.[17]

Making Decisions

The second task of the justices' weekly conferences is to discuss cases actually accepted and argued before the Court. Beginning the first Monday in October and lasting until June, the Court hears oral arguments in two-week cycles: two weeks of courtroom arguments followed by two weeks of reflecting on cases and writing opinions about them. Figure 16.5 shows the stages in this process.

Figure 16.5 The Supreme Court's Decision-Making Process

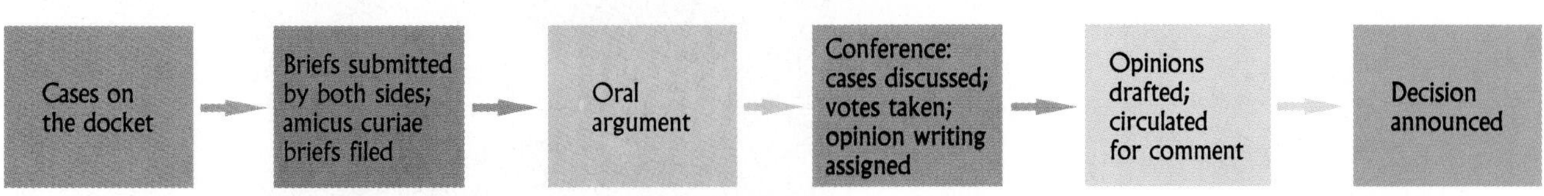

Before the justices enter the courtroom to hear the lawyers for each side present their arguments, they have received elaborately prepared written briefs from each party involved. They have also probably received several *amicus curiae* briefs from parties (often groups) who are interested in the outcome of the case but who are not formal litigants.

Amicus curiae briefs have another important role: The government, under the direction of the solicitor general, may submit them in cases in which it has an interest. For instance, a case between two parties may involve the question of the constitutionality of a federal law. The federal government naturally wants to have its voice heard on such matters, even if it is not formally a party to the case. These briefs are also a means to urge the Court to change established doctrine. For example, the Reagan administration frequently submitted *amicus curiae* briefs to the Court to try to change the law dealing with defendants' rights.

In most instances, the attorneys for each side have only a half-hour to address the Court. During this time they summarize their briefs, emphasizing their most compelling points. The justices may listen attentively, interrupt with penetrating or helpful questions, request information, talk to one another, read (presumably briefs), or simply gaze at the ceiling. After 25 minutes, a white light comes on at the lectern from which the lawyer is speaking, and five minutes later a red light signals the end of that lawyer's presentation, even if he or she is in midsentence. Oral argument is over.[18]

Back in the conference room, the Chief Justice, who presides over the Court, raises a particular case and invites discussion, turning first to the senior associate justice. Discussion can range from perfunctory to profound and from courteous to caustic. If the votes are not clear from the individual discussions, the Chief Justice may ask each justice to vote. Once a tentative vote has been reached, it is necessary to write an **opinion,** a statement of the legal reasoning behind the decision.

opinion

A statement of legal reasoning behind a judicial decision. The content of an opinion may be as important as the decision itself.

Opinion writing is no mere formality. In fact, the content of an opinion may be as important as the decision itself. Broad and bold opinions have far-reaching implications for future cases; narrowly drawn opinions may have little impact beyond the case being decided. Tradition in the Supreme Court requires that the Chief Justice, if in the majority, write the opinion or assign it to another justice in the majority. The Chief Justice often writes the opinion in landmark cases, as Earl Warren did in *Brown v. Board of Education* and Warren Burger did in *United States v. Nixon.* If the Chief Justice is part of the minority, the senior associate justice in the majority assigns the opinion. Drafts are then circulated among the majority, suggestions are made, and negotiations are conducted among the justices.[19] Votes can be gained or lost by the content of the opinion. An opinion that proves unacceptable to a clear majority is reworked and redrafted.

The content of a Supreme Court opinion may be as important as the decision itself, and justices may spend months negotiating a majority opinion. Here, William H. Rehnquist, Chief Justice of the Supreme Court, prepares a written opinion.

Justices are free to write their own opinions, to join in other opinions, or to associate themselves with part of one opinion and part of another. *Dissenting opinions* are those written by justices opposed to all or part of the majority's decision. *Concurring opinions* are those written not only to support a majority decision but also to stress a different constitutional or legal basis for the judgment. When the opinions are written and the final vote is taken, the decision is announced. At least six justices must participate in a case, and decisions are made by majority vote. If there is a tie (because of a vacancy on the Court or because a justice chooses not to participate), the decision of the lower court from which the case came is sustained. Five votes in agreement on the reasoning underlying an opinion are necessary for the logic to serve as precedent for judges of lower courts.

The vast majority of cases that reach the courts are settled on the principle of ***stare decisis*** ("let the decision stand"), meaning that an earlier decision should hold for the case being considered. All courts rely heavily on **precedent**—the way similar cases were handled in the past—as a guide to current decisions. Lower courts, of course, are expected to follow the precedents of higher courts in their decision making. If the Supreme Court, for example, rules in favor of the right to abortion under certain conditions, it has established a precedent that lower courts are expected to follow. Lower courts have much less discretion than the Supreme Court.

stare decisis

A Latin phrase meaning "let the decision stand." The vast majority of cases reaching appellate courts are settled on this principle.

precedents

How similar cases have been decided in the past.

The Supreme Court is in a position to overrule its own precedents, and it has done so more than 200 times.[20] One of the most famous of such instances occurred with *Brown* v. *Board of Education* (1954) (see Chapter 5), in which the court overruled *Plessy* v. *Ferguson* (1896) and found that segregation in the public schools violated the Constitution.

What happens when precedents are unclear? This is especially a problem for the Supreme Court, which is more likely than other courts to handle cases at the forefront of the law. Precedent is typically less firmly established on these matters. Moreover, the justices are often asked to apply to concrete situations the vague phrases of the Constitution ("due process of law," "equal protection," "unreasonable searches and seizures") or vague statutes passed by Congress. This ambiguity provides leeway for the justices to disagree (only about one-third of the cases in which full opinions are handed down are decided unanimously) and for their values to influence their judgment.

As a result, it is often easy to identify consistent patterns in the decisions of justices. For example, if there is division on the Court (indicating that precedent is not clear) and

"Call it 'legislating from the bench,' if you will, but on this occasion I should like to repeal the First Amendment."

You Are the Policymaker

The Debate Over Original Intentions

The most contentious issue involving the courts is the role of judicial discretion. According to Christopher Wolfe: "The Constitution itself nowhere specifies a particular set of rules by which it is to be interpreted. Where does one go, then, in order to discover the proper way to interpret the Constitution?"

Some have argued for a jurisprudence of **original intent** (sometimes referred to as *strict constructionism*). This view holds that judges and justices should attempt to determine the intent of the framers of the Constitution regarding a particular matter and decide cases in line with that intent. Such a view is popular with conservatives. Advocates of strict constructionism view it as a means of constraining the exercise of judicial discretion, which they see as the foundation of the liberal decisions of the past four decades, especially on matters of civil liberties, civil rights, and defendants' rights (discussed in Chapters 4 and 5).

They also see following original intent as the only basis of interpretation consistent with democracy. Judges, they argue, should not dress up constitutional interpretations with *their* views on "contemporary needs," "today's conditions," or "what is right." It is the job of legislators, not judges, to make such judgments.

Other jurists, such as former Justice William Brennan, disagree. They maintain that what appears to be deference to the intentions of the framers is simply a cover for making conservative decisions. Opponents of original intent assert that the Constitution is subject to multiple meanings by thoughtful people in different ages. Judges will differ in time and place about what they think the Constitution means. Thus, basing decisions on original intent is not likely to have much effect on judicial discretion.

In addition, Brennan and his supporters contend that the Constitution is not like a paint-by-numbers kit. Trying to reconstruct or guess the framers' intentions is very difficult. Recent key cases before the Supreme Court have concerned issues such as school busing, abortions, the Internet, and wire tapping, that the framers could not have imagined; there were no public schools or buses, no contraceptives or modern abortion techniques, and certainly no computers or electronic surveillance equipment or telephones in 1787.

The Founders embraced general principles, not specific solutions when they wrote the Constitution. They frequently lacked discrete, discoverable intent. Moreover, there is often no record of their intentions, nor is it clear whose intentions should count—those of the writers of the Constitution, those of the more than 1,600 members who attended the ratifying conventions, or those of the voters who sent them there. This problem grows more complex when you consider the amendments to the Constitution, which involve thousands of additional "framers."

Historian Jack N. Rakove points out that there is little historical evidence that the framers believed their intentions should guide later interpretations of the Constitution. In fact, there is some evidence for believing that Madison—the key delegate—left the Constitutional Convention bitterly disappointed with the results. What if Madison had one set of intentions but—like anyone working in a committee—got a different set of results?

The lines are drawn. On one side is the argument that any deviation from following the original intentions of the Constitution's framers is a deviation from principle, leaving unelected judges to impose their views on the American people. If judges do not follow original intentions, then on what do they base their decisions?

On the other side are those who believe that it is often impossible to discern the views of the framers, and that there is no good reason to be constrained by the views of the eighteenth century, which reflect a more limited conception of constitutional rights. In order to cope with current needs, they argue, it is necessary to adapt the principles in the Constitution to the demands of each era.

The choice here is at the very heart of the judicial process. If you were a justice sitting on the Supreme Court and were asked to interpret the meaning of the Constitution, what would *you* do?

Sources: Christopher Wolfe, *The Rise of Modern Judicial Review* (New York: Basic Books, 1986); Raoul Berger, *Government by Judiciary: The Transformation of the Fourteenth Amendment* (Cambridge, MA: Harvard University Press, 1977); Traciel V. Reid, "A Critique of Interpretivism and Its Claimed Influence upon Judicial Decision Making," *American Politics Quarterly* 16 (July 1988): 329–356; Jack N. Rakove, ed., *Interpreting the Constitution* (Boston: Northeastern University Press, 1990); and Arthur S. Miller, "In Defense of Judicial Activism," in Stephen C. Halpern and Charles M. Lamb, eds., *Supreme Court Activism and Restraint* (Lexington, MA: D.C. Heath, 1982).

you can identify a conservative side to the issue at hand, it is likely that Chief Justice William Rehnquist will be on that side. Ruth Bader Ginsburg may very well be voting on the other side of the issue. Liberalism and conservatism have several dimensions, including freedom, equality, and economic regulation. The point is that policy preferences do matter in judicial decision making, especially on the nation's highest court[21] (see "You Are the Policymaker: The Debate Over Original Intentions").

original intent

A view that the Constitution should be interpreted according to the original intent of the framers. Many **conservatives** support this view.

Once a decision is announced, copies of it are conveyed to the press as the decision is formally announced in open court. Media coverage of the Court remains primitive—short and shallow. Doris Graber reports that "much court reporting, even at the Supreme Court level, is imprecise and sometimes even wrong."[22] More important to the legal community, the decisions are bound weekly and made available to every law library and lawyer in the United States. There is, of course, an air of finality to the public announcement of a decision. In fact, however, even Supreme Court decisions are not self-implementing; they are actually "remands" to lower courts, instructing them to act in accordance with the Court's decisions.

Implementing Court Decisions

Reacting bitterly to one of Chief Justice Marshall's decisions, President Andrew Jackson is said to have grumbled: "John Marshall has made his decision; now let him enforce it." Court decisions carry legal, even moral, authority, but courts must rely on other units of government to enforce their decisions. **Judicial implementation** refers to how and whether court decisions are translated into actual policy, thereby affecting the behavior of others.

judicial implementation

How and whether court decisions are translated into actual policy, thereby affecting the behavior of others. The courts rely on other units of government to enforce their decisions.

You should think of any judicial decision as the end of one process—the litigation process—and the beginning of another process—the process of judicial implementation. Sometimes delay and stalling follow even decisive court decisions. There is, for example, the story of the tortured efforts of a young African American named Virgil Hawkins to get himself admitted to the University of Florida Law School. Hawkins' efforts began in 1949, when he first applied for admission, and ended unsuccessfully in 1958, after a decade of court decisions. Despite a 1956 order from the U.S. Supreme Court to admit Hawkins, continued legal skirmishing produced a 1958 decision by a U.S. district court in Florida ordering the admission of non-Whites but upholding the denial of admission to Hawkins himself. Other courts and other institutions of government can be roadblocks in the way of judicial implementation.

Charles Johnson and Bradley Canon suggest that implementation of court decisions involves several elements.[23] First, there is an *interpreting population*, heavily composed of lawyers and judges. They must correctly understand and reflect the intent of the original decision in their subsequent actions. Usually lower-court judges do follow the Supreme Court, but sometimes they circumvent higher-court decisions to satisfy their own policy interests.[24]

Second, there is an *implementing population*. Suppose the Supreme Court held (as it did) that prayers organized by school officials in the public schools are unconstitutional. The implementing population (school boards and school administrators) must then actually abandon prayers. Police departments, hospitals, corporations, government agencies—all may be part of the implementing population. With so many implementors, many of whom may disagree with a decision, there is plenty of room for "slippage" between what the Supreme Court decides and what actually occurs. Judicial decisions are more likely to be implemented smoothly if implementation is concentrated in the hands of a few highly visible officials, such as the president or state legislators.

participation
The Court and School Prayer

Third, every decision involves a *consumer population*. The potential "consumers" of an abortion decision are those who want abortions (and those who oppose them); the consumers of the *Miranda* decision (see Chapter 4) are criminal defendants and their attorneys. The consumer population must be aware of its newfound rights and stand up for them.

Virgil Hawkins' unsuccessful struggle to attend the all-White University of Florida Law School illustrates how judicial implementation can affect the impact of court decisions. The Supreme Court ordered the school to admit Hawkins in 1956, but the school and state refused to implement the ruling, and continued to appeal the case. Two years later a Florida district court again denied admission to Hawkins, although it did order the school's desegregation.

The federal courts lack a bureaucracy to implement their decisions. In fact, some of the Supreme Court's most controversial decisions, such as those dealing with school integration and school prayers, have been implemented only with great difficulty. What if the courts had a bureaucracy to enforce their decisions? Would justice be better served?

Congress and presidents can also help or hinder judicial implementation. The Supreme Court held in 1954 that segregated schools were "inherently unconstitutional" and the next year ordered public schools desegregated with "all deliberate speed." President Eisenhower refused to state clearly that Americans should comply with this famous decision in *Brown v. Board of Education,* which may have encouraged local school boards to resist the decision. Congress was not much help either; only a decade later, in the wake of the civil rights movement discussed in Chapter 5, did it pass legislation denying federal aid to segregated schools. Different presidents have different commitments to a particular judicial policy. After years of court and presidential decisions supporting busing to end racial segregation, the Reagan administration in December 1984 went before the Supreme Court and argued *against* school busing in a case in Norfolk, Va.

The fate and effect of a Supreme Court decision are complex and unpredictable. The implementation of any court decision involves many actors besides the justices, and the justices have no way of ensuring that their decisions and policies will be implemented. Courts have made major changes in public policies, however, not because their decisions are automatically implemented, but because the courts both reflect and help to determine the national policy agenda.[25]

The Courts and the Policy Agenda

Even though American courts and judges work largely alone and in isolation from daily contact with other political institutions, they do play a key role in shaping the policy agenda. Like all policymakers, however, the courts are choice-takers. Confronted with controversial policies, they make controversial decisions that leave some people winners and others losers. The courts have made policy about slavery and segregation, about corporate power and capital punishment, and about dozens of other controversial matters.

A Historical Review

Until the Civil War, the dominant questions before the Court concerned the strength and legitimacy of the federal government and slavery. These issues of nation building were resolved in favor of the supremacy of the national government. From the Civil War until 1937, questions of the relationship between the federal government and the economy predominated. During this period, the Court restricted the power of the federal government to regulate the economy. From 1938 to the present, the paramount issues before the Court have concerned personal liberty and social and political equality. In this era, the Court has enlarged the scope of personal freedom and civil rights and has removed many of the constitutional restraints on the regulation of the economy.

Few justices played a more important role in making the Court a significant national agenda setter than John Marshall, Chief Justice from 1801 to 1835. His successors have continued not only to respond to the political agenda but also to shape discussion and debate about it.

John Marshall and the Growth of Judicial Review. Scarcely was the government housed in its new capital when Federalists and Democrats clashed over the courts. In the election of 1800, Democrat Thomas Jefferson had beaten Federalist John Adams. Determined to leave at least the judiciary in trusted hands, Adams tried to fill it with Federalists. He is alleged to have stayed at his desk until nine o'clock signing commissions on his last night in the White House (March 3, 1801).

In the midst of this flurry, Adams appointed William Marbury to the minor post of justice of the peace in the District of Columbia. In the rush of last-minute business, however, Secretary of State John Marshall failed to deliver commissions to Marbury and 16 others. He left the commissions to be delivered by the incoming secretary of state, James Madison.

Madison and Jefferson were furious at Adams' actions and refused to deliver the commissions. Marbury and three others in the same situation sued Madison, asking the Supreme Court to order Madison to give them their commissions. They took their case directly to the Supreme Court under the Judiciary Act of 1789, which gave the Court original jurisdiction in such matters.

The new chief justice was none other than Adams' former secretary of state and arch-Federalist John Marshall, himself one of the "midnight appointments" (he took his seat on the Court barely three weeks before Adams' term ended). Marshall and his Federalist colleagues were in a tight spot. Threats of impeachment came from Jeffersonians fearful that the Court would vote for Marbury. Moreover, if the Court ordered Madison to deliver the commissions, he was likely to ignore the order, putting the nation's highest court at risk over a minor issue. Marshall had no means of compelling Madison to act.

The Court could also deny Marbury's claim. Taking that option, however, would concede the issue to the Jeffersonians and give the appearance of retreat in the face of opposition, thereby reducing the power of the Court.

Marshall devised a shrewd solution to the case of ***Marbury v. Madison.*** In February 1803, he delivered the unanimous opinion of the Court. First, Marshall and his colleagues argued that Madison was wrong to withhold Marbury's commission. The Court also found, however, that the Judiciary Act of 1789, under which Marbury had brought suit, contradicted the plain words of the Constitution about the Court's original jurisdiction. Thus Marshall dismissed Marbury's claim, saying that the Court, according to the Constitution, had no power to require that the commission be delivered.

Conceding a small battle over Marbury's commission (he did not get it), Marshall won a much larger war, asserting for the courts the power to determine what is and what is not constitutional. As Marshall wrote, "An act of the legislature repugnant to the Constitution is void," and "it is emphatically the province of the judicial department to say what the law is." The Chief Justice established the power of **judicial review,** the power of the courts to hold acts of Congress, and by implication the executive, in violation of the Constitution.

Marbury v. Madison was part of a skirmish between the Federalists on the Court and the Democratic-controlled Congress. Partly, for example, to rein in the Supreme Court, the Jeffersonian Congress in 1801 abolished the lower federal appeals courts and made the Supreme Court judges return to the unpleasant task of "riding circuit"—serving as lower-court judges around the country. This was an act of studied harassment of the Court by its enemies.

Marbury v. Madison

The 1803 case in which Chief Justice John Marshall and his associates first asserted the right of the **Supreme Court** to determine the meaning of the **U.S. Constitution.** The decision established the Court's power of **judicial review** over acts of Congress, in this case the Judiciary Act of 1789.

judicial review

The power of the courts to determine whether acts of Congress, and by implication the executive, are in accord with the U.S. Constitution. Judicial review was established by John Marshall and his associates in ***Marbury v. Madison.*** See also **judicial interpretation.**

John Marshall, Chief Justice from 1801 to 1835, established the Supreme Court's power of judicial review in the 1803 case *Marbury v. Madison.* In their ruling on the case, Marshall and his associates declared that the Court has the power to determine the constitutionality of congressional actions.

After *Marbury,* angry members of Congress, together with other Jeffersonians, claimed that Marshall was a "usurper of power," setting himself above Congress and the president. This view, however, was unfair. State courts, before and after the Constitution, had declared acts of their legislatures unconstitutional. In the *Federalist Papers,* Alexander Hamilton had expressly assumed the power of the federal courts to review legislation, and the federal courts had actually done so. *Marbury* was not even the first case to strike down an act of Congress; a lower federal court had done so in 1792, and the Supreme Court itself had approved a law after a constitutional review in 1796. Marshall was neither inventing nor imagining his right to review laws for their constitutionality.

The case also illustrates that the courts must be politically astute in exercising their power over the other branches. By in effect reducing its *own* power—the authority to hear cases such as Marbury's under its original jurisdiction—the Court was able to assert the right of judicial review in a fashion that the other branches could not easily rebuke.

More than any other power of the courts, judicial review has embroiled them in policy controversy. Before the Civil War the Supreme Court, headed by Chief Justice Roger Taney, held the Missouri Compromise unconstitutional because it restricted slavery in the territories. The decision was one of many steps along the road to the Civil War. After the Civil War, the Court was again active, this time using judicial review to strike down dozens of state and federal laws curbing the growing might of business corporations.

The "Nine Old Men." Never was the Court so controversial as during the New Deal. At President Roosevelt's urging, Congress passed dozens of laws designed to end the Depression. However, conservatives—most nominated by Republican presidents—who viewed federal intervention in the economy as unconstitutional and tantamount to socialism dominated the Court.

The Supreme Court began to dismantle New Deal policies one by one. The National Recovery Act was one of a string of anti-Depression measures. Although it was never particularly popular, the Court sealed its doom in *Schechter Poultry Corporation v. United States* (1935), declaring the Act unconstitutional because it regulated purely local business that did not affect interstate commerce.

Incensed, Roosevelt in 1937 proposed what critics called a "court-packing plan." Noting that the average age of the Court was over 70, Roosevelt railed against those "nine old men." Because Congress can determine the number of justices, he proposed that Congress expand the size of the Court, a move that would have allowed him to appoint additional justices sympathetic to the New Deal. Congress objected and never passed the plan. Indeed, it became irrelevant when two justices, Chief Justice Charles Evans Hughes and Associate Justice Owen Roberts, began switching their votes in favor of New Deal legislation. (One wit called it the "switch in time that saved nine.") Shortly thereafter Associate Justice William Van Devanter retired, and Roosevelt got to make the first of his many appointments to the Court.

The Warren Court. Few eras of the Supreme Court have been as active in shaping public policy as that of the Warren Court (1953–1969), presided over by Chief Justice Earl Warren. Scarcely had President Eisenhower appointed Warren when the Court faced the issue of school segregation. In 1954, it held that laws requiring segregation of the public schools were unconstitutional. Later it expanded the rights of criminal defendants, extending the right to counsel and protections against unreasonable search and seizure and self-incrimination (see Chapter 4). It ordered states to reapportion both their legislatures and their congressional districts according to the principle of one person, one vote, and it prohibited organized prayer in public schools. So active was the Warren Court that right-wing groups, fearing that it was remaking the country, posted billboards all over the United States urging Congress to "Impeach Earl Warren."[26]

The Burger Court. Warren's retirement in 1969 gave President Richard Nixon his hoped-for opportunity to appoint a "strict constructionist"—that is, one who interprets the Constitution narrowly—as Chief Justice. He chose Minnesotan Warren E. Burger, then a conservative judge on the District of Columbia Court of Appeals. As Nixon hoped, the Burger Court turned out to be more conservative

The Supreme Court frequently makes controversial decisions regarding important matters of politics and public policy. Critics often argue that unelected judges are making policy decisions that should be made by elected officials. Here demonstrators protest the Supreme Court's decisions regarding counting the ballots in the 2000 presidential election.

than the liberal Warren Court. It narrowed defendants' rights, though it did not overturn the fundamental contours of the *Miranda* decision. The conservative Burger Court, however, also wrote the abortion decision in *Roe v. Wade*, required school busing in certain cases to eliminate historic segregation, and upheld affirmative action programs in the *Weber* case (see Chapter 5). One of the most notable decisions of the Burger Court weighed against Burger's appointer, Richard Nixon. At the height of the Watergate scandal (see Chapter 13), the Supreme Court was called upon to decide whether Nixon had to turn his White House tapes over to the courts. It unanimously ordered him to do so in ***United States v. Nixon*** (1974), thus hastening the president's resignation.

United States v. Nixon

The 1974 case in which the Supreme Court unanimously held that the doctrine of executive privilege was implicit in the Constitution but could not be extended to protect documents relevant to criminal prosecutions.

The Rehnquist Court. In the late 1990s, the conservative nominees of Republican presidents, led by Chief Justice William Rehnquist, composed a clear Supreme Court majority. One justice, Harry Blackmun, even took the extraordinary step of speaking out publicly, declaring that the Supreme Court was "moving to the right . . . where it wants to go, by hook or by crook."[27] Needless to say, others saw the trend in the Court's decisions in a more positive light.[28]

However one evaluates the Court's current direction, the Rehnquist Court has not created a revolution in constitutional law. Instead, as discussed in Chapters 4 and 5, it has limited rather than reversed rights established by liberal decisions such as those regarding defendants' rights and abortion. Although its protection of the First Amendment rights of free speech and free press remains robust, the Court no longer sees itself as the special protector of individual liberties and civil rights for minorities (affirmative action laws are at risk). Instead, it has typically deferred to the will of the majority and the rules of the government. Most professional Supreme Court watchers expect this trend to continue.

timeline
Umpiring the Government

Understanding the Courts

Powerful courts are unusual; few nations have them. The power of American judges raises questions about the compatibility of unelected courts with a democracy and about the appropriate role for the judiciary in policymaking.

The Courts and Democracy

Announcing his retirement in 1981, Justice Potter Stewart made a few remarks to the handful of reporters present. Embedded in his brief statement was this observation: "It seems to me that there's nothing more antithetical to the idea of what a good judge should be than to think it has something to do with representative democracy." He meant that judges should not be subject to the whims of popular majorities. In a nation that insists so strongly that it is democratic, where do the courts fit in?

In some ways, the courts are not a very democratic institution. Federal judges are not elected and are almost impossible to remove. Indeed, their social backgrounds probably make the courts the most elite-dominated policymaking institution. If democracy requires that key policymakers always be elected or be continually responsible to those who are, then the courts diverge sharply from the requirements of democratic government.

As you saw in Chapter 2, the Constitution's framers wanted it that way. Chief Justice Rehnquist, a judicial conservative, put the case as follows: "A mere change in public opinion since the adoption of the Constitution, unaccompanied by a constitutional amendment, should not change the meaning of the Constitution. A merely temporary majoritarian groundswell should not abrogate some individual liberty protected by the Constitution."[29]

How You Can Make A Difference

Teen Court

Unknown to most college students, a branch of many state and local court systems known as "teen court" needs smart and ambitious volunteers. A teenage defendant (between the ages of 10 and 17) who has already pleaded guilty to a misdemeanor (curfew violation, smoking, trespassing, littering, larceny, disorderly conduct, etc.) can request to bypass the traditional juvenile court system and enter the teen court system. Though teen courts vary from city to city and state to state, this basic system remains fairly consistent. The bailiff, defense attorneys, prosecutors, and members of the jury are literally the defendant's peers—they are all teenagers. Usually, a local judge, lawyer, or other court official serves as the teen court judge. Since guilt has already been decided, the teen court focuses upon sentencing the defendant. After the prosecuting and defense "attorneys" present their cases, the jury members are usually allowed to question the defendant to gather enough information to make a fair ruling. Jurors are usually presented with a menu of sentencing options including community service, monetary restitution, a written essay, and/or a written apology to the victim. After deliberation, the jury announces its binding decision to the defendant and his or her parent(s). This is not a game but a serious procedure requiring training, maturity, and hard work.

These courts desperately need volunteers to help organize and train teenagers to correctly function within the court system said Peggy Jones, a former undergraduate student who helped develop the teen court system in northern Kentucky. Peggy took a primary role in recruiting and training high school students to participate in the program. This program put her in touch with lawyers, judges, and the court system for the first time. Her curiosity about law school soon blossomed into a firm determination to succeed. By working alongside the president of the Kentucky Bar Association, local judges, and lawyers, Peggy not only gained invaluable preparation for law school but also contacts and references that helped her law school application stand out from the other countless applications.

If teen courts interest you, contact your local, county, or state judicial system to see if a teen court is already in place. If not, you can follow Peggy's example by helping to develop one with the assistance and permission of local lawyers and judges. The American Probation and Parole Association with the National Youth Court Center conduct several training seminars per year for those interested in developing or enhancing a teen court system. You can also download an implementation guide that shows how to organize teen court, recruit volunteers, and develop a program model at www.youthcourt.net/peerjustice.

The courts are not entirely independent of popular preferences, however. Turn-of-the-century Chicago humorist Finley Peter Dunne had his Irish saloonkeeper character "Mr. Dooley" quip that "th' Supreme Court follows th' iliction returns." Many years later, political scientists have found that the Court usually reflects popular majorities.[30] Even when the Court seems out of step with other policymakers, it eventually swings around to join the policy consensus, as it did in the New Deal. A study of the period from 1937 to 1980 found that the Court was clearly out of line with public opinion only on the issue of prayers in public schools.[31]

Despite the fact that the Supreme Court sits in a "marble palace," it is not as insulated from the normal forms of politics as one might think. The two sides in the abortion debate flooded the Court with mail, targeted it with advertisements and protests, and bombarded it with 78 *amicus curiae* briefs in the *Webster v. Reproductive Health Services* (1989) case. Members of the Supreme Court are unlikely to cave in to interest group pressures, but they are aware of the public's concern about issues, and this awareness becomes part of their consciousness as they decide cases. Political scientists have found that the Court is more likely to hear cases for which interest groups have filed *amicus curiae* briefs.[32]

Courts can also promote pluralism. When groups go to court, they use litigation to achieve their policy objectives.[33] Both civil rights groups and environmentalists, for example, have blazed a path to show how interest groups can effectively use the courts to achieve their policy goals. The legal wizard of the NAACP's litigation strategy,

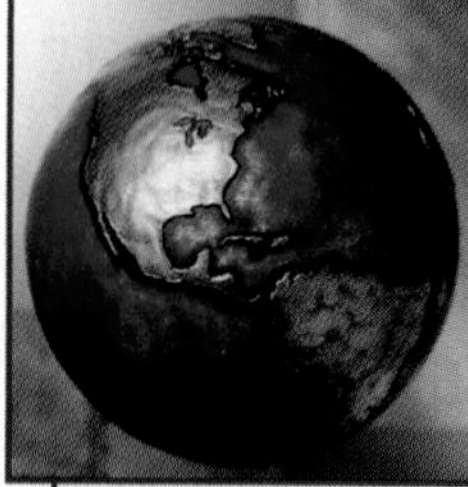

America in Perspective

Courts and Culture

The Japanese and Americans have many things in common. Both live in nations that are modern industrial giants with developed economies and complex societies. However, the role of the law and the judiciary in the daily life of the people of Japan is quite different from that in the United States.

The role of the courts in Japan is influenced by the prevailing attitude toward law and the court system. The Japanese typically find adversary proceedings distasteful and will resort to going to court only when all the preferred traditional forms of informal mediation and negotiation have failed. Most people prefer to settle disputes through a compromise agreement arrived at with the mediation of friends, relatives, or influential persons, rather than engage in litigation in courts.

The Japanese have traditionally preferred amicable and harmonious social relations, relations that would be jeopardized by clear-cut court decisions based on the assertion of individuals' legal rights and on the assignment of moral fault. They prefer to deemphasize conflict and the existence of disputes and to seek compromise solutions. The Japanese are also less likely to desire others to apply the universalistic standards that characterize the law. Instead, they favor participating in the settlement of disputes, applying their personal criteria for reconciling differences.

This attitude toward litigation is reflected in the small number of practicing lawyers in Japan. There are far fewer lawyers per capita in Japan than in the United States (about one-twentieth as many), and only about one-fourth as many civil suits per capita come to court in Japan as in the United States.

All is not well in the land of the rising sun, however. Some of the functions performed by American lawyers are handled in Japan by legal specialists and by graduates of law faculties who have knowledge of the law but who are not professionally trained as lawyers. Moreover, the increased tempo of life in modern Japan has brought greater use of courts and legal procedures, especially in commercial matters.

There is also more involved here than just the cultural preferences of potential litigants. The Japanese government has deliberately restricted access to the courts through a formidable system of procedural barriers. In addition, the number of courts and lawyers is purposely kept small to encourage Japanese citizens to resolve their differences in other forums.

Sources: Bradley M. Richardson and Scott C. Flanagan, *Politics in Japan* (Boston: Little, Brown, 1984), 59–60; Marc Galanter, "Reading the Landscape of Disputes: What We Know and Don't Know (and Think We Know) About Our Allegedly Contentious and Litigious Society," *UCLA Law Review* 31 (October 1983): 51–59; and Louis D. Hayes, *Introduction to Japanese Politics* (New York: Paragon House, 1992), 66–68.

comparative
Comparing Judiciaries

Thurgood Marshall, not only won most of his cases but also won for himself a seat on the Supreme Court. Almost every major policy decision these days ends up in court. Chances are good that some judge can be found who will rule in an interest group's favor. On the other hand, agencies and businesses commonly find themselves ordered by different courts to do opposite things. The habit of always turning to the courts as a last resort can add to policy delay, deadlock, and inconsistency (see "America in Perspective: Courts and Culture").

What Courts Should Do: The Scope of Judicial Power

The courts, Alexander Hamilton wrote in *The Federalist Papers*, "will be least in capacity to annoy or injure" the people and their liberties.[34] Throughout American history, critics of judicial power have disagreed. They see the courts as too powerful for their own—or the nation's—good. Yesterday's critics focused on John Marshall's "usurpations" of power, on the proslavery decision in *Dred Scott*, or on the efforts of the "nine old men" to kill off Franklin D. Roosevelt's New Deal legislation. Today's critics are never short of arguments to show that courts go too far in making policy.

Interest groups often use the judicial system to pursue their policy goals, forcing the courts to rule on important social issues. Some Hispanic parents, for example, have successfully sued local school districts to compel them to offer bilingual education.

Courts make policy on both large and small issues. In the last few decades, courts have made policies on major issues involving school busing, abortion, affirmative action, nuclear power, legislative redistricting, bilingual education, prison conditions, counting votes in the 2000 presidential election, and many other key issues.[35]

There are strong disagreements about the appropriateness of allowing the courts to have a policymaking role. Many scholars and judges favor a policy of **judicial restraint,** in which judges adhere closely to precedent and play minimal policymaking roles, leaving policy decisions strictly to the legislatures. These observers stress that the federal courts, composed of unelected judges, are the least democratic branch of government and question the qualifications of judges for making policy decisions and balancing interests. Advocates of judicial restraint believe that decisions such as those on abortion and prayer in public schools go well beyond the "referee" role they say is appropriate for courts in a democracy.

judicial restraint

A judicial philosophy in which judges play minimal policymaking roles, leaving that duty strictly to the legislatures.

On the other side are proponents of **judicial activism,** in which judges make bolder policy decisions, even charting new constitutional ground with a particular decision. Advocates of judicial activism emphasize that the courts may alleviate pressing needs—especially needs of those who are politically or economically weak—left unmet by the majoritarian political process.

judicial activism

A judicial philosophy in which judges make bold policy decisions, even charting new constitutional ground. Advocates of this approach emphasize that the courts can correct pressing needs, especially those unmet by the majoritarian political process.

It is important not to confuse judicial activism or restraint with liberalism or conservatism. In Table 16.5, you can see the varying levels of the Supreme Court's use of judicial review to void laws passed by Congress in different eras. In the early years of the New Deal, judicial activists were conservatives. During the tenure of Earl Warren as Chief Justice (1953–1969), activists made liberal decisions. It is interesting to note that the tenure of the conservative Chief Justice Warren Burger (1969–1986) and several conservative nominees of Republican presidents marked the most active use of judicial review in the nation's history.

The problem remains of reconciling the American democratic heritage with an active policymaking role for the judiciary. The federal courts have developed a doctrine of **political questions** as a means to avoid deciding some cases, principally those that involve conflicts between the president and Congress. The courts have shown no willingness, for example, to settle disputes regarding the War Powers Resolution (see Chapter 13).

political questions

A doctrine developed by the federal courts and used as a means to avoid deciding some cases, principally those involving conflicts between the president and Congress.

Similarly, judges typically attempt, whenever possible, to avoid deciding a case on the basis of the Constitution, preferring less contentious "technical" grounds. They also employ issues of jurisdiction, mootness (whether a case presents an issue of contention), standing, ripeness (whether the issues of a case are clear enough and evolved enough to serve as the basis of a decision), and other conditions to avoid adjudication of some politically charged cases. The Supreme Court refused to decide, for example, whether it was legal to carry out the war in Vietnam without an explicit declaration of war from Congress.

As you saw in the discussion of *Marbury v. Madison,* from the earliest days of the republic, federal judges have been politically astute in their efforts to maintain the legitimacy of the judiciary and to conserve their resources. (Remember that judges are typically recruited from political backgrounds.) They have tried not to take on too many politically controversial issues at one time. They have also been much more likely to find state and local laws unconstitutional (nearly 1,100) than federal laws (167, as shown in Table 16.5).

Another factor that increases the acceptability of activist courts is the ability to overturn their decisions. First, the president and the Senate determine who sits on the federal bench. Second, Congress, with or without the president's urging, can begin the process of amending the Constitution to overcome a constitutional decision of the Supreme Court. Although this process does not occur rapidly, it is a safety valve. The Eleventh Amendment in 1798 reversed the decision in *Chisolm v. Georgia,* which permitted an individual to sue a state in federal court; the Fourteenth Amendment in 1868 reversed the decision in *Dred Scott v. Sandford,* which held African Americans not to be citizens of the United States; the Sixteenth Amendment in 1913 reversed the decision in *Pollock v. Farmer's Loan and Trust Co.,* which prohibited a federal income tax; and the Twenty-sixth Amendment in 1971 reversed part of *Oregon v. Mitchell,* which voided a congressional act according 18- to 20-year-olds the right to vote in state elections.

Even more drastic options are available as well. Just before leaving office in 1801, the Federalists created a tier of circuit courts and populated them with Federalist judges; the Jeffersonian Democrats took over the reins of power and promptly abolished the entire level of courts. In 1869, the Radical Republicans in Congress altered the appellate jurisdiction of the Supreme Court to prevent it from hearing a case (*Ex parte McCardle*) that concerned the Reconstruction Acts. This kind of alteration has never recurred, although Congress did threaten to employ the method in the 1950s regarding some matters of civil liberties.

statutory construction

The judicial interpretation of an act of Congress. In some cases where statutory construction is an issue, Congress passes new legislation to clarify existing laws.

Finally, if the issue is one of **statutory construction,** in which a court interprets an act of Congress, then the legislature routinely passes legislation that clarifies existing laws and, in effect, overturns the courts.[36] In 1984, for example, the Supreme Court ruled in *Grove City College v. Bell* that when an institution receives federal aid, only the program or activity that actually gets the aid, not the entire institution, is covered by four federal

Table 16.5 Supreme Court Rulings in Which Federal Statutes Have Been Found Unconstitutional[a]

PERIOD	STATUTES VOIDED
1798–1864	2
1864–1910	33 (34)[b]
1910–1930	24
1930–1936	14
1936–1953	3
1953–1969	25
1969–1986	35
1986–present	31
TOTAL	167

[a]In whole or in part.

[b]An 1883 decision in the *Civil Rights Cases* consolidated five different cases into one opinion declaring one act of Congress void. In 1895, *Pollock v. Farmers Loan and Trust Co.* was heard twice, with the same result both times.

Source: From *The Judicial Process: An Introductory Analysis of the Courts of the United States, England, and France,* 7th ed., by Henry J. Abraham. Copyright 1993 by Henry J. Abraham. Used by permission of Oxford University Press, Inc. Updated by the authors.

Career Profile

Position: Clerk of the United States District Court, Sioux Falls, SD
Salary: $100,000-125,000
Benefits: Health, life, and retirement benefits.
Qualifications: Usually, a minimum requirement is a bachelor's degree. A Masters degree or law degree is recommended. Experience at deputy federal court clerk position or experienced trial court administrator usually required

Real People on the Job: Joe Haas

If you ever want to work in a position of authority within the legal system without actually practicing law or judging cases, then the job of head Clerk in the U.S. District Court system may be the right fit. It certainly is for Joe Haas. As a federal clerk, Joe oversees the budget of the court, manages judges' caseloads, deals with the press, supervises the court's staff, and handles all the filing and paperwork. In short, it's Joe's job to make sure that things run smoothly and efficiently for the judges in his courthouse. For example, Joe is currently managing four trials occurring at the same time. He must prepare the jury accommodations and make media preparation for all four trials even though one or more may be settled before going to trial.

Compared to other branches of the federal government, the judiciary is very decentralized. As such, Joe's position offers him plenty of opportunities to use his own initiative. He has nearly complete autonomy in managing the court. If someone needs a computer, he can order it with no problem. This autonomy also allows Joe to develop solutions to persistent problems within the judicial branch. To this end, one of Joe's long-term projects concerns easing the logjam of paperwork in the judicial system. For example, when a federal appeals court prepares to hear a case, the court must order transcripts of the original case. This can take weeks to accomplish. Joe is working to fix this problem by adopting a program driven by customer service and business models. Rather than faxing or mailing huge documents from one place to another, Joe has his staff optically scan transcripts so that a judge in St. Louis hearing an appeal of a trial from Sioux Falls can download the information off the Internet at the click of a button.

Although many judges, particularly Supreme Court justices, take on recent law school grads for one or two years to serve as their personal law clerks, there remains a great need for career clerks to administer the operation of the federal judiciary. In fact, career administrative clerks like Joe often do not have law degrees. Although Joe does in fact hold a law degree, he notes that today nearly 80% of all federal court clerks do not have law degrees. In fact, courts are starting to recognize the value of employees with business management skills. Thus, a Masters in Judicial Administration or Public Administration may become more useful to an aspiring clerk than a law degree. Starting out in the lower echelons of the federal clerk system at a salary of $35,000-45,000, a dedicated and talented clerk can move up the ranks to greater responsibilities and greater financial rewards. To find out more, check out the Federal Court Clerks Association at http://www.id.uscourts.gov/fcca.htm. For federal law clerk vacancies, go to the Federal Law Clerk Information System at https://lawclerks.ao.uscourts.gov/.

civil rights laws. In 1988 Congress passed a law specifying that the entire institution is affected. The description of the judiciary as the "ultimate arbiter of the Constitution" is hyperbolic; all the branches of government help define and shape the Constitution.

Summary

The American judicial system is complex. Sitting at the pinnacle of the judicial system is the Supreme Court, but its importance is often exaggerated. Most judicial policymaking and enforcement of laws take place in the state courts and the lower federal courts.

Throughout American political history, courts have shaped public policy with regard to the economy, liberty, equality, and, most recently, ecology. In the economic arena, until the time of Franklin D. Roosevelt, courts traditionally favored corporations, especially when government tried to regulate them. Since the New Deal, however, the courts have been more tolerant of government regulation of business, shifting much of their policymaking attention to issues of liberty and equality. From *Dred Scott* to *Plessy* to *Brown,* the Supreme Court has moved from a role of reinforcing discriminatory policy toward racial minorities to a role of shaping new policies for protecting civil rights. Most recently, environmental groups have used the courts to achieve their policy goals.

A critical view of the courts claims that they are too powerful for the nation's own good and are rather ineffective policymakers besides. Throughout American history, however, judges have been important agenda setters in the political system. Many of the most important political questions make their way into the courts at one time or another. The judiciary is an alternative point of access for those seeking to obtain public policy decisions to their liking, especially those who are not in the majority.

Once in court, litigants face judges whose discretion in decision making is typically limited by precedent. Nevertheless, on questions that raise novel issues (as do many of the most important questions that reach the Supreme Court), the law is less firmly established. Here there is more leeway and judges become more purely political players, balancing different interests and linked to the rest of the political system by their own policy preferences and the politics of their selection.

The unelected and powerful federal courts raise important issues of democracy and the scope of judicial power. Yet court decisions are typically consistent with public opinion and judges and justices have often used their power to promote democracy. Reconciling the American democratic heritage with an active policymaking role for the judiciary remains a matter of debate. The courts have been sensitive to the issue of their power and often avoid the most controversial issues, at least for a time. It has also been easier for opponents of court decisions to accept judicial power because it is possible to overturn judicial decisions.

Key Terms

standing to sue
class action suits
justiciable disputes
amicus curiae briefs
original jurisdiction
appellate jurisdiction
district courts
courts of appeal
Supreme Court
senatorial courtesy
solicitor general
opinion
stare decisis
precedent
original intent
judicial implementation
Marbury v. Madison
judicial review
United States v. Nixon
judicial restraint
judicial activism
political questions
statutory construction

For Further Reading

Abraham, Henry J. *Justices, Presidents, and Senators: A History of the U.S. Supreme Court Appointments from Washington to Clinton*. Lanham, MD: Rowmand and Littlefield, 1999. A readable history of the relationships between presidents and the justices they appointed.

Baum, Lawrence. *The Supreme Court*, 6th ed. Washington, D.C.: Congressional Quarterly Press, 1998. An excellent work on the operations and impact of the Court.

Ely, John Hart. *Democracy and Distrust*. Cambridge, MA: Harvard University Press, 1980. An appraisal of judicial review and an effort to create a balanced justification for the role of the courts in policymaking.

Epstein, Lee, and Joseph F. Kobylka. *The Supreme Court and Legal Change*. Chapel Hill: University of North Carolina Press, 1992. Examines how interest groups propelled issues regarding abortion and the death penalty to the Supreme Court, and how the way they framed their legal arguments affected outcomes on these issues.

Gates, John B., and Charles A. Johnson, eds. *The American Courts: A Critical Assessment*. Washington, D.C.: Congressional Quarterly Press, 1991. Useful essays covering many aspects of judicial politics.

Goldman, Sheldon. *Picking Federal Judges*. New Haven, CT: Yale University Press, 1997. The definitive work on backgrounds and the politics of recruiting lower court judges.

Howard, J. Woodford, Jr. *Courts of Appeals in the Federal Judicial System*. Princeton, NJ: Princeton University Press, 1981. A leading work on the federal courts of appeal.

Jacob, Herbert. *Law and Politics in the United States*, 2nd ed. Boston: HarperCollins, 1995. An introduction to the American legal system with an emphasis on linkages to the political arena.

Johnson, Charles A., and Bradley C. Canon. *Judicial Policies: Implementation and Impact*, 2nd ed. Washington, D.C.: Congressional Quarterly Press, 1999. One of the best overviews of judicial policy implementation.

O'Brien, David M. *Storm Center*, 3rd ed. New York: Norton, 1993. An overview of the Supreme Court's role in American politics.

Rowland, C. K., and Robert A. Carp. *Politics and Judgment in Federal District Courts*. Lawrence: University Press of Kansas, 1996. An important work on the operations of the federal district courts.

Segal, Jeffrey A., and Harold J. Spaeth. *The Supreme Court and the Attitudinal Model*. Cambridge: Cambridge University Press, 1993. Examines how the attitudes and values of justices affect their decisions.

Woodward, Bob, and Scott Armstrong. *The Brethren*. New York: Simon & Schuster, 1979. A gossipy "insider's" portrayal of the Supreme Court.

Internet Resources

www.supremecourtus.gov/
Official site of the U.S. Supreme Court with information about its operations.

supct.law.cornell.edu/supct/
Decisions of the Supreme Court, background, schedule, and rules of the Court; also includes backgrounds of the justices serving on the Court.

oyez.at.nwu.edu/oyez.html
Website that allows you to hear oral arguments before the Supreme Court.

www.courttv.com/cases/
Web site in which you can decide actual cases before the courts, then compare your decisions to those of the judges.

www.uscourts.gov/
Explains the organization, operation, and administration of federal courts.

www.nara.gov/education/teaching/conissues/separat.html
FDR's court-packing plan.

rodan.asu.edu/~george/vacancy
Describes the vacancy and appointment process.

Notes

1. Quoted in Lawrence C. Baum, *The Supreme Court*, 4th ed. (Washington, D.C.: Congressional Quarterly Press, 1992), 72.
2. Administrative Office of the United States Courts.
3. Quoted in J. Woodford Howard, Jr., *Courts of Appeals in the Federal Judicial System: A Study of the Second, Fifth, and District of Columbia Circuits* (Princeton, NJ: Princeton University Press, 1981), 101.
4. See Gary King, "Presidential Appointments to the Supreme Court: Adding Systematic Explanation to Probabilistic Description," *American Politics Quarterly* 15 (July 1987): 373–386.
5. Quoted in Nina Totenberg, "Will Judges Be Chosen Rationally?" *Judicature* 60 (August/September 1976): 93.
6. See John Schmidhauser, *Judges and Justices: The Federal Appellate Judiciary* (Boston: Little, Brown, 1978).
7. One study found, however, that judicial experience is not related to the congruence of presidential preferences and the justices' decisions on racial equality cases. See John Gates and Jeffrey Cohen, "Presidents, Supreme Court Justices, and Racial Equality Cases: 1954–1984," *Political Behavior* 10 (November 1, 1988): 22–35.
8. On the importance of ideology and partisanship considerations in judicial retirement and resignation decisions, see Deborah J. Barrow and Gary Zuk, "An Institutional Analysis of Turnover in the Lower Federal Courts, 1900–1987," *Journal of Politics* 52 (May 1990): 457–476.

9. Quoted in Henry J. Abraham, *Justices and Presidents: A Political History of Appointments to the Supreme Court*, 3rd ed. (New York: Oxford University Press, 1992), 266.
10. *Ibid.*, 70.
11. See, for example, the important role that African-American support played in the confirmation of Clarence Thomas even though he was likely to vote against the wishes of leading civil rights organizations. L. Marvin Overby, Beth M. Henschen, Julie Walsh, and Michael H. Strauss, "Courting Constituents: An Analysis of the Senate Confirmation Vote on Justice Clarence Thomas," *American Political Science Review* 86 (December 1992): 997–1,003.
12. On the impact of the background of members of the judiciary, see Robert A. Carp and C. K. Rowland, *Policymaking and Politics in the Federal District Courts* (Knoxville: University of Tennessee Press, 1983); Thomas G. Walker and Deborah J. Barrow, "The Diversification of the Federal Bench: Policy and Process Ramifications," *Journal of Politics* 47 (May 1985): 596–617; and C. Neal Tate, "Personal Attribute Models of the Voting Behavior of United States Supreme Court Justices: Liberalism in Civil Liberties and Economics Decisions, 1946–1978," *American Political Science Review* 75 (June 1981): 355–367.
13. Quoted in Nina Totenberg, "Behind the Marble, Beneath the Robes," *New York Times Magazine*, March 16, 1975, 37.
14. H. W. Perry, Jr., *Deciding To Decide: Agenda Setting in the United States Supreme Court* (Cambridge, MA: Harvard University Press, 1991); Doris Marie Provine, *Case Selection in the United States Supreme Court* (Chicago: University of Chicago Press, 1980); and Stuart H. Teger and Douglas Kosinski, "The Cue Theory of Supreme Court Certiorari Jurisdiction: A Reconsideration," *Journal of Politics* 42 (August 1980): 834–846.
15. Sidney Ulmer, "The Supreme Court's Certiorari Decisions: Conflict as a Predictive Variable," *American Political Science Review* (December 1984): 901–911.
16. See Rebecca Mae Salokar, *The Solicitor General* (Philadelphia: Temple University Press, 1992).
17. Each year, data on Supreme Court decisions can be found in the November issue of the *Harvard Law Review*.
18. A useful look at attorneys practicing before the Supreme Court is Kevin McGuire, *The Supreme Court Bar: Legal Elites in the Washington Community* (Charlottesville: University Press of Virginia, 1993).
19. See, for example, Forrest Maltzman and Paul J. Wahlbeck, "Strategic Policy Considerations and Voting Fluidity on the Burger Court," *American Political Science Review* 90 (September 1996): 581–592; Paul J. Wahlbeck, James F. Spriggs, II, and Forrest Maltzman, "Marshalling the Court: Bargaining and Accommodation on the United States Supreme Court," *American Journal of Political Science* 42 (January 1998): 294–315; James F. Spriggs II, Forrest Maltzman, and Paul J. Wahlbeck, "Bargaining on the U.S. Supreme Court: Justices' Responses to Majority Opinion Drafts," *Journal of Politics* 61 (May 1999): 485–506.
20. A. P. Blaustein and A. H. Field, "Overruling Opinions in the Supreme Court," *Michigan Law Review* 57, no. 2 (1957): 151; David H. O'Brien, *Constitutional Law and Politics*, 3rd ed. (W.W. Norton, 1997), 38.
21. See, for example, Jeffrey A. Segal and Harold J. Spaeth, *The Supreme Court and the Attitudinal Model* (Cambridge: Cambridge University Press, 1993); Jeffrey A. Segal and Albert O. Cover, "Ideological Values and the Votes of U.S. Supreme Court Justices," *American Political Science Review* 83 (June 1989): 557–566; Tracey E. George and Lee Epstein, "On the Nature of Supreme Court Decision Making," *American Political Science Review* 86 (June 1992): 323–337; and Jeffrey A. Segal and Harold J. Spaeth, "The Influence of *Stare Decisis* on the Votes of United States Supreme Court Justices," *American Journal of Political Science* 40 (November 1996): 971–1,003.
22. Doris Graber, *Mass Media and American Politics*, 5th ed. (Washington, D.C.: Congressional Quarterly Press, 1997), 309.
23. Charles A. Johnson and Bradley C. Canon, *Judicial Policies: Implementation and Impact*, 2nd ed. (Washington, D.C.: Congressional Quarterly Press, 1999), chap. 1. See also James F. Spriggs, II, "The Supreme Court and Federal Administrative Agencies: A Resource-Based Theory and Analysis of Judicial Impact," *American Journal of Political Science* 40 (November 1996): 1,122–1,151.
24. See Richard L. Pacelle, Jr., and Lawrence Baum, "Supreme Court Authority in the Judiciary," *American Politics Quarterly* 20 (April 1992): 169–191; and Donald R. Songer, Jeffrey A. Segal, and Charles M. Cameron, "The Hierarchy of Justice: Testing a Principal-Agent Model of Supreme Court-Circuit Court Interactions," *American Journal of Political Science* 38 (August 1994): 673–696.
25. However, see Gerald N. Rosenberg, *The Hollow Hope: Can Courts Bring About Social Change?* (Chicago: University of Chicago Press, 1991); Rosenberg questions whether courts have brought about much social change.
26. For an excellent overview of the Warren period by former Watergate special prosecutor and Harvard law professor Archibald Cox, see *The Warren Court* (Cambridge, MA: Harvard University Press, 1968).
27. *Washington Post* Weekly Review, October 1, 1984, 33.
28. On the Rehnquist Court, see David G. Savage, *Turning Right: The Making of the Rehnquist Supreme Court* (New York: Wiley, 1992).
29. William Rehnquist, "The Notion of a Living Constitution," in *Views from the Bench*, ed. Mark W. Cannon and David M. O'Brien (Chatham, NJ: Chatham House, 1985), 129. One study found, however, that judicial experience is not related to the congruence of presidential preferences and the justices' decisions on racial equality cases. See John Gates and Jeffrey Cohen, "Presidents, Supreme Court Justices, and Racial Equality Cases: 1954–1984," *Political Behavior* 10 (November 1, 1988): 22–35.
30. Richard Funston, "The Supreme Court and Critical Elections," *American Political Science Review* 69 (1975): 810; John B. Gates, *The Supreme Court and Partisan Realignment* (Boulder, CO: Westview, 1992); Thomas R. Marshall, "Public Opinion, Representation, and the Modern Supreme Court," *American Politics Quarterly* 16 (July 1988): 296–316; William Mishler and Reginald S. Sheehan, "The Supreme Court as a Countermajoritarian Institution? The Impact of Public Opinion on Supreme Court Decisions," *American Political Science Review* 87 (March 1993): 87–101; William Mishler

and Reginald S. Sheehan, "Public Opinion, the Attitudinal Model, and Supreme Court Decision Making: A Micro-Analytic Perspective," *Journal of Politics* 58 (February 1996): 169–200; and Roy B. Flemming and B. Dan Wood, "The Public and the Supreme Court: Individual Justice Responsiveness to American Policy Moods," *American Journal of Political Science* 41 (April 1997): 468–498.

31. David G. Barnum, "The Supreme Court and Public Opinion: Judicial Decision Making in the Post-New Deal Period," *Journal of Politics* 47 (May 1985): 652–662.
32. Gregory A. Caldeira and John R. Wright, "Organized Interests and Agenda Setting in the U.S. Supreme Court," *American Political Science Review* 82 (December 1988): 1, 109–1,128.
33. On group use of the litigation process, see Karen Orren, "Standing To Sue: Interest Group Conflict in the Federal Courts," *American Political Science Review* 70 (September 1976): 723–742; Karen O'Connor and Lee Epstein, "The Rise of Conservative Interest Group Litigation," *Journal of Politics* 45 (May 1983): 479–489; and Lee Epstein and C. K. Rowland, "Debunking the Myth of Interest Group Invincibility in the Courts," *American Political Science Review* 85 (March 1991): 205–217.
34. "Federalist No. 78" in Hamilton, Madison, and Jay, *The Federalist Papers*.
35. Examples of judicial activism are reported in a critical assessment of judicial intervention by Donald Horowitz, *The Courts and Social Policy* (Washington, D.C.: Brookings Institution, 1977).
36. William N. Eskridge, "Overriding Supreme Court Statutory Interpretation Decisions," *Yale Law Journal* 101 (1991): 331–455; and Joseph Ignagni and James Meernik, "Explaining Congressional Attempts To Reverse Supreme Court Decisions," *Political Research Quarterly* 10 (June 1994): 353–372. See also R. Chep Melnick, *Between the Lines: Interpreting Welfare Rights* (Washington, D.C.: Brookings Institution, 1994).

17 Economic Policymaking

Chapter Outline

Thomas Penfield Jackson is a federal district judge in Washington D.C. who was appointed to the federal bench in 1982 by President Ronald Reagan. Like all federal district judges, he makes $141,300 annually. William H. ("Bill") Gates, on the other hand, is a household name. With Paul Allen and Steve Ballmer, Gates cofounded Microsoft, the largest software company in the world, headquartered just outside Seattle, Wash. Though his wealth fluctuates with the value of his Microsoft stock, which ranges between $40 and 90 billion, he is the wealthiest individual in the world.

In August 1995, America Online, another big player in the high-tech economy, complained to the Justice Department that Microsoft was violating antitrust laws and behaving like a monopoly. Indeed, Microsoft produced the operating systems for 87.1 percent of all computers sold in the United States. AOL's complaint was that, by packaging its MSN Internet browser with its operating systems, Microsoft was dominating Internet access as well (and violating an earlier court order). The Justice Department sued Microsoft and the case ended up in the paneled courtroom of Judge Jackson.

Years of legal wrangling followed. Millions of pages of documents were produced for the Court. Company e-mails were subpoenaed. Bill Gates gave a videotaped deposition in which he appeared to many as overconfident and arrogant.

Microsoft, Judge Jackson finally decided, was indeed a monopoly. The judge began to put together what the law calls a "remedy." On June 7, 2000, Judge Jackson (waiting until after the stock market closed for the day) read his opinion, calling Microsoft and its executives "untrustworthy." Microsoft was, he continued, "unwilling to accept the notion that it broke the law." Judge Jackson ordered the division of Microsoft into two separate companies, which could compete with one another ("Micro" and "Soft," cartoonists imagined). Bill Gates was furious in private and barely concealed his anger in public. The decision proved, he said, that "the government can take away what you created if it turns out to be too popular." In what surely could not have been a coincidence, the Bill and Melinda Gates Foundation announced on the same day that their foundation would give away $1 billion dollars for minority scholarships over the next decade. The case then began its long travel through the federal appellate system. In February of 2001, the District of Columbia Court of Appeals heard oral arguments on Judge Jackson's decision. Several of the judges on that court were none too happy with Judge Jackson, who had given out extensive off-the-record interviews to reporters as he was hearing the case.

Microsoft, of course, is a leading edge of the New Economy. More information-oriented than manufacturing-oriented, the New Economy also poses new policy challenges. As you will see in this chapter, government involvement in the economy is nothing new. What is different, though, are the issues emerging from an information-based, instead of an industrial-based economy.

The Microsoft case connects to our common themes of democracy and the scope of government. Obviously, Americans want a vital and strong economy, one dominated by private decisions and private entrepreneurs. But they do not want a completely unregulated economy, one where the powerful become too powerful, as Microsoft was accused of being. Government in America regulates the economy, and liberals and conservatives debate about how government should use its democratic tools to regulate and manage the economy.

The parties also sharply disagree on the scope of government versus the private economy. Conservatives complain about the oppressive scope of government in relation to the private economy, about the high rate of taxes and the overly long arm of regulation. The bigger the public economy, the more they see government on the brakes and not the gas pedal. In every campaign, the connection between big government and the private economy is a central issue.

Source: The key events in the Microsoft case are summarized in Joel Brinkley and Steve Lohr, "Retracing the Missteps in the Microsoft Defense," the New York Times, June 9, 2000, 1.

Americans usually see politics and economics as two quite different subjects. Robert Reich, the Clinton Administration's first Secretary of Labor, has written that

> *Americans tend to divide the dimensions of our national life into two broad realms. The first is the realm of government and politics. The second is the realm of business and economics. . . . The choice is falsely posed. In advanced industrial nations like the United States, drawing such sharp distinctions between government and the market has ceased to be useful.*[1]

The view that politics and economics are closely linked is neither new nor unique. Both James Madison, the architect of the Constitution, and Karl Marx, the founder of Communist theory, argued that economic conflict was at the root of politics. Politics and economics are powerful, intertwined forces shaping public policies and the lives of everyone.

Americans also draw sharp distinctions between "our economy" and "the world economy." Thomas Friedman, the *New York Times'* world affairs correspondent, argues that this distinction is losing its meaning. To be sure, he says, "the United States is now the sole and dominant superpower," economically as well as militarily. Equally important today is what he calls the "Electronic Herd," consisting of "millions of investors moving money around the world at the click of a mouse."[2] Our new economy is also an international and global economy. Shortly after Judge Jackson's decision in the Microsoft monopoly case, economic regulators in the European Community were also considering charging Microsoft with illegal trade practices.

Government and the economy in the United States have always been closely linked. This chapter shows how and explores some of the key issues past, present and future.

Government and the Economy

capitalism

An economic system in which individuals and corporations, not the government, own the principal means of production and seek profits.

The collapse of the former Soviet Union has been described as the "triumph of capitalism." Unlike the Soviet system, where government planners controlled the supply and price of goods, the United States operates under **capitalism**—an economic system in which individuals and corporations own the principal means of production,

through which they seek to reap profits. In a purely capitalist economy, the government is strictly uninvolved in business affairs. As you shall see, the United States does not meet this standard. In fact, America actually has a **mixed economy**—a system in which the government, while not commanding the economy, is still deeply involved in economic decisions. Even in the U.S. Constitution, written in an agrarian era, key economic tasks were assigned Congress, including the power to regulate commerce and to coin money.

mixed economy

An economic system in which the government is deeply involved in economic decisions through its role as regulator, consumer, subsidizer, taxer, employer, and borrower.

Unemployment and Inflation

Economic problems create social problems. President Harry S. Truman once remarked that the most sensitive part of a voter's anatomy is the pocketbook. When the economy goes sour, the cry of "throw the rascals out" reverberates throughout the country; too much unemployment or inflation can increase unemployment among politicians.

The **unemployment rate** is the percentage of Americans seeking work who are unable to find it. Measuring how many and what types of workers are unemployed is one of the major jobs of the Bureau of Labor Statistics (BLS) in the Department of Labor. To carry out this task, the BLS conducts a random survey of the population every month. Unlike most of the surveys discussed in this book, the sample size is not a mere one or two thousand, but rather a massive 50,000 households. Therefore, policymakers can be assured that any change of over one-tenth of 1 percent is more than could possibly be attributed to sampling error. Most people are out of work for only a short time (which is why the connection between the poverty rate and the unemployment rate is weak). Even so, the official unemployment rate underestimates unemployment because it leaves out "discouraged workers," who have given up their job search altogether. Figure 17.1 shows what has happened to unemployment rates in recent decades.

unemployment rate

As measured by the Bureau of Labor Statistics (BLS), the proportion of the labor force actively seeking work but unable to find jobs.

The problem of **inflation**—the rise in prices for consumer goods—is the other half of policymakers' regular economic concern. For decades the government has also

inflation

The rise in prices for consumer goods.

Figure 17.1 Unemployment: Joblessness in America, 1960–2000

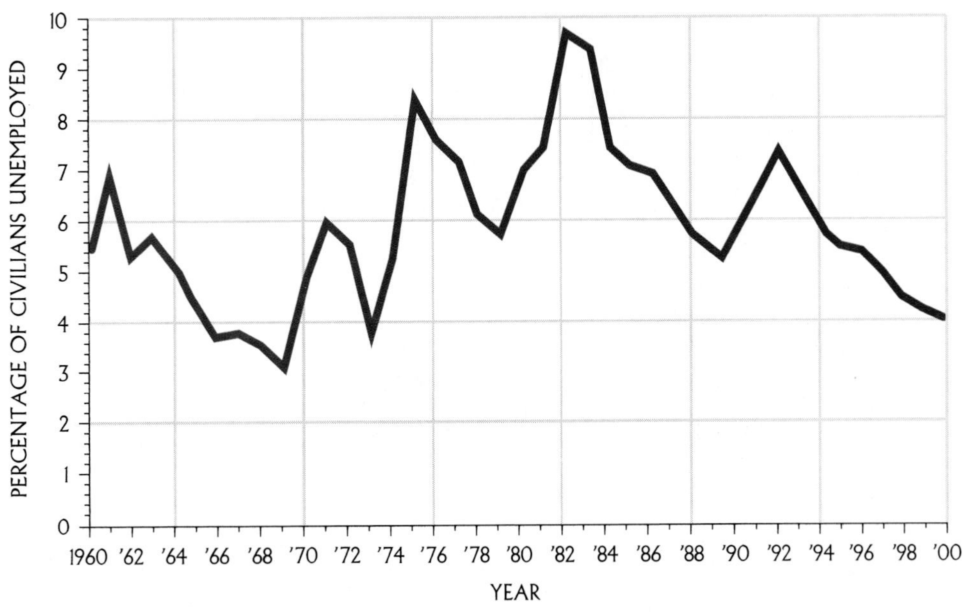

Source: Economic Report of the President, 2000 (Washington, D.C.: U.S. Government Printing Office, 2000).

consumer price index (CPI)

The key measure of inflation that relates the rise in prices over time.

kept tabs on inflation via the **consumer price index (CPI),** which measures the change in the cost of buying a fixed basket of goods and services. On a regular basis, the prices of 95,000 items from 22,000 stores are surveyed, as well as the cost of 35,000 rental units. Many economists and politicians believe that methods for calculating the CPI need to be revised in order to avoid overestimating inflation. It overestimates inflation because it does not take into account consumer shifts in buying habits. In the real world, if the price of beef goes up, consumer shifts to chicken, but the CPI ignores changes in people's buying habits. Inflation has risen sharply during three periods in recent decades, as you can see in Figure 17.2, much of which can be tied to soaring prices for energy.

The first inflationary shock occurred in 1973 in large part due to huge increases in oil prices resulting from the 1973 Arab oil embargo. After the Iranian Revolution of 1979, Americans once again faced long lines and higher prices at the gas pumps. The Persian Gulf War led to a moderate surge of inflation, as oil prices temporarily increased in possible anticipation of renewed shortages. The summer of 2000 and the winter of 2001, though, saw sharp spikes in the prices of gasoline and heating oil.

Few things are more worrisome to consumers and politicians alike than the combined effects of inflation and unemployment marching upward together. President Jimmy Carter coined the phrase "misery index" to signal the combined unemployment and inflation total. He used it to defeat Gerald Ford, on whose watch it soared. Ronald Reagan, though, used the same misery index in 1980 against Jimmy Carter. Little wonder that parties and politicians make the care and feeding of the economy one of their top priorities.

Elections and the Economy

People who are unemployed, worried about the prospect of being unemployed, or struggling with runaway inflation have an outlet to express some of their dissatisfaction—the polling booth. Ample evidence indicates that economic trends affect how voters make up their minds on election day, taking into consideration not just their own financial sit-

Figure 17.2 Inflation: Increases in the Cost of Living, 1960–2000

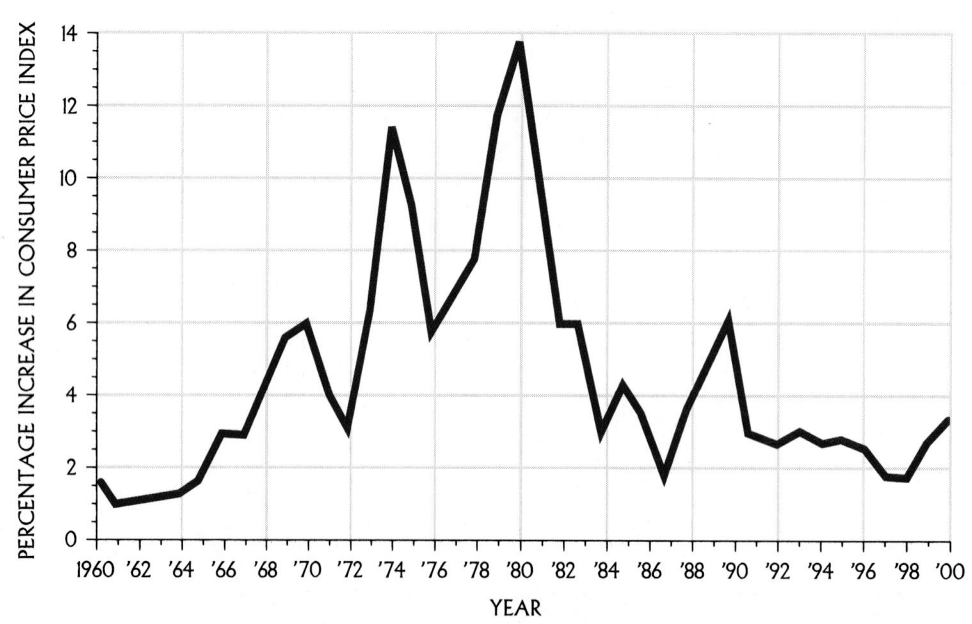

Source: Economic Report of the President, 2000 (Washington, D.C.: U.S. Government Printing Office, 2000).

uation but the economic condition of the nation as well. In a careful analysis of two decades of election study data, Roderick Kiewiet found that voters who experience unemployment in their family are more likely to support Democratic candidates.[3] It is not only a voter's personal experience with unemployment that benefits the Democrats; employed voters who feel that joblessness is a serious national problem lean strongly toward the Democratic Party. Concern over inflation, on the other hand, has had less impact on voter choices, according to Kiewiet. Michael Lewis-Beck and Tom Rice tracked the connection between unemployment and presidential elections and found a straightforward pattern: When unemployment rates are dropping, the president's party usually wins; when unemployment in on the rise, his party is in trouble.[4]

Political Parties and the Economy

Because voters are sensitive to economic conditions, the parties must pay close attention to those conditions when selecting their policies. Some years ago, Nobel laureate Paul Samuelson articulated a common belief about the two parties in the United States. "We tend to get our recessions during Republican administrations," he remarked. "The Democrats," he continued, "are willing to run with some inflation; the Republicans are not."[5] This observation leads to an interesting hypothesis about party behavior: Republicans are willing to risk higher unemployment and recession, whereas Democrats are willing to tolerate high inflation. Douglas Hibbs investigated this hypothesis as part of his influential analysis of economic policy in 20 advanced industrialized democracies. His general conclusion was that economic policies pursued by left-wing governments are broadly in accordance with the interests of working-class people whereas those of conservative right-wing governments tend to favor the interests of business and the wealthy.

Parties thus behave very much the way voters expect them to. In the United States, the Democratic coalition is made up heavily of groups who worry the most about unemployment—union members, minorities, and the poor. This gives the Democratic Party a special incentive to pursue policies designed to lower unemployment. On the other hand, the Republican coalition rests more heavily on a base of people who are most concerned about steady prices for their goods and services—business owners, managers, and professional people. Therefore, Republican administrations have taken stronger action to keep inflation down, even if this may lead to greater unemployment.

Politicians and parties exert enormous effort to control the economy. The impact of government on the economic system is substantial, but it is also sharply limited by a basic commitment to our free enterprise system. The following sections will introduce the economic tools the government possesses for guiding the economy, as well as the constraints on governmental control.

Instruments for Controlling the Economy

The time when government could ignore economic problems, confidently asserting that the private marketplace could handle them, has long passed, if it ever really existed. Especially since the Great Depression and the New Deal, government has been actively involved in steering the economy. When the stock market crash of 1929 sent unemployment soaring, President Herbert Hoover clung to **laissez-faire**—the principle that government should not meddle with the economy. In the next presidential election, Hoover was handed a crushing defeat by Franklin D. Roosevelt, whose New Deal programs experimented with dozens of new federal policies to put the economy back on track.

laissez-faire

The principle that government should not meddle in the economy.

Since the New Deal, policymakers have regularly sought to control the economy. The American political economy offers two important tools to guide the economy: monetary policy and fiscal policy.

Monetary Policy and "the Fed"

monetary policy

Based on **monetarism**, monetary policy is the manipulation of the supply of money in private hands by which the government can control the economy.

monetarism

An economic theory holding that the supply of money is the key to a nation's economic health. Monetarists believe that too much cash and credit in circulation produces inflation.

Federal Reserve System

The main instrument for making **monetary policy** in the United States. It was created by Congress in 1913 to regulate the lending practices of banks and thus the money supply. The seven members of its Board of Governors are appointed to 14-year terms by the president with the consent of the Senate.

One way the government can influence the overall operation of the economy is through **monetary policy,** that is, manipulation of the supply of money and credit in private hands. An economic theory called **monetarism** holds that the supply of money is the key to the nation's economic health. Monetarists believe that having too much cash and credit in circulation generates inflation. Essentially, they advise holding the growth in money supply to the rise in the gross domestic product, the total value of all the goods and services a nation produces. Politicians worry constantly about the money supply because it affects the rate of interest their constituents have to pay for home loans, new cars, starting up new businesses, and so on.

The main agency for making monetary policy is "the Fed," whose formal title is the Board of Governors of the **Federal Reserve System.** Created by Congress in 1913 to regulate the lending practices of banks and thus the money supply, the Federal Reserve System is intended to be formally beyond the control of the president and Congress. Its seven-member Board of Governors—appointed by the president and confirmed by the Senate—is expected to do its job without regard to partisan politics. Accordingly, members of the Fed are given 14-year terms designed to insulate them from political pressures.

The Fed has three basic instruments for controlling the money supply. First, the Fed sets discount rates for the money that banks borrow from Federal Reserve banks. If the Fed raises this rate, banks have to pass their increased costs along to their customers. Thus, fewer people will want to take out loans, and less money will be in circulation. Second, the Fed sets reserve requirements that determine the amount of money that banks must keep in reserve at all times. When the Fed increases this requirement, banks have less money to lend out and therefore charge their customers more for it. Third, the Fed can add to the money supply by selling bonds. Whereas raising the costs of borrowing money increases the risk of unemployment and recession, making more money available for borrowing increases the risk of inflation.

In sum, the amount of money available, interest rates, inflation, and the availability of jobs are all affected either directly or indirectly by the complicated financial dealings of the Fed. The Fed can profoundly influence the state of the economy; it is no wonder that it attracts the attention of politicians. With so much riding on its decisions, presidents quite naturally try to persuade the Fed to pursue policies in line with presidential plans for the country. Alan Greenspan did indeed lead the Fed to hold the line on interest rates, thus adding more evidence to the general finding that the Fed is responsive to the White House, though not usually to the extent of trying to influence election outcomes.[6] Nevertheless, even the chief executive can be left frustrated by the politically insulated decisions of the Fed. Some have called for more openness in its decision-making process, whereas others have proposed more direct political control of the Fed through shorter terms for its Board of Governors. In any event, whoever is chair of the Fed is bound to be one of the nation's most important figures, as you can see in "Making a Difference: Alan Greenspan."

Fiscal Policy: Keynesian Versus Supply-Side Economics

fiscal policy

The policy that describes the impact of the federal budget—taxes, spending, and borrowing—on the economy. Fiscal policy is almost entirely determined by Congress and the president, who are the budget makers.

Keynesian economic theory

The theory emphasizing that government spending and deficits can help the economy weather its normal ups and downs. Proponents of this theory advocate using the power of government to stimulate the economy when it is lagging.

How much of an annual deficit or surplus the government runs is another factor in determining the nation's economic health. **Fiscal policy** describes the impact of the federal budget—taxing, spending, and borrowing—on the economy. Unlike monetary policy, mostly the Congress and the president shape fiscal policy. The use of fiscal policy to stimulate the economy is most often associated with advocates of big, intrusive, government.

On the side of an activist government with a large scope is **Keynesian economic theory,** named after English economist John Maynard Keynes. Soon after the 1936 publication of his landmark book *The General Theory of Employment, Interest, and Money*, Keynesianism became the dominant economic philosophy in America. This

Making a Difference

Alan Greenspan

On December 5, 1996, the second most powerful man in the United States used two words—"irrational exuberance"—to hint at what might be going on in the soaring stock market. When the chairman of the Federal Reserve Board speaks, the world listens. The Japanese stock market was just opening when Alan Greenspan's remark's hit the news wires, and it plunged 3 percent—its largest drop of that year. Then, the European markets woke up to the same news, falling 4 percent in Germany and 2 percent in Britain. And finally, the New York Stock Exchange plunged 2 percent in its first 30 minutes of trading. All these markets interpreted Alan Greenspan's remark to mean that he thought the equities were overvalued and that the Fed might raise American interest rates to cool down escalating stock prices and prevent an inflationary spiral.

Such is the power that the chair of the Fed can exercise with a few choice words at any time. (Greenspan himself doesn't own any stocks to avoid a conflict of interest, but his wife, television newswoman Andrea Mitchell, does.) Unlike the president, the Fed doesn't have to get congressional support for actions that are likely to impact the economy. And unlike the Congress, the Fed deliberates in secret, making every public statement by its leader a potentially valuable clue as to how it might soon act.

Alan Greenspan was a kid from New York who became an American success story—but on Wall Street and not Main Street. Founding his own economic forecasting and consulting firm, he continued to work part-time on his Ph. D. in economics at New York University and finally finished it. He was appointed chairman of the nation's central bank in 1987. Few Fed chairs had more respect from liberals and conservatives alike. The New York stock market nearly doubled during his years on duty, and the high-tech stock market called the NASDAQ came to rival the old-line stock market. The new economy surged (and sometimes slumped), mutual fund investments exploded, and by 1999 9.7 million Americans could trade over the Internet. To Greenspan, inflation was Public Enemy Number One. According to his dogma, control inflation and investors will put their money into enterprises that will produce goods and services, people will be employed, and pensions will be secure. He made fighting inflation the Federal Reserve Board's top priority, and as you can see in Figure 17.2, he has been largely successful.

Source: On Greenspan's famous remark and the rise of the stock market, see Robert J. Shiller, *Irrational Exuberance* (Princeton, NJ: Princeton University Press, 2000).

John Maynard Keynes' influential economic theories encouraged the use of government spending to stimulate the economy during down periods.

How You Can Make a Difference

Fair Lending Practices

In the not too distant past, discrimination against religious and racial minorities in the financial and banking sector was common and obvious. The policy of redlining, for example, refers to the practice of loan officers who used to deny loans to applicants living in the boundaries of segregated or integrated neighborhoods that were marked by a red line on their office map. In the wake of the civil rights movement, things changed with the passage of federal laws such as the Home Ownership and Equity Protection Act (HOEPA), Community Reinvestment Act (CRA), and the Home Mortgage Disclosure Act (HMDA), which gave the Federal Reserve Board authority to stop such unfair lending practices.

Though blatant, old-style redlining may have been eradicated, many activist groups are looking for volunteers to help continue the fight against economic injustice in America. Instead of being rejected purely on the basis of color, these activists maintain that many Americans, particularly ethnic minorities in the inner cities, remain ignored or "unbanked" by reputable financial institutions and become victims of predatory lending practices. Nearly all advances in curbing these financial abuses were achieved in conjunction with such community activist organizations. For over 30 years, the Association of Community Organizations for Reform Now (ACORN) has conducted training sessions for organizing local communities to action and for providing technical financial assistance. The Woodstock Institute in Chicago (www.woodstockinst.org), for example, recently initiated a unique, permanent dialogue between community groups and federal bank regulators (including those from the Federal Reserve Board and Federal Deposit Insurance Corporation) to improve financial service to inner cities across the Midwest. The National Community Reinvestment Coalition (www.ncrc.org), a coalition of 640 community and regional organizations across the country, helps coordinate activity among the various organizations. Recently, the NCRC issued a nationwide call to action when the Federal Reserve revised HOEPA.

What can you do by contacting these groups? If you have accounting and financial skills, you can volunteer your services in a nearby area. Even if you can't balance your own checkbook, you can still write letters to congressmen and Federal Reserve officials on behalf of pending legislation and action that would aid the movement such as the proposed revisions of HOEPA highlighted by the NCRC. For the more ambitious, several organizations, most particularly ACORN, stage regional and national protest rallies to convince the public, governments, and financial institutions to change their attitudes and policies.

theory emphasized that government spending could help the economy weather its normal ups and downs, even if it meant running in the red. Keynes argued that government could spend its way out of the Depression by stimulating the economy through an infusion of money from government programs. If businesses were not able to expand, it would be up to the government to pick up the slack, he claimed. If there were no jobs available for people, the government should create some—building roads, dams, houses, or whatever seemed most appropriate. The key would be to get money back in the consumers' pockets, for if only few have money to buy goods, then little will be produced. Thus, the government's job would be to increase the demand when necessary; the supply would take care of itself.

So dominant was Keynesian thinking in government policymaking that Democrats and Republicans alike adhered to its basic tenets—until the Reagan Administration. Reagan's economic gurus proposed a radically different theory based on the premise that the key task for government economic policy is to stimulate the supply of goods, not their demand.[7] This theory has been labeled **supply-side economics.** To supply-siders, big government soaked up too much of the gross domestic product. By taxing too heavily, spending too freely, and regulating too tightly, government actually curtailed economic growth. Supply-side economists argued that incentives to invest, work harder, and save could be increased by cutting back on the scope of government, especially tax rates. Economist Arthur Laffer proposed (legend says he did so on the back of a cocktail napkin) a curve suggesting that the more government taxed, the less people worked, and thus the smaller the government's tax revenues. Cut the taxes, Laffer reasoned, and people would work harder and thereby stimulate the economy by producing a greater

supply-side economics

An economic theory advocated by President Reagan holding that too much income goes to taxes so too little money is available for purchasing, and the solution is to cut taxes and return purchasing power to consumers.

supply of goods. In its most extreme form, this theory held that by taking a smaller percentage of people's income, the government would actually get more total revenue as production increased.

Faced with the worst economic downturn since the Depression of the 1930s, Reagan and the supply-siders believed that cutting taxes would pull business out of its doldrums. During his first administration, Reagan fought for and won massive tax cuts, from which the wealthiest Americans profited the most. One cannot emphasize enough how this approach differed from the established Keynesian model. Rather than public works programs to stimulate demand, Americans got tax cuts to stimulate supply; rather than a fiscal policy that promoted bigger government, Americans got a policy that tried to reduce the scope of government. Whichever fiscal approach politicians favor, one formerly controversial issue is now agreed upon: It is the government's responsibility to use fiscal policy to try to control the economy. But like controlling the weather, this is much easier said than done.

Why does it matter?

When government in America taxes about a third of people's incomes, the issue of tax rates is always a lively political issue, especially at election time. Chances are that you will pay more of your lifetime income in taxes than for your housing, your food, or your education. Cutting taxes would leave more money in the hands of people and businesses for investment and job creation. Critics say tax cuts will lead to budget deficits. Should we cut taxes, especially when there is a budget surplus, on the grounds that "it's your money, not government's?" Or should we resist the urge to cut taxes until we are very sure that government can pay its bills?

Obstacles to Controlling the Economy

Some scholars argue that politicians manipulate the economy for short-run advantage to win elections. Edward Tufte writes, "When you think economics, think elections; when you think elections, think economics."[8] Tufte concluded that real disposable income (after taxes and inflation) tended to increase more at election time than at other times. In addition, transfer payments, such as Social Security and veterans' benefits, seemed more likely to increase just prior to an election.

This apparent ability of politicians to control economic conditions, precisely in order to facilitate their reelection is a neat trick if you can do it. However, controlling unemployment and inflation with precision is like stopping on an economic dime. All the instruments for controlling the economy are difficult to use. Even economists do not understand the workings of the economy well enough to understand always why the economy fluctuates as it does.

Politicians sometimes proclaim that they have the solution for economic prosperity. But even when such optimists have the ability to implement their programs, most policies must be decided upon a year or more before they will have their full impact on the economy. The president's budget, for example, is prepared many months in advance of its enactment into law. In addition, benefits such as Social Security are now

BY PETERS FOR THE DAYTON DAILY NEWS, OHIO

Many factors limit the American government's ability to control the economy. The 1973 OPEC oil embargo (in response to America's support of Israel in the Yom Kippur War) and the 1979 Iranian revolution led to increased oil prices, gas lines, inflation, and economic recession.

indexed—that is, they go up automatically as the cost of living increases. Thus it is hard to know what the economy will be like when the government's money is actually spent.

A ripple abroad, especially a crisis abroad, can ruin a government's best efforts to manage the economy. Importing half its oil from other nations, the United States is always vulnerable to troubles in the Middle East. High prices at the gasoline pump or heating oil shortages can be blamed on government. Bringing Arab and Israeli statesmen to the presidential retreat at Camp David, Md., has as much to do with American oil supplies as with our desire to see peace among peoples. American stock markets were vulnerable to a slumping Asian economy in the 1990s called the "Asian flu." Powerful as it is, the American government can do only so much to manage its own economy, and even less to manage others.

The American capitalist system imposes an additional restraint on controlling the economy. Because the private sector is much larger than the public sector, it dominates the economy. An increase in the price of raw materials or in the wages of union workers can offset a host of government efforts to control inflation. When two in three dollars spent in the economy are private dollars, what happens in the private economy can overwhelm policymakers' plans.

simulation
You Are Changing Tax Policy

The budgetary process also hinders fiscal policy. As you saw in Chapter 14, most of the budget expenditures for any year are "uncontrollable," that is, they are mandated by law and determined by the number of eligible beneficiaries. Given that law already mandates so much spending, it is very difficult to make substantial cuts. Coordinating economic policymaking is equally difficult. The president and Congress both have central roles in this process but they may not see eye to eye on taxes or spending, and neither may agree with the independent-minded Fed on the money supply. Like the rest of policymaking in the United States, the power to make economic policy is decentralized.

Arenas of Economic Policymaking

When the government spends one-third of America's gross domestic product and regulates much of the other two-thirds, its economic policies will surely provoke much debate. Liberals tend to favor active government involvement in the economy and higher taxes in order to smooth out the unavoidable inequality of a capitalist system. Conservatives maintain that the most productive economy is one in which the government exercises a hands-off policy of minimal regulation and taxation.

Liberal or conservative, most interest groups seek benefits, protection from unemployment, or safeguards against harmful business practices. Business, consumers, and labor are three of the major actors in, and objects of, government economic policy.

Business and Public Policy: Subsidies Amid Regulations

The corporation has long stood at the center of the American economy. Every year, *Fortune* magazine publishes a listing of the Fortune 500, the 500 largest industrial corporations in the United States. Their leaders are the giants of American business, controlling assets in the hundreds of billions of dollars. To elite theorists, they represent "monopoly capital," a concentration of wealth sufficient to shape both America's and the world's economy.[9] Indeed, the concentration of resources among the top 100 corporations has been increasing since 1950s. Corporate giants have also internationalized in the postwar period. Some **transnational corporations,** businesses with vast holdings in many countries—such as Microsoft, Coca-Cola, and AOL-Time/Warner—have annual budgets exceeding that of many foreign governments.

transnational corporations

Businesses wih vast holdings in many countries—such as Microsoft,Coca-Cola, and McDonald's—many of which have annual budgets exceeding that of many foreign governments.

The Changing Face of Corporate Capitalism. Since the early 1980s, a new form of entrepreneurship has flourished—merger mania. Conglomerates buying up and buying out other companies have spent billions. The massive publisher Time, Inc., merged with Warner's communications empire, and then Time-Warner and America Online proposed merging, stimulating regulatory debates in both the United States and Europe. The history of this textbook provides a telling example of how frequently companies are acquired these days. Little, Brown originally published the book. Then, Little, Brown's textbook division was taken over by Scott, Foresman, which in turn was taken over by HarperCollins. Now, as you can see, the book is being published by Addison Wesley Longman, which bought the textbook division of HarperCollins, Inc. Addison Wesley Longman itself is a part of an even larger publisher, the British Pearson Education group. With each merger, your authors find themselves confronted with an even bigger publishing house. What is true in publishing is true in nearly every sector of the economy.

Competition in today's economy is often about which corporations control access to, and the profits from, the new economy. On April 30, 2000, for example, millions of cable connections to ABC's network went dead, the result of a battle between two media giants, Disney (which owned ABC) and Time-Warner (which controlled many cable networks). To viewers who were eager to watch ABC's popular *Who Wants To Be a Millionaire* game show, it was more than a minor annoyance. It was, though, an important challenge to telecommunications policy in the new economy. Technically it was a battle over the Cable Act of 1992, which required broadcasters to negotiate coverage with cable companies. Time-Warner wanted more money to carry ABC ($300 million more) than Disney was prepared to pay. More importantly, the two media titans were battling for power over new technologies that would bring television, cable, and the Internet closer together in the coming years. Congress was furious, mostly at Time-Warner, and threatened to hold up its proposed merger with Internet giant AOL.

AOL is the richest, but not the only, Internet corporation. Amazon sells books on the Internet, and you can buy everything from airline tickets to groceries from a "dot com" company. Internet companies awash in a sea of red ink nonetheless attracted billions of dollars in investments (and often lost them as fast as they got them). Internet companies and supporters of this "new new economy" fought for, and won, a federal law exempting Internet commerce from state sales taxes. To the worry of governors and legislators, the more Americans bought their books, clothes, cars, and other goods on the Internet, the less states could collect for schools and highways.

In the old and the new economy, Americans have always been suspicious of concentrated power, whether it is in the hands of government or business. In both the old economy and the new, government policy has tried to control excess power in the corporate world. How government regulates business is a fertile source for conflict over economic policy.

Regulating Business. At the turn of the twentieth century, powerful corporate titans gobbled up control of entire industries. After they eliminated competitors, they could charge customers essentially whatever they wanted to. At the turn of the twentieth century, John D. Rockefeller's control of oil refining and processing was the most famous example. Rockefeller started in business in August 1855 at the age of 16, working out of Cleveland, Ohio. Four years later, he went into business for himself and by 1868—at the age of 32—was the largest oil refiner in the world, a monopolist beyond anyone we could imagine today. This was the era of the trusts, as monopolies were then called. Government regulation of business is at least as old as the first antitrust act, the Sherman Act of 1890. The purpose of **antitrust policy** is to ensure competition and prevent monopoly (control of a market by one company). Antitrust legislation permits the Justice Department to sue in federal court to break up companies that control too much of the market. It also generally prevents restraints on trade or limitations on competition, such as price fixing, by which corporations agree not to undercut one another's prices.[10]

antitrust policy

A policy designed to ensure competition and prevent monopoly, which is the control of a market by one company.

Because they are usually lengthy and expensive, antitrust suits are more often threatened than carried out. Some have lasted decades and cost millions of corporate and federal dollars. In one of the biggest pre-Microsoft cases, the government challenged AT&T's monopoly of long-distance phone services. After seven years of legal action, an out-of-court settlement with the corporate giant resulted in its agreement to sell 22 local operating organizations—the "baby bells." AT&T's stranglehold on long-distance pricing ended and competitors swarmed into the telephone and telecommunications market. The Microsoft case (which opened this chapter) is likely to be just as long and complex as the phone monopoly case. New technologies posed new problems for old antitrust policies. Today's corporations—or tomorrow's—may seek to control, not oil, but the Internet, or genetic codes, or media access.

Antitrust policy is hardly the only way business is regulated; Chapter 15 reviewed a variety of regulatory policies affecting businesses. Business owners and managers, especially in small businesses, complain constantly about regulation. Before they complain too much, they should remember some of the benefits they get from government.

Benefiting Business. Government has not always been just a silent partner in American business. In a few cases—namely Chrysler, Lockheed, and the nation's railroads—government loans or buyouts have made government an actual partner or owner in corporate America. When a crucial industry falls on hard times, it usually looks to the government for help in the form of subsidies, tax breaks, or loan guarantees. Similarly, local governments often try to entice employers to move to their community by offering the same sorts of benefits.

Throughout economic booms and busts, the Department of Commerce serves as a veritable storehouse of assistance for business. It collects data on products and markets through the Census Bureau, helps businesses export their wares, and protects inventions through the Patent Office. The Small Business Administration is the government's counselor, advisor, and loan maker to small businesses. Several agencies fund research that is valued by businesses involved with natural resources, transportation, electronics and computers, and health. In fact, the federal government is the principal source of research and development funding in the United States.

Calvin Coolidge's saying that "the business of America is business" rings particularly true when Republican administrations are in office, but some would argue that it applies almost all the time. One of the reasons why official Washington is so hospitable to business interests is that industry lobbyists in Washington are well organized and well funded (see Chapter 11). Businesses organized for lobbying have been around for years; consumer groups, by contrast, are a relatively new arrival on the economic policy stage.

Consumer Policy: The Rise of the Consumer Lobby

Years ago the governing economic principle of consumerism was "let the buyer beware." With a few exceptions, public policy ignored consumers and their interests. The first major consumer protection policy in the United States was the Food and Drug Act of 1906, which prohibited the interstate transportation of dangerous or impure foods and drugs. Today, the **Food and Drug Administration (FDA)** has broad regulatory powers over the manufacturing, contents, marketing, and labeling of food and drugs. It is the FDA's responsibility to ascertain the safety and effectiveness of new drugs before approving them for marketing in the United States.

Food and Drug Administration (FDA)

The federal agency formed in 1913 and assigned the task of approving all food products and drugs sold in the United States. All drugs, with the exception of tobacco, must have FDA authorization.

The FDA regulates presciption drugs, whose cost is soaring even faster than other medical costs. Which drugs the FDA approves and how fast they approve them generate conflict. Commissioner Dr. David Kessler's determination to regulate nicotine as a drug during the Clinton Administration also raised ire. The FDA reasoned that nicotine was a drug and tobacco products were its delivery system. Asserting this power would permit the FDA to regulate—even ban, the tobacco industry claimed—cigarettes. Tobacco companies fought this assertion of FDA authority in the courts—and won. The states, though, fought a civil action against tobacco companies and won a multibillion-dollar settlement.

Consumerism was a sleeping political giant until the 1960s, when self-proclaimed consumer activists such as Ralph Nader, who later ran for president on the Green Party ticket in 2000, awakened it. Uncovering clear cases of unsafe products and false advertising, these activists argued that it was the government's responsibility to be a watchdog on behalf of the consumer. As they garnered broad public support, the 1960s and 1970s saw a flood of consumer protection legislation. Created in 1972 by the Product Safety Act, the Consumer Product Safety Commission (CPSC) has broad powers to ban hazardous products from the market. Today the CPSC regulates the safety of items ranging from toys to lawn mowers.

Federal Trade Commission (FTC)

The independent regulatory agency traditionally responsible for regulating false and misleading trade practices. The FTC has recently become active in defending consumer interests through its truth-in-advertising rule and the Consumer Credit Protection Act.

The **Federal Trade Commission (FTC),** traditionally responsible for regulating trade practices, also jumped into the business of consumer protection in the 1960s and 1970s, becoming a defender of consumer interests in truth in advertising. It has made new rules about product labeling, exaggerated product claims, and the use of celebrities in advertising. For example, in 1997 the FTC ordered Jenny Craig Inc. to warn consumers

Budget cuts made during the 1980s left many independent regulatory agencies open to criticism from the consumer groups they were created to protect. Here, demonstrators protest FDA delays in testing and approving experimental drugs for AIDS patients.

that weight losses as a result of using their product are usually only temporary. The Congress has also made the FTC the administrator of the new Consumer Credit Protection Act. This act stipulates that whenever you borrow money, even if only by using a credit card, you must receive a form stating the exact amount of interest you must pay. The FTC enforces truth in lending through such forms and other means.

Labor and Government

National Labor Relations Act

A 1935 law, also known as the Wagner Act, that guarantees workers the right of **collective bargaining,** sets down rules to protect unions and organizers, and created the National Labor Relations Board to regulate labor-management relations.

collective bargaining

Negotiations between representatives of labor unions and management to determine pay and acceptable working conditions.

Taft-Hartley Act

A 1947 law giving the president power to halt major strikes by seeking a court injunction and permitting states to forbid requirements in labor contracts that force workers to join a union.

Throughout most of the nineteenth century and well into the twentieth, the federal government allied with business elites to squelch labor unions. The courts interpreted the antitrust laws as applying to unions as well as businesses. Until the Clayton Antitrust Act of 1914 exempted unions from antitrust laws, the mighty arm of the federal government was busier busting unions than trusts. Government lent its hand to enforcing "yellow dog contracts"—contracts that forced workers to agree not to join a union as a condition of employment.

The major turnabout in government policy toward labor took place during the New Deal. In 1935 Congress passed the **National Labor Relations Act,** often called the Wagner Act after its sponsor, Senator Robert Wagner of New York. The Wagner Act guaranteed workers the right of **collective bargaining**—the right to have labor union representatives negotiate with management to determine working conditions. It also established rules to protect unions and organizers. For example, under the Wagner Act, an employer cannot fire or discriminate against a worker who advocates unionizing.

After World War II, a series of strikes and a new Republican majority in Congress tilted federal policy somewhat back in the direction of management. The **Taft-Hartley Act** of 1947 continued to guarantee unions the right of collective bargaining, but it prohibited various unfair practices by unions as well. The act also gave the president power to halt major strikes by seeking a court injunction for an 80-day "cooling off" period. Most important, section 14B of the law permitted states to adopt what union opponents call **right to work laws.** Such laws forbid labor contracts from requiring workers to join

Unionization began in the late 1800s not only because of low wages, but because of working conditions for men, women, and children which we would call inhumane. Coal mining was then—and it is now—one of the most dangerous jobs in the country. Union power and membership grew for nearly a hundred years, but began to decline in the 1970s.

unions to hold their jobs. The effect of right to work laws is to subject unions to the free-rider problem (see Chapter 11); workers can enjoy the benefits of union negotiations without contributing dues to support the union. Subsequent public policies focused on union corruption. Stirred by revelations of the mismanagement of funds, racketeering, and violence by some unions, Congress tried to crack down by passing the Labor-Management Reporting and Disclosure Act, called the Landrum-Griffin Act, in 1959. The act enabled union members to exercise more control over their leaders and forbade ex-convicts from serving as union officials for five years after their release.

right-to-work law

A state law forbidding requirements that workers must join a union to hold their jobs. The Taft-Hartley Act of 1947 specifically permitted state right-to-work laws.

Unions have had some notable successes over the years, which have become staples of the American economy. First, partly as the result of successful union lobbying, the government provides unemployment compensation—paid for by workers and employers—to cushion the blows of unemployment. Second, since the New Deal, the government has guaranteed a minimum wage, setting a floor on the hourly wages earned by employees. No issue of economic policy more sharply divides the parties than the minimum wage. Democrats always argue for its increase (now $5.15 per hour), appealing in part to their core constituents. Republicans always argue that increasing it would lead employers to lay off, or not hire, low-paid workers.

Why does it matter?

The role of labor unions continues to be controversial in the United States. Union membership is declining. Workers in the new economy often prefer to get their benefits in the form of stock options than join with others as dues-paying union members. Many companies, including Microsoft, pay thousands of contract workers to do the company's business, some of it at home. Telecommuters are not very easy to unionize. Should government policy encourage unions to organize in the new economy just as it did in the old economy? How has the decline in union membership affected American workers and American politics? What difference would it make to you if unions were to totally disappear in the future?

New Economy, New Policy Arenas

The last few decades have seen a shift in focus from the old industrial economy to a new information economy. Three million Americans now work in technology-producing industries. Half of all adults own one or more computers. In a single three-year period (1996–1999), access to the Internet doubled. The number of individuals using the Internet for educational purposes is rising rapidly. With perhaps a bit of entrepreneurial exaggeration, John Chambers of Cisco claimed that "education over the Internet is going to be so big it is going to make email usage look like a rounding error."[11] Access to technology, though, is uneven. The old economy generated issues of income inequality, but the new economy involves issues of information inequality. As with income, the groups looking from the outside in on the information revolution are primarily minority Americans. In 1998, 32 percent of White households, but only 12 percent of Hispanic and 13 percent of Black households had access to the Internet.[12] Rural Americans also experience a gap in Internet availability. So do women. Men are about 12–13 percent more likely to use the Internet than women.[13]

The "new economy" signals technology, and Microsoft is one of its leading corporations. President Bill Clinton assembled a White House Conference on the New Economy, and Microsoft's Chairman Bill Gates (left) was one of the leading contributors, along with James Wolfensohn (right), president of the World Bank. This did not stop the Clinton administration from suing Microsoft, though, and seeking its breakup as a monopoly.

You Are the Policymaker

Should Government Help Close the Digital Divide?

By the end of 1999 the estimated value of commercial Internet activity was about $100 billion. Incredibly, economists estimated that it would double in the next year alone. The Internet created 1.2 million jobs in 1998 and that number was also soaring. Not only commerce, but also education, science, and innovation were Internet-driven. Being left behind in the digital age is like being stuck on the farm as the industrial age emerged. Access to the Internet often mirrors and reinforces other indicators of poverty. The college-educated population is 16 times more likely to have Internet access than those without high school degrees.

Today's Internet connections will seem slow in comparison to technologies already around the corner. Broadband connections—with speeds at least 1.5 megabites per second—will be 1,000 times faster than current dial-in modems. People who live a long way from the fiber-optic cables that provide Broadband service are out of luck. In Atlanta, the fiber-optic cables head north from downtown areas, and not south, with its heavy concentration of African Americans. Some low-population states and rural areas are being bypassed completely.

Telecommunications decisions in the United States are in the private sector. Government does not build fiber-optic cables; corporations expecting a profit do. Here is the problem: Unequal access to future technologies threatens to widen the digital divide between rich and poor, and urban and rural Americans. Companies argue that cables can't be laid where there are no profits to be made. Interest groups and some members of Congress—especially those from rural states and the West—think government should subsidize broadband cable just like it subsidized the Interstate Highway system. E-mail and the Internet, they argue, are the twenty-first century's equivalent of the postal service of the last century.

Yet we cannot afford to provide broadband access to every home, however isolated, in the country. Just as the Interstate Highways system bypassed some people, leaving small towns to die, broadband access may do the same. Government did not subsidize everyone's car just because mass transportation was important to making a living. Government doesn't subsidize people's Internet connections just because the Internet is an important educational technology. What do you think? Should government subsidize new technologies to make them more available to all Americans?

Source: "Who Will Get Connected?" *CQ Outlook*, March 11, 2000.

The racial and ethnic gaps are widening, not shrinking. This "digital divide" can also be a racial ravine. One policy issue involves the role of the government as new, faster technologies come to market. See "You Are the Policymaker: Should Government Help Close the Digital Divide?"

The policymaker at the turn of the twentieth century—facing questions of monopoly power and labor-management conflict—could hardly imagine the range of policy issues at the turn of the twenty-first century. Now, as then, though, policy arises from conflict between groups. As we invent new telecommunications technologies and decode the human genome, the long arms of government regulation and subsidies will continue to shape the economy.

Understanding Economic Policymaking

The minimum wage and unemployment compensation are just two of many economic policies that contradict Karl Marx's assumptions of how a capitalist system inevitably exploits ordinary workers. Looking at mid-nineteenth-century business practices, Marx saw an economic system in which working conditions were long, hard, and miserable. Most workers barely managed to earn a meager livelihood while the rich got richer off their labor. In a completely free economic system, there was no way to compel the owners of the factories to treat the workers better. Marx thought exploitation would continue, and even get worse. His radical solution was for the state to assume all power over the economy in a revolution of the proletariat (i.e., the workers). In the Communist sys-

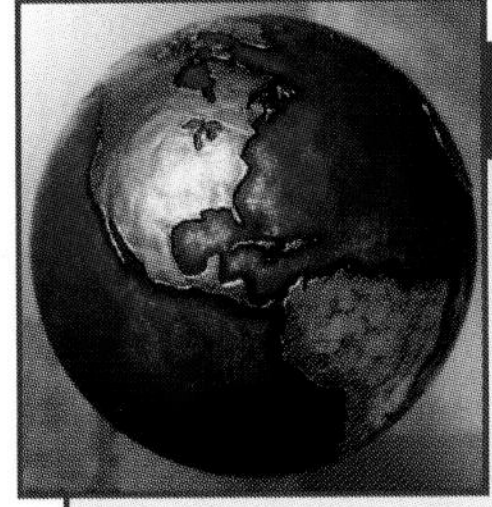

America in Perspective

The Soviet Economic Morass

What went wrong with the Soviet economy? The simplest answer is that having the national government make all the decisions on what to produce proved to be impractical and inefficient. Or as Mikhail Gorbachev, who tried to reform the system, once said, "It is an illusion to think that everything can be foreseen from the center within the framework of such a huge economy as ours."

The Communist economic system depended on the wisdom of central planners in Moscow to decide what was in the people's best interest to produce, as well as what the appropriate prices would be. The Soviet economy was a *command* economy. Annual national production quotas were drawn up for everything from tractors to tennis shoes, typically without any consideration of how much people wanted the specific goods. Each individual plant was then assigned the task of meeting a specific percentage of the national quota. Rather than a measure of success based on customer satisfaction and profit, the goal was merely to churn out the goods.

Quality was thereby regularly sacrificed for quantity, which often produced disastrous results. Tens of thousands of tractors would come off the assembly lines, but few spare parts would be made available. Millions of pairs of shoes were left on the shelves of stores because their sizes did not match the population's. Television sets were so shoddily made that they regularly blew up in people's living rooms, becoming the leading cause of household fires in the Soviet Union.

With an emphasis on production rather than profit, Soviet workers were given little incentive to make quality a priority. Absenteeism from the job was high, and morale was low. A favorite saying of the workers became "They pretend to pay us and we pretend to work." About the only incentive people had at the workplace was to steal. Many workers reportedly made up for their poor pay by pilfering goods at their plant. The common saying was "What belongs to everyone, belongs to no one, so why shouldn't it be mine?"

Today, the Russian economy has a per capita output similar to nations like Lebanon or Peru. Russia's health, Nicholas Eberstadt reports, is deteriorating rapidly. There are more deaths from heart disease in Russia than from all causes of death combined in the United States. Russia's health profile, he says, is worse than in many Third World countries. There are lessons for America's economic management in these grim stories. Though regulated, our economy is not a centrally planned one. Though Americans may debate about government regulation and the scope of government, almost all would agree that a centrally planned economy is a prescription for economic disaster.

The state-run economy of the former Soviet Union was so inefficient that there was shortages of virtually everything. Standing in line for goods in short supply became several hours a day.

Source: From Hedrick Smith, *The New Russians* (New York: Random House, 1990). Reprinted by permission of International Merchandising Corporation. The material on health is from Nicholas Eberstadt, "Russia: Too Sick to Matter?" *Policy Review* 95 (June and July 1999), 3–24.

tem envisioned by Marx, all the means of production would be owned by the state—in which each citizen would be an equal shareholder. In practice, however, the state-run economy of the Soviet Union did not provide the necessary incentives to get people to work productively (see "America in Perspective: The Soviet Economic Morass").

In America, however, solutions to many of the problems of a free enterprise economy were achieved through the democratic process. A large part of this effort involved expanding the scope of government, which conservatives would like to see at least partially rolled back in today's economy.

Democracy and Economic Policymaking

As the voting power of the ordinary worker grew, so did the potential for government regulation of the worst ravages of the capitalist system. Political pressure grew for action to restrict unfair business practices and to protect individual rights. Over time, the state assumed responsibility for setting the age at which one could work, determining the normal work week, establishing standards for safety on the job, protecting pension funds, and many other aspects of economic life. Just as the right of free speech is not interpreted so as to allow someone to shout "fire" in a crowded movie theater, so the right to free enterprise is no longer interpreted as giving businesses the right to employ 10-year-olds or to force employees to work in unsafe conditions. It is now generally agreed that the government should forbid such practices. Through the ballot box, Americans essentially decided to give up certain economic freedoms for the good of society as a whole.

It would be a vast exaggeration, however, to say that democracy regularly facilitates an economic policy that looks after general rather than specific interests. As you have seen throughout this text, the decentralized American political system often works against efficiency in government. In particular, groups that may be adversely affected by an economic policy have many avenues through which they can work to block it. Therefore, one of the consequences of democracy for economic policymaking is that it is difficult to make decisions that hurt particular groups or that involve short-term pain for long-term gain. Of course, this is the way most Americans presumably want it to be.

Economic Policymaking and the Scope of Government

What liberals and conservatives disagree about most when it comes to economic policymaking is the scope of government involvement in the economy. In general, liberals look to the writings of economists such as John Maynard Keynes and Robert Solow, whose works offer justification for an expanded role of government in stimulating the economy during times of recession. Conservatives, on the other hand, rely on Friedrich Hayek's influential theories on the free market and on Milton Friedman's arguments against government intervention. Whereas liberals focus on the imperfections of the market and what government can do about them, conservatives focus on the imperfections of government. For example, while liberals often propose job-training programs for unskilled workers, conservatives argue that businesses can create new jobs and prepare people for them if government will just stay out of the way.

Summary

In the United States, the political and economic sectors are closely intermingled. Although politicians have strong feelings about the economy and pay close attention to it, only scattered evidence indicates that they can successfully manipulate the economic situation at election time. The two parties do have different economic policies, particularly with respect to unemployment and inflation; Democrats try to curb unemployment more than Republicans, though they risk inflation in so doing, and Republicans are generally more concerned with controlling inflation. Two major instruments are available to government for managing the economy: monetary policy and fiscal policy. Democrats lean more toward Keynesian economics, which holds that government must stimulate greater demand, when necessary, with bigger government such as federal job programs. In contrast, many Republicans advocate supply-side economics, which calls for smaller government and tax cuts to increase the incentive to produce more goods.

Through public policy, government also regulates various sectors of the economy. It regulates business and offers some protection to consumers and to labor. These are issues of the old economy, and still very much issues today. In the twenty-first century, there are also new economic issues—access to information technology, for example—which public policy is just beginning to confront.

Career Profile

Position: Financial Services Analyst
Employer: Federal Reserve Board
Starting Salary Range: about $38,000 for BA, $45,000 for MA
Benefits: Alternative work schedule, telecommuting option, business casual dress, 13 days paid vacation per year, tuition assistance, technical training program
Qualifications: Training in finance, economics, public policy, or a related field is preferred. A bachelor's degree is usually the standard educational requirement, though a master's degree is advantageous. An understanding of at least two of these areas is required: finance, microeconomics, statistics, econometrics, electronic payments, and cost accounting

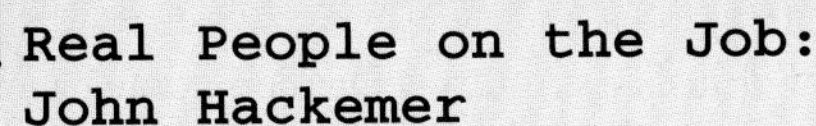

Real People on the Job: John Hackemer

Though Alan Greenspan's position is already taken, you can follow the example of John Hackemer by applying for a job at the center of America's financial universe—the Federal Reserve Board. John works in Washington D.C. as a financial services analyst in the Division of Reserve Bank Operations and Payment Systems overseeing the operation of the Federal Reserve Banks, researching issues concerning the global payments system, and developing payment system policies and regulations.

A large part of John's daily duties focus on the successful transfer of billions of dollars among depository institutions (e.g. banks, savings banks, and credit unions) through the U.S. payments system. When Citibank wants to shift $100 million to Wells Fargo, for example, it uses the Federal Reserve's Fedwire system to move money out of its account with the Federal Reserve Bank of New York, into Wells Fargo's account with the Federal Reserve Bank of San Francisco. Because institutions make many such moves every day, they often rely upon the Federal Reserve's "daylight" credit, short-term loans that must be repaid by the end of the day. As you can imagine, staying on top of these financial arrangements is not only extremely challenging but also vital to the continued confidence of America's banking and financial systems.

Recently, John was given the job of analyzing whether depository institutions' access to "daylight" credit from the Federal Reserve is sufficient to balance payment system efficiency with the credit risks posed to the Federal Reserve. To this end, John pores over the payment flows of participating banks and analyzes them in conjunction with extensions of credit. Using his background in statistics and finance, he builds models to answer questions about efficiency, liquidity, and risk. John thrives on the intellectual freedom required to tackle this problem. And when his work is incorporated into a policy adopted by the Federal Reserve Board, a sense of accomplishment and closure offers tremendous satisfaction to John and his colleagues.

As opposed to the cutthroat atmosphere within most Wall Street firms, John appreciates the collegiality and teamwork he finds at the Federal Reserve. The work environment is refreshing, stimulating, and open. Employee amenities include a gym, cafeteria, store, barber, dry-cleaning, tennis courts, and a host of other amenities not usually available to most workers in the corporate financial world. Also, to advance within his division, John does not need to hold a Ph.D. in economics. While economists naturally tend to dominate the research divisions that support the determination of monetary policy, including the setting of key interest rates, John, who possesses a master's degree, has high and realistic hopes of advancement within his division.

For more information on careers at the Federal Reserve Board, check their website at www.federalreserve.gov.

Key Terms

capitalism
mixed economy
unemployment rate
inflation
consumer price index (CPI)
laissez-faire
monetary policy
monetarism
Federal Reserve System
fiscal policy
Keynesian economic theory
supply-side economics
antitrust policy
Food and Drug Administration (FDA)
Federal Trade Commission (FTC)
National Labor Relations Act
collective bargaining
Taft-Hartley Act
right to work laws

For Further Reading

Carson, Robert B., Wade L. Thomas, and Jason Hecht. *Economic Issues Today: Alternative Approaches*, 6th ed. New York: M.E. Sharpe, 1999. Examines 16 separate economic policy questions from the conservative, liberal, and radical viewpoints.

Gilder, George. *Wealth and Poverty*. New York: Basic Books, 1981. A supply-sider's bible.

Greider, William. *Secrets of the Temple: How the Federal Reserve Runs the Country*. New York: Simon & Schuster, 1987. A book that demystifies the Fed.

Kiewiet, D. Roderick. *Macroeconomics and Micropolitics*. Chicago: University of Chicago Press, 1983. A good study of the electoral effects of economic issues.

Krugman, Paul. *Peddling Prosperity: Economic Sense and Nonsense in the Age of Diminished Expectations*. New York: Norton, 1994. A top economist traces how various economic theories have affected policymaking during the period of declining American economic growth.

Reich, Robert B. *The Work of Nations: Preparing Ourselves for 21st Century Capitalism*. New York: Knopf, 1991. Argues that education, communications, and transportation facilities are crucial to a country's economic success in our increasingly interdependent world.

Schultze, Charles L. *Memos to the President: A Guide Through Macroeconomics for the Busy Policymaker*. Washington, D.C.: Brookings Institution, 1992. A set of very readable memos explaining what politicians need to know about how the American economy works.

Stein, Herbert. *Presidential Economics*, 3rd ed. Washington, D.C.: American Enterprise Institute, 1994. The making of economic policy from FDR to Clinton.

Tufte, Edward R. *Political Control of the Economy*. Princeton, NJ: Princeton University Press, 1978. A bold argument that politicians manipulate the economy to their electoral advantage.

Weidenbaum, Murray L. *Business and Government in the Global Marketplace*, 6th ed. Englewood Cliffs, NJ: Prentice-Hall, 1998. An excellent text on how the private and public sectors interact.

Internet Resources

www.whitehouse.gov/WH/EOP/CEA/html/publications.html
Publications of the Council of Economic Advisors, such as the annual Economic Report of the President.

www.federalreserve.gov
Information about the activities of the Federal Reserve Board.

www.ftc.gov/ftc/consumer.htm
The Federal Trade Commission's consumer protection page.

www.usdoj.gov/atr/
The Department of Justice's Antitrust Division home page, where you can learn the latest about the Microsoft case.

Notes

1. Robert B. Reich, *The Next American Frontier* (New York: Penguin Books, 1983), 4–5.
2. Thomas Friedman, *The Lexus and the Olive Tree* (New York: Ferrar, Straus and Giroux, 1999), 11.
3. D. Roderick Kiewiet, *Macroeconomics and Micropolitics: The Electoral Effects of Economic Issues* (Chicago: University of Chicago Press, 1983).
4. Michael Lewis-Beck and Tom W. Rice, *Forecasting Elections* (Washington: Congressional Quarterly Press, 1992), 32–33.
5. Quoted in Douglas Hibbs, "Political Parties and Macroeconomic Policy," *American Political Science Review* 71 (December 1977): 1,467.
6. See William Greider, *Secrets of the Temple: How the Federal Reserve Runs the Country* (New York: Simon & Schuster, 1987); Nathaniel Beck, "Elections and the Fed: Is There a Political Monetary Cycle?" *American Journal of Political Science* 31 (February 1987): 194–216; and Nathaniel Beck, "Presidential Influence on the Federal

Reserve in the 1970s," *American Journal of Political Science* 26 (August 1982): 415–445.

7. One supply-side theory can be found in George Gilder, *Wealth and Poverty* (New York: Basic Books, 1981).
8. Edward R. Tufte, *Political Control of the Economy* (Princeton, NJ: Princeton University Press, 1978), 65.
9. The argument that the American economy is dominated by "monopoly capital" is common among Marxist economists. See, for example, James O'Connor, *The Fiscal Crisis of the State* (New York: St. Martin's, 1973).
10. For a good review of the history of antitrust issues, see Marc Allen Eisner, *Antitrust and the Triumph of Economics: Institutions, Expertise, and Policy Change* (Chapel Hill: University of North Carolina Press, 1991).
11. Cited in Peter Navarro, "Economics in the Cyberclassroom," *Journal of Economic Perspectives* 14 (Spring 2000), 119.
12. "Who Will Get Connected?" *Congressional Quarterly Outlook*, March 11, 2000, 12.
13. Bruce Bimber, "Measuring the Gender Gap on the Internet," *Social Science Quarterly* 81 (September 2000): 868–878.

18 Social Welfare Policymaking

Chapter Outline

Beginning in 1998, the federal government launched the largest mass mailing in history. It was a letter from Kenneth S. Apfel, commissioner of Social Security, to every single American paying Social Security taxes. The letter was entitled "Your Social Security Statement." The massive computers of the Social Security Administration in Baltimore, Md., generated millions of individualized letters reporting what each individual had paid year by year. The letters also reported estimated benefits. Based on what you had paid in so far, you could expect to receive—if you kept working until the retirement age—so many dollars per month.

About 75 million "Baby Boomers" will start retiring in about 2010. Chances are, they will live longer and healthier lives than any generation before—and run up even bigger costs for the Social Security system and its health-care cousin, Medicare.

Social Security, the most expensive public policy in the United States, began modestly enough as a

"pay-as-you-go" plan during Franklin Roosevelt's New Deal. At first it was "a deal that couldn't be beat."[1] The idea was that money in payroll taxes would have to come into the Treasury before money could go out to the beneficiaries. President Roosevelt wanted a plan so fiscally solid that "no damn politician can ever scrap my social security program." Over the years, Americans have tended to believe that their social security payments were just "getting out what I paid in." But that wasn't true even for the very first Social Security recipient, a woman named Ida May Fuller from Brattleboro, Vt. Her total contributions were a mere $22.54, but her lifetime benefits were $22,888.92 because she lived to a ripe old age. But Ida May Fuller's deal is no longer available. A young woman starting her career today at the age of, say, 22, will find that the biggest investment of her lifetime—bigger than housing, children, or any other personal costs—is Social Security. There will be only about one worker for every two recipients by the time she retires (in contrast to about one in 25 when the program began).

Yet even as big as it is, Social Security is far from the only social welfare policy in the United States. Social security helps mostly the elderly (though a third supports families of deceased workers and disabled Americans). There are also expensive and extensive national and state programs designed to help the poor.

One long-debated question about democracy in America is how much we owe to one another, to the poor, or to future generations. On the one hand, Social Security is the single most popular policy in America (95 percent of Americans favor it). Social Security is so popular that politicians fear to tread on it. Only in the 2000 election, and then very carefully, did one candidate seriously discuss rethinking Roosevelt's contract with America. The aged and aging, of course, are vigorous participants in American politics; the poor are not.

The scope of government in America is perhaps more directly determined by the aging of America than any other factor today. The government in Washington has grown in large part to pay for its social policies. The future of Social Security and other social programs is at the heart of the debate about the scope of American government. In this chapter, we will see why.

Americans pride themselves in their self-reliance and are deeply suspicious of government's efforts to redistribute wealth. But Americans differ widely in their economic success. Some people, of course, are rich and some are poor. Some work hard and some don't. Chances are that if people who worked hard always came out well economically, and the lazy ones did not, Americans would be comfortable with that. But economies are not that simple. Moreover, few nations have the enormous differences between the rich and poor that we have. Andrew Hacker reports that "among the world's modernized countries, the United States has the most glaring income gaps."[2] In this chapter we ask what causes these gaps and what government has tried to do about them. Equally important, we ask what role public policies play—and should play—in income, wealth, and poverty.

How Americans think about economic inequality influences how government provides assistance and support to specific groups in society through its **social welfare policies.** Who gets these benefits and what level of support is provided are issues that must be resolved by the political system. Political leaders, parties, interest groups, and voters all make collective decisions that impact the nature and distribution of poverty and the effectiveness of various social welfare programs.

social welfare policies

Policies that provide benefits to individuals, particularly those in need.

The Social Welfare Debate

It would be hard to think of a public policy that stimulates more argument and causes more confusion than social welfare. Here is one major confusion: Many Americans equate social welfare exclusively with government moneys given to the poor. Yet the government gives far more money to the nonpoor than to people below the "poverty line." Money paid out by the government to poorer Americans is dwarfed by Social Security payments alone. Few Americans have the slightest qualms about assisting older Americans with government programs (even though most retirees will get back in benefits many times what they put in). Handing out money to the poor may be another matter.

Social welfare policies consist of two kinds of programs. First are the **entitlement programs** (on entitlements, see pages 452–453 in Chapter 14). An entitlement is any benefit provided by law and regardless of need. The two biggest entitlement programs are Social Security and Medicare. You don't have to be poor to get an entitlement, nor does being rich disqualify you. Billionaires like Ross Perot and Bill Gates are entitled to Social Security benefits just like the rest of us.

entitlement programs

Government benefits that certain qualified individuals are entitled to by law, regardless of need.

means-tested programs

Government programs available only to individuals below a poverty line

Means-tested programs, on the other hand, provided benefits selectively only to people with specific needs. Here is where the political battleground lies. To be eligible for means-tested programs, people have to prove that they qualify for them. Entitlement programs are rarely controversial in America and often overwhelmingly popular. Means-tested programs generate powerful political controversy. Much of that conflict has to do with how people see the poor and the causes of poverty. People who see the poor as mostly shiftless and irresponsible are hostile to what they see as "government handouts" to the poor. If people see poverty, though, as largely beyond people's control, they are much more sympathetic to governmental assistance. Thus Americans have often distinguished between the "deserving poor" and the "undeserving poor." The deserving poor are victims of things they aren't responsible for: the loss of the breadwinner, disabilities, or poor economic opportunities. The undeserving poor have presumably created their own problems and don't need government's help.

Why does it matter?

Our views of the poor are likely to affect our views about the best policies for government. Americans have often distinguished between the "deserving" and the "undeserving" poor. The deserving poor are poor because of circumstances beyond their control. The undeserving poor are depicted as lazy, unwilling to work, and living off welfare benefits. These "pictures of the poor" shape our views of public policy toward the poor. How do politicians' views of the poor affect the kind of social welfare policies they favor? How do your own opinions about the poor influence your views about antipoverty programs?

A major study by Fay Lomax Cook and Edith Barrett found that people's attitudes toward government social welfare spending depends a lot on their images and opinions of the poor. "When recipients are seen as being in need, as wanting to be independent, and as not being at fault for their conditions," support for public programs is strong.[3] There is also evidence that some of Americans' opposition to welfare is rooted

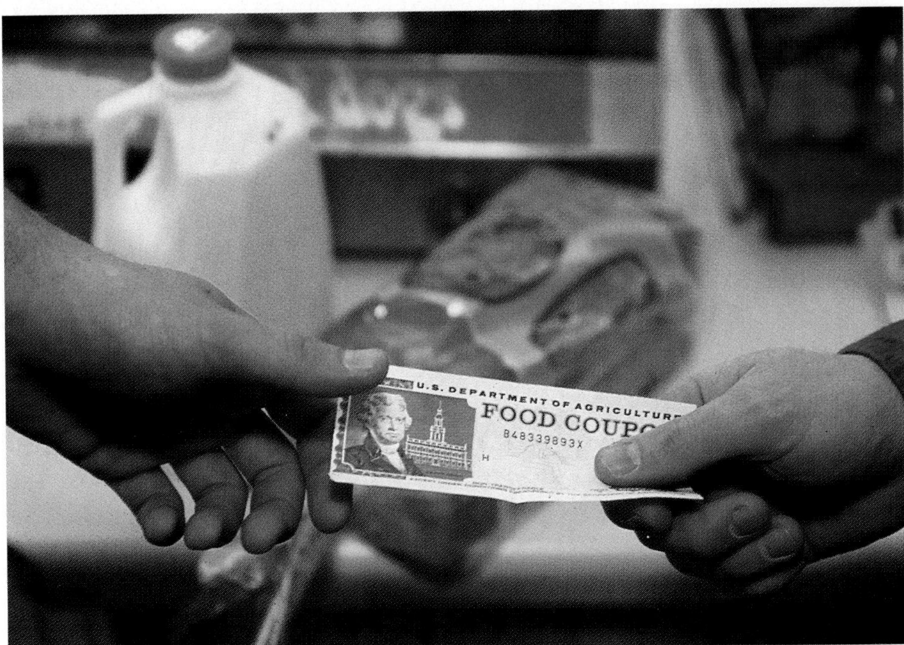

People who receive Food Stamps, and use them for buying groceries as shown here, must pass a means test in order to receive this government benefit.

in their attitudes toward African Americans. Using survey data, Martin Gilens found that Whites' welfare attitudes were strongly influenced by whether they viewed African Americans as lazy or not.[4] Negative views of African-American welfare mothers were more politically potent and generated greater opposition to welfare than comparative views of White welfare mothers. Understanding the debate regarding the causes of poverty is crucial to understanding the political debate over welfare programs.

Let's look, therefore, at who's rich, who's poor, who's in between—and what public policy has to do with income.

Income, Poverty, and Public Policy

Americans are a rich people. The United States once had the highest per capita income on earth. Switzerland, Denmark, Norway, and Japan outrank us in terms of per capita income, but most other countries have—by our standards—staggering costs of living. When we factor in purchasing power, only tiny Luxembourg ranks ahead of the United States. The Census Bureau reported that in 2000 the median American household income was $40,800—that is, half of American households made more, and half less than this amount. No industrialized country, though, has wider extremes of income than the United States.

Who's Getting What?

The novelist F. Scott Fitzgerald once wrote to his friend Ernest Hemingway, "The rich are different from you and me." "Yes," replied Hemingway, "they have more money." In fact, the distribution of income across segments of the American population is quite uneven. The concept of **income distribution** describes the share of national income earned by various groups in the United States. You can see in Table 18.1 how income distribution has changed in recent decades. During the 1960s and 1970s, the distribution of income was rather constant. The 1980s and 1990s, however, proved the old adage true: the rich get richer and the poor get poorer.

income distribution
The "shares" of the national income earned by various groups.

income
The amount of funds collected between any two points in time.

Although the words *income* and *wealth* might seem similar, they are not the same thing. **Income** is the amount of money collected between any two points in time;

The United States is a wealthy nation but one that also has tremendous inequality in wealth. In many parts of the country, affluent suburban neighborhoods can be found less than 10 miles away from poverty-stricken areas.

wealth

The amount of funds already owned.

wealth is the amount already owned, including stocks, bonds, bank accounts, cars, houses, and so forth. Studies of wealth display even more inequality than those of income: The top 1 percent of the wealth holders currently possesses about 37 percent of all American wealth. The assets held by the wealthiest 1 percent of Americans actually exceeded the net worth of those in the bottom 90 percent. In fact, the wealth of one man in the United States, Microsoft's Bill Gates, is equal to the total wealth of the bottom 40 percent of all Americans. In the New Economy, millionaires are fairly common. There are now 250 billionaires in the United States. At the other end of the line, the wealth of the median American household is $71,600. At the very end of the line are the poor in America.

Table 18.1 Who Gets What? Income Shares of American Households

The following table demonstrates how much of the nation's income is received by people within each quintile (or fifth) of the population. In other words, the 4.9 percent in 1960 means that people whose income placed them in the lowest 20 percent received just 4.9 percent of the nation's income in that year while the highest fifth got 42 percent.

INCOME QUINTILE	1960	1970	1980	1990	1999
Lowest fifth	4.9	5.5	5.1	4.6	3.7
Second fifth	11.8	12.0	11.6	10.8	9.0
Third fifth	17.6	17.4	17.5	16.6	15.0
Fourth fifth	23.6	23.5	24.3	23.8	23.0
Highest fifth	42.0	41.6	41.6	44.3	49.3

Source: U.S. Census Bureau.

Who's Poor in America?

Compared with most people in India or Haiti or Nigeria, poor Americans seem almost prosperous. Russia is a poor country by American standards, but it is not afflicted with the poverty of rural Mexico. Mexico City may look poor to an American visitor, but millions come there from the Mexican countryside seeking prosperity—relatively speaking. Poverty, of course, is always relative. But it would be scant comfort to poor Americans for politicians to tell them how well off they are in comparison to people in other countries, or, for that matter, to their own ancestors (in 1900 the average income was only $246 a year).

Making a Difference

Mollie Orshansky and the Origins of the Poverty Threshold

Mollie Orshansky was a fairly high-level research analyst with the Social Security Administration at a time when few women held influential positions in government. She had a personal concern with poverty based on her own family roots. Orshansky recalled spending a good deal of her childhood waiting in long lines to receive surplus food during the Depression. "If I write about the poor," she said, "I don't need a good imagination—I have a good memory."

A statistician by training, she realized that in order for 1960s politicians to do something about poverty, they first had to find a way to measure it. Early in her career, Orshansky worked for the Department of Agriculture, and she learned from her work there that a family barely managing to make ends meet spent roughly one-third of its money on food. She then took the cost of the Department of Agriculture's subsistence diet and multiplied it by three to set the poverty level. The federal government adopted this formula as its official measure of the poverty threshold in the mid-1960s, and has continued to update the formula every year by factoring in inflation.

Ironically, Orshansky never intended to create a formula that would last to this day. She believed that if spending habits changed, then the measurement of poverty ought to be adjusted accordingly. Today, some scholars believe that an income equal to three times a subsistence food budget leaves a family in need of many necessities—as the price of food has declined once inflation is taken into account. They call for the measurement of poverty to return to Mollie Orshansky's basic concept: If a struggling family today spends one-fifth of its income on food, then the poverty threshold should be five rather than three times its basic food budget. These scholars argue that poverty in recent years has been underestimated due to a slavish adherence to Orshansky's formula rather than her concept. If Mollie Orshansky were alive today, she would probably agree.

Source: John E. Schwarz and Thomas J. Volgy, *The Forgotten Americans: Thirty Million Working Poor in the Land of Opportunity* (New York: Norton, 1992).

poverty line

A method used to count the number of poor people, it considers what a family must spend for an "austere" standard of living.

To count the poor, the U.S. Bureau of the Census has established the **poverty line,** which takes into account what a family must spend to maintain an "austere" standard of living. This official statistic was designed by Mollie Orshansky during the 1960s (see "Making a Difference: Mollie Orshansky and the Origins of the Poverty Threshold"). For 1999, the Census Bureau defined a family of three as falling below the poverty level if it had an annual income below $13,470; that year 11.8 percent of all Americans were living in poverty.

A careful, decade-long study of 5,000 American families showed that poverty may be even more extensive than the poverty line suggests.[5] In this representative sample of American families, almost one-third were below the poverty level at least once during the decade. The official poverty counts tend to *underestimate* the seriousness of poverty in America. A count of the poor for one year can conceal millions who drop into and out of poverty. As many as 70 million Americans live so close to the poverty line that any crisis could push them into poverty. Divorce, the loss of a breadwinner, and the addition of a new mouth to feed can precipitate the fall below the poverty line. Rank and Hirschl looked at the overall incomes of Americans during their working lifetimes. An impressive 50.4 percent of all working Americans experienced at least a year of poverty during their lifetimes.[6]

Who's poor? Although the poor are a varied group, poverty is more common among some groups—African Americans, Hispanics, unmarried women, and inner-city residents—than among others. Figure 18.1 reports the characteristics of persons in America living below the poverty line. These characteristics are additive. Having one of these features tips the scale toward landing in poverty, two increases it further, and so on. But the nature of poverty in America has changed in the last few decades.

When Ida May Fuller received the first Social Security check, poverty was largely—not entirely—a problem for older Americans. For decades, though, the constant

Estimates vary, but most experts believe that around 1 million Americans—like this man across the street from the White House—are homeless. Cuts to government programs that funded low-income housing and unemployment benefits, in addition to the deinstitutionalization of the mentally ill, forced thousands of people out into the streets during the 1980s.

Figure 18.1 Poverty Rates for Persons With Selected Characteristics: 1999

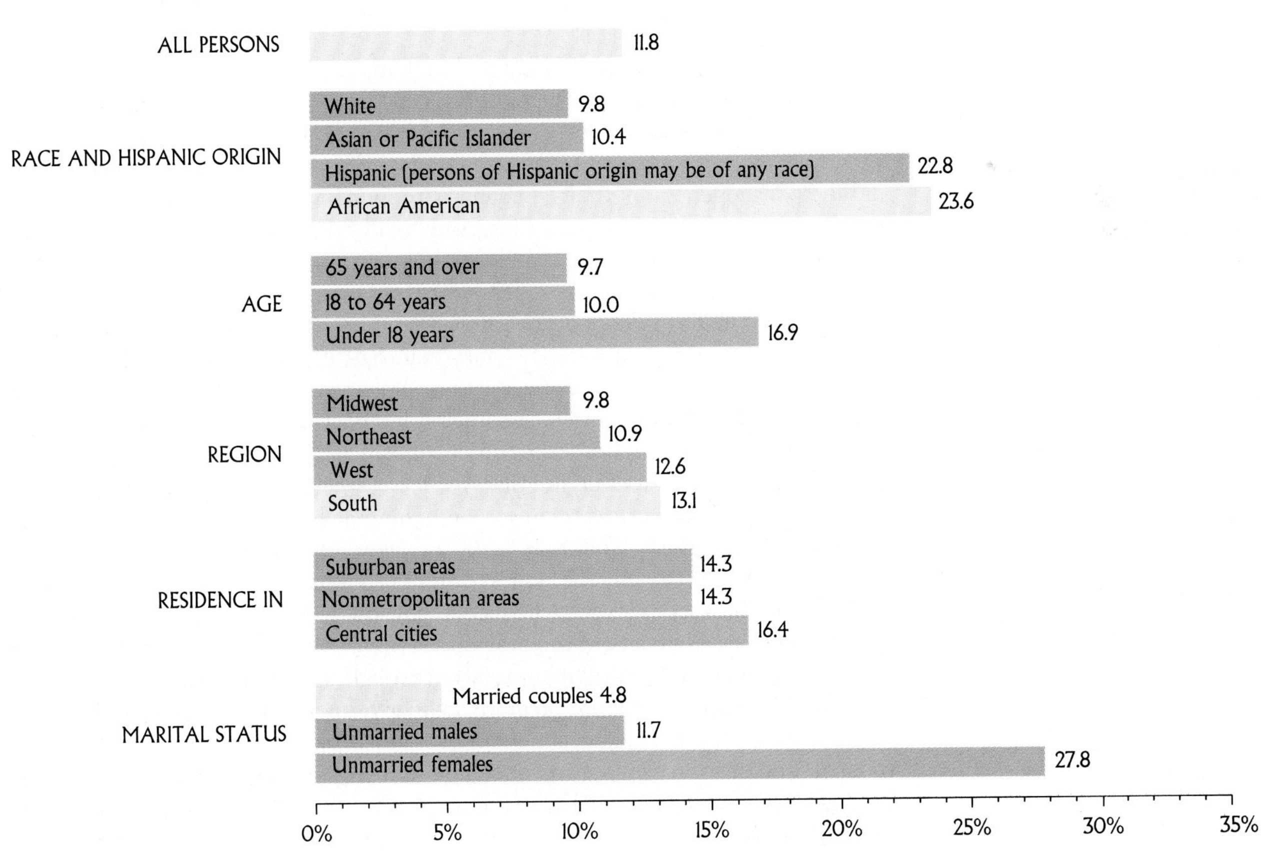

Source: U.S. Census Bureau.

expansion of the Social Security system and the increase in its benefits has significantly reduced poverty among the elderly. Unmarried women and their children now greatly outnumber the elderly among the ranks of the poor. Poverty scholar Harrell Rodgers entitled his study of contemporary poverty *Poor Women, Poor Children.*[7] Because of the high incidence of poverty among unmarried mothers and their children, experts on poverty often describe the problem today as the **feminization of poverty.** Having children out of wedlock, Rodgers says, is the "superhighway to poverty."[8] The unwed mother collecting welfare checks is among the most negative of all images of the poor. "Despite two decades of heated ideological controversy," Christopher Jencks says, "we don't know how much a father's absence (or a stepfather's presence) affects a child's social or emotional development. We do know, however, that not having a man in the house has serious economic consequences."[9]

feminization of poverty

The increasing concentration of poverty among women, especially unmarried women and their children.

What Part Does Government Play?

Conservatives and liberals in America tend to disagree on the reasons why some people are rich and others are poor. Conservatives may focus on work habits or the lack of a work ethic; liberals may point to factors beyond the ready control of individuals. One thing on which they can surely agree is this: When government spends a third of our Gross Domestic Product, it is bound to have an effect on income. Actually, politicians almost never directly debate about income distribution in America. Income distribution is hiding way off the political agenda. No party platform is likely to proclaim "If elected, we will make the rich richer and the poor poorer." Nor will one claim, "When we are elected, we will take from the rich in order to end poverty." There are two important ways in which government does indeed affect people's incomes. One is through its taxes; the other is through its expenditures.

Taxation. "Nothing," said Benjamin Franklin, "is certain in life but death and taxes." There are three general types of taxes, and each can affect citizens' incomes in a different way. A **progressive tax** takes a bigger bite from the incomes of the rich than from those of the poor; an example is charging millionaires 50 percent of their income and the poor 5 percent of theirs. Second, a **proportional tax** takes the same percentage from everyone, rich and poor alike. And finally, a **regressive tax** takes a higher percentage from those at lower income levels than from the well-to-do.

A tax is rarely advocated or defended because it is regressive, but some taxes do take a bigger bite from the poor than they do the rich. Chief among these is the sales tax from which many states derive more than half their revenues. A sales tax looks proportional—six percent of every purchase, for example, is taxed. However, since poor families spend more of their income on the necessities subject to the tax—food, clothing, and school supplies, for example—they wind up paying a higher percent of their incomes in taxes than do the rich.

In general, federal taxes are progressive (you only have to look at the rates on your tax forms to see this). The rich send a bigger proportion of their incomes to Washington than the poor. The richest fifth of taxpayers in 1999 paid about 29.1 percent of their incomes in taxes to the federal government. The poorest fifth paid about 4.6 percent of theirs. In fact, if you are poor enough, you can get money back from the government in lieu of paying income tax. Through the **Earned Income Tax Credit (EITC)**, the poorest of the poor receive a check from Washington instead of sending one. The EITC is a special tax benefit for working people who earn very low incomes. In 2000, workers who were raising one child in their home and had family incomes of less than $26,928 could get an EITC of up to $2,312. If Ms. Smith worked all or part of the year, but still remained poor and owed $660 in taxes, the Internal Revenue Service would refund her $660 and send her an additional check as well. The EITC may have done as much to alleviate poverty as all the other policy programs tried by the federal government.

progressive tax

A tax by which the government takes a greater share of the **income** of the rich than of the poor—for example, when a rich family pays 50 percent of its income in taxes and a poor family pays 5 percent.

proportional tax

A tax by which the government takes the same share of income from everyone, rich and poor alike—for example, when a rich family pays 20 percent and a poor family pays 20 percent.

regressive tax

A tax in which the burden falls relatively more heavily upon low-income groups than upon wealthy taxpayers. The opposite of a **progressive tax,** in which tax rates increase as income increases.

Earned Income Tax Credit

A "negative income tax" that provides income to very poor individuals in lieu of charging them federal income taxes.

Poverty in America is concentrated among a few groups. More than one-third of single parent, female-headed families, for example, live below the poverty line.

The main question about the effect of taxes on income is their net effect: The progressive federal tax compensates for regressive state taxes. Political scientist Benjamin Page demonstrated that the two cancel one another out, leaving the net effect of taxes on people's incomes, or **tax incidence**, in the United States proportional.[10]

tax incidence

The proportion of income a particular group pays in taxes.

Government Expenditures. The second way government can affect personal income is through the expenditure side of the ledger. Each year billions of government checks are mailed from federal computers to Social Security beneficiaries, retired government employees, veterans, and others. The government also provides "in kind" benefits, something with cash value that is not cash itself, such as food stamps, for example. A little more than 18 million people got food stamps in 1999 (down from 26.6 million in 1995). A low-interest loan for a college education is another in kind benefit. Together these benefits are called **transfer payments;** they transfer money from the federal treasury *directly* to individuals.

visual literacy
Where The Money Goes...

transfer payments

Benefits given by the government directly to individuals. Transfer payments may be either cash transfers, such as Social Security payments and retirement payments to former government employees, or in-kind transfers, such as food stamps and low-interest loans for college education.

The biggest chunk of transfer payments goes to elderly and other recipients of Social Security. The next biggest cut goes to Medicare payments (see the next chapter for a discussion of Medicare). The expansion of payments to the elderly has gone a long way in turning the elderly from one of our poorest groups to a group whose income is above average.

Table 18.2 summarizes the major government social welfare programs that affect our incomes. Social Security and Medicare are the two major entitlement programs. They are also the most costly social welfare programs. Unemployment payments also count as entitlement programs. Companies and their employees pay into these social insurance programs to provide income in case of job loss. The other programs are means tested and are available only to the poor or the very poor.

The Evolution of American Social Welfare Programs

For centuries, societies considered family welfare a private concern. Children were to be nurtured by their parents and, in turn, later nurture them in their old age. When children cast off their parents or when parents let their children go hungry, significant

Table 18.2 The Major Social Welfare Programs

PROGRAM	DESCRIPTION	BENEFICIARIES	FUNDING
The Entitlement Programs:			
Social Security	monthly payments; entitlement program	retired or disabled people and surviving members of their families	payroll tax on employees and employers
Medicare (Part A)	partial payment of cost of hospital care; entitlement	retired and disabled people	payroll taxes on employees and employers
Medicare (Part B)	voluntary program of medical insurance (pays physicians); entitlement	persons 65 or over and disabled Social Security beneficiaries	beneficiaries pay premiums
Unemployment Insurance (UI)	weekly payments; benefits vary by state; entitlement	workers who have been laid off and cannot find work	taxes on employers; states determine benefits
The Means-Tested Programs:			
Medicaid	medical and hospital aid; means-tested	the very poor	federal grants to state health programs
Food Stamps	coupons that can be used to buy food; means-tested	people whose income falls below a certain level	general federal revenues
Temporary Assistance to Needy Families (TANF)	payment; means-tested	families with children, either one-parent families or, in some states, two-parent families where the breadwinner is unemployed	paid partly by states and partly by the federal government
Supplementary Security Income (SSI)	cash payments; means-tested	elderly, blind, or disabled people whose income is below a certain amount	general federal revenues

social pressure was often enough to make people accept their proper family responsibilities. Governments took little responsibility for feeding and clothing the poor or anyone else. The life of the poor in America and elsewhere was grim almost beyond our imagining. In England, governments passed Poor Laws intended, historians argue, to make the life of the poor so miserable that people would do almost anything to avoid the specter, disgrace, and agony of poverty.[11] It was scarcely better in the United States.

After the turn of the century, however, America and other industrialized societies recognized the breakdown in these family-based support networks. With the growth of large, depersonalized cities and the requirements of the urban workplace, the old ways of thinking about the problems of the elderly and the poor seemed inadequate. The government was impelled to take a more active role in social welfare support. As with other major policy changes in America, these changes in the patterns of government support for the needy were incremental in nature, with key breakthroughs in policy direction coming at times of particular societal need or crisis.

The origins of social policies in America were, Theda Skocpol has argued, found in the pensions given to Civil War veterans and their families. Parties were eager to glean votes from these large and popular groups. By 1910, about 29 percent of American men (and many women) were receiving government pensions. At this time, the Civil War pensions consumed a hefty one-fifth to one-third of federal government expenditures.[12] Other countries were also adopting social welfare policies. The first major social welfare system began in Germany in the 1880s. Then, as now, social policy could be a way for a party to win votes. The Civil War veterans were generally happy to vote for the Republicans who brought them their pensions. Today's elderly are vigilant about keeping their social security payments growing, too.

The Evolution of Social Welfare Policy

No event has shaped American social welfare policy more than the Great Depression. Franklin Roosevelt's Administration initiated hundreds of New Deal programs in its efforts to help citizens like these jobless men. Government spending on social welfare has continued to grow, even during the Reagan Administration.

The New Deal and the Elderly

After the onset of the Great Depression in 1929, many Americans began to think that governments should do more to protect their citizens against the consequences of economic downturns.[13] External circumstances far beyond the control of individuals or their families began to be seen as major contributors to short- and long-term poverty and need. In 1935, the federal government responded to this change by passing one of the most significant pieces of social welfare legislation of all time—the Social Security Act. This act brought government into the equation of one generation's obligations to another. Never would middle-class family choices be quite the same. Adults could put their own children, instead of their parents, first.

The Social Security system works like this: Government taxes workers and their employers a percent of the employee's income up to a maximum. Both employee and employer contributions are paid into the Social Security Trust Fund. The Trust Fund keeps collecting money from workers, but begins to pay out when each worker retires. As long as there is more money paid in than going out, the Trust Fund stays in the black.

Later, in 1965, when the federal government adopted Medicare, adults were also freed from paying for their parents' medical expenses. Thus, the post-1965 generation of adults was the first to be substantially free of the ancient obligation of caring for its parents as well as for its children. "Substantially free" does not, of course, mean that millions of Americans have not dutifully filled in gaps left by Social Security or Medicare. The burden, though, is no longer theirs alone, for government benefits provide a crucial cushion.

President Johnson and the Great Society

In the 1960s, America experienced an outpouring of federal programs to help the poor and the elderly, to create economic opportunities for those at the lower rungs of the economic ladder, and to reduce discrimination against minorities. Many of these programs were established during the presidency of Lyndon B. Johnson (1963–1969), whose administration coined the term "The Great Society" for these policy initiatives. Johnson was a policy entrepreneur, initiating antipoverty programs, community development programs, Medicare, school-aid schemes, job-retraining programs, and a host of other public programs. Johnson declared a "war on poverty." During this period, government revenues were still growing and budget deficits were low. Although the Vietnam War eventually drained funds from Johnson's Great Society, many of the programs Ronald Reagan later railed against were set in place during the Johnson period. Richard Nixon, Johnson's Republican successor, carried on and even expanded many of them, as did Presidents Ford and Carter.

Many people believed that poverty was closely tied to race issues, and many of those who resisted desegregation also fought against antipoverty programs that were thought to disproportionately benefit racial minorities. In addition, the ability of the poor and their supporters to form strong political bases from which to demand government help was limited. Compared to the elderly, poor people were less organized and had lower turnout rates at the polls. On the positive side, minorities and the poor were becoming a more important constituency in the Democratic Party, which was beginning to pay more attention to the electoral demands of these groups.

Perhaps the most important element for the success of both program types, however, was strong presidential leadership. Making important changes in social welfare programs usually requires strong presidential commitment, and President Johnson provided it. He made these programs a centerpiece of his administration and worked to rally the Congress, public opinion, and major interest groups behind him. It is impossible to overestimate the role of political leadership, particularly by the president, in building the public and political coalitions needed to support new program initiatives in the area of social welfare policy. It was the active leadership of a subsequent president, Ronald Reagan, that helped build coalitions to move American social welfare programs in a different direction.

President Reagan and Limits to the Great Society

Unlike Presidents Nixon, Ford, and Carter—who largely accepted and even expanded some portions of the programs initiated by Johnson—President Reagan took a very different approach. The growing demands of defense spending and entitlement programs for the elderly had increased government deficits and threatened to stifle economic growth. Public support for some welfare programs was eroding, particularly among members of the traditional Democratic coalition. The working class and the middle- and upper-income groups were seeing their incomes threatened and were looking for places to cut government expenditures. It was possible, therefore, for Republicans to make some headway into the Democratic Party's constituency by taking a more restrictive stand on social welfare programs.

One thing that had not changed was the vulnerability of the poor. Their group bases of support were still smaller than those of the elderly—the poor were limited to the Democratic Party, which was becoming more divided on support for poverty and social welfare programs, and the poor's representation in the interest group system was as weak as ever. The elderly still had bipartisan support and strong electoral and interest group bases.

Just as in the Johnson era, the major actor was the president. In this case, President Reagan chose to target poverty programs as one major way to cut government spending. This action was consistent with his own ideological beliefs in less government and more self-sufficiency. The president set the tone, rallied public opinion, and worked to create congressional coalitions to support these efforts.

The Omnibus Budget Reconciliation Act (OBRA) of 1981 initiated many of the cuts President Reagan had sought. For example, OBRA included substantial cuts estimated to be about 14 percent in the AFDC program. These cuts resulted in an AFDC

In 1965, President Lyndon Johnson signed Medicare legislation into law. This program, which helps older Americans with their medical expenses, was first proposed more than a decade earlier by former President Harry Truman (right), who was invited to the signing.

caseload reduction of about 12 percent, with many who remained on the rolls receiving lower benefits.[14]

In this and subsequent policy battles, Democratic leaders in Congress worked to limit these cuts. The growth rates of many programs were reduced, benefits were slashed, program burdens were shifted to the states, and many previously eligible recipients were removed from the rolls. Still, the basic outlines of the original programs persisted throughout the Reagan and Bush Administrations. Ironically, it was not until a Democratic president committed to welfare reform was elected that a major overhaul of the welfare system was enacted.

Drawing by Dana Fardon; ©1992 *The New Yorker Magazine,* Inc.

Making a Difference: Welfare Reform

Welfare Reform in the 1990s

In the 1992 presidential election campaign, Bill Clinton promised to "end welfare as we know it," by providing two years of support—training, child care, and health care—in exchange for an agreement to return to work. The congressional Republican Party was even more enthusiastic about welfare reform than the new president. In 1994 Newt Gingrich, the new Republican Speaker of the House, launched a war not on poverty but on poverty programs. In August of 1996 the president and the congressional Republicans completed a welfare reform bill that received almost unanimous backing among congressional Republicans but that was opposed by half of congressional Democrats. The law bore the lofty name of the Personal Responsibility and Work Opportunity Reconciliation Act. The major provisions of this bill were: (1) each state would receive a *fixed* amount of money to run its own welfare programs, (2) people on welfare would have to find work within two years or lose all their benefits, and (3) a lifetime maximum of five years on welfare was set. Opponents of the bill expressed fears that these changes would push at least a million innocent children into poverty; proponents countered by asserting that millions would be lifted out of the culture of dependency and given the incentive to make something of their lives.

Symbolically, the welfare reform policies also changed the name of "welfare as we knew it." Cash payments to poor families were once called Aid to Families With Dependent Children (AFDC). After welfare reform, they were known as **Temporary Assistance to Needy Families** (TANF), today's name for the means-tested aid for the poorest of the poor. TANF benefits like AFDC are small and declining. The average recipient family collects about $363 monthly in TANF benefits.

Temporary Assistance to Needy Families

Once called "Aid to Families With Dependent Children," the new name for public assistance to needy families.

A hotly debated question has been how the revamped system will work now that the welfare safety net no longer exists to catch someone who has failed to find a job after being on welfare for two years. Between the Act's signing in 1996 until 2000, the number of welfare recipients declined from 12.2 million to 5.8 million, a drop of 53 percent. The Welfare Reform law stipulated that adults must be working in no fewer than 25 percent of the families on welfare, or else states would be subject to financial penalties at the start of 1999. Most states met this target, with the nationwide data showing that 28 percent of adults on the welfare rolls were engaged in some sort of

Crime, drugs, and poverty are a part of life for the urban underclass. Slogans like "just say no," which assume that addictions and other problems can be changed by a simple change in attitude, seem meaningless in the face of hostile urban environments dominated by gangs.

work activity by the end of 1998. Proponents of the reforms point to these figures as proof that the new system is working as intended. Opponents of these changes argue that the decline in the welfare rolls is due to the strong economic growth of recent years and warn of impending disaster the next time a recession strikes. Assessing which side proves to be right will be a key question in social welfare policymaking for years to come.[15]

Why does it matter?

Has the Welfare Reform Act of 1996 really "ended welfare as we know it," as President Clinton promised it would, or is it merely a minor change in the system? How do you think people who have been on welfare in recent years have reacted to the change? If you or a family member were at risk of poverty, would government assistance be a "handout" or a "helping hand"?

The Future of Social Welfare Policy

Political campaigns and congressional debates have increasingly focused on social welfare policy programs. The major point of disagreement concerns the extent to which social welfare programs work. Paying for social programs is the most expensive thing government does in America. Once "off limits" to politicians, even the future of Social Security is on the political agenda. Once Lyndon Johnson and Congress could enthusiastically endorse a "war on poverty." Today, critics say, we are launching a "war on the poor" instead.

The Entitlement Programs: Living on Borrowed Time?

The long-term sustainability of entitlement programs, particularly Social Security and Medicare, is a matter of much current debate. Indeed, as it stands now, the Social Security program is living on borrowed time. The Social Security Administration can make some very precise estimates. Here's the math. As the number of retirees grows, and their average benefit is constantly increased to cover the cost of living (called a Cost of Living Allowance), Social Security expenditures are going to increase. The more retirements and the more benefits, the higher the costs. At some point—about 2038 unless something changes—payouts will exceed income. Technically the Social Security system will be bankrupt. If this happens, Congress would have to use regular appropriations to pay out benefits to claimants as they retired. If taxes were not raised, a dollar, which would have gone to the military or the national parks, would have to be diverted to the retirees. Commission after commission, congressional committee after congressional committee, and expert after expert have concluded that the math doesn't lie.[16] No solution is a politically pleasant one. Cutting benefits to retirees is no more popular than raising taxes on working contributors. Hard choices lie ahead.

Like a sleeping giant, the issue of Social Security awoke in the election of 2000. Governor George W. Bush and the Republicans proposed diverting a small portion (the suggested figure was two percent) of Social Security contributions to private retirement funds. Each individual could, presumably, reduce his or her contribution to the Social Security system and instead put the money into a private account, a stock, a bond, or another investment. Chile, Great Britain, Australia, Poland, and Brazil have done just that. Democrats feared just what Franklin Roosevelt warned about, that some "damn politicians" were about to scrap the nearly sacred Social Security program. The problem, the Democrats emphasized, was that permitting people to divert money from the system, even for good reason, would merely hasten its bankruptcy.

The Means-Tested Programs: Do They Work?

The future of means-tested programs for the poor is another matter. Antipoverty programs have never been remotely as popular as programs for the elderly. The evidence that Social Security has lifted the elderly out of poverty is powerful. The evidence that

How You Can Make a Difference

Social Security Reform

Look at your last paycheck. Notice that line titled "FICA" with the comparatively large amount of money underneath it? That's your contribution to the Social Security Administration. Considering the increasingly larger percentage of people's income diverted to this federal program, the future of Social Security should be of vital interest to today's younger college students. Everyone agrees that the Social Security Administration requires reform in order to remain solvent when today's youth reach retirement age. There is little agreement, however, on exactly what kind of reform is needed.

One increasingly visible proposal advocated by Republicans as well as some Democrats is the partial privatization of Social Security funds. By privatization, this plan's advocates call for a small portion of the program's funds to be invested in private enterprise and the stock market. The Cato Institute, a venerable libertarian think tank, clearly states its opposition to the current trend and looks for more creative solutions. Their proposal at www.socialsecurity.org, similar to George W. Bush's campaign in 2000, looks beyond establishing mere solvency of the Social Security program and toward privatization. Individuals should be given a choice of investments while still keeping current beneficiaries' checks flowing.

Others, including most Democrats and progressive liberals, find this privatization too risky. The New Century Alliance for Social Security is an advocacy organization comprised of a broad coalition of labor groups (NEA and AFL-CIO), liberal academics, civil rights organizations, feminists, and environmentalists. Associated with this coalition, the Campaign for America's Future (www.ourfuture.org) distributes a handbook for antiprivatization advocates and a "Sign the Pledge" campaign to uncover which candidates oppose privatization of Social Security and Medicare. Also a member of the New Century Alliance, X-PAC (www.x-pac.org) targets college students and "Generation X" youth devoted to preserving Social Security protections for their generation. Rather than put forward any radical plans of their own, most of these progressive groups advocate spending budget surpluses on financing the Social Security system in order to maintain current benefits without changes that could hurt lower income and disabled Americans.

The future of this debate is undecided. You can enter this still fluid debate by joining one of these organizations, writing letters, and attending town hall meetings. Remember that FICA line on your next paycheck!

antipoverty programs have lifted the poor out of poverty is mixed at best. In one complex but important study, Reynolds and Smolensky tried to assess the impact of both taxes and expenditures on income distribution and concluded that government spending and taxing did little to make incomes more equal.[17] Equally disturbing, the actual incidence of poverty—the percentage of Americans below Mollie Orshansky's poverty line—has remained fairly constant since Lyndon Johnson first declared war on poverty in 1964.

Conservative economist Charles Murray has offered an influential and provocative argument that the social welfare programs of the Great Society and later administrations not only failed to curb the advance of poverty, but actually made the situation worse.[18] The problem, Murray maintained, was that these public policies discouraged the poor from solving their problems. He contended that the programs made it profitable to be poor, and discouraged people from pursuing means by which they could rise out of poverty. For example, Murray pointed out that poor couples could obtain more benefits if they weren't married; thus most would not marry, a decision that leads to further disintegration of the family.

Many scholars, however, have strongly criticized Murray's arguments and the program cuts emanating from them. Political scientist Arnold Vedlitz has argued that "the conservatives exaggerate both the expectations and intentions of the programs and denigrate their accomplishments. . . . The reality of these programs is that they were never designed to end poverty, presidential rhetoric to the contrary."[19] In a separate challenge to Murray's position, economists David Ellwood and Lawrence Summers showed not only that spending for the poor was relatively limited in these

You Are the Policymaker

Should Welfare Recipients Be Allowed To Save for Their Education?

Sandra Rosado of New Haven, Conn., had known poverty most of her young life, but she was determined to go to college. The oldest of eight children, she saved every dollar she could from her part-time job after school at a neighborhood community center. As one might expect, Sandra's mother was very proud of her. Sandra seemed well on her way to providing for herself rather than ending up on welfare like her mother.

When state officials became aware of Sandra's college savings, however, it soon became a bureaucratic nightmare for the Rosado family. For years the family had received welfare support from the Aid to Families With Dependent Children (AFDC)—now TANF—program. But because of Sandra's $4,900 bank account, welfare officials told them they were no longer eligible for welfare payments (federal law stipulates that recipients must not have liquid assets of over $1,000). Without the means to support her eight children, Mrs. Rosado asked if there were some way to get around this problem. The easiest way, she was told, was simply for Sandra to spend the money immediately. Rather than spending her money on a college education, Sandra ended up buying clothes, jewelry, shoes, and perfume.

The case of Sandra Rosado presents a difficult problem for policymakers. The rationale for the rule concerning assets is that the government should not be supporting people who have the means to support themselves. But to discourage poor people from saving for things like a college education only makes it more likely that they will continue indefinitely on the public dole. Critics thus charge that the rule is counterproductive in that it punishes welfare recipients when they exercise personal initiative and responsibility. They propose that welfare families be allowed to set up special bank accounts to be used only for educational purposes.

Assume the role of the policymaker. Should people on TANF be allowed to save money for purposes such as education, which will help them break their dependency on welfare? When you ponder this question, consider how a working-class family living from paycheck to paycheck might feel knowing that its tax dollars are going to support people with money in the bank. In addition to trying to provide the right incentives to people on welfare, there are also questions of fairness to all citizens involved in such a policy decision.

Sandra Rosado

programs but also that economic growth and recessions were responsible for much of the movement into and out of poverty during the post-1965 period.[20] Scholars such as Ellwood and Summers are much more likely to conclude that the Great Society programs contributed to easing the shocks to the American economic and social system caused by international oil crises, deindustrialization of the American economy, and increased foreign economic competition. Their position is that the poor would have been much worse off were it not for LBJ's safety net programs.

For those looking for the "right" answer, the evidence is clearly mixed. Scholars disagree on how beneficial the programs were and are. One of the soundest assessments comes from economist Rebecca Blank who warns about the fight on poverty: "Don't declare success too quickly." Very likely no one single strategy—the war on poverty, income subsidies, the Earned Income Tax Credit, welfare reform—can claim the credit for improving poverty. Having a strong economy is also a powerful help to the poor.[21]

Social Welfare Policy Elsewhere

The future of social welfare policies is just as complex and controversial in other democratic countries. Most industrial nations not only provide social policy benefits but also are usually more generous with them than the U.S. government. The scope of social benefits in health, child care, parental leave, unemployment compensation, and benefits to the elderly are far greater in European nations than in ours. Europeans often think of their countries as "welfare states," with all the generous benefits—and staggering taxes by U.S. standards—that this implies.

Other national governments and their citizens often take quite a different approach to the problems of poverty and social welfare. Americans tend to see poverty and social welfare needs as individual rather than governmental concerns, whereas European nations tend to support greater governmental responsibility for these problems. Also, Europeans often have a more positive attitude toward government, whereas Americans are more likely to distrust government action in areas such as social welfare policy.

Most Americans would be amazed at the range of social benefits in the average European country. French parents, for example, are guaranteed the right to put their toddlers in *crèches* (what we would call day care centers), regardless of whether the parents are rich or poor, at work or at home. French unemployment benefits are generous by American standards (and French unemployment rates are two to three times higher than ours). In many European countries, treatments at health spas come with free or low-cost government health care policies. For example, see America in Perspective, "Parental Leave Here and in Western Europe."

Still, there are huge costs to these generous welfare programs. Taxes commensurate with the benefits of social policy are common in Western European nations, where taxes far exceed those in the United States (see Chapter 14). Japan is the only nation with a developed economy that spends a smaller proportion of its Gross Domestic Product on social policies than does the United States, in part because the family's traditional role of supporting the elderly is still commonplace in Japan. Income taxes in European countries approach (or even exceed) 50 percent.

As in the United States, there has been a backlash against the welfare state in Europe. Margaret Thatcher was prime minister of Great Britain while Ronald Reagan was the American president. Like Reagan, she tried hard to roll back welfare benefits and cut taxes. Other countries have also experimented with privatization of social security in whole or in part. Chile took the lead in 1981, requiring every worker to invest at least 10 percent of his or her wages in a tax-free investment account; retirement funds piled up to $30 billion by 1999, but lost 25 percent of their value in a Chilean stock market crash. People and governments all around the world continue to debate social policy.

Understanding Social Welfare Policy

Discussing and debating social welfare policies is a very difficult task in a capitalist, democratic political system. Very few issues divide liberals and conservatives more sharply. Americans struggle to balance individual merit and the rewards of initiative with the reality of systemic inequalities and the need to provide support to many. Citizens disagree on how much government can or should do to even out the competition and protect those who are less able to compete.

Democracy and Social Welfare

There is an extensive social welfare system in every major democracy. Ours, in fact, is the least extensive of all. As with other policies, competing demands have to be resolved by government decision makers, but decision makers do not act in a vacuum. They are aligned with and pay allegiance to various groups in society. These groups include members of their legislative constituencies, members of their electoral coalitions, and members of their political party. Many of these

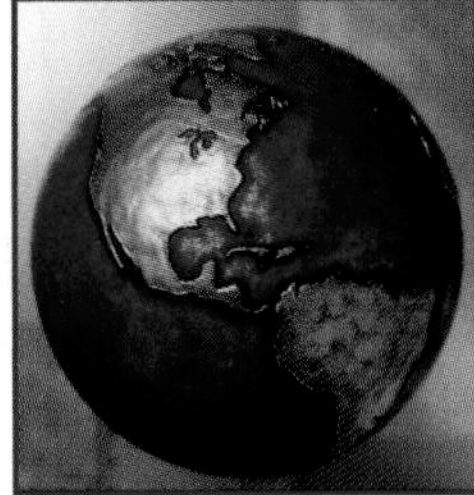

America in Perspective

Family Policies Here and in Western Europe

American politicians, liberal or conservative, rarely make a speech without talking about their commitment to "family values." This fuzzy phrase can mean many different things to many different people (perhaps that's why they say it). But Americans and Western Europeans have sharply different views about family policy. Every European country provides for generous (by U.S. standards) child care, usually at state expense. Parents can take *paid* leaves from their jobs to spend time with young children.

In the United States it took a major political struggle to permit *unpaid* leave for parents to tend to children or other family needs. One of the first laws passed under the Clinton Administration was the Family and Medical Leave Act. This law requires employers with 50 or more employees to provide workers with up to 12 weeks of unpaid leave for the birth or adoption of a child or for the illness of a close family member. To qualify, a person must have worked for the employer for at least a year and worked at least 1,250 hours during that year. However, an employer can deny unpaid leave to a worker who is among the company's top 10 percent in salary and whose leave would result in "substantial and grievous economic injury" to the business. President Clinton hailed the Family and Medical Leave Act as a landmark piece of legislation, whereas the majority of Republicans denounced it as yet another example of intrusive government.

This is what you could expect in some European countries if you wanted to take parental leave:

- **Belgium:** Three months of full-time leave or six months of part-time leave until the child is four. Payment of $482 a month during the leave.
- **Italy:** Ten months leave any time until the child is eight. The leave is extended by one month if the father takes at least three months. Pay is equivalent to 30 percent of earnings during the leave.
- **France:** Full-time leave until the child is three. For two or more children, the payment is $439 a month.
- **Norway:** Fifty-six weeks of full-time leave at 80 percent of earnings or 42 weeks of leave at full earnings.
- **Germany:** Full-time leave until the child is three. Payment of $292 a month until the child is two.

In the United States, about two of every three mothers with small children work. Even with larger employers, the best you can do in the United States is to get a short stint of unpaid leave. Child care policies here are thin in comparison to child care policies in Western European countries.

Source: The information on other countries' programs is reported in *USA Today*, July 12, 2000, 12A.

groups provide the financial assistance that the decision makers need to seek and retain political office.

In the social welfare policy arena, the competing groups are often quite unequal in terms of political resources. For example, the elderly are relatively well organized and often have the resources needed to wield significant influence in support of programs they desire. As a result, they are usually successful in protecting and expanding their programs. For the poor, however, influencing political decisions is more difficult. They vote less frequently and lack strong, focused organizations and money.

Although government benefits are difficult to obtain, especially for the poor, the nature of democratic politics also makes it difficult to withdraw them once they are established. Policymaking in the United States is very incremental in nature. Once put in place, policies develop a life of their own. They engage supporters in the public, in Congress, in the bureaucracy, and among key interest groups.

Tremendous pressures come from these supporters to keep or expand programs and to preserve them from elimination. These pressures persist even when the size and costs of programs seem to have grown beyond anything anyone might have originally envisioned. Despite a succession of presidents who have talked about the need for cuts in welfare, government now spends a larger share of the gross domestic product on social welfare policies than it did during the Johnson Administration in the 1960s.

Career Profile

Position: District Manager of Social Security Administration
Salary Range: $73,000-91,000
Benefits: Outstanding scholar recruitment, health benefits, retirement plan, flexible scheduling
Qualifications: Bachelor's degree, U.S. citizen, strong interpersonal and time management skills, and problem-solving ability

Real People on the Job: Gary Rehahn

Gary Rehahn works as the district manager for the Social Security office in Quincy, Ill. Because they oversee claims representatives, district managers must understand the system from all angles. Claims representatives meet with the public to explain eligibility requirements and to assist those applying for benefits. Most often, claims representatives must determine whether or not to approve a person's claim after examining evidence including wage earning records. Applicants include not only the better-known retirees and their survivors under Title II of the Social Security Act but also those applying under the Title XVI Supplemental Security Income program for aged, blind, or disabled persons. Because the federal government frequently modifies Social Security programs including the recent Senior Citizens' Freedom to Work Act, a nimble mind is required to keep up with these changes.

Being a manager within the Social Security Administration carries with it more than all the expected tasks of balancing use of resources and staff to provide efficient service. Thousands of people literally depend upon the effective function of his office to live from month to month. When older beneficiaries can no longer deal with benefits on their own, Gary and his claims representatives must search for a representative payee to ensure that money is distributed appropriately. Gary describes the job as one part lawyer, one part social worker, and one part accountant. In addition, Gary views his responsibilities as not only to current beneficiaries but also to all future applicants as well. If Gary and his workers do not get out and tell low-income, disabled, or elderly people about their eligibility for Social Security, often these people go without food or shelter. Thus he also acts as a public relations director within his region by working with local radio and television stations to educate potential applicants.

With 65,000 employees, the Social Security Administration is always looking for applicants, likely within your own region—either rural or urban. Like Gary, you will begin as a claims representative, the typical starting position for recent college graduates, starting at a salary of $22,819 and within four years rising to $46,018. Gary describes this four-year period as an apprenticeship. With a disproportionately high number of Social Security employees expected to retire within the next few years, Social Security will be needing many apprentices. The potential for advancement is high, especially considering that Social Security must expand to keep pace with the soon to be retiring Baby Boomer population. As the Baby Boomers grow older, so do the demand for services and for more claims representatives and managers. Increasingly, experts in the computer field are being sought out as well. While it's not an easy job, it is a rewarding and challenging job for college graduates interested in social welfare and social services.

For more information, see www.ssa.gov for information about the nearest regional office.

Social Welfare Policy and the Scope of Government

Conflicts and compromises over social welfare policy have given Americans a huge bureaucracy at all levels of government. Fifty years ago, the most important explanation for the growth of government was the need for a strong national defense. Today the explanation is the soaring cost of social programs. What is true in the United States is also true in every other democratic country: Government has gotten bigger as social welfare costs have grown. In part, this is because Americans and people elsewhere are simply living longer. Nearly a century ago, governments first committed themselves to relieving the family of some of the burden of the elderly. Benefits once given are not easily whittled back.

Large government programs, whether in the area of national defense or social welfare, require large organizations to administer them. The appropriate way to evaluate these administrative systems is not to focus on their scope or expense alone but rather to weigh these factors against the conduct of their mission, the goals and accomplishments of their programs, and the extent to which private, nongovernmental entities could realistically be depended on to help. Clearly, these are questions on which well-intentioned people can come to quite different conclusions.

Summary

There are two distinct paths our social policies have taken. First are the entitlement policies, dominated by Social Security and Medicare. In the United States, we spend more money on federal entitlements than on any other single thing the government does. Rich or poor, Americans are entitled to Social Security benefits by law. The other road includes the means-tested programs, government's expenditures for poorer Americans.

You have seen in this chapter that government action and inaction can play a major role in affecting the social welfare status of many poor and elderly Americans. Entitlement programs such as Social Security and Medicare have significantly improved the lot of the elderly, but these very costly programs threaten to grow ever larger and more expensive. Programs aimed more specifically at the poor cost less (and perhaps have accomplished less), but they seem likely to remain objects of political controversy for many years to come.

Social welfare programs, like other government policies, evolve slowly over time. Although there have been important watershed events and policies, such as Social Security in 1935 and the Great Society in the late 1960s, much of the growth and change in American social welfare policies has been incremental in nature, building on past policies, adding a little here, taking a little there.

As the century turned, social welfare policies were under fire more than any period since the New Deal. A Democratic president and a Republican Congress had already reformed welfare. Social Security seemed ripe for reassessment. Election 2000 saw the first debate in generations about the future of Social Security. Those debates will not be settled soon or easily.

Key Terms

social welfare policies
entitlement programs
means-tested programs
income distribution
income
wealth
poverty line
feminization of poverty
progressive tax
proportional tax
regressive tax
tax incidence
Earned Income Tax Credit
transfer payments
Temporary Assistance to Needy Families

For Further Reading

Blank, Rebecca. *It Takes a Nation: A New Agenda for Fighting Poverty.* Princeton NJ: Princeton University Press, 1998. One of the nation's most distinguished economists examines poverty.

Cook, Fay Lomax, and Edith J. Barrett. *Support for the American Welfare State.* New York: Columbia University Press, 1992. A comprehensive review of public opinion about social welfare.

Gilens, Martin. *Why Americans Hate Welfare: Race, Media, and the Politics of Antipoverty Policy.* Chicago: University of Chicago Press, 1999. Gilens argues that public opposition to welfare is fed by a combination of racial stereotypes and lack of information about the true nature of America's poor.

Handler, Joel F. *The Poverty of Welfare Reform.* New Haven, CT: Yale University Press, 1995. Handler exposes numerous myths regarding the welfare system and presents evidence to argue that past attempts to reform welfare have proved both ineffective and misguided.

Kelso, William A. *Poverty and the Underclass: Changing Perceptions of the Poor in America.* New York: New York University Press, 1994. An excellent analysis of the supporting evidence for numerous approaches to dealing with poverty.

Levy, Frank. *The New Dollars and Dreams: American Incomes and Economic Change.* New York: Russell Sage, 1999. A good review of recent data on income inequality.

Murray, Charles. *Losing Ground: American Social Policy, 1950–1980.* New York: Basic Books, 1984. A classic conservative argument that social policies have not worked and have actually made things worse.

Olasky, Marvin. *The Tragedy of Human Compassion.* Washington, D.C.: Regnery, 1992. Olasky is the guru of "compassionate conservatism," which George W. Bush used as a campaign slogan in 2000.

Patterson, James T. *America's Struggle Against Poverty, 1900–1994.* Cambridge, MA: Harvard University Press, 1994. A good review of the history of governmental programs to combat poverty.

Rodgers, Harrell, Jr. *American Poverty in a New Era of Reform.* New York: M.E. Sharpe, 2000. Discusses what has happened to poverty since the welfare reforms.

Schieber, Sylvester J., and John B. Shoven. *The Real Deal: The History and Future of Social Security.* New Haven CT: Yale University Press, 2000. An excellent analysis of the past, present, and future of Social Security.

Sharp, Elaine B. *The Sometime Connection: Public Opinion and Social Policy.* Albany, NY: SUNY Press, 1999. Investigates the complex links between public opinion and public policy.

Skocpol, Theda. *Social Policy in the United States.* Princeton, NJ: Princeton University Press, 1995. Skocpol takes a historical approach to social welfare programs.

Vedlitz, Arnold. *Conservative Mythology and Public Policy in America.* New York: Praeger, 1988. A good counterweight to Murray.

Wilson, William J. *When Work Disappears: The World of the Urban Poor.* New York: Knopf, 1996. Wilson has studied the urban underclass and the poorest of the poor.

Internet Resources

www.census.gov/hhes/www/poverty.html
Reports about poverty made available by the Census Bureau.

www.apwa.org
A good source of up-to-date information, articles and links about the progress of welfare reform from the American Public Welfare Association.

www.Heritage.org
The conservative Heritage Foundation provides a critique of the Census Bureau data on income distribution and poverty.

www.ssa.gov
The official site of the Social Security Administration, where you can learn about the history of the program and its current status.

www.welfare.info.com
The "Green Book" published every two years by the House Committee on Ways and Means, containing statistical information on all social welfare programs.

Notes

1. Sylvester J. Schieber and John B. Shoven, *The Real Deal: The History and Future of Social Security* (New Haven. CT: Yale University Press, 1999), chap. 7. The Ida May Fuller story is also from Schieber and Shoven.
2. Andrew Hacker, *Money: Who Has How Much and Why* (New York: Scribner, 1997), 52.
3. Fay Lomax Cook and Edith Barrett, *Support for the American Welfare State* (New York: Columbia University Press, 1992), 212.
4. Martin Gilens, "Race Coding and White Opposition to Welfare," *American Political Science Review*, 90 (1996): 593–604.
5. Greg J. Duncan and James N. Morgan, eds., *Five Thousand American Families* (Ann Arbor: University of Michigan Institute for Social Research, 1983).
6. Mark R. Rank and Thomas A. Hirschl, "Rags of Riches? Estimating the Probabilities of Poverty and Affluence Across the Adult American Life Span," *Social Science Quarterly*, March, 2002.
7. Harrell Rodgers, *Poor Women, Poor Children*, 3rd ed., (New York: M. E. Sharpe, 1996).
8. Harrell Rodgers, *American Poverty in a New Era of Reform* (New York: M. E. Sharpe, 2000), 207.

9. Christopher Jencks, *Rethinking Social Policy* (New York: Harper Collins, 1992), 130.
10. Benjamin Page, *Who Gets What from Government?* (Berkeley: University of California Press, 1983), chap. 3.
11. See, for example, Francis Fox Piven and Richard Cloward, *Regulating the Poor* (New York: Pantheon, 1971).
12. Theda Skocpol, *Social Policy in the United States* (Princeton, NJ: Princeton University Press, 1995), 259.
13. The origins of social security during the New Deal are traced in Sylvester J. Schieber and John B. Shoven, *The Real Deal,* Part I.
14. For a more detailed discussion of the impact of OBRA on cuts in social welfare programs, see Tom Joe and Cheryl Rogers, *By the Few for the Few: The Reagan Welfare Legacy* (Lexington, MA: Lexington Books, 1985), chap. 7.
15. One early assessment of the welfare reforms is Harrell Rodgers, Jr., *American Poverty in a New Era of Reform,* chap. 8.
16. For one rare but dissenting view, which argues that the Social Security "crisis" is exaggerated, partly by people who would profit from more private investment, see Dean Baker and Mark Weisbrot, *Social Security: The Phony Crisis* (Chicago: University of Chicago Press, 2000).
17. Morgan Reynolds and Eugene Smolensky, *Public Expenditures, Taxes, and the Distribution of Income* (New York: Academic Press, 1977).
18. Charles Murray, *Losing Ground: American Social Policy, 1950–1980* (New York: Basic Books, 1984). Marvin Olasky, the guru of "compassionate conservatism," makes a similar argument in his *Tragedy of Human Compassion* (Chicago: Regnery, 1992). Doing good for people, especially through government, Olasky argues, is bad for them.
19. Arnold Vedlitz, *Conservative Mythology and Public Policy in America* (New York: Praeger, 1988), chap. 6.
20. David T. Ellwood and Lawrence H. Summers, "Is Welfare Really the Problem?" *Public Interest* 83 (Spring 1986): 57–78.
21. Rebecca Blank, "Fighting Poverty: Lessons from Recent U.S. History," *Journal of Economic Perspectives* 14 (Spring 2000): 3–20.

19 Policymaking for Health Care and the Environment

Chapter Outline

Mildred Davis almost bled to death before she finally sought medical treatment. The custodian and security guard at a community center in Austin, Texas, lost four-and-a-half pints of blood while patrolling her area. Yet she deferred going to a doctor until she could no longer stand the pain. As a result, she had an emergency hysterectomy, after which she received a hospital bill for $8,000 and a doctor's bill for $2,000.

Why would Ms. Davis wait so long for health care? The answer is straightforward: she didn't have health insurance. "When you walk into a doctor's office, the first thing they say is: 'How will you pay? What insurance do you have?' I have to go to the bank before I go to the doctor."[1]

Health care, like a clean environment, has become a necessity for every American. Yet many people lack access to quality health care just as they suffer from polluted air and water. Tremendous technological advances have created both practical and moral problems for policymakers. New

issues must be dealt with. When medical researchers develop new techniques for prolonging life, everyone is pleased. Many of these new technologies, however, are amazingly expensive, and their cost has transformed the American medical system. The rapid growth of the American economy during the twentieth century has also brought pollution problems to the forefront of politics. Americans have become increasingly sensitive to the quality of the environment, but they find it difficult to determine who should pay to clean up toxic wastes and to make trade-offs between protecting an endangered species and saving jobs.

These policy issues pose new challenges to American democracy. How does the general public affect government decisions on such technically complex issues as determining standards for clean air and regulating pesticides? Does the complexity of such issues give special interests an advantage in the policymaking process? How can citizens compete with the wealth and expertise of organized interests in a battle over health care policy? How can elected officials make decisions about storing nuclear waste when no one wants it near them?

Technological change has also altered Americans' expectations regarding the scope of government. Demands for solutions to problems such as providing access to health care and controlling pollution have greatly expanded the scope of government policies. What *should* the role of government be in ensuring access to health care for all citizens? If treatments are expensive and budgets are tight, should government intervene to allocate health care? Or should it greatly expand its role to ensure that all citizens have adequate care? Should government impose restrictions on activities in the private sector in order to protect the environment?

Technology has brought important changes to the lives of Americans, and the quickened pace of change has made policymaking more complex. This chapter examines two related areas of public policy that are important to all Americans and that have been profoundly affected by technological developments: health care and the environment.

Health Care Policy

America's health policy paradox is this: As a nation we spend a far larger share of our national resources on health than any other industrialized country yet we are far from having the healthiest population. There are few things more important to people than their health. It is often said that Americans enjoy the best health care in the world, and some do. Americans, compared to people in other countries, pay a lot for their health care. Yet it is not clear whether they always get their money's worth. Unlike other countries, we do not have a government-run health care system. Nor do we have a completely private one. The system is vast, complex, and controversial.

The Health of Americans

Although Americans are generally healthy (which is to be expected given the country's wealth), health care statistics show that they still lag behind other countries in some key health care categories (see "America in Perspective: Health Care Spending, Life Expectancy and Infant Mortality Rates"). When the World Health Organization developed a complex measure of "healthy life expectancy," the United States fell behind almost every country in Europe, as well as Canada, Australia, Israel, and Japan.[2]

The average American has a life expectancy of 76 years—a high number, but one surpassed by citizens of most other developed nations. Despite advances in medical technology the average American does not live as long as the average Canadian. This difference may be due in part to lifestyle differences among adults. But what about the *infant mortality rate*—the proportion of babies who do not survive their first year of life—a common indicator of a nation's health? The chances in the United States of a baby dying in the first year of life are more than 50 percent higher than those of a baby born in Japan. Indeed, the United States ranks only eighteenth among the world's nations in infant mortality. The health care system in the United States may be part of the explanation.

The Cost of Health Care

American health care does not come cheap. The United States spends a higher proportion of its wealth on health care than any other country. Americans now spend more than $1 *trillion* annually on health care. Health expenditures are one of the largest single components of America's economy, accounting for *one-seventh* (14 percent) of the GDP. Canada, France, and Germany provide universal health care coverage for their citizens but spend only 8 to 10 percent of their GDPs on health care, and Britain and Japan spend only 7 percent for universal coverage.[3] Not only are costs high, they are increasing faster than any other good or service we purchase. We spend almost *three times* as much maintaining our health today as we did in 1983. In comparison, we spend only about half again as much on food and housing.

Costs are soaring on the private side of health care spending and also on the public side. As we saw in Chapter 14, 17 cents of every federal tax dollar goes for health care for the elderly and the poor. The costs of health care are a major obstacle to balancing the federal budget and to investing in the economy. As President Clinton said shortly before taking office, "If I could wave a magic wand tomorrow and do one thing for this economy, I would bring health costs in line with inflation . . . because . . . that would free more money for people to invest in the plants and the production and the jobs of the future."[4]

Why are health care expenditures in the United States so high? There are many reasons. American health providers have overbuilt medical care facilities (one-third of all hospital beds are vacant on any given day),[5] and doctors and hospitals have few incentives to be more efficient. New technologies, drugs, and procedures often add to

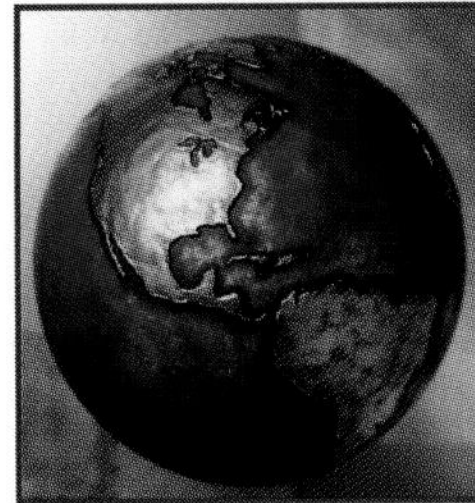

America in Perspective

Health Care Spending, Life Expectancy, and Infant Mortality Rates

Even though the United States is the wealthiest country and spends the most on health care, its citizens, however, do not enjoy the best health among the developed nations. This is America's health policy paradox.

COUNTRY	% OF GDP SPENT ON HEALTH	LIFE EXPECTANCY	INFANT MORTALITY RATE (DEATHS PER 1,000 BIRTHS)
United States	**14.0**	77.1	6.8
Germany	10.6	77.4	4.8
Britain	6.9	77.7	5.6
Italy	7.6	79.0	5.9
France	9.6	78.8	4.5
Canada	9.3	79.4	5.1
Japan	7.4	80.7	3.9

Source: U.S. Bureau of the Census, *Statistical Abstract of the United States,* 2000 (Washington, D.C.: U.S. Government Printing Office, 2001), 826, 828.

the cost of health care by addressing previously untreatable conditions or by providing better, but more expensive, care. Much of the money that Americans pay for health care goes to services like organ transplants, kidney dialysis, and other treatments that are not widely available outside the United States. These treatments also cost a lot—sometimes hundreds of thousands of dollars.

Because insurance companies and government programs pay for most health care expenses, most patients have no reason to ask for cheaper care—they do not directly face the full financial consequences of their care. Health care providers, such as physicians, are also insulated from competing with each other to offer less expensive care. In fact, with the rise in medical malpractice suits, doctors may be ordering extra tests, however expensive they may be, to ensure that they cannot be sued—an approach that is sometimes called "defensive medicine." Such practices drive up the costs of medical care for everyone. As doctors are hit with higher and higher costs for insurance against malpractice suits, they increase their fees to pay their premiums. Because insurance companies pay the bills, patients do not protest. However, increased costs associated with medical care are making insurance rates skyrocket, and one way or another, through taxes, insurance, or out of our own pockets, the consumer pays for it all.

What explains the contradiction between the high costs that Americans pay for health care—the highest costs in the world—and the fact that Americans are not the world's healthiest people? One explanation can be found in the way the American health care industry is organized.

Access to Health Care

Inequalities in health and health care are a serious problem in America. Americans spend large amounts of money on health (nearly $4,000 per person each year),[6] and the world's highest quality care is available to some citizens. Nevertheless, many poor and working Americans, like Mildred Davis, whom we met earlier in this chapter, are relegated to an inferior health care system because access to health insurance is not universal in the United States as it is in many countries.

Americans gain access to health care in a variety of ways. The most common means of access is through private plans. The traditional form of such a plan is a health insurance policy, in which a policyholder pays an annual premium and then is entitled to have the insurance company pay a certain amount of the cost of health care for the year. Today, many people contract with a **Health Maintenance Organization (HMO)** that directly provides all or most of a person's health care for a yearly fee. The government-subsidized Medicare program covers older Americans, and many of those living below the poverty line are covered by another government program, Medicaid (discussed in the next section). Some people must pay all their health care expenses out of their own pocket.

health maintenance organizations (HMOs)

Organizations contracted by individuals or insurance companies to provide health care for a yearly fee. Such network health plans limit the choice of doctors and treatments. About 60 percent of Americans are enrolled in HMOs or similar programs.

Health Insurance. Most Americans have health insurance of some kind (an individual policy or membership in an HMO), but more than 43 million people—16 percent of the population—are without health insurance coverage. In 1999, 15.5 percent of all Americans were without health insurance; 13.9 percent of all children went without insurance.[7] Millions of others are without health insurance for shorter periods.[8] Most of the uninsured are under 65 because nearly everyone 65 and older participates in Medicare, a government subsidized program discussed later in this chapter. Another 41 million individuals without private health insurance receive health care benefits from Medicaid, which helps those with very low incomes.[9] Nevertheless, many Americans simply go without proper health care. National polls have found that 39 percent of Americans reported not seeing a doctor for a medical problem because it would have cost too much.[10]

Getting and keeping health insurance are often linked to having a job, especially a high-paying job. Sixty-one percent of Americans get their health insurance from the workplace.[11] Often, the lack of health insurance is associated with short periods of unemployment. Moreover, part-time employees may not be eligible for employer insurance plans. Nevertheless, the majority of the nation's uninsured are full-time workers (and their families), most of whom work for companies with 100 or fewer employees and earn low wages. Their employers have to pay more for health insurance than do larger companies, mostly because health risks and marketing and administrative costs cannot be spread as broadly.

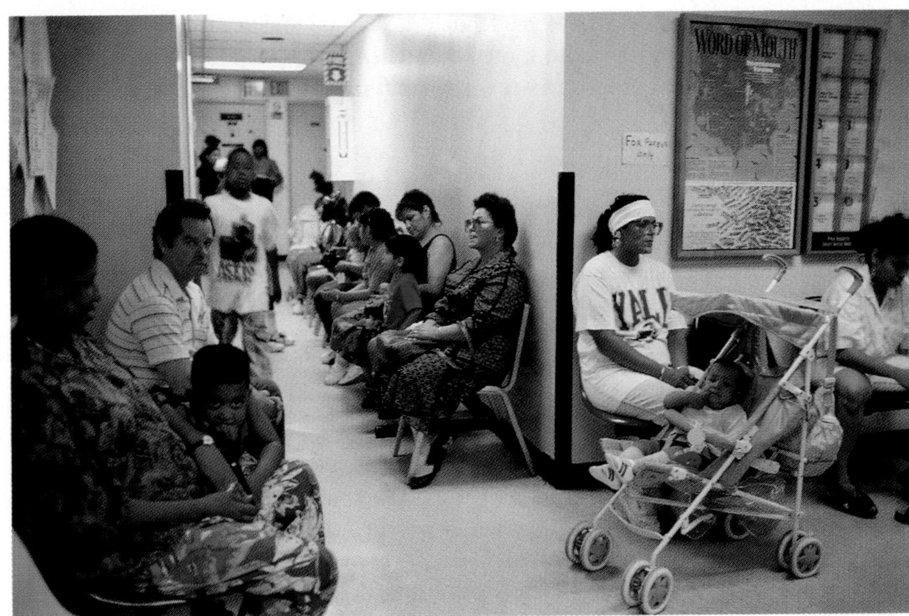

Access to health care is one of the greatest challenges to health care policy. The quality of health care varies substantially among Americans; so does the health of different groups in society.

Thus, many small companies find providing health insurance too costly.[12] In addition, some companies have cut back on benefits to dependents of workers. As a result, even if parents have coverage through their employers, their children may be uninsured.

Even when people have access to a group health insurance plan, they may have to pay a large share of the cost themselves. Six million workers are offered health insurance by their employers or unions and do not take it.[13] Many are like Rita Carillo, 26, who works as a customer service representative for a company that repairs appliances. She has the opportunity to participate in an employer health plan but cannot afford the premiums.[14] As a result, she remains uninsured.

Access to health insurance in the United States is also closely tied to race and income. One-third of Hispanic families went without health insurance in 1999, as did 21 percent of African-American and Asian families. Thirty-two percent of the poor lack health insurance, despite the existence of government-subsidized programs such as Medicaid and Medicare. The higher a family's income, the more likely it is that its members are insured.[15]

Discrepancies in access to health care are reflected in the health of different groups. Whites have an average life expectancy seven years longer than that of African Americans. For African-American males, life expectancy is seven years less than for white males and is lower than the averages in many Eastern European and less developed countries. Not all of this difference can be explained by variances in lifestyles and nutrition. Similarly, infant mortality rates among those with good insurance plans and a family doctor are very low. For those without insurance, the statistics are disturbing. African-American infant mortality is over twice as high as that for Whites.[16]

Tremendous advances have been made in the technology available to keep premature babies alive, but many pregnant women, especially in the nation's inner cities, lack the care that will ensure that their babies will be born healthy. Instead of having a family doctor (few doctors practice in poor neighborhoods), many of the nation's poor go only to hospital emergency rooms. Prenatal care is an important component in reducing health risks during the first year of life, but prenatal care is not available to all. Often, the availability of family doctors and routine hospital services are more important in determining the quality of a nation's health care than the most current medical and research equipment.

Even among those who have insurance, coverage is often incomplete. Especially for those with low-paying jobs, health insurance may not cover all their health needs.

About 20 million Americans have inadequate insurance and receive less and poorer quality health care than those with more comprehensive insurance. These individuals often postpone treatment until illnesses worsen and require more expensive emergency treatment.[17]

Managed Care. One of the biggest constraints on obtaining health insurance has been its cost. In recent years, private market forces have transformed the country's health care system dramatically. Approximately 160 million Americans are enrolled in health maintenance organizations (HMOs) or other forms of network health plans that limit the choice of doctors and treatments. Insurers choose HMOs or restricted physician lists for the provision of care, negotiate with physician groups and hospitals on fees and costs, and try to monitor most aspects of care to control unnecessary use. At least three-fourths of all doctors have signed contracts, covering at least some of their patients, to cut their fees and accept oversight of their medical decisions. Enrollment in managed care plans grew slowly in the 1970s, but more than tripled in the 1980s and doubled again in the 1990s. Today these plans insure about 60 percent of all Americans, representing about 85 percent of workers who receive health insurance.

Managed care grew on the strength of its claims to provide better service at a lower cost. Traditional insurance gave doctors incentives to provide additional, and perhaps unnecessary, services and no incentive to help patients get well. Doctors treated patients with little concern about cost, and insurance companies paid the bills with few questions asked. The more treatments doctors provided, the more money they made. Moreover, doctors insisted that patients be able to choose their own doctors without restrictions, which made it impossible to contract with groups of doctors to provide services more economically.

Managed care is intended to improve health care by focusing on prevention rather than treatment and by designating a single doctor as a patient's primary care provider rather than having patients treated by different specialists with no central coordination or oversight. This designation also helps to contain the health care costs that were driving up the cost of medical care and health insurance for patients and employers. These measures are designed to contain the costs of health care, but they have done nothing to ease the plight of those without health insurance. In addition, as we will see, they raise new questions about ensuring quality health care.

BY BORGMAN FOR THE CINCINNATI ENQUIRER

The Role of Government in Health Care

Medical care in the United States differs from that in most other democracies in one important way: the role that the government plays. The United States has the most thoroughly privatized medical care system in the developed world. National, state, and local governments pay for 46 percent of the country's total health bill, whereas the median for all industrialized countries is about 77 percent (see Figure 19.1). The government also subsidizes employer-provided health insurance with tax breaks worth about $77 billion per year, the benefits of which go disproportionately to affluent, highly paid workers.

Forty-six percent amounts to much more than most Americans realize. Many hospitals are connected to public universities, and much medical research is financed through the *National Institute of Health (NIH)*, for example. Further, the federal government pays for much of the nation's medical bill through the Medicare program for the elderly, the Medicaid program for the poor, and health care for veterans. More than 20,000 physicians work for the federal government, and nearly all the rest receive payments from it. The government thus plays an important health care role in America, though less so than in other countries.

Who pays for the rest of Americans' health care? Private insurance companies cover one-third, and Americans pay nearly one-fifth of their health care costs out of

Figure 19.1 Health Care Spending in Selected Democracies

As with many other areas of the economy, the role of government in health care is smaller in the United States than in comparable countries. The United States lacks national health insurance or a national health service to provide health care directly to those who need it. Still, the government accounts for over 46 percent of all money spent on health care in this country—a sizable percentage. In fact, the government is the largest single source of health care dollars, providing more funds than even private insurance companies.

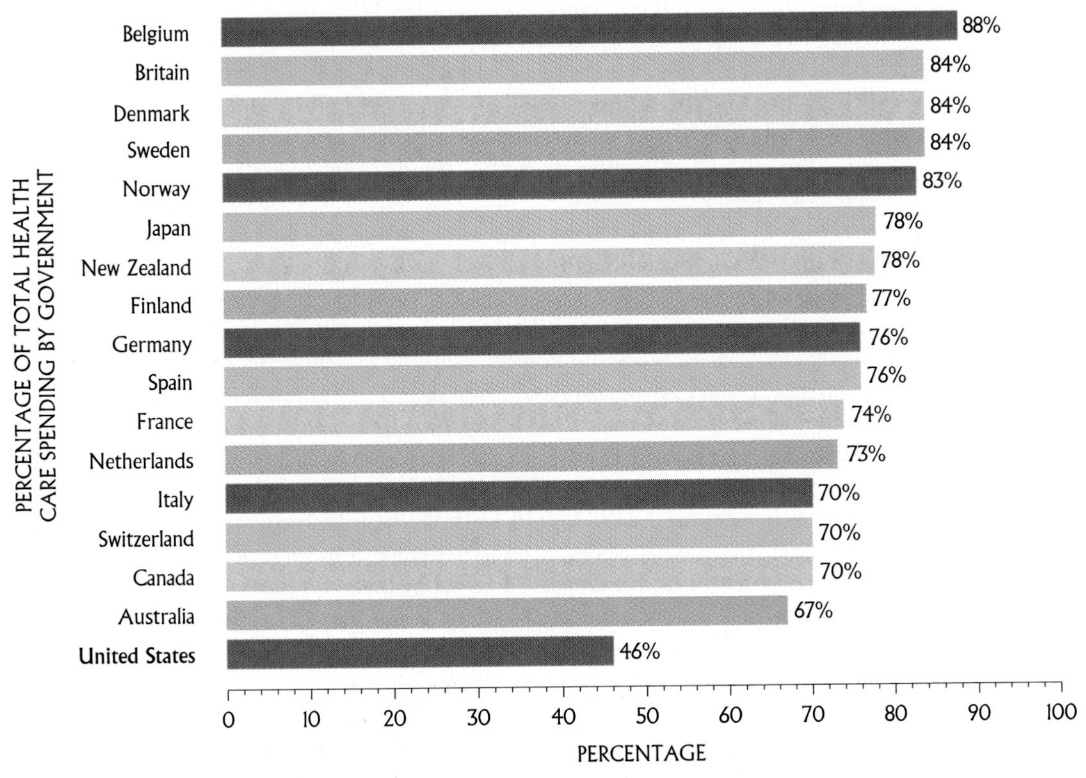

Source: U.S. Bureau of the Census, *Statistical Abstract of the United States, 2000* (Washington, D.C.: U.S. Government Printing Office, 2001), 828.

Figure 19.2 Who Pays Medical Costs? Government Versus Private Sources

Private insurance covers only a third of health care costs. Government programs pay for nearly half.

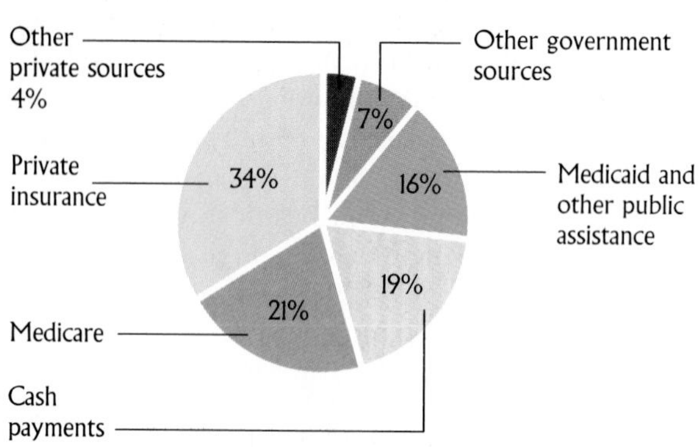

Source: U.S. Bureau of the Census, *Statistical Abstract of the United States, 2000* (Washington, D.C.: U.S. Government Printing Office, 2001), 111.

their own pockets (see Figure 19.2). Americans often think that insurance companies pay most health care costs, but in fact the government is more heavily involved than the private insurance industry.

national health insurance

A compulsory insurance program for all Americans that would have the government finance citizens' medical care. First proposed by President Harry S. Truman, the plan was soundly opposed by the American Medical Association.

Harry S. Truman was the first president to call for **national health insurance,** a compulsory insurance program to finance all Americans' medical care. The idea was strongly opposed by the American Medical Association, the largest physicians' interest group, which called this program *socialized medicine* because it would be run by the government. Although every other industrial nation in the world has adopted some form of national health insurance, the United States remains the exception.

Medicare

A program added to the Social Security system in 1965 that provides hospitalization insurance for the elderly and permits older Americans to purchase inexpensive coverage for doctor fees and other medical expenses.

Nonetheless, in 1965 Congress sought to rectify the special health care problems of elderly Americans by adopting **Medicare.** Medicare is part of the Social Security system and covers 40 million people. Part A of Medicare provides hospitalization insurance and short-term nursing care; Part B, which is voluntary, permits older Americans to purchase inexpensive coverage for doctor fees and other nonhospital medical expenses. Because the number of elderly Americans grows rapidly—and because the cost of medical care is growing just as fast (Medicare cost about $220 billion in 2000)—the funding of health care for the elderly is one of the country's most pressing public policy issues.

Like Social Security, Medicare costs are outrunning contributions to the Medicare Trust Fund. While Social Security is likely to last until about 2030, the safe horizon for Medicare is much shorter. By 2008, expenditures will outrun revenues. It is the most rapidly increasing component of the federal budget. Today it is about 12 percent of the federal budget. Without reform, it will soar to nearly 30 percent by 2030.[18] The cost squeeze, though, is here today. More and more hospitals, physicians, and insurance companies have abandoned Medicare patients because Medicare payments do not cover their costs. In the last few years, HMOs have cancelled programs covering nearly 750,000 patients.[19]

Medicaid

A public assistance program designed to provide health care for poor Americans. Medicaid is funded by both the states and the national government.

Not to be confused with Medicare is **Medicaid,** a program that is designed to provide health care for the poor and serves about 35 million people. Like other public assistance programs, Medicaid is funded by both the states and the national government (in 2000, the federal government alone spent $111 billion on Medicaid). Unlike Medicare, which goes to elderly Americans regardless of their income, Medicaid is a means-tested program. Medicaid is for the poorest of the poor (only 42 percent of people below the poverty line even qualify). Debates arise about the formulas for determining eligibility because people with low-paying jobs often are not eligible, whereas those on welfare may qualify. Thus, because of the loss of health benefits and the high cost of purchasing them privately, it may not pay to take a low-wage service job. Obviously, however, the government does not want to encourage people *not* to work. Like Medicare, the future of Medicaid is tenuous as costs soar. Insurers and providers who cannot afford Medicare patients cannot afford Medicaid patients either.

Government in America plays an important role in health care, even if it is less involved than in other countries. One way to explain the uneven access to health care in the United States is to look at those who make health care policy.

Policymaking for Health Care

In countries with national health care systems (or national health insurance), government policymakers have focused more on ensuring equality of care and on containing costs, especially administrative costs. In the United States, equality of care and cost containment have taken a back seat to technological advance. At times, competition among urban hospitals to provide the most advanced care has led to duplication of expensive equipment and thus higher health costs. As a result, Americans have high-tech, expensive, and unequal care.

Many lifesaving procedures are extremely expensive, so allocating their use involves complicated questions of public policy. Dollars spent on expensive procedures to save a few lives cannot be spent on other, equally pressing health needs. Thus, when the government allows Medicare payments for certain procedures, less money is available for rural hospitals, for health clinics in poor areas of the nation's cities, or for other problems.

Americans do not like to admit that "rationing" of medical care goes on all the time in our system.[20] Much rationing is informal; physicians and families quietly agree not to provide further care to a loved one. Some of it is formal. Medical boards have elaborate rules for allocating donated organs. When we ration openly and publicly, though, conflict erupts. Oregon took the lead on the issue of rationing health care, trying to set priorities for medical treatments under the Medicaid program, which is funded by both the state and the national government. In 1991, the state came up with a list of 709 treatments/conditions. The Oregon legislature agreed to fund 587 of these from its tight Medicaid budget. As a result, Oregon does not pay for some costly treatments that might save or merely prolong people's lives, but by doing so it can use its resources to provide medical care to a larger pool of people. Though Oregon's plan was controversial at first, evidence shows that it works well and that patient satisfaction is higher after the plan than it was before.[21]

One reason for uneven government and private health care policies involves the representation of interests. Powerful lobbying organizations representing hospitals, doctors, and the elderly want Medicare to pay for the latest techniques. Politicians hardly feel comfortable denying these lifesaving measures to those who may have voted them into office. On the other hand, many groups are unrepresented in government. Their health needs may not be met simply because no well-organized groups are insisting that the government meet them.

The elderly are now one of the most powerful voting and lobbying forces in American politics. Health care policy that favors the elderly is one of the results of this interest group activity. The American Association of Retired Persons (AARP) has grown from about 150,000 members in 1959 to more than 32 million today, making it the largest voluntary association in the world.[22] This single group now can claim to represent one American in eight and its numbers may swell as the baby boomer generation reaches retirement. It claims to speak with authority on all questions associated with the elderly.

For workers in low-paying service jobs that do not include health insurance, and for those who are unemployed and cannot afford private health insurance, there is no organization capable of exerting such influence in government. Because many of these people do not vote, the bias in representation is even greater. The groups that enjoy good health care coverage in the United States are largely those that are well organized to influence the government.

Why does it matter?

The United States, unlike most other developed nations, does not have national health insurance. Consider your health care costs now and over the next few years. You are probably healthy now, but how will you manage serious and perhaps unexpected health care costs? Would you and your family have greater access to health care if we adopted a national health care system? Would you receive better or worse quality of care under a policy of national health insurance?

Health care policymaking involves difficult ethical issues. For example, should limited federal funds be spent on the expensive, unproven, but potentially lifesaving artificial heart technology shown here? Or should public money be devoted to less dramatic medical procedures that could help many more Americans?

One group that is increasingly active in health care policymaking is business. Conflict between the government (which pays many medical bills) and private employers (who pay much of the insurance premiums for their employees) is increasing. Each side wants the other to assume more of the health care burden. For example, the government is saving money by forcing patients to exhaust their private insurance before allowing government programs to begin making payments. As the government reduces its payments in such ways, doctors and hospitals pass on their costs to those patients with private insurance. As private insurance rates increase, employers complain that they are paying inflated premiums for their workers to cover the costs of those who cannot pay or whose insurance provides only partial reimbursement for medical care. Employers then may attempt to reduce their burden by cutting out benefits that are covered by government programs.

Business groups are increasingly calling for relief in the health care field. For example, they complain that their foreign competitors avoid the high costs of private insurance premiums because governments, rather than employers, cover health insurance costs in many other countries. At the same time, employers defend the $77 billion tax break, or subsidy, that they receive for providing health insurance to their employees. Yet such insurance has high administrative costs, ties workers to a specific job rather than encouraging labor mobility, and continues to insulate people from the consequences of their health care costs.[23]

Insurance companies are also major players in health care policymaking. They have been making it more difficult for doctors and hospitals to pass along the costs of others' unpaid bills to them, causing a cost crunch for some institutions, including inner-city hospitals and trauma centers that serve the poor. In addition, the health insurance industry has a huge stake in the outcome of the debate on national health insurance. A program funded and run by the national government would leave insurance companies without a function (or a profit). Thus they are fighting to be seen as a viable alternative.

The Clinton Health Care Reform Plan. President Clinton made health care reform the centerpiece of his first administration. His five-pound, 1,342-page Health Security Act proposal was an effort to deal with the two great problems of health care policy: costs and access. The difficulties the president faced with this proposal reveal much about the challenge of reforming health care in America.

The president's main concern was guaranteeing health care coverage for all Americans. His plan would particularly have benefited people without any health insurance, but it would also have extended coverage for millions of others with inadequate health insurance.

Paying for the plan would have necessitated either broad-based taxes, which were politically unpalatable, or a requirement that employers provide health insurance for their employees or pay a premium into a public fund (which would also cover Medicaid and Medicare recipients). The president chose the employer insurance option, but the small business community was adamantly opposed to bearing the cost of providing health insurance. The president also proposed raising taxes on cigarettes, which angered the tobacco industry, and imposing a small tax on other large companies.

To contain health care costs, the administration would have required states to set up large consumer groups called "health alliances" to collect premiums, bargain with health plans, and handle payments. Most companies would have had to buy coverage through an alliance. The proposal would also have limited the annual increase in the price of health insurance premiums and capped government spending for Medicare (threatening the elderly) and Medicaid.

Because the White House reform plan for health care was bureaucratic and complicated, it was easy for opponents to label it a government takeover of the health care system. An aggressive advertising campaign mounted by the health insurance industry characterized the president's plan as being expensive and experimental, as providing lower-quality and rationed care, and as killing jobs. The health insurance industry's famous "Harry and Louise" ads—Harry and Louise mull over the Clinton plan around their kitchen and conclude, "There's got to be a better way"—were one of the most

Many Americans lack access to health care. President Clinton, appearing here at a rally in Minneapolis, made improved health care a centerpiece of his administration.

effective policy-oriented campaigns in history. After a long and tortuous battle, the plan died in Congress.

The Health Policy Issues Ahead. The massive effort by President Clinton failed, but health care issues remain high on the policy agenda. As managed care has come to dominate the provision of health care in the United States, its ability to deliver health care has been challenged, drawing attention from both state and federal lawmakers. Opponents charge that managed care's cost-cutting bureaucrats impose stifling rules on network physicians, block sick patients from seeing specialists, and delay or deny coverage for recommended treatments or medications—all to save money.

While Americans are fairly satisfied with their own health care, a careful analysis of public opinion surveys show that people think the nation's health care system needs a great deal of reform.[24] Most of these concerns focus on the very issues we have examined here: access and cost. A March 2000 Princeton Research Survey found that Americans were more worried about their ability to get affordable health care than any other aspect of their standard of living. Two-thirds of the people in a *Wall Street Journal* poll in 1999 thought that government should guarantee health insurance for everyone. The backlash against the perceived failures of manage care generated a wave of state legislative action to protect patients' rights. President Clinton proposed a "patients' bill of rights," which included a right to see the doctor of one's choice, obtain access to reasonable emergency care without prior authorization from a plan, secure the right to appeal a plan's refusal to provide medical treatments, attain easier access to out-of-network doctors, receive more information on their plan's regulations, and acquire the right to sue a plan for malpractice. Physicians, who typically side with Republicans, have been supportive of the Democrats' criticism of managed care. They chafe under the constraints of their organizations and resent the limits on their incomes. In 2000, the Republican Congress, however, killed President Clinton's patients' bill of rights.

The cost of medical care in general and prescription drugs in particular confronted Congress as the century turned. Prescription drug costs have grown by an annual average of 11 percent since 1992. The AARP and other lobbies for the elderly have pressured Congress to add prescription costs to Medicare, which now leaves them up to individuals. People near the Canadian border sometimes go to Canadian pharmacies for their prescriptions because the Canadian health care system subsidizes drug costs.

There is little doubt that government will continue to struggle with regulating the costs of health care and helping those who fall through the cracks of the American health care system. Alone among the industrialized nations, the United States lacks a national health insurance system. Our part-private, part-public system remains complex, confusing, and expensive.

Environmental Policy

One might think that such a cherished national treasure as the natural environment would be above politics. After all, public opinion analyst Louis Harris reported that "the American people's desire to battle pollution is one of the most overwhelming and clearest we have ever recorded in our . . . years of surveying public opinion."[25] Concern for the environment is further reflected in the rapid growth of environmental groups.

As in other areas, however, politics infuses itself into the debate over the environment. Attempts to control air quality or limit water pollution often affect political choices through their impact on business, economic growth, and jobs. And although Americans may be generally in favor of "doing something" about the environment, specific proposals to limit suburban growth, encourage carpooling, and limit access to national parks have met with strong resistance.

Economic Growth and the Environment

Environmental controls figure prominently in the debate about local and state economic development. As you saw in Chapter 3, the federal system puts the states in competition for economic advantage. States and cities pushing for large investments, such as a billion-dollar auto plant, spend millions of dollars. New business is a boon to the local and state economies as well as to the political fortunes of their politicians. Business elites can often argue that stringent pollution-control laws will drive businesses away by driving up their costs. On the other hand, states with lax pollution enforcement may find their citizens unhappy, and those businesses that move to their area may find employees unwilling to come along. Thus, state competition does not always work against pollution standards. In fact, sometimes states compete with each other to enforce tighter pollution and land use controls. In the process, they sometimes realize substantial direct savings as well.[26]

Concern for the environment and concern about economic development can overlap in complex ways. The Environmental Protection Agency (EPA), created in 1970, has had to deal with industrial pollution among other things. Congress required that the EPA set standards for "ambient air"—standards about just how clean the air had to be. States and localities were required to take policy actions to bring air cleanliness up to standards set by the EPA. Naturally, environmentalists insisted that *higher* standards be adopted for those areas with *cleaner* air. It would be silly, said environmentalists, to set standards so low in clean-air San Antonio that industries and autos might pollute it to the level of dirty-air Gary, Ind.

In 1977 Congress wrote some amendments to the Clean Air Act, formally requiring the "nondegradation" standard. A community could not, insisted the policy, permit "degradation" of its air quality, whether it started out with pristine air or the foulest air in the country. Suppose you wanted to locate a new plant in a community that had little pollution. You could not, said the law, worsen air quality there, even if the air was still better than that in 99 percent of the rest of the country. Thus, you would have to install expensive "scrubbers" or other expensive pollution abatement techniques if you used coal or other pollutants.

These damaged trees in Tennessee show the devastating effects of acid rain, which is formed when tall smokestacks at coal-burning plants belch pollution high into the atmosphere. Much of the acid rain caused by American industries actually falls in Canada; officials there estimate that more than 2,000 lakes have "died" as a result of acid rain.

The results of these amendments were predictable. Industries were discouraged from relocating in clean-air environments, mostly in the Sunbelt, because of the cost of doing so. Robert Crandall carefully analyzed the supporters of this clean-air amendment. Not surprisingly, they hailed mostly from urban, industrialized areas of the Northeast—the areas likely, without a nondegradation policy, to lose industry to the Sunbelt.[27] No doubt each vote was motivated by a sincere environmental concern. Still, environmental concern can often be mixed with an equal measure of self-interest.

Concern for the environment has increased greatly in the United States since the 1950s, when few environmental groups were around. Since then, growth in membership for many of the most important groups has been measured in the millions. Following the passage of important legislation in the early 1970s, these groups have gained important victories, and many of their goals are now part of the political mainstream.

Americans today are much more concerned about the environment than they were when President Reagan took office in 1981. Steadily increasing percentages of Americans are willing to see the government spend money to clean up and protect the environment. In one recent survey, 63 percent of those polled favored strong government action to protect the environment, including strict regulations against polluters.

Environmental Policies in America

In the early 1960s, environmental protection was not a prominent element of federal policy. What policy existed then focused largely on conservation and the national parks. Beginning in the last year of President Kennedy's tenure, Congress passed numerous bills that firmly established environmental protection as a national goal. Spearheading government efforts the **Environmental Protection Agency (EPA)** is now the nation's largest federal regulatory agency. The EPA has a wide-ranging mission; it is charged with administering policies dealing with land, air, and water quality.

Environmental Protection Agency (EPA)

An agency of the federal government created in 1970 and charged with administering all the government's environmental legislation. It also administers policies dealing with toxic wastes. The EPA is the largest federal independent regulatory agency.

National Environmental Policy Act (NEPA)

The law passed in 1969 that is the centerpiece of federal environmental policy in the United States. The NEPA established the requirements for **environmental impact statements.**

environmental impact statement (EIS)

A report required by the National Environmental Policy Act that specifies the likely environmental impact of a proposed action. NEPA requires that whenever any agency proposes to undertake a policy that impacts the environment, the agency must file a statement with the EPA.

Environmental Impacts. The centerpiece of federal environmental policy is the **National Environmental Policy Act (NEPA),** passed in 1969. This law required both government and private agencies to complete **environmental impact statements (EIS).** Every time an agency proposes to undertake a policy that is potentially disruptive to the natural environment, it must file an EIS with the Environmental Protection Agency, detailing possible effects of the policy. Big dams and small post offices, major port construction and minor road widening—proposals for all these projects must include an EIS.

Strictly speaking, an environmental impact statement was merely a procedural requirement. "In theory," says William Ophuls, "an agency can report that a proposed activity will cause the sky to fall . . . and still proceed with the project once it has satisfied the procedural requirements of the act."[28] In practice, the filing of impact statements alerted environmentalists to proposed projects. Environmentalists can then take agencies to court for violating the act's procedural requirements if the agencies file incomplete or inaccurate impact statements. Because environmental impacts are usually so complicated and difficult to predict, it is relatively easy to argue that the statements are either incomplete or inaccurate in some way. Agencies have often abandoned proposed projects to avoid prolonged court battles with environmental groups.

The law did not give environmental groups the right to stop any environmentally unsound activities, but it did give them the opportunity to delay construction so much that agencies simply give up. Chances are that many of the biggest public works projects of the past century—including the Hoover Dam, Kennedy Airport, Cape Canaveral's space facility, and most Tennessee Valley Authority projects—would not have survived the environmental scrutiny to which they would have been subject had they been undertaken after the NEPA was enacted. In any case, the NEPA has been an effective tool in preventing environmental despoliation.

Clean Air. Another landmark piece of legislation affecting the environment is the **Clean Air Act of 1970,** which charges the Department of Transportation (DOT) with the responsibility of reducing automobile emissions. You have probably met the Clean Air Act if you have bought a new car or even looked at one. Cars today use far cleaner fuels (and less of it) than before the Clean Air Act. For years after the act's passage, fierce battles raged between the automakers and the DOT about how stringent the requirements had to be. Automakers claimed it was impossible to meet DOT standards; the DOT claimed that automakers were deliberately dragging their feet in hopes that Congress would delay or weaken the requirements. In fact, Congress did weaken them, again and again. Still, the smaller size of American cars, the use of unleaded gasoline, and the lower gas consumption of new cars are all due in large part to DOT regulations. In 1990 Congress passed a reauthorization of the Clean Air Act, which significantly increased the controls on cars, oil refineries, chemical plants, and coal-fired utility plants. This bill was the strongest step forward in the fight to clean the air since the bill's original passage 20 years earlier. As a result of federal policies, air pollution from toxic organic compounds and sulfur dioxide has decreased substantially since 1970.

Clean Air Act of 1970

The law that charged the Department of Transportation (DOT) with the responsibility to reduce automobile emissions.

The Clean Air Act Amendments of 1990 also marked one of the most radical innovations in pollution control policy. Congress permitted utility companies to use emissions trading, essentially the right to buy and trade rights to pollute on the open market (there is even a market for these emissions credits on the Chicago Board of Trade). A utility generating cleaner fuel could "bank" its savings and sell them to other utilities around the country. Some environmentalists were horrified at these "licenses to pollute," but the evidence is that the trading program has helped reduce pollution rates.[29]

Clean Water. Congress acted to control pollution of the nation's lakes and rivers with the **Water Pollution Control Act of 1972.** This law was enacted in reaction to the tremendous pollution of northeastern rivers and the Great Lakes. Since its passage, water quality has improved dramatically. In 1972 only one-third of U.S. lakes and rivers were safe for fishing and drinking. Today, the fraction has doubled to two-thirds. Similarly, the number of waterfowl in U.S. waters has increased substantially. Our waters are cleaner today than before the Act. There is a problem with it: Federal laws only regulate "point sources"—places where pollutants can be dumped in the water, such as a paper mill along a river. What is hard to regulate is the most important cause of water pollution, "runoff" from streets, roads, fertilized lawns, and service stations.

Water Pollution Control Act of 1972

A law intended to clean up the nation's rivers and lakes. It requires municipal, industrial, and other polluters to use pollution control technology and secure permits from the **Environmental Protection Agency** for discharging waste products into waters.

Wilderness Preservation. In addition to protecting air and water, environmental policy literally aims to keep some parts of the environment intact. One component of the environment that has received special attention is wilderness—those areas that are largely untouched by human activities. Ever since the founding of the National Park system in 1916, the United States has been a world leader in wilderness preservation. Perhaps the most consistently successful environmental campaigns in the postwar era have been those aimed at preserving such wild lands.[30] There are now 378 national parks and 155 national forests. Still, only about 4 percent of the United States is now designated as wilderness, and half of that is in Alaska. The strains of overuse have forced our national parks to consider restricting the public's access to preserve them for future generations. In addition, wilderness areas—with the biological, recreational, and symbolic values they embody—come under increasing pressure from those, such as logging and mining interests, who stress the economic benefits lost by keeping them intact. At the end of the 2000 congressional session, Congress also provided $8 billion to restore Florida's Everglades to something closer to its previous ecological state.

participation
Federal Regulations and Mandates

The gray wolf is an endangered species. In 1995–96, the U.S. Fish and Wildlife Service reintroduced 31 gray wolves into Yellowstone National Park in an effort to reestablish its presence. They number 120 adults today. Environmentalists hail this effort as a great victory, but ranchers and farmers around Yellowstone complain that wolf packs will endanger their livestock.

Endangered Species. Preserving wilderness areas indirectly helps protect another part of the larger environment: wildlife. National policy protects wildlife in other, more direct ways as well. The **Endangered Species Act of 1973,** for example, created an endangered species protection program in the U.S. Fish and Wildlife Service. More important, the law required the government to actively protect each of the hundreds of species listed as endangered—regardless of the economic effect on the surrounding towns or region. Later, during the Reagan Administration, the act was amended to allow exceptions in cases of overriding national or regional interest. A cabinet-level committee, quickly labeled "The God Squad," was established to decide such cases. As EPA Chief William Reilly explained, "The God Squad is a group of people, of which I am a minor divinity, which has the power to blow away a species."[31] The God Squad has granted few exemptions to the Endangered Species Act so far, but because expanding human populations and growing economic demands increasingly threaten endangered species, it is likely to be called on more frequently in coming years to exercise its "divine" powers. You can think about the policy issues of saving species in "You Are the Policymaker: Should We Save All Endangered Species? Owls, Salamanders, and Economic Growth."

Endangered Species Act of 1973

This law requires the federal government to protect actively each of the hundreds of species listed as endangered—regardless of the economic effect on the surrounding towns or region.

Energy, the Environment, and Global Warming

Modern American society depends on the availability of abundant energy. Americans are used to getting their energy cheaply and easily. Producing the amounts of energy necessary to retain Americans' standard of living and accustomed patterns of life while at the same time preserving the environment has become increasingly difficult. Energy

You Are the Policymaker

Should We Save All Endangered Species? Owls, Salamanders and Economic Growth

Thirty years ago, Jeanette Sainz's daughter found an ugly black and ivory salamander on their ranch near Santa Barbara, Calif. that neither of them had seen before. Curious, Ms. Sainz took the new specimen to a local museum, which identified it as a tiger salamander, never before seen in that area. With that chance episode of scientific curiosity began one more battle over saving endangered species. In January 2000, the tiger salamander joined the ranks of endangered species, officially certified by the U.S. Fish and Wildlife Service on an emergency basis. Farmers, ranchers, or winegrowers who harmed the salamander or its habitat—which had not yet been fully identified—faced a year of jail time and a $50,000 fine.

Ms. Sainz, like many ranchers in Santa Barbara County, had been planning to convert her unprofitable ranch into vineyard. Some of her neighbors had already done so. Ms. Sainz' now felt that she was being punished for her scientific curiosity of years ago. Like many ranching families in scenic Santa Barbara, she was caught up in the peculiar politics of the Endangered Species Act.

Loggers in the Pacific Northwest had felt the same way when, on June 26, 1990, the spotted owl was identified as an endangered species. The Fish and Wildlife Service had identified 3,602 pairs of spotted owls inhabiting forests in Oregon, Washington, and California. Their habitat covered an area about the size of the state of Connecticut. The Fish and Wildlife Service itself—the enforcers of the Endangered Species Act—estimated that 32,436 jobs could be lost through reduced logging in the spotted owl's habitat.

The Endangered Species Act remains one of the nation's most controversial environmental laws. Sponsors may have envisioned the American bald eagle or the grizzly bear as symbols of our destruction of habitats and species. (These were sometimes called the "charismatic" species.) To critics, saving the bald eagle, America's symbol, was one thing. Saving tiger salamanders was something else.

Sometimes jobs and economic growth collide with the policy objective of protecting endangered species. You be the policymaker. Do we want to save every single species—there may be 100 million of them—from possible extinction? Do we want to put jobs ahead of species, or only some species? And if so, how do we play God with nature?

Sources: On the Endangered Species Act, see Richard Tobin, *The Expendable Future: U.S. Politics and the Protection of Environmental Diversity* (Durham, NC: Duke University Press, 1990). The story of Santa Barbara County is from James Sterngold, "California Wine Region Torn by Debate over Use of Land," the *New York Times*, April 1, 2000, A1. The spotted owl data are from "Owls, Trees and Jobs," the *New York Times*, April 2, 1994, A9.

issues continually present thorny problems for policymakers to resolve, and government is constantly involved in battles concerning what forms of energy the country should be producing, and from what sources.

Once Americans used wood, animals, water, and people power for energy. Today 87 percent of the nation's energy comes from coal, oil, and natural gas (see Figure 19.3). Americans search continually for new and more efficient sources of energy, both to increase supplies and to reduce pollution. Much of the research on new energy sources and efficiencies comes from the government in Washington.

Coal is America's most abundant fuel. An estimated 90 percent of the country's energy resources are in coal deposits—enough to last hundreds of years. Although coal may be the nation's most plentiful fuel, unfortunately it is also the dirtiest. It contributes to global warming (discussed later in this chapter) and smog, and it is responsible for the "black lung" health hazard to coal miners and for the soot-blackened cities of the Northeast. In addition, acid rain is traced to the burning of coal to produce electricity. Coal may be abundant, but most Americans do not want to rely on it exclusively for their energy needs. Coal accounts for only 23 percent of the energy Americans use.

Oil, which accounts for over 40 percent of the energy Americans use, is one of nature's nonrenewable resources. Some resources, such as the wind and solar energy, are renewable; that is, using them once does not reduce the amount left to be used in

Figure 19.3 Sources of America's Energy

Despite the technological advances of society, America still relies on traditional sources for its energy: coal, oil, and natural gas. Only 6 percent of our energy comes from renewable sources, mainly hydroelectricity and geothermal power.

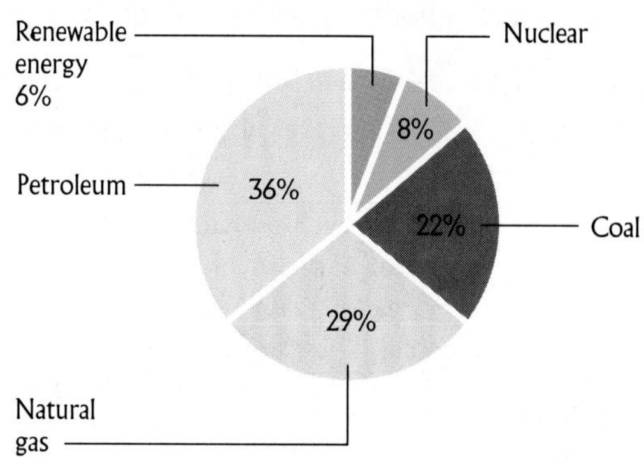

Source: Monthly Energy Review, December 2000.

the future. These things are constantly renewed by nature. Oil, coal, and other common sources of energy, however, are not renewable. Natural gas and petroleum are somewhat cleaner than coal (though they too contribute to global warming), but petroleum imports inevitably lead to oil spills.

The most controversial energy source is nuclear power. During the 1940s and 1950s, Americans were convinced that the technology that had ended World War II could be made to serve peaceful purposes. Nuclear scientists spoke enthusiastically about harnessing the atom to produce electricity that would be "too cheap to meter." These claims, however, were met with increasing skepticism in the light of huge cost overruns and the accidents at Three Mile Island and Chernobyl. The wave of environmental concern that developed in the late 1960s devastated the nuclear power industry, and no new nuclear power plants have been built in the United States since 1978.

The trade-offs between nuclear and other forms of energy emphasize many of the problems of politics in a high-tech age. Environmentalists dislike nuclear power because of radiation leaks in the mining, transportation, and use of atomic fuel; because of the enormous problem of nuclear waste disposal; and because of the inherent difficulty of regulating such complex technology. Defenders of nuclear energy argue that burning coal to generate electricity continues to blacken miners' lungs, causes acid rain that defoliates forests and kills lakes, adds to global warming, and creates other problems. Discussing energy policy in the United States, therefore, almost automatically means discussing environmental policy as well.[32]

Each source of energy poses potential risks to the environment. Even clean hydroelectric power plants flood large areas of land, which in turn affects the habitat of both plant and animal life. No form of electricity generation is perfect; but Americans want their lights to come on when they flip a switch. Policymakers must therefore determine the best combination of energy sources to use.

Recently, policymakers have shown more interest in conservation, renewable energy supplies, and alternative fuels. The 1992 energy bill, for example—the closest thing the United States has to a comprehensive national energy strategy—encourages the development of renewable energy sources and alternative "clean" fuels (such as methane and natural gas), mandates efficiency standards for buildings and home appliances, and encourages state utilities to reward conservation. The bill left many issues open, but it showed a new appreciation for the role that newer energy sources (and conservation) can play in improving the environment and reducing the United States' dependence on energy imports. The bill's passage also suggested that renewable and alternative energy sources, as well as conservation, are increasingly seen as compatible with continued economic growth.

American's long-standing expectation of abundant energy and rock-bottom prices was again put to the test as the twenty-first century began. High gasoline prices in the summer of 2000 were followed by hefty increases in the costs of natural gas during the cold winter of 2000–2001. Nowhere were the problems worse than in California, where "rolling brownouts"—temporary but planned disruptions of electric service—darkened homes, factories, and offices in 2001.

Global Warming. One of the most intractable and potentially most serious issues relating to energy and the environment is global warming. When fossil fuels (coal, oil, and natural gas—the remnants of ancient plants and animals) are burned, they produce carbon dioxide. It, along with smaller quantities of methane and other gases, collects in the atmosphere, wrapping the earth in an added layer of insulation and heating the climate. The "greenhouse effect" occurs when energy from the sun is trapped under the atmosphere and warms the earth as a result, much as in a greenhouse.[33]

Many scientists argue that the earth is warming at a rapid rate and will be between 2 and 6 degrees warmer by the year 2100. This may not seem like a major change, but the world is now only 5–9 degrees warmer than during the depths of the last ice age, 20,000 years ago. Scientists predict that if the warming trend is not reversed, seas will rise (gobbling up shorelines and displacing millions of people), severe droughts, rainstorms, heat waves, and floods will become more common, and broad shifts in climatic and agricultural zones will occur, bringing famine, disease, and pestilence to some areas.

There is no technology to control carbon emissions, so the only way to reduce greenhouse gases is to burn less fuel or find alternative sources of energy. In 1992, industrialized countries met in Rio de Janeiro and voluntarily agreed to cut greenhouse gas emissions to 1990 levels by the year 2000. None of the countries has come close to meeting these goals.

At the end of 1997, 150 nations met in Kyoto, Japan, and agreed in principle to require 38 industrial nations to reduce their emissions of greenhouse gases below 1990 levels by about 2010. The European Union would reduce emissions by 8 percent, the United States by 7 percent, and Japan by 6 percent. The less developed nations argue that rich countries got rich by burning coal and oil and still produce most of the emissions today. (The United States alone, with only 4 percent of the world's population, produces more than 20 percent of the gases that cause global warming.) Thus, the less developed nations say that developed nations should bear most of the burden in reducing global warming. Besides, less developed nations insist they are the ones who would be hurt worst by climate changes, and they are hard-pressed enough as it is.

Why does it matter?

Many scientists believe that global warming will have dire consequences for the entire world. Because of its advanced economic system, the United States produces a larger quantity of greenhouse gases per person than any other nation. At the same time, no other nation can force the United States to reduce its emissions. Do you have any responsibility to help reduce greenhouse gases, or is that a problem for the next generation? What are our responsibilities to other peoples? How much cost, if any, should you and other American people bear to benefit the rest of the world?

Opponents of the treaty in the United States fear that cutting greenhouse gases will cost a staggering sum. They also argue that it is unfair that the developed nations should bear the burden of cutting greenhouse emissions. After all, they say, less developed nations produce more emissions per dollar of gross domestic product than do developed countries. Adding ratification barrier is the fact that carbon dioxide lingers in the atmosphere for over 100 years and the benefits of reductions would not be felt for decades—but the costs would be immediate. In addition, not everyone is convinced that the earth's warming is the result of greenhouse gases. Scientific uncertainty in a technological age undermines efforts to deal with problems caused by technology. As a result of the conflicting views regarding global warming and the burden of reducing it, President Clinton never submitted the Kyoto treaty to the Senate and President Bush simply renounced it in 2001.

participation
America's Place in the World

Toxic Wastes

Long before the environmental movement was born, polluters created problems that are still unresolved. During the 1940s and 1950s, for example, before government oversight of toxic substances was as stringent as it is now, Hooker Chemical Company dumped toxic waste near the shores of the Love Canal in New York. Then in 1953, the company generously donated a 16-acre plot next to the canal to build a school. Thereafter, tons of chemicals, some in rotting barrels, were discovered, and children and adults later developed liver, kidney, and other health problems. With the company out of business, the level of contamination so great, and the identification of a huge number of other toxic waste dumps, popular outcry led to action in Washington.

Superfund

A fund created by Congress in 1980 to clean up hazardous waste sites. Money for the fund comes from taxing chemical products.

In 1980, Congress reacted to increased pressure to deal with toxic waste by establishing a **Superfund,** funded by taxing chemical products. The law established that those who polluted the land were responsible for paying to clean it up. A controversial retroactive liability provision holds companies liable even for legal dumping prior to 1980. The law also contains strict provisions for liability, under which the government can hold a single party liable for cleaning up an entire site that received waste from many sources.

The Comprehensive Environmental Response, Compensation, and Liability Act (the formal name of the Superfund law) has virtually eliminated haphazard dumping of toxic waste, but it has been less successful in cleaning up existing waste. Instead, the law has led to endless rounds of litigation. Large companies facing multimillion-dollar cleanup bills have tried to recover some of their costs by suing small businesses that had contributed to the hazardous waste. They have also been embroiled in protracted court fights with their insurers over whether policies written in the early 1980s cover Superfund-related costs.[34]

The federal government spends more than $11 billion annually to restore lands spoiled by chemical and radioactive wastes, about $2 billion of which comes from the Superfund. This is the fastest growing segment of the nation's environmental budget. The average cleanup takes 10 years and costs nearly $30 million. The EPA says that about 350 sites have been cleaned and that the most dangerous compounds have been removed from 3,300 more. Just 279 of the 1,296 sites on the EPA's priority list have been cleaned up; 64 of these are now so pristine that they have been taken off the list.

The EPA has found it more difficult to clean up toxic waste sites than it had hoped, however; workers find that the damage at some sites is so serious that they may never be cleaned satisfactorily. The effort is also hampered by the sheer number of sites requiring attention—more than 30,000—and by the limits of technology for cleaning up toxic compounds. Moreover, as it investigates more and more sites, the EPA finds that there are many more dangerous sites than it estimated. Equally troublesome, there is no consensus on how clean a contaminated site has to become (see "Making a Difference: Robert J. Martin, EPA's Quiet Man in the Middle"). In most cases, the EPA has chosen the strictest—and most expensive—standards, whether the site is to be used for a factory or a playground.

In the meantime, more carefully monitoring and regulating the use and disposal of hazardous wastes has implemented a series of governmental policies to prevent future disasters like Love Canal. Regulations mandated by the Resource Conservation and Recovery Act of 1977, for example, require "cradle-to-grave" tracking of many toxic chemicals, specify how these chemicals are to be handled while in use or in transit, and prescribe certain disposal techniques.[35]

Another serious environmental challenge is the disposal of nuclear waste, such as that from nuclear reactors and the production of nuclear weapons. It is necessary to protect not only ourselves but also the people of a distant future from radioactive materials. These wastes must be isolated for 10,000 years! At this point, 30,000 metric tons of highly radioactive nuclear waste are sitting in temporary sites around the country, most of them near nuclear power plants. Congress has studied, debated, and fretted for years over where to store the nation's nuclear waste. In the 1980s, Congress envisioned that spent nuclear fuel would be consolidated and permanently buried. It designated Yucca Mountain in Nevada as the provisional site in 1987. Questions about the safety and cost of the site and the vehement opposition from Nevada's congressional delegation have delayed the implementation of the plan. No state is eager to have a storage area for nuclear wastes within its boundaries, and there can be little doubt that cleaning up nuclear waste is going to take decades and cost billions of dollars.

Neighborhoods don't want to be the recipients of toxic and other wastes either. When minority communities see dumps, waste sites, or other environmental messes put in their neighborhood, they often see it as discrimination. "Environmental

Making a Difference

Robert J. Martin, EPA's Quiet Man in the Middle

Robert J. Martin's narrow office is tucked in the corner of a corridor of the Environment Protection Agency. The view is not much to look at, and his walls are decorated with photographs of his three children's soccer teams. In other words, one might define the office as a classic example of bureaucratic obscurity. Inside Washington, the 41-year-old lawyer remained virtually anonymous—until recently.

Martin is the ombudsman in EPA's Office of Solid Waste and Emergency Response. A watchdog group, the Project on Government Oversight recently honored Martin with its "Beyond the Headlines" award that recognizes little-noticed but high-impact work. Martin came to the Project's attention from people such as Marie Flickinger, the owner of a community newspaper in an industrial area of Houston where the EPA identified a so-called Superfund hazardous waste site and ordered it cleaned up. "That man saved this community," Flickinger said.

At issue was an abandoned facility that was once used by Monsanto Co. and other companies to store and reprocess chemical waste. Under the Superfund law, the companies were responsible for the cleanup. After years of studies and negotiations, EPA's Dallas office approved a plan to dispose of the site's contaminated soil by incineration. In the early 1990s, the companies constructed a $30 million incinerator to accomplish that task.

But Flickinger and other community activists, who had spent years arguing that the site was the source of an unusual number of birth defects and other health problems in a nearby subdivision, feared that digging up the soil and burning it would only spread the pollutants into the atmosphere and make the situation worse. They took their case to Martin, who launched his own investigation. Ultimately, Martin sided with Flickinger and her supporters.

Martin persuaded the EPA to approve an alternative plan to evacuate the subdivision and contain the pollutants by walling off the site. The incinerator was dismantled without ever being used.

With a staff of only four others, Martin estimates that his office handles about 4,000 complaints a year. These complaints range from unauthorized dumping in someone's backyard to serious oil spills and continuing problems at Superfund sites. Noting that he cannot compel other EPA officials to accept his findings and recommendations, Martin remarks, "I have no power." Perhaps this is true in a sense, but Robert Martin is certainly making a difference.

Source: Edward Walsh, "EPA's Quiet Man in the Middle: Watchdog Group Honors Ombudsman for Being Public's Voice," *Washington Post*, December 8, 1998, A19.

racism" is the targeting of unwanted land uses to minority neighborhoods. In 1982, a massive hazardous waste landfill was proposed for Warren County, N.C., almost two-thirds African American and the state's poorest county. The Congressional Black Caucus and the United Church of Christ joined protesting residents. This protest began to focus attention on where the worst environmental waste is placed.[36] Injustice, though, can be hard to prove. Landfills are put into areas with low-cost land, where poor and minority groups live. The calculation can be as much economic as racial. Still, groups that see themselves as the targets for the worst of our environmental pollution no longer sit idly by.

Making Environmental Policy

Nobody is against cleaning up the environment. The issue becomes a political question only because environmental concerns often conflict with equally legitimate concerns about foreign trade, economic growth, and jobs. Those who generate pollution do so in their efforts to make cars, to produce electricity, and to provide food and the consumer products that Americans take for granted. On federally owned land, including national parks and forests, there has long been a policy of multiple use whereby mining, lumbering, and grazing leases are awarded to private companies or ranchers at very low cost. Often the industries supported by these arrangements are important sources of jobs to otherwise depressed areas, and they may also lessen the country's dependence on foreign sources of oil and minerals.

Massive battles pitting lumbering interests against national and local environmental groups have raged in Alaska, where exports of lumber products to Japan provide jobs but decimate large parts of the Tongass National Forest. Similarly, harvesting old-growth timber on public lands has caused great concern in Oregon and Washington. In the Northwest and Alaska, environmentalists have complained that some of the few remaining large tracts of virgin forest, with trees hundreds of years old, are being felled by logging companies operating under generous lease agreements with the U.S. government, which owns the lands. Oil exploration on public lands and off shore in coastal waters also brings the goals of environmental protection and economic growth into conflict. In 1989, the spill of the *Exxon Valdez* off the coast of Alaska demonstrated the environmental risks of oil exploration.

One of the biggest changes in environmental policymaking in recent years is the increasing presence of new interest groups that complain about pollution and press for government action. Once, only a few conservation groups actively attempted to conserve public lands or oppose potentially damaging projects. Pollution was mostly seen as an inevitable product of economic growth; because Americans wanted jobs, they accepted the pollution that accompanied the businesses.

The 1960s and 1970s saw an explosion in the size and number of environmental interest groups.[37] Bosso reports two environmental groups (the National Wildlife Federation and the World Wildlife Fund) with more than a million members. The Sierra Club, Greenpeace, the National Audubon Society, the Natural Resources Defense Council, and others count half a million members each. Obviously, American environmental interest groups have sizable memberships.

In March of 1989, the *Exxon Valdez* ran aground off the southern coast of Alaska, spilling 11 million gallons of crude oil. Despite a $2 billion clean-up effort, the oil killed thousands of fish and animals and ruined miles of shoreline. No other single oil spill has drawn so much public attention to the environmental dangers of America's reliance on oil as an energy source.

How You Can Make a Difference

Protecting the Environment

"Think Globally, Act Locally" is a popular bumper sticker message for the environmental movement with good reason: Protecting the planet as a whole starts with the little things you do in your own community. For example, if your college doesn't have recycling bins next to the garbage cans, then a simple request to your student government representative or the student development office can make a small but significant difference. Collectively such acts have global consequences.

If your campus or community doesn't have an organization devoted to pursuing environmental concerns, then create one! If this sounds too intimidating, try consulting *A Beginner's Guide to Protecting the Planet* (www.foe.org/ptp/guide/organize). This guidebook promises "... straightforward information to help the beginner take action and make a difference on environmental issues." The manual illustrates the importance of choosing a worthwhile, winnable environmental issue that will result in improving people's lives. To do this, you need to set out both long-range and short-range goals. For example, a short-term goal may be to meet with the student development office on campus or the city council in your community. Another short-term goal might be to collect information using the Freedom of Information Act. With advice including tactics to influence the media and government, this guide is a vital companion to any effort at building a local environmental action group.

In fact, the Environmental Protection Agency (www.epa.gov) now considers these types of community-based organizations a necessary component of an effective environmental agenda. Traditionally, the EPA and other environmentalists have most heavily emphasized a "command and control" model that assumes that federal regulation is the key component in solving environmental problems. Increasingly, however, the EPA is arguing that local control proves far more efficient than federal control from Washington, D.C. Every community has unique and individual problems that require their own unique solution. For those interested in more closely engaging with the EPA locally, their website also provides access to the Resource Conservation and Recovery Act (RCRA) Public Participation Manual.

No group proudly announces that it is opposed to a clean environment. But there are many groups that oppose self-proclaimed environmentalists ("tree huggers," some sneer). They argue that the effects of environmental regulations on employment, economic growth, and international competitiveness must be part of the policymaking equation. Others, especially ranchers, miners, farmers, and loggers, demand inexpensive access to public land and the right to use their own property as they wish or else be compensated by government for being prohibited from doing so. In the West, groups that oppose the environmentalists often call themselves "wise use" advocates. Western proponents of mining interests formed People for the West. Republicans get a large share of their certain electoral votes from western states. Ranching, grazing, logging, and mining interests loom large in this coalition. George W. Bush was generous in his appointments of "wise use" westerners to key environmental posts. (Environmentalists thought this was leaving the fox to watch the henhouse.)

Widening opposition to potentially hazardous industrial facilities (such as toxic or nuclear waste dumps) has further complicated environmental policymaking in recent years. Local groups have often successfully organized resistance to planned development, rallying behind the cry "Not in My Back Yard." The so-called NIMBY phenomenon highlights another difficult dilemma in environmental policy: How can government equitably distribute the costs associated with society's seemingly endless demand for new technologies, some of which turn out to be environmentally threatening? If, for example, we are to use nuclear power to keep our lights on, the waste it produces must go in someone's backyard. But whose?

For all these reasons, government policies designed to clean up the environment are sure to be controversial, expensive, and debated for years to come.

Why does it matter?

Most Americans say "NIMBY"—not in my backyard—when government proposes locating unwanted waste dumps, toxic disposal sites, and other unhealthy land uses near their homes. Would you always oppose the placement of environmental hazards in your neighborhood? Should government give every neighborhood a veto over having to house wastes? If every community, even sparsely populated rural areas, had a veto, where would society dispose of its hazardous materials?

Understanding Health Care and Environmental Policy

The complex issues involved in making policy for health care and the environment pose many special problems in a democracy. These issues are difficult to understand when discussed in experts' terms, but most Americans do not want to leave them to "experts" to decide. This section discusses how democracies handle such issues and then considers the impact of these issues on the scope of government.

Democracy, Health Care, and Environmental Policy

Very few Americans actually understand how a nuclear power plant operates. Few know how to perform a heart operation. Does such ignorance mean that citizens should not be allowed to participate in the public policy debates concerning complex technologies? High-tech issues, more than any others, strain the limits of public participation in a democracy. Further, the issues associated with high technology are often so complex that many different levels of government—local, state, and national—become heavily involved. Whether it be the new ethical issues raised by machines and devices that can keep patients alive indefinitely—respirators, artificial kidneys, and the like—or whether it be the threats to public safety inherent in an accident at a nuclear power plant, governments are constantly called on to make decisions that involve tremendously complex technologies. Maintaining the right balance between public participation and technological competence is not an easy task.

High-technology issues make it especially difficult to include the public in a reasoned political debate. Often groups of specialists are the only ones who seem qualified to make decisions (and these specialists may have "special interest" in the issues on which they pass expert judgment). Still, in the United States, dramatic change has occurred. Environmental groups that once focused only on dramatic statements or loud protests now have their own staffs of scientists. Because knowledge is important in a highly complex debate, they have procured the resources to develop that knowledge. No longer are major public issues such as environmental pollution debated in the absence of well-informed groups looking out for the public interest.

Policymaking for technological issues seems to rely heavily on group representation. Individual citizens are unlikely to have the information or the resources to participate meaningfully because of the complexity of the debates. Interest groups—

Citizen action is a powerful force even on highly technical issues such as nuclear power. Here, protesters oppose the nuclear power plant in Shoreham, New Hampshire.

"I'm rather fortunate. I have no parents, so Medicare is no problem, and I have no children, so the environment is no problem."

Drawing by Handelsman ©1995 The New Yorker Magazine, Inc.

associations of professionals and citizens—play an active role in making the complicated decisions that will affect all Americans for generations.

The Scope of Government and Health Care and Environmental Policy

Americans do not hesitate to call for government to play a greater role in high-technology issues, and the scope of the federal government has grown in response to these demands. Medicare for the elderly, Medicaid for the poor, and tax subsidies for employer-provided health insurance are large, expensive public policies. Further efforts to reform health care will only increase the government's role. So will responses to health crises like the AIDS epidemic.

Similarly, in the past three decades, concerns for environmental protection have placed additional demands on the federal government (see Table 19.1). Americans like to think that nuclear power plants are inspected by federal officials to ensure safety. As the plants grow older, citizens might want more, not fewer, people working in this federal agency. When the *Exxon Valdez* spilled millions of gallons of oil into the waters off Alaska, no one complained about using the Coast Guard to coordinate the cleanup.

At the same time, important forces rein in the federal government. One of the principal reasons why President Clinton's health care proposal failed to pass Congress in 1994 was the public's fear of government health care regulations. The Republicans who took over Congress in 1995 are demanding that future health, safety, and environmental regulations be subjected to rigorous standards of evaluation. Thus, there is tension between demands for government services and protections and concerns about how government will provide those services and protections.

Summary

Americans live in an age driven by technology. Like so much in human history, technology brings its blessings and its curses. In particular, technology meets public policy in health care and the environment.

Table 19.1 The Revolution in Environmental Protection

In 1960 environmental protection was not a prominent feature of federal policy, which at that time focused largely on the establishment of parks. Things changed, however. Starting in 1963, Congress passed numerous bills that firmly established protection of the environment as one of the federal government's principal responsibilities.

MAJOR ENVIRONMENTAL PROTECTION LAWS	
1963	Clean Air Act
1964	Wilderness Act
1965	Highway Beautification Act
	Water Quality Act
1967	Air Quality Act
1968	Wild and Scenic Rivers Act
1969	National Environmental Policy Act
	Endangered Species Conservation Act
1970	Clean Air Act Amendments
	Water Quality Improvement Act
1972	Federal Water Pollution Control Act
	Marine Mammal Protection Act
	Marine Protection, Research, and Sanctuaries Act
	Coastal Zone Management Act
	Federal Environmental Pesticide Control Act
	Noise Control Act
1973	Endangered Species Act
1974	Safe Drinking Water Act
1976	Federal Land Policy and Management Act
	National Forest Management Act
	Resource Conservation and Recovery Act
	Toxic Substances and Control Act
1977	Clean Air Act Amendments
	Clean Water Act
	Surface Mining Control and Reclamation Act
1978	Outer Continental Shelf Lands Act Amendments
1980	Comprehensive Environmental Response, Compensation, and Liability Act
	Alaska National Interest Lands Conservation Act
1984	Hazardous and Solid Waste Amendments
1986	Safe Drinking Water Act Amendments
	Superfund Amendments and Reauthorization Act
1987	Water Quality Act
1988	Endangered Species Act Reauthorization
	Federal Insecticide, Fungicide, and Rodenticide Act Amendments
1990	Clean Air Act Reauthorization
1994	California Desert Protection Act
	Marine Mammal Protection Act Reauthorization
1996	Safe Drinking Water Act Amendments
	Overhaul of Pesticide Regulations
1997	Higher Standards for Clean Air

Health care already makes up one-seventh of America's GDP, and with increased technology, its costs will almost certainly continue to rise. These advances have improved health care, but tremendous problems also plague health care in America, including inadequate insurance coverage (or no coverage at all) for many people and ever-increasing costs for even routine medical attention. The paradox of health policy in the United States is that it spends more of its national income on health than other nations and is far from the healthiest.

Career Profile

Position: On-Scene Coordinator for EPA Emergency Response Teams
Starting Salary Range: $33,000-35,000
Benefits: Health and retirement, EPA-issued cellphones, Palm Pilots and laptop computers.
Qualifications: Except under unique circumstances, a bachelor's degree in the sciences (biology, chemistry, or engineering) is required. Interpersonal skills and decisive leadership abilities are mandatory

Real People on the Job: Jose Negron

In the middle of the night, a freight train running through your neighborhood suddenly derails. A tank car full of toxic chemicals ruptures and spews fumes into the air. Although local emergency, fire, and ambulance crews are the first to arrive, the Environmental Protection Agency's National Response Center, operating 24 hours a day and 365 days a year, receives a request to dispatch an Emergency Response Team to the accident site. In such a scenario, responsibility for the EPA's response will fall on an on-scene coordinator like Jose Negron.

During a toxic spill emergency, Jose coordinates with the local police and fire departments, as well as any other federal, state, and local agencies responding to the emergency. He establishes a mobile command post for the emergency complete with telecommunications equipment and computer databases.

In order to ensure an efficient command structure, Jose becomes the central point of control and authority. It's Jose's job to determine the exact nature of the toxic material in question and the health and environmental threats it poses. Typical toxic substances include gasoline, oil, chlorine, pesticides, and insecticides. Depending upon state regulations and requirements, a cleanup plan is then initiated. The most common EPA emergencies involve oil pipeline leaks. Most emergencies take anywhere from three days to a couple of weeks to clean up, depending upon the nature of substances involved.

While emergency cleanups are often dramatic, Jose spends most of his time on projects labeled as Critical Action Removals, hazardous waste sites that require immediate (but not emergency) attention from the EPA. When a marina in Kentucky caught fire, for example, the boats docked at the marina sank and their fuel and oil began seeping into the lake. Jose and his crew had to use scuba gear to eliminate the contaminants because the site was too far from the surface. At another site, discarded casings from batteries stripped for their lead content leached into the soil and created a toxic hazard. In these and other situations, Jose helps design the restoration plans, drainage solutions and relocation models to fix the problem. The EPA then calls on approved regional subcontractors who are qualified to assist in completing the mission.

Despite some similarities, each new site is unique and requires a new plan of attack to solve the contaminant problem. This very diversity, says Jose, is perhaps the best and most rewarding part of his job. He is constantly challenged to not only protect the environment but also to save lives. In this job, you can't be afraid of making decisions because countless agencies and workers depend upon your decision.

If you want to find out more about working for the Environmental Protection Agency, check http://www.epa.gov.

Americans are also increasingly concerned with the environment. Environmental issues will continue to cause the government to become involved in many aspects of daily life, and they often pit citizens' groups against important economic interests. The government has become very active in ensuring the quality of America's air, land, and water and in protecting wildlife. We are dependent on energy, but the most common sources of energy, coal and oil, cause many environmental and health problems. Nuclear power, once seen as a solution to the nation's energy needs, is at a virtual standstill because of the massive public fear of exposure to radioactivity, the high costs of the technology, and inconsistency in design and management.

In both of these public policy areas government is and will continue to be at the center of public debate. Furthermore, governmental activities can be expected to grow, rather than to decrease, in each of these areas. Finally, citizen participation has profoundly influenced government decisions. Voting and organizing interest group campaigns will continue to be important means of influencing health care and the environment.

Key Terms

health maintenance organizations (HMOs)
national health insurance
Medicare
Medicaid
Environmental Protection Agency (EPA)
National Environmental Policy Act (NEPA)
environmental impact statement (EIS)
Clean Air Act of 1970
Water Pollution Control Act of 1972
Endangered Species Act of 1973
Superfund

For Further Reading

Easterbrook, Gregg. *A Moment on the Earth: The Coming Age of Environmental Optimism.* New York: Viking, 1995. Stresses the successes of environmental protection.

Ginzberg, Eli, ed. *Critical Issues in U.S. Health Reform.* Boulder, CO: Westview, 1994. Examines many dimensions of reforming the U.S. health care system.

Gore, Albert. *Earth in the Balance: Ecology and the Human Spirit.* Boston: Houghton Mifflin, 1992. The former vice president presents a manifesto for protecting the environment.

Hird, John A. *Superfund: The Politics of Environmental Risk* (Baltimore: Johns Hopkins, 1994). An assessment of the Superfund and the politics of toxic wastes.

Landy, Marc K., Marc J. Roberts, and Stephen R. Thomas. *The Environmental Protection Agency,* expanded edition. New York: Oxford University Press, 1994. A critical evaluation of the EPA.

McCormick, John. *Reclaiming Paradise: The Global Environmental Movement.* Bloomington: Indiana University Press, 1989. A discussion of the origins and the explosive growth of the environmental movement worldwide.

Switzer, Jacqueline Vaughn. *Environmental Politics—Domestic and Global Dimensions.* New York: St. Martin's Press, 1994. A good overview of the politics of environmental policy.

Tobin, Richard. *The Expendable Future: U.S. Politics and the Protection of Biological Diversity.* Durham, NC: Duke University Press, 1990. The promise and problems of trying to protect endangered species.

Vig, Norman J., and Michael E. Kraft, eds. *Environmental Policy,* 4th ed. Washington, D.C.: Congressional Quarterly Press, 2000. Useful articles on a range of environmental policy issues.

Wilson, Edward O. *The Diversity of Life.* Cambridge, MA: Belknap Press, 1992. The dean of American biologists argues that human beings are in danger of precipitating a biological disaster, diminishing the world's biodiversity.

Internet Resources

www.census.gov/prod/3/98pubs/98statab/sasec3.pdf
Statistical Abstract of the United States data on Americans' health and health care policy.

www.census.gov/hhes/www/hlthins.html
Census Bureau data on health insurance coverage.

www.ahcpr.gov/consumer/hlthpln1.htm
Department of Health and Human Services' Agency for Health Care Policy and Reform provides a guide to choosing and using a health plan.

www.epa.gov/
Official site for the Environmental Protection Agency, which provides information on policies and current environmental issues.

www.sierraclub.org/
Web site for the Sierra Club, one of the most active environmental protection organizations.

www.epa.gov/superfund/sites/index.htm
Locate toxic waste sites in your state.

Notes

1. Robert Pear, "Policy Changes Fail To Fill Gap in Health Coverage," *New York Times*, August 9, 1998, 1, 18.
2. Barbara Crossette, "Americans Enjoy 70 Healthy Years, Behind Europe, U. N. Says," *New York Times*, June 5, 2000, A10.
3. *Statistical Abstract of the United States, 2000*, 828.
4. Quoted in Richard L. Berke, "Clinton Warns That Economy May Still Be Bad," *New York Times*, December 8, 1992, A13.
5. *Ibid.* 1998, 134.
6. *Ibid.*, 1998, 119.
7. Robert Pear, "Number of Insured up for First Time Since '87," *New York Times*, September 29, 2000, A16.
8. U.S. Bureau of the Census, *Current Population Reports: Who Loses Coverage and for How Long?* May 1996, 1.
9. *Statistical Abstract of the United States, 2000*, 116.
10. CBS News/*New York Times* Poll, reported in *The American Enterprise*, March/April 1992, 87. See also, Peter T. Kilborn, "The Uninsured Find Fewer Doctors in the House," *New York Times*, August 30, 1998, 14.
11. *Current Population Reports: Health Insurance Coverage: 1997*.
12. Julie Kosterlitz, "A Sick System," *National Journal*, February 15, 1992, 380.
13. *Current Population Reports: Health Insurance Coverage: 1997*.
14. Pear, "Policy Changes Fail To Fill Gap in Health Coverage," *New York Times*, 18.
15. John Budetti, et al., *Can't Afford To Get Sick: A Reality for Millions of Working Americans* (New York: Commonwealth Fund, 2000).
16. *Statistical Abstract of the United States, 2000*, 85, 88, 826.
17. Kosterlitz, "A Sick System," 376.
18. On Medicare's future, see Ronald Lee and Jonathan Skinner, "Will Aging Baby Boomers Bust the Federal Budget?" *Journal of Economic Perspectives* 13 (Winter 1999): 117–40.
19. Robert Pear, "More HMOs Exit Medicare and Cite Its Unprofitability," the *New York Times*, June 30, 2000, A1.
20. Robert Blank, *Rationing Medicine* (New York: Columbia University Press, 1988).
21. Howard M. Leichter, "The Poor and Managed Care in the Oregon Experience," *Journal of Health Politics, Policy and Law* 24 (October 1999): 1172–1184.
22. See the *Encyclopedia of Associations, 1999*, vol. 1, part 2 (Detroit: Gale Research, Inc., 1999), 1,322.
23. Edgar K. Browning and Jacqueline M. Browning, *Public Finance and the Price System*, 4th ed. (New York: Macmillan, 1994), 185–188.
24. These survey data are reported by the Economic Policy Institute in its "Take the Pulse Report" at epinet.org.
25. Louis Harris, *Washington Post*, January 15, 1982.
26. Jonathan Walters, "Land Use Laws and Hard Times," *Governing* 6 (October 1992): 25.
27. Robert Crandall, *Controlling Industrial Pollution* (Washington, D.C.: Brookings Institution, 1983).
28. William Ophuls, *Ecology and the Politics of Scarcity* (San Francisco: Freeman, 1977), 177.
29. Robert Stavins, "What Can We Learn from the Grand Policy Experiment? Positive and Normative Lessons from SO2 Allowance Trading," *Journal of Economic Perspectives* 12 (1998); see also A. Denny Ellerman, et al, *Markets for Clean Air: The U.S. Acid Rain Program* (Cambridge, MA: Cambridge University Press, 2000).
30. Samuel Hays, *Beauty, Health, Permanence* (New York: Cambridge University Press, 1987), 99.
31. Charles P. Alexander, "On the Defensive," *Time*, June 15, 1992, 35.
32. See John L. Campbell, *Collapse of an Industry: Nuclear Power and the Contradictions of U.S. Policy* (Ithaca, NY: Cornell University Press, 1988).
33. The global warming issue and the politics of climate are discussed in Lamont C. Hemple, "Climate Policy on the Installment Plan," in Norman J. Vig and Michael E. Kraft, eds. *Environmental Policy*, 4th ed., (Washington D.C.: Congressional Quarterly, 2000), chap. 13.
34. On implementing the Superfund law, see Thomas W. Church and Robert T. Nakamura, *Cleaning up the Mess: Implementation Strategies in Superfund* (Washington, D.C.: Brookings Institution, 1993).
35. On toxic waste and its politics, see John A. Hird, *Superfund: The Politics of Environmental Risk* (Baltimore: Johns Hopkins University Press, 1994).
36. Evan Ringquist, "Environmental Justice: Normative Concerns and Empirical Evidence," in Vig and Kraft, eds., *Environmental Policy*, chap. 11.
37. On environmental groups, see Christopher Bosso, "Environmental Groups and the New Political Landscape," in Vig and Kraft, eds., *Environmental Policy*, chap. 3. Group membership numbers are from Bosso.

Foreign and Defense Policymaking

20

Chapter Outline

In 1987, President Ronald Reagan stood before the historic Brandenburg Gate in a divided Berlin and challenged President Mikhail Gorbachev of the Soviet Union to tear down the Berlin Wall. Five years later, on June 17, 1992, Boris Yeltsin addressed a joint session of the U.S. Congress. When the burly, silver-haired president of the new Russian republic entered the House chamber, members of Congress greeted him with chants of "Bo-ris, Bo-ris" and hailed him with numerous standing ovations.

Yeltsin proclaimed to thunderous applause,

> The idol of communism, which spread everywhere social strife, animosity and unparalleled brutality, which instilled fear in humanity, has collapsed . . . I am here to assure you that we will not let it rise again in our land.

The Cold War that had been waged for two generations had ended, and the West, led by the United States, had won.

There was not much time to rejoice, however. The end of one set of challenges brought another to prominence. Now that Commu-

nism was no longer the principal threat to the security of the United States, what should our foreign policy goals be? What should be the role of the world's only remaining superpower? What should we do with our huge defense establishment, which had undergone an enormous increase in the 1980s?

The need to answer the question of the appropriate role of the national government in foreign and defense policy is more important, and perhaps more difficult, than ever. How should we deal with our former adversaries? Yeltsin's visit to the United States was not motivated primarily by a desire simply to bury the Cold War. He also signed an unprecedented arms control agreement with President Bush, discussed mutually beneficial trade, and sought aid for his ailing economy. At the same time, many of the former Communist nations of Eastern and Central Europe exhibited a frightening tendency to self-destruct in civil wars. In 1996, President Clinton proclaimed that "[t]here are times when only America can make the difference between war and peace, between freedom and repression, between hope and fear." Should the United States get involved in trying to end civil wars and the breakdown of political authority that results from the surfacing of long-suppressed ethnic, religious, and sectional conflicts?

And just how should we decide about national security policy? Should the American people delegate discretion in this area to officials who seem more at home with complex and even exotic issues of defense and foreign policy? Or should they and their representatives fully participate in the democratic policymaking process, just as they do in domestic policy? And can the public or its representatives in Congress or in interest groups have much influence on the elites who often deal in secrecy in national security policy?

The end of the Cold War has not lessened the importance of defense and foreign policy. New and complex challenges have emerged to replace the conflict with Communism. Most of these challenges are not traceable to a malevolent enemy who can be contained or defeated.

American Foreign Policy: Instruments, Actors, and Policymakers

foreign policy

A policy that involves choice-taking, like domestic policy, but additionally involves choices about relations with the rest of the world. The president is the chief initiator of foreign policy in the United States.

Foreign policy, like domestic policy, involves making choices—but the choices involved are about relations with the rest of the world. Because the president is the main force behind foreign policy, every morning the White House receives a highly confidential intelligence briefing that might cover monetary transactions in Tokyo, last night's events in some trouble spot on the globe, or Fidel Castro's health. The briefing is part of the massive informational arsenal the president uses to manage American foreign policy.

Instruments of Foreign Policy

The instruments of foreign policy are, however, different from those of domestic policy. Foreign policies depend ultimately on three types of tools: military, economic, and diplomatic. Among the oldest instruments of foreign policy are war and the threat of war. German General Karl von Clausewitz once called war a "continuation of politics by other means." As we learned in Chapter 13, the United States has been involved in only a few full-scale wars. It has often employed force to influence actions in other countries, however. Most of this influence has been close to home, in Central America and the Caribbean, as you can see in Figure 20.1.

Figure 20.1 U.S. Military Interventions in Central America and the Caribbean Since 1900

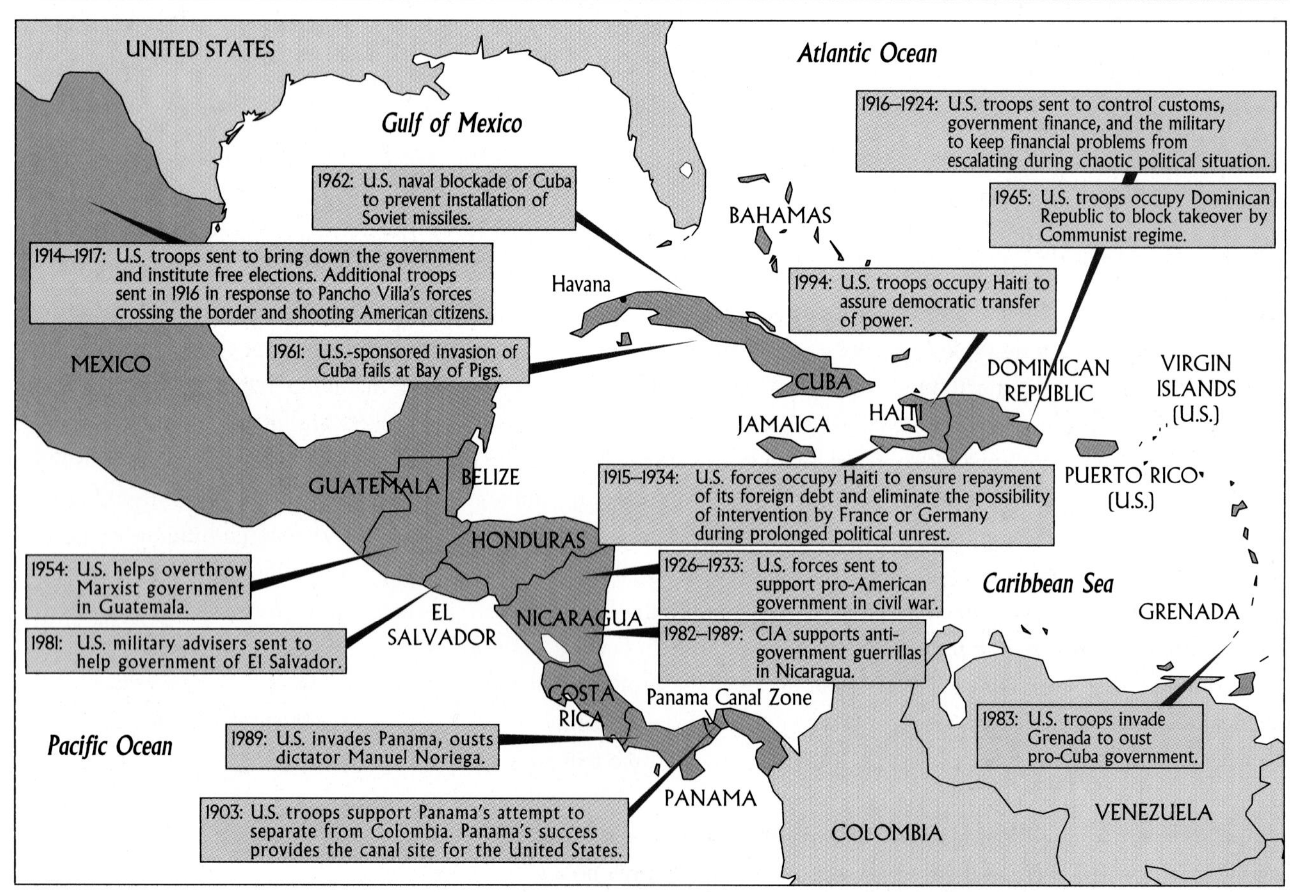

In recent years, the United States has continued to use force in limited ways around the world: to oppose ethnic cleansing in the Kosovo province of Yugoslavia, to prevent the toppling of the democratic government of the Philippines, to rescue the U.S. embassy in Somalia, to rescue stranded foreigners and protect our embassy in Liberia, to launch missile attacks on Baghdad in retaliation for an effort to assassinate former President Bush and the failure to provide United Nations weapons inspectors access to suspected weapons sites. The United States also employed military forces to aid the democratic transfer of power in Haiti and for humanitarian relief operations in Yugoslavia, Iraq, Somalia, Bangladesh, Russia, and Bosnia.

Today, economic instruments are becoming weapons almost as potent as those of war. The control of oil can be as important as the control of guns. Trade regulations, tariff policies, and monetary policies are other economic instruments of foreign policy. A number of recent studies have called attention to the importance of a country's economic vitality to its long-term national security.[1]

Diplomacy is the quietest instrument of influence. It is the process by which nations carry on relationships with each other. It often evokes images of ambassadors at chic cocktail parties, but the diplomatic game is played for high stakes. Sometimes national leaders meet in summit talks. More often, less prominent negotiators work out treaties covering all kinds of national contracts, from economic relations to the aid of stranded tourists.

Actors on the World Stage

If all the world's a stage, then there are more actors on it than ever before. More than 125 nations have emerged since 1945—nearly two dozen in the 1990s alone. Once foreign relations were almost exclusively transactions among nations in which military, economic, or diplomatic methods were used to achieve foreign policy goals. Nations remain the main actors in international politics, but today's world stage is more crowded.

International Organizations. Most of the challenges in international relations, ranging from peacekeeping and controlling weapons of mass destruction to protecting the environment and maintaining stable trade and financial networks, require the cooperation of many nations. It is not surprising that international organizations play an increasingly important role on the world stage.

The best-known international organization is the **United Nations (UN).** Housed in a magnificent skyscraper in New York City, the UN was created in 1945. Its members agree to renounce war and respect certain human and economic freedoms. The UN General Assembly is composed of 185 member nations. Each nation has one vote. Although not legally binding, General Assembly resolutions can achieve a measure of collective legitimization when a broad international consensus is formed on some matter concerning relations among states.

United Nations (UN)

Created in 1945, an organization whose members agree to renounce war and to respect certain human and economic freedoms. The seat of real power in the UN is the Security Council.

It is the *Security Council,* however, that is the seat of real power in the UN. Five of its 15 members (the United States, Great Britain, China, France, and Russia) are permanent members; the others are chosen from session to session by the General Assembly. Each permanent member has a veto over Security Council decisions, including any decisions that would commit the UN to a military peacekeeping operation. The Secretariat is the executive arm of the UN and directs the administration of UN programs. Composed of 8,700 international civil servants, it is headed by the secretary general. In addition to its peacekeeping function, the UN runs a number of programs focused on economic development and on health, education, and welfare.

Since 1948 there have been 53 United Nations peacekeeping operations, 40 of which were created by the Security Council between 1988 and 2000. In 1990, the UN Security Council backed resolutions authorizing an embargo on the shipment of goods to or from Iraq in an attempt to force its withdrawal from Kuwait. Later, it authorized the use of force to compel Iraq to withdraw. In 1992, the UN assisted famine relief in Somalia. More recently, it supported the return of the democratically elected president of Haiti and has been active, with only modest success, in trying to end the civil war in Bosnia-Herzegovina. In 2000 there were 14 UN missions under way in the Democratic Republic of the Congo, Sierra Leone, Western Sahara, East Timor, India/Pakistan, Tajikistan, the Golan Heights, Iraq/Kuwait, Lebanon, Bosnia-Herzegovina, Croatia, Cyprus, Georgia, Kosovo, and the Middle East generally.

The United States often plays the critical role in implementing UN policies. Although President Clinton envisioned an expanded role for UN peacekeeping operations at the beginning of his term, he later concluded that the UN is often not capable of making and keeping peace, particularly when hostilities among parties still exist. He also backtracked on his willingness to place American troops under foreign commanders—always a controversial policy.

The UN is only one of many international organizations. The International Monetary Fund, for example, helps regulate the chaotic world of international finance; the World Bank finances development projects in new nations; the World Trade Organization (WTO) attempts to regulate international trade; and the International Postal Union helps get the mail from one country to another.

Regional Organizations. *Regional organizations* have proliferated in the post-World War II era. These are organizations of several nations bound by a treaty, often for military reasons. The **North Atlantic Treaty Organization (NATO)** was created in 1949. Its members—the United States, Canada, most Western European nations, and Turkey—agreed to combine military forces and to treat a war against one as a war against all. During the Cold War, more than a million NATO troops (including about 325,000 Americans) were spread from West Germany to Portugal as a deterrent to foreign aggression. To counter the NATO alliance, the Soviet Union and its Eastern European allies formed the *Warsaw Pact.* The Warsaw Pact has since been dissolved, however, and the role of NATO has changed dramatically as the Cold War has thawed. In 1998, Poland, Hungary, and the Czech Republic, former members of the Warsaw Pact, became members of NATO. The current members of NATO are shown in Figure 20.2.

North Atlantic Treaty Organization (NATO)

Created in 1949, an organization whose members include the United States, Canada, most Western European nations, and Turkey, all of whom agreed to combine military forces and to treat a war against one as a war against all.

Regional organizations can be economic as well as military. The **European Union (EU)** is an economic alliance of the major Western European nations. The EU coordinates monetary, trade, immigration, and labor policies so that its members have become one economic unit, just as the 50 United States are an economic unit. Other economic federations exist in Latin America and Africa, although none is as unified as the EU.

European Union (EU)

An alliance of the major Western European nations which coordinates monetary, trade, immigration, and labor policies, making its members one economic unit. An example of regional organization.

Multinational Corporations. Chapter 17 discussed the potent *multinational corporations*, or MNCs. Today, a large portion of the world's industrial output comes from these corporations, and they account for more than one-fifth of the global economy.[2] Sometimes more powerful (and often much wealthier) than the governments under which they operate, MNCs have voiced strong opinions about governments, taxes, and business regulations. They have even linked forces with agencies such as the Central Intelligence Agency (CIA) to overturn governments they disliked. In the 1970s, for example, several of these corporations worked with the CIA to "destabilize" the democratically elected Marxist government in Chile; Chile's military overthrew the government in 1973. Even when they are not so heavy handed, MNCs are forces to be reckoned with in nearly all nations.

Nongovernmental Organizations (NGOs). *Groups* are also actors on the global stage. Churches and labor unions have long had international interests and activities. Today, environmental and wildlife groups such as Greenpeace have also proliferated. Ecological interests are active in international as well as in national politics. Groups interested in protecting human rights, such as Amnesty International, have also grown (see "Making a Difference: Jody Williams").

Not all groups, however, are committed to saving whales, oceans, or even people. Some are committed to the overthrow of particular governments and operate as ter-

Figure 20.2 NATO Membership

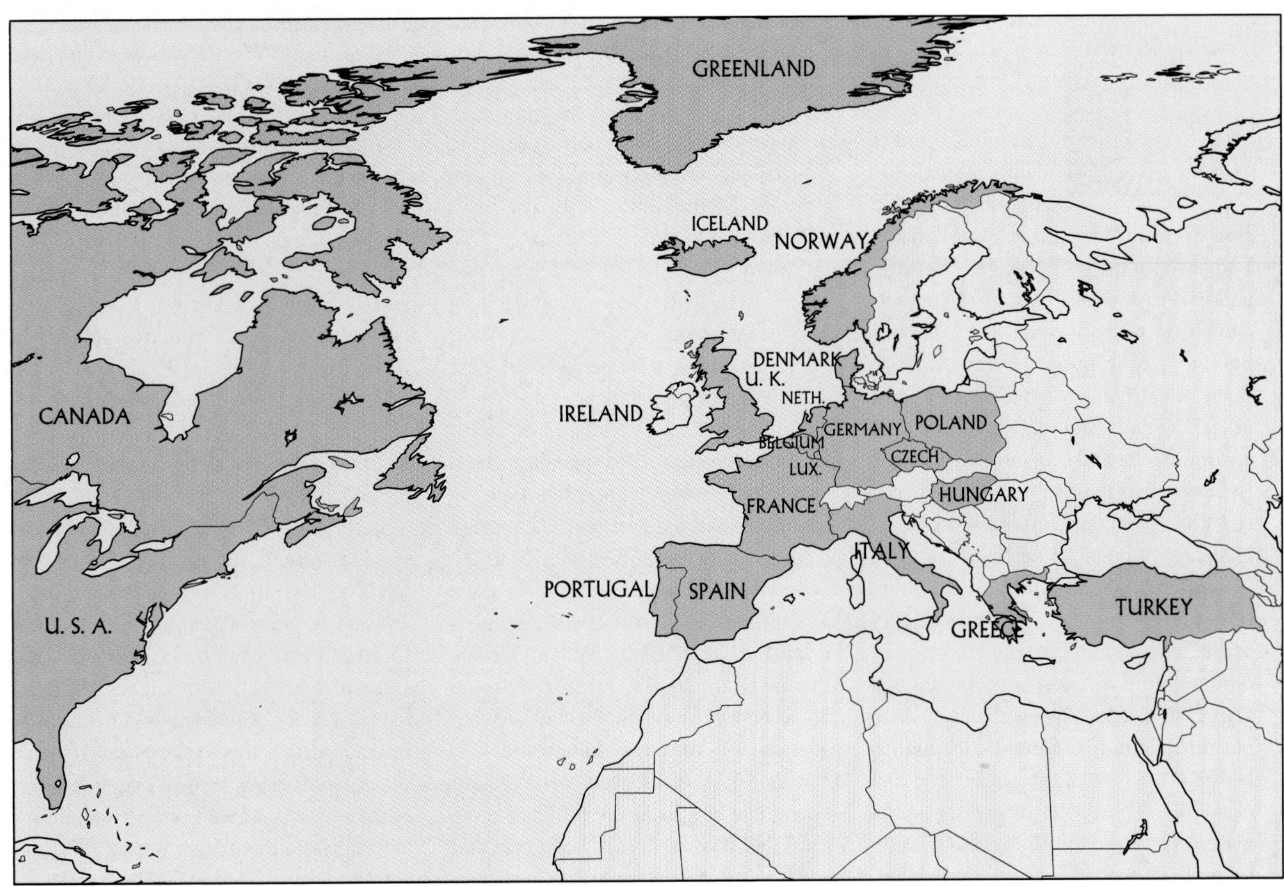

rorists around the world. Airplane hijackings, and assassinations, bombings, and similar terrorist attacks have made the world a more unsettled place. Conflicts within a nation or region thus spill over into world politics.

Individuals. Finally, *individuals* are international actors. The recent explosion of tourism sends Americans everywhere and brings to America legions of tourists from Japan, Europe, and the less-developed world. Tourism creates its own costs and benefits and thus always affects the international economic system. Tourism may enhance friendship and understanding among nations. However, more tourists traveling out of the country than arriving in the country can create problems with a country's balance of payments (discussed later in this chapter). In addition to tourists, growing numbers of students are going to and coming from other nations; they are carriers of ideas and ideologies. So are immigrants and refugees, who also place new demands on public services.

Just as there are more actors on the global stage than in the past, there are also more American decision makers involved in foreign policy problems.

The Policymakers

There are many policymakers involved with national security policy, but any discussion of foreign policymaking must begin with the president.

The President. The president, as you know from Chapter 13, is the main force behind foreign policy. As chief diplomat, the president negotiates treaties; as commander in chief of the armed forces, the president deploys American troops abroad.

Making a Difference

Jody Williams

Landmines are a daily threat in Afghanistan, Angola, Bosnia, Cambodia, Chechnya, Croatia, Iraq, Mozambigue, Nicaragua, Somalia, and dozens of other countries. Mines recognize no cease-fire and long after the fighting has stopped they continue to maim or kill. Mines also render large tracts of agricultural land unusable, wreaking environmental and economic devastation. Refugees returning to their war-ravaged countries often face this life-threatening obstacle to rebuilding their lives.

What makes landmines so abhorrent is the indiscriminate destruction they cause. Mines cannot be aimed. They lie dormant until a person or an animal triggers their detonating mechanism. Antipersonnel mines cannot distinguish between the footfall of a soldier and that of a child. Those who survive the initial blast usually require amputations, long hospital stays, and extensive rehabilitative services. In Cambodia alone there are over 35,000 amputees who were injured by landmines—and they are the survivors. Many others die in the fields from loss of blood or lack of transport to get medical help. Mine deaths and injuries in the past few decades total hundreds of thousands.

Jody Williams, a former schoolteacher and director of humanitarian relief efforts in Central America, decided to do something about the death and maiming caused by landmines. She became the founding coordinator of the International Campaign to Ban Landmines (ICBL), which was formally launched by six nongovernmental organizations (NGOs)—Handicap International, Human Rights Watch, Medico International, Mines Advisory Group, Physicians for Human Rights, and Vietnam Veterans of America Foundation—in October 1992. As coordinator, Ms. Williams oversaw the growth of the ICBL to more than 1,000 NGOs in over 75 countries and served as the chief strategist and spokesperson for the campaign.

Working in an unprecedented cooperative effort with governments, UN bodies, and the International Committee of the Red Cross, the ICBL has brought about tremendous change in a short period of time. In Ottawa, Canada, in December 1997, 122 countries signed a treaty that bans the use, production, stockpiling, and transfer of antipersonnel mines. The treaty became international law in March 1999, obtaining the signatures of an additional 11 nations.

In 1997, the Nobel Peace Prize was awarded to the ICBL and its coordinator, Jody Williams. In its announcement, the Norwegian Nobel Committee said the Campaign had changed a ban from "a vision to feasible reality." It also noted that by working with small and medium-sized countries, "this work has grown into a convincing example of an effective policy for peace that could prove of decisive importance to the international effort for disarmament . . ." Jody Williams made a difference.

The president also appoints U.S. ambassadors and the heads of executive departments (with the consent of the Senate), and he has the sole power to accord official recognition to other countries and receive (or refuse to receive) their representatives.

Some presidential foreign policy is made through the formal mechanisms of treaties or executive agreements. Both are written accords in which the parties agree to specific actions. Since the end of World War II, presidents have negotiated thousands of executive agreements but only about 800 treaties (see Table 20.1). They both have legal standing, but only treaties must be ratified by two-thirds of the Senate. Presidents usually find it more convenient to use executive agreements. Most executive agreements deal with routine and noncontroversial matters, but they have also been used for matters of significance such as ending the Vietnam War and arms control agreements.

The president combines constitutional prerogatives with greater access to information than other policymakers and can act with speed and secrecy if necessary. The White House is also advantaged by the president's role as a leader of Congress and the public and by his ability to commit the nation to a course of action. Presidents do not act alone in foreign policy, however. They are aided (and sometimes thwarted) by a huge national security bureaucracy. In addition, they must contend with the views and desires of Congress, which also wields considerable clout in the foreign policy arena—sometimes doing so in opposition to a president.

Table 20.1 Treaties and Executive Agreements Concluded By The United States, 1789–1998

YEARS	NUMBER OF TREATIES	NUMBER OF EXECUTIVE AGREEMENTS
1789–1839	60	27
1839–1889	215	238
1889–1929	382	763
1930–1932	49	41
1933–1944 (F. Roosevelt)	131	369
1945–1952 (Truman)	132	1,324
1953–1960 (Eisenhower)	89	1,834
1961–1963 (Kennedy)	36	813
1964–1968 (L. Johnson)	67	1,083
1969–1974 (Nixon)	93	1,317
1975–1976 (Ford)	26	666
1977–1980 (Carter)	79	1,476
1981–1988 (Reagan)	125	2,840
1989–1992 (Bush)	67	1,350
1993–1998 (Clinton)	168	1,647

Note: Number of treaties includes those concluded during the indicated span of years. Some of these treaties did not receive the consent of the U.S. Senate. Varying definitions of what comprises an executive agreement and their entry-into-force date make these numbers approximate.
Source: Harold W. Stanley and Richard G. Niemi, *Vital Statistics on American Politics*, 1999–2000 (Washington, D.C.: Congressional Quarterly Press, 2000), 329.

The Diplomats. The State Department is the foreign policy arm of the U.S. government. As the department's chief, the **secretary of state** (Thomas Jefferson was the first) has traditionally been the key advisor to the president on foreign policy matters. In over 300 overseas posts from Albania to Zimbabwe, the State Department staffs U.S. embassies and consulates, representing the interests of Americans. Once a dignified and genteel profession, diplomacy is becoming an increasingly dangerous job. The November 1979 seizure of the American embassy in Tehran and the 1998 bombing of the American embassy in Nairobi, Kenya are extreme examples of the hostilities that diplomats can face.

secretary of state
The head of the Department of State and traditionally a key advisor to the president on **foreign policy.**

The 27,700 people working in the State Department are organized into functional areas (such as economic and business affairs and human rights and humanitarian affairs) and area specialties (a section on Middle Eastern affairs, one on European affairs, and so on), each nation being handled by a "country desk." The political appointees who occupy the top positions in the department and the highly select members of the Foreign Service who compose most of the department are heavily involved in formulating and executing American foreign policy.

Many recent presidents have found the State Department too bureaucratic and intransigent. Even its colloquial name "Foggy Bottom," taken from the part of Washington where it is located, conjures up less than an image of cooperation. Some recent presidents have bypassed institutional arrangements for foreign policy decision making and have instead established more personal systems for receiving policy advice. Presidents Nixon and Carter, for example, relied more heavily on their special assistants for national security affairs (Henry Kissinger and Zbigniew Brzezinski, respectively) than on their secretaries of state. Foreign policy was thus centered in the White House and was often disconnected from what was occurring in the State Department. Critics, however, charged that this situation led to split-level government and chronic discontinuity in foreign policy.[3] President Reagan, by contrast, relied less on his assistants for national security affairs (six different men filled the job in eight

The secretary of state is typically the president's chief foreign policy advisor, presiding over a global bureaucracy of diplomats. Here, Colin Powell meets with South Korean President Kim Young-san.

years) and more on his Secretary of State, George Schultz, who was a powerful player. George Bush continued this pattern, appointing his closest friend, James Baker, as secretary of state. President Clinton also relied heavily on his secretaries of state, Warren Christopher and Madeleine Albright. George W. Bush appointed Colin Powell, one of the most admired people in America, as secretary of state. Powell is already the president's leading foreign policy adivsor.

The National Security Establishment. Foreign policy and military policy are closely linked. Thus the Department of Defense is a key foreign policy actor. Often called "the Pentagon" after the five-sided building in which it is located, the Defense Department was created after World War II. The U.S. Army, Navy, and Air Force were collected into one giant department, although they have never been thoroughly integrated and continue to plan and operate largely independently of one another. Reforms, made law under the Goldwater-Nichols Defense Reorganization Act of 1986, have increased interservice cooperation and centralization of the military hierarchy. The **secretary of defense** manages a budget larger than that of most nations and is the president's main civilian advisor on national defense matters.

secretary of defense

The head of the Department of Defense and the president's key advisor on military policy; a key **foreign policy** actor.

Joint Chiefs of Staff

The commanding officers of the armed services who advise the president on military policy.

The commanding officers of each of the services, along with a chairperson, constitute the **Joint Chiefs of Staff.** American military leaders are sometimes portrayed as aggressive hawks in policymaking, presumably eager to crush some small nation with a show of American force. Richard Betts carefully examined the Joint Chiefs' advice to the president in many crises and found them to be no more likely than civilian advisors to push an aggressive military policy. (The most hawkish advice, incidentally, came from the admirals. The most dovish advice came from the army generals and the Marine Corps.)[4] On several occasions during the Reagan administration, the president's uniformed advisors cautioned against aggressive actions—including the use of military force—favored by the State Department. The military was similarly conservative regarding the use of force against Iraq in 1991[5] and intervention in the civil wars in Eastern Europe. Steeped in the mythology of generals like George Patton and Curtis LeMay, many Americans would be surprised at the cautious attitudes of America's top military leaders today.

American foreign and military policies are supposed to be coordinated. The *National Security Council (NSC)* was formed in 1947 for this purpose. The NSC is

Both defense and diplomatic officials advise the president on national security policy. Here, President George W. Bush meets with Secretary of State Colin Powell and Secretary of Defense Donald Rumsfeld.

composed of the president, the vice president, the secretary of defense, and the secretary of state. The NSC staff is managed by the president's national security assistant—a position that first gained public prominence with the flamboyant, globe-trotting Henry Kissinger during President Nixon's first term.

Despite the coordinating role assigned to the NSC, conflict within the foreign policy establishment remains common. The NSC staff has sometimes competed with, rather than integrated, policy advice from cabinet departments—particularly State and Defense. It has also become involved in covert operations. A scandal erupted in November 1986 when NSC staff were found to be involved in a secret operation to sell battlefield missiles to Iran in return for Iranian help in gaining the release of hostages held by Iranian-backed terrorists in Lebanon. Some of the money from the sale was funneled secretly to anti-Communist rebels (called *Contras*) fighting the Nicaraguan government, despite a congressional ban on such aid.

The scandal, termed the Iran-Contra affair, resulted in the resignation of the president's assistant for national security affairs, Vice Admiral John Poindexter, and the sacking of a number of lower-level NSC officials, including Lieutenant Colonel Oliver North. North went from obscurity to national prominence overnight as he described his involvement in the affair before a televised congressional inquiry in 1987. Both Poindexter and North were subsequently convicted of felony charges related to the diversion of funds and misleading Congress, but their convictions were overturned because their testimony before Congress, given under conditions of immunity, was judged to have been used against them in court.

No discussion of the institutional structures of foreign policy would be complete without mention of the **Central Intelligence Agency (CIA).** "The Company," as the CIA is known to insiders, was created after World War II to coordinate American information- and data-gathering intelligence activities abroad and to collect, analyze, and evaluate its own intelligence. Technically, its budget and staff are secret; estimates put them at $3 billion and about 19,000 people.

Central Intelligence Agency (CIA)

An agency created after World War II to coordinate American intelligence activities abroad. It became involved in intrigue, conspiracy, and meddling as well.

The CIA plays a vital role in providing information and analyses necessary for effective development and implementation of national security policy. Most of its activities are uncontroversial because the bulk of the material it collects and analyzes comes from readily available sources such as government reports and newspapers. However, the CIA also collects information by espionage. Most people accept the necessity of this form of information collection when it is directed against foreign adversaries. However, in the 1970s it was discovered that at times the agency had also engaged in wiretaps, interception of mail, and the infiltration of interest groups—in the United States. These actions violated the CIA's charter, and revelations of spying on Americans who disagreed with the foreign policy of the administration badly damaged the agency's morale and external political support.

The CIA also has a long history of involvement in other nations' internal affairs. After the end of World War II, when Eastern European nations had fallen under Moscow's shadow and Western European nations were teetering, the CIA provided aid to anti-Communist parties in Italy and West Germany. It was no less busy in the developing countries, where, for example, it nurtured coups in Iran in 1953 and in Guatemala in 1954. The CIA has also trained and supported armies—the most notable, of course, in Vietnam. It subsidized Communist defectors, often in an extravagant style.

In the 1980s, a major controversy surrounded the CIA's activity in Central America, particularly in Nicaragua, where the dominant Marxist government developed close ties with the Soviet Union and Cuba and embarked on a massive military buildup. Determined to undermine the regime, the Reagan administration aggressively supported armed rebels (Contras). Congressional inquiries into the Iran-Contra affair suggested that the CIA, under Director William Casey, was quietly involved in covert operations to assist the Contra rebels.[6]

Reconciling covert activities with the principles of open democratic government remains a challenge for public officials. With the end of the Cold War, there is less pressure for covert activities and a climate more conducive to conventional intelligence gathering. Currently, Congress requires the CIA to inform relevant congressional committees promptly of current and anticipated covert operations. In the meantime, there is substantial debate on the role of the CIA in the post-Cold War era.

There are numerous other components of America's intelligence community. For example, the National Reconnaissance Office uses imagery satellites to monitor missile sites and other military activities around the world, and the National Security Agency is on the cutting edge of electronic eavesdropping capabilities.

After World War II, these military and foreign policy institutions steadily grew. As the American role on the world stage grew, so did the importance of these institutions as foreign policy instruments.

Congress. The U.S. Congress shares with the president constitutional authority over foreign and defense policy (discussed in Chapters 12 and 13). Congress has sole authority, for example, to declare war, raise and organize the armed forces, and appropriate funds for national security activities. The Senate determines whether treaties will be ratified and ambassadorial and cabinet nominations confirmed. The "power of the purse" (discussed in Chapter 14) and responsibilities for oversight of the executive branch give Congress considerable clout, and each year senators and representatives carefully examine defense budget authorizations.[7]

Congress's important constitutional role in foreign and defense policy is sometimes misunderstood. It is a common mistake among some journalists, executive officials, and even members of Congress to believe that the Constitution vests foreign policy decisions solely in the president. Sometimes this erroneous view leads to perverse results, such as the Iran-Contra affair that dominated the news in late 1986 and much of 1987. Officials at high levels in the executive branch "sought to protect the president's 'exclusive' prerogative by lying to Congress, to allies, to the public, and to one another." Louis Fisher suggests that such actions undermined the "mutual trust and close coordination by the two branches that are essential attributes in building a foreign policy that ensures continuity and stability."[8]

American Foreign Policy: An Overview

Throughout most of its history, the United States followed a foreign policy course called **isolationism.** This policy, articulated by George Washington in his Farewell Address, directed the country to stay out of other nations' conflicts, particularly

isolationism

A **foreign policy** course followed throughout most of our nation's history, whereby the United States has tried to stay out of other nations' conflicts, particularly European wars. Isolationism was reaffirmed by the Monroe Doctrine.

European wars. The famous *Monroe Doctrine,* enunciated by President James Monroe, reaffirmed America's inattention to Europe's problems but warned European nations to stay out of Latin America. The United States—believing that its own political backyard included Central and South America—did not hesitate to send marines, gunboats, or both to intervene in South American and Caribbean affairs. When European nations were at war, however, Americans relished their distance from the conflicts. So it was until World War I (1914–1918).

timeline
The Evolution of Foreign and Military Policy

In the wake of World War I, President Woodrow Wilson urged the United States to join the League of Nations, a forerunner to the United Nations. The U.S. Senate refused to ratify the League of Nations treaty, indicating that the country was not ready to abandon the long-standing American habit of isolationism. It was World War II, which forced the United States into a global conflict, that dealt a deathblow to American isolationism. At a conference in San Francisco in 1945, a charter for the United Nations was signed. The United States was an original signatory and soon donated land to house the United Nations permanently in New York City.

The Cold War

At the end of World War II, Germany and Japan were vanquished and much of Europe was strewn with rubble. The United States was unquestionably the dominant world power, both economically and militarily. It not only had helped to bring the war to an end but also had inaugurated a new era in warfare by dropping the first atomic bombs on Japan in August 1945. Because only the United States possessed nuclear weapons, Americans looked forward to an era of peace secured by their nuclear umbrella.

After World War II, the United States forged strong alliances with the nations of Western Europe. To help them rebuild their economies, the United States poured billions of dollars into war-ravaged European nations through an aid package known as the Marshall Plan—named after its architect, Secretary of State George C. Marshall. A military alliance was also forged; the creation of NATO in 1949 affirmed the mutual military interests of the United States and Western Europe, and NATO remains a cornerstone of American foreign and defense policy.

Containment Abroad and Anti-Communism at Home. Although many Americans expected cooperative relations with their wartime ally, the Soviet Union, they soon abandoned these hopes. There is still much dispute about how the Cold War between the United States and the Soviet Union started.[9] Even before World War II ended, some American policymakers feared that their Soviet allies were intent on spreading Communism not only to their neighbors but everywhere. All of Eastern Europe fell under Soviet domination as World War II ended. In 1946, Winston Churchill warned that the Russians had sealed off Eastern Europe with an "iron curtain."

Communist support of a revolt in Greece in 1946 compounded fears of Soviet aggression. Writing in *Foreign Affairs* in 1947, foreign policy strategist George F. Kennan proposed a policy of "containment."[10] His **containment doctrine** called for the United States to isolate the Soviet Union—to "contain" its advances and resist its encroachments—by peaceful means if possible, but with force if necessary. When economic problems forced Great Britain to decrease its support of Greece, the United States stepped in with the Truman Doctrine of helping other nations oppose Communism. The Soviet Union responded with the Berlin Blockade of 1948–1949, in which it closed off land access to West Berlin (which was surrounded by Communist East Germany). The United States and its allies broke the blockade by airlifting food, fuel, and other necessities to the people of the beleaguered city.

containment doctrine

A **foreign policy** strategy advocated by George Kennan that called for the United States to isolate the Soviet Union, "contain" its advances, and resist its encroachments by peaceful means if possible, but by force if necessary.

The fall of China to Mao Zedong's Communist-led forces in 1949 seemed to confirm American fears that Communism was a cancer spreading over the "free world." In the same year, the Soviet Union exploded its first atomic bomb. The invasion of pro-American South Korea by Communist North Korea in 1950 further fueled American

In 1963, President John Kennedy looked over the Berlin Wall, which the Soviet Union had built to separate Communist East Berlin from the western sectors of the city. The wall stood as the most palpable symbol of the Cold War for almost 30 years until it was torn down in 1989.

Cold War

War by other than military means usually emphasizing ideological conflict, such as that between the United States and the Soviet Union from the end of World War II until the 1990s.

McCarthyism

The fear, prevalent in the 1950s, that international Communism was conspiratorial, insidious, bent on world domination, and infiltrating American government and cultural institutions. It was named after Senator Joseph McCarthy and flourished after the Korean War.

fears of Soviet imperialism. President Truman said bluntly, "We've got to stop the Russians now" and sent American troops to Korea under United Nations auspices. The Korean War was a chance to put containment into practice. Involving China as well as North Korea, the war dragged on until July 27, 1953.

The 1950s were the height of the **Cold War;** though hostilities never quite erupted into armed battle, the United States and the Soviet Union were often on the brink of war. John Foster Dulles, secretary of state under Eisenhower, proclaimed a policy of "brinkmanship," in which the United States was to be prepared to use nuclear weapons in order to *deter* the Soviet Union and Communist China from taking aggressive actions.

Fear of Communism affected domestic as well as foreign policy. Those who subscribed to **McCarthyism** assumed that international Communism was conspiratorial, insidious, bent on world domination, and infiltrating American government and cultural institutions. Named after Senator Joseph McCarthy—who with flimsy evidence accused scores of prominent Americans and State Department officials of being Communists—McCarthyism flowered during the Korean War. Domestic policy in general was deeply affected by the Cold War and by anti-Communist fears. A burgeoning defense budget during the Korean War and later in the 1950s was another result of the Cold War.

The Swelling of the Pentagon. The Cold War ensured that military needs and massive national security expenditures would remain fixtures in the American economy. As early as 1947, aircraft manufacturers noted that the decline of military procurement after World War II would injure the industry; to avert dislocation, they launched a campaign to sell planes to the U.S. Air Force.[11] Thus were forged some of the first links between policymakers' perceptions of the Soviet threat and corporations' awareness of potential profits from military hardware. Generals and admirals believed that they needed weapons systems, and private industry was happy to supply them for a profit. Defense expenditures grew to be the largest component of the federal budget in the 1950s, consuming $13 of every $100 of the gross domestic product (GDP) by 1954. Large parts of this defense budget were spent on weapons supplied by giant companies such as Westinghouse, RCA, Western Electric, and General Motors.

The interests shared by the armed services and defense contractors produced what some call a *military-industrial complex.* The phrase was coined not by a left-wing critic of the military but by President Dwight D. Eisenhower, a former general. Elite theorists especially pointed to this tight alliance between business and government. Economist Seymour Melman wrote about *pentagon capitalism,* linking the military's drive to expand with the profit motives of private industry.[12] As the defense budget grew, so did the profits of aircraft producers and other defense contractors.

By the 1950s, the Soviet Union and the United States were engaged in an **arms race.** One side's weaponry goaded the other side to procure yet more weaponry, as one missile led to another. By the 1960s, the result of the arms race was a point of *mutual assured destruction (MAD)*, in which each side could annihilate the other, even after absorbing a surprise attack. Later sections of this chapter will examine efforts to control the arms race.

arms race

A tense relationship beginning in the 1950s between the Soviet Union and the United States whereby one side's weaponry became the other side's goad to procure more weaponry, and so on.

The Vietnam War. Even though it reached its peak during the 1960s, American involvement in Vietnam began much earlier. The Korean War and the 1949 victory of Communist forces in China fixed the U.S. government's attention on Asian Communism. In 1950, while the Korean War raged and just after the fall of Chiang Kai-shek in China, President Truman decided to aid France's effort to retain its colonial possessions in Southeast Asia.[13]

Aided by the new Communist government in China, the Vietnamese Communists finally defeated the French in a battle at Dien Bien Phu in 1954. The morning after the battle, peace talks among the participants and other major powers began in Geneva, Switzerland.

Though a party to the resultant agreements, the United States never accepted the Geneva agreement, which stipulated that national elections be held in Vietnam in 1956. Instead, it began supporting one non-Communist leader after another in South Vietnam, each seemingly more committed than the last to defeating Communist forces in the north.

Vietnam first became an election-year issue in 1964. President Lyndon B. Johnson, who had succeeded John F. Kennedy, was seeking his first full term and promised that he would not "send American boys to do an Asian boy's job" of defending the pro-American regime in South Vietnam. His Republican opponent, Barry Goldwater, advocated tough action in Vietnam; he promised to send American troops if necessary and even defoliate the jungles with chemicals so that the Communist guerrillas would have no place to hide.

There was a standing joke among Johnson's opponents after his victory in 1964: "They told me that if I voted for Goldwater, we'd have half a million American troops in Vietnam in four years. I did, and we do." Unable to contain the forces of the Communist guerillas and the North Vietnamese army with American military advisors, Johnson sent in American troops—more than 500,000 at the peak of the undeclared war. He dropped

The Vietnam War Memorial is one of Washington, D.C.'s most moving sights. Often called "The Wall," the memorial lists the names of more than 58,000 Americans killed during the Vietnam War.

more bombs on Communist North Vietnam than the United States had dropped on Germany in all of World War II. American troops and massive firepower failed to contain the North Vietnamese, however. At home, widespread protests against the war contributed to Johnson's decisions not to run for reelection in 1968 and to begin peace negotiations.

The new Nixon administration prosecuted the war vigorously, in Cambodia as well as in Vietnam, but also negotiated with the Vietnamese Communists. A peace treaty was signed in 1973, but no one expected it to hold. South Vietnam's capital, Saigon, finally fell to the North Vietnamese army in 1975. South and North Vietnam were reunited into a single nation, and Saigon was renamed Ho Chi Minh City, in honor of the late leader of Communist North Vietnam.

Looking back on the Vietnam War, few Americans think it was worthwhile. It divided our nation and made citizens painfully aware of the ability of the government to lie to them—and (perhaps worse) to itself. It reminded Americans that even a "great power" cannot prevail in a protracted military conflict against a determined enemy unless there is a clear objective and unless the national will is sufficiently committed to expend vast resources on the task.

The Era of Détente

Even while the Vietnam War was being waged, Richard Nixon—a veteran fighter of the Cold War—supported a new policy that came to be called *détente*. The term was popularized by Nixon's national security assistant and later secretary of state, Henry Kissinger.

détente

A slow transformation from conflict thinking to cooperative thinking in **foreign policy** strategy and policymaking. It sought a relaxation of tensions between the superpowers, coupled with firm guarantees of mutual security.

Détente represented a slow transformation from conflict thinking to cooperative thinking in foreign policy strategy. It sought a relaxation of tensions between the superpowers, coupled with firm guarantees of mutual security. The policy assumed that the United States and the Soviet Union had no long-range, irrevocable sources of conflict; that both had an interest in peace and world stability; and that a nuclear war was—and should be—unthinkable. Thus foreign policy battles between the United States and the Soviet Union were to be waged with diplomatic, economic, and propaganda weapons; the threat of force was downplayed.

One major initiative emerging from détente was the *Strategic Arms Limitation Talks (SALT)*. These talks represented a mutual effort by the United States and the Soviet Union to limit the growth of their nuclear capabilities, with each power maintaining sufficient nuclear weapons to deter a surprise attack by the other. The first SALT accord was signed by Nixon in 1972 and was followed by negotiations for a second agreement, SALT II. After six years of laborious negotiations, the agreement was finally signed and sent to the Senate by President Carter in 1979. The Soviet invasion of Afghanistan that year caused Carter to withdraw the treaty from Senate consideration, however, even though both he and Ronald Reagan insisted that they would remain committed to the agreement's limitations on nuclear weaponry.

The United States applied the philosophy of détente to the People's Republic of China as well as to the Soviet Union. After the fall of the pro-American government in 1949, the United States refused to extend diplomatic recognition to the world's most populous nation, recognizing instead the government in exile on the nearby island of Taiwan. As a senator in the early 1950s, Richard Nixon had been an implacable foe of "Red China," even suggesting that the Democratic administration had traitorously "lost" China. Nevertheless, two decades later it was this same Richard Nixon who, as president, first visited the People's Republic and sent an American mission there. President Jimmy Carter extended formal diplomatic recognition to China in November 1978. Since then, cultural and economic ties between the United States and China have increased greatly.

Not everyone favored détente, however. Few people saw more threats from the Soviet Union than did Ronald Reagan, who called it the "Evil Empire." He viewed the Soviet invasion of Afghanistan in 1979 as typical Russian aggression that, if unchecked, could only grow more common. He hailed anti-Communist governments everywhere and pledged to increase American defense spending.

The Reagan Rearmament

From the mid-1950s to 1981 (with the exception of the Vietnam War), the defense budget had generally been declining as a percentage of both the total federal budget and the GDP. In 1955, during the Eisenhower administration, the government was spending 61 percent of its budget for defense purposes, or about 10 percent of the GDP (the total value of all the goods and services produced annually by the United States). By the time President Reagan took office in 1981, less than 25 percent of the federal budget and 5.2 percent of the GDP were devoted to defense expenditures. These figures reflected a substantial cut indeed, although the decrease came about more because levels of social spending had increased than because military spending had declined. Still, Republican Richard Nixon used to boast that he was the first president in recent history who committed more of the national budget to social services than to military expenditures.

During his campaign for the presidency, Reagan argued that "we cannot negotiate arms control agreements that will slow down the Soviet military buildup as long as we let the Soviets move ahead of us in every category of armaments." According to Reagan, America faced a "window of vulnerability" because the Soviet Union was galloping ahead of the United States in military spending.

As president, Reagan was determined to reverse the trend of diminishing defense spending and proposed the largest peacetime defense spending increase in American history: a five-year defense buildup costing $1.5 trillion. The early days of the Reagan administration were the most critical in this defense spending buildup. The news came down to the Pentagon rank and file quickly: President Carter's last budget had proposed a large increase in defense spending, and the Reagan administration would add $32 billion on top of that. Defense officials were ordered to find places to spend more money.[14] These heady days for the Pentagon lasted only through the first term of Reagan's presidency, however. In his second term, concern over huge budget deficits brought defense spending to a standstill. After taking inflation into account, Congress appropriated no increase in defense spending at all from 1985 to 1988.

In 1983 President Reagan added another element to his defense policy—a new plan for defense against missiles. He called it the **Strategic Defense Initiative (SDI)**; critics quickly renamed it "Star Wars." Reagan's plans for SDI proposed creating a global umbrella in space, wherein computers would scan the skies and use various high-tech devices to destroy invading missiles. The administration proposed a research program that would have cost tens of billions of dollars over the next decade.

Strategic Defense Initiative (SDI)

Renamed "Star Wars" by critics, a plan for defense against the Soviet Union unveiled by President Reagan in 1983. SDI would create a global umbrella in space, using computers to scan the skies and high-tech devices to destroy invading missiles.

In the face of an onslaught of criticism regarding the feasibility of SDI, its proponents reduced their expectations about the size and capabilities of any defensive shield that could be erected over the next generation. Talk of a smaller system—capable of protecting against an accidental launch of a few missiles or against a threat by some third-world country with nuclear weapons—replaced the dream of an impenetrable umbrella over the United States capable of defeating a massive Soviet nuclear strike.

The Final Thaw in the Cold War

On May 12, 1989, in a commencement address at Texas A&M University, President Bush announced a new era in American foreign policy. He termed this era one "beyond containment"; the United States' goal would be more than containing Soviet expansion. Bush declared that it was time to seek the integration of the Soviet Union into the community of nations.

The Cold War ended as few had anticipated—spontaneously. Suddenly, the elusive objective of 40 years of post-World War II U.S. foreign policy—freedom and self-determination for Eastern Europeans and Soviet peoples and the reduction of the military threat from the East—occurred. Forces of change sparked by Soviet leader Mikhail Gorbachev led to a staggering wave of upheaval that shattered Communist

Beginning in 1989, Communism in the Soviet Union and in Eastern Europe suddenly began to crumble. The end of the Cold War between East and West reduced the threat of nuclear war between the superpowers, but it also left a host of difficult new national security issues in its wake. Here, soldiers remove a bust of Vladimir Lenin, the founder of Soviet Communism, from a Moscow military school.

regimes and the postwar barriers between Eastern and Western Europe. The Berlin Wall, the most prominent symbol of oppression in Eastern Europe, came tumbling down on November 9, 1989, and East and West Germany formed a unified, democratic republic. The former Soviet Union split into 15 separate nations, and non-Communist governments formed in most of them. Poland, Czechoslovakia (splitting into the Czech Republic and Slovakia), and Hungary established democratic governments, and reformers overthrew the old-line Communist leaders in Bulgaria and Rumania.

Events were unfolding so fast and in so many places at once that no one was quite sure how to deal with them. President Bush declared, "Every morning I receive an intelligence briefing, and I receive the best information available to any world leader today. And yet, the morning news is often overtaken by the news that very same evening."[15]

In 1989, reform seemed on the verge of occurring in China as well as in Eastern Europe. That spring in Tiananmen Square, the central meeting place in Beijing, thousands of students held protests on behalf of democratization. Unable to tolerate challenges to their rule any longer, the aging Chinese leaders forcibly—and brutally—evacuated the square, crushing some protestors under armored tanks. It is still not clear how many students were killed and how many others arrested, but the reform movement in China received a serious setback. This suppression of efforts to develop democracy sent a chill through what had been a warming relationship between the United States and the People's Republic of China (see "You Are the Policymaker: Defending Human Rights").

simulation
You are the President

Despite its risks and uncertainties, the Cold War was characterized by a stable and predictable set of relations among the great powers. Now international relations have entered an era of improvisation as nations struggle to come up with creative responses to changes in the global balance of power.

Almost everyone agrees that today's more cooperative, albeit more complicated, international environment portends an overhaul of the American national security infrastructure. Armed forces and alliances, defense industries, and budgets built up since World War II are being reassessed in light of the Cold War thaw.

The Politics of Defense Policy

The politics of national defense involves high stakes—the nation's security, for example. Domestic political concerns, budgetary limitations, and ideology all influence decisions on the structure of defense policy and negotiations with allies and adversaries. All public policies include budgets, people, and equipment. In the realm of

You Are the Policymaker

Defending Human Rights

Americans sat riveted to their television screens for several weeks in May and June of 1989 as they watched Chinese students and workers in Beijing's Tiananmen Square protest on behalf of greater democracy. This was heady stuff for the world's most populous country, apparently emerging from two generations of totalitarian rule.

For a time it looked as though China's rulers would accommodate demands for reform. On the night of June 3, however, the army violently crushed the democracy movement, killing hundreds—perhaps thousands—of protestors and beginning a wave of executions, arrests, and repression.

Westerners were shocked at the bloodshed and widely condemned the Chinese government. Regardless, in July and December 1989, President Bush sent his national security advisor Brent Scowcroft and Deputy Secretary of State Lawrence Eagleburger to meet secretly with Chinese leaders. Bush also lifted some economic sanctions against China. The president claimed he was not normalizing relations with China, but many political leaders criticized him for moral capitulation to the hard-line Communist leaders.

The president asked, "How else should nuclear powers deal with each other?" and pointed out that the United States maintains relations with many countries that have even more egregious records of human rights violations than China. In addition, Bush argued that keeping the lines of communication open would increase his ability to encourage the Chinese leaders to moderate their repression.

His critics responded, "How can you deal with immoral leaders who slaughter their own people for nonviolently advocating rights that Americans cherish? Is there no place for morality in international relations?"

President Clinton faced a similar dilemma. In his 1999 State of the Union message, he told the American people that stability in China could "no longer be bought at the expense of liberty." But then he added, "It's important not to isolate China. The more we bring China into the world, the more the world will bring change and freedom to China."

Both President Bush and President Clinton were also mindful of the potentially vast market that China provided for U.S. goods and services and the role the contribution that capitalism might make to political freedom. Their critics argued that we should sell out our principles for a greater market share.

If you were the president, what would *you* do?

national defense, these elements are especially critical because of the size of the budget and the bureaucracy, as well as the destructive potential of modern weapons.

At the core of defense policy is a judgment about what the United States will defend. The central assumption of current American defense policy is that the United States requires forces and equipment sufficient to fight two nearly simultaneous major regional conflicts. For example, our goal is to be ready to fight simultaneous aggression by a remilitarized Iraq against Kuwait and Saudi Arabia *and* aggression by North Korea against South Korea. A large military infrastructure is necessary to meet the two-war goal.

Defense Spending

Defense spending now makes up about one-sixth of the federal budget. Although this is a much smaller percentage than in earlier years (see Figure 20.3), vast sums of money and fundamental questions of public policy are still involved (see Chapter 14). Some scholars have argued that America faces a trade-off between defense spending and social spending. A nation, they claim, must choose between guns and butter, and more guns mean less butter. Evidence supporting the existence of such a trade-off is mixed, however. In general, defense and domestic policy expenditures appear to be independent of each other.[16] Ronald Reagan's efforts to increase military budgets while cutting back on domestic policy expenditures seem to have stemmed more from his own ideology than from any inevitable choice between the two.

Defense spending is a thorny political issue, entangled with ideological disputes. Conservatives fight deep cuts in defense spending, pointing out that many nations retain potent military capability and insisting that America maintain its readiness at a

Figure 20.3 Trends in Defense Spending

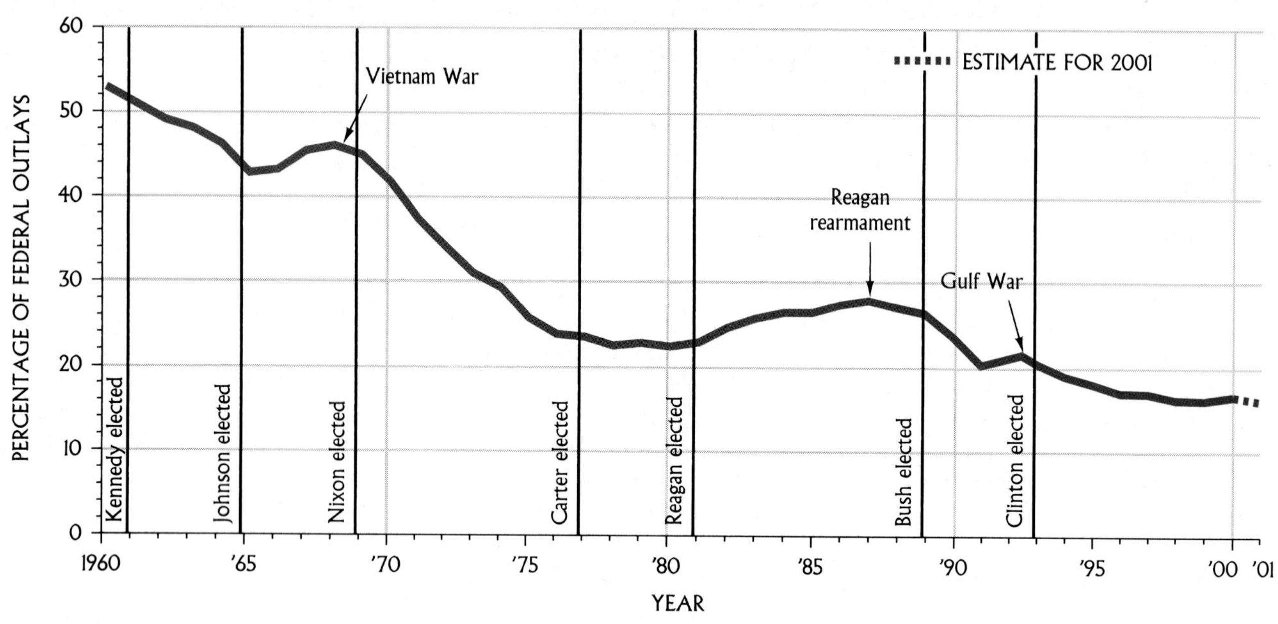

Source: Budget of the United States Government, Fiscal Year 2002: Historical Tables (Washington, D.C.: U.S. Government Printing Office, 2001), Table 3.1.

high level. They refer to the Gulf War to prove that wars on a significant scale are still possible. In addition, they attribute the collapse of Communism in Eastern and Central Europe to Western toughness and the massive increase in defense spending that occurred in the early 1980s. When the Soviet Union saw that it could not outspend the United States, they argue, it finally decided not to continue to allocate so much of its scarce resources to defense and to loosen its grip on Eastern Europe.

Liberals, on the other hand, maintain that the Pentagon wastes money and that the United States buys too many guns and too little butter. The most crucial aspect of national defense, they argue, is a strong economy, which is based on investments in "human capital" such as health and education. Liberals insist that the erosion of the Communist party's authority was well under way when Gorbachev rose to power. This erosion accelerated as *glasnost* (the Russian term for the new openness of society) made the party's failures a matter of public ridicule as democratization freed new forces to challenge the existing order. They contend that Gorbachev and his fellow reformers were responding primarily to internal, not external, pressures. Inadequacies and defects at the core of the Soviet economy—the inertia, wastefulness, and corruption inherent in the system—were the driving forces that brought change to the Soviet Union, not American defense spending.

Why does it matter?

In the post-Cold War era, the United States spends about one-sixth of its national budget on defense to support a large defense establishment. Does this establishment bias expenditures in favor of defense, even in the absence of a significant foreign threat?

In addition, scholars such as Paul Kennedy and David Calleo envision a new world order different from the bipolar dominance of the United States and the Soviet Union.[17] Kennedy warns of the historical dangers of "imperial overstretch," suggesting that great empires in a stage of relative economic decline vis-à-vis emerging powers accelerate their decline by clinging to vast military commitments.

Whatever its cause, the lessening of East-West tensions has given momentum to significant reductions in defense spending, what some call the *peace dividend*. Liberals are especially interested in restraining defense spending in order to allocate more funds to domestic programs.

Changing spending patterns is not easy, however. For example, military hardware developed during the lush years of the early 1980s has proven to be increasingly expensive to purchase and maintain. And when the assembly lines at weapons plants close down, submarine designers, welders, and others lose their jobs. These programs become political footballs as candidates compete over promises to keep weapons systems such as the *Seawolf* submarine or the *Osprey* helicopter in production. Ideology plays a crucial role in the basic decisions members of Congress make regarding defense spending, but once these decisions are made, liberal as well as conservative representatives and senators fight hard to help constituencies win and keep defense contracts.[18]

Personnel

The structure of America's defense has been based on a large standing military force and a battery of strategic nuclear weapons. The United States has nearly 1.4 million men and women on active duty and nearly 900,000 million in the National Guard and Reserves (see Table 20.2). About 260,000 active-duty troops are deployed abroad, mostly in Europe, Japan, and South Korea.[19] This is a very costly enterprise and one that frequently evokes calls to bring the troops home. Many observers believe that America's allies, especially prosperous nations such as Japan and Germany, should bear a greater share of common defense costs.

Cuts in defense spending have led to reduced numbers of active-duty personnel in the armed services. As a result, the military now relies much more heavily on National Guard and Reserve units to maintain national security (the "Total Force" concept). For example, the president mobilized National Guard units and sent them into active duty in Bosnia.

Weapons

To deter an aggressor's attack, the United States has relied on a triad of nuclear weapons: ground-based intercontinental ballistic missiles (ICBMs), submarine-launched ballistic missiles (SLBMs), and strategic bombers. Both the United States and Russia have thousands of large nuclear warheads. These weapons, like troops, are costly (each Stealth bomber costs over a *billion* dollars), and they pose obvious dangers to human survival. The total cost of building nuclear weapons has been $5.5 *trillion* dollars![20]

The rapid drive toward democracy in Eastern Europe, combined with Moscow's economic stagnation and the Pentagon's budgetary squeeze, pushed arms reduction inexorably onto the two superpowers' discussion agenda. Substantial progress has been made to end the arms race and what was known as "the balance of terror."

Table 20.2 Size of the Armed Forces

BRANCH	PERSONNEL[a]
Army	480,000
Navy	372,642
Air Force	357,000
Marines	172,600
Subtotal	**1,382,242**
Reserves	863,775
Total	**2,246,017**

[a]2001 estimates

Sources: Office of Management and Budget, *Budget of the United States Government, Fiscal Year 2002:* Appendix (Washington, D.C.: U.S. Government Printing Office, 2001), 245, 249.

The Trident submarine is one of the U.S. Navy's most sophisticated weapons. A key component of America's nuclear weapons triad, the Trident can launch missiles from the ocean's depths, where it is virtually invisible and invulnerable to enemy attack. Like most weapons systems, however, the submarines cost hundreds of millions of dollars more than planned.

During the May 1988 Moscow summit meeting, President Reagan and Mikhail Gorbachev exchanged ratified copies of a new treaty eliminating *intermediate-range nuclear forces (INF)*. Reagan, who had built his reputation on fervid anti-Communism and had denounced earlier arms control efforts (such as Jimmy Carter's SALT II agreement), became the first American president to sign a treaty to reduce current levels of nuclear weapons. Under the terms of the INF treaty, more than 2,500 nuclear weapons with ranges between 300 and 3,400 miles were to be destroyed.

Superpower relations continued to improve at a dizzying pace, accelerated by the dissolution of the Soviet Union. On November 19, 1990, the leaders of 22 countries signed a treaty reducing conventional armed forces in Europe. The treaty slashed forces in Europe by 40 percent—the Soviet Union was called on to remove the most troops. A related change occurred in 1991 as the Warsaw Pact, the military alliance tying Eastern Europe to the Soviet Union, was dissolved.

On July 31, 1991, shortly before Soviet hard-liners attempted a coup to remove President Gorbachev and other reformers from power, he and President Bush signed the *Strategic Arms Reduction Treaty (START)*—after nine years of negotiations. The treaty had the distinction of being the first accord mandating the elimination of

President Reagan and Soviet President Mikhail Gorbachev begin their 1988 summit meeting in Moscow. The two presidents later signed a treaty eliminating intermediate-range nuclear missiles from Europe. The INF treaty marked the first time an American president had agreed to reduce current levels of nuclear weapons.

strategic nuclear weaponry. (The INF treaty banned a whole class of shorter-flying nuclear arms.)

The significance of these changes was soon overshadowed by other events, however, as the democratization of Eastern Europe, the restructuring of the Soviet Union, and the deterioration of the Soviet economy substantially diminished both Russia's inclination and potential to threaten the interests of the United States and its allies. President Bush broke ground with his decision in the fall of 1991 to dismantle unilaterally some U.S. nuclear weapons, enticing President Gorbachev to follow suit shortly afterward. In January 1993, Presidents Bush and Yeltsin signed an agreement (START II) to cut the U.S. and Russian (including those of Ukraine, Belarus, and Kazakhstan) nuclear arsenals to a total of no more than 6,500 weapons by the year 2003—less than one-third of the 20,000 long-range nuclear weapons the two possessed at the time. Large, accurate ICBMs with multiple warheads (MIRVs) were banned altogether. The 3,500 strategic nuclear weapons that the United States is allowed under this agreement would be the smallest stockpile this country has possessed since the Kennedy administration of the early 1960s.

Nuclear weapons are the most destructive in America's arsenal, but they are by no means the only weapons. Jet fighters, aircraft carriers, and even tanks are extraordinarily complex and equally costly. The perception that space-age technology helped win the Gulf War in "100 hours" with few American casualties, in addition to the fact that producing expensive weapons provides jobs for American workers, means that high-tech weapons systems will continue to play an important role in America's defense posture.

Although progress has been made on reducing tensions between East and West, other international matters clamor for attention. Even the mightiest nation can be mired in intractable issues.

The New Global Agenda

The global agenda is changing rapidly. As military competition with the Communist powers has diminished, economic competition with the world has increased. The gap between domestic and foreign policy is increasingly obscure. Dealing with allies such as Japan and Germany on trade and finance is as crucial as negotiating arms reductions with Russia. Maintaining access to petroleum in the Middle East is more crucial than ever, and determining policy regarding the global environment has taken on new prominence.

Regardless of the standards one uses for measurement, the United States is the world's mightiest military power. Its very strength seems to belie an essential weakness, however. Events on the world stage often appear to counter the American script. In the long and controversial Vietnam War, 500,000 American troops were not enough. U.S. economic vulnerability has increased. Oil supply lines depend on a precarious Middle Eastern peace and on the safe passage of huge tankers through a sliver of water called the Strait of Hormuz. We sometimes appear to be losing the highly publicized "war on drugs" to an international network of wealthy drug lords called *narco-traficantes.* Perhaps most important of all, our economy is increasingly dependent on international trade, placing us at the mercy of interest rates in Germany and restrictive markets in Japan and China.

Public opinion polls find that in the post-Cold War era, Americans are more likely to perceive threats to their security from the economic competition of allies than from military rivalry with old adversaries.[21]

The Decreasing Role of Military Power

Harvard political scientist Stanley Hoffman likened the United States' plight to that of Jonathan Swift's fictional character, Gulliver, the traveler seized and bound by the tiny Lilliputians.[22] For Americans, as for Gulliver, merely being big and powerful is no guarantee of dominance. Time after time and place after place, so it seems, the American Gulliver is frustrated by the Lilliputians.

One explanation for America's tribulations is that the nation's supposed strong suit—military might—is no longer the primary instrument of foreign policy. Robert Keohane and Joseph Nye, in describing the diminishing role of military force in contemporary international politics, say that among the developed nations, "the perceived margin of safety has widened: fears of attack in general have declined, and fears of attacks by one another are virtually nonexistent."[23]

Today military power is losing much of its utility in resolving many international issues. "Force," argue Keohane and Nye, "is often not an appropriate way of achieving other goals (such as economic and ecological welfare) that are becoming more important" in world affairs.[24] Economic conflicts do not readily yield to nuclear weapons. America cannot persuade Arab nations to sell it cheap oil by bombing them, nor can it prop up the textile industry's position in world trade by resorting to military might. The United States is long on firepower at the very time when firepower is decreasing in its utility as an instrument of foreign policy.

Conflict among large powers, the threat of nuclear war, and the possibility of conventional war have certainly not disappeared, but grafted onto them are new issues. Former Secretary of State Henry Kissinger described the new era eloquently:

> *The traditional agenda of international affairs—the balance among major powers, the security of nations—no longer defines our perils or our possibilities. Now we are entering a new era. Old international patterns are crumbling; old slogans are uninstructive. The world has become interdependent in economics, in communications, in human aspirations.*[25]

Why does it matter?

The United States is the world's only superpower. What implications does this have for decisions regarding policing the world's hot spots? Would you want to serve in missions for peacekeeping and other humanitarian purposes? Or should we reserve our military resources for our own self-defense?

Despite these changes, military power remains an important element in U.S. foreign policy. The end of the Cold War emboldened local dictators and reignited age-old ethnic rivalries that had been held in check by the Soviet Union. The result is that the number of regional crises likely to pose a threat to peace has grown exponentially in the post-Cold War era. Thus, although the end of the Cold War gives the United States unprecedented freedom to act, its status as the only superpower has meant that Washington is the first place people look for help when trouble erupts, even in Europe's backyard as in the case of the territory of the former Yugoslavia. One of the nation's most difficult foreign policy problems is in deciding when to send U.S. troops to police the world's hot spots.

Economic Sanctions. An ancient tool of diplomacy, sanctions are nonmilitary penalties imposed on a foreign government in an attempt to modify its behavior. The penalties can vary broadly—a cutoff of U.S. aid, a ban on military sales, restrictions on imports, a denial of aircraft landing rights, a total trade embargo. The implied power behind sanctions is U.S. economic muscle and access to U.S. markets.

Economic sanctions are often a first resort in times of crises, as they are less risky than sending in troops. Sanctions are often the outgrowth of pressure from well-organized domestic political groups with ethnic, cultural, environmental, human rights, or religious grievances against a foreign regime. These groups and government officials want to curb unfair trade practices, end human rights abuses and drug trafficking, promote environmental initiatives, and stop terrorism.

There are examples of economic sanctions that accomplished the goals of their sponsors, such as the sanctions levied against South Africa in the mid-1980s that contributed to the demise of apartheid. Most experts, however, view these tools as having limited effect. The trade embargo that the United Nations placed on Iraq after its 1990 invasion of Kuwait has succeeded in isolating Iraq, diplomatically and economically, and prevented it from rebuilding its military to its former strength. Yet Saddam Hussein retains a firm grip on power.

Successful sanctions most often have broad international support, which is rare. Unilateral sanctions are doomed to failure. The sanctions leak and the real losers are U.S.

companies that are forced to abandon lucrative markets. They are quickly replaced by their competitors around the globe. When President Carter imposed a grain embargo on the Soviet Union in 1980 in retaliation for the Soviet invasion of Afghanistan, only U.S. farmers were hurt. The Soviet Union simply bought grain from elsewhere.

In addition, critics argue that sanctions are counterproductive because they can provoke a nationalist backlash. The decades-old sanctions against Cuba have not ousted Marxist dictator Fidel Castro, and the perennial threats of sanctions against China typically result in a hardening of China's attitude regarding human rights and other matters.

Nuclear Proliferation

The spread of technology has enabled the creation of nuclear weapons and the missiles to deliver them, encouraging U.S. officials to adopt a more assertive posture in attempting to deny these weapons of mass destruction to rogue states. American policymakers have sought to halt the spread of nuclear weapons since the signing of the Nuclear Non-Proliferation Treaty in 1968. The primary means of accomplishing this goal has been to encourage nations to agree that they would not acquire, or at least test, nuclear weapons. As you can see in Figure 20.4, only seven countries have declared that they have nuclear weapons capacities: the United States, Russia, Britain, France,

Figure 20.4 The Spread of Nuclear Weapons

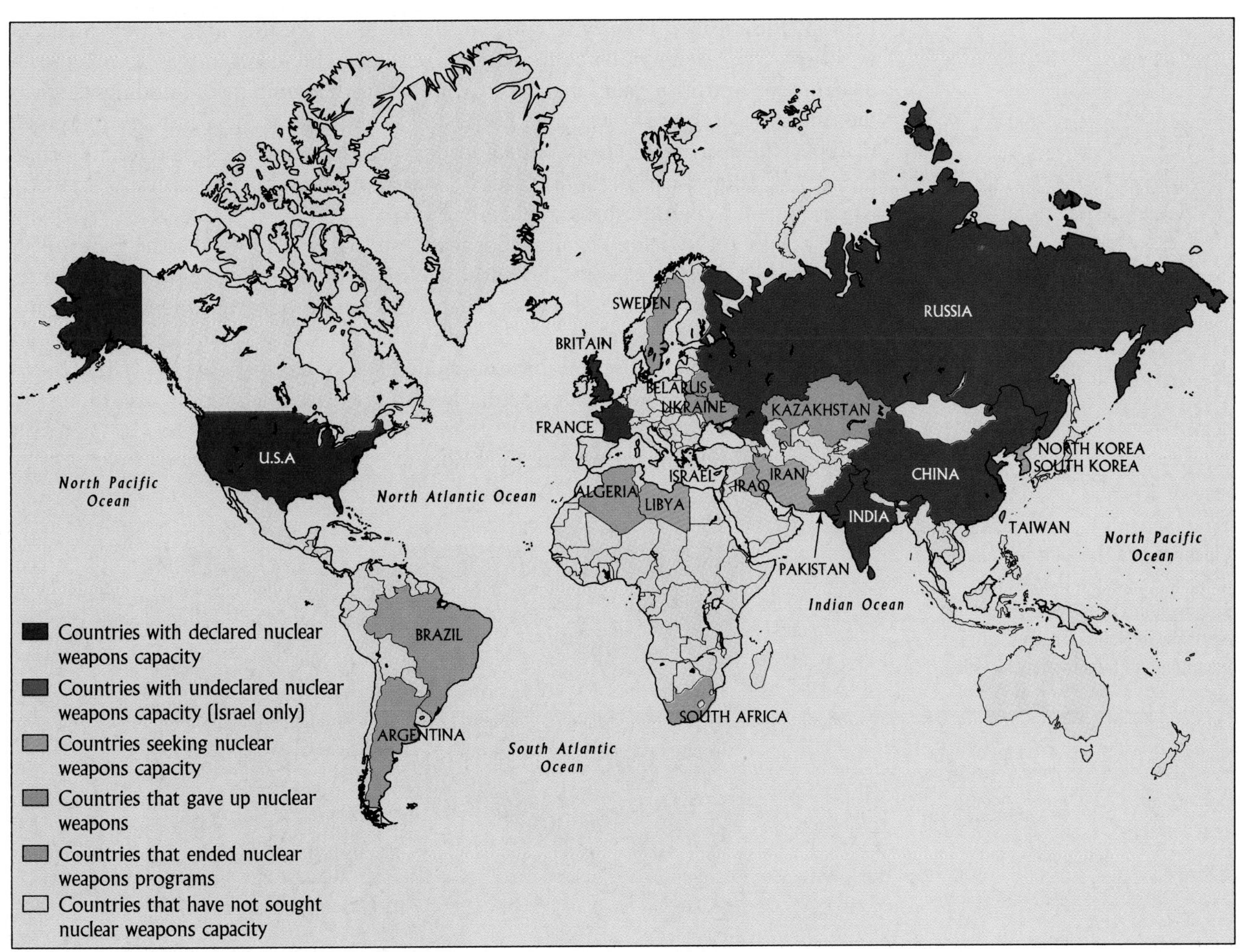

Source: Congressional Quarterly Weekly Report, May 23, 1998, 1366.

China, India, and Pakistan. Israel is widely suspected of having nuclear weapons. South Africa and three countries that used to be part of the Soviet Union, Belarus, Kazakhstan, and Ukraine, have given up nuclear weapons. Algeria, Argentina, Brazil, South Korea, Sweden, and Taiwan have ended their nuclear weapons programs.

Currently, policymakers are most concerned about countries who are actively seeking nuclear weapons capabilities: North Korea, Iran, Iraq, and Libya. These nations, frequently branded as "outlaw" states, pose serious threats to their neighbors, and perhaps to the United States as well. The United States has provided aid to North Korea in return for a promise to end its nuclear weapons program, but many doubt North Korea's compliance with the agreement. The United States has actively supported the UN weapons inspections of Iraq, which have faced continuous harassment and obstruction from Saddam Hussein. Our efforts regarding Iran and Libya have been less effective yet, as we lack diplomatic relations with those nations.

Other nations have serious security concerns when faced with hostile neighbors possessing nuclear weapons. When India resumed testing of nuclear weapons in 1998, neighboring Pakistan quickly tested its first nuclear weapons. Ending the proliferation of nuclear weapons will require resolving diplomatic tensions involving undeclared and nonnuclear states. In the meantime, the United States will focus on discouraging the deployment of nuclear weapons that have been developed.

Terrorism

Perhaps the most troublesome issue in the national security area is the spread of terrorism—the use of violence to demoralize and frighten a country's population or government. Terrorism takes many forms, including the bombing of buildings (such as the American embassy in Kenya in 1998) and ships (such as the *USS Cole* in Yemen in 2000), the assassinations of political leaders (as when Iraq attempted to kill former president George Bush in 1993), and the kidnappings of diplomats and civilians (as when Iranians took Americans hostage in 1979).

It is difficult to defend against terrorism, especially in an open society. Terrorists have the advantage of stealth and surprise. Improved security measures and better intelligence gathering can help. So, perhaps, can punishing governments and organizations that engage in terrorist activities. In 1986, the United States launched an air attack on Libya in response to Libyan-supported acts of terrorism; in 1993, the United States struck at Iraq's intelligence center in response to a foiled plot to assassinate former president George Bush; and in 1998, the United States launched an attack in Afghanistan on Osama bin Laden, the leader of a terrorist organization.

Diplomacy has become increasingly dangerous. Here a U.S. Marine stands guard at the American embassy in Nairobi, Kenya, after it was bombed by terrorists in 1998.

The International Economy

Once upon a time, nations took pains to isolate themselves from the world. They erected high barriers to fend off foreign products and amassed large armies to defend their borders against intruders. Times have changed. One key word describes today's international economy: **interdependency,** a mutual reliance in which actions reverberate and affect other people's economic lifelines. The health of the American economy depends increasingly on the prosperity of its trading partners and on the smooth flow of trade and finance across borders.

interdependency

Mutual dependency, in which the actions of nations reverberate and affect one another's economic lifelines.

The *International Monetary Fund (IMF)* is a cooperative international organization of 182 countries intended to stabilize the exchange of currencies and the world economy. From 1997 to 1998, the decline of currencies in a number of Asian countries, including South Korea, Thailand, Indonesia, and the Philippines, threatened to force these nations to default on their debts—and throw the international economy into turmoil in the process. To stabilize these currencies, the IMF, to which the United States is by far the largest contributor, arranged for loans and credits of more than $100 billion. The IMF's intervention seems to have been successful, but the necessity of making the loans dramatically illustrates the world's economic interdependence.

International Trade. Since the end of World War II, trade among nations has grown rapidly. U.S. exports and imports have increased tenfold since 1970 alone (see Figure 20.5). Among the largest U.S. exporters are grain farmers, producers of computer hardware and software, aircraft manufacturers, moviemakers, heavy construction companies, and purveyors of accounting and consulting services. Foreign tourist spending bolsters the U.S. travel, hotel, and recreation industries. American colleges

Figure 20.5 Exports and Imports

Since 1975, the United States has imported more than it has exported, resulting in a mounting trade deficit.

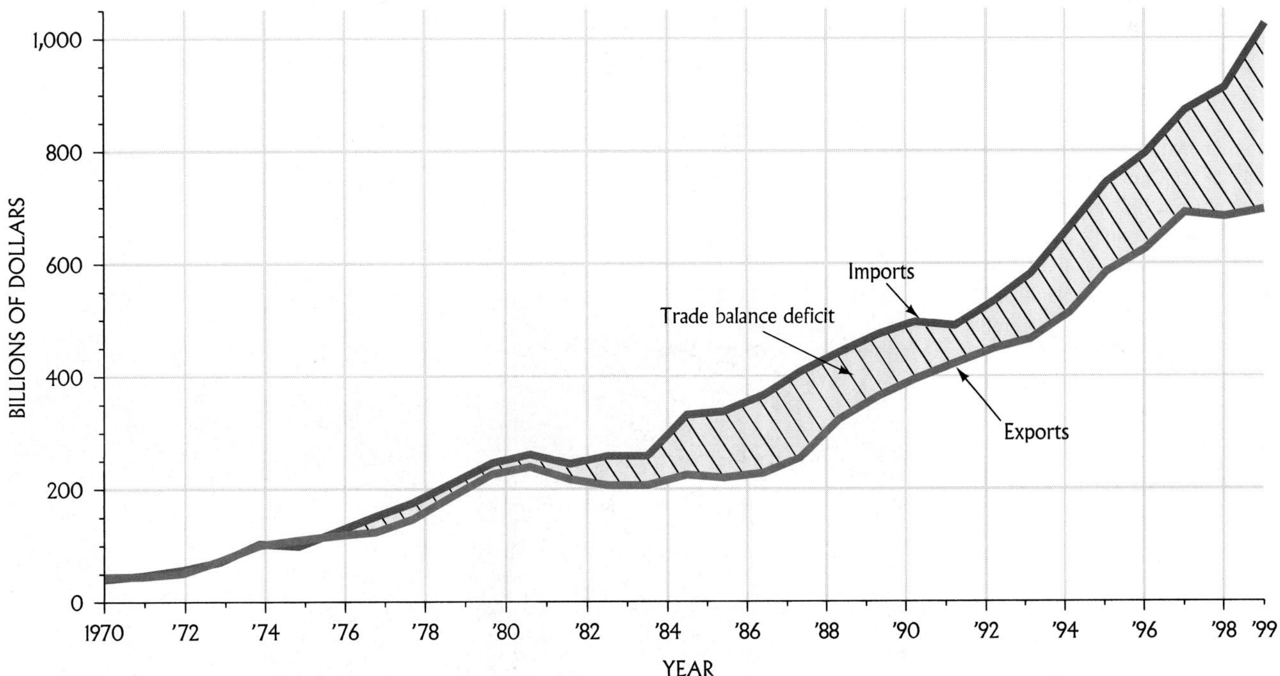

Source: U.S. Bureau of the Census, *Statistical Abstract of the United States, 2000* (Washington, D.C.: U.S. Government Printing Office, 2001), 794.

and universities derive a significant portion of their revenue from educating foreign students. The globalization of finances has been even more dramatic than the growth of trade. Worldwide computer and communications networks link financial markets in all parts of the globe instantaneously, making it easier to move capital across national boundaries but also increasing the probability that a steep decline in the Japanese stock market will send prices plummeting on Wall Street.

Coping with foreign economic issues is becoming just as difficult, and increasingly just as important, as coping with domestic ones. In a simpler time, the main instrument of international economic policy was the **tariff**, a special tax added to the cost of imported goods. Tariffs are intended to raise the price of imported goods and thereby protect American businesses and workers from foreign competition. Tariff making, though, is a game everyone can play. High U.S. tariffs encourage other nations to respond with high tariffs on American products. The high tariffs that the government enacted early in the Great Depression (and that some say aggravated this economic crisis) were the last of their kind. Since that time, the world economy has moved from a period of high tariffs and protectionism to one of lower tariffs and freer trade.

tariff

A special tax added to imported goods to raise the price, thereby protecting American businesses and workers from foreign competition.

However, nontariff barriers such as quotas, subsidies, and quality specifications for imported products are common means of limiting imports. The United States places quotas on the amount of steel that can be imported and negotiates voluntary limits on the importation of Japanese automobiles. Such policies do save American jobs, but they also raise the price of steel and automobiles that Americans buy. American and European subsidies for agricultural products have been an obstacle to negotiating tariff reductions.

Recently, substantial progress has been made in lowering barriers to trade. In 1992, President Bush signed the *North American Free Trade Agreement (NAFTA)* with Canada and Mexico, which would eventually eliminate most tariffs among North American countries. In 1993, after a heated battle, President Clinton obtained congressional passage of the legislation implementing the agreement.

President Clinton submitted an even more important agreement to Congress in 1994. The *General Agreement on Tariffs and Trade (GATT)* is the mechanism by which most of the world's nations negotiate widespread trade agreements. In 1994, 117 nations agreed to (1) reduce tariffs 38 percent for developed countries; (2) eliminate certain nontariff barriers and subsidies; (3) broaden GATT principles to areas such as trade in services, investment, and intellectual property rights; and (4) apply more effective disciplines

International trade is a controversial subject. Opponents believe that it undermines U.S. laws that protect the environment and workers rights, costs some employees their jobs, and encourages the exploitation of foreign workers. Proponents argue that everyone benefits from increased trade. Here Seattle police face protesters during a World Trade Organization meeting in 1999.

to agricultural trade. The GATT also included a charter to create a World Trade Organization (WTO) that would act as the arbiter of international trade disputes. In its last action, the 103rd Congress passed the legislation necessary to implement this agreement.

A persistent issue for the president is opening up foreign markets for U.S. goods and services. The White House is especially eager to open lucrative Japanese markets in areas such as automobiles, auto parts, telecommunications, insurance, and medical equipment. The United States lacks the influence to *demand* that these markets be opened, however. If we refuse to trade with another nation, that nation will deny *our* exports access to its markets, and United States consumers will lose access to its products. In addition, thousands of Americans now work in foreign-owned companies in the United States, such as Japanese automobile assembly plants. Although foreign investments and the creation of jobs are good for the United States, a by-product is that Americans have a stake in averting a trade crisis with investing nations. Those benefiting from Japanese investments, for example, may flock to Tokyo's side on some important issues.

Balance of Trade. Foreign products are not free. When Americans purchase foreign products, they send dollars out of the country. When an oil tanker arrives in Houston, dollars travel to Saudi Arabia. If other nations do not buy as many American products as Americans do of theirs, then the United States is paying out more than it is taking in. If the United States puts military bases in Germany, the money that soldiers spend for a night on the town goes into German pockets. When American tourists spend their dollars abroad, they carry American dollars away. All these instances combine to upset the **balance of trade:** the ratio of what a country pays for imports to what it earns from exports. When a country imports more than it exports, it has a balance-of-trade *deficit.* Year after recent year, the American balance of trade has been preceded by a minus sign, and the deficit for merchandise was more than $330 billion in 1999.[26]

balance of trade

The ratio of what is paid for imports to what is earned from exports. When more is imported than exported, there is a balance-of-trade deficit.

The excess of imports over exports decreases the dollar's buying power against other currencies, making Americans pay more for goods that they buy from other nations. This decline in the value of the dollar, however, also makes American products cheaper abroad, thereby increasing our exports. Since the late 1980s, the United States has experienced an export boom, exceeding $1 trillion in 2000.[27] Exports account for more than 10 percent of the GDP.

A poor balance of trade also exacerbates unemployment. Currently, 5 percent of all civilian employment in the United States is related to manufacturing exports. A substantial amount of white-collar employment—in the area of financial services, for example, is also directly tied to exports. The trade imbalance has caused not only dollars but also jobs to flow abroad. Because labor is cheaper in Mexico, Taiwan, Malaysia, and South Korea, products made there can be priced lower than American-made products. Sometimes American firms have shut down their domestic operations and relocated in countries where labor costs are lower. The AFL-CIO claims that hundreds of thousands of American jobs have been lost to foreign competition. Under a special act guaranteeing compensation to American workers who lose their jobs to foreign competition, the Department of Labor has aided thousands of workers. The Labor Department, however, would be the first to note that short-term aid is no substitute for a long-term job.

Even so, a cheaper dollar also makes the cost of American labor more competitive. In response to this and to criticism about the balance of trade, more foreign-owned companies are building factories in the United States—just as American companies have plants around the globe. Thus, many Hondas are made in the United States, and parts for some cars manufactured by General Motors are made abroad. The web of interdependency has become so tangled that it is increasingly difficult to define "imports."

In addition, the stability of the U.S. economy and the low value of the dollar have made the United States attractive to foreign investors, who buy everything from major motion picture studios to Rockefeller Center. Although advantages accrue to the

United States when investors pour money into the country, some fear that both profits and control will move outside our borders.

International Inequality and Foreign Aid

A major transformation in the international system over the past two decades has been the addition of North-South conflict to the old rivalries between East and West. Whereas the Cold War meant continuous conflict between the Soviet Union and the West, world politics today includes a growing conflict between rich and poor nations—the rich nations primarily being concentrated in the Northern Hemisphere, the poor nations in the Southern Hemisphere. You can see some differences among nations in Table 20.3.

The old expression "the rich get richer and the poor get poorer" describes fairly accurately the inequalities among nations today. The income gap between rich, industrialized nations and poor, less developed nations is widening rather than narrowing. One reason for the widening gap is that: "The rich get richer and the poor get children." While birthrates in the developed nations are leveling off, those in the poorer nations often outpace increases in these countries' gross domestic products. If a nation's GDP increases 3 percent but its birthrate increases 5 percent, the nation has to divide 3 percent more money among 5 percent more people.

Why does it matter?

The world economy is increasingly interdependent. In fact, citizens of the United States have more investments abroad than citizens of any other nation. Do these private investments force the national government to take risky actions in bailing out failing economies? Or does everyone benefit from strong economies abroad?

Less developed countries have responded to their poverty by borrowing money, and international banks have been willing participants in this debt dependency. Nations unable to pay the installments could simply refinance their debt, though naturally at ever-higher interest rates. Viewed from any perspective, the foreign debts of these governments are truly staggering, often amounting to large percentages of their gross domestic products. In 1994, the United States provided massive loan guarantees for Mexico to avoid a Mexican default on its foreign debt. The default would have resulted in a deep depression in the Mexican economy, the loss of a huge market for U.S. exports, massive losses for U.S. investors in Mexican bonds, and would have propelled thousands of illegal aliens across the U.S. border. Mexico, unlike most countries, repaid its loan—with interest—ahead of schedule.

There is another complication to the issue of international inequality. Not only are there wide gaps between rich and poor nations (international inequality), but there

Table 20.3 Rich Nations, Poor Nations

NATION	POPULATION (MILLIONS)	BIRTH RATE PER 1,000 POPULATION	GROSS DOMESTIC PRODUCT PER CAPITA $ (PURCHASING POWER PARITY)
Low-income			
Ethiopia	64.1	45.1	560
Bangladesh	129.2	25.4	1,470
Pakistan	141.6	32.1	2,000
Middle-income			
Algeria	31.2	23.1	4,700
Malaysia	21.8	25.3	10,700
Colombia	39.7	22.9	6,200
High-income			
United States	275.6	14.2	33,900
Japan	126.6	10.0	23,400
France	59.3	12.3	23,300

Source: Central Intelligence Agency, *The World Factbook 2000*.

are also big gaps between the rich and poor within less developed countries (intranational inequality). Every nation has income inequality. The poorer the nation, though, the wider the gap between rich and poor.[28] The poor in a poor country are doubly disadvantaged; their economic system produces little wealth, and a minority of elites receives most of the wealth that is produced.

Given that American policy has done little to alter income distribution at home, it is perhaps surprising to discover that American foreign policy has attempted to eliminate international inequalities. Less developed nations have claimed at various conferences that the developed nations have exploited their resources. Such nations have thus passed resolutions calling for a redistribution of the world's wealth. These requests have never received much sympathy in Washington.

Nevertheless, presidents of each party have pressed for aid to nations in the developing world. Aside from simple humanitarian concern for those who are suffering, presidents have wanted to stabilize nations that were friendly to the United States or that possessed supplies of vital raw materials. Sometimes aid has been given in the form of grants, but often it has taken the form of credits and loan guarantees to purchase American goods, loans at favorable interest rates, and forgiveness of previous loans. At other times, the United States has awarded preferential trade agreements for the sale of foreign goods in the United States.

A substantial percentage of foreign aid is in the form of military assistance and is targeted to a few countries the United States considers to be of vital strategic significance: Israel, Egypt, Turkey, and Greece have received the bulk of such assistance in recent years. Foreign aid programs have also assisted with agricultural modernization, irrigation, and population control. Food for Peace programs have subsidized the sale of American agricultural products to poor countries (and simultaneously given an economic boost to American farmers). Peace Corps volunteers have fanned out over the globe to provide medical care and other services in less developed nations.

Nevertheless, foreign aid has never been very popular with Americans. Lacking a constituency, the president's foreign aid requests are typically cut by Congress, which appropriated about $16.5 billion for foreign aid in fiscal year 2001. Moreover, many people believe that the provision of economic aid to other nations serves only to further enrich the few without helping the many within a poor nation. Although the United States donates more total aid (including military assistance) than any other country, it devotes a smaller share of its GDP to foreign economic development than any other developed nation (see "America in Perspective: Ranking Largess").

Since the thaw in the Cold War, the nations of Central and Eastern Europe, including Russia, have sought aid from the West. Some U.S. leaders have argued that failure to help these formerly Communist nations through the severe economic dislocations resulting from their transition to market economies could lead to the collapse of democracy there. Yet many complain bitterly that we need to spend our resources at home rather than abroad. The United States has given some aid to Russia, Poland, and a few of their neighbors, but much less than they requested.

The Global Connection, Energy, and the Environment

In an interdependent world, economic, military, and diplomatic issues increasingly share the foreign policy stage with issues of energy and the international environment.

Nothing symbolizes the global connection of energy and the environment as succinctly as massive oceangoing oil tankers. In 1946, the largest oil tanker was a mere 18,000 tons. Today the biggest tankers are 326,000 tons, and bigger ones are being designed. These tankers have made it possible to import half the oil Americans

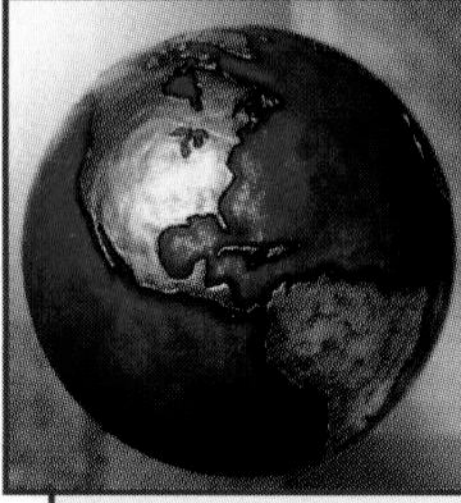

America in Perspective

Ranking Largess

The United States is the second largest donor of foreign aid, but it ranks lower than other industrialized nations in the percentage of its gross domestic product (GDP) that it spends on economic development aid for needy nations.

COUNTRY	TOTAL ECONOMIC AID (IN MILLIONS)	PERCENTAGE OF GDP
Denmark	1,724	1.00
Norway	1,370	.91
Netherlands	3,134	.79
Sweden	1,643	.70
France	5,494	.38
Switzerland	976	.35
Finland	402	.32
Belgium	753	.30
Canada	1,721	.28
New Zealand	134	.27
Germany	5,478	.26
Australia	981	.26
Austria	527	.26
United Kingdom	3,279	.23
Japan	9,358	.22
Italy	1,266	.11
United States	**9,135**	**.10**

Source: Organization for Economic Cooperation and Development, *OECD in Figures*, *2000 Edition,* Paris, 2000, 64–65.

now use, but they have also despoiled fisheries and beaches when they have spilled their contents.

Organization of Petroleum Exporting Countries (OPEC)

An economic organization, consisting primarily of Arab nations, that controls the price of oil and the amount of oil its members produce and sell to other nations.

Growing Energy Dependency. Most, though not all, of these tankers are sailing from nations of the **Organization of Petroleum Exporting Countries (OPEC)**—the organization that first made headlines in 1973 by responding to American support of Israel in the short war against Egypt by embargoing oil shipments to the United States and Western European nations.

The fuel shortages and long lines at gas stations that resulted from the 1973 oil embargo convincingly illustrated the growing dependency of world politics. More than half the world's recoverable reserves of oil lie in the Middle East; Saudi Arabia alone controls much of this resource. States such as Texas, Oklahoma, Louisiana, and Alaska produce considerable amounts of oil within the United States, but not enough to meet the country's needs. America imports more than 50 percent of its annual consumption of oil from other countries, particularly from the Middle East. The United States is not as dependent on foreign sources of oil as many European countries, like France or Italy, which have virtually no oil of their own, or like Japan, which also imports all of its oil. On the other hand, America's dependence on foreign oil is growing every year.

Fortunately for the U.S. economy, the era of scarce oil in the 1970s and early 1980s was followed by an oil glut. Prices sank as supplies increased; nations and businesses depending on oil income suffered a severe recession (as did oil-producing states

Figure 20.6 American Dependence on Foreign Oil

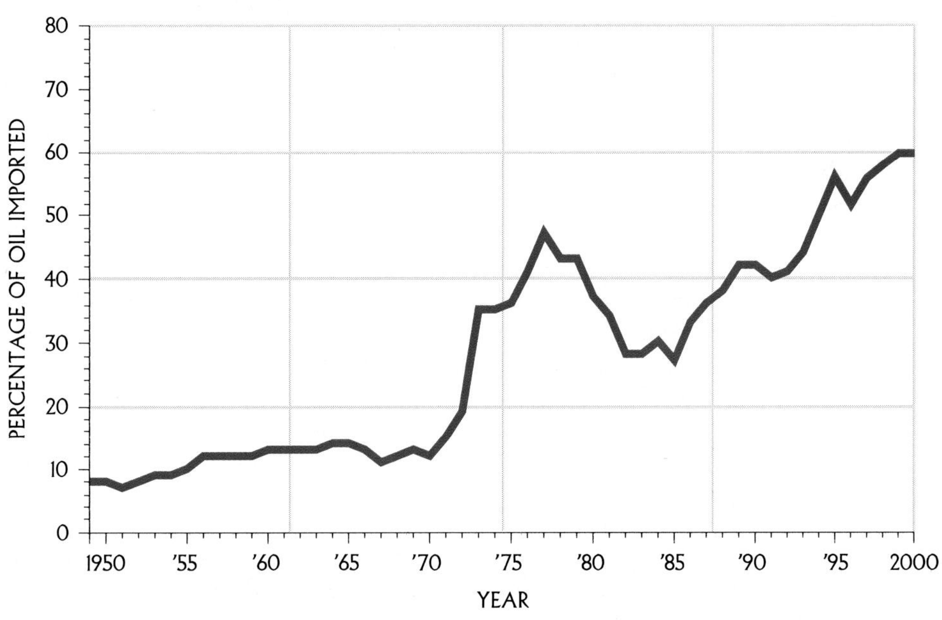

Dependency on imported oil decreased in the early 1980s, but by 1995 it had increased to more than half of the oil in the United States.

Source: Energy Information Administration, *Monthly Energy Review* (Washington, D.C.: U.S. Government Printing Office, various years).

such as Texas, Oklahoma, and Louisiana); oil millionaires went bankrupt; and discipline within the OPEC cartel crumbled. This abundance, of course, was a great boon to energy users. Speed limits on U.S. highways, which had been reduced in the 1970s to save energy, were raised in 1996.

Circumstances may again restrict the availability of oil, however, and the United States is vulnerable because it now imports more than half of the oil it uses (see Figure 20.6). America's decision to respond to Iraq's invasion of Kuwait in 1990 was based in large part by this dependence. Kuwait, although a small country, produces about 10 percent of the world's oil; its neighbor, Saudi Arabia, possesses about half the world's proven oil reserves. Following a UN embargo and ultimatum to Iraq to pull out of Kuwait, the United States and its allies poured forces into Saudi Arabia (more than half a million soldiers from the United States alone). The allied forces quickly defeated the Iraqis and liberated Kuwait. Yet Saddam Hussein remained in power, and the Middle East—and America's sources of foreign oil—remain unstable. In addition, OPEC limited the supply of oil, and thus increased its price, in 2000.

Environment and the World Commons. The oceans traveled by the supertankers are an important part of the world commons (areas shared by everyone). When a supertanker spills its oil on the beaches, it makes environmental headlines. Supertankers are hardly the only ecological problem in the world commons, however.

Almost every nation faces environmental dilemmas at least as severe as those facing America (see Chapter 19 for a discussion of America's environmental challenges). A nation's political ideology seems unrelated to its level of environmental despoliation. The formerly Communist nations of Central and Eastern Europe certainly rank among the worst offenders. The explosion of a nuclear reactor at Chernobyl contaminated a vast area not only within the USSR but in other European nations as well. Germany has poured as many chemicals into the Rhine as Americans have poured into their rivers. Underdeveloped nations almost always favor economic growth at the expense of ecological sensitivity. Environmentalists have cautioned less developed nations to think ecologically, but in places where economic development means the difference between starvation and salvation, most ecological pleas go unheard.

Global issues of environment and energy have crept slowly onto the nation's policy agenda. Recent concerns about the effects of fluorocarbons, found in many household products, on the earth's ozone layer have generated international studies and diplomatic discussions. Americans have bargained with other nations to restrict overfishing of some of the world's fishing areas; they have pressured the Japanese to eliminate whaling; they have shown their concern about pollution in the Rhine and the deforestation of the tropical rain forests.

Issues closer to home, however, are often harder to preach about. In 1992, President Bush refused to sign an international agreement on environmental protection, arguing that it would cost the United States jobs and that it failed to protect patent rights in newly developing industries. The Canadian government has become gravely concerned about acid rain, which originates from emissions in the United States. Rain containing more than 10 times the normal acidity falls on lakes in the northeastern United States and Canada. On the pH scale—a measure of acidity in which 7 represents neutral—the Adirondack lakes in northeastern New York consistently measure 5 (vinegar measures 3).

We saw in Chapter 19 that President Clinton did not agree to follow a specific timetable to reduce the threat of global warming (the United States produces one-fifth of the world's greenhouse gases). He did not submit the treaty the United States signed in Kyoto, Japan, in 1997 to the Senate. George W. Bush renounced the treaty in 2001. While the less developed nations argue that developed nations should bear most of the burden in reducing greenhouse gases, opponents of the treaty in the United States fear that cutting greenhouse gases will cost a staggering sum. Moreover, they question why the United States should undergo changes in its energy usage while there is still uncertainty regarding the cause of global warming.

participation
America's Place in the World

Issues such as acid rain and global warming have soured some goodwill between Americans and their neighbors, but global issues of the world commons have yet to become a major issue of U.S. foreign policy.

Understanding Foreign and Defense Policymaking

Foreign and defense policy are perhaps the most exotic arenas of public policy, dealing with issues and nations that are often far from America's shores. Nevertheless, the themes that have guided your understanding of American politics throughout *Government in America*—democracy and the scope of government—can also shed light on the topic of international relations.

Foreign and Defense Policymaking and Democracy

To some commentators, democracy has little to do with the international relations of the United States. Because domestic issues are closer to their daily lives and easier to understand, Americans are usually more interested in domestic policy than in foreign policy. This preference would seem to give public officials more discretion in making foreign policy. In addition, some say, those with the discretion are elites in the State Department and unelected military officers in the Pentagon.

There is little evidence, however, that policies at odds with the wishes of the American people can be sustained; civilian control of the military is unquestionable.

How You Can Make a Difference

Aid to Developing Nations

You don't have to work for the State Department or win a Nobel Peace Prize like Jody Williams to have an impact in foreign affairs. You can impact a government's policies through letter writing, protests, and other activist campaigns. Or, you can volunteer your time and money to organizations that champion international humanitarian aid and human rights. Do not underestimate the importance of these types of activism! Without people willing to take on larger, 'global' issues, Jody Williams' tireless efforts to eliminate landmines would have been in vain.

For the past 40 years, joining the Peace Corps as a volunteer has offered college students of any age perhaps the most exciting opportunity to impact and aid the larger world around them. First created by John F. Kennedy, the Peace Corps has grown into an organization supporting over 7,000 volunteers in 76 countries. After receiving intensive language courses and other training, volunteers serve in host countries for two years, sometimes in remote locations. They serve in local communities to improve education, stimulate economic activity, and work on basic programs to improve families' health. Along with business and natural science majors, liberal arts students (history, political science, sociology, English, and other majors) will find that they are in especially heavy demand in the Peace Corps. In addition to a small stipend to cover the basic necessities of life, the Peace Corps will pay for your transportation to and from your host country, as well as all medical and dental care. For more information, be sure to check out their website at www.peacecorps.gov.

Because so many other organizations exist, the following list is necessarily selective and representational. These organizations deal with issues as diverse as disaster relief, refugee assistance, human rights and the effects of war or political upheaval, and they all need volunteers and assistance:

CARE (www.care.org) first began as an operation to aid the survivors of World War II. It has expanded to become one of the largest private humanitarian aid organizations in both emergency aid and sustainable development.

The United Nations (www.un.org) sponsors a wide range of these organizations including UNICEF (www.unicef.org), which is selectively concerned with assisting children in need.

Groups dedicated to eradicating hunger include Food for Life Global (www.ffl.org) and Freedom from Hunger (www.freefromhunger.org).

The American Red Cross (www.crossnet.org) may have gained a reputation for its important blood drives, but its impact extends far beyond that one activity. It desperately needs volunteer college students willing to give up summer and Christmas vacations for disaster assistance. The American Red Cross website offers a special link for this purpose.

Amnesty International (www.amnesty.org) and Human Rights Watch (www.hrw.org) are the two premier organizations dedicated to policing governments and their agencies around the world in respect to human rights.

To check out more opportunities and a more extensive directory of humanitarian organizations, examine ReliefWeb at www.reliefweb.int.

When the American people hold strong opinions regarding international relations—as when they first supported and later opposed the war in Vietnam—policymakers are usually responsive. Citizens in democracies do not choose to fight citizens in other democracies, and studies have found that well-established democracies rarely go to war against one another.[29]

In addition, the system of separation of powers plays a crucial role in foreign as well as domestic policy. The president takes the lead on national security matters, but you saw in Chapter 12 that Congress has a central role in matters of international relations. Whether treaties are ratified, defense budgets appropriated, weapons systems authorized, or foreign aid awarded is ultimately at the discretion of the Congress—the government's most representative policymaking body. Specific issues such as the proper funding for the Strategic Defense Initiative rarely determine congressional elections, but public demands for and objections to policies are likely to be heard in Washington.

When it comes to the increasingly important arena of American international economic policy, pluralism is pervasive. Agencies and members of Congress, as well as their constituents, all pursue their own policy goals. For example, the Treasury Department and the Federal Reserve Board worry about the negative balance of trade, and the Department of Defense spends billions in other countries to maintain American troops abroad. The Departments of Agriculture and Commerce and their constituents—farmers and businesspeople—want to peddle American products abroad and generally favor freer trade. The Department of Labor and the unions worry that the nation may export not only products but also jobs to other countries where labor costs are low. Jewish citizens closely monitor U.S. policy toward Israel, whereas Greek Americans seek to limit military aid to Turkey, Greece's ancient rival. Even foreign governments hire lobbying firms and join in the political fray. As a result, a wide range of interests are represented in the making of foreign policy.

Foreign and Defense Policymaking and the Scope of Government

America's global connections as a superpower have many implications for how active the national government is in the realm of foreign policy and national defense. Treaty obligations to defend allies around the world, the nation's economic interests in an interdependent global economy, and pressing new questions on the global agenda—ranging from illicit drugs to environmental protection—demand government action.

By any standard, the scope of government in these areas is large. The national defense consumes about one-sixth of the federal government's budget and requires about 2.2 million civilian and military employees for the Department of Defense. Even though the United States has improved relations with Eastern and Central Europe, the United States will remain a superpower and continue to have political, economic, and military interests to defend around the world. As long as these interests remain, the scope of American government in foreign and defense policy will be substantial.

Summary

The world—its politics and its economics—intrudes on Americans more each year. This chapter examined America's global connections and the contours of its foreign policy.

The Cold War began shortly after World War II, when the containment doctrine became the basis of American foreign policy. The Cold War led to actual wars in Korea and Vietnam when the United States tried to contain Communist advances. With containment came a massive military buildup, resulting in what some people called the *military-industrial* complex. Gradually, containment has been balanced by détente and then friendship with many of our former adversaries. This trend has accelerated with the democratization of Central and Eastern Europe and the dissolution of the Soviet Union. Nevertheless, the United States maintains an enormous defense capability. Still, both foreign and defense policy are undergoing substantial reevaluation in response to the Cold War thaw that began in 1989.

Although the United States has great military power, many of the issues facing the world today are not military issues. Nuclear proliferation and terrorism present new challenges to national security, challenges not easily met by advanced weaponry. Interconnected issues of equality, energy, and the environment have also become important. The international economic system pulls the United States deeper and deeper into the world's problems as global interdependency and its own vulnerability become more apparent.

Career Profile

Position: Foreign Service Officer
Salary Range: $33,000-$49,000
Benefits: Health and retirement benefits, free overseas housing, vacation and home leave, language incentive pay for foreign language fluency
Qualifications: U.S. citizen between 20 and 59 years of age; college degree recommended but not required; must pass the Foreign Service Written and Oral Exams; security and medical clearances required; availability for worldwide assignments (including hardship postings), and a willingness to support and publicly defend U.S. foreign policy

Real People on the Job: Robert Blake

Nearly everyone who starts out as a Foreign Service officer in the U.S. State Department hopes one day to have Robert Blake's job. As a desk officer, Robert is on the cutting edge of U.S. foreign policy. The State Department assigns only one desk officer to each country that has diplomatic relations with the United States. These desk officers serve as the principal liaison between the American embassy in their assigned countries and the State Department in Washington D.C. Each report sent back to Washington by Foreign Service officers from around the world, cables about political, economic, and human rights issues, goes through a desk officer like Robert.

Most recently, Robert served as the desk officer for Turkey. When devastating earthquakes hit the country in 1999, Robert worked with the White House, the Agency for International Development and other agencies to coordinate U.S. aid to the Turkish government and people. He helped initiate the dispatch of search and rescue units to help locate survivors trapped in collapsed buildings.

Regardless of whether Robert is responding to an emergency like an earthquake or something less pressing like a minor trade dispute, it's his responsibility to do more than just make decisions that accurately reflect American foreign policy goals; he must also help to determine those very policy goals. To do his job effectively, he needs detailed information from the Foreign Service officers in his assigned country. As a former Foreign Service officer himself, he knows what it takes to obtain such information. The officer must read the official reports of foreign governments or follow regional developments in the local media. Also, the officer must cultivate personal relationships and friendships with the citizens of the country in which he or she is stationed.

For more information about careers in the Foreign Service, call 1-202-261-8888 or see the State Department website at www.state.gov.

Key Terms

foreign policy
United Nations (UN)
North Atlantic Treaty Organization (NATO)
European Union (EU)
secretary of state
secretary of defense
Joint Chiefs of Staff
Central Intelligence Agency (CIA)
isolationism
containment doctrine
Cold War
McCarthyism
arms race
détente
Strategic Defense Initiative (SDI)
interdependency
tariff
balance of trade
Organization of Petroleum Exporting Countries (OPEC)

For Further Reading

Calleo, David. *Beyond American Hegemony.* New York: Basic Books, 1987. An important study of America's role as a world power in an age of increasing economic interdependency and competition.

Hilsman, Roger. *The Politics of Policymaking in Defense and Foreign Affairs.* Englewood Cliffs, NJ: Prentice-Hall, 1987. An insightful analysis of how the American political system copes with defense and foreign policy problems.

Huntington, Samuel P. *The Clash of Civilizations and the Remaking of World Order.* New York: Simon & Schuster, 1996. Argues that civilizational identities built on religious empires of the past will be the source of international turmoil in the next century.

Kagan, Donald. *On the Origins of War and the Preservation of Peace.* New York: Doubleday, 1995. Provides insights gleaned from studying the origins of great wars.

Kennedy, Paul. *The Rise and Fall of the Great Powers.* New York: Random House, 1987. A provocative historical analysis of the interconnections between relative economic strength and military power.

Lieber, Robert J., ed. *Eagle Adrift: American Foreign Policy at the End of the Century.* New York: Longman, 1997. An excellent collection of articles on U.S. foreign policy in the post-Cold War era.

Lindsay, James M. *Congress and the Politics of U.S. Foreign Policy.* Baltimore: Johns Hopkins University Press, 1994. A useful discussion of the role of Congress in setting U.S. foreign policy.

Mueller, John. *Retreat from Doomsday: The Obsolescence of Major War.* New York: Basic Books, 1989. An insightful rethinking of defense policy.

Nye, Joseph S. *Bound To Lead.* New York: Basic Books, 1990. Argues that America is not in decline, but that American power faces serious challenges in an increasingly interdependent world.

Yergin, Daniel. *Shattered Peace: The Origins of the Cold War and the National Security State.* Boston: Houghton Mifflin, 1977. An excellent political history of the early years of the Cold War and containment.

Internet Resources

www.state.gov/
Information about the Department of State and current foreign policy issues.

www.defenselink.mil/
Information about the Department of Defense and current issues in national security policy.

www.odci.gov/cia/publications/factbook/index.html
The *CIA World Factbook.*

www.oecdwash.org/
The Organization for Economic Cooperation and Development (OECD) provides a wealth of economic information on the world's nations.

www.nato.int/
Contains background and activities of NATO.

www.un.org/
Background on the United Nations and its varied programs.

www.cfr.org
The Council on Foreign Relations is the most influential private organization in the area of foreign policy. Its website includes a wide range of information on foreign policy.

www1.whitehouse.gov/WH/EOP/NSC/html/nschome.html
Information about the members and functions of the National Security Council.

Notes

1. See, for example, Paul Kennedy, *The Rise and Fall of the Great Powers* (New York: Random House, 1987).
2. Raymond Vernon, *Storm over the Multinationals: The Real Issues* (Cambridge, MA: Harvard University Press, 1977); United Nations, *World Investment Report, 1998: Trends and Determinants, Overview* (New York: United Nations, 1998).
3. I. M. Destler, "National Security Management: What Presidents Have Wrought," *Political Science Quarterly* 95 (Winter 1980–1981): 573–588.
4. Richard Botts, *Soldiers, Statesmen, and Cold War Crises* (Cambridge, MA: Harvard University Press, 1977), 216, table A.
5. For more on decision making regarding the Gulf War, see Bob Woodward, *The Commanders* (New York: Simon & Schuster, 1991).
6. See Bob Woodward, *Veil: The Secret Wars of the CIA, 1981–1987* (New York: Simon & Schuster, 1987).
7. A good study of the role of Congress in setting U.S. foreign policy is James M. Lindsay, *Congress and the Politics of U.S. Foreign Policy* (Baltimore: Johns Hopkins University Press, 1994). Congress's role in the defense budget process is discussed in Ralph G. Carter, "Budgeting for Defense," in Paul E. Peterson, ed., *The President, Congress, and the Making of Foreign Policy* (Norman: University of Oklahoma Press, 1994).
8. Louis Fisher, "Executive-Legislative Revelations in Foreign Policy" (paper presented at the United States-Mexico Comparative Constituional Law Conference, Mexico City, June 17, 1998), 1.

9. An excellent treatment of the origins of the Cold War is Daniel Yergin, *Shattered Peace: The Origins of the Cold War and the National Security State* (Boston: Houghton Mifflin, 1977).
10. The article was titled "Sources of Soviet Conduct" and appeared in *Foreign Affairs* (July 1947), under the pseudonym X.
11. Yergin, *Shattered Peace*, 268.
12. Seymour Melman, *Pentagon Capitalism: The Political Economy of War* (New York: McGraw-Hill, 1970).
13. Stanley Karnow, *Vietnam: A History* (New York: Penguin Books, 1983), 43. Karnow's book is one of the best of many excellent books on Vietnam. See also Frances FitzGerald, *Fire in the Lake* (Boston: Little, Brown, 1972); and David Halberstam, *The Best and the Brightest* (New York: Random House, 1972).
14. Nicholas Lemann, "The Peacetime War," *Atlantic Monthly*, October 1984, 72.
15. Quoted in Andrew Rosenthal, "Striking a Defensive Tone, Bush Sees Virtue in Caution," *New York Times*, February 8, 1990, A10.
16. See, for example, Bruce Russett, "Defense Expenditures and National Well-Being," *American Political Science Review* 76 (December 1982): 767–777; William K. Domke, Richard C. Eichenberg, and Catherine M. Kelleher, "The Illusion of Choice: Defense and Welfare in Advanced Industrial Democracies, 1948–78," *American Political Science Review* 77 (March 1983): 19–35; and Alex Mintz, "Guns Versus Butter: A Disaggregated Analysis," *American Political Science Review* 83 (December 1989): 1,285–1,296.
17. Kennedy, *The Rise and Fall of the Great Powers*; and David Calleo, *Beyond American Hegemony: The Future of the Western Alliance* (New York: Basic Books, 1987). For a different view, see Joseph S. Nye, *Bound to Lead* (New York: Basic Books, 1990).
18. On the importance of ideology, see studies discussed in Robert A. Bernstein, *Elections, Representation, and Congressional Voting Behavior* (Englewood Cliffs, NJ: 1989), 70–76.
19. U.S. Department of Commerce, *Statistical Abstract of the United States, 2000* (Washington, D.C.: U.S. Government Printing Office, 2001), 368.
20. Stephen I. Schwartz, ed., *Atomic Audit: The Costs and Consequences of U.S. Nuclear Weapons Since 1940* (Washington, D.C.: Brookings Institutions, 1998).
21. John E. Reilly, ed., *American Public Opinion and U.S. Foreign Policy 1999*, (Chicago: Chicago Council on Foreign Relations, 1999).
22. Stanley Hoffman, *Gulliver's Troubles, or the Setting of American Foreign Policy* (New York: McGraw-Hill, 1968).
23. Robert O. Keohane and Joseph S. Nye, *Power and Interdependence*, 2nd ed. (New York: HarperCollins, 1989), 27.
24. *Ibid.*, 27–28.
25. *Ibid.*, 3.
26. *Statistical Abstract of the United States, 2000*, 794.
27. U.S. Department of Commerce, Bureau of the Census.
28. Michael Don Ward, *The Political Economy of Distribution: Equality Versus Inequality* (New York: Elsevier, 1978), 44.
29. See Bruce M. Russett, *Controlling the Sword* (Cambridge, MA: Harvard University Press, 1990), chap. 5; Thomas Hartley and Bruce M. Russett, "Public Opinion and the Common Defense: Who Governs Military Spending in the United States?" *American Political Science Review* 86 (December 1992): 905–915; Bruce M. Russett, *Grasping the Democratic Peace* (Princeton, NJ: Princeton University Press, 1993); Spencer R. Weart, *Never at War* (New Haven: Yale University Press, 1998); Michael D. Ward and Kristian S. Gleditsch, "Democratizing Peace," *American Political Science Review* 92 (March 1998): 51–62; and Paul R. Hensel, Gary Foertz, and Paul F. Diehl, "The Democratic Peace and Rivalries," *Journal of Politics* 62 (November 2000): 1173–1188.

21 The New Face of State and Local Government

Chapter Outline

Charles Jeff attends St. Ad Albert's Roman Catholic elementary school in Cleveland—but the taxpayers in Ohio pay for it.[1] Charles' family participates in an experimental program that gives *tuition vouchers* to parents so they can choose where to send their children to school. Tuition vouchers are a set amount of money given by the government to parents that can only be used to pay for public or private school tuition. Tuition vouchers and other "school choice" reforms have recently become important issues for state and local governments. School choice reforms are similar to a whole host of policy reforms designed to either devolve authority to state and local government, or to otherwise localize control over what government does.

Proponents of tuition vouchers argue that by giving parents a

choice in where they send their children to school, schools will have to pay more attention to the needs of students and their parents or risk losing students to competitive schools with better services. They argue that schools that are guaranteed students solely because of their location have no incentive to improve. Further, voucher advocates argue that it is unfair that rich families have the ability to choose which school their children attend, but poor families do not.

Tuition voucher programs are controversial, however. In fact, they generate vehement opposition from those who support the current public school system, including teachers' unions. Opponents argue that voucher systems will amount to little more than a subsidy for those already well off enough to send their children to private schools. They argue that voucher systems would actually decrease the quality of public schools, as top teachers and students with active and involved parents move to private schools, leaving public schools filled with those least likely to succeed.

The debate over school choice reforms is important for several reasons. Public education of children is the cornerstone of a responsible democracy. Not only is an educated electorate needed for making intelligent and informed choices in elections, but the public schools have also become the great socializing institution for American values, such as equality and meritorious advancement. The public schools are also the center of community life in many American neighborhoods, where people go to vote, meet their neighbors, work in community groups, and so forth.

Would a tuition voucher program, and the competitive system of public and private schools the program is meant to stimulate, enhance or detract from this democratic mission of education? If schools offered better education, would the electorate be better informed? If parents could select the schools they send their children to, would citizens mingle with those outside of their social, economic, and ethnic groups more or less frequently? Which is more compatible with democracy, having parents or public officials decide where children ought to be attending school? And who should decide how our tax dollars are spent—elected local officials or bureaucrats who are not directly accountable to taxpayers?

Tuition vouchers also raise the question about the scope of government. Elementary and secondary education have always been the responsibility of state and local governments in the United States. Advocates of tuition vouchers suggest we put education back into the private sector, with the government providing the money, but not the institutions, for education. Is this the proper role of government? And if education should no longer be provided by government, does that suggest that other sorts of services that state and local governments have historically provided—such as garbage collection and even police and fire protection—could be provided in other ways, such as by private contractors?

subnational governments

Another way of referring to state and local governments. Through a process of reform, modernization, and changing intergovernmental relations since the 1960s, subnational governments have assumed new responsibilities and importance.

State and local governments, or **subnational governments,** touch our lives every day. They pick up our garbage, educate us, keep us safe from criminals, and perform a myriad of other vital services. Odds are that you are attending a state or city university right now. You will drive home on locally maintained streets (and may perhaps be issued a speeding ticket from a local official). Subnational governments regulate a wide range of business activities, from generating electric power to cutting hair. The state government is also the single largest employer in every state; in aggregate, local governments employ even more people than do the states. So, as a consumer of government services, as a regulated businessperson, and/or as an employee, subnational governments are intimately involved in our lives.

Not long ago, however, some political observers predicted that state governments would cease to exist in the near future.[2] The states seemed to some like archaic accidents of history rather than meaningful political entities. For example, how could one possibly equate Wyoming, with less than half a million people and less than five people per square mile, to California with 32 million people and 190 people per square mile? What do Hawaii and Alaska have in common with Rhode Island and Louisiana as political entities? Some critics in the 1950s and 1960s thought, "not much." Further, a generation ago, state governments were ridiculed as being "horse and buggy" institutions in an era of space travel.[3] Their institutions were weak, outdated, resource-poor, and were simply not up to the task of running a modern state. The states were also seen by social liberals as obstacles to addressing the grievances of racial and ethnic minorities and urban dwellers—witness Governor George Wallace's stand against the racial integration of Alabama schools (Chapter 3). The federal government was seen as the modern engine of progressive policymaking, and the states were encouraged to step aside or get replaced.

But as Mark Twain said about his mistaken obituary, these reports of the death of the states were greatly exaggerated. Through a process of reform, modernization, and changing intergovernmental relations since the 1960s, subnational governments have become more vital to our democratic system than ever. They have assumed new and costly responsibilities in areas such as welfare, health, economic development, and criminal justice. States and localities have also gained importance as federal policymakers have confronted budgetary limits, and policymakers have recognized the virtues of grassroots democracy—of giving decision-making power to governments closer to the people.

In this chapter, we discuss subnational government with an eye toward two important characteristics: *revitalization* and *diversity*. Since the early 1960s, the states have become revitalized in their institutions, their personnel, and their role in the federal system.[4] State legislatures, governors' offices, courts, and even bureaucracies have undergone dramatic changes that have allowed them to move forward as strong and active players in the U.S. policymaking and governing process. The people involved in governing the states and localities are far more representative of their constituents than was previously the case, and they tend to be better educated, more professionalized, and more interested in policymaking. With the weight of the philosophical argument about where policymaking power should lie in the federal system swinging strongly toward the states for the past 30 years (Chapter 3), the federal government has provided the states and localities with increasing control over policymaking.

The second characteristic important to understanding subnational government in the United States is diversity. As anyone who has every traveled outside of their hometown knows, government, policy, and political behavior differ from place to place. For example, in California citizens can propose and pass laws through the ballot box; in Delaware they can't. On the freeways of New Jersey, you may legally drive no faster than 65 mph at most, whereas until recently in Montana, the only limit was your own judgment and the power of your car's engine. In South Dakota, almost twice the proportion of eligible voters vote as in Louisiana. To understand this diversity among the states is to understand the politics and history of the United States better. This also raises the important questions of why these differences exist and what effects these differences have.

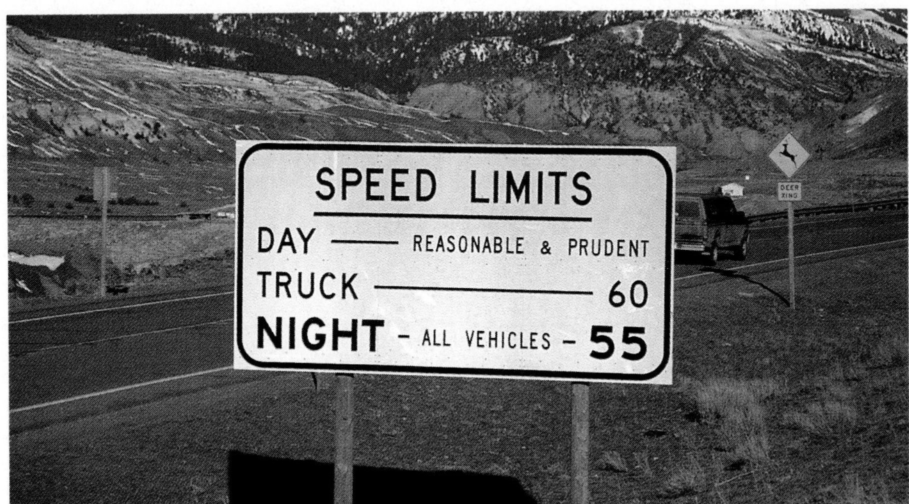

The long, straight, and empty freeways of Montana allowed policymakers there to set a speed limit that would be unthinkable on the crowded highways of New Jersey.

State Constitutions

Each state is governed by a separate and unique constitution that spells out the basic rules of that state's political game. Every state elects a governor as its chief executive officer, and most states have a legislature with two chambers like the Congress (except for Nebraska, which only has a senate). However, the states endow their governors with different powers and organize and elect their legislatures differently. Each state's constitution was written under unique historical conditions and with a unique set of philosophical principles in mind. Each is unique in its length and provisions. Some are modern documents; others were written over 100 years ago. The differences among these documents also reflect the diversity—social, economic, geographic, historic, and political—of the states.[5]

visual literacy
Explaining the Differences in State Laws

State constitutions are subordinate to the U.S. Constitution and the laws of the United States, but they take precedence over state law. State constitutions share many features in common with the U.S. Constitution. Both provide for separation of powers; the creation of executive, judicial, and legislative branches; means of taxation and finance; and all include a bill of rights. Figure 21.1 shows how the Texas state constitution arranges the state's governmental structure.

The key difference between the federal and state constitutions is that the state documents often provide far more detail about specific policies. The Oklahoma constitution, for example, requires that "stock feeding" be taught in public schools, and the South Dakota constitution authorizes a twine and cordage plant at its state penitentiary.[6] This level of specificity leads to constitutions that are long and sometimes confusing. Whereas the U.S. Constitution is a brief document of 8,700 words, state constitutions can be as long as Alabama's 220,000-word tome. In contrast, a few states try to stick to the point as closely as the federal constitution does—Vermont's constitution, adopted in 1793, is a model of brevity with only 6,880 words.

Why do some states try to embed specific policy into what is supposed to be a document detailing fundamental principles and government organization? It has long been argued that powerful interest groups have encouraged lengthy constitutions in order to protect their interests. It is far more difficult to amend a state constitution than to change a law, so policy advocates with the ability at a given time to place a policy statement in the constitution will do so in order to guard against its future repeal at a time when they might not be as strong politically. In states where one political party dominates politics, the lack of effective opposition leads to more protection for programs in the constitution.[7] Longer constitutions, it may also be argued, help limit government interference with Americans' valued individualism.

participation
Explore Your State Constitution

Figure 21.1 Government under the Texas State Constitution

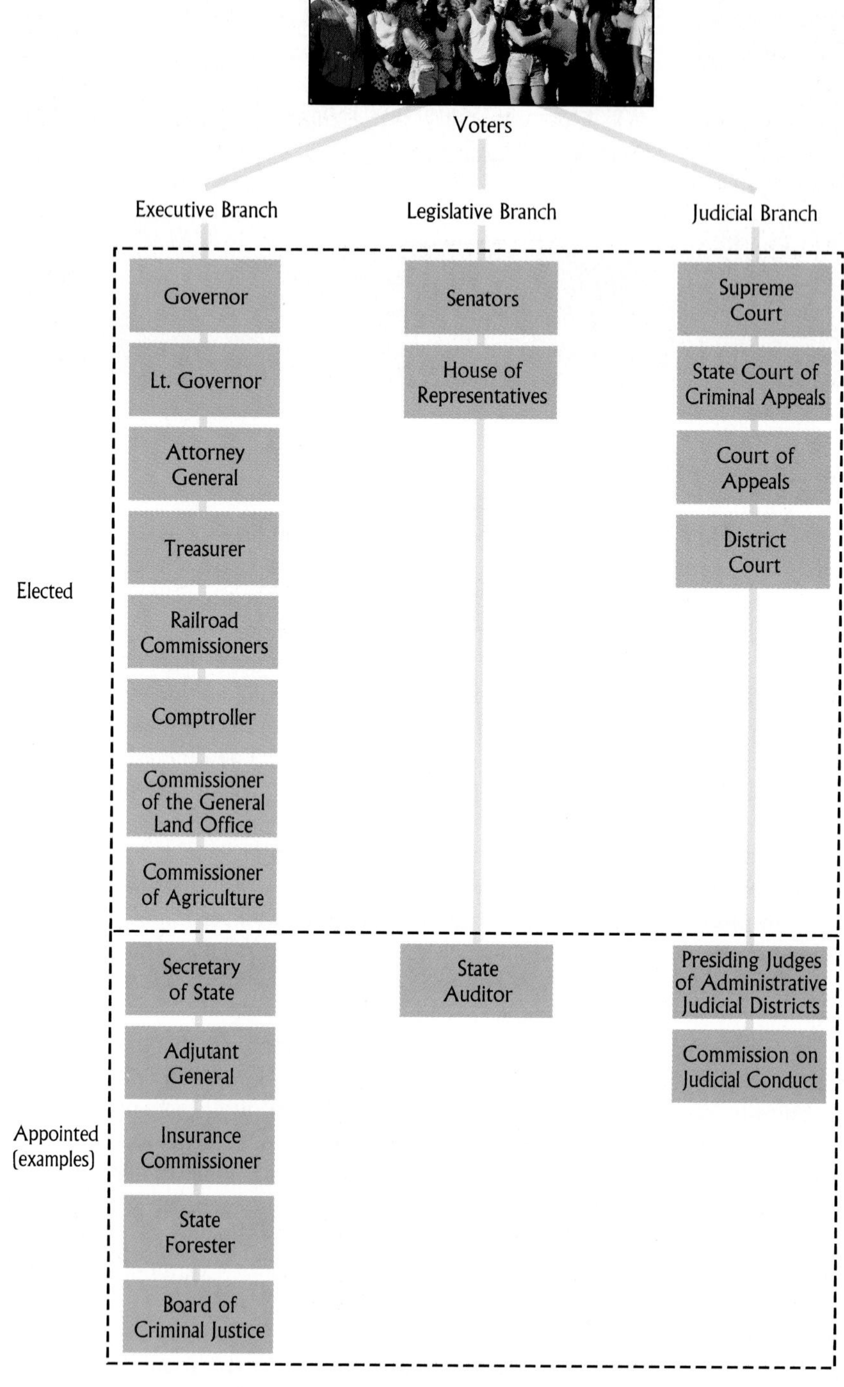

Amending State Constitutions

Periodically, a state considers changes to the rules of its political game. Most avoid the politically difficult process of writing an entirely new constitution. Massachusetts, for example, is governed by a constitution written in 1780. Mississippi, Nebraska, New York, and Utah are among 29 states that have nineteenth-century constitutions.

Although a few states have attempted to write entirely new constitutions since World War II (the most recent successful attempt being Georgia in 1983), most states have adapted their governing documents to the late twentieth century by the "cut and paste" method of constitutional amendment.

The most common way that state constitutions are amended is through a two-step process by which the legislature "proposes" an amendment (usually by passing a resolution to this effect by a vote of two-thirds of the legislature, and in 12 states doing so in two consecutive sessions) and a majority vote in the next general election "ratifies" it. Although this process makes constitutional amendment difficult, it is used every election year in most states, although often for minor issues regarding taxation and public debt. Between 1898 and 1998, 827 direct (from voters) and indirect initiatives (through legislature) for constitutional amendments were proposed, and 343 (42 percent) were approved by states' voters.[8] State constitutions can also be amended through a constitutional convention (although this is extremely rare).

State Elections

Most top-level state policymakers are elected to office. To an even greater extent than federal officials, state officials must achieve office through the ballot box and respond to the voters' preferences if they wish to remain there. At the federal level, voters can only elect one member of the executive branch (the president) while they can elect no one in the judicial branch. However, at the state level, voters usually have far more power to determine who governs them. For example, in California voters get to select eight statewide executive officers (including the governor, treasurer, and even the insurance commissioner and secretary of education), as well as many judges down to the trial court level.[9] Further, in many states voters are authorized to make law directly through the ballot box by using the direct democracy mechanisms we will discuss shortly.

Historically, state elections have been decided by the general political mood of the country or state, with those running for office having little ability to influence their own electoral fortunes. Voters cared little and knew less about state legislative or even gubernatorial races. But as the states have become more important and as their institutions have become more effective and respected in the past generation, average voters and political activists are giving more attention to state elections. As a result, state officials look more like their constituents, in terms of partisanship, ideology, and demographics.

Gubernatorial Elections

Gubernatorial races have increasingly become focused on individual candidates rather than party affiliations. Political scientists Barbara and Stephen Salmore call this the "presidentialization" of gubernatorial elections, since they have come to resemble the personality-focused mega-events that make up modern campaigns for the White House.[10] This has occurred because of the increasing importance of television and money to gubernatorial campaigns, and the decoupling of gubernatorial races from presidential races and state political party organizations.

Historically, most governors were elected during presidential years, either because their term of office was only two years, or because their four-year term coincided with that of the presidential term. But since the 1960s, most states have adopted a four-year gubernatorial term and shifted that term so that elections are held during nonpresidential election years. Today, only 9 of the 48 states that elect a governor for a four-year term hold their gubernatorial elections at the same time as presidential elections.[11]

The change means that the gubernatorial race is the "top of the ticket" in most states, which makes it more likely that voters will pay attention. Races are therefore more likely to be decided on what voters think about the candidates than on any "coattail effect" from the presidential race. This means that candidates for governor can no longer expect to garner much help from a popular presidential candidate for their party, nor can they assume any candidate's campaign suffers from an unpopular presidential candidate topping the ticket. Today, running for governor means running on your own.

In order to "run on their own," gubernatorial candidates have taken to television advertising in a big way, just as presidential candidates have, and largely for the same reasons. There are simply too many people in a state for a candidate to meet them all face to face. Gubernatorial candidates hire nationally known advertising agencies to develop slick ad campaigns. These campaigns are not cheap. The use of television is one of the main reasons why the costs of gubernatorial campaigns have skyrocketed. For elections between 1977 and 1980, the total cost of gubernatorial elections was $422.7 million (adjusted for 1997 dollars). That cost increased by 45 percent, to $611.8 million, for elections between 1994 and 1997. Although the largest states have some of the most expensive elections, if we adjust for the cost per general election vote, we find that the past five general elections have cost the most in Alaska, at $42.10 per vote, Hawaii, at $23.54 per vote, and West Virginia, at $16.58 per vote. However, collectively the elections in California and Texas have cost the most, with California averaging almost $51 million and Texas $44 million per election between 1980 and 1992.[12]

Most of this money has to be raised by the candidates themselves, further personalizing these races. At one time, state political party organizations had a strong hand in funding these campaigns and in selecting the party nominees for the general election. Those days are long gone in most states. With the advent of the direct primary for nominating party candidates, a person who wants to become governor must organize and fund a major campaign in the primary itself. Parties traditionally have stayed out of these intraparty races. By the time a candidate wins the primary, he or she has built a solid campaign organization and has little need for the party's help in the general election. Further, contributing money to a specific candidate can be more appealing than contributing to a party organization, so candidates tend to have more success in fundraising than state parties do.

One result of the personalization of gubernatorial elections has been that parties have a harder time predicting their success. Because voters now become familiar with gubernatorial candidates during campaigns, they more frequently vote based on their attitude toward the candidates rather than resorting to party loyalty. This can lead to ticket splitting and divided government, as citizens vote for less well-known state legislative candidates strictly based on their party affiliation.[13] We see the results of this when states whose voters are predominantly of one party elect governors of the other party. For example, in 1998, Massachusetts voters elected Republican Paul Cellucci to the governorship, even though registered Democrat voters outnumber registered Republicans nearly three to one and the state legislature is heavily dominated by Democrats. At the extreme, this has led to four Independent governors being elected in recent years. Two of these—Lowell Whicker of Connecticut and Walter Hickel of Alaska—were politicians formerly associated with a major party who challenged their parties' candidates in the general election due to intraparty squabbles. But the two governors currently serving—Angus King of Maine (Independent) and Jesse Ventura of Minnesota (Reform Party)—are truly independent of the Democratic and Republican parties and owe their election completely to the efforts of their personal campaign organizations.

State Legislative Elections

Of all state- and federal-level officials, state legislators face the smallest constituencies, ranging from less than 3,000 people in a New Hampshire House of Representatives district to almost 800,000 people in a California Senate district, but with an average size of about 140,000 for state senate districts and 50,000 for state house districts.[14] By comparison, governors and members of the U.S. House of Representatives need to respond to considerably more voters.

Throughout much of the twentieth century, state legislatures were horribly malapportioned, giving greater representation to rural areas than their population warranted. One hundred years ago, most state legislators represented rural areas because that was where people lived. However, by the early 1960s the population had become overwhelmingly urban. Since the legislative district boundaries had rarely changed, state legislatures continued to be dominated by rural politicians. The main reason for the underrepresentation of urban areas was that districts were often constructed on the basis of the boundaries of some local government, such as a county, regardless of how many people lived there. This meant that in many states, rural counties with a few thousand residents and urban counties with hundreds of thousands of residents all had the same representation in the state legislature.

In 1962, after decades of avoiding the issue, the U.S. Supreme Court ruled that the districts of the lower chamber of state legislatures must be based on the number of people living in them. This landmark decision in *Baker v. Carr* established the principle of "one person, one vote" in drawing up state house districts. Two years later, the Court ruled in *Reynolds v. Sims* that state senates must also be apportioned in this fashion.

These cases dramatically changed the face of state legislature. Gone was the rural dominance of these chambers. New representatives arrived from the central cities and suburbs. Urban and metropolitan area problems became the focus of state legislatures.

Periodic redrawing of legislative districts is required as population shifts. This is now done following every decennial census, further changing the composition of state legislatures. The late twentieth-century migration of citizens to the suburbs has resulted in new voting power for suburban metropolitan interests and a decline in the power of central cities in state capitals.

Ironically, although state legislators have smaller districts than any other state or federal elected officials, they are the least well known by voters. This is largely due to the historic lack of media coverage given to state legislatures and the lack of campaign resources of candidates for the office. The result is that races for state legislature, at least in general elections, have been decided on the basis of forces beyond candidates' control—party identification of district voters, and the parties' candidates in the race for governor and president.

But with the recent shifting of more policy responsibilities to the states and increases in state legislative salaries (discussed shortly) making the office both more important and attractive, campaigns for the state legislature have started to become more candidate centered, although not nearly to the extent that gubernatorial campaigns have. This "congressionalization" of state legislative races is encouraged by increased resources (mainly staff and time) for incumbent legislators to retain their seats, and increases in the activities of PACs at the state level willing to fund expensive campaigns.[15] Campaign costs skyrocketed for state legislative campaigns from the 1970s to 1990s, and continue to be high today, with competitive races in large states costing as much as $2 million. Although it is still possible to run a less closely contested campaign for the state legislature in a less populous state for only several thousand dollars, this is no longer the norm.[16]

Because of the need to raise and spend more money on these campaigns, incumbent legislators appear to be more advantaged than they used to be. Incumbents can use the resources and prestige of office both to enhance their visibility with their constituents and to attract campaign contributions from PACs and others interested in garnering favor in the legislature.[17] State legislative leaders also help incumbents through their own PACs and party funds in order to enhance their personal influence as leaders and the prospects of their party retaining or regaining control of their chamber.[18]

Partisan Competition, Legislative Turnover, and Term Limits. The 2000 elections continued the 20-year trend in state legislatures of increasing party competition, closer partisan splits, and changing party control (see Table 21.1). Although much of this change has occurred as a result of Republican gains in the South (for example, the South Carolina state house now has a majority of Republicans, as do both chambers of the Florida state legislature), even northern states have been experiencing increasingly close legislative party divisions. Democrats hold 51.5 percent of all seats in state legislatures, the smallest percentage since the New Deal, continuing a steady downward trend since the Watergate scandals buoyed the party's fortunes in the mid-1970s.[19]

Although some state legislative chambers have very lopsided partisan splits (for example, in the Idaho state senate Republicans hold 89 percent of the seats and in the Hawaii state senate Democrats hold 92 percent), there are more close splits today than there have been in the past. In 10 of the 50 state senates, there are three or fewer seats separating the parties. The Washington state house is the extreme case, with exactly 49 Republicans and 49 Democrats. This sort of partisan "tie" is not unique to Washington this year; nine states have been in the same position in the 1990s. And finally, seven chambers changed majority party control as a result of the 1998 election, which along with the eight chambers that switched as a result of the 1996 elections indicates a remarkable period of increasing party competition in the state legislatures.

Divided government exists when a single party does not control both chambers of the state legislature and the governor's office. With divided government, it is usually much more difficult for coherent policy action to take place because the parties that control the different components of state government have conflicting policy and electoral goals. Increased switching of party control and party competition has inevitably led to more divided control of state government than in the past, when party affiliation of voters within states was more stable and electorates more homogeneous.[20] After the 1998 elections, 26 states had divided government, approximately the same level as has been seen since the mid-1980s. In contrast, in 1946 only seven states had divided government. Minnesota has the most extreme case of divided government today, with its Senate controlled by Democrats, its House controlled by Republicans, and its governor (Jesse Ventura) a member of the Reform Party!

Increased party competition, divided government, and majority party switching in state legislatures has tended to increase legislative partisanship and polarize legislative deliberations, thereby making compromise harder to come by. If a minority party leader thinks he or she has a chance to become the majority party leader after the next election, he or she may take a vocal opposition to the current majority party on a tough policy choice rather than quietly negotiate a settlement. Further, this sort of swinging from party to party can lead to a lack of policy continuity in a state. On the other hand, high levels of party competition tend to make elected officials more attentive and responsive to voters.[21]

Aside from partisan change there is the question of turnover in state legislatures. Turnover levels—the rate that state legislators are replaced from election to election—give us an understanding both of how much experience and expertise state legislators have relative to other political actors in the states and how closely they are "connected" to their constituencies and the normal life of a state citizen. If some people, such as lobbyists and bureaucrats, work for many years in the policymaking process and state legislators serve for only a few years, the latter may be at a disadvantage. On the other hand, some argue that a significant amount of turnover is important for state legislatures, so that those bodies get fresh ideas on a regular basis and do not lose touch with the average citizen's concerns.

Recent history has shown that in any 10-year period, about 72 percent of state senate and 84 percent of state house legislative seats are turned over.[22] Thus, significant change in the people holding state legislative office is the norm. During the 1980s, New York had the lowest percent of changes in its Senate (38 percent), followed by Michigan (50 percent). Mississippi and West Virginia had the highest turnover in their

Table 21.1 The Balance of Power

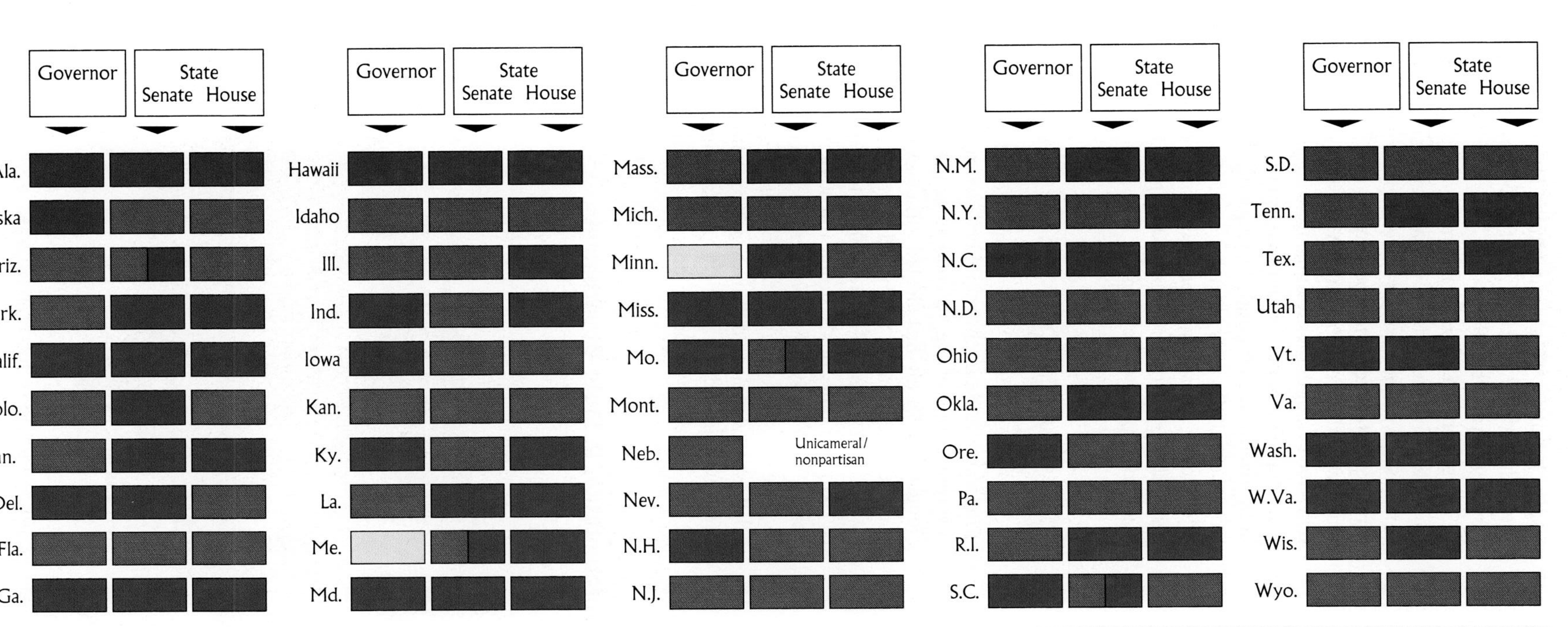

Source: Council of State Governments.

upper chambers: 94 percent. On the House side, Arkansas and Illinois had the lowest turnover with 49 percent, whereas Washington and West Virginia had 90 percent turnover during the 1980s.[23]

Regardless of these high turnover rates, in recent years voters in many states have attempted to increase turnover rates by legally restricting the number of terms a member may serve. Increasingly, voters appear to support the argument that professional, career-oriented legislators become so entrenched and difficult to unseat that they lose touch with their constituents and instead pander to special interests. Since 1990, 21 states have adopted term limits for state legislators, almost exclusively through direct democracy mechanisms (discussed shortly). However, three states have seen their term limits overturned in court, leaving only 18 term limit laws intact.[24] The number of terms permitted varies from state to state. For example, California limits its assembly (their lower house) members to six years and its senators to eight years in office, Colorado legislators are limited to eight consecutive years, and Oklahoma legislators may serve up to twelve years.[25]

The Changing Face of State Elected Officials

In November 1996, Washington state voters chose Gary Locke, the son of Chinese immigrants, as their governor. Locke became the first Asian American ever to be elected governor of one of the 48 contiguous states. Seven years before, Virginia voters made Douglas Wilder the first elected African-American governor. Although these two governors are exceptions to the rule that governors are White, married men who are often lawyers, state voters are increasingly electing a wider variety of people to state offices.

Women have made strong inroads into the governors' offices (see Figure 21.2). Before 1974, only a few women had ever been governors, and those were elected because they were married to a former governor who could not run again. But in 1974, Ella Grasso was elected to the governor's office of Connecticut in her own right. Dixie Lee Ray followed her in 1976 in Washington. Since 1976, nine women have been elected to the governorship in states as varied as Oregon, Kansas, and Kentucky, rep-

Figure 21.2 Female Representation in State Government

Percentage of females in the state legislature (2000):

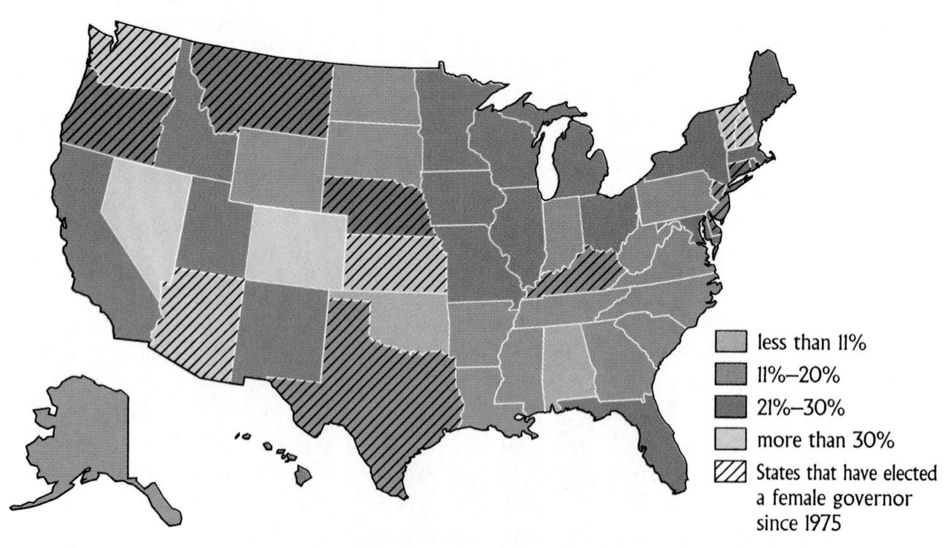

Source: National Conference of State Legislatures, "Women in State Legislatures 1999," www.ncsl.org/programs/legman/about/women.htm (January 3, 2000).

In 1998, women were elected to all five statewide executive offices in Arizona—governor, secretary of state, treasurer, superintendent of public instruction, and attorney general. The so-called "Fab Five" were sworn into office by another powerful Arizona female—U.S. Supreme Court Justice Sandra Day O'Connor.

resenting both the Democratic and Republican Parties. At least two prominent female governors—Ann Richards of Texas and Christine Whitman of New Jersey—have been mentioned as potential presidential candidates. In the 36 gubernatorial general elections held in 1998, nine had a female major party candidate, two of whom won the election (in Arizona and New Hampshire). Including Whitman, reelected governor of New Jersey in 1997, there are five female state governors in the United States today. Being female or a person of color is no longer a disqualification for being elected to a state's highest office.

State legislatures too have been looking more and more like the diverse population of the United States.[26] In 1999, 22 percent of all state legislators were women, a record number.[27] In 1969, only about 4 percent of state legislators were women. Four of the 49 speakers of the state houses were women in the 1997–1998 sessions. Although state legislatures varied widely in the percentage of women in them (from 41 percent in Washington state to only 8 percent in Alabama), there has been a steady increase in female representation across the country for the past 30 years.

In 1998, there were 579 state legislators of African-American descent—7 percent, a figure that has also been increasing steadily for 30 years.[28] Asians and Hispanics have also been increasing in their state legislative representation, primarily in Florida and the Western states that have significant percentages of these people in the voting public.

The less-than-representative percentage of women and ethnic minorities in state elected positions (although historically high) shows the slowness with which progress is made in this area, due at least in part to informal qualifications for higher level offices that can include experience at lower level offices. Women and minorities are making the inroads today in the state and local offices that may well lead to them being elected more frequently to federal positions in the future. For example, the sharp jump in the representation of women in the U.S. Senate in the 1990s was encouraged by increases in women being elected to state legislative positions in the 1970s and 1980s. Note that some of the states that traditionally had the highest rates of women in the state legislature (California, Washington, Maine, and Maryland) are those sending women to the U.S. Senate. Not only do lower level offices provide training and experience for those holding them, but voters also become "used to" voting for those who have historically been underrepresented in the ranks of elected officials. For instance,

Making a Difference

Charlene Marshall

Charlene Marshall always knew she wanted to help people who had a difficult time helping themselves; she just had to work awfully hard to do it. Marshall was born into poverty in a northern West Virginia coal town in the middle of the Great Depression. When she was five years old, her father was killed doing the best job an African-American man could get in the area—mining coal. At 17, her stepfather died the same way. Marshall not only faced numbing poverty and family crisis, but the legal segregation and pervasive racial prejudice that were the norm in the rural South at that time. For example, she had to travel to the opposite side of the state (a 24-hour drive in those pre-interstate highway days) to attend one of the only state colleges that admitted African Americans.

Marshall's first efforts at improving the lot of the underdog were as a steelworker's union official at a northern West Virginia manufacturing plant in the 1960s. Even though she was the first African-American woman to work at the plant, her skills at facilitating dialogue between adversaries made her a leader in achieving better conditions for workers there. She also worked actively in the local Democratic Party organization, during which time she even met John Kennedy.

After her plant closed, she took an administrative staff position at West Virginia University in Morgantown—the university that she could not attend as a young adult because of her race. In this position she was again active in union efforts to improve the lot of workers, successfully lobbying university administrators and the state legislature to, among other things, increase wages to at least the federal minimum wage.

A life of grassroots political activism finally spilled over into the electoral arena when in 1990 she was elected to the Morgantown city council, and subsequently as mayor of the city. As mayor, Marshall was instrumental in developing excellent relations between the city, the university, and local businesses, something that is rare in college towns. She worked hard on things that mattered to city residents — getting the streets properly paved, modernizing the housing code, and helping rid the city of dilapidated and abandoned buildings. Under her leadership, the city also stabilized its financial condition. She was also very active in pursuing the interest of the many university students in the city.

In 1998, Marshall was elected to the West Virginia House of Delegates (the lower house of the state legislature), the first African-American woman to do so in 48 years. She is currently serving on the Health and Human Resources Committee (among others), pursuing her lifelong commitment to helping improve people's lives.

someone from New Jersey who has twice voted for and been governed by a female governor might be less likely to be put off by a female presidential candidate in 2004 solely because of her gender.

Governors and the Executive Branch

In his first month as governor of California in 1999, Gray Davis went to Mexico City to meet with the Mexican president, something that Davis's predecessor, Pete Wilson, had never done in his eight years in office. In his capacity as governor, Davis was representing California to those outside the state who were yet important to it. Similarly, Wilson's decision not to cross the border was a conscious choice to represent the interests of Californians as he saw fit. Whereas Davis views Mexico as a trading partner and the ethnic homeland of a large portion of Californians, Wilson saw Mexico as a threat, primarily due to illegal immigration.

The contrast between these two governors' behavior toward Mexico highlights the modern role of the governor. Not only is the governor the chief executive officer of a state, with the responsibility to execute the laws passed by the legislature, but he or she is also the best-known state public official, to whom the public looks for leadership, assurance, conflict resolution, and policy initiatives. If administering public policy is the governor's main constitutional responsibility, then promoting his or her vision of what public policy ought to be is the modern governor's primary responsibility to the public.

To lead a state government successfully today, a governor must supplement his or her formal powers with more "informal" powers of persuasion. Here, California Gov. Gray Davis meets with Holocaust survivors at the Simon Wiesenthal Center.

The Job of Governor

Like presidents, governors are expected to wear many hats—sometimes fulfilling constitutionally assigned duties, sometimes performing political tasks. But the powers of governors are not always commensurate with citizens' expectations. State constitutions often hamstring a governor, dividing executive power among many different administrative actors and agencies. But a generation of modernization and reform has resulted in enhanced powers for governors by reducing the number of independently elected officials and independent boards and commissions in the state executive branch, as well as by enhancing governors' other formal powers.[29] These reforms have established clearer lines of authority and enhanced the governor's appointment, reorganization, and budgetary powers. Most states have also raised their governors' salaries and increased the term of office from two to four years, with the ability to obtain at least one more term. Nevertheless, the limited formal powers of governors make it very difficult for them to fulfill their responsibilities to the state without resorting to more "informal powers," such as the use of the media and public relations staff.

How powerful are the nation's governors? Political scientist Thad Beyle has devoted considerable attention to this subject. On the basis of an analysis of gubernatorial powers outlined in state constitutions and statutes, and in the strength of their party in their states' legislatures, he has rated each of the states' governor's institutional powers. Figure 21.3 displays this rating, based on the governor's ability to stay in office, make major appointments, prepare the state budget, veto legislation, and direct political parties. Seven states' governors—those in Hawaii, Maryland, New Jersey, New York, Ohio, Pennsylvania, and Utah—have very strong powers. Another 18 governors enjoy strong executive powers. Ten states accord their governors moderate powers. The remaining 15 states, including states as diverse as Massachusetts, California, and Nevada, give only weak powers to their governors.[30]

Extensive civil service and merit-based employment policies in most states diminish the governor's power. Although these systems seek to professionalize administration and safeguard programs against politicization, they limit the governor's ability to control the executive branch. Civil service rules require that the majority of state jobs be awarded competitively on the basis of qualifications; jobs cannot simply be given to a

Figure 21.3 Institutional Powers of the Governors

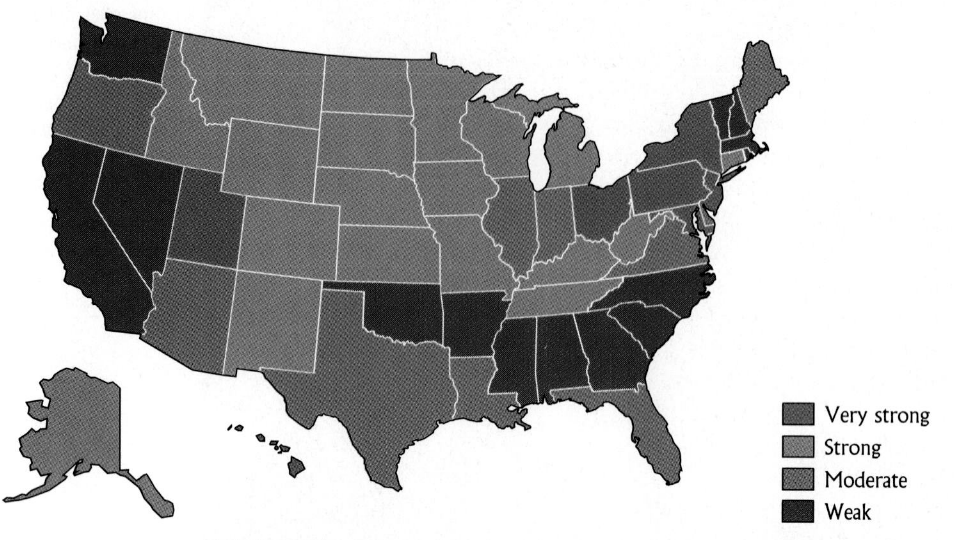

Source: Adapted from Thad Beyle, "The Governors," in Virginia Gray, Russell L. Hanson, and Herbert Jacob, eds., 7th ed., *Politics in the American States* (Washington, D.C.: Congressional Quarterly Press, 1999), 210–211.

governor's friends and political allies. Administrators protected by civil service status cannot be fired without good cause. But such protections also insulate the bureaucracy from gubernatorial control, even when the governor has legitimate policy preferences or concerns about an agency's performance.

Two of a governor's most important formal powers for controlling state government are the veto and the executive budget. The governor's veto is similar to that of the president—a governor can refuse to sign a bill passed by the state legislature, blocking it from becoming law. But in most states, the governor's veto power is far more potent than the president's. First, gubernatorial vetoes have been very difficult for state legislatures to override historically, and this remains true today.[31] Although state legislatures have become more aggressive in overriding vetoes in recent years, still less than 10 percent of gubernatorial vetoes are overridden.

line-item veto

The power possessed by 42 state governors to veto only certain parts of a bill while allowing the rest of it to pass into law.

Further, 42 state governors have the **line-item veto,** which allows them to veto only certain parts of a bill while allowing the rest of the bill to pass into law. This keeps the legislature from being able to "hold a bill hostage," forcing the governor to sign a popular bill even though it contains a provision that the governor thinks is unwise. This is especially useful on appropriations bills, allowing the governor to trim "pork barrel spending" as he or she sees fit. In Wisconsin, the governor is even allowed to veto individual words and letters from a bill, sometimes changing its basic meaning. In 1987, newly elected Governor Tommy Thompson used this power over 350 times on the budget passed by the Democratic state legislature.[32] With this power, a governor with a sizable minority in the legislature to support him or her can force or cajole the legislature into passing much of his or her agenda.

The governor also has the power to initiate the state budget process in almost all states. This allows the governor to set the agenda for what is by far the most important bill(s) of the state legislative session. The budget details how state tax dollars are going to be spent—it is where state public policy "puts up or shuts up." Although the legislature may amend and must pass the governor's proposal as it does any other bill, the limited staff and session time of most state legislatures, especially compared to that available to the governor, makes the massive budget sent by the governor difficult to change substantially. Further, since the governor has the ability to veto—and sometimes item veto—the budget passed by the legislature, he or she also has the last word in the process. This provides a governor the ability to gain help for his or her policy goals from both state legislators and bureaucrats interested in furthering their own policy goals through state spending.

To enhance their influence, governors supplement their formal institutional powers with more "personal powers."[33] A governor's real power depends on the way he or she uses character, leadership style, and persuasive abilities in conjunction with the formal prerogatives of the office. Building public support is an increasingly important part of the policymaking process. Public relations and media experts have become a key part of many governors' staffs. Although press coverage of state politics is intermittent at best, focusing on only the most salient controversies and such predictable events as the governor's State of the State address, a savvy governor can create media events and opportunities that enhance his or her popularity and political clout. Whether it is Governor Gray Davis visiting the president of Mexico (or Pete Wilson visiting a tightly guarded border south of San Diego), or Governor Tommy Thompson taking his office staff to Superior, Wis., for a "State Government Week," or Governor Cecil Underwood (of West Virginia) visiting scenes of disastrous flooding, the media image of a caring, active, busy governor can be parlayed into political clout with the legislature and executive agencies.

After languishing for most of the twentieth century as a political backwater office, where political hacks, business leaders, and other "good-time Charlies" went to cap off their careers before retiring to the country club, today's governors are politically savvy, active, and have strong policy agendas.[34] Modern governors are more likely to be bright, experienced, and capable of managing the diverse problems of a state. In addition to being better educated than their predecessors, recent governors have often had previous experience as a statewide elected official or held a federal position. For example, Idaho's Dirk Kempthorne was a U.S. Senator and Pennsylvania's Tom Ridge was a member of Congress; Donald Siegelman of Alabama, Gray Davis of California, and Frank O'Bannon of Indiana were lieutenant governors; and Bob Taft of Ohio, James Gilmore of Virginia, and Marc Racicot of Montana held other statewide executive positions.

Today's governors increasingly have the tools and skills to control state government and guide the state in the policy directions that they think are best. Demonstrating the esteem in which the modern governorship is held is the fact that in the last quarter of the twentieth century, the U.S. president has been a former governor in all but five years. In each presidential race in this period, at least one of the major party nominees was a sitting or former governor.

Other Executive Officers

Unlike the U.S. president, most governors must work with an array of independently elected executive branch officials in conducting the affairs of state government. At various times, these officials may assist or oppose the governor. State voters choose a **lieutenant governor** in 43 states. The governor and lieutenant governor are elected as a team in 24 states. In states where the governor and lieutenant governor are chosen independently, it is possible for the two top state executives to be political rivals or even members of different political parties. This can result in some real battles between them. For example, in 1990 when then-Governor (and Democrat) Michael Dukakis of Massachusetts left the state on an international trade mission, Republican Lieutenant Governor Evelyn Murphy initiated major cuts in public employment in an attempt to jump-start her floundering campaign for governor.[35] Perhaps in anticipation of such antics, when Steve Windom became the first Republican this century to be elected lieutenant governor of Alabama, the Democrat-dominated state legislature and Democratic governor promptly stripped the office of almost all its powers.[36] Most lieutenant governors have few formal duties aside from presiding over the state senate and being in the succession path for governor.

lieutenant governor

Often the second-highest executive official in state government, who is elected with the governor as a ticket in some states and is elected separately in others. She or he may have legislative and executive branch responsibilities.

Other major executive positions elected in some states include:

As the state's legal counsel, the attorney general watches out for the state's legal interests. In 1998, a group of state attorneys general successfully sued cigarette makers to recover their states' expenses related to smoking. Here, North Dakota Attorney General Heidi Heitkamp, along with the attorneys general from Oklahoma, New York, Colorado, Washington, Iowa, and Pennsylvania, holds a press conference about this lawsuit.

- Attorney General—the state's legal counsel and prosecutor (elected in 43 states)
- Treasurer—the manager of the state's bank accounts (elected in 38 states)
- Secretary of State—in charge of elections and record-keeping (elected in 36 states)
- Auditor—financial comptroller for the state (elected in 25 states)

Other officials elected in fewer states include education secretary and commissioners for land, labor, mines, agriculture, and utilities, among others.[37]

So many independent executives, commissions, and boards work within state governments that many politicians and scholars have called for major state government reorganization to allow governors more control and to increase efficiency generally. Every state has undertaken some kind of reorganization of the executive branch in the last decade. However, research shows that the expected benefits of reorganized state governments are not always achieved. Such reorganization seldom results in cost saving and efficiency—benefits often promised by its proponents.[38] Although state residents may value smaller governments, they enjoy having electoral control over the leaders of state executive branches.

State Legislatures

State legislatures are often easy targets for criticism. Their work is not well understood and the institution does not typically receive the public attention that the governor's office or federal institutions do. Further, up until a generation ago, state legislatures and legislators had a history of poor performance that still haunts them. At that time, they were "malapportioned, unrepresentative, dominated by their governors and/or special interests, and unable and unwilling to deal with the pressing issues of the day."[39]

But between 1965 and 1985, many state legislatures underwent a metamorphosis into more full-time, professional bodies—several like state-level congresses. According to political scientist Alan Rosenthal, "They increased the time they spent on their tasks; they established or increased their professional staffs; and they streamlined their procedures, enlarged their facilities, invigorated their processes, attended to their ethics, disclosed their finances, and reduced their conflicts of interest."[40] As a result, state legislatures are far more active, informed, representative, and democratic today than they were 40 years ago.

State legislatures serve the same basic function in the states as Congress does in the federal government, and they do it with the same basic mechanisms. State legislatures make almost all the basic laws of the state by approving identical bills in each of their two-chambered bodies (except in Nebraska's unicameral legislature). They appropriate the money that is needed for state government to function. They oversee the activities of the executive branch through confirming gubernatorial appointments, controlling the budgets of the agencies, and investigating complaints and concerns of citizens and the press. State legislators themselves attend closely to the needs of their constituents, whether through voting on bills in line with their constituents' interests or chasing down problems a citizen has with a driver's license.

Even more than U.S. congresspersons, members of the state legislature are at the front line of interaction between citizens and government. Because most state legislatures meet for only a limited number of months each year, and because state capitals are typically closer to their districts than Washington, D.C. is to the districts of most congresspersons, state legislators usually live among the people they represent. They are closely involved with their constituents not only at election time, but also throughout the year. They coach basketball and run restaurants; they teach school and preach at local churches; they are local attorneys and bankers. In short, the state legislature in almost all states comes closest to the sort of citizen-directed government envisioned by Thomas Jefferson over 200 years ago.

The reforms of the past generation designed to improve the efficiency and effectiveness of state legislatures are collectively called *legislative professionalism*.[41] That is, these are reforms designed "to enhance the capacity of the legislature to perform its role in the policymaking process with an expertise, seriousness, and effort comparable to that of other actors in the process."[42] Changes have been primarily in three areas. First, legislative sessions have been lengthened to give legislators more time to deal with the increasingly complex problems of the states. Before 1965, most state legislatures only met for several weeks each year, and many would only meet every other year. In 2000, 43 state legislatures had annual sessions, usually meeting for between three and five months, with a few (such as in Michigan, Massachusetts, and Wisconsin) meeting year-round.

The second legislative professionalism reform was to increase legislators' salaries so they could devote more of their time to considering the states' business, and less to their "regular" job. The idea was also that if service in the state legislature paid a living wage, legislators would have fewer conflicts of interest and a wider variety of people would be willing to serve. For instance, the only people who could afford to serve in the West Virginia state legislature in 1960 for a salary of $1,500 were those with either an outside source of income or who were independently wealthy. In 2000, the $53,581 an Illinois state representative earned could allow him or her to focus full-time on legislative duties.

The third major professionalism reform was the increase in the staff available to help legislators in their duties. Even since 1979 (after many of the big professionalism changes had already occurred), permanent state legislative staff has increased almost 60 percent.[43] By increasing their session length, salary, and staff, state legislatures have dramatically increased their ability to have an impact on the state policymaking process.

Not all the effects of this drive toward legislative professionalism are seen as good, and not all states have professionalized their legislatures to the same level. Some argue that professionalism leads to an overemphasis on reelection by state legislators, inflated campaign costs, and lack of leadership in the law-making process.[44] Legislative professionalism threatens the existence of the "citizen legislature," in which people leave their job for a couple of months each year to serve the state and inject some "common sense" into government. The recent spate of state term limits laws indicates the esteem in which many Americans hold this sort of nonprofessional state legislature. There is also some evidence that increased professionalism does not enhance even some of the

Figure 21.4 Legislative Professionalism

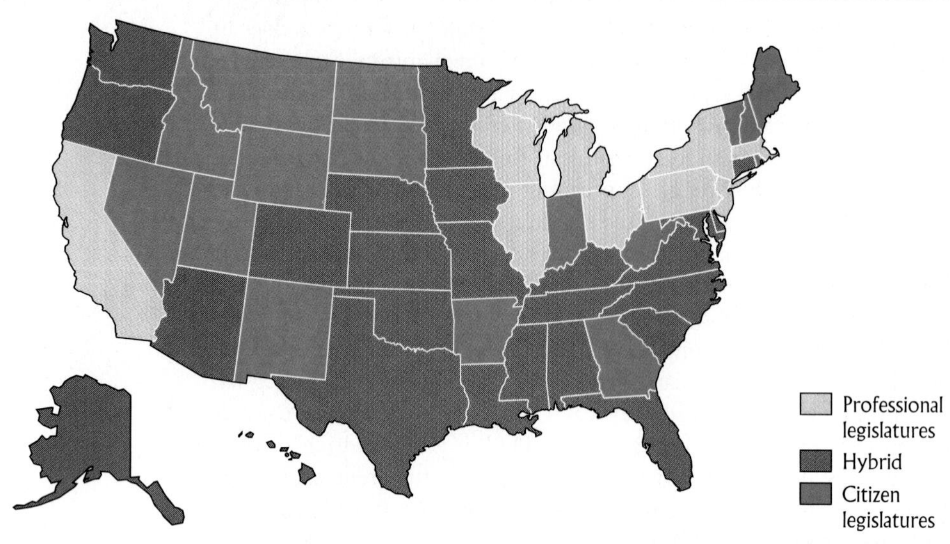

Source: Keith E. Hamm and Gary F. Moncrief, "Legislative Politics in the States," in Virginia Gray, Russell L. Hanson, and Herbert Jacob, eds., 7th ed., *Politics in the American States* (Washington, D.C.: Congressional Quarterly Press, 1999), 145.

aspects of the process that proponents argued it would, such as increasing membership diversity in state legislatures.[45]

It is also important to note that not all state legislatures are in any sense full-time, professional bodies. Members of the New Hampshire House of Representatives earn $200 for a two-year term, which consists of only one 30-day period of service in each year. These are clearly not professional legislators. On the other hand, across the border in Massachusetts, state legislators earn $46,410 and meet virtually the entire year. Figure 21.4 shows roughly which states have professionalized legislatures, which still have "citizen legislatures," and which have legislatures that are "hybrids," having some characteristics of both. Those states that have developed professional legislatures tend to be those with large and heterogeneous populations, that both need and can afford them, although there is a regional effect that may have to do with political preferences for a professional government.[46] Although this selective process makes it difficult to assess the independent effects of legislative professionalism, there is some evidence that more professionalism leads to more liberal welfare policy and perhaps more divided government in the states.[47]

We may now be seeing the beginning of a "deprofessionalizing" trend in some states, as some harken back to the Jeffersonian ideal of the citizen legislature. Term limits laws are the most obvious manifestation of this, but recent laws in California limiting legislative staffing and in Colorado limiting the powers of the legislative leadership may also signal that the legislative professionalism movement is cyclical.[48] The debate over state legislative professionalism may come down to the question of how a state ought to be governed—by people who are less informed about policy and politics than the other actors in the policymaking process (e.g., the governor, interest groups, bureaucrats) but who are closely connected to the people of the state, or by those whose expertise and resources in policy and politics is high, but who may spend most of their time in the capital, as do our U.S. Representatives.

State Court Systems

The organization of the states' courts reflects two major influences: (1) the model of organization set by the federal courts, and (2) the judicial preferences of each state's citizens as manifested in state constitutions and statutes. State courts are far more involved in administering justice than is the federal judiciary. Indeed, 99 percent of all litigation in the United States is settled in state courts.[49] Recent data show that state courts have 100 times the number of trials and hear five times more appeals than federal courts.[50] In addition, state court workloads have been increasing in both criminal and civil cases, forcing states to experiment with alternatives to trial courts, like mediation, arbitration, and plea bargaining, among others. The volume of cases heard by state courts is significant, but courts are also policymaking bodies. Particularly when the highest court in the state rules on a case, judges are more than just interpreting the law; they are often making policy in the same fashion as the U.S. Supreme Court.

Since World War II, many state court systems have undergone reforms designed to modernize and rationalize their procedures and structure, much like the reforms undergone in the states' governors' offices and legislatures. These include reforms both of organizational structure and judicial selection.

State Court Organization

State court systems often developed as a hodgepodge of individual courts set up at odd times and for odd reasons at the subnational level. Many states have low-level courts, such as justices of the peace or magistrate courts, whose presiding officials may not even be lawyers. Many states developed a variety of specialized courts to deal with specific judicial matters involving traffic, family, or taxes. These systems, which included courts that were completely independent of any higher authority, often led to confusion, duplication of effort, and unfair treatment of cases and people.

In the past generation, efforts have been made to consolidate and coordinate many state courts systems so that they parallel the federal system, discussed in Chapter 16. First, specialized courts have been consolidated and subsumed into trial courts with more general jurisdiction. These courts are usually established for county-sized areas and are the setting for most trials. They are known by a variety of labels—district courts, circuit courts, superior courts, and (in the case of New York) supreme courts. Judges assigned to these trial courts often work in only one county and specialize in criminal, juvenile, or civil litigation. A single judge presides over each case, and citizens may be called upon to serve as jurors and members of grand jury panels.

Many states have also moved toward coordinating their court systems through their court of last resort, usually called the state supreme court. Under a coordinated system, the state supreme court serves not only as the court of final appeal for all cases in the state court system, as does the U.S. Supreme Court in the federal system, but it also has the responsibility for administering and regulating the justice system in the state. This usually involves appointing a chief court administrator to handle the day-to-day budgeting, operations, and organization of all the courts in the state, and establishing boards to oversee and deal with complaints against lawyers and judges in the states.

A major innovation adopted by most states in the past 30 years is an *intermediate court of appeal*. Like federal appeals courts, states organize these courts on a regional basis and with judges working together in panels of three or more, with a majority deciding each case. No witnesses are called before appellate courts, and juries are not used. Instead, judges read briefs and hear arguments prepared by lawyers that address whether the law was appropriately applied at the trial court level and whether due process of law was followed. The job of judges at this level is not to determine the facts of a case but to interpret the laws and the state or national constitution as they apply to the case.

The organizational purpose of an intermediate court of appeal is to reduce the pressure on the state supreme court of the many "routine" appeals of trial court decisions. These are appeals that have few implications for state policy or procedure; they are appeals that primarily impact only the case at hand. An intermediate appeals court frees up the state supreme court to consider only those cases with statewide policy importance, again, much as the U.S. Supreme Court does. Twelve states, all with

Figure 21.5 Prototypical Modern State Court System

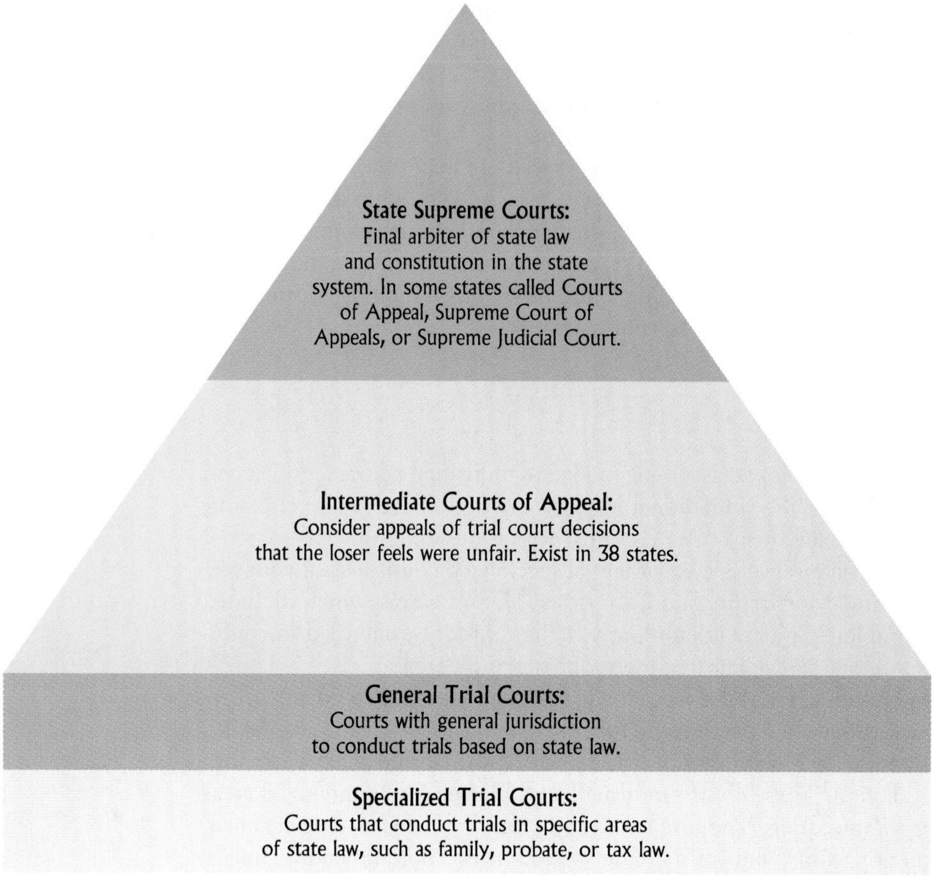

small populations, do not have intermediate courts of appeal,[51] so the appellate work in these states falls solely to the supreme court, reducing its ability to concentrate on making policy through judicial interpretation.

Selecting Judges

In contrast to federal judges, all of whom are appointed by the president for life, judges rise to the bench in the states in a variety of ways (see Table 21.2). These judicial selection mechanisms are each relics of values that were manifested in a series of reform movements over the past 200 years.

At the founding of the country, almost all state judges were appointed, as in the federal system, either by the governor or the state legislature, and 13 states still use this method of judicial selection for some or all of their judges. With the Jacksonian democratic impulse of the early to mid-nineteenth century, states began to select their judges by partisan ballot, just as other state officials were selected. Currently, 11 states select some or all of their judges this way. In the Progressive Era (1890–1920), reformers argued that to be administered fairly, justice should be nonpartisan because a judge elected on a party platform might be more biased in his or her decisions. Persuaded by this argument, many states changed their judicial selection mechanism to that of nonpartisan election, where candidates ran against one another but without a party label. Nineteen states still use nonpartisan elections to select some or all of their judges.

Electing judges remains both common and controversial. Minority groups and political parties have made allegations of bias in the judicial selection process. A 1994

Table 21.2 State Judicial Selection Mechanisms

APPOINTMENT	ELECTION	MERIT PLAN
By Governor: DE, ME, MD, MA, NH, NJ, NY, RI, VT	**Partisan:** AL, AR, IL, IN, MS, NY, NC, PA, TN, TX, WV	AK, AZ, CA, CO, FL, IN, IA, KS, MD, MO, NE, NM, OK, SD, TN, UT, WY
By Legislature: CT, HI, RI, SC, VA	**Nonpartisan:** AZ, CA, FL, GA, ID, KS, KY, LA, MI, MN, MT, NV, NM, ND, OH, OK, OR, SD, WA	

Source: Council of State Governments, *The Book of the States, 1998–99*, 135–137.
Note: States may appear more than once, since some states select different types of judges through different mechanisms. Minor local judges, such as justices of the peace, are not considered in this table.

federal court ruling held North Carolina's method of electing judges statewide to be biased against the Republican Party because most of the state's trial court judges were Democrats. In 1997, the Republican-controlled Illinois state legislature changed the state's supreme court districts to make it harder for Democrats to dominate in these elections. Legal interest groups challenged the law, and a court declared it unconstitutional, with little opposition from the state.

The most recent wave of judicial selection reforms since World War II has been 17 states adopting a hybrid system of appointment and election known as the **Merit Plan.**[52] In this system, the governor appoints the state's judges from a list of persons recommended by the state bar or a committee of jurists and other officials. Each appointed judge then serves a short "trial run" term, usually one year, in which citizens may assess the judge's performance. After this, an election is held in which voters are asked whether the judge should be retained in office—they simply vote "yes" or "no," not for one candidate or another. If voters approve retention by a majority vote (Illinois requires 60 percent), then the judge continues in office for a lengthy term (usually 6 to 12 years), after which another retention election is held if the judge wishes to continue serving. Few judges lose in this type of retention election, which raises the question of whether the Merit Plan's democratic component truly enhances responsiveness to citizens.

Merit Plan

Method for selecting state judges in which governors appoint persons based on the reccomenditions of a committee. After serving a short term, the judge then often faces a retention election.

Direct Democracy

A method of policymaking that is unique in the United States to subnational governments is "**direct democracy.**" Three procedures—the initiative, the referendum, and the recall—provide voters with ways that they can directly impact policymaking and the political process through the voting booth. One or more of these procedures is available in all but one state (Alabama); the referendum for ratifying constitutional amendments is especially common. The more proactive of these are less widely available—the initiative (24 states) and recall (17 states) (see Table 21.3). These procedures were developed in the Progressive Era largely in the western and midwestern states as a way to bring more "power to the people," by cutting out the middle persons in the policymaking system—political parties, politicians, and interest groups.

direct democracy

Government controlled directly by citizens. In some U.S. states, procedures such as the initiative, the referendum, and the recall give voters a direct impact on policymaking and the political process by means of the voting booth and can therefore be considered forms of direct democracy.

The **initiative** is the purest form of direct democracy. Although its details vary from state to state, the basic procedure is as follows. First, a citizen decides that he or she wants to see a law passed. The specific language of that proposal is then registered with a state official (typically the secretary of state), and permission to circulate a petition is given. The advocates of the proposal then try to get a specified number of eligible voters (typically 5–10 percent of those voting in the previous election) to sign a

initiative

A process permitted in some states whereby voters may place proposed changes to state law on the ballot if sufficient signatures are obtained on petitions calling for such a vote.

Table 21.3 Direct Democracy Mechanisms

INITIATIVE[a]	LEGISLATIVE REFERENDUM[b]	RECALL
AK, AZ, AR, CA, CO, FL, ID, IL, ME, MA, MI, MS, MO, MT, NE, NV, ND, OH, OK, OR, SD, UT, WA, WY	AZ, AR, CA, DE, ID, IL, KY, ME, MD, MA, MI, MO, MT, NE, NV, NM, ND, OH, OK, OR, SD, UT, WA	AK, AZ, CA, GA, ID, KS, LA, MI, MN, MT, NV, NM, ND, OR, SD, WA, WI

[a]These states have at least one of the several forms of initiative.
[b]All states except Alabama allow or require a referendum for state constitutional amendments. The states listed in this column also allow referenda on the passage of legislative issues that are not constitutional amendments.
Source: The Council of State Governments, *The Book of the States, 1998–99* (Lexington, KY: Council of State Governments, 1998), 210 and 224–225.

petition saying that they would like to see the proposal on the ballot. When the appropriate number of signatures has been verified, the proposal is placed on the next general election ballot for an approve/disapprove vote. If a majority of voters approve it, the proposal becomes law. Elected officials are bypassed in this way. However, elected officials can influence the outcome by endorsing or opposing a proposal. The impact depends on the popularity of the public official.[53]

The initiative allows for the adoption of policy that might otherwise be ignored or opposed by policymakers in the state legislature and governor's offices. The best example of this is the state legislative term limits movement of the 1990s. Since this policy would directly and negatively affect some state legislators, it is easy to see why such a policy would be difficult to pass through the state legislature. Of the 21 states that have passed such limits, only Louisiana does not have the initiative. Perhaps just as telling, of the 24 states that have the initiative in some form, only four (Alaska, Illinois, Mississippi, and North Dakota) have not passed term limits. Other sorts of ideas become state law through this process that might not otherwise do so, for good or ill. These include everything from a series of property tax limitations in many states in the 1970s and 1980s to recent initiatives allowing marijuana to be used for medical purposes in California and six other states. Some research even suggests that legislatures in states with the initiative may pass laws more in line with citizen preferences when the threat of citizen action through the initiative is present,[54] but other research disputes this finding.[55]

However, the initiative today does not always work exactly as its originators envisioned. There is considerable debate over the wisdom of making state law through citizen-initiated proposals. Constitutional amendments and legislation passed through initiative are often poorly drafted and may contain ambiguous or contradictory provisions. As a result, initiatives often create new problems, leading to lawsuits and court interpretation and eventually requiring corrective action by the legislature.

It is also unclear to what extent the initiative process empowers citizens or merely gives new tools to well-financed interest groups. In larger states, special interests can pay professional firms to gather the required number of signatures. Monied interests also have the advantage in mounting expensive television advertising campaigns. These ads can present voters with a biased or incomplete set of facts on an issue they would otherwise know little about. For example, in the 1998 California initiative campaign to legalize Indian tribal casinos, the gambling industry spent more than $71 million on *both sides* of the issue, with advertisements that were often confusing to citizens (Nevada casinos tried to block the plan, while those associated with the California-based interests advocated it).[56] In initiative and referendum campaigns, complex public policy questions too often are reduced to simplistic sloganeering. As Ann O' M. Bowman and Richard C. Kearney argue,

> *Seldom are issues so simple that a yes-or-no ballot question can adequately reflect appropriate options and alternatives. A legislative setting, in contrast, fosters the negotiation and*

Why does it matter?

Direct democracy has a special appeal to Americans, who believe in "government by the people." But is it always the best way to make public policy? What if all laws passed by a state legislature had to be approved by the voters? What differences in public policy would you expect to see? How would the policymaking process be different? Are there any types of policy that you would not like to see decided by a majority vote? Why?

California is a state known for its citizen-initiated policies. In 2000, Proposition 22 was passed by voters in this state to ban marrigaes bettween same-sex couples.

compromise that produce workable solutions. Legislatures are deliberative bodies, not instant problem solvers.[57]

A hybrid of legislative and direct democratic policymaking is the **referendum.** Unlike the initiative, which is proposed by a citizen or group, the referendum begins life as a legislative resolution. Typically, the state legislature deliberates on and passes the proposal in both chambers in identical form, as required for any bill to become law, but then instead of sending the bill to the governor for his or her approval, the proposal is presented to the voters in a general election. If a majority of the voters approve it, it becomes law; otherwise, it does not. In all states (except Alabama), this procedure is required for amendments to the state constitution, and in many subnational governments referenda are required for bond issues (government debt), tax changes, and other fiscal matters.

referendum

A state-level method of direct legislation that gives voters a chance to approve or disapprove legislation or a constitutional amendment proposed by the state legislature.

School bond referenda (votes to authorize borrowing to build or improve local schools) are often important and controversial issues in local elections. Recently, some local and state governments have asked taxpayers to foot the bill for new sports stadiums for big league teams via referendum bond issues. In 1998, Pittsburgh voters rejected building a new stadium to house the Steelers and Pirates, but in recent years voters in Seattle, Tampa, Cincinnati, and Cleveland have approved such measures.[58] Some state legislatures are also allowed to offer referenda on proposals at their option. This may be done to seek out the advice of the electorate on a fundamental issue, or it may be a way for legislators to sidestep the responsibility for a tough political decision.

The **recall** is different than the initiative or referendum because it is about elected officials rather than public policy. In essence, the recall allows voters to call a special election for a specific official in an attempt to throw him or her out of office before the end of his or her term. The process involves gathering signatures on a petition of voters in the jurisdiction of the official being recalled, much like an initiative. Once enough signatures are gathered, a special election is held, usually within three months, in which the official being recalled runs against any forthcoming challenger(s), if he or she desires to do so.

recall

A procedure that allows voters to call a special election for a specific official in an attempt to throw him or her out of office before the end of term. Recalls are only permitted in 17 states, seldom used because of their cost and disruptiveness, and rarely successful.

Needless to say, this is a drastic action and it is infrequently undertaken successfully. It is disruptive of the routine political process, traumatic for the official being recalled, and very costly for the jurisdiction having to hold the special election. Because of this, only 17 states allow for the recall, and these states make it difficult to undertake, with the required number of signatures being much higher than that required to place an initiative on the ballot. Historically, those who have been recalled have been accused of a serious breach of propriety, morals, or ethics, and often are local officials or judges serving long terms. For example, in 1982 a district judge in Madison, Wis., made the highly publicized and inflammatory statement that he thought a very young victim in a sexual assault case appeared promiscuous; the judge was recalled and removed from office.[59] However, in recent years, some state and local officials have been recalled for more policy-oriented reasons, such as for supporting Indian treaty rights in Wisconsin, tax increases in Michigan, and gun control in California. A recent case of a successful recall petition drive on a state official was against Wisconsin state Senator George Petak, who lost his seat in a 1996 recall vote. Petak faced the recall after casting the deciding vote for a %0.1 sales tax increase that would pay for a new sports stadium.[60]

timeline
The Initiative and the Referendum

State and Local Government Relations

In Chapter 3, you read about the concept of federalism, and how the nation's Founders tried to strike a balance between the powers of the central government and those of the states. This state-federal *intergovernmental relationship* has evolved in the past 200 years through statutes passed by Congress, constitutional amendments and their interpretation by the U.S. Supreme Court, civil war, and tradition. The relationship between the states and the federal government is both contentious and one of the defining characteristics of government in the United States.

The intergovernmental relationship between the states and their inferior governments—local governments—is no less important in defining how our government works. But this relationship is far less ambiguous and involves no balance and little interpretation.

Dillon's Rule

The idea that local governments have only those powers that are explicitly given them by the states. This means that local governments have very little discretion over what policies they pursue or how they pursue them. It was named for Iowa Judge John Dillon, who expressed this idea in an 1868 court decision.

The basic relationship is that local governments are totally subservient to the state government. According to **Dillon's Rule** (after Iowa Judge John Dillon, who expressed this idea in an 1868 court decision) local governments have only those powers that are explicitly given to them by the states. Dillon argued definitively that local governments were "creatures of the state," and that the state legislature gave local governments the "breath of life without which they cannot exist."[61] This means that local governments have very little discretion over which policies they pursue or how they pursue them. In fact, the states have been known to take away policymaking and administrative power from local governments completely, as when the state of West Virginia recently took over two school districts that state officials felt were run improperly. An extreme case of state usurpation of local power took place in 1997 when the Massachusetts state legislature actually *abolished* Middlesex County due to mismanagement and corruption![62]

Why does it matter?

State boundaries typically result from historical accidents rather than efforts to define regions that have similar interests and needs. For example, the people of the Florida panhandle probably have more in common with those of southern Alabama and Georgia than those of south Florida. But what if the states were reconstructed so as to make them more homogeneous internally, and therefore more different from one another? How do you think this would affect the delivery of public services in whatever 'new' state you might find yourself living in? How would it affect the nation as a whole?

The basis of this shocking imbalance of power is the U.S. Constitution. Although the Constitution discusses at length the role of the states and the relationship between the states and the central government, local governments are never explicitly mentioned. The establishment and supervision of local government has been interpreted to be one of the "reserve powers" for the states, under the Tenth Amendment of the Bill of Rights. The idea is that states have certain responsibilities and policy goals that they must fulfill, but sometimes the best way to do this is through local units of government they establish. For example, the states have the responsibility to educate children, but all states (except Hawaii) have opted to establish regional school districts to do this for the states. The states have the constitutional authority to establish (or abolish) local governments, define their responsibilities and powers, specify their organization, and mandate the way in which their officials are chosen.

Although local governments have no constitutional sovereignty, local government officials are certainly not powerless in their efforts to control their own destiny. But the power of local government arises from informal political clout rather than formal powers. First, many people feel more strongly connected to their local governments than to the state. After all, it is the local government officials they see most frequently—the police officer responding to an emergency call, the teacher in the school caring for their child, the city council member helping to get the potholes filled in the street. State offi-

How You Can Make a Difference

Direct Democracy

If you live in a state with direct democracy mechanisms such as initiative, recall, and referendum (see Table 21.3), you can get directly involved in shaping and passing legislation you support. Most people limit their participation to voting for or against a referendum or initiative, but you can do more by becoming a part of an initiative and referendum movement.

You can join the campaign staff of an initiative or, if you are very ambitious, you can start your own ballot initiative. Using the information found in the Initiative and Referendum Institute (www.iandrinstitute.org), you can discover the key steps to develop a ballot petition in your state. In Michigan, for example, after you decide on the legislation you want enacted, you then get the format of your initiative approved by the state (though this isn't required). Next, you must gather a sufficient number of valid signatures supporting the petition within 180 days in order to have it placed on the next statewide ballot. In 2000, a petition proposing a constitutional amendment in Michigan required 302,710 signatures.

The issues appearing on ballot initiatives are usually the controversial ones that state legislatures want to avoid out of fear of casting a vote that would offend potential supporters. In recent years, the hot topics have ranged from affirmative action, government benefits to illegal aliens, legalization of marijuana, vouchers and school choice, gun control, health care reform, bilingual education, homosexual marriage, and physician-assisted suicide. For a more detailed list of the issues in your state, check out the Initiative and Referendum Institute, Ballot Watch (www.ballotwatch.org) and Ballot.org.

No matter what issues interest you, becoming active in an initiative or a referendum ballot election can be one of the surest ways to directly change government and your surrounding world.

cials understand the sympathy (and political clout) these officials have among citizens, so they do not try to rile them without good reason. Further, local government officials of all stripes form interest groups to lobby state officials. In all states, organizations of local officials, such as the Wisconsin League of Municipalities or the Texas Association of Counties, are among the most powerful interest groups in the state capitol.[63]

Many cities have also managed to get state legislatures to grant them a degree of autonomy through a **local charter.** A charter is an organizational statement and grant of authority from the state to a local government, much like a state or federal constitution. States sometimes allow cities to write their own charters and to change them without permission from the state legislature, within limits. Today, this practice of **home rule** is widely used to organize and modernize city government.

local charter

An organizational statement and grant of authority from the state to a local government, much like a state or federal constitution. States sometimes allow municipalities to write their own charters and to change them without permission of the state legislature, within limits. See also **home rule.**

home rule

The practice by which municipalities are permitted by the states to write their own charters and change them without permission of the state legislature, within limits. Today this practice is widely used to organize and modernize municipal government. See also **local charter.**

Local Governments

The U.S. Bureau of the Census counts not only people but also governments. Its latest count revealed an astonishing 87,453 American local governments (see Table 21.4). In addition to being a citizen of the United States and of a state, the average citizen also resides within the jurisdiction of perhaps 10 to 20 local governments. The state of Illinois holds the current record for the largest number of local governments: 6,722 at the latest count. The six-county Chicago metropolitan area alone has more than 1,200 governments!

The sheer number of governments in the United States is, however, as much a burden as a boon to democracy. Citizens are governed by a complex maze of local governments—some with broad powers, others performing very specialized services. This plethora of local governments creates voter overload and ignorance, thereby defeating the democratic purpose of citizen control.

Table 21.4 Local Governments in the United States

TYPE OF GOVERNMENT	1962	1997	% CHANGE 1962–1997
All local governments	91,186	87,453	–4.1%
General-purpose governments:			
County	3,043	3,043	0.0%
Municipal	18,000	19,372	+7.6%
Township	17,142	16,629	–3.0%
Single-purpose governments:			
School district	34,678	13,726	–60.4%
Special district	18,323	31,683	+72.9%

Source: U.S. Bureau of the Census, *Statistical Abstract of the United States, 1999* (Washington, D.C.: U.S. Government Printing Office, 1999).

Types of Local Government

Local governments can be classified into five types based on their legal purpose and the scope of their responsibilities: counties, townships, municipalities, school districts, and special districts.

Counties. The largest geographic unit of government at the local level is the *county* government, although they are called "parishes" in Louisiana and "boroughs" in Alaska. Texas has the most counties with 254; Delaware and Hawaii have just 3 each. Los Angeles County serves the most people—over 8.8 million residents, whereas Loving County, Texas, serves only 140 residents.

County governments are administrative arms of state government. Typically, counties are responsible for keeping records of births, deaths, and marriages; establishing a system of justice and law enforcement; maintaining roads and bridges; collecting taxes; conducting voter registration and elections; and providing for public welfare and education. Rural residents more often rely on county governments for services because they have fewer local governments to turn to than city dwellers.

County governments usually consist of an elected *county commission*, the legislative body that makes policy, and a collection of "row officers," including sheriffs, prosecutors, county clerks, and assessors, who run county services. Some urban counties, such as Milwaukee County, St. Louis County, and Wayne (Detroit) County, now elect a county executive (like a mayor or governor). In some counties, such as Dade (Miami) County and Sacramento County, the county commission appoints a county administrator to take responsibility for the administration of county policies.

Townships. *Township* governments are found in only 20 states, including Maine, Michigan, New Hampshire, New York, Vermont, and Wisconsin. Most township governments have limited powers and primarily just assist with county services in rural areas; however, some, such as those in New England, function much like city governments. Voters typically elect a township board, a supervisor, and perhaps a very small number of other executives. Township officers oversee public highways and local law enforcement, keep records of vital statistics and tax collections, and administer elections. Most, however, lack the power to pass local ordinances since they serve as administrative extensions of the state and county governments.

Municipalities. Cities are more formally known as municipal governments or *municipalities*, and they supply most local programs and services for more than 19,275 communities in the United States. Municipalities typically provide police and fire protection, street maintenance, solid waste collection, water and sewer works, park and recreation services, and public planning. Some larger cities also run public hospitals and health programs, administer public welfare services, operate public transit and utilities, manage housing and urban development programs, and even run universities. Citizen satisfaction with the delivery of such services varies greatly.

Originally, many municipalities in the United States were run with a special form of direct democracy—the **town meeting.** Under this system, all voting-age adults in a community gathered once a year to make public policy, such as passing new local laws, approving a town budget, and electing a small number of local residents to serve as town officials. But as cities became too large for the town meeting style of governance, three modern forms of municipal government developed.

town meeting

A special form of direct democracy under which all voting-age adults in a community gather once a year to make public policy. Now only used in a few villages in upper New England.

Mayor-Council Government. In a typical mayor-council government (Figure 21.6), local residents elect a mayor and a city council. In "strong mayor" cities, such as New York City, the city council makes public policy, and the mayor and city bureaucrats who report to the mayor are responsible for policy implementation. Strong mayors may also veto actions of the city council. In "weak mayor" cities, most power is vested in the city council, which directs the activities of the city bureaucracy. The mayor serves as the presiding officer for city council meetings and as the ceremonial head of city government. Most mayor-council cities have this weak mayor form of governance because most of the numerous small cities of 10,000 or fewer residents use this system. San Diego is one major city that uses the weak mayor form of government.

Council-Manager Government. In this form of municipal government, voters elect a city council, and sometimes a mayor who often acts as both presiding officer and voting member of the council (see Figure 21.7). The council is responsible for setting policy for the city. The implementation and administration of the council's actions are placed in the hands of an appointed **city manager,** who is expected to carry out policy

city manager

An official appointed by the city council who is responsible for implementing and administering the council's actions. More than one-third of U.S. cities use the council-manager form of government.

Figure 21.6 Mayor-Council Government

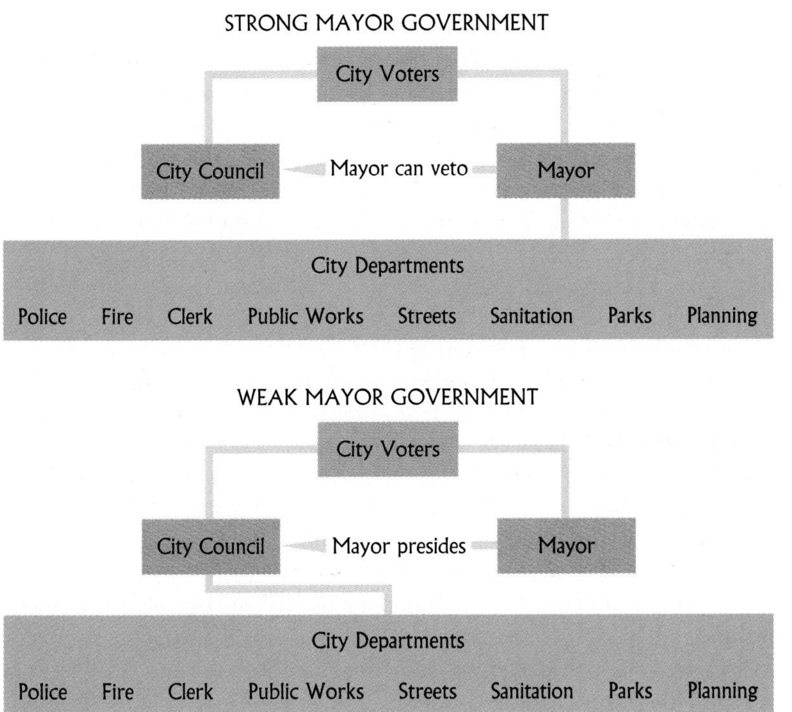

Figure 21.7 Council-Manager Government

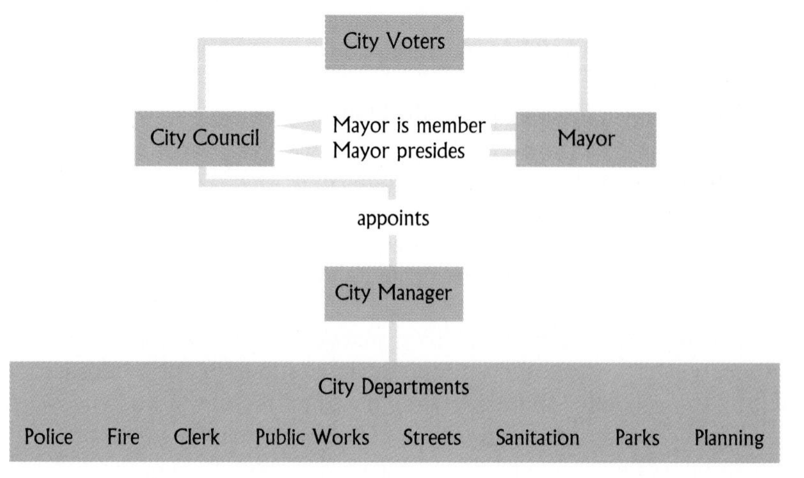

Figure 21.8 Commission Government

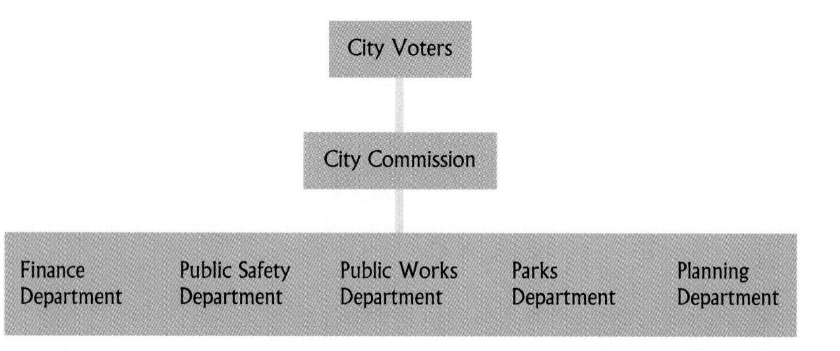

with the aid of city bureaucracy. More than one-third of cities use this form of government, including such major cities as Dallas, Kansas City, and Phoenix.

Commission Government. In commission government, voters elect a panel of city commissioners, each of whom serves as both legislator and executive (Figure 21.8). These officials make public policy just as city council members do in the other two forms of government. However, each member is also elected as a commissioner of a functional area of city government (for example, public safety), and bureaucrats report to a single commissioner. Among the few cities that still use a commission government are Vicksburg, Miss., and St. Petersburg, Fl.[64]

Most city council members and many mayors are elected in nonpartisan elections. Traditionally, city council members represented a district or ward of the city—a practice that permitted ward-based machine "party bosses" to control elections and try to create public policies that were good for individual wards, rather than for the city as a whole. Reformers advocated at-large city elections, with all members of the city council chosen by voters throughout the city. These at-large representatives could not create public policies to benefit only their own neighborhoods because they would have to answer to all the city's voters. A majority of cities use at-large elections today.

An unintended consequence of at-large elections is that they make it more difficult for minority group members to be elected to the city council. This is because African-American and other ethnic minorities in U.S. cities tend to live in more or less homogeneous neighborhoods—a legacy of official and unofficial housing segregation.

Therefore, although they may be a minority of the entire city's population (and so fail to generate a majority in at-large elections), they may be a majority in smaller sections of the city, and so could elect candidates to pursue their interests in district-based electoral systems. Cities that employ district elections may have a greater degree of representational equity for African Americans and Hispanics on city councils than cities that use at-large elections.[65]

School Districts. The nation's over 14,000 *school districts* are responsible for educating children. Although a few cities, counties, townships, and one state (Hawaii) operate schools, most school systems are run as independent local governments. Consolidation of small, often rural, districts into larger ones is the major reason for a nearly 60 percent drop in the number of school districts during the past 30 years.

In an independent school district, voters within a geographically defined area are responsible for their own public education system, including electing a board of education, selecting administrators and teachers, building and operating schools, designing and running education programs, and raising the revenues to meet a locally adopted school budget. Because the states are ultimately responsible for public education, state governments adopt general standards for education, mandate certain school programs, and provide a system of state financial assistance to public schools. But within the guidelines of state policy and the parameters of state funding, locally elected school boards and their appointed administrators deliver education services to the nation's children.

School districts have become the focus for many emotionally charged issues at the local level. Prayer in public schools, sex education, equity in school funding, charter schools, and lingering racial discrimination are just a few of the more explosive issues surrounding schools in the 2000s. For example, although the Supreme Court declared that states have a responsibility to eliminate discrimination in education in such important decisions as *Brown v. Board of Education* (1954) and *Swann v. Charlotte-Mecklenberg County Schools* (1971) (see Chapter 5), inequities in the public school systems persist, with racial minorities still encountering poorly funded public education in many instances. In fact, political scientists have discovered an extensive pattern of "second-generation discrimination"—a shortage of minority teachers "which leads to negative outcome for minority students."[66]

This inequity is coupled with a financial crisis in many public school systems. States have widely divergent school aid policies—some states are good providers to their neediest local schools, whereas others leave the financing responsibility largely to local districts.[67] Local revenue sources are disproportionately based on the local property tax—a policy choice that results in wealthier districts having an abundance of resources, while poorer districts have inadequate revenues for their schoolchildren. Schools around the country continue to struggle with providing quality education with limited resources.

Special Districts. The fastest growing form of local government in the United States is the *special district.* The last official count showed 31,555 of these independent, limited-purpose governments. Generally, special districts provide only a single service, such as flood control, waste disposal, fire protection, public libraries, or public parks. There is no standard model of special district government organization—the types of organizational arrangements are almost as plentiful as the number of districts. Some districts have elected policymaking boards; a governor or mayor appoints others. Special districts are highly flexible units of local government because their boundary lines can be drawn across the usual municipal, county, and township borders. By providing services on a larger scale, they help localities realize certain economies and efficiencies.

However, important questions about democracy are inherent in the growth of special districts. Special districts are, to a great extent, invisible governments; the local press rarely covers their operations, and there is little direct public participation in their decisionmaking. Most citizens do not even know who serves on these district boards or when the boards meet. As a result, the public has great difficulty holding special districts accountable.

Fragmentation, Cooperation, and Competition

Each governing body in a fragmented metropolis tends to look at problems from its own narrow perspective. As a result, local bodies fail to cooperate with one another and plan effectively for the region's future needs. For example, the development of an effective mass transit system is often hindered when not all communities are willing to share in financing a new metropolitan bus network or light rail system; or a narrowly focused special district devoted to maintaining the region's road network may not be willing to divert its funds to help finance new rail construction.

Traditionally, regional cooperation on specific policy areas has been undertaken through the use of special districts. For example, water and sewer needs transcend municipality borders, so special sewer and water districts have been set up in most metropolitan areas to coordinate the delivery of this service.

But there are limits to the number of special districts that can be established efficiently and the level of coordination that these districts can achieve. What can be done to coordinate a variety of public services in a metropolitan area? A few areas have developed "super-locals," institutional arrangements that act almost as general purpose governments for an entire region. Seattle, Miami, and Minneapolis-St. Paul each have a "metropolitan council" that serves such a function. For example, the Minneapolis-St. Paul Metropolitan Council operates the region's bus service, provides sewer and water services, operates a regional housing and development authority, and funds and plans regional parks and trails, all activities that cut across traditional local government physical and policy area boundaries. In 1970, Indianapolis took this idea to the extreme by expanding the boundaries of the city to include all of Marion County, which included the entire metropolitan area, thus allowing for the general coordination of most local government services.

Why does it matter?

The multitude of local governments with independent authority can make the delivery of public services in a metropolitan area inefficient, contentious, and just plain confusing. What if all government services in a metropolitan area were taken over by a single government entity, such as the county? Would government services be provided more effectively? Would better public policy result? How do you think such a change might affect your own interests as a student?

These examples of institutionalized regional coordination are the exceptions rather than the rule. For the most part, the prospects for promoting regional cooperation to correct the inequalities and coordination problems that result from metropolitan fragmentation have been dim. Generally speaking, the United States lacks the strong tradition of regional planning evident in Europe (see "America in Perspective: Urban Planning in Western Europe and the United States"). In large part, this reflects the strong localism inherent in American democracy. Americans prefer living in small, autonomous communities. Suburbanites, in particular, profess a preference for their small-scale, easy-to-reach government over more distant and bureaucratized metropolitan arrangements.

In the United States, there is a tradition (or perhaps a myth) of people being able to "vote with their feet," that is, of people moving to the place where the government's policies best reflect their values.[68] This exacerbates the problem of regional coordination because local governments in different parts of the same metropolitan area will sometimes offer very different services to their citizens. This often manifests itself as a conflict between city dwellers and suburbanites.

A good (if disturbing) example of this is seen in the conflict over the racial integration of the Milwaukee public schools. When its schools were ordered to desegregate in the 1970s and 1980s, many White families moved out of the school district into neighboring suburban districts. In a classic case of "White flight," White student enrollment in the Milwaukee Public Schools dropped rapidly. In response, the federal court that issued the original desegregation order then expanded its order to include other school districts within Milwaukee County, thus attempting to force a regional coordination for educational policy by judicial fiat and with the backing of the federal government. But again, many White families voted with their feet and left the county entirely, making the attempt at coordination a failure.

Other typical conflicts between the preferences and needs of suburbanites and city dwellers involve taxes, roads, and central city services. Many people move to the suburbs because property taxes are lower and land is cheaper. The denser population of an urban area causes a higher need for most local government services, and therefore a

Mass transit is one of the most visible services provided by local government, but the multiplicity of local governments in metropolitan areas makes coordination of service difficult.

higher tax burden. Regional coordination often looks to suburbanites as a way to get them to subsidize the taxes of the urban dwellers they left behind. Because suburbanites live more spread out and often far away from their jobs, they need plenty of good roads and highways on which to commute. But these roads are expensive (especially major highways cutting through urban areas, which can cost millions of dollars per mile to build and maintain). Urban dwellers would rather that more transportation money be spent on mass transit, which is economical for dense populations. Urban dwellers also complain that suburbanites drive into the central city each workday, using city services like roads, police, water, and so forth, and then take themselves and their tax dollars back to the suburbs at night. These examples offer the barest outline of the differences in preferences and viewpoints of people in different areas of a metropolis. It is easy to understand why coordination and cooperation are hard to come by.

Local governments are also engaged in serious competition for economic development. That is, they try to expand their tax base through commercial and residential development. Some analysts believe that cities are quite limited in their ability to control economic change within their borders, but local officials often believe that development policies are a community's lifeblood.[69] A business owner can simply threaten to leave a community or locate facilities in another town if he or she is unhappy with local policies. Thus, business owners and corporate officials have great leverage to extract concessions from local officials because no local government wants to face the loss of jobs or tax base. As a result, cities compete with one another for desirable business facilities by offering tax reductions, promises of subsidized infrastructure development, and other services demanded by business. This competition can increase antagonism among local governments and make coordination and cooperation difficult.

However, local governments can cooperate with one another when they find it in their mutual interest to do so. Central cities and suburbs are often willing, for instance, to share the costs of a new sewage disposal facility. They may also cooperate in ventures to attract a major new employer to the area, or to keep one, as in the case of the massive efforts by local governments in the Chicago metropolitan area to construct a new baseball stadium to keep the White Sox from leaving town in the late 1980s. Sometimes two or more governments may cooperate informally to share equipment and services. In many areas of the country, a **council of governments** (frequently referred to as a COG) exists wherein officials from various localities meet to discuss

council of governments (COG)

Councils in many areas of the country where officials from various localities meet to discuss mutual problems and plan joint, cooperative action.

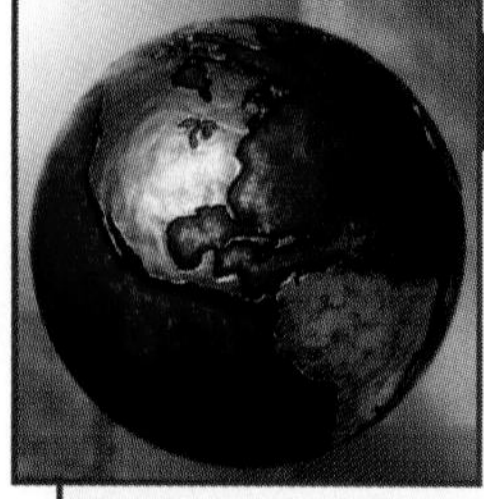

America in Perspective

Urban Planning in Western Europe and the United States

The nations of Western Europe play a much stronger role in guiding urban development than does the United States. Europe's strong planning has helped to preserve cities, control the pace of development, protect agricultural land and the environment, and minimize urban sprawl to a degree that is hardly imaginable in the United States. Typically, these urban planning actions are initiated by regional agencies that get their authority from the central government.

In Great Britain, planners prevented the overgrowth of London by encircling the city with a "green belt"—a designated area in which the countryside would be preserved and no new development permitted. The growth of the region's population was absorbed in planned "new towns" that were built some distance from the central city. The result was a mixture of city and countryside in a metropolitan area and the avoidance of American-style urban sprawl.

Faced with the prospect of excessive growth in Paris, France's national agency for development steered new industries into the suburbs and more distant cities. Still the lure of Paris proved attractive. In response, central government and regional planners built two new towns of high-rise office buildings, convention centers, and hotels in different spots just outside the city's borders. These towns became the main office centers of the metropolitan Paris area. High-rise residential new towns were built in a ring around Paris to absorb the area's rapidly growing population. These new commercial and residential centers were connected to the old city by a new commuter rail system.

The Netherlands has also relied on strong government planning and controls over land use to prevent the country's limited supply of land from being eaten up by rapid urbanization. Dutch planners saved valuable agricultural land and badly needed recreational space in a "green heart" in the midst of the metropolitan Amsterdam-The Hague-Rotterdam Randstad ("Ring City") area, one of the most densely populated areas in the world. Riding a train through the area today, you can easily see exactly where the city ends and the land designated for agricultural purposes begins. The planning boundaries are extremely clear and well guarded.

European planners now confront new problems. With the globalization of their economies, cities in Europe find that they are increasingly competing with one another for new business. As a result, spatial planning considerations are sometimes sacrificed in order to give a corporation a site it desires. Citizens' demands for individual homes of their own have also led to pressures for continued suburban development, sometimes compromising the integrity of regional land-use plans. Rush-hour traffic jams have become increasingly commonplace in major European metropolises.

Despite these new problems, European nations have been able to ward off the ills of uncontrolled growth. In the United States, by contrast, the private sector and the free market—not government—play the dominant role in deciding where growth will occur. Compared to Western Europe, regional planning in the United States is essentially toothless.

Sources: Peter Hall, *Urban and Regional Planning*, 2nd ed., London: Allen and Unwin, 1982; H. V. Savitch, *Post-Industrial Cities: Politics and Planning in New York, Paris, and London*, Princeton, NJ: Princeton University Press, 1988; and Myron A. Levine and Jan Van Weesep, "The Changing Nature of Dutch Urban Planning" in *Journal of the American Planning Association*, 54 (Summer 1988): 315–323.

mutual problems and plan joint, cooperative action. These COGs are often formally very weak, being underfunded, poorly staffed, and lacking in any real legislative or taxing power.

State and Local Finance Policy

When a state or local government approves its budget for the next year, the basic policy objectives of the government have also been approved. These objectives are contained in the taxing and spending plans that make up the budget. Lofty speeches can be made and bills passed into law, but without some significant and specific budgetary commitment, a policy will usually have little impact on citizens' lives. Taxpayers increasingly demand more accountability and efficiency from their subnational governments, forcing officials to squeeze services and programs out of limited revenue dollars. Figure 21.9 shows how state governments get their money and how they spend it.

Figure 21.9 State Government Revenues and Expenditures

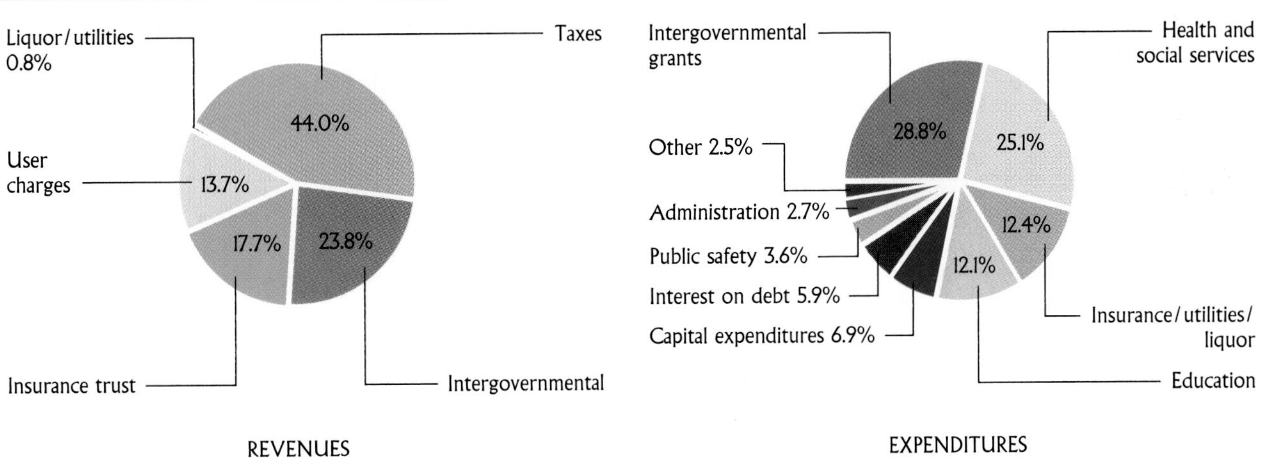

Source: U.S. Bureau of the Census, *Statistical Abstract of the United States, 2000* (Washington, D.C.: U.S. Government Printing Office, 2001).

State government revenues are derived from a variety of sources. States receive the largest share of revenue, 44 percent, from taxes. States' major sources of tax revenue are sales taxes, income taxes, and motor vehicle and fuel taxes. The second largest source of state revenue is intergovernmental revenue (23 percent)—almost all as grants from the federal government. The third major revenue source is state insurance programs (17 percent). Charges and fees for services such as state hospitals, college courses, and state parks have become an increasingly important source of revenue for states in the past 20 years (13 percent).

Changes in their constitutions over the past 40 years have given states wider access to income and sales taxes and other sources of revenue. Today, 45 states levy a general sales tax; Alaska, Delaware, Montana, New Hampshire, and Oregon are the only holdouts. Only seven states—Alaska, Florida, Nevada, South Dakota, Texas, Washington, and Wyoming—do not have a personal income tax, and New Hampshire and Tennessee have only a limited form of income tax. The modernization of state revenue structures gives the states new money to finance the public programs demanded by citizens.

How do states spend their money? Most of the states' money—about 47 percent—goes to operate state programs (in public safety, education, health and social services, etc.), construct state buildings, and provide direct assistance to individuals. Another 28 percent is allocated as aid to local governments. Since so much of the money that states spend is given to local governments (and since so much of the local governments' revenue comes from the states), the states have even more leverage over the locals than is given to them by Dillon's Rule.

Local government finances can be confusing because of the fragmentation of local governments and the varied ways in which states support and constrain their local authorities. This situation is primarily due to the different ways in which states and their local governments have sorted out the assignment of policy responsibilities among local governments. Figure 21.10 offers a snapshot of local government finances—combining county, city, township, school, and special district budgets—across the United States. Local governments receive their revenues from three main sources: taxes, user charges, and intergovernmental aid. Intergovernmental aid (primarily from the states) and "own source" taxes are now about equal in their contribution to local government revenue, again showing the great dependence of local governments on their states. Local taxes are mainly property taxes, but sales and income taxes also contribute to the revenue of some local governments. Charges on the users of certain services, such as libraries and recreation facilities, provide another 20 percent of local government revenue. They receive 8 percent of their revenue from

Figure 21.10 Local Government Revenues and Expenditures

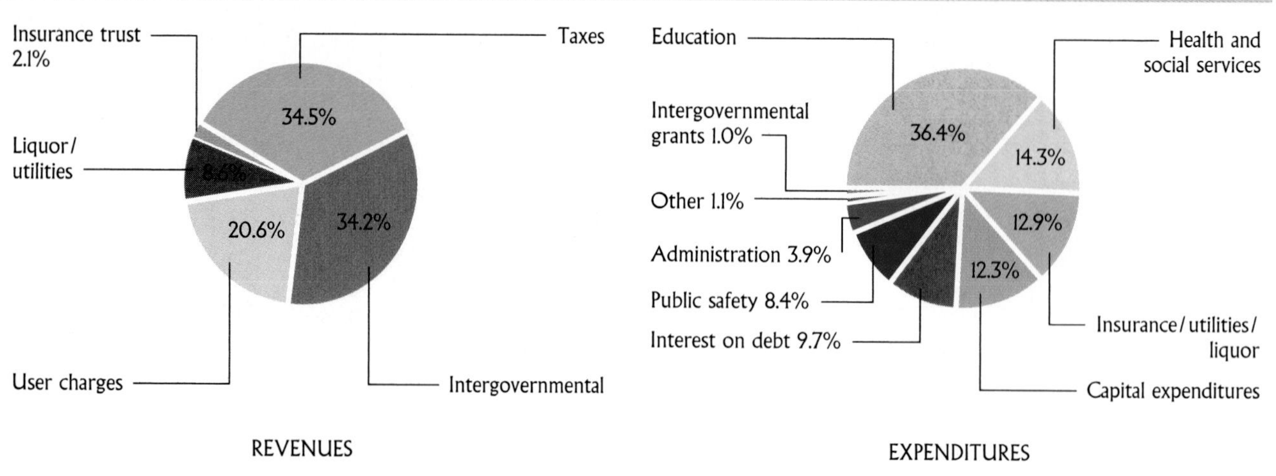

Source: U.S. Bureau of the Census, *Statistical Abstract of the United States, 2000* (Washington, D.C.: U.S. Government Printing Office, 2001).

the operation of municipally owned utilities and liquor sales. Compared to those in some other countries, U.S. local governments do not receive much revenue from the national government.

Local governments allocate their monies to a range of services, but the main areas are public education (36 percent), health and social services (14 percent), and public safety (8 percent). These are services that citizens need on a regular basis, and expect local governments to provide.

The difference between state and local expenditures reflects the distribution of public services between these levels of government that has developed over the course of the history of the United States. Local government is expected to provide two of the most important and broadly used services of all government in the United States—education and public safety (i.e., police and fire protection). State governments, on the other hand, are mainly in charge of making sure that the poorest of the state's citizens have their basic physical needs met. Further, the state is charged with gathering the state's resources and distributing them where they are most needed, via intergovernmental grants. While local governments are busy providing direct citizen service, the state governments can take a broader view to enhance equity in public service.

Understanding State and Local Governments

A full understanding of the complexity of subnational government cannot be gleaned from a single textbook chapter, but you should remember a few important points about these 85,000 governments.

Democracy at the Subnational Level

The very existence of so many governments to handle complex as well as ordinary—but needed—services, testifies to the health of our democracy. States have been willing to decentralize their governing arrangements to permit the creation of local governments to address citizens' policy demands. Today, local voters choose their own representatives to serve on county commissions, city councils, school boards, and some special district boards. As small legislatures elected from among the commu-

You Are the Policymaker

Should Your State Take a Chance on Gambling?

No one likes taxes, but government services have to be paid for somehow. In the 1980s and 1990s many states tried to earn money for state programs "painlessly" through legalized gambling. Thirty years ago, only Nevada allowed most forms of gambling; in some states children couldn't even enter a sweepstakes on the back of a cereal box. Today, many states not only allow a variety of types of gambling, they even sponsor and earn money from such activities. Various states run lotteries and allow casino and riverboat gambling, horse and dog racing, slot machines, video lottery, bingo, and other forms of what proponents call "gaming."

Suppose you are a state legislator faced with the question of legalizing gambling in your state in order to earn extra revenue without raising taxes. To what extent are you willing to accept the negative aspects of gambling in order to gain its monetary rewards?

States earn money from gambling in two main ways. First, states may run a gambling operation outright. State lotteries are the best example of this. States skim off as much as 50 percent of the receipts from lottery tickets, offering most of the rest as prize money. Second, states may earn money from gambling by taxing bets and winnings heavily, as is commonly done with casino and racetrack gambling.

This sort of revenue is a very attractive alternative to direct taxation as a way to help states fund public services. First, it is seen as a voluntary source of revenue, rather than mandatory taxation. Some characterize it as a "tax on stupidity." Second, some forms of gambling are argued to encourage economic development in a local area, thereby being a positive good aside from a source of revenue. The prosperity that some Native American tribes have gained through opening casinos (allowed by the federal government since 1988) is evidence in favor of this position. Third, there are those who view gambling as a harmless recreational activity that the state has no business banning anyway—why not make a little money on it?

Even though dozens of states have legalized and earned money from a wide variety of forms of gambling in the past 20 years, not all states have done so and not all people are convinced that it is good public policy. One argument against legalized gambling is that it is a regressive form of taxation because the people who gamble the highest proportions of their incomes are those who are relatively poor. There has been increasing concern about compulsive gambling, a psychological disorder akin to alcoholism that drives people to gamble incessantly. Like alcoholism, compulsive gambling can lead to financial ruin and the destruction of families. There are also those who argue that gambling is simply immoral, and that legalizing and especially encouraging it (as in state lottery TV commercials) leads people to pursue false hope and a destructive lifestyle. Finally, there is some debate as to just how much money a state can actually earn from gambling, now that it has become so commonplace in the United States.

As a state legislator, you must weigh the benefits of "painless" gambling revenue against the arguments of those who oppose it. Should your state legalize gambling? If so, what form should it adopt? Should it run a lottery? Should it allow casinos, and tax them? What difference does it make if neighboring states do or do not have legalized gambling? What would *you* do?

nity's residents, these governing bodies are usually the policymaking institutions closest and most open to all citizens. In many ways, local governments encourage individual participation in government and promote the value of individualism at the local level.

The states also operate in an open policymaking environment. Many of the most important of state officials are elected to office, far more than in the federal government. Direct primaries permit voters to select nominees for state offices. The recall even allows voters to oust an official from office before his or her term is over in about one-third of the states. The initiative and the referendum permit voters in many states to make policy or amend their state constitutions directly. In most states, voters have a far more direct role in selecting judges than is the case in the federal court system. And by the 1990s, subnational elections were putting officials into office who are far more representative of the U.S. population demographically than is the case in the federal government today or subnational governments in previous years.

Even so, subnational politics may not be as democratic as this initial assessment would seem to indicate. Politics at the state level is poorly covered by the media and, as a result, is relatively invisible to the public. Voters can hardly hold elected officials accountable if they know little about what is going on in the state capital. Even at the local level, there is little press coverage of anything other than the results of city council meetings or a mayor's actions—and that doesn't even happen regularly in smaller communities or in suburbs that lack their own daily newspaper.

When, as is often the case, only 30 to 35 percent of voters participate in statewide elections and fewer than 20 percent turn out for local elections, there are real concerns about the health of our grass-roots governments. In one effort to boost citizen participation, states have begun experimenting with "vote-by-mail" elections. Instead of having to show up on a specific day to cast a ballot, citizens in Oregon were able to mail in their ballots in 1996, and in 1998 Oregon voters passed an initiative making vote-by-mail "the only way to vote" for every election. Further, in a small number of cities, including Birmingham, Dayton, Portland, and St. Paul, vigorous programs of neighborhood democracy have been developed where citizen participation in public affairs goes far beyond voting. In these cities, neighborhood boards are given control over meaningful policy decisions and program resources, and their actions are not merely advisory. These cities also reward municipal officials who listen to the views of these neighborhood bodies. The experience in these and other cities shows that citizens will devote the considerable time necessary to participate in public affairs if they are convinced that participation is meaningful and that city officials are not just manipulating them.[70]

Competition between subnational governments for economic development also raises significant questions about democracy. As a result of this competition, state and local governments have subsidized business growth and economic development, often at the cost of slighting redistribution services and human resource needs. Business interests have substantial leverage in state and city affairs as a result of their ability to threaten to leave or locate facilities in another jurisdiction. The increasing importance of money in subnational elections has only added to the influence that special interests exert in state and local affairs.

Term limitations also raise questions about democracy. On the one hand, term limits can be seen as contributing to democracy by limiting the power of career politicians. Term limits thereby allow citizen government and permit new ideas to enter the policymaking process. This may be especially important with state legislative professionalism making public service more attractive and less of a financial hardship than it used to be. Yet, as we have seen, there is more turnover in state legislatures and city councils than is commonly believed. Also, term limitations may be regarded as undemocratic because they deny voters the ability to reelect a popular official. In legislatures term limits may negatively influence the legislative process.[71]

The workings of democracy are often difficult to see in the judicial branch of government. Because most citizens do not attend trials and only lawyers and judges are directly involved in the appeals process, the proceedings of the judiciary are seldom visible to the public until a significant case or decision is announced. This judicial process is not subject to quite the same scrutiny as the legislative and executive functions of state governments. Even though most state and local judges and justices must face the voters to gain or retain their positions, the lack of information that voters have about the judicial process makes the level of true democracy in this process suspect. Citizens will have to take more interest in the crucial role of courts in our democracy in order for courts to assume the same political importance in states as the other branches of government.

comparative
Comparing State and Local Governments

The Scope of Subnational Government

Growth in subnational government employment has proceeded at a pace exceeding that of the federal government for most of this century, as we learned in Chapter 15. Most of this growth has been driven by citizen demand for more government services. Although most American voters want their elected representatives to control the size of government, voters also want government to provide them with more and better programs.

Has the reform and professionalization of subnational government in the past generation made any difference for taxpayers? In most cases, it has not resulted in smaller government. By its very nature, legislative professionalism costs tax dollars and leads to a legislature that is more permanent and continuous. School district consolidation has occurred, reducing the overall number of local governments by nearly 7 percent in the past 30 years. This declining number of school districts come at a time of growing demand for more special district governments, which have increased by over 72 percent in three decades.

Most state governments have experimented with *sunset legislation*, which involves periodically reviewing agencies to control the growth of government and eliminate unneeded programs. States have also empowered their legislatures to review executive branch regulations and rules to ensure that citizens or businesses are not overregulated by government. These practices help limit the scope of governments.

But as citizen demand in the late twentieth century has led to growth and development in the areas of technology, communications, and public health and safety, subnational governments have had to grow, not diminish. More police, more health care providers, more computer technicians, and more social-welfare caseworkers have been needed to meet the expanding range of services and problems that confront people daily. Although some local governments are barely able to fulfill their basic responsibilities for public safety and maintenance of the local infrastructure, other cities and counties have become much more competent at managing local affairs. Indeed, recent research suggests that local governments often lead their states and the nation in devising innovative ways to deliver public services.[72]

In sum, with the greater responsibilities thrust upon them by the federal government and the demands of their citizens, subnational governments have responded by enhancing their capacity to provide services to their citizens. In the past 40 years, the enhancement of the capacity of the democratically elected officials in the states, especially the state legislators and governors, and the greater use of direct democracy mechanisms has led to subnational governments that are stronger and more effective than before, but also to ones that are more extensive and expensive.

Summary

Our nation's 50 states and its tens of thousands of local governments are responsible for most of the public policies with which we are most familiar: education, fire protection, police protection, highway maintenance, public welfare, public health, and trash collection. The states are a diverse group, but each has a government that makes, enforces, and interprets laws for its citizens. The structure for state governments is specified in state constitutions—some very long, others quite short. Citizens may modify these state constitutions when necessary to keep pace with changing demands of government.

State legislatures include elected representatives who make laws, appropriate money, oversee the executive branch, perform casework, and help manage conflict across the state. Legislators are increasingly diverse demographically, but most tend to be from a somewhat higher socioeconomic position than the majority of the people they represent. Significant turnover takes place in state legislatures, and voters in some states have ensured that this will continue by enacting term limits for their public officials.

The governors of our states are elected to administer public policy and to attend to citizen needs. Once in office, a governor directs a complex set of state government institutions and programs, conducts state affairs with other governors and the president, initiates much of the legislation that state legislatures will adopt, and helps manage conflict. Governors must often work with a number of other elected executive officials to produce public policy.

Career Profile

Position: Wildlife Supervisor at the Iowa Department of Natural Resources
Salary Range: $42,000-45,000
Benefits: Health, life, and dental insurance. Retirement plan. Continuing education tuition program. State vehicle provided.
Qualifications: Officially, only a two-year associate's degree is required. In practice, a bachelor or master of science degree in the biological sciences (biology, wildlife management, etc.) and superior interpersonal skills are expected. Beyond educational requirements, this highly competitive position requires at least six years as a state biologist or equivalent experience

Real People on the Job: Don Pfeiffer

If you want a job that combines a love for the outdoors and wildlife with challenging political and managerial components, then Don Pfeiffer's job as a regional wildlife supervisor for the state of Iowa may be a model to follow. Don, with his staff of 23 biologists, technicians, and office personnel, manages over 150,000 acres of state land wildlife habitat in southeast Iowa. Don and his team work to maintain wetlands, forests, and grasslands by planting trees, erecting artificial nest structures, and conducting wildlife and game animal census counts. When animals such as barn owls, whistling swans, and peregrine falcons native to a certain region become scarce, the threatened species are taken from one area of Iowa and reintroduced to a new location. Increasingly, Don must also keep track of predators like mountain lions, wolves, and black bears that are slowly reintroducing themselves to Iowa. All these actions aim to preserve a biological balance of wildlife in the state.

Not all of the job, however, is a scene from the Discovery Channel. He must also regulate public use of the wildlife habitat by maintaining roads, fences, and signs that allow the public to wisely use some of this land for hunting and recreation. Don also must spend quite a bit of time educating private landowners about what they can and cannot do on their land. Finally, Don is also responsible for evaluating the environmental impact of building proposals and coming up with solutions to preserve the ecological balance. For example, if a new road is going to destroy five acres of marshland, then Don must ensure that five acres of new marshland are created to counteract the effect.

For those who want to join the ranks of wildlife specialists, you should get started well before graduating from college. Summer internships with state, federal, or private wildlife management, environmental, and conservation organizations have become an unwritten expectation for applicants in this field. While the job requires dedication, physical fitness, and long hours, the thrills and freedoms of this job make this a highly competitive field in any state. For more information on the Iowa Department of Natural Resources, examine www.iowaaccess.org/government/dnr. Also check out Cyber-Sierra's government listings (federal, state, and local) for wildlife specialists at www.cyber-sierra.com/nrjobs/gov1.html.

The state court systems are similar in organization to federal courts. Most states have trial courts, intermediate courts of appeal, and a court of last resort; all have jurisdiction over both civil and criminal cases. Judges may attain office through appointment, election, or a hybrid of both known as the Merit Plan. The actions of state judges, especially those serving on the court of last resort, can affect policy significantly.

Local governments in the United States—municipalities, counties, townships, school districts, and special districts—were established by the states to decide on and administer policy in limited geographic and policy areas. Most cities are run by city councils with either a mayor or a city manager directing the day-to-day affairs of city bureaucracies. Counties and townships help states perform many local functions, such as record-keeping and the administration of justice. School districts run public schools, and special districts provide limited services for multiple communities. The existence of nearly 85,000 local governments indicates that democracy truly thrives at the local level in the United States.

Key Terms

subnational government
term limits
item veto
lieutenant governor
Merit Plan
direct democracy
initiative
referendum
recall
Dillon's Rule
local charter
home rule
town meeting
city manager
council of governments

For Further Reading

Beyle, Thad L. *Governors and Hard Times.* Washington, D.C.: Congressional Quarterly Press, 1992. A timely monograph on the modern governor by one of the country's leading experts.

The Council of State Governments. *The Book of the States,* (biannual). Lexington, KY: Council of State Governments. An overview of annual developments in state government.

Gray, Virginia, Russell L. Hanson, and Herbert Jacob, eds. *Politics in the American States: A Comparative Analysis,* 7th ed. Washington, D.C.: Congressional Quarterly Press, 1999. A superb collection of essays that review the empirical literature on state politics.

Hovey, Hal A., and Kendra A. Hovey. *CQ's State Fact Finder: Rankings Across America* (annual). Washington, D.C.: Congressional Quarterly Press. A data book with hundreds of state-by-state comparisons on economic, demographic, political, and policy variables.

Hedge, David M. *Governance and the Changing American States: Transforming American Politics.* Washington, D.C.: Congressional Quarterly Press, 1998. An in-depth and balanced assessment of the literature on the resurgence of state government institutions.

International City/County Management Association. *The Municipal Year Book.* Washington, D.C.: ICMA, annual. Excellent current affairs updates on local governments and informative directories on civic affairs and public officials.

Nelson, Albert J. *Emerging Influentials in State Legislatures: Women, Blacks, and Hispanics.* New York: Praeger Publishers, 1991. Explores the power of minority and women legislators by focusing on their representation, turnover, and influence within party leadership and as chairs of committees.

Rosenthal, Alan. *The Decline of Representative Democracy: Process, Participation, and Power in State Legislatures,* Washington, D.C.: Congressional Quarterly Press, 1997. A detailed examination and evaluation of the state legislatures at the end of the millennium by the leading analyst of those bodies.

Weber, Ronald E., and Paul Brace, eds. *American State and Local Politics: Directions for the 21st Century.* Chatham, NJ: Chatham House, 1999. A collection of essays by top scholars focusing on recent reforms and their implications.

Welch, Susan, and Timothy Bledsoe. *Urban Reform and Its Consequences: A Study in Representation.* Chicago: University of Chicago Press, 1988. An important review and analysis of urban government today.

Internet Resources

www.ezgov.com/portal/index.jsp/
Website of the Citizen Information Center with easy links to your state and local government as well as information on state and local politics.

www.statesnews.org/
Website of the Council of State Governments, with information on states and state public policies.

www.ncsl.org/
Website of the National Conference of State Legislatures, with information on state legislatures, elections, and members.

www.ncsc.dni.us/
Website of the National Center for State Courts with information on state courts.

www.nga.org/
Website of the National Governors' Association, with links to websites for each state.

www.usmayors.org/
U.S. Conference of Mayors website.

www.census.gov/
Website of the U.S. Census Bureau, with links to sites with data on states and local areas.

www.stateline.org/
Website of the Pew Center on the State, with lots of general and state-specific policy information.

Notes

1. David Masci, "School Choice Debate," *The Congressional Quarterly Researcher* (July 18, 1997).
2. Luther H. Gulick, "Reorganization of the State," *Civil Engineering* (August 1933): 420–421.
3. James N. Miller, "Hamstrung Legislatures," *National Civic Review* (May 1965): 178–187.
4. Ann O' M. Bowman and Richard C. Kearney, *The Resurgence of the States* (Englewood Cliffs, NJ: Prentice-Hall, 1986). For other important statements of the improved capacity of state governments to undertake innovative action, see David Osborne, *Laboratories of Democracy* (Boston: Harvard Business School Press, 1988); David B. Walker, *The Rebirth of Federalism* (Chatham, NJ: Chatham House, 1995); and David M. Hedge, *Governance and the Changing American States* (Boulder, CO: Westview, 1998).
5. See Daniel J. Elazar, "The Principles and Traditions Underlying American State Constitutions," *Publius: The Journal of Federalism* 12 (Winter 1982): 11–25.
6. Mavis Mann Reeves, *The Question of State Government Capability* (Washington, D.C.: Advisory Commission on Intergovernmental Relations, 1985), 38.
7. David C. Nice, "Interest Groups and State Constitutions: Another Look," *State and Local Government Review* 20 (Winter 1988): 21–27.
8. Initiative & Referendum Institute, *I & R Usage, 2000* (Washington, D.C.: Initiative & Referendum Institute, 2000).
9. The Council of State Governments, *The Book of the States, 1998–99 Edition*, 35–40 and 135–137.
10. Stephen A. Salmore and Barbara G. Salmore, "The Transformation of State Electoral Politics," in *The State of the States*, 3rd ed., Carl E. Van Horn, ed. (Washington, D.C.: Congressional Quarterly Press, 1996).
11. The Council of State Governments, *The Book of the States, 1998–99 Edition*, 17–18.
12. Thad Beyle, "The Governors," in *Politics in the American States*, 7th ed., Virginia Gray, Russell L. Hanson, and Herbert Jacob, eds. (Washington, D.C.: Congressional Quarterly Press, 1999), 196–199.
13. Salmore and Salmore, "The Transformation of State Electoral Politics," 52.
14. Note that not all lower chambers of state legislatures are called the "House of Representatives," although most are; we refer to them as such in this chapter to avoid confusion. The Council of State Governments, *The Book of the States, 1998–99 Edition*, 68, 454, 466.
15. Salmore and Salmore, "The Transformation of State Electoral Politics," 61.
16. Alan Rosenthal, *The Decline of Representative Democracy: Process, Participation, and Power in State Legislatures*, (Washington, D.C.: Congressional Quarterly Press, 1998), 179–180.
17. Keith E. Hamm and Gary F. Moncrief, "Legislative Politics in the States," in *Politics in the American States*, 7th ed., Virginia Gray, Russell L. Hanson, and Herbert Jacob, eds. (Washington, D.C.: Congressional Quarterly Press, 1999), 156–160.
18. Anthony Gierzynski, *Legislative Party Campaign Committees in the American States* (Lexington: University of Kentucky Press, 1992).
19. National Conference of State Legislatures, "NCSLnet: Democratic Share of Legislative Seats," www.ncsl.org/programs/legman/elect/demshare2000.htm, November 13, 2000.
20. Morris P. Fiorina, "Divided Government in the States," in *The Politics of Divided Government*, Gary Cox and Samuel Kernell, eds. (Boulder, CO: Westview, 1991).
21. V. O. Key, Jr., *Southern Politics in State and Nation* (New York: Knopf, 1949).
22. Keith E. Hamm and Gary F. Moncrief, "Legislative Politics in the States," in *Politics in the American States*, 7th ed., Virginia Gray, Russell L. Hanson, and Herbert Jacob, eds. (Washington, D.C.: Congressional Quarterly Press, 1999), 166.
23. Rich Jones, "The State Legislatures," in Council of State Governments, *The Book of the States, 1992–93*, 127.
24. National Conference of State Legislatures, "Term Limits for State Elected Officials," www.ncsl.org/programs/legman/about/termlim.htm, August 24, 2000.
25. Alan Rosenthal, "The Legislature: Unraveling of Institutional Fabric," in *The State of the States*, 3rd ed., Carl E. Van Horn, ed. (Washington, D.C.: Congressional Quarterly Press, 1996), 128.
26. Albert J. Nelson, *Emerging Influentials in State Legislatures: Women, Blacks, and Hispanics* (New York: Praeger, 1991).
27. Center for American Women and Politics, "Women in State Legislatures: Modest Gains Set New Record in 1998 Elections, Exciting Opportunities Lie Ahead," www.rci.rutgers.edu/~cawp/ legpress98.html, February 23, 1999.
28. David A. Bostis, "Black Elected Officials, 1994–1997," *Focus* magazine, (September 1998).
29. Nelson C. Dometrius, "Governors: Their Heritage and Future," in *American State and Local Politics: Directions for the 21st Century*, Ronald E. Weber and Paul Brace, eds. (Chatham, NJ: Chatham House, 1999).
30. Thad Beyle, "The Governors," in Virginia Gray, Russell L. Hanson, and Herbert Jacob, eds., 7th ed., *Politics in the American States* (Washington, D.C.: Congressional Quarterly Press, 1999), 210–211.
31. Charles W. Wiggins, "Executive Vetoes and Legislative Overrides in the American States," *Journal of Politics*, 42 (November 1980): 1111–1117.
32. Dennis Farney, "When Wisconsin Governor Wields Partial Veto, the Legislature Might As Well Go Play Scrabble," *Wall Street Journal*, (July 1, 1993).
33. Beyle, "Governors," 203–209.
34. Larry Sabato, *Goodbye to Good-Time Charlie: The American Governorship Transformed*, 2nd ed., (Washington, D.C.: Congressional Quarterly Press, 1983).
35. Ann O' M. Bowman and Richard C. Kearney, *State and Local Government*, 4th ed. (Boston: Houghton-Mifflin, 1999), 203–204.
36. Associated Press, "Alabama Lt. Governor Finds Nothing To Do," the *New York Times*, (February 17, 1999).
37. The Council of State Governments, *The Book of the States, 1998–99*, Table 2.10, 35–36.
38. Kenneth J. Meier, "Executive Reorganization of Government: Impact on Employment and Expenditures," *American Journal of Political Science* 24 (1980): 396–412.

39. Hedge, *Governance and the Changing American States,* 111.
40. Alan Rosenthal, "The Legislative Institution: Transformed and At Risk," in *The State of the States,* Carl Van Horn, ed. (Washington, D.C.: Congressional Quarterly Press, 1989), 69.
41. Joel A. Thompson and Gary E. Moncrief, "The Evolution of the State Legislature: Institutional Change and Legislative Careers," in *Changing Patterns in State Legislative Careers,* Gary E. Moncrief and Joel A. Thompson, eds. (Ann Arbor: University of Michigan Press, 1992).
42. Christopher Z. Mooney, "Measuring U.S. State Legislative Professionalism: An Evaluation of Five Indices," *State and Local Government Review,* 26 (Spring 1994): 70–71.
43. National Conference of State Legislatures, "Size of State Legislative Staff: 1979, 1988 and 1996—Permanent Staff (June 1996)," www.ncsl.org/programs/legman/about/stf1.htm, February 7, 1999.
44. Rosenthal, "The Legislative Institution: Transformed and At Risk."
45. Peverill Squire, "Legislative Professionalization and Membership Diversity in State Legislatures, *Legislative Studies Quarterly,* 17 (February 1992): 69–79.
46. Christopher Z. Mooney, "Citizens, Structures, and Sister States: Influences on State Legislative Professionalism," *Legislative Studies Quarterly,* 20 (February 1995): 47–68.
47. Phillip W. Roeder, "State Legislative Reform: Determinants and Policy Consequences," *American Politics Quarterly,* 7 (January 1979): 51–70; Morris P. Fiorina, "Divided Government in the American States: A Byproduct of Legislative Professionalism?" *American Political Science Review,* 88 (June 1994): 304–316.
48. Alan Rosenthal, *The Decline of Representative Democracy: Process, Participation, and Power in State Legislatures* (Washington, D.C.: Congressional Quarterly Press, 1998).
49. Melinda Gann Hall, "State Judicial Politics: Rules, Structures, and the Political Game," in *American State and Local Politics: Directions for the 21st Century.* Ronald E. Weber and Paul Brace, eds. (New York: Chatham House, 1999), 116.
50. Kenneth G. Pankey, Jr., "The State of the Judiciary," in *The Book of the States, 1992–93,* 210.
51. Delaware, Maine, Mississippi, Montana, Nevada, New Hampshire, North Dakota, Rhode Island, South Dakota, Vermont, West Virginia, and Wyoming.
52. Richard A. Watson and Rondal G. Downing, *The Politics of the Bench and Bar: Judicial Selection under the Missouri Nonpartisan Court Plan* (New York: John Wiley, 1969).
53. Shaun Bowler and Todd Donovan, *Demanding Choices: Opinion, Voting, and Direct Democracy,* (Ann Arbor: University of Michigan Press, 1998), 58–65.
54. Elisabeth R. Gerber, "Legislative Response to the Threat of Popular Initiatives," *American Journal of Political Science* 40 (February 1996): 99–128.
55. Edward L. Lascher, Jr., Michael G. Hagen, and Steven A. Rochlin, "Gun Behind the Door?: Ballot Initiatives, State Policies, and Public Opinion," *Journal of Politics* 58 (August 1996): 760–775.
56. Brett Pulley, "The 1998 Campaign: Special Interests; Gambling Proponents Bet $85 Million on Election," the *New York Times* (October 31, 1998).
57. Bowman and Kearney, *State and Local Government,* 125.
58. Richard Sandomir, "Stadiums Are Proposed, but Public Isn't Always Disposed To Pay Price," the *New York Times* (May 7, 1998).
59. Thomas E. Cronin, *Direct Democracy* (Cambridge, MA: Harvard University Press, 1989), 143.
60. Kenneth R. Lamke, "Petak Is Considering Race for Congress or State Senate," *Milwaukee Journal World,* (May 30, 1997).
61. *City of Clinton v. Cedar Rapids and Missouri RR Co.,* 24 Iowa 475 (1868), as quoted in Richard P. Nathan, "The Role of the States in American Federalism," in *The State of the States,* 2nd ed., Carl E. Van Horn, ed. (Washington, D.C.: Congressional Quarterly Press, 1993).
62. Don AuCoin and William F. Doherty, "House Votes To Pull Plug on Middlesex," *Boston Globe* (June 13, 1997), B12.
63. Clive S. Thomas and Ronald J. Hrebenar, "Interest Groups in the States," in *Politics in the American States,* 7th ed., Virginia Gray, Russell L. Hanson, and Herbert Jacob, eds. (Washington, D.C.: Congressional Quarterly Press, 1999).
64. *The Municipal Year Book, 1996,* (Washington, D.C.: International City/County Management Association, 1996).
65. Susan Welch, "The Impact of At-Large Elections on the Representation of Blacks and Hispanics," *The Journal of Politics,* 52 (November 1990): 1050–1076.
66. Kenneth J. Meier, Joseph Stewart, Jr., and Robert E. England, *Race, Class, and Education: The Politics of Second-Generation Discrimination* (Madison: University of Wisconsin Press, 1989).
67. John P. Pelissero and David R. Morgan, "Targeting Intergovernmental Aid to Local Schools: An Analysis of Federal and State Efforts," *Western Political Quarterly* 45 (1992): 985–999.
68. Thomas R. Dye, *American Federalism* (Lexington, MA: D.C. Heath, 1990).
69. Paul E. Peterson, *City Limits* (Chicago: University of Chicago Press, 1981).
70. Jeffrey Berry, Kent Portney, and Ken Thomson, *The Rebirth of Urban Democracy* (Washington, D.C.: Brookings Institution, 1993).
71. Daniel Diermeier. "Commitment, Deference, and Legislative Institutions," *American Political Science Review,* 89 (June, 1995): 344–355.
72. David Osborne and Ted Gaebler, *Reinventing Government: How the Entrepreneurial Spirit Is Transforming the Public Sector,* (Reading, MA: Addison-Wesley, 1992).

Appendix

The Declaration of Independence*

In Congress, July 4, 1776

*This text retains the spelling, capitalization, and punctuation of the original.

The Unanimous Declaration of the Thirteen United States of America

When in the Course of human events it becomes necessary for one people to dissolve the political bands which have connected them with another, and to assume among the powers of the earth, the separate and equal station to which the Laws of Nature and of Nature's God entitle them, a decent respect to the opinions of mankind requires that they should declare the causes which impel them to the separation.

We hold these truths to be self-evident, that all men are created equal, that they are endowed by their Creator with certain unalienable Rights, that among these are Life, Liberty and the pursuit of Happiness.—That to secure these rights, Governments are instituted among Men, deriving their just powers from the consent of the governed,—That whenever any Form of Government becomes destructive of these ends, it is the Right of the People to alter or to abolish it, and to institute new Government, laying its foundation on such principles and organizing its powers in such form, as to them shall seem most likely to effect their Safety and Happiness. Prudence, indeed, will dictate that Governments long established should not be changed for light and transient causes; and accordingly all experience hath shewn that mankind are more disposed to suffer, while evils are sufferable, than to right themselves by abolishing the forms to which they are accustomed. But when a long train of abuses and usurpations, pursuing invariably the same Object evinces a design to reduce them under absolute Despotism, it is their right, it is their duty, to throw off such Government, and to provide new Guards for their future security.

Such has been the patient sufferance of these Colonies; and such is now the necessity which constrains them to alter their former Systems of Government. The history of the present King of Great Britain is a history of repeated injuries and usurpations, all having in direct object the establishment of an absolute Tyranny over these States. To prove this, let Facts be submitted to a candid world.

He has refused his Assent to Laws, the most wholesome and necessary for the public good.

He has forbidden his Governors to pass Laws of immediate and pressing importance, unless suspended in their operation till his Assent should be obtained; and when so suspended, he has utterly neglected to attend to them.

He has refused to pass other Laws for the accommodation of large districts of people, unless those people would relinquish the right of Representation in the Legislature, a right inestimable to them and formidable to tyrants only.

He has called together legislative bodies at places unusual, uncomfortable, and distant from the depository of their Public Records, for the sole purpose of fatiguing them into compliance with his measures.

He has dissolved Representative Houses repeatedly, for opposing with manly firmness his invasions on the rights of the people.

He has refused for a long time, after such dissolutions, to cause others to be elected; whereby the Legislative Powers, incapable of Annihilation, have returned to the People at large for their exercise; the State remaining in the mean time exposed to all the dangers of invasion from without, and convulsions within.

He has endeavored to prevent the population of these States; for that purpose obstructing the Laws for Naturalization of Foreigners; refusing to pass others to encourage their migration hither, and raising the conditions of new Appropriations of Lands.

He has obstructed the Administration of Justice, by refusing his Assent to Laws for establishing Judiciary powers.

He has made Judges dependent on his Will alone, for the tenure of their offices, and the amount and payment of their salaries.

He has erected a multitude of New Offices, and sent hither swarms of Officers to harass our people, and eat out their substance.

He has kept among us, in times of peace, Standing Armies without the Consent of our legislatures.

He has affected to render the Military independent of and superior to the Civil power.

He has combined with others to subject us to a jurisdiction foreign to our constitution, and unacknowledged by our laws; giving his Assent to their Acts of pretended Legislation:

For quartering large bodies of armed troops among us:

For protecting them, by a mock Trial, from punishment for any Murders which they should commit on the Inhabitants of these States:

For cutting off our Trade with all parts of the world:

For imposing Taxes on us without our Consent:

For depriving us in many cases, of the benefits of Trial by Jury:

For transporting us beyond Seas to be tried for pretended offences:

For abolishing the free System of English Laws in a neighboring Province, establishing therein an Arbitrary government, and enlarging its Boundaries so as to render it at once an example and fit instrument for introducing the same absolute rule into these Colonies:

For taking away our Charters, abolishing our most valuable Laws, and altering fundamentally the Forms of our Governments:

For suspending our own Legislatures, and declaring themselves invested with power to legislate for us in all cases whatsoever.

He has abdicated Government here, by declaring us out of his Protection and waging War against us.

He has plundered our seas, ravaged our Coasts, burnt our towns, and destroyed the lives of our people.

He is at this time transporting large Armies of foreign Mercenaries to compleat the works of death, desolation and tyranny, already begun with circumstances of Cruelty & perfidy scarcely paralleled in the most barbarous ages, and totally unworthy the Head of a civilized nation.

He has constrained our fellow Citizens taken Captive on the high Seas to bear Arms against their Country, to become the executioners of their friends and Brethren, or to fall themselves by their Hands.

He has excited domestic insurrections amongst us, and has endeavored to bring on the inhabitants of our frontiers, the merciless Indian Savages, whose known rule of warfare, is an undistinguished destruction of all ages, sexes and conditions.

In every stage of these Oppressions We have Petitioned for Redress in the most humble terms: Our repeated Petitions have been answered only by repeated injury. A Prince, whose character is thus marked by every act which may define a Tyrant, is unfit to be the ruler of a free people.

Nor have We been wanting in attention to our British brethren. We have warned them from time to time of attempts by their legislature to extend an unwarrantable jurisdiction over us. We have reminded them of the circumstances of our emigration and settlement here. We have appealed to their native justice and magnanimity, and we have conjured them by the ties of our common kindred to disavow these usurpations, which would inevitably interrupt our connections and correspondence. They too have been deaf to the voice of justice and consanguinity. We must, therefore, acquiesce in the necessity, which denounces our Separation, and hold them, as we hold the rest of mankind, Enemies in War, in Peace Friends.

We, therefore, the Representatives of the United States of America, in General Congress, Assembled, appealing to the Supreme Judge of the world for the rectitude of our intentions, do, in the Name, and by Authority of the good People of these Colonies, solemnly publish and declare, That these United Colonies are, and of Right ought to be Free and Independent States; that they are Absolved from all Allegiance to the British Crown, and that all political connection between them and the State of Great Britain, is and ought to be totally dissolved; and that as Free and Independent States, they have full Power to levy War, conclude Peace, contract Alliances, establish Commerce, and to do all other Acts and Things which Independent States may of right do. And for the support of this Declaration, with a firm reliance on the protection of divine Providence, we mutually pledge to each other our Lives, our Fortunes and our sacred Honor.

John Hancock

NEW HAMPSHIRE
Josiah Bartlett,
Wm. Whipple,
Matthew Thornton.

MASSACHUSETTS BAY
Saml. Adams,
John Adams,
Robt. Treat Paine,
Elbridge Gerry.

RHODE ISLAND
Step. Hopkins,
William Ellery.

CONNECTICUT
Roger Sherman,
Samuel Huntington,
Wm. Williams,
Oliver Wolcott.

NEW YORK
Wm. Floyd,
Phil. Livingston,
Frans. Lewis,
Lewis Morris.

NEW JERSEY
Richd. Stockton,
Jno. Witherspoon,
Fras. Hopkinson,
John Hart,
Abra. Clark.

PENNSYLVANIA
Robt. Morris,
Benjamin Rush,
Benjamin Franklin,
John Morton,
Geo. Clymer,
Jas. Smith,
Geo. Taylor,
James Wilson,
Geo. Ross.

DELAWARE
Caesar Rodney,
Geo. Read,
Tho. M'kean.

MARYLAND
Samuel Chase,
Wm. Paca,
Thos. Stone,
Charles Caroll of
Carrollton.

VIRGINIA
George Wythe,
Richard Henry Lee,
Th. Jefferson,
Benjamin Harrison,
Thos. Nelson, jr.,
Francis Lightfoot Lee,
Carter Braxton.

NORTH CAROLINA
Wm. Hooper,
Joseph Hewes,
John Penn.

SOUTH CAROLINA
Edward Rutledge,
Thos. Heyward, Junr.,
Thomas Lynch, jnr.,
Arthur Middleton.

GEORGIA
Button Gwinnett,
Lyman Hall,
Geo. Walton.

The Federalist No. 10

James Madison

November 22, 1787

To the People of the State of New York.

Among the numerous advantages promised by a well constructed Union, none deserves to be more accurately developed than its tendency to break and control the violence of faction. The friend of popular governments, never finds himself so much alarmed for their character and fate, as when he contemplates their propensity to this dangerous vice. He will not fail therefore to set a due value on any plan which, without violating the principles to which he is attached, provides a proper cure for it. The instability, injustice and confusion introduced into the public councils, have in truth been the mortal diseases under which popular governments have every where perished; as they continue to be the favorite and fruitful topics from which the adversaries to liberty derive their most specious declamations. The valuable improvements made by the American Constitutions on the popular models, both ancient and modern, cannot certainly be too much admired; but it would be an unwarrantable partiality, to contend that they have as effectually obviated the danger on this side as was wished and expected. Complaints are every where heard from our most considerate and virtuous citizens, equally the friends of public and private faith, and of public and personal liberty; that our governments are too unstable; that the public good is disregarded in the conflicts of rival parties; and that measures are too often decided, not according to the rules of justice, and the rights of the minor party; but by the superior force of an interested and over-bearing majority. However anxiously we may wish that these complaints had no foundation, the evidence of known facts will not permit us to deny that they are in some degree true. It will be found indeed, on a candid review of our situation, that some of the distresses under which we labor, have been erroneously charged on the operation of our governments; but it will be found, at the same time, that other causes will not alone account for many of our heaviest misfortunes; and particularly, for that prevailing and increasing distrust of public engagements, and alarm for private rights, which are echoed from one end of the continent to the other. These must be chiefly, if not wholly, effects of the unsteadiness and injustice, with which a factious spirit has tainted our public administrations.

By a faction I understand a number of citizens, whether amounting to a majority or minority of the whole, who are united and actuated by some common impulse of passion, or of interest, adverse to the rights of other citizens, or to the permanent and aggregate interests of the community.

There are two methods of curing the mischiefs of faction: the one, by removing its causes; the other, by controlling its effects.

There are again two methods of removing the causes of faction: the one by destroying the liberty which is essential to its existence; the other, by giving to every citizen the same opinions, the same passions, and the same interests.

It could never be more truly said than of the first remedy, that it is worse than the disease. Liberty is to faction, what air is to fire, an aliment without which it instantly expires. But it could not be a less folly to abolish liberty, which is essential to political life, because it nourishes faction, than it would be to wish the annihilation of air, which is essential to animal life, because it imparts to fire its destructive agency.

The second expedient is as impracticable, as the first would be unwise. As long as the reason of man continues fallible, and he is at liberty to exercise it, different opinions will be formed. As long as the connection subsists between his reason and his self-love, his opinions and his passions will have a reciprocal influence on each other; and the former will be objects to which the latter will attach themselves. The diversity in the faculties of men from which the rights of property originate, is not less an insuperable obstacle to a uniformity of interests. The protection of these faculties is the first object of Government. From the protection of different and unequal faculties of acquiring property, the possession of different degrees and kinds of property immediately results: and from the influence of these on the sentiments and views of the respective proprietors, ensues a division of the society into different interests and parties.

The latent causes of faction are thus sown in the nature of man; and we see them every where brought into different degrees of activity, according to the different circumstances of civil society. A zeal for different opinions concerning religion, concerning Government and many other points, as well of speculation as of practice; an attachment to different leaders ambitiously contending for pre-eminence and power; or to persons of other descriptions whose fortunes have been interesting to the human passions, have in turn divided mankind into parties, inflamed them with mutual animosity, and rendered them much more disposed to vex and oppress each other, than to co-operate for their common good. So strong is this propensity of mankind to fall into mutual animosities, that where no substantial occasion presents itself, the most frivolous and fanciful distinctions have been sufficient to kindle their unfriendly passions, and excite their most violent conflicts. But the most common and durable source of factions, has been the various and unequal distribution of property. Those who hold, and those who are without property, have ever formed distinct interests in society. Those who are creditors, and those who are debtors, fall under a like discrimination. A landed interest, a manufacturing interest, a mercantile interest, a monied interest, with many lesser interests, grow up of necessity in civilized nations, and divide them into different classes, actuated by different sentiments and views. The regulation of these various and interfering interests forms the principal task of modern Legislation, and involves the spirit of party and faction in the necessary and ordinary operations of Government.

No man is allowed to be a judge in his own cause; because his interest would certainly bias his judgment, and, not improbably, corrupt his integrity. With equal, nay with greater reason, a body of men, are unfit to be both judges and parties, at the same time; yet, what are many of the most important acts of legislation, but so many judicial determinations, not indeed concerning the rights of single persons, but concerning the rights of large bodies of citizens, and what are the different classes of legislators, but advocates and parties to the causes which they determine? Is a law proposed concerning private debts? It is a question to which the creditors are parties on one side, and the debtors on the other. Justice ought to hold the balance between them. Yet the parties are and must be themselves the judges; and the most numerous party, or, in other words, the most powerful faction must be expected to prevail. Shall domestic manufactures be encouraged, and in what degree, by restrictions on foreign manufactures? are questions which would be differently decided by the landed and the manufacturing classes; and probably by neither, with a sole regard to justice and the public good. The apportionment of taxes on the various descriptions of property, is an act which seems to require the most exact impartiality; yet, there is perhaps no legislative act in which greater opportunity and temptation are given to a predominant party, to trample on the rules of justice. Every shilling with which they over-burden the inferior number, is a shilling saved to their own pockets.

It is in vain to say, that enlightened statesmen will be able to adjust these clashing interests, and render them all subservient to the public good. Enlightened statesmen will not always be at the helm: Nor, in many cases, can such an adjustment be made at all, without taking into view indirect and remote considerations, which will rarely prevail over the immediate interest which one party may find in disregarding the rights of another, or the good of the whole.

The inference to which we are brought, is, that the causes of faction cannot be removed; and that relief is only to be sought in the means of controlling its effects.

If a faction consists of less than a majority, relief is supplied by the republican principle, which enables the majority to defeat its sinister views by regular vote: It may clog the administration, it may convulse the society; but it will be unable to execute and mask its violence under the forms of the Constitution. When a majority is included in a faction, the form of popular government on the other hand enables it to sacrifice to its ruling passion or interest, both the public good and the rights of other citizens. To secure the public good, and private rights, against the danger of such a faction, and at the same time to preserve the spirit and the form of popular government, is then the great object to which our enquiries are directed: Let me add that it is the great desideratum, by which alone this form of government can be rescued from the opprobrium under which it has so long labored, and be recommended to the esteem and adoption of mankind.

By what means is this object attainable? Evidently by one of two only. Either the existence of the same passion or interest in a majority at the same time, must be prevented; or the majority, having such co-existent passion or interest, must be rendered, by their number and local situation, unable to concert and carry into effect schemes of oppression. If the impulse and the opportunity be suffered to coincide, we well know that neither moral nor religious motives can be relied on as an adequate control. They are not found to be such on the injustice and violence of individuals, and lose their efficacy in proportion to the number combined together; that is, in proportion as their efficacy becomes needful.

From this view of the subject, it may be concluded, that a pure Democracy, by which I mean, a Society, consisting of a small number of citizens, who assemble and administer the Government in person, can admit of no cure for the mischiefs of faction. A common passion or interest will, in almost every case, be felt by a majority of the whole; a communication and concert results from the form of Government itself; and there is nothing to check the inducements to sacrifice the weaker party, or an obnoxious individual. Hence it is, that such Democracies have ever been spectacles of turbulence and contention; have ever been found incompatible with personal security, or the rights of property; and have in general been as short in their lives, as they have been violent in their deaths. Theoretic politicians, who have patronized this species of Government, have erroneously supposed, that by reducing mankind to a perfect equality in their political rights, they would, at the same time, be perfectly equalized and assimilated in their possessions, their opinions, and their passions.

A republic, by which I mean a government in which the scheme of representation takes place, opens a different prospect, and promises the cure for which we are seeking. Let us examine the points in which it varies from pure democracy, and we shall comprehend both the nature of the cure and the efficacy which it must derive from the union.

The two great points of difference, between a democracy and a republic, are, first, the delegation of the government, in the latter, to a small number of citizens, elected by the rest; secondly, the greater number of citizens, and greater sphere of country, over which the latter may be extended.

The effect of the first difference is, on the one hand, to refine and enlarge the public views, by passing them through the medium of a chosen body of citizens, whose wisdom may best discern the true interest of their country, and whose patriotism and love of justice, will be least likely to sacrifice it to temporary or partial considerations. Under such a regulation, it may well happen, that the public voice, pronounced by the representatives of the people, will be more consonant to the public good, than if pronounced by the people themselves, convened for the purpose. On the other hand the effect may be inverted. Men of factious tempers, of local prejudices, or of sinister designs, may by intrigue, by corruption, or by other means, first obtain the suffrages, and then betray the interest of the people. The question resulting is, whether small or extensive republics are most favorable to the election of proper guardians of the public weal, and it is clearly decided in favor of the latter by two obvious considerations.

In the first place, it is to be remarked that, however small the republic may be, the representatives must be raised to a certain number, in order to guard against the cabals of a few; and that however large it may be, they must be limited to a certain number, in order to guard against the confusion of a multitude. Hence, the number of representatives in the two cases not being in proportion to that of the constituents, and being proportionally greatest in the small republic, it follows, that if the proportion of fit characters be not less in the large than in the small republic, the former will present a greater option, and consequently a greater probability of a fit choice.

In the next place, as each Representative will be chosen by a greater number of citizens in the large than in the small Republic, it will be more difficult for unworthy candidates to practise with success the vicious arts, by which elections are too often carried; and the suffrages of the people being more free, will be more likely to center on men who possess the most attractive merit, and the most diffusive and established characters.

It must be confessed, that in this, as in most other cases, there is a mean, on both sides of which inconveniences will be found to lie. By enlarging too much the number of electors, you render the representative too little acquainted with all their local circumstances and lesser interests; as by reducing it too much, you render him unduly attached to these, and too little fit to comprehend and pursue great and national objects. The Federal Constitution forms a happy combination in this respect; the great and aggregate interests being referred to the national, the local and particular, to the state legislatures.

The other point of difference is, the greater number of citizens and extent of territory which may be brought within the compass of Republican, than of Democratic Government; and it is this circumstance principally which renders factious combinations less to be dreaded in the former, than in the latter. The smaller the society, the fewer probably will be the distinct parties and interests composing it; the fewer the distinct parties and interests, the more frequently will a majority be found of the same party; and the smaller the number of individuals composing a majority, and the smaller the compass within which they are placed, the more easily will they concert and execute their plans of oppression. Extend the sphere, and you take in a greater variety of parties and interests; you make it less probable that a majority of the whole will have a common motive to invade the rights of other citizens; or if such a common motive exists, it will be more difficult for all who feel it to discover their own strength, and to act in unison with each other. Besides other impediments, it may be remarked, that where there is a consciousness of unjust or dishonorable purposes, communication is always checked by distrust, in proportion to the number whose concurrence is necessary.

Hence it clearly appears, that the same advantage, which a Republic has over a Democracy, in controlling the effects of faction, is enjoyed by a large over a small Republic—is enjoyed by the Union over the States composing it. Does this advantage consist in the substitution of Representatives, whose enlightened views and virtuous sentiments render them superior to local prejudices, and to schemes of injustice? It will not be denied, that the Representation of the Union will be most likely to possess these requisite endowments. Does it consist in the greater security afforded by a greater variety of parties, against the event of any one party being able to outnumber and oppress the rest? In an equal degree does the increased variety of parties, comprised within the Union, increase this security? Does it, in fine, consist in the greater obstacles opposed to the concert and accomplishment of the secret wishes of an unjust and interested majority? Here, again, the extent of the Union gives it the most palpable advantage.

The influence of factious leaders may kindle a flame within their particular States, but will be unable to spread a general conflagration through the other States: a religious sect may degenerate into a political faction in a part of the Confederacy but the variety of sects dispersed over the entire face of it, must secure the national Councils against any danger from that source: a rage for paper money, for an abolition of debts, for an equal division of property, or for any other improper or wicked project, will be less apt to pervade the whole body of the Union, than a particular member of it; in the same proportion as such a malady is more likely to taint a particular county or district, than an entire State.

In the extent and proper structure of the Union, therefore, we behold a Republican remedy for the diseases most incident to Republican Government. And according to the degree of pleasure and pride, we feel in being Republicans, ought to be our zeal in cherishing the spirit, and supporting the character of Federalists.

PUBLIUS

The Federalist No. 51

James Madison

February 6, 1788

To the People of the State of New York.

To what expedient then shall we finally resort for maintaining in practice the necessary partition of power among the several departments, as laid down in the constitution? The only answer that can be given is, that as all these exterior provisions are found to be inadequate, the defect must be supplied, by so contriving the interior structure of the government, as that its several constituent parts may, by their mutual relations, be the means of keeping each other in their proper places. Without presuming to undertake a full development of this important idea, I will hazard a few general observations, which may perhaps place it in a clearer light, and enable us to form a more correct judgment of the principles and structure of the government planned by the convention.

In order to lay a due foundation for that separate and distinct exercise of the different powers of government, which to a certain extent, is admitted on all hands to be essential to the preservation of liberty, it is evident that each department should have a will of its own; and consequently should be so constituted, that the members of each should have as little agency as possible in the appointment of the members of the others. Were this principle rigorously adhered to, it would require that all the appointments for the supreme executive, legislative, and judiciary magistracies, should be drawn from the same fountain of authority, the people, through channels, having no communication whatever with one another. Perhaps such a plan of constructing the several departments would be less difficult in practice than it may in contemplation appear. Some difficulties however, and some additional expense, would attend the execution of it. Some deviations therefore from the principle must be admitted. In the constitution of the judiciary department in particular, it might be inexpedient to insist rigorously on the principle; first, because peculiar qualifications being essential in the members, the primary consideration ought to be to select that mode of choice, which best secures these qualifications; secondly, because the permanent tenure by which the appointments are held in that department, must soon destroy all sense of dependence on the authority conferring them.

It is equally evident that the members of each department should be as little dependent as possible on those of the others, for the emoluments annexed to their offices. Were the executive magistrate, or the judges, not independent of the legislature in this particular, their independence in every other would be merely nominal.

But the great security against a gradual concentration of the several powers in the same department, consists in giving to those who administer each department, the necessary constitutional means, and personal motives, to resist encroachments of the others. The provision for defense must in this, as in all other cases, be made commensurate to the danger of attack. Ambition must be made to counteract ambition. The interest of the man must be connected with the constitutional right of the place. It may be a reflection on human nature, that such devices should be necessary to control the abuses of government. But what is government itself but the greatest of all reflections on human nature? If men were angels, no government would be necessary. If angels were to govern men, neither external nor internal controls on government would be necessary. In framing a government which is to be administered by men over men, the great difficulty lies in this: You must first enable the government to control the governed; and in the next place, oblige it to control itself. A dependence on the people is no doubt the primary control on the government; but experience has taught mankind the necessity of auxiliary precautions.

This policy of supplying by opposite and rival interests, the defect of better motives, might be traced through the whole system of human affairs, private as well as public. We see it particularly displayed in all the subordinate distributions of power; where the constant aim is to divide and arrange the several offices in such a manner as that each may be a check on the other; that the private interest of every individual, may be a sentinel over the public rights. These inventions of prudence cannot be less requisite in the distribution of the supreme powers of the state.

But it is not possible to give to each department an equal power of self defense. In republican government the legislative authority, necessarily, predominates. The remedy for this inconveniency is, to divide the legislature into different branches; and to render them by different modes of election, and different principles of action, as little connected with each other, as the nature of their common functions, and their common dependence on the society, will admit. It may even be necessary to guard against dangerous encroachments by still further precautions. As the weight of the legislative authority requires that it should be thus divided, the weakness of the executive may require, on the other hand, that it should be fortified. An absolute negative, on the legislature, appears at first view to be the natural defense with which the executive magistrate should be armed. But perhaps it would be neither altogether safe, nor alone sufficient. On ordinary occasions, it might not be exerted with the requisite firmness; and on extraordinary occasions, it might be prefidiously abused. May not this defect of an absolute negative be supplied, by some qualified connection between this weaker department, and the weaker branch of the stronger department, by which the latter may be led to support the constitutional rights of the former, without being too much detached from the rights of its own department?

If the principles on which these observations are founded be just, as I persuade myself they are, and they be applied as a criterion, to the several state constitutions, and to the federal constitution, it will be found, that if the latter does not perfectly correspond with them, the former are infinitely less able to bear such a test.

There are moreover two considerations particularly applicable to the federal system of America, which place that system in a very interesting point of view.

First. In a single republic, all the power surrendered by the people, is submitted to the administration of a single government; and usurpations are guarded against by a division of the government into distinct and separate departments. In the compound republic of America, the power surrendered by the people, is first divided between two distinct governments, and then the portion allotted to each, subdivided among distinct and separate departments. Hence a double security arises to the rights of the people. The different governments will control each other; at the same time that each will be controlled by itself.

Second. It is of great importance in a republic, not only to guard the society against the oppression of its rulers; but to guard one part of the society against the injustice of the other part. Different interests necessarily exist in different classes of citizens. If a majority be united by a common interest, the rights of the minority will be insecure. There are but two methods of providing against this evil: The one by creating a will in the community independent of the majority, that is, of the society itself, the other by comprehending in the society so many separate descriptions of citizens, as will render an unjust combination of a majority of the whole, very improbable, if not impracticable. The first method prevails in all governments possessing an hereditary or self appointed authority. This at best is but a precarious security; because a power independent of the society may as well espouse the unjust views of the major, as the rightful interests, of the minor party, and may possibly be turned against both parties. The second method will be exemplified in the federal republic of the United States. While all authority in it will be derived from and dependent on the society, the society itself will be broken into so many parts, interests and classes of citizens, that the rights of individuals or of the minority, will be in little danger from interested combinations of the majority. In a free government, the security for civil rights must be the same as for religious rights. It consists in the one case in the multiplicity of interests, and in the other, in the multiplicity of sects. The degree of security in both cases will depend on the number of interests and sects; and this may be presumed to depend on the extent of country and number of people comprehended under the same government. This view of the subject must particularly recommend a proper federal system to all the sincere and considerate friends of republican government: Since it shows that in exact proportion as the territory of the union may be formed into more circumscribed confederacies or states, oppressive combinations of a majority will be facilitated, the best security under the republican form, for the rights of every class of citizens, will be diminished; and consequently, the stability and independence of some member of the government, the only other security, must be proportionally increased. Justice is the end of government. It is the end of civil society. It ever has been, and ever will be pursued, until it be obtained, or until liberty be lost in the pursuit. In a society under the forms of which the stronger faction can readily unite and oppress the weaker, anarchy may as truly be said to reign, as in a state of nature where the weaker individual is not secured against the violence of the stronger: And as in the latter state even the stronger individuals are prompted by the uncertainty of their condition, to submit to a government which may protect the weak as well as themselves: So in the former state, will the more powerful factions or parties be gradually induced by a like motive, to wish for a government which will protect all parties, the weaker as well as the more powerful. It can be little doubted, that if the state of Rhode Island was separated from the confederacy, and left to itself, the insecurity of rights under the popular form of government within such narrow limits, would be displayed by such reiterated oppressions of factious majorities, that some power altogether independent of the people would soon be called for by the voice of the very factions whose misrule had proved the necessity of it. In the extended republic of the United States, and among the great variety of interests, parties and sects which it embraces, a coalition of a majority of the whole society could seldom take place on any other principles than those of justice and the general good; and there being thus less danger to a minor from the will of the major party, there must be less pretext also, to provide for the security of the former, by introducing into the government a will not dependent on the latter; or in other words, a will independent of the society itself. It is no less certain than it is important, notwithstanding the contrary opinions which have been entertained, that the larger the society, provided it lie within a practicable sphere, the more duly capable it will be of self government. And happily for the *republican cause*, the practicable sphere may be carried to a very great extent, by a judicious modification and mixture of the *federal principle*.

PUBLIUS

The Constitution of the United States of America*

*This text retains the spelling, capitalization, and punctuation of the original. Brackets indicate passages that have been altered by amendments.

(Preamble)

We the People of the United States, in Order to form a more perfect Union, establish Justice, insure domestic Tranquility, provide for the common defence, promote the general Welfare, and secure the Blessings of Liberty to ourselves and our Posterity, do ordain and establish this Constitution for the United States of America.

Article I.

(The Legislature)

Section 1. All legislative Powers herein granted shall be vested in a Congress of the United States, which shall consist of a Senate and House of Representatives.

Section 2. The House of Representatives shall be composed of Members chosen every second Year by the People of the several States, and the Electors in each State shall have the Qualifications requisite for Electors of the most numerous Branch of the State Legislature.

No person shall be a Representative who shall not have attained to the Age of twenty five Years, and been seven Years a Citizen of the United States, and who shall not, when elected, be an Inhabitant of that State in which he shall be chosen.

Representatives and direct [Taxes][1] shall be apportioned among the several States which may be included within this Union, according to their respective Numbers [which shall be determined by adding to the whole Number of free Persons, including those bound to Service for a Term of Years, and excluding Indians not taxed, three fifths of all other Persons].[2] The actual Enumeration shall be made within three Years after the first Meeting of the Congress of the United States, and within every subsequent Term of ten Years, in such Manner as they shall by Law direct. The Number of Representatives shall not exceed one for every thirty Thousand, but each State shall have at Least one Representative; and until such enumeration shall be made, the State of New Hampshire shall be entitled to chuse three, Massachusetts eight, Rhode-Island and Providence Plantations one, Connecticut five, New-York six, New Jersey four, Pennsylvania eight, Delaware one, Maryland six, Virginia ten, North Carolina five, South Carolina five, and Georgia three.

When vacancies happen in the Representation from any State, the Executive Authority thereof shall issue Writs of Election to fill such Vacancies.

[1] See Amendment XVI.
[2] See Amendment XIV.

The House of Representatives shall chuse their speaker and other Officers; and shall have the sole Power of Impeachment.

Section 3. The Senate of the United States shall be composed of two Senators from each State [chosen by the Legislature thereof],[3] for six Years; and each Senator shall have one Vote.

Immediately after they shall be assembled in Consequence of the first Election, they shall be divided as equally as may be into three Classes. The Seats of the Senators of the first Class shall be vacated at the Expiration of the second year, of the second Class at the Expiration of the fourth Year, and of the third Class at the Expiration of the sixth Year, so that one third may be chosen every second Year [and if Vacancies happen by Resignation, or otherwise, during the Recess of the Legislature of any State, the Executive thereof may make temporary Appointments until the next Meeting of the Legislature, which shall then fill such Vacancies].[4]

No Person shall be a Senator who shall not have attained to the Age of thirty Years, and been nine Years a Citizen of the United States, and who shall not, when elected, be an Inhabitant of that State for which he shall be chosen.

The Vice President of the United States shall be President of the Senate, but shall have no Vote, unless they be equally divided.

The Senate shall chuse their other Officers, and also a President pro tempore, in the Absence of the Vice President, or when he shall exercise the Office of President of the United States.

The Senate shall have the sole Power to try all Impeachments. When sitting for that Purpose, they shall be on Oath or Affirmation. When the President of the United States is tried, the Chief Justice shall preside: And no Person shall be convicted without the Concurrence of two thirds of the Members present.

Judgment in Cases of Impeachment shall not extend further than to removal from Office, and disqualification to hold and enjoy any Office of honor, Trust or Profit under the United States; but the Party convicted shall nevertheless be liable and subject to Indictment, Trial, Judgment and Punishment, according to Law.

Section 4. The Times, Places and Manner of holding Elections for Senators and Representatives, shall be prescribed in each State by the Legislature thereof; but the Congress may at any time by Law make or alter such Regulations, except as to the Places of chusing Senators.

[The Congress shall assemble at least once in every Year, and such Meeting shall be on the first Monday in December, unless they shall by Law appoint a different Day.][5]

[3] See Amendment XVII.
[4] See Amendment XVII.
[5] See Amendment XX.

Section 5. Each House shall be the Judge of the Elections, Returns and Qualifications of its own Members, and a Majority of each shall constitute a Quorum to do Business; but a smaller Number may adjourn from day to day, and may be authorized to compel the Attendance of absent Members, in such Manner, and under such Penalties as each House may provide.

Each House may determine the Rules of its Proceedings, punish its Members for disorderly Behaviour, and, with the Concurrence of two thirds, expel a Member.

Each House shall keep a Journal of its Proceedings, and from time to time publish the same, excepting such Parts as may in their judgment require Secrecy; and the Yeas and Nays of the Members of either House on any question shall, at the Desire of one fifth of those present, be entered on the Journal.

Neither House, during the Session of Congress, shall, without the Consent of the other, adjourn for more than three days, nor to any other Place than that in which the two Houses shall be sitting.

Section 6. The Senators and Representatives shall receive a Compensation for their Services, to be ascertained by Law, and paid out of the Treasury of the United States. They shall in all Cases, except Treason, Felony and Breach of the Peace, be privileged from Arrest during their Attendance at the Session of their respective Houses, and in going to and returning from the same; and for any Speech or Debate in either House, they shall not be questioned in any other Place.

No Senator or Representative shall, during the Time for which he was elected, be appointed to any civil Office under the Authority of the United States, which shall have been created, or the Emoluments whereof shall have been encreased during such time; and no Person holding any Office under the United States, shall be a Member of either House during his Continuance in Office.

Section 7. All Bills for raising Revenue shall originate in the House of Representatives; but the Senate may propose or concur with Amendments as on other Bills.

Every Bill which shall have passed the House of Representatives and the Senate, shall, before it becomes a Law, be presented to the President of the United States; If he approves he shall sign it, but if not he shall return it, with his Objections to that House in which it shall have originated, who shall enter the Objections at large on their Journal, and proceed to reconsider it. If after such Reconsideration two thirds of that House shall agree to pass the Bill, it shall be sent, together with the Objections, to the other House, by which it shall likewise be reconsidered, and if approved by two thirds of that House, it shall become a Law. But in all such Cases the Votes of both Houses shall be determined by yeas and Nays, and the Names of the Persons voting for and against the Bill shall be entered on the Journal of each House respectively. If any Bill shall not be returned by the President within ten Days (Sundays excepted) after it shall have been presented to him, the Same shall be a Law, in like Manner as if he had signed it, unless the Congress by their Adjournment prevent its Return, in which Case it shall not be a Law.

Every Order, Resolution, or Vote to which the Concurrence of the Senate and House of Representatives may be necessary (except on a question of Adjournment) shall be presented to the President of the United States; and before the Same shall take Effect, shall be approved by him, or being disapproved by him, shall be repassed by two thirds of the Senate and House of Representatives, according to the Rules and Limitations prescribed in the Case of a Bill.

Section 8. The Congress shall have Power To lay and collect Taxes, Duties, Imposts and Excises, to pay the Debts and provide for the common Defence and general Welfare of the United States; but all Duties, Imposts and Excises shall be uniform throughout the United States;

To borrow Money on the credit of the United States;

To regulate Commerce with foreign Nations, and among the several States, and with the Indian Tribes;

To establish a uniform Rule of Naturalization, and uniform Laws on the subject of Bankruptcies throughout the United States;

To coin Money, regulate the Value thereof, and of foreign Coin, and fix the Standard of Weights and Measures;

To provide for the Punishment of counterfeiting the Securities and current Coin of the United States;

To establish Post Offices and post Roads;

To promote the Progress of Science and useful Arts, by securing for limited Times to Authors and Inventors the exclusive Right to their respective Writings and Discoveries;

To constitute Tribunals inferior to the supreme Court;

To define and punish Piracies and Felonies committed on the high Seas, and Offences against the Law of Nations;

To declare War, grant Letters of Marque and Reprisal, and make Rules concerning Captures on Land and Water;

To raise and support Armies, but no Appropriation of Money to that Use shall be for a longer Term than two Years;

To provide and maintain a Navy;

To make Rules for the Government and Regulation of the land and naval Forces;

To provide for calling forth the Militia to execute the Laws of the Union, suppress Insurrections and repel Invasions;

To provide for organizing, arming, and disciplining, the Militia, and for governing such Part of them as may be employed in the Service of the United States, reserving to the States respectively, the Appointment of the Officers, and the Authority of training the Militia according to the discipline prescribed by Congress;

To exercise exclusive Legislation in all Cases whatsoever, over such District (not exceeding ten Miles square) as may, by Cession of particular States, and the Acceptance of Congress, become the Seat of the Government of the United States, and to exercise like Authority over all Places purchased by the Consent of the Legislature of the State in which the Same shall be, for the Erection of Forts, Magazines, Arsenals, dock-Yards, and other needful Buildings;—And

To make all Laws which shall be necessary and proper for carrying into Execution the foregoing Powers, and all other Powers vested by this Constitution in the Government of the United States, or in any Department or Officer thereof.

Section 9. The Migration or Importation of such Persons as any of the States now existing shall think proper to admit, shall not be prohibited by the Congress prior to the Year one thousand eight hundred and eight, but a Tax or duty may be imposed on such Importation, not exceeding ten dollars for each Person.

The Privilege of the Writ of Habeas Corpus shall not be suspended, unless when in Cases of Rebellion or Invasion the public Safety may require it.

No Bill of Attainder or ex post facto Law shall be passed.

[No Capitation, or other direct, Tax shall be laid, unless in Proportion to the Census or Enumeration herein before directed to be taken.][6]

No Tax or Duty shall be laid on Articles exported from any State.

No Preference shall be given by any Regulation of Commerce or Revenue to the Ports of one State over those of another; nor shall Vessels bound to, or from, one State, be obliged to enter, clear, or pay Duties in another.

No Money shall be drawn from the Treasury, but in Consequence of Appropriations made by Law; and a regular Statement and Account of the Receipts and Expenditures of all public Money shall be published from time to time.

No Title of Nobility shall be granted by the United States: And no Person holding any Office of Profit or Trust under them, shall, without the Consent of the Congress, accept of any present, Emolument, Office, or Title, of any kind whatever, from any King, Prince, or foreign State.

Section 10. No State shall enter into any Treaty, Alliance, or Confederation; grant Letters of Marque and Reprisal; coin Money; emit Bills of Credit; make any Thing but gold and silver Coin a Tender in Payment of Debts; pass any Bill of Attainder, ex post facto Law, or Law impairing the Obligation of Contracts, or grant any Title of Nobility.

No State shall, without the Consent of the Congress, lay any Imposts or Duties on Imports or Exports, except what may be absolutely necessary for executing its inspection Laws: and the net Produce of all Duties and Imposts, laid by any State on Imports or Exports, shall be for the Use of the Treasury of the United States; and all such Laws shall be subject to the Revision and Controul of the Congress.

No State shall, without the Consent of Congress, lay any Duty of Tonnage, keep Troops, or Ships of War in time of Peace, enter into any Agreement or Compact with another State, or with a foreign Power, or engage in War, unless actually invaded, or in such imminent Danger as will not admit of delay.

[6] See Amendment XVI.

Article II.

(The Executive)

Section 1. The executive Power shall be vested in a President of the United States of America. He shall hold his Office during the Term of four Years, and, together with the Vice President, chosen for the same Term, be elected, as follows.

Each State shall appoint, in such Manner as the Legislature thereof may direct, a Number of Electors, equal to the whole Number of Senators and Representatives to which the State may be entitled in the Congress; but no Senator or Representative, or Person holding an Office of Trust or Profit under the United States, shall be appointed an Elector.

[The Electors shall meet in their respective States, and vote by Ballot for two Persons, of whom one at least shall not be an Inhabitant of the same State with themselves. And they shall make a List of all the Persons voted for, and of the Number of Votes for each; which List they shall sign and certify, and transmit sealed to the Seat of the Government of the United States, directed to the President of the Senate. The President of the Senate shall, in the Presence of the Senate and House of Representatives, open all the Certificates, and the Votes shall then be counted. The Person having the greatest Number of Votes shall be the President, if such Number be a Majority of the whole Number of Electors appointed; and if there be more than one who have such Majority, and have an equal Number of Votes, then the House of Representatives shall immediately chuse by Ballot one of them for President; and if no Person have a Majority, then from the five highest on the List the said House shall in like Manner chuse the President. But in chusing the President, the Votes shall be taken by States, the Representation from each State having one Vote; A quorum for this Purpose shall consist of a Member or Members from two thirds of the States, and a Majority of all the States shall be necessary to a Choice. In every Case, after the Choice of the President, the Person having the greatest Number of Votes of the Electors shall be the Vice President. But if there should remain two or more who have equal Votes, the Senate shall chuse from them by Ballot the Vice President.][7]

The Congress may determine the Time of chusing the Electors, and the Day on which they shall give their Votes; which Day shall be the same throughout the United States.

No Person except a natural born Citizen, or a Citizen of the United States, at the time of the Adoption of this Constitution, shall be eligible to the Office of President; neither shall any Person be eligible to that Office who shall not have attained to the Age of thirty five Years, and been fourteen Years a Resident within the United States.

[In Case of the Removal of the President from Office, or of his Death, Resignation, or Inability to discharge the Powers and Duties of the said Office, the Same shall devolve on the Vice President, and the Congress may by Law provide for the Case of

[7] See Amendment XII.

Removal, Death, Resignation or Inability, both of the President and Vice President, declaring what Officer shall then act as President, and such Officer shall act accordingly, until the Disability be removed, or a President shall be elected.][8]

The President shall, at stated Times, receive for his Services, a Compensation, which shall neither be encreased nor diminished during the Period for which he shall have been elected, and he shall not receive within that Period any other Emolument from the United States, or any of them.

Before he enter on the Execution of his Office, he shall take the following Oath or Affirmation:—"I do solemnly swear (or affirm) that I will faithfully execute the Office of President of the United States, and will to the best of my Ability, preserve, protect and defend the Constitution of the United States."

Section 2. The President shall be Commander in Chief of the Army and Navy of the United States, and of the Militia of the several States, when called into the actual Service of the United States; he may require the Opinion, in writing, of the principal Officer in each of the executive Departments, upon any Subject relating to the Duties of their respective Offices, and he shall have Power to grant Reprieves and Pardons for Offences against the United States, except in Cases of Impeachment.

He shall have Power, by and with the Advice and Consent of the Senate, to make Treaties, provided two thirds of the Senators present concur; and he shall nominate, and by and with the Advice and Consent of the Senate, shall appoint Ambassadors, other public Ministers and Consuls, Judges of the supreme Court, and all other Officers of the United States, whose Appointments are not herein otherwise provided for, and which shall be established by Law: but the Congress may by Law vest the Appointment of such inferior Officers, as they think proper, in the President alone, in the Courts of Law, or in the Heads of Departments.

The President shall have Power to fill up all Vacancies that may happen during the Recess of the Senate, by granting Commissions which shall expire at the end of their next Session.

Section 3. He shall from time to time give to the Congress Information of the State of the Union, and recommend to their Consideration such Measures as he shall judge necessary and expedient; he may, on extraordinary Occasions, convene both Houses, or either of them, and in Case of Disagreement between them, with Respect to the Time of Adjournment, he may adjourn them to such Time as he shall think proper; he shall receive Ambassadors and other public Ministers; he shall take Care that the Laws be faithfully executed, and shall Commission all the Officers of the United States.

Section 4. The President, Vice President and all civil Officers of the United States, shall be removed from Office on Impeachment for, and Conviction of, Treason, Bribery, or other high Crimes and Misdemeanors.

[8] See Amendment XXV.

Article III.

(The Judiciary)

Section 1. The judicial Power of the United States, shall be vested in one supreme Court, and in such inferior Courts as the Congress may from time to time ordain and establish. The Judges, both of the supreme and inferior Courts, shall hold their Offices during good Behaviour, and shall, at stated Times, receive for their Services, a Compensation, which shall not be diminished during their Continuance in Office.

Section 2. The judicial Power shall extend to all Cases, in Law and Equity, arising under this Constitution, the Laws of the United States, and Treaties made, or which shall be made, under their Authority;—to all Cases affecting Ambassadors, other public Ministers and Consuls;—to all Cases of admiralty and maritime Jurisdiction;—to Controversies to which the United States shall be a Party;—to Controversies between two or more States; [—between a State and Citizens of another State;—][9] between Citizens of different States,—between Citizens of the same State claiming Lands under Grants of different States, [and between a State, or the Citizens thereof, and foreign States, Citizens or Subjects.][10]

In all Cases affecting Ambassadors, other public Ministers and Consuls, and those in which a State shall be Party, the supreme Court shall have original Jurisdiction. In all the other Cases before mentioned, the supreme Court shall have appellate Jurisdiction, both as to Law and Fact, with such Exceptions, and under such Regulations as the Congress shall make.

The Trial of all Crimes, except in Cases of Impeachment, shall be by Jury; and such Trial shall be held in the State where the said Crimes shall have been committed; but when not committed within any State, the Trial shall be at such Place or Places as the Congress may by Law have directed.

Section 3. Treason against the United States, shall consist only in levying War against them, or in adhering to their Enemies, giving them Aid and Comfort. No Person shall be convicted of Treason unless on the Testimony of two Witnesses to the same overt Act, or on Confession in open Court.

The Congress shall have Power to declare the Punishment of Treason, but no Attainder of Treason shall work Corruption of Blood, or Forfeiture except during the Life of the Person attainted.

Article IV.

(Interstate Relations)

Section 1. Full Faith and Credit shall be given in each State to the public Acts, Records, and judicial Proceedings of every other State. And the Congress may by general Laws prescribe the Manner in which such Acts, Records and Proceedings shall be proved, and the Effect thereof.

[9] See Amendment XI.
[10] See Amendment XI.

Section 2. The Citizens of each State shall be entitled to all Privileges and Immunities of Citizens in the several States.

A Person charged in any State with Treason, Felony, or other Crime, who shall flee from Justice, and be found in another State, shall on Demand of the executive Authority of the State from which he fled, be delivered up, to be removed to the State having Jurisdiction of the Crime.

[No Person held to Service or Labour in one State under the Laws thereof, escaping into another, shall, in Consequence of any Law or Regulation therein, be discharged from such Service or Labour, but shall be delivered up on Claim of the Party to whom such Service or Labour may be due.][11]

Section 3. New States may be admitted by the Congress into this Union; but no new State shall be formed or erected within the Jurisdiction of any other State; nor any State be formed by the Junction of two or more States, or Parts of States, without the Consent of the Legislatures of the States concerned as well as of the Congress.

The Congress shall have Power to dispose of and make all needful Rules and Regulations respecting the Territory or other Property belonging to the United States; and nothing in this Constitution shall be so construed as to Prejudice any Claims of the United States, or of any particular State.

Section 4. The United States shall guarantee to every State in this Union a Republican Form of Government, and shall protect each of them against Invasion, and on Application of the Legislature, or of the Executive (when the Legislature cannot be convened) against domestic Violence.

Article V.

(Amending the Constitution)

The Congress, whenever two thirds of both Houses shall deem it necessary, shall propose Amendments to this Constitution, or, on the Application of the Legislatures of two thirds of the several States, shall call a Convention for proposing Amendments, which, in either Case, shall be valid to all Intents and Purposes, as Part of this Constitution, when ratified by the Legislatures of three fourths of the several States, or by Conventions in three fourths thereof, as the one or the other Mode of Ratification may be proposed by the Congress; Provided that no Amendment which may be made prior to the Year One thousand eight hundred and eight shall in any Manner affect the first and fourth Clauses in the Ninth Section of the first Article; and that no State, without its Consent, shall be deprived of its equal Suffrage in the Senate.

Article VI.

(Debts, Supremacy, Oaths)

All Debts contracted and Engagements entered into, before the Adoption of this Constitution, shall be as valid against the United States under this Constitution, as under the Confederation.

This Constitution, and the laws of the United States which shall be made in Pursuance thereof; and all Treaties made, or which shall be made, under the Authority of the United States, shall be the supreme Law of the Land; and the Judges in every State shall be bound thereby, any Thing in the Constitution or Laws of any State to the Contrary notwithstanding.

The Senators and Representatives before mentioned, and the Members of the several State Legislatures, and all executive and judicial Officers, both of the United States and of the several States, shall be bound by Oath or Affirmation, to support this Constitution; but no religious Test shall ever be required as a Qualification to any Office or public Trust under the United States.

Article VII.

(Ratifying the Constitution)

The Ratification of the Conventions of nine States, shall be sufficient for the Establishment of this Constitution between the States so ratifying the Same.

Done in Convention by the Unanimous Consent of the States present the Seventeenth Day of September in the Year of our Lord one thousand seven hundred and Eighty seven and of the Independence of the United States of America the Twelfth. IN WITNESS whereof we have hereunto subscribed our Names.

Go. WASHINGTON
Presid't. and deputy from Virginia

Attest
William Jackson
Secretary

DELAWARE
Geo. Read
Gunning Bedford jun
John Dickinson
Richard Basset
Jaco. Broom

MASSACHUSETTS
Nathaniel Gorbam
Rufus King

CONNECTICUT
Wm. Saml. Johnson
Roger Sherman

NEW YORK
Alexander Hamilton

NEW JERSEY
Wh. Livingston
David Brearley
Wm. Paterson
Jona. Dayton

PENNSYLVANIA
B. Franklin
Thomas Mifflin
Robt. Morris
Geo. Clymer
Thos. FitzSimons
Jared Ingersoll
James Wilson
Gouv. Morris

NEW HAMPSHIRE
John Langdon
Nicholas Gilman

MARYLAND
James McHenry
Dan of St. Thos. Jenifer
Danl. Carroll

VIRGINIA
John Blair
James Madison Jr.

NORTH CAROLINA
Wm. Blount
Richd. Dobbs Spaight
Hu. Williamson

SOUTH CAROLINA
J. Rutledge
Charles Cotesworth Pinckney
Charles Pinckney
Pierce Butler

GEORGIA
William Few
Abr. Baldwin

[11] See Amendment XIII.

Articles in addition to, and amendment of the Constitution of the United States of America, proposed by Congress and ratified by the Legislatures of the several states, pursuant to the Fifth Article of the original Constitution.

(The first 10 amendments were passed by Congress on September 25, 1789, and were ratified on December 15, 1791.)

Amendment I—Religion, Speech, Assembly, Petition

Congress shall make no law respecting an establishment of religion, or prohibiting the free exercise thereof; or abridging the freedom of speech, or of the press; or the right of the people peaceably to assemble, and to petition the Government for a redress of grievances.

Amendment II—Right to Bear Arms

A well regulated Militia, being necessary to the security of a free State, the right of the people to keep and bear Arms, shall not be infringed.

Amendment III—Quartering of Soldiers

No Soldier shall, in time of peace be quartered in any house, without the consent of the Owner, nor in time of war, but in a manner to be prescribed by law.

Amendment IV—Searches and Seizures

The right of the people to be secure in their persons, houses, papers, and effects, against unreasonable searches and seizures, shall not be violated, and no warrants shall issue, but upon probable cause, supported by Oath or affirmation, and particularly describing the place to be searched, and the persons or things to be seized.

Amendment V—Grand Juries, Double Jeopardy, Self-incrimination, Due Process, Eminent Domain

No person shall be held to answer for a capital, or otherwise infamous crime, unless on a presentment or indictment of a Grand Jury, except in cases arising in the land or naval forces, or in the Militia, when in actual service in time of War or public danger; nor shall any person be subject for the same offence to be twice put in jeopardy of life or limb; nor shall be compelled in any criminal case to be a witness against himself, nor be deprived of life, liberty, or property, without due process of law; nor shall private property be taken for public use, without just compensation.

Amendment VI—Criminal Court Procedures

In all criminal prosecutions, the accused shall enjoy the right to a speedy and public trial, by an impartial jury of the State and district wherein the crime shall have been committed, which district shall have been previously ascertained by law, and to be informed of the nature and cause of the accusation; to be confronted with the witnesses against him; to have compulsory process for obtaining witnesses in his favor, and to have the assistance of counsel for his defence.

Amendment VII—Trial by Jury in Common-law Cases

In Suits at common law, where the value in controversy shall exceed twenty dollars, the right of trial by jury shall be preserved, and no fact tried by a jury, shall be otherwise re-examined in any Court of the United States, than according to the rules of the common law.

Amendment VIII—Bails, Fines, and Punishment

Excessive bail shall not be required, nor excessive fines imposed, nor cruel and unusual punishments inflicted.

Amendment IX—Rights Retained by the People

The enumeration in the Constitution, of certain rights, shall not be construed to deny or disparage others retained by the people.

Amendment X—Rights Reserved to the States

The powers not delegated to the United States by the Constitution, nor prohibited by it to the States, are reserved to the States respectively, or to the people.

Amendment XI—Suits Against the States (Ratified February 7, 1795)

The Judicial power of the United States shall not be construed to extend to any suit in law or equity, commenced or prosecuted against one of the United States by Citizens of another State, or by Citizens or Subjects of any Foreign State.

Amendment XII—Election of the President and Vice-President (Ratified June 15, 1804)

The Electors shall meet in their respective states, and vote by ballot for President and Vice-President, one of whom, at least, shall not be an inhabitant of the same state with themselves; they shall name in their ballots the person voted for as President, and in distinct ballots the person voted for as Vice-President, and they shall make distinct lists of all persons voted for as President, and of all persons voted for as Vice-President, and of the number of votes for each, which lists they shall sign and certify, and transmit sealed to the seat of the government of the United States, directed to the President of the Senate;—The President of the Senate shall, in the presence of the Senate and House of Representatives, open all the certificates and the votes shall then be counted;—The person having the greatest number of votes for President, shall be the President, if such number be a majority of the whole number of Electors appointed; and if no person have such majority, then from the persons having the highest numbers not exceeding three on the list of those voted for as President, the House of Representatives shall choose immediately, by ballot, the President. But in choosing the President, the votes shall be taken by states, the representation from each state having one vote; a quorum for this purpose shall consist of a member or members from two-thirds of the states, and a majority of all the states shall be necessary to a Choice. [And if the House of Representatives shall not choose a President whenever the right of choice shall devolve upon them, before the fourth day of March next following, then the Vice-President shall act as President, as in the case of the death or other constitutional disability of the President.][12]—The person having the greatest number of votes as Vice-President, shall be the Vice-President, if such number be a majority of the whole number of Electors appointed, and if no person have a majority, then from the two highest numbers on the list, the Senate shall choose the Vice-President; a quorum for the purpose shall consist of two-thirds of the whole number of Senators, and a majority of the whole number shall be necessary to a choice. But no person constitutionally ineligible to the office of President shall be eligible to that of Vice-President of the United States.

Amendment XIII—Slavery (Ratified on December 6, 1865)

Section 1. Neither slavery nor involuntary servitude, except as a punishment for crime whereof the party shall have been duly convicted, shall exist within the United States, or any place subject to their jurisdiction.

Section 2. Congress shall have power to enforce this article by appropriate legislation.

Amendment XIV—Citizenship, Due Process, and Equal Protection of the Laws (Ratified on July 9, 1868)

Section 1. All persons born or naturalized in the United States, and subject to the jurisdiction thereof, are citizens of the United States and of the State wherein they reside. No State shall make or enforce any law which shall abridge the privileges or immunities of citizens of the United States; nor shall any State deprive any person of life, liberty, or property, without due process of law; nor deny to any person within its jurisdiction the equal protection of the laws.

Section 2. Representatives shall be apportioned among the several States according to their respective numbers, counting the whole number of persons in each State, excluding Indians not taxed. But when the right to vote at any election for the choice of electors for President and Vice President of the United States, Representatives in Congress, the Executive and Judicial officers of a State, or the members of the Legislature thereof, is denied to any of the male inhabitants of such State, being twenty-one years of age, and citizens of the United States, or in any way abridged, except for participation in rebellion, or other crime, the basis of representation therein shall be reduced in the proportion which the number of such male citizens shall bear to the whole number of male citizens twenty-one years of age in such State.

Section 3. No person shall be a Senator or Representative in Congress, or elector of President and Vice President, or hold any office, civil or military, under the United States, or under any State, who, having previously taken an oath, as a member of Congress, or as an officer of the United States, or as a member of any State legislature, or as an executive or judicial officer of any State, to support the Constitution of the United States, shall have engaged in insurrection or rebellion against the same, or given aid or comfort to the enemies thereof. But Congress may by a vote of two-thirds of each House, remove such disability.

Section 4. The validity of the public debt of the United States, authorized by law, including debts incurred for payment of pensions and bounties for services in suppressing insurrection or rebellion, shall not be questioned. But neither the United States nor any State shall assume or pay any debt or obligation incurred in aid of insurrection or rebellion against the United States, or any claim for the loss or emancipation of any slave, but all such debts, obligations and claims shall be held illegal and void.

Section 5. The Congress shall have power to enforce, by appropriate legislation, the provisions of this article.

Amendment XV—The Right To Vote (Ratified on February 3, 1870)

Section 1. The right of citizens of the United States to vote shall not be denied or abridged by the United States or by any State on account of race, color, or previous condition of servitude.

Section 2. The Congress shall have power to enforce this article by appropriate legislation.

Amendment XVI—Income Taxes (Ratified on February 3, 1913)

The Congress shall have power to lay and collect taxes on incomes, from whatever source derived, without apportionment among the several States, and without regard to any census or enumeration.

Amendment XVII—Election of Senators (Ratified on April 8, 1913)

The Senate of the United States shall be composed of two Senators from each State, elected by the people thereof, for six years; and each Senator shall have one vote. The electors in each State shall have the qualifications requisite for electors of the most numerous branch of the State legislatures.

When vacancies happen in the representation of any State in the Senate, the executive authority of such State shall issue writs of

[12] Amendment XX.

election to fill such vacancies: *Provided*, That the legislature of any State may empower the executive thereof to make temporary appointments until the people fill the vacancies by election as the legislature may direct.

This amendment shall not be so construed as to affect the election or term of any Senator chosen before it becomes valid as part of the Constitution.

Amendment XVIII—Prohibition (Ratified on January 16, 1919)

Section 1. After one year from the ratification of this article the manufacture, sale, or transportation of intoxicating liquors within, the importation thereof into, or the exportation thereof from the United States and all territory subject to the jurisdiction thereof for beverage purposes is hereby prohibited.

Section 2. The Congress and the several States shall have concurrent power to enforce this article by appropriate legislation.

Section 3. This article shall be inoperative unless it shall have been ratified as an amendment to the Constitution by the legislatures of the several States, as provided in the Constitution, within seven years from the date of the submission hereof to the States by the Congress.[13]

Amendment XIX—Women's Right To Vote (Ratified on August 18, 1920)

The right of citizens of the United States to vote shall not be denied or abridged by the United States or by any State on account of sex.

Congress shall have power to enforce this article by appropriate legislation.

Amendment XX—Terms of Office, Convening of Congress, and Succession (Ratified February 6, 1933)

Section 1. The terms of the President and Vice President shall end at noon on the 20th day of January, and the terms of Senators and Representatives at noon on the 3d day of January, of the years in which such terms would have ended if this article had not been ratified; and the terms of their successors shall then begin.

Section 2. The Congress shall assemble at least once in every year, and such meeting shall begin at noon on the 3d day of January, unless they shall by law appoint a different day.

Section 3. If, at the time fixed for the beginning of the term of the President, the President elect shall have died, the Vice President elect shall become President. If a President shall not have been chosen before the time fixed for the beginning of his term, or if the President elect shall have failed to qualify, then the Vice President elect shall act as President until a President shall have qualified; and the Congress may by law provide for the case wherein neither a President elect nor a Vice President elect shall have qualified, declaring who shall then act as President, or the manner in which one who is to act shall be selected, and such person shall act accordingly until a President or Vice President shall have qualified.

Section 4. The Congress may by law provide for the case of the death of any of the persons from whom the House of Representatives may choose a President whenever the rights of choice shall have devolved upon them, and for the case of the death of any of the persons from whom the Senate may choose a Vice President whenever the right of choice shall have devolved upon them.

Section 5. Sections 1 and 2 shall take effect on the 15th day of October following the ratification of this article.

Section 6. This article shall be inoperative unless it shall have been ratified as an amendment to the Constitution by the legislatures of three-fourths of the several States within seven years from the date of its submission.

Amendment XXI—Repeal of Prohibition (Ratified on December 5, 1933)

Section 1. The eighteenth article of amendment to the Constitution of the United States is hereby repealed.

Section 2. The transportation or importation into any State, Territory, or possession of the United States for delivery or use therein of intoxicating liquors, in violation of the laws thereof, is hereby prohibited.

Section 3. This article shall be inoperative unless it shall have been ratified as an amendment to the Constitution by conventions in the several States, as provided in the Constitution, within seven years from the date of the submission hereof to the States by the Congress.

Amendment XXII—Number of Presidential Terms (Ratified on February 27, 1951)

No person shall be elected to the office of the President more than twice, and no person who has held the office of President, or acted as President, for more than two years of a term to which some other person was elected President shall be elected to the office of the President more than once. But this Article shall not apply to any person holding the office of President when this Article was proposed by the Congress, and shall not prevent any person who may be holding the office of President, or acting as President, during the term within which this Article becomes operative from holding the office of President or acting as President during the remainder of such term.

[13] Amendment XXI.

Amendment XXIII—Presidential Electors for the District of Columbia (Ratified on March 29, 1961)

Section 1. The District constituting the seat of Government of the United States shall appoint in such manner as the Congress may direct:

A number of electors of President and Vice President equal to the whole number of Senators and Representatives in Congress to which the District would be entitled if it were a State, but in no event more than the least populous State; they shall be in addition to those appointed by the States, but they shall be considered, for the purposes of the election of President and Vice President, to be electors appointed by a State; and they shall meet in the District and perform such duties as provided by the twelfth article of amendment.

Section 2. The Congress shall have power to enforce this article by appropriate legislation.

Amendment XXIV—Poll Tax (Ratified on January 23, 1964)

Section 1. The right of citizens of the United States to vote in any primary or other election for President or Vice President, for electors for President or Vice President, or for Senator or Representative in Congress, shall not be denied or abridged by the United States or any State by reason of failure to pay any poll tax or other tax.

Section 2. The Congress shall have power to enforce this article by appropriate legislation.

Amendment XXV—Presidential Disability and Vice Presidential Vacancies (Ratified on February 10, 1967)

Section 1. In case of the removal of the President from office or of his death or resignation, the Vice President shall become President.

Section 2. Whenever there is a vacancy in the office of the Vice President, the President shall nominate a Vice President who shall take office upon confirmation by a majority vote of both Houses of Congress.

Section 3. Whenever the President transmits to the President pro tempore of the Senate and the Speaker of the House of Representatives his written declaration that he is unable to discharge the powers and duties of his office, and until he transmits to them a written declaration to the contrary, such powers and duties shall be discharged by the Vice President as Acting President.

Section 4. Whenever the Vice President and a majority of either the principal officers of the executive departments or of such other body as Congress may by law provide, transmit to the President pro tempore of the Senate and the Speaker of the House of Representatives their written declaration that the President is unable to discharge the powers and duties of his office, the Vice President shall immediately assume the powers and duties of the office as Acting President.

Thereafter, when the President transmits to the President pro tempore of the Senate and the Speaker of the House of Representatives his written declaration that no inability exists, he shall resume the powers and duties of his office unless the Vice President and a majority of either the principal officers of the executive department or of such other body as Congress may by law provide, transmit within four days to the President pro tempore of the Senate and the Speaker of the House of Representatives their written declaration that the President is unable to discharge the powers and duties of his office. Thereupon Congress shall decide the issue, assembling within forty-eight hours for that purpose if not in session. If the Congress, within twenty-one days after receipt of the latter written declaration, or, if Congress is not in session, within twenty-one days after Congress is required to assemble, determines by two-thirds vote of both Houses that the President is unable to discharge the powers and duties of his office, the Vice President shall continue to discharge the same as Acting President; otherwise, the President shall resume the powers and duties of his office.

Amendment XXVI—Eighteen-year-old Vote (Ratified on July 1, 1971)

Section 1. The right of citizens of the United States, who are eighteen years of age or older, to vote shall not be denied or abridged by the United States or by any State on account of age.

Section 2. The Congress shall have power to enforce this article by appropriate legislation.

Amendment XXVII—Congressional Salaries (Ratified on May 18, 1992)

Section 1. No law varying the compensation for the services of the Senators and Representatives, shall take effect, until an election of Representatives shall have intervened.

Presidents of the United States

YEAR	PRESIDENTIAL CANDIDATES	POLITICAL PARTY	ELECTORAL VOTE	PERCENTAGE OF POPULAR VOTE
1789	**George Washington**	—	69	—
	John Adams		34	
	Others		35	
1792	**George Washington**	—	132	—
	John Adams		77	
	Others		55	
1796	**John Adams**	Federalist	71	—
	Thomas Jefferson	Democratic-Republican	68	
	Thomas Pinckney	Federalist	59	
	Aaron Burr	Anti-Federalist	30	
	Others		48	
1800	**Thomas Jefferson**	Democratic-Republican	73	—
	Aaron Burr	Democratic-Republican	73	
	John Adams	Federalist	65	
	C. C. Pinckney	Federalist	64	
	John Jay	Federalist	1	
1804	**Thomas Jefferson**	Democratic-Republican	162	—
	C. C. Pinckney	Federalist	14	
1808	**James Madison**	Democratic-Republican	122	—
	C. C. Pinckney	Federalist	47	
	George Clinton	Independent-Republican	6	
1812	**James Madison**	Democratic-Republican	128	—
	De Witt Clinton	Fusion	89	
1816	**James Monroe**	Democratic-Republican	183	—
	Rufus King	Federalist	34	
1820	**James Monroe**	Democratic-Republican	231	—
	John Q. Adams	Independent-Republican	1	
1824	**John Q. Adams**	National Republican	84	30.5
	Andrew Jackson	Democratic	99	
	Henry Clay	Democratic-Republican	37	
	W. H. Crawford	Democratic-Republican	41	
1828	**Andrew Jackson**	Democratic	178	56.0
	John Q. Adams	National Republican	83	
1832	**Andrew Jackson**	Democratic	219	55.0
	Henry Clay	National Republican	49	
	William Wirt	Anti-Masonic	7	
	John Floyd	Nullifiers	11	
1836	**Martin Van Buren**	Democratic	170	50.9
	William H. Harrison	Whig	73	
	Hugh L. White	Whig	26	
	Daniel Webster	Whig	14	
1840	**William H. Harrison***	Whig	234	53.0
	Martin Van Buren	Democratic	60	
	(John Tyler, 1841)			
1844	**James K. Polk**	Democratic	170	49.6
	Henry Clay	Whig	105	
1848	**Zachary Taylor***	Whig	163	47.4
	Lewis Cass	Democratic	127	
	(Millard Fillmore, 1850)			

Note: Presidents are shown in boldface.

*Died in office, succeeding vice president shown in parentheses.

YEAR	PRESIDENTIAL CANDIDATES	POLITICAL PARTY	ELECTORAL VOTE	PERCENTAGE OF POPULAR VOTE
1852	**Franklin Pierce**	Democratic	254	50.9
	Winfield Scott	Whig	42	
1856	**James Buchanan**	Democratic	174	45.4
	John C. Fremont	Republican	114	
	Millard Fillmore	American	8	
1860	**Abraham Lincoln**	Republican	180	39.8
	J. C. Breckinridge	Democratic	72	
	Stephen A. Douglas	Democratic	12	
	John Bell	Constitutional Union	39	
1864	**Abraham Lincoln***	Republican	212	55.0
	George B. McClellan	Democratic	21	
	(Andrew Johnson, 1865)			
1868	**Ulysses S. Grant**	Republican	214	52.7
	Horatio Seymour	Democratic	80	
1872	**Ulysses S. Grant**	Republican	286	55.6
	Horace Greeley	Democratic	**	
1876	**Rutherford B. Hayes**	Republican	185	47.9
	Samuel J. Tilden	Democratic	184	
1880	**James A. Garfield***	Republican	214	48.3
	Winfield S. Hancock	Democratic	155	
	(Chester A. Arthur, 1881)			
1884	**Grover Cleveland**	Democratic	219	48.5
	James G. Blaine	Republican	182	
1888	**Benjamin Harrison**	Republican	233	47.8
	Grover Cleveland	Democratic	168	
1892	**Grover Cleveland**	Democratic	277	46.0
	Benjamin Harrison	Republican	145	
	James B. Weaver	People's	22	
1896	**William McKinley**	Republican	271	51.0
	William J. Bryan	Democratic	176	
1900	**William McKinley***	Republican	292	51.7
	William J. Bryan	Democratic	155	
	(Theodore Roosevelt, 1901)			
1904	**Theodore Roosevelt**	Republican	336	56.4
	Alton B. Parker	Democratic	140	
1908	**William H. Taft**	Republican	321	51.6
	William J. Bryan	Democratic	162	
1912	**Woodrow Wilson**	Democratic	435	41.8
	Theodore Roosevelt	Progressive	88	
	William H. Taft	Republican	8	
1916	**Woodrow Wilson**	Democratic	277	49.2
	Charles E. Hughes	Republican	254	
1920	**Warren G. Harding***	Republican	404	60.3
	James M. Cox	Democratic	127	
	(Calvin Coolidge, 1923)			
1924	**Calvin Coolidge**	Republican	382	54.1
	John W. Davis	Democratic	136	
	Robert M. LaFollette	Progressive	13	

**Horace Greeley died between the popular vote and the meeting of the presidential electors.

YEAR	PRESIDENTIAL CANDIDATES	POLITICAL PARTY	ELECTORAL VOTE	PERCENTAGE OF POPULAR VOTE
1928	**Herbert C. Hoover**	Republican	444	58.2
	Alfred E. Smith	Democratic	87	
1932	**Franklin D. Roosevelt**	Democratic	472	57.4
	Herbert C. Hoover	Republican	59	
1936	**Franklin D. Roosevelt**	Democratic	523	60.8
	Alfred M. Landon	Republican	8	
1940	**Franklin D. Roosevelt**	Democratic	449	54.7
	Wendell L. Willkie	Republican	82	
1944	**Franklin D. Roosevelt**[*]	Democratic	432	53.4
	Thomas E. Dewey	Republican	99	
	(Harry S Truman, 1945)			
1948	**Harry S Truman**	Democratic	303	49.5
	Thomas E. Dewey	Republican	189	
	J. Strom Thurmond	States' Rights	39	
1952	**Dwight D. Eisenhower**	Republican	442	55.1
	Adlai E. Stevenson	Democratic	89	
1956	Dwight D. Eisenhower	Republican	457	57.4
	Adlai E. Stevenson	Democratic	73	
1960	**John F. Kennedy**[*]	Democratic	303	49.7
	Richard M. Nixon	Republican	219	
	(Lyndon B. Johnson, 1963)			
1964	**Lyndon B. Johnson**	Democratic	486	61.0
	Barry M. Goldwater	Republican	52	
1968	**Richard M. Nixon**	Republican	301	43.4
	Hubert H. Humphrey	Democratic	191	
	George C. Wallace	American Independent	46	
1972	**Richard M. Nixon**	Republican	520	60.7
	George S. McGovern	Democratic	17	
	(Gerald R. Ford, 1974)‡			
1976	**Jimmy Carter**	Democratic	297	50.1
	Gerald R. Ford	Republican	240	
1980	**Ronald Reagan**	Republican	489	50.7
	Jimmy Carter	Democratic	49	
	John Anderson	Independent	—	
1984	**Ronald Reagan**	Republican	525	58.8
	Walter Mondale	Democratic	13	
1988	**George Bush**	Republican	426	53.4
	Michael Dukakis	Democratic	112	
1992	**Bill Clinton**	Democratic	370	43.0
	George Bush	Republican	168	
	H. Ross Perot	Independent	—	
1996	**Bill Clinton**	Democratic	379	49.2
	Robert Dole	Republican	159	
	H. Ross Perot	Reform	—	
2000	**George W. Bush**	Republican	271	47.9
	Al Gore	Democratic	266	
	Ralph Nader	Green		
	Patrick J. Buchanan	Reform		

†Resigned

‡Appointed vice president

Party Control of the Presidency, Senate, and House of Representatives in the Twentieth Century

			Senate			House		
CONGRESS	YEARS	PRESIDENT	D	R	OTHER*	D	R	OTHER*
57th	1901–03	McKinley T. Roosevelt	29	56	3	153	198	5
58th	1903–05	T. Roosevelt	32	58	—	178	207	—
59th	1905–07	T. Roosevelt	32	58	—	136	250	—
60th	1907–09	T. Roosevelt	29	61	—	164	222	—
61st	1909–11	Taft	32	59	—	172	219	—
62d	1911–13	Taft	42	49	—	228‡	162	1
63d	1913–15	Wilson	51	44	1	290	127	18
64th	1915–17	Wilson	56	39	1	230	193	8
65th	1917–19	Wilson	53	42	1	200	216	9
66th	1919–21	Wilson	48	48‡	1	191	237‡	7
67th	1921–23	Harding	37	59	—	132	300	1
68th	1923–25	Coolidge	43	51	2	207	225	3
69th	1925–27	Coolidge	40	54	1	183	247	5
70th	1927–29	Coolidge	47	48	1	195	237	3
71st	1929–31	Hoover	39	56	1	163	267	1
72d	1931–33	Hoover	47	48	1	216‡	218	1
73d	1933–35	F. Roosevelt	59	36	1	313	117	5
74th	1935–37	F. Roosevelt	69	25	2	322	103	10
75th	1937–39	F. Roosevelt	75	17	4	333	89	13
76th	1939–41	F. Roosevelt	69	23	4	262	169	4
77th	1941–43	F. Roosevelt	66	28	2	267	162	6
78th	1943–45	F. Roosevelt	57	38	1	222	209	4
79th	1945–47	Truman	57	38	1	243	190	2
80th	1947–49	Truman	45	51‡	—	188	246‡	1
81st	1949–51	Truman	54	42	—	263	171	1
82d	1951–53	Truman	48	47	1	234	199	2
83d	1953–55	Eisenhower	47	48	1	213	221	1
84th	1955–57	Eisenhower	48‡	47	1	232‡	203	—
85th	1957–59	Eisenhower	49‡	47	—	234‡	201	—
86th†	1959–61	Eisenhower	64‡	34	—	283‡	154	—
87th	1961–63	Kennedy	64	36	—	263	174	—
88th	1963–65	Kennedy Johnson	67	33	—	258	176	—
89th	1965–67	Johnson	68	32	—	295	140	—
90th	1967–69	Johnson	64	36	—	248	187	—
91st	1969–71	Nixon	58‡	42	—	243‡	192	—
92d	1971–73	Nixon	55‡	45	—	255‡	180	—
93d	1973–75	Nixon Ford	57‡	43	—	243‡	192	—
94th	1975–77	Ford	61‡	38	—	291‡	144	—
95th	1977–79	Carter	62	38	—	292	143	—
96th	1979–81	Carter	59	41	—	277	158	—
97th	1981–83	Reagan	47	53	—	243‡	192	—
98th	1983–85	Reagan	46	54	—	269‡	166	—
99th	1985–87	Reagan	47	53	—	253‡	182	—
100th	1987–89	Reagan	55‡	45	—	258‡	177	—
101st	1989–91	Bush	55‡	45	—	260‡	175	—
102d	1991–93	Bush	56‡	44	—	267‡	167	1
103d	1993–95	Clinton	57	43	—	258	176	1
104th	1995–97	Clinton	46	54	—	202	232	1
105th	1997–99	Clinton	45	55	—	206	228	1
106th	1999–01	Clinton	45	55	—	211	223	1
107th	2001–03	Bush	50	49	1	212	221	2

*Excludes vacancies at beginning of each session. Party balance immediately following election.

†The 437 members of the House in the 86th and 87th Congresses are attributable to the at-large representative given to both Alaska (January 3, 1959) and Hawaii (August 21, 1959) prior to redistricting in 1962.

‡Chamber controlled by party other than that of the president.

D=Democrat R=Republican

Supreme Court Justices Serving in the Twentieth Century

NAME	NOMINATED BY	SERVICE
John M. Harlan	Hayes	1877–1911
Horace Gray	Arthur	1882–1902
Melville W. Fuller*	Cleveland	1888–1910
David J. Brewer	Harrison	1890–1910
Henry B. Brown	Harrison	1890–1906
George Shiras, Jr.	Harrison	1892–1903
Edward D. White	Cleveland	1894–1910
Rufus W. Peckham	Cleveland	1895–1909
Joseph McKenna	McKinley	1898–1925
Oliver W. Holmes	T. Roosevelt	1902–1932
William R. Day	T. Roosevelt	1903–1922
William H. Moody	T. Roosevelt	1906–1910
Horace H. Lurton	Taft	1910–1914
Edward D. White	Taft	1910–1921
Charles E. Hughes	Taft	1910–1916
Willis Van Devanter	Taft	1911–1937
Joseph R. Lamar	Taft	1911–1916
Mahlon Pitney	Taft	1912–1922
James C. McReynolds	Wilson	1914–1941
Louis D. Brandeis	Wilson	1916–1939
John H. Clarke	Wilson	1916–1922
William H. Taft	Harding	1921–1930
George Sutherland	Harding	1922–1938
Pierce Butler	Harding	1922–1939
Edward T. Sanford	Harding	1923–1930
Harlan F. Stone	Coolidge	1925–1941
Charles E. Hughes	Hoover	1930–1941
Owen J. Roberts	Hoover	1930–1945
Benjamin N. Cardozo	Hoover	1932–1938
Hugo L. Black	F. Roosevelt	1937–1971
Stanley F. Reed	F. Roosevelt	1938–1957
Felix Frankfurter	F. Roosevelt	1939–1962
William O. Douglas	F. Roosevelt	1939–1975
Frank Murphy	F. Roosevelt	1940–1949
Harlan F. Stone	F. Roosevelt	1941–1946
James F. Byrnes	F. Roosevelt	1941–1942
Robert H. Jackson	F. Roosevelt	1941–1954
Wiley B. Rutledge	F. Roosevelt	1943–1949
Harold H. Burton	Truman	1945–1958
Fred M. Vinson	Truman	1946–1953
Tom C. Clark	Truman	1949–1967
Sherman Minton	Truman	1949–1956
Earl Warren	Eisenhower	1953–1969
John M. Harlan	Eisenhower	1955–1971
William J. Brennan, Jr.	Eisenhower	1956–1990
Charles E. Whittaker	Eisenhower	1957–1962
Potter Stewart	Eisenhower	1958–1981

*Boldface type indicates service as chief justice.

NAME	NOMINATED BY	SERVICE
Byron R. White	Kennedy	1962–1993
Arthur J. Goldberg	Kennedy	1962–1965
Abe Fortas	Johnson	1965–1969
Thurgood Marshall	Johnson	1967–1991
Warren E. Burger	Nixon	1969–1986
Harry A. Blackmun	Nixon	1970–1994
Lewis F. Powell, Jr.	Nixon	1971–1987
William H. Rehnquist	Nixon	1971–1986
John Paul Stevens	Ford	1975–
Sandra Day O'Connor	Reagan	1981–
William H. Rehnquist	Reagan	1986–
Antonin Scalia	Reagan	1986–
Anthony M. Kennedy	Reagan	1988–
David H. Souter	Bush	1990–
Clarence Thomas	Bush	1991–
Ruth Bader Ginsburg	Clinton	1993–
Stephen G. Breyer	Clinton	1994–

Glossary

A

activation. One of three key consequences of electoral campaigns for voters, in which the voter is activated to contribute money or ring doorbells instead of just voting. See also **reinforcement** and **conversion.**

actual group. That part of the **potential group** consisting of members who actually join. See also **interest group.**

Adarand Constructors v. Pena. A 1995 Supreme Court decision holding that federal programs that classify people by race, even for an ostensibly benign purpose such as expanding opportunities for minorities, should be presumed to be unconstitutional. Such programs must be subject to the most searching judicial inquiry and can survive only if they are "narrowly tailored" to accomplish a "compelling governmental interest."

administrative discretion. The authority of administrative actors to select among various responses to a given problem. Discretion is greatest when routines, or **standard operating procedures,** do not fit a case.

advertising. According to David Mayhew, one of three primary activities undertaken by members of Congress to increase the probability of their reelection. Advertising involves contacts between members and their constituents between elections. See also **credit claiming** and **position taking.**

affirmative action. A policy designed to give special attention to or compensatory treatment to members of some previously disadvantaged group.

agenda. See **policy agenda.**

agents of socialization. Families, schools, television, peer groups, and other influences that contribute to **political socialization** by shaping formal and especially informal learning about politics.

Americans with Disabilities Act of 1990. A law passed in 1990 that requires employers and public facilities to make "reasonable accommodations" for people with disabilities and prohibits discrimination against these individuals in employment.

***amicus curiae* briefs.** Legal briefs submitted by a "friend of the court" for the purpose of raising additional points of view and presenting information not contained in the briefs of the formal parties. These briefs attempt to influence a court's decision.

Anti-Federalists. Opponents of the American Constitution at the time when the states were contemplating its adoption. They argued that the Constitution was a class-based document, that it would erode fundamental liberties, and that it would weaken the power of the states. See also **Federalists** and **U.S. Constitution.**

antitrust policy. A policy designed to ensure competition and prevent monopoly, which is the control of a market by one company.

appellate jurisdiction. The jurisdiction of courts that hear cases brought to them on appeal from lower courts. These courts do not review the factual record, only the legal issues involved. Compare **original jurisdiction.**

appropriations bill. An act of Congress that actually funds programs within limits established by **authorization bills.** Appropriations usually cover one year.

arms race. A tense relationship beginning in the 1950s between the Soviet Union and the United States whereby one side's weaponry became the other side's goad to procure more weaponry, and so on.

Articles of Confederation. The first constitution of the United States, adopted by Congress in 1777 and enacted in 1781. The Articles established a national legislature, the Continental Congress, but most authority rested with the state legislatures.

authorization bill. An act of Congress that establishes, continues, or changes a discretionary government program or an entitlement. It specifies program goals and maximum expenditures for discretionary programs. Compare **appropriations bill.**

B

balance of trade. The ratio of what is paid for imports to what is earned from exports. When more is imported than exported, there is a balance-of-trade deficit.

balanced budget amendment. A proposed amendment to the Constitution that would instruct Congress to hold a national convention to propose to the states a requirement that peacetime federal budgets be balanced. The amendment has been passed in varied forms by the legislatures of nearly two-thirds of the states.

Barron v. Baltimore. The 1833 Supreme Court decision holding that the **Bill of Rights** restrained only the national government, not the states and cities. Almost a century later, the Court first ruled in ***Gitlow v. New York*** that state governments must respect some **First Amendment rights.**

beats. Specific locations from which news frequently eminates, such as Congress or the White House. Most top reporters work a particular beat, thereby becoming specialists in what goes on at that location.

bicameral legislature. A legislature divided into two houses. The U.S. Congress and every American state legislature except Nebraska's are bicameral.

bill. A proposed law, drafted in precise, legal language. Anyone can draft a bill, but only a member of the House of Representatives or the Senate can formally submit a bill for consideration.

Bill of Rights. The first 10 amendments to the **U.S. Constitution,** drafted in response to some of the **Anti-Federalist** concerns. These amendments define such basic liberties as freedom of religion, speech, and press and offer protections against arbitrary searches by the police and being held without talking to a lawyer.

blanket primaries. Elections to select party nominees in which voters are presented with a list of candidates from all the parties. Voters can then select some Democrats and some Republicans if they like. See also **primaries.**

block grants. Federal grants given more or less automatically to states or communities to support broad programs in areas such as community development and social services. Compare **categorical grants.**

broadcast media. Television and radio, as compared with **print media.**

Brown v. Board of Education. The 1954 Supreme Court decision holding that school segregation in Topeka, Kans., was inherently unconstitutional because it violated the **Fourteenth Amendment's** guarantee of **equal protection.** This case marked the end of legal segregation in the United States. See also ***Plessy v. Ferguson.***

budget. A policy document allocating burdens (taxes) and benefits (expenditures). See also **balanced budget amendment.**

budget resolution. A resolution binding Congress to a total expenditure level, supposedly the bottom line of all federal spending for all programs.

bureaucracy. According to Max Weber, a hierarchical authority structure that uses task specialization, operates on the merit principle, and behaves with impersonality. Bureaucracies govern modern states.

C

cabinet. A group of presidential advisers not mentioned in the Constitution, although every president has had one. Today the cabinet is composed of 13 secretaries and the attorney general.

campaign strategy. The master game plan candidates lay out to guide their electoral campaign.

capitalism. An economic system in which individuals and corporations, not the government, own the principal means of production and seek profits. Pure capitalism means the strict noninterference of the government in business affairs. Compare **mixed economy.**

casework. Activities of members of Congress that help constituents as individuals; cutting through bureaucratic red tape to get people what they think they have a right to get. See also **pork barrel.**

categorical grants. Federal grants that can be used only for specific purposes, or "categories," of state and local spending. They come with strings attached, such as nondiscrimination provisions. Compare **block grants.**

caucus (congressional). A group of members of Congress sharing some interest or characteristic. Most are composed of members from both parties and from both houses.

caucus (state party). A meeting of all state party leaders for selecting delegates to the **national party convention.** Caucuses are usually organized as a pyramid.

censorship. Governmental regulation of media content.

census. A valuable tool for understanding demographic changes. The Constitution requires that the government conduct an "actual enumeration" of the population every 10 years. See also **demography.**

Central Intelligence Agency (CIA). An agency created after World War II to coordinate American intelligence activities abroad. It became involved in intrigue, conspiracy, and meddling as well.

chains. See **newspaper chains.**

checks and balances. An important part of the Madisonian model designed to limit government's power by requiring that power be balanced among the different governmental institutions. These institutions continually check one another's activities. This system reflects Madison's goal of setting power against power. See also **separation of powers.**

city manager. An offical appointed by the city council who is responsible for implementing and administrating the council's actions. More than one-third of U.S. cities use the council-manager form of government.

civic duty. The belief that in order to support democratic government, a citizen should always vote.

civil disobedience. A form of **political participation** that reflects a conscious decision to break a law believed to be immoral and to suffer the consequences. See also **protest.**

civil law. The body of law involving cases without a charge of criminality. It concerns disputes between two parties and consists of both statutes and **common law.** Compare **criminal law.**

civil liberties. The legal constitutional protections against government. Although our civil liberties are formally set down in the **Bill of Rights,** the courts, police, and legislatures define their meaning.

civil rights. Policies designed to protect people against arbitrary or discriminitory treatment by government officials or individuals.

Civil Rights Act of 1964. The law that made racial discrimination against any group in hotels, motels, and restaurants illegal and forbade many forms of job discrimination. See also **civil rights movement** and **civil rights policies.**

civil rights movement. A movement that began in the 1950s and organized both African Americans and Whites to end the policies of segregation. It sought to establish equal opportunities in the political and economic sectors and to end policies that erected barriers between people because of race.

civil rights policies. Policies that extend government protection to particular disadvantaged groups. Compare **social welfare policies.**

civil service. A system of hiring and promotion based on the **merit principle** and the desire to create a nonpartisan government service. Compare **patronage.**

class action suits. Lawsuits permitting a small number of people to sue on behalf of all other people similarly situated.

Clean Air Act of 1970. The law that charged the Department of Transportation (DOT) with the responsibility of reducing automobile emissions.

closed primaries. Elections to select party nominees in which only people who have registered in advance with the party can vote for that party's candidates, thus encouraging greater party loyalty. See also **primaries.**

coalition. A group of individuals with a common interest upon which every political party depends. See also **New Deal Coalition.**

coalition government. When two or more parties join together to form a majority in a national legislature. This form of government is quite common in the multiparty systems of Europe.

coattails. See **presidential coattails.**

Cold War. War by other than military means usually emphasizing ideological conflict, such as that between the United States and the Soviet Union from the end of World War II until the 1990s.

collective bargaining. Negotiations between representatives of labor unions and management to determine acceptable working conditions.

collective good. Something of value (money, a tax write-off, prestige, clean air, and so on) that cannot be withheld from a group member.

command-and-control policy. According to Charles Schultze, the existing system of **regulation** whereby government tells business how to reach certain goals, checks that these commands are followed, and punishes offenders. Compare **incentive system.**

commercial speech. Communication in the form of advertising. It can be restricted more than many other types of speech but has been receiving increased protection from the Supreme Court.

commission government. A form of municipal government in which voters elect individuals to serve as city commissioners who will have legislative responsibilities to approve city policies and executive responsibilities to direct a functional area of city government, such as public safety or public works. See also **mayor-council government** and **council-manager government.**

committee chairs. The most important influencers of the congressional agenda. They play dominant roles in scheduling hearings, hiring staff, appointing subcommittees, and managing committee bills when they are brought before the full house.

committees (congressional). See **conference committees, joint committees, select committees,** and **standing committees.**

common law. The accumulation of judicial decisions applied in **civil law** disputes.

comparable worth. The issue raised when women are paid less than men for working at jobs requiring comparable skill.

conference committees. Congressional committees formed when the Senate and the House pass a particular **bill** in different forms. Party leadership appoints members from each house to iron out the differences and bring back a single bill. See also **standing committees, joint committees,** and **select committees.**

Congressional Budget and Impoundment Control Act of 1974. An act designed to reform the congressional budgetary process. Its supporters hoped that it would also make Congress less dependent on the president's budget and better able to set and meet its own budgetary goals.

Congressional Budget Office (CBO). A counterweight to the president's **Office of Management and Budget (OMB).** The CBO advises Congress on the probable consequences of budget decisions and forecasts revenues.

Connecticut Compromise. The compromise reached at the Constitutional Convention that established two houses of Congress: the House of Representatives, in which **representation** is based on a state's share of the U.S. population, and the Senate, in which each state has two representatives. Compare **New Jersey Plan** and **Virginia Plan.**

consensus. Agreement. Consensus is reflected by an opinion distribution in which a large majority see eye to eye.

consent of the governed. According to John Locke, the required basis for government. **The Declaration of Independence** reflects Locke's view that governments derive their authority from the consent of the governed.

conservatives. Those who advocate **conservatism.** Compare **liberals.**

constitution. A nation's basic law. It creates political institutions, assigns or divides powers in government, and often provides certain guarantees to citizens. Constitutions can be either written or unwritten. See also **U.S. Constitution.**

constitutional convention. A method of amending a state constitution in which voters may approve the calling of a convention of state citizens to propose amendments to the state constitution; the proposals are submitted to state voters for approval. See also **initiative** and **legislative proposal.**

constitutional courts. Lower federal courts of original jurisdiction created by Congress by the Judiciary Act of 1789. Compare **legislative courts.**

consumer price index (CPI). The key measure of inflation that relates the rise in prices over time.

containment doctrine. A **foreign policy** strategy advocated by George Kennan that called for the United States to isolate the Soviet Union, "contain" its advances, and resist its encroachments by peaceful means if possible, but by force if necessary.

continuing resolutions. When Congress cannot reach agreement and pass appropriations bills, these resolutions allow agencies to spend at the level of the previous year.

convention. See **national party convention.**

conversion. One of three key consequences of electoral campaigns for voters, in which the voter's mind is actually changed. See also **reinforcement** and **activation.**

cooperative federalism. A system of government in which powers and policy assignments are shared between states and the national government. They may also share costs, administration, and even blame for programs that work poorly. Compare **dual federalism.**

council-manager government. A common form of government used by municipalities in which voters elect a city council (and possibly an independent mayor) to make public policy for the city. The city council, in turn, appoints a professional city manager to serve as chief executive of the city and to administer public policy. See also **mayor-council government** and **commission government.**

Council of Economic Advisors (CEA). A three-member body appointed by the president to advise the president on economic policy.

council of governments (COG). Councils in many areas of the country where officials from various localities meet to discuss mutual problems and plan joint, cooperative action.

county. A political subdivision of state government that has a set of government officers to administer some local services—

often on behalf of the state. Called a *parish* in Louisiana and a *borough* in Alaska. See also **county government.**

county government. A unit of local government that serves as the administrative arm of state government at the local level. It has many social service and record-keeping responsibilities. See also **county.**

court of last resort. The final appeals court in a state, often known as the state "supreme court."

courts. See **constitutional courts, legislative courts, district courts,** and **courts of appeal.**

courts of appeal. Appellate courts empowered to review all final decisions of district courts, except in rare cases. In addition, they also hear appeals to orders of many federal regulatory agencies. Compare **district courts.**

Craig v. Boren. In this 1976 Supreme Court decision, the Court determined that gender classification cases would have a "heightened" or "middle level" of scrutiny. In other words, the courts were to show less deference to gender classifications than to more routine classifications, but more deference than to racial classifications.

credit claiming. According to David Mayhew, one of three primary activities undertaken by members of Congress to increase the probability of their reelection. It involves personal and district service. See also **advertising** and **position taking.**

criminal law. The body of law involving a case in which an individual is charged with violating a specific law. The offense may be harmful to an individual or society and in either case warrants punishment, such as imprisonment or a fine. Compare **civil law.**

crisis. A sudden, unpredictable, and potentially dangerous event requiring the president to play the role of crisis manager.

critical election. An electoral "earthquake" whereby new issues emerge, new coalitions replace old ones, and the majority party is often displaced by the minority party. Critical election periods are sometimes marked by a national crisis and may require more than one election to bring about a new **party era.** See also **party realignment.**

cruel and unusual punishment. Court sentences prohibited by the **Eighth Amendment.** Although the Supreme Court has ruled that mandatory death sentences for certain offenses are unconstitutional, it has not held that the death penalty itself constitutes cruel and unusual punishment. See also ***Furman v. Georgia, Gregg v. Georgia,*** and ***McClesky v. Kemp.***

culture of poverty. Negative attitudes and values toward work, family, and success that condemn the poor to low levels of accomplishment. The view that there is a culture of poverty is most commonly held by **conservatives.**

D

Dartmouth College v. Woodward. The 1819 case in which the Supreme Court held that Dartmouth's charter, as well as the charter of any corporation, is a legal contract that cannot be tampered with by a government.

dealignment. See **party dealignment.**

debate. See **presidential debate.**

debt. See **federal debt.**

Declaration of Independence. The document approved by representatives of the American colonies in 1776 that stated their grievances against the British monarch and declared their independence.

deficit. An excess of federal **expenditures** over federal **revenues.** See also **budget.**

delegate. See **instructed delegate.**

democracy. A system of selecting policymakers and of organizing government so that policy represents and responds to the public's preferences.

democratic theory. See **traditional democratic theory.**

demography. The science of population changes. See also **census.**

Dennis v. United States. A 1951 Supreme Court decision that permitted the government to jail several American Communist Party leaders under the Smith Act, a law forbidding advocacy of the violent overthrow of the U.S. government.

deregulation. The lifting of restrictions on business, industry, and professional activities for which government rules had been established and that bureaucracies had been created to administer.

détente. A slow transformation from conflict thinking to cooperative thinking in **foreign policy** strategy and policymaking. It sought a relaxation of tensions between the superpowers, coupled with firm guarantees of mutual security.

Dillon's Rule. The idea that local governments have only those powers that are explicitly given them by the states. This means that local governments have very little discretion over what policies they pursue or how they pursue them. It was named for Iowa Judge John Dillon, who expressed this idea in an 1868 court decision.

direct democracy. Procedures such as the initiative, the referendum, and the recall, by which voters can have a direct impact on policymaking and the political process by means of the voting booth.

direct mail. A high-tech method of raising money for a political cause or candidate. It involves sending information and requests for money to people whose names appear on lists of those who have supported similar views or candidates in the past.

direct primaries. **Primaries** used to select party nominees for congressional and state offices.

district courts. The 91 federal courts of original jurisdiction. They are the only federal courts in which no trials are held and in which juries may be empaneled. Compare **courts of appeal.**

Dred Scott v. Sandford. The 1857 Supreme Court decision ruling that a slave who had escaped to a free state enjoyed no rights as a citizen and that Congress had no authority to ban slavery in the territories.

dual federalism. A system of government in which both the states and the national government remain supreme within their own spheres, each responsible for some policies. Compare **cooperative federalism.**

due process clause. Part of the **Fourteenth Amendment** guaranteeing that persons cannot be deprived of life, liberty, or property by the United States or state governments without due process of law. See also ***Gitlow v. New York.***

E

earned income tax credit. A "negative income tax" that provides income to very poor individuals in lieu of charging them federal tax.

efficacy. See **political efficacy.**

Eighth Amendment. The constitutional amendment that forbids **cruel and unusual punishment,** although it does not define this phrase. Through the **Fourteenth Amendment,** this **Bill of Rights** provision applies to the states.

elastic clause. The final paragraph of Article I, Section 8, of the Constitution, which authorizes Congress to pass all laws "necessary and proper" to carry out the enumerated powers. See also **implied powers.**

electioneering. Direct group involvement in the electoral process. Groups can help fund campaigns, provide testimony, and get members to work for candidates, and some form **political action committees (PACs).**

electoral college. A unique American institution created by the Constitution that provides for the selection of the president by electors chosen by the state parties. Although the electoral college vote usually reflects a popular majority, the winner-take-all rule gives clout to big states.

electoral mandate. A concept based on the idea that "the people have spoken." It is a powerful symbol in American electoral politics, according legitimacy and credibility to a newly elected president's proposals. See also **mandate theory of politics.**

elite. The upper class in a society that utilizes wealth for political power. According to the **elite and class theory** of government and politics, elites control policies because they control key institutions.

elite theory. A theory of government and politics contending that societies are divided along class lines and that an upper-class elite will rule, regardless of the formal niceties of governmental organization. Compare **hyperpluralism, pluralist theory,** and **traditional democratic theory.**

Endangered Species Act of 1973. This law requires the federal government to protect actively each of the hundreds of species listed as endangered—regardless of the economic effect on the surrounding towns or region.

Engel v. Vitale. The 1962 Supreme Court decision holding that state officials violated the **First Amendment** when they wrote a prayer to be recited by New York's schoolchildren. Compare ***School District of Abington Township, Pennsylvania v. Schempp.***

entitlement programs. Policies for which expenditures are uncontrollable because Congress has in effect obligated itself to pay X level of benefits to Y number of recipients. Each year, Congress's bill is a straightforward function of the X level of benefits times the Y number of beneficiaries. Social Security benefits are an example.

entrepreneur. See **political entrepreneur.**

enumerated powers. Powers of the federal government that are specifically addressed in the Constitution; for Congress, these powers are listed in Article I, Section 8, and include the power to coin money, regulate its value, and impose taxes. Compare **implied powers.**

environmental impact statement (EIS). A report filed with the **Environmental Protection Agency (EPA)** that specifies what environmental effects a proposed policy would have. The **National Environmental Policy Act** requires that whenever any agency proposes to undertake a policy that is potentially disruptive of the environment, the agency must file a statement with the EPA.

Environmental Protection Agency (EPA). An agency of the federal government created in 1970 and charged with administering all the government's environmental legislation. It also administers policies dealing with toxic wastes. The EPA is the largest federal **independent regulatory agency.**

equal opportunity. A policy statement about equality holding that the rules of the game should be the same for everyone. Most of our **civil rights** policies over the past three decades have presumed that equality of opportunity is a public policy goal. Compare **equal results.**

equal protection of the laws. Part of the **Fourteenth Amendment** emphasizing that the laws must provide equivalent "protection" to all people. As one member of Congress said during debate on the amendment, it should provide "equal protection of life, liberty, and property" to all a state's citizens.

equal results. A policy statement about equality holding that government has a duty to help break down barriers to **equal opportunity. Affirmative action** is an example of a policy justified as promoting equal results rather than merely equal opportunities.

Equal Rights Amendment. A constitutional amendment originally introduced in 1923 and passed by Congress in 1978 and sent to the state legislatures for ratification, stating that "equality of rights under the law shall not be denied or abridged by the United States or by any state on account of sex." Despite substantial public support and an extended deadline, the amendment failed to acquire the necessary support from three-fourths of the state legislatures.

establishment clause. Part of the **First Amendment** stating that "Congress shall make no law respecting an establishment of religion."

European Union (EU). An alliance of the major Western European nations that coordinates monetary, trade, immigration, and labor policies, making its members one economic unit. An example of a regional organization.

exclusionary rule. The rule that evidence, no matter how incriminating, cannot be introduced into a trial if it was not constitutionally obtained. The rule prohibits use of evidence obtained through **unreasonable search and seizure.**

executive agency. See **independent executive agency.**

executive orders. Regulations originating from the executive branch. Executive orders are one method presidents can use to control the bureaucracy; more often, though, presidents pass along their wishes through their aides.

exit poll. Public opinion surveys used by major media pollsters to predict electoral winners with speed and precision.

expenditures. Federal spending of **revenues.** Major areas of such spending are social services and the military.

extradition. A legal process whereby an alleged criminal offender is surrendered by the officials of one state to officials of the state in which the crime is alleged to have been committed.

F

facilitator. According to George Edwards, the effective leader who works at the margin of coalition building to recognize and exploit opportunities presented by a favorable configuration of political forces.

factions. Interest groups arising from the unequal distribution of property or wealth that James Madison attacked in ***Federalist Paper No. 10.*** Today's parties or interest groups are what Madison had in mind when he warned of the instability in government caused by factions.

federal debt. All the money borrowed by the federal government over the years and still outstanding. Today the federal debt is about $5 trillion.

Federal Election Campaign Act. A law passed in 1974 for reforming campaign finances. The act created the **Federal Election Commission (FEC),** provided public financing for presidential primaries and general elections, limited presidential campaign spending, required disclosure, and attempted to limit contributions.

Federal Election Commission (FEC). A six-member bipartisan agency created by the **Federal Election Campaign Act** of 1974. The FEC administers the campaign finance laws and enforces compliance with their requirements.

Federal Regulation of Lobbying Act. Passed in 1946, an act requiring congressional lobbyists to register and state their policy goals. According to the Supreme Court, the law applies only to groups whose "principal" purpose is **lobbying.**

Federal Reserve System. The main instrument for making **monetary policy** in the United States. It was created by Congress in 1913 to regulate the lending practices of banks and thus the money supply. The seven members of its Board of Governors are appointed to 14-year terms by the president with the consent of the Senate.

Federal Trade Commission (FTC). The **independent regulatory agency** traditionally responsible for regulating false and misleading trade practices. The FTC has re-cently become active in defending consumer interests through its truth-in-advertising rule and the Consumer Credit Protection Act.

federalism. A way of organizing a nation so that two levels of government have formal authority over the same land and people. It is a system of shared power between units of government. Compare **unitary government.**

Federalist Papers. A collection of 85 articles written by Alexander Hamilton, John Jay, and James Madison under the name "Publius" to defend the Constitution in detail. Collectively, these papers are second only to the **U.S. Constitution** in characterizing the framers' intents.

Federalists. Supporters of the **U.S. Constitution** at the time the states were contemplating its adoption. See also **Anti-Federalists** and **Federalist Papers.**

feminization of poverty. The increasing concentration of poverty among women, especially unmarried women and their children.

Fifteenth Amendment. The constitutional amendment adopted in 1870 to extend **suffrage** to African Americans.

Fifth Amendment. The constitutional amendment designed to protect the rights of persons accused of crimes, including protection against double jeopardy, **self-incrimination,** and punishment without due process of law.

filibuster. A strategy unique to the Senate whereby opponents of a piece of legislation try to talk it to death, based on the tradition of unlimited debate. Today, 60 members present and voting can halt a filibuster.

First Amendment. The constitutional amendment that establishes the four great liberties: freedom of the press, of speech, of religion, and of assembly.

fiscal federalism. The pattern of spending, taxing, and providing grants in the federal system; it is the cornerstone of the national government's relations with state and local governments. See also **federalism.**

fiscal policy. The policy that describes the impact of the federal budget—taxes, spending, and borrowing—on the economy. Unlike **monetary policy,** which is mostly controlled by the **Federal Reserve System,** fiscal policy is almost entirely determined by Congress and the president, who are the budget makers. See also **Keynesian economic theory.**

Food and Drug Administration (FDA). The federal agency formed in 1913 and assigned the task of approving all food products and drugs sold in the United States. All drugs, with the exception of tobacco, must have FDA authorization.

foreign policy. A policy that involves choice taking, like domestic policy, but additionally involves choices about relations with the rest of the world. The president is the chief initiator of foreign policy in the United States.

formula grants. Federal **categorical grants** distributed according to a formula specified in legislation or in administrative regulations.

Fourteenth Amendment. The constitutional amendment adopted after the Civil War that states, "No State shall make or enforce any law which shall abridge the privileges or immunities of citizens of the United States; nor shall any state deprive any person of life, liberty, or property, without due process of law; nor deny to any person within its jurisdiction the **equal protection of the laws.**" See also **due process clause.**

fragmentation. A situation in which responsibility for a policy area is dispersed among several units within the bureaucracy, making the coordination of policies both time consuming and difficult.

free exercise clause. A **First Amendment** provision that prohibits government from interfering with the practice of religion.

free-rider problem. The problem faced by unions and other groups when people do not join because they can benefit from the group's activities without officially joining. The bigger the group, the more serious the free-rider problem. See also **interest group.**

frontloading. The recent tendency of states to hold primaries early in the calendar in order to capitalize on media attention. At one time, it was considered advantageous for a state to choose its delegates late in the primary season so that it could play a decisive role. However, in recent years, votes cast in states that have held late primaries have been irrelevant given that one candidate had already sewn up the nomination early on.

full faith and credit clause. A clause in Article IV, Section 1, of the Constitution requiring each state to recognize the official documents and civil judgments rendered by the courts of other states.

G

gender gap. A term that refers to the regular pattern by which women are more likely to support Democratic candidates. Women tend to be significantly less conservative than men and are more likely to support spending on social services and to oppose the higher levels of military spending.

General Schedule rating. See **GS (General Schedule) rating.**

Gibbons v. Ogden. A landmark case decided in 1824 in which the Supreme Court interpreted very broadly the clause in Article I, Section 8, of the Constitution giving Congress the power to regulate interstate commerce, encompassing virtually every form of commercial activity. The commerce clause has been the constitutional basis for much of Congress's regulation of the economy.

Gideon v. Wainwright. The 1963 Supreme Court decision holding that anyone accused of a felony where imprisonment may be imposed, however poor he or she might be, has a right to a lawyer. See also **Sixth Amendment.**

Gitlow v. New York. The 1925 Supreme Court decision holding that freedoms of press and speech are "fundamental personal rights and liberties protected by the **due process clause** of the **Fourteenth Amendment** from impairment by the states" as well as the federal government. Compare ***Barron v. Baltimore.***

government. The institutions and processes through which **public policies** are made for a society.

governmental corporation. A government organization that, like business corporations, provides a service that could be provided by the private sector and typically charges for its services. The U.S. Postal Service is an example. Compare **independent regulatory agency** and **independent executive agency.**

governor. The elected chief executive of state government who directs the administration of state government and the implementation of public policy in the state.

Gramm-Rudman-Hollings. Named for its sponsors and also known as the Balanced Budget and Emergency Deficit Act, legislation mandating maximum allowable deficit levels each year until 1991, when the budget was to be balanced. In 1987, the balanced budget year was shifted to 1993, but the Act was abandoned in 1991.

grandfather clause. One of the methods used by Southern states to deny African Americans the right to vote. In order to exempt illiterate Whites from taking a literacy test before voting, the clause exempted people whose grandfathers were eligible to vote in 1860, thereby disenfranchising the grandchildren of slaves. The grandfather clause was declared unconstitutional by the Supreme Court in 1913. See also **poll taxes** and **white primary.**

grants. See **categorical grants** and **block grants.**

Gregg v. Georgia. The 1976 Supreme Court decision that upheld the constitutionality of the death penalty, stating that "It is an extreme sanction, suitable to the most extreme of crimes." The court did not, therefore, believe that the death sentence constitutes **cruel and unusual punishment.**

gross domestic product. The sum total of the value of all the goods and services produced in a nation.

GS (General Schedule) rating. A schedule for federal employees, ranging from GS 1 to GS 18, by which salaries can be keyed to rating and experience. See **civil service.**

H

Hatch Act. A federal law prohibiting government employees from active participation in partisan politics.

health maintenance organizations (HMOs). Organizations contracted by individuals or insurance companies to provide health care for a yearly fee. Such network health plans limit the choice of doctors and treatments. About 60 percent of Americans are enrolled in HMOs or similar programs.

high-tech politics. A politics in which the behavior of citizens and policymakers and the political agenda itself are increasingly shaped by technology.

home rule. The practice by which municipalities are permitted by the states to write their own charters and change them without permission of the state legislature, within limits. Today this practice is widely used to organize and modernize municipal government. See also **local charter.**

House Rules Committee. An institution unique to the House of Representatives that reviews all bills (except revenue, budget, and appropriations bills) coming from a House committee before they go to the full House.

House Ways and Means Committee. The House of Representatives committee that, along with the **Senate Finance Committee,** writes the tax codes, subject to the approval of Congress as a whole.

hyperpluralism. A theory of government and politics contending that groups are so strong that government is weakened. Hyperpluralism is an extreme, exaggerated, or perverted form of **pluralism.** Compare **elite and class theory, pluralist theory,** and **traditional democratic theory.**

I

ideology. See **political ideology.**

impacts. See **policy impacts.**

impeachment. The political equivalent of an indictment in criminal law, prescribed by the Constitution. The House of Representatives may impeach the president by a majority vote for "Treason, Bribery, or other high Crimes and Misdemeanors."

implementation. The stage of policymaking between the establishment of a policy and the consequences of the policy for the people whom it affects. Implementation involves translating the goals and objectives of a policy into an operating, ongoing program. See also **judicial implementation.**

implied powers. Powers of the federal government that go beyond those enumerated in the Constitution. The Constitution states that Congress has the power to "make all laws necessary and proper for carrying into execution" the powers enumerated in Article I. Many federal policies are justified on the basis of implied powers. See also ***McCulloch v. Maryland*,** **elastic clause,** and **enumerated powers.**

incentive system. According to Charles Shultze, a more effective and efficient policy than **command-and-control;** in the incentive system, market-like strategies are used to manage public policy.

income. The amount of funds collected between any two points in time. Compare **wealth.**

income distribution. The "shares" of the national income earned by various groups.

income tax. Shares of individual wages and corporate revenues collected by the government. The first income tax was declared unconstitutional by the Supreme Court in 1895, but the **Sixteenth Amendment** explicitly authorized Congress to levy a tax on income. See also **Internal Revenue Service.**

incorporation doctrine. The legal concept under which the **Supreme Court** has nationalized the **Bill of Rights** by making most of its provisions applicable to the states through the **Fourteenth Amendment.**

incrementalism. The belief that the best predictor of this year's **budget** is last year's budget, plus a little bit more (an increment). According to Aaron Wildavsky, "Most of the budget is a product of previous decisions."

incumbents. Those already holding office. In congressional elections, incumbents usually win.

independent executive agency. The government not accounted for by **cabinet** departments, **independent regulatory agencies,** and **government corporations.** Its administrators are typically appointed by the president and serve at the president's pleasure. The Veterans Administration is an example.

independent regulatory agency. A government agency responsible for some sector of the economy, making and enforcing rules supposedly to protect the public interest. It also judges disputes over these rules. The Interstate Commerce Commission is an example. Compare **government corporation** and **independent executive agency.**

individualism. The belief that individuals should be left on their own by the government. One of the primary reasons for the comparatively small scope of American government is the prominence of this belief in American political thought and practice.

industrial policy. An economic policy that advocates the federal government's support of key strategic industries, such as the making of computer chips, and protection of these industries from foreign competition by tariffs and other measures.

INF Treaty. The elimination of intermediate range nuclear forces (INF) through an agreement signed by President Reagan and Mikhail Gorbachev during the May 1988 Moscow summit. It was the first treaty to reduce current levels of nuclear weapons.

inflation. The rise in prices for consumer goods. Inflation hurts some but actually benefits others. Groups such as those who live on fixed incomes are particularly hard hit, while people whose salary increases are tied to the **consumer price index** but whose loan rates are fixed may enjoy increased buying power.

initiative. A process permitted in some states whereby voters may put proposed changes in the state constitution to a vote if sufficient signatures are obtained on petitions calling for such a referendum. See also **legislative proposal** and **constitutional convention.**

instructed delegate. A legislator who mirrors the preferences of his or her constituents. Compare **trustee.**

interdependency. Mutual dependency, in which the actions of nations reverberate and affect one another's economic lifelines.

interest group. An organization of people with shared policy goals entering the policy process at several points to try to achieve those goals. Interest groups pursue their goals in many arenas.

intergenerational equity. The issue of the distribution of government benefits and burdens among the generations and over time. Affected groups include children, the working and middle classes, and the elderly, all of whom are beneficiaries of public policies.

intergovernmental relations. The workings of the federal system—the entire set of interactions among national, state, and local governments.

Internal Revenue Service. The office established to collect federal **income taxes,** investigate violations of the tax laws, and prosecute tax criminals.

investigative journalism. The use of detective-like reporting to unearth scandals, scams, and schemes, putting reporters in adversarial relationships with political leaders.

iron triangles. Entities composed of bureaucratic agencies, interest groups, and congressional committees or subcommittees, which have dominated some areas of domestic policymaking. Iron triangles are characterized by mutual dependency, in which each element provides key services, information, or policy for the others.

isolationism. A **foreign policy** course followed throughout most of our nation's history, whereby the United States has tried to stay out of other nations' conflicts, particularly European wars. Isolationism was reaffirmed by the Monroe Doctrine.

issue. See **political issue.**

item veto. The power possessed by 42 state governors to veto only certain parts of a bill while allowing the rest of it to pass into law.

J

Joint Chiefs of Staff. The commanding officers of the armed services who advise the president on military policy.

joint committees. Congressional committees on a few subject-matter areas with membership drawn from both houses. See also **standing committees, conference committees,** and **select committees.**

judicial activism. A judicial philosophy in which judges make bold policy decisions, even charting new constitutional ground. Advocates of this approach emphasize that the courts can correct pressing needs, especially those unmet by the majoritarian political process.

judicial implementation. How and whether court decisions are translated into actual policy, affecting the behavior of others. The courts rely on other units of government to enforce their decisions.

judicial interpretation. A major informal way in which the Constitution is changed by the courts as they balance citizens' rights against those of the government. See also **judicial review.**

judicial restraint. A judicial philosophy in which judges play minimal policymaking roles, leaving that strictly to the legislatures. Compare **judicial activism.**

judicial review. The power of the courts to determine whether acts of Congress, and by implication the executive, are in accord with the **U.S. Constitution.** Judicial review was established by John Marshall and his associates in ***Marbury v. Madison.*** See also **judicial interpretation.**

jurisdiction. See **original jurisdiction** and **appellate jurisdiction.**

justiciable disputes. A constraint on the courts, requiring that a case must be capable of being settled by legal methods.

K

Keynesian economic theory. The theory emphasizing that government spending and deficits can help the economy weather its normal ups and downs. Proponents of this theory advocate using the power of government to stimulate the economy when it is lagging. See also **fiscal policy.**

Korematsu v. United States. A 1944 Supreme Court decision that upheld as constitutional the internment of more than 100,000 Americans of Japanese descent in encampments during World War II.

L

laissez-faire. The principle that government should not meddle in the economy. See also **capitalism.**

leak. See **news leak.**

legislative courts. Courts established by Congress for specialized purposes, such as the Court of Military Appeals. Judges who serve on these courts have fixed terms and lack the protections of **constitutional court** judges.

legislative oversight. Congress's monitoring of the bureaucracy and its administration of policy, performed mainly through hearings.

legislative proposal. A method of state constitutional revision in which the state legislature offers a proposed change to state voters for approval (or may be used to describe a bill proposed by a legislator). See also **constitutional convention** and **initiative.**

legislative turnover. The rate at which incumbent state legislators leave office by choice or by defeat during a bid for reelection.

legislative veto. The ability of Congress to override a presidential decision. Although the **War Powers Resolution** asserts this authority, there is reason to believe that, if challenged, the Supreme Court would find the legislative veto in violation of the doctrine of separation of powers.

legislators. The elected representatives of state citizens who serve in the state legislature and make public policy.

legitimacy. A characterization of elections by political scientists meaning that they are almost universally accepted as a fair and free method of selecting political leaders. When legitimacy is high, as in the United States, even the losers accept the results peacefully.

Lemon v. Kurtzman. The 1971 Supreme Court decision that established that aid to church-related schools must (1) have a secular legislative purpose (2) have a primary effect that neither advances nor inhibits religion and (3) not foster excessive government entanglement with religion.

libel. The publication of false or malicious statements that damage someone's reputation.

liberalism. A **political ideology** whose advocates prefer a government active in dealing with human needs, support individual rights and liberties, and give higher priority to social needs than to military needs.

lieutenant governor. Often the second-highest executive official in state government, who is elected with the governor as a ticket in some states and is elected separately in others. May have legislative and executive branch responsibilities.

limited government. The idea that certain things are out of bounds for government because of the **natural rights** of citizens. Limited government was central to John Locke's philosophy in the seventeenth century, and it contrasted sharply with the prevailing view of the divine rights of monarchs.

linkage institutions. The channels or access points through which issues and people's policy preferences get on the government's **policy agenda.** In the United States, elections, **political parties, interest groups,** and the **mass media** are the three main linkage institutions.

litigants. The **plaintiff** and the **defendant** in a **case.**

lobbying. According to Lester Milbrath, a "communication, by someone other than a citizen acting on his own behalf, directed to a governmental decisionmaker with the hope of influencing his decision."

local charter. An organizational statement and grant of authority from the state to a local government, much like a state or federal constitution. States sometimes allow municipalities to write their own charters and to change them without permission of the state legislature, within limits. See also **home rule.**

M

majority leader. The principal partisan ally of the Speaker of the House or the party's wheel horse in the Senate. The majority leader is responsible for scheduling bills, influencing committee assignments, and rounding up votes in behalf of the party's legislative positions.

majority rule. A fundamental principle of **traditional democratic theory.** In a democracy, choosing among alternatives requires that the majority's desire be respected. See also **minority rights.**

mandate. See **electoral mandate** and **mandate theory of elections.**

mandate theory of elections. The idea that the winning candidate has a mandate from the people to carry out his or her platforms and politics. Politicians like the theory better than political scientists do.

Mapp v. Ohio. The 1961 Supreme Court decision ruling that the Fourth Amendment's protection against **unreasonable searches and seizures** must be extended to the states as well as the federal government. See also **exclusionary rule.**

Marbury v. Madison. The 1803 case in which Chief Justice John Marshall and his associates first asserted the right of the **Supreme Court** to determine the meaning of the **U.S. Constitution.** The decision established the Court's power of **judicial review** over acts of Congress, in this case the Judiciary Act of 1789.

mass media. Television, radio, newspapers, magazines, and other means of popular communication. They are a key part of **high-tech politics.** See also **broadcast media** and **print media.**

mayor-council government. One of three common forms of municipal government in which voters elect both a mayor and a city council. In the weak mayor form, the city council is more powerful; in the strong mayor form, the mayor is the chief executive of city government. See also **council-manager government.**

McCarthyism. The fear, prevalent in the 1950s, that international communism was conspiratorial, insidious, bent on world domination, and infiltrating American government and cultural institutions. It was named after Senator Joseph McCarthy and flourished after the Korean War.

McCleskey v. Kemp. The 1987 Supreme Court decision that upheld the constitutionality of the death penalty against charges that it violated the **Fourteenth Amendment** because minority defendants were more likely to receive the death penalty that white defendants.

McCulloch v. Maryland. An 1819 Supreme Court decision that established the supremacy of the national government over state governments. In deciding this case, Chief Justice John Marshall and his colleagues held that Congress had certain **implied powers** in addition to the **enumerated powers** found in the Constitution.

McGovern-Fraser Commission. A commission formed at the 1968 Democratic convention in response to demands for reform by minority groups and others who sought better representation.

means-tested-programs. Government programs available only to individuals below a poverty line.

media events. Events purposely staged for the media that nonetheless look spontaneous. In keeping with politics as theater, media events can be staged by individuals, groups, and government officials, especially presidents.

Medicaid. A public assistance program designed to provide health care for poor Americans. Medicaid is funded by both the states and the national government. Compare **Medicare.**

Medicare. A program added to the Social Security system in 1965 that provides hospitalization insurance for the elderly and permits older Americans to purchase inexpensive coverage for doctor fees and other expenses. Compare **Medicaid.**

melting pot. The mixing of cultures, ideas, and peoples that has changed the American nation. The United States, with its history of immigration, has often been called a melting pot.

merit plan. A hybrid system of appointment and election used to select judges in 17 states. In this system the governor appoints the state's judges from a list of recommended persons; an appointed judge then serves a short "trial run" term, after which a retention election is held. If voters approve retention by a majority vote, then the judge continues in office for a lengthy term.

merit principle. The idea that hiring should be based on entrance exams and promotion ratings to produce administration by people with talent and skill. See also **civil service** and compare **patronage.**

Miami Herald Publishing Company v. Tornillo. A 1974 case in which the Supreme Court held that a state could not force a newspaper to print replies from candidates it had criticized, illustrating the limited power of government to restrict the **print media.** See ***Red Lion Broadcasting Company v. FCC.***

Miller v. California. A 1973 Supreme Court decision that avoided defining obscenity by holding that community standards be used to determine whether material is obscene in terms of appealing to a "prurient interest."

minority leader. The principal leader of the minority party in the House of Representatives or in the Senate.

minority majority. The emergence of a non-Caucasian majority, as compared with a white, generally Anglo-Saxon majority. It is predicted that, by about 2060, Hispanic Americans, African Americans, and Asian Americans together will outnumber white Americans.

minority rights. A principle of **traditional democratic theory** that guarantees rights to those who do not belong to majorities and allows that they might join majorities through persuasion and reasoned argument. See also **majority rule.**

Miranda v. Arizona. The 1966 Supreme Court decision that sets guidelines for police questioning of accused persons to protect them against **self-incrimination** and to protect their right to counsel.

mixed economy. An economic system in which the government is deeply involved in economic decisions through its role as regulator, consumer, subsidizer, taxer, employer, and borrower. The United States can be considered a mixed economy. Compare **capitalism.**

monetarism. An economic theory holding that the supply of money is the key to a nation's economic health. Monetarists believe that too much cash and credit in circulation produces inflation. See also **monetary policy.**

monetary policy. Based on **monetarism,** monetary policy is the manipulation of the supply of money in private hands by which the government can control the economy. See also the **Federal Reserve System,** and compare **fiscal policy.**

Motor Voter Act. Passed in 1993, this Act went into effect for the 1996 election. It requires states to permit people to register to vote at the same time they apply for drivers' licenses.

multinational corporations. Large businesses with vast holdings in many countries. Many of these companies are larger than most governments.

municipalities. Another name for *cities,* also known by the legal term *municipal corporations;* denotes a government created by charter granted from the state government or by home rule charter approved by local voters.

N

NAACP v. Alabama. The Supreme Court protected the right to assemble peaceably in this 1958 case when it decided the NAACP did not have to reveal its membership list and thus subject its members to harassment.

narrowcasting. As opposed to the traditional "broadcasting," the appeal to a narrow, particular audience by channels such as ESPN, MTV, and C-SPAN, which focus on a narrow particular interest.

national chairperson. One of the institutions that keeps the party operating between conventions. The national chairperson is responsible for the day-to-day activities of the party and is usually selected by the presidential nominee. See also **national committee.**

national committee. One of the institutions that keeps the party operating between conventions. The national committee is composed of representatives from the states and territories. See also **national chairperson.**

national convention. The meeting of party delegates every four years to choose a presidential ticket and write the party's platform.

National Environmental Policy Act (NEPA). The law passed in 1969 that is the centerpiece of federal environmental policy in the United States. The NEPA established the requirements for **environmental impact statements.**

national health insurance. A compulsory insurance program for all Americans that would have the government finance citizens' medical care. First proposed by President Harry S Truman, the plan has been soundly opposed by the American Medical Association.

National Labor Relations Act. A 1935 law, also known as the Wagner Act, that guarantees workers the right of **collective bargaining,** sets down rules to protect unions and organizers, and created the National Labor Relations Board to regulate labor management relations.

national party convention. The supreme power within each of the parties. The convention meets every four years to nominate the party's presidential and vice-presidential candidates and to write the party's platform.

national primary. A proposal by critics of the **caucuses** and **presidential primaries** systems who would replace these electoral methods with a nationwide **primary** held early in the election year.

National Security Council. An office created in 1947 to coordinate the president's foreign and military policy advisors. Its formal members are the president, vice president, **secretary of state,** and **secretary of defense,** and it is managed by the president's national security advisor.

NATO. See **North Atlantic Treaty Organization.**

natural rights. Rights inherent in human beings, not dependent on governments, which include life, liberty, and property. The concept of natural rights was central to English philosopher John Locke's theories about government, and was widely accepted among America's founding fathers. Thomas Jefferson echoed Locke's language in drafting the Declaration of Independence.

Near v. Minnesota. The 1931 Supreme Court decision holding that the **First Amendment** protects newspapers from **prior restraint.**

necessary and proper clause. See **elastic clause.**

New Deal Coalition. A **coalition** forged by the Democrats, who dominated American politics from the 1930s to the 1960s. Its basic elements were the urban working class, ethnic groups, Catholics and Jews, the poor, Southerners, African Americans, and intellectuals.

New Jersey Plan. The proposal at the Constitutional Convention that called for equal **representation** of each state in Congress regardless of the state's population. Compare **Virginia Plan** and **Connecticut Compromise.**

New York Times v. Sullivan. Decided in 1964, this case established the guidelines for determining whether public officials and public figures could win damage suits for libel. To do so, said the Court, such individuals must prove that the defamatory statements made about them were made with "actual malice" and reckless disregard for the truth.

news leak. A carefully placed bit of inside information given to a friendly reporter. Leaks can benefit both the leaker and the leakee.

newspaper chains. Newspapers published by massive media conglomerates that account for almost three-quarters of the nation's daily circulation. Often these chains control **broadcast media** as well.

Nineteenth Amendment. The constitutional amendment adopted in 1920 that guarantees women the right to vote. See also **suffrage.**

nomination. The official endorsement of a candidate for office by a **political party.** Generally, success in the nomination game requires momentum, money, and media attention.

nonrenewable resources. Minerals and other resources that nature does not replace when they are consumed. Many commonly used energy resources, such as oil and coal, are nonrenewable.

North Atlantic Treaty Organization (NATO). Created in 1949, an organization whose members include the United States, Canada, most Western European nations, and Turkey, all of whom agreed to combine military forces and to treat a war against one as a war against all. Compare **Warsaw Pact.**

O

Office of Management and Budget (OMB). An office that grew out of the Bureau of the Budget, created in 1921, consisting of a handful of political appointees and hundreds of skilled professionals. The OMB performs both managerial and budgetary functions, and although the president is its boss, the director and staff have considerable independence in the budgetary process. See also **Congressional Budget Office.**

Office of Personnel Management (OPM). The office in charge of hiring for most agencies of the federal government, using elaborate rules in the process.

Olson's law of large groups. Advanced by Mancur Olson, a principle stating that "the larger the group, the further it will fall short of providing an optimal amount of a collective good." See also **interest group.**

OPEC. See **Organization of Petroleum Exporting Countries.**

open primaries. Elections to select party nominees in which voters can decide on election day whether they want to participate in the Democratic or Republican contests. See also **primaries.**

opinion. A statement of legal reasoning behind a judicial decision. The content of an opinion may be as important as the decision itself.

Organization of Petroleum Exporting Countries (OPEC). An economic organization, consisting primarily of Arab nations, that controls the price of oil and the amount of oil its members produce and sell to other nations. The Arab members of OPEC caused the oil boycott in the winter of 1973–1974.

original intent. A view that the Constitution should be interpreted according to the original intent of the framers. Many **conservatives** support this view.

original jurisdiction. The jurisdiction of courts that hear a case first, usually in a trial. These are the courts that determine the facts about a case. Compare **appellate jurisdiction.**

oversight. The process of monitoring the bureaucracy and its administration of policy, mainly through congressional hearings.

P

PACs. See **political action committees (PACs).**

parliamentary governments. Governments, like the one in Great Britain, that typically select the political leader from membership in the parliament (the legislature).

participation. See **political participation.**

party. See **political party.**

party competition. The battle of the parties for control of public offices. Ups and downs of the two major parties are one of the most important elements in American politics.

party dealignment. The gradual disengagement of people and politicians from the parties, as seen in part by shrinking **party identification.**

party eras. Historical periods in which a majority of voters cling to the party in power, which tends to win a majority of the elections. See also **critical election** and **party realignment.**

party identification. A citizen's self-proclaimed preference for one party or the other.

party image. The voter's perception of what the Republicans or Democrats stand for, such as **conservatism** or **liberalism.**

party machines. A type of political party organization that relies heavily on material inducements, such as patronage, to win votes and to govern.

party neutrality. A term used to describe the fact that many Americans are indifferent toward the two major political parties. See also **party dealignment.**

party platform. A political party's statement of its goals and policies for the next four years. The platform is drafted prior to the party convention by a committee whose members are chosen in rough proportion to each candidate's strength. It is the best formal statement of what a party believes in.

party realignment. The displacement of the majority party by the minority party, usually during a **critical election period.** See also **party eras.**

patronage. One of the key inducements used by machines. A patronage job, promotion, or contract is one that is given for political reasons rather than for merit or competence alone. Compare **civil service** and the **merit principle.**

Pendleton Civil Service Act. Passed in 1883, an Act that created a federal **civil service** so that hiring and promotion would be based on merit rather than **patronage.**

per curiam decision. A court decision without explanation—in other words, without an **opinion.**

Planned Parenthood v. Casey. A 1992 case in which the Supreme Court loosened its standard for evaluating restrictions on abortion from one of "strict scrutiny" of any restraints on a "fundamental right" to one of "undue burden" that permits considerably more regulation.

plea bargaining. An actual bargain struck between the defendant's lawyer and the prosecutor to the effect that the defendant will plead guilty to a lesser crime (or fewer crimes) in exchange for the state's promise not to prosecute the defendant for a more serious (or additional) crime.

Plessy v. Ferguson. An 1896 Supreme Court decision that provided a constitutional justification for segregation by ruling that a Louisiana law requiring "equal but separate accommodations for the white and colored races" was not unconstitutional.

pluralist theory. A theory of government and politics emphasizing that politics is mainly a competition among groups, each one pressing for its own preferred policies. Compare **elite and class theory, hyperpluralism,** and **traditional democratic theory.**

pocket veto. A veto taking place when Congress adjourns within 10 days of having submitted a **bill** to the president, who simply lets it die by neither signing nor vetoing it. See also **veto.**

policy. See **public policy.**

policy agenda. According to John Kingdon, "the list of subjects or problems to which government officials, and people outside of government closely associated with those officials, are paying some serious attention at any given time."

policy differences. The perception of a clear choice between the parties. Those who see such choices are more likely to vote.

policy entrepreneurs. People who invest their political "capital" in an issue. According to John Kingdon, a policy entrepreneur "could be in or out of government, in elected or appointed positions, in interest groups or re-search organizations."

policy gridlock. A condition that occurs when no coalition is strong enough to form a majority and establish policy. The result is that nothing may get done.

policy impacts. The effects a policy has on people and problems. Impacts are analyzed to see how well a policy has met its goal and at what cost.

policy implementation. See **implementation.**

policymaking institutions. The branches of government charged with taking action on political issues. The U.S. Constitution established three policymaking institutions—the Congress, the presidency, and the courts. Today, the power of the bureaucracy is so great that most political scientists consider it a fourth policymaking institution.

policymaking system. The process by which political problems are communicated by the voters and acted upon by government policymakers. The policymaking system begins with people's needs and expectations for governmental action. When people confront government officials with problems that they want solved, they are trying to influence the government's policy agenda.

policy voting. Voting that occurs when electoral choices are made on the basis of the voters' policy preferences and on the basis of where the candidates stand on policy issues. For the voter, policy voting is hard work.

Political Action Committees (PACs). Funding vehicles created by the 1974 campaign finance reforms. A corporation, union, or some other interest group can create a PAC and register it with the **Federal Election Commission (FEC),** which will meticulously monitor the PAC's expenditures.

political culture. An overall set of values widely shared within a society.

political efficacy. The belief that one's **political participation** really matters—that one's vote can actually make a difference.

political ideology. A coherent set of beliefs about politics, public policy, and public purpose. It helps give meaning to political events, personalities, and policies. See also **liberalism** and **conservatism.**

political issue. An issue that arises when people disagree about a problem and a public policy choice.

political participation. All the activities used by citizens to influence the selection of political leaders or the policies they pursue. The most common, but not the only, means of political participation in a **democracy** is voting. Other means include **protest** and **civil disobedience.**

political party. According to Anthony Downs, a "team of men [and women] seeking to control the governing apparatus by gaining office in a duly constituted election."

political questions. A doctrine developed by the federal courts and used as a means to avoid deciding some cases, principally those involving conflicts between the president and Congress.

political socialization. According to Richard Dawson, "the process through which an individual acquires his [or her] particular political orientations—his [or her] knowledge, feelings, and evaluations regarding his [or her] political world." See also **agents of socialization.**

political system. A set of institutions and activities that link together people, politics, and policy.

politics. According to Harold Lasswell, "who gets what, when, and how." Politics produces authoritative decisions about public issues.

poll taxes. Small taxes, levied on the right to vote, that often fell due at a time of year when poor African-American sharecroppers had the least cash on hand. This method was used by most Southern states to exclude African Americans from voting registers. Poll taxes were declared void by the **Twenty-fourth Amendment** in 1964. See also **grandfather clause** and **white primary.**

polls. See **exit polls.**

pork barrel. The mighty list of federal projects, grants, and contracts available to cities, businesses, colleges, and institutions in the district of a member of Congress.

position taking. According to David Mayhew, one of three primary activities undertaken by members of Congress to increase the probability of their reelection. It involves taking a stand on issues and responding to constituents about these positions. See also **advertising** and **credit taking.**

potential group. All the people who might be **interest group** members because they share some common interest. A potential group is almost always larger than an actual group.

poverty line. A method used to count the number of poor people, it considers what a family would need to spend for an "austere" standard of living.

power. The capacity to get people to do something that they would not otherwise do. The quest for power is a strong motivation to political activity.

precedent. How similar cases have been decided in the past.

presidential approval. An evaluation of the president based on many factors, but especially on the predisposition of many people to support the president. One measure is provided by the Gallup Poll.

presidential coattails. The situation occurring when voters cast their ballots for congressional candidates of the president's party because they support the president. Recent studies show that few races are won this way.

presidential debate. A debate between presidential candidates. The first televised debate was between Richard Nixon and John Kennedy during the 1960 campaign.

presidential primaries. Elections in which voters in a state vote for a candidate (or delegates pledged to him or her). Most delegates to the **national party conventions** are chosen this way.

press conferences. Meetings of public officials with reporters.

press secretary. The person on the White House staff who most often deals directly with the press, serving as a conduit of information. Press secretaries conduct daily press briefings.

primaries. Elections that select candidates. In addition to **presidential primaries,** there are **direct primaries** for selecting party nominees for congressional and state offices and proposals for **regional primaries.**

print media. Newspapers and magazines, as compared with **broadcast media.**

prior restraint. A government's preventing material from being published. This is a common method of limiting the press in some nations, but it is usually unconstitutional in the United States, according to the **First Amendment** and as confirmed in the 1931 Supreme Court case of ***Near v. Minnesota.***

privacy. See **right to privacy.**

privileges and immunities clause. A clause in Article IV, Section 2, of the Constitution according citizens of each state most of the privileges of citizens of other states.

probable cause. The situation occurring when the police have reason to believe that a person should be arrested. In making the arrest, the police are allowed legally to search for and seize incriminating evidence. Compare **unreasonable searches and seizures.**

progressive tax. A tax by which the government takes a greater share of the **income** of the rich than of the poor—for example, when a rich family pays 50 percent of its income in taxes and a poor family pays 5 percent. Compare **regressive tax** and **proportional tax.**

project grants. Federal grants given for specific purposes and awarded on the basis of the merits of applications. A type of the **categorical grants** available to states and localities.

proportional representation. An electoral system used throughout most of Europe that awards legislative seats to political parties in proportion to the number of votes won in an election. Compare with **winner-take-all system.**

proportional tax. A tax by which the government takes the same share of income from everyone, rich and poor alike—for example, when a rich family pays 20 percent and a poor family pays 20 percent. Compare **progressive tax** and **regressive tax.**

protest. A form of **political participation** designed to achieve policy change through dramatic and unconventional tactics. See also **civil disobedience.**

public goods. Goods, such as clean air and clean water, that everyone must share.

public interest. The idea that there are some interests superior to the private interest of groups and individuals, interests we all have in common. See also **public interest lobbies.**

public interest lobbies. According to Jeffrey Berry, organizations that seek "a collective good, the achievement of which will not selectively and materially benefit the membership or activities of the organization." See also **lobbying** and **public interest.**

public opinion. The distribution of the population's beliefs about politics and policy issues.

public policy. A choice that **government** makes in response to a political issue. A policy is a course of action taken with regard to some problem.

R

random digit dialing. A technique used by pollsters to place telephone calls randomly to both listed and unlisted numbers when conducting a survey. See also **random sampling.**

random sampling. The key technique employed by sophisticated survey researchers, which operates on the principle that everyone should have an equal probability of being selected for the sample. See also **sample.**

rational-choice theory. A popular theory in political science to explain the actions of voters as well as politicians. It assumes that individuals act in their own best interest, carefully weighing the costs and benefits of possible alternatives.

realignment. See **party realignment.**

reapportionment. The process of reallocating seats in the House of Representatives every 10 years on the basis of the results of the census.

recall. A procedure that allows voters to call a special election for a specific official in an attempt to throw him or her out of office before the end of his or her term. Recalls are only permitted in 17 states, are seldom used because of their cost and disruptiveness, and are rarely successful.

reconciliation. A congressional process through which program authorizations are revised to achieve required savings. It usually also includes tax or other revenue adjustments.

Red Lion Broadcasting Company v. FCC. A 1969 case in which the Supreme Court upheld restrictions on radio and television broadcasting, such as giving adequate coverage to public issues and covering opposing views. These restrictions on the **broadcast media** are much tighter than those on the **print media** because there are only a limited number of broadcasting frequencies available. See ***Miami Herald Publishing Company v. Tornillo.***

Reed v. Reed. The landmark case in 1971 in which the Supreme Court for the first time upheld a claim of gender discrimination.

referendum. A state-level method of direct legislation that gives voters a chance to approve or disapprove legislation or a constitutional amendment proposed by the state legislature.

Regents of the University of California v. Bakke. A 1978 Supreme Court decision holding that a state university could not admit less qualified individuals solely because of their race. The Court did not, however, rule that such **affirmative action** policies and the use of race as a criterion for admission were unconstitutional, only that they had to be formulated differently.

regional primaries. A proposal by critics of the **caucuses** and **presidential primaries** to replace these electoral methods with a series of primaries held in each geographic region.

registration. See **voter registration.**

regressive tax. A tax in which the burden falls relatively more heavily upon low-income groups than upon wealthy taxpayers. The opposite of a **progressive tax,** in which tax rates increase as income increases.

regulation. The use of governmental authority to control or change some practice in the private sector. Regulations pervade the daily lives of people and institutions.

regulatory agency. See **independent regulatory agency.**

reinforcement. One of three key consequences of electoral campaigns for voters, in which the voter's candidate preference is reinforced. See also **activation** and **conversion.**

relative deprivation. A perception by a group that it is doing less well than is appropriate in relation to a reference group. The desire of a group to correct what it views as the unfair distribution of resources, such as income or government benefits, is a frequent motivator for political activism.

representation. A basic principle of **traditional democratic theory** that describes the relationship between the few leaders and the many followers.

republic. A form of government that derives its power, directly or indirectly, from the people. Those chosen to govern are accountable to those whom they govern. In contrast to a direct democracy, in which people themselves make laws, in a republic the people select representatives who make the laws.

responsible party model. A view favored by some political scientists about how parties should work. According to the model, parties should offer clear choices to the voters, who can then use those choices as cues to their own preferences of candidates. Once in office, parties would carry out their campaign promises.

retrospective voting. A theory of voting in which voters essentially ask this simple question: "What have you done for me lately?"

revenues. The financial resources of the federal government. The individual income tax and Social Security tax are two major sources of revenue. Compare **expenditures.**

right to privacy. According to Paul Bender, "the right to keep the details of [one's] life confidential; the free and untrammeled use and enjoyment of one's intellect, body, and private property . . . the right, in sum, to a private personal life free from the intrusion of government or the dictates of society." The right to privacy is implicitly protected by the **Bill of Rights.** See also **Privacy Act.**

right-to-work law. A state law forbidding requirements that workers must join a union to hold their jobs. State right-to-work laws were specifically permitted by the Taft-Hartley Act of 1947.

Roe v. Wade. The 1973 Supreme Court decision holding that a state ban on all abortions was unconstitutional. The decision forbade state control over abortions during the first trimester of pregnancy, permitted states to limit abortions to protect the mother's health in the second trimester, and permitted states to protect the fetus during the third trimester.

Roth v. United States. A 1957 Supreme Court decision ruling that "obscenity is not within the area of constitutionally protected speech or press."

S

sample. A relatively small proportion of people who are chosen in a survey so as to be representative of the whole.

sampling error. The level of confidence in the findings of a public opinion poll. The more people interviewed, the more confident one can be of the results.

Schenck v. United States. A 1919 decision upholding the conviction of a socialist who had urged young men to resist the draft during World War I. Justice Holmes declared that government can limit speech if the speech provokes a "clear and present danger" of substantive evils.

School District of Abington Township, Pennsylvania v. Schempp. A 1963 Supreme Court decision holding that a Pennsylvania law requiring Bible reading in schools violated the **establishment clause** of the **First Amendment.** Compare ***Engel v. Vitale.***

school districts. Units of local government that are normally independent of any other local government and are primarily responsible for operating public schools.

search warrant. A written authorization from a court specifying the area to be searched and what the police are searching for. The Fourth Amendment requires a search warrant to prevent **unreasonable searches and seizures.**

secretary of defense. The head of the Department of Defense and the president's key adviser on military policy; a key **foreign policy** actor.

secretary of state. The head of the Department of State and traditionally a key adviser to the president on **foreign policy.**

select committees. Congressional committees appointed for a specific purpose, such as the Watergate investigation. See also **joint committees, standing committees,** and **conference committees.**

selective benefits. Goods (such as information publications, travel discounts, and group insurance rates) that a group can restrict to those who pay their yearly dues.

selective perception. The phenomenon that people often pay the most attention to things they already agree with and interpret them according to their own predispositions.

self-incrimination. The situation occurring when an individual accused of a crime is compelled to be a witness against himself or herself in court. The **Fifth Amendment** forbids self-incrimination. See also ***Miranda v. Arizona.***

Senate Finance Committee. The Senate committee that, along with the **House Ways and Means Committee,** writes the tax codes, subject to the approval of Congress as a whole.

senatorial courtesy. An unwritten tradition whereby nominations for state-level federal judicial posts are not confirmed if they are opposed by the senator from the state in which the nominee will serve. The tradition also applies to courts of appeal when there is opposition from the nominee's state senator, if the senator belongs to the president's party.

Senior Executive Service (SES). An elite cadre of about 11,000 federal government managers, established by the Civil Service Reform Act of 1978, who are mostly career officials but include some political appointees who do not require Senate confirmation.

seniority system. A simple rule for picking **committee chairs,** in effect until the 1970s. The member who had served on the committee the longest and whose party controlled Congress became chair, regardless of party loyalty, mental state, or competence.

separation of powers. An important part of the **Madisonian model** that requires each of the three branches of government—executive, legislative, and judicial—to be relatively independent of the others so that one cannot control the others. Power is shared among these three institutions. See also **checks and balances.**

Shays' Rebellion. A series of attacks on courthouses by a small band of farmers led by revolutionary war Captain Daniel Shays to block foreclosure proceedings.

Simpson-Mazzoli Act. An immigration law, named after its legislative sponsors, that as of June 1, 1987, requires employees to document the citizenship of their employees. Civil and criminal penalties can be assessed against employers who knowingly employ illegal immigrants.

single-issue groups. Groups that have a narrow interest, tend to dislike compromise, and often draw membership from people new to politics. These features distinguish them from traditional **interest groups.**

Sixteenth Amendment. The constitutional amendment adopted in 1915 that explicitly permitted Congress to levy an **income tax.**

Sixth Amendment. The constitutional amendment designed to protect individuals accused of crimes. It includes the right to counsel, the right to confront witnesses, and the right to a speedy and public trial.

social policies. Policies that manipulate opportunities through public choice. They include policies related to income and policies related to opportunity.

Social Security Act. A 1935 law passed during the Great Depression that was intended to provide a minimal level of sustenance to older Americans and thus save them from poverty.

social welfare policies. Policies that provide benefits to individuals, particularly to those in need. Compare **civil rights policies.**

socialized medicine. A system in which the full cost of medical care is borne by the national government. Great Britain and the former Soviet Union are examples of countries that have socialized medicine. Compare **Medicaid** and **Medicare.**

soft money. Political contributions earmarked for party-building expenses at the grass-roots level (or for generic party advertising). Unlike money that goes to the campaign of a particular candidate, such party donations are not subject to contribution limits.

solicitor general. A presidential appointee and the third-ranking office in the Department of Justice. The solicitor general is in charge of the appellate court litigation of the federal government.

sound bites. Short video clips of approximately 15 seconds, which are typically all that is shown from a politician's speech or activities on the nightly television news.

Speaker of the House. An office mandated by the Constitution. The Speaker is chosen in practice by the majority party, has both formal and informal powers, and is second in line to succeed to the presidency should that office become vacant.

special districts. Limited-purpose local governments called *districts* or *public authorities* that are created to run a specific type of service, such as water distribution, airports, public transportation, libraries, and natural resource areas.

standard operating procedures. Better known as SOPs, these procedures are used by bureaucrats to bring uniformity to complex organizations. Uniformity improves fairness and makes personnel interchangeable. See also **administrative discretion.**

standing committees. Separate subject-matter committees in each house of Congress that handle **bills** in different policy areas. See also **joint committees, conference committees,** and **select committees.**

standing to sue. The requirement that **plaintiffs** have a serious interest in a **case,** which depends on whether they have sustained or are likely to sustain a direct and substantial injury from a party or an action of government.

stare decisis. A Latin phrase meaning "let the decision stand." The vast majority of cases reaching appellate courts are settled on this principle.

statutory construction. The judicial interpretation of an act of Congress. In some cases where statutory construction is an issue, Congress passes new legislation to clarify existing laws.

Strategic Defense Initiative (SDI). Renamed "Star Wars" by critics, a plan for defense against the Soviet Union unveiled by President Reagan in 1983. SDI would create a global umbrella in space, using computers to scan the skies and high-tech devices to destroy invading missiles.

street-level bureaucrats. A phrase coined by Michael Lipsky, referring to those bureaucrats who are in constant contact with the public and have considerable **administrative discretion.**

subgovernments. A network of groups within the American political system which exercise a great deal of control over specific policy areas. Also known as iron triangles, subgovernments are composed of interest group leaders interested in a particular policy, the government agency in charge of administering that policy, and the members of congressional committees and subcommittees handling that policy.

subnational governments. Another way of referring to state and local governments. Through a process of reform, modernization, and changing intergovernmental relations since the 1960s, subnational governments have assumed new responsibilities and importance.

suffrage. The legal right to vote, extended to African Americans by the **Fifteenth Amendment,** to women by the **Nineteenth Amendment,** and to people over the age of 18 by the **Twenty-sixth Amendment.**

Super Tuesday. Created by a dozen or so Southern states when they held their **presidential primaries** in early March 1988. These states hoped to promote a regional advantage as well as a more conservative candidate.

superdelegates. National party leaders who automatically get a delegate slot at the Democratic **national party convention.**

Superfund. A fund created by Congress in the late 1970s and renewed in the 1980s to clean up hazardous waste sites. Money for the fund comes from taxing chemical products.

supply-side economics. An economic theory, advocated by President Reagan, holding that too much income goes to taxes and too little money is available for purchasing and that the solution is to cut taxes and return purchasing power to consumers.

supremacy clause. Article VI of the Constitution, which makes the Constitution, national laws, and treaties supreme over state laws when the national government is acting within its constitutional limits.

Supreme Court. The pinnacle of the American judicial system. The Court ensures uniformity in interpreting national laws, resolves conflicts among states, and maintains national supremacy in law. It has both **original jurisdiction** and **appellate jurisdiction,** but unlike other federal courts, it controls its own agenda.

symbolic speech. Nonverbal communication, such as burning a flag or wearing an armband. The Supreme Court has accorded some symbolic speech protection under the **First Amendment.** See ***Texas v. Johnson.***

T

Taft-Hartley Act. A 1947 law giving the president power to halt major strikes by seeking a court injunction and permitting states to forbid requirements in labor contracts forcing workers to join a union. See also **right-to-work law.**

talking head. A shot of a person's face talking directly to the camera. Because this is visually unappealing, the major commercial networks rarely show a politician talking one-on-one for very long. See also **sound bites.**

tariff. A special tax added to imported goods to raise the price, thereby protecting American businesses and workers from foreign competition.

tax. See **proportional tax, progressive tax,** and **regressive tax.**

tax expenditures. Defined by the 1974 Budget Act as "revenue losses attributable to provisions of the federal tax laws which allow a special exemption, exclusion, or deduction." Tax expenditures represent the difference between what the government actually collects in taxes and what it would have collected without special exemptions.

tax incidence. The proportion of its income a particular group pays in taxes.

Temporary Assistance to Needy Families. Once called "Aid to Families with Dependent Children," the new name for public assistance to needy families.

Tenth Amendment. The constitutional amendment stating that "The powers not delegated to the United States by the Constitution, nor prohibited by it to the states, are reserved to the states respectively, or to the people."

term limits. Laws to restrict legislators from serving more than a fixed number of years or terms in office. Since 1990, 21 states have adopted term limits for state legislators. Although similar term limits have been proposed for federal legislators (senators and representatives), a constitutional amendment on term limitations has twice failed to pass Congress, and the Supreme Court ruled in 1995 that state-imposed term limits on members of Congress were unconstitutional.

Texas v. Johnson. A 1989 case in which the Supreme Court struck down a law banning the burning of the American flag on the grounds that such action was **symbolic speech** protected by the **First Amendment.**

third parties. Electoral contenders other than the two major parties. American third parties are not unusual, but they rarely win elections.

Thirteenth Amendment. The constitutional amendment passed after the Civil War that forbade slavery and involuntary servitude.

ticket-splitting. Voting with one party for one office and with another party for other offices. It has become the norm in American voting behavior.

town meeting. A special form of direct democracy under which all voting-age adults in a community gather once a year to make public policy. Now only used in a few villages in upper New England, originally many municipalities in the United States were run by town meeting. The growth of most cities has made them too large for this style of governance.

township. A political subdivision of local government that is found in 20 states and often serves to provide local government services in rural areas. It is a particularly strong form of local government—comparable to a municipality—in the Northeast.

traditional democratic theory. A theory about how a democratic government makes its decisions. According to Robert Dahl, its cornerstones are equality in voting, effective participation, enlightened understanding, final control over the agenda, and inclusion.

transfer payments. Benefits given by the government directly to individuals. Transfer payments may be either cash transfers, such as Social Security payments and retirement payments to former government employees, or in-kind transfers, such as food stamps and low-interest loans for college education.

transnational corporations. Businesses with vast holdings in many countries—such as Microsoft, Coca-Cola, and McDonald's—many of which have annual budgets exceeding that of many foreign governments.

trial balloons. An intentional **news leak** for the purpose of assessing the political reaction.

trial courts. The lowest tier in the trial court system, in which the facts of a case are considered. These courts hear both civil and criminal matters.

trustee. A legislator who uses his or her best judgment to make policy in the interests of the people. This concept was favored by Edmund Burke. Compare **instructed delegate.**

Twenty-fifth Amendment. Passed in 1951, the amend-ment that permits the vice president to become acting president if both the vice president and the president's cabinet determine that the president is disabled. The amendment also outlines how a recuperated president can reclaim the job.

Twenty-fourth Amendment. The constitutional amendment passed in 1964 that declared **poll taxes** void.

Twenty-second Amendment. Passed in 1951, the amendment that limits presidents to two terms of office.

U

uncontrollable expenditures. Expenditures that are determined by how many eligible beneficiaries there are for some particular program. According to Lance LeLoup, an expenditure is classified as uncontrollable "if it is mandated under current law or by a previous obligation." Three-fourths of the federal **budget** is uncontrollable. Congress can change uncontrollable expenditures only by changing a law or existing benefit levels.

unemployment rate. As measured by the Bureau of Labor Statistics (BLS), the proportion of the labor force actively seeking work but unable to find jobs.

unfunded mandates. When the federal government requires state and local action but does not provide the funds to pay for the action.

union shop. A provision found in some collective bargaining agreements requiring all employees of a business to join the union within a short period, usually 30 days, and to remain members as a condition of employment.

unitary government. A way of organizing a nation so that all power resides in the central government. Most governments today, including those of Great Britain and Japan, are unitary governments. Compare **federalism.**

United Nations (UN). Created in 1945, an organization whose members agree to renounce war and to respect certain human and economic freedoms. The seat of real power in the UN is the Security Council.

United States v. Nixon. The 1974 case in which the Supreme Court unanimously held that the doctrine of executive privilege was implicit in the Constitution but could not be extended to protect documents relevant to criminal prosecutions.

unreasonable searches and seizures. Obtaining evidence in a haphazard or random manner, a practice prohibited by the Fourth Amendment. Both **probable cause** and a **search warrant** are required for a legal and proper search for and seizure of incriminating evidence.

unwritten constitution. The body of tradition, practice, and procedure that is as important as the written constitution. Changes in the unwritten **constitution** can change the spirit of the Constitution. **Political parties** and **national party conventions** are a part of the unwritten constitution in the United States.

urban underclass. The poorest of the poor in America. These are the Americans whose economic opportunities are severely limited in almost every way. They constitute a large percentage of the Americans afflicted by homelessness, crime, drugs, alcoholism, unwanted pregnancies, and other endemic social problems.

U.S. Constitution. The document written in 1787 and ratified in 1788 that sets forth the institutional structure of U.S. government and the tasks these institutions perform. It replaced the Articles of Confederation. See also **constitution** and **unwritten constitution.**

V

veto. The constitutional power of the president to send a **bill** back to Congress with reasons for rejecting it. A two-thirds vote in each house can override a veto. See also **legislative veto** and **pocket veto.**

Virginia Plan. The proposal at the Constitutional Convention that called for *representation* of each state in Congress in proportion to that state's share of the U.S. population. Compare **Connecticut Compromise** and **New Jersey Plan.**

voter registration. A system adopted by the states that requires voters to register well in advance of election day. A few states permit election day registration.

Voting Rights Act of 1965. A law designed to help end formal and informal barriers to African-American **suffrage.** Under the law, federal registrars were sent to Southern states and counties that had long histories of discrimination; as a result, hundreds of thousands of African Americans were registered and the number of African-American elected officials increased dramatically.

W

War Powers Resolution. A law, passed in 1973 in reaction to American fighting in Vietnam and Cambodia, requiring presidents to consult with Congress whenever possible prior to using military force and to withdraw forces after 60 days unless Congress declares war or grants an extension. Presidents view the resolution as unconstitutional. See also **legislative veto.**

Water Pollution Control Act of 1972. A law intended to clean up the nation's rivers and lakes. It requires municipal, industrial, and other polluters to secure permits from the **Environmental Protection Agency** for discharging waste products into waters. According to the law, polluters are supposed to use "the best practicable [pollution] control technology."

Watergate. The events and scandal surrounding a break-in at the Democratic National Committee headquarters in 1972 and the subsequent cover-up of White House involvement, leading to the eventual resignation of President Nixon under the threat of **impeachment.**

wealth. The amount of funds already owned. Wealth includes stocks, bonds, bank deposits, cars, houses, and so forth. Throughout most of the last generation, wealth has been much less evenly divided than **income.**

whips. Party leaders who work with the **majority leader** or **minority leader** to count votes beforehand and lean on waverers whose votes are crucial to a **bill** favored by the party.

white primary. One of the means used to discourage African-American voting that permitted political parties in the heavily Democratic South to exclude African Americans from primary elections, thus depriving them of a voice in the real contests. The Supreme Court declared white primaries unconstitutional in 1941. See also **grandfather clause** and **poll taxes.**

winner-take-all system. An electoral system in which legislative seats are awarded only to the candidates who come in first in their constituencies. In American presidential elections, the system in which the winner of the popular vote in a state receives all the electoral votes of that state. Compare with **proportional representation.**

writ of certiorari. A formal document issued from the **Supreme Court** to a lower federal or state court that calls up a case.

writ of habeas corpus. A court order requiring jailers to explain to a judge why they are holding a prisoner in custody.

writ of mandamus. A court order forcing action. In the dispute leading to ***Marbury v. Madison,*** Marbury and his associates asked the **Supreme Court** to issue a writ ordering Madison to give them their commissions.

Z

Zurcher v. Stanford Daily. A 1978 Supreme Court decision holding that a proper **search warrant** could be applied to a newspaper as well as to anyone else without necessarily violating the **First Amendment** rights to freedom of the press.

Key Terms in Spanish

A
activation—acción y efecto de activar
actual group—grupo actual
administrative discretion—discreción administrativa
affirmative action—acción afirmativa
Americans with Disabilities Act of 1990—disposición legal de 1990 para ciudadanos americanos minusválidos
amicus curiae briefs—instrucciones, informes, de la competencia de amigos del senado.
Anti-Federalists—anti-federalistas
antitrust policy—política antimonopolio
appellate jurisdiction—jurisdicción apelatoria
appropriations bill—proyecto de ley de apropiación
arms race—carrera armamentista
Articles of Confederation—Artículos de la Confederación
authorization bill—estatuto de autorización

B
balance of trade—balance de intercambio comercial
beats—v. derrotar; recorrido de vigilancia policiaca
bicameral legislature—legislatura bi-camaral
Bill of Rights—proyecto de ley de derechos
bill—proyecto de ley; moción; cuenta
blanket primaries—cubiertas primarias
block grants—otorgamientos en conjunto
broadcast media—medios de transmisión
budget—presupuesto
budget resolution—resolución de presupuesto
bureaucracy—burocracia

C
cabinet—gabinete
campaign strategy—estrategia de campaña
capitalism—capitalismo
casework—trabajo de asistencia social
categorical grants—concesiones categorizadas
caucus—reunión del comité central o asamblea local de un partido
censorship—censura
census—censo
Central Intelligence Agency (CIA)—Agencia Central de Inteligencia
chains (newspaper chains)—cadena (cadenas periodísticas)
checks and balances—cheques y balances
city manager—aministrador de la ciudad
civic duty—deber cívico
civil disobedience—desobediencia civil
civil liberties—libertades civiles
civil rights—derechos civiles
Civil Rights Act of 1964—ley de Derechos Humanos de 1964
civil rights movement—movimiento de derechos civiles
civil service—administración pública
class action lawsuits—demanda colectiva
Clean Air Act of 1970—ley contra la contaminación del aire de 1970
closed primaries—primarias cerradas
coalition—coalición
coalition government—coalición de gobierno
cold war—guerra fría
collective bargaining—negociación colectiva
collective good—bienestar colectivo
command-and-control policy—política de ordenamiento y control
commercial speech—discurso comercial
committee chairs—presidentes de comité
comparable worth—valor comparable
conference committees—comités de conferencias
Congressional Budget and Impoundment Control Act of 1974—Ley del Presupuesto e Incautación del Congreso de 1974
Congressional Budget Office (CBO)—Oficina de Presupuesto del Congreso
Connecticut Compromise—Compromiso de Connecticut
consent of the governed—consentimiento del gobernado
conservatives—conservadores
Constitution—constitución
consumer price index (CPI)—índice de precios del consumidor
containment doctrine—doctrina o política de contención
continuing resolutions—resoluciones continuas
conversion—conversión
cooperative federalism—federalismo cooperativo
Council of Economic Advisors (CEA)—Consejo de Asesores Económicos
council of governments—consejo de gobiernos
courts of appeal—corte de apelación
crisis—crisis
critical election—elección crítica
cruel and unusual punishment—castigo cruel e inusual
culture of poverty—cultura de pobreza

D
Declaration of Independence—Declaración de Independencia
deficit—déficit
democracy—democracia
demography—demografía
deregulation—desregular, liberalizar
détente—relajación
Dillon's Rule—Regla de Dillon
direct democracy—democracia directa
direct mail—correo directo
district courts—juzgado de distrito
dual federalism—federalismo dual

E
Eighth Amendment—Octava Enmienda (constitucional)
elastic clause—cláusula flexible
electioneering—campaña electoral
electoral college—colegio electoral
elite theory—teoría de la élite

Endangered Species Act of 1973—Ley de Especies en Peligro de Extinción de 1973
entitlements—derechos
enumerated powers—poderes enumerados
Environmental Protection Agency (EPA)—Agencia de Protección al Ambiente
environmental impact statement (EIS)—declaración de impacto sobre el ambiente
Equal Rights Amendment—enmienda de Igualdad de Derechos
equal protection of the laws—igualdad de protección de la ley
establishment clause—cláusula de instauración
European Union (EU)—Unión Europea
exclusionary rule—regla de exclusión
executive orders—órdenes ejecutivas
exit poll—conteo de salida de votación
expenditures—gastos
extradition—extradición

F
factions—facciones
Federal Election Campaign Act—Ley de la Campaña Federal de Elección
Federal Election Commission (FEC)—Comisión Federal Electoral
Federal Reserve System—Sistema Federal de Reserva
Federal Trade Commission (FTC)—Comisión Federal de Comercio
federal debt—deuda federal
federalism—federalismo
Federalist Papers—Documentos Federalistas
Federalists—federalistas
Fifteenth Amendment—Quinceava Enmienda
Fifth Amendment—Enmienda Quinta
filibuster—intervención parlamentaria con objeto de impedir una votación
First Amendment—Enmienda Primera
fiscal federalism—federalismo fiscal
fiscal policy—política fiscal
Food and Drug Administration (FDA)—Departamento Administrativo de Alimentos y Estupefacientes
foreign policy—política extranjera
formula grants—fórmula de concesión
Fourteenth Amendment—Catorceava Enmienda
free exercise clause—cláusula de ejercicio libre
free-rider problem—problema de polizón
frontloading—carga frontal
full faith and credit—fe y crédito completo

G
gender gap—disparidad de género
government—gobierno
government corporations—corporaciones gubernamentales
gross domestic product—producto doméstico bruto
GS (General Schedule) rating—prorrateo programático general

H
Hatch Act—Ley Hatch
health maintenance organization (HMO)—Organización para el Manteniento de la Salud
high-tech politics—política sobre alta tecnología
home rule—regla de casa (local)
House Rules Committee—Comité de Reglas de la Cámara
House Ways and Means Committee—Comité de Formas y Medios de la Cámara
hyperpluralism—hiperpluralismo; pluralismo en exceso

I
impeachment—juicio de impugnación
implied powers—poderes implícitos
incentive system—sistema de incentivos
income—ingciones de enlace
incorporation doctrine—doctrina de incorporación
incrementalism—incrementalismo
incumbents—titular en función
independent executive agencies—agencias ejecutivas independientes
independent regulatory agency—agencia regulatoria independiente
industrial policy—política industrial
inflation—inflación
initiative—iniciativa
initiative petition—iniciativa de petición
interdependency—interdependencia
interest group—grupos de interés
intergovernmental relations—relaciones intergubernamentales
investigative journalism—periodismo de investigación
iron triangles—triángulos de acero
isolationism—aislacionismo
item veto—artículo de veto

J
Joint Chiefs of Staff—Junta de Comandantes de las Fuerzas Armadas (Estado Mayor)
joint committees—comisiones
judicial activisim—activismo judicial
judicial implementation—implementación judicial
judicial restraint—restricción judicial
judicial review—revisión judicial
justiciable disputes—conflictos enjuiciables

K
Keynesian economic theory—teoría económica keynesiana

L
laissez-faire—liberalismo económico
legislative oversight—descuido legislativo
legislative veto—Veto legislativo
legitimacy—legitimidad
libel—difamación, calumnia
liberals—liberales
lieutenant governor—lugarteniente del gobernador
limited government—gobierno limitado
linkage institutions—instituciones de enlace
lobbying—cabildeo
local charter—estatutos locales; fuero local

M
majority leader—líder de la mayoría
majority rule—gobil o
mandate theory of elections—mandato teórico de elecciones

mass media—medios de difusión (comunicación) masiva
McCarthyism—macartismo
McGovern-Fraser Commission—Comisión *McGovern-Fraser*
media event—evento de los medios de difusión (comunicación)
Medicaid—programa de asistencia médica estatal *Medicaid* para personas de bajos ingresos
Medicare—programa de asistencia médica estatal *Medicare* para personas mayores de 65 años
melting pot—crisol
merit plan—plan meritorio (por méritos)
merit principle—principio de mérito
minority leader—líder de la minoría parlamentaria
minority majority—majoria de la minoría
minority rights—derechos de las minorías
mixed economy—economía mixta
monetarism—monetarismo
monetary policy—política monetaria
Motor Voter Act—Ley para promoción del voto

N

narrowcasting—transmisión cerrada; monitoreo cerrado
National Environmental Policy Act (NEPA)—Ley de la Política Ambiental Nacional
National Labor Relations Act—Ley Nacional de Relaciones Laborales
National Security Council (NSC)—Consejo Nacional de Seguridad
national chairperson—director/a de comité nacional
national committee—comité nacional
national convention—convención nacional
national health insurance—seguro de salud nacional
national party convention—convención nacional del partido
national primary—primaria nacional
natural rights—derechos naturales
New Deal coalition—coalición para el Nuevo Tratado
New Jersey Plan—Plan de New Jersey
Nineteenth Amendment—Enmienda Diecinueve
nomination—nominación
North Atlantic Treaty Organization (NATO)—Tratado de las Organizaciones del Atlantico Norte

O

Office of Management and Budget (OMB)—Oficina de Gestión y Presupuesto
Office of Personnel Management (OPM)—Oficina de Gestión de Personal
Olson's law of large groups—ley de Olson de grandes grupos
open primaries—primarias abiertas
opinion—opinión
Organization of Petroleum Exporting Countries (OPEC)—Organización de Países Exportadores de Petróleo
original intent—intento original
original jurisdiction—jurisdicción original

P

party competition—competencia de partido
party dealignment—desalineamiento del partido
party eras—épocas del partido
party identification—identificación partidista
party image—imágen del partido
party machines—maquinaria partidista
party neutrality—neutralidad partidista
party platform—plataforma del partido
party realignment—realinación del partido
patronage—patrocinio
Pendleton Civil Service Act—Ley del Servicio Público de Pendleton
plea bargaining—negociación fiscal-defensa
pluralist theory—teoría pluralista
pocket veto—veto indirecto del presidente al no firmar dentro de los diez días establecidos
policy agenda—agenda política
policy entrepreneurs—política empresarial
policy gridlock—parálisis política
policy implementation—implementación política
policy voting—política de votación
policymaking institutions—instituciones de normatividad política
policymaking system—sistema de normatividad política
political action committees (PACs)—comités de acción política
political culture—cultura política
political efficacy—eficacia política
political ideology—ideología política
political issue—asunto político
political participation—participación política
political party—partido político
political questions—cuestiones políticas
political socialization—socialización política
politics—política
poll taxes—votación para impuestos
pork barrel—asignación de impuestos estatales para el beneficio de una cierta zona o grupo
potential group—grupo potencial
poverty line—límite económico mínimo para sobrevivencia
precedent—precedente
presidential coattails—acción a la sombra presidencial
presidential primaries—elecciones primarias presidenciales
press conferences—conferencias de prensa
print media—medios de comunicación impresos
prior restraint—restricción anterior
privileges and immunities—privilegios e inmunidades
probable cause—causa probable
progressive tax—impuesto progresivo
project grant—proyecto de concecsión
proportional representation—representación proporcional
proportional tax—impuesto proporcional
protest—n. protesta; v. protestar
public goods—bienes públicos
public interest lobbies—cabildeo por intereses públicos
public opinion—opinión pública
public policy—política pública

R

random sampling—muestreo aleatorio
random-digit dialing—llamadas con números aleatorios
rational-choice theory—teoría de selección racional
reapportionment—nueva distribución en la representación del congreso
recall—retirar
reconciliation—reconciliación
referendum—referendum
regional primaries—elecciones primarias regionales

regressive tax—impuesto regresivo
regulation—norma, regla
reinforcement—refuerzo
relative deprivation—privación relativa
representation—representación
republic—república
responsible party model—modelo de partido responsable
retrospective voting—votación retrospectiva
revenues—ingresos
right to privacy—derecho a la privacidad
right-to-work laws—leyes del derecho al trabajo

S
sample—muestra
sampling error—error de muestreo
search warrant—orden de cateo
secretary of defense—secretario de la defensa
secretary of state—secretario de estado
select committees—comités seleccionados
selective benefits—beneficios selectivos
selective perception—percepción selectiva
self-incrimination—auto incriminación
Senate Finance Committee—Comité Senatorial de Finanzas
senatorial courtesy—cortesía senatorial
Senior Executive Service—el de más alto rango en el servicio del ejecutivo
seniority system—sistema de antigüedad
separation of powers—separación de poderes
Shays' Rebellion—Rebelion de Shays
single-issue groups—grupos para una sola causa
Sixteenth Amendment—Enmienda Dieciséis
Sixth Amendment—Enmienda Sexta
Social Security Act—Ley de Seguridad Social
social welfare policies—políticas para el bien social
soft money—moneda débil, sin garantía
solicitor general—subsecretario de justicia
sound bites—segmentos de sonido
Speaker of the House—presidente de la cámara
standard operating procedures (SOPs)—procedimientos normales de operación
standing committees—comités permanentes
standing to sue—en posición de entablar demanda
stare decisis—variación de "decisión firme" o "decisión tomada"; la decisión se fundamenta en algo ya decidio.
statutory construction—construcción establecida por ley
Strategic Defense Initiative (SDI)—Iniciativa de Defensa Estratégica
street-level bureaucrats—burócratas de bajo nivel
subnational government—gobierno subnacional
subgovernments—subgobiernos
suffrage—sufragio
Super Tuesday—Super martes: día de votación en varios estados importantes.
superdelegates—superdelegados
Superfund—superfondo; fondo de proporciones mayores
supply-side economics—economía de la oferta
supremacy clause—cláusula de supremacía
Supreme Court—Suprema Corte
symbolic speech—discurso simbólico

T
Taft-Hartley Act—Ley de Taft-Hatley
talking head—busto parlante; presentador, entrevistador
tariff—tarifa
tax expenditures—gastos de impuesto
Tenth Amendment—Enmienda Décima
term limits—periodo límite
third parties—terceras personas
Thirteenth Amendment—Enmienda Treceava
ticket-splitting—votación de candidatos de diferentes partidos para diferentes cargos
town meeting—consejo municipal de vecinos
transfer payments—transferencia de pagos
transnational corporations—corporaciones transnacionales
trial balloons—globo de prueba; proponer algo para concer la reacción de alguien
Twenty-fifth Amendment—Enmienda veiticincoava
Twenty-fourth Amendment—Enmienda veiticuatrava
Twenty-second Amendment—Enmienda veintidoava

U
U.S. Constitution—Constitución de los Estados Unidos
uncontrollable expenditures—gastos incontrolables
unemployment rate—nivel de desempleo; porcentage de desempleo
union shop—empresa que emplea sólo trabajadores sindicalizados
unitary governments—estados/gobiernos unitarios
United Nations (UN)—Naciones Unidas
unreasonable searches and seizures—cateos y detenciones/ embargos irrazonables
urban underclass—urbanita de clase baja

V
veto—veto
Virginia Plan—Plan Virginia
voter registration—registro de votantes
Voting Rights Act of 1965—Ley de Derechos del Elector de 1965

W
War Powers Resolution—Resolución de Poderes de Guerra
Water Pollution Control Act of 1972—Ley para el Control de la Contaminación de Aguas de 1972
wealth—riqueza
whips—miembro de un cuerpo legislativo encargado de hacer observar las consignas del partido
white primary—primaria blanca/ sin novedad
winner-take-all system—sistema en el que el ganador toma todos los votos
writ of habeas corpus—un recurso de hábeas corpus

Acknowledgments

TEXT ACKNOWLEDGMENTS

"Stories Citizens Have Tuned In and Out"—By permission of Los Angeles Times Syndicate

"The Big Spending PACS" from the Center of Responsive Politics archived at www.opensecrets.org by permission of Center for Responsive Politics.

"The Inflated Importance of Iowa and New Hampshire in the Presidential Nomination Process" from *Media and Momentum*, 1987, by Gary R. Orren and Nelson W. Polsby. Copyright © Chatham House Publishers. Reprinted by permission.

"The Incumbency Factor in Congressional Elections" republished with permission Congressional Quarterly, from Norman J. Ornstein, Thomas E. Mann, and Michael J. Malbin, *Vital Statistics on Congress, 1995–1996*; permission conveyed through Copyright Clearance Center.

"Principal Offices in the White House," copyright © 1997 by St. Martins Press, Inc. from *Presidential Leadership*, Fourth Edition by George C. Edwards III and Stephen J. Wayne, reprinted with permission of Bedford/St. Martins Press, Inc.

"Supreme Court Rulings in Which Federal Statutes Have Been Found Unconstitutional" from *The Judicial Process: An Introductory Analysis of the Courts of the United States, England, and France*, Seventh Edition by Henry J. Abraham. Copyright © 1993 by Henry J. Abraham. Used by permission of Oxford University Press, Inc.

"America in Perspective" from *USA TODAY*, July 12, 2000, copyright © 2000, USA TODAY. Reprinted with permission.

"The Abortion Debate" from Gallup/CNN/USA Today Poll, January 13–16, 2000, reprinted by permission of The Gallup Poll.

"The Power 25" from *Fortune*, December 6, 1999, reprinted by permission of Fortune Magazine.

"Government by the People: The American Revolution and the Democratization of the Legislatures" by Jackson Turner Main in *The William and Mary Quarterly*, July 23, 1996, reprinted by permission of The Omohundro Institue of Early American History and Culture.

"America in Perspective: Citizens Show Little Knowledge of Geography," Copyright © November 9, 1989, reprinted by permission of *The New York Times*.

"Time Devoted to the Three Branches of Government on Network Television News" republished with permission Congressional Quarterly, from Doris A. Graber, *Mass Media and American Politics*, 5th Edition, 1997, reprinted by permission of Congressional Quarterly.

"Spending Time with the News" reprinted by permission of Pew Research Center for the People & The Press from their website; http://people-press.org/medsec3.htm.

"What Makes Someone an American?" from *American Identity and the Politics of Ethnic Change* by Jack Citrin, Beth A. Reingold and Donald P. Green in *Journal of Politics, 52:4*, reprinted by permission of Blackwell Publishers.

"Percentage of Groups Using Various Lobbying Techniques" from Kay L. Schlozman and John T. Tierney, *Organized Interests and American Democracy*, 1986. Reprinted by permission of Addison Wesley Educational Publishers, Inc.

"A Day in the Life of a Member of Congress" from *The Congressional Experience: A View From the Hill*, by David E. Price, copyright © 1992 by Westview Press, Inc., reprinted by permission of Westview Press, a member of Perseus Books, L.L.C.

"Presidential Success on Votes in Congress" from George C. Edwards III, "At the Margins: Presidential Leadership of Congress." Copyright © 1989 by Yale University Press. Reprinted by permission.

"A Full Day of Regulations" from "A Typical Day is Full of Rules" in *Chicago Tribune*, copyright © 1981 by Chicago Tribune Company. All rights reserved. Used with permission.

Excerpt from "The Death of an Iron Triangle" from Frank B. Baumgartner and Bryan D. Jones, *Agendas and Instability in American Politics*. Copyright © 1993 University of Chicago Press. Reprinted by permission.

"America in Perspective: The Soviet Economic Morass" from Hedrick Smith, *The New Russians*, 1990, Random House. Reprinted by permission of International Merchandising Corporation.

"The Spread of Nuclear Weapons" republished with permission Congressional Quarterly, from *Congressional Quarterly Weekly*, May 23, 1998; permission conveyed through Copyright Clearance Center.

"Treaties and Executive Agreements Concluded by the U.S. 1789–1996" from *Vital Statistics on American Politics 1999–2000* by Harold W. Stanley and Richard G. Niemi, reprinted by permission of CQ Press.

"American in Perspective: Urban Planning is Western Europe and the U.S." from *Urban and Regional Planning*, 2nd Edition by Peter Hall.

Savitch, H.V., *Post-Industrial Cities: Politics and Planning in New York, Paris, and London*, copyright © 1989 by Princeton University Press. Reprinted by permission of Princeton University Press.

Myron A. Levine and Jan Van Weesep, "The Changing Nature of Dutch Urban Planning" in *Journal of the American Planning Association*, 54, Summer 1988. Reprinted by permission of Journal of the American Planning Association.

"Institutional Powers of the Governors" from *Politics in the American States*, Fifth Edition. Copyright © 1990 by Virginia Gray, Herbert Jacobs, and Robert B. Alberton. Reprinted by permission of Addison-Wesley Educational Publishers, Inc.

Graphics, "Bush Counties" and "Gore Counties" from *The Washington Post*, copyright © 2001, The Washington Post. Reprinted with permission.

"Associations by Type" from Frank R. Baumgartner and Beth L. Leech, *Basic Interests: The Importance of Groups in Politics and Political Science*, 1998, Princeton University Press.

PHOTO ACKNOWLEDGMENTS

Page abbreviations are as follows: (T) top, (C) center, (B) bottom, (L) left, (R) right.

ICONS: Detail of an American Flag: Siede Preis/PhotoDisc; Earth: The Studio Dog/PhotoDisc; Crowd of Businesspeople in a Grandstand: Duncan Smith/PhotoDisc; United States Capitol Building: Jeremy Woodhouse/PhotoDisc; American Flag and Gavel: Al Riccio/PhotoDisc. 1: AP/Wide World Photos; 2: Mark Richards/PhotoEdit; 5: AFP/Corbis; 6: Bill Aron/PhotoEdit; 7: Reuters/Kevin Lemarque/Archive Photos; 8T: AP/Wide World Photos; 8B: Jim Argo/MercPix.com; 9: AFP/Corbis; 10: D. Young-Wolff/PhotoEdit; 12: Jane Rosett/Corbis Sygma; 13: AP/Wide World Photos; 14: Art by Jim Borgman. Reprinted with special permission of King Features Syndicate; 18: Ed Zurga/AP/Wide World Photos; 21: Owen Franklin/Corbis Sygma; 27: Paul Conklin/PhotoEdit; 30: U.S. Capitol Historical Society; 32L: Brown Brothers; 32R: National Archives and Records Administration; 36: Scribner's Popular History of the U.S., 1897; 37: Copyright Yale Universtiy Art Gallery; 38: New York Public Library, Astor, Lenox and Tilden Foundations; 40: DOONESBURY © G.B. Trudeau. Reprinted with permission of Universal Press Syndicate. All rights reserved; 41: The Granger Collection, New York; 46: Bob Daemmrich/The Image Works; 47L: AP/Wide World Photos; 47R: The White House Collection, copyright White House Historical Association; 47B: Frantz Jantzen/Collection of the Supreme Court of the United States; 48: National Geographic Photographer George Mobley/U.S. Capitol Historical Society; 49: Scott, Foresman and Company; 53: AP/Wide World Photos; 58: Drawing by Luckovich/Creators Syndicate; 61: David J. Phillip/AP/Wide World Photos; 65: Davis Barber/PhotoEdit; 67TL: Morton Beebe, S.F./Corbis; 67TC: UN Photo/M. Grant 185500/106L; 67TR: AP/Wide World Photos; 67B: Reuters NewMedia Inc./Corbis; 69: Mark Richards/PhotoEdit; 75: Stephen Frisch/Stock Boston, Inc.; 76: Scott, Foresman and Company; 77: George Eastman House/Lewis W. Hine/Archive Photos; 81: Renato Rotolo/Liaison Agency; 83: FRANK & ERNEST reprinted by permission of Newspaper Enterprise Association, Inc.; 89: Reuters/Pierre duCharme/Archive Photos; 91: Pete Erickson, Telegraph Herald/AP/Wide World Photos; 95: Robert Ginn/Unicorn; 96: Christopher Lingg/The Image Works; 101: Rob Crandall/Stock Boston, Inc.; 102: AP/Wide World Photos; 106T: ©The New Yorker Collection 1992 Robert Mankoff from cartoonbank.com. All Rights Reserved; 106B: AP/Wide World Photos; 108: Pool/Liaison Agency; 109: ©The New Yorker Collection 1991 Mischa Richter from cartoonbank.com. All Rights Reserved; 111: Corbis; 113: Corbis; 117: Brian Plonka/The Spokesman-Review; 121T: Michael Newman/PhotoEdit; 121B: Creators Syndicate & Johnny Hart; 123: Flip Schulke © 1964; 127: Mobile Press Register/Corbis Sygma; 130: Reuters/Pool/Archive Photos; 131: Corbis; 137: William Johnson/Stock Boston, Inc.; 140: AP/Wide World Photos/fls; 142: The Granger Collection, New York; 143: Bettmann/Corbis; 145: Bettmann/Corbis; 146: AP/Wide World Photos; 147: Scott, Foresman and Company; 150: AP/Wide World Photos; 151: ©Seattle Post-Intelligencer Collection; Museum of History and Industry/Corbis; 154: Mark Godfrey/The Image Works; 156: Reuters/Bettmann/Corbis; 157: Allan Tannenbaum/Corbis Sygma; 161: Mark Richards/PhotoEdit; 168: M. Reinstein/The Image Works; 173: Reuters NewMedia Inc./Corbis; 174: Allan J. Barnes; 175: Drawing by Jack Ohman. ©Tribune Media Services, Inc. All Rights Reserved. Reprinted with permission; 177: Bart Bartholomew/Black Star; 179: David Young-Wolff/PhotoEdit; 183: Bob Daemmrich/Stock Boston, Inc.; 186: Gail Machlis/Universal Press Syndicate; 188: Jon Feingersh/Corbis Stock Market; 197: Davidson/The Image Works; 198: Judi Siebens/*The Desert Sun*; 199T: Jeffrey Markowitz/Corbis Sygma; 199B: John Filo; 200: Bruce Brothers/Photo Researchers, Inc.; 203: Bob Daemmrich; 207: Jim Bourg/Liaison Agency/Getty Source; 209: Reuters/Bettmann/Corbis; 210: Bettmann/Corbis; 211: Milan Ryba/Globe Photos; 212: AP/Wide World Photos; 217: AP/Wide World Photos; 219B: Bettmann/Corbis; 219T: Scott, Foresman and Company; 220: © Tribune Media Services, Inc. All Rights Reserved. Reprinted with permission; 223: Bettmann/Corbis; 225: Don Wright/Miami News; 226: Larry Wright/©2000 *The Detroit News*; 227: AP/Wide World Photos; 228: David Young-Wolff/PhotoEdit; 229: © The New Yorker Collection 1989 Frank Modell from cartoonbank.com. All Rights Reserved; 230: Corbis Sygma; 235: AFP/Corbis; 237: David Burnett/Contact Press Images; 248: Bettmann/Corbis; 249: Bettmann/Corbis; 252L: THE PARTY GOES ON by Xandra Kayden/reprinted by permission of Basic Books, Inc. New York ,1985; 252R: THE PARTY GOES ON by Xandra Kayden/ reprinted by permission of Basic Books, Inc. New York ,1985; 253: Bob Daemmrich/The Image Works; 254: AFP/Corbis; 255: AP/Wide World Photos; 258: Greg Matheison/Corbis Sygma; 259: Rob Rogers for the *Pittsburgh Post-Gazette.* United Media; 261: Rodney White/AP/Wide World Photos; 265: Brooks Kraft/Corbis Sygma; 267: AP/Wide World Photos; 268: © National Enquirer/Liaison Agency; 269: Reuters NewMedia/Corbis; 270: AP/Wide World Photo; 271: Don Wright/*The Miami News*; 276: Howell/Liaison Agency; 277: www.hillary2000.org; 278: Karin Cooper/Liaison Agency; 280: AP/Wide World Photos; 284: AP/Wide World Photos; 285: ©1999 by Herblock in *The Washington Post*; 287: courtesy the authors; 288: AP/Wide World Photos; 290: Les Stone/Corbis Sygma; 291: Chris Usher/Corbis Sygma; 295: Liaison Agency/Getty Source; 297: John Novrok/PhotoEdit; 298: AP/Wide World Photos; 299: Library of Congress; 300: Mike Peters/© Tribune Media Services, Inc. All Rights Reserved. Reprinted with permission; 301: Gary I. Rothstein/AP/Wide World Photos; 304: Reuters/Mike Blake/Archive Photos; 309: Renault for *Sacramento Bee*, with acknowledgment to the Simpsons; 313: © The New Yorker Collection 1989 Jack Ziegler from cartoonbank.com. All Rights Reserved; 315: Doug Mills/AP/Wide World Photos; 316: Bettmann/Corbis; 318: SIPA Press; 321: AP/Wide World Photos; 322: Wayne Stayskal/©Tribune Media Services, Inc. All Rights Reserved. Reprinted with permission; 323: Jason Cohn/ZUMA Press. ©2000 by Jason Cohn; 327T: Bettmann/Corbis; 327B: Bettmann/Corbis; 331: Jim Borgman/Reprinted with special permission of King Features Syndicate; 335: AP/Wide World Photos; 336: Jim Borgman/Reprinted with special permission of King Features Syndicate; 339: Jeffrey Markowitz/Corbis Sygma; 341: AP/Wide World Photos; 342: Michael C. York/AP/Wide World Photos; 343T: Theo Westenberger/Liaison Agency; 343B: Michael DiBari Jr./AP/Wide World Photos 345T: Allan

Tannenbaum/Corbis Sygma; 348: Electronic Freedom Foundation; 353: Mark Wilson/Corbis Sygma; 357: AP/Wide World Photos; 358: Gunther/SIPA Press; 361: AP/Wide World Photos; 368L: AP/Wide World Photos; 368C: Brad Markel/Liaison Agency; 368R: AP/Wide World Photos; 371: Paul Conklin/Pictor; 373: Kamenko Pajic/AP/Wide World Photos; 376: Bob Daemmrich/The Image Works; 381: Catherine Karnow/Woodfin Camp & Associates; 383: © The New Yorker Collection 1996 J.B. Handelsman from cartoonbank.com. All Rights Reserved; 385: C-SPAN; 386: © The New Yorker Collection 1987 Dana Fradon from cartoonbank.com. All Rights Reserved; 388: Mark Wilson/Liaison Agency/ Newsmakers; 393: Chris Usher/Corbis Sygma; 395: AUTH/Universal Press Syndicate. All rights reserved; 396: AP/Wide World Photos; 396: AP/Wide World Photos; 396: AP/Wide World Photos; 396: AP/Wide World Photos; 396: AP/Wide World Photos; 396: AP/Wide World Photos; 396: AP/Wide World Photos; 396: AP/Wide World Photos; 396: AP/Wide World Photos; 397T: AP/Wide World Photos; 397B: Liaison Agency; 398: Alex Webb/Magnum Photos; 404T: J. Scott Applewhite/AP/Wide World Photos; 404B: Doug Mills/AP/Wide World Photos; 408: Reuters NewMedia Inc./Corbis; 411: Liaison Agency/Getty Source; 415: Terry Ashe/Liaison Agency; 416: TOLES © The Buffalo News. Reprinted with permission of Universal Press Syndicate. All rights reserved; 417: Stephen Jaffe /Archive Photos; 418: Bettmann/Corbis; 419: AP/Wide World Photos; 423: AP/Wide World Photos; 425: © The New Yorker Collection 1984 Jack Ziegler from cartoonbank.com. All Rights Reserved; 426: Wayne Miller/Magnum Photos; 428: AP/Wide World Photos; 429: AFP/ Corbis; 432: Joseph Sohm, ChromoSohm Inc./Corbis; 437: Allan Tannenbaum/Corbis Sygma; 441: Reuters/Mark Cardwell/Archive Photos; 444: Bettmann/Corbis; 447: Citizens For Tax Justice; 449: Randy Jolly/The Image Works; 450: Bettmann/Corbis; 460: Reuters/William Philpott/Archive Photos; 462: Ted Korodny/Corbis Sygma; 463: Reuters NewMedia Inc./Corbis; 467: Richard Pasley/Stock Boston, Inc; 473: DOONESBURY © G.B. Trudeau. Reprinted with permission of Universal Press Syndicate. All rights reserved; 478: Chuck Nacke/Woodfin Camp & Associates; 479: David H. Wells/The Image Works; 481: AP/Wide World Photos; 485: Bob Strong/SIPA Press; 488: Bettmann/Corbis; 489: Stayce Pick/Stock Boston, Inc.; 490: J. Pat Carter/AP/Wide World Photos; 493: Bettmann/Corbis; 498: NASA/The Image Works; 503: John Neubauer/Monkmeyer; 504: Bob Daemmrich/The Image Works; 505: Carl Iwasaki/TimePix; 507: John Ficara/Woodfin Camp & Associates; 511: Bob Daemmrich/The Image Works; 515: Reuters/Corbis; 516: AP/Wide World Photos; 518: Corbis Sygma; 522: Abe Franjndlich/Corbis Sygma; 523: © The New Yorker Collection 1992 J.B. Handelsman from cartoonbank.com. All Rights Reserved; 526: Bettmann/Corbis; 528: Supreme Court Historical Society; 529: Rob Crandall/The Image Works; 533: Bob Daemmrich/Stock Boston, Inc.; 535: Bob Daemmrich/The Image Works; 541: AP/Wide World Photos; 542: Walt Handelsman/©Tribune Media Services, Inc. All Rights Reserved. Reprinted with permission; 547T: Reuters/Archive Photos; 547B: Bettmann/Corbis; 549: Mike Peters/© Tribune Media Services, Inc. All Rights Reserved. Reprinted with permission; 550: Craig Aurness/Woodfin Camp & Associates; 553: Chuck Nacke/MercPix.com; 554: Library of Congress; 555: Robert Trippett/SIPA Press; 557: P. LeSegretain/Corbis Sygma; 559: Andy Sacks/Stone Images; 563: AP/Wide World Photos; 565: Brooks Kraft/Corbis Sygma; 566T: Bob Daemmrich; 566B: Bob Krist/Black Star; 567: Dan Wasserman/©Tribune Media Services, Inc. All Rights Reserved. Reprinted with permission; 569: Bettmann/Corbis; 571: Bob Daemmrich; 573: Bettmann/Corbis; 575T: Courtesy Lyndon Baines Johnson Library, Austin, TX; 575B: © The New Yorker Collection 1987 Dana Fradon from cartoonbank.com. All Rights Reserved; 576: Brendan Beirne/Stone Images; 582: David Falconer/Folio, Inc.; 587: David Ulmer/Stock Boston, Inc.; 589: George Danby/*The Bangor Daily News*, Maine; 591: Randy Matusow/Monkmeyer; 592: Art by Jim Borgman. Reprinted with special permission of King Features Syndicate; 596: D. Goldberg/Corbis Sygma; 597: Dennis Brack/Black Star; 599: Jenny Hager/The Image Works; 602: Pienee Lynn/Stone Images; 608: B. Nation/Corbis Sygma; 610: Allan Tannenbaum/Corbis Sygma; 611: © The New Yorker 1995 J.B. Handelsman from cartoonbank.com. All Rights Reserved; 613: Corbis; 617: Thomas Haley/SIPA Press; 622: AP/Wide World Photos; 624: Yonhap/AP/Wide World Photos; 625: AFP/Corbis; 628L: Bettmann/Corbis; 628R Tom Stoddart/Woodfin Camp & Associates; 629: Wally McNamee/Woodfin Camp & Associates; 632: Corbis; 636T: Jesse Nemerofsky–MercPix.com; 636B: Corbis; 640: AP/Wide World Photos; 642: Corbis Sygma; 651: Burhan Ozbilici/AP/Wide World Photos; 655: Paul Conklin/ Monkmeyer; 657: Steven Starr/Stock Boston, Inc.; 658: D. Young-Wolff/PhotoEdit; 665: AP/Wide World Photos; 666: AP/ Wide World Photos; 667: AFP/Corbis; 670: AP/Wide World Photos; 677: Paul Sakuma/AP/Wide World Photos; 685: Monika Graff/The Image Works; 692: Lynda Richardson/Corbis

Index

Note: Supreme Court rulings are indexed under the main heading *Supreme Court rulings* rather than under the individual subject of the ruling. Supreme Court cases are indexed under the main heading *Supreme Court cases* rather than alphabetically by case names. Text discussions of specific election years are indexed under elections. Page numbers with an n indicate endnotes.